MATHPOWER™ 11

WESTERN EDITION

MATHPOWER™11

WESTERN EDITION

MATHPOWER™ 10–12,
Western Edition, Authors

George Knill, B.Sc., M.S.Ed.
Hamilton, Ontario

Stella Ablett, B.Sc.
Vancouver, British Columbia

Cynthia Ballheim, B.Sc., M.A.
Calgary, Alberta

John Carter, B.Sc., M.Sc.
Toronto, Ontario

Eileen Collins, B.A., M.Ed.
Hamilton, Ontario

Eleanor Conrad, B.Sc.
Pugwash, Nova Scotia

Russel Donnelly, B.Sc., M.A.
Calgary, Alberta

Michael Hamilton, B.Sc., M.Sc.
St. Catharines, Ontario

Rosemary Miller, B.A.
Hamilton, Ontario

Alan Sarna, B.A.
Vancouver, British Columbia

Harold Wardrop. B.Sc.
Surrey, British Columbia

MATHPOWER™ 11
Western Edition, Consultants

Lois Edwards
Cochrane, Alberta

John Chapman
Oliver, British Columbia

Terry Clifford
Winnipeg, Manitoba

Bill Korytowski
Winnipeg, Manitoba

Petra Menz
Richmond, British Columbia

Darryl Smith
Edmonton, Alberta

Colleen Tong
Calgary, Alberta

McGraw-Hill
Ryerson

Toronto Montréal New York Burr Ridge Bangkok Bogotá Caracas
Lisbon London Madrid Mexico City Milan New Delhi
Seoul Singapore Sydney Taipei

McGraw-Hill
Ryerson Limited
A Subsidiary of The **McGraw-Hill** Companies

**COPIES OF THIS BOOK
MAY BE OBTAINED BY
CONTACTING:**

McGraw-Hill Ryerson Ltd.

WEBSITE:
http://www.mcgrawhill.ca

E-MAIL:
Orders@mcgrawhill.ca

TOLL FREE FAX:
1-800-463-5885

TOLL FREE CALL:
1-800-565-5758

**OR BY MAILING
YOUR ORDER TO:**

McGraw-Hill Ryerson
Order Department,
300 Water Street
Whitby, ON L1N 9B6

Please quote the ISBN and
title when placing your
order.

MATHPOWER™ 11
Western Edition

ISBN 0-07-552598-4

http://www.mcgrawhill.ca

7 8 9 10 TRI 8 7 6 5

Printed and bound in Canada

Canadian Cataloguing in Publication Data

Main entry under title:

Mathpower 11

Western ed.
Includes index.
ISBN 0-07-552598-4

1. Mathematics. 2. Mathematics - Problems, exercises, etc.
I. Knill, George, date. II Title: Mathpower eleven.

QA107.M37649 1999   510   C98-932309-9

PUBLISHER: Melanie Myers
EDITORIAL CONSULTING: Michael J. Webb Consulting Inc.
ASSOCIATE EDITORS: Sheila Bassett, Mary Agnes Challoner, Maggie Cheverie, Jean Ford, Janice Nixon
SENIOR SUPERVISING EDITOR: Carol Altilia
PERMISSIONS EDITORS: Jacqueline Donovan, Crystal Shortt
PRODUCTION COORDINATOR: Yolanda Pigden
ART DIRECTION: Wycliffe Smith Design Inc.
COVER DESIGN: Wycliffe Smith Design Inc., Dianna Little
INTERIOR DESIGN: Wycliffe Smith Design Inc.
ELECTRONIC PAGE MAKE-UP: Tom Dart/First Folio Resource Group, Inc.
COVER ILLUSTRATIONS: Clarence Porter
COVER IMAGE: Kaz Mori/The Image Bank

CONTENTS

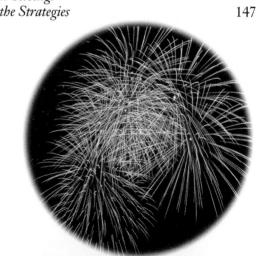

Using *MATHPOWER™ 11*, Western Edition

Each chapter contains several numbered sections.
In a typical numbered section, you find the following features.

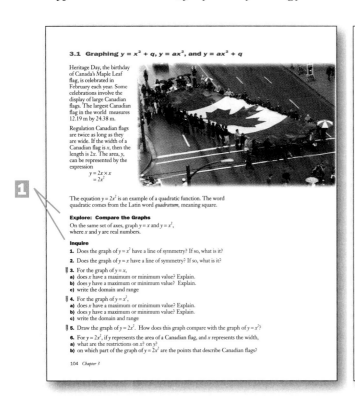

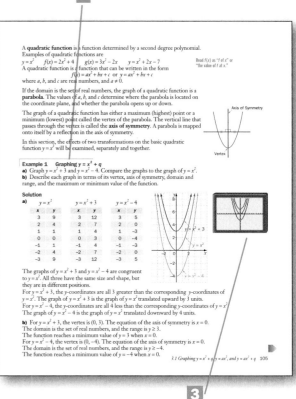

1 Explore and Inquire

You start with an exploration, followed by a set of inquire questions. The exploration and the inquire questions allow you to construct your own learning. Many explorations show how mathematics is applied in the world.

2 Examples

The examples show you how to use what you have learned.

3 Graphing Calculator Displays

These displays show you how technology can be used to solve problems.

4 Practice

By completing these questions, you practise what you have learned, so that you can stabilize your learning.

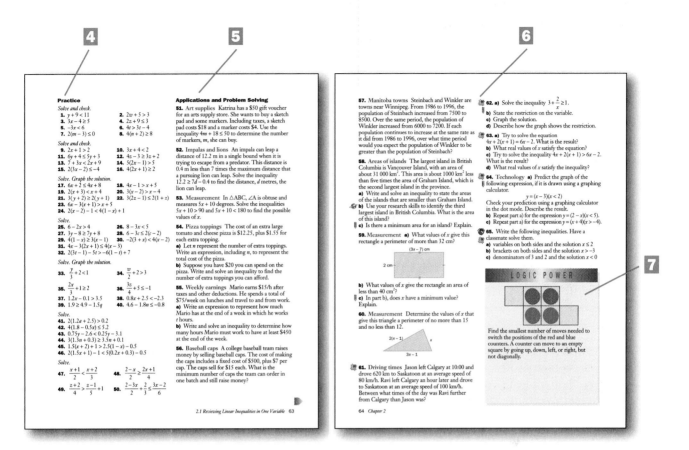

Practice

Solve and check.
1. $y + 9 < 11$
2. $2w + 5 > 3$
3. $3x - 4 \geq 5$
4. $2z + 9 \leq 3$
5. $-3x < 6$
6. $4r > 3t - 4$
7. $2(m - 3) \leq 0$
8. $4(n + 2) \geq 8$

Solve and check.
9. $2x + 1 > 2$
10. $3x + 4 < 2$
11. $6y + 4 \leq 5y + 3$
12. $4z - 3 \geq 3z + 2$
13. $7 + 3x < 2x + 9$
14. $5(2x - 1) > 5$
15. $2(3x - 2) \leq -4$
16. $4(2x + 1) \geq 2$

Solve. Graph the solution.
17. $6x + 2 \leq 4x + 8$
18. $4x - 1 > x + 5$
19. $2(x + 3) < x + 4$
20. $3(x - 2) > x - 4$
21. $3(y + 2) \geq 2(y + 1)$
22. $3(2z - 1) \leq 2(1 + z)$
23. $6x - 3(x + 1) > x + 5$
24. $2(x - 2) - 1 < 4(1 - x) + 1$

Solve.
25. $6 - 2x > 4$
26. $8 - 3x < 5$
27. $3y - 8 \geq 7y + 8$
28. $6 - 3c \leq 2(c - 2)$
29. $4(1 - x) \geq 3(x - 1)$
30. $-2(3 + x) < 4(x - 2)$
31. $4x - 3(2x + 1) \leq 4(x - 3)$
32. $2(3t - 1) - 5t > -6(1 - t) + 7$

Solve. Graph the solution.
33. $\frac{y}{3} + 2 < 1$
34. $\frac{w}{2} + 2 > 3$
35. $\frac{2x}{3} + 1 \geq 2$
36. $\frac{3z}{4} + 5 \leq -1$
37. $1.2x - 0.1 > 3.5$
38. $0.8x + 2.5 < -2.3$
39. $1.9 \geq 4.9 - 1.5q$
40. $4.6 - 1.8n \leq -0.8$

Solve.
41. $2(1.2a + 2.5) > 0.2$
42. $4(1.8 - 0.5x) \leq 5.2$
43. $0.75y - 2.6 < 0.25y - 3.1$
44. $3(1.3n + 0.3) \geq 3.5n + 0.1$
45. $1.5(x + 1) + 1 > 2.5(1 - x) - 0.5$
46. $2(1.5x + 1) - 1 < 5(0.2x + 0.3) - 0.5$

Solve.
47. $\frac{x+1}{2} < \frac{x+2}{3}$
48. $\frac{2-x}{2} \geq \frac{2x+1}{4}$
49. $\frac{z+2}{4} > \frac{z-1}{5} + 1$
50. $\frac{2-3x}{2} \leq \frac{3x-2}{6}$

Applications and Problem Solving

51. **Art supplies** Katrina has a $50 gift voucher for an arts supply store. She wants to buy a sketch pad and some markers. Including taxes, a sketch pad costs $18 and a marker costs $4. Use the inequality $4m + 18 \leq 50$ to determine the number of markers, m, she can buy.

52. **Impalas and lions** An impala can leap a distance of 12.2 m in a single bound when it is trying to escape from a predator. This distance is 0.4 m less than 7 times the maximum distance that a pursuing lion can leap. Solve the inequality $12.2 \geq 7d - 0.4$ to find the distance, d metres, the lion can leap.

53. **Measurement** In $\triangle ABC$, $\angle A$ is obtuse and measures $5x + 10$ degrees. Solve the inequalities $5x + 10 > 90$ and $5x + 10 < 180$ to find the possible values of x.

54. **Pizza toppings** The cost of an extra large tomato and cheese pizza is $12.25, plus $1.55 for each extra topping.
a) Let n represent the number of extra toppings. Write an expression, including n, to represent the total cost of the pizza.
b) Suppose you have $20 you can spend on the pizza. Write and solve an inequality to find the number of extra toppings you can afford.

55. **Weekly earnings** Mario earns $15/h after taxes and other deductions. He spends a total of $75/week on lunches and travel to and from work.
a) Write an expression to represent how much Mario has at the end of a week in which he works t hours.
b) Write and solve an inequality to determine how many hours Mario must work to have at least $450 at the end of the week.

56. **Baseball caps** A college baseball team raises money by selling baseball caps. The cost of making the caps includes a fixed cost of $500, plus $7 per cap. The caps sell for $15 each. What is the minimum number of caps the team can order in one batch and still raise money?

57. **Manitoba towns** Steinbach and Winkler are towns near Winnipeg. From 1986 to 1996, the population of Steinbach increased from 7500 to 8500. Over the same period, the population of Winkler increased from 6000 to 7200. If each population continues to increase at the same rate as it did from 1986 to 1996, over what time period would you expect the population of Winkler to be greater than the population of Steinbach?

58. **Areas of islands** The largest island in British Columbia is Vancouver Island, with an area of about 31 000 km². This area is about 1000 km² less than five times the area of Graham Island, which is the second largest island in the province.
a) Write and solve an inequality to state the areas of the islands that are smaller than Graham Island.
b) Use your research skills to identify the third largest island in British Columbia. What is the area of this island?
c) Is there a minimum area for an island? Explain.

59. **Measurement** a) What values of x give this rectangle a perimeter of more than 32 cm?

$(3x - 7)$ cm
2 cm

b) What values of x give the rectangle an area of less than 40 cm²?
c) In part b), does x have a minimum value? Explain.

60. **Measurement** Determine the values of x that give this triangle a perimeter of no more than 15 and no less than 12.

$2(x - 1)$ x
$3x - 1$

61. **Driving times** Jason left Calgary at 10:00 and drove 620 km to Saskatoon at an average speed of 80 km/h. Ravi left Calgary an hour later and drove to Saskatoon at an average speed of 100 km/h. Between what times of the day was Ravi further from Calgary than Jason was?

62. a) Solve the inequality $3 + \frac{2}{x} \geq 1$.
b) State the restriction on the variable.
c) Graph the solution.
d) Describe how the graph shows the restriction.

63. a) Try to solve the equation $4x + 2(x + 1) = 6x - 2$. What is the result?
b) What real values of x satisfy the equation?
c) Try to solve the inequality $4x + 2(x + 1) > 6x - 2$. What is the result?
d) What real values of x satisfy the inequality?

64. **Technology** a) Predict the graph of the following expression, if it is drawn using a graphing calculator.
$$y = (x - 3)(x < 2)$$
Check your prediction using a graphing calculator in the dot mode. Describe the result.
b) Repeat part a) for the expression $y = (2 - x)(x < 5)$.
c) Repeat part a) for the expression $y = (x + 4)(x > -4)$.

65. Write the following inequalities. Have a classmate solve them.
a) variables on both sides and the solution $x \leq 2$
b) brackets on both sides and the solution $x > -3$
c) denominators of 3 and 2 and the solution $x < 0$

LOGIC POWER

Find the smallest number of moves needed to switch the positions of the red and blue counters. A counter can move to an empty square by going up, down, left, or right, but not diagonally.

5 Applications and Problem Solving

These questions let you use what you have learned to solve problems, and to apply and extend what you have learned. The descriptors on many of the problems show connections to other disciplines, to other topics in mathematics, and to people's daily experiences.

6 Logos

The four logos indicate special kinds of problems or opportunities for research.

When you see this logo, you will be asked to demonstrate an understanding of what you have learned by writing about it in a meaningful way.

This logo signals that you will need to think critically when you answer a question.

This logo indicates an opportunity to work with a classmate or in a larger group to solve a problem.

For a problem with this logo, you will need to use your research skills to find information from the Internet, a print data bank, or some other source.

7 Power Problems

These problems are challenging and fun. They encourage you to reason mathematically.

Special Features of
MATHPOWER™ 11, Western Edition

Math Standard
There are 14 Math Standard pages before Chapter 1. By working through these pages, you will explore the mathematical concepts that citizens of the twenty-first century will need to understand.

Getting Started
A Getting Started section begins each chapter. This section reviews the mathematics that you will need to use in the chapter.

Mental Math
The Mental Math column in each Getting Started section includes a strategy for completing mental math calculations.

Problem Solving
The numerous ways in which problem solving is integrated throughout the book are described on pages xiv–xv.

Technology
Each chapter includes from one to four Technology sections. These sections allow you to explore the use of graphing calculators, geometry software, spreadsheets, and the Internet to solve problems. The use of technology is also integrated into many numbered sections and feature pages. The graphing calculator displays were generated using a TI-83 or a TI-92 calculator. The geometry software displays were generated using The Geometer's Sketchpad software.

Investigating Math
The explorations in the Investigating Math sections will actively involve you in learning mathematics, either individually or with your classmates.

Connecting Math and ...
Each chapter includes a Connecting Math section. In the explorations, you will apply mathematics to other subject areas, such as zoology, business, history, and astronomy.

Computer Data Bank
The Computer Data Bank sections are to be used in conjunction with the MATHPOWER™ 11, Western Edition, Computer Data Bank. In these sections, you will explore the power of a computer database program in solving problems. The explorations in these sections use ClarisWorks 4.0 and 5.0, Microsoft 4.0, and Microsoft Access 97 for Windows 95, and ClarisWorks 4.0 and 5.0 for Macintosh OS 7.0.

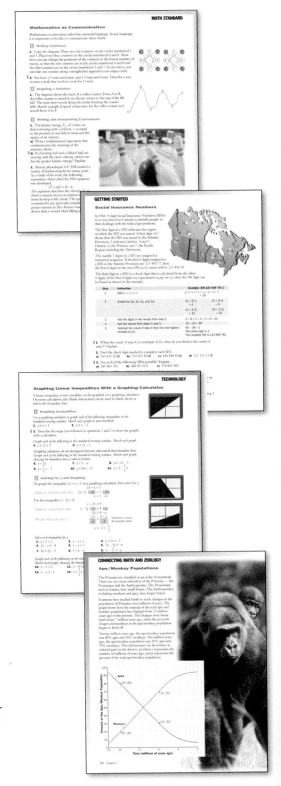

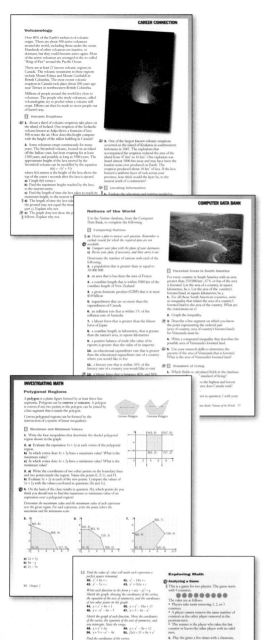

Career Connection

The explorations on the Career Connection pages will show you some applications of mathematics to the world of work.

Review/Chapter Check

Near the end of each chapter are sections headed Review and Chapter Check, which allow you to test your progress. The questions in each Review are keyed to section numbers in the chapter, so that you can identify any sections that require further study.

Exploring Math

At the end of the Review section in each chapter, the Exploring Math column includes an enrichment activity designed as a problem solving challenge.

Cumulative Review

Chapter 4, Chapter 8, and Chapter 9 end with cumulative reviews. The cumulative review at the end of Chapter 4 covers the work you did in Chapters 1–4. The cumulative review at the end of Chapter 8 covers Chapters 5–8, and the cumulative review at the end of Chapter 9 covers Chapters 1–9.

Data Bank

Problems that require the use of the Data Bank on pages 580–589 are included in a Data Bank box at the end of the Problem Solving: Using the Strategies page in each chapter.

Answers

On pages 591–642, there are answers to most of the questions in this book.

Glossary

The illustrated glossary on pages 643–651 explains mathematical terms.

Indexes

The book includes three indexes — an applications index, a technology index, and a general index.

Problem Solving in *MATHPOWER* ™ *11, Western Edition*

In whatever career you choose, and in other parts of your daily life, you will be required to solve problems. An important goal of mathematics education is to help you become a good problem solver.

George Polya was one of the world's best teachers of problem solving. The problem solving model he developed has been adapted for use in this book. The model is a guide. It will help you decide what to do when you "don't know what to do."

The problem solving model has the following four steps.

Understand the Problem

Read the problem and ask yourself these questions.
- What am I asked to find?
- Do I need an exact or approximate answer?
- What information am I given?
- What are the conditions or requirements?
- Is enough information given?
- Is there too much information?
- Have I solved a similar problem?

Think of a Plan

The main challenge in solving a problem is to devise a plan, or an outline of how to proceed. Organize the information and plan how to use it by deciding on a problem solving strategy. The following list of strategies, some of which you have used in previous grades, may help.

- Act out the problem.
- Look for a pattern.
- Work backward.
- Use a formula.
- Use logic.
- Draw and read graphs.
- Make an assumption.
- Guess and check.

- Use manipulatives.
- Solve a simpler problem.
- Use a diagram or flowchart.
- Sequence the operations.
- Use a data bank.
- Change your point of view.
- Use a table or spreadsheet.
- Identify extra information.

Carry Out the Plan

Estimate the answer to the problem. Choose the calculation method you will use to solve the problem. Then, carry out your plan, using paper and pencil, a calculator, a computer, or manipulatives. After solving the problem, write a final statement that gives the solution.

Look Back

Check your calculations in each step of the solution. Then, ask yourself these questions.
- Have I solved the problem I was asked to solve?
- Does the answer seem reasonable?
- Does the answer agree with my estimate?
- Is there another way to solve the problem?

Opportunities for you to develop your problem solving skills appear throughout this book.

In the first three chapters, there are nine numbered problem solving sections. Each section focusses on one strategy. The section provides an example of how the strategy can be used and includes problems that can be solved using the strategy.

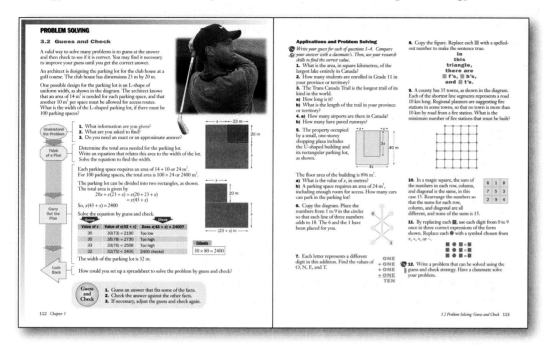

At the end of each chapter, you will find a section headed Problem Solving: Using the Strategies. Each of these sections includes a variety of problems that can be solved using different strategies. The section ends with problems contained in a Data Bank box. To solve the Data Bank problems, you can look up information in the Data Bank on pages 580–589, or you can use a data bank of your choice.

Every numbered section of the book includes the subheading Applications and Problem Solving. The problems under this subheading are related to that section and provide you with many opportunities to apply problem solving strategies.

Many numbered sections include Power Problems, which have been grouped into four types — Logic Power, Pattern Power, Number Power, and Word Power. These problems are challenging and fun.

Further problem solving opportunities are to be found in the Exploring Math columns. Each of these columns allows you to explore challenging mathematical ideas.

As described on pages xii–xiii, many special features in the book involve explorations. These features — including Math Standard, Technology, Investigating Math, Connecting Math, Computer Data Bank, and Career Connection sections — are filled with opportunities for you to refine your problem solving skills.

MATH STANDARD

Mathematics as Problem Solving

Solving problems in any career field follows a similar process to solving problems in mathematics. Practice in solving a variety of mathematics problems throughout this book will help you improve your problem solving ability.

1 Solving Problems

1. A school's debating team consists of four females and four males. The team captain is a female. The team is entered in a regional competition. However, each school is allowed to send only six team members, three males and three females, to the competition. The team captain must be among the members who compete. All other members are equally qualified to compete. How many possible combinations of members could make up the team that competes?

2. a) Copy and complete the square with numbers that will make it a magic square.

b) If columns two and four are interchanged, will the square still be a magic square? Explain your reasoning.

c) In your completed magic square, find pairs of numbers that add to 26. Describe the relationship between the positions of the pairs of numbers that add to 26.

17	24	1		15
		7	14	
4		13		22
	12	19	21	3
11	18		2	

3. You have a 5-L container and a 9-L container and plenty of water. You want exactly 6 L of water in the 9-L container. How can you use the two containers to measure exactly 6 L of water?

4. A cube is 20 cm on an edge.
a) How can you cut the cube into six identical pyramids?
b) What are the dimensions of each pyramid?

5. The sum of the numbers of sides of two convex polygons is 11, and the sum of the numbers of their diagonals is 14. Name the two types of polygons.

6. Twelve toothpicks are used to make a figure with 6 congruent regions, as shown. If one more toothpick is added, how can the toothpicks be rearranged to make another figure with 6 congruent regions?

Mathematics as Communication

Mathematics is sometimes called the universal language. In any language, it is important to be able to communicate ideas clearly.

1 Writing Solutions

1. Copy the diagram. Place two red counters on the circles numbered 1 and 3. Place two blue counters on the circles numbered 6 and 8. Show how you can change the positions of the counters in the fewest number of moves, so that the red counters are in the circles numbered 6 and 8 and the blue counters are in the circles numbered 1 and 3. In one move, you can take one counter along a straight line segment to an empty circle.

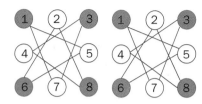

2. You have a 5-min sand timer and a 9-min sand timer. Describe a way to time a steak that needs to cook for 13 min.

2 Graphing a Solution

1. The diagram shows the track of a roller coaster. From A to B, the roller coaster is raised by an electric motor to the top of the lift hill. The train then travels along the tracks forming the coaster hills. Sketch a graph of speed versus time for the roller coaster as it travels from A to F.

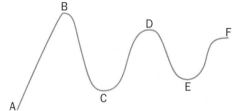

3 Writing and Interpreting Expressions

1. The kinetic energy, E_k, of a mass, m, that is moving with a velocity, v, is equal to the product of one half its mass and the square of its velocity.
a) Write a mathematical expression that communicates the meaning of the sentence above.
b) If a bowling ball and a billiard ball are moving with the same velocity, which one has the greater kinetic energy? Explain.

2. Muscle physiologist A.V. Hill studied a variety of human muscles for many years. As a result of his work, the following expression, often called the Hill equation, was developed.

$$(T + a)(V + b) = k$$

The equation describes the velocity, V, at which a muscle moves in relation to the tension, T, that the muscle must develop to lift a load. The symbols a, b, and k represent constants for any particular muscle. If a muscle must develop a greater tension to lift a heavier load, will the muscle move faster or slower than it would when lifting a lighter load?

MATH STANDARD

Mathematics as Reasoning

Every day you encounter problems, large and small, that require logical reasoning to solve. This book will help you increase your ability to reason logically.

1 Using Logic

1. Three nickels and three dimes are placed in three boxes so that there are two coins in each box. The total number of cents in each box is written on the top of the box. However, the tops of the boxes have been switched so that no box is labelled correctly.

Each box has a slot at the bottom so that, when you shake the box, one coin rolls out of the box. What is the minimum number of coins you must shake out of the boxes to determine the exact contents of each box?

2. Four people, one of whom was known to have won a lottery, made the following statements when questioned by a reporter.
Sofia: "Paolo won it."
Paolo: "Jeff won it."
Melissa: "I didn't win it."
Jeff: "Paolo lied when he said I won it."
a) If only one of the four statements is true, who won the lottery?
b) If only one of the four statements is false, who won the lottery?

2 Solving Problems

1. Adrienne's father is three times as old as Adrienne. In fifteen years, Adrienne's father will be twice as old as Adrienne. How old are Adrienne and her father now?

2. You have 17 coins in your pocket. They are all either dimes or quarters. If you have a total of $3.20, how many dimes and quarters do you have?

3. Jaleen is eleven years old, and her height is 155 cm. Her brother, Jamal, is eight years old, and his height is 149 cm. If Jaleen grows 2 cm a year and Jamal grows 3 cm a year, how old will each person be when they are both the same height?

Mathematical Connections

Mathematical connections can be found in such diverse fields as science, the arts, and sports. This book will explore many of these connections.

1 Animal Physiology

Animal physiologists have measured the average energy requirements of various mammals. The daily energy requirements and the body masses of some mammals are listed in the table.

Mammal	Average Body Mass (kg)	Average Daily Energy Requirements (kJ/day)
Mouse	0.0214	13.2
Guinea pig	0.451	144.4
Rabbit	2.37	422.7
Monkey	4.05	792.4
Chimpanzee	34.6	4 185.5
Human	58.5	4 897.1
Pig	122	5 148.2
Horse	440	7 785.1
Elephant	3620	61 526.9

1. Use the data in the table to calculate the average amount of energy per kilogram of body mass that each mammal uses.

2. How do you know from question 1 that the amount of energy required by a mammal does not depend only on its body mass?

3. What factors other than body mass might affect the energy requirements of a particular mammal?

2 Human Physiology

Physiologists can monitor heart rate and oxygen consumption while a person walks on a treadmill. During one treadmill test, the following results were obtained.

Heart Rate (beats/min)	Oxygen Consumption (L/min)
60	0.47
80	0.75
100	0.92
120	1.30
140	1.69
160	1.95

a) Plot the data on a scatter plot.

b) Describe the relationship between heart rate and oxygen consumption. Does the relationship appear to be linear?

c) Predict the oxygen consumption when the heart rate is 95 beats/min; 180 beats/min.

d) Predict the heart rate when the oxygen consumption is 1.2 L/min.

MATH STANDARD

Algebra

Much of the language of mathematics is algebra.

1 Writing and Evaluating Expressions

1. In 1996, the Royal Canadian Mint issued a sterling silver dollar to commemorate the discovery of the McIntosh apple, in 1811, by John McIntosh in Dundela, Ontario. The McIntosh apple is now grown in British Columbia, Ontario, Quebec, New Brunswick, Nova Scotia, and parts of the United States. The mass of the McIntosh silver dollar is 2.825 g less than 4 times the mass of a loonie.
a) Write an expression to represent the mass of the McIntosh silver dollar in terms of the mass of a loonie.
b) If the mass of a loonie is 7 g, what is the mass of the McIntosh silver dollar?
c) How much greater is the mass of a $25-roll of McIntosh dollars than the mass of a $25-roll of loonies?

2. The West Edmonton Mall houses an NHL-size ice arena called the Ice Palace. The approximate dimensions of the arena can be represented by the expressions $x + 6$ and $3x - 2$.
a) Write and expand an expression for the approximate area of the arena.
b) If x represents 20 m, what is the area of the arena?

3. a) Write and simplify an expression to represent the area of the shaded region.
b) If y represents 2 m, find the area of the shaded region.

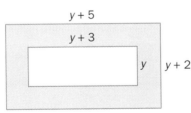

2 Simplifying Expressions

Simplify.

1. $\dfrac{6x + 2y}{9x + 3y}$

2. $\dfrac{x^2 - 25}{x^2 + 8x + 15}$

3. $\dfrac{2p^2 - 3p - 2}{3p^2 - 5p - 2}$

4. $\dfrac{x^2 - 9}{x^2 + 2x + 1} \times \dfrac{x^2 - x - 2}{x^2 - 4x + 3}$

5. $\dfrac{3a^2 - 5a - 2}{2a^2 + a - 1} \div \dfrac{3a^2 - 11a - 4}{2a^2 - 5a + 2}$

6. $\dfrac{3}{x^2 + 3x + 2} + \dfrac{2}{x^2 + 4x + 3}$

Functions

Functions are used to study relationships. Mathematical relationships often can be found using patterns.

1 Using Relationships

1. The fastest land animal in Canada is the pronghorn, found in the Prairies. The distance a pronghorn runs in a certain length of time is related to its speed. A pronghorn's speed can reach 95 km/h in short bursts.
a) Write an expression that shows the relationship between the distance travelled in a length of time and the speed.
b) What distance would a pronghorn, running at top speed, travel in 20 s? 1 min? 2.5 min? Express your answers to the nearest tenth of a metre.

2. The time, t seconds, it takes for an object to fall from a height of h metres is given by the following relationship.
$$t = \sqrt{h \div 4.9}$$
Hunlen Falls, in British Columbia, has a vertical drop of 253 m. How long would it take an object to fall this distance, to the nearest tenth of a second?

2 Using Patterns

1. The horizontal blue line through the red curve divides the curve into a maximum of 6 parts. Two horizontal lines divide the curve into a maximum of 11 parts.
a) How many parts will n horizontal lines produce?
b) How many parts will 150 horizontal lines produce?
c) How many horizontal lines are needed to produce 116 parts?

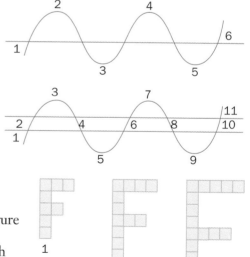

2. Each F-figure is made from squares of side 1 unit.
a) How many squares are in the 4th figure? 5th figure?
b) Write an expression for the number of squares in the nth figure in terms of n.
c) How many squares are in the 25th figure? 48th figure? 112th figure?

3. a) What is the perimeter of the 4th figure? 5th figure?
b) Write an expression for the perimeter of the nth figure in terms of n.
c) What is the perimeter of the 19th figure? 35th figure? 104th figure?

4. a) Write an expression for the perimeter in terms of the number of squares, s.
b) What is the perimeter of the figure with 84 squares? 148 squares?

MATH STANDARD

Geometry From a Synthetic Perspective

Geometry is the study of two-dimensional and three-dimensional shapes, their properties and relationships. The ability to see an object in two dimensions and picture it in your mind in three-dimensions is an advantage in such fields as art and architecture.

1 Folding a Net

Each of these two nets can be folded to form a cube. If you place each cube on a table with a blank face down and rotate the cube, the word CUBE is spelled out.

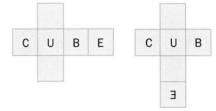

Copy each of the following nets. Write one of the letters C, U, B, and E on each of four faces, so that, when each net is folded into a cube and placed on a table, as in the examples above, the word CUBE is spelled out.

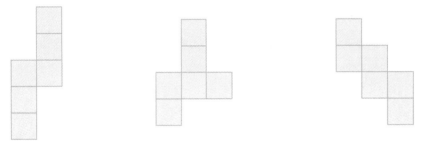

2 Architectural Models

Architects sometimes build models of a building or a group of buildings they are designing. It is important to know how a structure will appear from every angle. The stack of blocks represents a simple architectural model.

1. Draw an accurate view of the model from the right side.

2. Draw an accurate view of the model from the front.

3. Draw an accurate view of the model from the left side.

4. Draw an accurate view of the model from above. Since only the top cube of each column is shown in this view, write the total number of cubes in each column on your diagram.

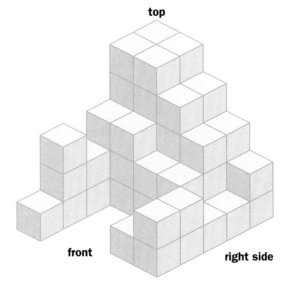

Geometry From an Algebraic Perspective

Applying algebraic transformations to simple
geometric figures makes geometry more dynamic.
Many problems can be solved by understanding
the connections between geometry and algebra.

1 Transforming a Triangle

$\triangle ABC$ has vertices
A(1, 3), B(4, 1), and
C(5, 4).

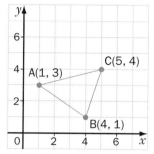

1. a) Use the
mapping
$(x, y) \rightarrow (-x, y)$ to
draw the image of
$\triangle ABC$, $\triangle A'B'C'$.
b) Write the
equation of the
reflection line that maps $\triangle ABC$ onto $\triangle A'B'C'$.

2. a) Use the mapping $(x, y) \rightarrow (x, -y)$ to draw
the image of $\triangle ABC$, $\triangle A''B''C''$.

b) Write the equation of the reflection line that maps $\triangle ABC$ onto $\triangle A''B''C''$.

3. a) Use the mapping $(x, y) \rightarrow (y, x)$ to draw the image of $\triangle ABC$, $\triangle A'''B'''C'''$.
b) Write the equation of the reflection line that maps $\triangle ABC$ onto $\triangle A'''B'''C'''$.

4. a) Use the mapping $(x, y) \rightarrow (y, -x)$ to draw the image of $\triangle ABC$, $\triangle A''''B''''C''''$.
b) Name the transformation that maps $\triangle ABC$ onto $\triangle A''''B''''C''''$.

2 Transforming a Non-Linear Relation

The graph of the non-linear relation $y = x^2 - 4$ is shown.

x	y
−3	5
−2	0
−1	−3
0	−4
1	−3
2	0
3	5

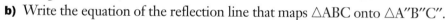

1. Copy the graph onto grid paper.

2. On the same set of axes, draw the image of $y = x^2 - 4$ after a reflection in the x-axis.

3. On the same set of axes, draw the image of $y = x^2 - 4$ after a rotation of $90°$
clockwise about the origin.

4. On the same set of axes, draw the image of $y = x^2 - 4$ after a rotation of $90°$
counterclockwise about the origin.

MATH STANDARD

Trigonometry

Trigonometry can be used to solve a wide variety of problems involving angles and triangles in many disciplines, including surveying and navigation.

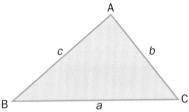

The three primary trigonometric ratios are

$$\sin A = \frac{\text{opposite}}{\text{hypotenuse}}$$

$$\cos A = \frac{\text{adjacent}}{\text{hypotenuse}}$$

$$\tan A = \frac{\text{opposite}}{\text{adjacent}}$$

The Law of Sines states that

$$\frac{\sin A}{a} = \frac{\sin B}{b} = \frac{\sin C}{c} \quad \text{or} \quad \frac{a}{\sin A} = \frac{b}{\sin B} = \frac{c}{\sin C}$$

The Law of Cosines states that

$$a^2 = b^2 + c^2 - 2bc \cos A$$
$$\text{or } b^2 = a^2 + c^2 - 2ac \cos B$$
$$\text{or } c^2 = a^2 + b^2 - 2ab \cos C$$

1 Finding Sides and Angles

1. Find x.

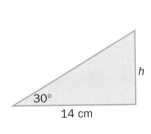

2. Find the length of the equal sides of the isosceles triangle.

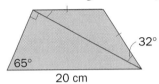

3. If you double the length of side h, will angle θ be double the original angle?

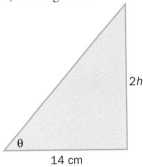

2 Problem Solving

1. During a night flight, the pilot of an aircraft saw the lights of a large city directly ahead and at an angle of depression of 14°. Exactly 1.5 min later, the pilot noticed that the same city lights were at an angle of depression of 22°. What was the altitude of the plane, to the nearest metre, if it was flying at a steady speed of 600 km/h?

2. Two hotels are located on the same side of a river. The hotels are on the bank of the river and are 2400 m apart. Across the river is the dock for two ferries to bring tourists to the hotels. The angles made by the riverbank and the lines drawn from the hotels to the dock, D, are shown.
a) How far is each hotel from the dock, to the nearest metre?
b) What is the width of this part of the river, to the nearest metre?

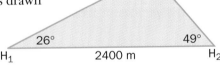

Statistics

Data in various forms reach us every day of our lives. It is important to be able to interpret the data correctly before making decisions.

1 Selecting Tires

Statistical analyses were done on the lifetimes of tires from two different tire manufacturers. The data shown in the table were collected.

Tires	Average Lifetime	Percent That Wear Out Before 80 000 km
Ajax	100 000 km	20%
Baron	90 000 km	5%

1. Which tires would you purchase?

2. Give reasons for your choice.

2 Purchasing Supplies

In a survey of 150 people, 30 said that they usually purchased popcorn when they went to a movie.

1. The manager of a theatre complex studied data from numbers of people attending four different, recent movies. From the data, the manager concluded that, at the next showing, the staff should expect 200 people for the movie in theatre one, 180 people in theatre two, 225 people in theatre three, and 175 people in theatre four. How many people should the staff expect to buy popcorn?

2. What additional data might help the manager make better decisions about purchasing and preparing popcorn?

3 Comparing Climates

Environment Canada has been collecting data on temperature and precipitation for many years. The bar graphs show the average temperature and amount of precipitation for each month of the year in several cities across Canada.

1. Which city has the greatest difference in average monthly temperatures? the least difference?

2. In which city does the amount of precipitation from month to month vary the most? the least?

3. In which city might an avid golfer choose to live? Why?

4. In which city might someone who loved to ski choose to live? Why?

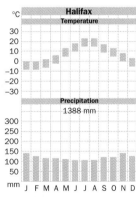

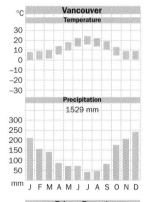

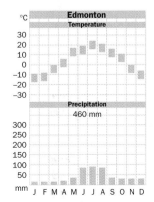

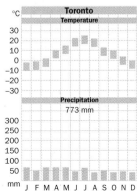

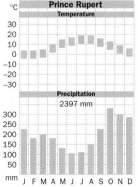

Probability

Probability is the mathematics of chance. Using probability, you can predict outcomes of events. Probability is frequently used in predicting the weather and evaluating risks involved in making investments.

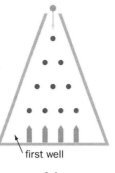

first well

1 Rolling Marbles

The marble game shown illustrates chance.
A marble is dropped through an opening at the top of the game. When the marble reaches each peg, there is an equal chance that it will go to the right or to the left.

1. How many paths lead into
a) the first well?
b) the second well?
c) the third well?
d) the fourth well?
e) the fifth well?

2. If you rolled 32 marbles into the opening of the game, how many would you expect to find in
a) the first well?
b) the second well?
c) the third well?
d) the fourth well?
e) the fifth well?

2 Rolling Dice

The tables show the outcomes when a regular pair of dice is rolled and when an irregular pair of dice is rolled.

Regular Dice

	⚀	⚁	⚂	⚃	⚄	⚅
⚀	2	3	4	5	6	7
⚁	3	4	5	6	7	8
⚂	4	5	6	7	8	9
⚃	5	6	7	8	9	10
⚄	6	7	8	9	10	11
⚅	7	8	9	10	11	12

Irregular Dice

	⚀	⚁	⚂	⚂	⚃	⚄
⚀	2	3	3	4	4	5
⚂	4	5	5	6	6	7
⚃	5	6	6	7	7	8
⚄	6	7	7	8	8	9
⚅	7	8	8	9	9	10
⚅	9	10	10	11	11	12

1. For each pair of dice, what is the probability of rolling 2? 3? 4? 5? 6? 7? 8? 9? 10? 11? 12?

2. What is the probability of rolling a double with each pair of dice?

Discrete Mathematics

The fundamental counting principle can help you determine the number of possible outcomes for a wide variety of situations. The principle states that, if there are m ways to make a first choice and n ways to make a second choice, then the number of ways to make both choices together is $m \times n$.

For example, to find the total number of two-digit numbers, multiply the number of possible choices for the first digit, of which there are 9, by the number of possible choices for the second digit, of which there are 10. The total number of two-digit numbers is 9×10 or 90.

1 Telephone Numbers

For many years, certain restrictions were placed on the digits that could be used in telephone numbers within Canada and the United States. These restrictions are illustrated here.

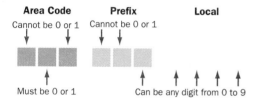

Area Code
Cannot be 0 or 1

Prefix
Cannot be 0 or 1

Local

Must be 0 or 1

Can be any digit from 0 to 9

1. Use these restrictions to answer the following questions.
a) What was the maximum number of area codes possible?
b) What was the maximum number of prefixes possible within one area code?
c) What was the maximum number of locals possible within one prefix?
d) What was the maximum number of telephone numbers possible within any one area code?
e) What was the maximum number of telephone numbers possible within Canada and the United States?

2. In recent years, some of the restrictions have been removed in certain regions of the two countries. Why? Use your research skills to find examples that illustrate these changes.

2 Selecting People

A club has 5 members: Aziz, Brenda, Eric, Justine, and Mala.
1. In how many ways is it possible to select a president and a treasurer?

2. In how many ways is it possible to select two people to attend a conference?

MATH STANDARD

Investigating Limits

Calculus is the mathematics of limits. Many problems in many fields of study, such as physics, chemistry, biology, and economics, can be solved by finding limiting values using calculus. The following activities will help you understand the concept of limits.

1 Finding the Value of a Function

Consider the function, $f(x) = \dfrac{x-3}{x^2 - 4x + 3}$.

1. Find $f(2)$ and $f(4)$.

2. Why is it not possible to find $f(3)$ by substituting $x = 3$ into $f(x)$?

3. Although you cannot find the exact value of the function when $x = 3$ by substitution, you can find the limiting value of the function as x approaches, or gets closer and closer, to 3. One way to find the limiting value is to substitute several values for x that are very close to 3. Copy and complete the tables by substituting the given values of x into the function. Use a calculator and record at least five decimal places.

x	f(x)	x	f(x)
2.5		3.5	
2.7		3.3	
2.9		3.1	
2.99		3.01	
2.999		3.001	

4. As x gets closer and closer to 3, what value does $f(x)$ approach?

5. State your answer to question 4 in mathematical terms by completing the following statement.

The limit of f(x) as x approaches 3 is ■.

6. Rewrite your answer to question 5 as a mathematical expression by filling in the blank.

$$\lim_{x \to 3} \frac{x-3}{x^2 - 4x + 3} = ■$$

8. Set up a table of values to find each of the following limits.

a) $\displaystyle\lim_{x \to 2} \frac{x^2 - 4}{x - 2} = ■$ **b)** $\displaystyle\lim_{x \to 1} \frac{x^2 - 4x + 3}{x - 1} = ■$

Mathematical Structure

The properties of numbers form an important component of mathematical structure. These properties help to tie all the strands of mathematics together.

1 **Investigating a Five-by-Five Grid**

1. Copy the following grid.

1	2	3	4	5
6	7	8	9	10
11	12	13	14	15
16	17	18	19	20
21	22	23	24	25

2. Choose any number in the first row and circle it. Then, cross out all the numbers in the same column below the circled number.

3. Circle any one of the remaining numbers in the second row. Then, cross out all the numbers in the same column above and below the circled number. Repeat this process for the third and fourth rows.

4. Circle the remaining number in the fifth row and cross out all the numbers in the same column above the circled number.

5. Add the five circled numbers and record the result.

6. Repeat steps 1 to 5 by circling a different number in the first row. How does the sum of the circled numbers compare with your result from step 5?

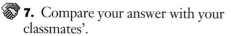 **7.** Compare your answer with your classmates'.

2 **Investigating Other Grids**

1. Repeat the steps above using the 6-by-6 grid shown.

2. What is the sum of the circled numbers?

3. What is the sum of the circled numbers on a 4-by-4 grid? a 3-by-3 grid?

3 **Explaining Results**

1. Choose one of the grids you used and explain why the sum of the circled numbers is always the same number.

1	2	3	4	5	6
7	8	9	10	11	12
13	14	15	16	17	18
19	20	21	22	23	24
25	26	27	28	29	30
31	32	33	34	35	36

Systems of Equations

T he World Heritage Committee of the United Nations Educational, Scientific, and Cultural Organization (UNESCO) has compiled a list of natural and cultural wonders. These World Heritage Sites are so significant that responsibility for their protection belongs not just to their home countries, but to the world. Some of these sites are the Pyramids, the Great Wall of China, and the Galapagos Islands.

Canada has heritage sites west of the Saskatchewan-Alberta border and east of the Ontario-Quebec border. If w represents the number of western sites, and e represents the number of eastern sites, the following equations show how the numbers of sites are related.

$$w + e = 12$$
$$w - 2e = 0$$

1. a) Use guess and check to find one value of w and one value of e that make both equations true. Express your answer as an ordered pair of the form (w, e).

b) How many of Canada's heritage sites are western sites? eastern sites?

2. a) Plot e versus w for the equation $w + e = 12$ and for the equation $w - 2e = 0$ on the same set of axes.

b) Find the coordinates of the point at which the two lines cross.

3. Compare the ordered pairs from questions 1a) and 2b).

4. Use your research skills to list Canada's heritage sites. Describe the location of each.

GETTING STARTED

Social Insurance Numbers

In 1964, 9-digit Social Insurance Numbers (SINs) were introduced in Canada to identify people in their dealings with the federal government.

The first digit in a SIN indicates the region in which the SIN was issued. A first digit of 1 shows that the SIN was issued in the Atlantic Provinces, 2 indicates Quebec, 4 and 5, Ontario, 6, the Prairies, and 7, the Pacific Region including the Territories.

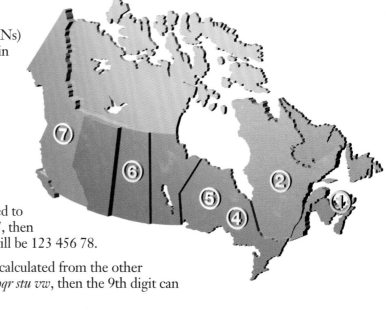

The middle 7 digits in a SIN are assigned in numerical sequence. If the first 8 digits assigned to a SIN in the Atlantic Provinces are 123 456 77, then the first 8 digits in the next SIN to be issued will be 123 456 78.

The final digit in a SIN is a check digit that is calculated from the other 8 digits. If the first 8 digits are represented as *pqr stu vw*, then the 9th digit can be found as shown in the example.

Step	Instruction	Example: SIN 123 456 78▇
1	Add $p + r + t + v$.	$p + r + t + v = 1 + 3 + 5 + 7$ $= 16$
2	Determine $2q$, $2s$, $2u$, and $2w$.	$2q = 2(2)$　　　　$2s = 2(4)$ $= 4$　　　　　　$= 8$ $2u = 2(6)$　　　$2w = 2(8)$ $= 12$　　　　　$= 16$
3	Add the digits in the results from step 2.	$4 + 8 + 1 + 2 + 1 + 6 = 22$
4	Add the results from steps 1 and 3.	$16 + 22 = 38$
5	Subtract the result of step 4 from the next highest multiple of 10.	$40 - 38 = 2$ The check digit is 2. The complete SIN is 123 456 782.

1. When the result of step 4 is a multiple of 10, what do you think is the result of step 5? Explain.

2. Find the check digit needed to complete each SIN.
a) 765 432 10▇　　**b)** 234 567 89▇　　**c)** 444 444 44▇　　**d)** 111 111 11▇

3. Are each of the following SINs possible? Explain.
a) 285 461 783　　**b)** 466 013 653　　**c)** 354 821 902

4. Devise a SIN in which the check digit is 7; 0.

5. If the number that results from step 4 of the example is represented by $10n + m$, the subtraction in step 5 can be represented by expression $10(n + 1) - (10n + m)$.
a) Simplify $10(n + 1) - (10n + m)$.
b) When the check digit is 0, what is the value of *m*? Explain.
c) Use the results from parts a) and b) to suggest a second way of completing step 5.

Warm Up

Simplify.
1. $3x + 2(1 - x)$
2. $4(x + 2) - 2x$
3. $2y - (5 - y)$
4. $-3(a - 1) - 2a$

Simplify.
5. $(2x + 3y) + (4x - 3y)$
6. $(3c - 4d) - (5c - 4d)$
7. $3(x + 2y) - 2(x + 3y)$
8. $5m - 2n + 5(n - m)$
9. $2x + y - z - (x - y - z)$
10. $p - 2q + 3r + 2(p + q - 2r)$

Solve.
11. $x + 3 = 11$
12. $c - 3 = -1$
13. $\dfrac{y}{3} = -2$
14. $2z = -10$
15. $6x - 1 = 11$
16. $\dfrac{m}{4} - 1 = 2$
17. $2(y + 3) = 5$
18. $4x - 2 = 2x + 1$
19. $\dfrac{t-1}{3} = 5 - t$
20. $\dfrac{2y+1}{3} = \dfrac{y-1}{2}$
21. $\dfrac{x}{2} + \dfrac{1}{3} = -\dfrac{1}{2}$
22. $2.5x + 6.4 = -3.6$
23. $3(x + 3) = -2(2x - 1)$
24. $0.2(4n + 1) = 0.5(n - 2)$

Solve for x.
25. $x + 3y = 11$
26. $5y - x = 8$
27. $x - 2y + 4 = 0$
28. $0.1x - 0.2y = 0.4$

Solve for y.
29. $2x + y = 3$
30. $x - y = 2$
31. $2x + 4y = -1$
32. $3x - 2y = 4$

Graph using a table of values.
33. $x + y = 5$
34. $y = 3x - 2$
35. $y = -x + 3$
36. $2x - y = 4$

Graph using the intercepts.
37. $x + y = 7$
38. $x - y = 4$
39. $2x + y = 8$
40. $3x - 2y = 6$

Graph using the slope and y-intercept.
41. $y = x - 2$
42. $y = -x + 1$
43. $y = 2x$
44. $y = -2x + 3$

Mental Math

Evaluating Expressions

Evaluate for $x = 3$ and $y = -2$.
1. $2x + y$
2. $3x + 4y$
3. $y - x$
4. $2x - 3y$
5. $x + 2y + 4$
6. $3x - 2y - 5$

Evaluate for $x = 2$, $y = 4$, and $z = -3$.
7. $x + y + 2z$
8. $2x - y - z$
9. $3x + y + 4z$
10. $y + z - x$
11. $x + 3y - 2z$
12. $4x - 2y + 3z$

Multiplying Special Pairs of Numbers

Suppose you want to multiply two 2-digit numbers whose first digits are the same and whose second digits add to 10. For 47×43, multiply 4 by the next whole number, 5. Then, affix the product of 7 and 3.
$4 \times 5 = 20$
$7 \times 3 = 21$
So, $47 \times 43 = 2021$

Estimate
$50 \times 40 = 2000$

Calculate.
1. 42×48
2. 83×87
3. 56×54
4. 71×79
5. 18×12
6. 65^2

To calculate 5.2×5.8 or 520×580, multiply 52 and 58. Then, place the decimal point.
$52 \times 58 = 3016$
So, $5.2 \times 5.8 = 30.16$
and $520 \times 580 = 301\,600$

Estimate
$500 \times 600 = 300\,000$

Calculate.
7. 3.4×3.6
8. 7.5^2
9. 2.2×2.8
10. 490×410
11. 970×930
12. 620×680

13. The following expressions represent two numbers whose first digits are the same and whose second digits add to 10.
$$10n + x \text{ and } 10n + 10 - x$$
a) Expand and simplify $(10n + x)(10n + 10 - x)$.
b) Explain why the rule for multiplying special pairs of numbers works.

INVESTIGATING MATH

Exploring Ordered Pairs and Solutions

1 Ordered Pairs and One Equation

An infinite number of ordered pairs satisfy the equation $3x + y = 7$. To see if the ordered pair $(-1, 10)$ satisfies the equation, substitute the values for x and y in the equation.

For $3x + y = 7$,
L.S. $= 3x + y$ R.S. $= 7$
    $= 3(-1) + 10$
    $= -3 + 10$
    $= 7$
Since L.S. = R.S., $(-1, 10)$ satisfies the equation.

1. Which of the ordered pairs satisfy the equation?
a) $x + y = 14$ $(1, 13), (-3, 12), (24, -10)$
b) $3x + y = 12$ $(-1, 14), (5, -3), (5, 0)$
c) $2x + 5y = -24$ $(-2, -4), (-3, 6), (-12, 0)$
d) $x - y = -1$ $(2, 3), (-1, -2), (-5, 6)$
e) $y = 3x - 4$ $(5, 10), (-2, -10), (-3, -12)$

2. Find the missing element of each ordered pair, so that the ordered pair satisfies the equation.
a) $x + y = 7$ $(4, \blacksquare), (-2, \blacksquare), (\blacksquare, -3), (\blacksquare, 9)$
b) $x - y = 5$ $(7, \blacksquare), (-4, \blacksquare), (\blacksquare, 6), (\blacksquare, -7)$
c) $2x + y = 9$ $(5, \blacksquare), (\blacksquare, -1), (-2, \blacksquare), (\blacksquare, -11)$
d) $y = 3x - 1$ $(2, \blacksquare), (\blacksquare, 8), (\blacksquare, -13), (-2, \blacksquare)$

2 Ordered Pairs and Two Equations

Two equations studied together are called a **system of equations**. The following is a system of equations.
$$x - y = 4$$
$$3x + 2y = 7$$

The solution to a system of equations is an ordered pair, or a set of ordered pairs, that satisfies both equations.
To check that the ordered pair $(3, -1)$ satisfies both equations, substitute the values for x and y in each equation.

For $x - y = 4$,
L.S. $= x - y$ R.S. $= 4$
  $= 3 - (-1)$
  $= 3 + 1$
  $= 4$
    L.S. = R.S.

For $3x + 2y = 7$,
L.S. $= 3x + 2y$ R.S. $= 7$
  $= 3(3) + 2(-1)$
  $= 9 - 2$
  $= 7$
    L.S. = R.S.

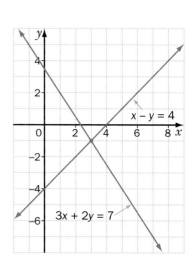

Since $(3, -1)$ satisfies both equations, the solution to the system is $(3, -1)$. The results are shown on the graph. Note that $(3, -1)$ is the only point that lies on both lines.

1. Identify the ordered pair that satisfies both equations.

a) $x + y = 3$ $(0, 3), (1, 2), (2, 1)$
$2x - y = 0$

b) $2x + y = -5$ $(-4, 3), (-8, 11), (-3, 1)$
$x + 5y = 2$

c) $y = 2x - 1$ $(2, 3), (1, 1), (-1, 6)$
$y = -x + 5$

d) $x + y = -2$ $(3, -4), (6, -8), (-7, 5)$
$3x + 2y = 2$

e) $y = \dfrac{1}{2}x - 4$ $(4, -2), (2, -3), (-2, -5)$
$y = 2x - 1$

f) $y = 2x + 15$ $(-4, 7), (7, -4), (-7, 1)$
$2x + y = -1$

2. Copy and complete each ordered pair so that it meets the stated condition.

a) $x + y = 1$ $(4, \blacksquare)$ satisfies the first equation but not the second.
$3x - y = 3$

b) $2x - y = -1$ $(\blacksquare, 3)$ satisfies the second equation but not the first.
$x + 2y = 12$

c) $y = 3x + 3$ $(\blacksquare, 0)$ satisfies both equations.
$y = 2x + 2$

d) $y = 4x - 3$ $(\blacksquare, \blacksquare)$ satisfies neither equation.
$y = -2x + 5$

 **3** **Problem Solving**

1. City elevations The two equations show the relationship between the elevation of Victoria, v metres, and the elevation of Prince Rupert, p metres.
$$v + p = 55$$
$$2v - p = -4$$

a) Find the missing element in the ordered pair $(17, \blacksquare)$, which satisfies both equations and is in the form (v, p).

b) State the elevation of each city.

2. Animal masses The two equations show how the average mass of a Canadian lynx, l kilograms, is related to the average mass of an Arctic wolf, w kilograms.
$$w - l = 24$$
$$2w - 5l = 0$$

a) Find the missing element in the ordered pair $(\blacksquare, 16)$, which satisfies both equations and is in the form (w, l).

b) State the average mass of each animal.

3. a) An infinite number of ordered pairs, including $(0, 1)$, $(1, 0)$, and $(2, -1)$, satisfy both equations. Explain why.
$$x + y = 1$$
$$2x + 2y = 2$$

b) Find two more ordered pairs that satisfy both equations.

4. No ordered pair satisfies both equations. Explain why.
$$y = 2x + 1$$
$$y = 2x + 3$$

1.1 Solving Systems of Linear Equations Graphically

A system of equations consists of two or more equations that are considered together. A solution to a system of equations must satisfy each equation in the system.

Explore: Use a Graph

At the Summer Olympics in Barcelona, Spain, the number of gold medals won by Canadian women, w, and the number of gold medals won by Canadian men, m, were related by the following equations.

$$w + m = 7$$
$$w - m = 1$$

a) Find three ordered pairs that satisfy the equation $w + m = 7$.
b) Plot the ordered pairs on a grid like the one shown and join the points.
c) Repeat steps a) and b) for $w - m = 1$, plotting the points on the same grid.

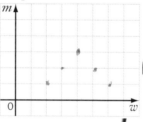

Inquire

1. How many ordered pairs satisfy
a) the equation $w + m = 7$?
b) the equation $w - m = 1$?

2. a) Which ordered pair appears to satisfy both equations?
b) How can you check that the ordered pair satisfies both equations?
c) Check the ordered pair in both equations.

3. How many of Canada's gold medals from Barcelona were won by
a) women?   **b)** men?

4. At the 1984 Summer Olympics in Los Angeles, the number of gold medals won by Canadian women and Canadian men were related by the following equations.

$$w + m = 10$$
$$m - w = 2$$

Use a graph to find the number of gold medals won by
a) Canadian women   **b)** Canadian men

5. Graph each pair of equations and find the coordinates of the point of intersection. Check that the ordered pair satisfies both equations.
a) $y = x + 2$ **b)** $x + y = 5$ **c)** $y = 2x - 3$
   $y = 8 - x$ $x - y = 7$ $y = -x + 6$

When you have found all the ordered pairs that satisfy two equations, such as $y = x + 2$ and $y = 8 - x$, you have solved a system of linear equations. In this section, you will study graphical solutions. Systems of equations can be graphed with a graphing calculator or manually. Manual methods include using tables of values, the intercepts, or the slope and y-intercept form of the equations.

Example 1   Using the Slope and y-Intercept Form ✳

Solve the system of equations graphically.

$$2x + y = 5 \quad (1)$$
$$x - 2y = 10 \quad (2)$$

(1) and (2) are used to name "equation one" and "equation two."

Solution

Write each equation in the slope and y-intercept form.

$$2x + y = 5 \qquad\qquad x - 2y = 10$$
$$y = -2x + 5 \qquad\qquad -2y = -x + 10$$
$$y = \frac{1}{2}x - 5$$

Method 1: Graphing manually

For the equation $y = -2x + 5$, the y-intercept is 5 and the slope is -2. Plot $(0, 5)$ and use the slope or the equation to find two other points, for example, $(-1, 7)$ and $(1, 3)$. Plot these two points and join the three points with a line.

For the equation $y = \frac{1}{2}x - 5$, the y-intercept is -5 and the slope is $\frac{1}{2}$. Plot $(0, -5)$.

Find and plot two other points, for example, $(2, -4)$ and $(-2, -6)$. Join the three points with a line.

The two lines appear to intersect at $(4, -3)$.

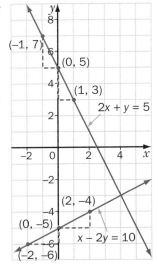

Method 2: Using a graphing calculator

Graph the equations in the standard viewing window.

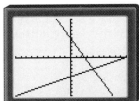

Use the Intersect operation to find the coordinates of the point of intersection.

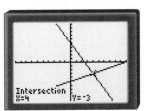

If your calculator does not have the Intersect operation, approximate values of the coordinates of the point of intersection can be found using the TRACE and ZOOM instructions.

The coordinates of the point of intersection appear to be $(4, -3)$.

Check $(4, -3)$ in (1).

L.S. $= 2x + y$ **R.S.** $= 5$
$\quad = 2(4) + (-3)$
$\quad = 8 - 3$
$\quad = 5$
$\qquad$ L.S. = R.S.

Check $(4, -3)$ in (2).

L.S. $= x - 2y$ **R.S.** $= 10$
$\quad = 4 - 2(-3)$
$\quad = 4 + 6$
$\quad = 10$
$\qquad$ L.S. = R.S.

The solution is $(4, -3)$.

Example 2   Using Intercepts

Solve the system of equations graphically.

$$4x + 3y = 12 \quad (1)$$
$$4x - y = 4 \quad (2)$$

Solution

It is convenient to use the intercepts for each equation.
For (1),
when $x = 0$, $y = 4$, so one point is $(0, 4)$;
when $y = 0$, $x = 3$, so another point is $(3, 0)$.
Plot the points and join them.
For (2),
when $x = 0$, $y = -4$, so one point is $(0, -4)$;
when $y = 0$, $x = 1$, so another point is $(1, 0)$.
Plot the points and join them.

The lines appear to intersect at $\left(\dfrac{3}{2}, 2\right)$.

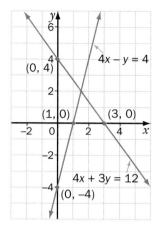

Check in (1).		Check in (2).	
L.S. $= 4x + 3y$	**R.S.** $= 12$	**L.S.** $= 4x - y$	**R.S.** $= 4$

$$\text{L.S.} = 4\left(\frac{3}{2}\right) + 3(2) \qquad\qquad \text{L.S.} = 4\left(\frac{3}{2}\right) - 2$$
$$= 6 + 6 \qquad\qquad\qquad\qquad\quad = 6 - 2$$
$$= 12 \qquad\qquad\qquad\qquad\qquad\quad = 4$$
$$\qquad \text{L.S.} = \text{R.S.} \qquad\qquad\qquad\quad \text{L.S.} = \text{R.S.}$$

The solution is $\left(\dfrac{3}{2}, 2\right)$.

Note that, before $\left(\dfrac{3}{2}, 2\right)$ is checked in Example 2, you do not know that the estimated coordinates of the point of intersection are correct. For example, if the correct x-coordinate was $\dfrac{29}{20}$, you might estimate it as $\dfrac{3}{2}$. A graphing calculator can distinguish between these possibilities.

Solving Example 2 by graphing the slope and y-intercept form in the standard viewing window of a graphing calculator gives the results shown.

The correct x-coordinate of the point of intersection is 1.5 or $\dfrac{3}{2}$. If the correct x-coordinate was $\dfrac{29}{20}$, the graphing calculator would display it as 1.45. However, as Example 3 will show, graphing a system on a graphing calculator does not always give an exact solution.

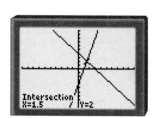

Example 3   Approximate Solutions

Use a graphing calculator to solve the system, to the nearest hundredth.

$$2x + 5y = -20 \quad (1)$$
$$5x - 3y = -15 \quad (2)$$

Solution

Write each equation in the slope and y-intercept form.

$$\begin{aligned} 2x + 5y &= -20 & 5x - 3y &= -15 \\ 5y &= -2x - 20 & -3y &= -5x - 15 \\ y &= -\frac{2}{5}x - 4 & y &= \frac{5}{3}x + 5 \end{aligned}$$

Graph the equations in the standard viewing window. Then, use the Intersect operation, or the TRACE and ZOOM instructions, to determine the approximate coordinates of the point of intersection.

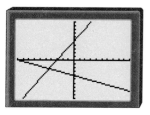 

It is impossible to tell whether the coordinates shown by the graphing calculator for the point of intersection are exact values. The decimals could continue beyond the maximum number of digits that the calculator displays. The solution is $(-4.35, -2.26)$, to the nearest hundredth.

Check in (1).

L.S. $= 2x + 5y$ **R.S.** $= -20$
$\doteq 2(-4.35) + 5(-2.26)$
$= -20$

L.S. $=$ **R.S.**

Check in (2).

L.S. $= 5x - 3y$ **R.S.** $= -15$
$\doteq 5(-4.35) - 3(-2.26)$
$= -14.97$

L.S. $\doteq$ **R.S.**

The check shows that the approximate solution is reasonable.

Note that, in Example 3, the graphs could be drawn manually and an approximate solution found by estimation. However, this method usually gives a less accurate approximation than a graphing calculator.

Example 4   Numbers of Solutions

Graph each system of equations and determine the number of solutions.

a) $y = 2x + 3$ $\quad (1)$ **b)** $x + y = 3$ $\quad (1)$
$\quad\ y = 2x - 4$ $\quad (2)$ $2x + 2y = 6$ $\quad (2)$

Solution

a) For (1), the y-intercept is 3 and the slope is 2. Plot $(0, 3)$. Find and plot another point on the line, for example, $(1, 5)$. For (2), the y-intercept is -4 and the slope is 2. Plot $(0, -4)$. Find and plot another point on the line, for example, $(1, -2)$. The lines are parallel and do not intersect. There is no solution to this system of equations.

Note that the lines have the same slope but different y-intercepts.

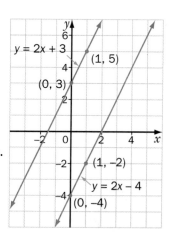

b) Use the intercepts to graph the lines.
For (1), two points are (0, 3) and (3, 0).
For (2), two points are (0, 3) and (3, 0).
The lines coincide. Each equation has the same graph. Two equations that have the same graph are called **equivalent equations**. Any ordered pair on the graph satisfies both equations. This system of equations has an infinite number of solutions.
Note that the lines have the same slope and the same intercepts.

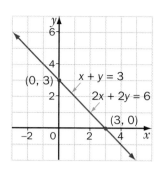

The graphs of two linear equations in two variables may intersect at one point, be parallel, or coincide.

Graphs of Lines	Slopes of Lines	Intercepts	Number of Solutions
Intersecting	Different	Different unless the lines intersect on one axis or at the origin	One
Parallel	Same	Different	None
Coincident	Same	Same	Infinitely many

Example 5 Analyzing Systems

Analyze each system to determine whether the system has one solution, no solution, or infinitely many solutions.

a) $2x + y = 6$ (1)
    $y - 8 = -2x$ (2)

b) $3x + y = 1$ (1)
    $6x + 2y = 2$ (2)

c) $2x + y - 4 = 0$ (1)
    $x + 2y - 6 = 0$ (2)

Solution

Before analyzing each system, express both equations in the form $y = mx + b$.

a) $y = -2x + 6$ (1)
    $y = -2x + 8$ (2)

b) $y = -3x + 1$ (1)
    $y = -3x + 1$ (2)

c) $y = -2x + 4$ (1)
    $y = -\frac{1}{2}x + 3$ (2)

Both lines have a slope of -2. Therefore, the lines are either parallel or they coincide. Since the y-intercepts are different, the lines must be parallel. The system has no solution.

Both lines have the same slope, -3, and the same y-intercept, 1. The two lines coincide. The system has infinitely many solutions.

The slopes of the lines are -2 and $-\frac{1}{2}$. The lines are not parallel and do not coincide. They intersect at a single point. The system has one solution.

Practice

Solve each system by graphing. Check your solutions.

1. $y = x - 4$
$y = 2 - x$

2. $x + y = 5$
$x - y = -7$

3. $x + 2y = 2$
$x + y = 3$

4. $x + 3y = -1$
$2x + 6y + 2 = 0$

5. $2x + y = 12$
$3x - 2y = 18$

6. $2x + y = -2$
$4x = y - 16$

7. $y = 2x - 3$
$2x - y = 5$

8. $2x + y = -5$
$3x - y = -5$

9. $2x - y = 5$
$y = x - 3$

10. $3x + y = -11$
$y = 2x + 4$

11. $3x + 4y - 16 = 0$
$x - 2y - 2 = 0$

12. $3x = y + 8$
$6x - 2y - 1 = 0$

13. $2x + 3y = 7$
$2x - 3y = 13$

14. $y = \frac{1}{2}x + 3$
$x = 2y - 6$

Solve by graphing. Check each solution.

15. $y = 4x$
$y = 2x + 1$

16. $2x - 2y - 1 = 0$
$x - 4y + 4 = 0$

17. $x + 2y = 0$
$x - 2y = -2$

18. $x + y = -1$
$3x - y = 7$

Solve each system, to the nearest tenth.

19. $3x + 2y = 3$
$2x + 10y = -5$

20. $x + 2y = 10$
$x - y = 5$

21. $2x + 3y - 7 = 0$
$3x - 5y - 13 = 0$

22. $y = -0.5x - 1$
$y = 0.25x + 1$

23. $y = 3$
$y = 2.58x - 3$

24. $y = 0.35x + 6.02$
$y = -3.22x - 3.12$

Without graphing, determine whether each system has one solution, no solution, or infinitely many solutions.

25. $2x + y = 5$
$4x + y = 9$

26. $3x - y = 0$
$6x - 2y = 3$

27. $x + y = 2$
$3x = 6 - 3y$

28. $x + 4y = 8$
$y + 2x = 0$

29. $2y = 3x - 1$
$8y - 4 = 12x$

30. $2y - x - 4 = 0$
$3x - 6y - 12 = 0$

Applications and Problem Solving

31. Geography The total number of states in Austria and Germany is 25. Germany has 7 more states than Austria. Solve the following system of equations graphically to find the number of states in each country.

$$a + g = 25$$
$$g = a + 7$$

32. Health clubs Phoenix Health Club charges a $200 initiation fee, plus $15 a month. Champion Health Club charges a $100 initiation fee, plus $20 a month. The costs of belonging to the clubs can be compared using the following equations.

Phoenix Cost: $\quad C = 200 + 15m$
Champion Cost: $\quad C = 100 + 20m$

a) Find the point of intersection of the two lines.
b) After how many months are the costs the same?
c) If you were to join a club for only a year, which club would be less expensive?

33. Nutrition The total mass of vitamin C in one apple and two peaches is 17 mg. The total mass of vitamin C in two apples and one peach is 13 mg. This information can be represented by the following system of equations.

$$a + 2p = 17$$
$$2a + p = 13$$

Graph the system to find the mass, in milligrams, of vitamin C in

a) one apple
b) one peach

34. Wind speeds The following equations relate the average wind speeds, in kilometres per hour, in Montreal and Victoria.

$$m - v = 5$$
$$2m = 3v$$

Solve the system graphically to find the average wind speed in each city.

35. Break-even point For a school reunion, students sell T-shirts. The cost of the T-shirts includes an $800 design and set-up charge plus $4 per T-shirt. The T-shirts sell for $20 each. The cost and the revenue can be represented by the following system of equations.

Dollar Cost: $\quad d = 800 + 4t$
Dollar Revenue: $\quad d = 20t$

a) Solve the system graphically.
b) The solution shows the **break-even point**, at which the cost and revenue are equal. How many T-shirts must the students sell to break even?
c) Suppose the students lose money. How many T-shirts are sold?
d) Suppose the students make a profit. How many T-shirts are sold?

36. Sea otters Sea otters are found along the shores of the North Pacific. Sea otters were almost extinct in 1910, because they had been over-hunted for their fine, silky brown fur. They are now protected by an international treaty. The two main populations of sea otters are along the coasts of California and Northern B.C.-Alaska. If n represents the approximate number of sea otters in the north, and s, the approximate number in the south, the following two equations show how these numbers are related.

$$n + s = 130\ 000$$
$$n = 25s$$

Solve the system of equations to find the approximate number of sea otters in each population.

37. Coordinate geometry The arms of an angle lie on the lines $y = \frac{2}{3}x + 7$ and $3x + 2y = -12$. What are the coordinates of the vertex of the angle?

38. Coordinate geometry The three lines $y = \frac{1}{3}x - 2$, $x - y = 4$, and $x + 3y = 4$ intersect to form a triangle. What are the coordinates of the vertices of the triangle?

39. Geometry Name the type of quadrilateral formed when the lines $x - y = -3$, $y = x - 2$, $y = -\frac{1}{2}x + 5$, and $x + 2y + 12 = 0$ intersect.

40. Inequalities Graph the equation $y = 2x + 3$. Use the graph to find three points that satisfy each of the following inequalities.
a) $y < 2x + 3$ **b)** $y > 2x + 3$

41. Write an equation that forms a system of equations with $x + y = 4$, so that the system has
a) no solution
b) infinitely many solutions
c) one solution

42. Solve each system by graphing.
a) $y = |x| + 2$ **b)** $y = x^2 - 1$
 $y = 2x - 1$ $y = x + 1$

43. Internet rates An Internet service provider offers three plans to its customers. The rates are as shown in the graph.

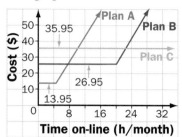

Interpret the graph to describe when each plan is
a) the least expensive **b)** the most expensive

44. Write a system of equations that has the point $(3, 2)$ as
a) the only solution
b) one of infinitely many solutions

45. If $(0, 3)$ and $(2, 4)$ are both solutions to a system of two linear equations, does the system have any other solutions? Explain.

46. Sketch a graph to represent a system of two equations with one solution, so that the two lines have
a) different x-intercepts and different y-intercepts
b) the same x-intercept but different y-intercepts
c) different x-intercepts but the same y-intercept
d) the same x-intercept and the same y-intercept

47. Technology For many systems solved graphically using a graphing calculator, the point of intersection does not fall within the standard viewing window.
a) Solve each of the following systems using a graphing calculator.
$y = -2x - 16$ $\quad$ $y = x - 24$ $\quad$ $y = x - 2$
$y = 4x + 59$ $\quad$ $y = -2x + 120$ $\quad$ $y = \frac{x}{2} - 10$

b) Describe how you found suitable values for the window variables in each case.
c) Compare your answers to part b) with those of your classmates.

Using the Databases

Use the *Vehicles, Nations, Craters, Olympics,* and *Parks* databases, from the Computer Data Bank, to complete the following.

a) *Devise a plan to answer each question. Remember to exclude records for which the required data are not available.*
b) *Compare your plan with the plans of your classmates.*
c) *Revise your plan, if necessary, and then carry it out.*

1 Seating Capacity of New Vehicles

1. How many vehicles seat more than 5 people?

2. Which type of vehicle occurs most frequently among the vehicles found in question 1?

3. Which of the vehicles found in question 1 is
a) the longest?   **b)** the lightest?
c) the most fuel efficient for city driving?
d) the least fuel efficient for highway driving?

2 Nations Around the World

1. Each nation is classified by the government type that best describes it. Fourteen government types are used, plus Other. How many nations have the same government type as
a) Canada?   **b)** Greenland?   **c)** China?

2. On which continent is each of the following government types most common?
a) constitutional monarchy   **b)** monarchy
c) transitional   **d)** military

3. Which of the six continents has the greatest variety of government types? the least variety? How many types are there for each of these two continents?

4. What is the average inflation rate for the nations in Europe?

5. Gross domestic product (GDP) measures the value of all goods and services produced in a nation. What is the average GDP for the nations in Africa?

6. Which continent has the greatest difference in literacy rates between the nations with the highest and the lowest literacy rates? What is the difference?

3 Locating Craters on Earth

1. On which continent is
a) the crater Teague?
b) the crater with the greatest diameter?
c) the oldest crater?
d) the crater with the highest rim?
e) the crater with the greatest difference between true and apparent depth?
f) the greatest number of craters that do not have both central peak dimensions available?

2. a) How many craters are on each continent?
b) Display the results of part a) in a graph.

4 Summer Olympics

1. Graph the winning distance by year for an event of your choice.

2. Write three questions for classmates to answer about your graph.

5 Camping in Western Canada

1. Which has more campsites and how many more — all the provincial parks in British Columbia or all the national parks in British Columbia?

2. Make the following assumptions about the national parks.
• All the parks have the same season — June 1 to September 30.
• The average daily occupancy rate for each park is 80% of campsites.
• The average daily charge per campsite for each park is $18.
What is the total campsite revenue for a season from the national parks in each province? from the national parks in all four provinces?

PROBLEM SOLVING

1.2 Use a Diagram

Diagrams provide insights that help you solve many problems. The following problem has been adapted from a two-thousand-year-old Chinese mathematics book called the *Chiu chang suan-shu*.

A tree trunk has a height of 20 m and a circumference of 3 m. An arrowroot vine winds seven times around the tree and reaches the top of the trunk. What is the length of the vine?

Understand the Problem

1. What information are you given?
2. What are you asked to find?
3. Do you need an exact or an approximate answer?

Think of a Plan

The vine winds seven times around the tree. Let the foot of the vine be fixed, and imagine that the tree is rotated seven times to the right along the ground. As the tree rotates, the vine unwinds. If the tree is perpendicular to the ground, the vine becomes the hypotenuse of a right triangle formed with the ground and the tree trunk. Find the length of the hypotenuse of the triangle.

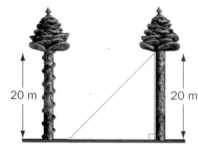

20 m   20 m

Carry Out the Plan

Let v metres represent the length of the vine. The circumference of the tree is 3 m. Each time the tree rotates, it moves 3 m along the ground. In seven rotations, the tree will move 7×3 or 21 m. Use the Pythagorean Theorem in the right triangle.

$v^2 = 21^2 + 20^2$
$\quad = 441 + 400$
$\quad = 841$
$v = \sqrt{841}$
$\quad = 29$

Estimate

$\boxed{\sqrt{900} = 30}$

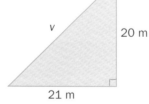

v 20 m

21 m

The length of the vine is 29 m.

Look Back

Does the answer seem reasonable?

Use a Diagram

1. Draw a diagram to represent the situation.
2. Use the diagram to solve the problem.
3. Check that the answer is reasonable.

Applications and Problem Solving

1. A staircase winds around the outside of a fire observation tower that is 60 m high. The diameter of the tower is 1.6 m, and the stairs wind around it 6 times. What is the length of the stairs, to the nearest metre?

2. If a 30 m long vine winds 5 times around a 22 m high tree trunk to reach the top, what is the radius of the trunk, to the nearest centimetre?

3. A train 100 m long travels at a speed of 90 km/h through a tunnel that is 400 m long. How much time, in seconds, does the train take to pass completely through the tunnel?

4. Three members of the Bold political party and three members of the Timid political party must cross a river in a boat that holds only two people at a time. Only one of the Timids and one of the Bolds know how to swim. For safety reasons, at least one of the swimmers must be in the boat each time it crosses the river. When there are Bolds and Timids on the same side of the river, the Bolds can never outnumber the Timids. How do the six people get across the river?

5. Two trains, each having an engine and 40 cars, are approaching each other on a single track from opposite directions. The track has a siding, as shown in the diagram. The siding can hold 20 cars and one engine. Engines can push or pull cars from either end. How can the trains pass each other?

6. The length and width of the floor of a room are each 10 m. The height of the room is 3 m. A spider, on the floor in a corner, sees a fly on the ceiling in the corner diagonally opposite. If the fly does not move, what is the shortest distance the spider can travel to reach the fly, to the nearest tenth of a metre?

7. A point P is inside rectangle ABCD. The length of PA is 5 cm, PB is 4 cm, and PC is 3 cm. Find the length of PD.

8. The coordinates of the endpoints of one diagonal of a square are (8, 11) and (4, 5). What are the coordinates of the endpoints of the other diagonal?

9. Each small square on a 2 by 2 grid must be painted red, black, or white. How many different ways of colouring are there, if rotations are not allowed?

10. A point P, in the plane of an equilateral triangle, is 4 cm, 6 cm, and 9 cm from the vertices of the triangle. What is the side length of the triangle?

11. The cube was made from 8 identical smaller cubes. One cube has been removed from one corner. Sketch the shape you would see if you looked at the shape along the diagonal from the missing corner D toward the opposite corner E.

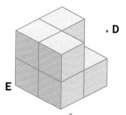

12. The toothpicks are arranged to make 5 identical squares.

Move 3 toothpicks to make 4 identical squares.

13. One patrol boat leaves the north shore of a lake at the same time as another patrol boat leaves the south shore of the lake. Each travels at a constant speed. The boats meet 500 m from the north shore. Each boat continues to the shore opposite where it started, and then turns around and heads back. The boats meet for the second time 200 m from the south shore. Find the distance across the lake from the north shore to the south shore.

14. Write a problem that can be solved using a diagram. Have a classmate solve your problem.

INVESTIGATING MATH

Translating Words Into Equations

Problem solving often involves the introduction of variables and the translation of information from words into equations.

1 Expressions in Two Variables

1. Numbers Let x represent the larger of two numbers and y the smaller. Write algebraic expressions for
a) the sum of the numbers
b) six times the larger plus two times the smaller
c) the larger subtracted from five times the smaller

2. Flying speed A plane flies at x kilometres per hour in still air. The wind speed is y kilometres per hour. Write algebraic expressions for the speed of the plane when it is flying
a) into the wind   **b)** with the wind

3. Fitness centre A fitness centre charges an initiation fee of $\$x$, plus a monthly charge of $\$y$. Write algebraic expressions to show how much it costs to be a member for
a) 7 months   **b)** 15 months

4. Swim meet Tickets to a college swim meet cost $10 for general admission and $5 for students. There were x general admission tickets and y student tickets sold. Write algebraic expressions for
a) the total number of tickets sold
b) the revenue, in dollars, from the general admission tickets
c) the revenue, in dollars, from the student tickets
d) the total revenue from all the tickets

5. Money Write algebraic expressions to show the value of x dimes and y quarters
a) in pennies   **b)** in dollars

6. Investments Traci invested $\$x$ at 7% and $\$y$ at 6%. Write algebraic expressions for
a) the total amount of money Traci invested
b) the interest Traci earned at 7% in one year
c) the interest Traci earned at 6% in one year
d) the total interest Traci earned in one year

2 Equations in Two Variables

Write an equation to describe each relation.

1.

x	y
2	6
5	3
−1	9

2.

x	y
9	4
−3	−8
2	−3

3.

x	y
3	8
4	15
5	24

4.

x	y
5	3
7	4
9	5

Introduce variables and translate each statement into an equation in two variables.

5. Basketball The sum of the length and the width of a basketball court is 40 m.

6. Supreme Court The difference between the total number of judges appointed to the Supreme Court of Canada and the number appointed from Quebec is 6.

7. Prime Ministers Indira Gandhi was the Prime Minister of India for 7 years less than twice the number of years that Margaret Thatcher was the Prime Minister of Great Britain.

8. Department store In a department that sells bicycles and tricycles, the total number of wheels is 61.

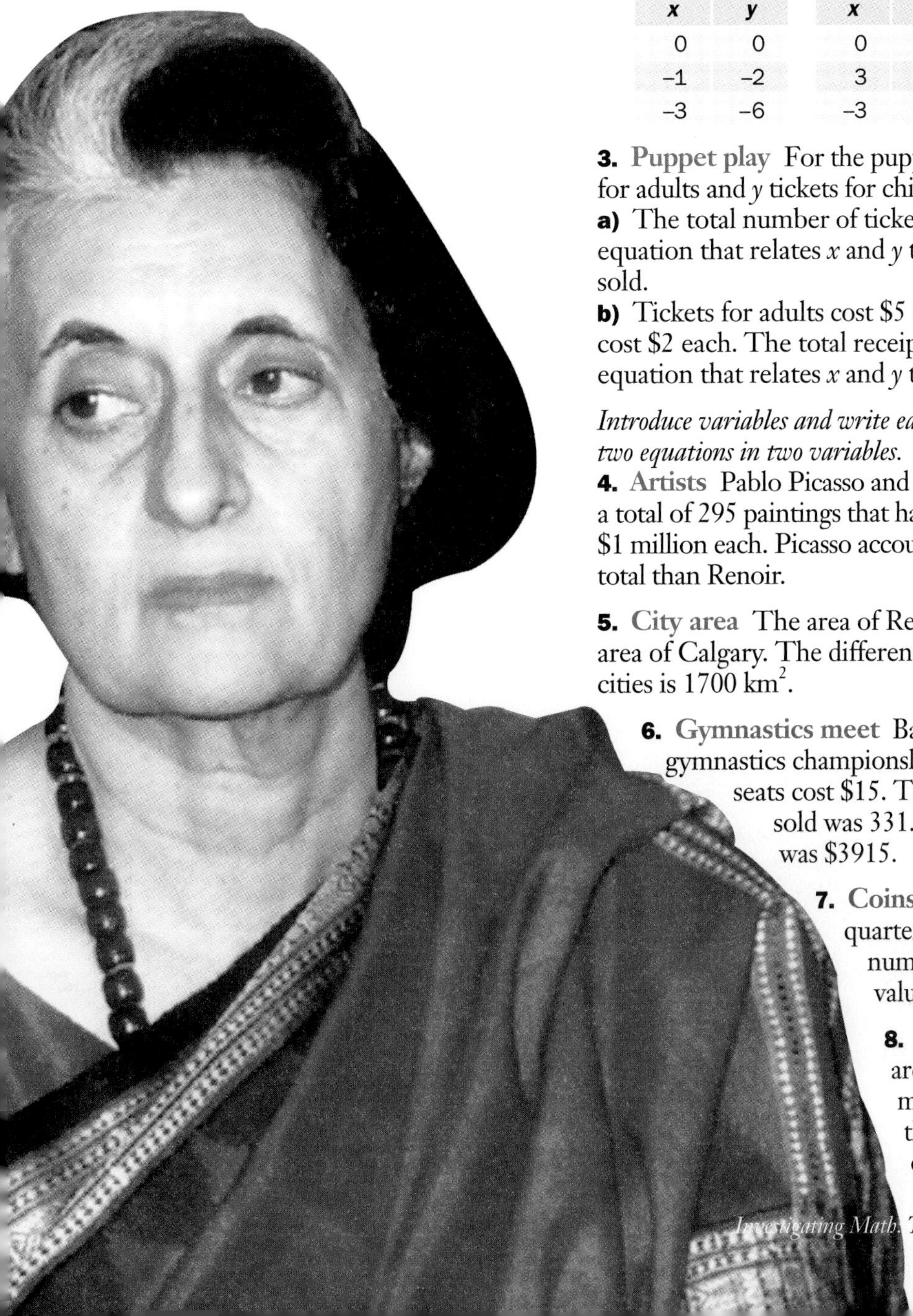

Write a system of equations for each pair of relations.

1.

x	y
2	5
-1	8
-2	9

x	y
2	-1
8	5
9	6

2.

x	y
0	0
-1	-2
-3	-6

x	y
0	-4
3	-1
-3	-7

3. Puppet play For the puppet play at the library, x tickets for adults and y tickets for children were sold.

a) The total number of tickets sold was 256. Write an equation that relates x and y to the total number of tickets sold.

b) Tickets for adults cost $5 each and tickets for children cost $2 each. The total receipts were $767. Write an equation that relates x and y to the total receipts.

Introduce variables and write each of the following as a system of two equations in two variables.

4. Artists Pablo Picasso and Auguste Renoir produced a total of 295 paintings that have sold for more than $1 million each. Picasso accounted for 11 more of this total than Renoir.

5. City area The area of Regina is two thirds of the area of Calgary. The difference in the areas of the two cities is 1700 km².

6. Gymnastics meet Balcony seats for the gymnastics championships cost $10, and floor-level seats cost $15. The total number of tickets sold was 331. The total revenue from sales was $3915.

7. Coins A newspaper box contains quarters and loonies. The total number of coins is 73. The total value of the coins is $37.

8. Measurement Two angles are supplementary. The measure of one angle is 4° less than three times the measure of the other angle.

INVESTIGATING MATH

Algebra Tiles and Substitution

Recall the meanings
of these algebra tiles.

1   **Representing Equations**

Write the equation represented by each balance scale.

1.   **2.**   **3.**

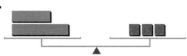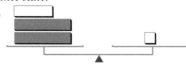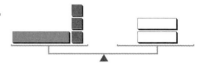

Use algebra tiles or a sketch to model each equation.
4. $x - y = -2$ **5.** $2x + 3y = 1$ **6.** $3y = 2 - x$

2   **Representing Systems of Equations**

For a system of equations, each equation is represented using a different balance scale.

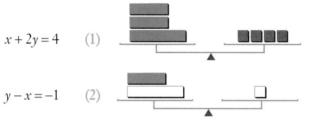

$x + 2y = 4$ (1)

$y - x = -1$ (2)

Use algebra tiles or sketches to model each system.
1. $x + y = -2$ **2.** $y - x = 3$ **3.** $2x = y - 2$
     $x - 2y = 1$ $3y + x = 5$ $3x = 2 - y$

3   **Solving Systems by Substitution, I**

Recall that zero can be represented by
two like quantities with opposite signs.
Each pair shown represents zero.
The balance scales represent a system
of equations, which can be solved by
substitution as shown.

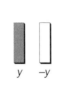

1   −1   x   −x   y   −y

 $3x + 2y = -1$ (1)

 $x = 1$ (2)

Since the variable x is already isolated in (2), use tiles to substitute 1
for x on the first balance scale.

 $3(1) + 2y = -1$
                        $3 + 2y = -1$

Isolate the variable y by adding three -1-tiles to each side.

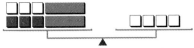

$$3 + 2y \boxed{+ (-3)} = -1 \boxed{+ (-3)}$$
$$3 + 2y - 3 = -1 - 3$$

Remove zero pairs.

$$2y = -4$$

Group tiles to show the value of the variable.

$$\frac{2y}{2} = \frac{-4}{2}$$

Show the result.

$$y = -2$$

So, the solution to the system is $(1, -2)$.

Use algebra tiles or sketches to solve each system.

1. $x + y = 3$ **2.** $2x - y = -1$ **3.** $x + 3y = 0$ **4.** $y = 2x - 2$
$\quad\ y = -1$ $\qquad\quad x = 1$ $\qquad\qquad x = -3$ $\qquad\quad y = 2$

4 Solving Systems by Substitution, II

The balance scales represent a system of equations.

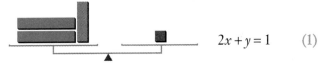

$$2x + y = 1 \qquad (1)$$

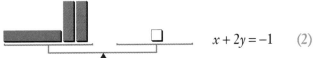

$$x + 2y = -1 \qquad (2)$$

To solve the system by substitution, first isolate a variable with a coefficient of 1.
In this case, you could solve (1) for y or solve (2) for x.
To solve (1) for y, isolate y by adding two $-x$-tiles to each side.

$$2x + y \boxed{+ (-2x)} = 1 \boxed{+ (-2x)}$$
$$2x + y - 2x = 1 - 2x$$

Remove zero pairs.

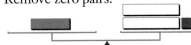

$$y = 1 - 2x$$

Investigating Math: Algebra Tiles and Substitution 19

Now, use tiles to substitute $1 - 2x$ for y in (2).

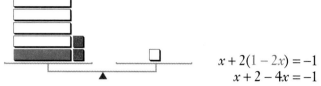

$$x + 2(1 - 2x) = -1$$
$$x + 2 - 4x = -1$$

Simplify by removing the zero pair from the left side.

$$-3x + 2 = -1$$

To isolate the variable x, first add three x-tiles to each side.

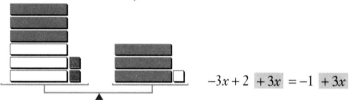

$$-3x + 2 \boxed{+ 3x} = -1 \boxed{+ 3x}$$

Remove zero pairs.

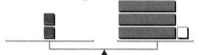

$$2 = -1 + 3x$$

Next, add one 1-tile to each side.

$$2 \boxed{+1} = -1 + 3x \boxed{+1}$$

Remove zero pairs.

$$3 = 3x$$

Group tiles to show the value of the variable.

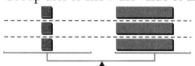

$$\frac{3}{3} = \frac{3x}{3}$$

Show the result.

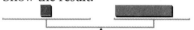

$$1 = x$$

So, $x = 1$. To find y, use tiles to substitute 1 for x in either (1) or (2). The result is $y = -1$. The solution to the system is $(1, -1)$.

Use algebra tiles or sketches to solve each system.

1. $x - 2y = 0$
  $2x + y = 5$

2. $x + y = 1$
  $x - y = 3$

3. $x - y = 1$
  $x - 2y = 2$

4. $x + 2y = 1$
  $2x - y = 2$

1.3 Solving Systems of Linear Equations by Substitution

The Siberian tiger and the Amur leopard are in danger of becoming extinct. Both animals are found in the Russian Far East. Two main reasons for their plight are poaching and the destruction of their habitat. Scientists and environmental groups are working to save the animals.

Explore: Use the Equations

Let t represent the approximate number of Siberian tigers that remain, and l, the approximate number of Amur leopards. The following equations show how the numbers of tigers and leopards are related.

$$t - 15l = 0 \qquad (1)$$
$$t + l = 480 \qquad (2)$$

 Describe in words the relationship shown by each equation.

Inquire

1. Use (1) to write an expression for t in terms of l.

2. a) What equation results when the expression from question 1 is substituted in (2)?
b) Solve the equation.

3. a) How can the value of the second variable be found?
 b) Find it.

4. What ordered pair satisfies the system of equations?

5. a) Use (2) to write an expression for one variable in terms of the other.
b) Substitute the expression from part a) in (1). Solve the resulting equation.
c) Find the value of the second variable.
d) Is the resulting ordered pair the same as in question 4?

6. What are the approximate numbers of
a) Siberian tigers?　　**b)** Amur leopards?

7. Solve each of the following systems of equations by substitution.
a) $2x - y = 0$　**b)** $x - 4y = 4$　**c)** $2x + y = 2$
　　$x + y = 15$　　　$x + 2y = 10$　　$3x + 2y = 1$

Solving a system of two equations in two variables by substitution involves solving one equation for one variable in terms of the other variable, and then substituting to create a third equation in one variable.

Example 1   Solving by Substitution

Solve. $x + 4y = 6$ (1)
$\quad\quad\,\, 2x - 3y = 1$ (2)

Solution

Since the coefficient of x in (1) is 1, solve (1) for x.
$$x + 4y = 6$$
$$x = 6 - 4y$$

At the point of intersection of the two lines, x must have the same value in both equations.

Substitute the expression $6 - 4y$ for x in (2).
$$2x - 3y = 1$$

Substitute: $2(6 - 4y) - 3y = 1$
Expand: $12 - 8y - 3y = 1$
Simplify: $-11y = -11$
$$y = 1$$

Substitute $y = 1$ in (2).
$$2x - 3y = 1$$
$$2x - 3(1) = 1$$
$$2x - 3 = 1$$
$$2x = 4$$
$$x = 2$$

The solution can be visualized graphically.

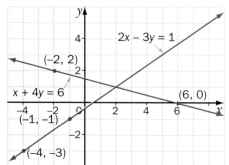

Check in (1).

L.S. $= x + 4y$ **R.S.** $= 6$
$\quad\,\, = 2 + 4(1)$
$\quad\,\, = 2 + 4$
$\quad\,\, = 6$
$\quad\quad\,$ L.S. = R.S.

Check in (2).

L.S. $= 2x - 3y$ **R.S.** $= 1$
$\quad\,\, = 2(2) - 3(1)$
$\quad\,\, = 4 - 3$
$\quad\,\, = 1$
$\quad\quad\,$ L.S. = R.S.

The solution is (2, 1).

When the coordinates of the point of intersection of two lines are not integers, it can be difficult to find the exact solution from a graph. Exact solutions can be found algebraically.

Example 2 Finding Exact Solutions

Solve.
$$5x - 3y - 2 = 0 \qquad (1)$$
$$7x + y = 0 \qquad (2)$$

Solution

The coefficient of y in (2) is 1.

Solve for y in (2).
$$7x + y = 0$$
$$y = -7x$$

Substitute for y in (1).

Write (1): $\qquad 5x - 3y - 2 = 0$

Substitute: $5x - 3(-7x) - 2 = 0$

Expand: $\qquad 5x + 21x - 2 = 0$

Simplify: $\qquad 26x - 2 = 0$

$$x = \frac{2}{26} \text{ or } \frac{1}{13}$$

Substitute $\frac{1}{13}$ for x in either of the original equations to find the value of y.

Substituting in (2) gives

$$7x + y = 0$$
$$7\left(\frac{1}{13}\right) + y = 0$$
$$\frac{7}{13} + y = 0$$
$$y = -\frac{7}{13}$$

Check in (1).

L.S. $= 5x - 3y - 2$ $\qquad$ **R.S.** $= 0$

$$= 5\left(\frac{1}{13}\right) - 3\left(-\frac{7}{13}\right) - 2$$
$$= \frac{5}{13} + \frac{21}{13} - 2$$
$$= \frac{26}{13} - 2$$
$$= 2 - 2$$
$$= 0$$

$\qquad$ L.S. = R.S.

Check in (2).

L.S. $= 7x + y$ $\qquad$ **R.S.** $= 0$

$$= 7\left(\frac{1}{13}\right) + \left(-\frac{7}{13}\right)$$
$$= \frac{7}{13} - \frac{7}{13}$$
$$= 0$$

$\qquad$ L.S. = R.S.

The solution is $\left(\frac{1}{13}, -\frac{7}{13}\right)$.

If a graphing calculator is used to solve Example 2, it is not clear that the coordinates of the point of intersection are exactly $\left(\frac{1}{13}, -\frac{7}{13}\right)$.

Graphing manually and estimating the solution from the graph is unlikely to give an accurate answer.

Example 3   Investing Money

Marie had $40 000 to invest. She invested part of it in bonds paying 4.2% per annum and the remainder in a second mortgage paying 6% per annum. If the total interest after one year was $1950, how much did Marie invest at each rate?

Solution

Let a represent the money invested at 4.2%.
Let b represent the money invested at 6%.

Using a table is helpful.

	Marie's Investments		
	at 4.2%	at 6%	Total
Money Invested ($)	a	b	40 000
Interest Earned ($)	0.042a	0.06b	1 950

Write the system of equations.
Money invested: $a + b = 40\ 000$ (1)
Interest earned: $0.042a + 0.06b = 1950$ (2)

Use substitution to solve the system.
From (1), $a + b = 40\ 000$
So $a = 40\ 000 - b$
Substitute for a in (2).
Write (2): $0.042a + 0.06b = 1950$
Substitute: $0.042(40\ 000 - b) + 0.06b = 1950$
Expand: $1680 - 0.042b + 0.06b = 1950$
Simplify: $1680 + 0.018b = 1950$
$$0.018b = 270$$
$$b = \frac{270}{0.018}$$
$$b = 15\ 000$$

Estimate

$300 \div 0.02 = 15\ 000$

Substitute for b in (1).
$$a + b = 40\ 000$$
$$a + 15\ 000 = 40\ 000$$
$$a = 25\ 000$$
Marie invested $25 000 at 4.2% and $15 000 at 6%.

Check, using the facts given in the problem.

Marie invested $40 000.
$$\$25\ 000 + \$15\ 000 = \$40\ 000$$

The investments earned $1950 in interest.
$$\$25\ 000 \times 0.042 + \$15\ 000 \times 0.06 = \$1950$$

Example 4   Mixing Solutions

A chemistry teacher needs to make 10 L of 42% sulfuric acid solution. The acid solutions available are 30% sulfuric acid and 50% sulfuric acid, by volume. How many litres of each solution must be mixed to make the 42% solution?

Solution

Let x represent the number of litres of 30% sulfuric acid solution.
Let y represent the number of litres of 50% sulfuric acid solution.

Organize the information in a table.

	Acid Solutions		
	30% acid	50% acid	42% acid
Volume of Solution (L)	x	y	10
Volume of Pure Acid (L)	0.3x	0.5y	0.42(10)

Write the system of equations.

| Solution: | $x + y = 10$ | (1) |
| Pure acid: | $0.3x + 0.5y = 4.2$ | (2) |

Solve the system by substitution.
From (1), $x + y = 10$
So $y = 10 - x$
Substitute for y in (2).

Write (2):	$0.3x + 0.5y = 4.2$
Substitute:	$0.3x + 0.5(10 - x) = 4.2$
Expand:	$0.3x + 5 - 0.5x = 4.2$
Simplify:	$5 - 0.2x = 4.2$
	$-0.2x = -0.8$
	$x = 4$

Substitute for x in (1).
$$x + y = 10$$
$$4 + y = 10$$
$$y = 6$$

So, 4 L of the 30% solution and 6 L of the 50% solution must be mixed to make the 42% solution.

Check against the given facts.

The total volume of 42% solution must be 10 L.
$$4 + 6 = 10$$

The 42% solution must contain 0.42(10) or 4.2 L of pure acid.
$$0.3(4) + 0.5(6) = 4.2$$

Practice

Solve each equation for x.

1. $x + 3y = 8$
2. $4y + x + 13 = 0$
3. $7y - x = -7$
4. $2y - x - 1 = 0$

Solve each equation for y.

5. $6x + y = 11$
6. $5x + y + 9 = 0$
7. $x - y = -2$
8. $3x - y + 4 = 0$

Solve each system of equations by substitution. Check each solution.

9. $x - y = 1$
$3x + y = 11$

10. $2x - y = 13$
$x + 2y = -6$

11. $3a + 4b = 15$
$a + b = 5$

12. $2x + 3y = 5$
$x - 4y = -14$

13. $2c - d + 2 = 0$
$3c + 2d + 10 = 0$

14. $4x - y = 3$
$6x - 2y = 5$

15. $a + 4b = 3$
$5b = -2a + 3$

16. $3e - f - 2 = 0$
$5e + 2f = 3$

17. $2x - 5y = 12$
$x + 10y = -9$

18. $x - 2y = 5$
$2x - 3y = 6$

19. $2r - s = 2$
$3r - 2s = 3$

20. $x + 3y = 0$
$3x - 6y = 5$

21. $5 = 2y - x$
$7 = 3y - 2x$

22. $x + 7y = 1$
$3x - 14y = -7$

23. $y = \dfrac{1}{2}x + 3$
$y = 5 - x$

24. $3x - 2y = -12$
$x - 4y = 8$

Applications and Problem Solving

25. Solve each system of equations by graphing and by substitution. Which method do you prefer? Why?

a) $x + y = 6$
$x - y = 42$

b) $2x + y = -4$
$4x + 3y = -6$

c) $2x + y = 5$
$2y = 2x + 1$

d) $6y + 3x = -4$
$x - 2y = -2$

26. Try to solve each system by substitution. Then, analyze each system to decide how many solutions it has. Describe how the number of solutions is related to the results when you try to solve by substitution.

a) $x - 4y = 8$
$2x - 8y = 8$

b) $y = 5 - 2x$
$3x = 2y + 11$

c) $x + y - 4 = 0$
$2x = 8 - 2y$

d) $x + y + 6 = 0$
$2x - y - 3 = 0$

e) $6x = 3y + 2$
$y - 2x + 4 = 0$

f) $y = 3x - 2$
$9x - 3y - 6 = 0$

27. Highest points The highest point in British Columbia, f metres above sea level, is on Fairweather Mountain. The highest point in Manitoba, b metres above sea level, is on Baldy Mountain. The heights are related by the following system of equations.

$$f - b = 3831$$
$$f = 6b - 329$$

a) Interpret each equation in words.
b) Solve the system of equations to find the height of each mountain.

28. Measurement Find the values of x and y.

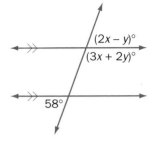

29. Simplify each system, and then solve it by substitution. Check each solution.

a) $2(x - 4) + y = 6$
$3x - 2(y - 3) = 13$

b) $2(x - 1) - 3(y - 3) = 0$
$3(x + 2) - (y - 7) = 20$

c) $2(3x - 1) - (y + 4) = -7$
$4(1 - 2x) - 3(3 - y) = -12$

30. Numbers The sum of two numbers is 752, and their difference is 174. What are the two numbers?

31. Measurement The rectangle has an area of m square units and a perimeter of $2m$ units. What is the value of x?

32. Bridge construction The longest cable suspension bridge in the world is the Akashi Kaikyo Bridge in Japan. It has one long span and two short spans. Each short span is half the length of the long span. The total length of the bridge is 3560 m. What is the length of each span?

33. Service calls ABC Plumbing charges $70 for a service call, plus $50/h for the time worked. Quality Plumbers charges $52 for a service call, plus $54/h. Describe the situations in which each company is cheaper.

34. Canadian birds The total number of species of owls and pigeons that raise their young in Canada is 17. Subtracting one from five times the number of species of pigeons gives the number of species of owls. Find the number of species of each bird that raise their young in Canada.

35. Measurement One of the acute angles in a right triangle measures 6° more than three times the other acute angle. What is the measure of each acute angle?

36. Theatre tickets The receipts from 550 people attending a play were $9184. The tickets cost $20 for adults and $12 for students. Find the numbers of adult tickets and student tickets sold.

37. Investing money Hakim invested $15 000. He put part of it in a term deposit that paid 4% per annum, and the remainder in a treasury bill that paid 5% per annum. After one year, the total interest was $690. How much did Hakim invest at each rate?

38. Driving distances Portage la Prairie is between Winnipeg and Brandon along the Trans-Canada Highway. The driving distance from Winnipeg to Brandon is 216 km. The distance from Portage la Prairie to Brandon is 36 km less than twice the distance from Winnipeg to Portage la Prairie. Find the distance from
a) Winnipeg to Portage la Prairie
b) Portage la Prairie to Brandon

39. Typing *Macbeth* It has been said that, given an infinite amount of time, a chimpanzee could eventually type the complete works of Shakespeare. For the play *Macbeth*, it has been calculated that a chimpanzee typing at a speed of 1 key/s would take x years to type the word "Macbet" and y years to type the word "Macbeth." The total time to type both words would be 348 years. The time to type "Macbeth" would be 28 times as long as than the time to type "Macbet." How many years would it take to type each word?

40. Vinegar solutions White vinegar is a solution of acetic acid in water. There are two strengths of white vinegar — a 5% solution and a 10% solution. How many millilitres of each solution must be mixed to make 50 mL of a 9% vinegar solution?

41. Gold jewellery Pure, or 24-carat, gold is very soft, so it is rarely used for jewellery. Most gold jewellery contains a certain percent of gold, mixed with cheaper metals that make it harder. Suppose a jewellery maker has some 18-carat gold, which contains 75% gold, and some 9-carat gold, which contains 37.5% gold. What mass of each should the jewellery maker melt and mix to make 150 g of 15-carat gold, which contains 62.5% gold?

42. Acid solutions What volume, in millilitres, of a 60% hydrochloric acid solution must be added to 100 mL of a 30% hydrochloric acid solution to make a 36% hydrochloric acid solution?

43. Road trips From his home in Banff, Dan drove to Jasper at an average speed of 75 km/h. From her home in Canmore, Ashley drove through Banff to Jasper at an average speed of 85 km/h. The distance from Canmore to Banff is 18 km. If Dan and Ashley left home at the same time,
a) after what length of time did Ashley overtake Dan?
b) how far were they from Banff when Ashley overtook Dan?

44. Fencing The sport of fencing has three main forms: sabre, foil, and épée. Sabre bouts take place within a rectangle of perimeter 52 m. Decide whether the perimeter and each of the following pieces of information are sufficient to allow you to find the dimensions of the rectangle. Explain your reasoning.
a) The sum of the length and the width is 26 m.
b) The length is twelve times the width.

45. Numbers The sum of the digits in a two-digit whole number is 14. The whole number is 8.5 times the ones digit. What is the whole number?

46. Three variables Use substitution to solve each system of equations. Write each solution as an ordered triple, (x, y, z).
a) $x + y + z = 3$
$y = 4x$
$z = -2x$

b) $2x - 3y + z = 10$
$x + 2z = 8$
$y + 4z = 11$

47. What value of m gives a system with no solution?
$$x(m - 1) - y + 6 = 0$$
$$2x + y - 3 = 0$$

48. What value of n gives a system with an infinite number of solutions?
$$2x - 4y - 4 = 0$$
$$y + 1 = nx$$

49. Write expressions for two numbers whose sum is q and whose difference is r.

PROBLEM SOLVING

1.4 Use a Data Bank

To solve some problems, you will need to retrieve information from a data bank.

An airline's operating cost for a flight depends on the type of aircraft used. Two measures of an aircraft's cost efficiency are:
• the cost of flying 1 km, or the operating cost per kilometre
• the cost of flying a passenger 1 km, or the cost per passenger-kilometre

A DC-10-10 flies 286 passengers from Vancouver to Winnipeg. Find
a) the total operating cost   **b)** the cost per kilometre   **c)** the cost per passenger-kilometre

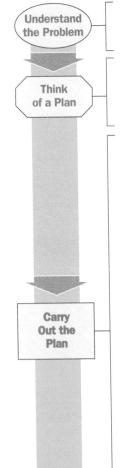

Understand the Problem
1. What information are you given?
2. What are you asked to find?
3. Do you need an exact or an approximate answer?

Think of a Plan
The total operating cost can be found from the number of hours the flight takes and the hourly cost of operating the plane. The measures of cost efficiency can then be found using the total operating cost, the distance flown, and the number of passengers.

Carry Out the Plan

a) A DC-10-10 flies 1862 km from Vancouver to Winnipeg at 801 km/h.

$$\text{Flying time} = \frac{\text{distance flown}}{\text{speed}}$$
$$= \frac{1862}{801}$$
$$\doteq 2.32$$

Estimate
$2000 \div 1000 = 2$

The flying time is about 2.32 h.
The hourly operating cost of a DC-10-10 is $7274/h.
Total operating cost = flying time × cost/hour
$$= 2.32 \times 7274$$
$$\doteq 16\ 876$$

Estimate
$2.5 \times 7000 = 17\ 500$

The total operating cost is about $16 876.

b) $\text{Cost per kilometre} = \dfrac{\text{total cost}}{\text{distance flown}}$
$$= \frac{16\ 876}{1862}$$
$$\doteq 9.06$$

Estimate
$16\ 000 \div 2000 = 8$

The operating cost per kilometre is about $9.06/km.

c) $\text{Cost per passenger-kilometre} = \dfrac{\text{operating cost per kilometre}}{\text{number of passengers}}$
$$= \frac{9.06}{286}$$
$$\doteq 0.032$$

Estimate
$9 \div 300 = 0.03$

The cost per passenger-kilometre is about $0.032.

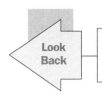

Look Back

Do the answers seem reasonable?
For the trip from Vancouver to Winnipeg, how does the cost of carrying one passenger compare with the cost of an airline ticket?

Use a Data Bank

1. Locate the information you need.
2. Solve the problem.
3. Check that your answer is reasonable.

Applications and Problem Solving

Where possible, use the Data Bank on pages 580-589 to solve the problems. For problems preceded by the logo, find information from another source, such as another print data bank or the Internet.

1. An L-1011-200 flew from Calgary to San Francisco with 288 passengers on board.
a) What was the airline's total operating cost?
b) What was the operating cost per kilometre?
c) What was the operating cost per passenger-kilometre?
d) If the plane left Calgary at 10:00, what was the local time in San Francisco when the plane landed?

2. An airline flying from Regina to Edmonton can use a DC-9-50 or a B737-100. Use the following to compare the efficiencies of the aircraft. State any assumptions you make.
a) the time of flight
b) the operating cost per kilometre
c) the operating cost per passenger-kilometre

3. For their summer vacation, Darla and Elise plan to drive from Winnipeg to Ottawa and then to Washington, D.C. Assume that they want to drive no more than 10 h/day, and that they will average 100 km/h. They would like to spend three full days in both Ottawa and Washington. They want to leave Winnipeg on the morning of July 5, which is a Saturday. Plan their trip, giving the places in which they should stop for the night. Include the dates spent in Ottawa and Washington, and the date they will arrive back in Winnipeg.

4. a) What is the projected increase in the number of children aged 5 to 14 in Canada from the year 2021 to the year 2041?
b) Estimate the number of new schools needed to accommodate the increase.
c) Estimate the number of additional teachers needed.

5. What is the shortest driving distance from Vancouver to Miami?

6. a) At the equator of which planet in our solar system is the speed of rotation about the planet's axis the greatest?
b) What is the greatest speed from part a), in kilometres per hour?
c) How does the speed from part b) compare with the speed of rotation at the Earth's equator? at the sun's equator?

7. Which Canadian province is the most crowded with people? the least crowded with people? Explain.

8. Use the Data Bank on pages 580–589 to write a problem. Have a classmate solve your problem.

WORD POWER

Which Canadian province meets both of these conditions?
• Its capital city has a name that is 50% vowels.
• The province borders a province with a name that is 50% vowels.

CAREER CONNECTION

Chemistry

In our daily lives, we experience a vast number of chemical reactions. Examples are as varied as leaves changing colour in the fall and iron nails rusting. A chef uses chemical reactions to cook you a meal, and your body uses chemical reactions to digest it. Chemical compounds, natural or synthetic, make up the clothing we wear, the materials used to build our homes, and the fuels that drive our cars and keep us warm in winter. Because chemical compounds are used in so many ways, and chemical reactions are so varied, chemists work in many situations to study and profit from them.

The chemical industry is very important to the Canadian economy. Examples of major industries include the potash industry in Saskatchewan, oil and gas in Alberta, and pulp and paper in British Columbia. Chemists are employed in these and other chemical industries, including pharmaceuticals, plastics, explosives, and fertilizers. Chemists are also involved in many other kinds of work, including forensic science and environmental protection.

1 Comparing Solubilities

Because many chemical reactions are carried out in solution, chemists often need to know the solubility of a substance. This is the maximum quantity of the substance that dissolves in a given quantity of solution. For many substances, solubility is related to temperature. In some cases, the relationship is approximately linear.

The table includes equations that model the solubilities of four substances in water. In each equation, s represents the solubility of the substance, in grams per 100 g of solution, and T represents the temperature in degrees Celsius from 0°C to 100°C.

Substance	Equation
sodium chloride	$s = 26 + 0.02T$
ammonium chloride	$s = 23 + 0.21T$
lithium sulfate	$s = 26 - 0.03T$
potassium iodide	$s = 56 + 0.11T$

1. a) Solve graphically or by substitution the system of equations for sodium chloride and ammonium chloride to find the temperature, to the nearest degree Celsius, at which their solubilities are equal.
b) What is the solubility of each substance, to the nearest gram per 100 g of solution, at this temperature?

2. Repeat question 1 using the system of equations for ammonium chloride and lithium sulfate.

3. a) Is the graph for potassium iodide parallel to any of the other three graphs?
b) Does the graph of potassium iodide intersect any of the other three graphs? Explain.

4. For which of the four substances does the solubility increase as the temperature increases? decrease as the temperature decreases? Explain how you know.

2 Locating Information

Use your research skills to find information about the following.

1. How and where are people trained for careers in chemistry?

2. Investigate a chemical that is important to the Canadian economy. How and where is it used?

3. Several Canadians have won Nobel Prizes in chemistry. Find information about the life and work of one of them.

Exploring Equivalence

1 Equivalent Forms

An equation has an infinite number of equivalent forms. For example, multiplying each term in the equation $x - 3 = 1$ by 2 gives the equivalent form $2x - 6 = 2$. The solution to both equations is the same, $x = 4$. Equations with the same solution are called **equivalent equations**.

1. Write three ordered pairs that satisfy the equation $x + y = 6$.

2. a) Multiply both sides of the equation $x + y = 6$ by 2.
b) Do the ordered pairs you found in question 1 satisfy the new equation?

3. a) Multiply both sides of the equation $x + y = 6$ by -3.
b) Do the ordered pairs you found in question 1 satisfy the new equation?

4. Are the three equations from questions 1, 2, and 3 equivalent? Explain.

5. Write three equations equivalent to each of the following equations.
a) $x - y = 2$
b) $2x + y = 7$
c) $y = 4x - 3$
d) $y = \dfrac{x + 5}{2}$

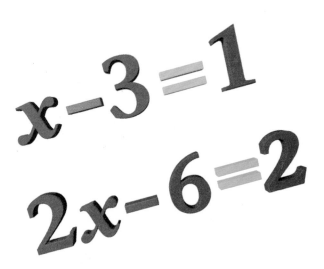

2 Equivalent Systems

Here are two systems of equations.

System A		System B	
$2x - y = 2$	(1)	$x = 3$	(1)
$x + y = 7$	(2)	$y = 4$	(2)

1. Graph the two equations in system A on the same set of axes. Find the point of intersection.

2. Repeat question 1 for system B.

3. a) In system A, multiply (1) by 2 and multiply (2) by -1. Call the resulting system of equations system C.
b) Graph system C and find the point of intersection.

4. Systems A, B, and C are called **equivalent systems**. Explain why.

5. Write a system of equations equivalent to the following system. Write each equation in your system in two variables.
$$x = 2$$
$$y = 1$$

3 Adding Equations

1. Graph the two equations on the same set of axes. Find the point of intersection.
$$x + 2y = 4 \qquad (1)$$
$$x - y = 1 \qquad (2)$$

2. Add (1) and (2) to form a new equation, (3), as follows.
a) Add the left side of (1) to the left side of (2). Simplify the expression.
b) Add the right side of (1) to the right side of (2).
c) Equate the results of parts a) and b).

3. Graph (3) on the same set of axes as (1) and (2). What do the three lines have in common?

4. Three systems of equations that can be formed from (1), (2), and (3) are: (1) and (2), (1) and (3), and (2) and (3). How are the three systems related? Explain.

5. How are systems P, Q, and R related? Explain.

System P	System Q	System R
$2x + 3y = 0$	$2x + 3y = 0$	$x - 3y = 9$
$x - 3y = 9$	$x = 3$	$x = 3$

INVESTIGATING MATH

Algebra Tiles and Equivalent Equations

1 Solving Systems by Addition

The balance scales represent a system of equations.

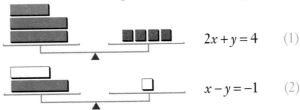

$$2x + y = 4 \qquad (1)$$

$$x - y = -1 \qquad (2)$$

Because the coefficients of y in the two equations are opposites, adding the equations will eliminate y.
The balance scale represents the sum of (1) and (2).

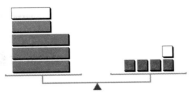

$$2x + y + (x - y) = 4 + (-1)$$
$$2x + x + y - y = 4 - 1$$

Remove zero pairs.

$$3x = 3$$

Group tiles to show the value of the variable.

$$\frac{3x}{3} = \frac{3}{3}$$

Show the result.

$$x = 1$$

So, $x = 1$.
To find y, use tiles to substitute 1 for x in either (1) or (2).
The result is $y = 2$.
So, the solution to the system is (1, 2).

Use algebra tiles or sketches to solve each system by addition.

1. $x + y = 3$
$2x - y = 3$

2. $y + 2x = 0$
$y - 2x = 4$

3. $2x + 3y = 3$
$x - 3y = -3$

4. $2y + 3x = 5$
$2y - 3x = -1$

2 Solving Systems by Subtraction

The balance scales represent a system of equations.

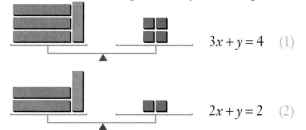

$3x + y = 4$ (1)

$2x + y = 2$ (2)

Because the coefficient of y in the two equations is the same, subtracting the equations will eliminate y. To subtract (2), add its opposite. The opposite of (2) can be represented by turning over the tiles that represent (2).

$-2x - y = -2$

Add (1) and the opposite of (2).

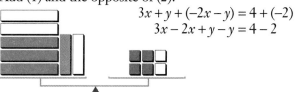

$$3x + y + (-2x - y) = 4 + (-2)$$
$$3x - 2x + y - y = 4 - 2$$

Remove zero pairs.

$x = 2$

So, $x = 2$.
To find y, substitute 2 for x in (1) or (2). The result is $y = -2$.
So, the solution is $(2, -2)$.

Use algebra tiles or sketches to solve each system by subtraction.

1. $2y + x = 4$
    $y + x = 3$

2. $x + 2y = 1$
    $3x + 2y = -1$

3. $2x + 3y = 6$
    $2x + y = 2$

4. $2y = 3x + 1$
    $y = 3x + 2$

3 Solving Systems by Multiplication

The balance scale represents a system of equations.

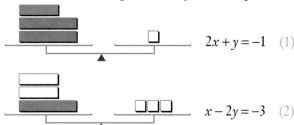

$2x + y = -1$ (1)

$x - 2y = -3$ (2)

Neither addition nor subtraction of (1) and (2) will eliminate a variable.
Multiply (1) or (2) by a suitable number to give an equivalent equation. Then, eliminate a variable.
Multiply (1) by 2.

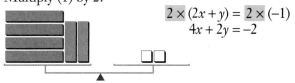

$$2 \times (2x + y) = 2 \times (-1)$$
$$4x + 2y = -2$$

Add the resulting equation and (2) to eliminate y.

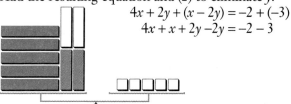

$$4x + 2y + (x - 2y) = -2 + (-3)$$
$$4x + x + 2y - 2y = -2 - 3$$

Remove zero pairs.

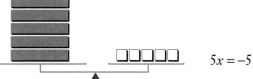

$5x = -5$

Grouping tiles gives $x = -1$, and substituting -1 for x in (1) or (2) gives $y = 1$.
So, the solution is $(-1, 1)$.

1. The above example was solved by first multiplying (1) by 2, and then eliminating y. Show a different solution that first uses multiplication, and then eliminates x.

Use algebra tiles or sketches to solve each system.

2. $x + 2y = 0$
    $2x + y = 3$

3. $3x + y = 3$
    $x - 2y = 1$

4. $3y = 2x - 2$
    $2y = x - 2$

Investigating Math: Algebra Tiles and Equivalent Equations   **33**

1.5 Solving Systems of Linear Equations by Elimination

The Beatles album *Anthology 1* was the first of three anthologies that traced their music from when the band formed in the late 1950s until it broke up in 1970.

Explore: Use the Equations

Let x represent the number of tracks on disc 1 of *Anthology 1*, and y represent the number of tracks on disc 2. The following system of equations shows how the numbers of tracks are related.

$$x + y = 60 \quad (1)$$
$$x - y = 8 \quad (2)$$

a) Interpret each equation in words.
b) Add the left sides of (1) and (2), and then simplify.
c) Add the right sides of (1) and (2).
d) Equate the answers from parts b) and c) to form a new equation.

Inquire

1. Solve the new equation from part d), above.

2. a) How can the value of the second variable be found?
b) Find it.

3. Which ordered pair satisfies the system of equations?

4. Check that the ordered pair satisfies both (1) and (2).

5. How many tracks are on each disc of *Anthology 1*?

6. Solve each system of equations using the above method.
a) $x + y = 17$ **b)** $x - y = 7$ **c)** $4x - 3y = 19$
  $x - y = 11$ $2x + y = 20$ $x + 3y = 1$

The method used to solve each of the above systems of equations is known as elimination, because equations were combined to eliminate a variable. Each system could also have been solved by substitution. The substitution method works well when at least one variable in one or both equations has a coefficient of 1 or -1. With other coefficients, substitution may lead to complicated equations, and it may be better to use the elimination method.

The elimination method uses the following properties of equality.

Since $4 = 4$ If $a = b$
and $3 = 3$ and $c = d$
then $4 + 3 = 4 + 3$ then $a + c = b + d$
and $4 - 3 = 4 - 3$ and $a - c = b - d$

Example 1   Solving by Addition
Solve by elimination.
$$3x + 2y = 19 \quad (1)$$
$$5x - 2y = 5 \quad (2)$$

Solution

Adding the equations eliminates the y terms and creates an equation with one variable.

Write (1):	$3x + 2y = 19$	(1)
Write (2):	$5x - 2y = 5$	(2)
Add (1) and (2):	$8x = 24$	
Solve for x:	$x = 3$	

Substitute 3 for x in (1) or (2).
Substituting in (1) gives

$$3x + 2y = 19$$
$$3(3) + 2y = 19$$
$$9 + 2y = 19$$
$$2y = 10$$
$$y = 5$$

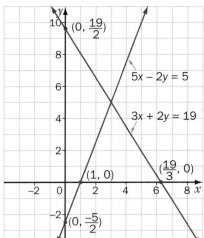

The solution can be visualized graphically.

Check in (1).

L.S. $= 3x + 2y$	**R.S.** $= 19$
$= 3(3) + 2(5)$	
$= 9 + 10$	
$= 19$	
L.S. = R.S.	

Check in (2).

L.S. $= 5x - 2y$	**R.S.** $= 5$
$= 5(3) - 2(5)$	
$= 15 - 10$	
$= 5$	
L.S. = R.S.	

The solution is $(3, 5)$.

Example 2   Solving by Subtraction or Addition

Solve by elimination.

| $4x + 3y = 5$ | (1) |
| $4x - 7y = 15$ | (2) |

Solution

Method 1: Solving by subtraction
Adding will not eliminate a variable.
Subtracting will.

Write (1):	$4x + 3y = 5$	(1)
Write (2):	$4x - 7y = 15$	(2)
Subtract (2) from (1):	$10y = -10$	
Solve for y:	$y = -1$	

Method 2: Solving by addition
Multiply (2) by -1 and add.

Write (1):	$4x + 3y = 5$	(1)
Multiply (2) by -1:	$-4x + 7y = -15$	(3)
Add (1) and (3):	$10y = -10$	
Solve for y:	$y = -1$	

Substitute -1 for y in (1).

$$4x + 3y = 5$$
$$4x + 3(-1) = 5$$
$$4x - 3 = 5$$
$$4x = 8$$
$$x = 2$$

Check in (1).

L.S. $= 4x + 3y$	**R.S.** $= 5$
$= 4(2) + 3(-1)$	
$= 8 - 3$	
$= 5$	
L.S. = R.S.	

Check in (2).

L.S. $= 4x - 7y$	**R.S.** $= 15$
$= 4(2) - 7(-1)$	
$= 8 + 7$	
$= 15$	
L.S. = R.S.	

The solution is $(2, -1)$.

Example 3 Solving Using Multiplication

Solve by elimination.

$$3x + 2y = 2 \qquad (1)$$
$$4x + 5y = 12 \qquad (2)$$

Solution

Neither addition nor subtraction will eliminate a variable. Use multiplication to write a system of equivalent equations, so that a variable can be eliminated by addition or subtraction.

Method 1: Eliminating y

Write (1):	$3x + 2y = 2$	(1)
Write (2):	$4x + 5y = 12$	(2)
Multiply (1) by 5:	$15x + 10y = 10$	(3)
Multiply (2) by –2:	$-8x - 10y = -24$	(4)
Add (3) and (4):	$7x = -14$	
Solve for x:	$x = -2$	

Substituting –2 for x in (1) gives $y = 4$.

Method 2: Eliminating x

Write (1):	$3x + 2y = 2$	(1)
Write (2):	$4x + 5y = 12$	(2)
Multiply (1) by 4:	$12x + 8y = 8^{*}$	(3)
Multiply (2) by –3:	$-12x - 15y = -36$	(4)
Add (3) and (4):	$-7y = -28$	
Solve for y:	$y = 4$	

Substituting 4 for y in (2) gives $x = -2$.

> To substitute, use your mental math skills.

Check in (1).

L.S. $= 3x + 2y$ **R.S.** $= 2$
$= 3(-2) + 2(4)$
$= -6 + 8$
$= 2$
     L.S. = R.S.

Check in (2).

L.S. $= 4x + 5y$ **R.S.** $= 12$
$= 4(-2) + 5(4)$
$= -8 + 20$
$= 12$
     L.S. = R.S.

The solution is (–2, 4).

Example 4 Solving Systems of Rational Equations

Solve.

$$\frac{x-3}{2} - \frac{y-5}{3} = 1 \qquad (1)$$

$$\frac{x+3}{2} + \frac{y-3}{4} = 1 \qquad (2)$$

Solution

To clear fractions, multiply each equation by its lowest common denominator.

Multiply (1) by 6:
$$6 \times \left(\frac{x-3}{2}\right) - 6 \times \left(\frac{y-5}{3}\right) = 6 \times 1$$

> The division bar is a grouping symbol. It acts as brackets.

$$3(x-3) - 2(y-5) = 6$$

Expand:
$$3x - 9 - 2y + 10 = 6$$

Simplify:
$$3x - 2y = 5 \qquad (3)$$

Multiply (2) by 4:
$$4 \times \left(\frac{x+3}{2}\right) + 4 \times \left(\frac{y-3}{4}\right) = 4 \times 1$$

$$2(x+3) + (y-3) = 4$$

Expand:
$$2x + 6 + y - 3 = 4$$

Simplify:
$$2x + y = 1 \qquad (4)$$

Multiply (4) by 2:
$$4x + 2y = 2 \qquad (5)$$

Write (3):
$$3x - 2y = 5 \qquad (3)$$

Add (5) and (3):
$$7x = 7$$

Solve for x:
$$x = 1 \qquad y = -1$$

Substituting 1 for x in (2) gives $y = -1$.

Check in (1).

L.S. $= \dfrac{x-3}{2} - \dfrac{y-5}{3}$ **R.S.** $= 1$

$= \dfrac{1-3}{2} - \dfrac{-1-5}{3}$

$= \dfrac{-2}{2} - \dfrac{-6}{3}$

$= -1 - (-2)$

$= -1 + 2$

$= 1$

     L.S. = R. S.

Check in (2).

L.S. $= \dfrac{x+3}{2} + \dfrac{y-3}{4}$ **R.S.** $= 1$

$= \dfrac{1+3}{2} + \dfrac{-1-3}{4}$

$= \dfrac{4}{2} + \dfrac{-4}{4}$

$= 2 + (-1)$

$= 2 - 1$

$= 1$

     L.S. = R. S.

The solution is $(1, -1)$.

Example 5   Riverboat Cruise

A riverboat took 2 h to travel 24 km down a river with the current and 3 h to make the return trip against the current. Find the speed of the boat in still water and the speed of the current.

Solution

Let b represent the speed of the boat in still water.
Let c represent the speed of the current.
Then, $b + c$ represents the speed of the boat travelling down the river with the current, and $b - c$ represents the speed of the boat travelling up the river against the current.

Use the formula distance = speed $\times$ time, and use a table to organize the given facts.

Direction	Distance (km)	Speed (km/h)	Time (h)	Equation
Down the river	24	$b + c$	2	$2(b + c) = 24$
Up the river	24	$b - c$	3	$3(b - c) = 24$

Solve the system to find the values of b and c.

$2(b + c) = 24$ (1)
$3(b - c) = 24$ (2)

Divide (1) by 2: $b + c = 12$ (3)
Divide (2) by 3: $b - c = 8$ (4)
Add (3) and (4): $2b = 20$
Solve for b: $b = 10$

Substituting 10 for b in (2) gives $c = 2$.

The speed of the boat in still water is 10 km/h, and the speed of the current is 2 km/h.

Check, using the facts given in the problem.
The speed of the boat travelling down the river is $10 + 2$ or 12 km/h.
The time to travel 24 km down the river is $24 \div 12$ or 2 h.
The speed of the boat travelling up the river is $10 - 2$ or 8 km/h.
The time to travel 24 km up the river is $24 \div 8$ or 3 h.

Example 6 Car Trip

Nicole drove 500 km from Edmonton to Lethbridge in $5\frac{1}{2}$ hours. She drove part of the

way at 100 km/h, and the rest of the way at 80 km/h. How far did she drive at each speed?

Solution

Let x represent the distance travelled at 100 km/h.
Let y represent the distance travelled at 80 km/h.

Organize the given information in a table.

Distance (km)	Speed (km/h)	Time (h)
x	100	$\dfrac{x}{100}$
y	80	$\dfrac{y}{80}$

Distance = speed × time,

so time = $\dfrac{\text{distance}}{\text{speed}}$.

Write a system of equations.

Total distance: $x + y = 500$ (1)

Total time: $\dfrac{x}{100} + \dfrac{y}{80} = \dfrac{11}{2}$ (2)

To clear the fractions in (2), multiply by the lowest common denominator.

Multiply (2) by 400: $400 \times \dfrac{x}{100} + 400 \times \dfrac{y}{80} = 400 \times \dfrac{11}{2}$

Simplify: $\qquad\qquad\qquad 4x + 5y = 2200$ (3)

Multiply (1) by -4: $\qquad\quad -4x - 4y = -2000$ (4)

Add (3) and (4): $\qquad\qquad\qquad\qquad y = 200$

Substituting 200 for y in (1) gives $x = 300$.

Nicole drove 300 km at 100 km/h, and 200 km at 80 km/h.

Check.
The total distance was $300 + 200$ or 500 km.

The total time was $\dfrac{300}{100} + \dfrac{200}{80}$ or $5\frac{1}{2}$ hours.

Practice

Solve each system of equations by elimination. Check each solution.

1. $4a - 3b = -10$
$2a + 3b = 22$

2. $5x + 2y = -11$
$3x + 2y = -9$

3. $4x + 9y = -7$
$4x + 3y = -13$

4. $2m - 3n = 12$
$5m - 3n = 21$

5. $2p + 3q = -1$
$2p - 3q = -7$

6. $6y - 5x = -7$
$2y - 5x = -19$

Solve each system by elimination. Check each solution. If there is not exactly one solution, does the system have no solution or infinitely many solutions?

7. $x + 2y = -3$
$2x + 3y = -4$

8. $8c - 3d = -10$
$2c - 5d = 6$

9. $4x + 3y = 15$
$8x - 9y = 15$

10. $3r + 2s = 5$
$9r + 6s = 7$

11. $2x - 3y = 2$
$5x + 6y = 5$

12. $4x - 3y = 5$
$8x - 6y = 10$

13. $3a + 2b = 16$
$2a + 3b = 14$

14. $3m + 4n = -1$
$4m - 5n = -22$

15. $5p + 3q = -19$
$2p - 5q = 11$

16. $2x - 3y = 15$
$5x - 2y = 10$

Solve by elimination. Check each solution.

17. $38 = 2x - 5y$
$75 = 7x - 3y$

18. $6x + 5y = 22$
$3y = 4x + 36$

19. $-3v = 2w - 34$
$-5v = 13 - 3w$

20. $3a - 7b - 13 = 0$
$4a - 5b - 13 = 0$

21. $6x - 5y = -3$
$2y - 9x = -1$

22. $3s + 4 = -4t$
$7s + 6t + 11 = 0$

23. $3c = 2 - 3d$
$5c = 3 - 2d$

24. $2d = 10 + 4e$
$3d = 15 + 6e$

25. $10x = 17 - 15y$
$15x = 25y - 3$

26. $4x - 5 = 2y$
$1 = 5y - 10x$

Solve by elimination. Check each solution.

27. $3(x + 2) - (y + 7) = -1$
$5(x + 1) + 4(y - 3) = -24$

28. $5(m - 3) + 2(n + 4) = 10$
$3(m + 4) - 4(n + 3) = -21$

29. $2(a - 4) + 5(b + 1) = 8$
$3(a - 1) - 2(b - 2) = -11$

30. $4(x - 1) - 3(y + 4) = -11$
$3(x + 4) + 5(y - 6) = -7$

Solve by elimination.

31. $\dfrac{x}{3} + \dfrac{y}{4} = 2$
$\dfrac{2x}{3} - \dfrac{y}{2} = 0$

32. $\dfrac{x-2}{3} + \dfrac{y+1}{5} = 2$
$\dfrac{x+2}{7} - \dfrac{y+5}{3} = -2$

33. $\dfrac{x+2}{6} - \dfrac{3(y+2)}{2} = 1$
$\dfrac{x-2}{2} + \dfrac{y-1}{3} = 0$

34. $\dfrac{5(x+2)}{6} + \dfrac{y+8}{9} = 6$
$\dfrac{2x+1}{3} - \dfrac{5y}{4} = \dfrac{7}{4}$

35. $0.3x - 0.5y = 1.2$
$0.7x - 0.2y = -0.1$

36. $1.7x + 3.5y = 0.01$
$0.6x + 1.2y = 0$

Applications and Problem Solving

In questions 37–42, state the method you would use to solve each system. Explain why you would choose each method.

37. $y = 6 - 3x$
$y = 2x + 1$

38. $2x - 5y = -1$
$3x + 5y = -14$

39. $4x + 3y = 15$
$x - 2y = 1$

40. $2x - 5y = 1$
$3x - 2y = -4$

41. $87x + 68y = 99$
$64x - 55y = 81$

42. $6x = 5y - 1$
$5x = 4y - 1$

43. Names of provinces Some provinces have names with First Nations origins. For example, "Saskatchewan" comes from "Kisiskatchewanisipi," the Cree name for the Saskatchewan River. If the number of provincial names with First Nations origins is a, and the number with other origins is b, the numbers are related by the following equations.
$$a + b = 10$$
$$3a - 2b = 0$$
a) Interpret each equation in words.
b) Find the number of provinces that have names with First Nations origins.

44. Human bones Babies and adults have different numbers of bones, because some bones fuse between birth and maturity. The average number of bones for an adult, a, and a baby, b, are related by the following equations.

$$\frac{a}{2} + \frac{b}{5} = 173$$
$$\frac{a}{3} + \frac{b}{6} = 127$$

Find the average numbers of bones for an adult and for a baby.

45. Measurement
Use the diagram to find the values of x and y.

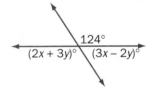

46. Numbers The mean of two numbers is 5. The sum of four times one number and three times the other is 2. Find the numbers.

47. Patrol boat It took a patrol boat 5 h to travel 60 km up a river against the current, and 3 h for the return trip with the current. Find the speed of the boat in still water and the speed of the current.

48. Flying speed A plane took 4 h to fly 2200 km from Saskatoon to Toronto with a tail wind. The return trip, with a head wind, took 5 h. Find the speed of the plane in still air and the wind speed.

49. Car trip Kareem took 5 h to drive 470 km from Regina to Medicine Hat. For part of the trip, he drove at 100 km/h. For the rest of the trip, he drove at 90 km/h. How far did he drive at each speed?

50. Sandwich prices At Lisa's Sandwich Shop, two chicken sandwiches and four cheese sandwiches costs $18. Five chicken sandwiches and six cheese sandwiches costs $34. Which type of sandwich is more expensive, and by how much?

51. Pool table The perimeter of a pool table is about 7.8 m. Four times the length equals nine times the width. What are the dimensions of the table, in metres?

52. Fitness Playing tennis burns energy at a rate of about 25 kJ/min. Cycling burns energy at about 35 kJ/min. Hans exercised by playing tennis and then cycling. He exercised for 50 min altogether and used a total of 1450 kJ of energy. For how long did he play tennis?

53. Connecting batteries When batteries are connected in series, the total electric potential, or voltage, is the sum of the voltages of the batteries.
a) Suppose you have two types of batteries. When you connect three of the first type in series with two of the second type, the total voltage is 21 V. Connecting two of the first type in series with four of the second type gives a total voltage of 30 V. What is the voltage of each type of battery?
b) How many different combinations of the two types of batteries connected in series would give a total voltage of 27 V?

54. Solve this system of equations by letting $a = \dfrac{1}{x}$ and $b = \dfrac{1}{y}$.

$$\frac{1}{x} + \frac{3}{y} = \frac{3}{4}$$
$$\frac{3}{x} - \frac{2}{y} = \frac{5}{12}$$

55. Coordinate geometry Find the coordinates of the vertices of a triangle whose sides lie on the following three lines.
$$2x + 5y - 16 = 0$$
$$4x - 3y - 6 = 0$$
$$3x + y + 2 = 0$$

56. Coordinate geometry Find A and B so that the points $(5, -3)$ and $(-3, 9)$ lie on the line $Ax + By - 9 = 0$.

57. For what values of the coefficients a and b is $(2, -1)$ the solution to the following linear system?
$$ax + by = -7$$
$$2ax - 3by = 1$$

58. For what value of c will each system have infinitely many solutions?
a) $2x - 6y = c$
  $6x - 18y = 30$
b) $cx - 4y = 14$
  $-9x + 6y = -21$

59. For what value of c will each system have no solution?
a) $x + 2y = 6$
  $cx - 4y = 8$
b) $cy + 1 = 5x$
  $9y + 8 = 15x$

60. The solution to a system of linear equations is $(2, 5)$. If each equation is multiplied by 3 to produce a new system, is the solution to the new system $(2, 5)$, $(6, 15)$, or another ordered pair? Explain.

61. Write a system of equations in the following form.
$$Ax + By = C$$
$$Dx + Ey = F$$
A, B, C, D, E, and F must be different integers, and the solution must be $(6, -5)$.

62. Write a system of linear equations that has:
• no coefficients equal to 0, 1, or -1
• integer coefficients and integer constants
• exactly one solution, as follows
a) $(2, 5)$ **b)** $(-4, 7)$ **c)** $\left(1, -\dfrac{2}{3}\right)$

63. Write a word problem that can be solved using a system of linear equations and has the solution $(7, 5)$. Have a classmate check that your problem gives the correct solution.

PATTERN POWER

1. Describe the pattern in words.

2. Find the missing number.

48	12	11	25
40	5	16	19
74	29	27	18
39	11	18	10
63		14	23

1.6 Solving Systems of Linear Equations in Three Variables

The ordered triple $(2, -1, 3)$ is a solution to the equation
$3x - 2y + 2z = 14$, since $3(2) - 2(-1) + 2(3) = 14$.
Other solutions include $(6, 3, 1)$, $(0, 0, 7)$, and $(4, -1, 0)$.
The equation $3x - 2y + 2z = 14$ is an equation in three
variables. Some problems can be solved using a
system of three equations in three variables.

Explore: Use the Equations

If the national art galleries and
museums are excluded, there are
28 major public art galleries and
museums in Canada. If c represents
the number in Central Canada, e, the
number in Eastern Canada, and w, the
number in Western Canada, the
following equations show how the
numbers of art galleries and museums
are related.

$$c + e + w = 28 \qquad (1)$$
$$c + e - w = 4 \qquad (2)$$
$$c - 2e + w = 10 \qquad (3)$$

Interpret each equation in words.

Inquire

1. a) Which variable is eliminated when (1) and (2) are added?
b) Add (1) and (2).

2. a) Which variable is eliminated when (2) and (3) are added?
b) Add (2) and (3).

3. Solve the pair of equations found from questions 1b) and 2b).

4. a) How can you find the value of the variable eliminated in questions 1a)
and 2a)?
b) What is the value of this variable?

5. How many public art galleries and museums are in each part of Canada?

6. a) How can you check that the solution is correct?
b) Check the solution.

7. Use the above method to solve the following systems of equations.
a) $x + y + z = 7$ **b)** $2a - b + c = 1$
$x + 3y - z = 9$ $a + b + c = 8$
$x - 2y + z = 1$ $a - b + c = 0$

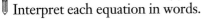

To solve a system of three equations in three variables, you can use elimination to
reduce the system to a system of two equations in two variables. Then, solve the
new system, and find the third variable by substitution.

Example 1 Solving by Elimination

Solve.
$$4x + y + z = 5 \qquad (1)$$
$$2x - y + 2z = 10 \qquad (2)$$
$$x - 2y - z = 2 \qquad (3)$$

Solution

Choose two pairs of equations, and eliminate the same variable from each pair. It does not matter which variable is eliminated first, but one choice may be more convenient than the others.

Eliminate z from (1) and (3).

Write (1):	$4x + y + z = 5$
Write (3):	$x - 2y - z = 2$
Add:	$5x - y = 7 \qquad (4)$

Eliminate z from (2) and (3).

Multiply (3) by 2:	$2x - 4y - 2z = 4$
Write (2):	$2x - y + 2z = 10$
Add:	$4x - 5y = 14 \qquad (5)$

The system has now been reduced to a system of two equations in two variables.

$$5x - y = 7 \qquad (4)$$
$$4x - 5y = 14 \qquad (5)$$

This system can be solved algebraically or graphically.

Method 1: Solving algebraically

Eliminate y from (4) and (5).

Multiply (4) by -5:	$-25x + 5y = -35$
Write (5):	$4x - 5y = 14$
Add:	$-21x = -21$
Solve for x:	$x = 1$

Substitute 1 for x in (4).

$$5(1) - y = 7$$
$$5 - y = 7$$
$$-y = 2$$
$$y = -2$$

Method 2: Using a graphing calculator

Solve (4) and (5) for y.

For (4), $y = 5x - 7$

For (5), $y = \dfrac{4x - 14}{5}$

Graph the equations in the standard viewing window.

Use the Intersect operation or the TRACE and ZOOM instructions to find the coordinates of the point of intersection.

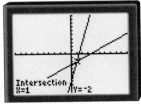

Substitute 1 for x and -2 for y in (1).

$$4(1) + (-2) + z = 5$$
$$2 + z = 5$$
$$z = 3$$

Check in (1).
L.S. $= 4x + y + z$ **R.S.** $= 5$
$= 4(1) + (-2) + 3$
$= 4 - 2 + 3$
$= 5$
     L.S. = R.S.

Check in (2).
L.S. $= 2x - y + 2z$ **R.S.** $= 10$
$= 2(1) - (-2) + 2(3)$
$= 2 + 2 + 6$
$= 10$
     L.S. = R.S.

Check in (3).
L.S. $= x - 2y - z$ **R.S.** $= 2$
$= 1 - 2(-2) - 3$
$= 1 + 4 - 3$
$= 2$
     L.S. = R.S.

The solution is $x = 1$, $y = -2$, and $z = 3$, or the ordered triple $(1, -2, 3)$.

You may find it easier to solve some systems of three equations in three variables by substitution, rather than by elimination.

Example 2   Staging a Musical

The longest running musical in the history of the theatre in Canada is *The Phantom of the Opera*. The total number of costumes, wigs, and pairs of shoes needed to stage the musical is 456. There are 80 more costumes than pairs of shoes. The number of pairs of shoes is two less than twice the number of wigs. Find the number of costumes, wigs, and pairs of shoes needed to stage the musical.

Solution

Let c represent the number of costumes, w represent the number of wigs, and p represent the number of pairs of shoes. Write a system of equations.

The total number of costumes, wigs, and pairs of shoes is 456: $\quad c + w + p = 456 \quad (1)$
There are 80 more costumes than pairs of shoes: $\quad\quad\quad\quad\quad c - p = 80 \quad (2)$
The number of pairs of shoes is two less than twice the number of wigs: $\quad p = 2w - 2 \quad (3)$

$$-2w + p = -2$$

Substitute $2w - 2$ for p in (2).
Substitute: $\quad\quad c - (2w - 2) = 80$
Expand: $\quad\quad\quad c - 2w + 2 = 80$
Simplify: $\quad\quad\quad\quad c - 2w = 78 \quad (4)$

Substitute $2w - 2$ for p in (1).
Substitute: $\quad c + w + (2w - 2) = 456$
Simplify: $\quad\quad\quad\quad c + 3w = 458 \quad (5)$

The system has now been reduced to a system of two equations in two unknowns.
This system can be solved by elimination or substitution.

$$c - 2w = 78 \quad (4)$$
$$c + 3w = 458 \quad (5)$$

Method 1: Solving by elimination

Write (5): $\quad\quad\quad\quad c + 3w = 458 \quad (5)$
Multiply (4) by −1: $\quad -c + 2w = -78 \quad (6)$
Add (5) and (6): $\quad\quad\quad 5w = 380$
Solve for w: $\quad\quad\quad\quad w = 76$

Method 2: Solving by substitution

From (4), $\quad\quad\quad\quad c - 2w = 78$
So, $\quad\quad\quad\quad\quad\quad\quad c = 78 + 2w$
Substitute $78 + 2w$ for c in (5).
Write (5): $\quad\quad\quad\quad\quad c + 3w = 458$
Substitute: $\quad (78 + 2w) + 3w = 458$
Simplify: $\quad\quad\quad\quad\quad 5w = 380$
Solve for w: $\quad\quad\quad\quad w = 76$

Substitute 76 for w in (3).
$$p = 2(76) - 2$$
$$= 152 - 2$$
$$= 150$$
Substitute 150 for p in (2).
$$c - 150 = 80$$
$$c = 230$$

So, 230 costumes, 76 wigs, and 150 pairs of shoes are needed to stage the musical.
Check using the facts given in the problem.
The total number of costumes, wigs, and pairs of shoes is 456. $\quad 230 + 76 + 150 = 456$
There are 80 more costumes than pairs of shoes. $\quad\quad\quad\quad\quad 230 - 150 = 80$
The number of pairs of shoes is two less than twice the number of wigs. $\quad 150 = 2(76) - 2$

Practice

Is the given ordered triple a solution to the given equation?

1. $3x + y - z = 7$ (2, 2, 1)
2. $4x - y - z = 8$ (3, –1, 4)
3. $5a - 2b + 3c = 24$ (2, –3, 3)
4. $3r + 4s - 2t = 17$ (–3, 0, 4)
5. $2x - 5y - 4z = 16$ (–1, –2, –2)
6. $3a - 3b - c = -6$ (–2, 1, –2)

Determine if the ordered triple is a solution to the system of equations.

7. $3x - 2y + 4z = 11$
$2x + 3y - z = 5$
$x + 4y - 3z = 3$ (1, 2, 3)

8. $4a - 3b - 2c = 31$
$7a - 3b + 5c = 26$
$5a - b - 4c = 28$ (3, –5, –2)

9. $4p - 3q - r = -2$
$5p + 4q + r = -7$
$2p - q - 3r = 4$ (–1, 0, –2)

10. $3u + v + w = 3$
$u - v - w = -2$
$2u + 3v - 4w = 10$ $\left(\dfrac{1}{2}, 2, -\dfrac{1}{2}\right)$

Solve and check.

11. $a + b + 3c = 12$
$2a + b + 3c = 14$
$a - b + 4c = 13$

12. $x + y + z = -1$
$2x + 3y - z = 5$
$3x - 2y - z = 0$

13. $3b + 4c + d = -1$
$b - 4c - 2d = 12$
$2b + 4c - 3d = 9$

14. $e + f + g = -6$
$e - 2f - 2g = 9$
$e + 3f + 4g = -19$

Solve and check.

15. $2x + 3y + z = 15$
$3x + 2y - z = 10$
$4x + y + 2z = 15$

16. $a + 2b + c = 0$
$3a - b - 2c = 11$
$2a + b - c = 3$

17. $5a + 2b - 3c = 11$
$3a - 5b + c = -13$
$a - 2b - c = 5$

18. $3r + 5s - t = 47$
$2r - s + 3t = -2$
$4r + s - 2t = 30$

19. $x - 2y + z + 9 = 0$
$2x + y - 3z + 3 = 0$
$x + 4y - 2z - 12 = 0$

20. $2r - 5s + 5t = 4$
$2r + 4s - 3t = -16$
$5r - 3s + 2t = -7$

21. $2r + 3s - 4t = -6$
$4r - 2s + 3t = 27$
$3r + 5s - 2t = 12$

22. $4x + 2y - 3z = 12$
$2x - 3y + 2z = 11$
$x + 5y + 4z = -20$

Solve and check.

23. $x + 3y + 2z = 1$
$2x - 3y - 4z = -5$
$3x + 6y - 2z = -2$

24. $2p - q - r = -1$
$2p - 3q + 5r = 3$
$p + 2q - 2r = -1$

25. $d + e - 2f = -5$
$3d - e - 4f = 11$
$2d + 4e + f = 4$

26. $3x - y + 2z = 4$
$2x + 2y - z = 19$
$4x - 2y - 3z = 35$

Solve each system of equations. Check each solution.

27. $x + y + z = 14$
$x - 2y = -4$
$z = 9$

28. $a - 2b - 3c = 0$
$b = 2$
$a + c = 0$

29. $2y - z = -13$
$2x = 12$
$3x + y = 13$

30. $r + s = 4$
$2q + 4r - s = -3$
$3r = -3$

Solve and check.

31. $t - u = 1$
$t + v = 2$
$v - u = 7$

32. $a + 2b = -3$
$4a - c = -10$
$3c - 2b = -6$

33. $p - q + 3r = -8$
$2q - r = 15$
$3p + 2r = -7$

34. $5x + 7y = -1$
$-2y + 3z = 9$
$7x - z = 27$

Solve and check.

35. $0.2a + 0.6b - 0.3c = 0.6$
$0.3a - 0.4b + 0.5c = 2.1$
$0.5a - 0.2b - 0.1c = 0.7$

36. $x + 0.5y + z = -8$
$0.2x - y + 1.5z = -4.6$
$0.05x + 0.02y - 0.1z = 0.21$

37. $\dfrac{x}{3} + \dfrac{y}{4} + \dfrac{z}{2} = 7$
$\dfrac{x}{6} + \dfrac{y}{2} + \dfrac{z}{6} = 6$
$\dfrac{x}{3} + \dfrac{y}{2} + \dfrac{z}{2} = 9$

38. $\dfrac{r}{2} - \dfrac{s}{3} + \dfrac{t}{6} = 2$
$\dfrac{r}{4} + \dfrac{s}{2} - \dfrac{t}{3} = -8$
$\dfrac{r}{2} + \dfrac{s}{3} + \dfrac{t}{4} = -1$

39. $5x + 2y - 3z = -1$
$10x - y + 6z = 6$
$5x + 3y + 9z = 7$

40. $3a - 12b - 2c = 5$
$4a - 3b + 8c = 5$
$6a + 9b + 16c = 4$

Applications and Problem Solving

41. Auto racing Jacques Villeneuve became the first Canadian to win the Formula One auto racing world championship. The points won by the first, second, and third place finishers were related by the following equations.

$$f + s + t = 159$$
$$s - t = 6$$
$$f = 2s - 3$$

a) Explain the meaning of each equation in words.
b) Solve the system to find the points won by the first, second, and third place finishers.

42. Measurement
Find the values of x, y, and z.

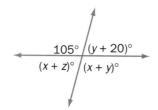

43. Numbers When three numbers are added in pairs, the sums of the pairs are 22, 39, and 45. What are the three numbers?

44. Integers The sum of three integers is 25. The first integer is four times the sum of the second and third. The second is twice the opposite of the third. What are the integers?

45. Measurement In $\triangle ABC$, the sum of $\angle A$ and $\angle B$ is 70° more than $\angle C$. The sum of $\angle B$ and $\angle C$ is 16° more than $\angle A$. What is the measure of each angle in the triangle?

46. Measurement In a triangle, the largest angle is 100° greater than the smallest angle. The largest angle is 3 times as large as the third angle. Find the measure of each angle.

47. Winter Olympics At the Winter Olympics in Lillehammer, Norway, the number of gold medals Canada won was half the number of silver medals. Canada won 3 silver medals for every 2 bronze medals it won. The total number of gold and bronze medals was one more than the number of silver medals.
a) How many medals of each type did Canada win?
b) Myriam Bédard won two of Canada's gold medals. Use your research skills to find the events she won.

48. Known moons The total number of known moons around Saturn, Uranus, and Neptune is 43. The total number of moons around Saturn and Neptune is 9 more than the number of moons around Uranus. Saturn has 2 moons more than twice the number of moons around Neptune. Find the number of moons each planet has.

49. Literature Canadian novelist Margaret Laurence (1926–1987) was born in Manitoba and spent much of her life in Canada. She also lived in England and in two countries in Africa. She spent $3\frac{1}{2}$ times as long in Canada as in England. She lived in England for 5 years longer than she lived in Africa. For how many years did she live in Canada?

50. Comic books Superman first appeared in *Action Comics* No. 1 (1938). *Detective Comics* No. 27 (1939) introduced Batman. *Whiz Comics* No. 1 (1940) was the first to feature Captain Marvel. In "near mint" condition, these three comic books have a total value of $338 000. The Superman comic book is worth $10 000 more than the Batman comic book. The Captain Marvel comic book is worth $74 000 less than the Batman comic book. Find the value of each comic book.

51. Counting bills There are $925 in $5, $10, and $20 bills in a cash register. There is a total of 71 bills. The number of $20 bills is 7 less than the total number of $5 bills and $10 bills. How many bills of each denomination are in the cash register?

52. Coastlines The total length of the coastlines of Canada, the United States, and Mexico is about 270 000 km. The Canadian coastline is 16 times the average length of the coastlines of the U.S. and Mexico. The U.S. coastline is 10 000 km longer than the Mexican coastline. Find the length of the coastline of each country, in kilometres.

53. Forests The total area of forested land in British Columbia, Alberta, and Manitoba is about 1 330 000 km². Alberta and Manitoba have equal areas of forested land. British Columbia has 90% as much forested land as Alberta and Manitoba combined. Find the area of forested land in each province, in square kilometres.

54. Investments Brandon invested $20 000. He invested part of the money in a term deposit paying 4% annual interest, three times as much in a government bond paying 5% annual interest, and the rest in a second mortgage paying 7% annual interest. If he earned a total of $1130 interest in one year, how much did he invest at each rate?

55. Rocket flight A rocket is fired down a practice range. The height of the rocket, h metres, depends on the time it has been in flight, t seconds, as shown in the equation.
$$h = at^2 + bt + c$$
After 10 s, the rocket reaches a height of 1500 m. The height is 2000 m after 20 s and 1500 m after 30 s. Find the values of a, b, and c.

56. Wildlife photographs Shana sells her wildlife photographs at county fairs. Her revenue, R dollars, is determined by the price, p dollars, she charges for each picture, as shown in the equation.
$$R = ap^2 + bp + c$$
At a price of $40, her revenue is $2900. At a price of $50, her revenue is $3000. At a price of $70, her revenue is only $2600. Find the values of a, b, and c.

57. Mixing alloys The table shows the composition of three alloys of copper, nickel, and zinc.

Alloy	Percent by Mass		
	Copper	Nickel	Zinc
X	50	40	10
Y	60	20	20
Z	70	10	20

What mass of each alloy should be melted and mixed to make 100 g of a new alloy that is 57% copper, 28% nickel, and 15% zinc, by mass?

58. Measurement Can the following equations describe the relationship between the side lengths in a triangle? Explain.
$$a + b + c = 13$$
$$b = 2a$$
$$a = c - 5$$

59. a) Describe the procedure you would use to solve this system of four equations in four unknowns.
$$w + x + y + z = 10$$
$$2w - x - y + 2z = 8$$
$$2w + 3x + 2y - z = 11$$
$$3w - 2x + y - 3z = -11$$
b) Solve the system.

60. Write a system of three different equations, so that no equations are equivalent, each equation has three variables, and the solution to the system is $(2, 3, -1)$.

61. Write a problem that can be solved using three equations in three variables. Have a classmate solve your problem.

LOGIC POWER

The cards are in a 2 by 3 arrangement.

Rearrange the cards so that all of the following statements are true.

- The cards are still in a 2 by 3 arrangement.
- The queens are not in the same column.
- One ace is below a black card. The other ace is above a diamond or a queen.
- The card in the middle of the top row is a king or a queen of the same suit as the card to the right.
- The card in the middle of the bottom row has the same suit as the card to the left.

Exploring Non-linear Systems With a Graphing Calculator

1 Graphing Non-linear Equations

The graphs of linear equations, such as $y = x + 3$, are straight lines. The graphs of non-linear equations are not straight lines.

1. Graph each of the following in the standard viewing window of your graphing calculator. Sketch each graph in your notebook.

a) $y = x^2$ **b)** $y = -x^2$
c) $y = x^2 - 4$ **d)** $y = 9 - x^2$
e) $y = x^2 - 2x - 8$ **f)** $y = -x^2 + 6x - 5$

2. a) How are the graphs in question 1 the same? How are they different?
b) In question 1, the coefficient of x^2 is either 1 or −1. How are the graphs related to the sign of this coefficient?

3. Repeat question 1 for each of the following.
a) $y = 2^x$ **b)** $y = -2^x$ **c)** $y = 2^x - 3$
d) $y = 1 - 2^x$ **e)** $y = 2 - 3^x$ **f)** $y = 4^x - 5$

4. How are the graphs in question 3 the same? How are they different?

5. Repeat question 1 for each of the following.
a) $y = x^3$ **b)** $y = -x^3$ **c)** $y = x^3 - 1$
d) $y = 8 - x^3$ **e)** $y = x^3 + 2x$ **f)** $y = -x^3 - x^2 + 6x$

6. How are the graphs in question 5 the same? How are they different?

2 Solving Systems Containing Non-linear Equations

As with systems of linear equations, systems containing non-linear equations can be solved by graphing the equations and finding the coordinates of the intersection point or points.

1. Solve each of the following systems graphically using a graphing calculator. Use the Intersect operation or the TRACE and ZOOM instructions to find the coordinates of the intersection points. Round to the nearest hundredth, when necessary.

a) $y = x^2 - 2$
     $y = 7$
b) $y = -x^2 + x$
     $y = x - 4$
c) $y = x^2 - 3x + 1$
     $y = 2x - 3$
d) $y = 3 - x^2$
     $y = 2 - x$

2. Repeat question 1 for the following systems.
a) $y = 2^x$ **b)** $y = -2^x$ **c)** $y = 2^x$ **d)** $y = 3^x$
    $y = 8$ $y = x - 3$ $y = -\dfrac{x}{2}$ $y = 2x + 2$

3. Repeat question 1 for the following systems.
a) $y = x^3 + 1$
    $y = 9$
b) $y = -x^3 + 1$
    $y = x - 9$
c) $y = x^3$
    $y = 4x$
d) $y = x^3 + 2x$
    $y = -x^2 + 3$

4. In questions 1–3, do you know that you have found all the intersection points of each system? Explain.

5. How many intersection points can you find for each of the following systems?
a) $y = x^2 + 1$ **b)** $y = 2x^2 - 4$ **c)** $y = 2^x + 1$
    $y = x - 2$ $y = 2(x^2 - 2)$ $y = -2^x - 1$
d) $y = x^3$ **e)** $y = x^2 - 1$ **f)** $y = 3^x + 1$
    $y = -x$ $y = -x^2 + 1$ $y = -x^2 + 4$

6. Patterns a) In the sequence 40, 44, 48, 52, ..., the value of term 1 is 40, the value of term 2 is 44, and so on. Write an equation you can use to find the value of a term from the term number.
b) Repeat part a) for the sequence 0, 2, 6, 12, 20,....
c) Graph both equations in the same viewing window. Which quadrant should you use? Explain.
d) Find the intersection point of the two graphs in this quadrant.
e) Interpret the meaning of the coordinates of the intersection point. Check your interpretation.

7. Population trends In 1999, when the world's population reached 6 billion, it was increasing by 1.4% per year. About 3 billion people were urban. The urban population was increasing by 2.5% per year. Let y represent population and x represent the number of years after 1999. If the trends continue, the world's population will be given by the equation
$$y = 6(1.014)^x$$
and the urban population by the equation
$$y = 3(1.025)^x$$
a) Graph both equations in the same viewing window.
b) Predict the year in which all the world's population will be urban.
c) Do you think that the prediction in part b) is valid? Explain.

PROBLEM SOLVING

1.7 Solve Fermi Problems

How many words does your daily newspaper print in a year? Estimation problems like this one are known as **Fermi problems**. They get their name from the physicist Enrico Fermi, who liked to pose them to his students at the University of Chicago. Solving a Fermi problem may require several estimates. Specify any assumptions you make to arrive at the estimates.

If the Royal Centre in Vancouver were hollow, about how many soccer balls would be needed to fill it?

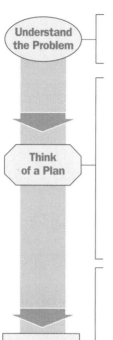

Understand the Problem

1. What information are you given?
2. What are you asked to find?
3. Do you need an exact or an approximate answer?

Think of a Plan

The problem is an example of a volume problem. The task is to estimate how many small objects are needed to fill a large object. The number of small objects, n, can be found using

$$n = (\text{large volume}) \div (\text{small volume})$$

Some information is missing from the problem. You can use your research skills to find that the Royal Centre has base dimensions of 40 m by 40 m, and a height of 140 m. A soccer ball has a diameter of about 22 cm.

Carry Out the Plan

Assume that the Royal Centre approximates a rectangular prism. Its volume is about $40 \times 40 \times 140$, or $224\,000$ m^3.

Assume that the soccer ball approximates a cube, with each edge 22 cm or 0.22 m. The volume of the cube is 0.22^3, or about 0.01 m^3.

So, $n \doteq \dfrac{224\,000}{0.01}$
$= 22\,400\,000$

About 22 000 000 soccer balls would be needed to fill the Royal Centre.

Look Back

Does the answer seem reasonable?
Is there a way to improve the estimate?

Solve Fermi Problems

1. Locate the information you need.
2. Decide what assumption(s) to make.
3. Estimate the solution to the problem.
4. Check that your estimate is reasonable.

Many Fermi problems will require you to use your research skills to locate missing information. You may use the Internet, or you may obtain the information in another way, such as looking it up in a reference book, measuring it, or asking an expert. The following Fermi problem is missing some information.

How many litres of gasoline does a family car use in a year?

The fuel efficiency of a car depends on several things, including the size of the car, where most of the driving is done — city or highway — and whether the transmission is manual or automatic.

Assume that the car is mid-sized, with an automatic transmission, that it is used mainly for city driving, and that it is driven about 25 000 km in a year. Research indicates that the car's fuel efficiency is about 12 L/100 km.

The car will use about $25\ 000 \times \dfrac{12}{100}$, or 3000 L of gasoline in a year.

Applications and Problem Solving

Locate any missing information. Then, solve each problem.

1. About how many dimes would it take to cover the floors of the hallways in your school?

2. Estimate the volume of one million loonies.

3. Estimate the number of litres of water that would be wasted if a drinking fountain ran continuously for a school year.

4. About how many basketballs would it take to fill your school?

5. About how many buildings of all types are there in your province?

6. About how many families in your province are connected to the Internet?

7. Estimate the total number of litres of milk Canadian students in grades 1 to 12 drink in a year.

8. Estimate the number of words your daily newspaper prints in a year.

9. About how many kilometres of sidewalk are there in your province?

10. About how long would it take to fill a community swimming pool with a garden hose?

11. Estimate the number of variety stores in Canada.

12. About how many people could stand in the West Edmonton Mall?

13. If the sun were hollow, about how many spheres the size of the Earth would fill it?

14. About how many movie theatres are there in Canada?

15. Estimate the number of tennis balls it would take to replace all the water in Lake Superior.

16. About how many televisions are there in Canada?

17. Estimate the number of advertising flyers delivered to homes in your province in a year.

18. If all the grade 11 students in Canada stood shoulder to shoulder, about how far would the line stretch?

19. Write a problem similar to question 1. Have a classmate solve your problem.

NUMBER POWER

You have 1023 coins. How can you place them in 10 bags so that, if you are asked for any number of coins from 1 to 1023, you can provide that number without opening a bag?

CONNECTING MATH AND ZOOLOGY

Ape/Monkey Populations

The Primates are classified as an order of mammals. There are two main suborders of the Primates — the Prosimians and the Anthropoidea. The Prosimians, such as lemurs, have small brains. The Anthropoidea, including monkeys and apes, have larger brains.

Scientists have studied fossils to track changes in the population of Primates over millions of years. The graph shows how the makeup of the total ape and monkey population has changed from 23 million years ago to the present. The changes were linear until about 7 million years ago, when the percents of apes and monkeys in the ape/monkey population began to level off.

Twenty million years ago, the ape/monkey population was 80% apes and 20% monkeys. Ten million years ago, the ape/monkey population was 30% apes and 70% monkeys. This information can be written as ordered pairs in the form (t, p) where t represents the number of millions of years ago, and p represents the percent of the total ape/monkey population.

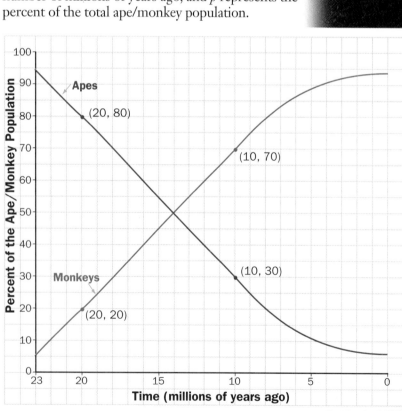

1 Interpreting the Graph

1. From the graph, estimate how many million years ago the ape and monkey populations were the same.

2. Estimate the percent of the ape/monkey population today that is made up of
a) apes   **b)** monkeys

3. Estimate the percent of the ape/monkey population 23 million years ago that was made up of
a) apes   **b)** monkeys

4. If the graphs had remained linear, estimate when apes would have become extinct.

2 Solving Algebraically

1. Use the coordinates of the four points shown on the graph to write an equation for the linear portion of each graph.

2. a) Solve the system of equations algebraically to find the intersection point of the two lines.
b) What do the coordinates of the intersection point represent?

3 Critical Thinking

1. Why are there no data for the ape/monkey population before 23 million years ago?

2. Give possible reasons why apes have not become extinct.

3. The line for apes falls from left to right, yet the slope is positive. The line for monkeys rises from left to right, yet the slope is negative. Explain these slopes.

4. Compare the absolute values of the slopes of the lines. Explain your results.

5. Does the graph show that there are more monkeys alive now than there were 23 million years ago? Explain.

Review

1.1 *Solve each system by graphing. Check your solutions.*

1. $y = x - 5$
$y = 3 - x$

2. $m + 2n = 2$
$3m + 2n = -6$

3. $x + y - 4 = 0$
$5x - y - 8 = 0$

4. $2x - y = -4$
$2x + y = 6$

Solve each system graphically, to the nearest tenth.

5. $4x + 3y = 1$
$4x - 3y = 14$

6. $3x + y = 1$
$x + 4y = 3$

Without graphing, determine whether each system has one solution, no solution, or infinitely many solutions.

7. $3c + d = 4$
$6c + 2d = 8$

8. $4x - 2y = 0$
$2x - y = 3$

9. $x + 5y = 9$
$x - y = 3$

10. $x + 2y - 7 = 0$
$3x + 6y - 14 = 0$

11. Deserts The two largest deserts in the world are the Sahara Desert and the Australian Desert. The sum of their areas is 13 million square kilometres. The area of the Sahara Desert is 5 million square kilometres more than the area of the Australian Desert. Solve the following system graphically to find the area of each desert, in millions of square kilometres.

$$s + a = 13$$
$$s = a + 5$$

12. Profit or loss A company manufactures and sell paddles. Its manufacturing costs are $500, plus $10 per paddle. The company sells the paddles for $18. The cost and revenue can be represented by the following system of equations.

Dollar Cost: $\quad d = 500 + 10p$
Dollar Revenue: $\quad d = 18p$

a) What does each variable represent?
b) Solve the system graphically.
c) How many paddles must be sold for the company to make a profit?

1.3 *Solve each system by substitution. Check each solution.*

13. $y = 6 - 2x$
$3x + 2y = 10$

14. $3x + y - 2 = 0$
$5x + 2y - 3 = 0$

15. $7 = b - 2a$
$4 = a + b$

16. $3m - 6n = 1$
$m + 3n = 2$

17. Lawn fertilizer One lawn fertilizer is 24% nitrogen, and another is 12% nitrogen. How much of each fertilizer should be mixed to obtain 100 kg of fertilizer that is 21% nitrogen?

Simplify each system, and then solve it by substitution. Check each solution.

18. $2(x - 1) + y = 2$
$3x - 4(y + 3) = 5$

19. $3(x + 1) - (y + 7) = -2$
$4x + 5(y - 3) = -6$

20. Buying bonds Li bought a Canada Savings Bond paying 5.5% interest and a provincial government bond paying 6.5% interest. She invested a total of $15 000 and earned $925 in interest in the first year. How much did she pay for each bond?

21. Canadian place names The two most common place names in Canada are Mount Pleasant and Centreville. A total of 31 places have these names. Triple the number of places named Centreville is 13 more than double the number of places named Mount Pleasant. How many places in Canada have each name?

1.5 *Solve each system of equations by elimination. Check each solution.*

22. $2x + 3y = 4$
$4x - 3y = -10$

23. $4a + 5b = -3$
$4a + 9b = 1$

24. $3x + 4y = 17$
$7x - 2y = 17$

25. $2x - 5y = 3$
$3x + 2y = 14$

Which method would you use to solve each system of equations? Explain. Then, solve and check each system.

26. $y = x - 1$
$y = 2x + 3$

27. $5x - y = 4$
$3x + y = 4$

28. $3m - 4n = 4$
$m + 6n = 5$

29. $4x + 7y = 10$
$3x - 5y = -13$

30. Car wash The Outdoors Club held a car wash to raise money. They washed cars for $5 each and vans for $7 each. They washed 45 vehicles and earned $243. How many of each type of vehicle did they wash?

Simplify and solve the system. Check the solution.

31. $3(x+1) - 4(y-1) = 13$
$5(x+2) + 2(y+3) = 0$

Solve. Check each solution.

32. $\dfrac{x}{3} + \dfrac{y}{2} = 3$

$\dfrac{x+3}{2} + \dfrac{y+1}{5} = 4$

33. $0.5x - 0.4y = 0.5$
$3x + 0.8y = 1.4$

34. **Tail wind** A small plane took 3 h to fly 960 km from Ottawa to Halifax with a tail wind. On the return trip, flying into the wind, the plane took 4 h. Find the wind speed and the speed of the plane in still air.

1.6 *Solve each system. Check each solution.*

35. $a + 2b + c = 1$
$a - b - c = 4$
$a - 2b - c = 3$

36. $x + y + z = 7$
$2x + 3y - z = 3$
$3x - 2y + 2z = 12$

37. $x + y + z = 8$
$x = 7$
$z - y = 3$

38. $2m - n = 6$
$m + 2l = 4$
$3l - n = 5$

39. **Geography** Of the 50 states in the United States, 17 share a border with Canada or Mexico. The number of states that do not share a border with another country is seven more than twice the number that share a border with Canada. How many states share a border with
a) Canada?
b) Mexico?
c) no other country?

40. **Reservoir capacities** The three largest reservoirs in Western Canada are Williston Lake and Kinbasket Lake in British Columbia, and Cross-Cedar Lake in Manitoba. The total capacity of these three reservoirs is 105 billion cubic metres. The capacity of Williston Lake is twice the total capacity of the other two reservoirs. The capacity of Cross-Cedar Lake is 40% of the capacity of Kinbasket Lake. Find the capacity of each reservoir, in billions of cubic metres.

Exploring Math

Tiling Squares With L-Shaped Triominoes

An L-shaped triomino is made up of 3 squares. You can make triominoes out of paper or linking cubes, or you can use a pencil to mark triominoes on a grid. A 4 by 4 grid cannot be tiled with triominoes,  because it has 16 squares. The grid can be tiled if one of the squares is removed, so that there are only 15 squares to be covered.

1. Copy the 4 by 4 grid, from which the indicated square has been removed. Tile the grid with 5 L-shaped triominoes. Show your solution by drawing the triomino shapes on your copy of the grid.

2. a) Are there locations from which a square can be removed from the 4 by 4 grid so that the grid cannot be tiled with 5 L-shaped triominoes?
b) To answer part a), what was the minimum number of locations you needed to try? Explain.

3. Using a 5 by 5 grid with one square removed and 8 L-shaped triominoes, find
a) the locations of the shaded square so that the grid can be tiled
b) the locations of the shaded square so that the grid cannot be tiled
c) the minimum number of locations you needed to try in order to answer parts a) and b)

4. Is it possible to tile a 3 by 3 grid with L-shaped triominoes? Explain.

Chapter Check

Solve each system by graphing. Check your solutions.

1. $y = x - 1$
$y = 2x - 5$

2. $x - y = 1$
$3x + 2y = -12$

3. $y = 4x + 4$
$x + 5y = -1$

4. $m + 5n + 9 = 0$
$3m - n - 5 = 0$

Solve each system graphically, to the nearest tenth.

5. $y = 2x + 5$
$y = -4x + 1$

6. $2x + 3y = 8$
$3x - 5y = 2$

7. Describe the graph of a system of equations with each number of solutions.

a) one

b) none

c) infinitely many

Solve each system by substitution. Check each solution.

8. $2x + y = 6$
$3x - 2y = 2$

9. $x + 2y + 2 = 0$
$2x - 6y + 9 = 0$

Solve each system by elimination. Check each solution.

10. $-2x + 5y = -3$
$2x - 3y = 1$

11. $3x + 2y = 8$
$2x + 3y = 7$

Solve each system by any method. Check each solution. If there is not exactly one solution, does the system have no solution or infinitely many solutions?

12. $5x - 3y = 9$
$2x - 5y = -4$

13. $3a + b - 4 = 0$
$2a - 10 = 3b$

14. $10x + 2 = 6y$
$5x = 3y - 1$

15. $x = 2 - 2y$
$y + \dfrac{1}{2}x = -1$

16. $\dfrac{x}{3} + \dfrac{y}{4} = -1$
$2x + y = -8$

17. $3p - 6q = 0$
$4p + q = 3$

18. $2x + 3y = -2$
$8x + 5y = -6$

19. $0.2x + 0.7y = 1.5$
$0.3x - 0.2y = 1$

Solve each system. Check your solution.

20. $x - y + z = 5$
$x - 2y = 2$
$2z + 1 = 7$

21. $p + q + 2r = 1$
$2p - q + r = -1$
$3p + q + r = 4$

22. **Hockey** The number of goals scored by a player's team less the number of goals scored against the player's team while the player is on the ice is the player's plus-minus statistic. One season, the plus-minus statistics of Eric Lindros, e, and Mike Modano, m, were related by the following equations. Solve the system graphically to find each player's plus-minus statistic.
$$e + 2m = 0$$
$$2e + 3m = 8$$

23. **Longest rivers** The Mackenzie, the longest river in Canada, is 1056 km longer than the Yukon, the second longest river. The total length of the two rivers is 7426 km. Find the length of each river.

24. **Granola mix** One type of granola is 30% fruit, and another type is 15% fruit. What mass of each type of granola should be mixed to make 600 g of granola that is 21% fruit?

25. **Frost-free days** The average number of frost-free days per year in Peace River, Alberta, is 18 less than in Yellowknife, Northwest Territories. Double the number of frost-free days in Peace River is 75 more than the number in Yellowknife. What is the average number of frost-free days per year in each community?

26. **Investments** Zach invested in a term deposit that paid 4% interest per annum and in a municipal bond that paid 6% interest per annum. If he invested a total of $13 000 and earned $700 interest in a year, how much did he invest at each rate?

27. **Flying speeds** A plane flew 3000 km from Calgary to Montreal with the wind in 5 h. The return flight into the wind took 6 h. Find the wind speed and the speed of the plane in still air.

28. **Canadian universities** There are 79 universities in Canada. The number in Western Canada is 5 more than the number in Eastern Canada. The number in Central Canada is double the number in Western Canada. How many universities are there in each part of Canada?

Using the Strategies

1. The number 13 can be written as the difference of two squares.
$$13 = 49 - 36$$
$$= 7^2 - 6^2$$
What other whole numbers between 10 and 20 can be written as the difference of two squares?

2. If there are exactly four Mondays in January, on what days of the week can January 31 not fall?

3. A large marching band was performing on a football field. First, the band formed a square. Then, the band formed a rectangle, so that the number of rows increased by 5. How many were in the band?

4. Copy the diagram. Show two ways of dividing the square along grid lines into 4 congruent parts, so that each part contains exactly one ✗.

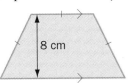

5. Each term in the following sequence is determined from the previous term only.
15, 26, 38, 67, 55, ...
Extend the sequence until you find the numbers that repeat. Which numbers repeat?

6. Estimate the number of ice cream cones the high school students in your province eat in a year.

7. The trapezoid has 3 equal sides. The length of the base is 2 cm less than the sum of the lengths of the three equal sides. The distance between the parallel sides is 8 cm. Find the area of the trapezoid.

8. If 3089 digits are used to number the pages in a book, beginning at page 1, how many pages are in the book?

9. What is the ones digit when 6317^{458} is written in standard form?

10. The 12 toothpicks have been arranged to make 3 identical squares.

How could you arrange the toothpicks to make 6 identical squares?

11. The vertices of a cube lie on a sphere of radius 5 cm. Find the volume of the cube, to the nearest tenth of a cubic centimetre.

12. Mark six points on a piece of paper, so that each point is 1 unit from exactly three other points.

1. If you worked for a charter airline and had to charter an aircraft to fly 240 passengers from Montreal to Mexico City, which type of aircraft would you choose? Explain.

2. If we assume that population increases are linear, the population of Canada for the years 1997 to 2025 can be modelled by the equation.
$$y = \frac{3}{14}x + 30$$
where y is the population, in millions, and x is the number of years since 1997.
For Uganda, the equation is
$$y = \frac{6}{7}x + 21$$
a) Explain why the equations model the population increases.
b) Use the equations to predict the year in which the population of Uganda will equal the population of Canada.

3. For the flag of each of the following provinces, estimate the percent that is blue and the percent that is yellow.
a) Newfoundland   **b)** British Columbia

CHAPTER 2

Linear Inequalities

The Pacific octopus is the largest species of octopus in the world. This giant can grow to over 100 kg and have a tentacle span of 9 m or more. Biologists are studying Pacific octopuses off the coast of Vancouver Island. Because the octopuses are bottom-dwellers, the biologists scuba dive to the seabed.

Scuba divers must be careful to avoid decompression sickness, or "the bends," when they return from high atmospheric pressure under water to normal atmospheric pressure at the surface. After spending too long in deep water, a scuba diver needs to undergo decompression by returning to the surface slowly, in stages.

The graph shows whether scuba divers need decompression after spending different lengths of time at various depths.

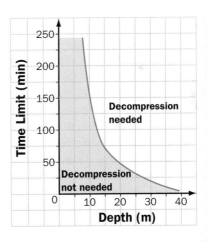

1. From the graph, estimate the maximum time a scuba diver can stay at each of the following depths without needing decompression.
a) 20 m **b)** 12 m **c)** 35 m

2. About how much longer can a scuba diver stay at a depth of 15 m than at a depth of 25 m without needing decompression?

3. Will a scuba diver need decompression after spending the given time at each depth?
a) 40 min at 12 m **b)** 100 min at 20 m **c)** 20 min at 24 m
d) 50 min at 24 m **e)** 30 min at 30 m **f)** 140 min at 10 m

4. The word *scuba* is an acronym. What words does it represent?

Frequency Ranges

The diagram shows one
cycle of a sound wave.

The frequency of a sound
wave is the number of waves that pass a given point in
one second. Frequency is measured in cycles per second
or hertz (Hz).

Low-pitched tones are produced by low-frequency
waves, and high-pitched tones by high-frequency waves.

The table gives the sound frequency ranges that can be
heard and produced by some animals.

Animal	Sound Frequency Range (Hz)	
	Heard	Produced
Dog	15–50 000	452–1080
Frog	50–10 000	50–8000
Cat	60–65 000	760–1520
Grasshopper	100–15 000	7000–100 000
Dolphin	150–150 000	7000–120 000
Robin	250–21 000	2000–13 000
Bat	1000–120 000	10 000–120 000

1. The expression $0 \leq x \leq 2$ is an example of a
compound inequality. It means that $x \geq 0$ and
$x \leq 2$. Write a compound inequality in the form
$\blacksquare \leq f \leq \blacktriangle$ for the following sound frequency ranges,
where f is the frequency, and $\blacksquare$ and $\blacktriangle$ are numbers.
a) the range heard by a robin
b) the range produced by a cat

2. Which animal in the table can
a) hear the greatest sound frequency range?
b) produce the greatest sound frequency range?
c) hear the smallest sound frequency range?
d) hear the second-smallest sound frequency range?
e) produce the smallest sound frequency range?
f) produce the second-smallest sound frequency range?

3. The sound frequency range produced by a guitar
is 82.4 Hz to 698 Hz. For a double bass, the values
are 41.2 Hz to 247 Hz. Can a robin hear
a) a guitar? **b)** a double bass?

4. a) Can a frog hear a bat?
b) Can a bat hear a frog?

5. a) Which animal in the table can produce some
sound frequencies that it is unable to hear?
b) About what percent of the frequency range this
animal can produce is it unable to hear?

6. A human can hear sound frequencies from
20 Hz to 20 000 Hz.
a) Write a compound inequality to show the range
of frequencies that satisfies both of the following
conditions.
• A human can hear the frequencies.
• A bat can produce the frequencies.
b) Of the range of frequencies a bat can produce,
what fraction can a human hear?

7. A human can produce sound frequencies from
80 Hz to 1100 Hz. A trained soprano singing voice
can produce frequencies from 262 Hz to 1046 Hz.
A trained bass singing voice can produce
frequencies from 82.4 Hz to 294 Hz.
a) If a bat were in an opera house during a duet
between a soprano and a bass, what would the bat hear?
b) If you spoke to a bat, would it hear you? Explain.

Warm Up

Identify which of the inequality signs $<$, $>$, $\leq$, or $\geq$ you would use to represent each of the following word phrases.

1. less than
2. more than
3. less than or equal to
4. greater than or equal to
5. no less than
6. at least
7. greater than
8. a maximum of
9. at most
10. fewer than
11. no more than
12. a minimum of

Use x as the variable and write an inequality represented by each graph.

13.
14.
15.
16.

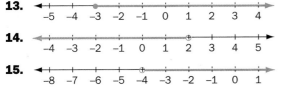

Use x as the variable and write a compound inequality represented by each graph.

17.
18.
19.
20.

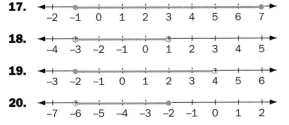

🖐 *How are the inequalities in each pair related? Explain.*
21. $x > 3$ and $3 < x$
22. $x \leq -2$ and $-2 \geq x$

🖐 *How are the compound inequalities in each pair related? Explain.*
23. $4 > x > 0$ and $0 < x < 4$
24. $-3 \leq x < 5$ and $5 > x \geq -3$

Mental Math

Equations and Inequalities

Copy and complete each ordered pair, so that it satisfies the given equation.

1. $x + y = 4$; (■, 1)   **2.** $y = x - 5$; (−2, ■)
3. $2x + y = 6$; (■, 2)   **4.** $x - 2y = -3$; (−1, ■)
5. $3x + 2y = -4$; (■, −2) **6.** $y = 2x - 1$; (■, 3)

For each inequality, write three different ordered pairs that include the given coordinate and that satisfy the inequality.

7. $x + y > 2$; (1, ■)   **8.** $y < x - 3$; (2, ■)
9. $x - y \geq -2$; (■, 1)   **10.** $y \geq 2 - x$; (■, 3)
11. $x - 2y < -3$; (1, ■) **12.** $2x + y \leq 3$; (−2, ■)

Squaring Two-Digit Numbers Beginning in 5

To square a two-digit number beginning in 5, add 25 to the ones digit. Then, affix the square of the ones digit.

For 57^2, $25 + 7 = 32$
$7^2 = 49$
So, $57^2 = 3249$

Estimate
$60^2 = 3600$

For 52^2, $25 + 2 = 27$
$2^2 = 04$
So, $52^2 = 2704$

Estimate
$50^2 = 2500$

Write 1^2 as 01, 2^2 as 04, and 3^2 as 09.

Calculate.
1. 58^2 **2.** 51^2 **3.** 56^2
4. 53^2 **5.** 55^2 **6.** 59^2

To calculate 5.7^2 or 570^2, find 57^2. Then, place the decimal point.
$57^2 = 3249$
So, $5.7^2 = 32.49$
and $570^2 = 324\,900$

Estimate
$6^2 = 36$
$600^2 = 360\,000$

Calculate.
7. 5.4^2 **8.** 540^2 **9.** 5.1^2
10. 520^2 **11.** 5.6^2 **12.** 590^2

Calculate.
13. 5.1×510 **14.** 530×5.3 **15.** 5.5×5500
16. 5800^2 **17.** 56×0.56 **18.** 0.57×5700

🧩 **19.** Let $50 + x$ represent a two-digit number
🖐 beginning in 5. Square this expression. Use the result to explain why the rule for squaring two-digit numbers beginning in 5 works.

2.1 Reviewing Linear Inequalities in One Variable

Long-track speed skater Catriona LeMay Doan from Saskatoon broke world records in both the 500-m and the 1000-m events on the same day in Calgary. We can describe her achievement in the form of an **inequality**. Her winning times were less than the old world records, or the old world records were greater than her winning times. A mathematical inequality may contain a symbol such as $<$, $\leq$, $>$, $\geq$, or $\neq$.

Event	Catriona's Time (s)	Old World Record (s)
500-m	37.90	38.69
1000-m	76.07	77.65

To solve an inequality, find values of the variable that make the inequality true. For example, the inequality $x + 2 > 7$ is true for $x = 5.1$, $x = 6$, $x = 7.25$, and all other real values of x greater than 5. These values are said to *satisfy* the inequality.

Explore: Solve the Inequalities

Passenger aircraft land at 240 km/h, but their speeds on their landing approaches are higher than this. When passenger aircraft descend for a landing, their speeds during descent are given by the inequalities $s - 320 \geq 0$ and $s - 320 \leq 80$, where s is the speed in kilometres per hour.
a) Solve the equations $s - 320 = 0$ and $s - 320 = 80$.
b) Solve the inequalities $s - 320 \geq 0$ and $s - 320 \leq 80$ using the same steps as you used in part a).

Inquire

1. What is the lowest speed at which a passenger aircraft can descend?

2. What is the highest speed at which a passenger aircraft can descend?

3. a) List the 3 greatest whole-number solutions for $s - 320 \leq 80$.
b) Use substitution to show that your 3 values from part a) satisfy both inequalities.

4. Solve each of the following inequalities using the same rules used to solve equations.
a) $4x + 7 < 15$ **b)** $7x + 2 > 23$
c) $0.8 + 1.3x > 7.3$ **d)** $\frac{1}{2}x - 5 < 3$

5. a) The table shows the results of various operations on both sides of the inequality $9 > 6$. Copy and complete the table by replacing each $\bullet$ with $>$ or $<$.

b) State the operations that reverse the direction of the inequality symbol.

Original Inequality	Operation	Resulting Inequality
$9 > 6$	Add 3	$9 + 3 \bullet 6 + 3$
$9 > 6$	Subtract 3	$9 - 3 \bullet 6 - 3$
$9 > 6$	Multiply by 3	$9 \times 3 \bullet 6 \times 3$
$9 > 6$	Multiply by –3	$9 \times (-3) \bullet 6 \times (-3)$
$9 > 6$	Divide by 3	$\frac{9}{3} \bullet \frac{6}{3}$
$9 > 6$	Divide by –3	$\frac{9}{-3} \bullet \frac{6}{-3}$

6. Test your statement from question 5b) by determining the results of the following operations.

	Inequality	Operation			Inequality	Operation
a)	$4 > -3$	Add 5		**b)**	$2 < 6$	Add -1
c)	$-3 < -1$	Subtract 2		**d)**	$-1 > -4$	Subtract -2
e)	$2 > -1$	Multiply by 4		**f)**	$-3 < -2$	Multiply by -3
g)	$4 > 3$	Multiply by 2		**h)**	$-4 < -3$	Multiply by -1
i)	$3 < 6$	Divide by 3		**j)**	$2 > -2$	Divide by -2
k)	$-4 < -2$	Divide by 2		**l)**	$-4 > -8$	Divide by -4

The results of performing operations on an inequality are summarized in the table. Similar results are observed for inequalities that include the symbols $<$, $\geq$, and $\leq$. These results and the methods you used to solve equations can be used to solve inequalities.

In the following examples and problems, assume that all variables represent real numbers.

Original Inequality	Operation	Resulting Inequality
$a > b$	Add c	$a + c > b + c$
$a > b$	Subtract c	$a - c > b - c$
$a > b$	Multiply by c, $c > 0$	$ac > bc$, $c > 0$
$a > b$	Multiply by c, $c < 0$	$ac < bc$, $c < 0$
$a > b$	Divide by c, $c > 0$	$\dfrac{a}{c} > \dfrac{b}{c}$, $c > 0$
$a > b$	Divide by c, $c < 0$	$\dfrac{a}{c} < \dfrac{b}{c}$, $c < 0$

Example 1　Solving an Inequality
Solve and check $3x - 2 < 13$.

Solution

Add 2 to both sides:

$$3x - 2 < 13$$
$$3x - 2 \;\boxed{+2}\; < 13 \;\boxed{+2}$$
$$3x < 15$$

Divide both sides by 3:
$$\frac{3x}{3} < \frac{15}{3}$$
$$x < 5$$

Check.
Try $x = 4$:　**L.S.** $= 3x - 2$　**R.S.** $= 13$
$$= 3(4) - 2$$
$$= 10$$
$$\text{L.S.} < \text{R.S.}$$

The solution is any real number less than 5.

Example 2　Solving and Graphing
Solve $2(3 - x) - 1 \geq 7$. Graph the solution.

Solution

Expand to remove brackets:

$$2(3 - x) - 1 \geq 7$$
$$6 - 2x - 1 \geq 7$$
$$5 - 2x \geq 7$$

Subtract 5 from both sides:
$$5 - 2x \;\boxed{-5}\; \geq 7 \;\boxed{-5}$$
$$-2x \geq 2$$

Divide both sides by -2:
$$\frac{-2x}{-2} \leq \frac{2}{-2}$$
$$x \leq -1$$

When you multiply or divide by a negative number, reverse the direction of the symbol.

The solution is any real number less than or equal to -1.

The graph is as shown. The closed dot at $x = -1$ shows that -1 is included in the solution.

Example 3 Solving an Inequality Involving Fractions

Solve $\dfrac{3x}{4} + \dfrac{x}{2} > 5$. Graph the solution.

Solution

The LCD is 4.

$$\frac{3x}{4} + \frac{x}{2} > 5$$

Multiply both sides by 4: $\boxed{4 \times}\left(\dfrac{3x}{4} + \dfrac{x}{2}\right) > \boxed{4 \times 5}$

$$3x + 2x > 20$$
$$5x > 20$$

Divide both sides by 5: $\dfrac{5x}{\boxed{5}} > \dfrac{20}{\boxed{5}}$

$$x > 4$$

The solution is any real number greater than 4.

The graph is as shown. The open dot at $x = 4$ shows that 4 is not included in the solution.

Check.

Try $x = 8$: **L.S.** $= \dfrac{3x}{4} + \dfrac{x}{2}$ **R.S.** $= 5$

$$= \frac{3(8)}{4} + \frac{8}{2}$$
$$= 6 + 4$$
$$= 10$$

L.S. > R.S.

```
  +---+---+---+---+---+---⊕---+---+---+---+---→
 -1   0   1   2   3   4   5   6   7   8
```

Example 4   Selling Hiking Staffs

Volunteers from a hiking association are selling hiking staffs as a fund raiser. The cost of making the staffs is a fixed overhead of $2000, plus $10 per staff. Each staff is sold for $30. What number of staffs must be sold for the revenue to exceed the cost?

Solution

Let x represent the number of staffs made and sold.
The cost of making the staffs, $C = 2000 + 10x$
The revenue from selling the staffs, $R = 30x$
For the revenue to exceed the cost, $R > C$
$$\text{so } 30x > 2000 + 10x$$

Method 1: Solving algebraically

$$30x > 2000 + 10x$$

Subtract $10x$ from both sides: $30x \boxed{-10x} > 2000 + 10x \boxed{-10x}$

$$20x > 2000$$

Divide both sides by 20: $\dfrac{20x}{\boxed{20}} > \dfrac{2000}{\boxed{20}}$

$$x > 100$$

Method 2: Solving graphically

Graph the cost equation and the revenue equation on the same set of axes.

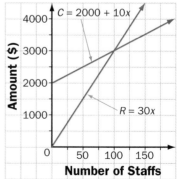

Over 100 staffs must be sold for the revenue to exceed the cost.

From the graph, $30x > 2000 + 10x$ when $x > 100$.

Practice

Solve and check.

1. $y + 9 < 11$ **2.** $2w + 5 > 3$

3. $3x - 4 \geq 5$ **4.** $2z + 9 \leq 3$

5. $-3x < 6$ **6.** $4t > 3t - 4$

7. $2(m - 3) \leq 0$ **8.** $4(n + 2) \geq 8$

Solve and check.

9. $2x + 1 > 2$ **10.** $3x + 4 < 2$

11. $6y + 4 \leq 5y + 3$ **12.** $4z - 3 \geq 3z + 2$

13. $7 + 3x < 2x + 9$ **14.** $5(2x - 1) > 5$

15. $2(3x - 2) \leq -4$ **16.** $4(2x + 1) \geq 2$

Solve. Graph the solution.

17. $6x + 2 \leq 4x + 8$ **18.** $4x - 1 > x + 5$

19. $2(x + 3) < x + 4$ **20.** $3(x - 2) > x - 4$

21. $3(y + 2) \geq 2(y + 1)$ **22.** $3(2z - 1) \leq 2(1 + z)$

23. $6x - 3(x + 1) > x + 5$

24. $2(x - 2) - 1 < 4(1 - x) + 1$

Solve.

25. $6 - 2x > 4$ **26.** $8 - 3x < 5$

27. $3y - 8 \geq 7y + 8$ **28.** $6 - 3c \leq 2(c - 2)$

29. $4(1 - x) \geq 3(x - 1)$ **30.** $-2(3 + x) < 4(x - 2)$

31. $4x - 3(2x + 1) \leq 4(x - 3)$

32. $2(3t - 1) - 5t > -6(1 - t) + 7$

Solve. Graph the solution.

33. $\dfrac{y}{3} + 2 < 1$ **34.** $\dfrac{w}{2} + 2 > 3$

35. $\dfrac{2x}{3} + 1 \geq 2$ **36.** $\dfrac{3z}{4} + 5 \leq -1$

37. $1.2x - 0.1 > 3.5$ **38.** $0.8x + 2.5 < -2.3$

39. $1.9 \geq 4.9 - 1.5q$ **40.** $4.6 - 1.8n \leq -0.8$

Solve.

41. $2(1.2a + 2.5) > 0.2$

42. $4(1.8 - 0.5x) \leq 5.2$

43. $0.75y - 2.6 < 0.25y - 3.1$

44. $3(1.3n + 0.3) \geq 3.5n + 0.1$

45. $1.5(x + 2) + 1 > 2.5(1 - x) - 0.5$

46. $2(1.5x + 1) - 1 < 5(0.2x + 0.3) - 0.5$

Solve.

47. $\dfrac{x + 1}{2} < \dfrac{x + 2}{3}$ **48.** $\dfrac{2 - x}{2} \geq \dfrac{2x + 1}{4}$

49. $\dfrac{z + 2}{4} > \dfrac{z - 1}{5} + 1$ **50.** $\dfrac{2 - 3x}{2} + \dfrac{2}{3} \leq \dfrac{3x - 2}{6}$

Applications and Problem Solving

51. Art supplies Katrina has a $50 gift voucher for an arts supply store. She wants to buy a sketch pad and some markers. Including taxes, a sketch pad costs $18 and a marker costs $4. Use the inequality $4m + 18 \leq 50$ to determine the number of markers, m, she can buy.

52. Impalas and lions An impala can leap a distance of 12.2 m in a single bound when it is trying to escape from a predator. This distance is 0.4 m less than 7 times the maximum distance that a pursuing lion can leap. Solve the inequality $12.2 \geq 7d - 0.4$ to find the distance, d metres, the lion can leap.

53. Measurement In $\triangle ABC$, $\angle A$ is obtuse and measures $5x + 10$ degrees. Solve the inequalities $5x + 10 > 90$ and $5x + 10 < 180$ to find the possible values of x.

54. Pizza toppings The cost of an extra large tomato and cheese pizza is $12.25, plus $1.55 for each extra topping.

a) Let n represent the number of extra toppings. Write an expression, including n, to represent the total cost of the pizza.

b) Suppose you have $20 you can spend on the pizza. Write and solve an inequality to find the number of extra toppings you can afford.

55. Weekly earnings Mario earns $15/h after taxes and other deductions. He spends a total of $75/week on lunches and travel to and from work.

a) Write an expression to represent how much Mario has at the end of a week in which he works t hours.

b) Write and solve an inequality to determine how many hours Mario must work to have at least $450 at the end of the week.

56. Baseball caps A college baseball team raises money by selling baseball caps. The cost of making the caps includes a fixed cost of $500, plus $7 per cap. The caps sell for $15 each. What is the minimum number of caps the team can order in one batch and still raise money?

57. Manitoba towns Steinbach and Winkler are towns near Winnipeg. From 1986 to 1996, the population of Steinbach increased from 7500 to 8500. Over the same period, the population of Winkler increased from 6000 to 7200. If each population continues to increase at the same rate as it did from 1986 to 1996, over what time period would you expect the population of Winkler to be greater than the population of Steinbach?

58. Areas of islands The largest island in British Columbia is Vancouver Island, with an area of about 31 000 km^2. This area is about 1000 km^2 less than five times the area of Graham Island, which is the second largest island in the province.
a) Write and solve an inequality to state the areas of the islands that are smaller than Graham Island.
b) Use your research skills to identify the third largest island in British Columbia. What is the area of this island?
c) Is there a minimum area for an island? Explain.

59. Measurement a) What values of x give this rectangle a perimeter of more than 32 cm?

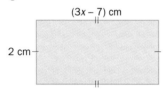
(3x – 7) cm

2 cm

b) What values of x give the rectangle an area of less than 40 cm^2?
c) In part b), does x have a minimum value? Explain.

60. Measurement Determine the values of x that give this triangle a perimeter of no more than 15 and no less than 12.

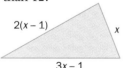
2(x – 1)

x

3x – 1

61. Driving times Jason left Calgary at 10:00 and drove 620 km to Saskatoon at an average speed of 80 km/h. Ravi left Calgary an hour later and drove to Saskatoon at an average speed of 100 km/h. Between what times of the day was Ravi further from Calgary than Jason was?

62. a) Solve the inequality $3 + \dfrac{2}{x} \geq 1$.
b) State the restriction on the variable.
c) Graph the solution.
d) Describe how the graph shows the restriction.

63. a) Try to solve the equation $4x + 2(x + 1) = 6x - 2$. What is the result?
b) What real values of x satisfy the equation?
c) Try to solve the inequality $4x + 2(x + 1) > 6x - 2$. What is the result?
d) What real values of x satisfy the inequality?

64. Technology a) Predict the graph of the following expression, if it is drawn using a graphing calculator.
$$y = (x - 3)(x < 2)$$
Check your prediction using a graphing calculator in the dot mode. Describe the result.
b) Repeat part a) for the expression $y = (2 - x)(x < 5)$.
c) Repeat part a) for the expression $y = (x + 4)(x > -4)$.

65. Write the following inequalities. Have a classmate solve them.
a) variables on both sides and the solution $x \leq 2$
b) brackets on both sides and the solution $x > -3$
c) denominators of 3 and 2 and the solution $x < 0$

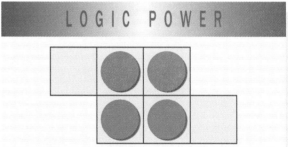

LOGIC POWER

Find the smallest number of moves needed to switch the positions of the red and blue counters. A counter can move to an empty square by going up, down, left, or right, but not diagonally.

Solving Inequalities With a Graphing Calculator

1 Displaying a Solution

Some graphing calculators can be used to display the solution to an inequality in one variable. To display the solution to $2x + 1 < 3x - 2$, enter the inequality as follows.

$$Y_1 = 2X + 1 < 3X - 2$$

Then, graph Y_1 in the standard viewing window using the dot mode.

1. Using paper and pencil, solve the inequality algebraically and graph the solution.

2. Compare your graph from question 1 with the way the calculator displays the solution.

3. Using the TRACE instruction, find the values of x in the solution.

4. Describe how each of the following can be used to give a more accurate answer than you found in question 3.
a) the ZOOM instruction   **b)** the TABLE and TABLE SETUP menus
c) changing the viewing window

5. a) Using the TRACE instruction, find the value of y for each value of x in the solution.
b) Explain why the graph of the solution does not lie on the x-axis.

6. Graph Y_1 using the connected mode instead of the dot mode. Explain why the dot mode should be used.

7. a) Modify the inequality by changing the $<$ symbol to $\leq$. Display the solution on the calculator.
b) Does the graphing calculator distinguish between $<$ and $\leq$? Explain.

2 Solving Inequalities

Display the solution to each of the following inequalities using a graphing calculator. In your notebook, sketch each display and describe how it should be modified to show the solution fully. State the solution to each inequality.

1. $2x + 3 \geq 7$

2. $3x - 1 < 8$

3. $2x - 3 > -x$

4. $5x + 8 \leq 4x + 5$

5. $-4x + 2 \leq -2$

6. $3x + 2 \geq 5x - 6$

7. $2(x - 3) \leq 4x - 2$

8. $3(x - 1) - x > 4(x + 1) - 1$

9. $\frac{2}{3}x \geq x - 1$

10. $\frac{3}{4}x + \frac{2}{3}x - \frac{5}{6} < 2(x - 1)$

11. $\frac{x - 1}{2} < \frac{x - 2}{3}$

12. $3 + \frac{x - 3}{6} \leq x$

13. $x - 2 \geq 3x - 1$

14. $4(x + 2) > 2(5 - x)$

15. Some graphing calculators have the capability to solve inequalities algebraically. If this type of calculator is available, use it to solve the inequalities in questions 1–14.

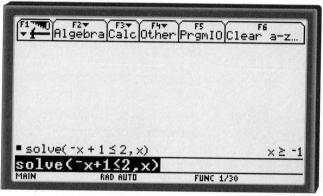

PROBLEM SOLVING

2.2 Solve a Simpler Problem

For some problems, a simpler or related problem may be easier to solve than the original problem. The solution to the simpler or related problem may give clues for solving the original problem.

At the end of a play, the 13 actors are introduced to the audience. The actors wait behind the curtain until their names are announced. The first actor introduced takes a spot on the stage facing the audience. The second actor introduced could stand on either side of the first actor. The third actor introduced could stand on either side of the two already on stage. The process continues for the remaining 10 actors. When introduced, each actor takes a position at one end of the line of actors. In how many different ways can the actors be lined up on the stage after all 13 have been introduced?

Understand the Problem

1. What information are you given?
2. What are you asked to find?
3. Do you need an exact or an approximate answer?

Think of a Plan

List the possible ways the first few actors could line up on the stage. Then, see if there is a pattern.

Carry Out the Plan

Actors	Possible Ways to Line Up								Number of Ways
A				A					1
A, B		AB				BA			2
A, B, C	CAB		ABC		CBA		BAC		4
A, B, C, D	DCAB	CABD	DABC	ABCD	DCBA	CBAD	DBAC	BACD	8

The numbers of ways are all powers of 2.
$1 = 2^0$, $2 = 2^1$, $4 = 2^2$, and $8 = 2^3$.
In each case, the exponent in the power of 2 is one less than the number of actors on stage.
For n actors, the number of ways is 2^{n-1}.
For 13 actors, the number of ways is 2^{13-1} or 2^{12} or 4096.

The actors can be lined up in 4096 different ways.

Look Back

Is there another way to solve the problem?

Solve a Simpler Problem

1. Break the problem into smaller parts.
2. Solve the problem.
3. Check that your answer is reasonable.

Applications and Problem Solving

1. Find the area of ABCDE.

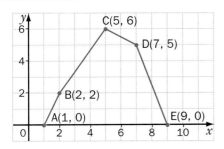

2. Evaluate.
$1 \times 2 - 2 \times 2 + 3 \times 2 - 4 \times 2 \ldots - 100 \times 2$

3. For how many whole numbers between 0 and 1000 does the sum of the digits equal 9?

4. Find the exact value of this difference.
$(5\ 555\ 555\ 555)^2 - (4\ 444\ 444\ 445)^2$

5. The first figure is made from one n-shape, the second from two n-shapes, the third from three n-shapes, and so on.

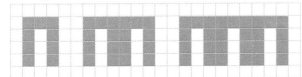

If the smallest squares on the grid measure 1 unit by 1 unit, what is the perimeter of the 60th figure?

6. Suppose you have a set of cards numbered consecutively from 1 to 100. You try to put the cards in pairs so that the sum of the numbers on the cards in each pair is 94. How many pairs will have a sum of 94?

7. Consider the following transformation on the number 119.
$$119 \rightarrow 1^2 + 1^2 + 9^2 = 83$$
$$83 \rightarrow 8^2 + 3^2 = 73$$
$$73 \rightarrow 7^2 + 3^2 = 58$$
$$58 \rightarrow 5^2 + 8^2 = 89$$
and so on
If this transformation is carried out on the number 42, what number results after 500 transformations?

8. How much more does a million dollars in toonies weigh than a million dollars in ten-dollar bills?

9. Without using a calculator, find the number of digits in the number n, if $n = 2^{23} \times 5^{19}$.

10. The whole numbers are arranged as follows.

Row	Number
1	1
2	2 3
3	4 5 6
4	7 8 9 10
5	11 12 13 14 15
and so on	

a) Write an expression for the last number in each row in terms of the row number.
b) What is the last number in the 38th row?
c) What number is in the 22nd column of the 56th row?

11. Evaluate.
$1 + 2 + 3 + \ldots + 1000 + \ldots + 3 + 2 + 1$

12. a) Find the number of triangles in each figure.

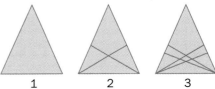

b) How many triangles are in the 17th figure? the 99th figure?

13. Write a problem that can be solved by solving a simpler problem. Have a classmate solve your problem.

NUMBER POWER

For the arithmetic series $2x + 6x + \ldots + 198x$, where x is an integer, what are
a) the two smallest values of x that make the sum a perfect square?
b) the two smallest positive values of x that make the sum a perfect cube?

INVESTIGATING MATH

Graphing Inequalities in the Coordinate Plane

The graph represents the inequality $x > 4$. The open dot shows that $x = 4$ does not satisfy the inequality. However, the point $x = 4$ is important because it is the **boundary point** that divides the number line into two parts or **regions**. In one region, the values of x satisfy $x > 4$, but in the other region they do not.

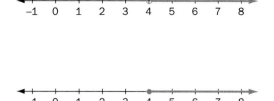

On the graph of $x \geq 4$, the point $x = 4$ is again the boundary point. The closed dot shows that $x = 4$ satisfies the inequality. The above ideas can be extended to graphs of inequalities in the coordinate plane.

1 Inequalities in One Variable

1. The graph represents the equation $x = 3$ in the coordinate plane.
a) Choose any point on the line $x = 3$ and record its coordinates.
b) Choose a second point directly to the left of your first point.
c) How does the y-coordinate of the second point compare with the y-coordinate of the first point?
d) How does the x-coordinate of the second point compare with the x-coordinate of the first point?

2. The graph represents the inequality $x \leq 3$. The line $x = 3$ is the **boundary line** that divides the coordinate plane into two parts or regions.
a) Do the points on the boundary line satisfy the inequality?
 b) Does the shaded region on the graph show points that satisfy the inequality or points that do not? Explain.

3. The graph represents the inequality $x < 3$. The line $x = 3$ is the boundary line.
a) Do the points on the boundary line satisfy the inequality?
b) How does the graph represent your answer to part a)?

4. Graph each inequality in the coordinate plane.
a) $x \geq 4$ **b)** $x > 5$ **c)** $x \leq 2$
d) $x < 1$ **e)** $x \geq -1$ **f)** $x < -3$

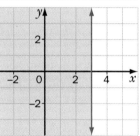

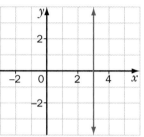

5. a) Graph the equation $y = 2$ in the coordinate plane.
b) Use the symbols $\leq$, $<$, $\geq$, and $>$ to write four inequalities for which the line $y = 2$ is the boundary line.
c) On separate grids, graph each of the four inequalities from part b) in the coordinate plane.
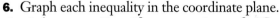 **d)** Explain why you graphed each inequality in the way you did.

6. Graph each inequality in the coordinate plane.
a) $y \geq 1$ **b)** $y \leq 0$ **c)** $y > -2$ **d)** $y < -3$

7. a) Graph the inequality $y \neq 6$.
b) Explain why you graphed the inequality in the way you did.

8. Graph each inequality in the coordinate plane.
a) $x - 2 \geq 0$ **b)** $y + 1 \leq 0$ **c)** $x + 2 < 0$ **d)** $y - 3 > 0$

2 Linear Inequalities in Two Variables

1. a) Graph the line $y = x + 2$, where x and y represent real numbers.
b) Choose any point on the line and record its coordinates.
c) Choose a second point directly above your first point and record its coordinates.
d) How does the x-coordinate of the second point compare with the x-coordinate of the first point?
e) How does the y-coordinate of the second point compare with the y-coordinate of the first point?
f) Do the coordinates of the second point satisfy the inequality $y \geq x + 2$? the inequality $y \leq x + 2$?
g) Would you shade above or below the boundary line to graph the inequality $y \geq x + 2$? Explain.
h) How would the graph of $y > x + 2$ differ from the graph of $y \geq x + 2$?

2. a) Graph the line $y = x - 1$, where x and y represent real numbers.
b) Choose any point on the line and record its coordinates.
c) Choose a second point directly below your first point and record its coordinates.
d) How does the x-coordinate of the second point compare with the x-coordinate of the first point?
e) How does the y-coordinate of the second point compare with the y-coordinate of the first point?
f) Do the coordinates of the second point satisfy the inequality $y \leq x - 1$? the inequality $y \geq x - 1$?
g) Would you shade above or below the boundary line to graph the inequality $y \leq x - 1$? Explain.
h) How would the graph of $y < x - 1$ differ from the graph of $y \leq x - 1$?

3. Graph each of the following inequalities for real values of the variables.
a) $y > -x + 1$ **b)** $y \leq -x + 1$
c) $y < -x + 1$ **d)** $y \geq -x + 1$
e) $y \leq 2x - 1$ **f)** $y > -2x + 3$
g) $y < \dfrac{x}{2} + 1$ **h)** $y \geq -1 - 3x$

4. On the graph of each of the following linear inequalities, in which x, y, ■, and ▲ represent real numbers, would you shade above the boundary line or below the boundary line?
a) $y < ■x + ▲$ **b)** $y \leq ■x + ▲$
c) $y > ■x + ▲$ **d)** $y \geq ■x + ▲$

5. Graph the inequality $y \neq x + 3$.

3 Restricting the Variables

The graph of $y \geq x - 2$, where x and y are real numbers, is shown.

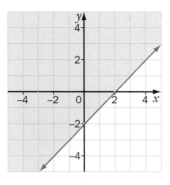

Suppose the possible lengths and widths of a rectangle are related by a similar inequality, $l \geq w - 2$.

The graph of $l \geq w - 2$ is shown. The graphs are different because, in a rectangle, the length and the width are restricted to values greater than zero. The graph of $l \geq w - 2$ does not include the points on the axes. Also, the graph does not extend below the x-axis or to the left of the y-axis.

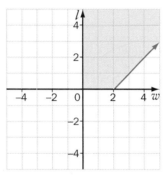

1. The graph represents the relationship between two negative real numbers, a and b, where $b < 2a - 3$.

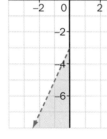

a) Describe how this graph is different from the graph of $y < 2x - 3$, where x and y are real numbers.
b) Explain why the graphs are different.

2. Graph each inequality.
a) $l \leq 2w + 3$, where l and w are the length and width of a rectangle
b) $m > n + 1$, where m and n are positive real numbers

3. Identify whether each of the following is represented by the graph shown, if x and y are real numbers. Explain.

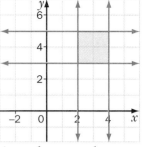

a) $y \geq x + 1, x \geq 2, y \geq 3$
b) $x > 2, x < 4, y > 3, y < 5$
c) $2 \leq x \leq 4, 3 \leq y \leq 5$
d) $x \geq 2, y \geq 3$

4. Graph each of the following, where x and y are real numbers.
a) $x > -1, y > -2$ **b)** $x \leq 0, y \geq 1$
c) $y > 2x, y \geq 0, x \geq 0$ **d)** $y \leq x - 1, x \leq 0$
e) $y \leq x - 1, y \leq 0$ **f)** $y \leq x - 1, x \leq 0, y \leq 0$

5. Reading habits Every weekday morning, Melanie spends between 20 min and 30 min reading the newspaper, and between 5 min and 15 min checking her e-mail messages. Graph newspaper reading time versus e-mail reading time to show the possible combinations of times she spends on these activities on a weekday morning.

6. Baseball A baseball has a cork centre encased in rubber, yarn, and cowhide. The circumference is permitted to be from 230 mm to 235 mm, and the mass from 142 g to 156 g. Graph mass versus circumference to show the values permitted for a baseball.

7. Measurement Determine the area of the region represented by each of the following.
a) $2 \leq y \leq 4, 1 \leq x \leq 3$
b) $0 \leq x \leq 2, -1 \leq y \leq 5$
c) $y \leq x, y \leq 8 - x, y \geq 3$
d) $y \leq x + 5, 0 \leq y \leq 9, 0 \leq x \leq 4$

Graphing Linear Inequalities With a Graphing Calculator

A linear inequality in two variables can be graphed on a graphing calculator. On some calculators, the Shade instruction can be used to shade above or below the boundary line.

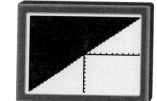

1 Graphing Inequalities

Use a graphing calculator to graph each of the following inequalities in the standard viewing window. Sketch each graph in your notebook.

1. $y \geq x + 1$ **2.** $y \leq x - 2$

3. Describe the steps you followed in questions 1 and 2 to draw the graphs with a calculator.

Graph each of the following in the standard viewing window. Sketch each graph.
4. $y \leq 2x + 3$ **5.** $y \geq 3x - 1$

Graphing calculators do not distinguish between solid and broken boundary lines. Graph each of the following in the standard viewing window. Sketch each graph, showing the boundary line as solid or broken.

6. $y > 2x$ **7.** $y < 3 - x$ **8.** $y \geq -2x - 1$

9. $y < \dfrac{1}{3}x - 1$ **10.** $y \leq 4(x - 1)$ **11.** $y > 2 - \dfrac{3}{2}x$

2 Solving for y and Graphing

To graph the inequality $2x + y < 3$ on a graphing calculator, first solve for y.
$$2x + y < 3$$

Subtract $2x$ from both sides: $2x + y \;-2x\; < 3 \;-2x$
$$y < 3 - 2x$$

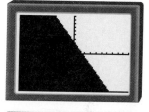

For the inequality $x - 2y \geq 4$,
$$x - 2y \geq 4$$

Subtract x from both sides: $x - 2y \;-x\; \geq 4 \;-x$
$$-2y \geq 4 - x$$

Divide both sides by -2: $\dfrac{-2y}{-2} \leq \dfrac{4 - x}{-2}$ Remember to reverse the inequality symbol.

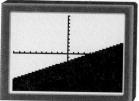

$$y \leq -2 + \dfrac{x}{2}$$

Solve each inequality for y.
1. $y + 2 > x$ **2.** $y - x < 1$ **3.** $y + 2x \leq -3$

4. $2y - x \geq -4$ **5.** $x - y < 3$ **6.** $2x - 3y \geq -6$

7. $3x \leq 2y - 2$ **8.** $1 > x - y$ **9.** $1 - \dfrac{y}{2} < -x$

Graph each of the following in the standard viewing window. Sketch each graph, showing the boundary line as solid or broken.

10. $y + 1 \leq x$ **11.** $y - 0.5x > 3$ **12.** $2x + 2y < 1$

13. $x - y \leq -1$ **14.** $x + \dfrac{1}{2}y \geq 0$ **15.** $-3 < 3x - 2y$

2.3 Graphing Linear Inequalities in Two Variables

When the equal sign in a linear equation in two variables is replaced with $<$, $>$, $\geq$, $\leq$, or $\neq$, a linear inequality in two variables results. The solution to such an inequality is the set of all the ordered pairs that make the inequality true.

Explore: Interpret the Data

For a CFL team, a game can end in a win, a loss, or a tie. Each team plays 18 league games in a season. If a team has x wins and y losses, the team's total number of wins and losses in a complete season is given by $x + y \leq 18$. In what situation is

a) $x + y = 18$?   **b)** $x + y < 18$?

Inquire

1. For the inequality $x - y \leq 2$, where x and y represent real numbers, use the intercepts to graph the boundary line $x - y = 2$.

2. Substitute $x = 0$ and $y = 0$ into $x - y \leq 2$ to determine whether the point $(0, 0)$ satisfies the inequality.

3. Using your result from question 2, decide whether to shade above or below the boundary line for the graph of $x - y \leq 2$. Explain your reasoning.

4. Solve $x - y \leq 2$ for y.

5. Using your result from question 4, decide whether to shade above or below the boundary line for the graph of $x - y \leq 2$.

6. Do your answers from questions 3 and 5 agree?

7. a) Graph the inequality $x + y \leq 18$ to represent the possible numbers of wins and losses for a CFL team in a complete season. Use shading for convenience, even though x and y are restricted to whole-number values.
b) How does the graph show the other restrictions on x and y?
c) Describe how you decided whether to shade above or below the boundary line.

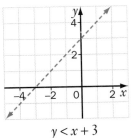

The graph of the linear equation $y = x + 3$, where x and y represent real numbers, divides the coordinate plane into two regions, or **half-planes**. The line is called the boundary line for the two regions. One region is described by $y > x + 3$, and the other by $y < x + 3$.

When $y = x + 3$ is the boundary line for an inequality, the line may be solid or broken. This depends on whether the line is included in the solution.

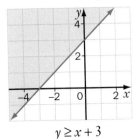

$y \geq x + 3$

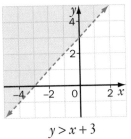

$y > x + 3$

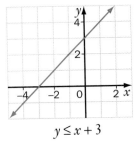

$y \leq x + 3$

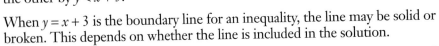

$y < x + 3$

Example 1 Boundary Lines in the Form $y = mx + b$

Graph $y \geq 2x + 1$.

Solution

Since $y \geq 2x + 1$ means $y > 2x + 1$ or $y = 2x + 1$, the boundary line is included in the solution. Using pencil and paper or a graphing calculator, graph the boundary line $y = 2x + 1$ as a solid line. To include points that satisfy $y > 2x + 1$, shade the region above the line.

Check.
Test the point $(0, 3)$, which is in the shaded region.

L.S. $= y$ **R.S.** $= 2x + 1$
$\quad\quad = 3 \quad\quad\quad\quad = 2(0) + 1$
$\quad\quad\quad\quad\quad\quad\quad\quad = 1$

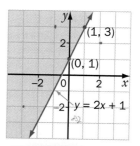

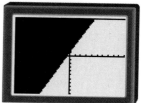

Since L.S. $>$ R.S., the point $(0, 3)$ satisfies the inequality $y \geq 2x + 1$. The correct side of the line has been shaded.

When y is isolated on the left side of an inequality, the inequality symbol shows which side of the boundary line to shade.
For $y > mx + b$ or $y \geq mx + b$, shade above the boundary line.
For $y < mx + b$ or $y \leq mx + b$, shade below the boundary line.

For some inequalities, such as $4x - 3y < -12$, the boundary line can be graphed using the intercepts. In this case, the inequality symbol does not directly show which side of the boundary line to shade.

Example 2 Boundary Lines in the Form $Ax + By = C$

Graph $4x - 3y < -12$.

Solution 1 Using the Intercepts and a Test Point

Since the inequality symbol is $<$, points on the boundary line are not included in the solution. Use the intercepts to draw the boundary line $4x - 3y = -12$ as a broken line.

Use $(0, 0)$ as the test point, and substitute $(0, 0)$ into the inequality.

For $4x - 3y < -12$,
L.S. $= 4(0) - 3(0)$ **R.S.** $= -12$
$\quad\quad = 0 \quad\quad\quad\quad\quad\quad = -12$

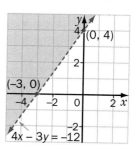

Since 0 is not less than -12, the point $(0, 0)$ does not satisfy the inequality. The point $(0, 0)$ is below the boundary line, so shade above the boundary line.

Note that $(0, 0)$ is usually chosen as the test point, if $(0, 0)$ does not lie on the boundary line. The coordinates $(0, 0)$ are the easiest values to substitute.

Solution 2　Solving for y

Solve the inequality for y.

$$4x - 3y < -12$$

Subtract $4x$ from both sides: $\quad 4x - 3y \boxed{-4x} < -12 \boxed{-4x}$

$$-3y < -12 - 4x$$

Divide both sides by -3: $\quad \dfrac{-3y}{-3} > \dfrac{-12 - 4x}{-3}$　Remember to reverse the inequality symbol.

$$y > 4 + \frac{4}{3}x$$

Draw the boundary line $y = \dfrac{4}{3}x + 4$ as a broken line. Because the inequality solved for y is $y > \dfrac{4}{3}x + 4$, shade above the boundary line.

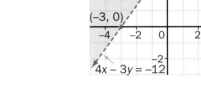

Check for both solutions.
Test the point $(-2, 4)$, which is in the shaded region.

In $4x - 3y < -12$,
L.S. $= 4(-2) - 3(4)$　**R.S.** $= -12$
$\quad\quad = -8 - 12$
$\quad\quad = -20$

Since L.S. < R.S., the point $(-2, 4)$ satisfies the inequality $4x - 3y < -12$.
So, the correct side of the line has been shaded.

Example 3　Buying Flowers

The library staff wants to plant flowers on the boulevard in front of the library. During a sale at the garden store, a flat of marigolds costs $5 and a flat of petunias costs $6. The store is paying the taxes. The library staff can spend a maximum of $60.
a) Write an inequality to describe the numbers of flats of marigolds and flats of petunias the library staff can buy.
b) What are the restrictions on the variables?
c) Graph the inequality.
d) Use the graph to find four possible combinations of flats of marigolds and flats of petunias the staff could buy. Assume that only whole numbers of flats can be bought.

Solution
a) Let m represent the number of flats of marigolds, and p represent the number of flats of petunias.
A flat of marigolds costs $5, so the cost of the marigolds is $5m$ dollars.
A flat of petunias costs $6, so the cost of the petunias is $6p$ dollars.
The maximum amount that can be spent is $60.
So, $5m + 6p \le 60$
b) The number of flats cannot be negative, so $m \ge 0$ and $p \ge 0$. Also, m and p must be whole numbers.

c) Because the inequality symbol is ≤, points on the boundary line are included in the solution. Use the intercepts to draw the boundary line $5m + 6p = 60$ as a solid line segment. As $m \geq 0$ and $p \geq 0$, the line segment should be drawn in the first quadrant.

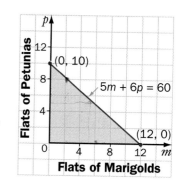

Decide whether to shade above or below the boundary line by using (0, 0) as a test point or by solving the inequality for p. Though the variables must be whole numbers, shade the entire region above or below the boundary line for convenience.

For $5m + 6p \leq 60$,
L.S. $= 5m + 6p$ **R.S.** $= 60$
$\qquad = 5(0) + 6(0)$
$\qquad = 0$

Since L.S. ≤ R.S., the point (0, 0) satisfies the inequality.
As the point (0, 0) is below the boundary line, shade below the boundary line.

d) The staff could spend $60 or less by choosing any whole-number values plotted on the boundary line or in the shaded region. Four examples are 10 flats of petunias and 0 flats of marigolds; 7 flats of marigolds and 0 flats of petunias; 6 flats of petunias and 2 flats of marigolds; or 4 flats of each.

Practice

Which of the given ordered pairs are solutions to the inequality?

1. $y \geq 3x - 5$
  (2, 2), (−1, −9), (1, −2), (0, 0)

2. $y < -2x + 4$
  (0, 0), (−3, 8), (4, −3), (2, 0)

3. $2x + 3y > 6$
  (0, 0), (3, 0), (5, −1), (−1, −2)

4. $3x - 4y \leq -12$
  (2, 5), (−4, 0), (0, 0), (−5, −1)

Graph each inequality.

5. $y \leq x - 2$ **6.** $y > x - 1$ **7.** $y > 2x - 1$
8. $y \leq 1 - 3x$ **9.** $y \geq 3x$ **10.** $y < 2x$

Graph each inequality.

11. $x + y > 5$ **12.** $x - y \leq -1$
13. $2x - y \geq 0$ **14.** $4x + y \leq 8$
15. $3x - 2y > -6$ **16.** $4x - 5y < 12$

Graph each inequality.

17. $x > y$ **18.** $2x \leq 3y$
19. $3x - 2 \geq y$ **20.** $10 < 5y - 4x$
21. $3x + 2y - 8 > 0$ **22.** $2x - 3y - 9 \leq 0$

Graph each inequality.

23. $y \geq \dfrac{1}{2}x + 1$

24. $y < 2 - \dfrac{x}{3}$

25. $y < \dfrac{1 - 3x}{2}$

26. $\dfrac{x}{2} + \dfrac{y}{3} \leq 1$

27. $\dfrac{x}{3} - \dfrac{y}{4} > \dfrac{1}{2}$

28. $\dfrac{2}{5}x + \dfrac{y}{2} \geq 2$

Given the restriction on the variables, graph each inequality.

29. $y > x - 2,\ x \geq 0,\ y \geq 0$
30. $x + y \geq 3,\ x \geq 0,\ y \geq 0$
31. $x - y \geq 1,\ x \leq 0,\ y \geq 0$
32. $y \leq 2 - 3x,\ x \geq 0,\ y \leq 0$
33. $2y + 3x < 6,\ x \geq 0,\ y \geq 0$
34. $4x - 5y < 20,\ x \leq 0,\ y \leq 0$

Applications and Problem Solving

35. Numbers Two positive real numbers, m and n, are related by the inequality $m - 3n \geq 6$.
a) What are the restrictions on m and n?
b) Graph the inequality.
c) Write three ordered pairs in the form (m, n) that satisfy the inequality.

36. Measurement The length of a rectangle, *l* metres, is greater than or equal to 1 m less than twice the width, *w* metres.
a) Write an inequality that describes the situation.
b) What are the restrictions on the length and width?
c) Graph *l* versus *w* for the inequality.
d) Write three ordered pairs in the form (*w*, *l*) that are possible dimensions of the rectangle.

37. Clothing sales A women's clothing store makes an average profit of $125 on each dress sold and $50 on each blouse. The manager's target is to make at least $500 a day on sales from dresses and blouses.
a) Write an inequality that represents the numbers of dresses and blouses that can be sold each day to reach the target.
b) What are the restrictions on the variables?
c) Graph the inequality.

38. World Cup soccer The teams that compete in the World Cup soccer tournament every four years are decided in the qualifying rounds. Canada plays 10 games in the qualifying rounds against teams from North America, Central America, and the Caribbean.
a) Write an inequality that relates the numbers of wins and ties to the number of games played by the Canadian team.
b) Graph the inequality, allowing for restrictions on the variables.
c) There are 3 points for a win and 1 point for a tie. Is it possible for a team to score 22 points? 29 points? Explain.

39. Book sizes The world's smallest book contains the children's story *Old King Cole!* The sum of the length and width of the book is only 2 mm. The pages must be turned with a needle.
a) Write an inequality in terms of the length and width to represent their sum, in millimetres, for all the other books in the world.
b) Graph the inequality.
c) Do you know that every point in the shaded region shows the dimensions of a real book? Explain.

40. Making appointments A lawyer schedules clients for half-hour or one-hour appointments. She meets with clients for, at most, 30 h in a week.
a) Write an inequality that represents the numbers of each type of appointment she may have in a week.
b) Graph the inequality.

41. Describe each graph in the coordinate plane.
a) $y < mx + b$ **b)** $y > mx + b$ **c)** $y \le mx + b$
d) $y \ge mx + b$ **e)** $y > b$ **f)** $y \le b$
g) $x < c$ **h)** $x \ge c$ **i)** $x \ne c$

42. Coordinate geometry Write an inequality that represents each graph.
a)

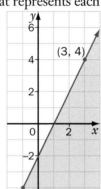

b)

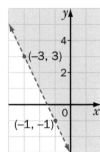

43. Graph each inequality.
a) $y \ne x + 4$ **b)** $y \not> x - 3$

44. a) Can you graph the inequality $x + y \ge 0$ using the intercepts? Explain.
b) Graph the inequality.

45. When graphing $x - 2y < 0$, could you use (0, 0) as the test point to decide which region to shade? Explain.

46. Graph each of the following.
a) $y \ge |x|$ **b)** $y < |x|$ **c)** $y > |x - 2|$
d) $|x + y| < 5$ **e)** $|y| \le 4$ **f)** $|x| > 3$

47. Write an inequality that is satisfied by the points (5, 7), (−1, 2), (3, −1), and (−5, −6). Compare your inequality with a classmate's.

Nations of the World

Use the *Nations* database, from the Computer Data Bank, to complete the following.

1 Comparing Nations

a) *Devise a plan to answer each question. Remember to exclude records for which the required data are not available.*
b) *Compare your plan with the plans of your classmates.*
c) *Revise your plan, if necessary, and then carry it out.*

Determine the number of nations with each of the following.
1. a population that is greater than or equal to 30 000 000

2. an area that is less than the area of France

3. a coastline length that is within 5000 km of the coastline length of New Zealand

4. a gross domestic product (GDP) that is at most $10 billion

5. expenditures that are no more than the expenditures of Canada

6. an inflation rate that is within 1% of the inflation rate of Australia

7. a labour force that is greater than the labour force of Japan

8. a coastline length, in kilometres, that is greater than the nation's area, in square kilometres

9. a positive balance of trade (the value of its exports is greater than the value of its imports)

10. an educational expenditure rate that is greater than the educational expenditure rate of a country where you would like to live

11. a literacy rate that is within 10% of the literacy rate of a country you would like to visit

12. a labour force that is between 40% and 50% of its population

13. an educational expenditure that is greater than $6 billion (Note: *Education Expenditure* is a percent of *Expenditures*.)

14. a gross domestic product (GDP) per capita that is less than the GDP per capita for Sweden

2 Forested Areas in South America

For every country in South America with an area greater than 250 000 km^2, 67% or less of the area is forested. Let the area of a country, in square kilometres, be x. Let the area of the country's forested land, in square kilometres, be y.
1. For all those South American countries, write an inequality that relates the area of a country's forested land to the area of the country. What are the restrictions on x?

2. Graph the inequality.

3. Describe a line segment on which you know the point representing the ordered pair (area of country, area of country's forested land) for Venezuela must lie.

4. Write a compound inequality that describes the possible area of Venezuela's forested land.

5. Use your research skills to determine the percent of the area of Venezuela that is forested. What is the area of Venezuela's forested land?

3 Standard of Living

1. Which fields or calculated fields in the database are strong indicators of standard of living?

2. Which countries have the highest and lowest standards of living? Where does Canada rank? Explain your reasoning.

3. Compare your answers to question 2 with your classmates' answers.

PROBLEM SOLVING

2.4 Use Logic

Logical thinking is a skill that can be improved with practice and applied in school, at work, and in everyday life.

Justine is a nature photographer. One day she drove from her cottage on the lake into town to get supplies. She left her cottage at 08:00, stopped several times to take pictures, and arrived in town at 15:00. She left for her cottage at 08:00 the next morning. She followed the same road back, stopped several times to take more pictures, and arrived at her cottage at 15:00. Show that there is one point on the road where Justine was exactly the same distance from her cottage at exactly the same time on both days.

Understand the Problem

1. What information are you given?
2. What are you asked to find?

Think of a Plan

On the same set of axes, draw graphs of Justine's two trips, showing the distance from her cottage versus the time of day.

Carry Out the Plan

Since she made several stops during each trip, the graphs will not be linear. The two graphs must intersect at some point.

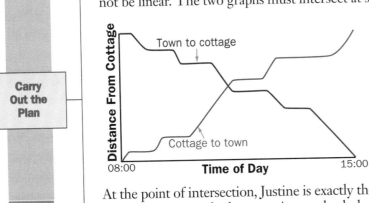

At the point of intersection, Justine is exactly the same distance from her cottage at exactly the same time on both days.

Look Back

Check that the solution agrees with the given information.

Could you solve the problem if, on the return trip, Justine left town at 10:00 and arrived at her cottage at 16:00? if she left town at 16:00 and arrived at her cottage at 21:00?

Use Logic

1. Organize the information.
2. Draw conclusions from the information.
3. Check that your answer is reasonable.

How can you measure 9 L of water using a 6-L pail and a 5-L pail?

One possible combination that equals 9 L is 5 L + 4 L. So, you could try to get 4 L of water in the 6-L pail and fill the 5-L pail.

1. Fill 5-L pail.

2. Empty 5-L pail into 6-L pail.

3. Fill 5-L pail.

4. Fill 6-L pail from 5-L pail.

5. Empty 6-L pail.

6. Empty 5-L pail into 6-L pail.

7. Fill 5-L pail.

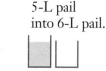 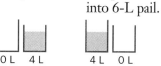

0 L   5 L   5 L   0 L   5 L   5 L   6 L   4 L   0 L   4 L   4 L   0 L   4 L   5 L

Is there another way to solve the problem?

Applications and Problem Solving

1. Three containers can hold 19 L, 13 L, and 7 L of water, respectively. The 19-L container is empty. The other two are full. How can you measure 8 L of water using no other container and no other water supply?

2. Three sportscasters, Aaron, Sandra, and Francois, predicted the winners of the same four hockey games on a Saturday night. Aaron said that Vancouver, Toronto, Edmonton, and Chicago would win. Sandra chose Montreal, Edmonton, Boston, and Toronto. Francois said that Calgary, Vancouver, Edmonton, and Montreal would win. No one chose Detroit to win. Which teams played each other?

3. In the system of equations, find the values of h and g.

$$a + b = c$$
$$c + d = e$$
$$a + e = f$$
$$f + g = h$$
$$h - e = 7$$
$$b + d + f = 30$$
$$a = 4$$

4. The numbers 1 to 6 are arranged so that the difference between a pair of numbers appears between and below the pair of numbers.

```
4  1  6
 3  5
  2
```

Use the same pattern to make a triangle with the numbers from 1 to 10. The 5 and the 7 have been placed for you.

```
■  ■  ■  ■
5  ■  ■
 ■  7
  ■
```

5. Suppose you start to write the whole numbers in words, starting at one. Remember that 101 is written "one hundred one." In what number will
a) the letter "a" appear for the first time?
b) the letter "b" appear for the first time?

6. There are 3 piles of toothpicks, one with 11 toothpicks, one with 7, and the third with 6. You are to get 8 toothpicks in each pile in 3 moves. In one move, you must add to any pile exactly as many toothpicks as it already has, and all the toothpicks added must come from one other pile.

7. The first time Tonya and Emma raced 20 km on bicycles, Emma was 2 km from the finish line when Tonya finished. The next day, Tonya agreed to start 2 km behind Emma, so that Tonya would ride 22 km and Emma, 20 km. If each of them rode at the same speed as she did during the first race, who won the second race?

8. Peter and Sharif travelled from Acton to Beamsville on foot. Peter walked half the distance and ran half the distance. Sharif walked half the time and ran half the time. If they walked at the same speed and ran at the same speed, who arrived in less time, or was it a tie?

9. Dylan is meeting his sister and four of her women friends for lunch. The five women are called Alicia, Rachel, Lani, Donna, and Casey. Three of the women are under 30 years old, and two are over 30. Two of the women are lawyers, and three are doctors. Alicia and Lani are in the same age group. Donna and Casey are in different age groups. Rachel and Casey have the same profession. Lani and Donna have different professions. Dylan's sister is a lawyer and is over 30. Who is Dylan's sister?

10. Write a problem similar to question 1, 6, or 9. Have a classmate solve your problem.

2.5 Solving Systems of Linear Inequalities

A solution to a system of linear equations in two variables is any ordered pair that satisfies all the equations in the system. Similarly, a solution to a system of linear inequalities in two variables is an ordered pair that satisfies all the inequalities in the system.

If the graphs of a system of inequalities overlap when drawn on the same grid, the region of overlap contains the solution to the system.

Explore: Draw a Graph

A hockey team has 8 games left to play and needs 10 points to make the playoffs. A win is worth 2 points, and a tie is worth 1 point.

Let x be the number of wins and y be the number of ties. The inequality $2x + y \geq 10$ relates the numbers of wins and ties to the number of points that will put the team into the playoffs.

The inequality $x + y \leq 8$ relates the numbers of wins and ties to the number of games left to play.

a) Graph the two inequalities on the same grid.

b) Use distinctive shading to show the region where the two graphs overlap.

Inquire

1. Why are all the solutions in the first quadrant?

2. a) Which segments on the boundary lines are made up of points that are included in the solution?
b) Is the point of intersection of the two boundary lines included in the solution?

3. a) Why are the ordered pairs in the solution made up of whole numbers?
b) List all the ordered pairs that satisfy both inequalities.

4. How many different combinations of wins and ties would put the hockey team into the playoffs?

If the graphs of inequalities overlap, the region of overlap is called the **intersection** of the graphs. If the variables are real numbers, the intersection includes infinitely many solutions to the system. Graphing is the most efficient way to show the solutions.

Example 1   Boundary Lines in the Form *y = mx + b*

Solve the system of inequalities by graphing.

$$y \geq 2x - 1$$
$$y < -x + 5$$

Solution

The solution contains the points in the intersection of the graphs of $y \geq 2x - 1$ and $y < -x + 5$.

Method 1: Graphing manually
Draw the boundary line
$y = 2x - 1$ for the first inequality.
The graph of $y \geq 2x - 1$ contains
the points on or above the line.

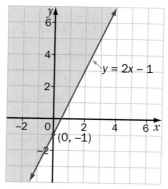

Method 2: Using a graphing calculator
In the standard viewing window, graph both lines, using the Shade instruction to shade above
$y = 2x - 1$ and below $y = -x + 5$.

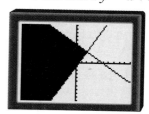

On the same set of axes, draw the
boundary line $y = -x + 5$ for the
second inequality.
This boundary line is not included
in the graph of $y < -x + 5$, so the
boundary line is broken.
The graph of $y < -x + 5$ contains
the points below the line.

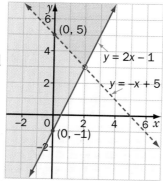

The calculator does not distinguish
between solid and broken
boundary lines. It also does not
draw the open dot at the point of
intersection. Copy the graph into
your notebook. Make the necessary
corrections, so that the graph
agrees with the final graph shown
for Method 1.

The intersection of the two graphs, shown in green, is the
solution to the system.
The point of intersection of the two boundary lines is shown as
an open dot. This indicates that the point of intersection is not
included in the solution to the system. The reason is that this
point is not included in the solution to $y < -x + 5$.

Check for both methods.
In both inequalities, test the point (0, 0), which is in the intersection.

For $y \geq 2x - 1$,
L.S. $= y$ **R.S.** $= 2x - 1$
$\quad = 0 \qquad \quad = 2(0) - 1$
$\qquad \qquad \quad = -1$
$\qquad$ L.S. $\geq$ R.S.

For $y < -x + 5$,
L.S. $= y$ **R.S.** $= -x + 5$
$\quad = 0 \qquad \quad = -(0) + 5$
$\qquad \qquad \quad = 5$
$\qquad$ L.S. $<$ R.S.

Since the point (0, 0) satisfies both inequalities, the region shaded
green is the solution to the system.

Example 2   Boundary Lines in the Form Ax + By = C

Solve the system of inequalities by graphing.

$$3x + 2y \leq 6$$
$$4x - 3y \geq 12$$

Solution 1   Using Intercepts and Test Points

Use the intercepts to draw the boundary line $3x + 2y = 6$ for the first inequality. The solution to this inequality includes the boundary line, so draw it as a solid line.

Use (0, 0) as the test point, and substitute (0, 0) into the first inequality.

For $3x + 2y \leq 6$,

L.S. $= 3x + 2y$ **R.S.** $= 6$
        $= 3(0) + 2(0)$
        $= 0$

Since $0 \leq 6$, the point (0, 0) satisfies the first inequality. As (0, 0) is below the boundary line, shade below the line.

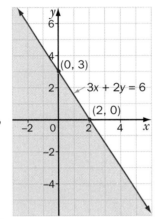

On the same set of axes, use the intercepts to draw the boundary line $4x - 3y = 12$ for the second inequality. The solution to this inequality includes the boundary line, so draw it as a solid line. Use (0, 0) as the test point, and substitute (0, 0) into the second inequality.

For $4x - 3y \geq 12$,

L.S. $= 4x - 3y$ **R.S.** $= 12$
        $= 4(0) - 3(0)$
        $= 0$

Since 0 is not greater than or equal to 12, the point (0, 0) does not satisfy the second inequality. As (0, 0) is above the boundary line, shade below the line.

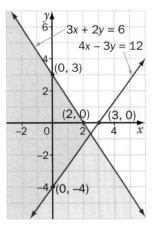

The region shaded in green is the solution to the system.

Solution 2   Solving for y

Solve each inequality for y.

For the first inequality, $3x + 2y \leq 6$, solving for y gives $y \leq -\dfrac{3}{2}x + 3$.

For the second inequality, $4x - 3y \geq 12$, solving for y gives $y \leq \dfrac{4}{3}x - 4$.

Graph the two boundary lines, $y = -\dfrac{3}{2}x + 3$ and $y = \dfrac{4}{3}x - 4$, on the same set of axes.

The solution to each inequality includes the boundary line, so draw each boundary line as a solid line. The inequality symbol is $\leq$ in each inequality solved for y, so shade below each boundary line.

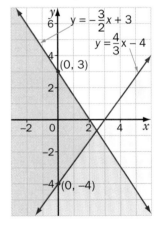

The region shaded in green is the solution to the system.

Check for both solutions.
In both of the original inequalities, test the point $(2, -3)$, which is in the intersection.

For $3x + 2y \le 6$,

L.S. $= 3x + 2y$ **R.S.** $= 6$
$= 3(2) + 2(-3)$
$= 6 - 6$
$= 0$

L.S. $\le$ R.S.

For $4x - 3y \ge 12$,

L.S. $= 4x - 3y$ **R.S.** $= 12$
$= 4(2) - 3(-3)$
$= 8 + 9$
$= 17$

L.S. $\ge$ R.S.

Since the point $(2, -3)$ satisfies both inequalities, the region shaded in green is the solution to the system.

Solving for y, as shown in Solution 2 of Example 2, is the first step in graphing a system of inequalities using a graphing calculator. Investigate whether a graphing calculator could be used to graph the system in Example 2.

Example 3   Target Heart Rates

To improve cardiovascular fitness, aerobics exercise should be performed with the heart rate, in beats per minute, in the appropriate target zone. The target zone is based on a person's maximum heart rate. The maximum rate is found by subtracting the person's age, in years, from 220.
Target zones are calculated for adults from 20 to 70 years old. During aerobics exercise, a person's heart rate should be no more than 80% of that person's maximum heart rate and no less than 70% of that person's maximum heart rate.

a) Write a system of inequalities that describes the target heart rate zone.
b) Graph the system.

Solution
a) Since the target heart rate depends on age, the target heart rate is the dependent variable, and age is the independent variable.
Let x represent age, in years, and y, the target heart rate, in beats per minute.

The minimum age used in the calculation is 20, so $x \ge 20$.
The maximum age used in the calculation is 70, so $x \le 70$.
The maximum heart rate is $220 - x$.

The target heart rate should be no more than 80% of the maximum, so $y \le 0.8(220 - x)$.
The target heart rate should be no less than 70% of the maximum, so $y \ge 0.7(220 - x)$.

The system of inequalities that describes the target heart rate zone is as follows.

$$y \le 0.8(220 - x)$$
$$y \ge 0.7(220 - x)$$
$$x \ge 20$$
$$x \le 70$$

b) On the same set of axes, graph the two inequalities that express y in terms of x. Allow for the restrictions on x.

Method 1: Graphing manually
Because y must be positive, and x values are from 20 to 70, the graph must be drawn in the first quadrant.

To graph $y \le 0.8(220 - x)$, shade below the solid boundary line $y = 0.8(220 - x)$ from $x = 20$ to $x = 70$.

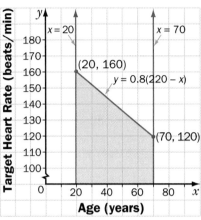

Method 2: Using a graphing calculator
The graph will not appear in the standard viewing window, so adjust the maximum and minimum values of x and y to suitable values. In the graph shown below, the window shows x-values from 20 to 70, and y-values from 100 to 170. Use the Shade instructions to shade above $y = 0.7(220 - x)$ and below $y = 0.8(220 - x)$.

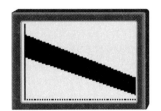

To graph $y \ge 0.7(220 - x)$, shade above the solid boundary line $y = 0.7(220 - x)$ from $x = 20$ to $x = 70$.

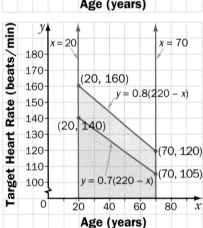

Check for both methods.
For each inequality that expresses y in terms of x, test the point (60, 120), which is in the intersection.

For $y \le 0.8(220 - x)$,
L.S. $= y$ **R.S.** $= 0.8(220 - x)$
     $= 120$ $= 0.8(220 - 60)$
                        $= 0.8(160)$
                        $= 128$
            L.S. $\le$ R.S.

For $y \ge 0.7(220 - x)$
L.S. $= y$ **R.S.** $= 0.7(220 - x)$
     $= 120$ $= 0.7(220 - 60)$
                        $= 0.7(160)$
                        $= 112$
           L.S. $\ge$ R.S.

Since the point (60, 120) satisfies both inequalities, the region shaded in green is the solution to the system.

Note that, in Example 3, the two inequalities that express y in terms of x could be written as the compound inequality $0.7(220 - x) \le y \le 0.8(220 - x)$.

Practice

Which of the given ordered pairs are solutions to the system of inequalities?

1. $y \geq 2x + 1$
$y \leq x + 2$
$(-1, 0), (0, 0), (3, 6), (-2, -2), (1, 3)$

2. $y < 3x - 2$
$y > -x + 3$
$(0, 0), (3, 0), (4, 2), (5, -1), (-1, -2)$

3. $y > 2x - 3$
$y \geq x - 1$
$(0, 0), (2, 3), (-1, -3), (2, 1), (-3, -3)$

4. $x + y \geq 1$
$x + y \leq 4$
$(0, 3), (0, 0), (4, -2), (0, 4), (-1, 1)$

5. $x - y < 2$
$2x - y > 3$
$(0, 0), (3, 2), (1, -1), (10, 9), (-1, -4)$

6. $3x - 2y < 6$
$2x - 3y \leq 0$
$(0, 0), (1, 0), (5, 4), (-4, -2), (-2, -3)$

Write a system of inequalities represented by each graph.

7.

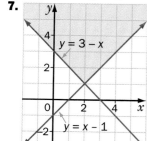

8.

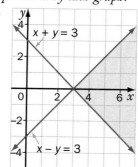

9.

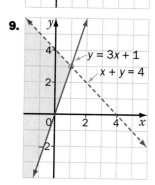

10.

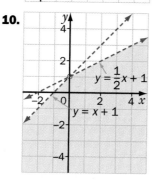

For questions 11–13, refer to the four regions formed when $y = x + 2$ and $y = 1 - x$ intersect, as shown in the graph.

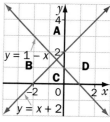

11. If both boundary lines are solid, as shown, write a system of inequalities whose solution is
a) region A   **b)** region B

12. Suppose both boundary lines are broken. Write a system of inequalities whose solution is
a) region C   **b)** region D

13. Suppose the boundary line $y = x + 2$ is solid, but the boundary line $y = 1 - x$ is broken. Write a system of inequalities whose solution is
a) region A   **b)** region D

Solve each system of inequalities by graphing.

14. $y \geq x + 2$
$y \leq -x + 2$

15. $y < x - 3$
$y > -x + 3$

16. $y \geq 3x$
$y < -2x + 4$

17. $y + 2 \geq 3x$
$y - 1 \leq 2x$

18. $y \leq \frac{1}{2}x + 3$
$y < x + 2$

19. $y \geq 2x - 1$
$y \geq x + 2$

Solve each system of inequalities by graphing.

20. $y \leq \frac{2}{3}x + 2$
$y \geq -\frac{1}{3}x + 5$

21. $y < -\frac{6}{5}x + 1$
$y < \frac{4}{5}x - 3$

22. $y \geq -\frac{1}{2}x - 5$
$y \geq \frac{2}{3}x + 2$

23. $y > \frac{3}{4}x + 7$
$y < -\frac{1}{2}x + 2$

24. $y < x - 4$
$y \geq -\frac{1}{2}x - 7$

25. $y \geq -\frac{1}{3}x + 1$
$y > \frac{3}{2}x + 1$

Solve each system of inequalities by graphing.

26. $x + 2y \leq 4$
$x + y \geq 1$

27. $2x + y > 2$
$3x + 2y < 6$

28. $x - y \geq 1$
$x - 2y \leq 2$

29. $x + y \geq 2$
$2x + y \geq 4$

30. $4x + y \leq 4$
$3x - 2y > 12$

31. $x - y + 1 < 0$
$2x + 3y + 6 \geq 0$

Solve each system of inequalities by graphing.

32. $x \geq 0$
$y \geq 0$

33. $x \geq 0$
$y \leq 0$

34. $x \leq 4$
$y > 5$

35. $x > 2$
$y < -3$

36. $y \leq x + 4$
$y \geq -1$

37. $y > -2x + 1$
$x \leq 2$

38. $x - y \leq 1$
$y \geq 3$

39. $x + y < 2$
$x < 1$

Solve each system of inequalities by graphing.

40. $y \geq x$
$x \geq 0$
$y \geq 0$

41. $y < -x$
$x \leq 0$
$y \geq 0$

42. $y \geq 2x + 1$
$y \leq x + 4$
$x \geq 0$
$y \geq 0$

43. $x + y < 2$
$x - y < 2$
$x \leq 0$

44. $x + 2y \leq 8$
$y \leq x + 1$
$x \geq 0$

45. $2x + y \leq 10$
$y - x \leq 2$
$x \geq 0$
$y \geq 0$

Applications and Problem Solving

46. Souvenirs Chandra can spend up to $120 on souvenir T-shirts from the Canada Games. She would like to buy at least 5 T-shirts to give to family and friends. The two styles of T-shirts cost $20 or $15 each.
a) Graph the following system of inequalities, where x represents the number of $20 T-shirts, and y represents the number of $15 T-shirts.
$$x + y \geq 5$$
$$20x + 15y \leq 120$$
b) Find how many T-shirts Chandra can buy at each price.

47. Hockey A hockey team needs at least 80 points to make the playoffs. The team plays 82 games, and gets 2 points for a win and 1 point for a tie. Let w be the number of wins, and t be the number of ties.
a) Write a system of inequalities to describe the values of w and t that will put a team into the playoffs.
b) What are the restrictions on the variables?
c) Solve the system by graphing.

48. Numbers The sum of two positive real numbers is less than 8 and greater than 4. Show all the possible values of the numbers graphically.

49. Buying pizza The volunteers who are organizing a walkathon have up to $90 to spend on pizza for lunch. They need to order at least 6 large pizzas for the group. Large pizzas cost $12 or $15 each. Write and solve a system of inequalities to determine how many pizzas can be ordered at each price.

50. Part-time jobs Manuel is a college student with two part-time jobs. He earns $10/h in a music store or $15/h in a warehouse. He needs to earn at least $180/week, but he cannot work more than 14 h/week. Write and solve a system of inequalities to determine how many hours he could work at each job in a week.

51. Which of the following does not have the same solution as the others? Explain.
a) $y \geq x - 1$
$y \leq 2x - 1$

b) $x - y \leq 1$
$2x - y \geq 1$

c) $x - y \geq 1$
$2x - y \leq 1$

d) $x - y \leq 1 \leq 2x - y$

52. Solve each system by graphing.
a) $y > -x + 2$
$x + y \leq -3$

b) $y \geq 2x + 1$
$2x - y \geq 3$

53. Graph each of the following systems. The variables represent real numbers.
a) $y \geq x + 4$
$y \leq 2x + 3$

b) $y < 3x - 1$
$y > 4x - 3$

c) $y \geq x + 2$
$2y \leq 2x + 4$

d) $y \leq 3 - x$
$2y \leq 6 - 2x$

e) $y > x + 3$
$2y > 2x + 6$

f) $y > 2x + 1$
$y < 2x + 1$

g) $y \geq 3x - 2$
$y \leq 3x - 1$

h) $y \geq x - 1$
$y \leq x - 2$

54. Use your results from question 53 to decide how many solutions a system of two inequalities can have, if the variables represent real numbers and the boundary lines are as follows. Explain.
a) They intersect in exactly one point.
b) They coincide and are solid.
c) They coincide and are broken.
d) They are parallel.

55. Without graphing, describe the solution to this system of inequalities.
$$2x + y > 1$$
$$y \leq -2x + 1$$

56. Coordinate geometry Write a system of inequalities that can be represented by each graph.

a)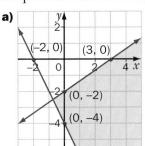

b)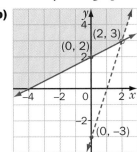

57. Technology Describe the advantages and disadvantages of using a graphing calculator to graph systems of inequalities.

58. Solve the system of inequalities.
$$y \le 2x + 3$$
$$y \le -x + 2$$
$$y \ge \frac{1}{3}x - 1$$

59. Measurement a) Write a system of inequalities whose solution is a rectangle and all the points inside it.
b) Calculate the area of the rectangle.

60. Measurement Determine the area of the region represented by each of the following systems of inequalities.

a) $y \ge 2x - 1$
$y \le 2x + 5$
$y \ge 1$
$y \le 3$

b) $x + y \ge -3$
$x - y \ge -2$
$x - 2 \le 0$
$x + 1 \ge 0$

61. Investing Toni wants to earn over $500 in interest by investing no more than $12 000 for one year. She wants to invest part of the money in a government bond paying 4% per annum, and the rest in a guaranteed investment certificate paying 5% per annum.
a) Write and graph a system of inequalities to represent the amounts that Toni can invest at each rate.
b) If she invests a whole number of dollars at each rate, what is the maximum amount she can invest at 4%? Explain.

62. Art gallery The floor of a room in an art gallery is defined by the following inequalities, where x and y are measured in metres.
$$x + y \le 8, y \le 6, x \le 7, x \ge 0, y \ge 0$$
a) What is the shape of the floor?
b) What is the area of the floor?

63. Fitness Sarah jogs at 10 km/h and walks at 6 km/h. On different days, she exercises for no less than half an hour and no more than an hour. She covers a distance of up to 8 km in a day.
a) Write and solve a system of inequalities to show the possible jogging distances and walking distances Sarah includes in one day's exercise.
b) Give three combinations of jogging distance and walking distance that satisfy the systems. Check each of your answers.

64. Technology Describe a suitable viewing window for graphing each of the following systems on your graphing calculator. Explain your reasoning.
a) $x + y \le 50$
$x - y \le 20$
b) $y \ge x - 9$
$y \le 2x + 5$
c) $y \ge 3x + 6$
$y \le 5x - 8$
$x \ge 0$
$y \ge 0$
d) $2x + 3y \ge -13$
$x + 2y \le 2$
$x \le 0$
$y \ge 0$

65. Nutrition Suppose you eat strawberries and cream for dessert. You have whipping cream, which is 35% fat, by mass, and cereal cream, which is 12% fat, by mass. You want to use at least 50 g of cream, but you do not want to eat more than 10 g of fat. The strawberries are fat-free.
a) Write a system of inequalities to represent the masses of whipping cream and cereal cream you could use.
b) What is the maximum mass of whipping cream you could use, to the nearest tenth of a gram?

66. Graph and describe each solution.
a) $|y| \le 4$
b) $|x| > 1$

67. The system is made up of one inequality and one equation.
$$x + y \le 8$$
$$y = 2x + 2$$
a) Draw a graph to show the points that make both sentences true.
b) Describe the solution in words.

2.6 Look for a Pattern

You can solve some problems by recognizing that a pattern exists and using it to make predictions.

The 7 by 5 jigsaw puzzle is made up of 35 pieces. There are 4 corner pieces, each with 2 straight edges. There are 16 side pieces, each with 1 straight edge. There are 15 inner pieces, each with no straight edges. Find the number of pieces of each type in a 35 by 30 jigsaw puzzle.

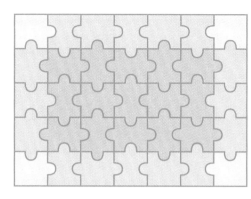

Understand the Problem

1. What information are you given?
2. What are you asked to find?
3. Do you need an exact or an approximate answer?

Think of a Plan

Look for a pattern in the number of pieces of each type in rectangular puzzles. Write the pattern algebraically and apply it to the 35 by 30 puzzle.

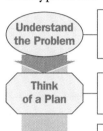

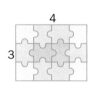

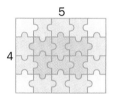

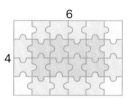

corner: 4
side: 6
inner: 2

corner: 4
side: 10
inner: 6

corner: 4
side: 12
inner: 8

corner: 4
side: 16
inner: 15

The number of corner pieces is always 4.
The number of side pieces can be found by finding the perimeter and subtracting 8, to allow for the dimensions of the 4 corner pieces.
So, for a puzzle with dimensions m by n, the number of side pieces is $2m + 2n - 8$.

Carry Out the Plan

Notice that the overall dimensions of the inner pieces are related to the dimensions of the puzzle. For an m by n puzzle, the dimensions of the inner pieces are $(m - 2)$ by $(n - 2)$. So, the number of inner pieces is $(m - 2)(n - 2)$.

Dimensions	
Whole Puzzle	Inner Pieces
4 by 3	2 by 1
5 by 4	3 by 2
6 by 4	4 by 2
7 by 5	5 by 3
m by n	$(m - 2)$ by $(n - 2)$

For a 35 by 30 puzzle, the number of corner pieces is 4.

If $m = 35$ and $n = 30$,
the number of side pieces $= 2m + 2n - 8$
$= 2(35) + 2(30) - 8$
$= 122$

Check.
$35 \times 30 = 1050$
$4 + 122 + 924 = 1050$

The number of inner pieces is $(m - 2)(n - 2) = (35 - 2)(30 - 2)$
$= 924$

So, a 35 by 30 jigsaw puzzle has 4 corner pieces, 122 side pieces, and 924 inner pieces.

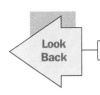

Look Back — How could you develop the formulas without first looking for a pattern?

Look for a Pattern
1. Use the given information to find a pattern.
2. Use the pattern to solve the problem.
3. Check that your answer is reasonable.

Applications and Problem Solving

1. a) Write expressions for the numbers of different types of pieces in any square jigsaw puzzle.
b) How many pieces of each type are in a square jigsaw puzzle with 1600 pieces?

2. How many jigsaw puzzle pieces of each type are there in a rectangular puzzle with 1147 pieces?

3. What is $33\,333\,333 \times 99\,999\,999$?

4. a) Copy and complete the following.
$$143 \times 14 = \blacksquare$$
$$143 \times 21 = \blacksquare$$
$$143 \times 28 = \blacksquare$$
$$143 \times 35 = \blacksquare$$
$$143 \times 42 = \blacksquare$$
b) Explain the pattern.
c) Use the pattern to predict 143×98. Check your prediction.

5. Find a rule that relates x and y. Then, copy and complete each table.

a)

x	y
1	10
2	14
3	18
4	22
9	■
■	98
52	■

b)

x	y
0	2
1	3
2	6
3	11
8	■
■	123
15	■

c)

x	y
0	−1
1	1
2	3
3	5
5	■
10	■
■	127

d)

x	y
1	2
3	3
5	4
7	5
11	■
■	20
99	■

6. Look for a pattern. Then, find the missing number.

43	51	16	24
19	13	45	39
56	61	21	26
24	44	29	■

7. a) How many asterisks are in the next diagram?

```
                        * * * *
              * * *     * * * *
      * *     * * *     * * * *
  *   * *     * * *     * * * *
  *   * *     * * *     * * * *
  1    2        3          4
```

b) Use the pattern to write an expression for the number of asterisks in the nth diagram.
c) How many asterisks are in the 30th diagram? the 50th diagram?

8. What is the remainder when 2^{75} is divided by 10?

9. What are the next two numbers in this sequence?
$$9 \quad 18 \quad 11 \quad 16 \quad 13 \quad 14 \quad 15 \quad 12$$

10. What number should appear in the final triangle?

2	1	6	4	0	■
	8	8	5	1	

11. For each of the following whole numbers, add all the digits. Then, add the digits in the result. Continue, if necessary, until you reach a result that is a single digit.
$$128 \quad 979 \quad 68\,576 \quad 2\,843\,976$$
a) How is the single-digit result related to the middle digit of the original number?
b) For each of the original numbers, add all the digits except the middle digit. What do you notice about the results?
c) Write a 9-digit number, an 11-digit number, and a 15-digit number that fit the same pattern.

INVESTIGATING MATH

Polygonal Regions

A **polygon** is a plane figure formed by at least three line segments. Polygons can be **convex** or **concave**. A polygon is convex if any two points in the polygon can be joined by a line segment that is inside the polygon.

Convex polygonal regions can be formed by the intersection of a system of linear inequalities.

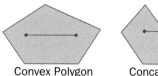

Convex Polygon   Concave Polygon

1 Maximum and Minimum Values

1. Write the four inequalities that determine the shaded polygonal region shown in the graph.

2. a) Evaluate the expression $3x + 2y$ at each vertex of the polygonal region.
b) At which vertex does $3x + 2y$ have a maximum value? What is the maximum value?
c) At which vertex does $3x + 2y$ have a minimum value? What is the minimum value?

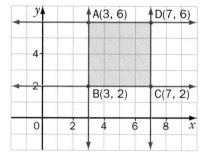

3. a) Write the coordinates of two other points on the boundary lines and two points inside the region. Name the points E, F, G, and H.
b) Evaluate $3x + 2y$ at each of the new points. Compare the values of $3x + 2y$ with the values you found in questions 2b) and 2c).

4. On the basis of the class results in question 3b), which points do you think you should test to find the maximum or minimum value of an expression over a polygonal region?

Determine the maximum value and the minimum value of each expression over the given region. For each expression, write the points where the maximum and the minimum occur.

5.
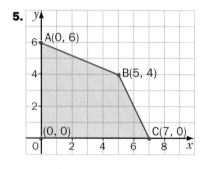

a) $2x + 3y$
b) $4x - y$
c) $2y - 3x$

6.
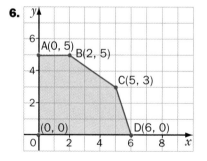

a) $4x + 2y$
b) $2x - 7y$
c) $5y - x$

7.
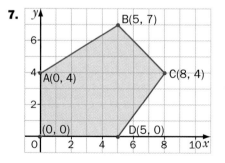

a) $3x + 4y$
b) $5x - 2y$
c) $3y - 2x$

2 Graphing Polygonal Regions, I

Graph each system of inequalities. Write the coordinates of the vertices of the polygonal region on the grid. Find the maximum and minimum values of the given expressions over the region.

1. $x \geq 1$
$x \leq 8$
$y \geq 2$
$y \leq 7$

a) $2x + 5y$
b) $y - 3x$

2. $x \geq 0$
$y \geq 0$
$x + y \leq 8$
$y \leq 6$

a) $x + 3y$
b) $x - 4y$

3. $x \geq 2$
$x \leq 10$
$y \leq 8$
$y \leq x$
$y \geq 0$

a) $4x + 5y$
b) $2x - 3y$

4. $x \geq 0$
$x \leq 8$
$y \geq 2$
$y \leq 9$
$y \leq x + 6$
$y \geq x - 3$

a) $2y - x$
b) $x - 3y$

3 Graphing Polygonal Regions, II

Graph each system of inequalities. Write the coordinates of the vertices of the polygonal region on the grid. Where necessary, solve the appropriate system of equations to determine a vertex. Find the maximum and minimum values of the given expressions over the region.

1. $x \geq 0$
$y \geq 0$
$2x + y \leq 8$
$x + 2y \leq 10$

a) $x + 4y$
b) $2x - 3y$

2. $x \geq 0$
$y \geq 0$
$y \leq x + 2$
$y \geq 2x - 6$

a) $x + 2y$
b) $x - 5y$

3. $x \geq 0$
$x \leq 5$
$y \geq 0$
$y \leq 0.5x + 5$
$y \leq -x + 8$

a) $2x + y$
b) $3y - x$

4. $y \leq x + 2$
$y \leq -2x + 20$
$y \geq -0.5x + 5$

a) $2x - y$
b) $3y - 2x$

4 Technology

1. Can you use a graphing calculator to graph polygonal regions? Explain.

2. How could you use a graphing calculator to find the vertices of the polygonal region defined by the following inequalities?

$$y \leq -\frac{1}{3}x + 5$$
$$y \leq -x + 7$$
$$y \geq x - 1$$
$$x \geq 0$$
$$y \geq 0$$

CONNECTING MATH AND BUSINESS

Linear Programming

Linear programming is a branch of mathematics that can be used in business applications. These include the maximizing of profits, the minimizing of costs, and the effective use of resources. The theory of linear programming was developed during World War II to help governments plan the use of money and materials.

1 Radio Advertising

Kim is holding a weekend sale at his clothing store. He has decided to advertise the sale on a radio station. He wants to run the advertisement at most 10 times, and does not want to spend more than $2400. For a thirty-second spot, the radio station charges $300 between 06:00 and 09:00, and $200 between 16:00 and 18:00. The station has 8000 listeners between 06:00 and 09:00, and 6000 listeners between 16:00 and 18:00. Kim wants to know how many times he should run the advertisement in each of these parts of the day to maximize the number of times the advertisement is heard.

Let x be the number of $300 spots Kim will choose, and y be the number of $200 spots. The following inequalities show the conditions, or **constraints**, that Kim must use.

$$\left. \begin{array}{l} x \geq 0 \\ y \geq 0 \end{array} \right\} \text{The number of advertisements cannot be negative.}$$

$x + y \leq 10$ The advertisement will run at most 10 times.

$300x + 200y \leq 2400$ Kim will not spend more than $2400.

1. Graph the system of inequalities. The resulting region is called the **feasible region**, because the ordered pairs (x, y) that satisfy the constraints are possible, or feasible, in this region.

2. Find the coordinates of each vertex of the feasible region.

3. The expression for the number of times the advertisement is heard is
$$8000x + 6000y$$
The aim is to maximize the value of this expression, which is called the **objective quantity**. Find the value of $8000x + 6000y$ at each vertex.

4. What is the maximum number of times the advertisement can be heard?

5. How many times should Kim run the advertisement in each part of the day?

2 More Business Applications

1. Book royalties Kyle's latest mystery novel is about to be published. His publisher predicts that 10 000 to 15 000 copies will be sold, some in hardcover and some in softcover.

a) Let the number of hardcover books sold be x, and the number of softcover books sold be y. Write two inequalities in terms of x and y to represent the possible numbers of books sold.

b) The publisher expects that 3000 to 4000 of the books sold will be hardcovers. Write two inequalities in terms of x to represent the possible numbers of hardcovers sold.

c) Graph the 4 inequalities from parts a) and b).

d) Find the coordinates of each vertex of the solution.

e) Kyle will earn a royalty of $3.00 for each hardcover sold, and $1.20 for each softcover sold. Write an expression in terms of x and y to represent Kyle's total royalties.

f) Evaluate the expression from part e) at each vertex to find the maximum amount and the minimum amount Kyle can expect to earn in royalties.

2. Part-time jobs Anna is a college student with two part-time jobs, one at a hardware store and the other at a fitness centre. She wants to work a minimum of 7 h/week at the hardware store and 5 h/week at the fitness centre. She does not want to work more than 15 h/week. The hardware store pays $15/h, and the fitness centre pays $13/h. How many hours should Anna work at each job every week to maximize her earnings?

3. Ski jackets Miki owns a store that sells outdoor wear. She wants to buy at most 20 ski jackets to sell. She has two styles to choose from. Mogul jackets cost $100 each, and Speed jackets cost $200 each. Miki does not want to spend more than $2800. She can make a profit of $50 on each Mogul jacket sold and $80 on each Speed jacket sold. If Miki can sell all the jackets she buys, how many of each style should she buy to maximize her profit?

4. Picnic tables The Sunshine Manufacturing Company makes two types of picnic table. The regular model takes 2 h at the cutting machine, and 2 h for assembly and finishing. The deluxe model takes 2 h at the cutting machine, and 5 h for assembly and finishing. There are a maximum of 22 machine-hours available each week, and a maximum of 40 assembly- and finishing-hours each week. The profit is $150 on a regular model and $200 on a deluxe model. How many of each model should be made in a week to maximize the profit?

5. Dishwashers You are the manager of the appliance department for a large department store. You need to order two types of dishwasher. The classic model costs you $250, and the profit is $50 for each one sold. The deluxe model costs you $300, and the profit is $100 for each one sold. Your target is to sell a minimum of 100 dishwashers and to make a total profit on dishwashers of at least $6000.

a) How many of each model should you order to minimize the cost?

b) Is it possible to use the feasible region to find a maximum cost? Explain.

Review

Solve and check.

1. $y + 3 < 9$
2. $3w + 4 > 10$
3. $2x - 5 \geq -7$
4. $4z - 5 \leq 3$
5. $-5k < 10$
6. $2t > t - 8$
7. $3(m - 2) \leq 6$
8. $2(n + 4) \geq 0$

Solve.

9. $3x + 2 > -10$
10. $5y + 1 < 1$
11. $7m + 3 \leq 6m + 2$
12. $3z - 8 > 2z + 3$
13. $9 + 5b < 6b + 1$
14. $4(2q - 1) > 4$
15. $3(2h - 2) \leq 6$
16. $2(4 - n) \geq 0$

Solve. Graph the solution.

17. $5m + 4 \leq 3m + 10$
18. $w + 2 > 6w - 8$
19. $2(x - 7) < x + 3$
20. $4(3z - 1) \leq 2(5 - z)$
21. $2(y - 3) + 1 \geq -4(2 - y) + 7$
22. $5n - 2(n + 3) - 1 < 2(n - 5) + 6$

Solve.

23. $\dfrac{x}{4} - 3 > -1$
24. $\dfrac{w}{3} + 5 \leq 2$
25. $1.9m + 2.4 < 6.2$
26. $3.3 - 2.6p \geq 8.5$
27. $\dfrac{x+1}{2} > \dfrac{5-x}{2} - 2$
28. $\dfrac{5-w}{4} \geq \dfrac{5-w}{5}$
29. $1.4(y + 3) + 6.1 > 2.5(1 - y)$
30. $3(1.2k + 2) - 12.6 \leq 5(0.3k + 0.8) - 2.2$

31. Fund-raising The symphony orchestra is holding a fund-raising banquet in a hotel. The hotel charges $200 for the banquet hall, plus $60 per person. Tickets are $100 each. How many tickets must be sold to raise more than $10 000?

32. Measurement A triangle has side lengths $2x + 1$, $2x + 3$, and $2x - 2$. What values of x give the triangle a perimeter of
a) 44 or more?   **b)** less than 56?

Which of the given ordered pairs are solutions to the inequality?

33. $y \geq 2x + 7$
   (2, 4), (−1, 6), (3, 13), (0, 0)

34. $y < -2x - 3$
   (0, 0), (−1, −5), (2, −9), (−2, 1)

Graph each inequality.

35. $y \leq 4x$
36. $y > -2x$
37. $y \geq x + 1$
38. $y < x - 3$
39. $y < 3x - 2$
40. $y \leq 3 - x$

Graph each inequality.

41. $x + y < -2$
42. $x - y \geq 3$
43. $2x - 3y \leq 0$
44. $2x + y > 3$
45. $2x - y + 3 \geq 0$
46. $6 < 3y + 2x$

Graph each inequality.

47. $y \leq \dfrac{1}{2}x - 3$
48. $y > 3 - \dfrac{x}{4}$
49. $y < \dfrac{x+3}{2}$
50. $\dfrac{x}{3} - \dfrac{y}{2} \geq 4$

Given the restriction on the variables, graph each inequality.

51. $y < x + 1, x \geq 0, y \geq 0$
52. $x + y \leq 4, x \geq 0, y \geq 0$
53. $2x - y > 3, x \leq 0, y \geq 0$
54. $y \geq 3 - 2x, x \geq 0, y \leq 0$

55. Fairground rides Rides at the county fair cost $2 or $3. Jamal can spend at most $18 on rides.
a) Write an inequality that represents the numbers of each type of ride Jamal can afford.
b) State any restrictions on the variables.
c) Graph the inequality.

56. Fitness classes Lia works part time leading fitness classes at a fitness centre. Level 1 Step classes are 40 min long, and Level 2 Step classes are 60 min long. Lia wants to work no more than 10 h a week.
a) Write an inequality that describes the numbers of each type of class Lia can lead in a week.
b) State any restrictions on the variables.
c) Graph the inequality.

Which of the given ordered pairs are solutions to the system of inequalities?

57. $y \geq x + 5$
   $y < 2x - 1$
   (0, 0), (10, 20), (0, 9), (15, 21)

58. $x + y < 1$
   $3x - y \leq 5$
   (5, 1), (0, −3), (−2, 1), (1, 5)

Write a system of inequalities represented by each graph.

59.

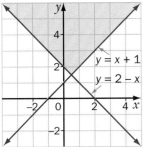

60.

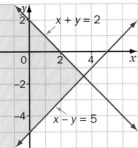

61.

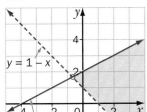

62.

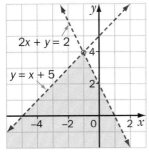

Solve each system by graphing.

63. $y \geq x + 3$
$y \leq 3 - x$

64. $y < 5 + x$
$y \leq x$

65. $y > 2x - 3$
$y \leq 3x$

66. $y < \frac{1}{2}x - 1$
$y < 3x - 1$

67. $y \leq \frac{3}{4}x - 1$
$y > 2 - \frac{1}{2}x$

68. $y \leq \frac{2}{3}x$
$y \geq \frac{1}{3}x - 1$

69. $2x + y > 1$
$x + 2y < 2$

70. $x + y \leq 2$
$x - y \leq 2$

71. $3x + 3y > 0$
$2x - 2y < 1$

72. $x + y - 3 \leq 0$
$-2x + y + 5 > 0$

73. Numbers The sum of two whole numbers is less than 12. The difference between the numbers is greater than or equal to 6. Write and solve a system of inequalities to determine the possible values of the two whole numbers.

Exploring Math

Midpoint Polygons

Line segments that join the midpoints of consecutive sides of a polygon form another polygon with the same number of sides.

The polygon with the midpoints as vertices can be called the midpoint polygon.

 Draw a midpoint polygon for each type of polygon in questions 1–15. Describe the midpoint polygon fully in each case.

1. scalene triangle
2. isosceles triangle
3. equilateral triangle
4. rectangle
5. square
6. rhombus
7. parallelogram
8. kite
9. trapezoid

10. isosceles trapezoid

11. quadrilateral with perpendicular diagonals

12. arrowhead

13. regular hexagon
14. irregular hexagon
15. convex quadrilateral with sides of different lengths, and with perpendicular diagonals of equal length

16. Similar polygons have the same shape but not necessarily the same size. Which of the above types of polygons are similar to their own midpoint polygons?

Use your results to predict whether each of the following is similar to its midpoint polygon. Then, test your prediction.
17. regular pentagon
18. irregular pentagon

Chapter Check

Solve and check.

1. $m - 8 < 9$ **2.** $3w - 2 > 10$

3. $2x + 5 \geq -1$ **4.** $4n - 10 \leq 2$

5. $-4k < 20$ **6.** $7t > 6t - 11$

Solve.

7. $2(m - 2) < -14$ **8.** $2z + 5 \geq z - 3$

9. $5h + 3 \leq 4h - 8$ **10.** $4y - 1 < 12 + 3y$

11. $3(x + 2) > -1(x - 2)$ **12.** $2z + 3 > 3z - 8$

Solve. Graph the solution.

13. $6m - 4 \leq 2m + 12$ **14.** $w + 3 > 7w - 9$

15. $5(g - 1) < 6g + 1$ **16.** $3(3z + 1) \leq -2(9 - z)$

17. $3(y - 1) + 10 \geq -5(2 - y) - 7$

18. $7n - 2(n + 5) - 1 < 2(n - 4) - 2$

Solve.

19. $\dfrac{x}{5} + 7 \geq 12$ **20.** $4 - \dfrac{m}{2} < \dfrac{1}{2}$

21. $6.8q - 2.9 < 3.9$ **22.** $4.9 - 8.2w \geq 0.8$

23. $\dfrac{h - 5}{3} + 4 > \dfrac{h}{2} + 1$ **24.** $\dfrac{k}{5} - \dfrac{2}{3} \leq \dfrac{4 + k}{3}$

25. $1.3p + 5.4 > 3.7 + 2.4p + 1.7$

26. $2.7(y - 2) < 3(0.2y + 2.1) - 1.2$

Which of the given ordered pairs are solutions to the inequality?

27. $y \leq 5 - x$
$(1, 1), (-1, 6), (7, -1), (0, 0)$

28. $y > 4x - 1$
$(0, 0), (-1, -5), (2, 5), (-2, -10)$

Graph each inequality.

29. $y > 5x$ **30.** $y \geq -x$ **31.** $y > x - 4$

32. $y \leq x + 1$ **33.** $y < 3x + 4$ **34.** $y \geq 2 - x$

Graph each inequality.

35. $x + y \geq 6$ **36.** $x - y < 2$

37. $3x - y \leq 0$ **38.** $3x + y > 6$

39. $4x - y + 5 \geq 0$ **40.** $8 < 3y - 2x$

Graph each inequality.

41. $y \leq \dfrac{1}{3}x - 1$ **42.** $y > 4 - \dfrac{x}{3}$

43. $y \geq \dfrac{2 - x}{3}$ **44.** $\dfrac{3}{4}x + \dfrac{2}{3}y < -1$

Given the restriction on the variables, graph each inequality.

45. $y < 1 - 2x, x \geq 0, y \geq 0$

46. $x + y \geq 6, x \geq 0, y \geq 0$

47. $x - 4y > 2, x \geq 0, y \leq 0$

48. $3x - y \leq -5, x \leq 0, y \geq 0$

49. Which of the given ordered pairs are solutions to the system of inequalities?
$$y \leq 5 - x$$
$$y > 3x$$
$$(0, 0), (3, -1), (1, 8), (-2, 3)$$

Solve each system by graphing.

50. $y > x - 2$ **51.** $y \leq 2x + 1$
     $y < 4 - x$ $y \leq x - 1$

52. $y \geq 3x - 1$ **53.** $y \leq \dfrac{1}{2}x + 1$
     $y > 3 - x$ $y > 2x$

54. $y \leq \dfrac{2}{3}x + 1$ **55.** $y < \dfrac{4}{5}x - 1$
     $y \geq -\dfrac{1}{2}x$ $y > 3 - \dfrac{1}{2}x$

56. $x + 3y < 2$ **57.** $2x + 4y \geq 5$
     $3x + y \leq 1$ $3x - y < 6$

58. $y \geq 5$ **59.** $x + 2y - 1 > 0$
     $y < 4$ $y \leq 3$

60. Reception cost The cost of a reception is $200, plus $25 per person. The total cost of the reception can be no more than $4000. Write and solve an inequality to determine the number of people who can be invited.

61. Buying snacks Rowena is responsible for buying apples, costing 40¢ each, and trail mix, costing $1 per package, for the junior rangers she is taking on a hike. She can spend, at most, $20.
a) Write an inequality that represents the numbers of apples and packages of trail mix that Rowena can buy.
b) Graph the inequality, allowing for restrictions on the variables.

62. Numbers The difference between two real numbers is less than 10 and greater than 6. Show all the possible values of the numbers graphically.

Using the Strategies

1. In this addition, the letters D, E, and F represent different digits. What are the values of D and F?

```
   D
   E
 + F
  DE
```

2. There are four red counters and four blue counters in a row.

You are allowed to move two adjacent counters at a time, without rotating them. In four moves, arrange the counters so that the colours alternate.

3. About how many litres of gasoline are used by all the cars in your province in a week?

4. In the system of equations, find the values of F and E.

$$A + B = C$$
$$C + D = E$$
$$A + E = F$$
$$B + D + F = 20$$
$$A = 4$$

5. The numbers at the corners of each square are related to the number in the middle of the square. The relationship is the same for all squares. Find the missing number.

```
12   4     7   8     9   10
  13          5          6
 8   5     2   6     3
```

6. The height, h, of a triangle is decreased by y. The base, b, is increased by x. The area of the new triangle is three times the area of the original triangle.
a) Write an expression for y in terms of the other variables.
b) If $h = 4$ and $b = 5$ in the original triangle, find a value of y and a value of x that make the expression true.

7. Suzanne, Beth, and Jasmin entered a 36-km bicycle race. Each of them kept a constant speed throughout the race. When Suzanne finished, Beth was 12 km from the finish line, and Jasmin was 18 km from the finish line. When Beth finished the race, how far from the finish line was Jasmin?

8. Five basketball players, A, B, C, D, and E, run onto the court in order from shortest to tallest. Each player after the first has a mass of 1 kg more than the player in front. The total of their masses is 310 kg.

E has a mass of 1 kg more than A.
B has a mass of 2 kg more than A.
C has a mass of 1 kg more than D.
E has a mass of 3 kg less than C.

What is the mass of each player?

9. Given that AC = BC, CD = CE, and ∠ACD = 50°, find the measure of ∠BDE.

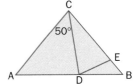

10. The two subtractions have the same answer.

```
  300        3XY
 -XY3       -300
```

Find the values of X and Y.

11. You have an unlimited number of 3¢ stamps and 5¢ stamps. What amounts of postage can you not make?

DATA BANK

1. Predict the first year in which India will have the greatest population of any country in the world. State your assumptions.

2. Omar and Sylvain are planning to drive from Saskatoon to New Orleans for Mardi Gras. They want to spend a day in Denver and a day in Austin on their way south, four days in New Orleans, and two days in Memphis on their way home. They will drive for no more than 11 h/day and will average 100 km/h while driving. Draw up a detailed itinerary that will allow Omar and Sylvain to complete the trip in the minimum number of days.

3. At which point is the geographical centre of Canada located? Explain your reasoning.

Quadratic Functions

A batted or thrown baseball, the water arcs from a fountain, the trails of rocks spewed from an erupting volcano, and the trails of rockets in a fireworks display all follow a curve that is sometimes called gravity's rainbow curve.

A red aerial flare fired from a boat in an emergency situation also traces gravity's rainbow curve. After the flare is fired, its height above the water is a function of the time since it was fired.

Suppose a red aerial flare is fired at an angle of 70° to the horizontal. The height of a flare fired at this angle can be modelled by the function

$$h = -5t^2 + 50t$$

where h is the height, in metres, and t is the time, in seconds, since the flare was fired.

Use the function to copy and complete the table.

Time (s)	Height (m)
0	0
1	45
2	
⋮	
10	

1. What is the maximum height reached by the flare?

2. After how many seconds does the flare reach its maximum height?

3. If the flare burns until it hits the water, for how many seconds does the flare burn?

4. The distance, d, to the horizon from a point above the Earth is given by the formula

$$d = \sqrt{2rh + h^2}$$

where r is the radius of the Earth, and h is the height of the point above the Earth. The radius of the Earth is about 6380 km. Use the maximum height of the flare, in kilometres, to find the maximum distance over which the flare can be seen, to the nearest kilometre.

5. List three events or situations, not mentioned above, that might be described by gravity's rainbow curve.

GETTING STARTED

Number Games

1. A result is found by choosing an integer, squaring it, subtracting the square from 400, and then adding 80 times the original integer.

a) Guess the value of the integer that gives the greatest result. Compare your guess with your classmates' guesses.

b) Choose an integer and calculate the result.

c) Repeat the calculation until you find the integer that gives the greatest result. Share your answer with your classmates. Who made the best guess in part a)?

d) Let the value of the integer that gives the greatest result be n. Copy and complete the table using the actual value of n.

e) Use the table to graph the result versus the starting integer.

f) Is there a least possible result? Explain.

g) Let the result be y and the original integer be x. Write an equation that expresses y in terms of x in the form $y = \blacksquare$.

Starting Integer	Result
n	
$n + 1$	
$n + 2$	
$n + 3$	
$n + 4$	
$n - 1$	
$n - 2$	
$n - 3$	
$n - 4$	

2. A result is found by choosing an integer, squaring it, adding the result to 1300, and then subtracting 70 times the original integer.

a) Guess the value of the integer that gives the least result. Compare your guess with your classmates' guesses.

b) Choose an integer and calculate the result.

c) Repeat the calculation until you find the integer that gives the least result. Share your answer with your classmates. Who made the best guess in part a)?

d) Let the value of the integer that gives the least result be n. Copy and complete the same table as above using the actual value of n.

e) Use the table to graph the result versus the starting integer.

f) Is there a greatest possible result? Explain.

g) Let the result be y and the original integer be x. Write an equation that expresses y in terms of x in the form $y = \blacksquare$.

3. Suppose you were asked to choose one of the following equations to calculate the amount of money you would win in a contest. In each equation, m represents an amount of money, in dollars, and n represents an integer.

$$m = 100 - n^2 + 50n \qquad m = 400 + n^2 - 20n$$

a) If the value of n were fixed at 25, which equation would you choose? Explain.

b) If you could choose your own value of n, which equation would you choose? Explain.

Warm Up

Write the domain and range of each relation.

1. (1, 2), (2, 4), (3, 6), (4, 8), (5, 10)
2. (5, 4), (8, 7), (12, 11), (15, 14), (28, 27)
3. (1, 1), (4, 1), (8, 1), (22, 1), (53, 1)

State whether each graph represents a function. Write the domain and range for each graph.

4. 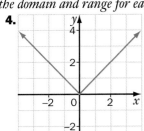   **5.**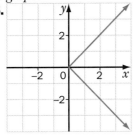

6. If $f(x) = 3x - 4$, find
a) $f(0)$ **b)** $f(1)$ **c)** $f(-1)$ **d)** $f(2)$
e) $f(-5)$ **f)** $f\left(\dfrac{2}{3}\right)$ **g)** $f(1.5)$ **h)** $f(25)$

7. If $f(x) = x^2$, find
a) $f(0)$ **b)** $f(1)$ **c)** $f(-1)$ **d)** $f(3)$
e) $f(-3)$ **f)** $f\left(\dfrac{1}{2}\right)$ **g)** $f\left(-\dfrac{1}{2}\right)$ **h)** $f(1.5)$

8. If $g(x) = x^2 + 4x - 1$, find
a) $g(0)$ **b)** $g(1)$ **c)** $g(-1)$ **d)** $g(2)$
e) $g(5)$ **f)** $g\left(\dfrac{1}{2}\right)$ **g)** $g(-3)$ **h)** $g(2.5)$

Copy and complete each of the following equations.

9. $2x^2 - 6x = 2(\rule{1cm}{0.3mm})$ **10.** $5x^2 + 10x = 5(\rule{1cm}{0.3mm})$
11. $-x^2 + 3x = -(\rule{1cm}{0.3mm})$ **12.** $-3x^2 - 12x = -3(\rule{1cm}{0.3mm})$
13. $4x^2 - 2x = 4(\rule{1cm}{0.3mm})$ **14.** $-2x^2 + 5x = -2(\rule{1cm}{0.3mm})$
15. $\dfrac{1}{2}x^2 - 7x = \dfrac{1}{2}(\rule{1cm}{0.3mm})$ **16.** $-\dfrac{1}{3}x^2 + x = -\dfrac{1}{3}(\rule{1cm}{0.3mm})$
17. $1.5x^2 - 9x = 1.5(\rule{1cm}{0.3mm})$
18. $0.4x^2 + 4x = 0.4(\rule{1cm}{0.3mm})$
19. $-2x^2 - 0.6x = -2(\rule{1cm}{0.3mm})$
20. $0.05x^2 + 3x = 0.05(\rule{1cm}{0.3mm})$
21. $\dfrac{2}{5}x^2 - x = \dfrac{2}{5}(\rule{1cm}{0.3mm})$
22. $-0.002x^2 + 0.06x = -0.002(\rule{1cm}{0.3mm})$

State the degree of each polynomial.

23. $2x + 1$ **24.** x^2
25. $y^2 - 3y + 6$ **26.** $2m^3 + m^2 - 9$
27. $3 - 5x^2 + 10x$ **28.** $4t^2 + t^4 - 3t$

Mental Math

Evaluating Expressions

Evaluate each expression for the given values of x.

1. $x^2 + 3$; $x = 2, 4, -2, -4$
2. $2x^2 - 1$; $x = 1, -1, 3, -3$
3. $x^2 + x$; $x = 1, -1, -3, 6$
4. $-x^2 + 2x$; $x = 1, -1, 3, -4$
5. $3x^2 - 4x$; $x = 2, -1, 3, \dfrac{1}{2}$
6. $x^2 - x - 3$; $x = 1, -2, 3, -3$
7. $(x + 2)^2 + 1$; $x = 1, -1, 3, -4$
8. $(x - 1)^2 - 4$; $x = 0, 1, -1, 4$

Multiplying in Two Steps

Numbers can be multiplied by rewriting the product and then multiplying in two steps.
To multiply 21×32, rewrite the product as
$(20 + 1) \times 32 = (20 \times 32) + (1 \times 32)$ **Estimate**
$\qquad\qquad = 640 + 32$ $\boxed{20 \times 30 = 600}$
$\qquad\qquad = 672$
To multiply 18×43, rewrite the product as
$(20 - 2) \times 43 = (20 \times 43) - (2 \times 43)$ **Estimate**
$\qquad\qquad = 860 - 86$ $\boxed{20 \times 40 = 800}$
$\qquad\qquad = 774$

Multiply in two steps.

1. 44×5 **2.** 87×7 **3.** 36×9
4. 11×13 **5.** 75×12 **6.** 67×15
7. 29×13 **8.** 25×26 **9.** 82×36
10. 102×25 **11.** 125×14 **12.** 203×19

To multiply 2.1×3.2, multiply 21×32. Then, place the decimal point.   **Estimate**
$21 \times 32 = 672$
$2.1 \times 3.2 = 6.72$ $\boxed{2 \times 3 = 6}$

Multiply in two steps.

13. 35×0.9 **14.** 57×1.8 **15.** 4.3×8.1
16. 0.12×0.24 **17.** 0.39×180 **18.** 0.73×0.25

19. Two two-digit numbers can be represented by the expressions $10x + y$ and $10m + n$.
a) Expand and simplify $(10x + y)(10m + n)$.
b) Expand and simplify $10x(10m + n) + y(10m + n)$.
c) Expand and simplify
$10(x + 1)(10m + n) - (10 - y)(10m + n)$.
d) Explain why the rules for multiplying in two steps work.

INVESTIGATING MATH

Exploring Transformations

In the following explorations, draw the graphs manually or use a graphing calculator.

1 Exploring y = |x|

1. Graph the function $y = |x|$.

2. Does the graph open up or down?

3. Why does the graph lie only in quadrants I and II?

4. The graph has a line of symmetry known as the **axis of symmetry**.
a) Where is the axis of symmetry?
b) What is the equation of the axis of symmetry?

5. The point at which the graph of $y = |x|$ intersects the axis of symmetry is called the **vertex** of the graph. What are the coordinates of the vertex?

6. For the function $y = |x|$, what is
a) the domain?　　**b)** the range?

2 Comparing y = |x| and y = |x| + q

1. Graph the following functions on the same set of axes.
a) $y = |x|$　　　　**b)** $y = |x| + 3$
c) $y = |x| - 7$

2. How are the three graphs the same? How are they different?

3. For each graph, write
a) the coordinates of the vertex
b) the equation of the axis of symmetry
c) the domain and the range

4. What translation maps the graph of $y = |x|$ onto the graph of
a) $y = |x| + 3$?　　　**b)** $y = |x| - 7$?

5. Without graphing, write the coordinates of the vertex, and the domain and range.
a) $y = |x| + 11$　　　**b)** $y = |x| - 10$
c) $y = |x| - 22$　　　**d)** $y = |x| + 44$

3 Comparing y = |x| and y = |x − p|

1. Graph the following functions on the same set of axes.
a) $y = |x|$　　　　**b)** $y = |x - 4|$
c) $y = |x + 6|$

2. For each graph, write
a) the coordinates of the vertex
b) the equation of the axis of symmetry
c) the domain and range

3. How is the graph of $y = |x|$ translated when x is replaced by
a) $x - 4$?　　　　　**b)** $x + 6$?

4. Without graphing, write the coordinates of the vertex and the equation of the axis of symmetry.
a) $y = |x - 9|$　　　**b)** $y = |x + 7|$
c) $y = |x - 11|$　　　**d)** $y = |x + 13|$

4 Comparing $y = |x|$ and $y = |x - p| + q$

1. Graph the following functions on the same set of axes.

a) $y = |x|$ **b)** $y = |x - 1| + 5$ **c)** $y = |x - 6| - 3$

2. For each graph, find
a) the coordinates of the vertex
b) the equation of the axis of symmetry
c) the domain and range

3. What translation maps the graph of $y = |x|$ onto the graph of

a) $y = |x - 1| + 5$?   **b)** $y = |x - 6| - 3$?

4. Graph the following functions on the same set of axes or in the same viewing window.

a) $y = |x|$ **b)** $y = |x + 5| + 6$ **c)** $y = |x + 8| - 7$

5. For each graph, write
a) the coordinates of the vertex
b) the equation of the axis of symmetry
c) the domain and range

6. What translation maps the graph of $y = |x|$ onto the graph of

a) $y = |x + 5| + 6$?   **b)** $y = |x + 8| - 7$?

7. Without graphing, write the coordinates of the vertex and the equation of the axis of symmetry.

a) $y = |x - 3| + 4$ **b)** $y = |x + 2| - 5$
c) $y = |x - 11| - 3$ **d)** $y = |x + 13| + 6$

5 Comparing $y = |x|$ and $y = a|x|$

1. Graph the following functions on the same set of axes.

a) $y = |x|$ **b)** $y = -|x|$ **c)** $y = 2|x|$
d) $y = -2|x|$ **e)** $y = 0.5|x|$ **f)** $y = -0.5|x|$

2. a) Which graphs open up? Which graphs open down?

b) What determines the direction of the opening?

3. For each graph, write
a) the coordinates of the vertex
b) the equation of the axis of symmetry
c) the domain and range

4. What transformation maps
$y = |x|$ onto $y = -|x|$?
$y = 2|x|$ onto $y = -2|x|$?
$y = 0.5|x|$ onto $y = -0.5|x|$?

5. How does the shape of the graphs of $y = 2|x|$ and $y = -2|x|$ compare with the shape of the graphs of $y = |x|$ and $y = -|x|$?

6. How does the shape of the graphs of $y = 0.5|x|$ and $y = -0.5|x|$ compare with the shape of the graphs of $y = |x|$ and $y = -|x|$?

6 Combining Transformations

Use your knowledge of transformations to sketch the graph of each of the following functions. For each graph, write
a) *the coordinates of the vertex*
b) *the equation of the axis of symmetry*
c) *the domain and range*
d) *the direction of the opening*
e) *a description of how the shape compares with the shape of $y = |x|$ or $y = -|x|$*

1. $y = 2|x| - 9$ **2.** $y = -3|x| + 7$
3. $y = -|x| - 2$ **4.** $y = 2|x - 3| + 6$
5. $y = -|x + 4|$ **6.** $y = -|x + 6| - 3$
7. $y = 0.5|x - 7|$ **8.** $y = -0.5|x - 5| - 8$

7 Exploring Intercepts

1. Sketch the graph of each of the following functions. Find the y-intercepts and any x-intercepts of each graph.

a) $y = |x| + 2$ **b)** $y = |x| - 3$
c) $y = |x - 1|$ **d)** $y = |x + 5|$
e) $y = |x - 2| + 3$ **f)** $y = |x - 3| - 1$
g) $y = |x + 1| + 4$ **h)** $y = |x + 3| - 2$
i) $y = 2|x|$ **j)** $y = 2|x - 1|$
k) $y = 3|x + 2|$ **l)** $y = -2|x|$
m) $y = -3|x + 1|$ **n)** $y = -2|x - 3|$
o) $y = -2|x| + 1$ **p)** $y = -3|x| - 2$
q) $y = 3|x - 2| + 1$ **r)** $y = 2|x + 3| - 4$
s) $y = -2|x - 1| + 3$ **t)** $y = -3|x + 1| - 2$

2. For an absolute value function of the form $y = a|x - p| + q$,
a) how many y-intercepts are there?
b) how many x-intercepts can there be?
c) is there a relationship between the number of x-intercepts and the value of p? the values of a and q? Explain.

3.1 Graphing $y = x^2 + q$, $y = ax^2$, and $y = ax^2 + q$

Heritage Day, the birthday of Canada's Maple Leaf flag, is celebrated in February each year. Some celebrations involve the display of large Canadian flags. The largest Canadian flag in the world measures 12.19 m by 24.38 m.

Regulation Canadian flags are twice as long as they are wide. If the width of a Canadian flag is x, then the length is $2x$. The area, y, can be represented by the expression

$$y = 2x \times x$$
$$= 2x^2$$

The equation $y = 2x^2$ is an example of a quadratic function. The word quadratic comes from the Latin word *quadratum*, meaning square.

Explore: Compare the Graphs

On the same set of axes, graph $y = x$ and $y = x^2$, where x and y are real numbers.

Inquire

1. Does the graph of $y = x^2$ have a line of symmetry? If so, what is it?

2. Does the graph of $y = x$ have a line of symmetry? If so, what is it?

3. For the graph of $y = x$,
a) does x have a maximum or minimum value? Explain.
b) does y have a maximum or minimum value? Explain.
c) write the domain and range

4. For the graph of $y = x^2$,
a) does x have a maximum or minimum value? Explain.
b) does y have a maximum or minimum value? Explain.
c) write the domain and range

5. Draw the graph of $y = 2x^2$. How does this graph compare with the graph of $y = x^2$?

6. For $y = 2x^2$, if y represents the area of a Canadian flag, and x represents the width,
a) what are the restrictions on x? on y?
b) on which part of the graph of $y = 2x^2$ are the points that describe Canadian flags?

A **quadratic function** is a function determined by a second degree polynomial.
Examples of quadratic functions are

$y = x^2$ $f(x) = 2x^2 + 4$ $g(x) = 3x^2 - 2x$ $y = x^2 + 2x - 7$

Read $f(x)$ as "f of x" or "the value of f at x."

A quadratic function is a function that can be written in the form

$$f(x) = ax^2 + bx + c \ \text{ or } \ y = ax^2 + bx + c$$

where a, b, and c are real numbers, and $a \neq 0$.

If the domain is the set of real numbers, the graph of a quadratic function is a
parabola. The values of a, b, and c determine where the parabola is located on
the coordinate plane, and whether the parabola opens up or down.

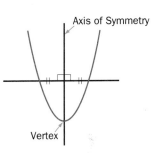

The graph of a quadratic function has either a maximum (highest) point or a
minimum (lowest) point called the vertex of the parabola. The vertical line that
passes through the vertex is called the **axis of symmetry**. A parabola is mapped
onto itself by a reflection in the axis of symmetry.

In this section, the effects of two transformations on the basic quadratic
function $y = x^2$ will be examined, separately and together.

Example 1   Graphing y = x² + q

a) Graph $y = x^2 + 3$ and $y = x^2 - 4$. Compare the graphs to the graph of $y = x^2$.
b) Describe each graph in terms of its vertex, axis of symmetry, domain and
range, and the maximum or minimum value of the function.

Solution

a)

$y = x^2$		$y = x^2 + 3$		$y = x^2 - 4$	
x	**y**	**x**	**y**	**x**	**y**
3	9	3	12	3	5
2	4	2	7	2	0
1	1	1	4	1	-3
0	0	0	3	0	-4
-1	1	-1	4	-1	-3
-2	4	-2	7	-2	0
-3	9	-3	12	-3	5

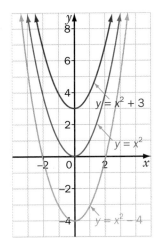

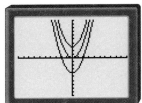

The graphs of $y = x^2 + 3$ and $y = x^2 - 4$ are congruent
to $y = x^2$. All three have the same size and shape, but
they are in different positions.

For $y = x^2 + 3$, the y-coordinates are all 3 greater than the corresponding y-coordinates of
$y = x^2$. The graph of $y = x^2 + 3$ is the graph of $y = x^2$ translated upward by 3 units.

For $y = x^2 - 4$, the y-coordinates are all 4 less than the corresponding y-coordinates of $y = x^2$.
The graph of $y = x^2 - 4$ is the graph of $y = x^2$ translated downward by 4 units.

b) For $y = x^2 + 3$, the vertex is (0, 3). The equation of the axis of symmetry is $x = 0$.
The domain is the set of real numbers, and the range is $y \geq 3$.
The function reaches a minimum value of $y = 3$ when $x = 0$.
For $y = x^2 - 4$, the vertex is (0, -4). The equation of the axis of symmetry is $x = 0$.
The domain is the set of real numbers, and the range is $y \geq -4$.
The function reaches a minimum value of $y = -4$ when $x = 0$.

Example 2   Graphing $y = ax^2$

Graph $y = 2x^2$, $y = \dfrac{1}{2}x^2$, $y = -x^2$, $y = -2x^2$, and $y = -\dfrac{1}{2}x^2$.

Compare the graphs to each other and to the graph of $y = x^2$.

Solution

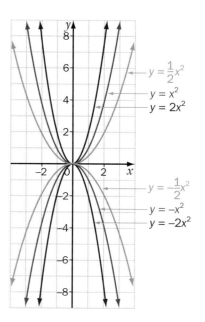

$y = x^2$

x	y
3	9
2	4
1	1
0	0
−1	1
−2	4
−3	9

$y = 2x^2$

x	y
3	18
2	8
1	2
0	0
−1	2
−2	8
−3	18

$y = \dfrac{1}{2}x^2$

x	y
3	4.5
2	2
1	0.5
0	0
−1	0.5
−2	2
−3	4.5

$y = -x^2$

x	y
3	−9
2	−4
1	−1
0	0
−1	−1
−2	−4
−3	−9

$y = -2x^2$

x	y
3	−18
2	−8
1	−2
0	0
−1	−2
−2	−8
−3	−18

$y = -\dfrac{1}{2}x^2$

x	y
3	−4.5
2	−2
1	−0.5
0	0
−1	−0.5
−2	−2
−3	−4.5

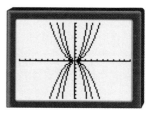

The y-coordinates of $y = -x^2$ are opposite to the corresponding y-coordinates of $y = x^2$. The graph of $y = -x^2$ is a reflection of the graph of $y = x^2$ in the x-axis.

For $a > 0$, the parabolas open up, and each vertex is the minimum point on the graph.

For $a < 0$, the parabolas open down, and each vertex is the maximum point on the graph.

In comparison with $y = x^2$, if $a > 1$ or $a < -1$, there is a stretch in the y-direction, and the parabola narrows.

The y-coordinates of $y = 2x^2$ are two times the corresponding y-coordinates of $y = x^2$.

The graph of $y = -2x^2$ is the graph of $y = 2x^2$ reflected in the x-axis, or the graph of $y = x^2$ reflected in the x-axis and then stretched vertically by a scale factor of 2.

In comparison with $y = x^2$, if $-1 < a < 1$, there is a shrink in the y-direction, and the parabola flattens.

The y-coordinates of $y = \dfrac{1}{2}x^2$ are half the corresponding y-coordinates of $y = x^2$.

The graph of $y = -\dfrac{1}{2}x^2$ is the graph of $y = \dfrac{1}{2}x^2$ reflected in the x-axis, or the graph of $y = x^2$ reflected in the x-axis and then shrunk vertically by a scale factor of $\dfrac{1}{2}$.

Example 3   Graphing $y = ax^2 + q$

Sketch the graph of $y = -2x^2 + 8$ and find
a) the coordinates of the vertex   **b)** the equation of the axis of symmetry
c) the domain and range   **d)** the maximum or minimum value
e) any intercepts

Solution
The graph of $y = -2x^2 + 8$ is the graph of $y = -2x^2$
translated 8 units upward.
a) The coordinates of the vertex are (0, 8).
b) The equation of the axis of symmetry is $x = 0$.
c) The domain is the set of real numbers.
The range is $y \le 8$.
d) The graph opens down, so the vertex is the
highest point on the graph. The maximum value of
the function is 8 when $x = 0$.
e) The graph crosses the y-axis at (0, 8), so the
y-intercept is 8. The graph appears to cross the x-axis
at (2, 0) and (−2, 0), so the x-intercepts are 2 and −2.

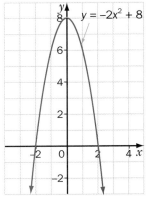

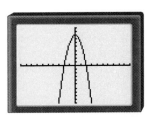

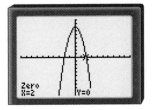

The Zero operation on a graphing calculator can be
used to find the values of the x-intercepts. Other graphing calculator methods
involve displaying a table of values or using the ZOOM and TRACE
instructions.

The above examples show that we can visualize the functions by identifying the
transformations shown in the general equation.

If $a < 0$, reflection in x-axis

$$y = ax^2 + q$$

vertical stretch   vertical translation

Example 4   Writing an Equation
A parabola with the vertex (0, −2) passes through the point (3, 1). Write an
equation for the parabola in the form $y = ax^2 + q$.

Solution
The vertex is translated 2 units downward from the vertex of $y = x^2$, so $q = -2$.
Substitute the coordinates (3, 1) into the equation $y = ax^2 - 2$ to find the value
of a.

$$y = ax^2 - 2$$
$$1 = a(3)^2 - 2$$
$$3 = 9a$$
$$\frac{1}{3} = a$$

So, an equation for the parabola is $y = \frac{1}{3}x^2 - 2$.

Example 5   St. Louis Gateway Arch

The stainless steel Gateway Arch in St. Louis, Missouri, has the shape of a **catenary**, which is a curve that approximates a parabola. If the curve is graphed on a grid with the origin on the ground directly below the top of the arch, the curve can be modelled by the function

$$h(d) = -0.02d^2 + 192$$

where $h(d)$ metres is the maximum height of the arch, and d metres is the horizontal distance from the centre of the arch.

a) Graph the shape of the arch.
b) Find the height of the arch.
c) Find the approximate width of the arch at the base.
d) Find the approximate height of the arch at a horizontal distance of 15 m from one end.

Solution

a) Draw the graph.

d	h(d)
0	192
20	184
40	160
60	120
80	64
90	30
–20	184
–40	160
–60	120
–80	64
–90	30

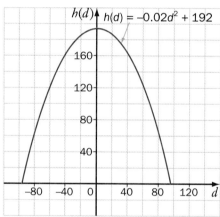

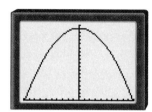

b) Since the origin is directly below the top of the arch, the maximum value of the function gives the height of the arch. The maximum value is 192, so the height of the arch is 192 m.

c) The width of the arch at the base is the distance from one d-intercept to the other. From the manual graph, the d-intercepts appear to be just less than 100 and just greater than –100, so the width of the arch is close to 200 m. A graphing calculator can give more accurate values for the d-intercepts of about 98 and –98. The width of the arch is about 196 m.

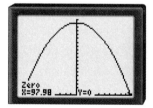

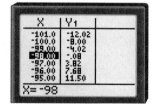

d) Because the curve has an axis of symmetry through the vertex, the height of the curve 15 units from either end is the same.
Since the positive d-intercept is about 98, the height of the curve 15 units from this end can be found by evaluating $h(d)$ when d is $98 - 15$ or 83.

$$h(d) = -0.02d^2 + 192$$
$$= -0.02(83)^2 + 192$$
$$\doteq 54$$

Estimate

$-0.02 \times 6400 = -128$
$-130 + 190 = 60$

So, the height of the arch at a horizontal distance of 15 m from one end is about 54 m.

Practice

Sketch the graph of each parabola and state
a) *the direction of the opening*
b) *the coordinates of the vertex*
c) *the equation of the axis of symmetry*
d) *the domain and range*
e) *the maximum or minimum value*

1. $y = x^2 + 5$ **2.** $y = x^2 - 2$
3. $y = -x^2 - 1$ **4.** $y = -x^2 + 3$
5. $y = 3x^2$ **6.** $y = -4x^2$
7. $y = 2 + x^2$ **8.** $f(x) = -1.5x^2$
9. $f(x) = -2x^2 - 3$ **10.** $f(x) = 0.5x^2 + 1$
11. $f(x) = -0.5x^2 + 7$ **12.** $f(x) + 6 = -3x^2$

Write one sentence that compares each pair of graphs.
13. $y = x^2$ and $y = x^2 - 4$
14. $y = -x^2$ and $y = -x^2 + 5$
15. $y = x^2$ and $y = 3x^2$
16. $y = -x^2$ and $y = -\frac{1}{3}x^2$
17. $y = 2x^2 + 7$ and $y = 2x^2 - 2$
18. $y = 0.25x^2$ and $y = -0.25x^2$

19. The four graphs represent the four equations $y = 2x^2 - 3$, $y = -2x^2 - 3$, $y = 2x^2 + 3$, and $y = -2x^2 + 3$. Match each graph with the correct equation.

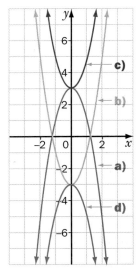

Without graphing each function, state
a) *the direction of the opening*
b) *the coordinates of the vertex*
c) *the domain and range*
d) *the maximum or minimum value*
20. $y = -5x^2$ **21.** $f(x) = x^2 - 11.4$
22. $y = -x^2 + 4.7$ **23.** $f(x) = 2x^2 - 3$
24. $f(x) = -2.9x^2 - 8.3$ **25.** $y - 9.9 = 1.6x^2$
26. $3.5 + 2.2x^2 = f(x)$ **27.** $4.3x^2 + y = -0.5$

Describe what happens to the point $(2, 4)$ on the graph of $y = x^2$ when each pair of transformations is applied to the parabola in the given order.
28. a vertical stretch of scale factor 2, followed by a vertical translation of 5
29. a reflection in the x-axis, followed by a vertical translation of 3
30. a reflection in the x-axis, followed by a vertical stretch of scale factor $\frac{1}{2}$
31. a vertical translation of –2, followed by a reflection in the x-axis

Sketch a graph of each parabola and state
a) *the coordinates of the vertex*
b) *any intercepts*
32. $y = x^2 - 9$ **33.** $y = x^2 + 1$
34. $y = -x^2 + 4$ **35.** $y = 2x^2 - 8$
36. $f(x) = 16 + x^2$ **37.** $f(x) = 18 - 2x^2$
38. $y = -3 - 3x^2$ **39.** $y = -5x^2 + 5$
40. $f(x) = -0.5x^2 + 8$ **41.** $f(x) = 0.25x^2 - 1$

Graph manually to estimate any x-intercepts, or use a graphing calculator to determine them to the nearest tenth.
42. $y = x^2 - 2$
43. $f(x) = -x^2 + 3$
44. $f(x) = x^2 + 6$
45. $y = 2x^2 - 10$
46. $f(x) = 8 - 4x^2$
47. $f(x) = 0.5x^2 - 3$

Write an equation for a parabola with the given vertex and given value of a.
48. $(0, 0)$; $a = 5$
49. $(0, 0)$; $a = -6$
50. $(0, -7)$; $a = -8$
51. $(0, 3)$; $a = 0.2$
52. $(0, -2.5)$; $a = 0.1$
53. $(0, 6.5)$; $a = -0.6$

Write an equation for the parabola with the given vertex and passing through the given point.
54. vertex $(0, 0)$; point $(2, 16)$
55. vertex $(0, 0)$; point $(-3, -18)$
56. vertex $(0, -7)$; point $(2, 5)$
57. vertex $(0, 3)$; point $(4, -13)$
58. vertex $(0, -5)$; point $(-4, -13)$
59. vertex $\left(0, \frac{3}{2}\right)$; point $(3, 3)$

Write an equation of the form $y = ax^2 + q$ *for each parabola.*

60.

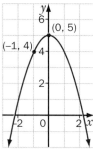

61.

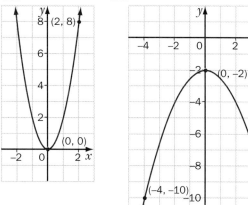

62.

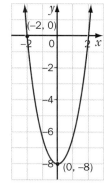

63.

Applications and Problem Solving

64. Find the value of c so that the parabola $y = -2x^2 + c$ passes through the point $(-3, -33)$.

65. If a function of the form $f(x) = ax^2 + q$ has an x-intercept of 7.5, what is the other x-intercept? Explain how you know.

66. A parabola with $x = 0$ as its axis of symmetry has a y-intercept of 6. One of its x-intercepts is 3. Write an equation for the parabola.

67. Geometry For triangles in which the base and height are equal,
a) write an equation that relates the area, A, to the height, h
b) graph A versus h
c) find the h- and A-intercepts
d) state the domain and range

68. a) Sketch a graph of $x = y^2$.
b) Find the domain and range of the relation.
c) Is the relation a function? Explain.

69. Golden Gate Bridge The road on the Golden Gate Bridge is supported by two towers and the two cables that join them. The distance between the towers is 1280 m. Suppose the curve of a cable is graphed on a grid, with the origin on the road at the centre of the bridge. The curve made by the cable is a catenary that can be approximately modelled by the quadratic function
$$h(d) = 0.000\,37d^2 + 2$$
where $h(d)$ metres is the height of the cable above the road, and d metres is the horizontal distance from the centre of the bridge.

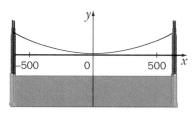

a) Graph the function.
b) What is the distance from the road to the lowest point of the cable?
c) What is the maximum height of the towers above the road, to the nearest ten metres?
d) At a horizontal distance of 200 m from the centre of the bridge, how high is the cable above the road, to the nearest metre?

70. Free fall For an object dropped from the top of a building, the approximate height of the object above the ground is given by the equation
$$h(t) = -5t^2 + d$$
where $h(t)$ metres is the height t seconds after the object is dropped, and d is the height from which it is dropped. Suppose an object is dropped 134 m, the height of the AGT Tower in Edmonton.
a) Graph $h(t)$ versus t for the falling object.
b) In which quadrant(s) did you draw the graph? Explain.
c) Use the graph to find how long the object takes to reach the ground, to the nearest tenth of a second.
d) On the moon, the approximate height of a falling object is given by the equation
$$h(t) = -0.8t^2 + d$$
If an object is dropped from a height of 134 m, how long does it take to reach the surface of the moon, to the nearest tenth of a second?

71. Graph $x + y = 4$ and $y = x^2 - 2$ on the same grid.
a) What are the coordinates of the intersection points?
b) Describe how you found the intersection points.

72. Inequality The area of the ground floor of a building is less than or equal to the area of the lot on which it is built.
a) For a square lot of side length s, write an inequality to express the area, A, of the ground floor of a building in terms of s.
b) Graph the inequality.

73. Find a and q so that a parabola $y = ax^2 + q$ passes through each pair of points.
a) $(-3, 11)$ and $(4, 18)$
b) $(3, -10)$ and $(-1, -2)$
c) $(1, -1)$ and $(2, 5)$
d) $(-4, -4)$ and $(2, 2)$

74. Confederation Bridge Building the Confederation Bridge from New Brunswick to Prince Edward Island was quite a challenge. The bridge is 12.9 km in length and has 44 main bridge spans, each 220 m wide. The arch of each main span is a parabola, with each end of the arch supported on a footing that raises it 40 m above sea level.

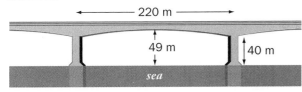

Write an equation for the arch, if the origin is placed
a) at the highest point of the arch
b) at sea level directly below the highest point of the arch

75. Patterns In the sequence $-2, 4, 14, 28, \ldots$, the number -2 is in position 1, the number 4 is in position 2, and so on.
a) Write an equation that relates each number, n, to its position, p, in the sequence.
b) Repeat part a) for the sequence $2, -4, -14, -28, \ldots$.
c) How are the graphs of n versus p for the two sequences related?

76. Geometry a) Write an equation that relates the area of a circle, A, to its radius, r.
b) Graph A versus r.
c) Does the graph have an axis of symmetry? Explain.
d) State the domain and range of the function.

77. Measurement
The 25 by 16 rectangle contains a square of side length s. The sides of the square are parallel to the sides of the rectangle.

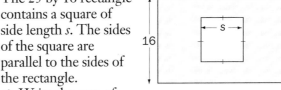

a) Write the area of the shaded region, A, as a function of s.
b) If no part of the square can be outside the rectangle, what is the maximum possible value of s?
c) Graph A versus s.
d) State the domain and range of the function.

78. Inequality Graph the inequality $2x^2 - y < 3$. Explain your reasoning.

79. For quadratic functions of the form $y = ax^2 + q$, where x and y are real numbers, describe any relationships between the values of a and q and
a) the number of y-intercepts
b) the number of x-intercepts

80. Technology For the equation $y = 0.5x^2$, state viewing window variables that produce the following views of the parabola. Compare your values with your classmates'.
a) a line with a positive slope
b) a line with a negative slope
c) a horizontal line

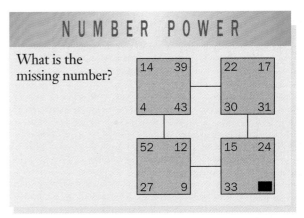

NUMBER POWER

What is the missing number?

14	39		22	17
4	43		30	31
52	12		15	24
27	9		33	■

PROBLEM SOLVING

3.2 Guess and Check

A valid way to solve many problems is to guess at the answer and then check to see if it is correct. You may find it necessary to improve your guess until you get the correct answer.

An architect is designing the parking lot for the club house at a golf course. The club house has dimensions 23 m by 20 m.

One possible design for the parking lot is an L-shape of uniform width, as shown in the diagram. The architect knows that an area of 14 m^2 is needed for each parking space, and that another 10 m^2 per space must be allowed for access routes. What is the width of the L-shaped parking lot, if there must be 100 parking spaces?

Understand the Problem

1. What information are you given?
2. What are you asked to find?
3. Do you need an exact or an approximate answer?

Think of a Plan

Determine the total area needed for the parking lot.
Write an equation that relates this area to the width of the lot.
Solve the equation to find the width.

Carry Out the Plan

Each parking space requires an area of $14 + 10$ or 24 m^2.
For 100 parking spaces, the total area is 100×24 or 2400 m^2.

The parking lot can be divided into two rectangles, as shown. The total area is given by
$$20x + x(23 + x) = x(20 + 23 + x)$$
$$= x(43 + x)$$
So, $x(43 + x) = 2400$

Solve the equation by guess and check.

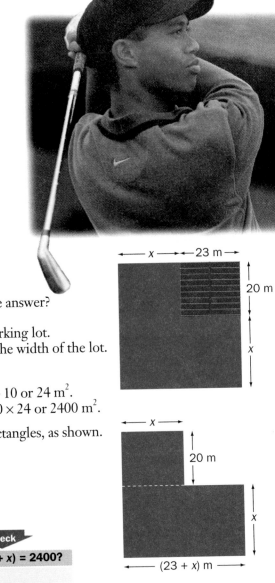

Guess		Check
Value of x	Value of x(43 + x)	Does x(43 + x) = 2400?
30	30(73) = 2190	Too low
35	35(78) = 2730	Too high
33	33(76) = 2508	Too high
32	32(75) = 2400	2400 checks!

Estimate

$30 \times 80 = 2400$

The width of the parking lot is 32 m.

Look Back

How could you set up a spreadsheet to solve the problem by guess and check?

Guess and Check

1. Guess an answer that fits some of the facts.
2. Check the answer against the other facts.
3. If necessary, adjust the guess and check again.

Applications and Problem Solving

1. What is the area, in square kilometres, of the largest lake entirely in Canada?

2. How many students are enrolled in Grade 11 in your province or territory?

3. The Trans Canada Trail is the longest trail of its kind in the world.
a) How long is it?
b) What is the length of the trail in your province or territory?

4. a) How many airports are there in Canada?
b) How many have paved runways?

5. The property occupied by a small, one-storey shopping plaza includes the U-shaped building and its rectangular parking lot, as shown.

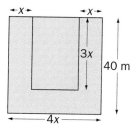

The floor area of the building is 896 m².
a) What is the value of x, in metres?
b) A parking space requires an area of 24 m², including enough room for access. How many cars can park in the parking lot?

6. Copy the diagram. Place the numbers from 1 to 9 in the circles so that each line of three numbers adds to 18. The 6 and the 1 have been placed for you.

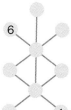

7. Each letter represents a different digit in this addition. Find the values of O, N, E, and T.

```
  ONE
+ ONE
+ ONE
+ ONE
  TEN
```

8. Copy the figure. Replace each ■ with a spelled-out number to make the sentence true.

In
this
triangle,
there are
■ f's, ■ h's,
and ■ t's.

9. A county has 35 towns, as shown in the diagram. Each of the shortest line segments represents a road 10 km long. Regional planners are suggesting fire stations in some towns, so that no town is more than 10 km by road from a fire station. What is the minimum number of fire stations that must be built?

10. In a magic square, the sum of the numbers in each row, column, and diagonal is the same, in this case 15. Rearrange the numbers so that the sums for each row, column, and diagonal are all different, and none of the sums is 15.

6	1	8
7	5	3
2	9	4

11. By replacing each ■, use each digit from 0 to 9 once in three correct expressions of the form shown. Replace each ● with a symbol chosen from ×, ÷, +, or −.

12. Write a problem that can be solved using the guess and check strategy. Have a classmate solve your problem.

3.3 Graphing $y = a(x - p)^2 + q$

A quadratic function can be written in several forms. One form is $y = a(x - p)^2 + q$, which is called the **standard form** of a quadratic function. Writing quadratic functions in this form helps in their analysis.

The Symphony of Fire is the largest offshore fireworks competition in the world. The fireworks are launched from barges anchored in Lake Ontario, close to Toronto. The fireworks are synchronized with a musical soundtrack. Competing countries are judged on the choice of music, the synchronization, and the visual display.

A function, written in standard form, that describes the path of one type of rocket in a fireworks display is

$$h(t) = -4.9(t - 5)^2 + 124$$

where $h(t)$ is the height of the rocket, in metres, and t is the time, in seconds, since it was launched.

Explore: Compare the Graphs

Graph each group of functions on the same set of axes. For each group of functions, complete a table like the one shown.

Group 1: **a)** $y = x^2$ **b)** $y = (x - 4)^2$ **c)** $y = (x + 3)^2$
Group 2: **a)** $y = (x - 4)^2$ **b)** $y = (x - 4)^2 + 2$ **c)** $y = (x - 4)^2 - 3$
Group 3: **a)** $y = (x + 3)^2$ **b)** $y = (x + 3)^2 + 5$ **c)** $y = (x + 3)^2 - 1$

Group 1	Function	Vertex	Axis of Symmetry
a)	$y = x^2$		
b)	$y = (x - 4)^2$		
c)	$y = (x + 3)^2$		

Inquire

1. For group 1, how is the graph of $y = x^2$ translated when x is replaced by
a) $x - 4$? **b)** $x + 3$?

2. Write the coordinates of the vertex and the equation of the axis of symmetry for each of the following functions.
a) $y = (x - 7)^2$ **b)** $y = (x + 9)^2$

3. For group 2, what translation maps the graph of $y = (x - 4)^2$ onto the graph of
a) $y = (x - 4)^2 + 2$? **b)** $y = (x - 4)^2 - 3$?

4. Write the coordinates of the vertex and the equation of the axis of symmetry for each of the following functions.

a) $y = (x - 7)^2 + 6$ **b)** $y = (x - 6)^2 - 5$

5. For group 3, what translation maps the graph of $y = (x + 3)^2$ onto the graph of

a) $y = (x + 3)^2 + 5$?   **b)** $y = (x + 3)^2 - 1$?

6. Write the coordinates of the vertex and the equation of the axis of symmetry for each of the following functions.

a) $y = (x + 9)^2 + 4$ **b)** $y = (x + 5)^2 - 7$

The graphs of $y = x^2$, $y = x^2 + 5$, $y = (x - 2)^2$, and $y = (x + 3)^2 - 4$ are shown. The graphs of $y = x^2 + 5$, $y = (x - 2)^2$, and $y = (x + 3)^2 - 4$ are congruent to $y = x^2$ but have different positions.

The graph of $y = x^2 + 5$ is the graph of $y = x^2$ translated 5 units upward. The graph of $y = (x - 2)^2$ is the graph of $y = x^2$ translated 2 units to the right. The graph of $y = (x + 3)^2 - 4$ is the graph of $y = x^2$ translated 3 units to the left and 4 units downward.

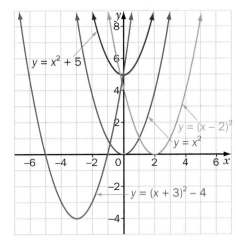

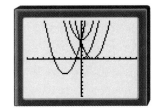

When using a graphing calculator, you may find it easier to keep track by adding one curve at a time to the viewing window and sketching each result.

The equations of all parabolas can be written in standard form.

Equation	Standard Form $y = a(x - p)^2 + q$	p	q	Vertex	Axis of Symmetry
$y = x^2$	$y = 1(x - 0)^2 + 0$	0	0	$(0, 0)$	$x = 0$
$y = x^2 + 5$	$y = 1(x - 0)^2 + 5$	0	5	$(0, 5)$	$x = 0$
$y = (x - 2)^2$	$y = 1(x - 2)^2 + 0$	2	0	$(2, 0)$	$x = 2$
$y = (x + 3)^2 - 4$	$y = 1(x + 3)^2 - 4$	-3	-4	$(-3, -4)$	$x = -3$

For a quadratic function written in the form $y = a(x - p)^2 + q$,
- the coordinates of the vertex are (p, q)
- the equation of the axis of symmetry is $x = p$

Comparing $y = a(x - p)^2 + q$ with $y = x^2$,
- if p is positive, the parabola is translated to the right p units
- if p is negative, the parabola is translated to the left p units
- if q is positive, the parabola is translated upward q units
- if q is negative, the parabola is translated downward q units

Example 1 Graphing When *a* > 0

Sketch the graph of $y = 2x^2$, $y = 2(x-4)^2$, and $y = 2(x+1)^2 + 4$. Describe each graph in terms of the direction of the opening, the vertex, the axis of symmetry, the domain and range, and the maximum or minimum value of the function.

Solution

The graph of $y = 2x^2$ opens up and has the vertex (0, 0).
The equation of the axis of symmetry is $x = 0$.
The domain is the set of real numbers, and the range is $y \geq 0$.
The function reaches a minimum value of $y = 0$ when $x = 0$.

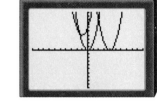

The graph of $y = 2(x-4)^2$ is the graph of $y = 2x^2$ translated to the right 4 units. The graph of $y = 2(x-4)^2$ opens up.
The vertex is (4, 0). The equation of the axis of symmetry is $x = 4$.
The domain is the set of real numbers, and the range is $y \geq 0$.
The function reaches a minimum value of $y = 0$ when $x = 4$.

The graph of $y = 2(x+1)^2 + 4$ is the graph of $y = 2x^2$ translated to the left 1 unit and upward 4 units. The graph of $y = 2(x+1)^2 + 4$ opens up.
The vertex is (−1, 4). The equation of the axis of symmetry is $x = -1$.
The domain is the set of real numbers, and the range is $y \geq 4$.
The function reaches a minimum value of $y = 4$ when $x = -1$.

Example 2 Graphing When *a* < 0

Sketch the graph of $y = -3x^2$, $y = -3(x+2)^2$, and $y = -3(x-5)^2 - 2$. Describe each graph in terms of the direction of the opening, the vertex, the axis of symmetry, the domain and range, and the maximum or minimum value of the function.

Solution

The graph of $y = -3x^2$ opens down and has the vertex (0, 0).
The equation of the axis of symmetry is $x = 0$.
The domain is the set of real numbers, and the range is $y \leq 0$.
The function reaches a maximum value of $y = 0$ when $x = 0$.

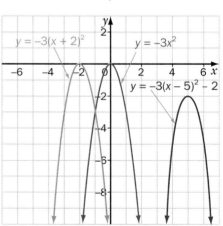

The graph of $y = -3(x+2)^2$ is the graph of $y = -3x^2$ translated to the left 2 units. The graph of $y = -3(x+2)^2$ opens down.
The vertex is (−2, 0). The equation of the axis of symmetry is $x = -2$.
The domain is the set of real numbers, and the range is $y \leq 0$.
The function reaches a maximum value of $y = 0$ when $x = -2$.

The graph of $y = -3(x-5)^2 - 2$ is the graph of $y = -3x^2$ translated to the right 5 units and downward 2 units.
The graph of $y = -3(x-5)^2 - 2$ opens down.
The vertex is (5, −2). The equation of the axis of symmetry is $x = 5$.
The domain is the set of real numbers, and the range is $y \leq -2$.
The function reaches a maximum value of $y = -2$ when $x = 5$.

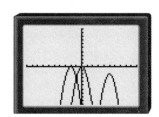

The chart summarizes how all parabolas, $y = a(x - p)^2 + q$, are obtained by transforming the function $y = x^2$.

$y = x^2$	Graph is a parabola.
$y = ax^2$	Reflects in the x-axis if $a < 0$. Stretches in the y-direction (narrows) if $a > 1$ or $a < -1$. Shrinks in the y-direction (flattens) if $-1 < a < 1$.
$y = a(x - p)^2$	Shifts p units to the right if p is positive. Shifts p units to the left if p is negative.
$y = a(x - p)^2 + q$ $y = a(x - p)^2 - q$	Shifts q units upward. Shifts q units downward.

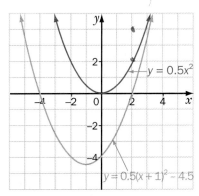

If $a < 0$,

reflection in x-axis → ... horizontal translation

$$y = a(x - p)^2 + q$$

vertical stretch or shrink ... vertical translation

Example 3   Locating Intercepts
Sketch the graph of $y = 0.5(x + 1)^2 - 4.5$ and find the intercepts.

Solution
Starting with $y = x^2$, shrink the graph by a factor of 0.5 in the y-direction to get $y = 0.5x^2$. Since a is positive, the parabola opens up.
Starting with $y = 0.5x^2$, shift the graph 1 unit to the left and 4.5 units downward to get $y = 0.5(x + 1)^2 - 4.5$.

The graph appears to cross the x-axis at $(-4, 0)$ and $(2, 0)$, so the x-intercepts appear to be -4 and 2. These values can also be found using a graphing calculator.

The manual graph appears to cross the y-axis at $(0, -4)$, so the y-intercept appears to be -4. The value can be found on a graphing calculator by displaying a table of values, or using the Value operation or the ZOOM and TRACE instructions. The y-intercept can also be found by substituting 0 for x in the equation.

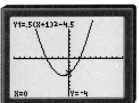

Example 4   Writing an Equation
a) Write an equation for the parabola with vertex $(-1, 4)$ and passing through the point $(-2, 2)$.
b) Find two other points on the graph.

Solution
a) The vertex is $(-1, 4)$, so $p = -1$ and $q = 4$.
Substitute in $y = a(x - p)^2 + q$
$$y = a(x - (-1))^2 + 4$$
$$y = a(x + 1)^2 + 4$$
The parabola passes through the point $(-2, 2)$, so substitute -2 for x and 2 for y.
$$2 = a(-2 + 1)^2 + 4$$
$$2 = a + 4$$
$$-2 = a$$
An equation for the parabola is $y = -2(x + 1)^2 + 4$.

b) When $x = 0$, $y = -2(0 + 1)^2 + 4$
$$= -2 + 4$$
$$= 2$$
When $x = 1$, $y = -2(1 + 1)^2 + 4$
$$= -8 + 4$$
$$= -4$$
Two other points on the graph are $(0, 2)$ and $(1, -4)$.

Example 5   Symphony of Fire

The path of one type of rocket at the Symphony of Fire is described by the function

$$h(t) = -4.9(t - 5)^2 + 124$$

where $h(t)$ is the height of the rocket, in metres, and t is the time, in seconds, since the rocket was fired.

a) What is the maximum height reached by the rocket? How many seconds after it was fired does the rocket reach this height?

b) How high was the rocket above the lake when it was fired?

Solution

a) The path of the rocket is a parabola in the form $y = a(x - p)^2 + q$, so the vertex is (p, q) or (5, 124).

Since a is negative, the parabola opens down. The vertex is the maximum point on the graph.

So, the rocket reaches a maximum height of 124 m after 5 s.

b) When the rocket was fired, $t = 0$ s.

Substitution into $h(t) = -4.9(t - 5)^2 + 124$ gives

$$\begin{aligned} h(t) &= -4.9(0 - 5)^2 + 124 \\ &= -4.9(25) + 124 \\ &= -122.5 + 124 \\ &= 1.5 \end{aligned}$$

So, the rocket was 1.5 m above the lake when it was fired.

Practice

Sketch each parabola and state

a) *the direction of the opening*

b) *the coordinates of the vertex*

c) *the equation of the axis of symmetry*

d) *the domain and range*

e) *the maximum or minimum value*

1. $y = (x + 5)^2$ **2.** $f(x) = -(x + 1)^2$

3. $y = (x - 3)^2$ **4.** $y = (x + 2)^2 + 4$

5. $f(x) = -(x - 2)^2 - 5$ **6.** $y = (x + 3)^2 - 5$

7. $f(x) = (x + 6)^2 + 2$ **8.** $f(x) = (x - 5)^2 - 4$

9. $y = -(x + 4)^2 + 3$ **10.** $f(x) = -(x - 6)^2 - 1$

Without sketching each parabola, state

a) *the direction of the opening*

b) *the coordinates of the vertex*

c) *the equation of the axis of symmetry*

d) *the domain and range*

e) *the maximum or minimum value*

11. $y = (x - 5)^2$ **12.** $y = -(x + 4)^2$

13. $f(x) = (x - 2)^2 + 1$ **14.** $f(x) = -(x + 1)^2 - 2$

For each parabola, state

a) *the direction of the opening*

b) *how the parabola is stretched or shrunk*

c) *the coordinates of the vertex*

d) *the equation of the axis of symmetry*

e) *the maximum or minimum value*

15. $y = 2(x - 1)^2$

16. $f(x) = -0.5(x + 7)^2$

17. $y = -2(x - 4)^2 + 7$

18. $y = 4(x + 3)^2 - 4$

19. $y = -3(x - 5)^2 + 6$

20. $f(x) = -0.4(x - 8)^2 - 1$

21. $y = \frac{1}{3}(x + 6)^2 - 7$

22. $f(x) = 0.5(x + 1)^2 - 5$

23. $y = 2.5(x + 1.5)^2 - 9$

24. $f(x) = -1.2(x - 2.6)^2 + 3.3$

25. The four graphs represent the four equations
$y = 3(x - 1)^2 + 2$,
$y = 3(x + 1)^2 - 2$,
$y = -3(x + 1)^2 + 2$, and
$y = -3(x - 1)^2 - 2$.
Match each graph with the correct equation.

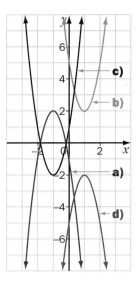

Sketch each parabola.
26. $y = (2 + x)^2$ **27.** $y = 3 + (x - 1)^2$
28. $m = (n + 2)^2 - 5$ **29.** $y - 4 = -2(3 + x)^2$
30. $-(r - 3)^2 = 1 - s$ **31.** $y + \dfrac{4}{5} = 3(x - 5)^2 + \dfrac{1}{5}$

Sketch each parabola and find
a) any intercepts
b) two other points on the graph
32. $y = (x - 2)^2$ **33.** $y = (x + 2)^2 - 9$
34. $y = (x - 3)^2 - 1$ **35.** $y = -(x + 2)^2 + 1$
36. $f(x) = -3(x + 2)^2 - 6$ **37.** $f(x) = 2(x + 1)^2 - 8$

Determine any x- and y-intercepts by graphing manually or using a graphing calculator. Round to the nearest tenth, if necessary.
38. $f(x) = (x + 1)^2 - 3$ **39.** $y = 2(x - 1)^2 - 4$
40. $f(x) = -4(x - 1)^2 + 1$ **41.** $y = -5(x + 3)^2 - 2$
42. $y = 4\left(x + \dfrac{1}{2}\right)^2$ **43.** $f(x) = -2\left(x - \dfrac{1}{3}\right)^2$
44. $y = 0.25(x + 4)^2$ **45.** $f(x) = -0.5(x + 3)^2 + 2$

Write an equation for the parabola with the given vertex and the given value of a.
46. $(7, 0)$; $a = 1$ **47.** $(-5, 0)$; $a = -1$
48. $(3, -5)$; $a = 2$ **49.** $(6, 7)$; $a = -3$
50. $(-1, -1)$; $a = -0.5$ **51.** $(-8, 9)$; $a = 1.5$

Write an equation that defines each parabola.
52. congruent to $y = x^2$; opens up; vertex at $(1, 5)$
53. congruent to $y = x^2$; opens down; vertex at $(-3, 0)$

54. congruent to $y = 3x^2$; minimum at $(4, -2)$
55. congruent to $y = 2x^2$; maximum at $(2, -3)$
56. congruent to $y = 0.4x^2$; opens up; vertex at $(-3, -3)$
57. congruent to $y = 5x^2$; minimum at $(4.5, 0)$
58. congruent to $y = 4x^2$; maximum on the x-axis; axis of symmetry $x = 3$
59. congruent to $y = 2x^2$; minimum value -6; axis of symmetry $x = -5$

Write an equation for the parabola with the given vertex and passing through the given point.
60. vertex $(-4, -5)$; point $(-2, -1)$
61. vertex $(3, 2)$; point $(1, -2)$
62. vertex $(1, 6)$; point $(3, 2)$
63. vertex $(-2, 3)$; point $(-1, 6)$
64. vertex $(-5, -3)$; point $(-3, -11)$
65. vertex $(6, 4)$; point $(8, 6)$

Write an equation for each parabola, given the vertex and the y-intercept.
66. vertex $(1, 2)$; y-intercept 4
67. vertex $(-2, 3)$; y-intercept -1
68. vertex $(2, -4)$; y-intercept -2
69. vertex $(-4, -1)$; y-intercept -5

Applications and Problem Solving

70. Determine the value of q so that the graph of $y = (x + 3)^2 + q$ passes through the point $(1, 20)$.

71. The vertex of a parabola is $(-2, -4)$. One x-intercept is 7. What is the other x-intercept?

72. The x-intercepts of a parabola are 5 and -7. What is the equation of the axis of symmetry? Explain.

73. Two points on a parabola are $(4, -1)$ and $(-10, -1)$. What is the equation of the axis of symmetry?

74. Aerial flares Red aerial miniflares are used by some boaters in an emergency. The path of one brand of flare, when fired at an angle of 70° to the horizontal, is modelled by the function
$$h(t) = -9(t - 3)^2 + 83$$
where $h(t)$ is the height, in metres, and t is the time, in seconds, since the flare was fired.
a) What is the maximum height of the flare?
b) For how many seconds does the flare burn before it hits the water?

Find a and q so that the given points lie on the parabola.

75. $y = a(x - 1)^2 + q$; $(2, 6)$, $(3, 12)$

76. $y = a(x + 3)^2 + q$; $(-5, -8)$, $(1, -20)$

77. $y = a(x - 4)^2 + q$; $(1, -13)$, $(-1, -45)$

78. Soccer The equation shows the height of a soccer ball, $h(d)$ metres, as a function of the horizontal distance, d metres, the ball travels until it first hits the ground.

$$h(d) = -0.025(d - 20)^2 + 10$$

a) What is the maximum height of the ball?

b) What is the horizontal distance of the ball from the kicker when it reaches its maximum height?

c) How far does the ball travel horizontally from when it is kicked until it hits the ground?

d) What is the height of the ball when it is 10 m horizontally from the kicker?

e) Would an opposing player positioned under the path of the ball 34 m from the kicker be able to head the ball? Explain.

f) If the origin were placed at the vertex of the parabola, what would the equation of the curve be?

79. Baseball The following function gives the height, $h(t)$ metres, of a batted baseball as a function of the time, t seconds, since the ball was hit.

$$h(t) = -6(t - 2.5)^2 + 38.5$$

a) What was the maximum height of the ball?

b) What was the height of the ball when it was hit?

c) How many seconds after it was hit did the ball hit the ground, to the nearest second?

d) Find the height of the ball 1 s after it was hit.

80. Touch football A touch football quarterback passed the ball to a receiver 40 m downfield. The path of the ball can be described by the function

$$h(d) = -0.01(d - 20)^2 + 6$$

where $h(d)$ is the height of the ball, in metres, and d is the horizontal distance of the ball from the quarterback, in metres.

a) What was the maximum height of the ball?

b) What was the horizontal distance of the ball from the quarterback at its maximum height?

c) What was the height of the ball when it was thrown? when it was caught?

d) If a defensive back was 2 m in front of the receiver, how far was the defensive back from the quarterback?

e) How high would the defensive back have needed to reach to knock down the pass?

81. Stopping distance The distance a car travels from when the driver decides to stop until the car comes to a stop is called the stopping distance. The stopping distance is a function of the speed of the car. For a car travelling on dry pavement, the stopping distance can be modelled by the function

$$d = 0.006(s + 15)^2 - 1.35$$

where d is the stopping distance, in metres, and s is the speed of the car, in kilometres per hour.

a) For this function, what is the domain? the range?

b) Find any s- and d-intercepts.

c) What is the stopping distance for a car travelling at 50 km/h? 100 km/h?

d) What is the speed limit in a school zone?

e) What is the stopping distance on dry pavement in a school zone?

82. Hunlen Falls The highest Canadian waterfall with a single leap is Hunlen Falls in British Columbia. If an object is thrown straight down from the height of Hunlen Falls with an initial velocity of 10 m/s, the height of the object above the ground can be modelled by the function

$$d(t) = -5(t + 1)^2 + 258$$

where $d(t)$ metres is the height of the object, and t seconds is the time for which the object has been falling.

a) Sketch a graph of the function.

b) Which part of the graph describes the falling object? Explain.

c) What is the height of the falls, in metres?

83. Pattern In a sports league, the number of games required for every team to play each of the other teams twice is shown in the table.

Number of Teams	2	3	4	5	6
Number of Games	2	6	12	20	30

The number of games, g, can be expressed as a function of the number of teams, t, as follows.

$$g = \left(t - \frac{1}{2}\right)^2 - \frac{1}{4}$$

a) Graph the function.

b) Find and interpret the t-intercepts.

c) Write the function in a different form by expanding, simplifying, and factoring the right-hand side.

d) Which form of the function would be easier to find from the pattern in the table? Explain.

84. a) Sketch the graphs of each pair of functions. Compare the parabolas in each pair.
$y = (x - 1)^2$ and $y = (1 - x)^2$
$y = (x - 4)^2 - 2$ and $y = (4 - x)^2 - 2$
b) Explain your results by expanding $(x - p)^2$ and $(p - x)^2$.

85. Systems of equations Graph $y = 3x + 3$ and $y = (x + 2)^2 - 3$ on the same set of axes. What are the coordinates of the intersection points? Describe how you found the intersection points.

86. The functions $y = m(x - 3)^2 + 1$ and $y = n(x - 2)^2 - 3$ are graphed on the same set of axes. How do m and n compare if the graphs both open up and
a) the graphs are congruent?
b) the first graph is narrower than the second?
c) the first graph is wider than the second?

87. Geometry The area of a square is 3 square units greater than the area of the square shown.
a) Write an equation that relates the area, A, of the larger square to the value of x.
b) Sketch a graph of A versus x.
c) What value of x results in the minimum area for the larger square?
d) What is the area of the smaller square when the larger square has its minimum area?

$x - 2$

e) If the area of the larger square were at least 3 square units more than the area of the smaller square, how would you graph A versus x for the larger square? Explain.

88. Write the equation of the image of $y = 3(x - 2)^2 + 1$ that results from
a) a reflection in the x-axis
b) a reflection in the y-axis
c) a reflection in the y-axis, followed by a reflection in the x-axis

89. Prime numbers No one has found a function that will generate all the prime numbers. The function $p(x) = (x + 0.5)^2 + 16.75$, where x is an integer, generates some prime numbers.
a) Find the three smallest prime numbers generated by the function.
b) What is the smallest composite number the function produces?

90. Astronomy British astronomer William Lassell used a telescope he built himself to discover a moon around Neptune in 1846, two moons around Uranus in 1851, and a moon around Saturn in 1858. The mirror from his telescope has a diameter of about 60 cm and a maximum depth of about 0.36 cm. A cross section of the mirror is in the shape of a parabola.

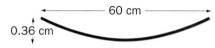

60 cm

0.36 cm

a) Suppose the origin of a coordinate grid is placed at the vertex, the y-axis is the axis of symmetry, and the units on the axes are centimetres. What are the coordinates of each end of the curve?
b) Write an equation for the curve.
c) Move the origin to the end that had two positive coordinates in part a). Write an equation for the curve.
d) Move the origin to the other end of the curve. Write an equation for the curve.
e) Determine the depth of the mirror at a horizontal distance of 20 cm from the vertex.

91. The points (0, 5), (3, 11), and (–2, 21) lie on a parabola. Write an equation for the parabola.

92. Technology For the equation $y = 2(x - 18.7)^2 + 54$, state viewing window variables that produce the following views of the parabola. Compare your values with your classmates'.
a) a line with a positive slope
b) a line with a negative slope
c) a vertical line

WORD POWER

Lewis Carroll invented a word game called doublets. The object of the game is to change one word to another by changing one letter at a time. You must form a real word each time you change a letter. The best solution has the fewest steps. Change the word RING to the word BELL by changing one letter at a time.

PROBLEM SOLVING

3.4 Work Backward

In some problems, you are given an end result and asked to find a fact that leads to the result. For this type of problem, working backward is a useful problem solving strategy.

Hailie, Monique, and Elena played a dice game. In the preliminary round, each player rolled two dice and added the two numbers rolled to give an initial number of points. Then, in each regular round, each player rolled one die. The person who rolled the lowest number in a regular round gave each of the other players enough points to double that player's points. In the event of a tie for lowest score, the round was repeated to decide a single loser. In the first three regular rounds, Hailie lost, and then Elena lost, and finally Monique lost. After the third regular round, Hailie had 8 points, Monique had 10 points, and Elena had 4 points. How many points did each player score in the preliminary round by rolling two dice?

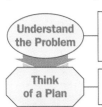

Understand the Problem

1. What information are you given?
2. What are you asked to find?
3. Do you need an exact or an approximate answer?

Think of a Plan

Set up a table and start with the number of points each player had at the end of the third round. Then, work backward.

Carry Out the Plan

At the end of the third round, the points for each player were as shown.

	Points		
After Round	**Hailie**	**Monique**	**Elena**
3	8	10	4

Monique was the last to lose, and she had to double the points of each of the other players. Since Hailie had 8 points, she must have had 4 points before Monique lost. Similarly, Elena must have had 2 points before Monique lost. Monique gave away a total of 6 points after she lost. So, at the end of the second round, before Monique lost, the points were as shown.

	Points		
After Round	**Hailie**	**Monique**	**Elena**
3	8	10	4
2	4	16	2

Elena lost the second round, so she gave Hailie 2 points and Monique 8 points. Elena gave away 10 points. At the end of the first round, before Elena lost, the points were as shown.

	Points		
After Round	**Hailie**	**Monique**	**Elena**
3	8	10	4
2	4	16	2
1	2	8	12

Hailie lost the first round, so she gave Monique 4 points and Elena 6 points. Hailie gave away 10 points. At the end of the preliminary round, before Hailie lost, the points were as shown.

	Points		
After Round	**Hailie**	**Monique**	**Elena**
3	8	10	4
2	4	16	2
1	2	8	12
Preliminary	12	4	6

So, in the preliminary round, Hailie scored 12 points, Monique scored 4 points, and Elena scored 6 points by rolling two dice.

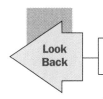

Look Back — Does the answer seem reasonable?
How could you check that the answer is correct?

Work Backward

1. Start with what you know.
2. Work backward to get an answer.
3. Check that your answer is reasonable.

Applications and Problem Solving

1. Scott, Ivan, and Enzo played the dice game described in the example. Ivan lost the first regular round. Then, Scott lost a round. Then, Enzo lost two rounds in a row. After these 4 rounds, Scott had 12 points, Ivan had 8 points, and Enzo had 1 point. How many points did each player score in the preliminary round?

2. Miki is a coin collector. She bought a rare coin from another collector. She paid the collector $750 in cash and borrowed the money for the balance. The loan was for one year at an annual interest rate of 8%. Her monthly payments were $247.50. How much did Miki pay the collector for the coin?

3. When the following transformations are applied to a point A in the given order, the final result is the point B(3, −2). Find the coordinates of point A.
    a reflection in the *x*-axis
    a horizontal translation of −1
    a vertical stretch of scale factor 2
    a vertical translation of 6
    a reflection in the *y*-axis

4. Copy the road map shown in the diagram. The numbers represent distances, in kilometres, between intersections.

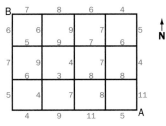

Starting at A, you are allowed to travel north or west. Find the shortest route from A to B.

5. A photocopier was set to enlarge an original to 150% of its size. A diagram was enlarged, the result was enlarged, and the new result was enlarged. The dimensions of the final result were 20.25 cm by 13.5 cm. What were the dimensions of the original diagram?

6. You are a travel agent. A local newspaper reporter has been assigned to cover the culmination of the United Nations Anniversary celebrations in New York City. The special session of the General Assembly will take place at the United Nations building on the fourth Tuesday in October. The session will start at 16:00 and end at 18:00. It will be followed by a reception for dignitaries and the press from 18:00 to 20:00. There is a press briefing at 15:00 on the day before the session. As the travel agent, your job is to use commercial transportation to get the reporter to the press briefing, the special session, and the reception, so that the reporter is away from home for as little time as possible. The reporter will look after hotel reservations and any taxis to and from airports, bus terminals, or train stations. Design an itinerary for the reporter's trip.

7. Design a dice game similar to the one described in the example. Give a classmate the rules and the final number of points for each player. Have your classmate find the number of points each player scored in the preliminary round.

8. Write another problem that can be solved by working backward. Have a classmate solve your problem.

COMPUTER DATA BANK

Jumping and Throwing Events

Use the *Olympics* database, from the Computer Data Bank, to complete the following.

1 Long Jump

In the long jump, the path of a jumper's centre of gravity can be modelled by a quadratic function. The jumper uses a takeoff angle, and horizontal and vertical speeds that will maximize the length of the jump. Theoretically, the takeoff angle would be 45° to the horizontal, and the horizontal and vertical speeds would be equal. However, since it is impossible for a jumper to achieve a vertical speed to match the horizontal speed attained in run-up, the actual take off angle is less than 45°.

A typical Olympic long jumper takes off at an angle of 22° to the horizontal, with a horizontal speed of 9.75 m/s and a vertical speed of 3.96 m/s. This combination raises the jumper's centre of gravity by 0.79 m at its maximum height, and carries the jumper's centre of gravity a horizontal distance of 7.92 m. This distance is typically about 0.65 m less than the actual distance of the long jump because the feet land ahead of the body's centre of gravity.

1. Sketch a graph of a parabolic path with a horizontal distance of 7.92 m and a maximum height of 0.79 m, where the horizontal axis is distance and the vertical axis is height.

2. What are the values of p and q in $y = a(x - p)^2 + q$ for the parabola you sketched?

3. a) How would you find the value of a?
b) What is the value of a, rounded to the nearest thousandth?

4. Devise a plan to model the path of each long jumper's centre of gravity as a quadratic function. Describe any calculation fields you would add.

5. Compare your plan with the plans of classmates. Revise your plan, if necessary, and then carry it out.

6. Sort the records from least to greatest value of a. Describe how you sorted in terms of the shape of the parabola representing the path of each long jumper's centre of gravity.

2 Winning Distances

1. Devise a plan to determine which winning distance or height is the greatest percent increase over the first winning distance or height for any one event, such as *Pole Vault, Men*. Describe any calculation fields you would add.

2. Compare your plan with the plans of your classmates. Revise your plan, if necessary, and then carry it out.

3. Determine which winning distance or height is the greatest percent increase over the first winning distance or height for each of four events.

4. Compare your results with the results of classmates who chose different events. Which event has the greatest improvement in performance? Use your research skills to determine why.

Algebra Tiles and Perfect Squares

1 Making Squares

The diagram shows how one x^2-tile, two x-tiles, and one 1-tile can be arranged to make a square. The area of the square can be expressed in expanded form as $x^2 + 2x + 1$. Since the side length of the square is $x + 1$, the area can also be expressed as the square of a binomial, $(x + 1)^2$. So, $x^2 + 2x + 1 = (x + 1)^2$.

1. Use algebra tiles or draw diagrams to make a square using the given tiles.

a) 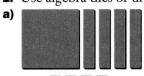   **b)**

2. Express the area of each square in question 1 in expanded form and as the square of a binomial. Then, use the two expressions to write an equation.

2 Completing the Square

The display represents the expression $x^2 + 8x$.

1. How many 1-tiles must be added to the display to complete the square?

2. Express the area of the square in expanded form and as the square of a binomial. Then, use the two expressions to write an equation.

3. Repeat questions 1 and 2 for the following displays.

a) 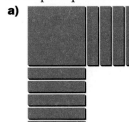   **b)**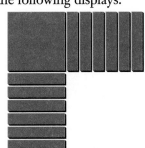

4. How is the number of 1-tiles added to each display in questions 1 and 3 related to the coefficient of the x-term in the expanded form?

5. To complete the square, how many 1-tiles must be added to a display that includes one x^2-tile and each of the following numbers of x-tiles?
a) 14   **b)** 16   **c)** 20   **d)** 30

6. For each case in question 5, write an equation like the one you wrote in question 2.

3.5 Graphing $y = ax^2 + bx + c$ by Completing the Square

The Canadian Space Agency (CSA) is involved in such programs as the Canadian Astronaut Program and the Space Science Program. The Space Science Program gives astronauts, such as Julie Payette, access to parabolic flight as part of their training, so that they can become accustomed to weightlessness. A modified DC-9 aircraft is used. It flies in parabolic arcs. One flight of the aircraft includes from 40 to 50 parabolas, each providing astronauts with a simulation of weightless conditions.

The parabolic path of the aircraft can be represented by the quadratic function
$$h(t) = -10t^2 + 300t + 9750$$
where $h(t)$ is the altitude of the aircraft, in metres, and t is the time, in seconds, since weightlessness was achieved.

The above equation is written in the **general form** of a quadratic function, $y = ax^2 + bx + c$. Because the analysis of quadratic functions is more convenient in the standard form $y = a(x - p)^2 + q$, a method for rewriting quadratic functions from the general form to the standard form is useful.

Explore: Look for a Pattern

Copy and complete the table by factoring each perfect square trinomial. The first row has been completed for you.

Trinomial, $x^2 + bx + c$	Value of b	Value of c	Factored Form, $(x - p)^2$	Value of p
$x^2 + 6x + 9$	6	9	$(x + 3)^2$	-3
$x^2 + 2x + 1$				
$x^2 + 10x + 25$				
$x^2 - 2x + 1$				
$x^2 - 8x + 16$				
$x^2 - 14x + 49$				

Inquire

1. The data in each row of the table can be used to write an equation in the form

$$x^2 + bx + c = (x - p)^2$$

If you know the value of b for a perfect square trinomial,
a) how can you find c?   **b)** how can you find p?

2. Use the results from question 1 to copy and complete the following equations for perfect squares. Then, state the value of p.

a) $x^2 + 12x + \blacksquare = (x + \blacktriangle)^2; p = \blacktriangledown$ **b)** $x^2 + 16x + \blacksquare = (x + \blacktriangle)^2; p = \blacktriangledown$
c) $x^2 - 20x + \blacksquare = (x - \blacktriangle)^2; p = \blacktriangledown$ **d)** $x^2 - 4x + \blacksquare = (x - \blacktriangle)^2; p = \blacktriangledown$
e) $x^2 + 1.6x + \blacksquare = (x + \blacktriangle)^2; p = \blacktriangledown$ **f)** $x^2 - 3x + \blacksquare = (x - \blacktriangle)^2; p = \blacktriangledown$

To graph a quadratic function in general form, a table of values can be used. For example, the function $y = x^2 + 2x - 3$ can be graphed using the table of values shown. Another method is to use the perfect square pattern to change the equation of a quadratic function from general form to standard form. The standard form can then be used to sketch the graph.

x	y
-4	5
-3	0
-2	-3
-1	-4
0	-3
1	0
2	5

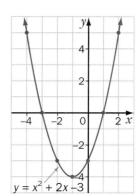

$y = x^2 + 2x - 3$

Example 1   Changing From General to Standard Form
a) Rewrite the equation $y = x^2 + 6x + 8$ in standard form.
b) Sketch the graph. Find the range and any intercepts.

Solution
a) First, determine what must be added to $x^2 + 6x$ to make it a perfect square trinomial. The square of half the coefficient of x is 9. Since 9 must be added to the original function, 9 must also be subtracted to keep the value of the function the same.

$$y = x^2 + 6x + 8$$

Add and subtract the square of half the coefficient of x: $= x^2 + 6x + 9 - 9 + 8$
Group the perfect square trinomial: $= (x^2 + 6x + 9) - 9 + 8$
Write the perfect square trinomial as the square of a binomial: $= (x + 3)^2 - 1$

The equation in standard form is $y = (x + 3)^2 - 1$.

b) The graph is a parabola that is congruent to $y = x^2$.
The graph opens up. The vertex is $(-3, -1)$. The range is $y \geq -1$.
The graph intersects the y-axis at $(0, 8)$, so the y-intercept is 8.
The graph appears to intersect the x-axis at $(-4, 0)$ and $(-2, 0)$,
so the x-intercepts appear to be -4 and -2.
Check the x-intercepts by substituting in $y = x^2 + 6x + 8$.

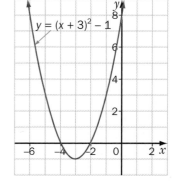

$y = (x + 3)^2 - 1$

For $(-4, 0)$
L.S. $= y$ **R.S.** $= x^2 + 6x + 8$
$= 0$ $= (-4)^2 + 6(-4) + 8$
            $= 16 - 24 + 8$
            $= 0$
    L.S. = R.S.

For $(-2, 0)$
L.S. $= y$ **R.S.** $= x^2 + 6x + 8$
$= 0$ $= (-2)^2 + 6(-2) + 8$
            $= 4 - 12 + 8$
            $= 0$
    L.S. = R.S.

The x-intercepts are -4 and -2.

Example 2   Completing the Square When $a \neq 1$

a) Express $y = 3x^2 - 12x + 11$ in standard form.

b) Sketch the graph. Find the maximum or minimum value of the function.

Solution

a) Factor the coefficient of x^2 from the first two terms.
Then, complete the square as you would for $a = 1$.

$$y = 3x^2 - 12x + 11$$

Group the terms containing x:
$$= [3x^2 - 12x] + 11$$

Factor the coefficient of x^2 from the first two terms:
$$= 3[x^2 - 4x] + 11$$

Complete the square inside the brackets:
$$= 3[x^2 - 4x + 4 - 4] + 11$$

Write the perfect square trinomial as the square of a binomial:
$$= 3[(x - 2)^2 - 4] + 11$$

Expand to remove the square brackets:
$$= 3(x - 2)^2 - 12 + 11$$

Simplify:
$$= 3(x - 2)^2 - 1$$

So, the equation in standard form is $y = 3(x - 2)^2 - 1$.

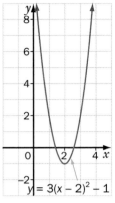

b) The graph is congruent to $y = 3x^2$.
The graph opens up, and its vertex is $(2, -1)$.
The minimum value is -1 when $x = 2$.

A way to verify that a parabolic function has been correctly rewritten from general form to standard form is to reverse the process. Another way is to graph both forms in the same viewing window of a graphing calculator. If the two forms are equivalent, you will see only one curve.

In some cases, completing the square requires the use of fractions.

Example 3   Completing the Square Using Fractions

Find the coordinates of the vertex of the function $y = 5x - 3x^2$.

Solution 1 Solving Algebraically

Rewrite the equation in standard form.

$$y = 5x - 3x^2$$
$$= -3x^2 + 5x$$
$$= [-3x^2 + 5x]$$
$$= -3\left[x^2 - \frac{5}{3}x\right]$$
$$= -3\left[x^2 - \frac{5}{3}x + \frac{25}{36} - \frac{25}{36}\right] \qquad \frac{1}{2} \times \frac{5}{3} = \frac{5}{6} \quad \left(\frac{5}{6}\right)^2 = \frac{25}{36}$$
$$= -3\left[\left(x - \frac{5}{6}\right)^2 - \frac{25}{36}\right]$$
$$= -3\left(x - \frac{5}{6}\right)^2 + \frac{25}{12}$$

The solution can be visualized graphically.

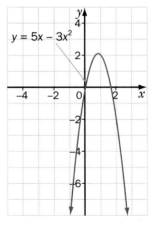

The vertex is $\left(\dfrac{5}{6}, \dfrac{25}{12}\right)$.

Solution 2 Using a Graphing Calculator

Because the equation can be input in either the general
form or the standard form, there is no need to rewrite
it. Graph the equation $y = 5x - 3x^2$ directly. The vertex
can be found using the Maximum operation or the
ZOOM and TRACE instructions. Note that, in this
case, the decimal values for the coordinates of the
vertex are not exact. The values obtained by rewriting
the equation in standard form in Solution 1 are exact.

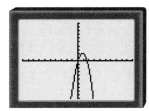 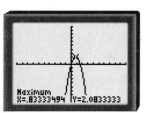

Example 4   Astronaut Training Flights

The parabolic path of an aircraft used to simulate weightlessness can be represented by
the quadratic equation
$$h(t) = -10t^2 + 300t + 9750$$
where $h(t)$ is the altitude of the aircraft, in metres, and t is the time, in seconds, since
weightlessness was achieved. Find
a) the maximum altitude reached by the aircraft
b) the number of seconds the aircraft takes to reach its maximum altitude after
weightlessness is achieved
c) the altitude of the aircraft when weightlessness is first achieved
d) the number of seconds the simulation of weightlessness lasts, if weightlessness is lost
at the same altitude as it is achieved

Solution

The solution can be visualized graphically.

Rewrite the equation in standard form.
$$\begin{aligned}
h(t) &= -10t^2 + 300t + 9750 \\
&= [-10t^2 + 300t] + 9750 \\
&= -10[t^2 - 30t] + 9750 \\
&= -10[t^2 - 30t + 225 - 225] + 9750 \\
&= -10[(t - 15)^2 - 225] + 9750 \\
&= -10(t - 15)^2 + 2250 + 9750 \\
&= -10(t - 15)^2 + 12\ 000
\end{aligned}$$

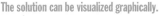
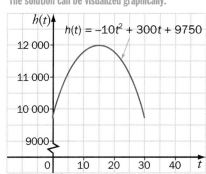

The graph is congruent to $h(t) = -10t^2$.
The graph opens down. The vertex is (15, 12 000).
a) The aircraft reaches a maximum altitude of 12 000 m.
b) The aircraft takes 15 s to reach its maximum altitude after weightlessness is achieved.
c) From the general form of the equation, $h = 9750$ when $t = 0$. So, the aircraft is at an
altitude of 9750 m when weightlessness is first achieved.
d) The equation of the axis of symmetry is $t = 15$, and (0, 9750) is one point on the
parabola. So, (30, 9750) is another point on the parabola. The simulation of
weightlessness lasts for 30 s.

In some problems involving maximum or minimum values, the function is not given. It must be found from the given information.

Example 5　Writing a Function
Find two numbers whose difference is 8 and whose product is a minimum.

Solution
The quantity to be minimized is the product, p, of two numbers. Let one number be n.
Since the difference between the two numbers is 8, the other number can be represented by $n - 8$ or $n + 8$.
Either expression can be used. In this example, we will use $n - 8$.
The product, p, is $n \times (n - 8)$, so $p = n^2 - 8n$
The function $p = n^2 - 8n$ is a parabola. It opens up and has a minimum value of p at the vertex.
To find the coordinates of the vertex, write the function in the standard form $y = a(x - p)^2 + q$.
$$\begin{aligned} p &= n^2 - 8n \\ &= n^2 - 8n + 16 - 16 \\ &= (n - 4)^2 - 16 \end{aligned}$$
The coordinates of the vertex are $(4, -16)$.
The function reaches a minimum value of -16 when $n = 4$.
If $n = 4$, then $n - 8 = 4 - 8$
$\qquad\qquad\qquad\quad = -4$

> Solve the problem using $n + 8$ to represent the difference. Compare the solutions.

So, the two numbers are 4 and -4.

Check against the given information.
The numbers differ by 8: $4 - (-4) = 8$
Their product is a minimum: The function $p = n^2 - 8n$ represents the products of all pairs of numbers whose difference is 8. The point $(4, -16)$ is the minimum point on the graph. So, -16, which is the product of 4 and -4, is the minimum product of two numbers whose difference is 8.

Example 6　Theatre Tickets
A theatre company has 300 season ticket subscribers. The board of directors has decided to raise the price of a season ticket from the current price of $400. A survey of the subscribers has determined that for every $20 increase in price, 10 subscribers would not renew their season tickets. What price would maximize the revenue from season tickets?

Solution
Let x represent the number of $20 increases. The cost of a season ticket will be $(400 + 20x)$.
The number of season tickets sold will be $(300 - 10x)$.
The revenue from ticket sales, $R(x)$, is (number of tickets sold) $\times$ (cost per ticket).
So, $R(x) = (300 - 10x)(400 + 20x)$
Find the maximum value of this function.
$$\begin{aligned} R(x) &= (300 - 10x)(400 + 20x) \\ &= 120\,000 + 6000x - 4000x - 200x^2 \\ &= -200x^2 + 2000x + 120\,000 \\ &= -200(x^2 - 10x) + 120\,000 \\ &= -200(x^2 - 10x + 25 - 25) + 120\,000 \\ &= -200(x - 5)^2 + 5000 + 120\,000 \\ &= -200(x - 5)^2 + 125\,000 \end{aligned}$$
The function reaches a maximum value of 125 000 when $x = 5$.
There should be five $20 increases to maximize the revenue.
So, a price of $500 would maximize the revenue from season tickets.

Practice

Find the value of c that will make each expression a perfect square trinomial.

1. $x^2 + 14x + c$ **2.** $x^2 - 12x + c$
3. $x^2 - 2x + c$ **4.** $x^2 + 18x + c$
5. $x^2 - 10x + c$ **6.** $x^2 + 20x + c$
7. $x^2 - 3x + c$ **8.** $x^2 + 5x + c$
9. $x^2 + x + c$ **10.** $x^2 - x + c$
11. $x^2 + 0.8x + c$ **12.** $x^2 - 0.05x + c$
13. $x^2 - 2.4x + c$ **14.** $x^2 + 13.7x + c$
15. $x^2 - \frac{2}{3}x + c$ **16.** $x^2 + \frac{x}{6} + c$

Write each function in the form $y = a(x - p)^2 + q$. Sketch the graph, showing the coordinates of the vertex, the equation of the axis of symmetry, and the coordinates of two other points on the graph.

17. $y = x^2 + 6x + 3$ **18.** $y = x^2 - 4x - 1$
19. $y = x^2 + 10x + 30$ **20.** $y = x^2 - 2x + 3$
21. $y = 28 + 12x + x^2$ **22.** $y = 12 - 8x + x^2$

23. The six graphs represent the six equations $y = x^2 + 4x$, $y = x^2 - 4x$, $y = -x^2 + 4x$, $y = -x^2 - 4x$, $y = x^2 - 4$, and $y = -x^2 + 4$. Match each graph with the correct equation.

a)
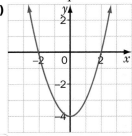

b)
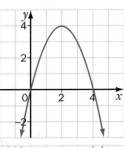

c)
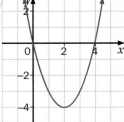

d)

e)

f)
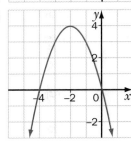

Sketch the graph of each function. Show the coordinates of the vertex, the equation of the axis of symmetry, and any intercepts. State the range.

24. $y = x^2 - 2x - 8$ **25.** $y = x^2 - 6x + 10$
26. $f(x) = x^2 + 4x$ **27.** $y = 40 - 12x + x^2$

Write each function in the form $y = a(x - p)^2 + q$. Sketch the graph, showing the coordinates of the vertex, the equation of the axis of symmetry, and the coordinates of two other points on the graph.

28. $y = -x^2 + 8x - 11$ **29.** $y = -x^2 - 8x - 7$
30. $y = -x^2 - 4x - 7$ **31.** $y = -2x - x^2$

Sketch the graph of each function. Show the coordinates of the vertex, the equation of the axis of symmetry, and any intercepts. State the range.

32. $y = -x^2 - 2x + 3$ **33.** $f(x) = -x^2 - 4x - 12$
34. $y = -x^2 + 8x - 12$ **35.** $y = 10x - 25 - x^2$

Without graphing each function, state whether it has a maximum or a minimum. Give the maximum or minimum value of the function.

36. $y = x^2 + 6x + 2$ **37.** $y = -x^2 - 4x + 1$
38. $f(x) = -x^2 + 8x$ **39.** $f(x) = x^2 - 12x + 36$
40. $m = n^2 + 10n - 5$ **41.** $h(t) = 4 - 6t - t^2$
42. $y - 21 = x^2 - 14x$ **43.** $d = 10k - 28 - k^2$

State the maximum or minimum value of y and the value of x when it occurs.

44. $y = 2x^2 + 4x + 3$ **45.** $y = -2x^2 + 20x - 44$
46. $y = -4x^2 - 24x - 29$ **47.** $y = -3x^2 + 18x - 28$
48. $y + 20x = 5x^2 + 18$ **49.** $y = 10x^2 - 20x + 12$
50. $y = 8x - 2x^2$ **51.** $y + 4x^2 = 8x - 4$

State the maximum or minimum value of y and the value of x when it occurs.

52. $y = x^2 + 3x + 1$ **53.** $y = x^2 - x - 2$
54. $y = -\frac{1}{3}x^2 + 2x + 4$ **55.** $y = -2x^2 + 3x - 2$
56. $y = -x^2 - 5x$ **57.** $y = 3x^2 - 0.6x + 1$
58. $y = -2x^2 - 0.8x - 2$ **59.** $y = 0.5x^2 + x + 2$
60. $y + 3x^2 - 4x = 0$ **61.** $y = 0.5x^2 - 0.6x$
62. $y + 4 = -x^2 + 1.8x$ **63.** $y = -0.003x^2 + 0.6x - 10$

Graph each function. Find any x-intercepts. Round to the nearest tenth, if necessary.

64. $y = 2x^2 + 7x$ **65.** $y = 3x^2 + 2x - 5$
66. $y = x^2 + \frac{2}{3}x + \frac{1}{9}$ **67.** $y = 4x^2 - 7$
68. $y = -2x^2 - 3x - 2$ **69.** $y = -0.7x^2 + 2x$

Applications and Problem Solving

70. Sketch the graph of each function. State any intercepts and the coordinates of the vertex.
a) $y = (x + 1)(x + 3)$
b) $y = (x + 2)(1 - x)$
c) $f(x) = (2x - 3)^2$
d) $r = (2s + 1)(s - 2)$
e) $y = (1 - 2x)(3 - 2x)$
f) $y = -3(x - 1)(x + 2)$

71. Number game A student is asked to do the following: "Choose any number and square it. Then, subtract eight times the original number. Then, add 35. Find the value of the original number that gives the least result."
a) If x is the original number and y is the result, write an equation that represents the instructions.
b) Find the original number that gives the least result.

72. Number game A student is asked to do the following: "Choose any number. Subtract ten times the original number and subtract the square of the original number from 375. Find the value of the original number that gives the greatest result."
a) If x is the original number and y is the result, write an equation that represents the instructions.
b) Find the original number that gives the greatest result.

73. Find two numbers whose difference is 10 and whose product is a minimum.

74. Find two numbers whose sum is 34 and whose product is a maximum.

75. Two numbers have a sum of 34. Find the numbers if the sum of their squares is a minimum.

76. Golf The path of the ball for many golf shots can be modelled by a quadratic function. The path of a golf ball hit at an angle of about 10° to the horizontal can be modelled by the function
$$h(d) = -0.002d^2 + 0.4d$$
where $h(d)$ is the height of the ball, in metres, and d is the horizontal distance the ball travels, in metres, until it first hits the ground.
a) What is the maximum height reached by the ball?
b) What is the horizontal distance of the ball from the golfer when the ball reaches its maximum height?
c) What distance does the ball travel horizontally until it first hits the ground?

77. Basketball The path of a basketball shot can be modelled by the equation
$$h(d) = -0.09d^2 + 0.9d + 2$$
where $h(d)$ is the height of the basketball, in metres, and d is the horizontal distance of the ball from the player, in metres.
a) What is the maximum height reached by the ball?
b) What is the horizontal distance of the ball from the player when it reaches its maximum height?
c) How far from the floor is the ball when the player releases it?

78. Gravity If a ball is thrown upward from a height of 2 m with an initial velocity of 10 m/s, its height, $h(t)$ metres, after t seconds is given by the equation
$$h(t) = -0.5gt^2 + 10t + 2$$
where g is a constant describing the acceleration of gravity. The table gives the value of g, rounded to the nearest whole number, for four planets.

Planet	Value of g (m/s^2)
Earth	10
Jupiter	25
Mars	4
Neptune	12

For each planet, calculate
a) the maximum height the ball would reach
b) how many seconds the ball would take to reach its maximum height

79. Brooklyn Bridge The Brooklyn Bridge in New York City is a suspension bridge that crosses the East River and connects Brooklyn to the island of Manhattan. If the origin is placed at the top of one of the cable-support towers, as shown, the shape of a cable that supports the main span can be modelled by the equation
$$h(d) = 0.0008d^2 - 0.384d$$
where $h(d)$ metres represents the height and d metres represents the horizontal distance.

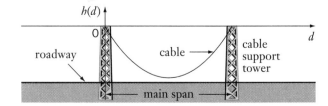

a) What is the vertical distance from the top of a support tower to the lowest point on a cable, to the nearest metre?
b) What is the length of the main span?
c) At a horizontal distance of 50 m from one end of the cable, how far is the cable below the top of the support towers, to the nearest metre?

80. Natural bridge A natural bridge is a stone arch formed over a river or stream. The longest natural bridge in the world is Rainbow Bridge in Utah. If the origin is placed at one end of the arch, the curve of the arch can be modelled by the equation
$$h(d) = -0.0425d^2 + 3.57d$$
where $h(d)$ metres represents the height and d metres represents the horizontal distance.

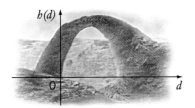

a) What is the width of the arch at the base?
b) What is the maximum height of the arch, to the nearest metre?
c) At a horizontal distance of 10 m from the vertex, what is the height of the arch, to the nearest metre?

81. Rectangular field A rectangular field is to be enclosed by 400 m of fence.
a) What dimensions will give a maximum area?
b) What is the maximum area?

82. Cattle pens A cattle farmer wants to build a rectangular fenced enclosure divided into five rectangular pens, as shown in the diagram.

A total length of 120 m of fencing material is available. Find the overall dimensions of the enclosure that will make the total area a maximum.

83. Rectangular corral A farmer wants to make a rectangular corral along the side of a large barn and has enough materials for 60 m of fencing. Only three sides must be fenced, since the barn wall will form the fourth side. What width of rectangle should the farmer use so that the maximum area is enclosed?

84. Amusement park An amusement park charges $8 admission and averages 2000 visitors per day. A survey shows that, for each $1 increase in the admission cost, 100 fewer people would visit the park.
a) Write an equation to express the revenue, $R(x)$ dollars, in terms of a price increase of x dollars.
b) Find the coordinates of the maximum point of this function.
c) What admission cost gives the maximum revenue?
d) How many visitors give the maximum revenue?

85. Fund-raising The Environmental Club sells sweatshirts as a fund-raiser. They sell 1200 shirts a year at $20 each. They are planning to increase the price. A survey indicates that, for every $2 increase in price, there will be a drop of 60 sales a year. What should the selling price be in order to maximize the revenue?

86. Measurement Determine the maximum area of a triangle, in square centimetres, if the sum of its base and its height is
a) 10 cm   **b)** 13 cm

87. Falling object The top of Harbour Centre, the tallest building in Vancouver, is 146 m above the ground. Suppose an object were thrown upward with an initial velocity of 24.5 m/s from this height. The height of the object above the ground, $h(t)$ metres, t seconds after being thrown, would be given by the equation
$$h(t) = -4.9t^2 + 24.5t + 146$$
a) What would be the maximum height of the object above the ground, to the nearest tenth of a metre?
b) From the time the object was thrown, how many seconds would it take to reach the ground, to the nearest tenth of a second?

88. Measurement The side length of a square is 10 cm. Four points on the square are joined to form an inner square, as shown.

Find the minimum area of the inner square, in square centimetres.

89. Parabolic skis A parabolic ski is narrower in the middle than it is at the ends. Each edge of the ski is parabolic. Assume that a coordinate grid is placed on the ski as shown.

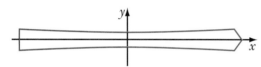

a) How are the coordinates of the two vertices related?
b) How are the values of a in the equations of the two parabolas related?
c) Use your research skills to find out why parabolic skis are used.

90. How is the graph of $y = ax^2 + bx + c$ affected if
a) $a = 0$?   **b)** $b = 0$?

91. Write an equation in general form for the parabola that passes through the points $(1, -4)$, $(-2, 5)$, and $(3, 0)$.

92. Write an equation in general form for the parabola that has x-intercepts of -1 and 3 and a y-intercept of 6.

93. When graphed on the same set of axes, do the graphs of $y = x^2 + 5x + 2$ and $y = x^2 + 5x + 3$ intersect? Explain.

94. If $f(x) = ax^2 + bx + c$, and $f(x) = f(-x)$ for all x, what is the value of b? Show your reasoning.

95. For the function $y = x^2 + 6x + k$, what value(s) of k will result in
a) one x-intercept?   **b)** two x-intercepts?
c) no x-intercept?

96. For the function $y = -2x^2 + 8x + k$, what value(s) of k will result in
a) one x-intercept?   **b)** two x-intercepts?
c) no x-intercept?

97. Technology For the function $y = -35x^2 + 60x - 52$, state viewing window variables that produce the following views of the parabola.
a) a line with a positive slope
b) a line with a negative slope
c) a horizontal line

98. Connections The cross sections of many reflectors and receiving dishes are parabolic. Examples include car headlights, microwave dishes, telescope mirrors, and parabolic microphones. Use your research skills to find out why a parabolic shape is used. Share your findings with your classmates.

99. Write an equation in general form that meets each of the following sets of conditions. Describe how you went about finding the equation. Have a classmate check that each of your equations meets the conditions.
a) congruent to $y = x^2$, two whole-number x-intercepts, vertex in the fourth quadrant
b) congruent to $y = -x^2$, one positive x-intercept and one negative x-intercept, vertex in the second quadrant
c) congruent to $y = 2x^2$, no x-intercepts, vertex in the first quadrant, y-intercept greater than 20
d) congruent to $y = -0.5x^2$, one x-intercept, y-intercept less than -6

PATTERN POWER

What is the next row in this table?

```
1
1 1
2 1
1 2 1 1
1 1 1 2 2 1
3 1 2 2 1 1
1 3 1 1 2 2 2 1
```

Exploring Patterns in $y = ax^2 + bx + c$

1 Relating $y = ax^2 + bx + c$ to the Axis of Symmetry

1. Copy and complete the table.

General Form $y = ax^2 + bx + c$	Value of a	Value of b	Value of c	Axis of Symmetry
a) $y = x^2 - 4x$				
b) $y = x^2 - 4x + 3$				
c) $y = x^2 + 6x$				
d) $y = x^2 + 6x - 5$				
e) $y = -x^2 + 8x$				
f) $y = -x^2 + 8x - 4$				
g) $y = 0.5x^2 - 3x$				
h) $y = 0.5x^2 - 3x + 2$				
i) $y = -2x^2 - 4x$				
j) $y = -2x^2 - 4x - 7$				

2. Is the equation for the axis of symmetry related to the value of c? Explain.

3. Describe how the equation for the axis of symmetry can be determined from the values of a and b.

4. Write an equation for the axis of symmetry in terms of a and b in the form $x = \blacksquare$.

5. Without graphing, write an equation for the axis of symmetry for each of the following.
a) $y = x^2 + 4x$
b) $y = x^2 - 16x$
c) $y = -x^2 - 12x$
d) $y = x^2 - 9x + 7$
e) $y = 2x^2 + 8x$
f) $y = -3x^2 - 12x - 3$
g) $y = 0.5x^2 + 2x - 1$
h) $y = -0.2x^2 + x - 9$
i) $y = -4x^2 - 24x + 11$
j) $f(x) = x^2 + 3x + 2$
k) $f(x) = 4x^2 - 6x - 3$
l) $f(x) = -0.75x^2 + 2x$

2 Relating $y = ax^2 + bx + c$ to $y = a(x - p)^2 + q$

1. An equation for the axis of symmetry gives one coordinate of the vertex. Which coordinate?

2. When you know one coordinate of the vertex, how can you find the other coordinate without graphing or completing the square?

3. Without graphing or completing the square, write the coordinates of the vertex for each of the following functions.
a) $y = x^2 + 6x + 4$
b) $f(x) = -x^2 - 12x - 1$
c) $y = 7x^2 - 14x$
d) $f(x) = 0.5x^2 + 10x$
e) $f(x) = -4x^2 - 6x - 5$
f) $y = -\frac{1}{3}x^2 + 2x - 4$

4. For the graph of an equation in the standard form $y = a(x - p)^2 + q$, how are the coordinates of the vertex related to p and q?

5. Describe how the value of p can be found from the values of a and b.

6. Write an equation for the value of p in terms of a and b in the form $p = \blacksquare$.

7. Use your results from questions 1–6 to describe a method for rewriting a quadratic equation from the general form $y = ax^2 + bx + c$ to the standard form $y = a(x - p)^2 + q$ without completing the square.

8. Without completing the square, rewrite each of the following equations in standard form.
a) $y = x^2 - 6x$
b) $f(x) = 2x^2 + 4x - 5$
c) $y = -5x^2 + 20x + 2$
d) $f(x) = -x^2 - 3x - 2$
e) $y = x^2 + 5x + 2$
f) $f(x) = 3x^2 - 3x$
g) $y = -1.5x^2 + 3x + 1$
h) $y = 0.4x^2 + x$

TECHNOLOGY

Graphing Calculators and Parabolic Functions

Parabolic functions can be graphed in either general or standard form using a graphing calculator.

1 Comparing Graphing Calculator and Manual Methods

Graph each of the following functions using a graphing calculator. For each function, determine the coordinates of the vertex and any intercepts. Round to the nearest tenth, where necessary. Identify cases in which you think it would be simpler to sketch the graph manually. Explain.

1. a) $y = x^2 + 5$ **b)** $f(x) = x^2 - 3$
c) $f(x) = -x^2 + 4$ **d)** $y = 8 - x^2$

2. a) $f(x) = 2x^2 - 9$ **b)** $y = 2 + 0.5x^2$
c) $12 = y + 3x^2$ **d)** $f(x) = 4 - 0.6x^2$

3. a) $y = (x - 2)^2 - 3$ **b)** $f(x) = 2(x + 2)^2 + 1$
c) $f(x) = 1 - (x + 3)^2$ **d)** $y = 6 - 0.5(x - 1)^2$
e) $y = 0.25(x - 4.5)^2$ **f)** $f(x) = -0.2(x + 5)^2$

4. a) $y = x^2 - 5x - 3$ **b)** $f(x) = -x^2 + 6x - 4$
c) $y = -x^2 - 2x + 5$ **d)** $y = -x^2 - 7x + 12.25$
e) $y + 2 = 2x^2 - 3x$ **f)** $y + 7x = -0.5x^2 - 3$

5. a) $y = x(3 - x)$ **b)** $f(x) = -x(x + 2)$
c) $f(x) = 0.1x(5 + x)$ **d)** $y = 0.25x(0.75 - x)$
e) $f(x) = 0.6x(x - 2.5)$ **f)** $\dfrac{y}{3.5} = -x(x + 1.8)$

6. Graph using a graphing calculator. Find the vertex and any intercepts in each case. Round to the nearest hundredth, where necessary.
a) $y = 0.3x^2 - 2.75x$ **b)** $y = 1.8x(1 - 2.8x)$
c) $f(x) = 1.1x^2 + 2.5x + 1$ **d)** $y = 0.8x + 0.8 - 0.71x^2$
e) $f(x) = 0.006x^2 + 3.5x$ **f)** $f(x) = 0.004\,13x^2 + 2x - 1.12$
g) $y = -2.36x^2 + 0.99x - 25$ **h)** $y + 0.052x^2 = 2.3 - 3.3x$

7. Describe the difficulties you might encounter if you tried to graph the function from question 6a) manually by first rewriting it in standard form.

8. Summarize the advantages and disadvantages of graphing calculator and manual methods for graphing parabolic functions.

Graph using a graphing calculator. Round answers to the nearest hundredth, where necessary, except as specified.

1. Basketball The height of a basketball, for a shot taken at a horizontal distance of 5 m from the hoop, can be modelled by the function
$$h(t) = -7.3t^2 + 8.25t + 2.1$$
where $h(t)$ is the height of the ball, in metres, and t is the time, in seconds, since the shot was taken. If the ball is in flight for 1 s, find
a) the height from which the ball was released
b) the maximum height reached by the ball
c) the height of the hoop

2. Cell culture In a nutrient medium, the rate of increase in the surface area of a cell culture could be modelled by the quadratic function
$$S(t) = -0.007t^2 + 0.05t$$
where $S(t)$ is the rate of increase in the surface area, in square millimetres per hour, and t is the time, in hours, since the culture began growing.
a) Find the maximum rate of increase in the surface area and the time taken to reach this maximum.
b) What was happening to the cells when the value of $S(t)$ became negative?
c) How long after the cells were placed in the medium did $S(t)$ become negative?

3. Measurement A rectangle has dimensions $0.7x$ and $5 - 3x$.
a) What is the maximum area of the rectangle?
b) What value of x gives the maximum area?

4. Natural bridge Owachomo Natural Bridge is found in Natural Bridges National Monument in Utah. If the origin is located at one end of the arch, the curve can be modelled by the equation
$$h(d) = -0.0429d(d - 54.9)$$
where $h(d)$ metres is the height of the arch, and d metres is the horizontal distance from the origin. Find, to the nearest tenth of a metre,
a) the maximum height of the arch
b) the width of the arch at the base
c) the height of the arch at a horizontal distance of 25 m from either end

5. Numbers Graph each pair of equations in the same standard viewing window. How are the graphs the same? How are they different? Explain.
a) $y = x^2 - 4$ and $y = |x^2 - 4|$
b) $y = x^2 - 4$ and $y = 4 - x^2$
c) $y = |x^2 - 4|$ and $y = |4 - x^2|$

PROBLEM SOLVING

3.6 Use a Table or Spreadsheet

Using a table or a spreadsheet is a powerful way to organize and manipulate data to solve problems. Nasif opened a boutique in a shopping mall to sell perfume and cologne. During the first month, his business lost $750. The profit that month could be expressed as –750. In the next month, the business lost $650, an improvement in performance of $100. At the end of the second month, the net financial position of the business could be expressed as –1400, since it had lost a total of $1400. The performance continued to improve by $100 each month for the first 20 months.

a) In which month did the net financial position first become positive?
b) Write a quadratic function that describes the net financial position in terms of the number of months.

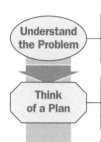

Understand the Problem

1. What information are you given?
2. What are you asked to find?
3. Do you need an exact or an approximate answer?

Think of a Plan

Use a table or a spreadsheet to calculate the profit and the net financial position at the end of each month. Use the maximum or minimum value of the net financial position to find the equation of the function.

Carry Out the Plan

a)

Month	Profit ($)	Net Financial Position ($)	Month	Profit ($)	Net Financial Position ($)
1	–750	–750	11	250	–2750
2	–650	–1400	12	350	–2400
3	–550	–1950	13	450	–1950
4	–450	–2400	14	550	–1400
5	–350	–2750	15	650	750
6	–250	–3000	16	750	0
7	–150	–3150	17	850	850
8	–50	–3200	18	950	1800
9	50	–3150	19	1050	2850
10	150	–3000	20	1150	4000

The net financial position first became positive in the 17th month.

b) The vertex is at the minimum value, –3200, of the function. The vertex is (8, –3200), so $p = 8$ and $q = -3200$. Substitute for p and q in $f(m) = a(m - p)^2 + q$, where $f(m)$ is the net financial position, and m is the number of months.
$$f(m) = a(m - 8)^2 - 3200$$
The parabola crosses the m-axis at (16, 0), so substitute 16 for m and 0 for $f(m)$ to find the value of a.
$$f(m) = a(m - 8)^2 - 3200$$
$$0 = a(16 - 8)^2 - 3200$$
$$0 = 64a - 3200$$
$$50 = a$$
The function is $f(m) = 50(m - 8)^2 - 3200$.

The solution can be visualized graphically.

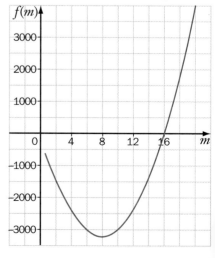

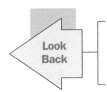
Does the answer seem reasonable?
How could you verify the assumption that the function is quadratic?
How could you set up a computer spreadsheet to calculate the net financial
position values shown in the table?

**Use
a Table or
Spreadsheet**

1. Organize the given information in a table or spreadsheet.
2. Complete the table or spreadsheet.
3. Find the answer from the table or spreadsheet.
4. Check that your answer is reasonable.

Applications and Problem Solving

1. Priya and Gustav opened a store to sell clothing
and equipment to campers, hikers, rock climbers,
and cross-country skiers. Priya and Gustav
projected that the business would lose $2100 in the
first month, and $1900 in the second month. They
thought that the business would continue to
improve by $200/month for the first two years.
a) Make a table of values showing the net financial
position at the end of each month.
b) In which month would the net financial position
of the business first become positive?
c) Assume that the graph is a quadratic function.
Write an equation to describe the net financial
position as a function of the number of months.

2. Priya and Gustav revised their projections from
question 1. They thought they could work more
and cut expenses to change their improvement in
performance from $200/month to $250/month for
the first two years. They assumed that the business
would still lose $2100 in the first month. Repeat
question 1 using the new projections. Find how
many months sooner the net financial position of
the business would first become positive.

3. The items in a vending machine all sell for
$1.00, $1.50, $2.00, or $3.00. The machine can
accept quarters, loonies, and toonies. How many
combinations of coins must the machine be
programmed to accept?

4. Some versions of chess do not use the usual 8 by
8 chessboard. Find the total number of squares of
all sizes on each of the following chessboards.
a) Capablanca's chess, played on a 10 by 8 board
b) wildebeest chess, played on an 11 by 8 board

5. A rocket was fired into the air. Without the
effect of gravity, it would have travelled upward
49 m every second. However, because its upward
motion was slowed by gravity, its height at the end
of the first second was 4.9 m less than 49 m. In each
second after the first, the rocket travelled upward
9.8 m less than in the previous second.
a) Make a table of values showing the height of the
rocket at the end of each second.
b) After how many seconds was the rocket at its
maximum height?
c) What was the maximum height?
d) Assume that the graph is a quadratic function.
Write an equation describing the height of the
rocket as a function of the time since it was fired.
e) What are the domain and range of this function?

6. How many scalene triangles, with side lengths
that are whole numbers of centimetres, have no
side longer than 10 cm?

7. During the summer, Tara earns $12/h cutting
lawns and $16/h painting houses. In how many
different ways can she earn $432 in a week, if she
works a whole number of hours at each job?

8. Ray earns $3000/month, after taxes and other
deductions. He decides to save for a car by saving
25% of the total money he has on payday each
month. At the end of the first month, he saves 25% of
$3000 or $750. At the end of the second month, he
has the $3000 he receives on payday, plus the $750 he
already saved, so he increases his total savings to 25%
of $3750. He continues in this way for ten more
months. Is this a good way to save for a car? Explain.

9. Write a problem that can be solved using a table
or spreadsheet. Have a classmate solve your
problem.

CONNECTING MATH AND HISTORY

Galileo's Experiments on Gravity

1 Falling Objects

Aristotle believed that, when an object was dropped from a certain height, the speed at which it fell depended on how heavy it was. Galileo pointed out that, if this were true, a 100-kg stone would fall 100 times faster than a 1-kg stone. In other words, if a 100-kg stone and a 1-kg stone were dropped from a height of 100 m at the same time, the 1-kg stone would fall only 1 m by the time the 100-kg stone hit the ground. Galileo knew that this idea could easily be disproved by experiment.

Galileo discovered that, in the absence of resistance from the air or another medium, all objects fall at the same rate. The speed of a falling object increases steadily as it falls, as shown by the approximate values in the table. The rate of increase in the speed is known as the acceleration of the object.

Elapsed Time (s)	Total Distance Fallen (m)	Instantaneous Speed (m/s)
0	0	0
1	5	10
2	20	20
3	45	30
4	80	40

The diagram at the right shows the motion of an object during the first 4 s of a free fall. Notice that, though the speed of the object was 10 m/s at the end of the first second, the object did not fall 10 m in the first second. The reason is that the object was not travelling at 10 m/s for the whole second.

0 s		
1 s	5 m	← Distance fallen in first second
2 s	15 m	← Distance fallen in next second
3 s	25 m	
4 s	35 m	

1. Use the patterns to write the next two rows in the table.

2. Let the total distance fallen be f metres and the elapsed time be t seconds. Write an equation of the form $f = \blacksquare t^{\blacktriangle}$, where $\blacksquare$ and $\blacktriangle$ represent whole numbers.

3. Use your equation to determine the distance an object falls in 7 s; 8 s.

4. From the table, what is the rate of increase in the instantaneous speed each second? The result is the acceleration due to gravity, g, expressed in metres per second per second (symbol m/s/s or m/s^2).

5. How is the value of $\blacksquare$ from your equation in question 2 related to the value of g?

6. Objects falling through the air approximately obey the equation for a certain length of time. Then, the instantaneous speed reaches a constant value, known as the terminal velocity. Use your research skills to find the factors that affect the terminal velocity. Find approximately how far, and for how long, an object falls in air before it reaches its terminal velocity.

2 The Path of a Cannonball

After Galileo determined the acceleration due to gravity, he tackled another problem of his day, the path of a cannonball. To do this, he combined two ideas.

1. Without considering the effect of gravity, Galileo pictured a cannonball fired upward so that the projected height of the cannonball would increase by 30 m/s. The equation that relates the projected height, H metres, to the elapsed time, t seconds, is

$$H = 30t$$

a) Copy and complete the table.
b) Graph H versus t.

Time, t (s)	Projected Height, H (m)
0	0
1	30
2	
3	
4	
5	
6	

2. Galileo then considered the other component, the downward change in the height of the cannonball from the effect of gravity. He reasoned that the actual height, h, of the cannonball would be the projected height, H, minus the downward change, f, resulting from gravity.

$$h = H - f$$

a) Copy and complete the table.

Time, t (s)	Projected Height, H (m)	Downward Change from Gravity, f (m)	Actual Height, h (m)
0	0	0	0
1	30	5	25
2			
3			
4			
5			
6			

b) Draw the graph of actual height, h, versus time, t, on the same grid as the graph in question 1.
c) What was the maximum height reached by the cannonball?
d) How many seconds after it was fired did the cannonball reach this height?
e) In the equation $h = H - f$, substitute for H and f to write an equation in which h is expressed in terms of t.
f) Use the equation to find the height of the cannonball after 2.6 s; 4.8 s.
g) For how many seconds was the cannonball airborne before it hit the ground?

3. a) Write an equation that expresses h in terms of t for a cannonball fired upward at 50 m/s.
b) Find the maximum height reached by the cannonball.
c) Find the time the cannonball took to reach its maximum height.
d) Find the height of the cannonball after 7.2 s.
e) For how many seconds was the cannonball airborne before it hit the ground?

3 Distance Travelled by a Cannonball

A cannon could be aimed correctly if the height of the tallest barrier that a cannonball would clear and the horizontal distance a cannonball would travel were known. Before the work of Galileo, the calculations were impossible.

1. The path of a cannonball is determined by the angle the cannon makes with the ground, $\angle A$, and the muzzle velocity, v, which equals the initial speed of the cannonball.

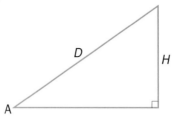

a) Let the straight-line distance the cannonball would travel in the absence of gravity be D. Use a trigonometric ratio to write an expression for the projected height, H, in terms of D and $\angle A$.

b) Substitute for H and f in the equation $h = H - f$, so that h is expressed in terms of D, $\angle A$, and t.

c) Since distance = velocity × time, the distance D can be expressed as $D = vt$. Substitute for D to write an equation that expresses h in terms of v, $\angle A$, and t.

2. A cannonball is fired at a velocity of 80 m/s at an angle of 30° to the ground.

a) What is the height of the cannonball, in metres, after 3 s?

b) If the cannonball takes 7 s to reach a 10-m wall, will the cannonball clear the top of the wall?

c) Graph h versus t to find the maximum height of the cannonball and the length of time it is airborne.

3. The horizontal distance, d, a cannonball travels before it hits the ground depends on v and $\angle A$.

a) Use the diagram to write an equation that expresses d in terms of D and $\angle A$.

b) Substitute the expression vt for D.

c) Use your equation from part b) and your answer to question 2c) to find the horizontal distance travelled by a cannonball fired with a muzzle velocity of 80 m/s at an angle of 30° to the ground. Round your answer to the nearest metre.

4. A cannonball was fired with a muzzle velocity of 60 m/s at an angle of 50° to the ground. The time of flight was found to be about 9.2 s. Calculate the horizontal distance travelled by the cannonball and the maximum height of the cannonball, to the nearest metre.

5. If a cannon makes an angle of 30° with the ground and it fires cannonballs with a muzzle velocity of 70 m/s, can it hit a target 500 m away? Show your reasoning.

6. The equation from question 3b) made it possible for the first time to calculate the muzzle velocity of a cannon. To do this, the time of flight and the angle the cannon made with the ground were measured.

a) Solve the equation from question 3b) for v.

b) A cannonball took 12.5 s to travel a horizontal distance of 400 m from a cannon that made an angle of 60° with the ground. What was the muzzle velocity of the cannon?

Volcanology

Over 80% of the Earth's surface is of volcanic origin. There are about 500 active volcanoes around the world, excluding those under the ocean. Hundreds of other volcanoes are inactive, or dormant, but they could become active again. Most of the active volcanoes are arranged in the so-called "Ring of Fire" around the Pacific Ocean.

There are at least 21 known volcanic regions in Canada. The volcanic mountains in these regions include Mount Edziza and Mount Garibaldi in British Columbia. The most recent volcanic eruption in Canada took place about 200 years ago near Terrace in northwestern British Columbia.

Millions of people around the world live close to volcanoes. The people who study volcanoes, called volcanologists, try to predict when a volcano will erupt. Efforts can then be made to move people out of harm's way.

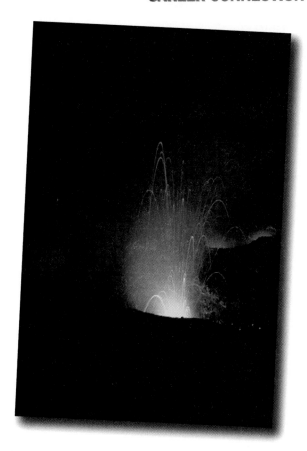

1 Volcanic Eruptions

1. About a third of volcanic eruptions take place on the island of Iceland. One eruption of the Icelandic volcano known as Askja threw a fountain of lava 500 m into the air. How does this height compare with the height of the tallest building in Canada?

2. Some volcanoes erupt continuously for many years. The Stromboli volcano, located on an island off the Italian coast, has been erupting for at least 2500 years, and possibly as long as 5000 years. The approximate height of the lava ejected by the Stromboli volcano can be modelled by the equation
$$h(t) = -5t^2 + 55t$$
where $h(t)$ metres is the height of the lava above the top of the crater t seconds after the lava is ejected.
a) Graph $h(t)$ versus t.
b) Find the maximum height reached by the lava, to the nearest metre.
c) Find the length of time the lava takes to reach its maximum height, to the nearest tenth of a second.
d) The length of time the lava takes to fall back to the ground may not equal the time you found in part c). Explain why not.
e) The graph does not show the path that the lava follows. Explain why not.

3. One of the largest known volcanic eruptions occurred on the island of Krakatoa in southwestern Indonesia in 1883. The explosions that accompanied the eruption reduced the area of the island from 47 km² to 16 km². One explosion was heard almost 5000 km away and may have been the loudest noise ever produced on Earth. The eruption produced about 18 km³ of lava. If the lava formed a uniform layer of rock across your province, how thick would the layer be, to the nearest tenth of a centimetre?

2 Locating Information

1. Explore the education and training needed to become a volcanologist. Also, find out who employs volcanologists and where they work.

2. Use your research skills to locate Canada's volcanic regions. How far is the closest one from where you live?

Review

3.1 *Write one sentence that compares each pair of graphs.*
1. $y = x^2$ and $y = x^2 - 3$ **2.** $y = -x^2$ and $y = -4x^2$

Sketch the graph of each parabola and state
a) *the direction of the opening*
b) *the coordinates of the vertex*
c) *the equation of the axis of symmetry*
d) *the domain and range*
e) *the maximum or minimum value*
f) *any intercepts*
  3. $y = x^2 + 4$ **4.** $y = -x^2 - 2$
  5. $f(x) = 0.5x^2$ **6.** $f(x) = -3x^2 + 3$

Without graphing each function, state
a) *the direction of the opening*
b) *the coordinates of the vertex*
c) *the domain and range*
d) *the maximum or minimum value*
  7. $y = -4x^2$ **8.** $y = -x^2 + 3.5$
  9. $f(x) = -2x^2 - 7$ **10.** $3 + 0.2x^2 = f(x)$

Estimate any x-intercepts, or use a graphing calculator to determine them to the nearest tenth.
11. $y = x^2 - 7$ **12.** $f(x) = -x^2 + 2$
13. $f(x) = x^2 + 1$ **14.** $y = 2x^2 - 9$

Write an equation for a parabola with
15. vertex $(0, 0)$ and $a = 2$
16. vertex $(0, -2)$ and $a = -3$
17. vertex $(0, 0)$, passing through $(-2, -20)$
18. vertex $(0, -5)$, passing through $(5, 20)$

19. Xiaoshang Bridge The Xiaoshang Bridge over the Xiaoji River in Henan Province, China, was built in 584. It is one of the oldest surviving stone arch bridges. Suppose the curve of the arch is graphed on a grid, with the origin on the river directly under the centre of the arch. The arch can be modelled by the function
$$h(d) = -0.06d^2 + 2.13$$
where $h(d)$ metres is the height of the arch, and d metres is the horizontal distance from the centre of the arch.
a) What is the maximum height of the arch?
b) If the ends of the arch are at the level of the river, how wide is the arch, to the nearest metre?
c) At a horizontal distance of 2 m from one end of the arch, how high is the arch, to the nearest tenth of a metre?

3.3 *Sketch each parabola and state*
a) *the direction of the opening*
b) *how the parabola is stretched or shrunk, if at all*
c) *the coordinates of the vertex*
d) *the equation of the axis of symmetry*
e) *the domain and range*
f) *the maximum or minimum value*
20. $y = -2(x - 3)^2 + 1$ **21.** $f(x) = (x + 7)^2 - 2$
22. $y = 0.5(x + 1)^2 + 5$ **23.** $y = -(x + 3)^2 - 1$

Without sketching each parabola, state
a) *the direction of the opening*
b) *how the parabola is stretched or shrunk, if at all*
c) *the coordinates of the vertex*
d) *the equation of the axis of symmetry*
e) *the domain and range*
f) *the maximum or minimum value*
24. $f(x) = (x + 1)^2 - 1$ **25.** $f(x) = -4(x - 1)^2$
26. $y = -2(x - 4)^2 - 3$ **27.** $y = 0.25(x + 2)^2 + 1$

Sketch each parabola and find
a) *the coordinates of the vertex*
b) *the maximum or minimum value*
c) *any intercepts*
d) *two other points on the graph*
28. $y = (x - 3)^2$ **29.** $y = (x + 2)^2 - 4$
30. $y = 2(x - 3)^2 - 8$ **31.** $y = -(x + 2)^2 + 9$

Estimate any x-intercepts, or use a graphing calculator to determine them to the nearest tenth.
32. $f(x) = (x + 2)^2 - 5$ **33.** $y = -2(x - 1)^2 + 3$

Write an equation that defines each parabola.
34. vertex $(3, 4)$; $a = 2$
35. congruent to $y = x^2$; opens up; vertex $(2, -3)$
36. congruent to $y = 2x^2$; minimum value -4; axis of symmetry $x = -3$
37. vertex $(1, 3)$; passing through $(2, -1)$
38. vertex $(-2, 1)$; y-intercept 3

39. Baseball The height, $h(t)$ metres, of a batted baseball as a function of the time, t seconds, since the ball was hit can be modelled by the function
$$h(t) = -2.1(t - 2.4)^2 + 13$$
a) What was the maximum height of the ball?
b) What was its height when it was hit, to the nearest tenth of a metre?
c) How many seconds after it was hit did the ball hit the ground, to the nearest tenth of a second?
d) What was the height of the ball, to the nearest tenth of a metre, 1 s after it was hit?

3.5 *Find the value of c that will make each expression a perfect square trinomial.*

40. $x^2 + 8x + c$ **41.** $x^2 - 14x + c$
42. $x^2 - 5x + c$ **43.** $x^2 + 0.6x + c$

Write each function in the form $y = a(x - p)^2 + q$. Sketch the graph, showing the coordinates of the vertex, the equation of the axis of symmetry, and the coordinates of two other points on the graph.

44. $y = x^2 + 4x + 1$ **45.** $y = x^2 - 10x + 15$
46. $y = -x^2 - 6x - 5$ **47.** $y = 3 - 4x - x^2$

Sketch the graph of each function. Show the coordinates of the vertex, the equation of the axis of symmetry, and any intercepts. State the range.

48. $y = x^2 + 6x$ **49.** $y = x^2 - 8x + 12$
50. $y + 9 = -x^2 - 4x$ **51.** $f(x) = 15 + 8x + x^2$

Find the coordinates of the vertex.

52. $y = x^2 - 5x + 3$ **53.** $y = -x^2 + x - 4$
54. $y = -3x^2 - 12x - 9$ **55.** $y = 2x^2 + 6x + 15$
56. $f(x) = 4x^2 + 2x - 1$ **57.** $y + 1.5x = -0.5x^2$

Graph each function. Find any x-intercepts. Round to the nearest tenth, if necessary.

58. $y = 2x^2 + 6x + 5$ **59.** $y = -3x^2 + 2x + 1$
60. $y = x^2 + 0.5x$ **61.** $y = 5 - 2x^2$

62. Basketball The path of a basketball shot can be modelled by the equation
$$h(d) = -0.125d^2 + d + 2.5$$
where $h(d)$ is the height of the basketball, in metres, and d is the horizontal distance of the ball from the player, in metres.
a) Find the maximum height reached by the ball.
b) What is the horizontal distance of the ball from the player when it reaches its maximum height?
c) How far from the floor is the ball when the player releases it?

63. Integers Find two integers whose difference is 12 and whose product is a minimum.

64. Rectangular fence A rectangular field is to be enclosed by 600 m of fence.
a) What dimensions will give a maximum area?
b) What is the maximum area?

Exploring Math

Analyzing a Game

This is a game for two players. The game starts with 9 counters.

The rules are as follows.
• Players take turns removing 1, 2, or 3 counters.
• A player cannot remove the same number of counters as the other player removed in the previous turn.
• The winner is the player who takes the last counter or leaves the other player with no valid turn.

1. Play the game a few times with a classmate, taking turns to go first. Describe the winning strategy for the player who goes first.

2. Now start the game with 8 counters. Describe any strategy with which the first player or the second player can always win.

3. If the starting number of counters is 1, 2, or 3, the player who goes first can always win. Copy and complete the table for games starting with 4, 5, and 6 counters, and so on, up to 13 counters. Use F for the player who goes first, and S for the player who goes second.

Starting Number of Counters	1	2	3	4	5	6	7
Player Who Can Always Win	F	F	F				
Starting Number of Counters	8	9	10	11	12	13	
Player Who Can Always Win							

4. When the game starts with 14 counters,
a) which player can always win?
b) what should the winning player's first move be?
c) why would this move guarantee a win?

5. Repeat question 4 for a game that starts with 16 counters.

6. Which player can always win when the game starts with each of the following numbers of counters?
a) 49 **b)** 200 **c)** 810 **d)** 960

Chapter Check

Sketch the graph of each parabola and state
a) *the direction of the opening*
b) *the coordinates of the vertex*
c) *the equation of the axis of symmetry*
d) *the domain and range*
e) *the maximum or minimum value*
  1. $y = x^2 - 1$ **2.** $y = -x^2 + 5$
  3. $f(x) = -2.5x^2$ **4.** $f(x) = -x^2 - 3$

Estimate any x-intercepts, or determine them to the nearest tenth using a graphing calculator.
  5. $y = x^2 + 3$ **6.** $f(x) = -x^2 + 10$
  7. $f(x) = 8 - 3x^2$ **8.** $y = 0.5x^2 - 3$

Write an equation for a parabola with
  9. vertex $(0, 0)$ and $a = -4$
  10. vertex $(0, -3)$ and $a = -0.5$
  11. vertex $(0, 0)$, passing through $(-2, 12)$
  12. vertex $(0, -5)$, passing through $(3, 13)$

Without sketching each parabola, state
a) *the direction of the opening*
b) *how the parabola is stretched or shrunk, if at all*
c) *the coordinates of the vertex*
d) *the equation of the axis of symmetry*
e) *the domain and range*
f) *the maximum or minimum value*
  13. $f(x) = (x + 3)^2 - 1$ **14.** $f(x) = 3(x - 1)^2$
  15. $y = -2(x - 5)^2 - 2$ **16.** $y = -0.5(x + 2)^2 + 3$

Sketch each parabola and find
a) *the coordinates of the vertex*
b) *the maximum or minimum value*
c) *any intercepts*
d) *two other points on the graph*
  17. $y = (x - 1)^2$ **18.** $y = (x + 1)^2 - 4$
  19. $y = (x - 5)^2 - 9$ **20.** $y = -2(x + 6)^2 + 18$

Estimate any x-intercepts or determine them to the nearest tenth using a graphing calculator.
  21. $y = 2(x + 2)^2 - 9$ **22.** $f(x) = -(x - 2)^2 + 3$

Write an equation that defines each parabola.
  23. congruent to $y = x^2$; opens up; vertex $(-3, 1)$
  24. congruent to $y = 2x^2$; maximum value 4; axis of symmetry $x = -5$
  25. vertex $(1, 4)$; passing through $(3, -4)$
  26. vertex $(-3, 1)$; y-intercept 5

Write each function in the form $y = a(x - p)^2 + q$. Sketch the graph, showing the coordinates of the vertex, the equation of the axis of symmetry, and the coordinates of two other points on the graph.
  27. $y = x^2 + 8x + 8$ **28.** $y = x^2 - 8x + 9$
  29. $y = 5 - 4x + x^2$ **30.** $y = -x^2 - 10x - 4$

Sketch the graph of each function. Show the coordinates of the vertex, the equation of the axis of symmetry, and any intercepts. State the range.
  31. $y = x^2 + 8x + 2$ **32.** $y = x^2 - 10x$
  33. $y = -x^2 - 6x - 10$ **34.** $f(x) = 6x + x^2 + 11$

Find the coordinates of the vertex.
  35. $y = x^2 - 7x + 1$ **36.** $y = -x^2 + x + 12$
  37. $y = -4x^2 - 8x + 5$ **38.** $y = 2x^2 + 5x + 5$

39. Entrance arch A park has an arch over its entrance. The curve of the arch can be graphed on a grid, with the origin on the path directly under the centre of the arch. The arch can be modelled by the function
$$h(d) = -1.17d^2 + 3$$
where $h(d)$ metres is its height, and d metres is the horizontal distance from the centre of the arch.
a) What is the maximum height of the arch?
b) If the ends of the arch are at the level of the path, how wide is the arch, to the nearest tenth of a metre?
c) At a horizontal distance of 0.5 m from the centre of the arch, how high is the arch, to the nearest tenth of a metre?

40. Flare The height, $h(t)$ metres, of a flare as a function of the time, t seconds, since the flare was fired from a boat is given by the function
$$h(t) = -5.25(t - 4)^2 + 86$$
a) What was the maximum height of the flare?
b) What was its height when it was fired?
c) How many seconds after it was fired did the flare hit the water, to the nearest second?

41. Riverboat cruise The captain of a riverboat cruise charges $36 per person, including lunch. The cruise averages 300 customers a day. The captain is considering increasing the price. A survey of customers indicates that for every $2 increase, there would be 10 fewer customers. What increase in price would maximize the revenue?

Using the Strategies

1. Some books are stored in 5 boxes, labelled A, B, C, D, and E. The total mass of A and B is 24 kg, of B and C is 27 kg, of C and D is 23 kg, of D and E is 16 kg, and of A, C, and E is 32 kg. What is the mass of each box?

2. Three soccer teams, the Astros, the Bears, and the Colts played each other once. The table gives some of the resulting statistics.

Team	Games Played	Won	Lost	Tied	Goals For	Goals Against
Astros	2			1	2	4
Bears	2				3	7
Colts	2	2				1

a) Copy and complete the table.
b) Find the final score of each game.

3. A checker starts on the lower left square of the board shown. The middle square of the board has been removed. The checker can move in two directions, to the right and up. How many different paths are there for the checker to move from the bottom left square to the top right square?

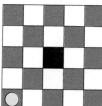

4. About how many hours do all the grade 11 students in Canada spend on the telephone in a year?

5. Every day at noon, one ship leaves Halifax for Lisbon. At exactly the same time every day, one ship leaves Lisbon for Halifax. Each crossing takes exactly 6 days. The ships send each other a radio message when they meet. In one crossing, how many radio messages will the ship from Halifax send to ships from Lisbon?

6. Damon rode his bicycle to school from his home at 9 km/h and arrived 10 min late. The next day, he left home at the same time, but he rode at 12 km/h and arrived 10 min early. What is the distance from Damon's home to the school?

7. Copy the diagram. Complete it by placing four odd numbers in the empty squares so that the sum of each row, column, and diagonal is 48.

	22	
4	16	28
	10	

8. What is the last digit when the following product is written in standard form?
$$(3^1)(3^2)(3^3)\ldots(3^{298})(3^{299})(3^{300})$$

9. The leader of a marching band has decided that the band must be able to form a rectangle. The leader has also decided that the number of band members marching on the outside edges of the rectangle must be the same as the number of band members marching in the interior.
a) What are the possible numbers of band members?
b) Show algebraically that you have found the only solutions.

10. The mean of a set of numbers is 53. The size of the set is increased by adding half as many numbers as are already in the set. The new set has a mean of 58.
a) What is the mean of the numbers that are added to the original set?
b) Does the answer depend on the number of numbers in the original set? Explain.

DATA BANK

1. A coordinate grid is placed on the cross section of the dish of the larger telescope at the Palomar Observatory as shown.

a) Write an equation for the curve.
b) Find the depth of the dish, in centimetres, at a horizontal distance of 1.5 m from the vertex.

2. Estimate the first year in which the number of Canadians 75 years of age or older will equal the number of Canadians under 10 years of age.

3. Which Canadian province has the greatest ratio of the number of trees to the number of people? What assumptions have you made?

CHAPTER 4

Quadratic and Polynomial Equations

For ocean waves, the wavelength is the distance from one wave crest to the next.

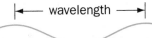

|←——— wavelength ———→|

In deep water, the speed of a wave, s metres per second, is approximately related to the wavelength, l metres, by the following equation.

$$s^2 = 1.6l$$

1. Substitute 10 for l to represent a wavelength of 10 m. What is the resulting equation?

2. What values of s satisfy your equation from question 1?

3. Which of the values of s you found in question 2 has no meaning for the speed of a wave? Explain.

4. What is the speed of a wave with a wavelength of 10 m?

5. Find the speed of a wave with a wavelength of
a) 2.5 m   **b)** 22.5 m   **c)** 0.9 m

GETTING STARTED

Investigating Patterns in Fibonacci Numbers

Many spirals occur in nature. In some cases, there are two opposing sets of spirals on the same object, with one set radiating clockwise, and the other radiating counterclockwise.

Examples include the following opposing sets.
• on a pine cone, 5 spirals and 8 spirals formed by the scales
• on a pineapple, 8 spirals and 13 spirals formed by the bumps
• on a daisy, 21 spirals and 34 spirals formed by the florets

The numbers of spirals in each of the above pairs are consecutive terms in a sequence discovered around A.D.1200 by an Italian mathematician, Leonardo Fibonacci. The first 12 terms in the Fibonacci sequence are shown below.

$$t_1 = 1 \quad t_2 = 1 \quad t_3 = 2 \quad t_4 = 3 \quad t_5 = 5 \quad t_6 = 8$$
$$t_7 = 13 \quad t_8 = 21 \quad t_9 = 34 \quad t_{10} = 55 \quad t_{11} = 89 \quad t_{12} = 144$$

Aside from t_1 and t_2, each term in the sequence is found by adding the two preceding terms. The general term, t_n, of the Fibonacci sequence is given by

$$t_n = t_{n-1} + t_{n-2}$$

1 The Sum of Consecutive Squares

1. Choose any two consecutive Fibonacci numbers, square them, and add the squares. Repeat for three more consecutive pairs.

2. For each pair you chose, how are the term numbers related to the term number of the result?

3. Use your findings to write the term that results from
a) $t_9^2 + t_{10}^2$
b) $t_{21}^2 + t_{22}^2$

4. Generalize your findings by copying and completing the following statement.
$$t_n^2 + t_{n+1}^2 = \blacksquare$$

2 The Difference Between Alternate Squares

1. Choose two alternate Fibonacci numbers, such as t_3 and t_5, square them, and subtract the smaller square from the larger. Repeat for three more alternate pairs.

2. For each pair you chose, how are the term numbers related to the term number of the result?

3. Generalize your findings by copying and completing the following statement.
$$t_{n+2}^2 + t_n^2 = \blacksquare$$

3 Four Consecutive Fibonacci Numbers

1. Choose any four consecutive Fibonacci numbers. How are the first and last numbers related to the difference between the squares of the middle two numbers? Repeat for three more sets of four consecutive numbers.

2. Generalize your findings.

Warm Up

Factor each polynomial, if possible.

1. $3x^2 - 3x$ **2.** $4x^2y + 10xy^2$
3. $y^2 + 8y + 7$ **4.** $s^2 - s - 6$
5. $m^2 - 7m - 12$ **6.** $c^2 + 10c + 25$
7. $x^2 - 6x + 7$ **8.** $4a^2 - 1$
9. $3v^2 + 11v - 4$ **10.** $4x^2 - 20x + 25$
11. $2t^2 - 26t + 24$ **12.** $25x^2 + 36$

Use guess and check to find two solutions to each equation.

13. $x^2 = 1$ **14.** $x^2 - 9 = 0$
15. $2x^2 = 8$ **16.** $3y^2 - 75 = 0$
17. $x^2 - x = 0$ **18.** $m^2 + 2m = 0$
19. $3x^2 + 12x = 0$ **20.** $4z^2 = 12z$

Simplify.

21. $\sqrt{20}$ **22.** $\sqrt{54}$ **23.** $\sqrt{60}$
24. $\sqrt{96}$ **25.** $2\sqrt{18}$ **26.** $5\sqrt{48}$
27. $7\sqrt{72}$ **28.** $4\sqrt{52}$ **29.** $7\sqrt{99}$
30. $\dfrac{\sqrt{50}}{5}$ **31.** $\dfrac{\sqrt{300}}{10}$ **32.** $\dfrac{3\sqrt{32}}{6}$
33. $\sqrt{9+16}$ **34.** $\sqrt{25+15}$
35. $\sqrt{36-16}$ **36.** $\dfrac{3-\sqrt{12}}{2}$
37. $\dfrac{-5+\sqrt{9}}{4}$ **38.** $\dfrac{4+\sqrt{20}}{2}$
39. $\dfrac{4+\sqrt{16+20}}{2}$ **40.** $\dfrac{-2-\sqrt{4+24}}{6}$

Divide using long division.

41. $(x^2 + 3x + 2) \div (x + 1)$
42. $(x^2 - 5x + 5) \div (x - 2)$
43. $(2x^2 + 7x + 5) \div (2x + 5)$
44. $(3x^2 + 2x - 4) \div (x - 1)$
45. $(x^3 - 2x^2 - 14x - 5) \div (x - 5)$
46. $(4x^3 + x^2 + 8x + 4) \div (x^2 + 2)$

Divide using synthetic division.

47. $(3x^2 + x - 4) \div (x - 1)$
48. $(5x^2 + 4x - 1) \div (x + 1)$
49. $(2x^3 + 3x^2 - 3) \div (2x - 1)$
50. $(3x^3 - 11x^2 + 8x + 7) \div (3x + 1)$

Mental Math

Simplifying and Evaluating Square Roots

Simplify, if possible.

1. $\sqrt{8}$ **2.** $\sqrt{18}$
3. $\sqrt{15}$ **4.** $\sqrt{12}$
5. $\sqrt{22}$ **6.** $\sqrt{24}$
7. $\sqrt{27}$ **8.** $\sqrt{44}$
9. $\sqrt{45}$ **10.** $\sqrt{50}$
11. $\sqrt{63}$ **12.** $\sqrt{80}$

Evaluate, if possible.

13. $\sqrt{49}$ **14.** $\sqrt{-9}$
15. $\sqrt{121}$ **16.** $\sqrt{25+56}$
17. $\sqrt{36-20}$ **18.** $\sqrt{64-28}$
19. $\sqrt{16+4(12)}$ **20.** $\sqrt{10^2 - 36}$
21. $\sqrt{7^2 + 32}$ **22.** $\sqrt{3^2 - 4(2)(-2)}$
23. $\sqrt{8^2 - 4(3)(-3)}$ **24.** $\sqrt{7^2 - 4(2)(3)}$

Subtracting in Two Steps

To subtract $92 - 53$, first subtract 50, and then subtract 3.

$92 - 50 = 42$
$42 - 3 = 39$
So, $92 - 53 = 39$

Estimate
$90 - 50 = 40$

Subtract.

1. $48 - 23$ **2.** $56 - 31$
3. $75 - 21$ **4.** $43 - 15$
5. $72 - 33$ **6.** $84 - 48$
7. $100 - 36$ **8.** $103 - 42$
9. $121 - 34$ **10.** $144 - 58$
11. $169 - 88$ **12.** $182 - 99$

Adapt the method to subtract the following. Describe how you adapted the method.

13. $3.6 - 1.7$ **14.** $4.2 - 2.3$
15. $6.4 - 3.8$ **16.** $16.2 - 5.4$
17. $22.5 - 4.9$ **18.** $30 - 13.3$
19. $470 - 120$ **20.** $670 - 290$
21. $830 - 540$ **22.** $920 - 450$
23. $1100 - 570$ **24.** $1320 - 440$

4.1 Solving Quadratic Equations by Graphing

Canada's rich history in soccer includes the gold medal at the 1904 Olympic Games in St. Louis. Today, many Canadians play professional soccer around the world. Many others play in amateur leagues.

The path of one kick of a soccer ball can be modelled by the function
$$h(d) = -0.025d^2 + d$$
where $h(d)$ metres is the height of the ball, and d metres is the horizontal distance of the ball from the place on the ground where it was kicked. One way to find the horizontal distance the ball travels before it first hits the ground is to graph the function and find the d-intercepts.

Since the height of the ball is 0 m when it is kicked and when it hits the ground, we can substitute 0 for $h(d)$. When the ball is kicked and when it first hits the ground, the following equation is true.
$$-0.025d^2 + d = 0$$

So, another way to find the horizontal distance the ball travels before it first hits the ground is to solve this equation.

The equation $-0.025d^2 + d = 0$ is an example of a **quadratic equation**. Quadratic equations are equations in the form $ax^2 + bx + c = 0$, where a, b, and c are real numbers and $a \neq 0$.

The graph of the quadratic function $y = ax^2 + bx + c$ represents all the ordered pairs (x, y) that satisfy the function. When solving the quadratic equation $ax^2 + bx + c = 0$, we are interested only in the values of x that make the expression $ax^2 + bx + c$ equal to zero.

Explore: Interpret the Graphs

Draw the graphs of $y = 2x - 3$ and $y = x^2 - 2x - 3$ on the same set of axes or in the same viewing window of a graphing calculator. Find the x- and y-intercepts for each graph.

Inquire

1. For the linear function $y = 2x - 3$, a related linear equation is $2x - 3 = 0$. For which point on the graph of $y = 2x - 3$ is the x-coordinate the solution to $2x - 3 = 0$? Explain.

2. For the quadratic function $y = x^2 - 2x - 3$, a related quadratic equation is $x^2 - 2x - 3 = 0$. For which points on the graph of $y = x^2 - 2x - 3$ are the x-coordinates solutions to $x^2 - 2x - 3 = 0$? Explain.

3. a) Graph $y = x^2 + x - 6$.   **b)** Find the x-intercepts.
c) Do the x-intercepts satisfy the equation $x^2 + x - 6 = 0$?

4. Solve each quadratic equation by graphing.
a) $x^2 - 2x - 8 = 0$ **b)** $x^2 + 3x - 4 = 0$ **c)** $x^2 + 2x + 1 = 0$

The solutions of the quadratic equation $ax^2 + bx + c = 0$ are known as the **zeros** of the quadratic function $f(x) = ax^2 + bx + c$. The real zeros are the x-intercepts of the parabola $y = ax^2 + bx + c$, since the value of y is zero for points on the x-axis. The x-intercepts are called the real solutions, or real **roots**, of the quadratic equation.

Example 1　Solving by Graphing

Solve $2x^2 + 5x - 3 = 0$ by graphing.

Solution 1　Graphing Manually

Use a table of values to plot the graph.

x	y
1	4
0	-3
-1	-6
-2	-5
-3	0
-4	9

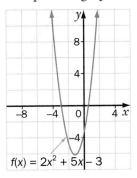

$f(x) = 2x^2 + 5x - 3$

The graph appears to intersect the x-axis at $\left(\dfrac{1}{2}, 0\right)$ and $(-3, 0)$. The x-intercepts are the real zeros of the function $f(x) = 2x^2 + 5x - 3$, since $f(x) = 0$ for these values of x.

So, $2x^2 + 5x - 3 = 0$ when $x = \dfrac{1}{2}$ and $x = -3$.

Solution 2　Using a Graphing Calculator

Graph the function in the standard viewing window. The values of the x-intercepts can be found using the Zero operation or the ZOOM and TRACE instructions, or by displaying a table of values.

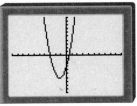

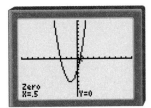

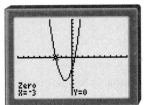

The x-intercepts are the real zeros of the function $f(x) = 2x^2 + 5x - 3$.

So, $2x^2 + 5x - 3 = 0$ when $x = \dfrac{1}{2}$ and $x = -3$.

Check for Solution 1 and Solution 2.

For $x = \dfrac{1}{2}$,

L.S. $= 2x^2 + 5x - 3$　　R.S. $= 0$
$= 2\left(\dfrac{1}{2}\right)^2 + 5\left(\dfrac{1}{2}\right) - 3$
$= 0$

For $x = -3$,

L.S. $= 2x^2 + 5x - 3$　　R.S. $= 0$
$= 2(-3)^2 + 5(-3) - 3$
$= 0$

The roots of the equation $2x^2 + 5x - 3 = 0$ are $\dfrac{1}{2}$ and -3.

The equation in Example 1 has two different or distinct roots. Some quadratic equations do not have distinct roots.

Example 2　Two Equal Roots

Solve $x^2 - 6x = -9$ by graphing.

Solution

Rewrite the equation in the form $ax^2 + bx + c = 0$.
$$x^2 - 6x = -9$$
So, $x^2 - 6x + 9 = 0$
Graph the related quadratic function $y = x^2 - 6x + 9$.
The graph meets the x-axis at one point, $(3, 0)$.
The x-intercept is 3, so the root is 3.

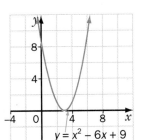

$y = x^2 - 6x + 9$

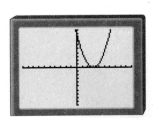

In Example 2, there are actually two roots. Each root equals 3. These equal roots are sometimes called a **double root**.

Example 3   No Real Roots
Solve $2x^2 + x + 2 = 0$ by graphing.

Solution
Graph the related quadratic function $y = 2x^2 + x + 2$.
The graph of the function does not intersect the x-axis.
The quadratic equation has no real solutions.

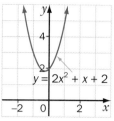

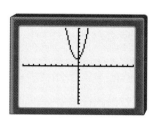

The following graphs show the three possible outcomes when solving a quadratic equation.

two distinct real roots   *two equal real roots*   *no real roots*

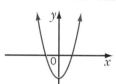   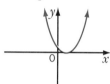   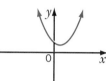

Example 4   Soccer
The function $h(d) = -0.025d^2 + d$ models the height, $h(d)$ metres, of one kick of a soccer ball as a function of the horizontal distance, d metres, from the place on the ground where the ball was kicked. By graphing, find the horizontal distance the ball travels before it first hits the ground.

Solution
Solve the equation $-0.025d^2 + d = 0$ by
graphing the function $h(d) = -0.025d^2 + d$.
The d-intercepts are $(0, 0)$ and $(40, 0)$.
The roots of the equation are 0 and 40.
The ball was kicked at $d = 0$. It hits the
ground at $d = 40$.
So, the ball travels a horizontal distance of
40 m before it first hits the ground.

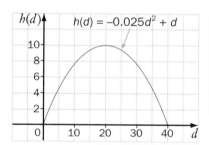

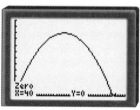

Example 5   Measurement
The width of a rectangle is 2 m less than the length. The area
of the rectangle is 48 m². Find the dimensions of the rectangle.

Solution
Let the length be x and the width be $x - 2$.
The area is $x(x - 2)$. The area is known to be 48 m².
So, $x(x - 2) = 48$
$\qquad x^2 - 2x = 48$
$x^2 - 2x - 48 = 0$
Graph the function $A = x^2 - 2x - 48$.

The intercepts are $(-6, 0)$ and $(8, 0)$.
The roots of the equation are -6 and 8.
The length of a rectangle cannot be negative, so the
root -6 is rejected.
The length of the rectangle is 8 m, and the width is $8 - 2$ or 6 m.

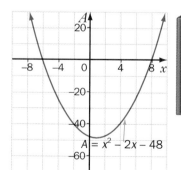

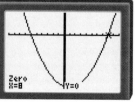

Example 6 Solving Graphically in Two Ways
Solve the equation $x^2 + 2x = 8$ by graphing.

Solution 1 Graphing a Related Function
Rewrite the equation so that one side equals zero.
Then, graph a related function and find the zeros of
the function.
$$x^2 + 2x = 8$$
$$x^2 + 2x - 8 = 0$$

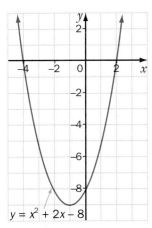

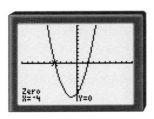

The roots are -4 and 2.

Solution 2 Graphing a Related System
Graph the following system of equations.
Find the intersection points.
$$y = x^2 + 2x$$
$$y = 8$$

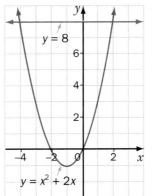

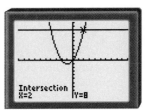

The intersection points are $(-4, 8)$ and $(2, 8)$.
The roots are the x-coordinates of the
intersection points.
The roots are -4 and 2.

Check for Solution 1 and Solution 2.

For $x = -4$,
L.S. $= x^2 + 2x$ R.S. $= 8$
$= (-4)^2 + 2(-4)$
$= 16 - 8$
$= 8$

For $x = 2$,
L.S. $= x^2 + 2x$ R.S. $= 8$
$= (2)^2 + 2(2)$
$= 4 + 4$
$= 8$

The roots of the equation $x^2 + 2x = 8$ are -4 and 2.

Practice

Solve by graphing a related function.

1. $x^2 + x - 6 = 0$
2. $x^2 - 5x + 4 = 0$
3. $x^2 + 6x + 5 = 0$
4. $x^2 + 4x + 4 = 0$
5. $0 = x^2 - 2x + 2$
6. $x^2 + 4x = 5$
7. $x^2 - 4 = 0$
8. $3x + x^2 = 0$
9. $9 - x^2 = 0$
10. $x^2 = 4x - 7$
11. $-x^2 + 2x - 1 = 0$
12. $-x^2 - 9 = 0$
13. $-x^2 + 5x = 0$
14. $-2 = x - x^2$

Solve by graphing a related system of equations.
15. $x^2 - 6x = -9$
16. $x^2 + 3x = 4$
17. $-5 = x^2 - 4x$
18. $-x^2 + 3x = 2$

*Solve by graphing. Round each answer to the nearest
tenth, if necessary.*

19. $2x^2 - x - 3 = 0$
20. $2x^2 - 5x - 3 = 0$
21. $4x^2 - 11x + 9 = 0$
22. $0 = 4x^2 + 4x + 1$
23. $-2x^2 + 5x = 0$
24. $-3x^2 - 7x + 5 = 0$
25. $6x^2 - 5x = 4$
26. $9a^2 - 48a + 64 = 0$
27. $40x^2 = 10 - 9x$
28. $3 = 2x + 7x^2$
29. $0.5x^2 - x - 3 = 0$
30. $0.02x^2 - 0.03x + 7 = 0$
31. $1.07x^2 + 3.5x = 0$
32. $-0.36n^2 - 1 = 1.2n$

Solve by graphing.

33. $(x - 2)^2 - 1 = 0$
34. $(x + 1)^2 - 4 = 0$
35. $(x + 2)^2 + 1 = 0$
36. $(x - 3)^2 = 0$
37. $-(1 - x)^2 = 0$
38. $4(x + 1)^2 - 1 = 0$
39. $0 = -2(p - 1)^2$
40. $0.1(q + 3)^2 = 1.6$

4.1 Solving Quadratic Equations by Graphing 155

Applications and Problem Solving

41. Measurement The width of a rectangle is 1 m less than the length. The area is 72 m². Find the width and the length.

42. Soccer The function $h(d) = -0.04d^2 + 0.8d$ models the height of a soccer ball, $h(d)$ metres, in terms of the horizontal distance, d metres, from where the ball was kicked on the ground. How far does the ball travel horizontally until it first hits the ground?

43. Football During a field goal attempt, the function $h(d) = -0.02d^2 + 0.9d$ models the height, $h(d)$ metres, of a football in terms of the horizontal distance, d metres, from where the ball was kicked. Find the horizontal distance the ball travels until it first hits the ground.

44. Measurement The length of a rectangle is 5 cm greater than twice the width. The area is 33 cm². Find the dimensions.

45. Measurement The hypotenuse of a right triangle measures 10 m. One leg of the triangle is 2 m longer than the other. Find the lengths of the legs.

46. Measurement The hypotenuse of a right triangle has a length of 13 cm. The sum of the lengths of the two legs is 17 cm. Find the lengths of the legs.

47. Measurement The height of a triangle is 2 m more than the base. The area is 17.5 m². Find the length of the base.

48. Fenced field The area of a rectangular field is 2275 m². The field is enclosed by 200 m of fencing. What are the dimensions of the field?

49. Basketball court The width of a basketball court is 1 m more than half the length. If the area of the court is 364 m², find the length and the width.

50. Measurement The diagonal of a rectangle is 8 cm. The length of the rectangle is 1.6 cm more than the width. Find the dimensions of the rectangle.

51. Integers The sum of the squares of two consecutive even integers is 452. Find the integers.

52. Canadian flag The Unity Flag is one of the largest Canadian flags. The length is twice the width, and the area is 167.2 m². Find the dimensions of the Unity Flag, to the nearest tenth of a metre.

53. Integers The sum of the squares of three consecutive positive integers is 194. Find the integers.

54. Factored form a) The left side of the equation $(x - 4)(x + 3) = 0$ is in factored form. Expand and simplify the left side.
b) Solve the resulting equation by graphing.
c) How are the roots of the equation related to the two numerical terms in the factored form of the equation?

55. a) Solve the equation $3x^2 - 4 = 5x - 2$ in two ways by graphing a related function and a related system of equations.
b) Which method do you prefer? Explain.
c) Is your answer to part b) affected by whether you graph manually or use a graphing calculator?

56. Repeat question 55 for the equation $x^2 - 3x = -x^2 + 2$.

57. For what values of c will the equation $x^2 + c = 0$ have
a) two distinct real roots? **b)** two equal real roots?
c) no real roots?

58. For what values of c will the equation $x^2 + 14x + c = 0$ have
a) two equal real roots? **b)** two distinct real roots?
c) no real roots?

59. For what values of b will the equation $x^2 + bx + 25 = 0$ have
a) two equal real roots? **b)** two distinct real roots?
c) no real roots?

60. For the equation $x^2 + bx = 0$,
a) what value of b will give two equal real roots?
b) when there are two distinct real roots, what does one of them always equal? how is the other root related to b?

61. For the quadratic function $y = x^2 - 9$, determine the values of x such that
a) $y \geq 7$ **b)** $y \leq 16$

4.2 Solving Quadratic Equations by Factoring

Any quadratic equation can be written in the form $ax^2 + bx + c = 0$, where $a \neq 0$. In the equation $x^2 + 3x + 2 = 0$, $a = 1$, $b = 3$, and $c = 2$. The equation $2x^2 = 5$ can be written as $2x^2 - 5 = 0$. In this case, $a = 2$, $b = 0$, and $c = -5$.

Recall that, when a number is multiplied by zero, the result is always zero. For example, $3 \times 0 = 0$, $0 \times (-7) = 0$, and $0 \times 0 = 0$.

The **zero product property** states that, if the product of two real numbers is zero, then one or both of the numbers must be zero.

Thus, if $ab = 0$, then $a = 0$, or $b = 0$, or $a = 0$ and $b = 0$.

You will be able to solve some quadratic equations by writing them in the form $ax^2 + bx + c = 0$, and then factoring and setting each factor equal to zero. For the equation $x^2 + 2x - 3 = 0$, factoring results in the equation $(x + 3)(x - 1) = 0$.
Thus, $x + 3 = 0$ or $x - 1 = 0$
$$x = -3 \quad \text{or} \quad x = 1$$

Explore: Solve an Equation

Maureen Griffin and Heather Landymoore won a bronze medal for Canada in the team épée fencing event at the Pan-American Games in Mar Del Plata, Argentina. Épée competitions are held on a rectangular strip whose length is 12 m greater than its width. The area of the strip is 28 m^2.
a) Let the width be x metres. Write an expression for the length in terms of x.
b) Write an expression for the area in terms of x.
c) Write an equation that relates the known area to the expression you wrote in part b).

Inquire

1. Write your equation from part c), above, in the form $ax^2 + bx + c = 0$.

2. Factor the left side of the equation.

3. a) Solve the equation for x.
b) State the width and the length of the strip.

4. Solve each of the following equations by factoring.
a) $x^2 + 5x + 6 = 0$ **b)** $x^2 - 3x - 4 = 0$ **c)** $x^2 + 2 = 3x$

Example 1 Solving by Factoring
Solve and check $x^2 + 7x + 12 = 0$.

Solution

$$x^2 + 7x + 12 = 0$$

Factor the left side: $(x + 4)(x + 3) = 0$

Use the zero product property: $x + 4 = 0$ or $x + 3 = 0$

$$x = -4 \quad \text{or} \quad x = -3$$

Check.

For $x = -4$,

L.S. $= x^2 + 7x + 12$ **R.S.** $= 0$
$= (-4)^2 + 7(-4) + 12$
$= 16 - 28 + 12$
$= 0$

For $x = -3$,

L.S. $= x^2 + 7x + 12$ **R.S.** $= 0$
$= (-3)^2 + 7(-3) + 12$
$= 9 - 21 + 12$
$= 0$

The solutions are -4 and -3.

You can visualize the solution by graphing $y = x^2 + 7x + 12$.

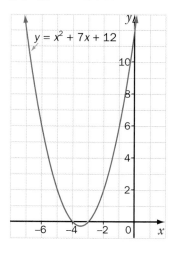

Example 2 Solving by Factoring
Solve and check $2x^2 + 3 = 5x + 1$.

Solution

$$2x^2 + 3 = 5x + 1$$

Write in the form $ax^2 + bx + c = 0$: $2x^2 - 5x + 2 = 0$

Factor the left side: $(2x - 1)(x - 2) = 0$

Use the zero product property: $2x - 1 = 0$ or $x - 2 = 0$

$$2x = 1 \quad \text{or} \quad x = 2$$

$$x = \frac{1}{2}$$

Check.

For $x = \frac{1}{2}$,

L.S. $= 2x^2 + 3$ **R.S.** $= 5x + 1$
$= 2\left(\frac{1}{2}\right)^2 + 3$ $= 5\left(\frac{1}{2}\right) + 1$
$= 2\left(\frac{1}{4}\right) + 3$ $= 2\frac{1}{2} + 1$
$= 3\frac{1}{2}$ $= 3\frac{1}{2}$

For $x = 2$,

L.S. $= 2x^2 + 3$ **R.S.** $= 5x + 1$
$= 2(2)^2 + 3$ $= 5(2) + 1$
$= 2(4) + 3$ $= 10 + 1$
$= 11$ $= 11$

The roots are $\frac{1}{2}$ and 2.

You can visualize the solution by graphing $y = 2x^2 - 5x + 2$.

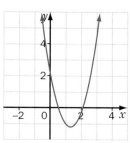

If $c = 0$, a quadratic equation simplifies to $ax^2 + bx = 0$. In this case, one of the roots is 0.

Example 3   Factoring When $c = 0$

Solve $3x^2 + 5x = 0$.

Solution

$$3x^2 + 5x = 0$$

Remove the common factor: $x(3x + 5) = 0$

Use the zero product property: $x = 0$ or $3x + 5 = 0$

$$3x = -5$$
$$x = -\frac{5}{3}$$

The roots are 0 and $-\dfrac{5}{3}$.

You can visualize the solution by graphing $y = 3x^2 + 5x$.

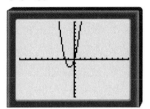

In rational equations that have the variable in the denominator, the value of the variable must be restricted because division by zero is not defined. For example, solving the equation $\dfrac{1}{x} = \dfrac{3}{2x}$ gives $2x = 3x$, so $x = 0$. However, the original equation is not defined at $x = 0$, so the equation has no solution. The solutions to rational equations with the variable in the denominator should be checked by substitution.

Example 4   Solving Rational Equations

Solve and check $\dfrac{2}{x+1} + \dfrac{5}{x-1} = -6$.

Solution

To clear the fractions, multiply by the lowest common denominator.

$$\frac{2}{x+1} + \frac{5}{x-1} = -6$$

Multiply both sides by $(x + 1)(x - 1)$: $2(x - 1) + 5(x + 1) = -6(x + 1)(x - 1)$

Expand and simplify: $2x - 2 + 5x + 5 = -6(x^2 - 1)$

$$7x + 3 = -6x^2 + 6$$

Write in the form $ax^2 + bx + c = 0$: $6x^2 + 7x - 3 = 0$

Factor the left side: $(2x + 3)(3x - 1) = 0$

Use the zero product property: $2x + 3 = 0$ or $3x - 1 = 0$

$$x = -\frac{3}{2} \quad \text{or} \quad x = \frac{1}{3}$$

Check.

Substituting $x = -\dfrac{3}{2}$ and $x = \dfrac{1}{3}$ into the original equation verifies the solutions.

The roots are $-\dfrac{3}{2}$ and $\dfrac{1}{3}$.

$3, -1$

Example 5　Dimensions of a Soccer Pitch

The length of a soccer pitch is 20 m less than twice its width.
The area of the pitch is 6000 m². Find its dimensions.

Solution

Draw a diagram.
Let w metres represent the width of the pitch.
Then, the length of the pitch is represented by $2w - 20$.
The area of the pitch is represented by $w(2w - 20)$ or $2w^2 - 20w$.
Since the area is 6000 m²,

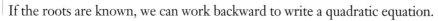

$$2w^2 - 20w = 6000$$

Write in the form $ax^2 + bx + c = 0$: $\quad 2w^2 - 20w - 6000 = 0$
Remove the common factor: $\qquad 2(w^2 - 10w - 3000) = 0$
Divide both sides by 2: $\qquad\quad w^2 - 10w - 3000 = 0$
Factor the left side: $\qquad\qquad (w - 60)(w + 50) = 0$
Use the zero product property: $\qquad w - 60 = 0 \text{ or } w + 50 = 0$
$$w = 60 \quad \text{or} \quad w = -50$$

The width of the pitch cannot be negative, so $w = -50$ is rejected.
Thus, the width of the pitch is 60 m.
The length of the pitch is $2(60) - 20$ or 100 m.
The dimensions of the pitch are 100 m by 60 m.
Check.
$100 \times 60 = 6000$

If the roots are known, we can work backward to write a quadratic equation.

Example 6　Writing an Equation

Write a quadratic equation whose roots are $-\dfrac{1}{2}$ and $\dfrac{4}{3}$.

Solution

If $\quad x = -\dfrac{1}{2}$ $\qquad$ If $\quad x = \dfrac{4}{3}$

$\qquad 2x = -1$ $\qquad\qquad\quad 3x = 4$

$\quad 2x + 1 = 0$ $\qquad\qquad 3x - 4 = 0$

So, $\quad (2x + 1)(3x - 4) = 0$
$\qquad\quad 6x^2 - 8x + 3x - 4 = 0$
$\qquad\qquad\quad 6x^2 - 5x - 4 = 0$

A quadratic equation whose roots are $-\dfrac{1}{2}$ and $\dfrac{4}{3}$ is $6x^2 - 5x - 4 = 0$.

Practice

Find the values of the variable that satisfy each equation.

1. $(x + 1)(x + 2) = 0$ $\qquad$ **2.** $(x + 3)(x - 1) = 0$
3. $(x - 5)(x - 5) = 0$ $\qquad$ **4.** $(x - 2)(x + 3) = 0$
5. $(2x + 1)(x - 3) = 0$ $\qquad$ **6.** $(3x + 4)(2x - 1) = 0$
7. $x(x + 9) = 0$ $\qquad\qquad$ **8.** $x(4 - x) = 0$

Write each equation in the form $ax^2 + bx + c = 0$.

9. $x^2 - 6 = 2x$ $\qquad\qquad$ **10.** $2y^2 - 3y = -2$
11. $3(z^2 + 1) = -4z$ $\qquad$ **12.** $(x + 1)^2 = 4$
13. $4m^2 = 3m$ $\qquad\qquad\quad$ **14.** $2(x^2 - 1) = x$

Write each equation in the form $ax^2 + bx + c = 0$.

15. $\dfrac{x^2}{2} + \dfrac{x}{3} = 1$

16. $2x^2 - \dfrac{x+1}{4} = 3$

17. $x - 1 = \dfrac{4}{x+1}$

18. $\dfrac{2}{y-1} + \dfrac{1}{y+2} = -3$

19. $t + \dfrac{3}{2} - \dfrac{4}{2t} = 0$

20. $\dfrac{2x}{3} + \dfrac{1}{x} = \dfrac{2}{5}$

Solve and check.

21. $n^2 + 7n + 12 = 0$

22. $y^2 - 3y + 2 = 0$

23. $x^2 - x - 6 = 0$

24. $a^2 - 8a + 16 = 0$

25. $0 = p^2 + 2p - 35$

26. $m^2 - 7m = 18$

Solve and check.

27. $2a^2 + 3a - 2 = 0$

28. $3s^2 - 4s + 1 = 0$

29. $2t^2 + 11t + 5 = 0$

30. $3x^2 + 7x - 6 = 0$

31. $0 = 4m^2 - 4m - 3$

32. $10y^2 - 16y = -6$

Solve.

33. $x^2 + 2x = 0$

34. $y^2 - 3y = 0$

35. $3m^2 + 2m = 0$

36. $5n^2 - 8n = 0$

37. $5t^2 - 20t = 0$

38. $0 = 4x + 3x^2$

Solve.

39. $x^2 - 2x - 11 = 4$

40. $w^2 + 30 = 9 + 10w$

41. $3p^2 + 8p - 9 = 2p$

42. $4t^2 = 12t - 9$

43. $5r^2 = 2r$

44. $(x-6)^2 - 8x = 0$

45. $(a+4)^2 = 4$

46. $(b-3)^2 = 9$

Solve and check.

47. $x - 1 = \dfrac{2}{x}$

48. $x - 2 = 4 - \dfrac{5}{x}$

49. $\dfrac{x^2}{4} - \dfrac{x}{3} = \dfrac{1}{3}$

50. $a = \dfrac{a-6}{a+6}$

51. $x + 2 = \dfrac{4}{x-1}$

52. $\dfrac{5y}{y^2 - 4} = 3$

53. $\dfrac{2}{s+3} - \dfrac{3}{s-2} = 2$

54. $1 + \dfrac{2x}{x+4} = \dfrac{3}{x-1}$

Write a quadratic equation with the given roots.

55. $-5, -3$

56. $2, 2$

57. $3, -3$

58. $4, -\dfrac{1}{2}$

59. $\dfrac{1}{3}, \dfrac{2}{3}$

60. $-\dfrac{3}{2}, \dfrac{1}{4}$

61. $0, -5$

62. $0, \dfrac{4}{3}$

Solve.

63. $2x(x-2) + x(x+1) = 0$

64. $x(2x-3) + 4(x+1) = 2(3+2x)$

65. $k^2 + (k+1)^2 + (k+2)^2 = 29$

66. $(2z+1)(2z-1) + 12 = 4(z+5) - 10$

67. $3(x-2)(x+1) - 2(x-1)^2 = 4$

68. $5g(g-4) + 48 = 2g(g+3)$

Applications and Problem Solving

69. Thrown object An object is thrown upward at a speed of 9 m/s from a height of 2 m. The height of the object, $h(t)$ metres, above the ground is approximately related to the time, t seconds, since the object was thrown by the function

$$h(t) = -5t^2 + 9t + 2$$

a) Substitute the value of $h(t)$ when the object hits the ground.

b) Solve the equation to find the time the object takes to hit the ground.

70. Numbers Two numbers differ by 6. If the numbers are squared and then added, the result is 146. What are the numbers?

71. Integers Two consecutive integers are added. The square of the sum is 361. What are the integers?

72. Numbers A number increased by 1 is multiplied by the same number decreased by 2 to give a result of 4. What is the number?

73. Numbers The product of two consecutive even numbers is 288. What are the numbers?

74. Integers When the square of an integer is added to ten times the integer, the sum is zero. What is the integer?

75. Measurement The area of the rectangle is 36 cm². What are its dimensions?

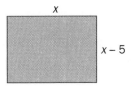

76. Numbers The sum of a number and its reciprocal is $\dfrac{13}{6}$. What is the number?

77. Numbers A number equals 2 divided by 1 less than the same number. What is the number?

78. Tenpin bowling A tenpin bowling lane is 17 m longer than it is wide. The area of the lane is 18 m^2. What are the dimensions of the lane?

79. Triple jump The takeoff board for the triple jump has an area of 2440 cm^2. The length of the board is 102 cm greater than the width. Find the dimensions of the board.

80. Carpets A rectangular carpet and a square carpet have equal areas. The square carpet has a side length of 4 m. The length of the rectangular carpet is 2 m less than three times its width. Find the dimensions of the rectangular carpet.

81. Measurement The hypotenuse of a right triangle is 17 cm long. One leg of the triangle is 7 cm longer than the other leg. Determine the lengths of the legs.

82. Geometry A regular polygon with n sides has $\dfrac{n(n-3)}{2}$ diagonals. Find the number of sides of a regular polygon that has 44 diagonals.

83. Measurement The rectangle has a perimeter of 5 units. Find the value of x.

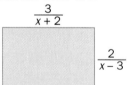

84. Area rug An area rug has a central 5 m by 3 m rectangle in a mosaic pattern, with a plain border of uniform width around it. The total area of the rug is 24 m^2. Find the width of the border.

85. Currency In Britain, people refer to their paper money as notes. A five-pound note is worth 5 pounds sterling. The length of a five-pound note is 5 mm less than twice the width. The area is 9450 mm^2.
a) Find the dimensions of a five-pound note.
b) How do the dimensions compare with those of a Canadian $20 bill?

86. Visualization a) Solve the equation $x^2 + 6x + 9 = 0$ by graphing. How many roots do there appear to be?
b) Solve the same equation by factoring. How many roots are there? How are they related?

87. Write a quadratic equation whose roots are p and q.

88. Solve for x.
a) $x^2 + 5xy + 4y^2 = 0$ **b)** $2x^2 - 5xy - 3y^2 = 0$
c) $4x^2 - 4xy + y^2 = 0$ **d)** $\dfrac{2x^2}{5} + \dfrac{7xy}{10} - \dfrac{y^2}{5} = 0$
e) $5x^2 + xy = 0$ **f)** $3x^2 - 7xy = 0$

89. a) Write a quadratic equation whose roots are $\dfrac{2}{3}$ and $-\dfrac{1}{2}$.
b) Is it possible to write another quadratic equation with the same roots? Explain.

90. If -3 is one root of the equation $3x^2 + mx + 3 = 0$,
a) what is the value of m?
b) what is the other root?

91. Write quadratic equations that can be solved by factoring and that have the following roots. Have a classmate solve your equations.
a) two roots that equal the same negative integer
b) two distinct roots that are positive integers
c) two distinct roots, one a positive fraction and the other a negative integer

PATTERN POWER

1. Describe the pattern in words.

11	14	8	20
19	18	2	15
28	0	19	8
12	12	10	22
15	13	4	

2. Find the missing number.

4.3 Quadratic Equations — The Square Root Principle

A quadratic equation of the form $ax^2 + bx + c = 0$, $a \neq 0$, simplifies to $ax^2 + c = 0$ when $b = 0$. The following are examples of quadratic equations in which $b = 0$.

$$x^2 - 1 = 0 \qquad -3y^2 + 27 = 0 \qquad 2x^2 = 8$$

Recall that you can solve an equation by performing the same operations on both sides. To solve the quadratic equation $x^2 = 25$ for x, you can take the square root of both sides.

$$x^2 = 25 \qquad \text{Read } \pm \text{ as "plus or minus."}$$
$$\pm\sqrt{x^2} = \pm\sqrt{25}$$
$$\pm x = \pm 5$$

There seem to be four cases to consider, but we can show that there are only two.

$x = 5$ or $-x = -5$ or $x = -5$ or $-x = 5$

$\qquad x = 5 \qquad\qquad\qquad x = -5$

Thus, the two cases are $x = 5$ or $x = -5$, which can be written as $x = \pm 5$.

There are two solutions, 5 and –5, since $(5)^2 = 25$ and $(-5)^2 = 25$.

Explore: Use the Diagram

Canada has many interesting archaeological sites, including the 7500-year-old L'Anse Amour burial site in southern Labrador. Before archaeologists begin to dig up a site, they divide it into a grid of congruent squares.

The diagram shows a site divided into a grid of 16 squares. The side length of each small square on the grid is represented by x.

Write an expression in terms of x for
a) the side length of the whole site   **b)** the area of the site

Inquire

1. A site divided into 16 squares has an area of 144 m². Write an equation that relates this area to the expression you wrote in b), above.

2. Isolate x^2 on one side of the equation.

3. Solve the resulting equation for x.

4. Must either value of x be rejected? Explain.

5. A site divided into a 10 by 10 grid has an area of 400 m². Write and solve an equation to find the side length of each small grid square.

6. A chessboard is made up of 64 small squares. Let s represent the side length of each small square.
a) Write an expression in terms of s for the area of the chessboard.
b) If the area of a chessboard is 576 cm², what is the value of s?
c) If the area of a chessboard is 784 cm², what is the value of s?

7. Solve each equation.

a) $x^2 = 36$ **b)** $y^2 = 49$ **c)** $w^2 = 121$

d) $2n^2 = 8$ **e)** $4t^2 = 100$ **f)** $50r^2 = 72$

Example 1 Solving When $a = 1$, $b = 0$

Solve and check $x^2 - 14 = 155$.

Solution 1 Taking the Square Root

$$x^2 - 14 = 155$$

Add 14 to both sides: $x^2 = 169$

Take the square root of both sides: $x = \pm 13$

Solution 2 Solving by Factoring

$$x^2 - 14 = 155$$

Subtract 155 from both sides: $x^2 - 169 = 0$

Factor the left side: $(x + 13)(x - 13) = 0$

Use the zero product property: $x + 13 = 0$ or $x - 13 = 0$

$$x = -13 \quad \text{or} \quad x = 13$$

Check for both solutions.

For $x = 13$,

L.S. $= x^2 - 14$ **R.S.** $= 155$
$= (13)^2 - 14$
$= 169 - 14$
$= 155$

For $x = -13$,

L.S. $= x^2 - 14$ **R.S.** $= 155$
$= (-13)^2 - 14$
$= 169 - 14$
$= 155$

The roots are 13 and −13.

Example 2 Solving When $a \neq 1$, $b = 0$

For the quadratic equation $9y^2 - 21 = 0$,

a) find the exact solutions

b) calculate the solutions, to the nearest hundredth

Solution

a)

$$9y^2 - 21 = 0$$

Divide both sides by 3: $3y^2 - 7 = 0$

Add 7 to both sides: $3y^2 = 7$

Divide both sides by 3: $y^2 = \dfrac{7}{3}$

Take the square root of both sides: $y = \pm\sqrt{\dfrac{7}{3}}$

Rationalize the denominator: $= \pm\dfrac{\sqrt{21}}{3}$ $\dfrac{\sqrt{7}}{\sqrt{3}} \times \dfrac{\sqrt{3}}{\sqrt{3}} = \dfrac{\sqrt{21}}{3}$

The exact solutions are $\dfrac{\sqrt{21}}{3}$ and $\dfrac{-\sqrt{21}}{3}$.

b) $\dfrac{\sqrt{21}}{3} \doteq 1.53$

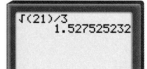

The solutions are 1.53 and −1.53, to the nearest hundredth.

Example 3   Square of a Binomial on One Side

Solve and check $(x + 3)^2 = 16$.

Solution

$$(x + 3)^2 = 16$$

Take the square root of both sides: $x + 3 = \pm 4$

Solve for x: $x + 3 = 4$ or $x + 3 = -4$

$$x = 1 \quad \text{or} \quad x = -7$$

Check.

For $x = 1$,   For $x = -7$,

L.S. $= (1 + 3)^2$ R.S. $= 16$ L.S. $= (-7 + 3)^2$ R.S. $= 16$

$\quad = 4^2$ $\quad = (-4)^2$

$\quad = 16$ $\quad = 16$

The roots are 1 and –7.

Example 4   Canada's Olympic Swimming Medals

In the first 96 years of the modern Olympics, Canada won many medals in swimming events. Twenty-five more than twice the square of the number of gold medals equalled the square of the number of silver medals. Canada won 15 silver medals. How many gold medals did Canada win?

Solution

Let g represent the number of gold medals. Twenty-five more than twice the square of this number is represented by $2g^2 + 25$. Canada won 15 silver medals. The square of 15 is 225. Solving the equation $2g^2 + 25 = 225$ gives the number of gold medals Canada won.

$$2g^2 + 25 = 225$$

Subtract 25 from both sides: $2g^2 = 200$

Divide both sides by 2: $g^2 = 100$

Take the square root of both sides: $g = \pm 10$

Since Canada could not have won a negative number of gold medals, the negative root is rejected.

So, Canada won 10 gold medals.

Practice

Solve.

1. $x^2 = 81$

2. $3z^2 = 192$

3. $4d^2 = 25$

4. $\dfrac{a^2}{2} = 8$

Solve and check.

5. $x^2 - 25 = 0$

6. $y^2 + 12 = 48$

7. $n^2 + 4 = 20$

8. $m^2 - 7.5 = 92.5$

9. $1.3 = x^2 + 0.3$

10. $1.25 + z^2 = 1.5$

11. $\dfrac{z^2 - 1}{5} = 7$

12. $2 = \dfrac{4 + x^2}{10}$

Solve and check.

13. $2x^2 - 32 = 0$

14. $3x^2 + 2 = 29$

15. $4x^2 + 5 = 21$

16. $125 = 3y^2 - 22$

17. $2x^2 - 0.42 = 2$

18. $10c^2 + 2.2 = 7.1$

19. $\dfrac{3y^2 + 7}{2} = 5$

20. $\dfrac{1 - 5n^2}{4} = -31$

Find the solutions, to the nearest hundredth.

21. $v^2 - 15 = 0$

22. $m^2 + 15 = 35$

23. $12 + x^2 = 52$

24. $10 - z^2 = 4$

25. $5k^2 - 67 = 18$

26. $4t^2 - 50 = -2$

27. $2a^2 - 6 = 14$

28. $73 - 3d^2 = 34$

29. $7x^2 - 3 = 1$

30. $-2 = 12 - 5d^2$

31. $\dfrac{x^2}{2} - \dfrac{1}{3} = 0$

32. $\dfrac{y^2 - 3}{4} = \dfrac{7}{2}$

Find the exact solutions.

33. $x^2 = 12$

34. $y^2 - 75 = 0$

35. $w^2 - 23 = 22$

36. $z^2 - 21 = -3$

37. $43 = 3 + 5g^2$

38. $2y^2 + 14 = 230$

39. $3t^2 + 14 = 19$

40. $10x^2 - 11 = 5$

41. $5 - 2p^2 = 4$

42. $-19 = 7 - 8n^2$

43. $\dfrac{2x^2}{3} = 3$

44. $2 - \dfrac{m^2}{5} = -\dfrac{1}{4}$

Solve and check.

45. $(x - 1)^2 = 0$

46. $(y + 2)^2 = 9$

47. $(z + 1)^2 = 1$

48. $(3 - c)^2 - 16 = 0$

49. $\left(x + \dfrac{1}{2}\right)^2 = \dfrac{1}{4}$

50. $\left(m - \dfrac{1}{3}\right)^2 = \dfrac{4}{9}$

51. $(2x - 3)^2 = 25$

52. $(1 - 2g)^2 = 49$

53. $3(b + 5)^2 - 8 = 4$

54. $-2(4t - 1)^2 + 72 = 0$

55. $\dfrac{(a + 2)^2}{4} = 16$

56. $\dfrac{(2n - 1)^2}{3} - 27 = 0$

Solve.

57. $(3y + 2)^2 = 0$

58. $(4m - 1)^2 = 49$

59. $(2k + 7)^2 = 4$

60. $9 - (3 - 5a)^2 = 0$

61. $(2s - 1)^2 = 0.25$

62. $1.21 = (10b + 1)^2$

63. $2(2x + 1)^2 = 0.98$

64. $\dfrac{(6z - 1)^2}{3} - 3 = 0$

Find the exact solutions. Then, calculate the solutions, to the nearest hundredth.

65. $(x - 5)^2 = 3$

66. $8 = (w + 3)^2$

67. $(3z - 1)^2 = 5$

68. $(4r + 3)^2 = 20$

69. $4(y + 3)^2 + 3 = 10$

70. $\dfrac{1}{2}(2n - 5)^2 - 3 = 6$

Applications and Problem Solving

71. Garden a) A garden has an area of 28 m². It contains a square flower bed and 19 m² of lawn. Write and solve an equation to find the dimensions of the flower bed.

b) Subtracting the square of a number from 28 gives a result of 19. Write and solve an equation to find the number.

c) Explain why your answers from parts a) and b) are different.

72. Integers Three times the square of an integer is 432. Find the integer.

73. Integers Eighteen more than the square of an integer is 43. What is the integer?

74. Alberta flag The length of an Alberta flag is twice the width.

a) Let w represent the width. Write an expression to represent the length.

b) Write an expression to represent the area.

c) Write and solve an equation to find the dimensions of an Alberta flag with an area of 800 cm².

75. Falling object The height, h metres, of a falling object is related to the time, t seconds, the object has been falling by the formula
$$h = -4.9t^2 + d$$
where d metres is the initial height of the object above the ground. The Bankers Hall building in Calgary is 196 m tall. Express the time an object takes to reach the ground from this height

a) as an exact number of seconds

b) to the nearest tenth of a second

76. Pendulum The period of a pendulum is the time it takes to swing back and forth once. The period, T seconds, is approximately related to the length of the pendulum, l metres, by the following equation.
$$T^2 = 4l$$

a) What is the period of a pendulum with a length of 1 m?

b) The longest pendulum in North America is in Portland, Oregon. The pendulum has a length of 27.4 m. What is the period of the pendulum, to the nearest tenth of a second?

77. Integers Four less than twice the square of an integer is 28. Find the integer.

78. Numbers Adding 1.25 to three times the square of a number gives 20. Find the number.

79. Numbers Seventy-one reduced by three times the square of a number is 50. Calculate the number, to the nearest hundredth.

80. Integers Squaring three less than an integer gives 289. What is the integer?

81. Numbers The sum of a number and its reciprocal is five times the number. What is the number?

82. Numbers The sum of half the square of a number and one fifth the square of the number is 10.
a) Find the exact value of the number.
b) Calculate the number, to the nearest hundredth.

83. Provinces Adding 19 to the square of the number of provinces in South Africa gives the square of the number of provinces in Canada. How many provinces are there in South Africa?

84. Governors General Manitoba-born Edward Schreyer and Saskatchewan-born Jeanne Sauvé each served as Canada's Governor General. Subtracting 10 from the square of the number of years in Edward Schreyer's term gives the number of years in Jeanne Sauvé's term. Jeanne Sauvé served as Governor General for 6 years. For how many years did Edward Schreyer serve as Governor General?

85. Photograph When a 1 cm wide frame is placed around a square photograph, the total area of the photograph and the frame is 169 cm². What are the dimensions of the photograph?

86. Measurement The surface area of a cube is 73.5 cm². Find the length of one edge.

87. Measurement Find the dimensions of both squares in each diagram. The area of the shaded region is given in each case.

a)

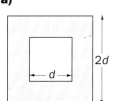

b)

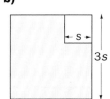

Shaded area = 48 cm²   Shaded area = 72 cm²

88. Solve.
a) $3(2x^2 + 5) = 5(3x^2 - 2)$
b) $2y(y - 1) - y(y - 2) - 9 = 0$
c) $3(x + 2) = (x + 1)(2x + 1)$
d) $(2x - 1)(2x - 3) = -4(2x - 5)$
e) $2(a + 1)(a + 3) = (a + 4)^2$
f) $\dfrac{(m - 1)^2}{2} - \dfrac{(m - 2)^2}{4} = 0$

g) $(2n + 3)^2 = (3n + 2)^2$
h) $(4z - 3)(z - 2) = (z - 6)(z - 5)$
i) $-5(x - 1)(x + 2) = (3x - 1)(2x - 1)$

89. Find each solution. Round each solution to the nearest tenth, if necessary.
a) $\dfrac{3}{x^2 - 1} = 1$
b) $3y + \dfrac{2}{y} = 4y$
c) $\dfrac{4}{z + 2} = z - 2$
d) $\dfrac{x}{2} + \dfrac{2}{3x} = 2x$
e) $\dfrac{1}{(a - 2)^2} = 4$
f) $\dfrac{3}{2} - \dfrac{1}{(x + 1)^2} = -\dfrac{3}{4}$

90. Can you solve the equation $\dfrac{3(x^2 + 1) - 9}{x^2 - 2} = 1$? Explain.

91. Measurement The area of the shaded square is 36 cm². Calculate
a) the side length of the larger square, to the nearest tenth of a centimetre
b) the area of the larger square

92. Inequalities Investigate the solutions to the following inequalities. Graph the solutions on a number line.
a) $x^2 < 9$
b) $x^2 \geq 25$

93. Is there a real number such that 15 more than the square of the number equals 11? Explain.

94. Write two problems similar to questions 72, 73 or 77–82. Have a classmate solve your problems.

WORD POWER

Change the word SILK to the word WORM by changing one letter at a time. You must form a real word each time you change a letter. The best solution has the fewest steps.

4.4 Solving Quadratic Equations by Completing the Square

The process of completing the square, which was used to graph quadratic functions, can also be used to solve quadratic equations.

In Roman times, a city forum was a large open space surrounded by buildings. It provided a meeting place and a centre for public life.

The Roman city of Pompeii was destroyed by the eruption of Mount Vesuvius in A.D. 79, but a coating of ash protected the city's buildings and streets. The continuing excavation of Pompeii allows visitors to see how citizens of the Roman Empire lived.

Explore: Use a Diagram

The forum in Pompeii was a rectangle whose length was 120 m greater than the width.

a) Let the width of the forum be x. Write an expression in expanded form to represent the area of the forum.

b) The area of the forum was 6400 m^2. Write an equation with the expression from part a) on the left side and the numerical value of the area on the right side.

Inquire

1. a) Add a number to the left side of the equation to make the left side a perfect square.

b) Why must this number also be added to the right side of the equation?

2. Write the left side as the square of a binomial, and simplify the right side.

3. Take the square root of both sides.

4. Solve for x.

5. Should either value of x be rejected? Explain.

6. For the forum in Pompeii, what was
a) the width?   **b)** the length?

7. Solve the following equations using the above method.
a) $x^2 + 4x = 12$ **b)** $x^2 - 2x = 3$ **c)** $x^2 + 6x = -8$

Most quadratic equations cannot be solved by factoring. The related quadratic functions can be graphed to find the x-intercepts, but exact solutions cannot always be found by this method.

The algebraic method of completing the square gives exact solutions to a quadratic equation. One of the steps in the process involves using the square root principle.

A quadratic equation can be solved using the square root principle if the equation is expressed in the form
$$(x + m)^2 = d$$
$$\text{or } x^2 + 2mx + m^2 = d$$

Example 1   Completing the Square
Solve $x^2 - 6x - 27 = 0$ by completing the square.

Solution

$$x^2 - 6x - 27 = 0$$

Add 27 to both sides:
Add the square of half the coefficient of x to both sides:

$$x^2 - 6x = 27$$
$$x^2 - 6x \boxed{+9} = 27 \boxed{+9}$$
$$x^2 - 6x + 9 = 36$$

Write the left side as the square of a binomial:
Take the square root of both sides:
Solve for x:

$$(x - 3)^2 = 36$$
$$x - 3 = \pm 6$$
$$x - 3 = 6 \text{ or } x - 3 = -6$$
$$x = 9 \quad \text{or} \quad x = -3$$

The roots are 9 and –3.

The solution to Example 1 can be visualized graphically.

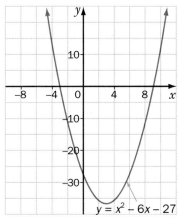

$y = x^2 - 6x - 27$

Example 2 Irrational Roots
Solve and check $x^2 + 8x + 11 = 0$.

Solution

$$x^2 + 8x + 11 = 0$$

Subtract 11 from both sides:
$$x^2 + 8x = -11$$

Add the square of half the coefficient of x to both sides:
$$x^2 + 8x + 16 = -11 + 16$$

$$x^2 + 8x + 16 = 5$$

Write the left side as the square of a binomial:
$$(x + 4)^2 = 5$$

Take the square root of both sides:
$$x + 4 = \pm\sqrt{5}$$

Solve for x:
$$x + 4 = \sqrt{5} \quad \text{or} \quad x + 4 = -\sqrt{5}$$
$$x = -4 + \sqrt{5} \quad \text{or} \quad x = -4 - \sqrt{5}$$

Check.
For $x = -4 + \sqrt{5}$,

$$\begin{aligned}
\textbf{L.S.} &= (-4 + \sqrt{5})^2 + 8(-4 + \sqrt{5}) + 11 \qquad \textbf{R.S.} = 0\\
&= 16 - 8\sqrt{5} + 5 - 32 + 8\sqrt{5} + 11\\
&= 32 - 8\sqrt{5} - 32 + 8\sqrt{5}\\
&= 0
\end{aligned}$$

$(-4 + \sqrt{5})(-4 + \sqrt{5}) = 16 - 4\sqrt{5} - 4\sqrt{5} + 5$

For $x = -4 - \sqrt{5}$,

$$\begin{aligned}
\textbf{L.S.} &= (-4 - \sqrt{5})^2 + 8(-4 - \sqrt{5}) + 11 \qquad \textbf{R.S.} = 0\\
&= 16 + 8\sqrt{5} + 5 - 32 - 8\sqrt{5} + 11\\
&= 32 + 8\sqrt{5} - 32 - 8\sqrt{5}\\
&= 0
\end{aligned}$$

$(-4 - \sqrt{5})(-4 - \sqrt{5}) = 16 + 4\sqrt{5} + 4\sqrt{5} + 5$

The roots are $-4 + \sqrt{5}$ and $-4 - \sqrt{5}$.

If the coefficient of x^2 is not 1, divide each term of the equation by the coefficient of x^2 before completing the square.

Example 3 Solving When $a \neq 1$
Find the roots of $2x^2 - 5x - 1 = 0$, to the nearest hundredth.

Solution

$$2x^2 - 5x - 1 = 0$$

Divide both sides by 2:
$$x^2 - \frac{5}{2}x - \frac{1}{2} = 0$$

Add $\frac{1}{2}$ to both sides:
$$x^2 - \frac{5}{2}x = \frac{1}{2}$$

Complete the square:
$$x^2 - \frac{5}{2}x + \frac{25}{16} = \frac{1}{2} + \frac{25}{16}$$

Write the left side as the square of a binomial:
$$\left(x - \frac{5}{4}\right)^2 = \frac{33}{16}$$

Take the square root of both sides:
$$x - \frac{5}{4} = \pm\frac{\sqrt{33}}{4}$$

Solve for x:
$$x = \frac{5}{4} \pm \frac{\sqrt{33}}{4}$$

The exact roots are $\dfrac{5+\sqrt{33}}{4}$ and $\dfrac{5-\sqrt{33}}{4}$.

The roots are 2.69 and -0.19, to the nearest hundredth.

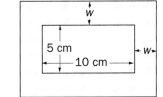

Estimate
$\sqrt{33} \doteq 6$
$\dfrac{5+6}{4} \doteq 3 \qquad \dfrac{5-6}{4} = -\dfrac{1}{4}$

```
(5+√(33))/4
           2.686140662
(5-√(33))/4
           -.186140662
```

Example 4   Framing a Picture
A picture that measures 10 cm by 5 cm is to be surrounded by a mat before being framed. The width of the mat is to be the same on all sides of the picture. The area of the mat is to be twice the area of the picture. What is the width of the mat?

Solution
Draw a diagram. Let the width of the mat be w cm.
Then, $w > 0$. Write and solve an equation to find w.
The dimensions of the picture plus the mat are
$(10 + 2w)$ by $(5 + 2w)$.
The total area is 3×50 or 150 cm^2.
So, $(10 + 2w)(5 + 2w) = 150$

$$(10 + 2w)(5 + 2w) = 150$$

Expand the left side: $\qquad 50 + 20w + 10w + 4w^2 = 150$

Simplify: $\qquad 4w^2 + 30w = 100$

Divide both sides by 4: $\qquad w^2 + \dfrac{15}{2}w = 25$

Complete the square: $\qquad w^2 + \dfrac{15}{2}w + \dfrac{225}{16} = 25 + \dfrac{225}{16}$

Write the left side as the square of a binomial: $\qquad \left(w + \dfrac{15}{4}\right)^2 = \dfrac{625}{16}$

Take the square root of both sides: $\qquad w + \dfrac{15}{4} = \pm\dfrac{25}{4}$

Solve for w: $\qquad w = -\dfrac{15}{4} + \dfrac{25}{4}$ or $w = -\dfrac{15}{4} - \dfrac{25}{4}$

$$= \dfrac{10}{4} \qquad\qquad = -\dfrac{40}{4}$$

$$= \dfrac{5}{2} \qquad\qquad = -10$$

The root -10 is rejected, since $w > 0$.

So, $w = \dfrac{5}{2}$

The width of the mat is 2.5 cm.

Check.
The overall dimensions of the mat and the picture are about
$10 + 2(2.5)$ by $5 + 2(2.5)$, or 15 cm by 10 cm.
The total area is about 15×10 or 150 cm^2.
The area of the mat is $150 - 50$ or 100 cm^2, which is twice the area of the picture.

Recall the Steps

Understand the Problem

Think of a Plan

Carry Out the Plan

Look Back

Practice

State the value of k that makes each expression a perfect square trinomial. Then, write the trinomial as the square of a binomial.

1. $x^2 + 2x + k$ **2.** $x^2 + 10x + k$

3. $t^2 - 8t + k$ **4.** $w^2 - 14w + k$

5. $m^2 + 3m + k$ **6.** $x^2 + 7x + k$

7. $p^2 - 5p + k$ **8.** $q^2 - 11q + k$

9. $x^2 + \dfrac{4}{3}x + k$ **10.** $d^2 - \dfrac{2}{3}d + k$

11. $x^2 - \dfrac{1}{2}x + k$ **12.** $r^2 + \dfrac{r}{5} + k$

13. $x^2 + 1.4x + k$ **14.** $x^2 - 0.06x + k$

Solve.

15. $(x + 3)^2 = 9$ **16.** $(x - 10)^2 - 1 = 0$

17. $(p + 1)^2 = \dfrac{1}{9}$ **18.** $(x + 2)^2 = \dfrac{9}{4}$

19. $(s - 1)^2 = 8$ **20.** $(y - 4)^2 - 12 = 0$

21. $4 = \left(x + \dfrac{1}{2}\right)^2$ **22.** $\left(x - \dfrac{1}{3}\right)^2 = \dfrac{7}{9}$

23. $\left(a + \dfrac{3}{4}\right)^2 = \dfrac{3}{16}$ **24.** $\left(c + \dfrac{3}{2}\right)^2 = \dfrac{3}{8}$

25. $(n - 0.5)^2 = 1.21$ **26.** $(x + 0.4)^2 - 0.01 = 0$

Solve by completing the square. Express solutions in simplest radical form.

27. $x^2 + 6x + 4 = 0$ **28.** $w^2 - 4w - 11 = 0$

29. $t^2 + 8t - 7 = 0$ **30.** $x^2 - 10x = 3$

31. $d^2 = 7d - 9$ **32.** $0 = x^2 - 5x + 2$

33. $x - 3 = -x^2$ **34.** $4 + y^2 = 20y$

Solve by completing the square. Express solutions in simplest radical form.

35. $2x^2 + 8x + 5 = 0$ **36.** $3x^2 - 6x + 2 = 0$

37. $4t^2 + 10t + 5 = 0$ **38.** $3m^2 + 4m = 2$

39. $6x^2 + 3x - 2 = 0$ **40.** $0 = 3w^2 - 5w - 2$

41. $2x - 6 = -5x^2$ **42.** $1 - 2z = 5z^2$

43. $\dfrac{1}{2}x^2 + x - 13 = 0$ **44.** $0.3y^2 - 0.2y = 0.3$

Solve. Round solutions to the nearest hundredth.

45. $x^2 + 2x - 1 = 0$ **46.** $x^2 - 4x + 1 = 0$

47. $w^2 + 2w - 5 = 0$ **48.** $d^2 + d = 7$

49. $0 = 2r^2 - 8r + 3$ **50.** $5x^2 = 4 - 10x$

51. $7x + 4 = -2x^2$ **52.** $\dfrac{2}{3}x^2 - 2x - 3 = 0$

53. $\dfrac{1}{4}n^2 + n = -\dfrac{1}{8}$ **54.** $1.2x^2 - 3x - 6 = 0$

Applications and Problem Solving

55. The Olympeion The enormous temple Olympeion was constructed in Athens, Greece, in 174 B.C. The base of the temple is a rectangle with a perimeter of 300 m. The area of the base is 4400 m². What are the dimensions of the base?

56. Measurement The base of a triangle is 2 cm more than the height. The area of the triangle is 5 cm². Find the base, to the nearest tenth of a centimetre.

57. Measurement The length of a rectangle is 2 m more than the width. The area of the rectangle is 20 m². Find the dimensions of the rectangle, to the nearest tenth of a metre.

58. Measurement The length and width of a rectangle are 6 m and 4 m. When each dimension is increased by the same amount, the area of the new rectangle is 50 m². Find the dimensions of the new rectangle, to the nearest tenth of a metre.

59. Skating rink A rectangular skating rink measures 40 m by 20 m. It is to be doubled in area by extending each side by the same amount. Determine how much each side should be extended, to the nearest tenth of a metre.

60. Measurement A triangle has a height of 6 cm and a base of 8 cm. If the height and the base are both decreased by the same amount, the area of the new triangle is 20 cm². What are the base and height of the new triangle, to the nearest tenth of a centimetre?

61. Integers The sum of an integer and its square is 210. Find the integer.

62. Measurement A square of side length $x + 1$ has an area of 6 square units. Find the value of x, to the nearest hundredth.

63. Numbers The sum of two numbers is 14, and their product is 37. What are the numbers
a) in simplest radical form?
b) to the nearest thousandth?

64. Numbers Subtracting a number from half its square gives a result of 13. Express the possible values of the number in simplest radical form.

65. Television screens The size of a television screen or a computer monitor is usually stated as the length of the diagonal. A screen has a 38-cm diagonal. The width of the screen is 6 cm more than the height. Find the dimensions of the screen, to the nearest tenth of a centimetre.

66. Solve. Express each solution in simplest radical form.
a) $x(x + 3) = 2x(x + 5) + 1$
b) $3(n - 1)^2 = (n + 1)(2n + 1)$
c) $\dfrac{1}{2}(r + 2)^2 = \dfrac{1}{3}(2r - 1)^2$
d) $(4x - 1)(3x + 7) = (5x - 1)(2x + 3) - 6$

67. Solve each equation. Express each solution in simplest radical form. State any restrictions on the variable.
a) $\dfrac{3}{x} - \dfrac{4}{2x} = x + 1$
b) $\dfrac{3}{2z + 1} = z - 3$
c) $\dfrac{2y}{y^2 - 15} = 3$
d) $\dfrac{1}{x + 1} + \dfrac{2}{x - 1} = 4$

68. Football The function $h(t) = -5t^2 + 20t + 2$ gives the height of a thrown football as a function of the time, t seconds, since it was thrown. The ball hit the ground before a receiver could get near it.
a) How long was the ball in the air, to the nearest tenth of a second?
b) For how many seconds was the height of the ball at least 17 m?

69. Selling bread A bakery sells 50 loaves a day of a particular bread at $1.50 a loaf. Research indicates that, for every 10¢ increase in the price, 2 fewer loaves would be sold.
a) Show that the following equation can be solved to find the number of 10¢ increases that will result in a daily income of $80.00 from this type of bread.
$$0.2x^2 - 2x + 5 = 0$$
b) Solve the equation to find the number of 10¢ increases.
c) What is the new price of a loaf of bread?
d) What prices would give a daily income of at least $79.20?

70. For what values of k is $x^2 + kx + \dfrac{49}{4}$ a perfect square trinomial?

71. Solve each equation for x by completing the square.
a) $x^2 + 2x = k$
b) $kx^2 - 2x = k$
c) $x^2 = kx + 1$

72. Write a quadratic equation with the given roots.
a) $\sqrt{5}$ and $-\sqrt{5}$
b) $3 + \sqrt{2}$ and $3 - \sqrt{2}$
c) $-1 + 2\sqrt{3}$ and $-1 - 2\sqrt{3}$
d) $3 + \dfrac{\sqrt{13}}{2}$ and $3 - \dfrac{\sqrt{13}}{2}$

73. Find the values of k that make $x^2 + (k + 7)x + (7k + 1)$ a perfect square trinomial.

74. Solve $x^2 + bx + c = 0$ for x by completing the square.

PATTERN POWER

Find the missing number.

4.5 The Quadratic Formula

Canadians Phillipe LaRoche and Lloyd Langlois won silver and bronze medals for Canada in the freestyle skiing aerials competition at the Winter Olympics in Lillehammer, Norway. In this competition, jumpers are judged in three categories: air, form, and landing. In the air category, points are awarded for the takeoff, height, and distance.

The path of one skier from the top of the kicker (ramp) to the landing point can be modelled by the function
$$h(d) = -0.2d^2 + 2.5d + 8$$
where $h(d)$ is the height in metres above the landing point, and d is the horizontal distance from the kicker.

Since $h(d) = 0$ when the skier lands, solving the equation
$$-0.2d^2 + 2.5d + 8 = 0$$
gives the horizontal distance from the kicker to the landing point.

This equation, and all other quadratic equations, can be solved using a formula developed by solving the quadratic equation $ax^2 + bx + c = 0$ by completing the square.

Explore: Describe the Steps

The following steps show how completing the square is used to solve $ax^2 + bx + c = 0$. Describe what takes place in each step of the general case. Use the example as a guide.

Step	General Case $ax^2 + bx + c = 0$	Example $2x^2 + 3x - 1 = 0$
1	$x^2 + \dfrac{b}{a}x + \dfrac{c}{a} = 0$	$x^2 + \dfrac{3}{2}x - \dfrac{1}{2} = 0$
2	$x^2 + \dfrac{b}{a}x = -\dfrac{c}{a}$	$x^2 + \dfrac{3}{2}x = \dfrac{1}{2}$
3	$x^2 + \dfrac{b}{a}x + \dfrac{b^2}{4a^2} = \dfrac{b^2}{4a^2} - \dfrac{c}{a}$	$x^2 + \dfrac{3}{2}x + \dfrac{9}{16} = \dfrac{9}{16} + \dfrac{1}{2}$
4	$\left(x + \dfrac{b}{2a}\right)^2 = \dfrac{b^2}{4a^2} - \dfrac{c}{a}$	$\left(x + \dfrac{3}{4}\right)^2 = \dfrac{9}{16} + \dfrac{1}{2}$
5	$\left(x + \dfrac{b}{2a}\right)^2 = \dfrac{b^2 - 4ac}{4a^2}$	$\left(x + \dfrac{3}{4}\right)^2 = \dfrac{9 + 8}{16}$
6	$x + \dfrac{b}{2a} = \pm\sqrt{\dfrac{b^2 - 4ac}{4a^2}}$	$x + \dfrac{3}{4} = \pm\sqrt{\dfrac{17}{16}}$
7	$x + \dfrac{b}{2a} = \pm\dfrac{\sqrt{b^2 - 4ac}}{2a}$	$x + \dfrac{3}{4} = \pm\dfrac{\sqrt{17}}{4}$
8	$x + \dfrac{b}{2a} - \dfrac{b}{2a} = -\dfrac{b}{2a} \pm \dfrac{\sqrt{b^2 - 4ac}}{2a}$	$x + \dfrac{3}{4} - \dfrac{3}{4} = -\dfrac{3}{4} \pm \dfrac{\sqrt{17}}{4}$
9	$x = -\dfrac{b}{2a} \pm \dfrac{\sqrt{b^2 - 4ac}}{2a}$	$x = -\dfrac{3}{4} \pm \dfrac{\sqrt{17}}{4}$
10	$x = \dfrac{-b \pm \sqrt{b^2 - 4ac}}{2a}$	$x = \dfrac{-3 \pm \sqrt{17}}{4}$

In the general case, the roots are $x = \dfrac{-b + \sqrt{b^2 - 4ac}}{2a}$ and $x = \dfrac{-b - \sqrt{b^2 - 4ac}}{2a}$.

In the example, the roots are $x = \dfrac{-3 + \sqrt{17}}{4}$ and $x = \dfrac{-3 - \sqrt{17}}{4}$.

Inquire

1. What are the values of a, b, and c in the equation $x^2 + 3x + 2 = 0$?

2. Using the values from question 1, evaluate

a) $b^2 - 4ac$ **b)** $\sqrt{b^2 - 4ac}$ **c)** $\dfrac{-b + \sqrt{b^2 - 4ac}}{2a}$ **d)** $\dfrac{-b - \sqrt{b^2 - 4ac}}{2a}$

3. Check that the answers to questions 2c) and 2d) are the roots of $x^2 + 3x + 2 = 0$.

4. Use the same method to solve the following quadratic equations.
a) $x^2 + 4x + 3 = 0$ **b)** $x^2 + x - 12 = 0$ **c)** $x^2 + 4x - 5 = 0$

A quadratic equation written in the form $ax^2 + bx + c = 0$, $a \neq 0$, can be solved using the **quadratic formula**, that is,

$$x = \dfrac{-b \pm \sqrt{b^2 - 4ac}}{2a}$$

Example 1   Rational Roots
Solve $3x^2 + 5x - 2 = 0$.

Solution
For $3x^2 + 5x - 2 = 0$, $a = 3$, $b = 5$, and $c = -2$.
Substitute these values into the quadratic formula.

$$x = \dfrac{-b \pm \sqrt{b^2 - 4ac}}{2a}$$

$$= \dfrac{-5 \pm \sqrt{5^2 - 4(3)(-2)}}{2(3)}$$

$$= \dfrac{-5 \pm \sqrt{25 + 24}}{6}$$

$$= \dfrac{-5 \pm \sqrt{49}}{6}$$

$$= \dfrac{-5 \pm 7}{6}$$

The solution can be visualized graphically.

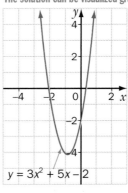

$y = 3x^2 + 5x - 2$

So, $x = \dfrac{-5 + 7}{6}$ or $x = \dfrac{-5 - 7}{6}$

$\qquad = \dfrac{2}{6} \qquad\qquad = -\dfrac{12}{6}$

$\qquad = \dfrac{1}{3} \qquad\qquad = -2$

The roots are $\dfrac{1}{3}$ and -2.

Example 2   Irrational Roots
Solve and check $x^2 - 2x - 1 = 0$.

Solution

For $x^2 - 2x - 1 = 0$, $a = 1$, $b = -2$, and $c = -1$.

The solution can be visualized graphically.

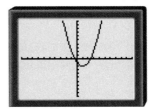

$$x = \frac{-b \pm \sqrt{b^2 - 4ac}}{2a}$$

$$= \frac{-(-2) \pm \sqrt{(-2)^2 - 4(1)(-1)}}{2(1)}$$

$$= \frac{2 \pm \sqrt{8}}{2}$$

$$= \frac{2 \pm 2\sqrt{2}}{2}$$

$$= 1 \pm \sqrt{2}$$

Check.

For $x = 1 + \sqrt{2}$,
L.S. $= x^2 - 2x - 1$ **R.S.** $= 0$
$= (1 + \sqrt{2})^2 - 2(1 + \sqrt{2}) - 1$
$= 1 + 2\sqrt{2} + 2 - 2 - 2\sqrt{2} - 1$
$= 0$

For $x = 1 - \sqrt{2}$,
L.S. $= x^2 - 2x - 1$ **R.S.** $= 0$
$= (1 - \sqrt{2})^2 - 2(1 - \sqrt{2}) - 1$
$= 1 + 2\sqrt{2} + 2 - 2 - 2\sqrt{2} - 1$
$= 0$

The roots are $1 + \sqrt{2}$ and $1 - \sqrt{2}$.

To use the quadratic formula, rewrite quadratic equations in the form $ax^2 + bx + c = 0$, if necessary.

Example 3   Variable in the Denominator
Solve $\dfrac{2}{x+1} + \dfrac{3}{x-2} = \dfrac{2x^2}{x^2 - x - 2}$, to the nearest hundredth.

Solution

$$\frac{2}{x+1} + \frac{3}{x-2} = \frac{2x^2}{x^2 - x - 2}$$

Factor $x^2 - x - 2$:

$$\frac{2}{x+1} + \frac{3}{x-2} = \frac{2x^2}{(x+1)(x-2)}$$

Multiply both sides by $(x+1)(x-2)$: $2(x-2) + 3(x+1) = 2x^2$
Expand: $2x - 4 + 3x + 3 = 2x^2$
Simplify: $-2x^2 + 5x - 1 = 0$
Multiply by -1: $2x^2 - 5x + 1 = 0$

Solving using the quadratic formula gives $x = \dfrac{5 \pm \sqrt{17}}{4}$.

$\dfrac{5 + \sqrt{17}}{4} \doteq 2.28$ $\dfrac{5 - \sqrt{17}}{4} \doteq 0.22$

Estimate		
$\sqrt{17} \doteq 4$	$\dfrac{5+4}{4} = 2.25$	$\dfrac{5-4}{4} = 0.25$

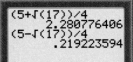

To the nearest hundredth, the roots are 2.28 and 0.22.

Example 4   Travelling Speed

A band's equipment truck travelled from Calgary to Spokane, a distance of 720 km. On the return trip, the average speed was increased by 10 km/h. If the total driving time for the round trip was 17 h, what was the average speed from Calgary to Spokane?

Solution

Let x represent the average speed from Calgary to Spokane.
Then, the average speed from Spokane to Calgary was $x + 10$ km/h.
Organize the information in a table.

Trip	Distance (km)	Speed (km/h)	Time (h)
Calgary to Spokane	720	x	$\dfrac{720}{x}$
Spokane to Calgary	720	$x + 10$	$\dfrac{720}{x + 10}$

The total time for the round trip was 17 h, so
$$\frac{720}{x} + \frac{720}{x+10} = 17$$

Multiply both sides by $x(x + 10)$: $720(x + 10) + 720x = 17x(x + 10)$
Expand: $720x + 7200 + 720x = 17x^2 + 170x$
Simplify: $1440x + 7200 = 17x^2 + 170x$
$$0 = 17x^2 - 1270x - 7200$$

For $17x^2 - 1270x - 7200$, $a = 17$, $b = -1270$, and $c = -7200$.

$$x = \frac{-b \pm \sqrt{b^2 - 4ac}}{2a}$$

$$= \frac{-(-1270) \pm \sqrt{(-1270)^2 - 4(17)(-7200)}}{2(17)}$$

$$= \frac{1270 \pm \sqrt{2\,102\,500}}{34}$$

$$= \frac{1270 \pm 1450}{34}$$

So, $x = \dfrac{2720}{34}$ or $x = -\dfrac{180}{34}$

$\qquad = 80 \qquad\qquad = -\dfrac{90}{17}$

```
(-1270)²-4(17)(-
7200)
           2102500.000
√(Ans)
           1450.000000
```

Estimate

$2700 \div 30 = 90$

The equation can be solved by factoring, but the factors may be difficult to find
$17x^2 - 1270x - 7200 = (17x + 90)(x - 80)$

Since $x > 0$, the root $-\dfrac{90}{17}$ is rejected.

The average speed from Calgary to Spokane was 80 km/h.

Check.
At 80 km/h, the trip from Calgary to Spokane took $\dfrac{720}{80}$ or 9 h.

From Spokane to Calgary, the average speed was $80 + 10$ or 90 km/h.

The time taken from Spokane to Calgary was $\dfrac{720}{90}$ or 8 h.

The total driving time for the round trip was $9 + 8$ or 17 h.

Example 5   Freestyle Aerials

Solve the equation $-0.2d^2 + 2.5d + 8 = 0$ for d, the horizontal distance from the kicker to the landing point, to the nearest metre.

Solution

For $-0.2d^2 + 2.5d + 8 = 0$, $a = -0.2$, $b = 2.5$, and $c = 8$.

$$d = \frac{-b \pm \sqrt{b^2 - 4ac}}{2a}$$

$$= \frac{-2.5 \pm \sqrt{(2.5)^2 - 4(-0.2)(8)}}{2(-0.2)}$$

$$= \frac{-2.5 \pm \sqrt{6.25 + 6.4}}{-0.4}$$

$$= \frac{-2.5 \pm \sqrt{12.65}}{-0.4}$$

So, $d \doteq -3$ or $d \doteq 15$

Since the distance is positive, the root -3 is rejected.

The horizontal distance from the kicker to the landing point is 15 m, to the nearest metre.

Practice

Solve using the quadratic formula.

1. $x^2 + 6x + 5 = 0$
2. $x^2 + 2x - 8 = 0$
3. $x^2 - 2x - 3 = 0$
4. $x^2 - 12x + 35 = 0$
5. $x^2 + 4x + 4 = 0$
6. $y^2 - 2y + 1 = 0$

Solve using the quadratic formula. Check your solutions.

7. $2x^2 - 3x + 1 = 0$
8. $5x^2 - 14x - 3 = 0$
9. $2x^2 - 5x - 12 = 0$
10. $9x^2 - 6x + 1 = 0$
11. $8x^2 + 6x - 9 = 0$
12. $6x^2 - x = 2$
13. $4x^2 - 9 = 0$
14. $0 = 4x^2 + 16x + 15$
15. $2x^2 - 5x = 0$
16. $3w^2 + 11w = -10$

Solve using the quadratic formula. Check your solutions.

17. $x^2 + 4x + 2 = 0$
18. $x^2 - 6x - 1 = 0$
19. $x^2 - 4x + 1 = 0$
20. $x^2 - 2x - 1 = 0$

Solve using the quadratic formula. Express answers in simplest radical form.

21. $x^2 + 4x + 1 = 0$
22. $z^2 - z - 4 = 0$
23. $7x^2 - 2x - 2 = 0$
24. $0 = x^2 + x - 1$
25. $2x^2 = 3 - 8x$
26. $a^2 - a - 5 = 0$
27. $4x = 5 - 4x^2$
28. $4 = m^2 - 2m$
29. $3r^2 - 4 = 0$
30. $0 = -3x^2 + 4x + 1$

Solve. Express answers as integers or as decimals, to the nearest tenth.

31. $5x^2 = 8x$
32. $2x^2 + 3x = 5x^2 - 1$
33. $\frac{x^2}{2} - x - \frac{5}{2} = 0$
34. $2c(c - 3) = 7$

35. $(n - 4)(n - 2) = 12$
36. $2(x - 2)(x + 1) - (x + 3) = 0$
37. $(6x - 1)(x + 5) = 15x - 9$
38. $(3x - 1)(x - 4) = (2x - 5)(x + 2)$
39. $(2d + 3)(d - 2) = (d + 9)(d - 3) + 16$
40. $3g^2 - (5g + 1)(2g - 3) = 3$

Solve. Round answers to the nearest hundredth.

41. $0.1x^2 + 0.4x - 0.3 = 0$
42. $0.25x^2 - x - 1.5 = 0$
43. $0.17y^2 - 0.2y = 0.03$
44. $1.2n^2 = 1.4n + 1$
45. $0.1 = -2.2x^2 - 2.4x$
46. $0.04a^2 + 0.1a + 0.05 = 5$

Solve. Express answers as integers or as decimals, to the nearest hundredth.

47. $\frac{15}{x} - \frac{15}{x - 2} = -2$
48. $\frac{100}{x} + \frac{100}{x + 5} = 9$
49. $\frac{3}{x} + \frac{4}{x + 3} = 1$
50. $\frac{2}{x - 3} + \frac{3}{x + 2} = 1$

Solve. Express radical solutions in simplest radical form.

51. $\frac{2x}{3} - \frac{1}{3} = \frac{2}{x}$
52. $\frac{2}{m^2} + \frac{3}{m} = -1$
53. $\frac{x}{x + 3} = \frac{2x}{x - 4}$
54. $\frac{x - 3}{x + 4} = \frac{x + 3}{2x - 1}$

55. $\dfrac{t}{t-1}+\dfrac{t}{t+2}=3$ **56.** $\dfrac{2}{x-1}-\dfrac{1}{x+1}=\dfrac{x^2}{x^2-1}$

57. $\dfrac{2}{x^2+6x+8}+\dfrac{3}{x^2+5x+4}=\dfrac{x}{x^2+3x+2}$

58. $\dfrac{2x+1}{x^2-4x+3}-\dfrac{3x+2}{x^2+x-2}=\dfrac{4}{x^2-x-6}$

Applications and Problem Solving

59. Peace Tower a) Find the width, in metres, of the Canadian flag on the Peace Tower in Ottawa by solving the equation $8w^2+18w-81=0$.
b) The height of the Peace Tower is 90 m. If an object is thrown downward at 5 m/s from this height, the time, t seconds, the object takes to reach the ground can be found by solving the equation $-4.9t^2-5t+90=0$. Find the time taken, to the nearest tenth of a second.

60. Natural bridge Sipapu Natural Bridge is in Utah. Find the horizontal distance, in metres, across this natural arch at the base by solving the equation $-0.04x^2+3.28x=0$.

61. Mackinac Bridge The Mackinac Bridge is one of the longest suspension bridges in the world. This bridge spans the 8 km wide Straits of Mackinac, where Lake Huron and Lake Michigan meet. Find the length of the main span, to the nearest ten metres, by solving the equation $0.000\,31x^2-0.36x=0$.

62. Numbers If 4 times the square of a number is 81, what is the number?

63. Hedge maze The world's largest hedge maze is in the grounds of an English country house known as Longleat. The rectangular maze has 2.7 km of paths flanked by 16 180 yew trees. The length of the rectangle is 60 m more than the width. The area of the rectangle is 6496 m^2. What are the dimensions of the rectangle?

64. Flying speed A plane flew 4200 km from Glasgow to Halifax into a head wind. With a tail wind, the plane flew 100 km/h faster on the return trip. The total flying time from Glasgow to Halifax and back was 13 h. What was the flying speed from Glasgow to Halifax?

65. Numbers Subtracting a number from its square gives 600. Find the number.

66. Driving speed The driving distance from Winnipeg to Billings, Montana, is 1200 km. A moving van made the round trip in 31 h, excluding the time taken to load and unload the van. The average speed from Winnipeg to Billings was 5 km/h slower than the average speed for the return trip to Winnipeg. What was the average speed from Winnipeg to Billings?

67. Integers The sum of the squares of two consecutive odd integers is 1570. Find the integers.

68. Hiking If Terry had hiked 0.5 km/h faster, he would have taken 1 h less to complete a 15-km hike. What was Terry's hiking speed?

69. Framing a photograph A photograph measuring 16 cm by 12 cm is to be surrounded by a mat before framing. The width of the mat is to be the same on all sides of the photograph. The area of the mat is to equal the area of the photograph. Find the width of the mat, to the nearest tenth of a centimetre.

70. Jogging Petra jogged 9 km in an hour. She covered the last 4 km at a speed that was 2 km/h slower than her speed over the first 5 km. What was her speed over the first 5 km?

71. Measurement The hypotenuse of a right triangle measures 20 cm. The sum of the lengths of the other two sides is 28 cm. Find the lengths of these two sides.

72. Lidless box A rectangular piece of tin 50 cm by 40 cm is made into a lidless box of base area 875 cm^2 by cutting squares of equal sizes from the corners and bending up the sides. Find
a) the side length of each removed square
b) the volume of the box

73. Numbers Find a number if the sum of three times the number and 4 times its square is
a) 0   **b)** 22   **c)** $-\dfrac{1}{2}$

74. Patrol boat A patrol boat took 2.5 h for a round trip 12 km upriver and 12 km back. The speed of the current was 2 km/h. What was the speed of the boat in still water?

75. Cropping a photograph If part of a photograph is used to fill an available space in a book or magazine, the photograph is said to be cropped. A photograph that was originally 15 cm by 10 cm is cropped by removing the same width from the top and the left side. Cropping reduces the area by 46 cm^2. What are the dimensions of the cropped photograph?

76. Estimation a) Estimate the side length of a square that has the same area as a circle of radius 10 cm.
b) Check your estimate by finding the side length of the square, to the nearest hundredth of a centimetre.

77. Retail sales A sporting goods store sells 90 ski jackets in a season for $200 each. Each $10 decrease in the price would result in 5 more jackets being sold.
a) Find the number of jackets sold and the selling price to give revenues of $17 600 from sales of ski jackets.
b) What is the lowest price that would produce revenues of at least $15 600? How many jackets would be sold at this price?

78. Reasoning a) The following steps show another method for deriving the quadratic formula. Write a description of each step.

Step	General Case $ax^2 + bx + c = 0$
1	$4a^2x^2 + 4abx + 4ac = 0$
2	$4a^2x^2 + 4abx + 4ac + b^2 = b^2$
3	$4a^2x^2 + 4abx + b^2 = b^2 - 4ac$
4	$(2ax + b)^2 = b^2 - 4ac$
5	$2ax + b = \pm\sqrt{b^2 - 4ac}$
6	$2ax = -b \pm \sqrt{b^2 - 4ac}$
7	$x = \dfrac{-b \pm \sqrt{b^2 - 4ac}}{2a}$

b) Is the technique of completing the square used in this method? Explain.
c) Illustrate each of the steps using the example $3x^2 + 2x - 4 = 0$. Simplify the result of step 7 of this example.

79. Measurement The height of a triangle is 2 units more than the base. The area of the triangle is 10 square units. Find the base, to the nearest hundredth.

80. Pattern Two points can be connected by a maximum of one line segment. Three non-collinear points can be connected by a maximum of three line segments.
a) Find the maximum number of line segments that can connect four non-collinear points; five non-collinear points.
b) Write an equation of the form $s = \blacksquare$ that relates the maximum number of line segments, s, to the number of non-collinear points, p.
c) Find the number of non-collinear points that can be connected by a maximum of 55 line segments.
d) Is it possible for a set of non-collinear points to be connected by a maximum of 40 line segments? Explain.

81. If a quadratic equation can be solved by factoring, what do you know about $b^2 - 4ac$?

82. If a quadratic equation appears to have one root, that is, it has two equal real roots, what do you know about $b^2 - 4ac$?

83. Measurement A cylinder has a height of 5 cm and a surface area of 100 cm^2. Find the radius of the cylinder, to the nearest tenth of a centimetre.

84. Solve each equation for x.
a) $2x^2 + 17xy + 8y^2 = 0$ **b)** $x^2 + 2xy - y^2 = 0$

85. Write a quadratic equation that has each pair of roots.
a) $\dfrac{1}{4}$ and $-\dfrac{3}{10}$ **b)** $3 + \sqrt{5}$ and $3 - \sqrt{5}$
c) $\dfrac{1+2\sqrt{3}}{2}$ and $\dfrac{1-2\sqrt{3}}{2}$

86. Write two problems that can be solved using quadratic equations. Check that the roots of each equation are real. Then, have a classmate solve your problems.

87. Describe the methods you know for solving quadratic equations. Describe the advantages and disadvantages of each method, and indicate when you would use it. Compare your conclusions with those of your classmates.

4.6 Complex Numbers

The computer-generated image shown is called a fractal. Fractals are used in many ways, such as making realistic computer images for movies and squeezing high definition television (HDTV) signals into existing broadcast channels. Meteorologists use fractals to study cloud shapes, and seismologists use fractals to study earthquakes. To understand how fractals are generated, we need to extend our understanding of numbers.

In mathematics, it is convenient to find the square roots of negative numbers, as well as positive numbers. So mathematicians have invented a number defined as the principal square root of negative one. This number, i, is the **imaginary unit**, with the properties
$$i = \sqrt{-1} \text{ and } i^2 = -1$$

In general, if x is a positive real number, then $\sqrt{-x}$ is a **pure imaginary number**, which can be defined as follows.
$$\sqrt{-x} = \sqrt{-1} \times \sqrt{x}$$
$$= i\sqrt{x}$$

The expression $i\sqrt{x}$ has the property that $\left(i\sqrt{x}\right)^2 = i^2 \times \left(\sqrt{x}\right)^2$
$$= -1 \times x$$
$$\text{so } \left(i\sqrt{x}\right)^2 = -x$$

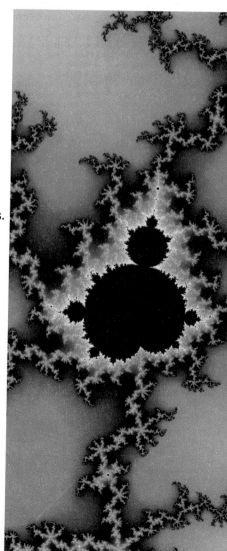

For example, $\left(i\sqrt{5}\right)^2 = i^2 \times \left(\sqrt{5}\right)^2$
$$= -1 \times 5$$
$$= -5$$

Numbers such as i, $i\sqrt{6}$, $2i$, and $-3i$ are examples of pure imaginary numbers. Despite their name, these numbers are just as real as real numbers.

Explore: Use the Definitions
Recall that some radicals can be simplified as follows.
$$\sqrt{12} = \sqrt{4} \times \sqrt{3}$$
$$= 2\sqrt{3}$$
Similarly, $\sqrt{-2} = \sqrt{-1} \times \sqrt{2}$ and $\sqrt{-12} = \sqrt{-1} \times \sqrt{12}$
$$= i\sqrt{2} \qquad\qquad\qquad = i \times \sqrt{4} \times \sqrt{3}$$
$$= 2i\sqrt{3}$$
Simplify each of the following radicals using the imaginary unit, i.
a) $\sqrt{-3}$ **b)** $\sqrt{-9}$ **c)** $\sqrt{-16}$ **d)** $\sqrt{-8}$ **e)** $\sqrt{-20}$

Inquire
1. Describe how to simplify square roots of negative numbers.

2. Simplify each of the following.
a) $\sqrt{-10}$ **b)** $\sqrt{-18}$ **c)** $\sqrt{-28}$ **d)** $\sqrt{-50}$

3. Since $3i \times 3i = 9i^2 = 9(-1) = -9$, evaluate each of the following.
a) $5i \times 5i$ **b)** $2i \times 3i$ **c)** $(-2i) \times (-2i)$
d) $(-3i) \times (-4i)$ **e)** $2i \times (-5i)$ **f)** $(-3i) \times 6i$

The sum of a real number and a pure imaginary number is called a **complex number**. Examples of complex numbers include $5 + 2i$ and $4 - 3i$. Complex numbers are used in applications of mathematics to engineering, physics, electronics, and many other areas of science.

A complex number is a number in the form $a + bi$, where a and b are real numbers and i is the imaginary unit. We call a the **real part** and bi the **imaginary part** of a complex number.

If $b = 0$, then $a + bi = a$. So, a real number, such as 5, can be thought of as a complex number, since 5 can be written as $5 + 0i$.

If $a = 0$, then $a + bi = bi$. Numbers of the form bi, such as $7i$, are pure imaginary numbers. Complex numbers in which neither $a = 0$ nor $b = 0$ are referred to as **imaginary numbers**. The following chart summarizes the complex number system.

Complex Numbers

$$a \quad + \quad bi$$

real part   imaginary part

Complex Numbers, C
$C = a + bi$, where a and b are real numbers and $i^2 = -1$

Restriction	Type	Examples
$b = 0$	real number	$5, \sqrt{2}, -1, \frac{3}{2}$
$a = 0$	pure imaginary number	$7i, -3i, i\sqrt{2}$
$a, b \neq 0$	imaginary number	$4 + 3i, 3 - 2i$

Example 1 Simplifying Expressions
Simplify.

a) $\sqrt{-24}$ **b)** $\sqrt{-45y^3}$ **c)** $2(-3i)^2$

Solution

a)
$$\begin{aligned}
\sqrt{-24} &= \sqrt{-1} \times \sqrt{24} \\
&= i \times \sqrt{4} \times \sqrt{6} \\
&= i \times 2 \times \sqrt{6} \\
&= 2i\sqrt{6}
\end{aligned}$$

b)
$$\begin{aligned}
\sqrt{-45y^3} &= \sqrt{-1} \times \sqrt{45} \times \sqrt{y^3} \\
&= i \times \sqrt{9} \times \sqrt{5} \times \sqrt{y^2} \times \sqrt{y} \\
&= i \times 3 \times \sqrt{5} \times y \times \sqrt{y} \\
&= 3iy\sqrt{5y}
\end{aligned}$$

c)
$$\begin{aligned}
2(-3i)^2 &= 2 \times (-3i) \times (-3i) \\
&= 2 \times 9 \times i^2 \\
&= 18 \times (-1) \\
&= -18
\end{aligned}$$

To add or subtract complex numbers, combine like terms; that is, combine the real parts and combine the imaginary parts.

Example 2 Adding and Subtracting Complex Numbers
Simplify.
a) $(6 - 3i) + (5 + i)$ **b)** $(2 - 3i) - (4 - 5i)$

Solution

a)
$$\begin{aligned}
(6 - 3i) + (5 + i) &= 6 - 3i + 5 + i \\
&= 6 + 5 - 3i + i \\
&= 11 - 2i
\end{aligned}$$

b)
$$\begin{aligned}
(2 - 3i) - (4 - 5i) &= 2 - 3i - 4 + 5i \\
&= 2 - 4 - 3i + 5i \\
&= -2 + 2i
\end{aligned}$$

Complex numbers can be multiplied using the distributive property.

Example 3   Multiplying Complex Numbers

Simplify.

a) $(1 - 2i)(4 + 3i)$ **b)** $(1 - 4i)^2$

Solution

a) $(1 - 2i)(4 + 3i) = 4 + 3i - 8i - 6i^2$
$= 4 - 5i - 6i^2$
$= 4 - 5i - 6(-1)$
$= 4 - 5i + 6$
$= 10 - 5i$

b) $(1 - 4i)^2 = (1 - 4i)(1 - 4i)$
$= 1 - 4i - 4i + 16i^2$
$= 1 - 8i + 16(-1)$
$= 1 - 8i - 16$
$= -15 - 8i$

Use FOIL to multiply the complex numbers.

An equation may have a solution in one set of numbers but not in another. For example, the equation $x + 1 = 0$ has no solution in the set of whole numbers. However, it has a solution, $x = -1$, in the set of integers. Similarly, the equation $x^2 - 2 = 0$ has no solution in the set of rational numbers. However, it has two solutions, $x = \pm\sqrt{2}$, in the set of real numbers.

The equation $x^2 + 1 = 0$ has no solution in the set of real numbers. An attempt to solve the equation gives
$$x^2 = -1$$
$$\text{and } x = \pm\sqrt{-1}$$

Since $i = \sqrt{-1}$, the solutions of the equation $x^2 + 1 = 0$ can be written as i and $-i$. These solutions are in the set of pure imaginary numbers. Many quadratic equations have roots that are pure imaginary or imaginary numbers.

All quadratic functions have two zeros, that is, two values of the independent variable that make the value of the function equal to zero. If the graph of a quadratic function intersects the x-axis, the zeros of the function are real zeros, that is, they are real numbers. If there are two real zeros, they can be distinct or equal. If the graph of a quadratic function does not intersect the x-axis, the function has two imaginary zeros. The three possibilities are shown in the graphs.

two distinct real zeros

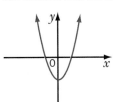

two equal real zeros

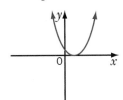

two imaginary zeros

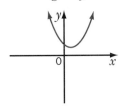

The quadratic equations that correspond to the functions shown in the graphs have two distinct real roots, two equal real roots, and two imaginary roots.

Example 4 Solving Using the Square Root Principle

Solve and check $2x^2 + 32 = 0$.

Solution

$$2x^2 + 32 = 0$$

Subtract 32 from both sides: $\qquad 2x^2 = -32$

Divide both sides by 2: $\qquad x^2 = -16$

Take the square root of both sides: $\qquad x = \pm\sqrt{-16}$

Simplify: $\qquad x = \pm\sqrt{-1} \times \sqrt{16}$

$$x = \pm 4i$$

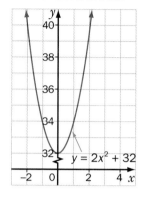

Note that the graph of $y = 2x^2 + 32$ does not intersect the x-axis.

Check.

For $x = 4i$,

L.S. $= 2x^2 + 32$ $\qquad$ **R.S.** $= 0$
$= 2(4i)^2 + 32$
$= 2 \times 16 \times i^2 + 32$
$= 2 \times 16 \times (-1) + 32$
$= -32 + 32$
$= 0$

For $x = -4i$,

L.S. $= 2x^2 + 32$ $\qquad$ **R.S.** $= 0$
$= 2(-4i)^2 + 32$
$= 2 \times 16 \times i^2 + 32$
$= 2 \times 16 \times (-1) + 32$
$= -32 + 32$
$= 0$

The roots are $4i$ and $-4i$.

Example 5 Solving Using the Quadratic Formula

Solve $x^2 - 2x + 3 = 0$.

Solution

$x^2 - 2x + 3 = 0$

Use the quadratic formula: $\qquad x = \dfrac{-b \pm \sqrt{b^2 - 4ac}}{2a}$

$$= \dfrac{-(-2) \pm \sqrt{(-2)^2 - 4(1)(3)}}{2(1)}$$

$$= \dfrac{2 \pm \sqrt{4 - 12}}{2}$$

$$= \dfrac{2 \pm \sqrt{-8}}{2}$$

Use the definition of i: $\qquad = \dfrac{2 \pm i\sqrt{8}}{2}$

Simplify: $\qquad = \dfrac{2 \pm 2i\sqrt{2}}{2}$

$$= 1 \pm i\sqrt{2}$$

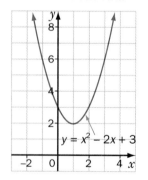

Note that the graph of $y = x^2 - 2x + 3$ does not intersect the x-axis.

The roots are $1 + i\sqrt{2}$ and $1 - i\sqrt{2}$.

Example 6   Solving Quartic Equations

Solve $2x^4 + x^2 - 6 = 0$.

Solution

Factor the left side:

$$2x^4 + x^2 - 6 = 0$$
$$(2x^2 - 3)(x^2 + 2) = 0$$

Use the zero product property:

$$2x^2 - 3 = 0 \quad \text{or} \quad x^2 + 2 = 0$$
$$x^2 = \frac{3}{2} \quad \text{or} \quad x^2 = -2$$

Take the square root of both sides:

$$x = \pm\sqrt{\frac{3}{2}} \quad \text{or} \quad x = \pm\sqrt{-2}$$

Simplify:

$$x = \pm\frac{\sqrt{6}}{2} \quad \text{or} \quad x = \pm i\sqrt{2}$$

The solutions are $\dfrac{\sqrt{6}}{2}$, $-\dfrac{\sqrt{6}}{2}$, $i\sqrt{2}$, and $-i\sqrt{2}$.

Functions that generate some fractals are in the form $f(z) = z^2 + c$, where c is a complex number. Fractals are created by **iteration**, which means that the function $f(z)$ is evaluated for some input value of z, and then the result is used as the next input value, and so on.

Example 7   Fractals

Find the first three output values for $f(z) = z^2 + 2i$.

Solution

Use $z = 0$ as the first input value:

$$f(z) = z^2 + 2i$$
$$f(0) = 0^2 + 2i$$
$$= 2i$$

Use $z = 2i$ as the second input value:

$$f(2i) = (2i)^2 + 2i$$
$$= 4i^2 + 2i$$
$$= -4 + 2i$$

Use $z = -4 + 2i$ as the third input value:

$$f(-4 + 2i) = (-4 + 2i)^2 + 2i$$
$$= 16 - 16i + 4i^2 + 2i$$
$$= 16 - 16i - 4 + 2i$$
$$= 12 - 14i$$

The first three output values are $2i$, $-4 + 2i$, and $12 - 14i$.

Practice

Simplify.

1. $\sqrt{-9}$ **2.** $\sqrt{-25}$ **3.** $\sqrt{-81}$

4. $\sqrt{-5}$ **5.** $\sqrt{-13}$ **6.** $\sqrt{-23}$

7. $\sqrt{-12}$ **8.** $\sqrt{-40}$ **9.** $\sqrt{-54}$

10. $-\sqrt{-4}$ **11.** $-\sqrt{-20}$ **12.** $\sqrt{-25y}$

13. $\sqrt{-36x^2}$ **14.** $\sqrt{-18x^4}$ **15.** $\sqrt{-20z^5}$

16. $\left(\sqrt{-6}\right)^2$ **17.** $\sqrt{(-6)^2}$ **18.** $\sqrt{-40x^5 y^3}$

Simplify.

19. i^3 **20.** i^4 **21.** i^5

22. $4i \times 5i$ **23.** $5i^2$ **24.** $-i^7$

25. $3(-2i)^2$ **26.** $i(4i)^3$ **27.** $(3i)(-6i)$

28. $\left(i\sqrt{2}\right)^2$ **29.** $-\left(i\sqrt{5}\right)^2$ **30.** $\left(i\sqrt{6}\right)\left(-i\sqrt{6}\right)$

31. $\left(2i\sqrt{3}\right)^2$ **32.** $\left(-5i\sqrt{2}\right)^2$ **33.** $\left(4i\sqrt{5}\right)\left(-2i\sqrt{5}\right)$

Simplify.

34. $(4 + 2i) + (3 - 4i)$ **35.** $(2 - 5i) + (1 - 6i)$

36. $(3 - 2i) - (1 + 3i)$ **37.** $(6 - i) - (5 - 7i)$

38. $(4 + 6i) + (7i - 6)$ **39.** $(i - 8) + (4i - 3)$

40. $(9i - 6) - (10i - 3)$ **41.** $(3i + 11) - (6i - 13)$
42. $2(1 - 7i) + 3(4 - i)$ **43.** $-3(2i - 4) - (5 + 6i)$

Simplify.
44. $2(4 - 3i)$ **45.** $3i(1 + 2i)$
46. $-4i(3 - 5i)$ **47.** $2i(3i^2 - 4i + 2)$
48. $(2 - 4i)(1 + 3i)$ **49.** $(3 + 4i)(3 - 5i)$
50. $(3i - 1)(4i - 5)$ **51.** $(1 - 5i)(1 + 5i)$
52. $(1 + 2i)^2$ **53.** $(4i - 3)^2$
54. $(i - 1)^2$ **55.** $(i^2 - 1)^2$

Solve and check.
56. $x^2 + 9 = 0$ **57.** $3x^2 + 12 = 0$
58. $y^2 + 20 = 0$ **59.** $6n^2 + 72 = 0$
60. $-2x^2 - 16 = 0$ **61.** $-5x^2 - 90 = 0$

Solve.
62. $x^2 + 2x + 2 = 0$ **63.** $x^2 - 4x + 8 = 0$
64. $z^2 + 5z + 8 = 0$ **65.** $n^2 - 3n + 3 = 0$
66. $x^2 - x + 7 = 0$ **67.** $-y^2 + 3y - 9 = 0$
68. $2x^2 + 3x + 3 = 0$ **69.** $3m^2 - 4m = -2$
70. $5x^2 + 5x + 2 = 0$ **71.** $4y - 1 = 5y^2$

Solve.
72. $\dfrac{x^2}{2} - \dfrac{x^2}{3} = -1$ **73.** $\dfrac{1}{x^2 + 2} = 1$

74. $\dfrac{3}{1 - x} = x$ **75.** $\dfrac{2}{x - 2} + 1 = \dfrac{1}{x - 1}$

76. $\dfrac{2x - 1}{x} = \dfrac{3x + 5}{2}$ **77.** $\dfrac{3}{x^2 - 1} = \dfrac{4}{x^2 - 4}$

Solve.
78. $x^4 - 8x^2 + 16 = 0$ **79.** $x^4 + 2x^2 + 1 = 0$
80. $x^4 + 3x^2 - 4 = 0$ **81.** $t^4 - 5t^2 + 6 = 0$
82. $y^4 - y^2 - 6 = 0$ **83.** $3r^4 - 5r^2 + 2 = 0$?
84. $2x^4 + 5x^2 + 3 = 0$ **85.** $2x^4 + x^2 = 6$
86. $4a^4 - 1 = 0$ **87.** $9x^4 - 4x^2 = 0$

Applications and Problem Solving

88. Numbers Numbers of the form $a + bi$ and $a - bi$, where a and b are real numbers, are known as **complex conjugates**.
a) Determine the product $(a + bi)(a - bi)$. Is the product real or imaginary?
b) Evaluate $(5 + 7i)(5 - 7i)$.
c) Express the number 25 as the product of complex conjugates in two different ways, with a and b both natural numbers.

89. Fractals Find the first three output values for each function. Use $z = 0$ as the first input value.
a) $f(z) = z^2 + i$ **b)** $f(z) = z^2 - i$
c) $f(z) = z^2 + 3i$ **d)** $f(z) = z^2 + 2 + i$

90. Pattern a) Simplify i^2, i^3, i^4, i^5, i^6, i^7, i^8, i^9, i^{10}, i^{11}, and i^{12}.
b) Describe the pattern in the values.
c) Describe how to simplify i^n, where n is a whole number.
d) Simplify i^{48}, i^{94}, i^{85}, and i^{99}.

91. Find the values of s and t that make the equations true.
a) $6 + 12i = 2s + 3ti$
b) $3s - 2t + i(2s + 3t) = 11 + 3i$
c) $s + 3t + 2si - ti = 5 + 3i$

92. Technology a) Graph the equation $y = x^2 - 2x + 2$ on a graphing calculator.
b) Describe the results when you try to find the zeros of the function using the Zero operation.
c) Repeat part b) for another quadratic function with imaginary roots.

93. Write a quadratic equation that has each pair of roots.
a) $2i$ and $-2i$ **b)** $1 + i$ and $1 - i$
c) $\dfrac{3 + 2i}{2}$ and $\dfrac{3 - 2i}{2}$

94. Rocket The height of a rocket fired upward from the ground at 50 m/s is given approximately by the expression $-5t^2 + 50t$, where t seconds is the time since the rocket was launched. Does a rocket fired upward at 50 m/s reach each of the following heights? If so, after how many seconds is the rocket at the given height?
a) 45 m **b)** 125 m **c)** 150 m

95. Is it possible for a quadratic equation to have one real root and one imaginary root? Explain.

96. Solve each of the following equations. State the relationship between the number of roots and the highest power of the variable in each case.
a) $x - 2 = 0$ **b)** $x^2 - x - 2 = 0$
c) $x^3 - x^2 - 2x = 0$ **d)** $x^4 - x^2 - 2 = 0$
e) $x^5 - x^3 - 2x = 0$

97. Integers The square of the product of two consecutive even integers is 28 224. Find the integers.

4.7 The Discriminant

The quadratic formula states that the roots of $ax^2 + bx + c = 0$ are

$$x = \frac{-b + \sqrt{b^2 - 4ac}}{2a} \text{ and } x = \frac{-b - \sqrt{b^2 - 4ac}}{2a}$$

The quantity under the radical sign, $b^2 - 4ac$, is called the **discriminant** of the quadratic equation. The discriminant is useful in determining the nature of the roots of $ax^2 + bx + c = 0$ without solving the equation.

Two Canadians, Ethel Catherwood and Duncan McNaughton, have won Olympic high jump gold medals. The path that high jumpers follow from takeoff to landing is a parabola.

The path of one jump can be modelled by the function
$$h(d) = -2d^2 + 4d$$
where $h(d)$ metres is the height of the jumper, and d metres is the horizontal distance of the jumper from the point of takeoff. If the height of the bar is 2.1 m, the equation $2.1 = -2d^2 + 4d$ can be solved to see if the jumper will clear the bar. The discriminant can also be used.

Explore: Complete the Table

Copy and complete the table by solving each equation using the quadratic formula. When deciding the type of solutions, choose between the following three possibilities:
real and distinct, real and equal, and imaginary.

Equation	Type of Solutions	Value of $b^2 - 4ac$
$x^2 + 2x + 1 = 0$		
$x^2 + 6x + 9 = 0$		
$x^2 + 4x + 3 = 0$		
$x^2 + 6x + 7 = 0$		
$x^2 + 5x + 7 = 0$		
$x^2 + 6x + 10 = 0$		

Inquire

1. State the type of roots obtained in each of the following cases. Explain why this type is obtained.
 a) $b^2 - 4ac = 0$ **b)** $b^2 - 4ac > 0$ **c)** $b^2 - 4ac < 0$

2. a) Write the equation $2.1 = -2d^2 + 4d$ in the form $ax^2 + bx + c = 0$ and find the value of the discriminant.
 b) Use the value of the discriminant to decide if the high jumper will clear the bar. Explain your reasoning.

3. When $b^2 - 4ac > 0$, what determines whether the roots are rational or irrational? Explain.

The relationships between the value of the discriminant, the solutions to a quadratic equation, and the graph of the related quadratic function can be summarized as follows.

Value of the Discriminant	Type of Solutions for $ax^2 + bx + c = 0$	Graph of Related Function $y = ax^2 + bx + c$	
$b^2 - 4ac > 0$	real and distinct		or
$b^2 - 4ac = 0$	real and equal		or
$b^2 - 4ac < 0$	imaginary		or

Example 1   Nature of the Roots

Without solving each equation, determine the nature of the roots.
a) $2x^2 + 3x - 10 = 0$ **b)** $9x^2 - 12x + 4 = 0$ **c)** $3x^2 - 7x + 5 = 0$

Solution

a) In $2x^2 + 3x - 10 = 0$,
$a = 2$, $b = 3$, and $c = -10$.
$b^2 - 4ac = (3)^2 - 4(2)(-10)$
$= 9 + 80$
$= 89$
Since $b^2 - 4ac > 0$, there are two distinct real roots.

b) In $9x^2 - 12x + 4 = 0$,
$a = 9$, $b = -12$, and $c = 4$.
$b^2 - 4ac = (-12)^2 - 4(9)(4)$
$= 144 - 144$
$= 0$
Since $b^2 - 4ac = 0$, there are two equal real roots.

c) In $3x^2 - 7x + 5 = 0$,
$a = 3$, $b = -7$, and $c = 5$.
$b^2 - 4ac = (-7)^2 - 4(3)(5)$
$= 49 - 60$
$= -11$
Since $b^2 - 4ac < 0$, there are two imaginary roots.

Example 2   Working Backward

For what values of k does the quadratic equation $x^2 + 10x + k = 0$ have
a) two distinct real roots?   **b)** two equal real roots?   **c)** two imaginary roots?

Solution

In the equation $x^2 + 10x + k = 0$, $a = 1$, $b = 10$, and $c = k$, so $b^2 - 4ac = 10^2 - 4(1)(k)$
$= 100 - 4k$

a) For two distinct real roots,
$b^2 - 4ac > 0$
$100 - 4k > 0$
$100 > 4k$
$25 > k$
There are two distinct real roots when $k < 25$.

b) For two equal real roots,
$b^2 - 4ac = 0$
$100 - 4k = 0$
$100 = 4k$
$25 = k$
There are two equal real roots when $k = 25$.

c) For two imaginary roots,
$b^2 - 4ac < 0$
$100 - 4k < 0$
$100 < 4k$
$25 < k$
There are two imaginary roots when $k > 25$.

Example 3   Fencing a Garden

A rectangular garden has an area of 324 m². Is it possible to enclose the garden on all four sides using 70 m of fencing?

Solution

Let one side of the rectangle measure x metres.
If 70 m of fencing were used, the other dimension of the rectangle would be $(35 - x)$ metres.
The dimensions would be related to the area by the following equation.

$$x(35 - x) = 324$$

Expand: $$35x - x^2 = 324$$
Write in the form $ax^2 + bx + c = 0$: $$0 = x^2 - 35x + 324$$

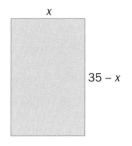

In the equation $x^2 - 35x + 324 = 0$, $a = 1$, $b = -35$, and $c = 324$.
Determine the discriminant.

$$\begin{aligned}
b^2 - 4ac &= (-35)^2 - 4(1)(324) \\
&= 1225 - 1296 \\
&= -71
\end{aligned}$$

Because the discriminant is negative, there are no real solutions to the equation $x^2 - 35x + 324 = 0$. So, it is not possible to enclose the 324-m² rectangular garden on all four sides using 70 m of fencing.

Practice

Use the discriminant to determine the nature of the roots.

1. $x^2 - 8x + 16 = 0$
2. $x^2 - x - 5 = 0$
3. $x^2 + 3x + 10 = 0$
4. $y^2 + 2y + 7 = 0$
5. $x^2 - 16 = 0$
6. $4x^2 - 12x + 9 = 0$
7. $3x^2 - x + 4 = 0$
8. $2x^2 + x - 5 = 0$
9. $5x^2 + 7x = 0$
10. $12a^2 - a + 6 = 0$

Without solving each equation, determine the nature of the roots.

11. $w^2 + 5 = 3w$
12. $3 - 5t = t^2$
13. $25 + x^2 = -10x$
14. $9n^2 = 5n$
15. $9 = -4x^2$
16. $16y^2 = 8y - 1$

Determine the nature of the roots.

17. $0.5x^2 + 4x + 4 = 0$
18. $(x + 1)(x - 2) = 4$
19. $4(x^2 - 5x + 5) = -5$
20. $2(y^2 + 3) = 4y$
21. $4 = (p - 5)^2$
22. $\dfrac{1}{3}x^2 + \dfrac{1}{2}x - 1 = 0$
23. $\dfrac{x - 1}{2} - x^2 = 3$

24. $\dfrac{3x - 1}{3} - \dfrac{2x + 1}{2} = x^2$
25. $3x^2 - \sqrt{2}x + 1 = 0$
26. $\sqrt{5}x^2 + 7x + 2\sqrt{5} = 0$

Without graphing, state the number of points in which each function intersects the x-axis.

27. $y = x^2 + x - 1$
28. $f(x) = 3x^2 - 2x + 4$
29. $f(x) = 6x^2 - 7x + 2$
30. $y = 16x^2 + 24x + 9$
31. $f(x) = -x^2 + 5x - 8$
32. $y = -4x^2 + 4x - 1$

Determine the value(s) of k that give the type of solution indicated.

33. $x^2 - 6x + k = 0$; equal real roots
34. $kx^2 - 2x + 1 = 0$; distinct real roots
35. $x^2 + 4x - 2k = 0$; imaginary roots
36. $2kx^2 - 4x + 3 = 0$; distinct real roots
37. $3kx^2 - 3x + 1 = 0$; imaginary roots
38. $m^2 + 4km + 1 = 0$; equal real roots
39. $(k + 1)x^2 - 2x - 3 = 0$; imaginary roots
40. $2x^2 + 5x - 2(k - 1) = 0$; distinct real roots
41. $3x^2 - 4x + 2(k + 2) = 0$; imaginary roots
42. $y^2 + (k + 2)y + 2k = 0$; equal real roots

43. For what values of m does the equation $mx^2 + 4x - 3 = 0$ have roots that are
a) real and distinct?
b) real and equal?
c) imaginary?

Applications and Problem Solving

44. Numbers Are there two real numbers that have a sum of 31 for each of the following products? If so, find the real numbers.
a) 240   **b)** 300   **c)** $\dfrac{385}{4}$

45. Building a fence Is it possible to build a fence on three sides of a 100-m² rectangular piece of land so that the total length of the fence is as follows? If so, what are the dimensions of the piece of land?
a) 30 m   **b)** 25 m

46. Measurement Is it possible for a rectangle with a perimeter of 44 cm to have each of the following areas? If so, find the dimensions of the rectangle.
a) 125 cm²   **b)** 121 cm²   **c)** 117 cm²

47. Thrown object The height, $h(t)$ metres, of an object thrown upward from the top of an 80-m cliff at 20 m/s is approximately related to the time, t seconds, since the object was thrown, by the function
$$h(t) = -5t^2 + 20t + 80$$
Will the object reach a height of 100 m? Explain.

48. Book sales A publishing company expects to sell 5000 copies of a new book at $30 each. The company expects that 500 more books would be sold for each price reduction of $2.
a) To give revenues of $156 000 from book sales, how many books must be sold and at what price?
b) Is it possible for the company to make $160 000 in revenues from book sales? Explain your solution algebraically and by graphing the appropriate function.
c) What selling prices of $30 or less would give revenues of at least $150 000?

49. In the quadratic equation $ax^2 + bx + c = 0$, what is the nature of the roots if $ac < 0$? Explain.

50. Probability Suppose you rolled a die and used the result as the value of k in the equation $y = 2x^2 + 5x + k$. What is the probability that the equation would have imaginary roots?

51. Numbers Are there two imaginary numbers with a sum of $19i$ and a product of 150? If so, find them.

52. a) Under what conditions is one root of $ax^2 + bx + c = 0$ the reciprocal of the other?
b) Check your answer to part a) by solving two equations that meet the conditions.

53. Determine the value(s) of k that give the type of solution indicated.
a) $x^2 + kx + 16 = 0$; distinct real roots
b) $x^2 + (k + 2)x + 2k = 0$; equal real roots
c) $2x^2 + kx + 2 = 0$; imaginary roots

54. Systems of equations Without graphing, determine whether the graphs of the equations in each system intersect in the Cartesian plane. If so, find the intersection points.
a) $y = 4x^2 + 6x + 7$ **b)** $y = 2x^2 - 3x + 2$
   $y = -2x + 4$ $y = 3x - 4$

55. For the equation $2x^2 - mx + 3 = 0$, find the values of m for which
a) the roots of the equation would not be real
b) one root would be double the other

PATTERN POWER

Subtracting 9 from the two-digit positive integer 21 results in the reversal of the digits to give 12.
1. List all two-digit positive integers for which the digits are reversed when you subtract 9.

2. Find all the two-digit positive integers for which the digits are reversed when you subtract
a) 18   **b)** 27   **c)** 36

3. Describe the pattern in words.

4. Use the pattern to find all the two-digit positive integers for which the digits are reversed when you subtract
a) 54   **b)** 72

Package Design

There are many examples of packages all around us. Packages are designed to protect and preserve their contents. Careful consideration is given to the colour and shape of a package to encourage us to purchase the product it contains.

Many types of materials, such as glass, plastic, and cardboard, are used to create all types of packages. Package designers must understand the properties of these materials, the processes by which packages are formed from these materials, and the consequences to the environment when these types of packaging materials are discarded.

Before manufacturing a package, a package designer creates a series of sketches of potential designs and presents them to clients. Often a package design is needed that can be sized to accommodate different amounts of the same materials, while still retaining the same visual impact.

1 Defining the Dimensions of a Package

Rosa is asked to design a package that can be used for different sizes of the same material. The package is to be constructed of cardboard, have the shape of a rectangular prism, and have tabs 2 cm deep for gluing the package together.

Rosa decides to design a box whose dimensions are approximately in the golden ratio. The net shows her initial design.

Glue Tabs

1.6^2x 1.6^2x

$1.6x$

x x x

2

The total surface area of the net, including the tabs, is given by
$$SA = 2x(1.6x) + 2(1.6x)(1.6^2x) + 2x(1.6^2x) + 4(2x) + 3(2)(1.6^2x) + 2(1.6x)$$
$$= 16.512x^2 + 31.68x$$
The volume of the package is given by
$$V = x(1.6x)(1.6^2x)$$
$$= 4.096x^3$$

1. Rosa's client would like to produce two different box sizes, one to hold 1 L of material and one to hold 1.5 L of material.
a) Use this information and the formula for the volume of the package to calculate the required dimensions of the two boxes. Round values to the nearest tenth of a square centimetre, if necessary.
b) What is the surface area of the material required to construct each size of box?

2. Rosa's client needs packages that will use at most 750 cm^2 of packaging material. Use the formula for the surface area to calculate the maximum dimensions of the package. Round answers to the nearest tenth of a square centimetre, if necessary.

2 Locating Information

Use your research skills to answer the following questions.
1. What skills are required to design the structure of a package?

2. What skills are required to design the appearance of a package?

3. How do colour and shape help make a package attractive to a buyer?

4. What education and training is required to become a package designer?

5. What types of companies require the skills of a package designer?

INVESTIGATING MATH

Sum and Product of the Roots

1 Exploring the Relationships

1. Solve each equation. Then, copy and complete the table. The first row has been completed for you.

Equation	Roots	Sum of Roots	Product of Roots	Value of a	b	c
a) $x^2 + 5x + 6 = 0$	−3, −2	−5	6	1	5	6
b) $x^2 - 9x + 20 = 0$						
c) $x^2 + 4x - 12 = 0$						
d) $2x^2 - 7x + 3 = 0$						
e) $2x^2 + 3x + 1 = 0$						
f) $3x^2 + 7x - 6 = 0$						
g) $x^2 + 8x = 0$						
h) $x^2 - 16 = 0$						

Work with a classmate to check your completed table.

2. For each equation, compare the values of the variables a, b, and c with the sum of the roots. Which two variables determine the sum of the roots?

3. Write an expression for the sum of the roots in terms of the two variables you found in question 2.

4. For each equation, compare the values of the variables a, b, and c with the product of the roots. Which two variables determine the product of the roots?

5. Write an expression for the product of the roots in terms of the two variables you found in question 4.

6. Without solving, find the sum and the product of the roots of each equation.
a) $x^2 + 6x + 8 = 0$ **b)** $x^2 - 3x - 4 = 0$ **c)** $2x^2 - 3x - 5 = 0$
d) $5y^2 + 9y = 0$ **e)** $4x^2 + 2x + 9 = 0$ **f)** $3n^2 + 2n = 8$
g) $2x^2 = -9$ **h)** $-2x^2 - 3x - 4 = 0$ **i)** $-4x^2 + 3x - 1 = 0$

2 Using Algebra

From the quadratic formula, the roots of a quadratic equation are given by the equations

$$r_1 = \frac{-b + \sqrt{b^2 - 4ac}}{2a} \text{ and } r_2 = \frac{-b - \sqrt{b^2 - 4ac}}{2a}$$

1. a) Add the above equations to write an equation in the form $r_1 + r_2 = \blacksquare$. Then, simplify the right-hand side of the equation.
b) Compare the simplified equation to your result from question 3 of *Exploring the Relationships*.

2. a) Multiply the above equations to write an equation in the form $r_1 \times r_2 = \blacksquare$. Then, simplify the right-hand side of the equation.
b) Compare the simplified equation to your result from question 5 of *Exploring the Relationships*.

3. Dividing a quadratic equation $ax^2 + bx + c = 0$ by a produces the equation

$$x^2 + \frac{b}{a}x + \frac{c}{a} = 0$$

Explain why we can write any quadratic equation in the form $x^2 - (\text{sum of roots})x + (\text{product of roots}) = 0$.

3 Working Backward

One way to work backward to find a quadratic equation from its roots is to use the sum and the product of the roots.

For example, suppose the roots of a quadratic equation are 2 and $-\frac{1}{2}$.

The sum of the roots is $\frac{3}{2}$, and the product of the roots is -1.

A quadratic equation can be written in the form
$$x^2 - (\text{sum of roots})x + (\text{product of roots}) = 0$$
$$\text{so } x^2 - \frac{3}{2}x - 1 = 0$$

Multiplying by 2 to eliminate the fraction gives $2x^2 - 3x - 2 = 0$

1. Write a quadratic equation with the following sum and product of the roots, and with integral values of a, b, and c.

a) sum: 2; product: 3   **b)** sum: -1; product: 5   **c)** sum: -2; product: -2

d) sum: 0; product: -3 **e)** sum: -4; product: 0   **f)** sum: 3; product: $\frac{1}{4}$

g) sum: $\frac{1}{2}$; product: 1   **h)** sum: $-\frac{2}{3}$; product: $-\frac{1}{2}$ **i)** sum: $-\frac{2}{5}$; product: $\frac{3}{10}$

2. Write a quadratic equation with the following roots and with integral values of a, b, and c.

a) 3 and 5   **b)** 4 and -1 **c)** $\frac{2}{3}$ and -3 **d)** $-\frac{1}{2}$ and 0

e) $\frac{3}{4}$ and $\frac{3}{4}$ **f)** $\frac{1}{3}$ and $-\frac{1}{3}$ **g)** $\sqrt{5}$ and $-\sqrt{5}$ **h)** $1 + \sqrt{2}$ and $1 - \sqrt{2}$

i) $2 + 3\sqrt{2}$ and $2 - 3\sqrt{2}$ **j)** $2i$ and $-2i$ **k)** $1 + 3i$ and $1 - 3i$ **l)** $\frac{2+\sqrt{3}}{2}$ and $\frac{2-\sqrt{3}}{2}$

4 Problem Solving

1. One root of the equation $12x^2 + 5x + k = 0$ is $\frac{1}{4}$. Find
a) the other root   **b)** the value of k

2. If the roots of $3x^2 + mx - 36 = 0$ are integers, what are the possible integral values of m?

3. For the equation $2x^2 + kx + 9 = 0$, find the values of k for which one root would be half the other.

4. If 2 is one root of $5x^2 + bx + 8 = 0$, what is the value of b?

5. Without solving the given equation, write an equation whose roots could be obtained by subtracting 1 from each root of $x^2 - 4x - 6 = 0$.

6. If $-\frac{1}{2}$ is one root of $2x^2 + 3x + c = 0$, what is the value of c?

7. For the equation $3kx^2 - 2(k - 1)x + 8 = 0$, find k when
a) the sum of the roots is 0   **b)** the sum of the roots is 4
c) the product of the roots is -6 **d)** the sum of the roots equals the product of the roots

8. a) Show that the following equation is true for the roots r_1 and r_2 of the equation $ax^2 + bx + c = 0$.
$$\frac{1}{r_1} + \frac{1}{r_2} = -\frac{b}{c}$$

b) What are the restrictions on r_1, r_2, and c?

CONNECTING MATH AND ESTHETICS

The Golden Ratio

Esthetics is a branch of philosophy that deals with our appreciation of beauty in such fields as art, music, and nature. Mathematical ideas can be appreciated and applied esthetically. Consider, for example, the following historical quotations.

> The mathematical sciences particularly exhibit order, symmetry, and limitation; and these are the greatest forms of the beautiful.
> Aristotle (384–322 B.C.)

> Geometry has two great treasures: one is the theorem of Pythagoras; the other is the division of a line into extreme and mean ratio. The first we compare to a measure of gold; the second we may name as a precious jewel.
> Johannes Kepler (A.D. 1571–1630)

The precious jewel Kepler wrote about is called the **golden ratio**. It is a number that is usually represented by the Greek letter phi (ϕ). This is the first letter in the name of Phidias, a Greek sculptor who used the golden ratio extensively in his work. The number ϕ satisfies the following proportion.

$$\frac{1}{\phi} = \frac{\phi}{1+\phi}$$

The golden ratio can be represented by a **golden rectangle**, in which the ratio of the length to the width is ϕ. Many people have found the shape of a golden rectangle esthetically pleasing, and it has been widely used in art and architecture. For example, the golden rectangle can be found in the abstract art of the Dutch painter Piet Mondrian, 1872–1944. The work shown is called *Place de la Concorde*.

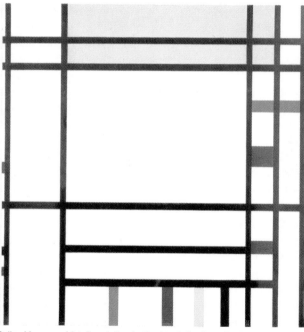

Dallas Museum of Art, Foundation for the Arts Collection, gift of the James H. and Lillian Clark Foundation

A golden rectangle has dimensions that satisfy the following proportion.

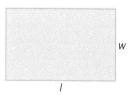

$$\frac{w}{l} = \frac{l}{w+l}$$

To find the golden ratio, let the width, w, of the rectangle be 1 unit. Then,

$$\frac{1}{l} = \frac{l}{1+l}$$

Multiplying by the common denominator $l(1 + l)$ gives

$$1 + l = l^2$$
$$\text{or } l^2 - l - 1 = 0$$

1 Investigating ø

1. For the equation $l^2 - l - 1 = 0$, the positive root, expressed in radical form, is the exact value of the golden ratio, ϕ.

a) Solve the equation. Leave the exact value of ϕ in radical form.

b) Use your calculator to evaluate ϕ, to the nearest thousandth.

c) Use the approximate value of ϕ to identify golden rectangles in Piet Mondrian's *Place de la Concorde*.

2. a) Square the exact value of ϕ. Simplify the result and leave it in radical form.

b) Use your calculator to evaluate ϕ^2, to the nearest thousandth.

c) How is the approximate value of ϕ^2 related to the approximate value of ϕ?

d) Subtract the exact value of ϕ from the exact value of ϕ^2. Compare the result with your answer to part c).

3. a) Find the exact value of $\dfrac{1}{\phi}$. Express your answer in radical form with a rational denominator.

b) Use your calculator to evaluate $\dfrac{1}{\phi}$, to the nearest thousandth.

c) How is the approximate value of $\dfrac{1}{\phi}$ related to the approximate value of ϕ?

d) Subtract the exact value of $\dfrac{1}{\phi}$ from the exact value of ϕ. Compare the result with your answer to part c).

4. Use the exact value of ϕ to show each of the following.

a) $\phi = \dfrac{1}{\phi - 1}$ **b)** $\phi = 2 - \dfrac{1}{\phi^2}$

5. Sequence a) For the sequence $t_1 = 1$, $t_2 = \phi$, $t_3 = \phi^2$, $t_4 = \phi^3$, $t_5 = \phi^4$, ..., write expressions for t_6, t_{22}, and t_n.

b) Use the exact value of ϕ to write the sum $t_1 + t_2$ in radical form.

c) Which term in the sequence equals the sum found in part b)?

d) Use the exact value of ϕ to write the sum $t_2 + t_3$ in radical form.

e) Which term in the sequence equals the sum found in part d)?

f) Use the pattern to predict the term that is the sum of $t_3 + t_4$; $t_8 + t_9$; $t_n + t_{n+1}$.

g) Name another sequence in which terms are generated using the pattern you used in part f).

2 Geometry and ø

1. The base of the square ABCD has been bisected at E. With centre E and radius EC, an arc is drawn to cut AB extended at F. Let the length AB be 2 units.

Show that $\dfrac{AF}{AB} = \phi$.

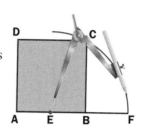

2. In $\triangle ABC$, $\angle B = 90°$, and AB = 2BC. With centre C and radius CB, an arc is drawn to cut AC at D. With centre A and radius AD, an arc is drawn to cut AB at E.

Show that $\dfrac{AB}{AE} = \phi$

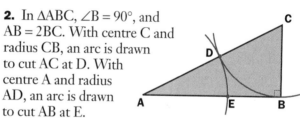

3. The diagram shows a regular pentagon of side length one unit. Three vertices are named as shown. Use the law of cosines, as follows, to find the length of the diagonal BC, to the nearest thousandth.

$$a^2 = b^2 + c^2 - 2bc \cos A$$

Compare the result to ϕ.

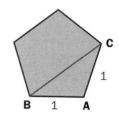

4. A golden triangle is an isosceles triangle in which the ratio of the length of one of the equal sides to the length of the base is the golden ratio. Describe how you could modify the construction method in question 1 to construct a golden triangle. Explain your reasoning.

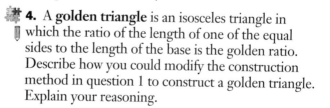

3 Fibonacci Numbers and ø

1. Sequence An approximation of ϕ can be found in the Fibonacci numbers,

$$1, 1, 2, 3, 5, 8, 13, 21, \ldots$$

The ratios of consecutive pairs of Fibonacci numbers converge to the golden ratio, ϕ. The ratio of the two consecutive Fibonacci numbers 13 and 21 gives $\dfrac{21}{13} = 1.615\,384\ldots$, which correctly shows the first three digits of ϕ. Which two consecutive Fibonacci numbers correctly show the first six digits of ϕ?

2. The following continued fraction also converges to the golden ratio.

$$1 + \cfrac{1}{1 + \cfrac{1}{1 + \ldots}}$$

a) Simplify. $1 + \cfrac{1}{1 + \cfrac{1}{1+1}}$

b) Simplify. $1 + \cfrac{1}{1 + \cfrac{1}{1 + \cfrac{1}{1 + \cfrac{1}{1+1}}}}$

c) Describe how numbers found in the simplification of the continued fraction are related to the Fibonacci numbers.

d) Write the continued fraction that equals $\dfrac{34}{21}$.

3. Sequence Aside from the first two terms, each term in the Fibonacci sequence is found by adding the two preceding terms. Suppose the first two terms of a sequence are natural numbers chosen at random, and subsequent terms are found using the same rule used in the Fibonacci sequence.
a) Write the first 10 terms of the sequence that begins 2, 5, ...
b) Determine the ratio of each pair of successive terms. To what value do the ratios converge?
c) Repeat parts a) and b) for a sequence that begins with two natural numbers of your choice.

4 ø in Architecture, Design, and Nature

1. Parthenon The Parthenon is in Athens, Greece. The width of the Parthenon and its height at the apex are approximately in the golden ratio. If the width is about 29 m, what is its height at the apex, to the nearest metre?

2. Great Pyramid The Great Pyramid of Cheops has a height of 146 m. The square base has a side length of 230 m. How does the slant height of a face compare with half the side length of the base?

3. Canadian money A Canadian $5 bill measures 152 mm by 70 mm. Compare the length of a diagonal of the bill, AC, with the length of a diagonal of half the bill, BC.

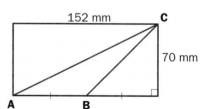

4. Nature Use your research skills to find examples of the golden ratio in nature.

Solving Quadratic Equations With a Graphing Calculator

1 Solving Algebraically

You have seen how a graphing calculator can be used to solve a quadratic equation graphically.

Complete the following with a graphing calculator that has the capability to solve quadratic equations algebraically.

Solve.

1. $x^2 - 3x - 4 = 0$

2. $x^2 + 3x - 10 = 0$

3. $x^2 + 6x + 5 = 0$

4. $y^2 - 7y + 6 = 0$

5. $x^2 - 16x + 64 = 0$

6. $n^2 - 0.49 = 0$

7. $2x^2 + x = 1$

8. $6p^2 - 5p - 6 = 0$

9. $7x^2 = -3x$

10. $(3x + 4)(x + 1) = 2$

11. $0.1x^2 + 0.2x - 1.5 = 0$

12. $2.7s^2 + 8.1s = 10.8$

13. $\dfrac{x^2}{2} - \dfrac{x}{3} = \dfrac{4}{3}$

14. $\dfrac{x^2 + 1}{5} + \dfrac{1 - x^2}{3} = x$

15. $\dfrac{4z^2}{3} - 3(z^2 - 5) = \dfrac{z - 3}{2}$

Solve.

16. $x^2 + 4x - 7 = 0$

17. $a^2 - 6a + 4 = 0$

18. $x^2 - 5x = -2$

19. $2x^2 + 7x - 12 = 0$

20. $3t^2 + 5t + 1 = 0$

21. $0.3x^2 - 2.3 = 1.2x$

22. $1.5k^2 + 6.2k - 11 = 0$

23. $(x + 2)(x - 3) = 5$

24. $5(2x^2 - 5) = -2(4 - x)$

25. $\dfrac{w^2}{4} + \dfrac{w}{2} = 1$

26. $\dfrac{x + 7}{5} - \dfrac{3 - x}{2} = \dfrac{x^2}{4}$

27. $\dfrac{3b - 4}{6} - \dfrac{3b^2}{4} = 2(2b - 3)$

28. $\dfrac{2}{x - 3} = -x$

29. $\dfrac{4}{x^2 - 3} = \dfrac{2}{3}$

30. $\dfrac{3y}{y - 1} + \dfrac{4}{y - 2} = 0$

2 Nature of the Roots

1. a) Solve $x^2 + 2x + 13 = 0$ algebraically with paper and pencil.

b) Try to solve $x^2 + 2x + 13 = 0$ algebraically with your graphing calculator. If you are able to find the imaginary roots, describe your method.

Solve algebraically with a graphing calculator, if possible. If your graphing calculator does not solve the equation algebraically, solve it by another method.

2. $2x^2 - 5x + 3 = 0$

3. $4x^2 + 6x + 5 = 0$

4. $2x^2 + \dfrac{x^2 + 1}{2} = \dfrac{1}{5}$

5. Solve each of the following equations algebraically using pencil and paper, and then using a graphing calculator. Compare the solutions from the two methods. Can your calculator deal with a situation in which some roots are real and some roots are imaginary?

a) $x^3 + x = 0$

b) $x^4 - 1 = 0$

c) $x^4 - 2x^2 - 15 = 0$

4.8 The Remainder Theorem

Canadian Catherine Bond-Mills won the bronze medal in the heptathlon at the Commonwealth Games in Victoria, British Columbia. In the heptathlon, athletes compete in seven events. One of them is the shot-put.

For a certain "put," the function $h(t) = -5t^2 + 8t + 2$ describes the height of the shot, $h(t)$ metres, as a function of the time, t seconds, since it was released.

Explore: Discover the Relationship

Divide each polynomial in the table by the given divisor of the form $x - b$. Also, evaluate $P(b)$. Copy and complete the table. Check your completed table with a classmate.

	Polynomial, $P(x)$	Divisor, $x - b$	Quotient	Remainder	$P(b)$
1.	$x^2 - 7x + 16$	$x - 3$			$P(3) = \blacksquare$
2.	$2x^2 + 3x - 8$	$x - 2$			$P(2) = \blacksquare$
3.	$3x^2 + 8x + 4$	$x + 2$			$P(-2) = \blacksquare$
4.	$x^3 + 3x^2 - 3x - 2$	$x - 1$			$P(1) = \blacksquare$
5.	$x^3 - 6x - 6$	$x + 2$			$P(-2) = \blacksquare$
6.	$2x^3 - x^2 - 2x + 3$	$x + 1$			$P(-1) = \blacksquare$

Inquire

1. When each polynomial is divided by $x - b$, what is the relationship between the remainder and the value of $P(b)$?

2. Without dividing each polynomial, how could you find the remainder given by each of the following divisors?
a) $x - 4$ **b)** $x + 3$

3. Without dividing, find the remainder when $x^3 + 2x^2 - 7x - 2$ is divided by
a) $x - 1$ **b)** $x + 1$ **c)** $x - 2$ **d)** $x + 3$

4. When a divisor is a factor of a polynomial, what is the remainder? Explain.

5. a) What is the remainder when the polynomial that represents the height of the shot, $-5t^2 + 8t + 2$, is divided by $t - 1$?
b) What does this remainder represent?

The division of polynomials by divisors of the form $x - b$, as in the exploration on the previous page, can be generalized as follows.

If a polynomial $P(x)$ is divided by $x - b$, and the division is continued until the remainder is a constant R, then

$$\text{Dividend} = (\text{Divisor})(\text{Quotient}) + \text{Remainder}$$

So, if the quotient is $Q(x)$, the following division statement is true for all values of x.

$$P(x) = (x - b) \times Q(x) + R$$

Substitute b for x: $\quad P(b) = (b - b) \times Q(b) + R$

Simplify: $\qquad\qquad P(b) = 0 \times Q(b) + R$

$$P(b) = R$$

This relationship between $P(b)$ and R is expressed in the **remainder theorem**, which can be stated as follows.

> When a polynomial $P(x)$ is divided by $x - b$, and the remainder is a constant, then the remainder is $P(b)$.

Example 1   Finding a Remainder

Find the remainder when the polynomial $2x^3 - 4x^2 + 3x - 6$ is divided by $x + 2$.

Solution

In the remainder theorem, the divisor is written in the form $x - b$.
So, $x + 2$ becomes $x - (-2)$.
The remainder theorem states that, when $2x^3 - 4x^2 + 3x - 6$ is divided by $x - (-2)$, the remainder is $P(-2)$.

Let $P(x) = 2x^3 - 4x^2 + 3x - 6$.

$$P(-2) = 2(-2)^3 - 4(-2)^2 + 3(-2) - 6$$
$$= -16 - 16 - 6 - 6$$
$$= -44$$

The remainder is -44.

Using the remainder theorem is an alternative to carrying out the division.

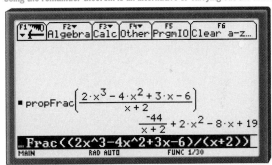

Example 2   Finding a Coefficient

When the polynomial $y^3 - ky^2 + 17y + 6$ is divided by $y - 3$, the remainder is 12. What is the value of k?

Solution

Let $P(y) = y^3 - ky^2 + 17y + 6$.

$$P(3) = (3)^3 - k(3)^2 + 17(3) + 6$$
$$= 27 - 9k + 51 + 6$$
$$= -9k + 84$$

From the remainder theorem, $P(3)$ is the remainder from the division by $y - 3$, so $P(3) = 12$.

So, $\quad 12 = -9k + 84$
$\qquad -72 = -9k$
$\qquad\quad 8 = k$

The value of k is 8.

Example 3   Using a System of Linear Equations

When the polynomial $P(x) = 3x^3 + mx^2 + nx - 7$ is divided by $x - 2$, the remainder is -3. When the polynomial is divided by $x + 1$, the remainder is -18. What are the values of m and n?

Solution

Use the given information to write a system of linear equations.

$$P(x) = 3x^3 + mx^2 + nx - 7$$
$$P(2) = 3(2)^3 + m(2)^2 + n(2) - 7$$
$$= 24 + 4m + 2n - 7$$
$$= 4m + 2n + 17$$

From the remainder theorem, we know that $P(2) = -3$.

So, $\quad -3 = 4m + 2n + 17$
$$-20 = 4m + 2n$$
$$-10 = 2m + n$$

So, $2m + n = -10$ (1)

$$P(x) = 3x^3 + mx^2 + nx - 7$$
$$P(-1) = 3(-1)^3 + m(-1)^2 + n(-1) - 7$$
$$= -3 + m - n - 7$$
$$= m - n - 10$$

From the remainder theorem, we know that $P(-1) = -18$.

So, $\quad -18 = m - n - 10$
$$-8 = m - n$$

So, $m - n = -8$ (2)

Solve the system of linear equations.

$$2m + n = -10 \quad (1)$$
$$m - n = -8 \quad (2)$$

Add (1) and (2): $3m = -18$

Solve for m: $m = -6$

Substitute -6 for m in (1).

$$2m + n = -10$$
$$2(-6) + n = -10$$
$$-12 + n = -10$$
$$n = 2$$

Check in (1).   Check in (2).

L.S. $= 2m + n$ **R.S.** $= -10$ **L.S.** $= m - n$ **R.S.** $= -8$
$= 2(-6) + 2$ $\qquad\qquad\qquad\qquad = -6 - 2$
$= -12 + 2$ $\qquad\qquad\qquad\qquad\quad\; = -8$
$= -10$

The value of m is -6, and the value of n is 2.

The remainder theorem can be extended to include divisors in which the coefficient of x is not 1. Dividing $2x^2 - 5x + 4$ by $2x - 3$ gives a remainder of 1, as shown.

$$\begin{array}{r} x - 1 \\ 2x - 3 \overline{)\, 2x^2 - 5x + 4} \\ \underline{2x^2 - 3x} \\ -2x + 4 \\ \underline{-2x + 3} \\ 1 \end{array}$$

This remainder can also be found by evaluating $P\left(\dfrac{3}{2}\right)$.

$$P\left(\frac{3}{2}\right) = 2\left(\frac{3}{2}\right)^2 - 5\left(\frac{3}{2}\right) + 4$$

$$= 2\left(\frac{9}{4}\right) - \frac{15}{2} + 4$$

$$= \frac{9}{2} - \frac{15}{2} + 4$$

$$= -3 + 4$$

$$= 1$$

In general, if $P(x)$ is divided by $ax - b$, and the division is continued until the quotient is $Q(x)$ and the remainder is a constant R, then the following division statement is true for all values of x.

$$P(x) = (ax - b) \times Q(x) + R$$

Substitute $\dfrac{b}{a}$ for x: $P\left(\dfrac{b}{a}\right) = \left(a \times \dfrac{b}{a} - b\right) \times Q\left(\dfrac{b}{a}\right) + R$

Simplify: $P\left(\dfrac{b}{a}\right) = 0 \times Q\left(\dfrac{b}{a}\right) + R$

$$P\left(\frac{b}{a}\right) = R$$

Thus, a more general form of the remainder theorem is as follows.

When a polynomial $P(x)$ is divided by $ax - b$, and the remainder is a constant, then the remainder is $P\left(\dfrac{b}{a}\right)$.

Example 4   Dividing When $a \neq 1$ in $ax - b$

Find the remainder when $2x^3 + 3x^2 - 7x - 3$ is divided by $2x + 5$.

Solution

Let $P(x) = 2x^3 + 3x^2 - 7x - 3$.

$$P\left(-\frac{5}{2}\right) = 2\left(-\frac{5}{2}\right)^3 + 3\left(-\frac{5}{2}\right)^2 - 7\left(-\frac{5}{2}\right) - 3$$

$$= 2\left(-\frac{125}{8}\right) + 3\left(\frac{25}{4}\right) + \frac{35}{2} - 3$$

$$= -\frac{125}{4} + \frac{75}{4} + \frac{70}{4} - 3$$

$$= \frac{20}{4} - 3$$

$$= 2$$

The remainder is 2.

Example 5　Area of a Rectangle

The area, $A(w)$, of a rectangle is represented by the expression $3w^2 - 5w + 7$, where w is the width.

a) Find the remainder when the expression is divided by $3w - 4$.

b) Interpret the remainder.

Solution

a) From the remainder theorem, when $A(w)$ is divided by $3w - 4$, the remainder equals $A\left(\dfrac{4}{3}\right)$.

$$A(w) = 3w^2 - 5w + 7$$

$$A\left(\frac{4}{3}\right) = 3\left(\frac{4}{3}\right)^2 - 5\left(\frac{4}{3}\right) + 7$$

$$= \frac{16}{3} - \frac{20}{3} + 7$$

$$= \frac{16 - 20 + 21}{3}$$

$$= \frac{17}{3}$$

b) When the width is $\dfrac{4}{3}$ units, the area of the rectangle is $\dfrac{17}{3}$ square units.

Practice

For $P(x) = 2x^2 - 3x - 2$, find the following.
 1. $P(1)$　　**2.** $P(0)$　　**3.** $P(2)$　　**4.** $P(-2)$

For $P(x) = x^3 + x^2 + x - 3$, find the following.
 5. $P(1)$　　**6.** $P(-1)$　　**7.** $P(0)$　　**8.** $P(-3)$

For $f(x) = x^3 - 2x^2 + 3x + 4$, find the following.
 9. $f(1)$　　**10.** $f(-1)$　　**11.** $f(-2)$　　**12.** $f(3)$

For $g(y) = 2y^3 - 3y^2 + 5$, find the following.
 13. $g(-2)$　　**14.** $g(4)$　　**15.** $g(0)$　　**16.** $g\left(\dfrac{1}{2}\right)$

Use the remainder theorem to determine the remainder when each polynomial is divided by $x - 2$.
 17. $x^2 - 5x - 3$　　　　**18.** $2x^2 + x - 10$
 19. $x^3 + 2x^2 - 8x + 1$　　**20.** $x^3 - 3x^2 + 5x - 2$
 21. $3x^3 - 12x - 2$　　　**22.** $2x^3 + 3x^2 - 9x - 10$

Use the remainder theorem to determine the remainder when $2x^3 - x^2 - 4x - 4$ is divided by each binomial.
 23. $x - 1$　　**24.** $x + 1$　　**25.** $x - 2$　　**26.** $x + 3$

Use the remainder theorem to determine the remainder for each division.
 27. $(x^2 + 2x + 4) \div (x - 2)$
 28. $(4n^2 + 7n - 5) \div (n + 3)$
 29. $(x^3 + 2x^2 - 3x - 1) \div (x - 1)$
 30. $(x^3 + 6x^2 - 3x^2 - x + 8) \div (x + 1)$

 31. $(2w^3 + 3w^2 - 5w + 2) \div (w + 3)$
 32. $(y^3 - 8) \div (y + 2)$
 33. $(x^3 + x^2 + 3) \div (x + 4)$
 34. $(1 - x^3) \div (x - 1)$
 35. $(m^4 - 2m^3 + m^2 + 12m - 6) \div (m - 2)$
 36. $(2 - 3t + t^2 + t^3) \div (t - 4)$
 37. $(2y^4 - 3y^2 + 1) \div (y - 3)$
 38. $(2 - x + x^2 - x^3 - x^4) \div (x + 2)$
 39. $\left(3x^2 - \sqrt{2}x + 3\right) \div \left(x + \sqrt{2}\right)$
 40. $(2r^4 - 4r^2 - 9) \div \left(r - \sqrt{3}\right)$

Use the remainder theorem to determine the remainder for each division.
 41. $(2x^2 + 5x + 7) \div (2x - 3)$
 42. $(6p^2 + 5p - 4) \div (3p + 4)$
 43. $(x^3 + 2x^2 - 4x + 1) \div (2x - 1)$
 44. $(2y^3 + y^2 - 6y + 3) \div (2y + 1)$
 45. $(9m^3 - 6m^2 + 3m + 2) \div (3m - 1)$
 46. $(8t^3 + 4t^2 - 19) \div (2t + 3)$

For each dividend, find the value of k if the remainder is 3.
 47. $(kx^2 + 3x + 1) \div (x + 2)$
 48. $(x^3 + x^2 + kx - 17) \div (x - 2)$
 49. $(x^3 + 4x^2 - x + k) \div (x - 1)$
 50. $(x^3 + kx^2 + x + 2) \div (x + 1)$

51. When the polynomial $4x^3 + mx^2 + nx + 11$ is divided by $x + 2$, the remainder is -7. When the polynomial is divided by $x - 1$, the remainder is 14. What are the values of m and n?

52. The polynomial $px^3 - x^2 + qx - 2$ has no remainder when divided by $x - 1$, and a remainder of -18 when divided by $x + 2$. Find the values of p and q.

53. The polynomial $3x^3 + vx^2 - 5x + w$ has a remainder of -1 when divided by $x + 2$, and a remainder of 109 when divided by $x - 3$. What are the values of v and w?

Applications and Problem Solving

54. The divisions $(2x^3 + 4x^2 - kx + 5) \div (x + 3)$ and $(6y^3 - 3y^2 + 2y + 7) \div (2y - 1)$ have the same remainder. Find the value of k.

55. When $ka^3 - 3a^2 + 5a - 8$ is divided by $a - 2$, the remainder is 22. What is the remainder when $ka^3 - 3a^2 + 5a - 8$ is divided by $a + 1$?

56. Measurement The area, $A(h)$, of a triangle is represented by the expression $h^2 + 0.5h$, where h is the height.
a) Find the remainder when the expression is divided by $2h - 7$.
b) Interpret the remainder.

57. Numbers The product of two numbers is represented by the expression $6n^2 - 5n + 8$, where n is one of the numbers.
a) Find the remainder when the expression is divided by $2n + 1$.
b) Interpret the remainder.

58. Suspension bridge The main span of the Tsing Ma Bridge in Hong Kong is the longest span of any suspension bridge in the world. If the origin is placed on the roadway of the main span, below the lowest point on a support cable, the shape of the cable can be modelled by the function
$$h(d) = 0.0003d^2 + 2$$
where $h(d)$ metres is the height of the cable above the roadway, and d metres is the horizontal distance from the lowest point on the cable.
a) Find the remainder when $0.0003d^2 + 2$ is divided by $d - 500$.

b) Find the remainder when $0.0003d^2 + 2$ is divided by $d + 500$.
c) Compare the results from parts a) and b). Use the graph of the function $h(d) = 0.0003d^2 + 2$ to explain your findings.

59. Hammer throw The hammer throw is an Olympic throwing event. The path of the hammer in one throw can be modelled by the function
$$h(d) = -0.017d^2 + 1.3d + 2.5$$
where $h(d)$ metres is the height of the hammer, and d metres is the horizontal distance of the hammer from the point where it was released.
a) Divide the polynomial $-0.017d^2 + 1.3d + 2.5$ by $d - 50$.
b) Interpret the remainder from part a).
c) Divide the polynomial $-0.017d^2 + 1.3d + 2.5$ by $d - 80$.
d) Does the remainder from part c) have any meaning for the hammer throw? Explain.

60. When $x^2 + 5x + 7$ is divided by $x + k$, the remainder is 3. Find k.

61. When the polynomial $bx^2 + cx + d$ is divided by $x - a$, the remainder is zero.
a) What can you conclude from this result?
b) Write an equation that expresses a in terms of b, c, and d.

62. A polynomial, $P(x)$, is divided by $x - b$ to give a quotient, $Q(x)$, and a remainder, R.
a) Predict the quotient and the remainder when $P(x)$ is divided by $b - x$.
b) Use an example with a non-zero remainder to test your prediction.
c) Use the division statements for the division by $x - b$ and the division by $b - x$ to explain your findings.

63. Working backward Write a polynomial that satisfies each set of conditions. Have a classmate check that the polynomial satisfies the conditions.
a) a quadratic polynomial that gives a remainder of -4 when it is divided by $x - 3$
b) a cubic polynomial that gives a remainder of 3 when it is divided by $x + 2$
c) a quartic polynomial that gives a remainder of 1 when it is divided by $2x - 1$

4.9 The Factor Theorem

Easter Island, also known as Rapa Nui, belongs to Chile. The island is in the Pacific Ocean, about 3700 km west of Chile. Easter Island is important to archeologists because of the gigantic statues found there. The statues consist of large heads, with elongated noses and ears. The construction of the statues started about 1800 years ago. They were carved from rectangular prisms made of volcanic rock. About 100 of the 600 original statues remain.

Several statues were carved from prisms whose volumes can be represented by the expression $x^3 - 9x^2 + 20x$, where x metres is the height of each prism. Factoring the expression $x^3 - 9x^2 + 20x$ will give the other dimensions of each prism.

For the integer 6, the factors over the integers are 1, 2, 3, 6, –1, –2, –3, and –6. The factors all divide 6 to give a remainder of 0. This concept can be applied to polynomials. For example, the polynomial $x^2 - 5x + 6$ can be factored as follows. $x^2 - 5x + 6 = (x - 2)(x - 3)$

The remainder theorem can be used to find the remainder when $x^2 - 5x + 6$ is divided by each of its factors.

$$P(x) = x^2 - 5x + 6 \qquad P(x) = x^2 - 5x + 6$$
$$P(2) = 2^2 - 5(2) + 6 \qquad P(3) = 3^2 - 5(3) + 6$$
$$= 4 - 10 + 6 \qquad\qquad = 9 - 15 + 6$$
$$= 0 \qquad\qquad\qquad = 0$$

Thus, as with integers, dividing a polynomial by one of its factors gives a remainder of zero.

Explore: Discover the Relationship

Copy the table. Complete it by using the remainder theorem to find the remainder for each division. Determine which binomials are factors of each given polynomial.

	Polynomial, $P(x)$	Divisor, $x - b$	Remainder, $P(b)$	Factor? (Yes or No)
1.	$x^3 + x^2 - 4x - 4$	$x + 1$	0	y
2.	$x^3 + x^2 - 4x - 4$	$x - 1$	-6	n
3.	$x^3 + x^2 - 4x - 4$	$x - 2$	0	y
4.	$x^3 + x^2 - 4x - 4$	$x + 2$	0	y
5.	$x^3 + x^2 - 4x - 4$	$x + 3$	-10	n
6.	$x^3 + 2x^2 - 5x - 6$	$x + 1$	0	y
7.	$x^3 + 2x^2 - 5x - 6$	$x - 2$	0	y
8.	$x^3 + 2x^2 - 5x - 6$	$x - 3$	24	n
9.	$x^3 + 2x^2 - 5x - 6$	$x + 3$	0	y
10.	$x^3 + 2x^2 - 5x - 6$	$x + 4$	-18	n
11.	$x^3 + 2x^2 - 5x - 6$	$x - 5$	144	n
12.	$x^3 + 2x^2 - 5x - 6$	$x + 6$	-120	0

Inquire

1. When a binomial is a factor, is its constant term a factor of the constant term of the polynomial? If so, explain why.

2. If the constant term of a binomial is a factor of the constant term of the polynomial, is the binomial always a factor?

3. a) What are the possible values of b for the binomial factors, $x - b$, of $x^3 + 2x^2 - 13x + 10$?
b) Test the possible values of b to find the three binomial factors of $x^3 + 2x^2 - 13x + 10$.
c) Multiply the three binomial factors to check that their product is $x^3 + 2x^2 - 13x + 10$.

4. a) Factor the expression $x^3 - 9x^2 + 20x$ to find the dimensions of the rectangular prisms used for some of the statues on Easter Island.
b) Use the remainder theorem to check your answers to part a).
c) If x represents 6 m, what were the dimensions of each rectangular prism?

The following synthetic division shows the result when the polynomial $x^3 - 6x^2 + 7x + 6$ is divided by $x - 3$.

$$
\begin{array}{r|rrrr}
3 & 1 & -6 & 7 & 6 \\
  &   & 3 & -9 & -6 \\
\hline
  & 1 & -3 & -2 & 0
\end{array}
$$
←The remainder is 0.

The remainder theorem can also be used to find the remainder.
$$P(x) = x^3 - 6x^2 + 7x + 6$$
$$P(3) = (3)^3 - 6(3)^2 + 7(3) + 6$$
$$= 27 - 54 + 21 + 6$$
$$= 0$$

The division statement is as follows.
$$\text{Dividend} = \text{Quotient} \times \text{Divisor} + \text{Remainder}$$
$$x^3 - 6x^2 + 7x + 6 = (x^2 - 3x - 2) \times (x - 3) + 0$$

The remainder is 0, so $x - 3$ is a factor of $x^3 - 6x^2 + 7x + 6$.

The above example illustrates the **factor theorem**, which is a special case of the remainder theorem. The factor theorem can be stated as follows.

A polynomial $P(x)$ has $x - b$ as a factor if and only if $P(b) = 0$.

The factor theorem can be established as follows.
If a polynomial $P(x)$ has $x - b$ as a factor, then
$$P(x) = (x - b) \times Q(x)$$
Substitute b for x: $\quad P(b) = (b - b) \times Q(b)$
Simplify: $\qquad\qquad P(b) = 0$
Conversely, if $P(b) = 0$, then, by the remainder theorem, the remainder is 0 when $P(x)$ is divided by $x - b$, that is, $x - b$ is a factor of $P(x)$.
The factor theorem can be used to find or verify a factor of a polynomial.

Example 1   Verifying a Factor $x - b$

Show that $x + 2$ is a factor of $x^3 + 5x^2 + 2x - 8$.

Solution

From the factor theorem, if $x + 2$ is a factor of $P(x) = x^3 + 5x^2 + 2x - 8$, then $P(-2) = 0$.

$P(-2) = (-2)^3 + 5(-2)^2 + 2(-2) - 8$

$\qquad = -8 + 20 - 4 - 8$

$\qquad = 0$

Since $P(-2) = 0$, $x + 2$ is a factor of $x^3 + 5x^2 + 2x - 8$.

When attempting to factor a polynomial, it is helpful to know which values of b to try. The **integral zero theorem,** which can be expressed as follows, lets you decide.

> If $x = b$ is an integral zero of a polynomial $P(x)$ with integral coefficients, then b is a factor of the constant term of the polynomial.

If $x = b$ is an integral zero of a polynomial, then $x - b$ is a factor of the polynomial. Therefore, we can use the factors of the constant term of the polynomial to look for factors of the polynomial.

Example 2   Factoring Using the Integral Zero Theorem

Factor $x^3 + 3x^2 + 13x - 15$.

Solution

Find a factor by evaluating $P(x)$ for values of x that equal the possible values of b. The possible values of b are the factors of 15, which are $\pm 1, \pm 3, \pm 5,$ and ± 15.

The factors of 15 and −15 are the same.

$P(x) = x^3 + 3x^2 - 13x - 15$

$P(1) = 1^3 + 3(1)^2 - 13(1) - 15$

$\qquad = -24$

$P(-1) = (-1)^3 + 3(-1)^2 - 13(-1) - 15$

$\qquad = -1 + 3 + 13 - 15$

$\qquad = 0$

Since $P(-1) = 0$, $x + 1$ is a factor of $x^3 + 3x^2 - 13x - 15$.
Use synthetic division to find another factor.

An alternative is to divide using a suitable graphing calculator.

$$
\begin{array}{r|rrrr}
-1 & 1 & 3 & -13 & -15 \\
   &   & -1 & -2 & 15 \\
\hline
   & 1 & 2 & -15 & 0 \\
\end{array}
$$

Another factor is $x^2 + 2x - 15$.
So, $x^3 + 3x^2 - 13x - 15 = (x + 1)(x^2 + 2x - 15)$.
Factoring $x^2 + 2x - 15$ gives $(x - 3)(x + 5)$.
So, $x^3 + 3x^2 - 13x - 15 = (x + 1)(x - 3)(x + 5)$.

You can check the answer by expanding the factors to give the original polynomial.

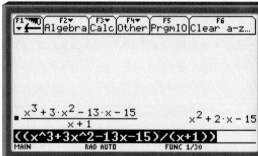

The factors of the polynomial $x^3 + 3x^2 - 13x - 15$ could have been found by graphing the corresponding function $P(x) = x^3 + 3x^2 - 13x - 15$. The x-intercepts appear to be 3, −1, and −5. These are the real zeros of the function. Using these zeros and the zero product property, the polynomial can be written in factored form, as follows.

$$P(x) = (x - 3)(x + 1)(x + 5)$$

Visualize the factors.

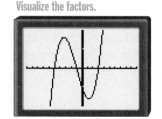

Example 3   Factoring a Polynomial

Factor $x^3 - 1$.

Solution

The factors of 1 are ± 1.

$P(x) = x^3 - 1$

$P(1) = 1^3 - 1$

$\quad\quad = 0$

Therefore, $x - 1$ is a factor of $x^3 - 1$.

Use synthetic division to find another factor.

```
1 |  1    0    0   -1        Note that x³ – 1 can be written as x³ + 0x² + 0x – 1.
  |       1    1    1
     1    1    1    0
```

Another factor of $x^3 - 1$ is $x^2 + x + 1$.

The expression $x^2 + x + 1$ cannot be factored.

So, $x^3 - 1 = (x - 1)(x^2 + x + 1)$.

Example 4   Bank Vault

A bank vault is built in the shape of a rectangular prism. Its volume, $V(w)$, is related to the width, w, of the doorway by the equation $V(w) = w^3 + 7w^2 + 16w + 12$.

a) Factor the expression $w^3 + 7w^2 + 16w + 12$.

b) If $w = 1$ m, what are the dimensions of the bank vault?

Solution

a) The factors of 12 are ± 1, ± 2, ± 3, ± 4, ± 6, and ± 12.

Because the dimensions of a bank vault are greater than the width of the doorway, test the negative factors of 12 first. Any factors of $w^3 + 7w^2 + 16w + 12$ that result will be of the form $w + n$, where n is a positive integer.

$V(w) = w^3 + 7w^2 + 16w + 12$

$V(-1) = (-1)^3 + 7(-1)^2 + 16(-1) + 12$ Use your mental math skills to complete the calculations.

$\quad\quad = 2$

$V(-2) = (-2)^3 + 7(-2)^2 + 16(-2) + 12$

$\quad\quad = 0$

So, $w + 2$ is a factor of $w^3 + 7w^2 + 16w + 12$.

Use synthetic division to find another factor.

```
-2 |  1    7    16   12
   |     -2  -10  -12
      1    5    6    0
```

So, $w^3 + 7w^2 + 16w + 12 = (w + 2)(w^2 + 5w + 6)$

Factoring $w^2 + 5w + 6$ gives $(w + 2)(w + 3)$.

So, the factors of $w^3 + 7w^2 + 16w + 12$ are $w + 2$, $w + 2$, and $w + 3$.

b) The dimensions of the bank vault are $w + 2$, $w + 2$, and $w + 3$.

So, if $w = 1$ m, the dimensions are 3 m by 3 m by 4 m.

The factor theorem can be extended to include polynomials in which the coefficient of the highest-degree term is not 1.

If a polynomial $P(x)$ has $ax - b$ as a factor, then

$$P(x) = (ax - b) \times Q(x)$$

Substitute $\dfrac{b}{a}$ for x: $\quad P\left(\dfrac{b}{a}\right) = [a\left(\dfrac{b}{a}\right) - b] \times Q\left(\dfrac{b}{a}\right)$

Simplify: $\quad P\left(\dfrac{b}{a}\right) = 0$

Conversely, if $P\left(\dfrac{b}{a}\right) = 0$, then, by the remainder theorem, the remainder is 0 when $P(x)$ is divided by $ax - b$, that is, $ax - b$ is a factor of $P(x)$.

Thus, a polynomial $P(x)$ has $ax - b$ as a factor if and only if $P\left(\dfrac{b}{a}\right) = 0$.

Example 5 Verifying a Factor $ax - b$, $a \neq 1$.

Verify that $2x - 3$ is a factor of $2x^3 - 5x^2 - x + 6$.

Solution

If $2x - 3$ is a factor of $P(x) = 2x^3 - 5x^2 - x + 6$, then $P\left(\dfrac{3}{2}\right) = 0$.

$$
\begin{aligned}
P\left(\dfrac{3}{2}\right) &= 2\left(\dfrac{3}{2}\right)^3 - 5\left(\dfrac{3}{2}\right)^2 - \dfrac{3}{2} + 6 \\
&= 2\left(\dfrac{27}{8}\right) - 5\left(\dfrac{9}{4}\right) - \dfrac{3}{2} + 6 \\
&= \dfrac{27}{4} - \dfrac{45}{4} - \dfrac{3}{2} + 6 \\
&= \dfrac{27 - 45 - 6 + 24}{4} \\
&= 0
\end{aligned}
$$

Since $P\left(\dfrac{3}{2}\right) = 0$, $2x - 3$ is a factor of $2x^3 - 5x^2 - x + 6$.

When attempting to factor a polynomial, it is helpful to know which values of a and b to try. The **rational zero theorem**, as follows, lets you decide.

If $x = \dfrac{b}{a}$ is a rational zero of a polynomial $P(x)$ with integral coefficients,

then b is a factor of the constant term of the polynomial, and a is a factor of the coefficient of the highest-degree term in the polynomial.

If $x = \dfrac{b}{a}$ is a rational zero of a polynomial, then $ax - b$ is a factor of the polynomial.

Therefore, we can use the factors of the constant term of the polynomial and the factors of the coefficient of the highest-degree term in the polynomial to look for factors of the polynomial.

Example 6 Factoring Using the Rational Zero Theorem

Factor $3x^3 - 4x^2 - 5x + 2$ completely.

Solution
If $3x^3 - 4x^2 - 5x + 2$ has a factor $ax - b$, then b is a factor of the constant term, which is 2, and a is a factor of the coefficient of x^3, which is 3.
The factors of 2 are $\pm1, \pm2$. The factors of 3 are ±1 and ±3.
Find a factor by evaluating $P(x)$ for x values that equal the possible values of $\dfrac{b}{a}$.

The possible ratios $\dfrac{b}{a}$ are $\dfrac{1}{1}, \dfrac{1}{-1}, \dfrac{-1}{1}, \dfrac{-1}{-1}, \dfrac{1}{3}, \dfrac{1}{-3}, \dfrac{-1}{3}, \dfrac{-1}{-3}, \dfrac{2}{1}, \dfrac{2}{-1}, \dfrac{-2}{1}, \dfrac{-2}{-1}, \dfrac{2}{3}, \dfrac{2}{-3}, \dfrac{-2}{3},$ and $\dfrac{-2}{-3}$.

Because some of these ratios are equal, the possible values of $\dfrac{b}{a}$ are $1, -1, 2, -2, \dfrac{1}{3}, -\dfrac{1}{3}, \dfrac{2}{3},$ and $-\dfrac{2}{3}$.

It is easier to test the integral values of $\dfrac{b}{a}$ first.

$$P(x) = 3x^3 - 4x^2 - 5x + 2$$
$$P(1) = 3(1)^3 - 4(1)^2 - 5(1) + 2$$
$$= -4$$
$$P(-1) = 3(-1)^3 - 4(-1)^2 - 5(-1) + 2$$
$$= 0$$

Since $P(-1) = 0$, $x + 1$ is a factor of $3x^3 - 4x^2 - 5x + 2$.
Use synthetic division to find another factor.

$$
\begin{array}{r|rrrr}
-1 & 3 & -4 & -5 & 2 \\
   &   & -3 & 7 & -2 \\
\hline
   & 3 & -7 & 2 & 0
\end{array}
$$

$3x^3 - 4x^2 - 5x + 2 = (x + 1)(3x^2 - 7x + 2)$
$3x^2 - 7x + 2$ can be factored as $(x - 2)(3x - 1)$.
So, $3x^3 - 4x^2 - 5x + 2 = (x + 1)(x - 2)(3x - 1)$.

The values of $\dfrac{b}{a}$ in the factors are $-1, 2,$ and $\dfrac{1}{3}$.
Note that they were all listed earlier as possible values.

The factors of the polynomial $3x^3 - 4x^2 - 5x + 2$ could have been found by graphing the corresponding function, $P(x) = 3x^3 - 4x^2 - 5x + 2$, on a graphing calculator. We know from the factors of the polynomial that one of the zeros of the function is $\dfrac{1}{3}$. The graphing calculator gives an approximate decimal value of this zero. The algebraic method shown in Example 6 leads to exact values of the zeros.

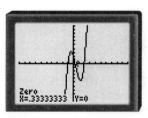

Practice

Use the factor theorem to determine whether each polynomial has a factor of $x - 1$.

1. $x^3 - 3x^2 + 4x - 2$
2. $2x^3 - x^2 - 3x - 2$
3. $3x^3 - x - 3$
4. $2x^3 + 4x^2 - 5x - 1$
5. $x^4 - 3x^3 + 2x^2 - x + 1$
6. $4x^4 - 2x^3 + 3x^2 - 2x + 1$

State whether each polynomial has a factor of $x + 2$.

7. $5x^2 + 2x + 4$
8. $x^3 + 2x^2 - 3x - 6$
9. $3x^3 + 2x^2 - 7x + 2$
10. $x^4 - 2x^2 + 3x - 4$
11. $x^4 + 3x^3 - x^2 - 3x + 6$
12. $3x^4 + 5x^3 + 3x - 2$

State whether each polynomial has a factor of $x - 4$.

13. $3x^2 - 7x - 20$

14. $x^3 - 5x^2 + 3x + 4$

15. $2x^3 - 3x^2 - 5x + 4$

16. $-x^4 + 3x^3 + 5x^2 - 16$

17. $x^4 - 2x^3 - 8x^2 + 3x - 4$

18. $2x^4 - 5x^3 - 7x^2 - 21x + 4$

Show that the binomial is a factor of the first polynomial.

19. $x^3 + 2x^2 + 2x + 1; x + 1$

20. $x^3 - 3x^2 + 4x - 4; x - 2$

21. $m^3 - 3m^2 + m - 3; m - 3$

22. $x^3 + 7x^2 + 17x + 15; x + 3$

23. $2r^3 + 4r^2 - 3r - 6; r + 2$

24. $x^4 + 5x^3 + 2x^2 + 7x - 15; x + 5$

Determine whether the second polynomial is a factor of the first polynomial.

25. $4x^2 + 3x - 8; x - 3$

26. $6x^2 - 17; x + 1$

27. $2y^3 - 5y^2 + 2y + 1; y - 1$

28. $x^3 - 6x - 4; x + 2$

29. $6x^4 + 2x^3 - 3x^2 - 1; x + 1$

30. $t^3 + t^2 - t - 1; t - 1$

State whether each polynomial has a factor of $2x - 1$.

31. $6x^2 + 5x - 4$ **32.** $4x^2 + 8x - 7$

33. $2x^3 - x^2 - 6x + 3$ **34.** $2x^3 + 9x^2 + 3x - 4$

35. $2x^4 - x^3 + 3x - 1$ **36.** $-4x^3 + 4x^2 + x - 1$

State whether each polynomial has a factor of $2x + 3$.

37. $6x^2 + 8x - 3$ **38.** $4x^2 + 8x + 3$

39. $2x^3 + 3x^2 + 4x + 6$ **40.** $6x^3 + 9x^2 + 2x - 3$

41. $2x^4 + 3x^3 - 4x - 9$ **42.** $-2x^3 - 3x^2 + 2x + 3$

Show that the binomial is a factor of the first polynomial.

43. $2x^3 + x^2 + 2x + 1; 2x + 1$

44. $2x^3 - 3x^2 - 2x + 3; 2x - 3$

45. $3y^3 + 8y^2 + 3y - 2; 3y - 1$

46. $6n^3 - 7n^2 + 1; 3n + 1$

47. $3x^3 - 4x^2 - x + 2; 3x + 2$

48. $3x^4 - 2x^3 + 12x - 8; 3x - 2$

Determine whether the binomial is a factor of the first polynomial.

49. $8x^2 + 2x - 1; 2x - 1$

50. $3x^3 - x^2 - 3x + 1; 3x - 1$

51. $2x^3 + 11x^2 + 7x + 1; 2x + 1$

52. $4n^3 - 3n^2 - 5n - 1; 4n + 1$

53. $2x^3 - 3x^2 - 3; 2x - 3$

54. $2x^3 - 3x^2 - 8x + 5; 2x + 5$

Factor completely.

55. $x^3 - 6x^2 + 11x - 6$ **56.** $x^3 + 8x^2 + 19x + 12$

57. $x^3 - 2x^2 - 9x + 18$ **58.** $x^3 + 4x^2 + 2x - 3$

59. $z^3 + z^2 - 22z - 40$ **60.** $x^3 + x^2 - 16x - 16$

61. $x^3 - 2x^2 - 6x - 8$ **62.** $k^3 + 6k^2 - 7k - 60$

63. $x^3 - 27x + 10$ **64.** $x^3 + 4x^2 - 15x - 18$

Factor.

65. $2x^3 - 9x^2 + 10x - 3$

66. $4y^3 - 7y - 3$

67. $3x^3 - 4x^2 - 17x + 6$

68. $3x^3 - 2x^2 - 12x + 8$

69. $2x^3 + 13x^2 + 23x + 12$

70. $2x^3 - 3x^2 + 3x - 10$

71. $6x^3 - 11x^2 - 26x + 15$

72. $4p^3 + 8p^2 - p - 2$

73. $6w^3 + 16w^2 - 21w + 5$

74. $4x^3 + 3x^2 - 4x - 3$

Applications and Problem Solving

75. Filing cabinet The volume, $V(h)$, of a filing cabinet can be represented by the expression $h^3 - 2h^2 + h$, where h is the height of the cabinet.

a) Factor the expression $h^3 - 2h^2 + h$.

b) If the height is 1.5 m, state the other dimensions of the cabinet.

76. Squash court The volume, $V(l)$, of a squash court can be represented approximately by the expression $3l^3 - l^2 - 4l$, where l is the length from the front wall to the back wall.

a) Factor the expression $3l^3 - l^2 - 4l$.

b) If l is about 4.6 m, find the other dimensions of the court.

77. Garage A garage is built in the shape of a rectangular prism. The volume, $V(h)$, can be represented by the expression $3h^3 + 8h^2 + 3h - 2$, where h is the height of the garage door.

a) Factor the expression $3h^3 + 8h^2 + 3h - 2$.

b) If the height of the door is 2 m, find the dimensions of the garage.

78. Factor.

a) $x^4 + 4x^3 - 7x^2 - 34x - 24$

b) $x^5 + 3x^4 - 5x^3 - 15x^2 + 4x + 12$

79. Factor.

a) $8x^3 + 4x^2 - 2x - 1$

b) $8x^3 - 12x^2 - 2x + 3$

80. Integers The product of four integers is $x^4 + 6x^3 + 11x^2 + 6x$, where x is one of the integers. How are the integers related?

81. Verify that $x + y$ is a factor of $x^2(y^2 - 1) - y^2(1 + x^2) + x^2 + y^2$.

82. The following polynomials each have a factor of $x - 3$. What is the value of k in each case?
a) $kx^3 - 10x^2 + 2x + 3$
b) $4x^4 - 3x^3 - 2x^2 + kx - 9$

83. Packing crates A shipping company uses two sizes of packing crate. Each dimension of the larger size is x metres longer than the corresponding dimension of the smaller size. The volume, $V(x)$, of the larger size can be represented by the expression $x^3 + 7x^2 + 16x + 12$. Find the dimensions of the smaller size.

84. For $P(x) = 3x^3 + 7x^2 - 22x - 8$, $P(2) = 0$, $P(-4) = 0$, and $P\left(-\dfrac{1}{3}\right) = 0$.
a) Find three factors of the polynomial.
b) Are there any other factors? Explain.

85. The polynomial $6x^3 + mx^2 + nx - 5$ has a factor of $x + 1$. When the polynomial is divided by $x - 1$, the remainder is -4. What are the values of m and n?

86. Show that $x - a$ is a factor of the polynomial $x^3 - ax^2 + bx^2 - abx + cx - ac$.

87. Measurement The edge length of a cube is $2x - 1$ units. The volume of a larger cube is $8x^3 + 12x^2 + 6x + 1$. How do the edge lengths of the two cubes compare?

88. Patterns Factor the polynomials in parts a) to f).
a) $x^3 - 1$ **b)** $x^3 + 1$
c) $x^3 - 27$ **d)** $x^3 + 64$
e) $8x^3 - 1$ **f)** $64x^3 + 1$
g) Use the results to decide whether $x + y$ or $x - y$ is a factor of $x^3 + y^3$. State the other factor.
h) Use the results to decide whether $x + y$ or $x - y$ is a factor of $x^3 - y^3$. State the other factor.
i) Use your findings to factor $8x^3 + 125$; $27x^3 - 64$.
j) Use your findings to factor $x^6 + y^9$.

89. a) Is $x + 1$ a factor of $x^{100} - 1$? Is $x - 1$? Explain.
b) Is $x + 1$ a factor of $x^{99} + 1$? Is $x - 1$? Explain.

90. Measurement Two spheres have different radii. The radius of the smaller sphere is r. The volume, $V(r)$, of the larger sphere is related to the radius of the smaller sphere by the equation $V(r) = \dfrac{4}{3}\pi(r^3 + 9r^2 + 27r + 27)$. What is the radius of the larger sphere?

91. Patterns Determine whether $x + y$ and $x - y$ are factors of each of the following.
a) $x^4 + y^4$ **b)** $x^4 - y^4$
c) $x^5 + y^5$ **d)** $x^5 - y^5$
e) $x^6 + y^6$ **f)** $x^6 - y^6$
g) $x^7 + y^7$ **h)** $x^7 - y^7$
i) Write a rule for deciding whether $x + y$ and $x - y$ are factors of $x^n + y^n$ and $x^n - y^n$.
j) Use your rule to write two factors of $x^8 - y^8$.
k) Use your rule to write a factor of $x^{11} + y^{11}$.

92. In $ax^3 + bx^2 - cx - d$, the values of a, b, c, and d are integers with no common factors. If the zeros of $ax^3 + bx^2 - cx - d$ are integers, what are the possible values of a? Explain.

93. a) If $x - 1$ is a factor of $ax^3 + bx^2 + cx + d$, what is the value of $a + b + c + d$? Explain. Use your result to decide whether $x - 1$ is a factor of each of the following polynomials.
b) $3x^3 + 5x^2 - 6x - 2$
c) $2x^3 - 9x^2 - x - 8$
d) $-5x^3 + 4x + 1$

LOGIC POWER

On the circuit board, draw 4 wires to connect A to A′, B to B′, C to C′, and D to D′, so that no wires cross and no part of any wire lies outside the board.

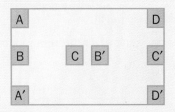

TECHNOLOGY

Exploring Polynomial Functions With a Graphing Calculator

Quadratic functions are functions of degree 2. They are also called second-degree functions. Quadratic functions have two zeros, that is, two values of the variable that make the value of the function zero. The corresponding quadratic equations can have two real roots or two imaginary roots. If the roots are real, they can be distinct or equal.

When working with functions of degree greater than 2, it is helpful to know that a function of degree n has n zeros. For example, a cubic function, such as $y = x^3 + 3x^2 - 3x - 4$, has three zeros. Cubic functions are also called third-degree functions.

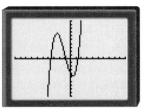

A quartic function, such as $y = x^4 - 6x^2 - x + 3$, has four zeros. Quartic functions are also called fourth-degree functions.

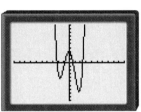

1 Cubic or Third-Degree Functions and Equations

1. Graph each cubic function in the standard viewing window. Sketch the graphs in your notebook.
a) $y = x^3 + 2x^2 - 3x - 4$ **b)** $y = x^3 + 2x^2 - 4x - 8$
c) $y = x^3 - 2x^2 - 2x - 3$ **d)** $y = x^3 - 3x^2 + 3x - 1$
e) $y = -x^3 - 3x^2 + x + 3$ **f)** $y = -x^3 + 3x^2 - 5x + 6$
g) $y = -x^3 + x^2 + 5x + 3$ **h)** $y = -x^3 + 3x^2 - 3x + 1$

2. Using the graphs from question 1, describe the general shape of the graphs of cubic functions.

3. How is the shape of the graph of a cubic function different from the shape of the graph of a quadratic function?

4. The general form of a cubic function is $y = ax^3 + bx^2 + cx + d$, where $a \neq 0$. Describe how the graphs of cubic functions where a is positive differ from those where a is negative.

5. What does the value of d represent in a cubic function?

6. a) Graph the cubic function $y = x^3 - 2x^2 - 5x + 6$. Find the x-intercepts by using the Zero operation, displaying a table of values, or using another suitable method. Sketch the graph and label the x-intercepts.
b) Do the x-intercepts from part a) satisfy the related cubic equation $x^3 - 2x^2 - 5x + 6 = 0$? Explain.

7. The real roots of a cubic equation are the x-intercepts of the related cubic function. How many real roots are there for the cubic equation that corresponds to each cubic function graphed in question 1?

8. State the possible numbers of each of the following types of roots for a cubic equation. Sketch a graph to illustrate each possibility.
a) distinct real roots
b) equal real roots
c) imaginary roots

9. Can a cubic equation have no real roots? Explain.

2 Quartic or Fourth-Degree Functions and Equations

1. Graph each quartic function in the standard viewing window. Sketch the graphs in your notebook.
a) $y = x^4 - 5x^2 + 2x + 2$
b) $y = x^4 + 3x^3 - x - 3$
c) $y = x^4 + 2x^3 + 2x + 6$
d) $y = x^4 - 4x^3 + 6x^2 - 4x + 1$
e) $y = x^4 - 2x^2 + 1$
f) $y = -x^4 + 5x^2 + 4$
g) $y = -x^4 + x^3 + 3x^2 - 2x - 5$
h) $y = -x^4 - 5x^3 - 5x^2 + 5x + 6$
i) $y = -x^4 + 3x^3 + 3x^2 - 7x - 6$
j) $y = -x^4 - 4x^3 - 5x^2 - 4x - 4$

2. Using the graphs from question 1, describe the shape of the graphs of quartic functions.

3. How is the shape of the graph of a quartic function different from the shape of the graph of a cubic function? a quadratic function?

4. The general form of a quartic function is $y = ax^4 + bx^3 + cx^2 + dx + e$, where $a \neq 0$. Describe how the graphs of quartic functions where a is positive differ from those where a is negative.

5. What does the value of e represent in a quartic function?

6. a) Graph the quartic function $y = x^4 + x^3 - 7x^2 - x + 6$. Sketch the graph and label the x-intercepts.
b) Do the x-intercepts from part a) satisfy the related quartic equation $x^4 + x^3 - 7x^2 - x + 6 = 0$? Explain.

7. The real roots of a quartic equation are the x-intercepts of the related quartic function. How many real roots are there for the quartic equation that corresponds to each quartic function graphed in question 1?

8. State the possible numbers of each of the following types of roots for a quartic equation. Sketch a graph to illustrate each possibility.
a) distinct real roots   **b)** equal real roots
c) imaginary roots

9. If a quartic equation has only equal real roots, must all four roots be the same? Explain.

3 Quintic or Fifth-Degree Functions

1. The function $y = x(x^2 - 1)(x^2 - 4)$ is a fifth-degree function or **quintic function**. Explain why.

2. Where does the graph of $y = x(x^2 - 1)(x^2 - 4)$ intersect the x-axis? Explain without graphing.

3. Sketch a predicted shape for the graph of $y = x(x^2 - 1)(x^2 - 4)$.

4. a) Graph $y = x(x^2 - 1)(x^2 - 4)$ in the standard viewing window. Sketch the graph and label the x-intercepts.
b) Describe the similarities and differences between your prediction and the actual graph.

5. Graph each of the following functions in the standard viewing window. Describe and explain the numbers of distinct real roots, equal real roots, and imaginary roots in each case.
a) $y = (x^2 - x - 2)(x^2 - 1)(x + 1)$
b) $y = (x^2 + x - 2)(x^2 - 1)(x + 1)$
c) $y = x^2(x^2 + 1)(x - 2)$
d) $y = (x - 1)^2(x - 4)^2(3 - x)$

4 Functions in the Form $y = x^n$

1. a) Graph $y = x^2$, $y = x^4$, and $y = x^6$ in the same standard viewing window.
b) How do the shapes of the three graphs compare?
c) What point(s) with integral coefficients do all three graphs have in common?
d) How is your answer to part c) related to the solutions to the equations $x^2 = 0$, $x^4 = 0$, and $x^6 = 0$?

2. a) Graph $y = x^3$, $y = x^5$, and $y = x^7$ in the standard viewing window.
b) How do the shapes of the three graphs compare?
c) What point(s) with integral coefficients do all three graphs have in common?
d) How is your answer to part c) related to the solutions to the equations $x^3 = 0$, $x^5 = 0$, and $x^7 = 0$.

4.10 Solving Polynomial Equations

Tutankhamun was born about 1343 B.C. He became king of ancient Egypt when he was only nine years old. Tutankhamun's tomb remained hidden for over 3000 years, until archeologists discovered it in 1922. The tomb is in the Valley of the Kings, in the desert west of the Nile River.

When the tomb was discovered, it contained hundreds of objects. These included many hollow boxes that had been built to hold valuables, such as gold statues. One of the boxes, in the shape of a rectangular prism, had a volume of about 45 m³. The width and the height of the box were approximately equal, and the length of the box was 2 m greater than the width.

The volume, $V(x)$, of the box, where x is the width, can be expressed as follows.

$$V = l \times w \times h$$
$$V(x) = (x + 2) \times x \times x$$
$$= x^2(x + 2)$$

So, $V(x) = x^3 + 2x^2$

The volume was 45 m³, so

$$x^3 + 2x^2 = 45$$

or $x^3 + 2x^2 - 45 = 0$

The equation $x^3 + 2x^2 - 45 = 0$ is an example of a **cubic equation**, also known as a third-degree equation.

Explore: Interpret the Graph

a) Draw the graph of $y = x^3 - 3x^2 - x + 3$.
b) What are the x-intercepts?
c) What is the y-intercept?
d) Label the intercepts on the graph.

Inquire

1. For the cubic function $y = x^3 - 3x^2 - x + 3$, the corresponding cubic equation is $x^3 - 3x^2 - x + 3 = 0$. Which points on the graph have x-coordinates that are the solutions to this equation? Explain.

2. a) Factor the left side of the equation $x^3 - 3x^2 - x + 3 = 0$ completely.
b) How can you use the factors to find the solutions to the equation?

3. Solve the following equations by factoring.
a) $x^3 - x^2 - 4x + 4 = 0$
b) $x^3 - 2x^2 - 5x + 6 = 0$
c) $x^3 - 7x - 6 = 0$
d) $x^3 - 7x^2 + 15x - 9 = 0$

The solutions of the quadratic equation $ax^2 + bx + c = 0$ are the zeros of the quadratic function $f(x) = ax^2 + bx + c$. The real zeros are the x-intercepts of the parabola $y = ax^2 + bx + c$, since the value of y is zero for these real values of x. Therefore, the x-intercepts are the real solutions, or real roots, of the quadratic equation.

Methods for solving quadratic equations include graphing, factoring, completing the square, and using the quadratic formula. Graphing does not always give the exact values of real roots. Some polynomial equations can be solved by factoring or by graphing. Again, graphing does not always give exact values of real roots. A method that gives exact real and imaginary roots for polynomial equations involves using the integral zero theorem or the rational zero theorem.

Example 1   Solving Equations With a Common Factor
Solve and check $x^3 - 4x = 0$.

Solution 1 Removing the Common Factor

$$x^3 - 4x = 0$$
Remove the common factor: $\qquad\qquad x(x^2 - 4) = 0$
Factor the binomial: $\qquad\qquad x(x - 2)(x + 2) = 0$
Use the zero product property: $\quad x = 0$ or $x - 2 = 0$ or $x + 2 = 0$
$$x = 2 \quad \text{or} \quad x = -2$$

Solution 2 Graphing
Graph the function $y = x^3 - 4x$ manually or using a graphing calculator. Find the x-intercepts.

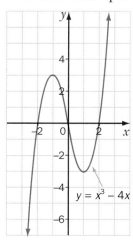

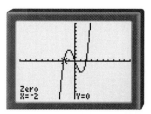

The x-intercepts appear to be -2, 0, and 2.

Check for Solution 1 and Solution 2.

For $x = 0$,
L.S. $= x^3 - 4x$ **R.S.** $= 0$
$\quad = 0^3 - 4(0)$
$\quad = 0$

For $x = 2$,
L.S. $= x^3 - 4x$ **R.S.** $= 0$
$\quad = 2^3 - 4(2)$
$\quad = 0$

For $x = -2$,
L.S. $= x^3 - 4x$ **R.S.** $= 0$
$\quad = (-2)^3 - 4(-2)$
$\quad = 0$

The roots are 0, 2, and -2.

Example 2   Finding Integral Roots
Solve $x^3 + 3x^2 - 4 = 0$.

Solution 1 Using the Integral Zero Theorem
The left side has no common factor.
Use the integral zero theorem.
The factors of 4 are ±1, ±2, and ±4.
Let $P(x) = x^3 + 3x^2 - 4$.
$$P(1) = 1^3 + 3(1)^2 - 4$$
$$= 0$$
So, $x - 1$ is a factor of $x^3 + 3x^2 - 4$.
Rewrite $x^3 + 3x^2 - 4$ as $x^3 + 3x^2 + 0x - 4$.
Synthetic division gives $x^2 + 4x + 4$ as another factor.

So, $x^3 + 3x^2 - 4 = (x - 1)(x^2 + 4x + 4)$
$$= (x - 1)(x + 2)(x + 2)$$
So, $x - 1 = 0$ or $x + 2 = 0$ or $x + 2 = 0$
$x = 1$ or $x = -2$ or $x = -2$
The roots are 1, −2, and −2.

Solution 2 Graphing
Graph the function $y = x^3 + 3x^2 - 4$ manually or using a graphing calculator. Find the x-intercepts.

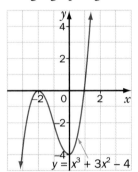

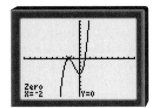

The x-intercepts appear to be −2 and 1.
There are two roots equal to −2. Checking by substitution verifies that the roots are 1, −2, and −2.

Example 3   Finding Rational Roots
Solve $3x^3 + 8x^2 + 3x - 2 = 0$.

Solution 1 Using the Rational Zero Theorem
The left side has no common factor.
Use the rational zero theorem.
In a factor $ax - b$, the possible values of $\dfrac{b}{a}$ are
$1, -1, 2, -2, \dfrac{1}{3}, -\dfrac{1}{3}, \dfrac{2}{3}$, and $-\dfrac{2}{3}$.
Let $P(x) = 3x^3 + 8x^2 + 3x - 2$.
$$P(1) = 3(1)^3 + 8(1)^2 + 3(1) - 2$$
$$= 12$$
$$P(-1) = 3(-1)^3 + 8(-1)^2 + 3(-1) - 2$$
$$= 0$$
So, $x + 1$ is a factor of $3x^3 + 8x^2 + 3x - 2$.
Synthetic division gives $3x^2 + 5x - 2$ as another factor.

So, $3x^3 + 8x^2 + 3x - 2 = (x + 1)(3x^2 + 5x - 2)$
$$= (x + 1)(x + 2)(3x - 1)$$
Since $(x + 1)(x + 2)(3x - 1) = 0$
$x + 1 = 0$ or $x + 2 = 0$ or $3x - 1 = 0$
$x = -1$ or $x = -2$ or $x = \dfrac{1}{3}$
The roots can be checked by substitution.
The roots are $-1, -2$, and $\dfrac{1}{3}$.

Solution 2 Graphing
Graph the function $y = 3x^3 + 8x^2 + 3x - 2$ manually or using a graphing calculator.
Find the x-intercepts.

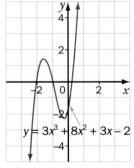

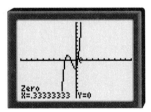

The x-intercepts appear to be −1, −2, and approximately $\dfrac{1}{3}$.

Checking by substitution verifies that the roots are $-1, -2$, and $\dfrac{1}{3}$.

Example 4 Finding Irrational Roots

For the equation $x^3 - 4x^2 + 2x + 3 = 0$.

a) Find the exact solutions.

b) Evaluate the solutions, rounded to the nearest hundredth, if necessary.

Solution Using the Quadratic Formula

a) Use the integral zero theorem.

The factors of 3 are ±1 and ±3.

Let $P(x) = x^3 - 4x^2 + 2x + 3$

$$P(1) = 1^3 - 4(1)^2 + 2(1) + 3$$
$$= 2$$
$$P(-1) = (-1)^3 - 4(-1)^2 + 2(-1) + 3$$
$$= -4$$
$$P(3) = 3^3 - 4(3)^2 + 2(3) + 3$$
$$= 0$$

So, $x - 3$ is a factor.

Find another factor by synthetic division.

```
3 | 1   -4    2    3
  |       3   -3   -3
  -----------------------
    1   -1   -1    0
```

$x^3 - 4x^2 + 2x + 3 = (x - 3)(x^2 - x - 1)$ and $(x - 3)(x^2 - x - 1) = 0$

The polynomial $x^2 - x - 1$ cannot be factored over the integers.

However, the quadratic formula can be used to solve $x^2 - x - 1 = 0$.

$x - 3 = 0$ or $x^2 - x - 1 = 0$
$x = 3$

$$x = \frac{-b \pm \sqrt{b^2 - 4ac}}{2a}$$
$$= \frac{1 \pm \sqrt{1 + 4}}{2}$$
$$= \frac{1 \pm \sqrt{5}}{2}$$

The exact solutions are 3, $\dfrac{1 + \sqrt{5}}{2}$, and $\dfrac{1 - \sqrt{5}}{2}$.

b) The two irrational solutions in part a) can be evaluated to the nearest hundredth.

The solutions are 3, −0.62, and 1.62, to the nearest hundredth.

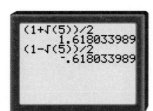

Note that approximate values of the irrational roots in Example 4 can be found by graphing $y = x^3 - 4x^2 + 2x + 3$. However, the exact values of irrational roots cannot be found by graphing.

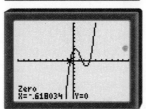

Example 5 Finding Imaginary Roots

Solve $x^3 = -1$.

Solution

$$x^3 = -1$$
$$x^3 + 1 = 0$$

Use the integral zero theorem to factor $x^3 + 1$.

The factors of 1 are ± 1.

Let $P(x) = x^3 + 1$.

$$P(1) = 1^3 + 1$$
$$= 2$$
$$P(-1) = (-1)^3 + 1$$
$$= 0$$

So, $x + 1$ is a factor.

Use synthetic division to find another factor.

$$
\begin{array}{r|rrrr}
-1 & 1 & 0 & 0 & 1 \\
   &   & -1 & 1 & -1 \\
\hline
   & 1 & -1 & 1 & 0
\end{array}
$$

Another factor is $x^2 - x + 1$, which cannot be factored further.

So, $x^3 + 1 = (x + 1)(x^2 - x + 1)$ and $(x + 1)(x^2 - x + 1) = 0$

$$x + 1 = 0 \quad \text{or} \quad x^2 - x + 1 = 0$$
$$x = -1$$

$$x = \frac{-b \pm \sqrt{b^2 - 4ac}}{2a}$$

$$= \frac{1 \pm \sqrt{1 - 4}}{2}$$

$$= \frac{1 \pm \sqrt{-3}}{2}$$

$$= \frac{1 \pm i\sqrt{3}}{2}$$

The imaginary zeros of $y = x^3 + 1$ cannot be found graphically.

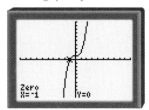

The roots are -1, $\dfrac{1 + i\sqrt{3}}{2}$, and $\dfrac{1 - i\sqrt{3}}{2}$.

Example 6 Tutankhamun's Tomb

Solve the equation $x^3 + 2x^2 - 45 = 0$ to find the dimensions of one of the boxes found in Tutankhamun's tomb, where the width and the height of the box are each x metres, and the length is $x + 2$ metres.

Solution

The factors of 45 are ± 1, ± 3, ± 5, ± 9, ± 15, and ± 45.

It is apparent that ± 1 and ± 45 will not make $P(x) = 0$.

Let $P(x) = x^3 + 2x^2 - 45$.

$$P(3) = 3^3 + 2(3)^2 - 45$$
$$= 27 + 18 - 45$$
$$= 0$$

So, $x - 3$ is a factor of $x^3 + 2x^2 - 45$.
Use synthetic division to find another factor.

$$\begin{array}{r|rrrr} 3 & 1 & 2 & 0 & -45 \\ & & 3 & 15 & 45 \\ \hline & 1 & 5 & 15 & 0 \end{array}$$

Another factor is $x^2 + 5x + 15$, which cannot be factored further.
$x^3 + 2x^2 - 45 = (x - 3)(x^2 + 5x + 15)$
So, $(x - 3)(x^2 + 5x + 15) = 0$

$$x - 3 = 0 \quad \text{or} \quad x^2 + 5x + 15 = 0$$
$$x = 3$$

$$x = \frac{-b \pm \sqrt{b^2 - 4ac}}{2a}$$
$$= \frac{-5 \pm \sqrt{25 - 60}}{2}$$
$$= \frac{-5 \pm \sqrt{-35}}{2}$$
$$= \frac{-5 \pm i\sqrt{35}}{2}$$

The roots $x = \dfrac{-5 + i\sqrt{35}}{2}$ and $x = \dfrac{-5 - i\sqrt{35}}{2}$ are imaginary and are rejected. So, $x = 3$.

The width and the height of the box are each 3 m, and the length is 5 m.

Practice

Solve.

1. $(x + 1)(x - 4)(x + 5) = 0$
2. $(y - 2)(y - 7)(y + 6) = 0$
3. $x(x + 3)(x - 8) = 0$
4. $(x + 6)(x - 3)^2 = 0$

Solve and check.

5. $x^3 + x^2 - 6x = 0$ **6.** $x^3 + 7x^2 + 12x = 0$
7. $x^3 - 4x^2 + 4x = 0$ **8.** $n^3 - 9n = 0$

Solve and check.

9. $x^3 + 3x^2 - x - 3 = 0$
10. $x^3 - 3x^2 - 4x + 12 = 0$
11. $a^3 + 2a^2 - 7a + 4 = 0$
12. $t^3 - 3t^2 - 16t + 48 = 0$
13. $x^3 - 4x^2 + x + 6 = 0$
14. $x^3 - 4x^2 - 3x + 18 = 0$
15. $x^3 - 6x^2 + 11x - 6 = 0$
16. $m^3 + 5m^2 - m - 5 = 0$
17. $x^3 + 2x^2 - 19x - 20 = 0$
18. $x^3 - x^2 - 16x - 20 = 0$

Solve and check.

19. $0 = x^3 - 9x^2 + 15x - 7$
20. $x^3 - 5x^2 = 12x - 36$
21. $k^3 - 19k = 30$
22. $x^3 - 4x^2 - 17x = -60$
23. $0 = w^3 - 5w^2 + 2w + 8$
24. $7x - 5x^2 = 3 - x^3$
25. $y(y^2 + 8y + 13) = -6$
26. $x^3 = x(x + 10) + 8$

Solve.

27. $(2x + 1)(x - 1)(x - 3) = 0$
28. $(4x + 1)(3x - 1)(x + 1) = 0$
29. $(3x - 2)(2x - 1)^2 = 0$
30. $g(g - 4)(5g + 2) = 0$

Solve and check.

31. $2x^3 - 3x^2 - 2x = 0$
32. $3x^3 - 10x^2 + 3x = 0$
33. $9z^3 - 4z = 0$
34. $16x^3 + 8x^2 + x = 0$

Solve.

35. $2x^3 + 9x^2 + 10x + 3 = 0$
36. $3x^3 - 8x^2 + 7x - 2 = 0$
37. $5x^3 - 7x^2 - 8x + 4 = 0$
38. $2d^3 - 3d^2 - 12d - 7 = 0$
39. $4x^3 + 8x^2 - 7x - 5 = 0$
40. $2x^3 - 13x^2 + 16x - 5 = 0$
41. $3x^3 + 2x^2 - 7x + 2 = 0$
42. $8n^3 - 26n^2 + 5n + 3 = 0$

Solve.

43. $2x^3 - 11x^2 + 12x = -9$
44. $9x^3 + 18x^2 = 4x + 8$
45. $6y^3 + 29y - 12 = 23y^2$
46. $x^2(2x - 1) = 2x - 1$

a) *Find the exact roots.*
b) *Evaluate the roots. Round to the nearest hundredth, if necessary.*

47. $x^3 - 8x = 0$
48. $s^3 - 10s + 3 = 0$
49. $x^3 - 6x^2 + 6x + 8 = 0$
50. $0 = x^3 + 3x^2 - 15x - 25$
51. $v^3 + 5v^2 = 18$
52. $x(x + 4)(x + 1) = 4$

Find the exact roots.

53. $2x^3 - 25x = 0$
54. $4x^3 - 8x^2 - 5x + 10 = 0$
55. $3d^3 - 4d^2 - 4d + 5 = 0$
56. $3x^3 + 11x^2 + 3x - 9 = 0$
57. $16 = 2x^3 + 9x^2$
58. $5b^3 - 11b^2 - 17b + 15 = 0$

Find the exact roots.

59. $x^3 + x = 0$
60. $x^3 + x + 2 = 0$
61. $x^3 - 3x^2 + 4x - 4 = 0$
62. $y^3 = -8$
63. $x^3 + x^2 = 6x - 4$
64. $c^3 + 8c^2 + 10c = 25$

Find the exact roots.

65. $3n^3 + 9n^2 + 10n + 4 = 0$
66. $5x^3 + 3x = 0$
67. $0 = 2x^3 - 8x^2 + 5x - 20$
68. $3x^3 - 7x^2 + 6x = 2$
69. $2m^3 + 7m^2 + 11m + 10 = 0$
70. $4x^3 = 9x^2 + 7x + 6$

Applications and Problem Solving

Solve.

71. $8x^3 - 12x^2 + 6x - 1 = 0$
72. $18x^3 + 15x^2 - 4x - 4 = 0$
73. $30x^3 + 19x^2 - 1 = 0$
74. $12y^3 - 4y^2 - 27y + 9 = 0$
75. $3x^3 + 8x^2 = 1$
76. $8a^3 + 27 = 0$

Solve.

77. $\dfrac{x^3}{2} - \dfrac{x}{3} = 0$

78. $x^3 - \dfrac{13x^2}{4} + x = -3$

79. $1 - \dfrac{1}{x} = \dfrac{1}{x^3} - \dfrac{1}{x^2}$

80. $\dfrac{2}{x-2} - \dfrac{1}{x-1} = x$

81. One root of each equation is -2. Evaluate k and find the other roots.
a) $x^3 + kx^2 - 10x - 24 = 0$
b) $3x^3 + 4x^2 + kx - 2 = 0$

82. If $x^3 - 4x^2 + kx = 0$,
a) what value of k results in two equal roots?
b) what are the roots for this value of k?

83. Write an equation that has the given roots. Is there more than one possible answer in each case? Explain.
a) $2, -1, 5$
b) $3, -2, -4$
c) $1, 1 + \sqrt{2}, 1 - \sqrt{2}$
d) $2, -1 + i, -1 - i$

84. **Integers** Find three consecutive integers with a product of -504.

Solve each of the following quartic equations.

85. $x^4 - 4x^3 + x^2 + 6x = 0$
86. $x^4 + 2x^3 - 7x^2 - 8x + 12 = 0$
87. $t^4 - 2t^3 - 11t^2 + 12t + 36 = 0$
88. $x^4 - 4x^2 + 3 = 0$
89. $x^4 - x^3 - 10x^2 + 10x + 12 = 0$
90. $x^4 - 1 = 0$
91. $2x^4 + 5x^3 + 3x^2 - x - 1 = 0$
92. $4p^4 - 8p^3 - 3p^2 + 5p + 2 = 0$

93. Measurement
The dimensions of a rectangular solid are shown. The volume of the solid is 42 cm³. Find its dimensions.

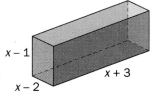

94. Packaging A toothpaste box has square ends. The length is 12 cm greater than the width. The volume of the box is 135 cm³. What are the dimensions of the box?

95. Encyclopedia A box holds the two CD-ROMs and the instruction manual for a multimedia encyclopedia. The width of the box is 15 cm greater than the height. The length of the box is 20 cm greater than the height. The volume of the box is 2500 cm³. Find the dimensions of the box.

96. Measurement A rectangular prism has dimensions 10 cm by 10 cm by 5 cm. When each dimension is increased by the same amount, the new volume is 1008 cm³. What are the dimensions of the new prism?

97. Solve $x^5 + 3x^4 - 5x^3 - 15x^2 + 4x + 12 = 0$.

98. Scaffold construction Two Scottish construction workers broke the world record for scaffold construction by building a two-storey scaffold in 25 min 53 s. The volume occupied by the scaffold was 100 m³. The length of the scaffold was four times the height. The width was 4 m less than the height. Find the dimensions of the scaffold.

99. Write a cubic equation that has a real root of 7 and two imaginary roots.

100. Suppose that 5, 2, and −3 are the solutions to a cubic equation. Sketch a graph of the corresponding cubic function. Is there more than one possible graph? Explain.

101. Container port A freight station at the Kwai Chung container port in Hong Kong is an enormous building in the shape of a rectangular prism. The length approximately equals the width. The length is about three times the height. The volume of the building is about 0.009 km³. Find the approximate dimensions of the building, in metres.

102. Brick dimensions Bricks used in building construction come in various sizes. For one size of brick, the height is two thirds of the width. The length is 2 cm more than twice the width. The volume of the brick is 1080 cm³. Find the dimensions of the brick.

103. Sandbox Selena and Carlos are building a sandbox for their community day care centre. The box is 12 times as wide as it is deep, and 1 m longer than it is wide. It holds 3 m³ of sand when full. What are the dimensions of the sandbox, in metres?

104. a) Write a cubic function with x-intercepts of $\sqrt{5}, -\sqrt{5}$, and −1, and a y-intercept of −5.
b) Write a cubic function with the same zeros as the equation in part a), but with a y-intercept of −10. Explain your reasoning.

105. If a polynomial equation of degree n has exactly one real root, what can you conclude about the value of n? Explain.

106. Decide whether each of the following statements is always true, sometimes true, or never true. Explain your reasoning.
a) A cubic equation has two real roots and one imaginary root.
b) A cubic equation has three roots.
c) A quartic equation has four imaginary roots.
d) A cubic equation has one rational root and two irrational roots.
e) A quartic equation has four equal irrational roots.
f) A quadratic equation has two equal imaginary roots.

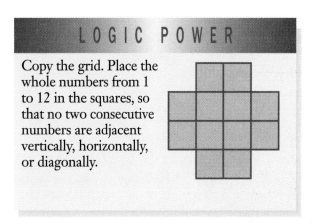

LOGIC POWER

Copy the grid. Place the whole numbers from 1 to 12 in the squares, so that no two consecutive numbers are adjacent vertically, horizontally, or diagonally.

TECHNOLOGY

Solving Polynomial Equations With a Graphing Calculator

1 Solving Algebraically

You have seen how a graphing calculator can be used to solve a polynomial equation graphically. Complete the following with a graphing calculator that has the capability to solve polynomial equations algebraically.

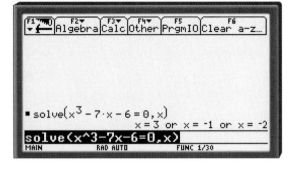

Solve.

1. $x^3 + 6x^2 - x - 30 = 0$

2. $x^3 - 7x^2 - 66x + 432 = 0$

3. $x^4 + 5x^3 - 13x^2 - 53x + 60 = 0$

4. $y^4 + 13y^3 + 49y^2 + 27y = 90$

5. $2x^3 + 17x^2 + 40x + 25 = 0$

6. $3x^2(6x + 13) = 13x + 14$

7. $4x^4 - 24x^3 + 31x^2 + 6x - 8 = 0$

8. $72a^4 + 169a^2 - 55a + 6 = 198a^3$

Solve. Express the roots as integers or as decimals, to the nearest hundredth.

9. $x^3 + 2x^2 - 2x - 4 = 0$

10. $2x^3 - 13x^2 + 13x + 11 = 0$

11. $n^4 - 8n^2 = -15$

12. $5x^4 - 10x^3 - 31x^2 + 2x + 6 = 0$

13. $\dfrac{2x^3 - 5x^2}{6} = 5x - 9$

14. $\dfrac{k^4 + k^3}{2} = \dfrac{k^2 + k}{5}$

15. In questions 1–14, how do you know that the calculator found all the roots of each equation?

2 Nature of the Roots

1. Solve each of the following equations with pencil and paper, and then solve algebraically with a graphing calculator. Use the pencil-and-paper method to state all the roots. Compare these roots with the roots shown by the calculator. Describe any limitations of the calculator.

a) $(x + 1)^3 = 0$ **b)** $x^3 - x^2 - 3x - 9 = 0$ **c)** $x^3 - 10x^2 + 33x - 36 = 0$

2. Use your results from question 1 to decide what to do when a graphing calculator does not show all the roots you expect for a polynomial equation.

Solve.

3. $(z + 1)^4 = 0$

4. $2x^3 + 5x^2 - 4x - 12 = 0$

5. $6x^3 - 7x^2 + 8x = 3$

6. $9w^4 - 6w^3 - 17w^2 + 12w - 2 = 0$

7. $x^5 - x^4 - x + 1 = 0$

8. $x^4 + 3x^2 + 2 = 0$

3 Problem Solving

1. Integers The product of four consecutive even integers is 48 384. What are the integers?

2. The Louvre There is a large glass pyramid in front of a famous art gallery, the Louvre, in Paris. Each side of the square base is about 14 m longer than the height of the pyramid. The volume of the pyramid is about 8575 m^3. Find the side length of the base and the height of the pyramid.

Exploring Finite Differences

The **method of finite differences** can be used to find an equation of a polynomial function from the values of the variables. The method involves examining the differences in values of the dependent variable for successive changes in the independent variable.

For the function $y = 3x + 4$, the dependent variable is y, since its value depends on the independent variable, x.

$y = 3x + 4$

x	y	Difference in y-values
0	4	
		$7 - 4 = 3$
1	7	
		$10 - 7 = 3$
2	10	

1 **Exploring Linear Functions, $y = mx + b$**

1. Copy and complete the tables for the following linear functions. Note that the differences between successive y-values are found by subtracting the first y-value from the second y-value, the second y-value from the third y-value, and so on.

a) $y = 2x + 5$

x	y	Difference
0	5	
		$7 - 5 = 2$
1	7	
2		
3		
4		

b) $y = 4x - 2$

x	y	Difference
0	-2	
		$2 - (-2) = 4$
1	2	
2		
3		
4		

c) $y = -3x + 1$

x	y	Difference
0	1	
		$-2 - 1 = -3$
1	-2	
2		
3		
4		

2. How are the differences you calculated for each function related to the equation of the function?

3. Where does the constant term for each equation occur in the table of values?

4. Use finite differences to write an equation for each function.

a)

x	y
0	3
1	5
2	7
3	9

b)

x	y
0	-4
1	1
2	6
3	11

c)

x	y
0	2
1	-4
2	-10
3	-16

d)

x	y
0	5
1	4.5
2	4
3	3.5

5. a) Copy and complete the table for the general linear function by subtracting the first value of y from the second value of y, and so on.

b) For any linear function, why are the differences between successive y-values the same?

$y = mx + b$

x	y	Difference
0	b	
1	m + b	
2	2m + b	
3		
4		

2 Exploring Quadratic Functions, $y = ax^2 + bx + c$

1. Copy and complete the tables for the following quadratic functions.

a) $y = x^2 + x + 1$

x	y	Difference 1st	Difference 2nd
0	1		
		2	
1	3		2
		4	
2	7		
3			
4			

b) $y = 2x^2 - x + 5$

x	y	Difference 1st	Difference 2nd
0	5		
1	6		
2			
3			
4			

c) $y = 3x^2 + 2x - 1$

x	y	Difference 1st	Difference 2nd
0			
1			
2			
3			
4			

2. What is true about the second difference values in each table?

3. What is the relationship between the second difference and the value of a for each function?

4. a) Copy and complete the table for the general quadratic function by subtracting the first value of y from the second value of y, and so on.

b) Using the results from part a) and the tables you completed in question 1, describe how you can use a table of finite differences to calculate the values of a, b, and c.

$y = ax^2 + bx + c$

x	y	Difference 1st	Difference 2nd
0	c		
		$a + b$	
1	$a + b + c$		
		$3a + b$	
2	$4a + 2b + c$		
3	$9a + 3b + c$		
4	$16a + 4b + c$		

5. a) Copy and complete the difference table.
b) Find c.
c) Find a.
d) Find b.
e) Write an equation for the quadratic function.

x	y	Difference 1st	Difference 2nd
0	1		
1	6		
2	15		
3	28		
4	45		

6. Write an equation for each function.

a)

x	y
0	3
1	6
2	11
3	18
4	27

b)

x	y
0	-2
1	1
2	12
3	31
4	58

c)

x	y
0	4
1	5
2	2
3	-5
4	-16

d)

x	y
0	0
1	3
2	4
3	3
4	0

3 Exploring Cubic Functions, $y = ax^3 + bx^2 + cx + d$

1. Copy and complete the table for the following cubic functions.

a) $y = x^3 - x^2 + 2x + 1$

x	y	1st	2nd	3rd
0	1			
		2		
1	3			
2				
3				
4				
5				

(Difference columns: 1st, 2nd, 3rd)

b) $y = 2x^3 - 3x - 4$

x	y	1st	2nd	3rd
0				
1				
2				
3				
4				
5				

(Difference columns: 1st, 2nd, 3rd)

2. a) For a cubic function, in which column are the differences equal?
b) What is the relationship between the third difference and the value of a?

3. a) Copy and complete the table for the general cubic function $y = ax^3 + bx^2 + cx + d$ by subtracting the second value of y from the first value of y, and so on.

$y = ax^3 + bx^2 + cx + d$

x	y	1st	2nd	3rd
0	d			
		a + b + c		
1	a + b + c + d			
2	8a + 4b + 2c + d			
3				
4				

(Difference columns: 1st, 2nd, 3rd)

b) Using the results from part a) and the tables you completed in question 1, describe how you can use a table of finite differences to calculate the values of a, b, c, and d.

4. a) Copy and complete the difference table.
b) Find a.
c) Find b.
d) Find c.
e) Find d.
f) Write an equation for the cubic function.

x	y	Difference		
		1st	**2nd**	**3rd**
0	–2			
1	–5			
2	–4			
3	7			
4	34			

5. Write an equation for each function.

a)

x	y
0	3
1	2
2	11
3	36
4	83

b)

x	y
0	2
1	8
2	28
3	74
4	158

c)

x	y
0	–4
1	0
2	6
3	8
4	0

d)

x	y
0	–8
1	–6
2	–22
3	–74
4	–180

4 Problem Solving

Write an equation for each function.

1.

x	y
0	7
1	5
2	5
3	7
4	11

2.

x	y
0	6
1	4
2	2
3	0
4	–2

3.

x	y
0	–1
1	0
2	9
3	32
4	75

4.

x	y
0	5
1	2
2	–1
3	–4
4	–7

5.

x	y
0	2
1	7
2	22
3	47
4	82

6.

x	y
0	0
1	7
2	20
3	27
4	16

7.

x	y
0	0
1	–7
2	–4
3	27
4	104

8.

x	y
0	–5
1	–4
2	–9
3	–20
4	–37

Copy and complete each table. Write an equation for each function.

9.

x	y	1st	2nd	3rd
0				
1	4			
2	7			
3	10			
4	13			
5				

10.

x	y	1st	2nd	3rd
0				
1	0			
2	3			
3	8			
4	15			
5	24			

11.

x	y	1st	2nd	3rd
0				
1				
2				
3	−15			
4	−29			
5	−47			
6	−69			

12.

x	y	1st	2nd	3rd
0				
1	2			
2	9			
3	28			
4	65			
5	126			

13.

x	y	1st	2nd	3rd
0				
1	0			
2	10			
3	42			
4	108			
5	220			

14.

x	y	1st	2nd	3rd
0				
1				
2	13			
3	14			
4	5			
5	−20			
6	−67			

15. Letter pattern Each diagram consists of asterisks arranged in an m-shape.

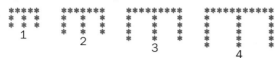

a) Write an equation in the form $n = \blacksquare$ that relates the number of asterisks, n, to the diagram number, d.

b) Predict the number of asterisks in the fifteenth diagram.

c) Which diagram contains 131 asterisks?

16. Stacking boxes A toy store employee stacks boxes in a triangular shape. The diagrams show the number of boxes in the top 5 layers.

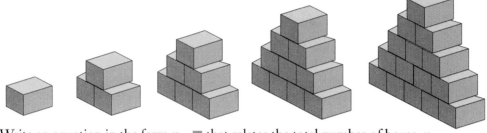

a) Write an equation in the form $n = \blacksquare$ that relates the total number of boxes, n, to the total number of layers, l.

b) How many boxes are needed to build 10 layers?

c) How many layers are there if the total number of boxes is 105?

17. Sequence Predict the next three terms in the following sequence.
12, 11, 6, −3, −16, −33,…

18. Sequence The first five numbers in a sequence are −2, 9, 44, 115, and 234.

a) Write an equation in the form $n = \blacksquare$ that relates each number, n, to its position, p, in the sequence.

b) In which position in the sequence is the number 999?

c) Calculate the tenth number in the sequence.

19. Volume pattern The volumes of the first six rectangular prisms in a pattern are 6 cm^3, 24 cm^3, 60 cm^3, 120 cm^3, 210 cm^3, and 336 cm^3.

a) Write an equation in the form $V = \blacksquare$ that relates the numerical value of each volume, V, to the position, p, in the pattern.

b) In which position in the pattern is the prism with a volume of 1320 cm^3?

c) Calculate the volume of the twentieth rectangular prism in the pattern.

d) Factor the right-hand side of the equation you wrote in part a).

e) Assume that each rectangular prism has dimensions that are whole numbers of centimetres. Use the factors from part d) to suggest possible dimensions for each of the first six rectangular prisms. Explain your reasoning.

f) Are the dimensions you gave in part e) the only possible whole-number dimensions that fit the pattern? Explain.

Exploring Regression With a Graphing Calculator

The analysis of the relationship between a dependent variable and one or more independent variables is known as **regression**. The relationship is usually expressed as an equation.

1 Linear Functions

The general form for a linear function is $y = ax + b$. The linear regression instruction on a graphing calculator determines an equation of a linear function if at least two points on the graph are known. For example, if the points $(-1, -7)$ and $(3, 5)$ are entered, the linear regression instruction gives the values $a = 3$ and $b = -4$, so the equation is $y = 3x - 4$.

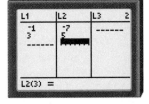

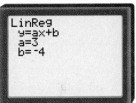

1. Use the linear regression instruction to write an equation for the line that contains each pair of points. Then, graph the function.
a) $(1, 6), (-4, -4)$ **b)** $(-3, 5), (0, 2)$ **c)** $(1, -1), (2, -13)$ **d)** $(-6, -5), (6, 1)$
2. Sequence The first two numbers in a linear sequence are 5 and −3.
a) Write a linear equation of the form $n = $ ■ that relates each number, n, to its position, p, in the sequence.
b) Find the seventeenth number in the sequence.
c) Find the position of the number −267 in the sequence.

2 Quadratic Functions

The general form for a quadratic function is $y = ax^2 + bx + c$. The quadratic regression instruction on a graphing calculator determines an equation of a quadratic function if at least three points on the graph are known. For example, if the points $(-2, -7), (2, 9)$, and $(4, 29)$ are entered, the quadratic regression instruction gives the values $a = 1$, $b = 4$, and $c = -3$, so the equation is $y = x^2 + 4x - 3$.

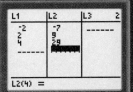

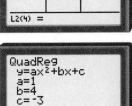

1. Use the quadratic regression instruction to write an equation for the parabola that contains each set of points. Then, graph the function.
a) $(-1, 6), (2, 0), (5, 12)$ **b)** $(-3, 9), (1, -3), (4, 30)$
c) $(-2, -1), (0, 9), (3, -21)$ **d)** $(1, 2), (2, -4), (3, -18)$

2. Sequence The first three numbers in a quadratic sequence are 3, 17, and 39.
a) Write a quadratic equation of the form $n = $ ■ that relates each number, n, to its position, p, in the sequence.
b) Find the eighth number in the sequence.
c) Find the position of the number 597 in the sequence.

3. Sequence The first three numbers in a quadratic sequence are $\dfrac{16}{9}, \dfrac{49}{9}$, and $\dfrac{100}{9}$.

Write a quadratic equation of the form $n = $ ■ that relates each number, n, to its position, p, in the sequence. If your calculator gives a decimal approximation for a, b, or c, use the most likely fraction in the equation. Then, check the equation by substitution.

4. a) Describe an algebraic method for writing an equation of a quadratic function, given the coordinates of three points on its graph. Why do you need to know at least three points?
b) Use your method from part a) to write an equation for the function that contains the points $(-1, 2), (1, -2)$, and $(2, -1)$.

3 Cubic Functions

The general form for a cubic function is $y = ax^3 + bx^2 + cx + d$. The cubic regression feature on a graphing calculator determines the equation of a cubic function if at least four points on the graph are known. If the points $(-4, -19)$, $(-2, 5)$, $(0, -3)$ and $(3, 30)$ are entered, the cubic regression feature gives the values $a = 1$, $b = 2$, $c = -4$, and $d = -3$, so the equation is $y = x^3 + 2x^2 - 4x - 3$.

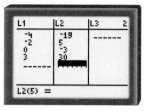

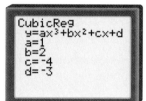

1. Use the cubic regression instruction to write an equation for the cubic function that contains each set of points. Then, graph the function.
a) $(-3, -49)$, $(-1, -1)$, $(2, -4)$, $(5, 47)$
b) $(-2, -7)$, $(0, -1)$, $(1, 5)$, $(2, 21)$
c) $(-4, 37)$, $(0, 5)$, $(2, 1)$, $(3, -19)$
d) $(-4, 118)$, $(-2, 14)$, $(2, -2)$, $(4, -106)$

2. Sequence The first four numbers in a cubic sequence are -6, 8, 46, and 120.
a) Write a cubic equation of the form $n = \blacksquare$ that relates each number, n, to its position, p, in the sequence.
b) Find the sixth number in the sequence.
c) Find the position of the number 15 992 in the sequence.

4 Using Finite Differences

1. Sequences Use the method of finite differences to decide whether each sequence is linear, quadratic, or cubic. Then, write an equation for the sequence.
a) $-4, -1, 2, 5, 8$ **b)** $0, 11, 46, 117, 236$ **c)** $-9, -21, -41, -69, -105$

2. Honeycomb pattern The cross section of a honeycomb can be thought of as a central regular hexagon surrounded by a ring of six more hexagons, surrounded by a ring of twelve more hexagons, and so on. Think of the central hexagon as ring 1, the ring of six hexagons as ring 2, and so on.
a) Record the total numbers of hexagons in the first ring, in the first two rings, in the first three rings, and in the first four rings.
b) Use the method of finite differences to determine whether the relationship between the number of hexagons and the number of rings is linear, quadratic, or cubic.
c) Write an equation of the form $h = \blacksquare$ that relates the number of hexagons, h, to the number of rings, r.
d) Find the total number of hexagons in the first ten rings.
e) How many rings contain a total of 631 hexagons?

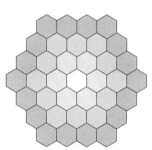

3. Stack of oranges Oranges are stacked in the shape of a square pyramid. There is one orange in the top layer and four oranges in the second layer, for a total of five oranges in the top two layers.
a) Find the total number of oranges in the top three layers, the top four layers, and the top five layers.
b) Determine whether the relationship between the number of oranges and the number of layers is linear, quadratic, or cubic.
c) Write an equation of the form $n = \blacksquare$ that relates the number of oranges, n, to the number of layers, l. Check the equation by substitution.
d) Find the total number of oranges in the top ten layers.

4. a) Predict the minimum number of points you would need to know on the graph of a quartic function in order to write an equation for the function.
b) Write an equation for a quartic function, calculate some points, and test your prediction.

5 Scatter Plots and Lines of Best Fit

A graphing calculator can be used to draw a scatter plot and its line of best fit. This line is called a **regression line**. The calculator will also write an equation for the regression line. The data represented by the line can be studied by using the TRACE instruction or the Value operation, or by displaying a table of values for the points on the line.

1. The table gives the total number of members of the Canadian Armed Forces, to the nearest thousand, for each year from 1990 to 1996. In the table, 1990 is represented by year 0.

Year	Total Armed Forces (thousands)
0	88
1	87
2	85
3	78
4	76
5	72
6	61

a) Draw a scatter plot and a regression line for the data.
b) Use the regression line to estimate the number of members of the Armed Forces in 2004, to the nearest thousand.
c) If the trend continues, predict the year in which Canada will have no Armed Forces.
d) Do you think that the prediction in part c) is valid? Explain.
e) Determine the slope of the regression line.
f) What does the slope represent for these data?

2. The table gives the total amount spent in Canada on education in six different years.

Year	Education Spending (billions of dollars)
1971	8
1976	15
1981	25
1986	37
1991	53
1996	58

a) Let 1971 be year 0, 1976 be year 5, 1981 be year 10, and so on. Draw a scatter plot and a regression line for the data.
b) Use the regression line to estimate the amounts spent on education in 1983 and in 1990, to the nearest billion dollars.
c) Use the data to predict the amount that will be spent on education in 2011, to the nearest billion dollars.
d) Do you think that the prediction in part c) is valid? Explain.
e) Determine the slope of the regression line.
f) What does the slope represent for these data?

Review

4.1 Solve by graphing.

1. $x^2 + 2x - 3 = 0$ **2.** $-x^2 - 4x = 5$
3. $-x^2 - 3x + 4 = 0$ **4.** $4x - 4 = x^2$
5. $x^2 + 19 = 8x$ **6.** $x^2 + 6x + 5 = 0$
7. $9x = 18 + x^2$ **8.** $4x^2 - 12x + 9 = 0$
9. $9 - 4x^2 = 0$ **10.** $2x^2 + x = 15$

11. Measurement The length of a rectangle is 5 cm more than the width. The area is 36 cm^2. What are the dimensions of the rectangle?

4.2 Solve by factoring.

12. $x^2 + 3x - 28 = 0$ **13.** $y^2 - 5y + 6 = 0$
14. $g^2 + 7g + 10 = 0$ **15.** $2x^2 + 5x = 3$
16. $2n^2 = 27 - 15n$ **17.** $8k^2 - 3k = 0$
18. $3w(w - 4) + w + 4(w + 1) = 0$

Solve and check.

19. $x + 3 = \dfrac{4}{x}$ **20.** $x + 2 = \dfrac{x + 2}{x - 2}$

Write a quadratic equation with the given roots.

21. $5, -1$ **22.** $\dfrac{1}{2}, 4$

23. Curling The playing surface in the game of curling is a rectangular sheet of ice with an area of about 225 m^2. The width is about 40 m less than the length. Find the approximate dimensions of the playing surface.

4.3 Solve and check.

24. $q^2 - 11 = 14$ **25.** $18 + b^2 = 82$
26. $(x - 2)^2 = 81$ **27.** $2(n + 3)^2 = 98$

Find and check the exact solutions.

28. $p^2 - 1 = 49$ **29.** $3r^2 + 1 = 37$
30. $-2 = 38 - 5v^2$ **31.** $\dfrac{x^2}{9} = \dfrac{1}{2}$

32. Lakes and islands Three of the world's ten largest islands are in Canada. This number is one less than the square of the number of the world's ten largest lakes that are entirely in Canada. How many of the world's ten largest lakes are entirely in Canada?

4.4 Solve by completing the square. Express radical solutions in simplest radical form.

33. $x^2 - 2x - 8 = 0$ **34.** $n^2 + 8n + 5 = 0$
35. $t^2 + 5t + 1 = 0$ **36.** $x^2 = 3x + 2$

37. $5x = x^2 - 9$ **38.** $3 = a^2 + 3a$
39. $0 = 3z^2 + 5z + 1$ **40.** $2x - 5 + 6x^2 = 0$
41. $-1 = \dfrac{1}{2}y^2 - 2y$ **42.** $0.6x^2 - 0.5x = 0.1$

43. Pool and deck A rectangular swimming pool measuring 10 m by 4 m is surrounded by a deck of uniform width. The combined area of the deck and the pool is 135 m^2. What is the width of the deck?

4.5 Solve using the quadratic formula. Express radical solutions in simplest radical form.

44. $n^2 + n - 42 = 0$ **45.** $2x^2 + 3 = 7x$
46. $7g^2 + 2 = 9g$ **47.** $4m^2 = 3 + 4m$
48. $k^2 - 10k = 9$ **49.** $0 = q^2 + 6q + 6$
50. $8w^2 = 9 + 3w$ **51.** $4 = 5x + 3x^2$

Solve. Express answers as integers or as decimals, to the nearest hundredth.

52. $6x^2 + x - 4 = 0$ **53.** $1.2x^2 + 0.5x - 0.3 = 0$

Solve. Express radical solutions in simplest radical form.

54. $\dfrac{3}{k - 1} + \dfrac{4}{k} = 2$ **55.** $\dfrac{2}{t + 2} - \dfrac{1}{t - 2} = -1$

56. Flying speeds A plane flew 5200 km from London to Montreal into a head wind. With a tail wind, the plane flew 150 km/h faster on the return trip. The total flying time from London to Montreal and back was 14.5 h. What was the flying speed from London to Montreal?

4.6 Simplify.

57. $\sqrt{-49}$ **58.** $\sqrt{-18}$ **59.** $\sqrt{-56y^3}$

60. $2(-5i)^2$ **61.** $i(2i)^3$ **62.** $\left(i\sqrt{3}\right)^2$
63. $(7 + 3i) + (5 - 6i)$ **64.** $(9 - 2i) - (11 + 4i)$
65. $(5i - 3)(2i + 5)$ **66.** $(2 - 3i)^2$

Solve.

67. $x^2 + 16 = 0$ **68.** $-5y^2 - 45 = 0$
69. $x^2 + 2x + 7 = 0$ **70.** $x^2 - 5x = -9$
71. $0 = 4x^2 + 4x + 3$ **72.** $3m^2 - 2m + 4 = 0$
73. $4x^4 - 19x^2 - 5 = 0$ **74.** $9x^4 - 4 = 0$

75. Fractals Using $z = 0$ as the first input value, find the first three output values for $f(z) = z^2 - 2i$.

4.7 *Determine the nature of the roots.*
  76. $b^2 - 5b + 6 = 0$ **77.** $6v^2 + 3 = 8v$
  78. $9p^2 - 12p + 4 = 0$ **79.** $(y + 3)(y - 2) = 5$
  80. $-\dfrac{x^2}{9} = 2x + 9$ **81.** $2(n^2 + 6) = 7n$

Determine the value(s) of k that give the type of solution indicated.
  82. $x^2 + 3x + k = 0$; distinct real roots
  83. $kx^2 - 5x + 2 = 0$; equal real roots
  84. $2x^2 + 3x + k = 0$; imaginary roots

  85. Measurement Is it possible for a rectangle with a perimeter of 46 cm to have an area of 120 cm²? If so, find the dimensions of the rectangle.

4.8 *Use the remainder theorem to determine the remainder for each division.*
  86. $(x^2 + 5x - 8) \div (x - 2)$
  87. $(3m^2 + 7m + 1) \div (m + 3)$
  88. $(g^3 - 5g^2 - 3g + 1) \div (g + 1)$
  89. $(2a^2 + 5a + 11) \div (2a - 1)$
  90. $(8y^3 + 12y^2 - 4y + 5) \div (2y + 3)$

For each polynomial, find the value of k if the remainder is −1.
  91. $(x^3 - 4x^2 + kx - 2) \div (x - 1)$
  92. $(x^3 - 3x^2 - 6x + k) \div (x + 2)$

4.9 *Show that the binomial is a factor of the first polynomial.*
  93. $z^3 - 2z^2 - 5z + 6$; $z - 1$
  94. $s^4 + 4s^3 - 9s^2 - 16s + 20$; $s + 2$
  95. $2w^3 - w^2 - 4w + 3$; $2w + 3$
  96. $3x^3 + 17x^2 + 18x - 8$; $3x - 1$

Factor.
  97. $x^3 - x^2 - 5x - 3$ **98.** $x^3 + 5x^2 + 3x - 4$
  99. $2x^3 - x^2 - 2x + 1$ **100.** $3y^3 + 13y^2 - 16$

.10 *Solve and check.*
  101. $y^3 = 9y$ **102.** $n^3 - 3n - 2 = 0$
  103. $3v^2 + 11v = 2v^3 + 6$ **104.** $3a^3 - 2 = 8a^2 - 7a$

Find the exact roots.
  105. $x^3 - 3x^2 + x + 1 = 0$ **106.** $4y^3 - 19y = 6$
  107. $x^3 + x^2 + 16x + 16 = 0$
  108. $n^3 - n^2 = 2n + 12$

  109. Packaging A cereal box is a rectangular prism with a volume of 2500 cm³. It is 4 times as wide as it is deep, and 5 cm taller than it is wide. What are the dimensions of the box?

Exploring Math

Investigating the Argand Plane

Complex numbers can be represented geometrically in the complex plane, often called the Argand plane. On an Argand plane, the horizontal axis is the real axis, and the vertical axis is the imaginary axis. The complex number $2 + 3i$ is represented by a line segment from the origin to the point $(2, 3)$. Real numbers, such as 4, are written in the form $4 + 0i$ and are represented by segments

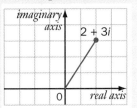

on the real axis. Pure imaginary numbers, such as $5i$, are written in the form $0 + 5i$ and are represented by segments on the imaginary axis.

Multiplying the complex number $4 + 3i$ by i results in another complex number.
  $i(4 + 3i) = -3 + 4i$
The segment for $-3 + 4i$ has the same length as the segment for $4 + 3i$.

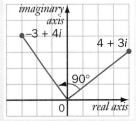

The segment for $-3 + 4i$ has been rotated 90° counterclockwise from the segment for $4 + 3i$.

1. Draw a line segment to show the result when $4 + 3i$ is multiplied by each of the following. Describe each transformation carried out.
  a) i^2 **b)** i^3 **c)** i^4 **d)** 2   **e)** 3   **f)** 4

2. a) Draw the line segments for $4 + 2i$ and $-2 + 3i$ on the same axes.
  b) Add $4 + 2i$ and $-2 + 3i$.
  c) On the axes used in part a), draw the segment for the complex number found in part b).
  d) Draw the parallelogram whose vertices are the origin and the other endpoints of the three segments.
  e) Describe how a parallelogram can be used to model the sum of two complex numbers.

3. Model each addition on an Argand plane.
  a) $(2 + 3i) + (3 - 5i)$ **b)** $(-3 + 4i) + (-4 + 3i)$
  c) $(-2 + 4i) + (0 - 6i)$ **d)** $(2 - 2i) + (-5 + 2i)$

Chapter Check

Solve by graphing.
1. $x^2 + 2x - 8 = 0$
2. $-x^2 + 3 = 2x$
3. $2x^2 + 5 = 11x$
4. $-2x^2 - 3x = 4$

Solve by factoring and check.
5. $q^2 + 2q - 15 = 0$
6. $w^2 + 24 = 11w$
7. $2k^2 + 7k = 4$
8. $9x^2 = 3x + 2$
9. $x - 2 = \dfrac{6}{x} - 3$
10. $p - 4 = \dfrac{p - 10}{p + 2}$

Write a quadratic equation with the given roots.
11. $0, -4$
12. $-\dfrac{1}{2}, \dfrac{3}{4}$

Find and check the exact solutions.
13. $x^2 + 11 = 155$
14. $8n^2 - 14 = 0$
15. $(a + 5)^2 - 6 = 30$
16. $3(y - 4)^2 = 12$

Solve by completing the square. Express each irrational solution in simplest radical form, and to the nearest hundredth.
17. $x^2 - 8x = -16$
18. $y^2 - 3y - 18 = 0$
19. $3t^2 = 2t + 7$
20. $2x = 5x^2 - 1$

Solve using the quadratic formula. Express radical solutions in simplest radical form.
21. $2x^2 + 8 + 8x = 0$
22. $2 = -7p - 5p^2$
23. $0 = 18w^2 + 9w - 2$
24. $12d^2 = 5d + 3$
25. $3v + 7 = v^2$
26. $8c = 1 + 5c^2$
27. $3x^2 = -3 - 7x$
28. $\dfrac{4}{t - 1} - \dfrac{5t}{t + 2} = 3$

Solve, to the nearest hundredth.
29. $3x^2 - 11x + 2 = 0$
30. $0.3z^2 - 0.6z = 0.8$

Simplify.
31. $\sqrt{-36}$
32. $\sqrt{-48}$
33. $5(-3i)^2$
34. $(8 - 3i) + (5 - 5i)$
35. $(7 + 2i) - (9 - 6i)$
36. $(6 - 3i)(2 + 5i)$
37. $(1 - 7i)(1 + 7i)$

Solve and check.
38. $p^2 = -18$
39. $y^2 + 1 = 0$
40. $11x^2 + 44 = 0$
41. $v^2 - 5v + 7 = 0$
42. $2k^2 + 3k + 5 = 0$
43. $2h^4 + 5h^2 - 3 = 0$

Determine the nature of the roots.
44. $m^2 + 2m + 5 = 0$
45. $5y^2 = 3y + 1$
46. $8(2w^2 - 3w) = -9$
47. $3a^2 + 4 = 8a$

Determine the value(s) of k that give the type of solution indicated.
48. $x^2 - 5x + k = 0$; distinct real roots
49. $kx^2 - 4x + 1 = 0$; imaginary roots

Use the remainder theorem to determine the remainder for each division.
50. $(m^2 + 3m - 4) \div (m - 3)$
51. $(p^3 + 4p^2 - 2p + 5) \div (p + 5)$
52. $(9x^2 - 6x + 1) \div (3x - 1)$
53. $(4v^3 + v^2 - 12v - 5) \div (4v + 1)$

54. When the polynomial $3x^3 + mx^2 + nx + 2$ is divided by $x - 2$, the remainder is -8. When the polynomial is divided by $x + 3$, the remainder is -88. What are the values of m and n?

Show that the binomial is a factor of the first polynomial.
55. $x^3 - 5x^2 - x + 5$; $x - 5$
56. $y^4 - 4y^3 - 5y^2 + 36y - 36$; $y + 3$
57. $3n^3 + n^2 - 38n + 24$; $3n - 2$
58. $4b^3 - 5b^2 - 23b + 6$; $4b - 1$

Factor completely.
59. $x^3 + 2x^2 - 21x + 18$
60. $3x^3 - 10x^2 - 9x + 4$

Find the exact roots.
61. $p^3 + 4p^2 + 4p = 0$
62. $x^3 - 3x^2 = 4x - 12$
63. $0 = b^3 + 2b^2 - 4b - 8$
64. $m^3 - 5m = 5m^2 - 1$
65. $x^3 + 4x^2 + 9x + 10 = 0$
66. $3w^3 - 28w^2 = 8 - 33w$

67. **Cribbage board** The area of a cribbage board is 270 cm², and the length is 17 cm greater than the width. What are the dimensions of the board?

68. **Landscaping** A rectangular lawn measuring 8 m by 4 m is surrounded by a flower bed of uniform width. The combined area of the lawn and the flower bed is 165 m². What is the width of the flower bed?

69. **Patrol boat** A patrol boat took 3.2 h for a round trip of 18 km upstream and 18 km back again. The speed of the current was 3 km/h. What was the speed of the boat in still water?

Using the Strategies

1. After the preliminary games in a bowling tournament, the top four bowlers have a playoff. In the first playoff game, player 4 bowls player 3. The loser gets the fourth-place prize, and the winner bowls player 2 in the second game. The loser of the second game gets the third-place prize, and the winner bowls player 1 in the final game. The loser of the final game gets the second-place prize, and the winner gets the first-place prize. In how many different orders can the bowlers finish the tournament?

2. The diagram shows the first four rectangles in a pattern.

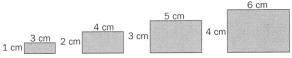

a) What is the area of the fifth rectangle? the 20th rectangle? the nth rectangle?
b) What is the width of a rectangle with an area of 1935 cm^2? 3480 cm^2? 9999 cm^2?

3. Rashad started the 780-km drive from Vancouver to Prince George at 09:00. His average speed was 80 km/h. Three hours later, Tyson left Prince George for Vancouver. He drove at 70 km/h on the same highway. How far from Vancouver, and at what time of day, did they meet?

4. The side lengths of a triangle are $x + 2$, $8 - x$, and $4x - 1$. What value, or values, of x make the triangle isosceles?

5. You are given a standard die labelled from 1 to 6. How can you label a second die using only the numbers 0, 1, 2, 3, 4, 5, and 6 so that, when you roll both dice, the totals from 1 to 12 are equally likely?

6. Each letter in the box represents a different number. The sums of four columns and four rows are given. Find the missing sums.

A	A	A	C	B	25
B	A	B	B	C	17
C	B	B	C	A	20
C	C	D	C	A	24
D	A	A	D	D	▨
21	25	19	20	▨	

7. Estimate the total number of CDs owned by the high school students in your province.

8. Suppose that a hop, a step, and a jump each have a specific length. Suppose p hops equals q steps, r jumps equals s hops, and t jumps equals x metres. How many steps does one metre equal?

9. The height of a triangle is 12 cm. The side lengths are consecutive whole numbers of centimetres. The area of the triangle is a whole number of square centimetres. What are the side lengths?

10. Find the missing letter in the pattern.

C	G	N	▨	V	W
4	7	3	5	1	6

11. The ninth term of a geometric sequence is 40. The twelfth term of the sequence is 5. What is the first term of the sequence?

12. Jessica and Danielle were each given a card with a whole number written on it. Each person did not know the other person's number, but they were told that the product of the two numbers was 15, 20, 24, or 28. The object was to determine the number on the other person's card. They both thought about the problem for some time, and then Jessica said that she could not determine Danielle's number. After hearing this, Danielle said: "Then I know what the numbers are!" What were the numbers? Explain your reasoning.

DATA BANK

1. a) Which of the aircraft listed in the Data Bank uses the least fuel per kilometre flown?
b) Is the aircraft you found in part a) the most fuel-efficient aircraft in the Data Bank? Explain.

2. Write two problems using data from the Data Bank. Have a classmate solve your problems.

3. Which Canadian province has
a) the most fresh water?
b) the most fresh water per person?

Chapter 1

Solve by graphing. Check your solutions.

1. $y = 3x + 1$
$y = 4x + 15$

2. $4x + y = -1$
$6x - y = 6$

Solve each system by substitution. Check each solution.

3. $x + 4y = 3$
$2x + 5y = 3$

4. $2a + b = 2$
$3a - 2b = 3$

Solve each system by elimination. Check each solution. If there is not exactly one solution, does the system have no solution or infinitely many solutions?

5. $8a - 3b = 10$
$7a + 3b = 20$

6. $5x - 8y = 12$
$10x - 16y = 24$

7. $2x - 3y = 6$
$5x - 4y = 1$

8. $5p + 8q = 4$
$3p + 10q = 5$

Solve and check.

9. $a + b + c = 10$
$a + b = 9$
$a - b = 1$

10. $3x + y + z = 8$
$x - 2y - z = -7$
$2x + y + 2z = 9$

11. Nutrition The total mass of calcium in one nectarine and three plums is 16 mg. The total mass of calcium in two nectarines and one plum is 17 mg. This information can be represented by the following system.

$$n + 3p = 16$$
$$2n + p = 17$$

Graph the system to find the mass of calcium, in milligrams, in
a) one nectarine **b)** one plum

12. Selling produce Portobello mushrooms sell for $6.60/kg and shiitake mushrooms sell for $11.00/kg. Find the mass of each type of mushroom in 1-kg bags selling for $8.36.

13. River patrol It took a patrol boat 3 h to travel 48 km up a river against the current and 2 h for the return trip with the current. Find the speed of the boat in still water and the speed of the current.

14. Golf course An 18-hole golf course has par 3, par 4, and par 5 holes. The total par for the course is 71. The number of par 3 holes plus twice the number of par 5 holes is one less than the number of par 4 holes. Find the number of holes of each par.

Chapter 2

Solve and check.

1. $n + 5 < 2$
2. $2w - 3 > 9$
3. $4(d - 3) \geq 8$
4. $5k - 8 \leq 7 + 2k$
5. $2(m - 3) - 5 > 3(4 - m) + 2$
6. $\dfrac{y}{4} - 3 \geq -5$
7. $\dfrac{2}{3}x + 5 \leq 1$
8. $1.3h - 0.2 > 3.7$
9. $9.2 - 5.8p < -2.4$
10. $\dfrac{q + 1}{2} \leq \dfrac{5 + q}{3}$
11. $\dfrac{c + 2}{4} - \dfrac{1}{2} > \dfrac{3c}{8}$

Graph each inequality.

12. $y \geq 7 - x$
13. $x + y < -3$
14. $2x - y \leq 5$
15. $9 - x + 3y > 4$
16. $y < \dfrac{3}{4}x - 1$
17. $\dfrac{x}{2} - \dfrac{y}{5} \geq 1$

Which of the given ordered pairs are solutions to the system of inequalities?

18. $x - y > 2$
$2x + y > 1$
$(1, 6), (0, 0), (3, -1), (-1, -8), (5, 3)$

Solve each system of inequalities by graphing.

19. $y < x + 3$
$y > x$

20. $y \leq 5$
$y > x - 2$

21. $y < \dfrac{1}{2}x - 1$
$y < 2x$

22. $x + y \leq 3$
$x - y \leq 0$

23. $2x + y > 5$
$2x - 3y < 1$

24. $x + 2y - 4 \leq 0$
$y - 3x + 1 \geq 0$

25. Island areas The largest island in the Maritime Provinces is Cape Breton Island, with an area of 10 300 km². This area is 900 km² less than twice the area of the second largest island. Write and solve an inequality to state the areas of the islands other than Cape Breton Island.

26. Scheduling appointments A financial planner schedules clients for 1-h and 2-h appointments. She consults with clients for, at most, 35 h each week.
a) Write an inequality to represent the numbers of each length of appointment she can make in a week.
b) Graph the inequality.

27. Rectangle dimensions The perimeter of a rectangle is greater than 18 cm but less than 22 cm. Show all the possible values for the length and width of the rectangle graphically.

Chapter 3

Sketch the graph of each parabola and state
a) the direction of the opening
b) the coordinates of the vertex
c) the equation of the axis of symmetry
d) the domain and range
e) any intercepts

1. $y = -2x^2$ **2.** $f(x) = x^2 - 3$
3. $f(x) = (x + 3)^2$ **4.** $f(x) = -(x - 2)^2 + 1$
5. $y = 0.5(x - 4)^2 + 3$ **6.** $y = -3(x + 5)^2 - 2$

Determine any x-intercepts and y-intercepts by graphing manually or using a graphing calculator. Round to the nearest tenth, if necessary.

7. $y = (x + 3)^2 - 2$ **8.** $f(x) = -0.5(x - 4)^2 + 1$

Write an equation that defines each parabola.

9. vertex $(0, -4)$; $a = 1$
10. congruent to $y = 2x^2$; maximum value 5; axis of symmetry $x = 1$
11. vertex $(5, 4)$; passing through $(4, 3)$
12. vertex $(-1, 2)$; y-intercept 4

Write each function in the form $y = a(x - p)^2 + q$. Sketch the graph, showing the coordinates of the vertex, the equation of the axis of symmetry, and the coordinates of two other points on the graph.

13. $y = -x^2 - 2x - 3$ **14.** $y = 0.5x^2 - 4x + 1$

15. Arch bridge A bridge over a river is arch shaped. Suppose the curve of the arch is graphed on a grid, with the origin on the river directly under the centre of the arch. The arch can be modelled by the function
$$h(d) = -0.05d^2 + 18.2$$
where $h(d)$ metres is the height of the arch, and d metres is the horizontal distance from the centre of the arch.
a) What is the maximum height of the arch?
b) If the ends of the arch are at the level of the river, how wide is the arch, to the nearest metre?
c) At a horizontal distance of 3 m from one end of the arch, how high is the arch, to the nearest tenth of a metre?

16. Admission fee A museum has an admission fee of $14 and averages 300 visitors per day. The museum board decides to raise the fee. Research indicates that for every $1 increase, there would be 10 fewer visitors per day. What admission fee would maximize the revenue?

Chapter 4

Solve by graphing.
1. $2x^2 - x - 3 = 0$ **2.** $-x^2 + 7x = 12$

Solve. Express radical solutions in simplest radical form.
3. $m^2 - 7 = 29$ **4.** $2(w - 3)^2 = 50$
5. $2x^2 = 4 + 7x$ **6.** $12 = d + d^2$
7. $9g^2 + 1 = 6g$ **8.** $2p^2 + p + 1 = 0$
9. $c + 9 + c^2 = 0$ **10.** $b^2 + 2b = 48$
11. $3x^2 + 10 + 17x = 0$ **12.** $3w^2 = 2w + 4$
13. $x - 2 = \left(i\sqrt{3}\right)$ **14.** $n^2 + 4n - 4 = 0$

Determine the nature of the roots.
15. $12x^2 - 11x + 2 = 0$ **16.** $4(x^2 + x) = -1$
17. $3y^2 + 5 = 4y$ **18.** $5t^2 + 3t = 8$

Solve. Round answers to the nearest hundredth.
19. $21x^2 + 11x - 2 = 0$ **20.** $5x^2 = 3x + 9$

21. Write a quadratic equation with roots 3 and $-\dfrac{1}{2}$.

22. Determine the values of k that give imaginary roots for $kx^2 - 3x + 1 = 0$.

Use the remainder theorem to determine the remainder for each division.
23. $(v^3 - 4v^2 + 5v - 2) \div (v - 1)$
24. $(6p^3 + p^2 + 9p + 5) \div (2p + 1)$

Factor completely.
25. $x^3 - 8x^2 + 11x + 20$
26. $4x^3 - 11x^2 - 6x + 9$

Find the exact roots.
27. $0 = q^3 - 5q^2 + 7q - 2$
28. $g^3 - 11g^2 + 24g + 36 = 0$
29. $w^3 + 4w = 3w^2 + 2$
30. $2y^3 - 18y + 9 = y^2$

31. Measurement The area of a triangle is 24 cm². Its height is 2 cm more than its base. Determine the base and the height.

32. Driving speed A delivery truck spent 15.5 h driving from its warehouse in Edmonton to a customer in Dawson Creek and back. Its average speed driving the 600 km to Dawson Creek was 5 km/h slower than its average speed on the return trip. What was the average speed on the return trip?

Planet	Mean Radius of Orbit, R (m)	Period of Orbit, T (s)	R^3 (m³)	T^2 (s²)	$\frac{R^3}{T^2}$ (m³/s²)
Mercury	5.79×10^{10}	7.60×10^6			
Venus	1.08×10^{11}	1.94×10^7			
Earth	1.49×10^{11}	3.16×10^7			
Mars	2.28×10^{11}	5.94×10^7			
Jupiter	7.78×10^{11}	3.74×10^8			
Saturn	1.43×10^{12}	9.30×10^8			
Uranus	2.87×10^{12}				
Neptune	4.50×10^{12}				
Pluto		7.82×10^9			

Functions

The great German mathematician and scientist Johannes Kepler (1571-1630) is best known for his work in astronomy. For example, it was Kepler who found that the planets move around the sun in elliptical orbits, not circular orbits. He believed that the sun somehow controlled the motions of the planets, but he thought that the attraction between the sun and the planets was magnetic. Sir Isaac Newton (1642-1727) showed that the attraction was gravitational.

Kepler's work was limited to part of the solar system. Only six planets were known in his time. Neptune, Uranus, and Pluto were discovered later.

In one of his most famous discoveries, Kepler described how the average distance of a planet from the sun, or the mean radius of orbit, is related to the time the planet takes to orbit the sun, or the period of orbit.

1. Copy the table. Complete the first six rows by calculating the values of R^3, T^2, and the ratio $\dfrac{R^3}{T^2}$.

2. a) What do you notice about the values of $\dfrac{R^3}{T^2}$ for planets in the solar system?

b) Determine the mean value of $\dfrac{R^3}{T^2}$.

3. Let $\dfrac{R^3}{T^2} = k$, where k is known as the Kepler constant.

a) Solve the equation for T.
b) Use the equation solved for T to calculate the periods of the orbits of Uranus and of Neptune. Use a data bank to check your answers.

4. a) Solve the equation $k = \dfrac{R^3}{T^2}$ for R.

b) Use the equation solved for R to calculate the mean radius of the orbit of Pluto. Use a data bank to check your answer.

Designing With Functions

1. The design is made up of straight lines. The window variables used are Xmin = 0, Xmax = 12, Ymin = 0, and Ymax = 6.

a) Determine the equations of the functions used to create the design.

b) Use a graphing calculator to recreate the design on screen by entering the functions that you defined.

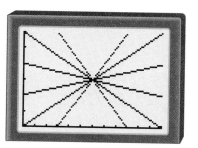

2. The design is made up of parabolas. The window variables used are Xmin = −4, Xmax = 4, Ymin = 0, and Ymax = 16.

a) Determine the equations of the functions used to create the design.

b) Use a graphing calculator to recreate the design on screen.

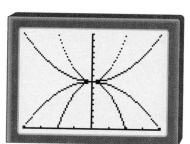

3. The design is made up of straight lines and parabolas. The window variables used are Xmin = −3, Xmax = 3, Ymin = 0, and Ymax = 36.

a) Determine the equations of the functions used to create the design.

b) Use a graphing calculator to recreate the design on screen.

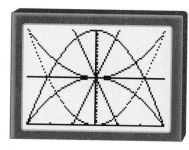

4. Design an image made up of parabolas and straight lines. Have a classmate determine the equations of the defining functions.

Warm Up

Simplify.

1. $(3x + 2) + (2x - 1)$

2. $(3x^2 - 2x - 1) + 2(4x - 3)$

3. $3(5x + 4) - (2x - 3)$

4. $(2x - 4) - (x^2 + 2x - 1)$

5. $(x + 1)(3x - 2)$

6. $(2x - 1)(x^2 - 3x + 2)$

7. $(x^2 - 3x + 2) \div (x - 1)$

8. $(3x^2 + 4x - 4) \div (x + 2)$

Simplify.

9. $(2\sqrt{x} - 1) + 2(\sqrt{x} + 1)$

10. $-2(3\sqrt{x} + 2) - (2\sqrt{x} - 5)$

11. $(\sqrt{x} + 1)(3\sqrt{x} - 1)$

12. $(4\sqrt{x} - 3)(1 - 2\sqrt{x})$

13. $(\sqrt{x} + 2)^2$

14. $(3\sqrt{x} - 1)^2$

15. $(\sqrt{x} + 1) \div (\sqrt{x} - 1)$

16. $(2\sqrt{x} - 1) \div (\sqrt{x} + 2)$

Solve for y.

17. $x - 2 = 3y$

18. $x = \dfrac{2}{y + 2}$

19. $x = \dfrac{3}{y} - 5$

20. $x = \dfrac{3}{1 - y} + 2$

State the degree of each function.

21. $y = x^2 + 3x - 1$

22. $y = 3x^4 - 5$

23. $y = 4 - x$

24. $y = 3$

Evaluate.

25. $|-4|$

26. $|3 - 4|$

27. $|(-2) \times (-3)|$

28. $|3| \times |-3|$

29. $|-2| + |4|$

30. $|3| - |-5|$

Solve.

31. $4x + 3 = 5$

32. $\dfrac{x}{3} + 4 = 2$

33. $\dfrac{3}{x} = -2$

34. $\dfrac{x - 3}{2} = -1$

35. $\dfrac{4}{x + 1} = \dfrac{1}{3}$

36. $-2 = \dfrac{3}{2x - 1}$

State the restrictions on the variable in each expression.

37. $\dfrac{3}{x}$

38. $\dfrac{5}{x - 1}$

39. $\dfrac{3x + 1}{2x + 1}$

40. $\dfrac{x + 1}{x^2}$

41. $\dfrac{3x}{x^2 - 9}$

42. $\dfrac{x - 4}{x^2 - x - 6}$

Mental Math

Evaluating Functions

1. If $g(x) = 2x^2 - x - 5$, find

a) $g(0)$　　**b)** $g(2)$　　**c)** $g(-3)$

2. If $f(x) = \sqrt{x + 3} - 4$, find

a) $f(1)$　　**b)** $f(6)$　　**c)** $f(13)$

3. If $g(x) = |x + 1| + 2$, find

a) $g(0)$　　**b)** $g(6)$　　**c)** $g(-8)$

4. If $f(x) = \dfrac{2}{x - 3}$, find

a) $f(1)$　　**b)** $f(0)$　　**c)** $f(-5)$

Dividing Using Compatible Numbers

To divide 209 by 11, rewrite the dividend so that 11 divides into it more easily.

$$209 \div 11 = (220 - 11) \div 11$$
$$= (220 \div 11) - (11 \div 11)$$
$$= 20 - 1 \text{ or } 19$$
$$345 \div 15 = (300 + 45) \div 15$$
$$= (300 \div 15) + (45 \div 15)$$
$$= 20 + 3 \text{ or } 23$$

Divide.

1. $96 \div 4$　　**2.** $132 \div 12$　　**3.** $135 \div 15$

4. $143 \div 11$　　**5.** $198 \div 22$　　**6.** $228 \div 19$

7. $156 \div 13$　　**8.** $406 \div 14$　　**9.** $306 \div 17$

10. $550 \div 25$　　**11.** $437 \div 23$　　**12.** $312 \div 26$

To divide 20.9 by 11, first divide 209 by 11, and then place the decimal point.

$20.9 \div 11 = 1.9$

To divide 3450 by 15, first divide 345 by 15, and then place the decimal point.

$3450 \div 15 = 230$

Divide.

13. $13.2 \div 11$　　**14.** $15.6 \div 12$　　**15.** $28.5 \div 15$

16. $5.46 \div 26$　　**17.** $6.75 \div 75$　　**18.** $2400 \div 15$

19. $6380 \div 29$　　**20.** $5290 \div 23$　　**21.** $984 \div 2.4$

22. a) Complete the following divisions.

$mx \div x$

$(m + n)x \div x - nx \div x$

$(m - n)x \div x + nx \div x$

b) Explain how the divisions are related to the method shown above.

5.1 Operations With Functions

Archeologists from the University of British Columbia and Brigham Young University have discovered the world's oldest known ballpark in southern Mexico. The ballpark was built by the Mokaya Indians about 3500 years ago. It is believed that the game *tlatchli* was played there. Two teams played this game with a hard rubber ball, which they tried to move to the opposite end of the playing surface without touching the ball with their hands, feet, or head.

Paso de la Amada, Mound 7, Ballcourt

Schematic Cross Section

The area of the playing surface in the ballpark can be represented by the function $A(x) = 11x^2 - 8x - 3$, and the width by $w(x) = x - 1$, where x is a distance, in metres.

Explore: Complete the Table

For the functions $p(x) = 2x + 1$ and $q(x) = x - 1$, x belongs to the domain of both functions. We can perform operations on the functions. For example,

$$p(x) + q(x) = (2x + 1) + (x - 1) \qquad p(x) - q(x) = (2x + 1) - (x - 1)$$
$$= 3x \qquad\qquad\qquad\qquad = x + 2$$

For the functions $f(x) = x^2 + x$ and $g(x) = x + 1$, x belongs to the domain of both functions. Copy the table. Complete the table by first writing expressions in simplest form for a new function, $h(x)$, that results from each operation. Then, find $h(4)$.

	Operation	Resulting Function, $h(x)$	$h(4)$
A	$f(x) + g(x)$	$h(x) = \blacksquare$	
B	$f(x) - g(x)$	$h(x) = \blacksquare$	
C	$f(x) \times g(x)$	$h(x) = \blacksquare$	
D	$\dfrac{f(x)}{g(x)}$	$h(x) = \blacksquare$	

Inquire

1. Calculate $f(4)$ and $g(4)$.

2. Calculate each of the following.

a) $f(4) + g(4)$ **b)** $f(4) - g(4)$ **c)** $f(4) \times g(4)$ **d)** $\dfrac{f(4)}{g(4)}$

3. How do the values of $h(4)$ in A, B, C, and D compare with the values found in question 2?

4. In D, what are the restrictions on the function $g(x)$? on the variable x? Explain.

5. How do the ways in which functions are combined compare with the ways in which real numbers are added, subtracted, multiplied, and divided?

6. Given that $p(x) = 2x^2 + 4x$ and $q(x) = 2x$, write a function $r(x)$ that results from each operation.

a) $p(x) + q(x)$ **b)** $p(x) - q(x)$ **c)** $q(x) - p(x)$ **d)** $p(x) \times q(x)$ **e)** $\dfrac{p(x)}{q(x)}$

7. a) Use the functions for the area and the width of the world's oldest known ballpark to write a function for the length, $l(x)$.

b) If x is 7 m, what are the dimensions of the ballpark?

Operations on any two functions, f and g, both defined on the real numbers, R, can be used to define new functions as follows, provided that x is in the domain of f and in the domain of g.

The *sum* of f and g: $(f + g)(x) = f(x) + g(x)$
The *difference* of f and g: $(f - g)(x) = f(x) - g(x)$
The *product* of f and g: $(fg)(x) = f(x)g(x)$

The *quotient* of f and g: $\left(\dfrac{f}{g}\right)(x) = \dfrac{f(x)}{g(x)}$, where $g(x) \neq 0$

Note that, in the definition of the quotient $\dfrac{f}{g}$, division by 0 is not defined.

Example 1   Linear Functions
For the functions $f(x) = 3x - 5$ and $g(x) = 4 - x$, the domain is the set of real numbers. Write an expression in simplest form for each of the following functions. State any restrictions on the variable.

a) $(f + g)(x)$ **b)** $(f - g)(x)$ **c)** $(fg)(x)$ **d)** $\left(\dfrac{f}{g}\right)(x)$

Solution

a) $(f + g)(x) = f(x) + g(x)$
$\qquad = 3x - 5 + 4 - x$
$\qquad = 2x - 1$

b) $(f - g)(x) = f(x) - g(x)$
$\qquad = 3x - 5 - (4 - x)$
$\qquad = 3x - 5 - 4 + x$
$\qquad = 4x - 9$

c) $(fg)(x) = f(x) \times g(x)$
$\qquad = (3x - 5)(4 - x)$
$\qquad = 12x - 20 - 3x^2 + 5x$
$\qquad = -3x^2 + 17x - 20$

d) $\left(\dfrac{f}{g}\right)(x) = \dfrac{3x - 5}{4 - x}, \ x \neq 4$

Example 2   Evaluating Combined Functions
For the functions $f(x) = 5x - 1$ and $g(x) = 2x$, the domain is the set of real numbers. Find

a) $(f + g)(3)$ **b)** $(f - g)(-2)$ **c)** $(fg)(0)$ **d)** $\left(\dfrac{f}{g}\right)(5)$

Solution

a) $(f + g)(x) = f(x) + g(x)$
$\qquad = 5x - 1 + 2x$
$\qquad = 7x - 1$
$(f + g)(3) = 7(3) - 1$
$\qquad = 20$

b) $(f - g)(x) = f(x) - g(x)$
$\qquad = 5x - 1 - 2x$
$\qquad = 3x - 1$
$(f - g)(-2) = 3(-2) - 1$
$\qquad = -7$

c) $(fg)(x) = f(x) \times g(x)$
$\qquad = (5x - 1)(2x)$
$\qquad = 10x^2 - 2x$
$(fg)(0) = 10(0)^2 - 2(0)$
$\qquad = 0$

d) $\left(\dfrac{f}{g}\right)(x) = \dfrac{5x - 1}{2x}, x \neq 0$

$\left(\dfrac{f}{g}\right)(5) = \dfrac{5(5) - 1}{2(5)}$

$\qquad = \dfrac{12}{5}$

The sum of two functions can be found graphically by adding the values of the y-coordinates.

Example 3 Graphing the Sum of Two Functions

Given $f(x) = 2x + 1$ and $g(x) = 1 - x$, where x is a real number, use their graphs to graph the sum $(f + g)(x)$.

Solution

Make a table of values for $f(x)$ and $g(x)$. Graph these functions on the same set of axes.

Then, for each value of x, add the values of $f(x)$ and $g(x)$ to find the value of $(f + g)(x)$. Graph the ordered pairs for $(f + g)(x)$ and join them with a line.

x	f(x)	g(x)	(f + g)(x)
-3	-5	4	-1
-2	-3	3	0
-1	-1	2	1
0	1	1	2
1	3	0	3
2	5	-1	4
3	7	-2	5

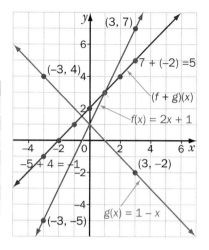

Example 4 Linear and Quadratic Functions

For the functions $f(x) = x^2 - 5x + 4$ and $g(x) = x - 1$, the domain is the set of real numbers. Write an expression in simplest form for each of the following functions. State any restrictions on the domain.

a) $(f + g)(x)$ **b)** $(f - g)(x)$ **c)** $(fg)(x)$ **d)** $\left(\dfrac{f}{g}\right)(x)$

Solution

a) $(f + g)(x) = f(x) + g(x)$
$= (x^2 - 5x + 4) + (x - 1)$
$= x^2 - 4x + 3$

The solutions can be visualized graphically.

 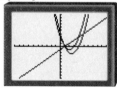

b) $(f - g)(x) = f(x) - g(x)$
$= (x^2 - 5x + 4) - (x - 1)$
$= x^2 - 5x + 4 - x + 1$
$= x^2 - 6x + 5$

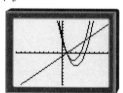 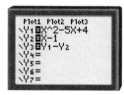

c) $(fg)(x) = f(x) \times g(x)$
$= (x^2 - 5x + 4)(x - 1)$
$= x^3 - x^2 - 5x^2 + 5x + 4x - 4$
$= x^3 - 6x^2 + 9x - 4$

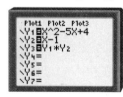 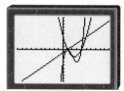

d) $\left(\dfrac{f}{g}\right)(x) = \dfrac{f(x)}{g(x)}$
$= \dfrac{x^2 - 5x + 4}{x - 1}$
$= \dfrac{(x - 4)(x - 1)}{x - 1}$
$= x - 4, x \neq 1$

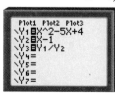 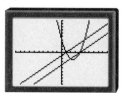

Note that, in part d) of Example 4, displaying a table of values for $\left(\dfrac{f}{g}\right)(x)$ shows the restriction on the variable.

By adjusting the window variables on your graphing calculator, you may be able to see a break in the graph of $\left(\dfrac{f}{g}\right)(x)$ at $x = 1$.

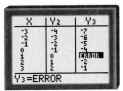 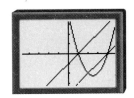

A **rational function** is defined as $f(x) = \dfrac{P(x)}{Q(x)}$, where $P(x)$ and $Q(x)$ are polynomials, and $Q(x) \neq 0$.

Example 5　Rational Functions

If $f(x) = \dfrac{x}{x-2}$ and $g(x) = \dfrac{x}{x+5}$, find each of the following functions. State any restrictions on the variable.

a) $(f+g)(x)$　　**b)** $\left(\dfrac{f}{g}\right)(x)$　　**c)** $(fg)(x)$

Solution

a) $(f+g)(x) = f(x) + g(x)$

$$= \frac{x}{x-2} + \frac{x}{x+5}$$

Rewrite using the LCD, and then simplify.

The LCD is $(x-2)(x+5)$

$$\frac{x}{x-2} + \frac{x}{x+5} = \frac{x(x+5)}{(x-2)(x+5)} + \frac{x(x-2)}{(x-2)(x+5)}$$

$$= \frac{x(x+5) + x(x-2)}{(x-2)(x+5)}$$

$$= \frac{x(2x+3)}{(x-2)(x+5)}$$

$$= \frac{2x^2 + 3x}{(x-2)(x+5)}, \; x \neq 2, \; -5$$

b) $\left(\dfrac{f}{g}\right)(x) = \dfrac{f(x)}{g(x)}$

$$= \frac{\dfrac{x}{x-2}}{\dfrac{x}{x+5}}$$

$$= \frac{x}{x-2} \times \frac{x+5}{x}$$

$$= \frac{x(x+5)}{x(x-2)}$$

$$= \frac{x+5}{x-2}, \; x \neq 0, \; 2, \; -5$$

c) $(fg)(x) = f(x) \times g(x)$

$$= \frac{x}{x-2} \times \frac{x}{x+5}$$

$$= \frac{x^2}{(x-2)(x+5)}, \; x \neq 2, \; -5$$

Radical functions include variables that appear in a radicand. Examples include $f(x) = \sqrt{x} + 1$, $g(x) = \sqrt{x-3} - 2$, and $f(x) = \sqrt[3]{x}$, but not $g(x) = x + \sqrt{2}$.

Example 6 Radical Functions

Given the functions $f(x) = 2\sqrt{x} - 3$ and $g(x) = \sqrt{x} + 1$, write each of the following functions in simplest form. State the domain of each new function.

a) $(f+g)(x)$ **b)** $(f-g)(x)$ **c)** $(fg)(x)$ **d)** $\left(\dfrac{f}{g}\right)(x)$

Solution

a) $(f+g)(x) = f(x) + g(x)$
$= 2\sqrt{x} - 3 + \sqrt{x} + 1$
$= 3\sqrt{x} - 2, \ x \geq 0$

b) $(f-g)(x) = f(x) - g(x)$
$= 2\sqrt{x} - 3 - (\sqrt{x} + 1)$
$= 2\sqrt{x} - 3 - \sqrt{x} - 1$
$= \sqrt{x} - 4, \ x \geq 0$ The domain is the set of non-negative real numbers.

c) $(fg)(x) = f(x) \times g(x)$
$= (2\sqrt{x} - 3)(\sqrt{x} + 1)$
$= 2x + 2\sqrt{x} - 3\sqrt{x} - 3$
$= 2x - \sqrt{x} - 3, \ x \geq 0$

d) $\left(\dfrac{f}{g}\right)(x) = \dfrac{f(x)}{g(x)}$
$= \dfrac{2\sqrt{x} - 3}{\sqrt{x} + 1}$
$= \dfrac{(2\sqrt{x} - 3)(\sqrt{x} - 1)}{(\sqrt{x} + 1)(\sqrt{x} - 1)}$ Rationalize the denominator.
$= \dfrac{2x - 5\sqrt{x} + 3}{x - 1}, \ x \geq 0, \ x \neq 1$

Example 7 Other Combinations of Functions

Given $f(x) = 2x^2 + 3x$ and $g(x) = 5 - x$, find
a) $4f(x)$ **b)** $2g(x) - f(x)$ **c)** $(gg)(x)$

Solution

a) $4f(x) = 4(2x^2 + 3x)$
$= 8x^2 + 12x$

b) $2g(x) - f(x) = 2(5 - x) - (2x^2 + 3x)$
$= 10 - 2x - 2x^2 - 3x$
$= 10 - 5x - 2x^2$

c) $(gg)(x) = g(x) \times g(x)$
$= (5 - x)(5 - x)$
$= 25 - 10x + x^2$

Example 8 Weekly Earnings

Alicia works as a veterinary assistant. She earns \$14/h for her regular 35 h/week and \$21/h for overtime. She always works at least 35 h/week.
a) Write two functions to represent Alicia's regular pay, $r(x)$, and her overtime pay, $v(x)$, where x is the total number of hours worked in a week.
b) Write and simplify a function to represent Alicia's total pay, $t(x)$.
c) Use the function from part b) to find Alicia's total earnings in a week in which she works 46 h.

Solution

a) Alicia's pay for the first 35 h/week is 14×35 or 490.
So, $r(x) = 490$
Alicia's pay for overtime hours is $21(x - 35)$, where $x \geq 35$.
So, $v(x) = 21(x - 35)$

Alicia always works at least 35 h/week, so her regular pay is independent of the total hours worked.

b) Alicia's total pay is represented by the sum of $r(x)$ and $v(x)$.

$$t(x) = r(x) + v(x)$$
$$= 490 + 21(x - 35)$$
$$= 490 + 21x - 735$$
$$= 21x - 245$$

c) $t(x) = 21x - 245$
$$= 21(46) - 245$$
$$= 721$$

Estimate
$20 \times 50 = 1000$
$1000 - 250 = 750$

In a week in which she works 46 h, Alicia's total earnings are \$721.

Practice

For each pair of functions, f and g, find

a) $(f+g)(x)$ **b)** $(f-g)(x)$ **c)** $(fg)(x)$ **d)** $\left(\dfrac{f}{g}\right)(x)$

Write each function in simplest form and state any restrictions on the variable.

1. $f(x) = 3x - 4$ and $g(x) = x + 6$
2. $f(x) = x + 8$ and $g(x) = 2x + 3$
3. $f(x) = x - 5$ and $g(x) = 2x - 1$
4. $f(x) = 2x - 4$ and $g(x) = x - 2$
5. $f(x) = 10$ and $g(x) = -5x$
6. $f(x) = 9$ and $g(x) = -4x - 5$
7. $f(x) = 3x$ and $g(x) = -3x$
8. $f(x) = x - 5$ and $g(x) = x$

For each of the following pairs of functions, f and g, find

a) $(f+g)(3)$ **b)** $(f-g)(-1)$ **c)** $(fg)(2)$ **d)** $\left(\dfrac{f}{g}\right)(-2)$

9. $f(x) = x - 3$ and $g(x) = x + 4$
10. $f(x) = 2x + 3$ and $g(x) = x - 1$
11. $f(x) = 3x + 5$ and $g(x) = x$
12. $f(x) = -x$ and $g(x) = x + 1$
13. $f(x) = 3x + 6$ and $g(x) = x + 1$

Given f(x) and g(x), use their graphs to graph $(f+g)(x)$.

14. $f(x) = x + 4$ and $g(x) = 2 - x$
15. $f(x) = x - 3$ and $g(x) = -x + 3$
16. $f(x) = 2x - 1$ and $g(x) = 1 - 2x$

Given f(x) and g(x), use their graphs to graph $(f-g)(x)$.

17. $f(x) = x + 3$ and $g(x) = 1 - x$
18. $f(x) = x - 2$ and $g(x) = -x + 4$
19. $f(x) = -2x$ and $g(x) = x$

For each pair of functions, f and g, find

a) $(f+g)(x)$ **b)** $(f-g)(x)$ **c)** $(fg)(x)$ **d)** $\left(\dfrac{f}{g}\right)(x)$

Write each function in simplest form and state any restrictions on the variable.

20. $f(x) = x^2$ and $g(x) = x - 1$
21. $f(x) = x^2 - 1$ and $g(x) = x + 4$
22. $f(x) = 3x - 1$ and $g(x) = 2x^2$
23. $f(x) = 2x^2 - 3$ and $g(x) = 2x + 5$
24. $f(x) = x$ and $g(x) = x^2 + 1$
25. $f(x) = 2x^2 - 4x$ and $g(x) = 2x$
26. $f(x) = x^2 - 2x + 1$ and $g(x) = x - 1$
27. $f(x) = -2x^2$ and $g(x) = 3x$
28. $f(x) = 2x^2 + 3x - 5$ and $g(x) = 2x + 5$
29. $f(x) = 12$ and $g(x) = x^2 - 3x + 2$
30. $f(x) = 4x^2 - 1$ and $g(x) = 2x - 1$

For each of the following pairs of functions, f and g, find

a) $(f+g)(-1)$ **b)** $(f-g)(2)$ **c)** $(fg)(0)$ **d)** $\left(\dfrac{f}{g}\right)(3)$

31. $f(x) = x^2$ and $g(x) = x$
32. $f(x) = x^2 + 2$ and $g(x) = 2x$
33. $f(x) = 3x - 1$ and $g(x) = -x^2$
34. $f(x) = 1 - x$ and $g(x) = 1 - x^2$
35. $f(x) = 2x^2 - 4x$ and $g(x) = x - 2$

For each pair of functions, f and g, find

a) $(f+g)(x)$ **b)** $(f-g)(x)$ **c)** $(fg)(x)$ **d)** $\left(\dfrac{f}{g}\right)(x)$

Write each function in simplest form and state any restrictions on the domain.

36. $f(x)=\dfrac{1}{x+1}$ and $g(x)=\dfrac{1}{x}$

37. $f(x)=\dfrac{2}{x+3}$ and $g(x)=\dfrac{3}{x-2}$

38. $f(x)=\dfrac{x}{x-1}$ and $g(x)=\dfrac{x}{x-4}$

39. $f(x)=\dfrac{x}{x-4}$ and $g(x)=\dfrac{2x}{x+4}$

For each pair of functions, f and g, find

a) $(f+g)(x)$ **b)** $(f-g)(x)$ **c)** $(fg)(x)$ **d)** $\left(\dfrac{f}{g}\right)(x)$

Write each function in simplest form and state any restrictions on the domain.

40. $f(x)=3\sqrt{x}$ and $g(x)=\sqrt{x}$

41. $f(x)=\sqrt{x}+3$ and $g(x)=2\sqrt{x}$

42. $f(x)=\sqrt{x}-2$ and $g(x)=\sqrt{x}+2$

43. $f(x)=2\sqrt{x}-1$ and $g(x)=\sqrt{x}+1$

44. Given $f(x)=2x-3$ and $g(x)=4-x$, find
a) $3f(x)+2g(x)$ **b)** $3g(x)-2f(x)$ **c)** $(ff)(x)$

45. Given $f(x)=3-x^2$ and $g(x)=x^2+2$, find
a) $3f(x)+2g(x)$ **b)** $3g(x)-f(x)$ **c)** $2(fg)(x)$

46. Given $f(x)=2x^2$ and $g(x)=x+3$, find
a) $2f(x)-3g(x)$ **b)** $g(x)-4f(x)$ **c)** $(gg)(x)$

47. Given $f(x)=x^2-1$ and $g(x)=x^2-1$, find
a) $2g(x)-4f(x)$ **b)** $3g(x)-f(x)$ **c)** $2\left(\dfrac{f}{g}\right)(x)$

For each set of functions, find $f(x)+g(x)-h(x)$.
48. $f(x)=7$, $g(x)=-3x$, and $h(x)=4x^2$
49. $f(x)=3x-3$, $g(x)=x+5$, and $h(x)=6-x$
50. $f(x)=2x^2-5x-3$, $g(x)=5x^2-9$, and $h(x)=4x-3$

For each set of functions, find $f(x)-g(x)+\dfrac{1}{2}h(x)$.

51. $f(x)=9$, $g(x)=4x$, and $h(x)=2x^2$
52. $f(x)=2x-1$, $g(x)=x-3$, and $h(x)=4-6x$
53. $f(x)=x^2-6x-4$, $g(x)=5x^2-9$, and $h(x)=2x-6$

Applications and Problem Solving

54. Weekly earnings Joseph works as a security guard. He earns \$12/h for his regular 37.5 h/week and \$15/h for overtime. He works some overtime every week.
a) Write two functions to represent Joseph's regular pay, $r(x)$, and his overtime pay, $p(x)$, where x is the total number of hours worked in a week.
b) Write and simplify a function to represent Joseph's total pay, $t(x)$.
c) What is the domain of the function from part b)? Explain.
d) Use the function from part b) to find Joseph's total earnings for a week in which he works 43 h.

55. The function f is the set of ordered pairs $(-1, 2)$, $(0, 1)$, $(1, 2)$, and $(2, 5)$. The function g is the set of ordered pairs $(-1, -1)$, $(0, 2)$, $(2, 8)$.
a) Calculate $(f+g)(0)$.
b) Calculate $(g-f)(-1)$.
c) Calculate $(fg)(2)$.
d) Is it possible to calculate $(f-g)(1)$? Explain.

56. Tennis court The area of a tennis court can be represented approximately by the function $A(x)=10x^2+3x-1$, and the length by $l(x)=5x-1$, where x is a distance, in metres.
a) Write and simplify a function, $w(x)$, to represent the width of a tennis court.
b) If x represents 5 m, what is the approximate width of a tennis court?

57. Window area The dimensions of a window are shown in the diagram.
a) Write a function, $r(x)$, to represent the area of the rectangular part.
b) Write a function, $c(x)$, to represent the area of the semicircular part.
c) Write a function in simplest form to represent the area of the whole window, $w(x)$.

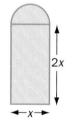

58. Measurement The area, $A(x)$, of a square can be represented by the expression $4x^2 + 4x + 1$. The area, $B(x)$, of a smaller square can be represented by the expression $x^2 - 2x + 1$. The difference between these areas represents the area of a rectangle.
a) Write a function, $C(x)$, to represent the area of the rectangle.
b) If each dimension of the rectangle is a function of x, what are the possible dimensions of the rectangle?

59. Great Pyramid Many Egyptian pyramids were built with similar shapes. For these pyramids, the original height can be approximately represented by the function $h(x) = 0.63x$, where x is the side length of the square base.
a) Write a function to represent the area of the base, $B(x)$.
b) Write and simplify a function to represent the volume of the pyramid, $V(x)$.
c) For the Great Pyramid of Cheops, the side length of the base is 230 m. Calculate the original volume of the pyramid, to the nearest thousand cubic metres.

60. Fencing a field a) Write a function to represent the area of a square field, $A(s)$, where s represents the side length.
b) Write a function to represent the perimeter of the field, $P(s)$.
c) What is the domain of the functions $A(s)$ and $P(s)$? Explain.
d) Use operations on the functions $A(s)$ and $P(s)$ to obtain a function in simplest form to represent the area to perimeter ratio, $r(s)$.
e) If the area to perimeter ratio for a square field is 5 m, find the length of fencing needed to enclose the field and the area of the field.

61. Measurement A cylinder has a radius r.
a) Write a function to represent the area of the base, $B(r)$.
b) If the height is three times the radius, write a function to represent the height, $h(r)$.
c) Write and simplify a function to represent the volume, $V(r)$.
d) If the radius is 7 cm, determine the volume of the cylinder, to the nearest cubic centimetre.

62. Compact disc Let r centimetres represent the radius of a compact disc, measured from the centre of the hole. The radius of the hole itself is $\frac{r}{8}$ centimetres.
a) Write a function to represent the area, $A(r)$, of one side of a compact disc, including the hole.
b) Write a function to represent the area, $B(r)$, of the hole.
c) Write and simplify a function, $C(r)$, to represent the area of one side of the disc, excluding the hole.
d) If r represents 6 cm, what is the area of one side of the disc, excluding the hole, to the nearest square centimetre?

63. If $m(x) = 4x + 1$ and $n(x) = 3x^2 - x - 2$, describe two methods for finding $(m + n)(3)$.

64. a) For each of the following pairs of functions, find $(f - g)(1)$ and $(g - f)(1)$. Describe how the two values are related in each case.
$$f(x) = 2x + 3 \text{ and } g(x) = 4x - 1$$
$$f(x) = 2x^2 - 4 \text{ and } g(x) = 5 - 4x^2$$
b) Find $(f - g)(1)$ and $(g - f)(1)$ for the following pair of functions. Are the two values related in the same way as you found in part a)? Explain.
$$f(x) = 3x^2 - 2 \text{ and } g(x) = -x + 2$$
c) Describe how the values of $(f - g)(x)$ and $(g - f)(x)$ are related for equal real values of x.

65. For the functions $f(x) = 2x - 1$ and $g(x) = 3x + 2$, how does the value of $(fg)(x)$ compare with the value of $(gf)(x)$ for a given value of x? Explain.

66. If $h(x) = (fg)(x)$, what can you conclude about $f(x)$ and $g(x)$ when $h(x) = 0$? Explain.

67. For each set of functions, explain why $\left(\dfrac{f}{g}\right)(x)$ is not the same function as $h(x)$.

a) $f(x) = 6x^2$, $g(x) = 2x$, and $h(x) = 3x$
b) $f(x) = x^2 - x$, $g(x) = x$, and $h(x) = x - 1$
c) $f(x) = x^2 + 7x - 18$, $g(x) = x + 9$, and $h(x) = x - 2$

68. Given the functions $f(x) = x + 1$ and $g(x) = 2x$, graph $(f - g)(x)$ and $(g - f)(x)$. Describe how the two graphs are related.

69. Spreadsheet On the spreadsheet shown, cell B1 defines the function f, and cell C1 defines the function g.

	A	B	C	D
1		=2*A1+3	=A1^2–4	
2	1			
3	–1			
4	2			
5	–2			

a) The values entered in column A are values of a variable, x. Write the functions $f(x)$ and $g(x)$.
b) Column D is to include values of $(f+g)(x)$. What should be entered in cell D1?
c) Copy and complete the spreadsheet.

70. If $a(x)$ is a quadratic function and $b(x)$ is a linear function, is each of the following functions linear, quadratic, or neither? Explain.
a) $(a+b)(x)$ **b)** $(a-b)(x)$
c) $(b-a)(x)$ **d)** $(ab)(x)$

71. Working backward Determine two functions f and g such that $(f+g)(x) = 5x-2$ and $(f-g)(x) = x+12$.

72. a) Find $(fg)(x)$ for the functions $f(x) = x+2$ and $g(x) = x-2$.
b) How do the domain and range of $(fg)(x)$ compare with the domain and range of $f(x) = x+2$ and $g(x) = x-2$? Explain.

73. The graphs of $f(x)$ and $g(x)$ are shown.

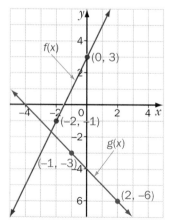

If $h(x) = (f+g)(x)$, write the function $h(x)$ in simplest form.

74. The graphs of $f(x)$ and $g(x)$ are shown.

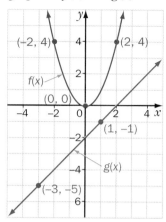

If $h(x) = (f+g)(x)$, write the function $h(x)$ in simplest form.

75. If $f(x)$ and $(f+g)(x)$ were graphed on the same set of axes, how could the graphs be used to draw the graph of $g(x)$?

76. If $f(x) = 3x-4$ and $g(x) = 2x$, find $f(g(x))$.

77. Given $f(x) = 3x-1$ and $g(x) = 2-x$, describe a manual method of graphing $(f+g)(x)$ that is different from the method in Example 3. Compare your method with your classmates'.

NUMBER POWER

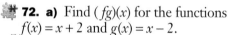

Copy the diagram. Replace each letter with a whole number so that the numbers in individual sectors, or the sums of numbers in two or more adjacent sectors, give all whole numbers from 1 to 19. A replacement number may be used more than once.

5.2 Composition of Functions

Explore: Use the Formulas

Rohana took a trip to Greece and Italy to see the ancient ruins in both countries.

a) Before leaving home, she converted $1000 Canadian to Greek drachmas. The function $g(d) = 220d$ converted dollars to drachmas, where g was the number of drachmas and d was the number of dollars. How many drachmas did she receive?

b) When Rohana left Greece for Italy, she converted 120 000 drachmas to Italian lira. The function $l(g) = 6g$ converted drachmas to lira. How many lira did she receive?

c) While in Italy, Rohana converted $200 Canadian directly to lira. How many lira did she receive?

Inquire

1. Write a function in the form $l(d) = \blacksquare d$ that converts Canadian dollars directly to Italian lira.

2. Write a function that converts lira to drachmas.

3. Write a function that converts drachmas to Canadian dollars.

4. Write a function that converts lira directly to Canadian dollars.

5. The function $f(d) = 4d$ converts Canadian dollars to French francs. The function $j(f) = 23f$ converts French francs to Japanese yen.
a) Write a function that converts Canadian dollars directly to yen.
b) Write a function that converts yen directly to Canadian dollars.

As well as combining functions by addition, subtraction, multiplication, and division, we can combine functions by a method called composition.

> For two functions, f and g, both defined on the real numbers, R, the **composition** is defined as
> $$(f \circ g)(x) = f(g(x))$$
> The domain of f must include the range of g.

$(f \circ g)(x)$ and $f(g(x))$ are both read as "f of g of x."

The composition of two functions, $f(g(x))$, is a new function, $h(x)$, found by substituting g into f. The new function is sometimes called a **composite function**. The functions found in Inquire questions 1, 4, and 5 are composite functions. Each of these functions is the composition of two other functions.

One way to think of a composition is in terms of a mapping.

The notation $f \circ g$ means that the map g is performed first, and the map f is performed second.

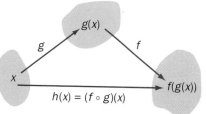

Note that, in the definition of the composition of functions, $f \circ g$, the domain of f must include the range of g. If this condition is not met, the composition is not defined. It does not exist.

Example 1   Compositions as Mappings
The functions f and g are the following sets of ordered pairs.
$f = \{(3, 5), (2, 4), (1, 4), (-1, -3)\}$
$g = \{(6, 3), (2, -1), (0, 2), (-2, 1)\}$
Find each of the following, if it exists.
a) $f \circ g$ **b)** $g \circ f$

Solution
Use arrow diagrams to represent the mappings.
a) For $f \circ g$, map g first, and then f.

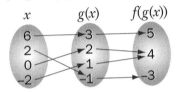

b) For $g \circ f$, map f first, and then g.

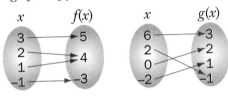

The outputs from g are acceptable inputs for f.
$f \circ g = \{(6, 5), (2, -3), (0, 4), (-2, 4)\}$

The outputs from f are not acceptable inputs for g.
So, $g \circ f$ does not exist.

You can evaluate the composition of two functions as follows.

1   1. Evaluate the inner function $g(x)$ first.

$$f(g(x))$$

2   2. Use the output from the inner function as the input for the outer function $f(x)$.

Example 2   Evaluating a Composition
If $f(x) = 4x + 1$ and $g(x) = 5x$, find the following.
a) $(f \circ g)(2)$ **b)** $(g \circ f)(2)$

Solution
a) $g(x) = 5x$
         $g(2) = 5(2)$
         $= 10$
     $(f \circ g)(2) = f(g(2))$
                 $= f(10)$
                 $= 4(10) + 1$
                 $= 41$

b) $f(x) = 4x + 1$
         $f(2) = 4(2) + 1$
         $= 9$
     $(g \circ f)(2) = g(f(2))$
                 $= g(9)$
                 $= 5(9)$
                 $= 45$

Example 3   Writing a Composite Function

If $f(x) = x^2 - 3$ and $g(x) = 2x - 1$, write the following functions.

a) $f \circ g$ **b)** $g \circ f$

Solution

The solution can be visualized graphically.

a) $f \circ g = f(g(x))$

$\qquad = f(2x - 1)$

$\qquad = (2x - 1)^2 - 3$

$\qquad = 4x^2 - 4x + 1 - 3$

$\qquad = 4x^2 - 4x - 2$

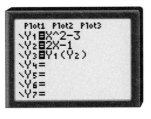

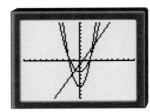

b) $g \circ f = g(f(x))$

$\qquad = g(x^2 - 3)$

$\qquad = 2(x^2 - 3) - 1$

$\qquad = 2x^2 - 6 - 1$

$\qquad = 2x^2 - 7$

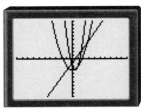

Notice that, in Example 3, $f(x)$ is a quadratic function and $g(x)$ is a linear function. The functions $f \circ g$ and $g \circ f$ are both quadratic.

Notice also, in Example 3, that $f \circ g \neq g \circ f$. Recall that the order was not important for the addition and multiplication of functions, because $f + g = g + f$ and $fg = gf$. But, in combining f and g by composition to find $f \circ g$ or $g \circ f$, the order is usually important. There are exceptions, such as $f(x) = 2x$ and $g(x) = 3x$, since $f(g(x)) = 2(3x)$ and $g(f(x)) = 3(2x)$

$\qquad\qquad = 6x \qquad\qquad\quad = 6x$

Two functions combined by composition need not be different. We can determine the composition of a function with itself.

Example 4   Composition of a Function With Itself

For $h(x) = 2x - 5$, find

a) $(h \circ h)(-6)$ **b)** $(h \circ h)(x)$

Solution

a) $(h \circ h)(-6) = h(h(-6))$

$\qquad\qquad = h(2(-6) - 5)$

$\qquad\qquad = h(-17)$

$\qquad\qquad = 2(-17) - 5$

$\qquad\qquad = -34 - 5$

$\qquad\qquad = -39$

b) $(h \circ h)(x) = h(h(x))$

$\qquad\qquad = h(2x - 5)$

$\qquad\qquad = 2(2x - 5) - 5$

$\qquad\qquad = 4x - 10 - 5$

$\qquad\qquad = 4x - 15$

Note that $(h \circ h)(x) \neq (hh)(x)$.

$(hh)(x) = h(x) \times h(x)$

$\qquad\quad = (2x - 5)^2$

$\qquad\quad = 4x^2 - 20x + 25$

Example 5   Compositions Involving a Radical Function

Given that $f(x) = \sqrt{x-1}$ and $g(x) = 2x$, find

a) $(f \circ g)(x)$ and $(g \circ f)(x)$

b) the domains of f, g, $f \circ g$, and $g \circ f$

c) the ranges of $f \circ g$ and $g \circ f$

Solution

a)
$$
\begin{aligned}
(f \circ g)(x) &= f(g(x)) \\
&= f(2x) \\
&= \sqrt{2x-1}
\end{aligned}
\qquad
\begin{aligned}
(g \circ f)(x) &= g(f(x)) \\
&= g(\sqrt{x-1}) \\
&= 2\sqrt{x-1}
\end{aligned}
$$

b) The functions in a composition are defined on the real numbers. Therefore, the domain of f is $x \geq 1$, since $x - 1 \geq 0$.
The domain of g is the set of real numbers.
The domain of $f \circ g$ is $x \geq \dfrac{1}{2}$, since $2x - 1 \geq 0$.
The domain of $g \circ f$ is $x \geq 1$, since $x - 1 \geq 0$.

c) The range of $f \circ g$ is the set of real numbers ≥ 0.
The range of $g \circ f$ is the set of real numbers ≥ 0.

Absolute value functions include variables within absolute value symbols. Examples include $f(x) = |x| + 1$, $g(x) = 2|x|$, and $f(x) = -|x + 3|$, but not $g(x) = x - |-2|$.

Example 6   Compositions Involving an Absolute Value Function

Given $f(x) = \sqrt{-x}$, $x \neq 0$, and $g(x) = |x|$, $x \neq 0$, does $f \circ g$ exist?

Solution 1
For $g(x) = |x|$, $x \neq 0$, the domain is all non-zero real numbers, and the range is all positive real numbers.

For $f(x) = \sqrt{-x}$, $x \neq 0$, the domain is all negative real numbers.
Since the range of g is not included in the domain of f, the composition $f \circ g$ is not defined.

Solution 2
Consider what $f \circ g$ would be if it were defined.
$$
\begin{aligned}
f \circ g &= f(g(x)) \\
&= f(|x|) \\
&= \sqrt{-|x|}
\end{aligned}
$$

Since the value of $|x|$ will always be positive, the value of $-|x|$ under the square root sign will always be negative. However, the functions f and g in the composition are defined on the real numbers, so the outputs from g are not acceptable inputs for f. Therefore, the composition $f \circ g$ does not exist.

Note that, if Example 6 did not include the restriction $x \neq 0$, $f \circ g$ would be defined for $x = 0$. The absolute value of 0 is 0, and 0 is an acceptable input for f.

Example 7   Compositions Involving a Rational Function

Given $f(x) = x + 1$ and $g(x) = \dfrac{1}{x-1}$, write and simplify the following.

State any restrictions on the variable.

a) $f \circ g$ **b)** $g \circ f$

Solution

a) $(f \circ g)(x) = f(g(x))$

$\quad = f\left(\dfrac{1}{x-1}\right)$

$\quad = \dfrac{1}{x-1} + 1$

$\quad = \dfrac{1 + x - 1}{x - 1}$

$\quad = \dfrac{x}{x-1}, \ x \neq 1$

b) $(g \circ f)(x) = g(f(x))$

$\quad = g(x + 1)$

$\quad = \dfrac{1}{x + 1 - 1}$

$\quad = \dfrac{1}{x}, \ x \neq 0$

In applications of functions, some variables depend on variables that, in turn, depend on other variables. The composition of functions can often be useful in this situation.

Example 8   Depreciation of Cars

Most new cars quickly go down in value or depreciate. The value of a new car after one year can be expressed as $v_1(c) = 0.8c$, where c is the original cost price. The value of the car after two years can be expressed as the function $v_2(v_1) = 0.85v_1$.

a) Find $(v_2 \circ v_1)(c)$. Interpret the meaning of this composite function.
b) If a new car costs $50 000, find its value after two years.

Solution

a) $(v_2 \circ v_1)(c) = v_2(v_1(c))$

$\quad\quad\quad\quad\quad = v_2(0.8c)$

$\quad\quad\quad\quad\quad = 0.85(0.8c)$

$\quad\quad\quad\quad\quad = 0.68c$

The function $(v_2 \circ v_1)(c)$ expresses the value of the car after two years as a function of the original cost price, c, that is, $v_2 = 0.68c$.

b) If a new car costs $50 000, its value after two years is given by

$\quad v_2 = 0.68c$

$\quad\quad = 0.68(50\ 000)$

$\quad\quad = 34\ 000$

So, the value of the car after two years is $34 000.

Practice

The functions f and g are defined by the arrow diagrams.

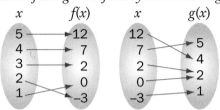

Use the arrow diagrams to state the following.
1. $g(f(5))$ **2.** $g(f(3))$ **3.** $g(f(1))$ **4.** $g(f(4))$
5. $f(g(12))$ **6.** $f(g(2))$ **7.** $f(g(7))$ **8.** $f(g(-3))$

9. For the arrow diagrams used in questions 1–8, write each of the following as a set of ordered pairs.
a) $g \circ f$ **b)** $f \circ g$

The functions f and g are the given sets of ordered pairs. Use arrow diagrams to find each of the following, if it exists.

a) $f \circ g$ **b)** $g \circ f$ **c)** $f \circ f$ **d)** $g \circ g$
10. $f = \{(3, 7), (0, 4), (-1, -3), (-2, -4)\}$
   $g = \{(2, 3), (1, 0), (0, -1), (-1, -2)\}$
11. $f = \{(8, 2), (6, 3), (5, 0), (1, 4), (-1, -1)\}$
   $g = \{(5, 7), (3, 8), (0, -1), (-2, 3), (-5, 0)\}$

If f(x) = x + 3 and g(x) = 2x, find
12. $f(g(3))$ **13.** $g(f(2))$
14. $(f \circ g)(4)$ **15.** $(g \circ f)(4)$

If f(x) = 2x − 3 and g(x) = 4x, find
16. $(f \circ g)(-2)$ **17.** $(g \circ f)(-2)$

If f(x) = 4 − 5x and g(x) = 1 − x, find
18. $(f \circ g)(3)$ **19.** $(g \circ f)(3)$

If f(x) = 2x − 1 and g(x) = x + 4, find
20. $(f \circ g)(x)$ **21.** $(g \circ f)(x)$

Find $(f \circ g)(x)$ and $(g \circ f)(x)$ in simplest form for each pair of functions.
22. $f(x) = 5x$ and $g(x) = 100 - x$
23. $f(x) = x^2$ and $g(x) = 12 - x$
24. $f(x) = 9$ and $g(x) = x + 4$
25. $f(x) = 3x$ and $g(x) = x^2$
26. $f(x) = 10 - x$ and $g(x) = 20 - x$
27. $f(x) = 15 - x$ and $g(x) = 15 - x$
28. $f(x) = -x$ and $g(x) = x^2$
29. $f(x) = x^2 - 2$ and $g(x) = 3x + 1$
30. $f(x) = 1 - x$ and $g(x) = 2x^2 + 3$
31. $f(x) = 4 - x^2$ and $g(x) = 2x - 1$

Find $(f \circ g)(x)$ and $(g \circ f)(x)$ in simplest form for each pair of functions.
32. $f(x) = |x|$ and $g(x) = 3x$
33. $f(x) = |x + 1|$ and $g(x) = x - 1$
34. $f(x) = \sqrt{x}$ and $g(x) = x + 1$
35. $f(x) = 2x - 1$ and $g(x) = \sqrt{2x}$

36. For $h(x) = x + 3$, find
a) $(h \circ h)(5)$ **b)** $(h \circ h)(x)$

37. For $g(x) = 3x - 4$, find
a) $(g \circ g)(-1)$ **b)** $(g \circ g)(x)$

38. For $f(x) = x^2$, find
a) $(f \circ f)(-1)$ **b)** $(f \circ f)(x)$

39. For $f(x) = 2 - x$, find
a) $(f \circ f)(3)$ **b)** $(f \circ f)(x)$

Use the functions $h(x) = 3x$ and $k(x) = (x - 1)^2$ to find each of the following.
40. $k(h(-1))$ **41.** $h(k(-1))$
42. $(k \circ h)(4)$ **43.** $(h \circ k)(4)$
44. $(k \circ k)(-2)$ **45.** $(h \circ h)(-2)$
46. $(h \circ k)(x)$ **47.** $(k \circ h)(x)$
48. $(h \circ h)(x)$ **49.** $(k \circ k)(x)$

Find each of the following composite functions, if it exists. Give the range of each composite function that exists.
50. $f \circ g$ for $f(x) = \sqrt{-x}$, $x < 0$, and $g(x) = |2x|$
51. $h \circ g$ for $g(x) = \sqrt{x}$ and $h(x) = 3x + 2$
52. $h \circ k$ for $h(x) = \sqrt{x} - 1$ and $k(x) = |x|$
53. $k \circ k$ for $k(x) = \sqrt{-2x}$, $x \le 0$
54. $f \circ g$ for $f(x) = 2 - x$ and $g(x) = |x - 1|$
55. $g \circ f$ for $f(x) = \sqrt{-x^2}$ and $g(x) = 2x$
56. $g \circ f$ for $f(x) = \sqrt{x}$ and $g(x) = x^2 + 1$
57. $f \circ g$ for $f(x) = \sqrt{-x^2} - 1$ and $g(x) = 2x$

Given f(x) and g(x), write and simplify $f \circ g$ and $g \circ f$. State any restrictions on the variable.
58. $f(x) = \dfrac{1}{x}$ and $g(x) = -x$

59. $f(x) = \dfrac{1}{x^2}$ and $g(x) = -x$

60. $f(x) = \dfrac{1}{x + 2}$ and $g(x) = 3 - x$

61. $f(x) = \dfrac{x}{x - 2}$ and $g(x) = 2x$

62. Given that $f(x) = \sqrt{x}$ and $g(x) = 3x$, find
a) $(f \circ g)(x)$ and $(g \circ f)(x)$
b) the domains of f, g, $f \circ g$, and $g \circ f$
c) the ranges of $f \circ g$ and $g \circ f$

63. Given that $h(x) = \sqrt{x}$ and $k(x) = x - 2$, find
a) $(h \circ k)(x)$ and $(k \circ h)(x)$
b) the domains of h, k, $h \circ k$, and $k \circ h$
c) the ranges of $h \circ k$ and $k \circ h$

64. If $h(x) = \sqrt{x+1}$ and $k(x) = 4x$, find
a) $(h \circ k)(x)$ and $(k \circ h)(x)$
b) the domains of h, k, $h \circ k$, and $k \circ h$
c) the ranges of $h \circ k$ and $k \circ h$

65. If $f(x) = \sqrt{x-2}$ and $g(x) = x^2 - 2$, find
a) $(f \circ g)(x)$ and $(g \circ f)(x)$
b) the domains of f, g, $f \circ g$, and $g \circ f$
c) the ranges of $f \circ g$ and $g \circ f$

66. If $h(x) = \dfrac{1}{x}$ and $k(x) = 5x$, find
a) $(h \circ k)(x)$ and $(k \circ h)(x)$
b) the domains of h, k, $h \circ k$, and $k \circ h$
c) the ranges of $h \circ k$ and $k \circ h$

67. If $f(x) = \dfrac{1}{x-1}$ and $g(x) = x - 1$, find
a) $(f \circ g)(x)$ and $(g \circ f)(x)$
b) the domains of f, g, $f \circ g$, and $g \circ f$
c) the ranges of $f \circ g$ and $g \circ f$

68. If $f(x) = 2x$ and $g(x) = |x|$, find
a) $(f \circ g)(x)$ and $(g \circ f)(x)$
b) the domains of f, g, $f \circ g$, and $g \circ f$
c) the ranges of $f \circ g$ and $g \circ f$

Applications and Problem Solving

69. Foreign currency exchange The function $p(d) = 0.5d$ converts Canadian dollars to Irish punts. The function $s(p) = 16p$ converts Irish punts to Austrian schillings.
a) Write a function that converts Canadian dollars directly to Austrian schillings.
b) How much is $1000 Canadian in Austrian schillings?
c) Write a function that converts Austrian schillings directly to Canadian dollars.
d) How much is 1000 schillings in Canadian dollars?

70. Vehicle depreciation A sports utility vehicle depreciates 20% in the first year and 10% in each year after the first.
a) Write a function $v_1(c)$ to describe the value after one year in terms of the original cost, c.
b) Write a function $v_2(v_1)$ to describe the value of the vehicle after two years in terms of its value after one year.
c) Write the functions $v_3(v_2)$ and $v_4(v_3)$ to describe its value after three years and four years in terms of the previous year's value.
d) Write a function to describe the value of the vehicle after four years in terms of its original cost.
e) If the original cost was $65 000, what is the value of the vehicle after four years?
f) If the value of a sports utility vehicle after four years is $30 618, what was its original cost?

71. Measurement The square and the smaller rectangle have a common side, as shown. The area of the square is x square units.

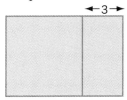

a) Write a function, $l(x)$, that represents the side length, l, of the square in terms of its area.
b) Write a function, $r(l)$, that represents the area of the smaller rectangle in terms of the side length of the square.
c) Write a function, $r(x)$, that represents the area of the smaller rectangle in terms of the area of the square.
d) If the area of the square is 25 square units, what is the area of the smaller rectangle?
e) If the area of the smaller rectangle is 24 square units, what is the area of the square?

72. Measurement a) Express the area of a square as a function of its side length.
b) Express the side length of a square as a function of the length of a diagonal.
c) Express the area of a square as a function of the length of a diagonal.
d) If the length of a diagonal of a square is 12 cm, what is the area of the square?

73. Speed of sound The speed of sound in air is about 330 m/s.
a) Write a function $d(t)$ to represent the distance, d metres, a sound travels from a source in terms of the time, t seconds, since the sound was made.
b) Write a function $A(d)$ to represent the circular area, $A(d)$ square metres, within a distance d metres of the source of a sound.
c) Write a function $A(t)$ to represent the circular area, A square metres, within which a sound can be heard within t seconds of the sound being made.
d) Calculate the area within which the sound can be heard within 0.1 s of a car backfiring. Round your answer to the nearest ten square metres.
e) If a sound is loud enough, how long does it take for the sound to be heard over an area of 1 km²? Round your answer to the nearest tenth of a second.

74. Sales bonus Connor earns a 3% bonus on all sales he makes over $250 000 in a year. His total sales are d dollars and $d > 250 000$.
a) Let $s(d)$ be the amount of Connor's sales over $250 000. Write a function that expresses $s(d)$ in terms of his total sales.
b) Let $p(s)$ be the amount of Connor's bonus. Write a function that expresses $p(s)$ in terms of Connor's sales over $250 000.
c) Find the composition $(p \circ s)(d)$.
d) Explain the meaning of the composite function from part c).
e) If Connor's sales one year are $375 000, calculate his bonus.

75. Foreign currency exchange The function $i(c) = 2.5c$ converts Canadian dollars to Israeli shekels. The function $n(i) = 2i$ converts Israeli shekels to Norwegian krones. The function $b(n) = 5n$ converts Norwegian krones to Belgian francs. The function $s(b) = 25b$ converts Belgian francs to South Korean won.
a) Write a composite function to convert Canadian dollars to South Korean won.
b) Write a composite function to convert Belgian francs to Canadian dollars.
c) Write a composite function to convert Norwegian krones to Israeli shekels.

d) Write a composite function to convert Israeli shekels to South Korean won.
e) How much is $500 Canadian worth in each of the other currencies?

76. Gasoline costs If a vehicle has a gasoline consumption of 9 L/100 km, it uses gasoline at a rate of 0.09 L/km.
a) Write the function $g(d)$ that describes the quantity of gasoline used, g litres, in terms of the distance driven, d kilometres.
b) The cost of gasoline, c dollars, can be described by the function $c(g) = \blacksquare g$, where $\blacksquare$ represents the average cost, in dollars, of a litre of gasoline where you live. Use the local cost of gasoline to write the function $c(g)$.
c) Write a function that expresses the cost of gasoline in terms of the distance driven.
d) How much would it cost to drive the vehicle described above a distance of 850 km?
e) Write a function that expresses the distance driven as a function of the cost of gasoline.
f) How far could you drive the vehicle on $30 worth of gasoline?

77. Measurement a) Write a function, $s(p)$, that expresses the side length, s, of an equilateral triangle in terms of its perimeter, p.
b) Write a function, $A(s)$, that expresses the area of an equilateral triangle in terms of its side length.
c) Write a function, $A(p)$, that expresses the area of an equilateral triangle in terms of its perimeter.
d) For an equilateral triangle with a perimeter of 30 cm, calculate the area, to the nearest square centimetre.

78. Markup A retailer marked up some merchandise 200% above her cost to get her selling price. For an end-of-season sale, she discounted the selling price by 75%.
a) Write a function that describes the discounted price as a function of the original cost.
b) Is the discounted price more or less than her cost?
c) For what markup would a 75% discount give a sale price that equals the cost?

79. If $f(x) = \dfrac{x+1}{x}$, $x \neq 0$, find $f \circ f$.

Find two functions, f and g, both containing the variable x, to make the following true.

80. $f \circ g = 3x$

81. $f \circ g = 2x + 2$

82. $f \circ g = \dfrac{1}{x - 4}$

83. $f \circ g = x^2 - 2x + 2$

84. Given that $f(x) = px - q$, $g(x) = rx - t$, and $f \circ g = g \circ f$, write an expression for t in terms of p, q, and r.

85. Given $f(x) = x^2 - 2$ and $g(x) = 2x + 1$, find any values of x for which $f(g(x)) = g(f(x))$.

86. Compare the ranges of $(f \circ g)(x)$ and $(g \circ f)(x)$ for the functions $f(x) = -x$ and $g(x) = x^2$.

87. Sale price During an end-of-season sale, a clothing store sold its winter stock at a 30% discount. Federal and provincial sales taxes added 15% to the selling price.
a) Write a function that expresses the selling price in terms of the regular price.
b) Write a function that expresses the total cost, including taxes, in terms of the selling price.
c) Write a function that expresses the total cost, including taxes, in terms of the regular price.
d) Mark bought a sweatshirt with a regular price of $50. How much did he pay, including taxes?

88. Employee discount a) Jacob works in a hardware store. He gets an employee discount of 20% on all merchandise. Write a function, $j(r)$, to show the price Jacob pays in terms of the regular price, r.
b) Some items in the store are on sale at 40% off. Write a function, $s(r)$, to show the sale price in terms of the regular price.
c) Find the composite functions $j(s(r))$ and $s(j(r))$. Explain the meaning of each composite function.
d) If Jacob buys a hammer with a regular price of $40 at the sale price, does the order of the composition matter? Explain.
e) Suppose Jacob buys an electric kettle priced at $50, which is not on sale. He claims his employee discount, and he has a manufacturer's discount coupon worth $5. Write a function, $m(r)$, to show the manufacturer's discount price in terms of the regular price. Then, find the composite functions $j(m(r))$ and $m(j(r))$. Does the order of the composition matter? Explain.

89. Measurement a) Write a function to represent the area of a circle in terms of the radius.
b) Write a function to represent the radius of a circle in terms of the circumference.
c) Write a function to represent the area of a circle in terms of the circumference.
d) For a circle with a circumference of 100 cm, what is the area, to the nearest square centimetre?

90. Is the composition of functions commutative? Explain.

91. Given $f(x) = 2x + 1$ and $h(x) = 3 - 2x$, determine a function $g(x)$ that makes $f \circ g = h$.

92. Decide whether each of the following statements is always true, sometimes true, or never true. Explain.
a) The composition of two linear functions is a linear function.
b) The product of two linear functions is a linear function.
c) The composition of two quadratic functions is a quadratic function
d) A function equals its composition with itself.

93. Write two functions, $f(x)$ and $g(x)$, that give $(f \circ g)(x) = 2x^2 - 1$.

94. Create two functions, $f(x)$ and $g(x)$, such that $(f \circ g)(x) = (g \circ f)(x)$.

95. Use the functions $f(x) = 5x$, $g(x) = x + 9$, and $h(x) = 3$ to find each of the following.
a) $(h \circ g \circ f)(x)$ **b)** $(g \circ f \circ h)(x)$
c) $(f \circ g \circ h)(x)$ **d)** $(f \circ f \circ f)(x)$
e) $(f \circ g \circ f)(x)$ **f)** $(g \circ g \circ g)(x)$

96. Find a function, $f(x)$, for which the product with itself, $(ff)(x)$, and the composition with itself, $f(f(x))$, are equal.

97. Technology a) Given that $f(x) = \sqrt{-x}$, use a graphing calculator to graph $f \circ f$ in the standard viewing window. Do there seem to be any points on the graph?
b) Display a table of values for $f \circ f$. Describe and explain your findings.
c) Explain your observation in part a).

TECHNOLOGY

Exploring Reflections With Geometry Software

Complete the following activities using geometry software. If suitable software is not available, use grid paper.

A reflection is defined by a reflection line or mirror line. An original point and its reflection image are the same distance from the reflection line. The line segment that joins a point and its reflection image is perpendicular to the reflection line.

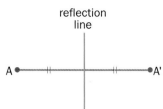

1 Reviewing Reflections

1. Construct a triangle with vertices (–1, 2), (4, 4), and (5, 1).

2. Reflect the triangle in the x-axis and determine the coordinates of the vertices of its image.

3. Reflect the original triangle in the y-axis and determine the coordinates of the vertices of its image.

4. Write a rule for finding the coordinates of the image of the point (x, y) after a reflection in
a) the x-axis   **b)** the y-axis

5. Identify the reflection line that reflects
a) (1, 3) onto (–1, 3)
b) (–2, –5) onto (–2, 5)

2 Exploring the Mapping $(x, y) \rightarrow (y, x)$

For the mapping $(x, y) \rightarrow (y, x)$, the coordinates of the original point, (x, y), are interchanged to give the coordinates of the image point, (y, x).

1. Graph the line $y = x$.

2. Plot the points (6, 2) and (2, 6). Join these points with a line segment.

3. Construct the point of intersection of the line segment and the line $y = x$. Find the coordinates of the point of intersection.

4. Measure the distance from the point of intersection to the point (6, 2), and the distance from the point of intersection to the point (2, 6). How do the distances compare?

5. Measure the angles formed by the intersection of the line and the line segment.

6. Measure the slope of the line and the line segment.

7. Are the line and the line segment perpendicular? Explain using the measured angles and slopes.

8. Is the point (6, 2) the reflection image of the point (2, 6) in the line $y = x$? Explain.

9. Repeat questions 1–8 using the points (3, –5) and (–5, 3), instead of (6, 2) and (2, 6).

10. For the mapping $(x, y) \rightarrow (y, x)$, what is the reflection line?

11. When a triangle with vertices (1, 4), (–2, 5), and (–3, –4) is reflected in the line $y = x$, what are the coordinates of the vertices of the image?

3 Problem Solving

1. a) How many squares meet all of the following conditions? The area is 16 square units, one vertex lies at the origin, and the square is its own reflection image in the line $y = x$.
b) What are the slopes of the sides of the squares from part a)?

2. a) Do any rectangles that are not squares meet all the conditions in question 1a)? Explain.
b) If a rectangle that is not a square is its own reflection image in the line $y = x$, what can you conclude about the slopes of the sides of the rectangle?

5.3 Inverse Functions

Inverse functions are a special class of functions that *undo* each other. Mappings for two inverse functions,

$f(x) = 2x + 1$ and $g(x) = \dfrac{x-1}{2}$, are shown.

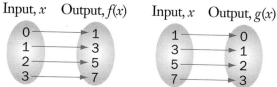

Notice that the output of the first function, $f(x)$, becomes the input for the second function, $g(x)$. The function $g(x)$ undoes what $f(x)$ does. The ordered pairs of $g(x)$ can be found by switching the coordinates in each ordered pair of $f(x)$.

Explore: Complete the Table

The Paralympic Games, which were first held in Rome in 1960, have become the world's second-largest sporting event, after the Olympic Games. At the Paralympics held in Atlanta, over 4000 competitors represented 120 countries. Canada finished seventh in the medal standings with 24 gold, 21 silver, and 24 bronze medals. Among the Canadians who won gold medals were wheelchair racers Chantal Petitclerc and Jeff Adams.

Wheelchair races are held over various distances, from 100 m to the marathon. The table includes data for some of the events that are held on a 400-m track. Copy and complete the table.

Distance, d (km)	Number of Laps, n
5	
3	
1.5	
	2
	1
	0.5

Inquire

1. a) Write a function in the form $d(n) = \blacksquare n$, where d is the distance of the race, in kilometres, and n is the number of laps.
b) What operation does the function $d(n)$ perform on each input value?
c) List the ordered pairs of the function $d(n)$.

2. a) Write a function in the form $n(d) = \blacksquare d$, where n is the number of laps and d is the distance of the race, in kilometres.
b) What operation does the function $n(d)$ perform on each input value?
c) List all the ordered pairs of the function $n(d)$.

3. How can the ordered pairs of $n(d)$ be obtained from the ordered pairs of $d(n)$?

4. Are $d(n)$ and $n(d)$ inverse functions? Explain.

5. How does the domain of each function compare with the range of the other?

6. Write the composite functions $d \circ n$ and $n \circ d$ in simplest form and explain the results.

7. Find the inverse, $g(x)$, of each of the following functions.
a) $f(x) = 2x$ **b)** $f(x) = \dfrac{3x}{4}$ **c)** $f(x) = x + 2$ **d)** $f(x) = x - 4$

A relation is a set of ordered pairs. The inverse of a relation can be found by interchanging the domain and the range of the relation.

Relation
(–3, 4), (0, 7), (2, 9)

Inverse Relation
(4, –3), (7, 0), (9, 2)

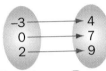

Domain Range

Domain Range

A function is a special relation. For each element in the domain of a function, there is exactly one element in the range. If the inverse of a function $f(x)$ is also a function, it is called the inverse function of $f(x)$. This inverse function is denoted by $f^{-1}(x)$. The notation f^{-1} is read as "the inverse of f" or "f inverse."

Note that the –1 in f^{-1} is *not* an exponent, so $f^{-1} \neq \dfrac{1}{f}$.

Example 1 Interchanging Coordinates
a) Find the inverse f^{-1} of the function f whose ordered pairs are $\{(-2, -8), (0, -2), (3, 4), (4, 7)\}$.
b) Graph both functions.

Solution
a) Switch the first and second coordinates of each ordered pair.
$f^{-1} = \{(-8, -2), (-2, 0), (4, 3), (7, 4)\}$

b) The graph of f is shown in red and the graph of f^{-1} is shown in blue. Note that switching the x- and y-coordinates reflects the function f in the line $y = x$. So, the graph of f^{-1} is the reflection of the graph of f in the line $y = x$.

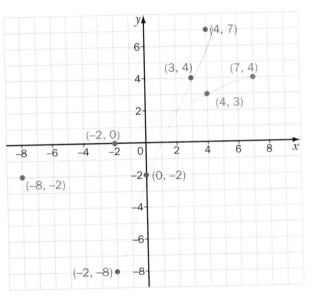

One way to find the inverse of a function is to reverse the operations that the function specifies.

The function $f(x) = 2x + 3$ means: Multiply x by 2, and then add 3.
Reversing the operations means: Subtract 3 from x, and then divide the result by 2.

So, the inverse function of $f(x)$ is $f^{-1} = \dfrac{x - 3}{2}$.

Let $x = 6$ and check that the inverse function undoes the other function.

Input   Multiply by 2   Add 3   Output
$f(x) = 2x + 3$ 6   ⟶   12   ⟶   15

Output   Divide by 2   Subtract 3   Input
6   ⟵   12   ⟵   15 $f^{-1}(x) = \dfrac{x - 3}{2}$

The functions $f(x) = 2x + 3$ and $f^{-1}(x) = \dfrac{x-3}{2}$ are inverses, because one function undoes the other.

One way to reverse the operations that a function specifies is to interchange the variables.

Example 2   Interchanging Variables

Find the inverse of the function $f(x) = 3x - 4$.

Solution

$$f(x) = 3x - 4$$

Replace $f(x)$ with y: $y = 3x - 4$

Interchange x and y: $x = 3y - 4$

Solve for y: $x + 4 = 3y$

$$\frac{x+4}{3} = y$$

So, $f^{-1}(x) = \dfrac{x+4}{3}$.

In Example 2, you could check that f^{-1} is the inverse of f by checking that f^{-1} undoes f. This means that, if $f(a) = b$, then $f^{-1}(b) = a$.

Using $x = 0$ gives,

$$f(x) = 3x - 4 \quad \text{and} \quad f^{-1}(x) = \frac{x+4}{3}$$

$$f(0) = 3(0) - 4 \qquad f^{-1}(-4) = \frac{-4+4}{3}$$

$$= -4 \qquad\qquad\qquad = 0$$

To check that f^{-1} undoes f for all values of the variable, take the composition of f and f^{-1}. To verify that f^{-1} is the inverse of f, the composition must be taken both ways, since the composition of functions is not commutative.

$$(f \circ f^{-1})(x) = f(f^{-1}(x)) \qquad\qquad (f^{-1} \circ f)(x) = f^{-1}(f(x))$$

$$= f\left(\frac{x+4}{3}\right) \qquad\qquad\qquad\qquad = f^{-1}(3x - 4)$$

$$= \frac{3(x+4)}{3} - 4 \qquad\qquad\qquad\qquad = \frac{3x - 4 + 4}{3}$$

$$= x + 4 - 4 \qquad\qquad\qquad\qquad\qquad = \frac{3x}{3}$$

$$= x \qquad\qquad\qquad\qquad\qquad\qquad\qquad = x$$

In general, two functions $f(x)$ and $g(x)$ are inverses of each other if and only if $(f \circ g)(x) = x$ and $(g \circ f)(x) = x$.

Example 3   Verifying Inverses

Determine if the functions in each pair are inverses of each other.

a) $f(x) = 2x - 7$ and $g(x) = 7x + 2$

b) $f(x) = 2x - 5$ and $g(x) = \dfrac{x+5}{2}$

Solution

Two functions, $f(x)$ and $g(x)$, are inverses of each other if and only if $f \circ g = x$ and $g \circ f = x$.

a) $(f \circ g)(x) = f(g(x))$
$\qquad\qquad = f(7x + 2)$
$\qquad\qquad = 2(7x + 2) - 7$
$\qquad\qquad = 14x + 4 - 7$
$\qquad\qquad = 14x - 3$

For $f(x)$ and $g(x)$ to be inverses, both compositions $f \circ g$ and $g \circ f$ must equal x. Because $(f \circ g)(x) \neq x$, there is no need to find $(g \circ f)(x)$.

The two functions $f(x) = 2x - 7$ and $g(x) = 7x + 2$ are not inverses of each other.

b)
$$f \circ g = f(g(x)) \qquad\qquad g \circ f = g(f(x))$$
$$= f\left(\frac{x+5}{2}\right) \qquad\qquad = g(2x - 5)$$
$$= 2\left(\frac{x+5}{2}\right) - 5 \qquad\qquad = \frac{2x - 5 + 5}{2}$$
$$= x + 5 - 5 \qquad\qquad\qquad = \frac{2x}{2}$$
$$= x \qquad\qquad\qquad\qquad = x$$

The two functions $f(x) = 2x - 5$ and $g(x) = \dfrac{x+5}{2}$ are inverses of each other.

Example 4   Inverse of a Linear Function

Is the inverse of $y = 4x + 3$ a function?

Solution

First, find the inverse of $y = 4x + 3$.

Interchange x and y:　　$x = 4y + 3$
Solve for y:　　　　　　$x - 3 = 4y$
$$\frac{x-3}{4} = y$$

The inverse of $y = 4x + 3$ is $y = \dfrac{x-3}{4}$.

The inverse is a function, since only one y-value can be found for each x-value.

In Example 4, the inverse function can be written in the slope and y-intercept form $y = mx + b$.

$$y = \frac{x}{4} - \frac{3}{4}$$

The inverse function is linear, with a slope of $\frac{1}{4}$

and a y-intercept of $-\frac{3}{4}$.

If we graph the functions $y = 4x + 3$ and $y = \frac{x}{4} - \frac{3}{4}$

on the same axes, or in the same viewing window of a graphing calculator, we see two straight lines that are reflections of each other in the line $y = x$.

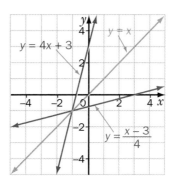

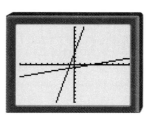

Example 5 Inverse of a Quadratic Function

a) Find the inverse of $f(x) = x^2 - 1$.
b) Graph $f(x)$ and its inverse.
c) Is the inverse of $f(x)$ a function?
d) Determine the domain and the range of $f(x)$ and its inverse.

Solution

a)

$$f(x) = x^2 - 1$$

Replace $f(x)$ with y: $y = x^2 - 1$

Interchange x and y: $x = y^2 - 1$

Isolate y: $x + 1 = y^2$

Take the square root of both sides: $\pm\sqrt{x+1} = y$

The inverse is $f^{-1}(x) = \pm\sqrt{x+1}$.

b) The graphs of $f(x)$ and f^{-1} are shown.

To graph $f^{-1}(x) = \pm\sqrt{x+1}$ manually,

graph the two branches $y = \sqrt{x+1}$

and $y = -\sqrt{x+1}$.

To graph f and f^{-1} on a graphing calculator, use the DrawInv or equivalent instruction. You can use DrawInv without finding an equation for f^{-1}.

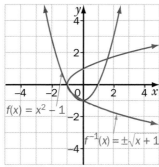

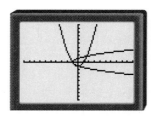

Recall that, if you can draw a vertical line that intersects a graph in more than one point, the graph does not represent a function.

c) For the inverse function f^{-1}, there are two values of y for each value of x, except $x = -1$.
In other words, f^{-1} does not pass the vertical line test. So, the inverse f^{-1} is not a function.

d) For $f(x) = x^2 - 1$, the domain is the set of real numbers. The range is the set of real numbers, $y \geq -1$.

For $f^{-1}(x) = \pm\sqrt{x+1}$, the domain is the set of real numbers, $x \geq -1$. The range is the set of real numbers.

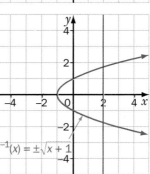

Example 6 Restricting the Domain of $f(x)$

a) Find the inverse of $f(x) = x^2 + 2$.

b) Graph $f(x)$ and its inverse.

c) Is the inverse of $f(x)$ a function? If not, restrict the domain of $f(x)$ so that its inverse is a function.

Solution

a)

$$f(x) = x^2 + 2$$

Replace $f(x)$ with y: $\quad y = x^2 + 2$

Interchange x and y: $\quad x = y^2 + 2$

Isolate y: $\quad x - 2 = y^2$

Take the square root of both sides: $\quad \pm\sqrt{x - 2} = y$

So, $f^{-1}(x) = \pm\sqrt{x - 2}$.

b) The graphs of f and f^{-1} are shown.

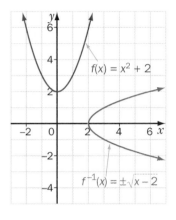

c) The inverse does not pass the vertical line test.
So, the inverse f^{-1} is not a function.
The inverse function has two branches, $y = \sqrt{x - 2}$ and $y = -\sqrt{x - 2}$.

The graph of one branch would pass the vertical line test. So, if the domain of f is restricted so that f^{-1} has only one branch, then f^{-1} will be a function.

For example, restricting the domain of $f(x)$ to real values of $x \geq 0$ would result in an inverse function $f^{-1}(x) = \sqrt{x - 2}$. The graphs are as shown.

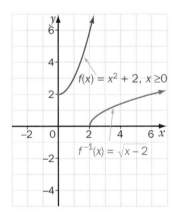

In Example 6c), note that there are infinitely many restrictions on the domain of f that would produce an inverse that is a function. The restriction $f(x) = x^2 + 2$, $x \leq 0$, would give the inverse function $f^{-1}(x) = -\sqrt{x - 2}$.

Each of the following restrictions on the domain of f would restrict the graph of the inverse function to a part of one branch.

$f(x) = x^2 + 2$, $x \geq 1$ $\qquad$ $f(x) = x^2 + 2$, $x > 3$
$f(x) = x^2 + 2$, $x < -1$ $\qquad$ $f(x) = x^2 + 2$, $x \leq -4$

Care is needed in restricting the domain of f, because there are also infinitely many restrictions that would produce an inverse that is not a function. An example is $f(x) = x^2 + 2$, $x \leq 3$. This restriction would result in all of the lower branch and part of the upper branch of $f^{-1}(x) = \pm\sqrt{x - 2}$. So, f^{-1} would not pass the vertical line test and would not be a function.

Example 7   Inverse of a Rational Function

Find the inverse of $y = \dfrac{1}{x+1}$.

Solution

$$y = \frac{1}{x+1}$$

Interchange x and y: $\qquad\qquad x = \dfrac{1}{y+1}$

Multiply both sides by $y + 1$: $\qquad (y+1)x = 1$

Divide both sides by x: $\qquad\qquad y+1 = \dfrac{1}{x}$

Solve for y: $\qquad\qquad\qquad y = \dfrac{1}{x} - 1$

The inverse is $y = \dfrac{1}{x} - 1$.

Example 8   Car Rental

The cost of renting a car for a day is a flat rate of $40, plus a charge of $0.10 per kilometre driven.

a) Let r dollars be the total rental cost and d kilometres be the distance driven. Write the function $r(d)$ to represent the total cost of a one-day rental.
b) Find the inverse of the function.
c) What does the inverse represent?
d) Give an example of how the inverse could be used.

Solution
a) $r(d) = 0.1d + 40$

b) Substitute y for r and x for d: $\qquad y = 0.1x + 40$
Interchange x and y: $\qquad\qquad\qquad x = 0.1y + 40$
Solve for y: $\qquad\qquad\qquad\qquad\quad x - 40 = 0.1y$

$$\frac{x - 40}{0.1} = y$$
$$10(x - 40) = y$$
$$10x - 400 = y$$

Because x and y were interchanged, x represents r and y represents d in the inverse. So the inverse is $d(r) = 10r - 400$.   Note that solving $r = 0.1d + 40$ for d gives the inverse.

c) The inverse shows the distance that can be driven for a given rental cost.

d) The distance that can be driven for a total rental cost of $48 for a day is given by
$d = 10(48) - 400$
$\quad = 480 - 400$
$\quad = 80$
So, a distance of 80 km can be driven for a total rental cost of $48.

Note that the use of the inverse cannot include values of $r < 40$, since $40 is the minimum daily rate and the distance driven cannot be negative.

Practice

Given the ordered pairs of each function, find the inverse, and graph the function and its inverse.

1. $f = \{(0, 2), (1, 3), (2, 4), (3, 5)\}$

2. $g = \{(-1, -3), (1, -2), (3, 4), (5, 0), (6, 1)\}$

Given the ordered pairs of each function, find the inverse, and state whether the inverse is a function.

3. $f = \{(-2, 3), (-1, 2), (0, 0), (4, -2)\}$

4. $g = \{(4, -2), (2, 1), (1, 3), (0, -2), (-3, -3)\}$

Solve each equation for x.

5. $y = 3x + 2$

6. $2x + 3y = 12$

7. $y = 3 - 4x$

8. $y = \dfrac{x + 3}{4}$

9. $y = \dfrac{x}{2} - 5$

10. $y = x^2 + 3$

Find the inverse of each function.

11. $f(x) = x - 1$

12. $f(x) = \dfrac{x}{2}$

13. $f(x) = x + 3$

14. $f(x) = \dfrac{4}{3}x$

15. $f(x) = 2x + 1$

16. $f(x) = \dfrac{x + 2}{3}$

17. $g(x) = \dfrac{5}{2}x - 4$

18. $h(x) = 0.2x + 1$

Find the inverse of each function. Graph the function and its inverse.

19. $y = x + 2$

20. $y = 4x$

21. $y = 3x - 2$

22. $y = x$

23. $y = 3 - x$

24. $y = \dfrac{x - 2}{3}$

Find the inverse of each function and determine whether the inverse is a function.

25. $f(x) = 2x - 5$

26. $f(x) = \dfrac{x + 3}{4}$

27. $f(x) = \dfrac{x}{4} + 3$

28. $f(x) = 5 - x$

Determine if the functions in each pair are inverses of each other.

29. $f(x) = x + 5$ and $g(x) = x - 5$

30. $f(x) = 7x$ and $g(x) = \dfrac{x}{7}$

31. $f(x) = 2x - 1$ and $g(x) = \dfrac{x + 1}{2}$

32. $f(x) = x - 3$ and $g(x) = 3 - x$

33. $f(x) = \dfrac{x}{3} - 4$ and $g(x) = 3x - 4$

34. $g(x) = \dfrac{x}{3} - 5$ and $h(x) = 3x + 5$

35. $h(x) = \dfrac{x - 8}{4}$ and $k(x) = 4(x + 2)$

For each of the following functions,
a) *find the inverse of $f(x)$*
b) *graph $f(x)$ and its inverse*
c) *determine the domain and range of $f(x)$ and its inverse*

36. $f(x) = x^2 - 3$

37. $f(x) = x^2 + 1$

38. $f(x) = -x^2$

39. $f(x) = -x^2 - 1$

40. $f(x) = (x - 2)^2$

41. $f(x) = (x + 1)^2$

Sketch the graph of the inverse of each function.

42.

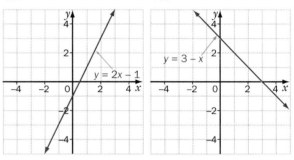

43.

44.

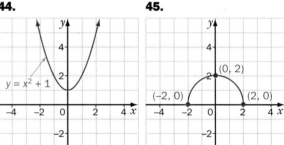

45.

46.

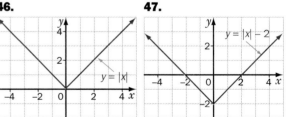

47.

Determine if the functions in each pair are inverses of each other.

48. $y = x^2 - 3$ and $y = \sqrt{x+3}$

49. $y = x^2 + 1$ and $y = \sqrt{x+1}$

Find the inverse of each function. If the inverse is a function, determine the domain and range of the inverse.

50. $y = 2x - 3$ **51.** $y = 2 - 4x$

52. $y = 3(x - 2)$ **53.** $y = \dfrac{1}{2}(x - 6)$

54. $y = x^2$ **55.** $y = x^2 + 2$

56. $y = x^2 - 4$ **57.** $y = 2x^2 - 1$

58. $y = (x - 3)^2$ **59.** $y = (x + 2)^2$

For each of the following functions,
a) *find the inverse of $f(x)$*
b) *graph $f(x)$ and its inverse*
c) *determine the domain and range of $f(x)$ and its inverse*

60. $f(x) = x^2, x \geq 0$ **61.** $f(x) = x^2 - 2, x \geq 0$

62. $f(x) = x^2 + 4, x \leq 0$ **63.** $f(x) = 3 - x^2, x \geq 0$

64. $f(x) = (x - 4)^2, x \geq 4$

65. $f(x) = (x + 3)^2, x \leq -3$

Find the inverse of each of the following functions.

66. $y = \dfrac{1}{x}$ **67.** $y = \dfrac{1}{x} + 2$

68. $y = \dfrac{1}{3 + x}$ **69.** $y = \dfrac{1 - x}{x + 2}$

70. $y = \dfrac{x}{x + 2}$ **71.** $y = \dfrac{x + 1}{x}$

Find the inverse of each of the following functions.

72. $y = \sqrt{x}$ **73.** $y = \sqrt{x - 2}$

74. $y = \sqrt{3 - x}$ **75.** $y = \sqrt{x^2 + 9}$

For each of the following functions,
a) *find the inverse f^{-1}*
b) *graph $f(x)$ and its inverse*
c) *restrict the domain of f so that f^{-1} is also a function*
d) *with the domain of f restricted, sketch a graph of f and f^{-1}*
e) *state the domain and range of f and f^{-1}*

76. $f(x) = x^2 + 3$ **77.** $f(x) = 2x^2$

78. $f(x) = x^2 - 1$ **79.** $f(x) = -x^2$

80. $f(x) = 1 - x^2$ **81.** $f(x) = (x - 2)^2$

82. $f(x) = (4 - x)^2$ **83.** $f(x) = -(x + 5)^2$

Applications and Problem Solving

84. Measurement a) Let x represent the radius of a circle. Write a function $f(x)$ to express the circumference in terms of the radius.
b) Find the inverse of this function.
c) Is the inverse a function?
d) What does the inverse represent?

85. Measurement a) Let x represent the radius of a sphere. Write a function $f(x)$ to express the surface area in terms of the radius.
b) Find the inverse of this function.
c) Determine the domain and range of the inverse.
d) Is the inverse a function?
e) What does the inverse represent?

86. Van Rental The cost of renting a van for one day is a flat rate of $50, plus a variable rate of $0.15/km.
a) Write a function to express the total cost of a one-day rental, $c(d)$ dollars, in terms of the distance driven, d kilometres.
b) Determine the inverse of the function.
c) What does the inverse represent?
d) What is the domain of the inverse?

87. Retail Sales A sale at an appliance store advertised that all appliances were being sold at 30% off the original selling price.
a) Write a function that gives the sale price as a function of the original selling price.
b) Find the inverse of this function.
c) What does the inverse represent?

88. Foreign currency exchange One day, the Canadian dollar was worth US$0.70.
a) Write a function that expresses the value of the US dollar, u, in terms of the Canadian dollar, c.
b) Find the inverse. Round the coefficient to the nearest hundredth.
c) Use the inverse to convert US$150 to Canadian dollars.

89. Number trick Marta asked Chen to choose a number. She then told him to add 6, multiply the result by 8, subtract 10, and finally divide by 2. Marta asked Chen for his answer, and he said 63. She then told him that the number he chose was 11. Use inverse functions to explain how she knew the number he chose.

90. Geology The approximate temperature, in degrees Celsius, of rocks beneath the surface of the Earth can be found by multiplying their depth, in kilometres, by 35 and adding 20 to the product.
a) Let d kilometres represent the depth of some rocks. Write a function $T(d)$ that expresses the Celsius temperature of the rocks in terms of their depth.
b) Write the inverse function.
c) At what depth do rocks have a temperature of 90°C?

91. Weekly wages Jana works at a clothing store. She earns $400 a week, plus a commission of 5% of her sales.
a) Write a function that describes Jana's total weekly earnings as a function of her sales.
b) Find the inverse of this function.
c) What does the inverse represent?
d) One week, Jana earned $575. Calculate her sales that week.

92. Measurement The measure of an interior angle, i, of a regular polygon is related to the number of sides n by the function $i(n) = 180 - \dfrac{360}{n}$.
a) Determine the measure of an interior angle of a regular heptagon.
b) Find the inverse of the function.
c) Use the inverse to identify the regular polygon with interior angles of 144°.

93. Falling object If an object is dropped from a height of 80 m, its approximate height, $h(t)$ metres, above the ground t seconds after being dropped is given by the function $h(t) = -5t^2 + 80$.
a) Graph the function.
b) Find and graph the inverse.
c) Is the inverse a function? Explain.
d) What does the inverse represent?
e) After what length of time is the object 35 m above the ground?
f) How long does the object take to reach the ground?

94. Meteorology The function $d(t) = \sqrt[3]{830t^2}$ relates the diameter, d kilometres, of a hurricane or tornado to the length of time it lasts, t hours.
a) What is the restriction on the value of t?
b) Find the inverse of the function.
c) Is the inverse a function? Explain.

d) If a hurricane has a diameter of 100 km, how long does it last, to the nearest hour?

95. Is the inverse of $f(x) = |x|$ a function? If not, restrict the domain of f so that f^{-1} is a function.

96. Horizontal line test The vertical line test can be used to decide whether a graph represents a function.
a) How can a horizontal line test be used to decide whether the inverse of a function is also a function?
b) Without graphing the inverse, decide whether the inverse of $f(x) = x^3$ is a function.

97. Write four functions that are their own inverses.

98. The function f includes the ordered pair (2, 3). Can f^{-1} include each of the following ordered pairs? Explain.
a) (3, 4)   **b)** (4, 2)

99. Coordinate geometry Find the area of the figure formed by the intersection of $f(x) = 4 - x$, $g(x) = 12 - 3x$, and g^{-1}.

100. a) Is the relation $y = k$, where k is a constant, a function? Explain.
b) Is the inverse of $y = k$ a function? Explain.

101. What is the inverse of the inverse of a function? Explain.

102. Number trick a) Write a number trick problem similar to the one in question 89.
b) Use inverse functions to determine how to solve it.
c) Have a classmate solve your problem.

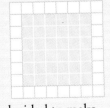

LOGIC POWER

Ryan ordered tiles to make a patio. He wanted a 6 by 6 square of green tiles surrounded by a single row of white tiles to give an 8 by 8 patio, as shown.

When the tiles arrived, Ryan decided to make a rectangular patio, with the white tiles in the centre surrounded by a single row of green tiles. What were the dimensions of the new patio?

New Vehicles

Use the *Vehicles* database, from the Computer Data Bank, to complete the following.

1 The "Average" Vehicle

There are 9 types of vehicles in the database — small car, medium car, large car, luxury car, sports/sporty car, coupe, minivan, sport-utility vehicle, and pickup truck.

1. For each of the following measurements, predict the order of the types of vehicles from greatest to least average.

a) mass   **b)** length
c) width   **d)** engine power
e) highway fuel efficiency   **f)** city fuel efficiency

2. Devise a plan to determine the order of the types of vehicles from greatest to least average for each measurement in question 1. Remember to exclude vehicles for which the data are not available.

3. Compare your plan with the plans of your classmates. Revise your plan, if necessary, and then, work together to carry it out.

4. Compare the results with your predictions, and then compare the orders of the types of vehicles for the six measurements. Are you surprised by any of your findings? Explain.

2 Acceleration Times

Many of the vehicles in the database were road tested to measure times to accelerate from 0 km/h to 48 km/h, and from 0 km/h to 96 km/h.

1. Which two of the given fields do you think have the greatest impact on acceleration times? Explain your reasoning.

2. For how many vehicles are both acceleration times available?

3. Which vehicle(s) took the least time to accelerate to each speed?

4. The theoretical time to accelerate is a function of mass and engine power. How does this statement compare with your answer to question 1?

The theoretical time, t seconds, to accelerate from 0 km/h to 48 km/h is given by

$$t = \frac{48^2 \times \text{mass}}{6024.67 \times \text{power}}.$$

The theoretical time, t seconds, to accelerate from 0 km/h to 96 km/h is given by

$$t = \frac{96^2 \times \text{mass}}{10\,378.64 \times \text{power}}.$$

In both formulas, mass is measured in kilograms and power is measured in horsepower, symbol hp.

5. Devise a plan to determine the percent of vehicles for which the theoretical time, t seconds, to accelerate from 0 km/h to 48 km/h is within 0.5 s of the road-tested time.

6. Compare your plan with the plans of your classmates. Revise your plan, if necessary, and then carry it out.

7. Determine the percent of vehicles for which the theoretical time, t seconds, to accelerate from 0 km/h to 96 km/h is within 1.0 s of the road-tested time.

3 Buying a Vehicle

1. Which vehicles have a highway fuel efficiency of 7.5 L/100 km or better, have seating for at least 5 people, and are not minivans or small cars?

2. Set at least four criteria for a vehicle someone you know might want to buy. Then, find the vehicles that match the criteria.

3. What other fields would be of interest to people wanting to buy a vehicle?

TECHNOLOGY

Exploring Polynomial Functions With a Graphing Calculator

The quadratic, cubic, and quartic functions you have seen are all examples of polynomial functions. The graph of a polynomial function is **continuous**, that is, there are no breaks in the graph. You can trace the graph without lifting your pencil.

The degree of a function is determined by the largest exponent of its variable. The equation $y = 4x^3 + 2x^2 - 3x + 1$ is a cubic function or a function of degree 3.

The graph of the cubic function $y = 2x^3 - 6x - 1$ is shown. The graph has a peak at $(-1, 3)$ and a valley at $(1, -5)$. The point $(-1, 3)$ is called a **relative maximum** of the function. This point does not have the greatest y-coordinate of any point of the function, but no nearby points have a greater y-coordinate. The point $(-1, 3)$ is the highest point on the graph among nearby points. Similarly, the point $(1, -5)$ is called a **relative minimum** of the function. It is the lowest point on the graph among nearby points. Relative maximums and relative minimums are known as **turning points** of graphs.

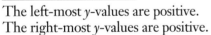

The **end behaviour** of the graph of a function describes the sign of the values of $f(x)$ for the left-most and right-most parts of the graph. Polynomial functions can have four types of end behaviour.

The graph of $y = x^3 - 1$ has no peaks or valleys, so it does not have a relative maximum or a relative minimum.

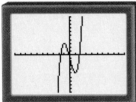

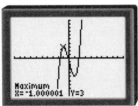

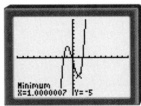

The left-most y-values are positive.
The right-most y-values are positive.

The left-most y-values are negative.
The right-most y-values are negative.

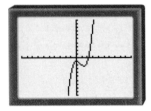

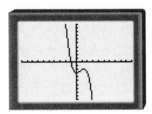

The left-most y-values are negative.
The right-most y-values are positive.

The left-most y-values are positive.
The right-most y-values are negative.

1 Analyzing Functions

1. Graph each of the following functions. Copy and complete the table.

	Function	Degree	End Behaviour	Observed Number of Turning Points
a)	$y = x + 2$			
b)	$y = -3x + 1$			
c)	$y = x^2 - 4$			
d)	$y = -2x^2 + 3x + 2$			
e)	$y = x^3 - 3x$			
f)	$y = -x^3 + 2x - 1$			
g)	$y = 2x^3 + 3$			
h)	$y = -x^3 - 4x$			
i)	$y = x^4 - 4x^2 + 5$			
j)	$y = -x^4 + 4x^2 + x - 2$			
k)	$y = x^4 + 2x^2 + 1$			
l)	$y = x^5 - 2x^4 - 3x^3 + 5x^2 + 4x - 1$			
m)	$y = x^5 - 2$			
n)	$y = -x^5 + 4x^3 + 2$			
o)	$y = x(x + 1)^2(x + 4)^2 + 5$			

2. The coefficient of the highest-order term in a polynomial is known as the **leading coefficient**. For two functions with the same degree, how does the sign of the leading coefficient affect the end behaviour of the graph?

3. Functions whose degree is an even number are called **even-degree functions**.
a) How do the end behaviours of even-degree functions compare?
b) Test your conjecture by graphing functions of even-degree higher than 4.

4. Functions whose degree is an odd number are called **odd-degree functions**.
a) How do the end behaviours of odd-degree functions compare?
b) Test your conjecture by graphing functions of odd-degree higher than 5.

5. a) What appears to be the maximum possible number of turning points for a linear function? a quadratic function? a cubic function? a quartic function?
b) What appears to be the relationship between the degree of a function and the maximum number of turning points?

c) If a graph of a function has five turning points, what is the minimum possible order of the function?

2 Sketching Graphs of Polynomial Functions

Sketch a graph of a polynomial function that satisfies each of the following sets of conditions.
1. an even-degree function with two relative maximums and one relative minimum

2. an even-degree function with two relative minimums and one relative maximum

3. an odd-degree function with two relative maximums and two relative minimums, and with the left-most y-values negative

4. an odd-degree function with three relative maximums and three relative minimums, and with the right-most y-values negative

5. an even-degree function with four relative maximums and three relative minimums

5.4 Polynomial Functions and Inequalities

At the start of a roller-coaster ride, an electric motor
raises the train to the top of the lift hill. Then,
the train is allowed to fall under gravity.
The train speeds up enough to carry it over
the coaster hills.

Explore: Draw a Graph

As a train descends the lift hill and then
climbs the first coaster hill, the function
$h(d) = 0.01d^2 - 1.2d + 60$, $d \leq 100$,
models the height, $h(d)$ metres, of the
train above the ground as a function of
the horizontal distance, d metres, the
train travels. Copy and complete the
table of values. Then, graph the function.
Alternatively, graph the function using a
graphing calculator.

d (m)	$h(d)$ (m)
0	60
20	40
40	28
50	25
60	24
70	25
80	28
100	40

Inquire

1. Between the lift hill and the first coaster hill,
how far above the ground is the train at its
lowest point?

2. For the function $h(d) = 0.01d^2 - 1.2d + 60$, $d \leq 100$,
what is
a) the domain?   **b)** the range?

3. What is the degree of the function?

4. Does the function have any real zeros? Explain.

5. Is the function continuous? Explain.

The function $h(d) = 0.01d^2 - 1.2d + 60$, $d \leq 100$, is an
example of a quadratic function. A quadratic function is
a special case of a general type of function called a **polynomial function**.

A polynomial function is an equation of the form $f(x) = a_n x^n + a_{n-1} x^{n-1} + \ldots + a_1 x^1 + a_0$,
where the coefficients a_n, a_{n-1}, ..., a_1, a_0 represent real numbers, a_n is not zero, and the
exponents are non-negative integers.

The following
are examples
of polynomial
functions.

Function	Example	Degree	
Constant	$f(x) = 5$	0	5 can be written as $5x^0$.
Linear	$f(x) = 3x + 5$	1	
Quadratic	$f(x) = x^2 + 3x - 4$	2	
Cubic	$f(x) = x^3 - x^2 + 2x - 1$	3	
Quartic	$f(x) = 2x^4 - 3x^3 + 7$	4	
Quintic	$f(x) = 3x^5 + x^3 - 4x + 2$	5	
General	$f(x) = a_n x^n + a_{n-1} x^{n-1} + \ldots + a_1 x^1 + a_0$	n	

Example 1 Identifying Polynomial Functions

Determine whether each function is a polynomial function. Justify your conclusion. If the function is a polynomial function, determine its degree.

a) $y = 3^x + 11$ **b)** $y = \dfrac{2}{3}x^4 - 5x^3 - 12x + 0.56$ **c)** $y = 3x^{-2} + 4x^2 - 6$

d) $y = 2x^3 - 4x + \sqrt{8}$ **e)** $y = 5 + 4x + \dfrac{1}{x}$ **f)** $y = 2\sqrt{x^3} + x^4$

Solution

a) The function $y = 3^x + 11$ is not a polynomial function, because, in the power 3^x, the variable is the exponent, not the base.

b) The function $y = \dfrac{2}{3}x^4 - 5x^3 - 12x + 0.56$ is a polynomial function, because all the coefficients are real numbers, and the exponents in the powers of x are non-negative integers. The degree is 4.

c) The function $y = 3x^{-2} + 4x^2 - 6$ is not a polynomial function, because, in the term $3x^{-2}$, the variable has an exponent that is a negative integer.

d) The function $y = 2x^3 - 4x + \sqrt{8}$ is a polynomial function, because all the coefficients are real numbers, and the exponents in the powers of x are non-negative integers. The degree is 3.

e) The function $y = 5 + 4x + \dfrac{1}{x}$ is not a polynomial function, because the term $\dfrac{1}{x}$ cannot be written in the form x^n, where n is a non-negative integer.

f) The function $y = 2\sqrt{x^3} + x^4$ is not a polynomial function, because the term $2\sqrt{x^3}$ cannot be written in the form x^n, where n is a non-negative integer.

For every polynomial expression, such as $x^3 + 4x^2 - 2x + 3$, we can write a corresponding polynomial function, in this case $f(x) = x^3 + 4x^2 - 2x + 3$. Every polynomial function that includes a variable has a value, or values, of the variable for which the corresponding value of the function is 0. These value(s) of the variable are the zeros of the function and the solutions to the corresponding equation $f(x) = 0$ or $y = 0$. The **real zeros** of a function are the x-intercepts of its graph.

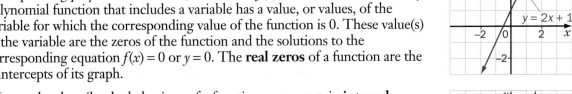

We can also describe the behaviour of a function over a certain **interval**, which is a restricted set of values of a variable. For example, for the function $y = 2x + 1$, we can state that $1 \le y \le 3$ over the interval $0 \le x \le 1$.

Some graphs of polynomial functions have symmetry. The graph of $y = x^3$ is symmetric about the origin. A 180° rotation about the origin maps the graph of $y = x^3$ onto itself.

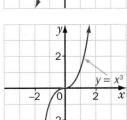

The graph of $y = x^2 + 1$ is symmetric about the y-axis. A reflection in the y-axis maps the graph of $y = x^2 + 1$ onto itself.

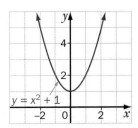

Example 2   Interpreting a Graph

Given the graph of the polynomial function $f(x) = x^4 - 3x^3 - x^2 + 3x$, determine

a) the domain and the range of $f(x)$
b) the real zeros of $f(x)$
c) the y-intercept
d) the intervals where $f(x) > 0$
e) the approximate coordinates of any relative maximums or relative minimums
f) any symmetry

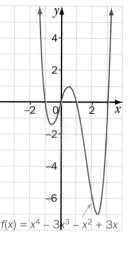

$f(x) = x^4 - 3x^3 - x^2 + 3x$

Solution

a) The domain is the set of real numbers.
The lowest point on the graph has a y-coordinate of about -7.
So, the approximate range is the real numbers, $y \geq -7$.
b) The real zeros are the x-intercepts, -1, 0, 1, and 3.
c) The y-intercept is 0.
d) The intervals where $f(x) > 0$ are the sets of x-values for which the graph is above the x-axis. From the graph, the intervals where $f(x) > 0$ are $x < -1$, $0 < x < 1$, and $x > 3$.
e) From the graph, $f(x)$ has a local maximum at about $(0.5, 1)$, and local minimums at about $(-0.5, -1.5)$ and $(2.5, -7)$.
f) The graph has no symmetry.

Using the Minimum operation on a graphing calculator gives the y-coordinate of the lowest point as about -6.9.

A graphing calculator gives the approximate coordinates as $(0.5, 0.9)$, $(-0.6, -1.4)$, and $(2.3, -6.9)$, respectively.

Example 3   Graphing a Quartic Function

a) Graph $y = x^2(x^2 - 4)$.
b) Find the domain, range, any zeros, and the y-intercept. Describe the symmetry.

Solution

a) Graph the function manually or using a graphing calculator.

x	y
-3	45
-2	0
-1.5	-3.9375
-1	-3
0	0
1	-3
1.5	-3.9375
2	0
3	45

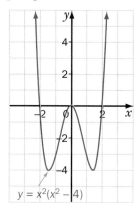

$y = x^2(x^2 - 4)$

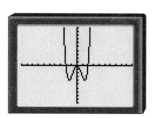

Finding the lowest y-value using a graphing calculator is more reliable than estimating from the manual graph.

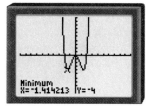

Minimum
X=-1.414213 Y=-4

The domain is the set of real numbers.
The range is $y \geq -4$.
The zeros are -2, 0, and 2.
The y-intercept is 0.
The graph is symmetric about the y-axis.

Graphing a polynomial function manually is easier if the function is written in factored form.

Example 4   Graphing a Function in Factored Form
Graph the function $f(x) = (x + 4)(x + 1)(x - 1)$. Determine
a) the real zeros of $f(x)$
b) the domain and the range of $f(x)$
c) the y-intercept
d) the intervals where $f(x) \leq 0$
e) any symmetry
f) the end behaviour

Solution
First use the factors to find the real zeros, or x-intercepts, of the function.
Plot the corresponding points.
Since $f(x) = 0$ when $x = -4$, $x = -1$, or $x = 1$, three points on the graph are $(-4, 0)$, $(-1, 0)$, and $(1, 0)$.
Now find values of the function that are between or beyond the zeros to find other points on the graph.

x	y
−5	−24
−4	0
−3	8
−2	6
−1	0
0	−4
1	0
2	18

To graph the function on a graphing calculator, you can leave the function in factored form.

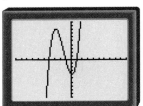

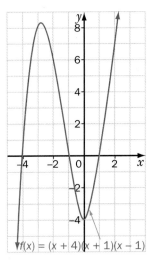

a) The real zeros are −4, −1, and 1.
b) The domain and range are the set of real numbers.
c) The y-intercept is −4.
d) The function $f(x) \leq 0$ where the graph is on or below the x-axis.
The intervals where $f(x) \leq 0$ are $x \leq -4$ and $-1 \leq x \leq 1$.
e) There is no symmetry.
f) The left-most y-values are negative. The right-most y-values are positive.

The real zeros of polynomial functions, or the real roots of polynomial equations, may be distinct or equal. Recall that two equal roots of an equation are sometimes called a double root.

Example 5　Equal Roots
a) Graph the function $f(x) = 2x^3 + 5x^2$.
b) Verify that the equation $f(x) = 0$ has two roots that equal 0.

Solution
a) Graph the function $y = 2x^3 + 5x^2$ manually or using a graphing calculator.

x	y
−3	−9
−2	4
−1	3
0	0
1	7

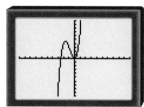

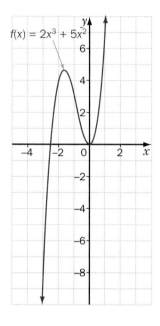

b) The appearance of the graph suggests that the equation $f(x) = 0$ has a double root $x = 0$.

To verify this, solve the equation $2x^3 + 5x^2 = 0$.
$$2x^3 + 5x^2 = 0$$
Factor the left side completely:　$x(x)(2x + 5) = 0$
Use the zero product property:　$x = 0$ or $x = 0$ or $2x + 5 = 0$
$$x = -\frac{5}{2}$$

The roots are 0, 0, and $-\dfrac{5}{2}$, so the equation $f(x) = 0$ has two roots that equal 0.

The graph of the function $f(x) = x^2 - 2x - 8$ is shown.
The real zeros of the function are −2 and 4. When $x < -2$, the function is positive.
When $-2 < x < 4$, the function is negative. When $x > 4$, the function is positive. As this example indicates, the value of a polynomial function can change sign only at a real zero.

When the real zeros are put in order on the x-axis, they divide the x-axis into intervals. In each interval, the function is either entirely positive or entirely negative.

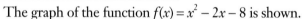

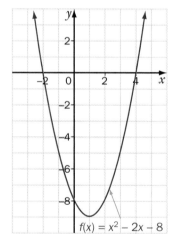

$f(x) = x^2 - 2x - 8$

Note that not all functions change sign at a real zero. An example is the function $f(x) = x^2 - 6x + 9$, which has a double root $x = 3$. In this example, the value of the function is positive in the intervals on both sides of $x = 3$.

The sign changes of polynomial functions can be used to solve polynomial inequalities. The real zeros of the polynomial function are the **critical numbers** of the inequality. The intervals of the polynomial function give the **test intervals** of the inequality, in which points on a number line are tested to determine if they satisfy the inequality.

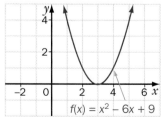

$f(x) = x^2 - 6x + 9$

Example 6 Solving a Quadratic Inequality

Solve $x^2 + x < 6$.

Solution 1 Using Test Intervals

$$x^2 + x < 6$$
$$x^2 + x - 6 < 0$$

Factor the left side: $(x + 3)(x - 2) < 0$

The zeros of the polynomial $f(x) = (x + 3)(x - 2)$ are -3 and 2, so the critical numbers of the inequality are -3 and 2. There are three test intervals, $x < -3$, $-3 < x < 2$, and $x > 2$.

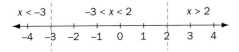

Choose a point on the number line in each test interval and determine the sign of $(x + 3)(x - 2)$.

In the test interval $x < -3$, use the point -4.
$$(x + 3)(x - 2) = (-4 + 3)(-4 - 2)$$
$$= (-1)(-6)$$
$$= 6$$
So, $(x + 3)(x - 2)$ is not less than zero in this interval.

In the test interval $-3 < x < 2$, use the point 0.
$$(x + 3)(x - 2) = (0 + 3)(0 - 2)$$
$$= (3)(-2)$$
$$= -6$$
So, $(x + 3)(x - 2)$ is less than zero in this interval.

In the test interval $x > 2$, use the point 3.
$$(x + 3)(x - 2) = (3 + 3)(3 - 2)$$
$$= (6)(1)$$
$$= 6$$
So, $(x + 3)(x - 2)$ is not less than zero in this interval.

The two points that have not been tested are the critical numbers -3 and 2. These numbers are zeros of the equation $(x + 3)(x - 2) = 0$, or $x^2 + x = 6$, so they do not satisfy the inequality $x^2 + x < 6$ and they are not included in the solution.

Since $(x + 3)(x - 2) < 0$ in the interval $-3 < x < 2$, the solution to $x^2 + x < 6$ is $-3 < x < 2$.

The solution to Example 6 can be graphed on a number line.

Solution 2 Solving Graphically

$$x^2 + x < 6$$
$$x^2 + x - 6 < 0$$

Graph the function $f(x) = x^2 + x - 6$.

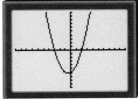

$f(x) < 0$ when the graph is below the x-axis. The graph is below the x-axis when $-3 < x < 2$. So, the solution is $-3 < x < 2$.

Example 7 Solving a Cubic Inequality

Solve $x^3 + 3x^2 - x - 3 \geq 0$.

Solution 1 Using Test Intervals

Use the integral zero theorem to factor $x^3 + 3x^2 - x - 3$.

$f(x) = x^3 + 3x^2 - x - 3$

$f(1) = (1)^3 + 3(1)^2 - 1 - 3$

$\qquad = 1 + 3 - 1 - 3$

$\qquad = 0$

Therefore $x - 1$ is a factor of $x^3 + 3x^2 - x - 3$.
Use synthetic division to find another
factor.

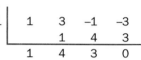

Another factor is $x^2 + 4x + 3$.
Factoring $x^2 + 4x + 3$ gives $(x + 3)(x + 1)$.
So, $x^3 + 3x^2 - x - 3 = (x + 3)(x + 1)(x - 1)$.

The zeros of the polynomial $f(x) = (x + 3)(x + 1)(x - 1)$ are -3, -1, and 1, so these are the critical numbers. There are four test intervals, $x < -3$, $-3 < x < -1$, $-1 < x < 1$, and $x > 1$.

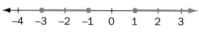

Choose a point on the number line in each test interval and determine the sign of $(x + 3)(x + 1)(x - 1)$. In the test interval $x < -3$, use the point -4.

$(x + 3)(x + 1)(x - 1) = (-1)(-3)(-5)$

$\qquad\qquad\qquad\qquad = -15$

So, $(x + 3)(x + 1)(x - 1)$ is not greater than or equal to 0 in this interval.

In the test interval $-3 < x < -1$, use the point -2.

$(x + 3)(x + 1)(x - 1) = (1)(-1)(-3)$

$\qquad\qquad\qquad\qquad = 3$

So, $(x + 3)(x + 1)(x - 1)$ is greater than or equal to 0 in this interval.

In the test interval $-1 < x < 1$, use the point 0.

$(x + 3)(x + 1)(x - 1) = (3)(1)(-1)$

$\qquad\qquad\qquad\qquad = -3$

So, $(x + 3)(x + 1)(x - 1)$ is not greater than or equal to 0 in this interval.

In the test interval $x > 1$, use the point 2.

$(x + 3)(x + 1)(x - 1) = (5)(3)(1)$

$\qquad\qquad\qquad\qquad = 15$

So, $(x + 3)(x + 1)(x - 1)$ is greater than or equal to 0 in this interval

The three points that have not been tested are the critical numbers -3, -1, and 1. These numbers are zeros of the equation $(x + 3)(x + 1)(x - 1) = 0$, or $x^3 + 3x^2 - x - 3 = 0$, so they satisfy the inequality $x^3 + 3x^2 - x - 3 \geq 0$ and are included in the solution.

Combining the results from the second and fourth intervals with the critical numbers gives the solution $-3 \leq x \leq -1$ or $x \geq 1$.

Solution 2 Solve Graphically

Graph the function
$f(x) = x^3 + 3x^2 - x - 3$.

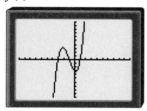

$f(x) \geq 0$ when the graph is on or above the x-axis.
The graph is on or above the x-axis when $-3 \leq x \leq -1$ or $x \geq 1$.
So, the solution is $-3 \leq x \leq -1$ or $x \geq 1$.

The solution to Example 7 can be graphed on a number line.

Example 8   Two Thrown Objects

Parts of the Stikine Canyon in British Columbia are 80 m high. A stone is thrown downward from one of these parts with a speed of 15 m/s. The height of the stone, $h(t)$ metres, above the floor of the canyon is given by the function $h(t) = 80 - 15t - 5t^2$, where t seconds is the time since the stone was thrown. At the same time as the stone is thrown, a ball is thrown upward from the floor of the same part of the canyon at 25 m/s. The height of the ball, $g(t)$ metres, is given by the function $g(t) = 25t - 5t^2$. Find the time period for which the stone is above the ball.

Solution 1   Comparing the Graphs

Graph both functions on the same axes or in the same viewing window of a graphing calculator. Draw the graph in the first quadrant, because neither the time nor the height above the canyon floor can be negative.

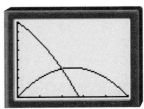

Determine the point of intersection of the graphs.

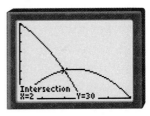

The objects are at the same height of 30 m after 2 s. Before this time, the graph of $h(t)$ is above the graph of $g(t)$, so $h(t) > g(t)$ or
$80 - 15t - 5t^2 > 25t - 5t^2$
So, the stone is above the ball for the time period $0 \le t < 2$ seconds.

Solution 2   Solving Algebraically

When the stone is above the ball, $h(t) > g(t)$.

Therefore, $80 - 15t - 5t^2 > 25t - 5t^2$
Simplify: $80 - 40t > 0$
                    $2 - t > 0$
Solve for t: $t < 2$ Note the sign reversal.

So, the stone is above the ball at times up to 2 s after they were both thrown, that is, since $t = 0$. So, the stone is above the ball for the time period $0 \le t < 2$ seconds.

Note that the above algebraic method of solving for t was used because the simplified inequality is linear. If the simplified inequality were quadratic or cubic, a method similar to those shown in Examples 6 or 7 could be used to solve it.

Practice

Determine whether each function is a polynomial function. Justify your conclusion. If the function is a polynomial function, determine its degree.

1. $y = 2x^5 - 3x - 4$

2. $y = 2x^2 - 4x^{-1} + 7$

3. $y = 7 - 4x + \dfrac{1}{x^2}$

4. $y = 3x^4 + 0.005x^3 - \sqrt{6}$

5. $y = \sqrt{x} + x^5 - 7x^6$

6. $y = (x - 5)(x - 7)(x + 4)$

7. $y = 4x^6 + 2^x - 11$

8. $y = 3ix^3 + 9$

Use the graph to determine the domain and range, the approximate coordinates of any relative maximums or relative minimums, and the y-intercept of each polynomial function.

9.

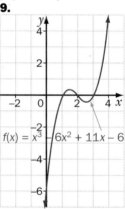

$f(x) = x^3 - 6x^2 + 11x - 6$

10.

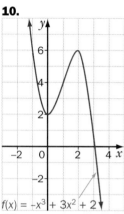

$f(x) = -x^3 + 3x^2 + 2$

11.

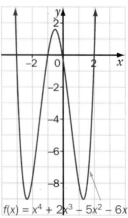

$f(x) = x^4 + 2x^3 - 5x^2 - 6x$

12.

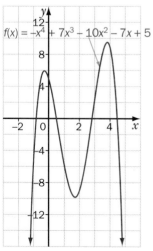

$f(x) = -x^4 + 7x^3 - 10x^2 - 7x + 5$

Use the graph to identify the real zeros of the polynomial function, and the intervals where $f(x) \geq 0$ and where $f(x) < 0$. Round answers to the nearest tenth, if necessary.

13.

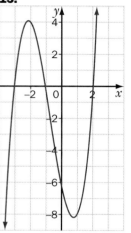

14.

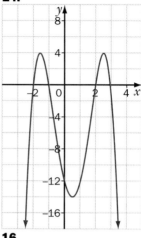

15.

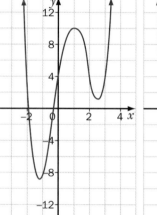

16.

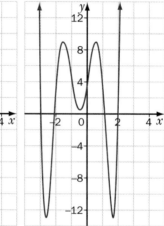

Graph each of the following functions and determine
a) the domain and range
b) any real zeros, to the nearest tenth, if necessary
c) the y-intercept
d) the approximate coordinates of any relative maximums or relative minimums
e) any symmetry
f) the end behaviour

17. $f(x) = x^2(x^2 - 4)$

18. $f(x) = x^2(x - 3)$

19. $y = -x(x^2 - 9)$

20. $y = x^2(x^2 + 4)$

21. $g(x) = -x^3 + 4x^2$

22. $y = x^3 - 3x^2 - 2x$

23. $y = x^3 + 2x^2 - x - 2$

24. $k(x) = x^3 + 3x + 4$

25. $y = x^4 + 5$

26. $y = -x^4 + 6$

27. $y = x^5 - 4x^3$

28. $f(x) = -x^5 + 4x^2$

29. $h(x) = x(x - 2)(x + 2)$
30. $y = (x - 1)(x + 1)^2$
31. $f(x) = (x - 3)(x - 2)(x + 1)$
32. $f(x) = (x - 2)(x - 1)(x + 1)(x + 2)$

Graph each of the following functions and determine
a) *the domain and range*
b) *any real zeros*
c) *the y-intercept*
d) *the intervals where $f(x) > 0$ and $f(x) \leq 0$*
e) *any symmetry*
f) *the end behaviour*
33. $f(x) = (x - 4)(x + 1)(x - 2)$
34. $f(x) = -(x + 3)(x - 2)(x + 1)$
35. $f(x) = x(x - 3)(x + 2)(x - 1)$
36. $f(x) = -x(x - 1)(x + 3)(x + 3)$

Graph each of the following functions. Verify that each function has the given equal roots.
37. $f(x) = 3x^3 - 4x^2$; two roots that equal 0
38. $g(x) = x^4 + 2x^3 + x^2$; two roots that equal 0 and two roots that equal -1
39. $h(x) = x^3 - 3x^2 + 3x - 1$; three roots that equal 1
40. $k(x) = x^5 - 6x^4 + 12x^3 - 8x^2$; two roots that equal 0 and three roots that equal 2

Solve each inequality.
41. $(x + 1)(x - 3) > 0$ **42.** $(x - 3)(x + 2) < 0$
43. $(3x + 1)(x + 1) \geq 0$ **44.** $(2x - 1)(2x + 3) \leq 0$

Solve each inequality. Graph each solution on a number line.
45. $x^2 + x - 12 > 0$ **46.** $x^2 - 3x \leq 10$
47. $x^2 - 4x > -4$ **48.** $2x^2 - 7x + 3 \geq 0$

Solve each inequality.
49. $(x - 1)(x + 1)(x + 2) < 0$
50. $x(x - 2)(x - 2) \geq 0$
51. $x(2x + 1)(x - 3) > 0$
52. $(2x - 1)(x + 1)(x - 2) \leq 0$

Solve each inequality.
53. $x^3 - 9x < 0$
54. $x^3 - 2x^2 - x + 2 \geq 0$
55. $x^3 - x^2 - 17x \leq 15$
56. $2x^3 - x^2 - 6x > 0$

Applications and Problem Solving

57. Technology The inequality $x^2 + x < 6$ was solved in Example 6. Another solution method is to graph $Y_1 = X^2 + X - 6 < 0$ using a graphing calculator. Solve each of the following by this method.
a) $x^2 + x - 2 \leq 0$ **b)** $x^2 + 3x + 2 > 0$
c) $x^3 + 3x^2 - x - 3 < 0$ **d)** $x^3 + 6x^2 + 11x + 6 \geq 0$

58. Estimation Use the graphs of two functions f and g to identify the approximate intervals where each of the following is true. Estimate to the nearest tenth, if necessary.
a) $f(x) \leq g(x)$ **b)** $f(x) > g(x)$

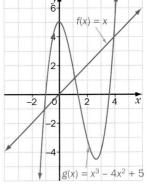

c) $f(x) \geq g(x)$ **d)** $f(x) < g(x)$

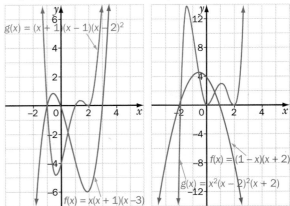

59. a) Graph the functions $y = x(x - 2)(x + 1)$ and $y = 3x(x - 2)(x + 1)$.
b) Compare and contrast the graphs.

60. Ravine The cross section of part of a ravine can be approximately modelled by the function
$$h(x) = x^3 - 6x^2 + 4x + 20, \ 0 \le x \le 5$$
where $h(x)$ metres is the height and x metres is the width of the ravine.
a) Graph the function using the given domain and a suitable range.
b) Find the vertical distance between the highest and lowest points on this part of the ravine, to the nearest metre.

61. Measurement a) For a cylinder whose height is twice the radius, write a function to express the volume, V, in terms of the radius, r.
b) Graph the function.
c) Determine the domain and range of the function.

62. Measurement a) The solid is made from 3 cubes, each having an edge length of x.
a) Write a function $A(x)$ that represents the surface area and a function $V(x)$ that represents the volume. Graph the functions.

b) For what value of x will the surface area and volume have the same numerical value?
c) For what values of x will the numerical value of the surface area be greater than the numerical value of the volume? less than the numerical value of the volume?
d) Describe how the graph of $A(x) - V(x)$ can be used to answer parts b) and c).

63. Fireflies The rate of flow of light energy is measured in lumens, which are represented by the symbol lm. For example, a 100-W incandescent light bulb emits about 1750 lm. The rate, $L(t)$ lumens, at which a firefly produces light energy is related to the air temperature, t degrees Celsius, by the function
$$L(t) = 10 + 0.3t + 0.4t^2 - 0.01t^3$$
a) What is a realistic domain for the function?
b) Graph the function.
c) Use your graph to find the rate at which a firefly produces light energy at 25°C. Round your answer to the nearest 10 lm.
d) At what temperature, to the nearest degree Celsius, do fireflies produce light energy at the greatest rate?

64. Heating and ventilation The size of a heating and ventilation system needed for a building depends on the volume of air that the system must circulate. A warehouse has a length that is 5 m more than its width. The height is 2 m less than the width.
a) Write a polynomial function to represent the volume of the warehouse in terms of the width.
b) What is the domain of the function?
c) Graph the function.
d) Using the graph, estimate the volume of air in a warehouse with a width of 20 m.
e) A particular system is capable of heating and ventilating a volume of up to 25 000 m³. Estimate the maximum width of a warehouse in which the system could be used, if the warehouse obeys the function from part a).

65. a) Describe the zeros and the end behaviour of the functions $y = x$, $y = x^2$, $y = x^3$, $y = x^4$, $y = x^5$, and $y = x^6$.
b) Describe how the graph of $y = x^n$, where n is a whole number greater than or equal to 1, depends on the nature of n.

66. Measurement The length of a rectangle is 5 cm more than the width. Find the possible dimensions of the rectangle, if the area must be at least 84 cm².

67. Graph $y = x^2 - 2$ and $y = x$ on the same set of axes. Explain how you can use these graphs to sketch the graph of $y = x + x^2 - 2$.

68. Graph $y = x^3 + 2$ and $y = x$ on the same set of axes. Explain how you can use these graphs to sketch the graph of $y = x - (x^3 + 2)$.

69. Lidless box A box with no lid is made from an 11 cm by 9 cm piece of tin. A square of side length x centimetres is removed from each corner, and the sides of the box are folded up.

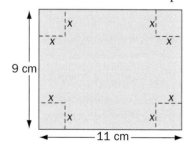

a) Write a function that expresses the volume of the box, $V(x)$ cubic centimetres, in terms of x.
b) Graph the function over a reasonable domain.
c) Find the value of x that gives the maximum volume. Round your answer to the nearest tenth of a centimetre.
d) Find the maximum volume of the box, to the nearest cubic centimetre.
e) For what values of x is the volume less than 65 cm³? Estimate values to the nearest tenth of a centimetre, if necessary.

70. Manufacturing trailers A company that manufactures trailers estimates that the annual cost, $C(x)$ dollars, of manufacturing x trailers is given by the function
$$C(x) = 200\,000 + 100x + 5x^2$$
The company's annual revenue, $R(x)$ dollars, from sales of the trailers is given by
$$R(x) = 8000x - 0.02x^3$$
a) Graph both functions using the domain $0 \le x \le 700$ and the range $0 \le y \le 2\,000\,000$.
b) What is the minimum number of trailers that must be manufactured for the company to make a profit?
c) What is the maximum number of trailers that the company can manufacture and still make a profit?
d) Write an equation to represent the profit function $P(x)$.
e) Graph the profit function. Use the graph to determine the maximum profit the company can make, to the nearest ten thousand dollars, and the number of trailers that must be manufactured to give this profit.
f) How do the graphs show that profits can never be greater than revenues?
g) Can the company make a profit if costs are greater than revenues? if costs are greater than profits? Explain.

71. Physics A triangular prism can be used to refract light and separate white light into its component colours.
a) Write a polynomial function to represent the volume, $V(x)$ cubic centimetres, of any equilateral triangular prism with all edges x centimetres long.

b) What is the domain for this function?
c) Graph the function.
d) For a prism with all the edges 5 cm long, what is the volume, to the nearest cubic centimetre?
e) Find the edge length, to the nearest tenth of a centimetre, for a prism of volume 20 cm³.

72. Draw the inverse of each of the following functions manually or using a graphing calculator. State whether each inverse is a function.
a) $y = x^3$ **b)** $y = x^4$

73. Measurement
a) Solve the inequality $(x + 3)(x + 1)(x - 1) > 0$.
b) A rectangular prism has the dimensions shown. Determine the possible values of x for the rectangular prism.
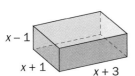
c) Compare your answers from parts a) and b), and explain any differences.

74. In standard form, write three quadratic inequalities that have no solution over the real numbers.

75. Write a quadratic inequality with each of the following solutions.
a) $-1 \le x \le 2$ **b)** $x < -\dfrac{1}{2}$ or $x > 4$

76. Find the solutions that satisfy both $x^2 + 4x - 5 > 0$ and $x^2 + 6x - 7 \le 0$.

77. Designing with functions
a) Identify the polynomial functions that were used to draw this diagram of a child's pushcart.

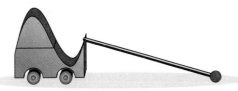

b) Create the diagram on the screen of a graphing calculator.
c) Use polynomial functions to create a design for a car or an object of your choice. Challenge a classmate to discover the polynomial functions you used.

TECHNOLOGY

Exploring Functions With Two Equal Roots

1 Verifying Equal Roots

The function $f(x) = x^3 - 2x^2 + k$ has two roots that equal 0 when $k = 0$.
The graph of $y = x^3 - 2x^2$ suggests that this is so.
The equal roots can be verified by solving the equation $x^3 - 2x^2 = 0$.

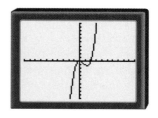

$$x^3 - 2x^2 = 0$$
$$x(x)(x - 2) = 0$$
$$x = 0 \text{ or } x = 0 \text{ or } x - 2 = 0$$
$$x = 2$$

So, there are two roots that equal 0.

Zero is not the only value of k for which the function $f(x) = x^3 - 2x^2 + k$ has two equal roots.
The graph of $y = x^3 - 2x^2 + \frac{32}{27}$ suggests that there are two roots that equal approximately $\frac{4}{3}$.

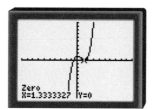

We can verify that there are two equal roots when $k = \frac{32}{27}$ by solving the equation $x^3 - 2x^2 + \frac{32}{27} = 0$.

Multiplying by 27 gives the equation $27x^3 - 54x^2 + 32 = 0$.

You can solve this equation with your graphing calculator, if it has the capability. Alternatively, factor using the factor theorem.
The factors of 32 are ±1, ±2, ±4, ±8, ±16, and ±32.
The factors of 27 are ±1, ±3, ±9, and ±27.

The many possible values of $\frac{b}{a}$ in factors of the form $ax - b$ include $1, \frac{1}{3}, \frac{4}{3}, -\frac{2}{9}$, and so on.

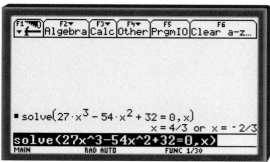

This calculator shows two roots, but we expect three for a cubic equation. The graph of the function suggests that there are two roots that equal $\frac{4}{3}$.

From the graph, there seem to be two equal roots close to $\frac{4}{3}$ when $k = \frac{32}{27}$, so test $\frac{4}{3}$ as a possible value of $\frac{b}{a}$.

$$f(x) = x^3 - 2x^2 + \frac{32}{27}$$
$$f\left(\frac{4}{3}\right) = \left(\frac{4}{3}\right)^3 - 2\left(\frac{4}{3}\right)^2 + \frac{32}{27}$$
$$= \frac{64}{27} - \frac{32}{9} + \frac{32}{27}$$
$$= \frac{64}{27} - \frac{96}{27} + \frac{32}{27}$$
$$= 0$$

Since $f\left(\frac{4}{3}\right) = 0$, $x - \frac{4}{3}$ or $3x - 4$ is a factor.

Use synthetic division or long division, or divide using a graphing calculator to find another factor. To use synthetic division to divide $27x^3 - 54x^2 + 32$ by $3x - 4$, rewrite $3x - 4$ as $3\left(x - \dfrac{4}{3}\right)$.

Divide by $\left(x - \dfrac{4}{3}\right)$.

$$
\begin{array}{r|rrrr}
\frac{4}{3} & 27 & -54 & 0 & 32 \\
 & & 36 & -24 & -32 \\
\hline
 & 27 & -18 & -24 & 0
\end{array}
$$

So, $\dfrac{27x^3 - 54x^2 + 32}{\left(x - \dfrac{4}{3}\right)} = 27x^2 - 18x - 24$

Now divide by 3.
$$\dfrac{27x^3 - 54x^2 + 32}{3\left(x - \dfrac{4}{3}\right)} = \dfrac{27x^2 - 18x - 24}{3}$$

$$\dfrac{27x^3 - 54x^2 + 32}{3x - 4} = 9x^2 - 6x - 8$$

Another factor is $9x^2 - 6x - 8$.

So, $27x^3 - 54x^2 + 32 = (3x - 4)(9x^2 - 6x - 8)$
$9x^2 - 6x - 8$ can be factored.
$9x^2 - 6x - 8 = (3x - 4)(3x + 2)$
$27x^3 - 54x^2 + 32 = (3x - 4)(3x - 4)(3x + 2)$
Since $(3x - 4)(3x - 4)(3x + 2) = 0$,

$3x - 4 = 0$ or $3x - 4 = 0$ or $3x + 2 = 0$

$x = \dfrac{4}{3}$ or $x = \dfrac{4}{3}$ or $x = -\dfrac{2}{3}$

So, two roots equal $\dfrac{4}{3}$ when $k = \dfrac{32}{27}$.

Verify that each of the following functions has two equal roots for the given non-zero value of k.

1. $f(x) = x^3 - x^2 + k;\ k = \dfrac{4}{27}$

2. $f(x) = x^3 - 3x^2 + k;\ k = 4$

3. $f(x) = x^3 - 4x^2 + k;\ k = \dfrac{256}{27}$

 **2**   **Investigating Patterns**

1. a) Examine the non-zero values of k that give two equal roots for the four functions in the previous exploration. Write an equation of the form $k(c) = \blacksquare$ to express the value of k in terms of c, the coefficient of x^2.

b) Use the equation from part a) to predict a non-zero value of k for which the function $f(x) = x^3 + x^2 + k$ has two equal roots. Verify that there are two equal roots for this value of k.

2. a) Copy the table. Complete it by recording the values of the roots for each function in the previous exploration. The roots found for the function in the example have been recorded for you. Describe any patterns in the roots.

Function	Roots
$f(x) = x^3 - x^2 + \dfrac{4}{27}$	
$f(x) = x^3 - 2x^2 + \dfrac{32}{27}$	$\dfrac{4}{3}, \dfrac{4}{3}, -\dfrac{2}{3}$
$f(x) = x^3 - 3x^2 + 4$	
$f(x) = x^3 - 4x^2 + \dfrac{256}{27}$	

b) Predict a non-zero value of k for which the function $f(x) = x^3 - 5x^2 + k$ has two equal roots.
c) Predict the roots of the function that has the value of k from part b).
d) Use substitution to verify the values of the roots. Graph the function to show that the equal roots have the value you predicted.

5.5 Absolute Value Functions, Equations, and Inequalities

The integers 5 and –5 are different. However, when they are graphed on a number line, they are the same distance from 0.

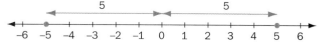

We say that 5 and –5 have the same **absolute value**. The absolute value of any number is its distance from the origin on a number line. The absolute value of 5 is 5, and the absolute value of –5 is 5.
$$|5| = 5 \text{ and } |-5| = 5$$

For any real number x,
if x is positive or zero, the absolute value of x is x, or
$$|x| = x, \text{ if } x \geq 0$$
if x is negative, the absolute value of x is the opposite of x, or
$$|x| = -x, \text{ if } x < 0$$

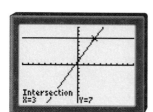

For a space shuttle launch, the time from the start of the countdown to liftoff is about 360 min. To meet the mission objectives and stay within safety guidelines, the shuttle must be launched within a certain time period. The following equation represents the maximum and minimum times that can be taken to launch the shuttle
$$|t - 360| = 5$$
where t minutes is the time after the start of the countdown.
The equation $|t - 360| = 5$ is an example of an **absolute value equation**, which is an equation with a variable within the absolute value symbol.

Explore: Interpret the Graphs

One way to solve the equation $2x + 1 = 7$ is to graph the two functions $y = 2x + 1$ and $y = 7$. The x-coordinate of the point where the graphs intersect is the solution to the equation $2x + 1 = 7$. The solution is 3. Solve the following equations by graphing manually or using a graphing calculator.

a) $|x + 2| = 5$ **b)** $|x - 3| = 4$ **c)** $|x + 5| = 2$ **d)** $|x - 6| = 3$

Inquire

1. a) How could you verify that your solutions are correct?
b) Verify your solutions.

2. Why does each equation have two solutions?

3. Solve the following equations by guess and check.
a) $|x - 6| = 11$ **b)** $|x + 9| = 10$ **c)** $|x + 17| = 1$ **d)** $|3 - x| = 8$

4. Solve the equation $|t - 360| = 5$ to find the maximum and minimum times, in minutes, that can be taken to launch the shuttle after the start of the countdown.

5. a) Try to solve the equation $|x + 1| = -2$ graphically.
b) Explain why the left side of the equation can never equal the right side.

Example 1   Solving an Absolute Value Equation

Solve $|2x - 3| = 5$.

Solution 1   Solving Algebraically

From the definition of absolute value, $|2x - 3| = 5$ means $2x - 3 = 5$ or $-(2x - 3) = 5$.

Consider both cases.

$$2x - 3 = 5 \quad \text{or} \quad -(2x - 3) = 5$$
$$2x = 8 \qquad\qquad -2x + 3 = 5$$
$$x = 4 \qquad\qquad -2x = 2$$
$$\qquad\qquad\qquad x = -1$$

Solution 2   Solving Graphically

Graph the functions $y = |2x - 3|$ and $y = 5$ manually on the same set of axes or in the same standard viewing window of a graphing calculator.

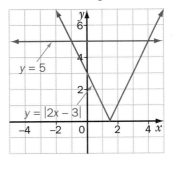

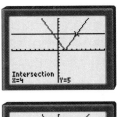

The graphs intersect at $(4, 5)$ and $(-1, 5)$.
So, $x = 4$ or $x = -1$.

Check for both solutions.

For $x = 4$,
L.S. $= |2x - 3|$ **R.S.** $= 5$
$\quad = |2(4) - 3|$
$\quad = |5|$
$\quad = 5$

For $x = -1$,
L.S. $= |2x - 3|$ **R.S.** $= 5$
$\quad = |2(-1) - 3|$
$\quad = |-5|$
$\quad = 5$

The solution is $x = 4$ or $x = -1$.

It is important to check the solutions to absolute value equations that are solved algebraically. If a solution found algebraically does not satisfy the original equation, the solution is known as an **extraneous solution** or **extraneous root**.

Example 2   Extraneous Solution

Solve $|x - 4| = 2x + 1$.

Solution

$$x - 4 = 2x + 1 \quad \text{or} \quad -(x - 4) = 2x + 1$$
$$-x = 5 \qquad\qquad -x + 4 = 2x + 1$$
$$x = -5 \qquad\qquad -3x = -3$$
$$\qquad\qquad\qquad x = 1$$

Check.

For $x = -5$,
L.S. $= |x - 4|$ **R.S.** $= 2x + 1$
$\quad = |-5 - 4|$ $= 2(-5) + 1$
$\quad = |-9|$ $= -9$
$\quad = 9$

For $x = 1$,
L.S. $= |x - 4|$ **R.S.** $= 2x + 1$
$\quad = |1 - 4|$ $= 2(1) + 1$
$\quad = |-3|$ $= 3$
$\quad = 3$

The solution $x = 1$ checks, but the solution $x = -5$ is extraneous.
The solution is $x = 1$.

Note that if Example 2 is solved graphically, the graph gives only the solution $x = 1$.

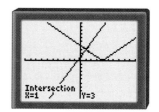

To solve equations in which two absolute value symbols appear, but there are no non-zero constant terms, use the definition of absolute value to eliminate the absolute value symbols.

If $|n| = |x|$, then $n = |x|$ or $-n = |x|$

If $n = |x|$,
then $n = x$ or $n = -x$

If $-n = |x|$,
then $-n = x$ or $-n = -x$
and $n = -x$ or $n = x$

Notice that there are four cases, but they can be reduced to two, $n = x$ or $n = -x$.

Example 3 Equations With Two Absolute Value Symbols
Solve $|x + 2| - |3x - 10| = 0$.

Solution 1 Solving Algebraically
Rewrite the equation with one absolute value symbol on each side of the equal sign.
$$|x + 2| - |3x - 10| = 0$$
$$|x + 2| = |3x - 10|$$
$x + 2 = 3x - 10$ or $x + 2 = -(3x - 10)$
$-2x = -12$ \qquad $x + 2 = -3x + 10$
$x = 6$ \qquad\qquad $4x = 8$
\qquad\qquad\qquad $x = 2$

Solution 2 Solving Graphically
Graph the function $y = |x + 2| - |3x - 10|$.
Find the x-intercepts.

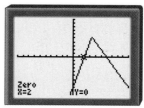 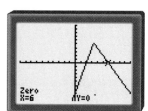

The graph intersects the x-axis at $(2, 0)$ and $(6, 0)$.
So, $x = 2$ or $x = 6$.

Check for both solutions.
For $x = 6$,
L.S. $= |x + 2| - |3x - 10|$ \qquad **R.S.** $= 0$
$= |6 + 2| - |3(6) - 10|$
$= |8| - |8|$
$= 8 - 8$
$= 0$

For $x = 2$,
L.S. $= |x + 2| - |3x - 10|$ \qquad **R.S.** $= 0$
$= |2 + 2| - |3(2) - 10|$
$= |4| - |-4|$
$= 4 - 4$
$= 0$

The solution is $x = 6$ or $x = 2$.

The algebraic method of solving absolute value equations containing two absolute value symbols changes when the equation also includes a non-zero constant term. There can be several solutions to this type of equation.

Example 4   Equations With Two Absolute Value Symbols and a Constant

Solve $|x + 1| + |x - 3| = 6$.

Solution 1   Solving Algebraically

To determine the intervals to be considered, graph the points for which $x + 1$ and $x - 3$ are positive or negative. The points -1 and 3 are the critical numbers.

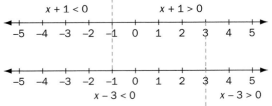

There are three intervals to consider, $x < -1$, $-1 < x < 3$, and $x > 3$.

When $x < -1$, both $x + 1$ and $x - 3$ are negative. In this interval, the equation becomes

$$-(x + 1) + [-(x - 3)] = 6$$
$$-(x + 1) - (x - 3) = 6$$
$$-x - 1 - x + 3 = 6$$
$$-2x + 2 = 6$$
$$-2x = 4$$
$$x = -2$$

When $-1 < x < 3$, $x + 1$ is positive and $x - 3$ is negative. In this interval, the equation becomes

$$(x + 1) + [-(x - 3)] = 6$$
$$x + 1 - (x - 3) = 6$$
$$x + 1 - x + 3 = 6$$
$$4 = 6$$

This result is not true, so in this interval there are no solutions.

When $x > 3$, $x + 1$ and $x - 3$ are both positive. In this interval, the equation becomes

$$(x + 1) + (x - 3) = 6$$
$$x + 1 + x - 3 = 6$$
$$2x - 2 = 6$$
$$2x = 8$$
$$x = 4$$

The two points that have not been tested are the critical numbers, -1 and 3. Substitution into $|x + 1| + |x - 3| = 6$ shows that these points do not satisfy the equation, so they are not included in the solution.

Substituting $x = -2$ or $x = 4$ into the original equation checks. So, the solution is $x = -2$ or $x = 4$.

Solution 2   Solving Graphically

Graph $y = |x + 1| + |x - 3|$ and $y = 6$.

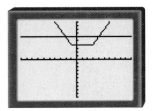

The graphs intersect at $(-2, 6)$ and $(4, 6)$. So, $x = -2$ and $x = 4$.

An **absolute value inequality** is an inequality that has a variable within the absolute value symbol.

Example 5   Solving Absolute Value Inequalities

Solve $|x - 2| \leq 5$.

Solution 1   Solving Algebraically

From the definition of absolute value, $|x - 2| \leq 5$ means $(x - 2) \leq 5$ or $-(x - 2) \leq 5$.

Consider both cases.

$$(x - 2) \leq 5 \quad \text{or} \quad -(x - 2) \leq 5$$
$$x - 2 \leq 5 \qquad\qquad -x + 2 \leq 5$$
$$x \leq 7 \qquad\qquad\quad -x \leq 3$$
$$\qquad\qquad\qquad\qquad x \geq -3$$

These results can be combined into the statement $-3 \leq x \leq 7$.

Solution 2   Solving Graphically

One way to solve $|x - 2| \leq 5$ graphically is to graph $y = |x - 2|$ and $y = 5$ to find the values of x for which $|x - 2| \leq 5$.

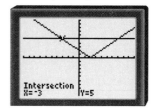 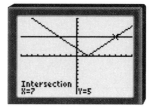

The graph of $y = |x - 2|$ is on or below the graph of $y = 5$ when $-3 \leq x \leq 7$.
So, $|x - 2| \leq 5$ when $-3 \leq x \leq 7$.

Substituting $x = -3$ or $x = 7$, or any value between them, into the original inequality checks.
So, the solution is all real numbers in the interval $-3 \leq x \leq 7$.

The solution can be graphed on a number line.

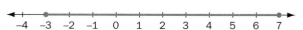

Example 6   Inequalities With Two Absolute Value Symbols

Solve $|x + 3| < |x - 4|$.

Solution 1   Solving Algebraically

To determine the intervals to be considered, graph the points for which $x + 3$ and $x - 4$ are positive or negative. The points -3 and 4 are the critical numbers.

There are three intervals to consider, $x < -3$, $-3 < x < 4$, and $x > 4$.

When $x < -3$, both $x + 3$ and $x - 4$ are negative. In this interval, the inequality becomes

$$-(x + 3) < -(x - 4)$$
$$-x - 3 < -x + 4$$
$$-3 < 4$$

This result is true, so in the interval $x < -3$ all values of the variable satisfy the inequality.

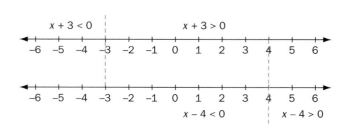

When $-3 < x < 4$, $x + 3$ is positive and $x - 4$ is negative.
In this interval, the inequality becomes
$$(x + 3) < -(x - 4)$$
$$x + 3 < -x + 4$$
$$2x < 1$$
$$x < \frac{1}{2}$$

In this interval, values of $x < \frac{1}{2}$ satisfy the inequality.

When $x > 4$, $x + 3$ and $x - 4$ are both positive.
In this interval, the inequality becomes
$$x + 3 < x - 4$$
$$3 < -4$$

This result is not true, so in this interval there are no solutions.

Combining the results from the first two intervals gives $x < \frac{1}{2}$.

The two points that have not been tested are the critical numbers -3 and 4.
Substitution into $|x + 3| < |x - 4|$ shows that -3 satisfies the inequality,
but 4 does not. The solution includes -3, but not 4.

So, the solution is all real numbers in the interval $x < \frac{1}{2}$.

Solution 2   Solving Graphically
Graph $y = |x + 3|$ and $y = |x - 4|$ on the same axes or in the same viewing
window. Find the values of x for which the graph of $y = |x + 3|$ is below the
graph of $y = |x - 4|$.

When $x = 0.5$, $|x + 3| = |x - 4|$.
The graph of $y = |x + 3|$ is below the graph of $y = |x - 4|$ when $x < 0.5$.

The solution is $x < \frac{1}{2}$.

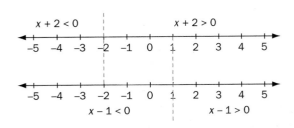

The solution can be graphed on a number line.

Example 7   Inequalities With Two Absolute Value Symbols and a Constant
Solve $|x + 2| + |x - 1| > 3$.

Solution 1   Solving Algebraically
To determine the intervals to be considered,
graph the points for which $x + 2$ and $x - 1$ are
positive or negative. The points -2 and 1 are the
critical numbers.

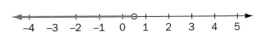

There are three intervals to consider,
$x < -2$, $-2 < x < 1$, and $x > 1$.

When $x < -2$, both $x + 2$ and $x - 1$ are negative.
In this interval, the inequality becomes
$$-(x + 2) + [-(x - 1)] > 3$$
$$-(x + 2) - (x - 1) > 3$$
$$-x - 2 - x + 1 > 3$$
$$-2x - 1 > 3$$
$$-2x > 4$$
$$x < -2$$

When $-2 < x < 1$, $x + 2$ is positive or zero and $x - 1$ is negative.
In this interval, the inequality becomes
$$(x + 2) + [-(x - 1)] > 3$$
$$x + 2 - (x - 1) > 3$$
$$x + 2 - x + 1 > 3$$
$$3 > 3$$

This result is not true, so in this interval there are no solutions.

When $x > 1$, $x + 2$ and $x - 1$ are both positive.
In this interval, the inequality becomes
$$(x + 2) + (x - 1) > 3$$
$$x + 2 + x - 1 > 3$$
$$2x + 1 > 3$$
$$2x > 2$$
$$x > 1$$

Combining the results from the first and third intervals gives $x < -2$ or $x > 1$.
The two points that have not been tested are the critical numbers -2 and 1.
Substitution into $|x + 2| + |x - 1| > 3$ shows that neither point satisfies
the inequality, and so neither is included in the solution.
The solution is all real numbers in the intervals $x < -2$ or $x > 1$.

Solution 2   Solving Graphically
Graph $y = |x + 2| + |x - 1|$ and $y = 3$ in the same viewing window.
Find the values of x for which the graph
$y = |x + 2| + |x - 1|$ is above the graph of $y = 3$.
The graphs are coincident in the interval $-2 \leq x \leq 1$.
The graph of $y = |x + 2| + |x - 1|$ is above the graph of $y = 3$
when $x < -2$ or $x > 1$.
The solution is $x < -2$ or $x > 1$.

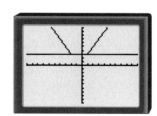

An **absolute value function** is a function that has a variable within the absolute value
symbol.

In Examples 1 to 7, above, each Solution 2 included the graph of at least one absolute
value function.

Example 8   Graphing an Absolute Value Function
Graph $f(x) = |x - 2| - 3$ and determine the values of x for which $f(x) > 0$.

Solution

Graph the function $y = |x - 2| - 3$ manually or using a graphing calculator.

x	y
-2	1
-1	0
0	-1
1	-2
2	-3
3	-2
4	-1
5	0
6	1

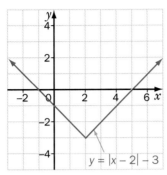

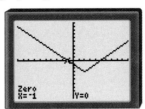

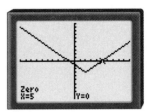

So, $f(x) > 0$ when $x < -1$ or $x > 5$.

Example 9   Graphing the Absolute Value of a Quadratic Function

a) Graph $y = |x^2 - 4|$.

b) Determine the domain and range.

c) Determine the values of any zeros.

d) Describe any symmetry.

Solution

a) Graph the function $y = |x^2 - 4|$ manually or using a graphing calculator.

x	y
-3	5
-2	0
-1	3
0	4
1	3
2	0
3	5

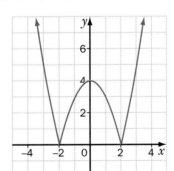

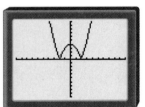

b) The domain is the set of real numbers. The range is the set of real numbers, $y \geq 0$.

c) The zeros are 2 and −2.

d) The graph is symmetric about the y-axis.

Example 10   Normal Body Temperature

The normal body temperature for a human is 37°C. An adult's body temperature is usually no more than about 0.5°C from this value. Write and solve an absolute value inequality to describe this range of temperatures.

Solution

The range of body temperatures, T degrees Celsius, can be described by the inequality $|T - 37| \leq 0.5$.

So, $T - 37 \leq 0.5$ or $-(T - 37) \leq 0.5$

$T \leq 37.5$ $-T + 37 \leq 0.5$

$-T \leq -36.5$

$T \geq 36.5$

Combining these results gives $36.5 \leq T \leq 37.5$.

Each temperature in this range is no more than 0.5°C from 37°C.

The range of temperatures is 36.5°C to 37.5°C.

Practice

Solve and check.

1. $|x| = 3$

2. $|y| - 4 = 0$

3. $|x| + 5 = 0$

4. $|x - 2| = 9$

5. $|n + 8| = 20$

6. $|3 - x| = 11$

7. $5 = |t + 5|$

8. $|2 + m| - 15 = 0$

9. $-4 - |x + 6| = 0$

10. $|2 - x| = -1$

Solve and check.

11. $|2x - 1| = 7$

12. $|3x + 2| = 8$

13. $|3 - 2z| = 7$

14. $|2 - 3x| - 8 = 0$

15. $|4x - 3| + 7 = 0$

16. $|2(x + 1)| = 4$

17. $|-2(x - 1)| = 2$

18. $9 = |0.5a + 1|$

19. $\left|\dfrac{x}{3} - \dfrac{1}{2}\right| = 1$

20. $\left|\dfrac{2x + 1}{3}\right| = 5$

Solve and check.

21. $|x| = x + 2$

22. $|y| = 3 - y$

23. $|p + 1| = p - 1$

24. $|x - 2| = x$

25. $|x + 3| = 2x$

26. $2x - 3 = |x - 3|$

27. $|3x - 2| = x - 4$

28. $|1 - 2x| = x + 2$

29. $|3(x - 6)| = x$

30. $2(x + 3) = |2(x - 1)|$

31. $\left|\dfrac{x}{3} - 1\right| = 6 - 2x$

32. $\dfrac{k}{2} + 3 = |3k - 3|$

Solve.

33. $|2x| = |x + 4|$

34. $|3w - 1| = |3w|$

35. $|x + 3| = |x - 3|$

36. $|x - 5| = |5x - 3|$

37. $|3d - 7| = |4 - d|$

38. $|x - 6| - |4x + 6| = 0$

39. $|2(x + 1)| = -|2(x - 1)|$

40. $\left|\dfrac{x + 1}{2}\right| = \left|\dfrac{x + 2}{3}\right|$

Solve.

41. $|x + 1| + |x - 1| = 4$

42. $|x - 2| + |x + 3| = 5$

43. $|c + 2| + |c - 3| = -2$

44. $|x - 4| - |x + 5| = 6$

45. $|m + 6| - 2 = |m + 4|$

46. $|2n - 1| + |n - 5| = 8$

47. $|x + 5| = 2 - |3x + 2|$

48. $\left|\dfrac{x}{3} - 1\right| + \left|\dfrac{x}{3} + 1\right| = 2$

Solve. Graph the solution.

49. $|x| < 2$

50. $|x| \geq 5$

51. $|y| - 1 > 4$

52. $|x| + 3 \leq 2$

53. $|2g| < 10$

54. $12 \leq |6x|$

55. $|4a| - 6 > 14$

56. $|x - 4| > 8$

57. $|x + 5| + 3 \geq 0$

58. $|2x - 7| \geq 0$

59. $|1 - 2x| > 5$

60. $|-2(3 - x)| < 10$

61. $\left|\dfrac{x}{2} + 1\right| \leq 3$

62. $2 < |0.5(z - 1)|$

Solve. Graph the solution.

63. $|x - 1| < |x - 3|$

64. $|x + 2| > |x - 4|$

65. $|x + 6| - |x + 8| \leq 0$

66. $|x - 7| - |x + 3| \geq 0$

67. $|x - 3| - |x - 2| < 0$

68. $|x + 1| + |x - 1| < 0$

69. $|2x - 1| < |x - 2|$

70. $|3b + 2| \geq |b + 4|$

71. $|3(x + 1)| \leq |3 - x|$

72. $|2x + 5| > |0.5x - 2|$

Solve. Graph the solution.

73. $|x + 1| + |x - 1| \leq 6$

74. $|x + 2| + |x - 4| > 8$

75. $|a - 3| - |a + 5| \leq 2$

76. $|x + 3| + |x - 1| > 10$

77. $|w + 4| + |4 - w| > 7$

78. $|x - 5| + |x - 3| < 9$

79. $|2x - 5| + |3x - 1| \geq 1$

80. $|4y + 2| - |2y - 5| \leq -1$

81. $|2(x + 3)| - |5 - 2x| < 2$

82. $\left|\dfrac{x + 1}{2}\right| + \left|\dfrac{x + 3}{2}\right| \geq 3$

Graph each function and
a) *determine the domain and range*
b) *determine the values of any zeros*
c) *determine the values of x for which $f(x) \geq 0$*
d) *describe any symmetry*

83. $f(x) = |x + 2| - 4$

84. $f(x) = |x - 3| - 5$

85. $f(x) = |x + 2| + 1$

86. $f(x) = -|x - 5|$

87. $f(x) = 3 - |x + 4|$

88. $f(x) = |2x + 3| - 2$

89. $f(x) = |3(1 - x)| - 3$

90. $f(x) = -\left|\dfrac{x}{2} - 1\right| + 4$

Graph each function and
a) *determine the domain and range*
b) *determine the values of any real zeros*
c) *determine the values of x for which $y > 0$*
d) *describe any symmetry*

91. $y = |x^2 - 1|$

92. $y = -|x^2 - 9|$

93. $y = |x^2 - 4| - 4$

94. $y = |x^2 - 2x|$

95. $y = -|x^2 + 6x|$

96. $y = |x(x + 3)|$

97. $y = \left|\dfrac{x^2}{2} - 1\right| - 7$

98. $y = |x^2 - x - 12|$

Applications and Problem Solving

99. Launch window The launch window for a satellite is the set of times within which it must be launched to meet its objectives. The launch window for a weather satellite is represented by the inequality $|t - 360| \leq 20$, where t minutes is the time from the start of the countdown to the launch. If the countdown starts at 01:00, at what times can the satellite be launched?

100. Environment A scientist was monitoring the temperature of a holding tank containing fish to be released into a river. In one 12-h period, the highest temperature was 10.4°C and the lowest temperature was 7.6°C. Write an absolute value equation that can be used to report the highest temperature and the lowest temperature.

101. Biology Green plants live in the ocean at depths described by the absolute value inequality
$$|15 - d| \leq 15$$
where d is the depth, in metres. Solve the inequality to find the depths at which green plants live in the ocean.

102. Astronomy The distance of the Earth from the sun changes at different times of the year. The maximum and minimum distances of the Earth from the sun can be represented by the equation
$$|d - 149.5| = 2.5$$
where d is measured in millions of kilometres. Solve the equation to find the maximum and minimum distances of the Earth from the sun.

103. Chemistry An equation that describes the maximum and minimum temperatures at which a chemical compound is a liquid under normal conditions is
$$|T - 50| = 50$$
where T is the temperature in degrees Celsius. Identify the chemical compound.

104. Construction The cross section of the sloping roof of a house is represented on a coordinate grid so that the points representing the bottom of the roof lie on the x-axis. The equation of the function describing the cross section is
$$h(x) = -|x| + 4$$
where $h(x)$ metres is the height of the roof and x metres is the horizontal distance from the centre of the roof. What is the width of the bottom of the roof?

105. Rolling dice Two dice are rolled and the outcomes are added. Write an absolute value inequality to describe the possible whole-number sums, s.

106. Measurement Two sides of a triangle have lengths of 3 cm and 8 cm. The possible lengths of the third side, s centimetres, can be described by the following absolute value inequality.
$$|s - 8| < 3$$
a) Solve the inequality and graph the possible lengths of the third side.
b) Explain why the length of the third side is restricted to the values represented by the inequality.
c) Does the absolute value inequality $|s - 3| < 8$ describe the possible values of s? Explain.
d) Does the absolute value inequality $|8 - s| < 3$ describe the possible values of s?

107. Inverses Graph the following functions and their inverses. Interpret the results with respect to the line $y = x$.
a) $y = |x|$ **b)** $y = |x + 1|$ **c)** $y = |x - 2|$

108. How do the graphs of the functions $y = |x - a|$ and $y = |a - x|$ compare, where a is a constant?

109. For what values of m does $m|x| = |mx|$?

110. Technology Some graphing calculators can be used to graph the solution to an absolute value equation directly.
a) Solve $|x - 1| + |x + 5| = 6$ algebraically and graph the solution manually.
b) Enter the equation into your graphing calculator as follows.
$$Y_1 = abs(X - 1) + abs(X + 5) = 6$$
With the calculator in the dot mode, graph Y_1 in the standard viewing window.
c) Does your calculator graph the correct solution on the number line $y = 1$?
d) How can you decide whether the endpoints of the graph are included in the solution?

111. Technology If possible, use the graphing calculator method from question 110 to solve each of the following.
a) $|x + 2| + |x - 3| = 5$ **b)** $|x - 4| + |x + 3| = 7$
c) $|x - 2| = |x + 4| + 6$ **d)** $|2x + 1| - |2x - 3| = 4$
e) $|2x + 1| - |2x - 3| = -4$

112. Technology Some graphing calculators can be used to graph the solution to an absolute value inequality directly.
a) Solve $|x - 1| \le 4$ algebraically and graph the solution manually.
b) Enter the inequality into your graphing calculator as follows.
$$Y_1 = \text{abs}(X - 1) \le 4$$
c) With the calculator in the dot mode, graph Y_1 in the standard viewing window.
d) Does your calculator graph the correct solution on the number line $y = 1$?
d) How can you decide whether the endpoints of the graph are included in the solution?

113. Technology If possible, use the graphing calculator method from question 112 to solve each of the following.
a) $|2x - 4| \ge 0$
b) $|2x - 3| > 5$
c) $|x - 2| + |x + 2| < 6$
d) $|3x + 1| \le |2x - 1|$
e) $|4x + 2| - |2x - 4| \ge 1$

114. How are the graphs of the functions in each pair related?
a) $y = x + 2$ and $y = |x + 2|$
b) $y = 2x - 1$ and $y = |2x - 1|$
c) $y = x^2 + 4$ and $y = |x^2 + 4|$
d) $y = x^2 - 1$ and $y = |x^2 - 1|$
e) $y = f(x)$ and $y = |f(x)|$

115. Coordinate geometry Write an equation for the absolute value function whose vertex is $(0, 1)$, if the point $(-3, 7)$ is on the graph of the function.

116. Working backward Write an absolute value inequality that has each of the following solutions.

a)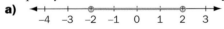

b)

c)

d)

117. Without testing intervals or graphing, state the solution to the inequality $|x + 1| < -|2x - 1|$. Explain your reasoning.

118. For the graph of $y = m|x|$, where m is a real number, state the values of m for which each of the following statements is true for the smaller angle, a, formed by the two arms.
a) $a = 90°$ **b)** $0° < a < 90°$ **c)** $90° < a < 180°$

119. Is the statement $|f(x)| = f(|x|)$ always true, sometimes true, or never true? Use examples to explain your answer.

120. a) Solve $|x - 2| + |x - 2| = 6$ by the method shown in Example 4.
b) Solve $|x - 2| = 3$ by the method shown in Example 1.
c) Compare the solutions from parts a) and b).
d) Suggest a method for simplifying an equation that includes the absolute value of the same expression more than once.
e) Solve $3|x - 1| = 9$.
f) Solve $-2|x + 3| = -4$.
g) Solve $|x + 4| + |x + 4| = 2$.
h) Solve $|3x - 2| - 3 = 1 - |3x - 2|$.
i) Solve $2|2x + 1| - |2x + 1| = 3$.
j) Solve $|3 - 2x| + |3 - 2x| = 9 - |3 - 2x|$.

121. Solve graphically.
a) $|x^2 - 9| = x^2 - 9$ **b)** $|x^2 - 9| \le x^2 - 9$
c) $|x^2 - 9| > x^2 - 9$

122. Technology By testing different values of k graphically, use a graphing calculator to determine the values of k for which each of the following equations has no solution.
a) $|x^2 - 4| = kx - 2$ **b)** $|x^2 - 9| = -x + k$
c) $|x^2 - k| = -x^2 + 4$

123. a) Graph $y \ge |x^2|$.
b) On the same axes, graph $y = x + 2$.
c) Use the graphs to solve the following system.
$$y \ge |x^2|$$
$$y = x + 2$$

124. Write an absolute value equation with each of the following solutions. Have a classmate solve your equations.
a) no solution
b) exactly two non-zero integral solutions
c) exactly one non-zero integral solution

5.6 Rational Functions, Equations, and Inequalities

How brightly an object is illuminated by a light depends on the distance of the object from the light. The brightness or illuminance of the object increases closer to the light and decreases farther from the light. Illuminance is measured in units known as lux (symbol, lx).

One of the most important aspects of making a television show is the lighting. Maintaining an even brightness on the performers is critical. In the studio, technicians check the brightness of a moving performer, because the performer's distance from each light is changing. The director can adjust the types and positions of the lights to maintain an even brightness.

For one type of light, the brightness can be determined using the function

$$l(d) = \frac{100}{d^2}$$

where $l(d)$ is the brightness or illuminance, in lux, and d is the distance from the light, in metres.

Explore: Draw a Graph

a) Copy and complete the table of values for $y = \frac{1}{x}$.

x	$\frac{1}{4}$	$\frac{1}{3}$	$\frac{1}{2}$	1	2	3	4
y							
x	$-\frac{1}{4}$	$-\frac{1}{3}$	$-\frac{1}{2}$	−1	−2	−3	−4
y							

b) Draw the graph of $y = \frac{1}{x}$.

Inquire

1. Why does the graph of $y = \frac{1}{x}$ appear only in the first and third quadrants?

2. What is the domain of this function?

3. Copy and complete the following tables of values for the function $y = \frac{1}{x}$.

Table 1

x	1	10	100	1000
y				
x	1	0.1	0.01	0.001
y				

Table 2

x	−1	−10	−100	−1000
y				
x	−1	−0.1	−0.01	−0.001
y				

4. For the branch of the graph represented by Table 1,
a) as x increases in value, what happens to the value of y?
b) will y ever reach 0? Explain.
c) as x decreases in value, what happens to the value of y?
d) will y ever reach a maximum? Explain.

5. For the branch of the graph represented by Table 2,
a) as x decreases in value, what happens to the value of y?
b) will y ever reach 0? Explain.
c) as x increases in value, what happens to the value of y?
d) will y ever reach a minimum? Explain.

6. a) Draw the graph of $l(d) = \dfrac{100}{d^2}$. Determine the domain and range of the function.

b) What is the illuminance 5 m from the light?
c) How far from the light is the illuminance 25 lx?

A **rational function** is a function of the form $f(x) = \dfrac{g(x)}{h(x)}$, where $g(x)$ and $h(x)$ are

polynomials and $h(x) \neq 0$. The above function, $l(d) = \dfrac{100}{d^2}$, is an example of a rational

function. The following are other examples.

$$f(x) = \frac{1}{x-2} \qquad f(x) = \frac{x}{x+1} \qquad f(x) = \frac{x^2}{(x-3)(x+2)}$$

Since rational functions are expressed in fraction form, the denominator cannot equal zero. The domain of a rational function cannot include the zeros of the denominator, since the function is not defined for these values. Near these values, the graphs of rational functions have features not found in the graphs of polynomial functions, which are continuous curves.

The graph of $f(x) = \dfrac{1}{x-2}$ is shown.

x	f(x)	x	f(x)
2.1	10	1.9	−10
3	1	1	−1
10	0.125	0	−0.5
50	0.021	−10	−0.08833
100	0.0102	−50	−0.019
1000	0.001	−100	−0.0098
		−1000	−0.001

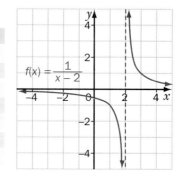

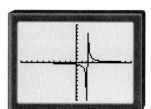

The function is not defined when $x = 2$, because the denominator cannot equal 0.

A line that a curve approaches more and more closely is called an **asymptote**. Asymptote comes from the Greek word asymptōtos, which means "not meeting." Each example of an asymptote in this book is a line that a curve never touches or crosses. The line $x = 2$ is a **vertical asymptote** of the graph of $f(x)$. Since there is a break in the graph of $f(x)$ at $x = 2$, we say the graph is **discontinuous** at $x = 2$.

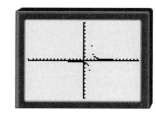

Now consider how $f(x)$ behaves for large values of the absolute value of x, $|x|$.

If $x = 10\,000$, $f(10\,000) = \dfrac{1}{9998}$
$\doteq 0.0001$

If $x = -10\,000$, $f(-10\,000) = \dfrac{1}{-10\,002}$
$\doteq -0.0001$

As $|x|$ increases, $f(x)$ gets closer to 0.
The graph of $f(x)$ approaches the graph of $y = 0$ but never touches it.
The line $y = 0$ is called a **horizontal asymptote** of the graph.

The domain of $f(x) = \dfrac{1}{x-2}$ is the set of real numbers, $x \neq 2$.

The range is the set of real numbers, $y \neq 0$.

Example 1   Asymptotes

Graph $f(x) = \dfrac{x}{x+1}$.

Determine the equations of any asymptotes.
State the domain and range.

Solution
The function is not defined when $x + 1 = 0$
$$x = -1$$
There is a vertical asymptote at $x = -1$.
Graph the line $x = -1$.
Determine the coordinates of points on both sides of the asymptote to find the shape
of the graph. Then, draw the graph.

Right Side of Asymptote		Left Side of Asymptote	
x	**f(x)**	**x**	**f(x)**
−0.9	−9	−1.1	11
−0.5	−1	−1.5	3
0	0	−2	2
1	0.5	−10	1.11
10	0.909	−100	1.01
100	0.99	−1000	1.001
1000	0.999		

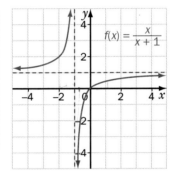

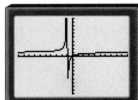

As $|x|$ increases, $f(x)$ gets closer to 1.
The graph of $f(x)$ approaches the graph of $y = 1$ but never touches it.
The line $y = 1$ is a horizontal asymptote of the graph of $f(x)$.
The domain of $f(x)$ is the set of real numbers, $x \neq -1$.
The range of $f(x)$ is the set of real numbers, $y \neq 1$.

In Example 1, the function $f(x) = \dfrac{x}{x+1}$ is discontinuous because of the break
at the vertical asymptote. The graphs of some rational functions may have **point
discontinuity**, where the break occurs at a single point in the graph.

Example 2   Point Discontinuity

a) Graph $f(x) = \dfrac{x^2 - 4}{x - 2}$.

b) If $g(x) = x + 2$, how does its graph differ from the graph of $f(x)$?

c) State the domain and range of $f(x)$.

Solution

a) For the function $f(x)$, $x \neq 2$.

x	y
-2	0
-1	1
0	2
1	3
2	not defined
3	5
4	6

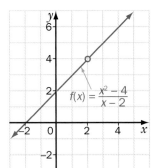

b) The graph of $f(x)$ is a line with an open circle at $(2, 4)$, because $x \neq 2$. The rest of the graph is the graph of the line $g(x) = x + 2$, because the expression $\dfrac{x^2 - 4}{x - 2}$ simplifies to $\dfrac{(x - 2)(x + 2)}{x - 2}$, or $x + 2$, when $x \neq 2$. So, the graph of $g(x) = x + 2$ is the same as the graph of $f(x) = \dfrac{x^2 - 4}{x - 2}$, except that the graph of $g(x)$ is continuous. It does not have an open circle at $(2, 4)$.

c) The domain of $f(x)$ is the set of real numbers, $x \neq 2$. The range of $f(x)$ is the set of real numbers, $y \neq 4$.

In Example 2a), graphing $y = \dfrac{x^2 - 4}{x - 2}$ on a graphing calculator may or may not show a break in the graph when $x = 2$. You may need to adjust the window variables to see the break. Displaying a table of values will show that the function is not defined for $x = 2$.

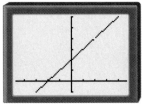
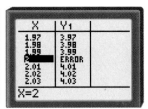

Note from Examples 1 and 2 that, unlike many other types of functions you have studied, there is not a single shape that describes the graphs of all rational functions. The shape of the graph of any rational function depends on the degrees of the polynomials in the numerator and in the denominator.

Example 3 Inverse of a Rational Function

a) Graph the inverse of $y = \dfrac{x}{x - 2}$.
b) Determine the domain and range of the inverse.

Solution

a) Determine the equation of the inverse of $y = \dfrac{x}{x - 2}$.

Interchange x and y: $x = \dfrac{y}{y - 2}$

Solve for y: $x(y - 2) = y$
$$xy - 2x = y$$
$$xy - y = 2x$$
$$y(x - 1) = 2x$$
$$y = \dfrac{2x}{x - 1}$$

Graph the inverse.

b) The line $x = 1$ is a vertical asymptote of the graph.
The line $y = 2$ is a horizontal asymptote of the graph.
The domain of the inverse is the set of real numbers, $x \neq 1$.
The range of the inverse is the set of real numbers, $y \neq 2$.

Note that, in Example 3a), you could graph the inverse of $y = \dfrac{x}{x-2}$ with a

graphing calculator using the DrawInv or equivalent instruction. To do this, you do not need to find the equation of the inverse.

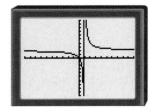

Example 4 Comparing Polynomial and Rational Functions

a) Graph $y = x^2 - 1$ and determine the zeros of this function.

b) Use the zeros of $y = x^2 - 1$ to determine the vertical asymptotes of $y = \dfrac{1}{x^2 - 1}$.

c) Compare the graphs of $y = x^2 - 1$ and $y = \dfrac{1}{x^2 - 1}$ with respect to the domain, range, symmetry, zeros, and asymptotes.

Solution

a) Graph $y = x^2 - 1$.
The zeros of the function are 1 and -1.

b) Since the zeros of $y = x^2 - 1$ are 1 and -1, the denominator of $y = \dfrac{1}{x^2 - 1}$ will be zero when $x = 1$ or

$x = -1$. So, the domain of $y = \dfrac{1}{x^2 - 1}$ is the set of real

numbers, $x \neq 1, -1$. The equations of the vertical asymptotes are $x = 1$ and $x = -1$.

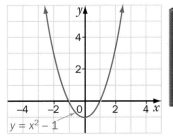

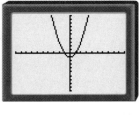

c) To graph $y = \dfrac{1}{x^2 - 1}$ manually, first draw the two vertical asymptotes, $x = 1$

and $x = -1$. Determine other points on both sides of each asymptote to find the shape of the graph. Then, draw the graph.

x	y		x	y		x	y
1	not defined		0	−1		−1	not defined
1.1	4.76		0.5	−1.33		−1.1	4.76
2	0.33		−0.5	−1.33		−2	0.33
10	0.01		0.9	−5.26		−10	0.01
100	0.0001		−0.9	−5.26		−100	0.0001

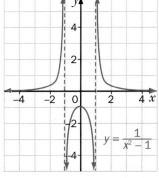

Use a table to compare the two graphs.

	Function	
	$y = x^2 - 1$	$y = \dfrac{1}{x^2 - 1}$
Domain	real numbers	real numbers, $x \neq 1, -1$
Range	$y \geq -1$	$y \leq -1$ or $y \geq 0$
Symmetry	about y-axis	about y-axis
Zeros	1, −1	none
Asymptotes	none	$x = 1, x = -1, y = 0$

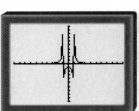

Equations that include rational expressions are called **rational equations**. Examples include the following.

$$\frac{4}{x} = 1 \qquad \frac{x^2}{x-1} = 4 \qquad \frac{x+1}{x+2} = \frac{x-3}{x+3}$$

Example 5   Solving Rational Equations

Solve $\dfrac{2x}{x+3} + \dfrac{x}{x-3} = \dfrac{18}{x^2-9}$.

Solution 1   Solving Algebraically

$$\frac{2x}{x+3} + \frac{x}{x-3} = \frac{18}{x^2-9}$$

Factor $x^2 - 9$:

$$\frac{2x}{x+3} + \frac{x}{x-3} = \frac{18}{(x-3)(x+3)}$$

The LCD is $(x-3)(x+3)$.

Multiply both sides by $(x-3)(x+3)$: $(x-3)(x+3) \times \left[\dfrac{2x}{x+3} + \dfrac{x}{x-3}\right] = (x-3)(x+3) \times \left[\dfrac{18}{(x-3)(x+3)}\right]$

$$2x(x-3) + x(x+3) = 18$$

Expand the left side: $2x^2 - 6x + x^2 + 3x = 18$

Simplify: $3x^2 - 3x - 18 = 0$

Divide both sides by 3: $x^2 - x - 6 = 0$

Factor the left side: $(x-3)(x+2) = 0$

$$x - 3 = 0 \quad \text{or} \quad x + 2 = 0$$
$$x = 3 \quad \text{or} \quad x = -2$$

Solution 2   Solving Graphically

Graph the equations $y = \dfrac{2x}{x+3} + \dfrac{x}{x-3}$ and $y = \dfrac{18}{x^2-9}$ in the same viewing window of a graphing calculator. Use the Intersect or equivalent operation to find the x-coordinates of any points of intersection. Test the three intervals $x < -3$, $-3 < x < 3$, and $x > 3$. There is one point of intersection, $(-2, -3.6)$.

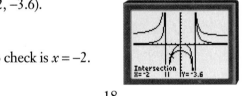

The x-coordinate of this point is -2.

Check both values for Solution 1. For Solution 2, the only value to check is $x = -2$.

For $x = 3$,

L.S. is not defined because $\dfrac{x}{x-3}$ is not defined.

R.S. is not defined because $\dfrac{18}{x^2-9}$ is not defined.

For $x = -2$,

$$\begin{aligned} \textbf{L.S.} &= \frac{2x}{x+3} + \frac{x}{x-3} \\ &= \frac{2(-2)}{-2+3} + \frac{-2}{-2-3} \\ &= \frac{-4}{1} + \frac{-2}{-5} \\ &= -4 + \frac{2}{5} \\ &= -\frac{18}{5} \end{aligned}$$

$$\begin{aligned} \textbf{R.S.} &= \frac{18}{x^2-9} \\ &= \frac{18}{(-2)^2-9} \\ &= \frac{18}{4-9} \\ &= -\frac{18}{5} \end{aligned}$$

So, $x = 3$ is an extraneous solution.
The solution is $x = -2$.

Example 6 Driving Speeds

A car and a bus left Regina at the same time. The car drove 480 km west to Calgary. The bus drove 570 km east to Winnipeg. The bus travelled 15 km/h faster than the car. The car and the bus arrived at their destinations at the same time. Find the speed of the car and the speed of the bus.

Solution

Use the relationship distance = speed × time or $\text{time} = \dfrac{\text{distance}}{\text{speed}}$.
Set up a table.

Vehicle	Distance (km)	Speed (km/h)	Time (h)
Car	480	s	$\dfrac{480}{s}$
Bus	570	s + 15	$\dfrac{570}{s+15}$

Because the times taken were equal, $\dfrac{480}{s} = \dfrac{570}{s+15}$.

Solve the rational equation. The LCD is $s(s + 15)$.

Multiply both sides by the LCD: $s(s+15) \times \dfrac{480}{s} = s(s+15) \times \dfrac{570}{s+15}$

$$480(s+15) = 570s$$

Expand the left side: $\qquad 480s + 7200 = 570s$

Solve for s: $\qquad\qquad 7200 = 90s$

$$80 = s$$

The speed of the car was 80 km/h. The speed of the bus was 95 km/h.

Use the calculated speeds to check that the times taken were the same.
$480 \div 80 = 6 \qquad 570 \div 95 = 6$
So, both trips took 6 h.

Inequalities that include rational expressions are called **rational inequalities**.

Example 7 Solving Rational Inequalities

Solve $\dfrac{x^2 - 2x - 8}{x - 1} \geq 0$.

Solution 1 Using Test Intervals

$$\dfrac{x^2 - 2x - 8}{x - 1} \geq 0$$

Factor the numerator of the left side: $\dfrac{(x-4)(x+2)}{x-1} \geq 0$

The numerator is zero when $x = 4$ or $x = -2$.
The denominator is zero and the inequality is not defined when $x = 1$.
So the critical numbers are -2, 1, and 4.
There are four test intervals.

$x < -2 \quad | \quad -2 < x < 1 \quad | \quad 1 < x < 4 \quad | \quad x > 4$

(number line: $-4 \quad -3 \quad -2 \quad -1 \quad 0 \quad 1 \quad 2 \quad 3 \quad 4 \quad 5 \quad 6$)

In the test interval $x < -2$, use the point $x = -3$.

L.S. $= \dfrac{x^2 - 2x - 8}{x - 1}$ **R.S.** $= 0$

$= \dfrac{(-3)^2 - 2(-3) - 8}{-3 - 1}$

$= -\dfrac{7}{4}$

In the test interval $-2 < x < 1$, use the point $x = 0$.

L.S. $= \dfrac{x^2 - 2x - 8}{x - 1}$ **R.S.** $= 0$

$= \dfrac{(0)^2 - 2(0) - 8}{0 - 1}$

$= 8$

In the test interval $1 < x < 4$, use the point $x = 2$.

L.S. $= \dfrac{x^2 - 2x - 8}{x - 1}$ **R.S.** $= 0$

$= \dfrac{(2)^2 - 2(2) - 8}{2 - 1}$

$= -8$

In the test interval $x > 4$, use the point $x = 5$.

L.S. $= \dfrac{x^2 - 2x - 8}{x - 1}$ **R.S.** $= 0$

$= \dfrac{(5)^2 - 2(5) - 8}{5 - 1}$

$= \dfrac{7}{4}$

So, $\dfrac{x^2 - 2x - 8}{x - 1} > 0$ in the intervals $-2 < x < 1$ and $x > 4$.

The three points that have not been tested are the critical numbers -2, 1, and 4.

It was already shown by factoring that $\dfrac{x^2 - 2x - 8}{x - 1} = 0$ when $x = -2$ or $x = 4$.

So, -2 and 4 satisfy the inequality $\dfrac{x^2 - 2x - 8}{x - 1} \geq 0$ and are included in the solution.

So, the solution is $-2 \leq x < 1$ or $x \geq 4$.

Note that the point $x = 1$ is not included in the solution, because the restriction on the variable is $x \neq 1$.

Solution 2   Solving Graphically

Graph the function $y = \dfrac{x^2 - 2x - 8}{x - 1}$.

Find the values of x for which the graph of
$y = \dfrac{x^2 - 2x - 8}{x - 1}$ is on or above the x-axis.

The graph crosses the x-axis at $x = -2$ and $x = 4$.
The left branch of the graph approaches but never touches the graph of the asymptote $x = 1$.
So, the left branch is on or above the x-axis when $-2 \leq x < 1$.
The right branch of the graph is on or above the x-axis when $x \geq 4$.
So, the solution is $-2 \leq x < 1$ or $x \geq 4$.

The solution to Example 7 can be graphed on a number line.

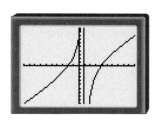

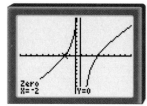

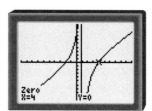

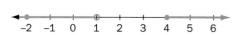

Example 8 Inequalities With Two Rational Terms

Solve $\dfrac{3}{x+1} < \dfrac{x}{2}$.

Solution 1 Using Test Intervals

The inequality is not defined when $x = -1$, so this is one of the points used to determine the test intervals.

To find the other points, solve the equation $\dfrac{3}{x+1} = \dfrac{x}{2}$.

The LCD is $2(x + 1)$.

Multiply both sides by the LCD: $2(x+1) \times \dfrac{3}{x+1} = 2(x+1) \times \dfrac{x}{2}$

$$6 = x(x+1)$$

Expand the right side: $6 = x^2 + x$

$$0 = x^2 + x - 6$$

Factor the right side: $0 = (x+3)(x-2)$

$$x + 3 = 0 \quad \text{or} \quad x - 2 = 0$$
$$x = -3 \quad \text{or} \quad x = 2$$

The points -3, -1, and 2 are the critical numbers
So, there are four test intervals.

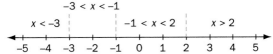

In the test interval $x < -3$, use the point $x = -4$.

L.S. $= \dfrac{3}{x+1}$ R.S. $= \dfrac{x}{2}$

$= \dfrac{3}{-4+1}$ $= \dfrac{-4}{2}$

$= -1$ $= -2$

In the test interval $-3 < x < -1$, use the point $x = -2$.

L.S. $= \dfrac{3}{x+1}$ R.S. $= \dfrac{x}{2}$

$= \dfrac{3}{-2+1}$ $= \dfrac{-2}{2}$

$= -3$ $= -1$

In the test interval $-1 < x < 2$, use the point $x = 0$.

L.S. $= \dfrac{3}{x+1}$ R.S. $= \dfrac{x}{2}$

$= \dfrac{3}{0+1}$ $= \dfrac{0}{2}$

$= 3$ $= 0$

In the test interval $x > 2$, use the point $x = 5$.

L.S. $= \dfrac{3}{x+1}$ R.S. $= \dfrac{x}{2}$

$= \dfrac{3}{5+1}$ $= \dfrac{5}{2}$

$= \dfrac{1}{2}$

So, $\dfrac{3}{x+1} < \dfrac{x}{2}$ in the interval $-3 < x < -1$ or the interval $x > 2$.

The three points that have not been tested are the critical numbers -3, -1, and 2.

Substitution into $\dfrac{3}{x+1} < \dfrac{x}{2}$ shows that the points -3, -1, and 2 do not satisfy the

inequality and are not included in the solution.
The solution is $-3 < x < -1$ or $x > 2$.

Solution 2   Solving Graphically

Graph the functions $y = \dfrac{3}{x+1}$ and $y = \dfrac{x}{2}$.

Find the values of x for which the graph of $y = \dfrac{3}{x+1}$
is below the graph of $y = \dfrac{x}{2}$.

The graphs intersect when $x = -3$ and $x = 2$.

The left branch of the graph $y = \dfrac{3}{x+1}$ approaches
but never touches the asymptote $x = -1$.

The graph of $y = \dfrac{3}{x+1}$ is below the graph of

$y = \dfrac{x}{2}$ when $-3 < x < -1$ or $x > 2$.

The solution is $-3 < x < -1$ or $x > 2$.

The solution to Example 8 can be graphed on a number line.

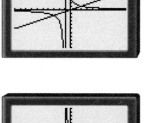

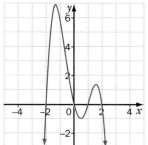

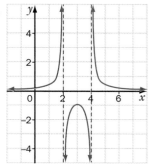

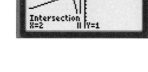

Practice

📝 *Determine whether each function is a rational function,
a polynomial function, or some other type of function.
Justify your conclusion.*

1. $y = x^5 + 2x^3 - 0.6$

2. $y = \dfrac{4}{x-2}$

3. $y = 1 - 2x^3$

4. $y = |x - 6| + 2$

5. $y = \dfrac{2x+1}{x^2 - 7x + 12}$

6. $y = \sqrt{2x^3} + 4x$

7. $y = (x + 5)^{-1}$

8. $y = 3^x + 4$

📝 *Which of the following graphs could be graphs of
polynomial functions and which could be graphs of
rational functions? Explain.*

9.

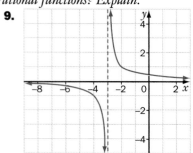

10.

11.

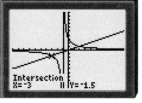

12.

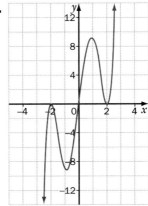

Graph each of the following functions and determine
a) *the equations of any asymptotes*
b) *the domain and range*

13. $f(x) = \dfrac{1}{x-1}$

14. $f(x) = \dfrac{1}{x+1}$

15. $g(x) = \dfrac{1}{x-3}$

16. $f(x) = \dfrac{1}{x+4}$

17. $f(x) = \dfrac{2}{x+3}$

18. $k(x) = \dfrac{3}{x-2}$

19. $h(x) = \dfrac{4}{5-x}$

20. $f(x) = \dfrac{-2}{2-x}$

Graph each of the following functions and determine
a) *the equations of any asymptotes*
b) *the domain and range*

21. $f(x) = \dfrac{x}{x+2}$

22. $f(x) = \dfrac{x}{x-1}$

23. $f(x) = \dfrac{x}{x+3}$

24. $g(x) = \dfrac{2x}{x+1}$

25. $f(x) = \dfrac{3x}{x-2}$

26. $k(x) = \dfrac{-3x}{x-2}$

Graph each of the following functions and determine the domain and range.

27. $f(x) = \dfrac{x^2-4}{x+2}$

28. $f(x) = \dfrac{9-x^2}{x-3}$

29. $g(x) = \dfrac{x^2+2x+1}{x+1}$

30. $f(x) = \dfrac{x^2-4x+4}{x-2}$

31. $f(x) = \dfrac{x^2-x-6}{x-3}$

32. $h(x) = \dfrac{x^2+3x+2}{x+2}$

Graph the inverse of each function and determine
a) *the equations of any asymptotes*
b) *the domain and range of the inverse*

33. $f(x) = \dfrac{2}{x-1}$

34. $y = \dfrac{1}{x+2}$

35. $f(x) = \dfrac{x+1}{x}$

36. $g(x) = \dfrac{x-2}{x}$

37. $y = \dfrac{x}{x-3}$

38. $f(x) = \dfrac{x}{x+1}$

39. $f(x) = \dfrac{-x}{x-2}$

40. $k(x) = \dfrac{2x}{x+2}$

41. $y = \dfrac{3x}{2x-1}$

42. $f(x) = \dfrac{3-2x}{x}$

For each pair of functions,
a) *graph the first function and determine its zeros*
b) *use the zeros to determine the vertical asymptotes of the second function*
c) *compare the graphs of the functions, considering the domain, range, symmetry, zeros, and asymptotes*

43. $y = x+3$ and $y = \dfrac{1}{x+3}$

44. $y = x-5$ and $y = \dfrac{1}{x-5}$

45. $f(x) = x^2-4$ and $g(x) = \dfrac{1}{x^2-4}$

46. $f(x) = 1-x^2$ and $g(x) = \dfrac{1}{1-x^2}$

47. $h(x) = x^2+2x$ and $k(x) = \dfrac{1}{x^2+2x}$

48. $y = x^2-x-2$ and $y = \dfrac{1}{x^2-x-2}$

Solve and check.

49. $\dfrac{2}{x} = \dfrac{x+1}{3}$

50. $\dfrac{x}{x-1} = \dfrac{1}{x+3}$

51. $\dfrac{3}{y-4} = \dfrac{y+1}{2}$

52. $\dfrac{a}{a-1} = \dfrac{2a}{a-2}$

53. $\dfrac{2}{3t+2} = \dfrac{t}{t-1}$

54. $\dfrac{2x}{x-1} = \dfrac{3x}{2x-2}$

Solve.

55. $\dfrac{4}{x} - \dfrac{3}{x+1} = 1$

56. $\dfrac{12}{m-2} - \dfrac{6}{m-3} = 1$

57. $\dfrac{6}{x+3} + \dfrac{x}{x-3} = 1$

58. $1 + \dfrac{1}{n-1} = \dfrac{n}{n-1}$

59. $\dfrac{x^2}{x-1} - \dfrac{3x}{x-1} = -4$

60. $\dfrac{x+2}{2x+1} - \dfrac{x}{3} = \dfrac{3}{4x+2}$

61. $\dfrac{2}{y+3} = \dfrac{y-2}{2y} + \dfrac{2}{5}$

62. $\dfrac{1}{x-2} = \dfrac{x+1}{3x-6} - \dfrac{5x}{6}$

Solve.

63. $\dfrac{3}{x^2} + \dfrac{4}{x} = -1$

64. $\dfrac{5r}{r^2-9} = 2$

65. $\dfrac{8}{x^2-16} + 1 = \dfrac{1}{x-4}$

66. $\dfrac{x+4}{x} + \dfrac{16}{x^2-4x} = \dfrac{-3}{x-4}$

67. $\dfrac{d+2}{d+3} + \dfrac{3}{d^2+3d} = \dfrac{1}{d}$

68. $\dfrac{1}{k+4} - \dfrac{2}{k^2+3k-4} = \dfrac{1}{k-1}$

69. $\dfrac{2x+2}{x^2+2x-15} + \dfrac{2}{x-3} = \dfrac{1}{x+5}$

70. $\dfrac{1}{2x^2+3x+1} = \dfrac{2}{2x+1} - \dfrac{1}{x+1}$

71. $\dfrac{1}{3z-1} + 1 = \dfrac{6}{3z^2-4z+1}$

Solve, to the nearest tenth.

72. $\dfrac{1}{x} + \dfrac{3}{x+4} = 2$

73. $\dfrac{3}{x^2-4} + \dfrac{1}{2} = \dfrac{4}{x-2}$

74. $\dfrac{2}{s^2+5s+4} - 1 = \dfrac{1}{s+1}$

75. $\dfrac{x-1}{x-2} - \dfrac{x+1}{1-x} = -1$

76. $\dfrac{2}{3g-1} = \dfrac{1}{3g-2} - 1$

Solve. Graph the solution.

77. $\dfrac{x}{x-5} > 0$

78. $\dfrac{x+4}{x-1} \geq 0$

79. $\dfrac{y-3}{y+5} < 0$

80. $\dfrac{x-7}{x-2} \geq 0$

81. $\dfrac{x+2}{x+3} > 0$

82. $\dfrac{m+6}{m+1} \leq 0$

83. $\dfrac{x^2+2x+1}{x+1} \leq 0$

84. $\dfrac{x^2+6x+9}{x-5} > 0$

85. $\dfrac{a^2-2a-15}{a-1} < 0$

86. $\dfrac{x^2-5x+4}{x+2} > 0$

87. $\dfrac{x^2+6x+8}{x-3} \geq 0$

88. $\dfrac{n^2-5n-6}{n+1} \leq 0$

Solve. Graph the solution.

89. $5 + \dfrac{1}{x} \leq \dfrac{11}{x}$

90. $\dfrac{1}{x+1} > \dfrac{2}{x+2}$

91. $\dfrac{3}{2k-1} \geq \dfrac{4}{1-k}$

82. $1 + \dfrac{2}{x-1} \leq \dfrac{2}{3}$

93. $\dfrac{5}{2x-3} > \dfrac{3}{3-2x}$

94. $\dfrac{4}{c+3} < c$

95. $\dfrac{4w}{w+1} > w+1$

96. $x-1 \leq \dfrac{6}{x-2}$

Applications and Problem Solving

Graph each of the following functions and determine
a) *the equations of any asymptotes*
b) *the domain and range*

97. $f(x) = \dfrac{1}{x^2+x-6}$

98. $f(x) = \dfrac{-1}{x^2+6x+8}$

99. $g(x) = \dfrac{1}{4x^2-9}$

100. $f(x) = \dfrac{1}{x^2+3x-4}$

101. $f(x) = \dfrac{-1}{x^2+6x+9}$

102. $k(x) = \dfrac{1}{2x^2-7x+3}$

Solve.

103. $\dfrac{x^2+5x+4}{x^2-6x-7} \le 0$

104. $\dfrac{x^2-7x+12}{x^2-11x+30} \ge 0$

105. $\dfrac{3x}{x-1} > \dfrac{4x}{x-4}$

106. $\dfrac{x}{x+1} < \dfrac{2x}{x-2}$

Solve. Graph the solution.

107. $|x| > \dfrac{1}{x}$

108. $|x-2| > \dfrac{3}{x}$

109. Numbers Dividing 4 less than the square of a number by 2 more than the number gives a result of 12. Find the number.

110. Numbers Find the values of x in the numbers x, $x+1$, and $x+2$ such that the reciprocal of the smallest number equals the sum of the reciprocals of the other two.

111. Driving speeds Laura and Mariko arranged to meet in Kamloops at noon. Laura drove 300 km from Banff. Mariko drove 320 km from Prince George. They left home at the same time and both arrived in Kamloops on time. Laura drove 5 km/h slower than Mariko.
a) At what speed did each of them drive?
b) At what time did they leave home?

112. Fitness Jason ran 4 km/h faster than Gersh walked. Jason ran 15 km in the time Gersh took to walk 9 km. What were their speeds?

113. Mixtures A 250-g tin of mixed nuts contains 40% cashews, by mass. The mixed nuts are placed in a bowl. What mass of cashews must be added to make the contents of the bowl 60% cashews?

114. Commuting To get to work, Laurie drives 30 km to a train station, and then travels 45 km on the train. The average speed of the train is 25 km/h more than his average driving speed. If the trip takes a total of 1 h, find Laurie's average driving speed, to the nearest kilometre per hour.

115. River currents The speed of the current in a river was 5 km/h. A boat travelled 10 km upstream and 10 km downstream in a total of 6 h. What was the speed of the boat in still water, to the nearest tenth of a kilometre per hour?

116. Measurement The base area, B, of a rectangular prism is its volume divided by its height. For one prism, $B = \dfrac{x^3+6x^2+11x+6}{x+3}$. If B measures 12 square units, what is the value of x?

117. Decide whether each of the following functions is a rational function. Explain your reasoning.

a) $f(x) = \dfrac{\sqrt{x+3}}{x}$

b) $g(x) = \dfrac{x+\sqrt{3}}{x}$

118. Electric circuit Electric resistance is measured in ohms, symbol Ω. In the electrical circuit shown, two resistors, R_1 and R_2, are connected in parallel. The equivalent resistance, R ohms, of the two resistors, is given by the equation $\dfrac{1}{R} = \dfrac{1}{R_1} + \dfrac{1}{R_2}$.

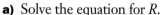

a) Solve the equation for R.
b) Solve the equation for R_1.
c) Solve the equation for R_2.
d) If R is 8 Ω and R_1 is 12 Ω, find R_2.

119. Numbers The sum of a number and twice its reciprocal is 3. What is the number?

120. Compare the graphs of the functions $y = \dfrac{x}{x^2-1}$ and $y = \dfrac{x^2-1}{x}$, considering the domain, range, symmetry, zeros, and asymptotes.

121. Solve.

a) $\dfrac{x+1}{x} = \dfrac{x-1}{2x} - \dfrac{1}{x+2}$

b) $x+4 = \dfrac{6-x}{x^2}$

c) $\dfrac{1}{x^2} = \dfrac{x^2}{5x^2-4}$

122. Solve $\dfrac{1}{x} + \dfrac{1}{y} = z$ for x.

123. Solve $\dfrac{x-c}{x-d} = \dfrac{d-x}{c-x}$ for x.

124. Technology Some graphing calculators can be used to graph the solution to a rational inequality directly.
a) Solve the rational inequality $\dfrac{x+1}{x-3} < 0$ algebraically and graph the solution manually.
b) Enter the inequality into your graphing calculator as follows.
$$Y_1 = (X + 1)/(X - 3) < 0$$
With the calculator in the dot mode, graph Y_1 in the standard viewing window.
c) Does your calculator graph the correct solution on the number line $y = 1$?
d) How can you decide whether the endpoints of the graph are included in the solution?

125. Technology If possible, use the graphing calculator method from question 124 to solve each of the following.
a) $\dfrac{x-2}{x+4} \geq 0$

b) $\dfrac{x-4}{x^2 - 3x + 2} \leq 0$

c) $\dfrac{x^2 - 6x + 8}{x^2 + x - 2} > 0$

d) $\dfrac{4x}{2x - 1} < 1 - x$

e) $\dfrac{3x}{x+1} \geq \dfrac{x+2}{x}$

126. Doppler effect The sound produced by a moving object, such as the siren on a fire truck, changes as the source moves toward you or away from you. This is an example of the Doppler effect. The frequency of the sound that you hear, f hertz, is given by the following function.
$$f = \dfrac{f_s}{1 \pm \dfrac{u}{v}}$$
where f_s hertz is the frequency of the source sound, v metres per second is the speed of the source sound in air, and u metres per second is the speed at which the source is moving.

a) Suppose the speed of the source sound in air is approximately 343 m/s, and the source sound is a fire-truck siren with a frequency of 310 Hz. Substitute these values and simplify the function.
b) Why does the function have the $\pm$ sign?
c) You are standing on a street corner as the fire truck travels down the street at a speed of 14 m/s. What siren frequency do you hear, to the nearest hertz, as the fire truck approaches the corner? leaves the corner? Explain your reasoning.

127. a) Graph the function
$$f(x) = \dfrac{x^3 + 6x^2 + 11x + 6}{(x+1)(x+2)}.$$

b) If $g(x) = x + 3$, how does its graph differ from the graph of $f(x)$?

128. If $\dfrac{m}{2x+1} - \dfrac{n}{3x-2} = \dfrac{4x-5}{6x^2 - x - 2}$, find the values of m and n.

129. Write an equation of a rational function whose domain is all the real numbers except 2 and whose range is all the real numbers except -5.

LOGIC POWER

Six students—Alicia, Brenda, Corinne, Derek, Erik, and Felipe—each answered all six questions on a test. There were two multiple-choice questions, with choices A, B, C, or D, and four true or false (T or F) questions. The students answered the questions as follows.

Alicia	D	D	F	T	F	T
Brenda	C	C	F	T	F	F
Corinne	A	A	T	T	T	T
Derek	B	B	F	F	F	T
Erik	B	C	T	F	T	F
Felipe	D	A	F	F	T	T

If no two students got the same number of correct answers, did any student get six correct answers?

Exploring Rational Functions With a Graphing Calculator

Graphing calculators are useful for analyzing complex rational functions. When graphing these functions, make sure that all the important features of the graph are shown, including the end behaviour. The end behaviour of some functions may indicate whether there are horizontal asymptotes.

Some calculators in the connected mode will draw a line connecting the separate parts of the graph. This can be avoided by using the dot mode. The graphs of $y = \dfrac{2}{x-4}$ show the effect of changing the mode.

Connected Mode   *Dot Mode*

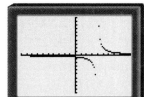

Note that displaying appropriate tables of values for very large absolute values of x can help you to find horizontal asymptotes. The table of values shown represents $y = \dfrac{2}{x-4}$ for large absolute values of x.

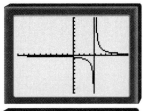

1 Exploring Rational Functions

Graph each of the following functions with a graphing calculator. Sketch the graph in your notebook, and indicate any asymptotes or point discontinuity. Determine the domain, range, and any real zeros. Describe any symmetry.

1. $y = \dfrac{x^2}{x^2 - 4}$ **2.** $y = \dfrac{x^2 - 4}{x^2}$ **3.** $y = \dfrac{x^2}{x^2 + 2x + 1}$ **4.** $y = \dfrac{x^2}{x^2 + 1}$

5. $y = \dfrac{x^2 + 2}{x^2}$ **6.** $y = \dfrac{x^2}{x^2 - 9}$ **7.** $y = \dfrac{x^2 - 1}{x^2}$ **8.** $y = \dfrac{x^2 + 1}{x^2 - 1}$

9. $y = \dfrac{x^2 - 1}{x^2 + 1}$ **10.** $y = \dfrac{x^2 + 4x + 4}{x^2}$ **11.** $y = \dfrac{x^2 - 4}{(x - 1)^2}$ **12.** $y = \dfrac{x^2}{x^2 - 4x + 3}$

13. How is the graph of $y = \dfrac{x^2 - 1}{x^2 - 1}$ different from the graph of $y = 1$? Explain.

2 Exploring Transformations of Rational Functions

1. Graph each of the following.

a) $y = \dfrac{x^2}{x^2 - 16}$ **b)** $y = \dfrac{x^2}{x^2 - 16} + 2$ **c)** $y = \dfrac{x^2}{x^2 - 16} - 4$

2. What effect does adding or subtracting a constant to $y = \dfrac{x^2}{x^2 - 16}$ have on the graph?

3. Graph each of the following.

a) $y = \dfrac{-x^2}{x^2 - 16}$ **b)** $y = \dfrac{-x^2}{x^2 - 16} + 2$ **c)** $y = \dfrac{-x^2}{x^2 - 16} - 4$

4. Describe the transformation that relates the graphs from
a) questions 1a) and 3a)   **b)** questions 1b) and 3b)   **c)** questions 1c) and 3c)

5.7 Radical Functions, Equations, and Inequalities

If a force is suddenly applied to a water surface, waves are generated. A pebble dropped into a puddle sends out waves in concentric circles. In the ocean, the same effect can be produced on a much larger scale by an earthquake, a volcanic eruption, or a landslide. The waves leaving such an event contain huge amounts of energy and move at a high speed. They are called tsunami waves.

Explore: Draw a Graph

The speed of a tsunami wave is a function of the depth of the water. The speed can be modelled by the function
$$s = 3\sqrt{d}$$
where s is the speed of the wave, in metres per second, and d is the depth of the water, in metres. Graph the function.

Inquire

1. What is the domain of the function? Explain.
2. What is the range? Explain.
3. In 100-m deep water, what is the speed of a tsunami wave
a) in metres per second?
b) in kilometres per hour?
4. The average depth of the Pacific Basin is 4600 m. What is the speed of a tsunami wave in this depth of water
a) to the nearest metre per second?
b) to the nearest kilometre per hour?

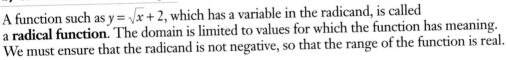

A function such as $y = \sqrt{x} + 2$, which has a variable in the radicand, is called a **radical function**. The domain is limited to values for which the function has meaning. We must ensure that the radicand is not negative, so that the range of the function is real.

Example 1 Graphing a Radical Function
Graph each function and determine the domain and range.
a) $y = \sqrt{x+1}$ b) $y = -\sqrt{x-1}$

Solution
Graph each function manually or using a graphing calculator.
If you graph manually, use convenient values of x in the table of values.

a)

x	y
−1	0
0	1
3	2
8	3
15	4

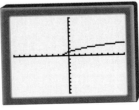

Since the radicand must not be negative, the domain is $x \geq -1$.
The range is $y \geq 0$.

b)

x	y
1	0
2	−1
5	−2
10	−3
17	−4

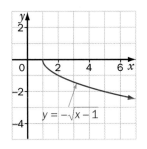

$y = -\sqrt{x-1}$

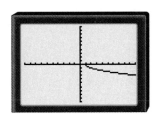

The domain is $x \geq 1$, and the range is $y \leq 0$.

An equation such as $\sqrt{x+1}+2=4$, in which a variable appears in the radicand, is called a **radical equation**. The algebraic solution of radical equations is based on the fact that, if two real numbers are equal, their squares are equal.

For example,
since $\sqrt{4} = 2$
then $(\sqrt{4})^2 = 2^2$
and $\quad 4 = 4$

The converse statement is that, if the squares of two real numbers are equal, the numbers are equal. This converse is not necessarily true. For example, $(-4)^2 = (4)^2$, but $-4 \neq 4$.

Example 2   Solving a Radical Equation

Solve and check $\sqrt{x+1}+3=5$.

Solution 1   Solving Algebraically

$$\sqrt{x+1}+3=5$$

Isolate the radical: $\quad \sqrt{x+1} = 2$

Square both sides: $\quad (\sqrt{x+1})^2 = 2^2$
Simplify: $\qquad\qquad\quad x+1 = 4$
$$x = 3$$

Solution 2   Solving Graphically

Graph the functions $y = \sqrt{x+1}+3$ and $y = 5$.

Find the x-coordinate of the point of intersection.

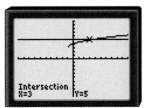

The graphs intersect at $(3, 5)$.
The x-coordinate of the point of intersection is 3.

Check.
L.S. $= \sqrt{x+1}+3$ $\quad$ **R.S.** $= 5$
$\quad = \sqrt{3+1}+3$
$\quad = \sqrt{4}+3$
$\quad = 5$

The solution is $x = 3$.

Example 3 Extraneous Solution

Solve $x = \sqrt{x + 10} + 2$.

Solution 1 Solving Algebraically

$$x = \sqrt{x + 10} + 2$$

Isolate the radical: $x - 2 = \sqrt{x + 10}$

Square both sides: $(x - 2)^2 = (\sqrt{x + 10})^2$

$$x^2 - 4x + 4 = x + 10$$

Simplify: $x^2 - 5x - 6 = 0$

Factor the left side: $(x - 6)(x + 1) = 0$

$$x - 6 = 0 \ \text{ or } \ x + 1 = 0$$

$$x = 6 \quad \text{ or } \quad x = -1$$

Solution 2 Solving Graphically

Graph the functions
$y = \sqrt{x + 10} + 2$ and $y = x$.
Find the x-coordinate of the
point of intersection.

The graphs intersect at $(6, 6)$.
The x-coordinate of the
point of intersection is 6.

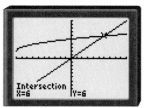

Check both values for Solution 1. For Solution 2, the only value to check is $x = 6$.
The solution $x = -1$ does not check, so it is an extraneous solution.
The solution is $x = 6$.

Note that extraneous solutions are sometimes introduced when both sides of an equation are squared.
For example, the equation $x = 3$ has one solution, 3.
Squaring both sides of the equation gives $x^2 = 9$.
The equation $x^2 = 9$ has two solutions, 3 and -3.
However, -3 is not a solution to the original equation.
Squaring both sides of $x = 3$ introduces an extraneous solution to $x = 3$, namely -3.
Note that, when the equation in Example 3 is solved algebraically, an extraneous solution is introduced.
Solving the same equation graphically does not introduce an extraneous solution.

Example 4 Equations With Two Radicals

Solve $\sqrt{4x + 5} - \sqrt{2x - 1} = 2$.

Solution 1 Solving Algebraically

$$\sqrt{4x + 5} - \sqrt{2x - 1} = 2$$

Isolate the radical $\sqrt{4x + 5}$: $\sqrt{4x + 5} = \sqrt{2x - 1} + 2$

Square both sides: $\left(\sqrt{4x + 5}\right)^2 = \left(\sqrt{2x - 1} + 2\right)^2$

$$\left(\sqrt{4x + 5}\right)^2 = \left(\sqrt{2x - 1} + 2\right)\left(\sqrt{2x - 1} + 2\right)$$

$$4x + 5 = 2x - 1 + 4\sqrt{2x - 1} + 4$$

Isolate the radical $4\sqrt{2x - 1}$: $2x + 2 = 4\sqrt{2x - 1}$

Divide both sides by 2: $x + 1 = 2\sqrt{2x - 1}$

Square both sides: $(x + 1)^2 = \left(2\sqrt{2x - 1}\right)^2$

$$(x + 1)^2 = 4(2x - 1)$$

Expand: $x^2 + 2x + 1 = 8x - 4$

Simplify: $x^2 - 6x + 5 = 0$

Factor: $(x - 5)(x - 1) = 0$

$$x - 5 = 0 \ \text{ or } \ x - 1 = 0$$

$$x = 5 \quad \text{ or } \quad x = 1$$

Solution 2   Solving Graphically

Graph the functions $y = \sqrt{4x+5} - \sqrt{2x-1}$ and $y = 2$.

If you use a graphing calculator, adjust the window variables to show the points of intersection.

Find the x-coordinates of the points of intersection.

The x-coordinates of the points of intersection are 1 and 5.

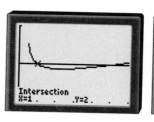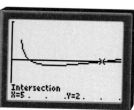

Check for Solution 1 and Solution 2.

For $x = 5$,

L.S. $= \sqrt{4x+5} - \sqrt{2x-1}$	**R.S.** $= 2$
$= \sqrt{4(5)+5} - \sqrt{2(5)-1}$	
$= \sqrt{25} - \sqrt{9}$	
$= 2$	

For $x = 1$,

L.S. $= \sqrt{4x+5} - \sqrt{2x-1}$	**R.S.** $= 2$
$= \sqrt{4(1)+5} - \sqrt{2(1)-1}$	
$= \sqrt{9} - \sqrt{1}$	
$= 2$	

The solutions are 5 and 1.

Example 5   Approximate Solutions

Find the roots of $\sqrt{x+9} = 1 + \sqrt{2-x}$, to the nearest tenth.

Solution 1   Solving Algebraically

$$\sqrt{x+9} = 1 + \sqrt{2-x}$$

Square both sides:

$$\left(\sqrt{x+9}\right)^2 = \left(1 + \sqrt{2-x}\right)^2$$

$$x + 9 = 1 + 2\sqrt{2-x} + 2 - x$$

Isolate the radical: $2x + 6 = 2\sqrt{2-x}$

Divide both sides by 2: $x + 3 = \sqrt{2-x}$

Square both sides: $x^2 + 6x + 9 = 2 - x$

Simplify: $x^2 + 7x + 7 = 0$

The left side does not factor.

Use the quadratic formula:

$$x = \frac{-b \pm \sqrt{b^2 - 4ac}}{2a}$$

$$= \frac{-7 \pm \sqrt{7^2 - 4(1)(7)}}{2(1)}$$

$$= \frac{-7 \pm \sqrt{21}}{2}$$

$$x \doteq -1.2 \text{ or } -5.8$$

Estimate

$\sqrt{21} \doteq 5$ $\dfrac{-7+5}{2} = -1$ $\dfrac{-7-5}{2} = -6$

Solution 2   Solving Graphically

Graph the functions $y = \sqrt{x+9}$ and $y = 1 + \sqrt{2-x}$.

Find the x-coordinate of the point of intersection.

The x-coordinate of the point of intersection is -1.2, to the nearest tenth.

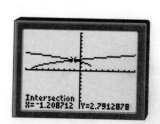

Check both values for Solution 1. For Solution 2, the only value to check is $x \doteq -1.2$.

For $x \doteq -1.2$,

L.S. $= \sqrt{x+9}$	R.S. $= 1 + \sqrt{2-x}$
$\doteq \sqrt{-1.2+9}$	$\doteq 1 + \sqrt{2-(-1.2)}$
$\doteq \sqrt{7.8}$	$\doteq 1 + \sqrt{3.2}$
$\doteq 2.8$	$\doteq 1 + 1.8$
	$\doteq 2.8$

For $x \doteq -5.8$,

L.S. $= \sqrt{x+9}$	R.S. $= 1 + \sqrt{2-x}$
$\doteq \sqrt{-5.8+9}$	$\doteq 1 + \sqrt{2-(-5.8)}$
$\doteq \sqrt{3.2}$	$\doteq 1 + \sqrt{7.8}$
$\doteq 1.8$	$\doteq 1 + 2.8$
	$\doteq 3.8$

The solution $x \doteq -5.8$ does not check. It is an extraneous solution.
The solution is $x \doteq -1.2$, to the nearest tenth.

Example 6   Tsunami Waves

The speed of a tsunami wave in the ocean is related to the depth of the water by the equation

$$s = 3\sqrt{d}$$

where s is the speed of the wave, in metres per second, and d is the depth of the water, in metres. What is the depth of the water, to the nearest metre, if the speed of a tsunami wave is 10 m/s?

Solution 1   Using Substitution

$$s = 3\sqrt{d}$$

Substitute for s: $\qquad 10 = 3\sqrt{d}$

Divide both sides by 3: $\qquad \dfrac{10}{3} = \sqrt{d}$

Square both sides: $\qquad \dfrac{100}{9} = d$

Evaluate d: $\qquad 11 \doteq d$

Estimate

$100 \div 10 = 10$

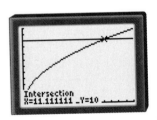

Solution 2   Solving Graphically

Graph $y = 3\sqrt{d}$ and $y = 10$ manually or graph $y = 3\sqrt{x}$ and $y = 10$ using a graphing calculator.

If you use a graphing calculator, adjust the window variables to show the point of intersection. Find the x-coordinate of the point of intersection. The x-coordinate of the point of intersection is 11, to the nearest whole number.

If the speed of a tsunami wave is 10 m/s, the depth of the water is 11 m, to the nearest metre.

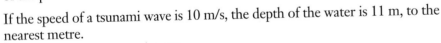

An inequality in which a variable appears in the radicand is called a **radical inequality**. A radical inequality can be solved in ways that are similar to the ways used with radical equations. However, squaring both sides of some inequalities introduces false statements. For example, $-3 < 1$, but it is not true that $(-3)^2 < 1^2$, since $(-3)^2 = 9$ and $1^2 = 1$. It is important to check the algebraic solutions to radical inequalities to make sure that no solutions are extraneous.

Example 7   Solving a Radical Inequality

Solve $\sqrt{x-1} - \sqrt{5-x} > 0$.

Solution 1   Solving Algebraically

$$\sqrt{x-1}-\sqrt{5-x}>0$$

Isolate the radicals: $\qquad\qquad \sqrt{x-1}>\sqrt{5-x}$

Square both sides: $\qquad\qquad x-1>5-x$

Simplify: $\qquad\qquad\qquad\quad 2x>6$

Divide both sides by 2: $\qquad\quad x>3$

Check that 3 is a root of the corresponding equation $\sqrt{x-1}-\sqrt{5-x}=0$.

L.S. $=\sqrt{x-1}-\sqrt{5-x}$ **R.S.** $=0$

$\qquad =\sqrt{3-1}-\sqrt{5-3}$

$\qquad =0$

So, 3 is a real solution of the corresponding equation and is not an extraneous solution. It can be used to decide the test intervals. Because the radicands cannot be negative, the restrictions on the variable in the original inequality are $x\geq 1$ and $x\leq 5$. So, the test intervals are $1\leq x<3$ and $3<x\leq 5$.

```
                    ┊1 ≤ x < 3┊3 < x ≤ 5┊
   ◄─┼──┼──┼──┼──┼──┼──┼──┼──┼──┼──┼──►
    -3  -2  -1   0   1   2   3   4   5   6   7
```

Choose a number in each test interval and test it in the original inequality $\sqrt{x-1}-\sqrt{5-x}>0$.

In the test interval $1\leq x<3$, use the point $x=2$.

L.S. $=\sqrt{x-1}-\sqrt{5-x}$ **R.S.** $=0$

$\qquad =\sqrt{2-1}-\sqrt{5-2}$

$\qquad \doteq -0.7$

The left side is not greater than the right side, so the original inequality is not satisfied in this interval.

In the test interval $3<x\leq 5$, use the point $x=4$.

L.S. $=\sqrt{x-1}-\sqrt{5-x}$ **R.S.** $=0$

$\qquad =\sqrt{4-1}-\sqrt{5-4}$

$\qquad \doteq 0.7$

The left side is greater than the right side, so the original inequality is satisfied in this interval.

Solution 2   Solving Graphically

Graph the function $y=\sqrt{x-1}-\sqrt{5-x}$.

Find the values of x for which the graph of $y=\sqrt{x-1}-\sqrt{5-x}$ is above the x-axis.

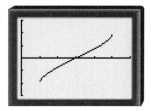

The graph crosses the x-axis at $x=3$.

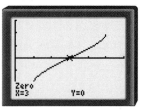

Displaying a table of values or using the Value operation shows that the maximum value of x for a point on the graph is 5.

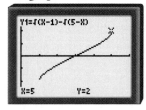

The graph is above the x-axis when $3<x\leq 5$.

So, the solution is $3<x\leq 5$.

It was shown in the check for an extraneous root that $x=3$ satisfies the equation $\sqrt{x-1}-\sqrt{5-x}=0$. So, $x=3$ does not satisfy the inequality $\sqrt{x-1}-\sqrt{5-x}>0$.

The solution is $3<x\leq 5$.

The solution to Example 7 can be graphed on a number line.

Example 8   Extraneous Roots

Solve $x \geq \sqrt{x-2} + 4$.

Solution 1   Using Test Intervals

$$x \geq \sqrt{x-2} + 4$$

Isolate the radical: $\qquad x - 4 \geq \sqrt{x-2}$

Square both sides: $\qquad x^2 - 8x + 16 \geq x - 2$

Simplify: $\qquad x^2 - 9x + 18 \geq 0$

Factor the left side: $\qquad (x-3)(x-6) \geq 0$

The corresponding radical equation, $x = \sqrt{x-2} + 4$, is equivalent to the equation $(x-3)(x-6) = 0$, which has the roots $x = 3$ and $x = 6$.

Check whether the roots are extraneous before deciding the test intervals.

For $x = 3$,

L.S. $= x$ **R.S.** $= \sqrt{x-2} + 4$
$\quad = 3 \qquad\qquad = \sqrt{3-2} + 4$
$\qquad\qquad\qquad\quad = 5$

For $x = 6$,

L.S. $= x$ **R.S.** $= \sqrt{x-2} + 4$
$\quad = 6 \qquad\qquad = \sqrt{6-2} + 4$
$\qquad\qquad\qquad\quad = \sqrt{4} + 4$
$\qquad\qquad\qquad\quad = 6$

The solution $x = 3$ is extraneous and is rejected.

So, the solution $x = 6$ is used to determine the test intervals.

Because the radicand cannot be negative in the original inequality, the variable is restricted to $x \geq 2$.

There are two test intervals, $2 \leq x < 6$ and $x > 6$.

Choose a number in each test interval and test it in the original inequality, $x \geq \sqrt{x-2} + 4$.

In the test interval $2 \leq x < 6$, use the point $x = 3$.

L.S. $= x$ **R.S.** $= \sqrt{x-2} + 4$
$\quad = 3 \qquad\qquad = \sqrt{3-2} + 4$
$\qquad\qquad\qquad\quad = 5$

The left side is not greater than or equal to the right side, so the original inequality is not satisfied in this interval.

In the test interval $x > 6$, use the point $x = 11$.

L.S. $= x$ **R.S.** $= \sqrt{x-2} + 4$
$\quad = 11 \qquad\qquad = \sqrt{11-2} + 4$
$\qquad\qquad\qquad\quad = 7$

The left side is greater than or equal to the right side, so the original inequality is satisfied in this interval.

As shown in the above check for extraneous roots, $x = 6$ satisfies the equation $x = \sqrt{x-2} + 4$.

Therefore, $x = 6$ also satisfies the inequality $x \geq \sqrt{x-2} + 4$. So, $x \geq \sqrt{x-2} + 4$ is true for $x = 6$ or $x > 6$. The solution is $x \geq 6$.

Solution 2   Solving Graphically

Graph the functions $y = x$ and $y = \sqrt{x-2} + 4$.

Find the values of x for which the graph of $y = x$ is on or above the graph of $y = \sqrt{x-2} + 4$.
The graphs intersect when $x = 6$.

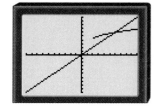 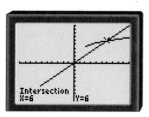

The graph of $y = x$ is on or above the graph of $y = \sqrt{x-2} + 4$ when $x \geq 6$.

The solution is $x \geq 6$.

The solution to Example 8 can be graphed on a number line.

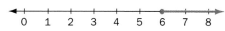

Example 9   Radical Inequalities Including Rational Expressions

Solve $\sqrt{x-2} < \dfrac{x}{x-3}$.

Solution 1   Using Test Intervals

$$\sqrt{x-2} < \frac{x}{x-3}$$

Case I: If $x > 3$, $x - 3 > 0$

Multiply both sides by $x - 3$: $\quad (x-3) \times \sqrt{x-2} < (x-3) \times \dfrac{x}{x-3}$

Simplify: $\qquad\qquad\qquad\qquad (x-3)\sqrt{x-2} < x$

Square both sides: $\qquad\qquad\quad (x-3)^2(x-2) < x^2$

Simplify: $\qquad\qquad\qquad\quad (x^2 - 6x + 9)(x-2) < x^2$

$$x^3 - 8x^2 + 21x - 18 < x^2$$
$$x^3 - 9x^2 + 21x - 18 < 0$$

Case II: If $x < 3$, $x - 3 < 0$
$$(x-3)\sqrt{x-2} > x$$

Then using the same steps as in case I,
$$(x-6)(x^2 - 3x + 3) > 0$$
$$\therefore x > 6$$

But $x < 3$ and $x > 6$ has no intersection, so this case yields no solution.

Use the integral zero theorem to find a factor of $x^3 - 9x^2 + 21x - 18$.
$$f(6) = 6^3 - 9(6)^2 + 21(6) - 18$$
$$= 0$$

So, $x - 6$ is a factor.
Use synthetic division to find another factor.

```
6 |  1   -9   21   -18
  |       6  -18    18
  ----------------------
     1   -3    3     0
```

Another factor is $x^2 - 3x + 3$, which cannot be factored further.
So, $x^3 - 9x^2 + 21x - 18 = (x-6)(x^2 - 3x + 3)$.

Check that $x = 6$ is a root of $\sqrt{x-2} = \dfrac{x}{x-3}$.

Since the discriminant is negative, the roots of the equation $x^2 - 3x + 3 = 0$ are imaginary.

Because both sides were squared in a previous step, check whether the root is extraneous.

L.S. $= \sqrt{x-2}$ R.S. $= \dfrac{x}{x-3}$
$\quad = \sqrt{6-2}$ $\qquad = \dfrac{6}{6-3}$
$\quad = 2$ $\qquad\qquad = 2$

So, $x = 6$ is not an extraneous root. It can be used to decide the test intervals.

Also, $\sqrt{x-2}$ is defined for $x \geq 2$, and $\dfrac{x}{x-3}$ is not defined at $x = 3$.

The three test intervals are $2 \leq x < 3$, $3 < x < 6$, and $x > 6$.

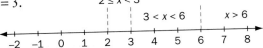

Choose a number in each test interval and test it in the original inequality $\sqrt{x-2} < \dfrac{x}{x-3}$.

In the test interval $2 \leq x < 3$, use the point $x = 2.5$.

$$\textbf{L.S.} = \sqrt{x-2} \qquad \textbf{R.S.} = \dfrac{x}{x-3}$$
$$= \sqrt{2.5-2} \qquad\qquad = \dfrac{2.5}{2.5-3}$$
$$\doteq 0.7 \qquad\qquad\qquad = -5$$

The left side is not less than the right side, so the original inequality is not satisfied in this interval.

In the test interval $3 < x < 6$, use the point $x = 4$.

$$\textbf{L.S.} = \sqrt{4-2} \qquad \textbf{R.S.} = \dfrac{4}{4-3}$$
$$\doteq 1.4 \qquad\qquad\qquad = 4$$

The left side is less than the right side, so the original inequality is satisfied in this interval.

In the test interval $x > 6$, use the point $x = 7$.

$$\textbf{L.S.} = \sqrt{7-2} \qquad \textbf{R.S.} = \dfrac{7}{7-3}$$
$$= \sqrt{5} \qquad\qquad\qquad = \dfrac{7}{4}$$
$$\doteq 2.2$$

The left side is not less than the right side, so the original inequality is not satisfied in this interval.

It was shown in the check for an extraneous root that $x = 6$ satisfies the equation $\sqrt{x-2} = \dfrac{x}{x-3}$.

So, $x = 6$ does not satisfy the inequality $\sqrt{x-2} < \dfrac{x}{x-3}$. The inequality is not defined when $x = 3$.

The solution is $3 < x < 6$.

Solution 2   Solving Graphically

Graph $y = \sqrt{x-2}$ and $y = \dfrac{x}{x-3}$ on the same axes or in the same viewing window.

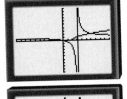

Find the values of x for which the graph of $y = \sqrt{x-2}$ is below the graph of $y = \dfrac{x}{x-3}$.

The graph of $y = \sqrt{x-2}$ is below the graph of $y = \dfrac{x}{x-3}$ between the asymptote at $x = 3$ and the point of intersection of the two graphs.
At the point of intersection, $x = 6$.
So, the solution is $3 < x < 6$.

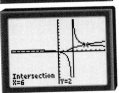

The solution to Example 9 can be graphed on a number line.

Practice

Graph each function and determine the domain and range.

1. $y = \sqrt{x+2}$

2. $y = \sqrt{3-x}$

3. $y = \sqrt{2x+1}$

4. $y = \sqrt{3-2x}$

5. $y = \sqrt{0.5x+4}$

6. $y = \sqrt{2x}$

7. $y = \sqrt{3(x-1)}$

8. $y = \sqrt{-0.5(x+1)}$

9. $y = -\sqrt{x+3}$

10. $y = -\sqrt{2-x}$

Graph each function and determine the domain and range.

11. $y = \sqrt{x+3}+1$

12. $y = \sqrt{x+1}-5$

13. $y = \sqrt{x-4}-2$

14. $y = \sqrt{2-x}-3$

15. $y = \sqrt{3x}-4$

16. $y = \sqrt{2x+5}+2$

17. $y = \sqrt{2(1-x)}+3$

18. $y = -\sqrt{x+2}+2$

19. $y = -\sqrt{5-x}+1$

20. $y = -\sqrt{2x}-3$

21. $y = -\sqrt{2x-1}-1$

22. $y = -\sqrt{\dfrac{1}{2}(x-2)}+5$

Solve and check.

23. $\sqrt{x} = 5$

24. $\sqrt{x}-2 = 0$

25. $\sqrt{x+3} = 0$

26. $\sqrt{y+1} = 2$

27. $\sqrt{3-m} = 4$

28. $\sqrt{1-x}+2 = 0$

29. $\sqrt{2x+1} = 3$

30. $\sqrt{4-3x}-2 = 0$

31. $\sqrt{x-3}+6 = 2$

32. $\sqrt{\dfrac{z}{3}}+1+2 = 4$

33. $\sqrt{4(x+3)} = 6$

34. $\sqrt{0.5(3x-2)}+2 = 1$

35. $2\sqrt{x-1}-2 = 8$

36. $-3\sqrt{x+2}+4 = 1$

Solve and check.

37. $\sqrt{x+1} = \sqrt{x+7}$

38. $\sqrt{2-x} = \sqrt{x-2}$

39. $\sqrt{2x-5} = \sqrt{x+2}$

40. $\sqrt{a+6}-\sqrt{3-2a} = 0$

41. $\sqrt{\dfrac{x}{2}+8} = \sqrt{4x+1}$

42. $\sqrt{4(p+1)} = \sqrt{2p+3}$

43. $\sqrt{3+w} = 2\sqrt{w-3}$

44. $\sqrt{y+3}-3\sqrt{y-1} = 0$

Solve.

45. $\sqrt{x-5} = 9-\sqrt{x+4}$

46. $\sqrt{x+2}-\sqrt{x+5} = 3$

47. $\sqrt{y-4}+1 = \sqrt{y+1}$

48. $\sqrt{x}-\sqrt{x-5} = 5$

49. $\sqrt{d}-2 = \sqrt{d-16}$

50. $\sqrt{3x-5}-\sqrt{3x} = -1$

Solve.

51. $x-\sqrt{x+2} = 0$

52. $\sqrt{r+4}+8 = r$

53. $3 = \sqrt{x+3}+\sqrt{x}$

54. $\sqrt{x-1}+3-x = 0$

55. $\sqrt{4+2x} = 1-\sqrt{3+x}$

56. $\sqrt{2-n}+2 = 1+\sqrt{3+n}$

57. $\sqrt{3g-2}-1 = 2\sqrt{g}$

58. $\sqrt{x-5}-\sqrt{2x+7} = -3$

59. $\sqrt{3(v+1)} = \sqrt{v+2}+1$

Find the roots, to the nearest tenth.

60. $\sqrt{2x+1}-x = 0$

61. $\sqrt{m+3} = -m$

62. $2\sqrt{x+1}+x = 1$

63. $\sqrt{x-2} = x-3$

64. $\sqrt{k+1}+5 = 2k$

65. $x\sqrt{3}+4 = x$

66. $\sqrt{w+5} = \sqrt{3-w}+1$

67. $\sqrt{x^2-4} = 2x-10$

Solve. Graph the solution.

68. $\sqrt{x+1} < 3$

69. $\sqrt{2-x} \geq 2$

70. $\sqrt{2x+5} \leq 3$

71. $\sqrt{4-3x} \geq -2$

Solve. Graph the solution.

72. $\sqrt{x}-\sqrt{7-x} \leq 0$

73. $\sqrt{x+2}-\sqrt{4-x} > 0$

74. $\sqrt{n+3} \geq \sqrt{9-n}$

75. $\sqrt{t+2}-\sqrt{t-2} > 0$

76. $\sqrt{2y+1} \leq \sqrt{y-3}$

77. $\sqrt{2(x+1)}-\sqrt{2-x} \geq 0$

Solve.

78. $\sqrt{1-x}+3 \geq x$

79. $\sqrt{2(x+3)}+1 < x$

80. $\sqrt{-(1+2x)}-x > 2$

81. $d \leq \sqrt{2(3-d)}+3$

82. $\sqrt{2x-1}+2 > x$

83. $\sqrt{2x-1} < 3x-1$

84. $\sqrt{5-x}-\sqrt{x} < 1$

85. $\sqrt{c}+\sqrt{c+21} < 7$

86. $3+\sqrt{x-4} \geq \sqrt{x+11}$

87. $\sqrt{3u+1}-\sqrt{u-1} < 2$

Solve.

88. $\sqrt{x} \geq x$

89. $\sqrt{y} > \dfrac{y}{3}$

90. $\sqrt{x} \leq \dfrac{1}{x}$

91. $\sqrt{x} > \dfrac{4}{x-2}$

92. $\sqrt{n} \geq \dfrac{2}{n-3}$

93. $\dfrac{4}{x} > \sqrt{2x}$

94. $\sqrt{3x} < \dfrac{2}{2-x}$

95. $\sqrt{x+2} > \dfrac{x}{x+2}$

96. $\sqrt{x+2} < \dfrac{x}{x+2}$

97. $\sqrt{m+1} \geq \dfrac{m}{m+1}$

98. $\dfrac{1}{x+3} > \sqrt{x+3}$

99. $\sqrt{x+2} \leq \dfrac{1}{x+2}$

100. $\dfrac{1}{2-t} < \sqrt{t-2}$

101. $\sqrt{x-3} > \dfrac{x}{2-x}$

Applications and Problem Solving

102. Decide whether each of the following functions is a rational function or a radical function. Explain your reasoning.

a) $y = \dfrac{2x^2}{x-1}$

b) $y = \dfrac{2(x-1)}{x^2}$

c) $y = \sqrt{2x^3}$

d) $y = \dfrac{\sqrt{2x^3}}{x+3}$

e) $y = \dfrac{\sqrt{x}+x^2}{2x^3-4}$

f) $y = \dfrac{x^2-\sqrt{3}}{2x^3+4}$

103. Solve graphically, to the nearest tenth.

a) $\sqrt{3-x} > \sqrt{x+2}-2$

b) $\sqrt{1-2x}+x < -3$

c) $\sqrt{2x-1}+\sqrt{x+1} \geq 5$

d) $\sqrt{x+3}-\sqrt{2(x+4)} \leq -2$

104. Graph each function and determine the domain and range.

a) $y = \sqrt{x^2-4}$

b) $y = -\sqrt{x^2-4}$

c) $y = \sqrt{9-x^2}$

d) $y = -\sqrt{9-x^2}$

105. Solve.

a) $\sqrt{6+\sqrt{x}} = 3$

b) $\sqrt{x+\sqrt{x+3}} = 3$

c) $\sqrt{x+\sqrt{x-2}} = 2$

106. Graph $y = \sqrt{x}$ and $y = -\sqrt{x}$ on the same axes. How are the graphs the same? How are they different?

107. Baseballs and tennis balls The radius, r, of a sphere is related to the surface area, A, by the equation $r = \dfrac{1}{2}\sqrt{\dfrac{A}{\pi}}$.

a) The surface area of a baseball is about 172 cm^2. Find the radius of a baseball, to the nearest tenth of a centimetre.

b) The radius of a tennis ball is about 3.3 cm. Find the surface area, to the nearest square centimetre.

108. Find the inverse of each of the following radical functions. Are the inverses also functions? Explain.

a) $y = \sqrt{x}$

b) $y = \sqrt{x+2}$

c) $y = \sqrt{x-1}+2$

109. Solve algebraically.

a) $\sqrt{x+2} = \sqrt{x}+\sqrt{2}$

b) $\sqrt{x-2} = \sqrt{x}-\sqrt{2}$

c) $\sqrt{2-x} = \sqrt{2}-\sqrt{x}$

110. Coordinate geometry Two vertices of a rectangle ABCD are A(2, 1) and B(7, 1). The length of each diagonal is 13 units. What are the coordinates of C and D?

111. Coordinate geometry In isosceles triangle ABC, AC = BC. The coordinates of two vertices are A(−4, 3) and B(8, 3). The perimeter of the triangle is 32 units. Find the coordinates of point C.

112. Geometric mean The geometric mean of two numbers is the square root of their product. The geometric mean of 2 and 8 is $\sqrt{2 \times 8}$, which is $\sqrt{16}$ or 4.
a) Find the geometric mean of 9 and 16.
b) The geometric mean of 5 and another number is 15. Find the other number.

113. Coordinate geometry Given two points on the y-axis, A(0, −9) and B(0, 16), and a point P on the x-axis, such that PA + PB = 35, find the coordinates of P.

114. Coordinate geometry Given △PXY, with vertices X(−6, 0) and Y(15, 0), and with P on the y-axis such that PY is 7 units longer than PX, find the coordinates of P.

115. Transformations Graph $y = \sqrt{x}$ and each of the following pairs of functions on the same axes. Describe how the constants affect the position of the graph.
a) $y = \sqrt{x+5}$ and $y = \sqrt{x-5}$
b) $y = \sqrt{x}+3$ and $y = \sqrt{x}-3$
c) $y = \sqrt{x+5}+3$ and $y = \sqrt{x+5}-3$
d) $y = \sqrt{x-5}+3$ and $y = \sqrt{x-5}-3$

116. Transformations Using your results from question 115, describe how the effects of the constants on the graph of $y = \sqrt{x}$ compare with their effects on the graph of $y = x^2$. For example, compare the graphs of $y = \sqrt{x+5}$ and $y = (x+5)^2$, and compare the graphs of $y = \sqrt{x+5}+3$ and $y = (x+5)^2+3$.

117. The graphs of the following three radical functions intersect in a single point. Find the value of k algebraically.
$$y = \sqrt{3+x} \qquad y = \sqrt{4-2x} \qquad y = \sqrt{0.5x+k}$$

118. Numbers The square root of three less than a number is 12. What is the number?

119. Pendulum The period, P, of a pendulum is the time, in seconds, it takes to complete one back-and-forth swing. The period is related to the length of the pendulum by the equation $P = 0.2\sqrt{l}$, where l represents the length of the pendulum, in centimetres.
a) What is the period of a pendulum with a length of 25 cm?
b) What is the length, in metres, of a pendulum with a period of 4 s?

120. Numbers The square root of four less than a number is at least 5. Write and solve an inequality to find the possible values of the number, n.

121. Measurement a) Write an equation to express the area, A, of an equilateral triangle in terms of the side length, s.
b) Solve the equation for s.
c) For an equilateral triangle of area 250 cm², what is the side length, to the nearest centimetre?

122. Numbers The square root of two more than a number is at most 10. Write and solve an inequality to find the possible values of the number, n.

123. If $a^2 = b^2$, does a = b? Explain.

124. Explain why you should always check the solutions to a radical equation or a radical inequality.

125. Hot-air balloon A hot-air balloon has an altitude of 200 m. Let d metres represent the horizontal distance of the balloon from an observer, and L metres represent the straight-line distance from the observer to the balloon.
a) Write an equation to express d as a function of L.
b) What is the domain of the function?
c) Graph the function.
d) Find d(250) and interpret the result.

126. Car speeds The approximate speed of a car before it brakes suddenly and skids is a function of the length of the tire marks it leaves on the road. For a dry road, the equation of the function is
$$s(d) = 13\sqrt{d}$$
where d is the length of the tire marks, in metres, and $s(d)$ is the speed of the car, in kilometres per hour, before the brakes are applied.
a) Graph the function.
b) State a reasonable domain and range for the function.
c) If a car travelling at 100 km/h brakes suddenly and skids, what is the length of the tire marks, to the nearest metre?

127. Velocity of sound Near the surface of the Earth, the velocity of sound in air, V kilometres per hour, is approximately related to the temperature, T degrees Celsius, by the following equation.
$$V = 72\sqrt{T + 273}$$
a) Graph the function.
b) On the hottest day ever recorded in Canada, the air temperature reached 45°C at Midale and Yellowgrass, Saskatchewan. Find the velocity of sound in air at this temperature, to the nearest 10 km/h.
c) At what temperature, to the nearest degree Celsius, does sound have a velocity of 1200 km/h in air?

128. Viewing distance The distance you can see across the Earth's surface from an aircraft is a function of the altitude of the aircraft.

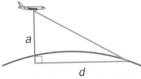

The equation of the function is $d(a) = \sqrt{10\ 000a - a^2}$, where a kilometres is the altitude, and d kilometres is the distance you can see across the Earth's surface.
a) Graph the function.
b) Give a reasonable domain and range for the function.
c) What distance, to the nearest kilometre, could you see from an aircraft flying at an altitude of 10 000 m?
d) What are the four largest cities or towns you could see if you were in an aircraft 10 000 m above your school?

129. Gravity The time, t seconds, an object takes to reach the ground when dropped from a height of h metres is given by the following equation.
$$t = \sqrt{\frac{h}{4.9}}$$
If an object takes 4 s to reach the ground, from what height was it dropped, to the nearest metre?

130. Solve.
a) $\sqrt{x+1} + \dfrac{2}{\sqrt{x+1}} = \sqrt{x+6}$

b) $\sqrt{x} + \sqrt{x-7} = \dfrac{21}{\sqrt{x-7}}$

131. Technology Some graphing calculators can be used to graph the solution to a radical inequality directly.
a) Solve the radical inequality $\sqrt{x-1} < 2$ algebraically and graph the solution manually.
b) Enter the inequality into your graphing calculator as follows.
$$Y_1 = \sqrt{(X-1)} < 2$$
With the calculator in the dot mode, graph Y_1 in the standard viewing window.
c) Does your calculator graph the correct solution on the number line $y = 1$?
d) How can you decide whether the endpoints of the graph are included in the solution?

132. Technology If possible, use the graphing calculator method from question 131 to solve each of the following.
a) $\sqrt{x+1} \geq 0$
b) $\sqrt{x-3} + \sqrt{x+2} \leq 5$
c) $2x - \sqrt{3x+3} < 1$
d) $-4x - 9 \geq \sqrt{3 - 2x}$
e) $\dfrac{5}{\sqrt{4x+5}} > 1$
f) $\sqrt{x} \leq x$
g) $\sqrt{5x} < \dfrac{1}{1-x}$
h) $\sqrt{x+4} \geq \dfrac{x}{x+4}$
i) $\sqrt{x+2} > \dfrac{x}{3-x}$

133. Paper folding A sheet of paper is folded so that the upper left corner touches a point on the bottom edge of the paper.

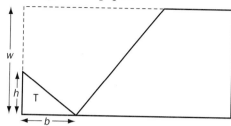

Label the triangle formed in the bottom left corner, T, the base of the triangle, b, the height of the triangle, h, and the width of the sheet of paper, w, as shown.

a) Write an equation that expresses b in terms of w and h.
b) Write an equation that expresses the area, A, of triangle T in terms of w and h.
c) If the width of the paper is 10 cm, write and simplify an equation that expresses the area, A, in terms of h.
d) Graph the function from part c).
e) Determine the domain and range of the function from part c).
f) What value of h, to the nearest tenth of a centimetre, gives the maximum area of triangle T?
g) What is the maximum area of triangle T, to the nearest tenth of a square centimetre?

134. Write a radical inequality with each of the following solutions.
a) $2 \le x < 11$ **b)** $-7 < x \le 2$

135. What is the domain of the function
$$y = \frac{\sqrt{x+2}}{x^2 - 2x + 1}?$$ Explain why.

136. Solve $\dfrac{1}{1-x} + \dfrac{1}{1+\sqrt{x}} = \dfrac{1}{1-\sqrt{x}}$.

137. Solve $\dfrac{3}{\sqrt{x+6}} = \dfrac{1}{\sqrt{x+6}} + \dfrac{1}{\sqrt{x-6}}$.

138. a) Suggest a way of factoring $x + 2\sqrt{x} + 1$.
b) Solve $x - 2\sqrt{x} + 1 = 0$ algebraically by first factoring the left side.
c) Solve $x - 5\sqrt{x} + 6 = 0$.
d) Solve $x - \sqrt{x} - 12 = 0$.
e) Solve $x + 6\sqrt{x} + 8 = 0$.

139. In the method used to solve a radical equation, both sides of the equation are squared to remove the radicals. Explain why radicals are isolated before both sides are squared.

140. Solve algebraically.
a) $\sqrt[3]{x+3} + 2 = 4$ **b)** $\sqrt[3]{2x-1} - 3 = -4$
c) $\sqrt[3]{x-2} > -1$ **d)** $\sqrt[3]{4-6x} - 1 \le 3$

141. Radicals that continue forever, such as $\sqrt{2 + \sqrt{2 + \sqrt{2 + \sqrt{2 + \ldots}}}}$, are called continued radicals.

a) Explain why $x = \sqrt{2 + \sqrt{2 + \sqrt{2 + \sqrt{2 + \ldots}}}}$ can be written as $x = \sqrt{2 + x}$.

b) Evaluate $\sqrt{2 + \sqrt{2 + \sqrt{2 + \sqrt{2 + \ldots}}}}$.

c) Evaluate $\sqrt{6 + \sqrt{6 + \sqrt{6 + \sqrt{6 + \ldots}}}}$.

d) Evaluate $\sqrt{12 - \sqrt{12 - \sqrt{12 - \sqrt{12 - \ldots}}}}$.

NUMBER POWER

Copy the diagram. Place one number in each circle so that the following conditions are met.
• Each number is a 2, 3, 4, 5, 6, 7, 8, 9, or 10.
• No two numbers are the same.
• The products of the three numbers that lie in a line are all the same.

CONNECTING MATH AND ASTRONOMY

Gravitational Forces

The weight of an object is the force of gravitational attraction acting on the object. For example, on the Earth, the weight of an object is the gravitational force of attraction between the object and the Earth.

Newton's law of gravitation states that the force of gravitational attraction, F newtons, between two objects is given by the formula

$$F = G\frac{m_1 m_2}{d^2}$$

where G is the gravitational constant, 6.673×10^{-11} N·m^2/kg^2, m_1 and m_2 are the masses of the objects, in kilograms, and d is the distance between the centres of the objects, in metres. The unit of force is the newton, with the symbol N. One newton equals 1 kg·m/s^2.

Weight and mass are often spoken of as if they are the same. In fact, they are different. Because the weight of an object is a gravitational force, the weight varies with the location of the object in the universe. For example, the same object has a lower weight on the moon than it does on the Earth. By contrast, the mass of an object is a measure of the quantity of matter in the object. Therefore, any object has the same mass on the moon as it has on the Earth. A mass is measured in grams or a multiple of grams, such as kilograms.

For an object on the surface of the Earth, the distance between the centre of the object and the centre of the Earth is approximately equal to the radius of the Earth, because the Earth is far larger than the object. The radius of the Earth is about 6370 km or 6.37×10^6 m.

1 The Earth and the Moon

1. The mass of the Earth is about 5.97×10^{24} kg. Calculate the weight of a 1-kg mass on the Earth's surface, to the nearest tenth of a newton.

2. Write an equation that relates the weight of any object on the Earth's surface, W newtons, to the mass of the object, m kilograms, in the form $W = \blacksquare m$, where $\blacksquare$ is a number.

3. What is the weight, to the nearest newton, of a 60-kg person on the Earth's surface?

4. The radius of the moon is about 1740 km, and the mass of the moon is about 7.34×10^{22} kg. Calculate the weight of a 1-kg mass on the moon's surface, to the nearest tenth of a newton.

5. Write an equation that relates the weight of any object on the moon's surface, W newtons, to the mass of the object, m kilograms, in the form $W = \blacksquare m$, where $\blacksquare$ is a number.

6. What is the weight, to the nearest newton, of a 60-kg person on the moon's surface?

7. For the women's 100-m hurdles race, the ten hurdles are set to a height of 0.84 m. To run an equivalent race on the moon, how high should the hurdles be, to the nearest tenth of a metre?

8. To escape the Earth's gravitational pull, a spacecraft must reach or exceed the escape velocity. The escape velocity, v metres per second, for the Earth is given by the formula $v = \sqrt{\dfrac{2Gm}{r}}$, where G is the gravitational constant, m is the mass of the Earth in kilograms, and r is the radius of the Earth in metres. What is the escape velocity for the Earth
a) to the nearest 100 m/s?
b) to the nearest 100 km/h?

9. Use the formula $v = \sqrt{\dfrac{2Gm}{r}}$ to find the escape velocity from the moon
a) to the nearest 100 m/s?
b) to the nearest 100 km/h?

10. If the Earth began to shrink but its mass stayed the same, what would happen to the weight of an object on the Earth's surface? Explain.

11. At what distance from the Earth's surface does the weight of a spacecraft equal 25% of its weight on the Earth?

2 Planets and the Sun

1. Copy the table, which gives the radii and masses of some planets and the sun. Complete the table by calculating the weight, to the nearest tenth of a newton, of a 1-kg mass on the surface of each.

Planet/ Star	Radius (km)	Mass (kg)	Weight of 1-kg Mass (N)
Mars	3397	6.42×10^{23}	
Jupiter	71 942	1.9×10^{27}	
Saturn	60 268	5.68×10^{26}	
Pluto	1162	1.26×10^{22}	
Sun	696 000	1.99×10^{30}	

2. For the men's 110-m hurdle race, the ten hurdles are set to a height of 1.067 m. To run an equivalent race on each of the following planets, how high should the hurdles be, to the nearest tenth of a metre?
a) Jupiter
b) Pluto

3. If the sun were a planet, could you lift your math textbook on the sun? Explain.

4. What is the escape velocity, to the nearest hundred metres per second, for a spacecraft launched from
a) Mars?
b) Saturn?

5. a) Solve $F = G\dfrac{m_1 m_2}{d^2}$ for d.

b) For a planet not listed in the table, a 1-kg mass on the planet's surface would have a weight of 11.2 N. The planet has a mass of 1.03×10^{26} kg. Use the equation you found in part a) to find the radius of this planet, to the nearest hundred kilometres.

6. a) Solve $F = G\dfrac{m_1 m_2}{d^2}$ for m_1.

b) For a planet not listed in the table, a 1-kg mass on the planet's surface would have a weight of 3.7 N. The planet has a radius of 2440 km. Use the equation you found in part a) to find the mass of this planet, in kilograms. Express your answer in scientific notation, with the decimal part rounded to the nearest tenth.

7. A black hole is thought to be the result of a star collapsing under the force of its own gravity. As the star collapses, the same quantity of matter occupies a smaller and smaller volume. The force of gravity a black hole exerts becomes so strong that light cannot escape from it. This is why a black hole appears black. A black hole with the same mass as the Earth would have a radius of about 0.4 cm, or 0.004 m. Calculate the weight, in newtons, of a 1-kg mass on the surface of a black hole that has the same mass as the Earth. Assume that the 1-kg mass is an iron sphere with a radius of about 3 cm, or 0.03 m. Express the answer in scientific notation. Round the decimal part to the nearest tenth.

Review

5.1 *For each pair of functions, f and g, find*

a) $(f+g)(x)$ **b)** $(f-g)(x)$ **c)** $(fg)(x)$ **d)** $\left(\dfrac{f}{g}\right)(x)$

Write each function in simplest form and state any restrictions on the variable.

1. $f(x) = 2x + 5$ and $g(x) = 3 - x$
2. $f(x) = 9x^2 - 1$ and $g(x) = 3x - 1$
3. $f(x) = \dfrac{x}{x-2}$ and $g(x) = \dfrac{3}{x}$
4. $f(x) = 1 - 2\sqrt{x}$ and $g(x) = \sqrt{x} + 2$

For each pair of functions, f and g, find

a) $(f+g)(2)$ **b)** $(f-g)(-3)$ **c)** $(fg)(-1)$ **d)** $\left(\dfrac{f}{g}\right)(1)$

5. $f(x) = 1 - x$ and $g(x) = 2x + 1$
6. $f(x) = x^2 + 3x - 10$ and $g(x) = x - 2$

7. Use the graphs of the functions f and g, in question 5, to graph $(g - f)(x)$.

8. Given $f(x) = x^2 - 1$ and $g(x) = 3 - 2x$, find
a) $f(x) + 3g(x)$ **b)** $2(gg)(x)$ **c)** $2f(x) - (fg)(x)$

5.2 *If $f = \{(4, 5), (-2, -1), (3, 4), (-1, 0)\}$ and $g = \{(-2, -1), (-4, -2), (6, 3), (8, 4)\}$, use arrow diagrams to find each of the following, if it exists.*
9. $f \circ g$ **10.** $g \circ f$ **11.** $f \circ f$ **12.** $g \circ g$

If $f(x) = x^2$ and $g(x) = 5 - x$, find
13. $(f \circ g)(-1)$ **14.** $g(f(3))$
15. $(g \circ g)(0)$ **16.** $f(f(-2))$

If $f(x) = 2x - 1$ and $g(x) = 3 - x^2$, find
17. $f \circ g$ **18.** $g \circ f$ **19.** $f \circ f$ **20.** $g \circ g$

For each of the following pairs of functions, find
a) $(f \circ g)(x)$, if it exists
b) $(g \circ f)(x)$, if it exists
c) *the domain and range of f, g, f ∘ g, and g ∘ f*
21. $f(x) = \sqrt{x+2}$ and $g(x) = 3x$
22. $f(x) = 3x + 1$ and $g(x) = |-x|$

23. Given $h(x) = \dfrac{x}{x-1}$ and $k(x) = \dfrac{1}{x^2}$, write and simplify $h \circ k$ and $k \circ h$. State any restrictions on the variable.

5.3 **24.** $f = \{(-1, 5), (3, -2), (2, 2), (0, 3)\}$
a) Graph the function and its inverse.
b) Is the inverse a function? Explain.

Find the inverse of each function.
25. $f(x) = 4x + 2$ **26.** $f(x) = x^2 - 5$
27. $k(x) = (x + 7)^2$ **28.** $g(x) = \dfrac{2}{3-x}$

Determine if the functions in each pair are inverses of each other.
29. $f(x) = 5x - 1$ **30.** $h(x) = 2x + 8$
$\quad g(x) = \dfrac{x+1}{5}$ $\quad k(x) = 8 - \dfrac{1}{2}x$

31. a) Find the inverse of $f(x) = 3 - x^2$.
b) Graph $f(x)$ and its inverse.
c) Restrict the domain of f so that f^{-1} is also a function.
d) With the domain of f restricted, sketch a graph of each function.
e) State the domain and range of each function.

5.4 *Determine whether each function is a polynomial function. Justify your conclusion. If the function is a polynomial function, determine its degree.*
32. $y = \sqrt{x} + x^2$ **33.** $y = 2^x$
34. $y = \dfrac{3}{x} - x^3$ **35.** $y = 4 - x + 3x^2 - x^3$

Graph each of the following functions and determine
a) *the domain and range*
b) *any real zeros and the y-intercept, to the nearest tenth, if necessary*
c) *the approximate coordinates of any relative maximums or relative minimums*
d) *the intervals where $f(x) > 0$ and $f(x) < 0$*
e) *any symmetry and the end behaviour*
36. $y = (x^2 - 9)(x^2 - 1)$ **37.** $y = x^5 + 3x^2 - 2$
38. $y = x(x - 1)(x + 1)(x - 2)$ **39.** $y = -x^3 + 2x + 1$

Solve each inequality.
40. $x(x + 3) > 0$ **41.** $x^3 < 2x^2 - 3$

5.5 *Solve and check.*
42. $|4 - n| = 7$ **43.** $|p - 8| = 3p + 4$
44. $|a + 2| = |2a - 4|$ **45.** $|k + 1| + |k - 3| = 8$

Solve. Graph the solution.
46. $|x - 3| > 7$ **47.** $|3q + 2| \geq 8$
48. $|x - 5| < |x + 2|$ **49.** $|d + 1| + |d - 1| \leq 4$

Graph each function and
a) *determine the domain and range*
b) *determine the values of any real zeros*
c) *determine the values of x for which f(x) ≥ 0*
d) *describe any symmetry*
50. $f(x) = |3 - x| - 2$ **51.** $f(x) = -|x + 1| + 5$
52. $f(x) = |x^2 - 1| - 3$ **53.** $f(x) = |x^2 - 4| - 2$

.6 *Graph each function and determine*
a) *the equations of any asymptotes*
b) *the domain and range*

54. $f(x) = \dfrac{2}{3 - x}$ **55.** $g(x) = \dfrac{x}{x + 4}$

56. $f(m) = \dfrac{m^2 - 9}{m - 3}$ **57.** $f(p) = \dfrac{p^2 - 2p - 8}{p + 2}$

58. Graph the inverse of $y = \dfrac{x}{2 - x}$. Determine the

equation of any asymptotes, the domain and range.

59. a) Graph $y = x^2 - 4x$ and determine its zeros.
b) Use the zeros from part a) to determine the

vertical asymptotes of $y = \dfrac{1}{x^2 - 4x}$.

c) Compare the graphs of the functions,
considering the domain, range, symmetry, zeros,
and asymptotes.

Solve and check.

60. $\dfrac{1}{y^2 - 4} = \dfrac{1}{y + 2}$ **61.** $\dfrac{b}{b - 2} = \dfrac{b}{5}$

Solve. Graph the solution.

62. $\dfrac{n - 8}{n + 3} \geq 0$ **63.** $\dfrac{3}{x - 3} < \dfrac{4}{4 + x}$

.7 *Graph each function and determine the domain and range.*
64. $y = \sqrt{x + 2} + 4$ **65.** $y = 3 - \sqrt{x - 1}$

Solve and check.

66. $\sqrt{x + 1} + 2 = 6$ **67.** $m = -\sqrt{m + 6}$
68. $\sqrt{v + 3} = \sqrt{2v + 1}$ **69.** $\sqrt{a + 1} + 1 = \sqrt{a + 3}$

Solve. Graph the solution.

70. $4 - d < \sqrt{d + 2}$ **71.** $\sqrt{n + 3} \geq \sqrt{1 - n}$

72. $\sqrt{2x} \leq \dfrac{x}{2}$ **73.** $\sqrt{w + 3} > \dfrac{1}{w + 3}$

Exploring Math

The Game of Pong Hau K'i

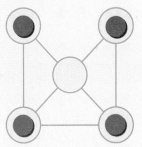

A board game for two players is called Pong Hau K'i in China and Ou-moul-ko-no in Korea. The game board is made up of five circles joined by seven line segments. One player has two red counters placed on the upper circles. The other player has two blue counters placed on the lower circles.

One player, the owner of either the red counters or the blue counters, moves a counter along a line segment to an adjacent empty circle. The other player then moves a counter. The players continue to take turns moving one counter at a time along a line segment to an adjacent empty circle.

The object of the game is to block your opponent's counters, so that your opponent does not have a move.

1. a) Play the game several times, taking turns to make the first move.
b) Is there a winning strategy for the player who makes the first move? Explain.
c) Is it better to have the red counters or the blue counters? Explain.

2. a) Modify the game by placing the counters on any four of the five circles before the start of the game. Decide which colour each of you will play and who will place the first counter. After the first counter is placed, the other player places a counter. The players, in the same order, then each place their second counters. Decide who will make the first move. Play the modified game several times.
b) Is it better to be the first player or the second player to place a counter? Explain.
c) Is it better to make the first move or the second move? Explain.

Chapter Check

For each pair of functions, f and g, find

a) $(f+g)(x)$ **b)** $(f-g)(x)$ **c)** $(fg)(x)$ **d)** $\left(\dfrac{f}{g}\right)(x)$

Write each function in simplest form and state any restrictions on the variable.

1. $f(x) = 4x - 1$ and $g(x) = 2 - x$

2. $f(x) = x^2 + 8x + 15$ and $g(x) = x + 5$

3. $f(x) = \dfrac{2}{x+2}$ and $g(x) = \dfrac{x}{x-1}$

4. $f(x) = \sqrt{x} + 3$ and $g(x) = 3\sqrt{x} - 1$

For each pair of functions, f and g, find

a) $(f+g)(-2)$ **b)** $(g-f)(3)$ **c)** $(fg)(2)$ **d)** $\left(\dfrac{f}{g}\right)(-1)$

5. $f(x) = x + 4$ and $g(x) = 3x - 1$

6. $f(x) = x^2 + x - 12$ and $g(x) = x + 4$

Given $f(x) = 25 - x^2$ and $g(x) = 5 - x$, find

7. $2f(x) + 3(g)(x)$ **8.** $(gg)(x) \div f(x)$

If $f(x) = (x - 1)^2$ and $g(x) = -x$, find the following.

9. $(f \circ g)(-2)$ **10.** $g(f(5))$ **11.** $(f \circ f)(-3)$

If $h(x) = 5 - x$ and $k(x) = x^2 + 2$, write the following functions.

12. $h \circ k$ **13.** $k \circ h$ **14.** $h \circ h$ **15.** $k \circ k$

For each of the following pairs of functions, find

a) $(f \circ g)(x)$, if it exists

b) $(g \circ f)(x)$, if it exists

c) the domain and range of f, g, $f \circ g$, and $g \circ f$

16. $f(x) = x - 2$ and $g(x) = \sqrt{3x}$

17. $f(x) = |x - 1|$ and $g(x) = \sqrt{x}$

18. Given $f(x) = \dfrac{1}{x}$ and $g(x) = x + 3$, write and simplify $f \circ g$ and $g \circ f$. State any restrictions on the variable.

a) Find the inverse of each function.

b) Is the inverse a function? Explain.

19. $f(x) = 5x + 2$ **20.** $h(x) = 3x^2 - 2$

Determine if the functions in each pair are inverses of each other.

21. $f(x) = \dfrac{x}{2} + 1$ and $g(x) = 2x - 1$

22. $h(x) = \dfrac{1}{2}x^2 + 1$, $x \geq 0$, and $k(x) = \sqrt{2x - 2}$

332 *Chapter 5*

Graph each of the following functions and determine
a) the domain and range
b) any real zeros and the y-intercept
c) the approximate coordinates of any relative maximums or relative minimums
d) the intervals where $f(x) > 0$ and $f(x) < 0$
e) any symmetry and the end behaviour

23. $y = (x - 3)(x + 1)(2x - 1)$ **24.** $y = (x^2 - 4)^2$

Solve each inequality. Graph each solution on a number line.

25. $-x(x - 1)(2x + 3)(x + 3) \geq 0$ **26.** $x^3 < 3x$

Graph each function and
a) determine the domain and range
b) determine the values of any real zeros
c) determine the values of x for which $f(x) \geq 0$
d) describe any symmetry

27. $f(x) = -|x - 4| + 3$ **28.** $f(x) = |x^2 - 9| - 2$

Graph each function and determine
a) the equations of any asymptotes
b) the domain and range

29. $f(x) = \dfrac{5}{2 - x}$ **30.** $g(x) = \dfrac{x^2 + 5x - 6}{x - 1}$

31. a) Graph $y = 3 + x$ and determine its zeros.
b) Use the zeros from part a) to determine the vertical asymptotes of $y = \dfrac{1}{3 + x}$.
c) Compare the graphs of the functions, considering the domain, range, symmetry, zeros, and asymptotes.

Solve and check.

32. $|t| = 2t - 9$ **33.** $|m - 5| - 1 = 3m$
34. $|v - 3| = |3v + 2|$ **35.** $|x - 1| + |x + 4| = 7$
36. $\dfrac{1}{z-1} = \dfrac{3}{z+5}$ **37.** $\dfrac{-c}{c^2 - 2} = \dfrac{1}{c}$
38. $\sqrt{p - 3} + 5 = 7$ **39.** $\sqrt{a + 5} + 1 = a$
40. $\sqrt{2z + 3} = \sqrt{3 - 2z}$ **41.** $\sqrt{x + 3} - 1 = \sqrt{3x - 2}$

Solve. Graph the solution.

42. $|b - 3| > 5$ **43.** $|2g - 1| < g + 4$
44. $|x + 1| \geq |x - 3|$ **45.** $|e + 5| + |e + 2| \leq 5$
46. $\dfrac{v + 3}{v - 3} \leq 0$ **47.** $\dfrac{b + 1}{3} > \dfrac{2}{b}$
48. $\sqrt{q + 4} + 2 < q$ **49.** $\sqrt{4x} \geq \dfrac{2}{x}$

Using the Strategies

1. You have 12 rods, each 13 units long. They are to be cut into pieces measuring 3, 4, and 5 units. The resulting pieces will be assembled into 13 triangles, each with sides of 3, 4, and 5 units. How should the rods be cut?

2. Five friends shared a table for dinner. Each ordered something to drink, an entrée, and a dessert. Brenda and Ms. Burns ordered milk, Betty and Ms. Brown ordered coffee, and Ms. Baker ordered juice. Brenda and Ms. Blue ordered steak. Bonnie and Ms. Baker ordered lamb. For dessert, Bonnie and Ms. Black had apple pie, while Barbara and Ms. Baker had cheesecake. The other friend had fruit salad. Who ordered salmon for an entrée, and what did Beth have to eat?

3. The letters R, S, and T represent integers. Find the possible values of R, S, and T.

$$R + S - T = 8$$
$$R \times S \times T = 48$$
$$R - S - T = 0$$

4. a) What is the quotient when any three-digit number whose digits are the same is divided by the sum of its digits?
b) Explain why the quotient is always the same.
c) Is there a constant quotient for four-digit numbers whose digits are the same? for five-digit numbers? for numbers with any number of digits? Explain.

5. Orly and her friends organized a fund-raising walk for charity. Without stopping, they walked on a level road, then up a hill, back down the hill, and then back to the start along the level road. The walk took six hours. Their speed was 4 km/h on the level road, 3 km/h up the hill, and 6 km/h down the hill. How far did they walk?

6. Each school sent one player to a handball tournament. Each player played every other player at the tournament three times. In total, 63 games were played. How many players were in the tournament?

7. You have a four-wheel drive all-terrain truck, and you need to make a 27 000-km trip. Each tire can be used for 12 000 km. The four tires on the truck are new, and you have five new tires in the back of the truck. How can you use the nine tires to complete the trip?

8. There are twenty marbles in a bag. There are eight yellow marbles, seven purple marbles, and five green marbles. If your eyes are closed, what is the maximum number of marbles you can take from the bag to be certain that you will leave in the bag at least four marbles of one colour and at least three marbles of a second colour?

9. The numbers in the Fibonacci sequence are 1, 1, 2, 3, 5, 8, 13, …. Is it possible to construct a triangle with sides whose lengths are all different Fibonacci numbers? Explain.

10. The length of each side of an equilateral triangle is 2 cm. The midpoints of the sides are joined to form an inscribed equilateral triangle. If this process is continued without end, find the sum of the perimeters of the triangles.

11. About how many high school students in your province have a driver's licence?

D A T A   B A N K

1. Bella drove from Winnipeg to Saskatoon by way of Regina. She stopped for a short visit at her sister's house between Regina and Saskatoon. Because of this visit, her average speed from Regina to Saskatoon was 30 km/h less than her average speed from Winnipeg to Regina. The journey took 10 h altogether. What was Bella's average speed from Winnipeg to Regina and from Regina to Saskatoon?

2. Write two problems using data from the Data Bank. Have a classmate solve your problems.

3. Determine the speed at which Calgary revolves around the Earth's axis, to the nearest ten kilometres per hour.

CHAPTER 6

Reasoning

As people age, their sleep requirements change dramatically. Newborn babies sleep for short periods at a time, but many times throughout the day. As children develop, the sleep pattern gradually becomes one uninterrupted period of sleep per day. As adults age, they sometimes revert to earlier patterns of sleeping a few hours during the night and napping during the day.

The graph shows the typical sleep patterns for five stages of human development.

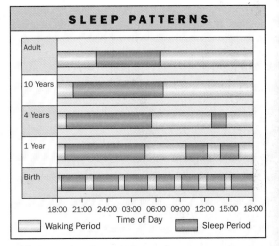

SLEEP PATTERNS

Time of Day

Waking Period · Sleep Period

1. At what times of the day would you expect
a) an adult and a 10-year-old both to be awake?
b) a 1-year-old and a 4-year-old both to be asleep?
c) a newborn and a 10-year-old both to be asleep?

2. At what times of the day would you expect a newborn, but not a 4-year-old, to be awake?

3. In a family consisting of two adults, a 4-year-old, and a 1-year-old, at what times would you expect the entire family to be
a) awake?   **b)** asleep?

4. Selina and Viktor were asked to give the times at which they expect an adult or a 10-year-old to be asleep. Selina's answer was 20:00 to 07:00. Viktor's answer was 20:00 to 23:00 and 06:30 to 07:00. How did Selina and Viktor each interpret the word "or"?

Patterns and Logical Reasoning

1 Patterns and Observations

Consider the following card trick.

Step 1: From a well-shuffled deck of 52 cards, select one of the top 11 cards and note its position number from the top of the deck. Now, count out these 11 cards face down, one after the other, thus reversing their position. Put the cards back on top of the deck.

Step 2: Take 16 cards from the bottom of the deck, and place them on the top of the deck.

Step 3: Count out the cards one at a time, beginning the count with the number one greater than the original position number of your card from the top of the deck. Count until you reach 28. The 28th card will be the card you selected in Step 1.

In the trick above, if you select one of the top 15 cards in Step 1, and take 20 cards from the bottom in Step 2, then in Step 3 your chosen card will the 36th card. If you repeat the trick again using the top 10 cards in Step 1 and 14 cards in Step 2, then in Step 3 your chosen card will be the 25th card.

1. What will be the position of your chosen card in Step 3, if you use 7 cards in Step 1 and 12 cards in Step 2?

2. Describe the position of your chosen card in Step 3, if you use n cards in Step 1 and y cards in Step 2.

3. Use the following steps to show why the trick works.
a) If you select n of the top cards and your card is in the xth position, in what position is your card after you reverse the positions of the cards?
b) If you transfer y cards from the bottom of the deck to the top, in what position is your card now?
c) If you start counting the cards, beginning the count with the number $x + 1$, what is the position of your card now?

2 Using Logical Reasoning

Three friends, Mike, Hari, and Carl, each have a sister. The girls are Amy, Sarah, and Tia. The six friends play mixed doubles tennis, but no boy ever partners his sister. In one match, Mike and Amy played Carl and Tia. In another match, Sarah partnered Carl, and Hari partnered Tia.

1. Copy and complete the following table to determine the name of each boy's sister. Mark X in a cell where you know that the boy and girl cannot be brother and sister, and ✓ in a cell where you can conclude that they are brother and sister.

	Amy	Tia	Sarah
Mike			
Carl			
Hari			

2. The same logic problem could be solved by considering all possible cases, as follows.

Possibility	1	2	3	4	5	6
Mike	Amy	Amy	Sarah	Sarah	Tia	Tia
Carl	Tia	Sarah	Tia	Amy	Sarah	Amy
Hari	Sarah	Tia	Amy	Tia	Amy	Sarah

Now use the information to eliminate possibilities.

3. Which possibilities does the first match eliminate? Why?

4. Which possibilities does the second match eliminate? Why?

5. What are the correct brother–sister names?

3 A Logic Challenge

Five siblings, Andrew, Barb, Carys, Dianne, and Erik, are all at a cottage on a lake. The following facts are observed one afternoon.
- If Andrew is swimming, so is his twin sister Barb.
- Either Dianne or Erik, or both of them, are swimming.
- Either Barb or Carys, but not both, are swimming.
- Dianne and Carys are either both swimming or both not swimming.
- If Erik is swimming, then so are Andrew and Dianne.

Who is swimming and who is not?

Mental Math

Complementary and Supplementary Angles

What is the measure of the complementary angle to each of the following?

1. 60°   **2.** 20°   **3.** 45°   **4.** 15°
5. 40°   **6.** 72°   **7.** 51°   **8.** 83°
9. 24°   **10.** 4°   **11.** 33°   **12.** 68°

What is the measure of the supplementary angle to each of the following?

13. 110°   **14.** 50°   **15.** 45°   **16.** 40°
17. 115°   **18.** 75°   **19.** 105°   **20.** 95°
21. 63°   **22.** 112°   **23.** 18°   **24.** 59°

Adding a Column of Numbers

To add the numbers shown, first add the numbers in the tens column. To the result, add the numbers in the ones column one at a time.

	35		30
	21		20
	49	⇒	40
	60		60
	+ 87		+ 80
			230

$230 + 7 = 237$; $237 + 0 = 237$; $237 + 9 = 246$;
$246 + 1 = 247$; $247 + 5 = 252$.
So, the sum is 252.

Add.

1. 11	**2.** 38	**3.** 77	**4.** 93	**5.** 56
19	41	65	14	58
23	92	84	28	80
51	17	17	55	11
+ 46	+ 33	24	40	29
		+ 32	59	91
			62	44
			+ 71	35
				+ 36

Describe how you could modify the method to complete each of the following. Then, add.

6. 2.3	**7.** 9.9	**8.** 110	**9.** 330	**10.** 102
7.5	0.4	430	520	201
6.6	1.8	230	980	333
4.1	5.7	580	590	407
+ 3.2	9.2	750	400	522
	+ 4.3	+ 290	+ 190	+ 690

6.1 Inductive Reasoning and Conjecturing

Inductive reasoning is the type of reasoning in which a pattern is observed in a set of data and the pattern is used to make an educated guess, or generalization, about the data. The generalization is called a **conjecture**. Most scientific inquiries begin with inductive reasoning.

The Bermuda Triangle, in the southeastern Atlantic Ocean, is a region bounded by imaginary lines that join Bermuda, Miami, and San Juan, Puerto Rico. This region is noted for a high incidence of losses of ships, small boats, and aircraft. In the past, when there was no explanation for the disappearances, people used inductive reasoning to conclude that something supernatural was the cause. This belief was held for many years.

Inductive reasoning, however, does not always prove something to be true. Recent investigations of the Bermuda Triangle have proved that the disappearances can be attributed to various factors. Among them are these facts: magnetic compasses in this area point up to 20° from magnetic north, the powerful Gulf Stream constantly moves the many reefs in the area, and the unpredictable weather, with sudden local thunderstorms and water spouts, often spells disaster.

Explore: Perform an Experiment

a) Draw acute triangle ABC on a piece of paper.
Label the vertices inside the triangle.
b) Extend BC to D to make exterior ∠ACD.
c) Cut out the triangle and the exterior angle as shown.

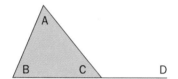

d) Tear off ∠A and ∠B, which are the interior and opposite angles, and place them in the exterior angle as shown.
e) Repeat steps 1 to 4 for △ABC where ∠B = 90°; where ∠B is obtuse.

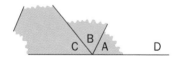

Inquire

1. Write a conjecture about the sum of the interior angles of a triangle.
2. Write a conjecture about the relationship between an exterior angle of a triangle and the sum of the two interior and opposite angles.
3. Compare your conjectures with those of your classmates.
4. Describe a similar procedure you could use to make a conjecture about the sum of the interior angles of a quadrilateral.
5. Use your procedure from question 4 to perform an experiment with quadrilaterals.
6. Write a conjecture about the sum of the interior angles of a quadrilateral.
7. Use your conjectures to find the measures of the indicated angles.

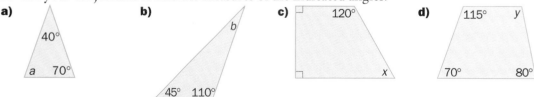

a) 40°, a 70°

b) b, 45° 110°

c) 120°, x

d) 115°, y, 70°, 80°

The conjectures made in Inquire questions 1 and 2 are stated below as theorems, which will be proved in a later section. A **theorem** is a statement that can be proved by reasoning logically from other true statements.

Triangle Angle Sum Theorem
The sum of the interior angles of a triangle is 180°.

Exterior Angle Theorem
The exterior angle of a triangle is equal to the sum of the interior and opposite angles.

Example 1   Alternate Angles

Draw a pair of parallel lines and a transversal. Measure and record the sizes of alternate angles 1 and 2. Repeat for several other pairs of parallel lines and different transversals. Make a conjecture about the alternate angles when a transversal intersects two parallel lines.

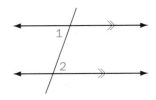

Solution
The table shows the results obtained from 5 different pairs of parallel lines and transversals.

			Test		
Angle	I	II	III	IV	V
$\angle 1$	52°	75°	36°	44°	115°
$\angle 2$	52°	75°	35°	44°	115°

The pattern in these results suggests that the measures of $\angle 1$ and $\angle 2$ are the same. In test III, the difference in the measures of $\angle 1$ and $\angle 2$ is only 1°, and probably can be explained as a measurement error.

Based on these results, a conjecture can be made that, when a transversal intersects two parallel lines, the alternate angles are equal.

Example 2   Number Theory

Use the patterns shown to make a conjecture. Try some numbers of your own to test the conjecture.

a)
$$1 + 3 = 4$$
$$3 + 5 = 8$$
$$5 + 7 = 12$$
$$7 + 9 = 16$$
$$9 + 11 = 20$$
$$11 + 13 = 24$$

b)
$$2^2 - 1^2 = 3$$
$$3^2 - 2^2 = 5$$
$$4^2 - 3^2 = 7$$
$$5^2 - 4^2 = 9$$
$$6^2 - 5^2 = 11$$
$$7^2 - 6^2 = 13$$

Solution
a) The pattern shows the sums of consecutive pairs of odd numbers.
Conjecture: The sum of two consecutive odd numbers is an even number.
Second conjecture: The sum of consecutive odd numbers is a multiple of 4.
Some other sums are: $13 + 15 = 28$, $25 + 27 = 52$, $101 + 103 = 204$.
Both of the conjectures made above are true for these sums.
b) The pattern shows the differences in the squares of pairs of consecutive whole numbers.
Conjecture: The difference in the squares of two consecutive whole numbers is equal to the sum of the whole numbers.
Some other differences are: $10^2 - 9^2 = 19$, $13^2 - 12^2 = 25$, $15^2 - 14^2 = 29$.
The conjecture is true for these differences.

Example 3　Sequences

The diagrams show the number of fence posts used to enclose square regions. The fence posts are placed one metre apart.

Make a conjecture about the number of fence posts needed to enclose a square region with side length s metres. Test your conjecture for a square with side length 6 m.

Solution

The numbers of fence posts for different side lengths form a sequence.

Side Length (m)	1	2	3	4
Number of Posts	4	8	12	16

Conjecture: The number of posts needed to enclose a square region is 4 times the side length. For a square with side length s metres, the number of posts is $4s$.

The diagram shows that a square with side length 6 m uses 24 posts.

Since $24 = 4 \times 6$, the conjecture is true for $s = 6$.

Practice

In questions 1–6, use the given data to make a conjecture. In each case, write two more examples that demonstrate your conjecture.

1. $1^2 = 1$
  $11^2 = 121$
  $111^2 = 12\ 321$
  $1111^2 = 1\ 234\ 321$

2. $1 = 1$
  $1 + 3 = 4$
  $1 + 3 + 5 = 9$
  $1 + 3 + 5 + 7 = 16$

3. $3^2 - 1^2 = 8$
  $5^2 - 3^2 = 16$
  $7^2 - 5^2 = 24$
  $9^2 - 7^2 = 32$

4. $12 \times 11 = 132$
  $43 \times 11 = 473$
  $26 \times 11 = 286$
  $56 \times 11 = 616$

5. $12 + 21 = 33$
  $38 + 83 = 121$
  $25 + 52 = 77$
  $64 + 46 = 110$

6. $2 \times 9 = 18$
  $22 \times 9 = 198$
  $222 \times 9 = 1998$
  $2222 \times 9 = 19\ 998$

7. Measurement Draw two lines that intersect at a point. Measure and record the size of each of the four angles at the point of intersection. Repeat for several other pairs of intersecting lines. Make a conjecture concerning the measures of opposite angles.

8. Measurement Draw a triangle large enough for its angles to be measured. Record the measure of each angle and the length of the side opposite the angle. Repeat for at least 5 different triangles. Make a conjecture describing how
a) the location of the longest side is related to the location of the largest angle
b) the location of the shortest side is related to the location of the smallest angle

9. Measurement Draw a large triangle. Bisect two of the sides of your triangle. Join the two midpoints. Measure angles and lengths to decide how the line segment joining the midpoints seems to be related to the third side of the triangle. Repeat the measurements on at least 4 different shapes of triangles. Make two conjectures concerning how the line segment joining the midpoints of two sides of a triangle is related to the third side.

10. Pattern Examine the following table.

Row	Numbers	Row Sum
1	1	1
2	2 3 4	1 + 8
3	5 6 7 8 9	8 + 27
4	10 11 12 13 14 15 16	27 + 64
5	17 18 19 20 21 22 23 24 25	64 + 125

a) Make a conjecture about the sum of the numbers in the nth row.
b) Show that your conjecture is true for the sixth row.

Applications and Problem Solving

11. Calendar patterns Select any month from a calendar. Choose a rectangular array of numbers that is at least 2 by 2. Make a conjecture about how the sums of the two pairs of numbers at opposite corners of your array compare. Test your conjecture on other rectangular arrays within the same month and in other months.

12. Cross-stitch A popular form of embroidery involves crossing one stitch over another to form an X-shape, called a cross-stitch. Cross-stitches were used to form the following three figures.

Make a conjecture about the number of cross-stitches in a figure that has a diagonal made from n cross-stitches.

13. Sequences Each of the following sequences is arithmetic or geometric, or it has some other kind of pattern. Predict the next two terms in each sequence.
a) 3, 12, 48, 192, ...
b) 17, 24, 31, 38, ...
c) 1, 2, 2, 4, 8, 32, ...
d) A, C, F, J, O, ...
e) C, E, F, H, I, K, L, ...

14. Goldbach's conjecture In 1742, Christian Goldbach sent a letter to the famous Swiss mathematician Leonard Euler. Goldbach proposed that every even number greater than 4 can be expressed as the sum of two odd primes. This conjecture has never been proved or disproved. Express 98 as the sum of two odd primes.

15. Geometry One line segment is required to join two points in a plane. Three line segments are required to join every pair of points when there are 3 points in a plane.

a) How many line segments are required to join every pair of points when there are 4 points in a plane?
b) Continue the pattern and make a conjecture about the number of line segments required to join every pair of points when there are n points in a plane.

16. Chemistry Hydrocarbons consist of combinations of carbon (C) and hydrogen (H). Alkanes are one type of hydrocarbons. The molecular structure of the first four straight-chain alkanes are shown.

Methane (CH_4)   Ethane (C_2H_6)

Propane (C_3H_8)   Butane (C_4H_{10})

a) The fifth straight-chain alkane is pentane (C_5H_{12}). Draw a sketch of the molecular structure of pentane.
b) Write a conjecture about the relationship between the number of hydrogen atoms and the number of carbon atoms in a straight-chain alkane.

17. Pendulum The period of a pendulum is the time it takes to complete a back-and-forth swing. Galileo observed that the period of a pendulum depends on the length of the pendulum. The table shows the results of some experiments with pendulums.

Length of Pendulum (cm)	Approximate Period (s)
25	1
100	2
225	3
400	4
625	5

Make a conjecture about the relationship between the period and the length of the pendulum.

18. Cutting pizzas If you make 1 straight cut across a pizza, you have 2 pieces of pizza. With 2 straight cuts, the maximum number of pieces you have is 4.

a) What is the maximum number of pieces you can obtain with 3 straight cuts?
b) Continue the pattern and make a conjecture about the maximum number of pieces you can obtain with k cuts.
c) Does the shape of the pizza make any difference to your answer? Explain.

19. Sequence Make a conjecture about the next three terms in the following sequence.
1, 2, 6, 10, 4, 5, 9, 3, ...
Explain your reasoning.

20. Fibonacci sequence In the Fibonacci sequence $t_1 = t_2 = 1$ and $t_k = t_{k-1} + t_{k-2}$ for $k \geq 3$.
a) Write the first 12 terms of the Fibonnaci sequence.
b) Find the values of the following sums.
$t_2 + t_4$
$t_2 + t_4 + t_6$
$t_2 + t_4 + t_6 + t_8$
$t_2 + t_4 + t_6 + t_8 + t_{10}$
c) Make a conjecture about the sum of
$t_2 + t_4 + t_6 + ... + t_{2k}$.

21. Measurement Draw a pair of parallel lines and a transversal. Label the angles formed as shown.

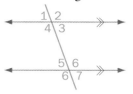

Measure and record the size of each angle. Collect similar data from at least 3 other students.
a) Make a conjecture about how the measures of corresponding angles 3 and 7 are related. Which other pairs of angles are corresponding angles? Are their measures related in the same way?
b) Make a conjecture about how the measures of co-interior angles 3 and 6 are related. Which other pair of angles are co-interior angles? Are their measures related in the same way?

22. Pattern a) Examine the pattern in the following equations.
$$1 \triangle 2 = 3$$
$$2 \triangle 1 = 4$$
$$5 \triangle 2 = 15$$
$$2 \triangle 5 = 12$$
Make a conjecture about the meaning of the symbol $\triangle$.
b) Make up a pattern using a symbol of your own choice. Give your pattern to a classmate to solve.

NUMBER POWER

In the diagram, each letter represents a number. The numbers outside the square show the sums of each row, three of the columns, and one diagonal. What is the sum of the second column?

A	B	B	C	20
B	A	C	C	21
B	C	C	A	21
D	D	A	D	25
21	■	21	23	25

6.2 Analyzing Conjectures Using Examples and Counterexamples

It is important to be cautious when making conjectures. They may or may not be true. To demonstrate that a conjecture is false, you need describe only one **counterexample**, which is an example for which the conjecture is false.

Many years ago, people thought the Earth was flat. Whenever a ship left on a voyage of exploration and never returned, it was believed that the ship had fallen off the edge of the Earth. The flat-Earth conjecture was believed by many until Ferdinand Magellan's ship arrived back in Portugal on September 6, 1522, after taking three years to sail around the world. This trip was seen as a counterexample to the conjecture that the Earth was flat.

Explore: Look for a Pattern

When 2 points are placed on the circumference of a circle and joined, 2 regions are formed.

When 3 points are placed on the circle, and each point is joined to every other point, 4 regions are formed.

When 4 points are used, 8 regions are formed.

a) Make a prediction about the number of regions formed when 5 points are used.
b) Use a diagram to check your prediction. Is your prediction valid?
c) Make a conjecture by writing a formula to give the number of regions formed when n points are used. Compare your formula with a classmate's.

Inquire

1. How can you test whether your formula is valid?

2. Use your formula to find the number of regions formed when 6 points are used.

3. Use a diagram to check your answer.

4. a) What conclusion can you make about your conjecture for finding the maximum number of regions formed?
b) Is it possible to modify your formula so that there are no counterexamples? Explain.

5. Give a counterexample to show that each of the following conjectures is false.
a) If you live in a country bordering the United States, then you live in Canada.
b) If a quadrilateral has four right angles, then it is a square.
c) A heavier-than-air mechanically driven vehicle that flies is an airplane.
d) Odd whole numbers less than 10 are prime.

Example 1   Finding a Counterexample in Number Theory
Consider the conjecture:
The sum of two prime numbers is an even number.
a) Give two examples for which the conjecture is true.
b) Give one counterexample that shows the conjecture is false.

Solution
a) The numbers 3 and 5 are both prime numbers, and $3 + 5 = 8$.
The numbers 7 and 11 are both prime numbers, and $7 + 11 = 18$.

b) The numbers 2 and 3 are both prime numbers, and $2 + 3 = 5$.
Since 5 is an odd number, the conjecture that the sum of two prime numbers is an even number is false.

Example 2   Analyzing a Conjecture in Geometry
Consider the conjecture:
In any isosceles triangle, all three angles are acute.
a) Draw two examples of triangles for which the conjecture holds.
b) Draw one counterexample that shows the conjecture is not true.

Solution
a)

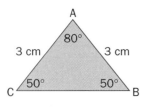

b)

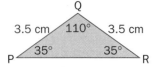

Since $\angle Q$ is obtuse, this counterexample shows the conjecture is not true.

Example 3 Analyzing a Conjecture From a Graph

Nima used a graphing calculator to graph the function $y = x^x$, using the standard viewing window. Based on the graph, she made the conjecture that x^x is not defined for $x < 0$.

a) Give one example that shows that Nima's conjecture is reasonable.
b) Find one counterexample to show that Nima's conjecture is false.
c) Suggest how Nima might check her original conjecture using the graphing calculator.

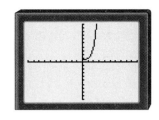

Solution

a) When $x = -0.5$, try to evaluate $(-0.5)^{-0.5}$.

$$(-0.5)^{-0.5} = (-0.5)^{-\frac{1}{2}}$$
$$= \frac{1}{\sqrt{-0.5}}$$

The square root of a negative number is not defined, so Nima's conjecture seems reasonable.

b) When $x = -1$, evaluate $(-1)^{-1}$.

$$(-1)^{-1} = \frac{1}{-1}$$
$$= -1$$

When $x = -1$, the value of x^x is defined, so Nima's conjecture is false.

c) Nima could explore the graph a little closer by changing the domain.

Using the Zoom In instruction reveals some points to the left of the y-axis.

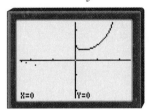

Changing the viewing window variables to Xmin: -4.7 and Xmax: 4.7 reveals more points.

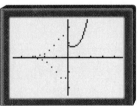

Practice

Give two examples that support each conjecture, and then one counterexample that shows the conjecture is false.

1. Multiples of 4 are divisible by 8.
2. The sum of two perfect squares is an even number.
3. The difference between consecutive pairs of perfect squares is a prime number.
4. The square root of a number is smaller than the number.
5. If $a^2 + b^2$ is even, then a and b are both even.
6. For any real number n, $\sqrt{n^2} = n$.
7. In the Cartesian plane, if the x-coordinate of a point is positive, then the point is in the first quadrant.

Draw a diagram illustrating each of the following conjectures. Then, draw a counterexample diagram showing the conjecture is not true.

8. The altitude from a vertex to the opposite side of a triangle lies within the triangle.
9. In a quadrilateral, if two angles are right angles, then the quadrilateral is a rectangle.
10. If line segments AB and BC have the same length, then B is the midpoint of line segment AC.
11. If ∠APB and ∠BPC are adjacent acute angles, then ∠APC is an obtuse angle.
12. If two opposite angles of a quadrilateral both measure 90°, then the quadrilateral is a rectangle.

Applications and Problem Solving

13. Geography Give a counterexample to this conjecture:
All provinces of Canada share a border with the United States.

14. Biology Give a counterexample to each of the following conjectures.
a) All birds can fly.
b) All cats are born with a tail.

15. Number theory Milo proposed the following conjecture:
If a, b, c, and d are any real numbers such that $a < b$ and $c < d$, then $ac < bd$.
a) Give two examples for which the conjecture is true and one counterexample.
b) For what set of numbers is the conjecture true?

16. Geometry Danielle conjectured that the diagonals of a parallelogram bisect the angles.
a) Draw two parallelograms for which the conjecture is true. Draw one counterexample.
b) For what type(s) of parallelograms is Danielle's conjecture true?

17. Measurement Marisa conjectured that if the diameter of a circle is doubled, then its area is doubled.
a) Provide one numerical example that shows Marisa's conjecture is not true.
b) Show algebraically that the conjecture can never be true.

18. Prime numbers Prime numbers have fascinated mathematicians for centuries.
a) One conjecture is that the sum of the sequence of powers of 2, that is, $1 + 2 + 2^2 + \ldots + 2^n$, where n is a whole number, is always a prime number. Provide two examples that support this conjecture. Then, find one counterexample.
b) Another conjecture is that $2^n - 1$, where n is a natural number, is always a prime number. Provide two examples that support this conjecture. Then, find one counterexample.
c) A conjecture for a prime number generator is $n^2 - n + 41$. Provide two examples that support this conjecture. Then, find one counterexample.

19. Geometry Draw one polygon for which the following conjecture is true, and draw one counterexample:
If a polygon has three congruent interior angles, then it has three congruent sides.

20. Prime numbers Consider the following conjecture:
The sum and the difference of two prime numbers are never both perfect squares.
a) Give two examples that support this conjecture and one counterexample.
b) Can you find more than one counterexample? If you think not, explain your reasoning.

21. Technology a) Use the standard viewing window of a graphing calculator to display the graph of $y = x^{-x}$. Use the graph to make a conjecture about the range of the relation.
b) Without graphing, find a counterexample that shows your conjecture is false.
c) Describe at least two different ways that you could use your graphing calculator to find a counterexample to the original conjecture.

PATTERN POWER

1. Describe the pattern in words.

14	21	35	18
27	17	52	12
9	16	34	
10	3	28	6
22	19	25	11

2. Find the missing number.

6.3 Deductive Reasoning

In the inductive reasoning process, observations of cases and patterns are used to make a conjecture about the general situation. However, inductive reasoning does not guarantee that the conjecture is true for all cases. It is necessary to prove a conjecture in order to state that it is true for all cases.

Deductive reasoning, or logical reasoning, is the process of demonstrating that, if certain statements are true, then other statements follow from them.

Lewis Carroll, whose real name was Charles Dodgson, was a mathematics professor at Oxford University. He enjoyed composing logic puzzles and intertwining them in the stories he wrote. The following excerpt is from *Alice's Adventures in Wonderland*.

"If I eat one of these cakes," she thought, "it's sure to make some change in my size; and, as it can't possibly make me larger, it must make me smaller..."

Explore: Use Inductive and Deductive Reasoning

Inductive Reasoning

Draw 3 different pairs of intersecting lines and label each angle, as shown.

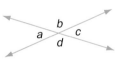

Measure each angle in your diagrams, and copy and complete the table.

	Angle			
	a	**b**	**c**	**d**
Diagram 1				
Diagram 2				
Diagram 3				
Diagram 4				

Deductive Reasoning

In the diagram, two lines EF and GH intersect at O. The angles have been labelled a, b, c, and d.

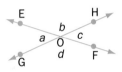

a) Copy and complete each statement.
Since $\angle$GOH is a straight angle, $a + b = \blacksquare°$.
Since $\angle$EOF is a straight angle, $c + b = \blacksquare°$.
b) Write an equation that compares $a + b$ and $c + b$.
c) Subtract the common angle from both sides.
d) Write the resulting equation.

Inquire

1. From the inductive reasoning exploration, what conjecture can you make about the opposite angles formed when two lines intersect?
2. Can you be sure that your conjecture is valid for all pairs of intersecting lines? Explain.
3. Why is the deductive reasoning valid for all pairs of intersecting lines?
4. Use deductive reasoning to prove that $b = d$.
5. Determine the measures of the indicated angles.

a)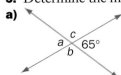

b)

c)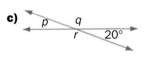

6. When Alice made her statement, she was using deductive reasoning. What statements did she believe to be true, and what statement followed from them?

Inductive reasoning does not prove that a conjecture is true for all cases. Instead, it gives a conjecture that might be true for all cases. However, it is usually impossible to test all cases to see whether there is a counterexample.

In the deductive reasoning exploration and Inquire question 4, it was proved deductively that, when two lines intersect, the opposite angles are equal. There is no counterexample for something that has been proved by deductive reasoning. We can now state the following theorem.

Opposite Angles Theorem
When two lines intersect, the opposite angles are equal.

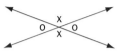

Example 1   Comparing Inductive and Deductive Reasoning
a) Choose a number. Double it. Add 5. Add your original number. Add 7. Divide by 3. Subtract your original number. Repeat this sequence of steps four times, starting with different numbers. Make a conjecture about the final number.
b) Prove your conjecture using deductive reasoning.

Solution
a)

	Trial			
	I	II	III	IV
Choose a number:	3	5	0	8
Double it:	6	10	0	16
Add 5:	11	15	5	21
Add the original number:	14	20	5	29
Add 7:	21	27	12	36
Divide by 3:	7	9	4	12
Subtract the original number:	4	4	4	4

Conjecture: The final number is always 4.

b) Let n represent the number chosen.

Choose a number:	n
Double it:	$2n$
Add 5:	$2n + 5$
Add the original number:	$2n + 5 + n = 3n + 5$
Add 7:	$3n + 5 + 7 = 3n + 12$
Divide by 3:	$(3n + 12) \div 3 = 3(n + 4) \div 3$
Subtract the original number:	$n + 4 - n$
Result:	4

Therefore, whatever number is chosen, the final number is always 4.

Example 2   Using Deductive Reasoning
Prove that if two angles are equal, then their supplements are equal.

Solution
In the figure, prove that if $x = y$, then $a = b$.
Supplementary angles are two angles whose sum is 180°.
So, $a + x = 180°$
and $b + y = 180°$
Since both sums equal 180°, $a + x = b + y$.
So, if $x = y$, then $a = b$.
In general, if two angles are equal, then their supplements are equal.

Theorem
If two angles are equal, then their supplements are equal.

Example 3   Deductive Reasoning in Number Theory
Prove that the difference between the squares of two odd numbers is always divisible by 4.

Solution

If k is any whole number, then $2k$ is an even number, and so $2k + 1$ must be an odd number.
Let $2k + 1$, where k is a whole number, represent the first odd number.
Let $2n + 1$, where n is a whole number, represent the other odd number.
Then, the difference between the squares of the two odd numbers is
$$(2n + 1)^2 - (2k + 1)^2 = 4n^2 + 4n + 1 - (4k^2 + 4k + 1)$$
$$= 4n^2 + 4n + 1 - 4k^2 - 4k - 1$$
$$= 4(n^2 + n - k^2 - k)$$
So, the difference between the squares of two odd numbers is a composite number, the product of 4 and some other number. Therefore, the difference between the squares of two odd numbers is always divisible by 4.

Practice

Write the conclusion that can be deduced using each pair of statements.

1. Paulette lives in Medicine Hat. Medicine Hat is in Alberta.

2. Every animal has a heart. All dogs are animals.

3. Stella is taller than Mario. Mario is taller than Annisa.

4. The sum of any two consecutive whole numbers is an odd number. The whole numbers 11 and 12 are consecutive.

5. The diagonals of a parallelogram bisect each other. PQRS is a parallelogram.

6. The diagonals of a rhombus intersect at right angles. KLMN is a rhombus.

7. If a triangle has two equal sides, then it has two equal angles. △ABC has two equal sides.

8. a) Choose a number. Triple the number. Add 2. Add the original number. Add 2. Divide by 4. Subtract 1. Repeat this sequence of steps four times, starting with different numbers. Make a conjecture about the final number.
b) Prove your conjecture using deductive reasoning.

Applications and Problem Solving

9. Numbers a) Prove that the sum of any two odd numbers is an even number.
b) Prove that the product of any two odd numbers is an odd number.

10. Integers Prove that the sum of any three consecutive integers is a multiple of 3.

11. Numbers Prove that the absolute value of the difference between the squares of consecutive whole numbers is equal to the sum of the two numbers.

12. Geometry Two rectangles have the same area, but different base lengths. What can be deduced about their heights?

13. Geometry If the diagonals of a quadrilateral are perpendicular, then the quadrilateral is a kite, a rhombus, or a square. If a quadrilateral is a rhombus or a square, then its diagonals bisect each other. The diagonals of quadrilateral PQRS are perpendicular but do not bisect each other. What can you conclude about quadrilateral PQRS? Explain.

14. Integers Prove that the product of any two consecutive integers is an even number.

15. Numbers Prove that, if n is an odd number and n is not 1, then $n^2 - 1$ is always divisible by 8.

16. Geometry Prove that, if two angles are equal, then their complements are equal.

17. Geometry PQRS is a square and △QRT is equilateral. Prove that △RST is isosceles.

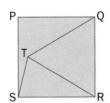

18. Geometry In a right triangle, if a perpendicular is drawn from the right angle to the hypotenuse, prove that each of the smaller triangles formed is similar to the original triangle.

19. Geometry Prove that, if exactly one altitude of a triangle bisects the opposite side, then the triangle is isosceles.

6.4 The Connecting Words *And, Or,* and *Not*

Proving theorems in mathematics involves making logical connections between statements and their conclusions. A **statement** is a sentence that is either true or false.

Consider the following sentences.
A. Sir John A. Macdonald was Canada's first prime minister.
B. Sir John A. Macdonald was not Canada's first prime minister.
C. Sir John A. Macdonald will always be known as Canada's best prime minister.
Sentence A is a statement because it is true.
Sentence B is a statement because it is false.
Sentence C is not a statement. It is an opinion, and is neither true nor false.

A **compound statement** is a statement formed by connecting one or more statements with a connective, such as *and, or, not,* ... .

> Curtis is 18 years old.   (1)
> Curtis has brown eyes.   (2)

The two statements could be combined to form compound statements, as follows.

> Curtis is 18 years old, and he has brown eyes.
> Curtis is 18 years old, or he has brown eyes.

The word *not* is used to form the **negation** of a statement. The negation of statement (1) would be as follows.

> Curtis is not 18 years old.

Explore: Compound Statements With *And* and *Or*

In everyday usage, *and* is inclusive.
> Mark is in grade 11, and he attends Westbrook High School.

Similarly in mathematics,
> 9 is an integer, and it is greater than 0.

In everyday usage, *or* can be inclusive or exclusive.
> I think I have a nickel or a dime in my pocket.

This inclusive use means I could have a nickel or a dime or both in my pocket.
> At 17:00 today, Barbara will be at home or at the arena.

This exclusive use means Barbara will be at home or at the arena, but not at both.

In mathematics, *or* is always inclusive.
> For the equation $x^2 - 5x + 6 = 0$, $x = 3$ or $x = 2$.

This inclusive use means the solution is $x = 3$ or $x = 2$, so both 3 and 2 are solutions to the equation.

a) Write an everyday-usage example of the inclusive use of *or*.
b) Write an everyday-usage example of the exclusive use of *or*.
c) Write a mathematical example of the use of *or*.
d) Write a mathematical example of the use of *and*.

Inquire

1. Which of the following sentences are statements?
a) February is the third month of the year.
b) May is the fifth month of the year.
c) September is the best month of the year.
d) 5 is not a factor of 25.
e) $x < y$.
f) The sum of the first eleven whole numbers is 55.
g) All families need a pet.
h) 56 is a multiple of 7.

2. In each of the following sentences, is the use of *or* inclusive or exclusive? Explain.
a) The package will be delivered on Tuesday or Wednesday.
b) Sophia likes movies that are animated or musical.
c) I plan to buy a car that is red or white.
d) x is a multiple of 5, or x is a multiple of 9.
e) y is a factor of 15, or y is a factor of 40.

For a compound statement containing *and* to be true, all component statements must be true.

Example 1   Compound Statements Using *And*
What values of x make the following compound statement true?
      x is a factor of 24, and x is a factor of 30.

Solution
The factors of 24 are 1, 2, 3, 4, 6, 8, 12, and 24.
The factors of 30 are 1, 2, 3, 5, 6, 10, 15, and 30.
The compound statement is true for factors that satisfy both statements.
The values of x that make the compound statement true are 1, 2, 3, and 6.

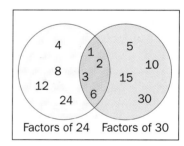

The solution to Example 1 can be visualized using a **Venn diagram**. This is a diagram that uses overlapping circles inside a rectangle to model statements.

In the Venn diagram shown, the interior of the rectangle represents all numbers. The factors of 24 and the factors of 30 are written within the two circles inside the rectangle. The numbers that are factors of 24 and factors of 30 are written within the region of overlap of the two circles.

A number line often provides a useful tool for visualizing the meanings of compound statements.

Example 2   Graphing Compound Statements Using *And*
Use a number line to show the set of numbers that satisfies each compound statement. In each case, n is a real number.
a) $n < 3$ and $n \geq -3$ **b)** $n < 0$ and $n < -2$

Solution
a) To show $n < 3$, use an open circle at 3, and draw a line to the left of the circle to indicate numbers less than 3.

To show $n \geq -3$, use a closed dot at 3, and draw a line to the right of the dot to indicate numbers greater than -3.

The combined statement $n < 3$ and $n \geq -3$ describes the numbers represented by both inequalities, that is, the numbers between 3 (exclusive) and -3 (inclusive), as shown.

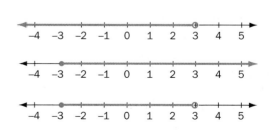

b) $n < 0$ and $n < -2$

This graph on the number line represents $n < 0$.

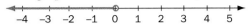

This graph on the number line represents $n < -2$.

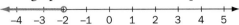

The combined statement $n < 0$ and $n < -2$ describes the numbers represented by both inequalities, as shown below.

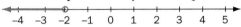

Example 3   Compound Statements Using *Or*

What values of y make the following compound statement true?

   y is a factor of 15, or y is a factor of 20.

The solution can be visualized using a Venn diagram.

Solution

The factors of 15 are 1, 3, 5, and 15.

The factors of 20 are 1, 2, 4, 5, 10, and 20.

The compound statement is true for factors that satisfy either statement or both statements.

The values of y that make the compound statement true are 1, 2, 3, 4, 5, 10, 15, and 20.

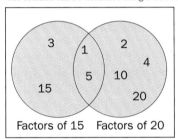

Factors of 15   Factors of 20

Example 4   Graphing a Compound Statement Using *Or*

Use a number line to show the set of numbers that satisfies the following statement, where n is a real number.

   $n < 3$ or $n < -2$

Solution

This graph on the number line represents $n < 3$.

This graph on the number line represents $n < -2$.

The combined statement $n < 3$ or $n < -2$ describes the numbers represented by one inequality or the other, or by both inequalities, as shown below.

Example 5   Statements Using *Not*

Use a number line to show the set of numbers that satisfies
the following statement, where n is a real number.

$$n \not< 3$$

$\not<$ means "is not less than"

Solution

$n \not< 3$ is the negation of $n < 3$ and represents the values of n
that are not less than 3. In other words, $n \not< 3$ represents the
numbers 3 and greater, as shown below.

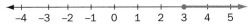

Example 6   Interpreting a Venn Diagram

The Venn diagram displays the results of a survey of
100 families regarding technology in their homes.
C represents the number of families with a computer.
V represents the number of families with a VCR.
F represents the number of families with a fax machine.
S represents all the families surveyed.

a) What percent of the families have a computer at home?
b) How many families have all three machines in their homes?
c) How many families have none of the machines in their homes?
d) How many families do not have a fax machine?
e) How many families have a computer and a VCR?
f) What fraction of the families have a computer or a fax machine?

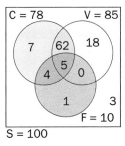

Solution

a) 78 of 100, or 78%, of the families surveyed have a computer at home.
b) The number of families with all three machines is the number in the overlap
of all three circles. So, 5 families have all three machines.
c) The number of families with none of the machines is the number outside all
three circles. So, 3 families have none of the machines.
d) The number of families without a fax machine is the total number of families
surveyed minus the number with a fax machine, that is, 100 – 10, or 90.
So, 90 families do not have a fax machine.
e) The number of families with a computer and a VCR is the number in the
overlap of the circles labelled C and V. There are 62 + 5, or 67, families with a
computer and a VCR.
f) The number of families with a computer or a fax machine is the number of
families with a computer or a fax machine or both. The total of the numbers
within circle C, circle F, or both is 62 + 7 + 1 + 0 + 4 + 5, or 79. The fraction
of the families with a computer or a fax machine is $\dfrac{79}{100}$.

Example 7   Drawing a Venn Diagram

Each member of a sports club plays at least one of soccer, rugby, or tennis.
The following information is known.
43 members play tennis, 11 play tennis and rugby, 7 play tennis and soccer,
6 play soccer and rugby, 84 play rugby or tennis, 68 play soccer or rugby,
and 4 play all three sports.
a) Display the information in a Venn diagram.
b) How many members does the club have?

Solution

a) Draw three overlapping circles and label them to represent
each of the three sports.
To place the numbers, start with the overlap of all three circles.
The number in this overlap is the number of people who play all
three sports. So, write 4 in the overlap.
Next, since 11 members play tennis and rugby, 11 − 4 members
play tennis and rugby, but not all three sports. Write 7 in the
overlap of the T and R circles.
Similarly, 6 − 4 gives 2 members who play soccer and rugby, and
7 − 4 gives 3 who play tennis and soccer.

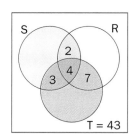

Then, since 43 members play tennis, 43 − 4 − 7 − 3 = 29.
Thus, 29 members play only tennis.
Because 84 members play rugby or tennis, the total of the numbers
in the R and T circles is 84.
Since 84 − 7 − 4 − 3 − 29 − 2 = 39, there are 39 members who play
only rugby.

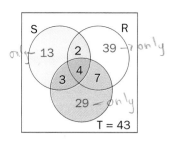

Similarly, for the S and R circles, 68 − 3 − 4 − 2 − 7 − 39 = 13, so 13
members play only soccer.

b) The total of the numbers inside the circles can be found as follows.
43 + 39 + 2 + 13 = 97
Therefore, the club has 97 members.

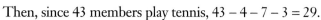

Practice

State whether each sentence is a statement.
  1. Ottawa is the capital of Canada.
  2. Is it raining?
  3. The moon is made of green cheese.
  4. Roses are better than tulips.
  5. No animals lay eggs.

*What whole-number values of x make each of the
following compound statements true?*
  6. x is a factor of 18, and x is a factor of 30.
  7. x is less than 10, and x is an even number.
  8. x is an odd number, and x is a factor of 12.
  9. x is a perfect square, and x is less than 50.
  10. x is a prime number, and x is less than 20.

*What whole-number values of y make each of the
following compound statements true?*
  11. y is a factor of 18, or y is a factor of 24.
  12. y is a factor of 12, or y is less than 10.
  13. y is an even prime number, or y is a factor of 6.
  14. y is zero, or y is a factor of 15.
  15. y is an odd number less than 12, or y is a factor
of 18.

Show each solution set on a number line.
  16. $n < 3$ and $n > -3$ **17.** $n < 3$ and $n < -3$
  18. $n \le -3$ and $n > 3$ **19.** $n \ge 5$ and $n > 2$
  20. $n \ge -2$ and $n \le 2$ **21.** $n < 0$ and $n \ge 4$
  22. $n < -2$ and $n > 3$ **23.** $n \le -1$ and $n \le -4$

Show each solution set on a number line.

24. $n > 5$ or $n < 3$ **25.** $n \leq -2$ or $n > 5$

26. $n < 3$ or $n < 2$ **27.** $n < 3$ or $n > 3$

28. $n \geq -2$ or $n > 5$ **29.** $n < 0$ or $n \geq 4$

30. $n \leq 3$ or $n > 6$ **31.** $n \geq -2$ or $n \leq 4$

Write a compound statement using inequalities and the word *and* to describe each solution set.

32.
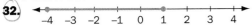

33.

34.
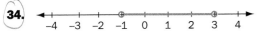

35.

Write a compound statement using inequalities and the word *or* to describe each solution set.

36.

37.

38.

39.

Write the negation of each statement.

40. Paulo lives in Edmonton.
41. The number 3 is the smallest prime number.
42. All isosceles triangles have 3 acute angles.
43. Ben is older than Katerina.
44. Deepak is telling the truth.
45. The Canucks won their game last night.

46. Use a circle, F, to represent the set of multiples of 5, and an overlapping circle, E, to represent the set of even numbers. Enclose the circles in a rectangle, T, representing the natural numbers less than or equal to 25. Place each natural number that is less than or equal to 25 in its appropriate position on your diagram.

The Venn diagram shows the natural numbers less than 20.
E represents even numbers.
O represents odd numbers.
P represents prime numbers.
Use the diagram to answer questions 47–50.

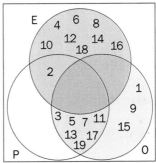

47. List the numbers less than 20 that are odd and prime.
48. List the numbers that are even or prime.
49. List the odd numbers that are not prime.
50. Why is the overlap of all three circles empty?

51. Of the 28 students in a class, 12 have a part-time job, 22 have a part-time job or do regular volunteer work, and 4 of the students have a part-time job and do regular volunteer work.
a) Display the data in a Venn diagram.
b) How many of the students do not have a part-time job or do not do regular volunteer work?

Applications and Problem Solving

52. Show the solution set for each situation on a number line.
a) Children who are more than 2 years old and less than 5 years old are allowed to attend preschool.
b) Admission to the museum is free to people who are less than 5 years old or 65 years old or older.
c) If you earn more than $29 000 and less than $39 000 per year, then you are taxed at rate B.

53. Write an inequality that is the negation of $n \geq 4$.

54. Show the solution set for each compound statement on a number line.
a) $n > 5$ or $n \not< 3$ **b)** $n \not< 2$ or $n \not> -2$
c) $n < 4$ and $n \not< 0$ **d)** $n \not\leq 3$ or $n < -3$
e) $n \not> 5$ and $n \not\leq -4$ **f)** $n > -2$ and $n \not\geq -1$

55. Write the compound inequality $-1 \leq x < 4$ as a compound statement.

56. Winter sports The Venn diagram displays the results of a recent survey of the members of an outdoors club. All members of the club participate in at least one of the three activities.
SK represents skiing.
S represents skating.
SB represents snowboarding.

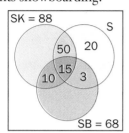

a) How many members does the club have?
b) How many members ski and skate?
c) How many members do not ski?
d) How many members do not skate or snowboard?

57. Course selections In a high school, there are 130 grade 11 students. Currently, 82 students are taking math, 27 are taking math and physics, 25 are taking math and chemistry, 20 are taking chemistry and physics, 110 are taking math or chemistry, and 87 are taking chemistry or physics. Eleven students are taking all three courses.
a) Draw a Venn diagram to display the information.
b) How many students are taking math or physics?
c) How many students are taking none of these three courses?

58. Music camp Each student at a music camp plays at least one of the following instruments: violin, piano, or saxophone. It is known that 6 students play all three instruments, 163 play piano, 36 play piano and violin, 13 play piano and saxophone, 11 play saxophone and violin, 208 play violin or piano, and 98 play saxophone or violin.
a) Display the information in a Venn diagram.
b) How many students are there at the camp?

59. Write a compound statement consisting of two inequalities, combined with the word *or*, for which the solution is the entire number line.

60. Write a compound statement consisting of two inequalities, combined with the word *and*, for which the solution is the number 5.

61. If possible, write a compound statement consisting of two inequalities, combined with the word *or*, for which there is no solution. Explain your answer.

62. If possible, write a compound statement consisting of two inequalities, combined with the word *and*, for which each of the following is true. Explain each answer.
a) The solution is the entire real number line.
b) There is no solution.

63. Blood types Human blood is classified as A, B, AB, or O. Type A has antigen A, type B has antigen B, type AB has both antigens, and type O has neither. Blood is also classified as Rh-positive or Rh-negative, depending on whether it contains the Rh factor. Blood tests on a group of 100 patients give these results.
36 patients have antigen A, 32 have antigen B, 83 are Rh-positive, 11 have antigens A and B, 28 have antigen A and are Rh-positive, 27 have antigen B and are Rh-positive, and 9 have antigens A and B and are Rh-positive.
a) Draw a Venn diagram with three overlapping circles to represent antigens A and B, and the Rh factor. Record the data in appropriate parts of your diagram.
b) How many patients have blood type A and are Rh-negative?
c) How many patients must be O positive?
d) Make up another question related to these data, and give it to a classmate to solve.

W O R D   P O W E R

Change the word FOOT to the word NOTE by changing one letter at a time. You must form a real word each time you change a letter. The best solution has the fewest steps.

Logic and Internet Search Engines

The Internet contains a great wealth of information. An Internet **search engine** is a software tool used to help you locate specific information quickly.

Search engines allow you to refine your searches using **Boolean operations**, that is, using the words *AND*, *OR*, and *NOT*. Some search engines use the symbols & or + for the word *AND*, and other symbols for the other words. Check the *Help* menu to find the symbols that your favourite search engine uses. In the following examples, the Boolean operators are capitalized for clarity. In practice, use only lower case. One search engine, for instance, uses only lower case unless you want the search to be case sensitive. If you search for *Mathematics*, you will get only the documents that have the word Mathematics with the first letter capitalized.

Consider the following searches.

The search, *mathematics* AND *magic*, returns all the documents containing the word *mathematics* and the word *magic*. The words do not have to be together. If you want words to appear together as an exact phrase, then enclose them in quotes, as in "mathematics magic." This search returns considerably fewer hits than the previous search.

The search *mathematics* OR *magic* returns all the documents containing the word *mathematics* or the word *magic*, perhaps hundreds of thousands of hits. This is probably not the search you really want.

The search *mathematics* AND NOT *magic* returns all the documents containing the word *mathematics* but not the word *magic*. Some search engines insist you use the word NOT with the word AND in their advanced search. Other search engines allow you to put a minus (–) sign immediately in front of the word, as in *mathematics–magic*.

If you want to force a grouping, you can use parentheses, as in *mathematics* AND (*cards* OR *tricks*). This returns all the documents that contain the word *mathematics* and either the word *cards* or *tricks* or both.

1 Comparing Searches

Consider the following searches.
A) mathematics AND cards
B) mathematics OR magic
C) mathematics AND (cards OR magic)
D) mathematics OR (cards AND magic)
E) (mathematics AND cards) OR (mathematics AND magic)
F) mathematics AND NOT magic
G) mathematics AND NOT (magic OR cards)
H) mathematics AND (cards AND magic)
I) (mathematics OR cards) OR magic

1. Which search would return the least number of hits? the greatest number of hits?

2. Explain why searches C and E would yield exactly the same number of hits.

3. Which of the given searches would yield the same number of hits as the search (mathematics OR cards) AND (mathematics OR magic)?

4. Why are the parentheses unnecessary in searches H and I?

2 Making Up Searches

1. Make up a search that is equivalent to search G from Exploration 1.

2. Make up a search using Boolean operations on a subject of your choice. Carry out the search, and then modify it to find the most efficient way of locating the information you want. Describe to your classmates the effects that various Boolean operations had on the results of your search.

The following extract is from Lewis Carroll's
Alice's Adventures in Wonderland.

"Then you should say what you mean," the March
Hare went on.

"I do," Alice hastily replied; "at least — at least
I mean what I say — that's the same thing, you
know."

"Not the same thing a bit!" said the Hatter. "Why,
you might just as well say that 'I see what I eat' is
the same thing as 'I eat what I see'!"

"You might just as well say," added the March
Hare, "that 'I like what I get' is the same thing as
'I get what I like'!"

"You might just as well say," added the
Dormouse, which seemed to be talking in its
sleep, "that 'I breathe when I sleep' is the same
thing as 'I sleep when I breathe'!"

As the extract shows, when you turn a statement
around, the result may not be a true statement.

When a compound statement is written in an
If...then form, it is called a **conditional
statement**.

Conditional statement: If a polygon is a pentagon,
then it has exactly five sides.

A conditional statement consists of two parts,
a **hypothesis** and a **conclusion**.
The hypothesis is the part following "If."
In the above example, "a polygon is a pentagon"
is the hypothesis.
The conclusion is the part following "then."
In the above example, "it has exactly five sides"
is the conclusion.

The **converse** of a conditional statement is written
by interchanging the order of the hypothesis and
the conclusion.

Conditional statement: If a polygon is a pentagon, then it has exactly five sides.

Converse: If a polygon has exactly five sides, then it is a pentagon.

Explore: Interpret the Statement

The following is a conditional statement.

If $x = 2$, then $x^2 = 4$.

a) What is the hypothesis of this statement?
b) What is the conclusion?
c) Is the conditional statement true?
d) Write the converse of the conditional statement.
e) What is the hypothesis of the converse?
f) What is the conclusion?
g) Is the converse true? Explain.

Inquire

1. To prove that a conjecture is not true, you need to find only one counterexample. How can this approach be used to show that one of the above conditional statements is not true?
2. Using the statement "If $x = 2$, then $x^2 = 4$," write a new conditional statement by replacing each equality symbol with a *less than* symbol.
3. Is the new conditional statement true? Explain.
4. Write the converse of the new conditional statement.
5. Is the converse true? Explain.

When a conditional statement and its converse are both true, they can be combined in an *if and only if* statement or **biconditional statement**.

Definitions are always considered to be biconditional.

Conditional statement: If an angle is a right angle, then its measure is 90°.
Converse: If the measure of an angle is 90°, then it is a right angle.
Biconditional statement: An angle is a right angle if and only if its measure is 90°.

The **contrapositive** of a conditional statement is formed by negating the hypothesis and the conclusion of the converse of the conditional statement.

Contrapositive: If the measure of an angle is not 90°, then it is not a right angle.

Example 1   Writing Conditional, Converse, and Contrapositive Statements

Consider the Pythagorean Theorem.
In $\triangle ABC$, $\angle C$ is $90°$.

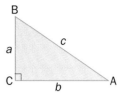

a) Write the Pythagorean Theorem as a conditional statement.
b) Write the converse of the Pythagorean Theorem.
c) Write the contrapositive.

Solution
a) The hypothesis is: In $\triangle ABC$, $\angle C$ is $90°$.
The conclusion is: $a^2 + b^2 = c^2$.
The Pythagorean Theorem can be expressed as a conditional statement, as follows.
If, in $\triangle ABC$, $\angle C$ is $90°$, then $a^2 + b^2 = c^2$.
b) To write the converse, interchange the hypothesis and the conclusion, as follows.
If $a^2 + b^2 = c^2$, then, in $\triangle ABC$, $\angle C$ is $90°$.
c) To write the contrapositive, negate the hypothesis and the conclusion in the converse.
If $a^2 + b^2 \neq c^2$, then, in $\triangle ABC$, $\angle C$ is not $90°$.

In the case of the Pythagorean Theorem, the conditional statement, its converse, and the contrapositive are all true.
The following example shows a situation where they are not all true.

Example 2   Determining the Truth of Statements

Consider the following conditional statement.
        If $\angle A$ is acute, then $\angle A = 30°$.
a) Is the conditional statement true?
b) Write the converse and decide whether it is true.
c) Write the contrapositive. Is it true?

Solution
a) There are many counterexamples to this conditional statement.
For instance, $\angle A = 45°$. The hypothesis is true, but the conclusion is not.
Therefore, the conditional statement is not true.
b) Interchanging the hypothesis and the conclusion gives the following converse.
If $\angle A = 30°$, then $\angle A$ is acute.
The converse is true.
c) Write the contrapositive by negating the hypothesis and the conclusion of the converse.
        If $\angle A \neq 30°$, then $\angle A$ is not acute.
As a counterexample to this conjecture, choose any other acute angle, such as $\angle A = 25°$. The conclusion is false.
Therefore, the contrapositive is not true.

Example 3   Reasoning With Inequalities

Consider the following conditional statement.
If $x > 0$, then $x^2 > 0$.
a) Is the conditional statement true?
b) Write the converse. Is it true?
c) Write the contrapositive. Is it true?

Solution
a) If $x > 0$, then x^2 is a positive number. The square of a positive number is always a positive number.
Therefore, the conditional statement is true.
b) *Converse:* If $x^2 > 0$, then $x > 0$.
One counterexample occurs when $x = -3$.
For $x = -3$, $x^2 = 9$, but $-3 \not> 0$.
Therefore, the converse statement is not true.
c) *Contrapositive:* If $x^2 \not> 0$, then $x \not> 0$.
The contrapositive can also be expressed in the following form.
If $x^2 \le 0$, then $x \le 0$.
The contrapositive is true because there is, in fact, only one case when the hypothesis, $x^2 \not> 0$, occurs. This is when $x = 0$. When $x = 0$, the conclusion of the contrapositive, $x \not> 0$ is true.
Therefore, the contrapositive is true.

Example 4   Reasoning in Number Theory
Consider the following statement.
Multiples of 4 are always multiples of 8.
a) Write the statement in *If…then* form. Is it true?
b) Write the converse. Is it true?
c) Write the contrapositive. Is it true?

Solution
a) If a number is a multiple of 4, then it is a multiple of 8.
Counterexample: 12 is a multiple of 4, but not a multiple of 8.
So, the statement is not true.
b) If a number is a multiple of 8, then it is a multiple of 4.
So, the converse statement is true.
c) If a number is not a multiple of 8, then it is not a multiple of 4.
Counterexample: 12 is not a multiple of 8, but it is a multiple of 4.
So, the contrapositive statement is not true.

Practice
Write each statement in If…then form.
1. Opposite angles are equal.
2. Canadians who are at least 18 years old may vote.
3. A quadrilateral is a polygon.
4. All prime numbers greater than 2 are odd numbers.
5. An angle that measures 90° has a sine of 1.
6. The diagonals of a rectangle bisect each other.
7. People who live in Moose Jaw live in Saskatchewan.
8. A right triangle has two acute angles.

Write each definition as a biconditional statement.
9. A pentagon is a polygon with exactly five sides.
10. A rational number is a number that can be expressed as the quotient of two integers.
11. A prime number has no factors other than itself and one.
12. An isosceles triangle has two sides of equal length.
13. A perfect square trinomial is one that can be factored as the square of a binomial.

Write the converse of each conditional statement. Is the converse true? Provide a counterexample, if appropriate, to justify your conclusion.

14. If $x = 6$, the $x^2 = 36$.

15. If $x = -4$, then $|x| = 4$.

16. If n is an even number, then $n + 1$ is an odd number.

17. If a rectangle has 4 equal sides, then it is a square.

18. If a triangle has three equal sides, then it is equilateral.

19. If a quadrilateral has one pair of opposite sides that are parallel, then it is a trapezoid.

20. If the equation of a line is $y = 3x + 1$, then the slope of the line is 3.

Determine whether each of the following conditional statements is true. Then, write the converse and the contrapositive statements, and determine whether each of them is true.

21. If $x = -4$, then $x^2 = 16$.

22. If $x = 3$, then $|x| = 3$.

23. If n is even, then $2n + 1$ is odd.

24. If n is a multiple of 6, then n is a multiple of 3.

25. If x^2 is an odd number, then x is an odd number.

26. If a quadrilateral is a rectangle, then its diagonals are equal.

27. If $3x - 5 = 16$, then $x = 7$.

Applications and Problem Solving

28. a) Is the following conditional statement true?
    If $x < 0$, then $x^2 > 0$.
b) What is the converse? Is it true?
c) What is the contrapositive? Is it true?

29. Consider the conditional statement:
    If $a^2 = b^2$, then $a = b$.
a) Is the conditional statement true?
b) Write the converse. Is it true?
c) Write the contrapositive. Is it true?

30. Coordinate geometry If the endpoints of line segment AB are A(3, 8) and B(7, 12), then the midpoint of AB is M(5, 10).
a) Is this statement true?
b) Write the converse. Is it true? If not, provide a counterexample.

31. Advertising Advertisers sometimes use faulty logic. Consider the following statement.
"People who eat at Tooleys have good taste, and we know you have good taste..."
a) What do the advertisers want you to think?
b) Why is their logic incorrect?
c) How should the statement be rewritten?

32. Algebra From the integral zero theorem, the following statement is true. If $x - p$ is a factor of $x^2 + bx + c$, then p is a factor of c.
a) Write the converse. Provide a counterexample to show that the converse is not true.
b) Write the contrapositive. Do you think it is true?

33. Write an example of each of the following.
a) a true conditional statement and its true converse
b) a false conditional statement and its true converse
c) a true conditional statement and its false converse
d) a false conditional statement and its false converse

34. Given a true conditional statement, can you conclude that either the converse or the contrapositive must be true? Give reasons and examples to support your answer.

NUMBER POWER

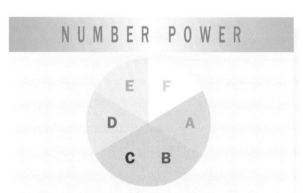

Copy the diagram. Replace each letter with a whole number so that the numbers in individual sectors, or the sums of numbers in two or more adjacent sectors, give all the whole numbers from 1 to 25. A replacement number may be used more than once.

Testing *If...then* Statements Using a Graphing Calculator

If...then statements are either true or false. In computer language, or Boolean algebra, a true statement is denoted by a 1 and a false statement by a 0. Consider the following statement.

If $x^2 \geq 6x - 5$, then $x \leq 1$ or $x \geq 5$.

A graphing calculator can be used to verify that the statement is true.

Graph $Y_1 = X^2 \geq 6X - 5$ in the standard viewing window.
Use the Value operation to test various values of x and see whether the y-value is 0 or 1.

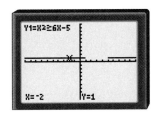
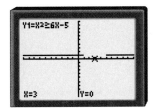

On the first screen shown, the x-value is -2 and the y-value is 1. This y-value shows that the x-value -2 makes the statement true. If you test a value of x greater than 1 and less than 5, such as $x = 3$ in the second screen, the y-value is 0. This y-value shows that, for the x-value 3, the statement is false. Continuing to find values of y for more values of x shows that if $x^2 \geq 6x - 5$, then $x \leq 1$ or $x \geq 5$.

1 Testing *If...then* Statements

Use a graphing calculator to test the truth of the following statements.

1. If $3x - 5 \leq -2x + 20$, then $x \geq 5$.

2. If $4x - 3 > 7x - 15$, then $x < 4$.

3. If $7x - 2 \leq 4x + 10$, then $x \leq 4$.

4. If $x^2 < 10x - 16$, then $x < 2$ and $x < 8$.

5. If $x^2 > -3x + 10$, then $x > -5$ and $x < 2$.

6. If $10x^2 - 6x \geq 19x$, then $x \leq 0.4$ or $x \geq 1.5$.

7. If $5x^2 + 17x < 12$, then $x > -4$ and $x < \dfrac{3}{5}$.

8. If $|x - 2| \geq 3$, then $x \leq -1$ or $x \geq 5$.

9. If $\left| \dfrac{2x}{3} - 5 \right| < 1$, then $x > 6$ and $x < 9$.

10. If $\left| \dfrac{1 - 2x}{3} \right| > 5$, then $x < -7$ or $x > 8$.

11. If $\dfrac{3}{x - 2} > 1$, then $x > 2$ and $x < 5$.

12. If $\dfrac{1}{x} + \dfrac{3}{4x} < \dfrac{7}{2}$, then $x > 0$ and $x < \dfrac{1}{2}$.

2 Solving Inequalities

Solve each inequality. Write the solution as an If...then statement.
Then, verify your result using a graphing calculator.

1. $12 - 3x \geq 23 - 14x$

2. $4x - 13 \leq -3x + 8$

3. $x^2 < x - 20$

4. $x^2 > -3x + 18$

5. $\dfrac{8}{x - 3} > 4$

6. $\dfrac{5}{x + 4} \leq 2$

Reviewing Congruent Triangles

Two triangles are **congruent** if and only if their corresponding parts are congruent.

The chart gives the theorems that prove that two triangles are congruent.

Theorem	**Example**	
If three sides of one triangle are congruent to the corresponding three sides of another triangle, the triangles are congruent.		$\triangle ABC \cong \triangle DEF$ (SSS)
If two sides and the contained angle of one triangle are congruent to the corresponding two sides and the contained angle of another triangle, the triangles are congruent.		$\triangle PQR \cong \triangle STU$ (SAS)
If two angles and the contained side of one triangle are congruent to the corresponding two angles and the contained side of another triangle, the triangles are congruent.		$\triangle KLM \cong \triangle NOP$ (ASA)

1 Congruent Triangles

For each pair of triangles,
a) *list three pairs of corresponding parts that are congruent*
b) *state the reason why the triangles are congruent*
c) *list the other parts that are congruent because the triangles are congruent*

1.
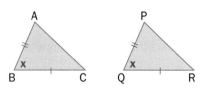

2.
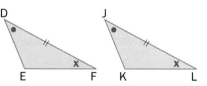

3.
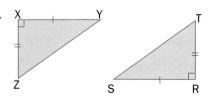

4.
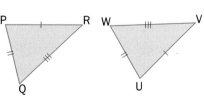

2 Triangles with Common Points and Sides

For each pair of triangles with all vertices named,
a) *list three pairs of corresponding parts that are congruent*
b) *state the reason why the triangles are congruent*
c) *list the other parts that are congruent because the triangles are congruent*

1.

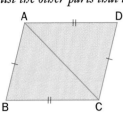

2.

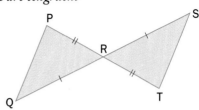

3.

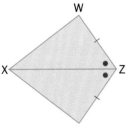

4.

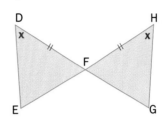

5.

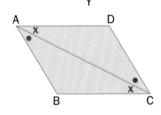

6.

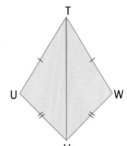

7.

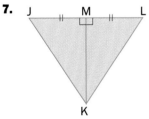

8.

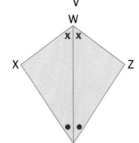

9.

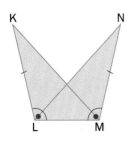

10.

6.6 Direct and Indirect Proof

When you have eliminated the impossible, whatever remains, however improbable, must be the truth.

Sherlock Holmes
The Sign of Four

The method of **direct proof** begins with given information and deductively reaches a conclusion.

In **indirect proof**, also known as proof by contradiction, the desired conclusion is assumed to be false. If this assumption leads to a contradiction, then it can be concluded that the assumption was incorrect and the desired conclusion is true.

Explore: Indirect Proof

Prove that the bisector of an angle of a scalene triangle cannot be perpendicular to the base.

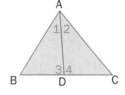

Draw scalene △ABC and draw the bisector of ∠A, AD. Mark the angles with numbers, as shown.

Since we want to prove that AD is not perpendicular to BC, assume that AD is perpendicular to BC.

Inquire

1. Why does ∠1 = ∠2?
2. Why does ∠3 = ∠4?
3. Why are △ABD and △ACD congruent?
4. How are AB and AC related?
5. What type of triangle is △ABC? What fact does this deduction contradict?
6. Is the bisector of an angle of a scalene triangle perpendicular to the base? Explain.
7. Use an indirect proof to prove that, if $x^2 = 5x$, then $x \neq 2$.
8. Does the above statement made by Sherlock Holmes illustrate indirect proof? Explain.

Steps for Writing an Indirect Proof

a) State all the possibilities.
b) Assume the negation of what you want to prove is true.
c) Reason correctly from the given information until a contradiction of a known theorem, postulate, or given fact is reached.
d) State that what was assumed to be true in step b) is false. Therefore, it follows that one of the other possibilities is true.
e) Repeat steps b) to d), until the one remaining possibility is the desired conclusion.

You have made conjectures previously, using inductive reasoning, about the relationships between parallel lines, transversals, alternate angles, corresponding angles, and co-interior angles on the same side of the transversal. However, inductive reasoning does not guarantee that these conjectures are true for all cases. The following two examples use indirect proof to prove the conjectures.

Example 1   Parallel Lines
Prove that if a transversal intersects two lines, making the alternate angles equal, the lines are parallel.

Solution
Given two lines, l_1 and l_2, and a transversal, t, intersecting l_1 and l_2 at A and B.
Given $\angle 1 = \angle 2$.
Prove that $l_1 \parallel l_2$.
Use indirect proof.
There are two possibilities.
Either l_1 and l_2 are parallel, or l_1 and l_2 are not parallel and they intersect.

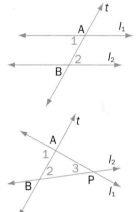

Assume that lines l_1 and l_2 are not parallel and they intersect at P.
Label $\angle APB$ as $\angle 3$.
$\angle 1$ is an exterior angle of $\triangle ABP$.
By the Exterior Angle Theorem, $\angle 1 = \angle 2 + \angle 3$.
Therefore, $\angle 1 \neq \angle 2$.
But it was given that $\angle 1 = \angle 2$.
Therefore, the assumption that the lines l_1 and l_2 are not parallel is false.
So, $l_1 \parallel l_2$.

> ***Theorem***
> If a transversal intersects two lines, making the alternate angles equal, then the lines are parallel.

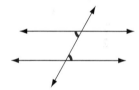

A **corollary** is a theorem that follows easily from a previously proved theorem.

The following are two corollaries to the above theorem.

> ***Corollary***
> If a transversal intersects two lines, making the corresponding angles equal, then the lines are parallel.

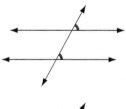

> ***Corollary***
> If a transversal intersects two lines, making the co-interior angles on the same side of the transversal supplementary, then the lines are parallel.

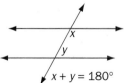

$x + y = 180°$

The theorem on the previous page and the two corollaries can be summarized as follows.

Transversal Parallel Lines Theorem
• If a transversal intersects two lines, making the alternate angles equal, then the lines are parallel.
• If a transversal intersects two lines, making the corresponding angles equal, then the lines are parallel.
• If a transversal intersects two lines, making the co-interior angles on the same side of the transversal supplementary, then the lines are parallel.

In order to prove the converse of the Transversal Parallel Lines Theorem, we first state the Parallel Line Postulate. Postulates, or **axioms**, are accepted to be true without proof.

Parallel Line Postulate
Through a given point, there is at most one line parallel to a given line.

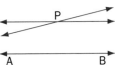

Example 2   Proving a Converse
Prove that, if a transversal intersects two parallel lines, the alternate angles are equal.

Solution
Given two parallel lines, l_1 and l_2, and a transversal, t, intersecting l_1 and l_2 at A and B.
Prove that $\angle 1 = \angle 2$.
Use indirect proof.
There are two possibilities.
Either $\angle 1 = \angle 2$ or $\angle 1 \neq \angle 2$.

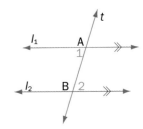

Assume that $\angle 1 \neq \angle 2$.
Therefore, there must exist a line l_3 through A, such that $\angle 3 = \angle 2$.
Since $\angle 3$ and $\angle 2$ are alternate angles and $\angle 3 = \angle 2$, then, $l_3 \parallel l_2$, by the Transversal Parallel Lines Theorem.
But, it is given that $l_1 \parallel l_2$.
So, by the Parallel Line Postulate, l_3 cannot be parallel to l_2.
Therefore, the assumption that $\angle 1 \neq \angle 2$ is false.
So, $\angle 1 = \angle 2$.

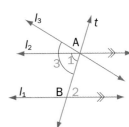

Converse
If a transversal intersects two parallel lines, the alternate angles are equal.

The following are corollaries of the converse.

Corollary
If a transversal intersects two parallel lines, the corresponding angles are equal.

Corollary
If a transversal intersects two parallel lines, the co-interior angles on the same side of the transversal are supplementary.

The converse and the two corollaries can be summarized as follow.

Converse of the Transversal Parallel Lines Theorem
- If a transversal intersects two parallel lines, the alternate angles are equal.
- If a transversal intersects two parallel lines, the corresponding angles are equal.
- If a transversal intersects two parallel lines, the co-interior angles on the same side of the transversal are supplementary.

Example 3   Triangle Angle Sum
Given $\triangle ABC$, prove that $\angle A + \angle B + \angle C = 180°$.

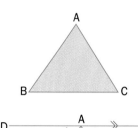

Solution
Draw a line, DE, through A, parallel to BC.
Label the angles 1, 2, and 3, as shown.
Since $\angle B$ and $\angle 1$ are alternate angles, $\angle B = \angle 1$, by the
Transversal Parallel Lines Theorem.
Similarly, $\angle C = \angle 3$.
Since $\angle DAE$ is a straight angle, $\angle 1 + \angle 2 + \angle 3 = 180°$.
So, in $\triangle ABC$, $\angle A + \angle B + \angle C = 180°$.

Triangle Angle Sum Theorem
The sum of the interior angles of a triangle is 180°.

A corollary to the Triangle Angle Sum Theorem is the Third Angle Theorem.

Third Angle Theorem
If two angles of one triangle are congruent to two angles of a second triangle, then the third angles of the triangles are congruent.

This theorem leads to another way to prove that two triangles are congruent.

Example 4   Angle-Angle-Side Congruence
Given $\triangle ABC$ and $\triangle DEF$, where $\angle A = \angle D$, $\angle B = \angle E$, and $CA = FD$, prove that
$\triangle ABC \cong \triangle DEF$.

Solution
Since $\angle A = \angle D$ and $\angle B = \angle E$, by the
Third Angle Theorem, $\angle C = \angle F$.
In $\triangle ABC$ and $\triangle DEF$,
$\angle A = \angle D$
$\angle C = \angle F$
$CA = FD$
Therefore, $\triangle ABC \cong \triangle DEF$ (ASA)

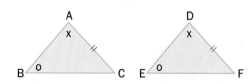

Angle-Angle-Side Congruence Theorem (AAS)
If two angles and a non-contained side of one triangle are congruent to the
corresponding two angles and a side of another triangle, the triangles are congruent.

Example 5   Exterior Angles
Given △ABC and exterior angle ACE.
Prove that ∠ACE = ∠A + ∠B.

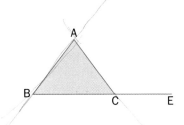

Solution
Since ∠BCE is a straight angle, ∠ACB + ∠ACE = 180°.
By the Triangle Angle Sum Theorem, ∠A + ∠B + ∠ACB = 180°.
Therefore, ∠ACB + ∠ACE = ∠A + ∠B + ∠ACB.
So, ∠ACE = ∠A + ∠B.

> **Exterior Angle Theorem**
> The exterior angle of a triangle is equal to the sum of the interior and
> opposite angles.

Example 6   Isosceles Triangles
Given isosceles triangle ABC, with AB = AC, prove that ∠B = ∠C.

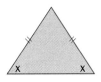

Solution
Draw the median, AD, from A to BC.
In △ABD and △ACD,
since AD is a median, BD = DC.
It is given that AB = AC.
AD = AD
So, △ABD ≅ △ACD (SSS)
Therefore, ∠B = ∠C.

The result of Example 6 is called the Isosceles Triangle Theorem.
Its converse is also true.

> **Isosceles Triangle Theorem**
> In any isosceles triangle, the angles opposite the equal sides are equal.
>
> **Converse of the Isosceles Triangle Theorem**
> If two angles of a triangle are equal then the sides opposite those two
> angles are equal.

Example 7   Triangle Medians
Use indirect proof to prove that the medians of a triangle cannot bisect each other.

Solution
In △ABC, AM is the median from A to BC, and CN is the median from C to AB.
The medians intersect at D.
There are two possibilities.
Either AM and CN bisect each other at D, or AM and CN do not bisect each
other at D.

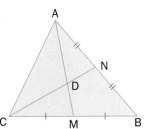

Assume that AM and CN do bisect each other at D.
Therefore, DA = DM and DC = DN.
In △AND and △CMD,
DA = DM and DC = DN
∠NDA = ∠CDM, by the Opposite Angles Theorem.
So, △AND ≅ △MCD (SAS).
Therefore, ∠AND = ∠MCD.
So, AB ∥ CB, by the Transversal Parallel Lines Theorem.
But, AB and CB are not parallel, since they intersect at B.
So, the assumption that AM and CN bisect each other at D is false.
Therefore, AM and CN do not bisect each other at D.
Therefore, the medians of a triangle cannot bisect each other.

Example 8   Scalene Triangle
In △ABC, ∠ABC is obtuse, and BD is the median from B to AC.
If BD is not an altitude, use indirect proof to prove that △ABC
is scalene.

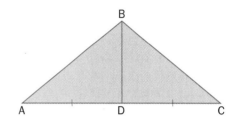

Solution
Assume that △ABC is not scalene.
There are two possibilities.
Either △ABC is an equilateral triangle or
△ABC is an isosceles triangle.

Case 1: Assume that △ABC is an equilateral triangle.
Therefore, each of the interior angles is 60°.
But we are given that ∠ABC is obtuse, which means that it is greater than 90°.
Therefore, the assumption that △ABC is an equilateral triangle is false.

Case 2: Assume that △ABC is isosceles.
Therefore, by the Isosceles Triangle Theorem, angles opposite the equal sides are equal.
Since ∠ABC is obtuse, the only possible equal angles are ∠A and ∠C.
If ∠A = ∠C, then AB = CB, by the converse of the Isosceles Triangle Theorem.
In △ABD and △CBD,
DA = DC, because BD is a median.
AB = CB
BD = BD
Therefore, △ABD ≅ △CBD (SSS).
So, ∠BDA = ∠BDC.
But, ∠BDA + ∠BDC = 180°.
Therefore, ∠BDA = ∠BDC = 90°.
So, BD is an altitude, which contradicts the given fact that BD is not an altitude.
Therefore, the assumption that △ABC is an isosceles triangle is false.

So, since △ABC is neither equilateral nor isosceles, △ABC is scalene.

Practice

*Using the method of indirect reasoning, what would be
your first assumption in trying to prove the following?*
1. In a group of 13 people, at least 2 people were
born in the same month.
2. There is no greatest whole number.
3. The sum of two odd integers is an even integer.
4. Suspect A is not guilty of the crime.

Use indirect reasoning to prove each of the following.
5. If the product of two natural numbers is greater
than 100, then at least one of the numbers is greater
than 10.
6. A handful of coins has a value of $2.25. There
are only dimes and quarters. Prove that there is an
odd number of quarters.
7. If the product of two numbers is 0, then at least
one of the numbers must be 0.
8. A triangle can have, at most, one obtuse angle.
9. If n is an integer such that n^2 is an even number,
then n is an even number.
10. If the sum of two numbers is less than 50, then
one of the numbers is less than 25.

Applications and Problem Solving

11. Use the method of indirect proof to show that,

if $a > 0$ and $b > 0$, then $a + b \neq \sqrt{a^2 + b^2}$.

12. Prove indirectly that, if x and y are positive
integers such that their product is an odd number,
then both x and y are odd numbers.

13. In $\triangle PQR$, PA is an altitude from P to QR and
$QA \neq AR$. Prove indirectly that $PQ \neq PR$.

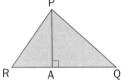

14. Use the method of indirect proof to show that
there is only one perpendicular from a point, P, to a
line.

15. a) Prove that the angle sum of a triangle ABC
is 180° by extending side BC to D, and
constructing a line CE that is parallel to AB.
b) Use the same diagram to prove that an exterior
angle of a triangle is equal to the sum of the two
opposite interior angles.

16. In the figure, $\angle ACD = 110°$, and $\angle B = 40°$.
Prove that $\triangle ABC$ is isosceles.

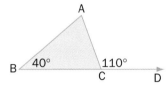

17. Prove that if two angles of one triangle are
respectively congruent to two angles of another
triangle, then the third angles are congruent.

18. Prove that the sum of the acute angles in a
right triangle is 90°.

19. Prove that the angle sum of any convex
quadrilateral is 360°.

20. Given lines l_1, l_2, and l_3 in a plane. If line l_1 is
perpendicular to line l_3, and line l_2 is perpendicular
to line l_3, prove that line l_1 is parallel to line l_2.

NUMBER POWER

When the following magic square is written
using only whole numbers, which of the
numbers from 1 to 10 is not used?

$x + 5$	$x - 2$	$x + 3$
x	$x + 2$	$x + 4$
$x + 1$	$x + 6$	$2x - 5$

Western Parks

Use the *Parks* database, from the Computer Data Bank, to complete the following.

 **a)** *Devise a plan to answer each question. Remember to exclude records for which the required data are not available.*
b) *Compare your plan with the plans of your classmates.*
c) *Revise your plan, if necessary, and then carry it out.*

1 True or False

In each conditional statement, is each conclusion true or false? Correct any false conclusions.
1. If you are in Spruce Woods Park, then you are in Manitoba, you can go swimming and hiking, and firewood is available.

2. If you are in Juniper Beach Park, then you are in a provincial park in British Columbia, with wheelchair access and 60 campsites, but no hiking trails.

3. If you are in Cypress Hills Park, you are in either Alberta or Saskatchewan.

4. If you are in Aspen Beach Park, then you are in a national park, with an area of 214 ha, and you can launch a boat and go fishing.

2 Facilities

1. What fraction of the parks in each province have fishing, but not boat launching?

2. Which provincial parks in Manitoba have firewood, showers, and more than 250 campsites?

3. How many parks have an area greater than the area of Elk Falls Park, have day use, but do not have wheelchair access?

4. How many parks have swimming and fishing, and are in British Columbia or Manitoba?

5. In which province do the greatest fraction of provincial and national parks have firewood and at least 50 campsites, but no showers?

3 Hiking Trails

There are more than 3000 km of hiking trails in British Columbia's provincial parks. What fraction of the provincial parks in British Columbia with hiking trails have day use?

4 Campsite Density

1. Which 6 parks in your province have the greatest campsite density, that is, the most campsites per hectare?
2. Use a bar graph to display the campsite densities of the 6 parks from question 1.

5 National Parks

Over 44% of the national parks in Canada are in the two westernmost provinces. What is the total area of all the national parks in British Columbia and Alberta? the average area?

6 Planning a Visit

1. a) Identify several parks that you are not familiar with, but would consider visiting for a day or part of a day.
b) What information in the database is important for you to know before your visits?
c) What other information would you like to know about the parks before you visit them?
d) Use your research skills to find this information.

2. Assume that you can go camping for 10 days next summer in one of the national parks in the Rockies.
a) What information, other than that given in the database, do you want to know about the park before your visit?
b) Use your research skills to find this information.

CONNECTING MATH AND COMPUTERS

Sorting Networks

One of the most time-consuming tasks a computer does is sort information, especially numbers. Consider the following representation of a sorting network.

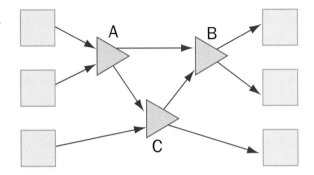

The numbers to be sorted start at the square nodes on the left and move along the lines until they reach the triangular nodes, where they are compared. The larger number comes out of the top of the triangle, and the smaller number comes out of the bottom. This process is repeated until the numbers reach the square nodes at the right. If the sorting network is designed properly, the numbers are sorted, with the largest number at the top and the smallest number at the bottom.

1 Determining the Output

Use the sorting network above. Suppose the numbers 2, 7, and 18 are in the three squares at the left, with 2 at the top, 7 in the middle, and 18 at the bottom.

1. a) Which two numbers are being compared at node A?
b) Which two numbers are being compared at node B?
c) Which two numbers are being compared at node C?
d) Are the numbers sorted properly?

2. Repeat question 1, with the three numbers to be sorted being x, y, and z, where $y < z < x$. At the start, x is in the top node, y is in the middle node, and z is in the bottom node.

2 More Complicated Sorting Networks

Use the following two networks.

Network 1

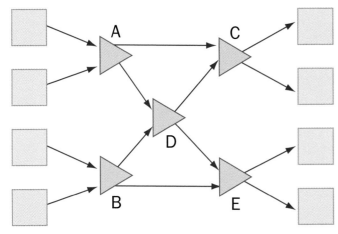

Network 2

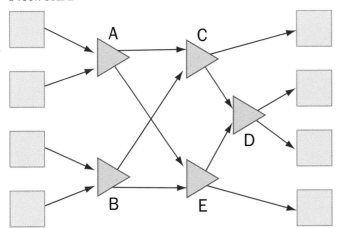

Suppose the numbers to be sorted, from top to bottom, are 5, 22, 29, and 51.
1. Use Network 1.
a) Which two numbers are being compared at node A?
b) Which two numbers are being compared at node B?
c) Which two numbers are being compared at node D?
d) Which two numbers are being compared at node C?
e) Which two numbers are being compared at node E?

2. Does Network 1 sort the numbers correctly?

3. Repeat the sorting process using Network 2. Does it sort the numbers correctly?

4. Design a different network to sort four numbers. Test your network using four different numbers.

Review

6.1 **1. Pattern a)** Simplify each expression and determine the pattern.

$$9 \times 1 - 1 = \blacksquare$$
$$9 \times 21 - 1 = \blacksquare$$
$$9 \times 321 - 1 = \blacksquare$$
$$9 \times 4321 - 1 = \blacksquare$$

b) Use inductive reasoning to find the value of
$$9 \times 987\ 654\ 321 - 1$$

2. In a stack of linking cubes, with 3 cubes per layer, each layer can be either red or green. Red layers cannot be adjacent. Green layers can be adjacent. The two possibilities for a single layer are as follows.

The three possibilities for a stack of two layers are as follows.

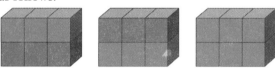

How many possibilities are there for a stack of 10 layers?

3. Sequences Predict the next two terms in each sequence.
a) 2, 5, 11, 23, 47, …
b) 4, 10, 28, 82, …
c) 1, 3, 3, 9, 27, 243, …
d) 1, 4, 7, 11, 14, 17, 21, …

6.2 *Provide one example that supports each of the following conjectures, and then give one counterexample for each conjecture.*
4. A point lies in the third quadrant if its *y*-coordinate is negative.
5. Even numbers are divisible by 4.
6. If the distance from A to P is the same as the distance from P to B, then P is the midpoint of AB.
7. For all real numbers n, n^2 is positive.
8. If two opposite sides of a quadrilateral are parallel, and one interior angle is 90°, then the quadrilateral is a rectangle.

6.3 *Write the conclusion that can be made using each pair of statements.*
9. All numbers that are divisible by 12 are also divisible by 6.
96 is divisible by 12.
10. Angles greater than 180° are called reflex angles.
∠R measures 220°.
11. Every Saturday, Miko goes swimming.
Tomorrow is Saturday.
12. In an equilateral triangle, each of the three angles measures 60°.
△KLM is an equilateral triangle.

13. Numbers a) Choose a number. Double it. Subtract 3. Add the original number. Divide by 3. Add 1.
Try this sequence of steps several times, starting with different numbers. Make a conjecture about the result.
b) Prove your result, using deductive reasoning.

14. Integers Prove deductively that the sum of any four consecutive integers is a multiple of 2.

6.4 *Show the solution set for each compound statement on a number line. In each statement, n is any real number.*
15. $n > -2$ and $n \le 0$
16. $n \le 8$ and $n < 5$
17. $n \le -3$ and $n > 4$
18. $n > 3$ and $n \le 4$
19. $n > 4$ or $n \le -1$
20. $n \le -1$ or $n < -3$
21. $n < -4$ or $n \ge 3$
22. $n \ge -2$ or $n > 3$

23. Cars Of 40 new cars in a dealership, 18 have air conditioning, 5 have air conditioning and a CD-player, and 28 have air conditioning or a CD-player.
a) Display the information in a Venn diagram.
b) How many cars do not have air conditioning or a CD-player?

24. Sports Two hundred people were surveyed about their participation in sports.
54 play hockey
73 play basketball
45 play tennis
22 play hockey and basketball
12 play hockey and tennis
16 play tennis and basketball
10 play all three sports
a) Display the information in a Venn diagram.
b) How many of the group play hockey but neither of the other sports?

c) What percent of the group plays either basketball or tennis?

d) How many do not play any of the sports?

6.5 *Write the converse and the contrapositive of each conditional statement. Decide whether each of the three statements is true, and provide a counterexample for any statement that is not true.*

25. If a prime number is greater than 2, then it is odd.

26. If a polygon has three sides, then it is a triangle.

27. In $\triangle XYZ$, if $\angle X + \angle Y < 90°$, then the triangle is obtuse.

28. If $x^2 > 0$, then $x > 0$.

6.6 **29.** In $\triangle ABC$, AB is extended to D, and AC is extended to E. $\angle DBC = \angle ECB$. Prove that $\triangle ABC$ is isosceles.

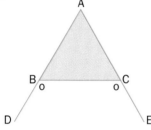

30. In $\triangle ABC$, AC = BC. BC is extended to D, and CE is parallel to BA. Prove that EC bisects $\angle ACD$.

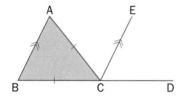

Use the method of indirect proof to prove each of the following.

31. No angle in a right triangle is obtuse.

32. Zero has no reciprocal.

33. If $x \neq 0$, then $\dfrac{1}{x} \neq 0$.

Exploring Math

Mathematical Induction

The principle of mathematical induction is another method of proving that a conjecture is true. Mathematical induction is often likened to the domino effect or to climbing a ladder. It works as follows.

Prove that the sum of the first n natural numbers is $\dfrac{n(n+1)}{2}$.

Conjecture: $S_n = \dfrac{n(n+1)}{2}$, where S_n is the sum of the first n natural numbers.

Step 1: Show that the conjecture is true when $n = 1$. When $n = 1$, the sum of the first natural number is $\dfrac{1(1+1)}{2}$ or 1.

Therefore, the conjecture is true when $n = 1$.

Step 2: Assume the conjecture is true for $n = k$. Then, show that the formula is true for $n = k + 1$.

$$1 + 2 + 3 + \ldots + k = \frac{k(k+1)}{2} \quad (1)$$

Add $k + 1$ to both sides of equation (1).

$$1 + 2 + 3 + \ldots + k + (k+1) = \frac{k(k+1)}{2} + (k+1)$$
$$= \frac{k(k+1) + 2(k+1)}{2}$$
$$= \frac{(k+1)(k+2)}{2}$$
$$= \frac{(k+1)[(k+1)+1]}{2}$$
$$= S_{k+1}$$

Therefore, the sum of the first n natural numbers is $\dfrac{n(n+1)}{2}$.

1. Use the principle of mathematical induction to prove the following conjectures. In each, n is a natural number.

a) the sum of the first n odd numbers is n^2

b) $n(n + 3)$ is even   **c)** $2n > n$

2. Use the principle of mathematical induction to prove that the nth term of the arithmetic sequence $a, a + d, a + 2d, \ldots$ is given by $a + (n - 1)d$.

Chapter Check

1. a) Predict the next two lines in the pattern.
$$2 + 1 \times 9 = 11$$
$$3 + 12 \times 9 = 111$$
$$4 + 123 \times 9 = 1111$$
$$5 + 1234 \times 9 = 11\,111$$
b) Test your predictions, using a calculator.

2. Two rays with a common endpoint form one angle, $\angle APB$.

Three rays with a common endpoint form 3 angles, $\angle APB$, $\angle APC$, and $\angle BPC$.

a) How many angles are formed by four rays? by five rays?
b) Make a conjecture about the number of angles formed by n rays.
c) Test your conjecture for six rays.

Give one example where each of the following conjectures holds, and then provide one counterexample to show that the conjecture is not always true.
3. All months have 31 days.
4. If n is a prime number, then $n + 1$ is an even number.
5. If $x < y < z$, then $yz < xy$.
6. If $\angle XPY + \angle YPZ = 180°$, then $\angle XPZ$ is a straight angle.

7. Describe the difference between inductive reasoning and deductive reasoning.

8. Farm animals A farm has only cows and chickens. The animals are normal in every way. Prove that there must be an even number of feet.

What conclusion can be made, using deductive reasoning, if each statement in the following pairs is true?
9. People who drive over the speed limit are likely to get a speeding ticket.
Marcel drives over the speed limit.
10. A person aged 13 to 19 is a teenager.
Sonya is 15 years old.
11. If both the x- and y-coordinates of a point are negative, then the point is in the third quadrant. The point P has coordinates $(-3, -4)$.

What values of n make each compound statement true?
12. n is a factor of 18, and n is a factor of 20.
13. n is an even number, and n is a factor of 12.
14. n is an odd number less than 12, or n is a factor of 12.
15. n is a multiple of 3 that is less than 20, or n is a factor of 24.

Write the converse and the contrapositive of each conditional statement. Decide whether each of the three statements is true, and provide a counterexample for any statement that is not true.
16. If a and b are consecutive natural numbers, then $a + b$ is an odd number.
17. If $\triangle ABC$ is a right triangle, then it contains two acute angles.
18. If $x^2 = 25$, then $x = 5$.

19. Lines l_1 and l_2 are parallel. Make a conjecture about the sum of the exterior angles on the same side of a transversal, t. Prove your conjecture.

20. Use the method of indirect proof to prove that the two equal angles in an isosceles triangle are acute.

Using the Strategies

1. The number 13 is a prime number in which the two digits are different. Reversing the digits gives 31, another prime number. How many other pairs of numbers containing two different digits, like 13 and 31, are both prime?

2. About how much time does it take for 500 cars to pass through an intersection during rush hour, if the intersection has stoplights?

3. A cyclist rode up a hill at 4 km/h and back down the same route at 12 km/h. If she made the ride without stopping, what was her average speed for the entire ride?

4. The sum of the lengths of the sides of a right triangle is 18 cm. The sum of the squares of the lengths of the sides is 128 cm^2. What is the area of the triangle?

5. The net shown is folded to make a cube. Name the face that will be opposite the face labelled A.

6. There were five books in a series. The books were published at six-year intervals. The year the fifth book was published, the sum of the five publication years was 9970. In what year was the first book published?

7. The number 144 is a perfect square. The sum of the digits of 144 is 9, which is also a perfect square. How many other three-digit numbers have this property?

8. A gift shop began selling cards on May 1. On May 2, it sold 3 more cards than it did on May 1. This pattern continued, with the shop selling 3 more cards each day than on the previous day. The shop was open every day for 9 straight days. At the end of the day on May 9, it had sold a total of 171 cards in the 9 days. How many cards did the shop sell on May 7?

9. You can use a balance scale, and a 1-g mass, a 3-g mass, and a 9-g mass to determine the masses of objects. How many different masses can be determined, if the objects and the given masses can be placed on either pan?

10. A dog is tethered to the side of a house, 5 m from the corner, as shown. The rope is 20 m long. Over what area can the dog run, to the nearest square metre?

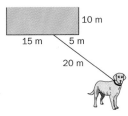

11. How many triangles are there in this figure?

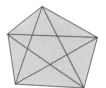

D A T A   B A N K

1. Assume that a coordinate grid is superimposed on a cross section of the telescope at the Max-Planck Institute, as shown. What is the vertical depth of the dish at a horizontal distance of 20 m toward the vertex from the outer edge? Round your answer to the nearest tenth of a metre.

2. Naomi is in Paris, France, on business. She needs to arrange a conference call with two of her colleagues. One is at head office in Vancouver. The other is in Sydney, Australia. For what time of day, Paris time, should Naomi arrange the conference call? Explain your reasoning.

3. a) Use data from the Data Bank on pages 580-589 to predict the world's population in the year 2100. State any assumptions you make.
b) Use your research skills to find out whether the predictions made by experts agree with your prediction. Give reasons for any differences.

CHAPTER 7

The Circle

Because of the nature of materials, architecture is primarily the art of straight lines. However, throughout history, architects have found ways to include circles and other curves in their designs. Some cities began as circles. Many old stone monuments, arches, and amphitheatres are circles or semicircles.

The circle and other curves were, and still are, important parts of architecture and other types of design. Dome structures are round. Ferris wheels and carousels are circles. Vehicles travel on circular wheels and turn on curves, not on right angles.

Some of our knowledge of the circle and other curves comes from the work of early Greek mathematicians. One of them, Apollonius of Perga, lived from about 245 to 190 B.C. and earned the title The Great Geometer. He studied various geometric shapes, including the circle and the parabola. His ideas are still used in such fields as astronomy and rocketry.

One of the circle problems that Apollonius posed was as follows.

Given three fixed non-overlapping circles, draw another circle that touches them all.

There are eight solutions to this problem. In the two solutions shown, the red circle touches each of the three fixed non-overlapping blue circles. The word *touches* is interpreted to mean that two circles intersect in exactly one point.

Draw the other six solutions.

GETTING STARTED

Geometry

1 **Angle Relationships**

Use the theorems that were proved in Chapter 6 to find the measures of the indicated angles.

1.

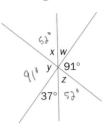

2.

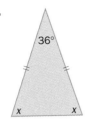

3.

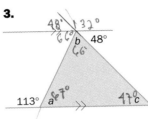

4.

5.

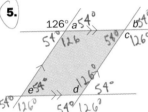

6.

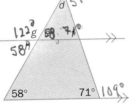

7.

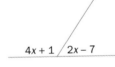

8.

Find the value of x in each of the following.

9.

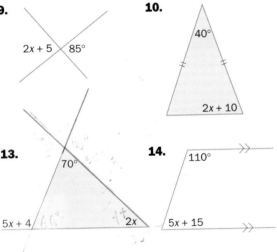

$2x + 5$ $85°$

10.

$40°$

$2x + 10$

11.

$4x + 1$ $2x - 7$

12.

x

$2x + 5$

$3x - 1$

13.

$70°$

$5x + 4$ $2x$

14.

$110°$

$5x + 15$

15.

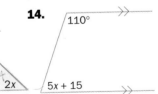

$2x - 1$

$2x - 8$ $x + 4$

16.

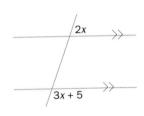

$2x$

$3x + 5$

2 Congruent Triangles

Recall that there are four theorems that can be used to prove two triangles congruent.

Side-Side-Side (SSS)
Side-Angle-Side (SAS)
Angle-Side-Angle (ASA)
Angle-Angle-Side (AAS)

For the indicated triangles,
a) *write the reason why the triangles are congruent*
b) *list the other equal parts*

1.

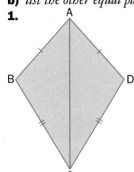

$\triangle ABC$ and $\triangle ADC$

2.

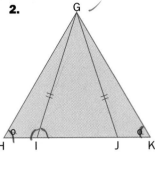

$\triangle GHI$ and $\triangle GKJ$

3.

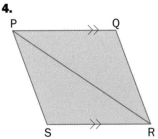

$\triangle DEF$ and $\triangle HGF$

4.

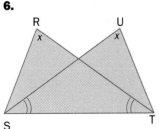

$\triangle PQR$ and $\triangle RSP$

5.

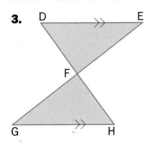

$\triangle ABD$ and $\triangle CDB$

6.

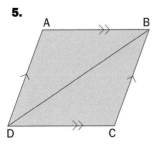

$\triangle RST$ and $\triangle UTS$

Mental Math

Angle Measures

Find the measures of the indicated angles.

1.

2.

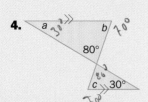

3.

4.

Adding the First *n* Whole, Even, or Odd Numbers

To add the first n whole numbers, multiply n by $n + 1$ and divide by 2.
So, $1 + 2 + 3 + \ldots + 9 = 9 \times 10 \div 2 = 45$

Calculate.
1. $1 + 2 + 3 + \ldots + 11$ **2.** $1 + 2 + 3 + \ldots + 49$
3. $1 + 2 + 3 + \ldots + 100$ **4.** $1 + 2 + 3 + \ldots + 1000$

5. Describe how the method can be modified to find the sum of the first n even numbers.

Calculate.
6. $2 + 4 + 6 + \ldots + 14$ **7.** $2 + 4 + 6 + \ldots + 20$
8. $2 + 4 + 6 + \ldots + 50$ **9.** $2 + 4 + 6 + \ldots + 100$

10. Add the following.
a) $1 + 3$ **b)** $1 + 3 + 5$
c) $1 + 3 + 5 + 7$ **d)** $1 + 3 + 5 + 7 + 9$

11. Use your results from question 10 to suggest a method for adding the first n odd numbers.

Calculate.
12. $1 + 3 + 5 + \ldots + 17$ **13.** $1 + 3 + 5 + \ldots + 99$

14. The sum, S_n, of an arithmetic series is given by
$$S_n = \frac{n}{2}[2a + (n-1)d]$$
where n is the number of terms, a is the first term, and d is the common difference. Use the formula to show why the methods for adding the first n whole, even, or odd numbers work.

INVESTIGATING MATH

Using the Equality Properties of Real Numbers

Recall the properties of real numbers shown in the table. These properties are used in geometric proofs.

In the table, a, b, and c represent real numbers.

Property	Statement
Addition property	If $a = b$, then $a + c = b + c$.
Subtraction property	If $a = b$, then $a - c = b - c$.
Multiplication property	If $a = b$, then $ac = bc$.
Division property	If $a = b$ and $c \neq 0$, then $\dfrac{a}{c} = \dfrac{b}{c}$.
Substitution property	If $a = b$, then a may replace b or b may replace a in any statement.
Transitive property	If $a = b$ and $b = c$, then $a = c$.
Symmetric property	If $a = b$, then $b = a$.
Reflexive property	$a = a$
Distributive property	$a(b + c) = ab + ac$

1 Writing Reasons

The table gives statements that include relationships between the lengths of line segments and the measures of angles. Copy the table. Complete the Reasons column by using one or more of the above properties to explain why each statement is true.

	Statement	Reason(s)
1.	If AB = CD, then AB + EF = CD + EF.	addition property
2.	If FG = PQ and FG = ST, then PQ = ST.	transitive property
3.	If XY = WZ, then XY − AB = WZ − AB.	substraction property
4.	If 2JK = 30 cm, then JK = 15 cm.	division property
5.	If ∠G = ∠K, then 3∠G = 3∠K.	multiplicatio property
6.	2(AB + BC) = 2AB + 2BC	distributive property
7.	If ∠A = 75° and ∠D = 75°, then ∠A = ∠D.	transitive property
8.	∠PQR = ∠PQR	reflexive property
9.	If ∠S = ∠T and ∠T = 90°, then ∠S = 90°.	transitive property
10.	If 90° = ∠DEF, then ∠DEF = 90°.	symmetric property
11.	If AB = BC and AB = 5 cm, then BC = 5 cm.	symmetric property, transitive property
12.	If UV − AB = XY − AB, then UV = XY.	addition property
13.	If ∠A + ∠B = 180° and ∠B + ∠C = 180°, then ∠A = ∠C.	substraction property, symmetric property
14.	If ∠C + ∠D = 180° and ∠C = ∠D, then ∠C = 90° and ∠D = 90°.	substitutio property, division property, transitive property
15.	If MN − PQ = 2 cm and PQ = 3 cm, then MN = 5 cm.	substitution property, addition property

2 Solving Equations

Solve each of the following equations, showing each step in the process. Beside each statement in your solution, write the reason that justifies the statement.

1. $2x - 3 = 19$ **2.** $4x + 1 = 33$ **3.** $\dfrac{5x + 1}{2} = 8$ **4.** $x + 2 = 5 - x$ **5.** $4(x - 1) = x - 5$

7.1 Geometric Proofs

The ideal reasoner would, when he has once been shown a single fact in all its bearing, deduce from it not only all the chain of events which led up to it, but also all the results which would follow from it.

Sherlock Holmes, *The Five Orange Pips*

Sherlock Holmes was the legendary detective created by Sir Arthur Conan Doyle in the late 1800s. Holmes used deductive and logical reasoning to solve mysteries.

Deductive reasoning was also used by Greek scholars, such as Euclid, interested in proving properties of geometric figures. The study of geometry in this chapter is closely related to the work of these scholars.

A set of statements and reasons is called a **proof**. The following can be used as reasons in a proof.
• given information
• definitions
• properties of real numbers
• previously proved theorems
• postulates or axioms

Theorems are statements that have been proved. **Postulates**, also known as **axioms**, are statements that are accepted to be true without proof. An example of a postulate is: "Through any two points, there is exactly one line."

Explore: Complete the Proof

Copy and complete the proof by writing the reason for each statement beside the statement.

Given: AE = CE; ED = EB
Prove: AD ‖ BC
Proof:

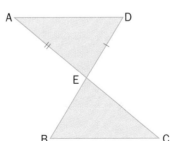

Statements	**Reasons**
In △AED and △CEB,	
a) AE = CE	
b) ED = EB	
c) ∠AED = ∠CEB	
d) △AED ≅ △CEB	
e) ∠DAE = ∠BCE	
f) AD ‖ BC	

Inquire

1. In line e) of the proof, what information tells you that
∠DAE = ∠BCE and not that ∠DAE = ∠CBE?

2. In line e) of the proof, what other pair of angles could have been
used to prove the lines AD and BC parallel? Explain.

3. Copy the diagram used in the proof and join AB and DC. Write a
proof to prove that AB = CD and AB ‖ CD. Compare your proof with
a classmate's.

The following steps can be used for most geometric proofs.
- Draw a diagram and mark the given information on the diagram.
- Analyze the given information and the diagram.
- Analyze what is to be proved.
- Use the analyses to plan a logical progression from the given
information to what is to be proved.

As you have seen, one way to record the statements and reasons for a
proof is to use two columns, with statements on the left and reasons on
the right. This method, called a **two-column proof**, is used in the
following example.

Example 1   Two-Column Proof

Given: BA = BC; BD = BE
Prove: ∠ABD = ∠CBE
Plan: Identify the equal angles in the isosceles triangles.
          Then, establish other equal angles.

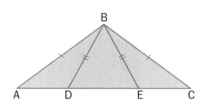

Proof:

Statements	Reasons
BD = BE	Given
∠BDE = ∠BED	Isosceles Triangle Theorem
∠BDA = ∠BEC	Supplements of equal angles are equal.
BA = BC	Given
∠BAD = ∠BCE	Isosceles Triangle Theorem
∠ABD = ∠CBE	Third Angle Theorem

Another method of writing a proof is called a **flow-chart proof** or a
flow proof. A flow-chart proof uses statements written in boxes, with
the reasons written under the statements. Arrows are used to show how
the statements are connected. This method of proof is shown in
Example 2.

Example 2   Flow-Chart Proof

Prove that any point on the perpendicular bisector of a line segment is equidistant from the endpoints of the segment.

Given: DC, the perpendicular bisector of AB
        Point P, any point on DC
Prove: PA = PB
Plan: Join PA and PB. Prove that △PAC ≅ △PBC.
Proof:
In △PAC and △PBC,

| AC = BC |
Definition

| ∠ACP = ∠BCP | ⟶ | △PAC ≅ △PBC | ⟶ | PA = PB |
Definition   SAS   Congruent Triangles

| PC = PC |
Reflexive property

The result of the proof in Example 2 is called the Perpendicular Bisector Theorem.
The converse of this theorem is also true.

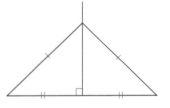

> ### Perpendicular Bisector Theorem
> Any point on the perpendicular bisector of a line segment is equidistant from the endpoints of the segment.
>
> ### Converse
> Any point equidistant from the endpoints of a line segment lies on the perpendicular bisector of the segment.

A third type of proof is called a **paragraph proof** or **informal proof**. In a paragraph proof, statements and reasons are written informally in a paragraph. The steps in a paragraph proof are the same as those in a two-column proof and in a flow-chart proof.

Example 3   Paragraph Proof

Given: AB = CD; AD = CB
Prove: AD || BC
Plan: Join AC and prove the triangles congruent.
Proof:
In △ADC and △CBA, it is given that AB = CD and AD = CB.
CA = AC by the reflexive property, so △ADC ≅ △CBA by SSS.
Since the triangles are congruent, ∠DAC = ∠BCA.
Therefore, AD || BC by the Transversal Parallel Lines Theorem.

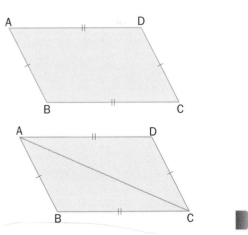

Example 4 Overlapping Triangles

Given: ∠PRT = ∠PSQ; PR = PS
Prove: RT = SQ
Plan: Separate the two triangles and mark the given information.
Prove the triangles congruent.

Proof:

Statements	**Reasons**
In △PRT and △PSQ,	
∠PRT = ∠PSQ	Given
PR = PS	Given
∠TPR = ∠QPS	Reflexive property
△PRT ≅ △PSQ	ASA
RT = SQ	Congruent triangles

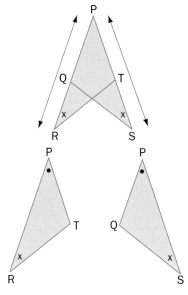

You already know the SSS, SAS, and ASA congruence theorems.
The following example proves another congruence theorem for triangles.

Example 5 Hypotenuse-Side Congruence

Prove that, if the hypotenuse and one side of one right
triangle are congruent to the hypotenuse and one side of
another right triangle, the triangles are congruent.

Given: △ABC and △DEF are right triangles.
AB = DE; CA = FD
Prove: △ABC ≅ △DEF
Plan: Use the Pythagorean Theorem to prove that BC = EF.
Then, prove the triangles congruent by SSS.
Proof: Let AB = DE = s and CA = FD = t.

Statements	**Reasons**
In △ABC, $t^2 = s^2 + BC^2$	Pythagorean Theorem
$BC^2 = t^2 - s^2$	Subtraction property
In △DEF, $t^2 = s^2 + EF^2$	Pythagorean Theorem
$EF^2 = t^2 - s^2$	Subtraction property
∴ $BC^2 = EF^2$	Transitive property Recall that ∴ means "therefore."
and BC = EF	Definition of square root
In △ABC and △DEF,	
BC = EF	Proved
AB = DE	Given
CA = FD	Given
∴ △ABC ≅ △DEF	SSS

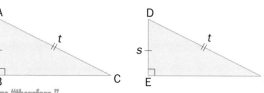

Hypotenuse-Side Congruence Theorem (HS)
If the hypotenuse and one side of one right triangle are
congruent to the hypotenuse and one side of another right
triangle, the triangles are congruent.

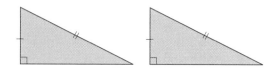

Example 6   Radio Tower

A radio tower, AB, is perpendicular to the ground. Four cables, AC, AD, AE, and AF, support the tower and have the same length. Prove that ∠ADB = ∠AEB.

Given: AB ⊥ CE; AB ⊥ DF   ⊥ means "is perpendicular to."
          AC = AD = AE = AF
Prove: ∠ADB = ∠AEB
Plan: Prove that △ADB and △AEB are congruent.
Proof:
In △ADB and △AEB,

| ∠DBA = ∠EBA = 90° |
Definition of
perpendicular

| AD = AE | → | △ADB ≅ △AEB | → | ∠ADB = ∠AEB |
Given   HS   Congruent triangles

| BA = BA |
Reflexive property

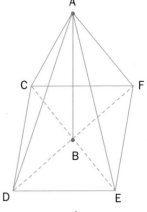

Practice

In questions 1–4, copy and complete each proof.

1. *Given:* AD is perpendicular to BC;
              D is the midpoint of BC.
    Prove: ∠B = ∠C

Proof:

Statements

In △ABD and △ACD,
BD = CD
∠BDA = ∠CDA
AD = AD
△ABD ≅ △ACD
∠B = ∠C

Reasons

Definition of midpoint
Definition of perpendicular
reflexive property
SAS
Congruent triangles

2. *Given:* BD = CD
              ∠ABD = ∠ACD
    Prove: AB = AC

Proof:

Statements	**Reasons**
BD = CD	Given
∠DBC = ∠DCB	Isosceles Triangle Theorem
∠ABD = ∠ACD	Given
∠ABD + ∠DBC = ∠ACD + ∠DCB	addition property
∠ABC = ∠ACB	
AB = AC	Substitution property
	Isosceles triangle Theorem

3. *Given:* PQ || SR
QT = ST
Prove: TP = TR

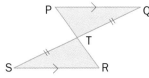

Proof:

Statements	**Reasons**
In △PQT and △RST,	
QT = ST	
▓▓▓▓▓▓▓	Opposite Angles Theorem
∠P = ∠R	▓▓▓▓▓▓▓
▓▓▓▓▓▓▓	AAS
TP = TR	▓▓▓▓▓▓▓

4. *Given:* Circle with centre O
Radii OA and OB
∠OAC = ∠OBC = 90°
Prove: AC = BC
Proof:

Statements	**Reasons**
In △AOC and △BOC,	
∠OAC = ∠OBC = 90°	▓▓▓▓▓▓▓
▓▓▓▓▓▓▓	Reflexive property
OA = OB	▓▓▓▓▓▓▓
△AOC ≅ △BOC	▓▓▓▓▓▓▓
AC = BC	▓▓▓▓▓▓▓

5. *Given:* AD = AE
DB = EC
Prove: BE = CD

6. *Given:* CA = CE
∠A = ∠CDB
∠E = ∠CBD
Prove: △CBD is isosceles.

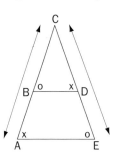

7. *Given:* QR = QT
SR = ST
Prove: ∠QRS=∠QTS

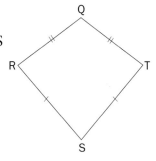

8. *Given:* ∠1 = ∠2
∠3 = ∠4
AB = AE
Prove: △ACD is isosceles.

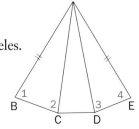

9. *Given:* DE = DG
FE = FG
Prove: EH = GH

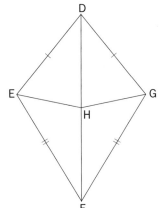

10. *Given:* LM ⊥ JK
KN ⊥ JL
MK = NL
Prove: △JKL is isosceles.

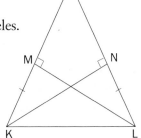

Applications and Problem Solving

11. Prove that the opposite angles and the opposite sides of a parallelogram are equal.

12. Prove that the diagonals of a parallelogram bisect each other.

13. Given that WZ || XY and WZ = XY, write a flow-chart proof to prove that WX = ZY and WX || ZY.

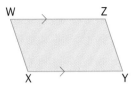

14. Prove that if the diagonals of a quadrilateral bisect each other, the quadrilateral is a parallelogram.

15. Three-dimensional geometry Determine which of the following conditions provide enough information to prove that △ABC ≅ △ADC. Give reasons for your answers.

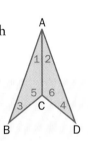

a) ∠1 = ∠2 and ∠5 = ∠6
b) AB = AD and ∠5 = ∠6 = 90°
c) ∠1 = ∠2 and AB = AD
d) ∠5 = ∠6 and AB = AD
e) ∠1 = ∠2 and ∠3 = ∠4
f) AB = AD and BC = DC

16. Two circles, with centres A and B, intersect at P and Q. Prove that PQ ⊥ AB.

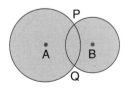

17. ∠DEF is any angle and GE is the bisector of the angle. Point P is any point on the bisector. Prove that P is equidistant from the arms of the angle.

18. Three-dimensional geometry Given that AD ⊥ BD, AD ⊥ CD, and △ABC is equilateral, prove that BD = CD.

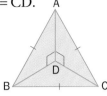

19. Ladder A ladder, AB, is leaning against a wall. The top of the ladder slides down the wall to the position represented by CD. If ∠BAE = ∠CDE, prove that AE = ED.

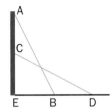

20. Flag pole The flag pole, FP, is perpendicular to the ground. Three cables, FA, FB, and FC, support the pole. The angles that the cables make with the ground at A, B, and C are congruent. Prove that the three cables have the same length.

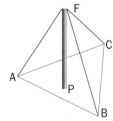

21. Write a paragraph proof to prove that any point, P, equidistant from the endpoints of any line segment, AB, lies on the perpendicular bisector of the segment.

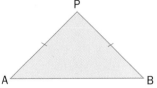

22. Surveying AB is the distance across a pond.

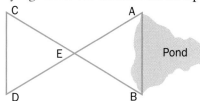

Describe how to locate the points C, D, and E so that the distance AB can be found by measuring the distance CD.

23. Show that if three angles of one triangle are congruent to three angles of another triangle, the triangles are not necessarily congruent.

24. Coordinate geometry Plot the points A(1, 1), B(–7, –1), C(–4, –4), and D(–1, –7), and join them to form △ABC and △ADC. Prove that △ABC ≅ △ADC using the Hypotenuse-Side Congruence Theorem.

25. Coordinate geometry △ABC has vertices A(0, 4), B(0, 0), and C(5, 0). △PQR has vertices P(–2, 2), Q(–2, –3), and R(–6, –3). Determine if △ABC ≅ △PQR.

26. Coordinate geometry △RST has vertices R(3, 3), S(–1, 5), and T(1, –1). △DEF has vertices D(2, 1), E(6, 3), and F(–2, 3). Is △RST ≅ △DEF?

27. Algebra Given △ABC ≅ △DEF, ∠B = $x + 25$, ∠D = $2x - 5$, and ∠C = 40°.
a) Find the value of x.
b) Find the measure of each angle in each triangle.

28. A rhombus is a quadrilateral with four equal sides. Prove that
a) a rhombus is a parallelogram
b) the diagonals intersect at right angles
c) the diagonals bisect the angles at the vertices of the rhombus

29. Given that the four sides of quadrilateral ABCD are congruent to the four sides of quadrilateral PQRS, are the two quadrilaterals necessarily congruent? Explain.

30. Probability The following six statements describe the two triangles.

| ∠A = ∠D | ∠B = ∠E | ∠C = ∠F |
| AB = DE | BC = EF | CA = FD |

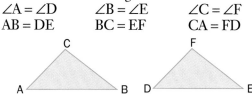

There are twenty ways of choosing a group of three statements from the six statements. What is the probability that a set of three statements chosen at random will ensure that the triangles are congruent?

31. Show that if two sides and the non-contained angle of one triangle are congruent to the corresponding two sides and non-contained angle of another triangle, the triangles are not necessarily congruent.

32. PQRS is any quadrilateral. Quadrilateral ABCD is formed by joining the midpoints of the sides of quadrilateral PQRS. Prove that ABCD is a parallelogram.

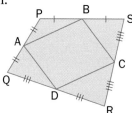

33. In isosceles trapezoid ABCD, AB = DC and AD ∥ BC. Prove that ∠B = ∠C and ∠A = ∠D.

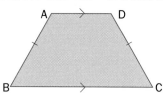

34. In the kite ABCD, AD = AB and DC = BC. Prove that the area of ABCD is $\frac{1}{2}$(AC)(DB).

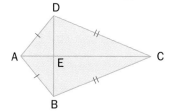

Terrestrial Craters

Use the *Craters* database, from the Computer Data Bank, to complete the following.

1 Simple and Complex Craters

A simple crater is a small crater with a bowl shape. The vertical cross section through the middle of a simple crater is nearly parabolic. A complex crater is distinguished from a simple crater by its wall terraces, central peak, and flat floors.

1. How could you determine which craters in the database are simple and which are complex using the above information?

2. How many craters of each type are in the database?

2 Simple Craters

1. Which crater in Canada has a diameter of 2.44 km and an apparent depth of 0.34 km?

2. Sketch a graph of the parabolic shape of the cross section of that crater, where the diameter is on the horizontal axis and the apparent depth is on the vertical axis.

3. What are the values of p and q in $y = a(x - p)^2 + q$ for the parabola you sketched?

4. a) How would you find the value of a?
b) What is the value of a, rounded to the nearest thousandth?

5. Devise a plan to model the cross section of each simple crater as a quadratic function. Remember to exclude records for which the required data are not available. Describe any calculation fields you would add.

6. Compare your plan with the plans of your classmates. Revise your plan, if necessary, and then carry it out.

7. Sort the records from least to greatest value of a. Describe how you sorted in terms of the shape of the parabola representing each simple crater.

3 Simple Crater Characteristics

Geologists studying both terrestrial and lunar craters have made the following generalizations about simple craters.
• The true depth of a simple crater is about 20% of the crater's diameter.
• The rim height of a simple crater is about 4% of the crater's diameter.

1. Devise a plan to check the validity of these generalizations using the database. Remember to exclude records for which the required data are not available. Describe any calculation fields you would add.

2. Compare your plan with the plans of your classmates. Revise your plan, if necessary, and then carry it out. Which crater most closely matches both generalizations? Explain your choice.

4 Complex Crater Characteristics

Geologists studying both terrestrial and lunar craters have made the following generalizations about complex craters.
• The central peak diameter is about 22% of the crater's diameter.
• The central peak height is about 8% of the crater's diameter.

1. Devise a plan to check the validity of these generalizations using the database. Remember to exclude records for which the required data are not available. Describe any calculation fields you would add.

2. Compare your plan with the plans of your classmates. Revise your plan, if necessary, and then carry it out. Which generalizations appear more valid from the database — those about simple craters or those about complex craters? Explain.

TECHNOLOGY

Exploring Chord Properties With Geometry Software

Complete the following explorations using geometry
software or a graphing calculator with geometry capabilities.
If suitable technology is not available, complete the
equivalent paper-and-pencil explorations on page 395.

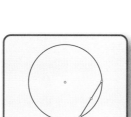
chord

A **chord** is a line segment joining two points on a circle.

1 Perpendicular Bisector of a Chord

1. Construct a circle.

2. Construct a chord of the circle.

3. Construct the midpoint of the chord.

4. Construct a line perpendicular to the chord
through its midpoint. Where is the centre of
the circle in relation to this perpendicular?
Compare your findings with those of your classmates.

5. Move an endpoint of the chord around the circumference
to change the chord to different lengths. In each case, where
is the centre of the circle in relation to the perpendicular?
Compare your findings with those of your classmates.

6. Write a statement about the location of the centre of a
circle in relation to the perpendicular bisector of a chord.

2 Perpendicular From the Centre of a Circle to a Chord

1. Construct a circle.

2. Construct a chord of the circle.

3. Construct a line perpendicular
to the chord through the centre of
the circle.

4. Construct the point of
intersection of the chord and the perpendicular line.

5. Measure the distance from the point of intersection to
each endpoint of the chord. How are the distances related?
Compare your findings with those of your classmates.

6. Move an endpoint of the chord around the circumference
to change the chord to different lengths. How are the
distances from the point of intersection to the endpoints of
the chord related in each case? Compare your findings with
those of your classmates.

7. Write a statement about the perpendicular from the
centre of a circle to a chord.

3 Line Segment From the Centre of a Circle to the Midpoint of a Chord

1. Construct a circle.

2. Construct a chord
of the circle.

3. Construct the
midpoint of the
chord.

4. Construct a line segment from the
midpoint of the chord to the centre of
the circle.

5. Measure the angles formed at the
midpoint. What do you notice about the
measures of the angles? Compare your
findings with those of your classmates.

6. Move an endpoint of the chord
around the circumference to change the
chord to different lengths. What do you
notice about the measures of the angles
in each case? Compare your findings
with those of your classmates.

7. Write a statement about the line
segment from the centre of a circle to the
midpoint of a chord.

Exploring Chord Properties

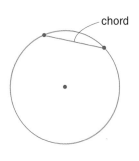

chord

Complete the following paper-and-pencil explorations using paper folding, a Mira, or a ruler and compasses.

A **chord** is a line segment joining two points on a circle.

1 Perpendicular Bisector of a Chord

1. Draw a circle.

2. Draw a chord of the circle.

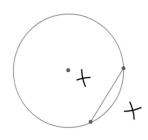

3. Construct the perpendicular bisector of the chord.

4. Where is the centre of the circle in relation to the perpendicular bisector?

5. Repeat steps 1 to 4 with another circle.

6. Compare your findings with those of your classmates.

7. Write a statement about the location of the centre of a circle in relation to the perpendicular bisector of a chord.

2 Perpendicular From the Centre of a Circle to a Chord

1. Draw a circle.

2. Draw a chord of the circle.

3. Construct the perpendicular from the centre of the circle to the chord.

4. Measure the distance from the point of intersection to each endpoint of the chord.

5. How are the distances related?

6. Repeat steps 1 to 5 with another circle.

7. Compare your findings with those of your classmates.

8. Write a statement about the perpendicular from the centre of a circle to a chord.

3 Line Segment From the Centre of a Circle to the Midpoint of a Chord

1. Draw a circle.

2. Draw a chord of the circle.

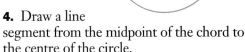

3. Construct the midpoint of the chord.

4. Draw a line segment from the midpoint of the chord to the centre of the circle.

5. Measure the angles formed at the midpoint.

6. What do you notice about the measures of the angles?

7. Repeat steps 1 to 6 with another circle.

8. Compare your findings with those of your classmates.

9. Write a statement about the line segment from the centre of a circle to the midpoint of a chord.

7.2 Chord Properties

A **circle** is the set of all points in the plane whose distance from a given point O is a given positive number, *r*. The point O is called the **centre** of the circle, and *r* is called the **radius**. A **chord** is a line segment that joins two points on the circle. A **diameter** is a chord that passes through the centre of the circle. A **secant** is a line that contains a chord.

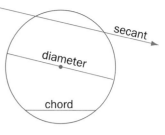

Since 1944, Canadair has manufactured thousands of aircraft for contracts in Canada and around the world. Planes built by Canadair are used to transport passengers and cargo, and as air ambulances.

The fuselage is the body of an aircraft where the passengers sit. On a circular cross section of the fuselage, the width of the floor forms a chord of the circle. The width of the floor is important in determining the maximum number of seats in the aircraft. Chord properties can be used to find the width of the floor.

Explore: Use a Diagram

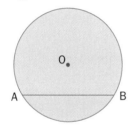

Draw a circle, centre O, to represent the cross section of the fuselage, and a horizontal chord, AB, to represent the width of the floor. From the centre of the circle draw a perpendicular to the chord at P. Join OA.

One model of Canadair aircraft has an internal radius of 1.285 m. The vertical distance from the middle of the floor to the ceiling is 1.88 m. Copy and complete the diagram, labelling the known distances.

Inquire

1. What kind of triangle have you drawn in your diagram?

2. What theorem can be used to relate the side lengths of this triangle?

3. Find the side lengths of the triangle.

4. What is the width of the floor, to the nearest hundredth of a metre?

In this section, theorems related to chords will be proved and applied.

Example 1   Perpendicular Bisector of a Chord

Prove that the perpendicular bisector of a chord contains the centre of the circle.

Given: Circle with centre O; chord AB
   l, the perpendicular bisector of AB.
Prove: O is a point of *l*.
Plan: Join OA and OB.
   Use the converse of the Perpendicular Bisector Theorem.

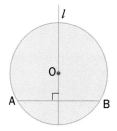

Proof:

Statements	Reasons
l is the perpendicular bisector of AB.	Given
OA = OB	Radii of a circle
O is a point of *l*.	Converse of the Perpendicular Bisector Theorem

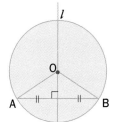

The theorem proved in Example 1 can be stated as follows.

> ### Theorem
> The perpendicular bisector of a chord contains the centre of the circle.

A **corollary** is a theorem that follows easily from a previously proved theorem. A corollary to the above theorem follows.

> ### Corollary
> The perpendicular bisectors of two non-parallel chords intersect at the centre of the circle.

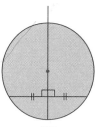

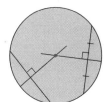

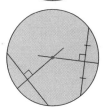

Example 2   Perpendicular From the Centre to a Chord

Prove that the perpendicular from the centre of a circle to a chord bisects the chord.

Given: Circle with centre O; chord AB; OC ⊥ AB.
Prove: AC = CB
Plan: Join OA and OB. Prove that △OAC ≅ △OBC.

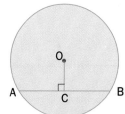

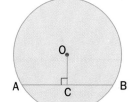

Proof:
In △OAC and △OBC,

$\boxed{\text{OA} = \text{OB}}$
Radii of a circle

$\boxed{\text{OC} = \text{OC}}$ $\longrightarrow$ $\boxed{\triangle\text{OAC} \cong \triangle\text{OBC}}$ $\longrightarrow$ $\boxed{\text{AC} = \text{BC}}$
Reflexive property   HS   Congruent triangles

$\boxed{\angle\text{OCA} = \angle\text{OCB}}$
Right angles, since OC ⊥ AB.

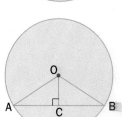

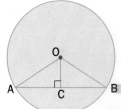

Since, in Example 2, AB was any chord, we can state the following theorem.

Theorem
The perpendicular from the centre of a circle to a chord bisects the chord.

Corollary
The line segment joining the centre of a circle and the midpoint of a chord is perpendicular to the chord.

The above theorems can be referred to collectively as the Chord Perpendicular Bisector Theorem, as follows.

Chord Perpendicular Bisector Theorem
• The perpendicular bisector of a chord contains the centre of the circle.
• The perpendicular bisectors of two non-parallel chords intersect at the centre of the circle.
• The perpendicular from the centre of a circle to a chord bisects the chord.
• The line segment joining the centre of a circle and the midpoint of a chord is perpendicular to the chord.

Example 3   Finding a Radius
A hemispherical pot is used for a hanging basket. The width of the surface of the soil is 30 cm. The maximum depth of the soil is 10 cm. Find the radius of the pot.

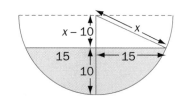

Solution
Label the diagram with the known information.
Let x represent the radius in centimetres.
The width of the soil surface is a chord, and the maximum depth is part of the perpendicular bisector of the chord.
Using the Pythagorean Theorem,
$$x^2 = (x - 10)^2 + 15^2$$
$$x^2 = x^2 - 20x + 100 + 225$$
$$20x = 325$$
$$x = 16.25$$
The radius of the pot is 16.25 cm.

Example 4   Congruent Chords
Prove that, if two chords in a circle are congruent, they are equidistant from the centre of the circle.

Given: Circle with centre O; AB = CD
Prove: AB and CD are equidistant from O.
Plan: Draw perpendiculars OE and OF to AB and CD.
           Join OA and OC.
           Prove $\triangle OAE \cong \triangle OCF$.

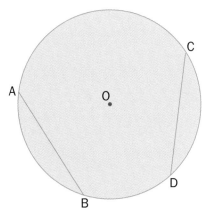

Proof:

Statements	**Reasons**
AB = CD	Given
$\frac{1}{2}$ AB = $\frac{1}{2}$ CD	Division property
AE = $\frac{1}{2}$ AB	Chord Perpendicular Bisector Theorem
CF = $\frac{1}{2}$ CD	Chord Perpendicular Bisector Theorem
∴ AE = CF	Substitution property
In △OAE and △OCF,	
AE = CF	Proved
OA = OC	Radii of a circle
∠AEO = ∠CFO	Definition of perpendicular
△OAE ≅ △OCF	HS
OE = OF	Congruent triangles
∴ AB and CD are equidistant from O.	

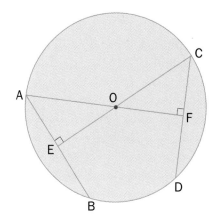

The following theorem was proved in Example 4.

Congruent Chords Theorem
If two chords are congruent, they are equidistant from the centre of a circle.

The converse of this theorem is also true.

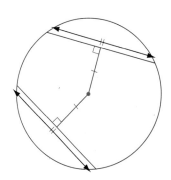

Converse
If two chords are equidistant from the centre of a circle, the chords are congruent.

Example 5   Equal Chords
Given: Circle centre O; DE = FG; DE and FG intersect at R.
Prove: OR bisects ∠DRG.
Plan: Draw perpendiculars from O to DE at A and from O to FG at B.
           Prove △OAR ≅ △OBR

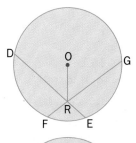

Proof:

Statements	**Reasons**
In △OAR and △OBR,	
OA = OB	Congruent Chords Theorem
RO = RO	Reflexive property
∠OAR = ∠OBR	Definition of perpendicular
△OAR ≅ △OBR	HS
∠ARO = ∠BRO	Congruent triangles
OR bisects ∠DRG	Definition of angle bisector

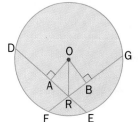

Practice

For questions 1–4, O is the centre of the circle. Decide whether each statement is true or false. Give reasons for your answer.

1.

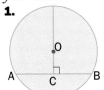

AC = CB

2. A

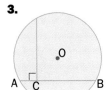

∠OCA = ∠OCB = 90°

3.

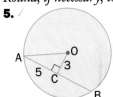

AC = CB

4. C

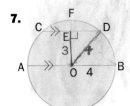

AB = FE

For questions 5–16, O is the centre of the circle. All lengths are in centimetres. Find the required lengths. Round, if necessary, to the nearest tenth of a centimetre.

5.

a) AO   **b)** AB

6.

AB

7.

a) EF   **b)** CD

8.

a) OA   **b)** CD

9.

a) OC   **b)** AB

10.

a) OC   **b)** AB

11.

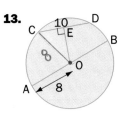

a) AB   **b)** FD

12.

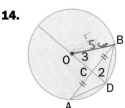

a) OA   **b)** CD

13.

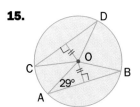

OE

14.

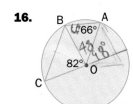

a) BC   **b)** BD

15.

∠OCD

16.

a) ∠AOB   **b)** ∠OCB

Applications and Problem Solving

17. A chord that is 10 cm long is 12 cm from the centre of a circle. Find the length of the radius.

18. The diameter of a circle is 20 cm. A chord is 8 cm from the centre. How long is the chord?

19. A chord is 12 cm long and the diameter of the circle is 16 cm. What is the distance between the chord and the centre of the circle? Round your answer to the nearest tenth of a centimetre.

20. If the diameter of a circle, AB, is perpendicular to a chord, CD, at E, prove that △ACD is isosceles.

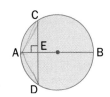

21. Write a two-column proof to prove that the line segment joining the centre of a circle and the midpoint of a chord is perpendicular to the chord.

22. Given three non-collinear points on a circle, describe how to find the centre of the circle using the three points.

23. AB and CD are two parallel chords in a circle, on the same side of the centre of the circle. AB is 10 cm long and CD is 14 cm long. Find the radius of the circle, if the perpendicular distance between the chords is 3 cm. Round your answer to the nearest tenth of a centimetre.

24. AB and CD are two parallel chords in a circle, on opposite sides of the centre of the circle. AB is 4 cm long and CD is 6 cm long. Find the radius of the circle, if the perpendicular distance between the chords is 5 cm. Round your answer to the nearest tenth of centimetre.

25. Road tunnel A road tunnel under a river is built inside a cylinder of radius 5.35 m. The road surface, AB, is 1.85 m above the lowest point of the cylinder. What is the width of the road, to the nearest hundredth of a metre?

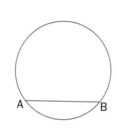

26. Water pipe A circular water pipe has a radius of 24 cm. If the maximum depth of the water in the pipe is 36 cm, find the width of the water surface, to the nearest tenth of a centimetre. What assumption did you make?

27. Water pipe A circular water pipe has a radius of 15 cm. If the width of the water surface in the pipe is 20 cm, find the maximum depth of the water, to the nearest tenth of a centimetre. What assumption did you make?

28. Draw a circle and two non-congruent chords. Is the shorter chord or the longer chord closer to the centre of the circle? Justify your answer.

29. A chord is the perpendicular bisector of a radius. If the radius is 30 cm, what is the length of the chord, to the nearest centimetre?

30. Two circles with centres A and B have the same radius. The circles intersect at C and D. If AB = 16 cm and CD = 12 cm, what is the radius of each circle?

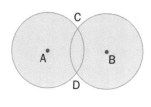

31. Write a paragraph proof to prove that the perpendicular bisectors of two non-parallel chords intersect at the centre of the circle.

32. Write a flow-chart proof to prove that, if two chords are equidistant from the centre of a circle, the chords are congruent.

33. Simon wants to hammer a square peg into a round hole. If the hole has a radius of 10 cm, will a square peg with a side length of 15 cm fit? Why or why not?

34. A circle has a radius of 20 cm. How many chords of the same length as the radius can be drawn parallel to a given diameter? Explain.

35. Write a two-column proof for the following. In the diagram, O is the centre of the circle and AB = CD. Prove that AE = ED and BE = CE.

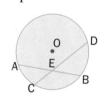

36. Three-dimensional geometry A sphere has centre O. The radius of the sphere is 12 cm. A plane intersects the sphere, forming a circle with centre P and radius 8 cm. How far is the plane from the centre of the sphere, to the nearest tenth of a centimetre?

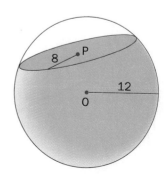

TECHNOLOGY

Exploring Properties of Angles in a Circle Using Geometry Software

Complete the following explorations using geometry software. If suitable software is not available, complete the equivalent paper-and-pencil explorations on pages 406–407.

A chord divides a circle into two arcs.

The smaller arc is a **minor arc**, and the larger arc is a **major arc**. Unless otherwise stated, any arc referred to in this text will be a minor arc.

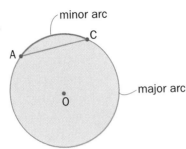

A **central angle** has its vertex at the centre of a circle, and two radii form the arms. Central angle AOC is described as **subtended** by the chord AC and by the arc AC.

An **inscribed angle** has its vertex on the circle, and two chords form the arms. Inscribed angle ABC is also described as subtended by the chord AC and by the arc AC.

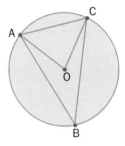

1 Central Angles Subtended by Equal Arcs

1. Construct a circle by centre and point. Show the label of the point.

2. Construct two other points on the circle, and an arc between them.

3. Measure the length of the arc.

4. Construct two other points on the circle, and an arc between them.

5. Measure the length of the arc.

6. Move an endpoint of one arc until the arc is the same length as the other arc.

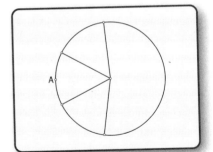

7. Construct and measure the central angle subtended by each arc. How are the measures of the angles related? Compare your findings with those of your classmates.

8. Move the centre or the point used to construct the circle to change the circle to different sizes. How are the measures of the central angles subtended by equal arcs related in each case? Compare your findings with those of your classmates.

9. Write a statement about how the measures of central angles subtended by equal arcs compare.

2 Inscribed Angles Subtended by the Same Arc

1. Construct a circle by centre and point. Show the label of the point.

2. Construct two other points on the circle, and an arc between them.

3. Construct another point on the circle.

4. Using the point from step 3 as the vertex, construct and measure the inscribed angle subtended by the arc from step 2.

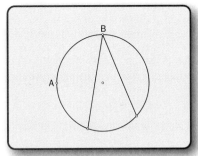

5. Move the vertex of the inscribed angle around the part of the circumference that is not on the arc to change the arms of the angle to different positions. What do you notice about the measure of the inscribed angle? Compare your findings with those of your classmates.

6. Move the centre or the point used to construct the circle to change the circle to different sizes. Repeat step 5 with circles of different sizes. What do you notice about the measure of the inscribed angle in each case? Compare your findings with those of your classmates.

7. Move an endpoint of the arc to change the arc to different lengths. Repeat steps 5 and 6 with arcs of different lengths. What do you notice about the measure of the inscribed angle for each arc length? Compare your findings with those of your classmates.

8. Write a statement about how the measures of inscribed angles subtended by the same arc compare.

3 Inscribed Angles Subtended by Equal Arcs

1. Construct a circle by centre and point. Show the label of the point.

2. Construct two other points on the circle, and an arc between them.

3. Measure the length of the arc.

4. Construct two other points on the circle, and an arc between them.

5. Measure the length of the arc.

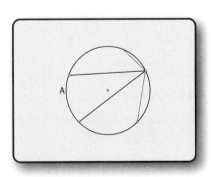

6. Move an endpoint of one arc until the arc is the same length as the other arc.

7. Construct another point on the circle.

8. Using the point from step 7 as the vertex, construct and measure the inscribed angle subtended by one of the arcs.

9. Using the same point from step 7 as the vertex, construct and measure the inscribed angle subtended by the other arc. How are the measures of the angles related? Compare your findings with those of your classmates.

10. Move the vertices of the inscribed angles around the part of the circumference that is not on the arcs to change the arms of the angles to different positions. How are the measures of the inscribed angles related in each case? Compare your findings with those of your classmates.

11. Move the centre or the point used to construct the circle to change the circle to different sizes. Repeat step 10 with circles of different sizes. How are the measures of the inscribed angles related in each case? Compare your findings with those of your classmates.

12. Write a statement about how the measures of inscribed angles subtended by equal arcs compare.

4 Angles Inscribed in a Semicircle

1. Construct a circle by centre and point. Show the label of the point.

2. To construct a semicircle, construct a line through the centre and the point on the circle, and construct the other point of intersection of the circle and the line.

3. Construct another point on the circle.

4. Using the point from step 3 as the vertex, construct and measure the angle inscribed in the semicircle. What is the measure of the inscribed angle? Compare your findings with those of your classmates.

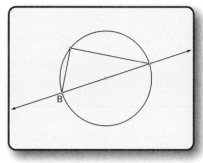

5. Move the vertex of the inscribed angle around the circumference to change the arms of the angle to different positions. What is the measure of the inscribed angle in each case? Compare your findings with those of your classmates.

6. Move the centre or the point used to construct the circle to change the circle to different sizes and the semicircle to different positions. What is the measure of the inscribed angle in each case? Compare your findings with those of your classmates.

7. Repeat step 5 with circles of different sizes. What is the measure of the inscribed angle in each case? Compare your findings with those of your classmates.

8. Write a statement about how the measures of angles inscribed in a semicircle are related.

5 Central and Inscribed Angles Subtended by the Same Arc

1. Construct a circle by centre and point. Show the label of the point.

2. Construct two other points on the circle, and an arc between them.

3. Construct and measure the central angle subtended by the arc.

4. Construct another point on the circle.

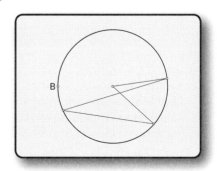

5. Using the point from step 4 as the vertex, construct and measure the inscribed angle subtended by the arc. How are the measures of the central and inscribed angles related? Compare your findings with those of your classmates.

6. Move an endpoint of the arc to change the arc to different lengths. How are the measures of the central and inscribed angles related in each case? Compare your findings with those of your classmates.

7. Move the centre or the point used to construct the circle to change the circle to different sizes. Repeat step 6 with circles of different sizes. How are the measures of the central and inscribed angles related in each case? Compare your findings with those of your classmates.

8. Write a statement about how central and inscribed angles subtended by the same arc are related.

6 Opposite Angles of a Cyclic Quadrilateral

1. Construct a circle by centre and point. Show the label of the point.

2. Construct four other points on the circle.

3. Using the points from step 2 as vertices, construct a quadrilateral. This quadrilateral is known as a cyclic quadrilateral because its vertices lie on a circle.

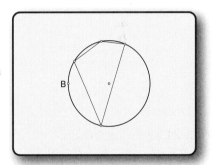

4. Measure each pair of opposite angles in the quadrilateral. How are the measures of the opposite angles related? Compare your findings with those of your classmates.

5. Move a vertex to change the quadrilateral to different shapes. How are the measures of the opposite angles related in each case? Compare your findings with those of your classmates.

6. Move the centre or the point used to construct the circle to change the circle to different sizes. Repeat step 5 with circles of different sizes. How are the measures of the opposite angles related in each case? Compare your findings with those of your classmates.

7. Write a statement about how the opposite angles of a cyclic quadrilateral compare.

7 Applying to Chords

Review Exploration 4. You constructed a diameter in order to construct a semicircle. As a result, the statement you wrote about angles inscribed in a semicircle applies to inscribed angles subtended by a chord, the diameter.

1. Consider your statements from the other explorations. Do you think they would apply to chords as well as arcs? Explain.

2. Repeat Explorations 1–3 and 5 for chords instead of arcs to test your conclusions from question 1.

INVESTIGATING MATH

Exploring Properties of Angles in a Circle

Complete the following paper-and-pencil explorations.

A chord divides a circle into two **arcs**.

The smaller arc is a **minor arc**, and the larger arc is a **major arc**. Unless otherwise stated, any arc referred to in this text will be a minor arc.

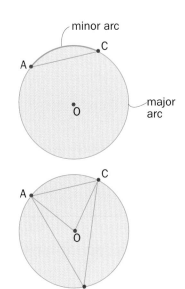

A **central angle** has its vertex at the centre of a circle, and two radii form the arms. Central angle AOC is described as **subtended** by the chord AC and by the arc AC.

An **inscribed angle** has its vertex on the circle, and two chords form the arms. Inscribed angle ABC is also described as subtended by the chord AC and by the arc AC.

1 Central Angles Subtended by Equal Arcs

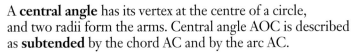

1. Draw a circle.

2. Mark two arcs equal in length on the circle.

3. Construct and measure the central angle subtended by each arc.

4. How are the measures of the angles related?

5. Repeat steps 1 to 4 with another circle.

6. Compare your findings with those of your classmates.

7. Write a statement about how the measures of central angles subtended by equal arcs compare.

2 Inscribed Angles Subtended by the Same Arc

1. Draw a circle.

2. Mark an arc on the circle.

3. Construct and measure three inscribed angles subtended by the arc.

4. What do you notice about the measures of the angles?

5. Repeat steps 1 to 4 with another circle.

6. Compare your findings with those of your classmates.

7. Write a statement about how the measures of inscribed angles subtended by the same arc compare.

3 Inscribed Angles Subtended by Equal Arcs

1. Draw a circle.

2. Mark two arcs equal in length on the circle.

3. Construct and measure an inscribed angle subtended by each arc.

4. How are the measures of the angles related?

5. Repeat steps 1 to 4 with another circle.

6. Compare your findings with those of your classmates.

7. Write a statement about how the measures of inscribed angles subtended by equal arcs compare.

4 Angles Inscribed in a Semicircle

1. Draw a circle.

2. Draw a diameter of the circle.

3. Construct and measure three angles inscribed in the semicircle.

4. What are the measures of the angles?

5. Repeat steps 1 to 4 with another circle.

6. Compare your findings with those of your classmates.

7. Write a statement about how the measures of angles inscribed in a semicircle are related.

5 Central and Inscribed Angles Subtended by the Same Arc

1. Draw a circle.

2. Mark an arc on the circle.

3. Construct and measure the central angle subtended by the arc.

4. Construct and measure an inscribed angle subtended by the arc.

5. How are the measures of the central and inscribed angles related?

6. Repeat steps 1 to 5 with another circle.

7. Compare your findings with those of your classmates.

8. Write a statement about how the measures of the central and inscribed angles subtended by the same arc are related.

6 Opposite Angles of a Cyclic Quadrilateral

1. Draw a circle.

2. Construct a quadrilateral with its vertices on the circle. This quadrilateral is known as a cyclic quadrilateral.

3. Measure each pair of opposite angles in the quadrilateral.

4. How are the measures of the opposite angles related?

5. Repeat steps 1 to 4 with another circle.

6. Compare your findings with those of your classmates.

7. Write a statement about how the measures of the opposite angles of a cyclic quadrilateral compare.

7 Applying to Chords

Review Exploration 4. By constructing a diameter, you constructed a semicircle. As a result, the statement you wrote about angles inscribed in a semicircle applies to inscribed angles subtended by a chord, the diameter.

1. Consider your statements from the other explorations. Do you think they would apply to chords as well as arcs? Explain.

2. Repeat Explorations 1–3 and 5 for chords instead of arcs to test your conclusions from question 1.

7.3 Angles in a Circle

Manon Rheaume was the goaltender for the Canadian women's national hockey team in two of the years that the team won the gold medal at the world championships.

Explore: Draw a Diagram

For one drill during a hockey practice, four players stand on an imaginary circle in front of the net. The net forms a chord of the imaginary circle. The players take turns shooting, trying to score on the goaltender.

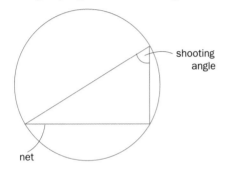

The diagram shows the shooting angle that one player might have on the net.
a) Draw your own diagram to show four players at different points on the circle.
b) Draw the shooting angle for each player.
c) Measure each shooting angle.

Inquire

1. How do the four shooting angles compare?

2. How could you move one of the players off the circle so that she has
a) a larger shooting angle?   **b)** a smaller shooting angle?

In the Technology section on pages 402–405, or the Investigating Math section on pages 406–407, you discovered that, when an inscribed angle and a central angle are subtended by the same arc, the measure of the central angle appears to be twice the measure of the inscribed angle. The following example proves that the central angle is exactly twice the measure of the inscribed angle.

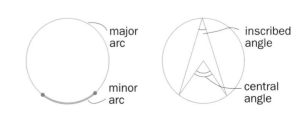

Example 1   Angles in a Circle

Prove that the measure of the central angle is equal to twice the measure of the inscribed angle subtended by the same arc.

Given: Circle with centre O; $\angle ABC$, an inscribed angle; $\angle AOC$, a central angle
Prove: $\angle AOC = 2\angle ABC$

Plan: Consider the three possibilities.

Case 1   O is on an arm of $\angle ABC$.
Plan: Compare central and inscribed angles using the Isosceles Triangle Theorem and the Exterior Angle Theorem.

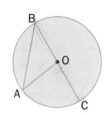

Proof:

Statements	Reasons
$OA = OB$	Radii of a circle
$\angle ABC = \angle BAO$	Isosceles Triangle Theorem
$\angle AOC = \angle ABC + \angle BAO$	Exterior Angle Theorem
$\angle AOC = \angle ABC + \angle ABC$	Substitution property
$\quad = 2\angle ABC$	
$\frac{1}{2}\angle AOC = \angle ABC$	Division property

Alternate Proof:

$$x = y$$
$$m = x + y$$
$$m = x + x$$
$$m = 2x$$
$$x = \frac{1}{2}m$$

Case 2   O is in the interior of $\angle ABC$.
Plan: Draw the diameter DOB. Use the result of Case 1 to compare the central and inscribed angles.

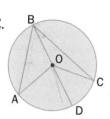

Proof:

Statements	Reasons
$\angle ABD = \frac{1}{2}\angle AOD$	Case 1
$\angle CBD = \frac{1}{2}\angle COD$	Case 1
$\angle ABC = \angle ABD + \angle CBD$	D is in the interior of $\angle ABC$.
$\angle ABC = \frac{1}{2}\angle AOD + \frac{1}{2}\angle COD$	Substitution property
$\angle ABC = \frac{1}{2}(\angle AOD + \angle COD)$	Distributive property
$\angle AOC = \angle AOD + \angle COD$	D is in the interior of $\angle AOC$.
$\angle ABC = \frac{1}{2}\angle AOC$	Substitution property

Alternate Proof:

$$x = \frac{1}{2}m$$
$$y = \frac{1}{2}n$$
$$x + y = \frac{1}{2}m + \frac{1}{2}n$$
$$x + y = \frac{1}{2}(m + n)$$

Case 3 O is outside $\angle ABC$.
Plan: Draw the diameter DOB.
Use the result of Case 1 to
compare the central and
inscribed angles.

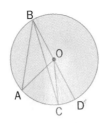

Proof:

Statements	**Reasons**
$\angle ABD = \dfrac{1}{2}\angle AOD$	Case 1
$\angle CBD = \dfrac{1}{2}\angle COD$	Case 1
$\angle ABC = \angle ABD - \angle CBD$	C is in the interior of $\angle ABD$.
$\angle ABC = \dfrac{1}{2}\angle AOD - \dfrac{1}{2}\angle COD$	Substitution property
$\angle ABC = \dfrac{1}{2}(\angle AOD - \angle COD)$	Distributive property
$\angle AOC = \angle AOD - \angle COD$	C is in the interior of $\angle AOD$.
$\angle ABC = \dfrac{1}{2}\angle AOC$	Substitution property

Alternate Proof:

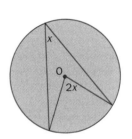

$$x = \dfrac{1}{2}m$$

$$y = \dfrac{1}{2}n$$

$$x - y = \dfrac{1}{2}m - \dfrac{1}{2}n$$

$$x - y = \dfrac{1}{2}(m - n)$$

The following theorem was proved in Example 1.

Angles in a Circle Theorem, Part 1
The measure of the central angle is equal to twice the measure
of the inscribed angle subtended by the same arc.

Example 2   Inscribed Angles
Prove that inscribed angles subtended by the same arc are congruent.

Given: Inscribed angles $\angle ABD$ and $\angle ACD$ subtended by the same arc AD.
Prove: $\angle ABD = \angle ACD$
Plan: Use the fact that both subtended angles have the same central angle.
Draw the central angle, $\angle AOD$.

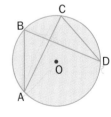

Proof:

Statements	**Reasons**
$\angle ABD = \dfrac{1}{2}\angle AOD$	Angles in a Circle Theorem
$\angle ACD = \dfrac{1}{2}\angle AOD$	Angles in a Circle Theorem
$\angle ABD = \angle ACD$	Transitive property

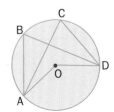

Corollary
Inscribed angles subtended by the same arc are congruent.

Corollary
Inscribed angles subtended by equal arcs are congruent.

Example 3   Angle in a Semicircle
Prove that the angle inscribed in a semicircle is a right angle.

Given: Diameter AC; inscribed angle, $\angle ABC$
Prove: $\angle ABC = 90°$
Plan: Consider the diameter AC as a central angle, $\angle AOC$. Use the fact that AOC is a straight line.

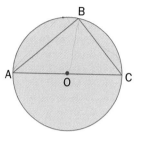

Proof:

$\boxed{\angle ABC = \dfrac{1}{2}\angle AOC}$
Angles in a Circle
Theorem

$\boxed{\angle AOC = 180°}$
Straight angle

$\boxed{\angle ABC = \dfrac{1}{2}(180°)}$
Substitution property

$\boxed{\angle ABC = 90°}$

Corollary
The angle inscribed in a semicircle is a right angle.

The results of Examples 1, 2, and 3 can be referred to collectively as the Angles in a Circle Theorem.

Angles in a Circle Theorem
• The measure of the central angle is equal to twice the measure of the inscribed angle subtended by the same arc.
• Inscribed angles subtended by the same arc, or by equal arcs, are congruent.
• The angle inscribed in a semicircle is a right angle.

Example 4   Finding Angle Measures
Determine the measures of angles 1 and 2.

Solution
$\angle 2 = 70°$, since $\angle BAC$ and $\angle BDC$ are subtended by the same arc, BC.
$\angle 1 + \angle 2 = 105°$, the measure of the exterior $\angle DCE$ of $\triangle BCD$.
$\therefore \; \angle 1 = 105° - 70°$
$\qquad = 35°$
So, $\angle 1 = 35°$ and $\angle 2 = 70°$.

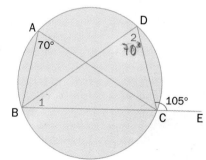

Example 5 Finding Angle Measures

The centre of the circle is O. Determine the measures of ∠BAC, ∠CBD, and ∠BOC.

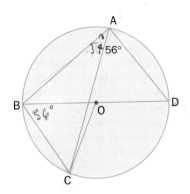

Solution

∠BAD = 90°, since ∠BAD is an angle in a semicircle.

∴ ∠BAC = 90° − 56°
  = 34°

∠CBD = ∠CAD, since they are both subtended by the arc CD.

∴ ∠CBD = 56°

∠BOC is a central angle subtended by the same arc as ∠BAC.

∴ ∠BOC = 2∠BAC
  = 68°

So, ∠BAC = 34°, ∠CBD = 56°, and ∠BOC = 68°.

Practice

Name the inscribed angles that are subtended by the arc BEC.

1.

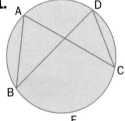

2.

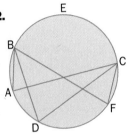

The centre of the circle is O.
a) *Name three angles subtended by the minor arc AB.*
b) *Name two angles subtended by the minor arc CD.*

3.

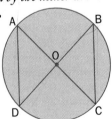

4.

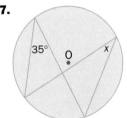

▯ *The centre of each circle is O. Find the degree measure of x. Explain your reasoning.*

5.

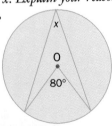

6.

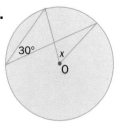

7.

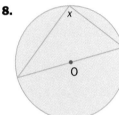

8.

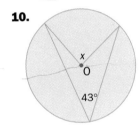

9.

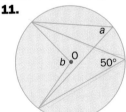

10.

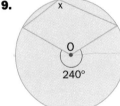

Find the measures of the indicated angles.

11.

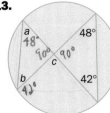

12.

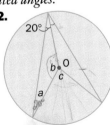

13.

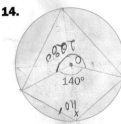

14.

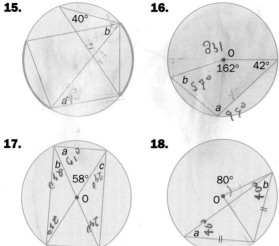

15.

16.

17.

18.

✏️ *Find the measures of the indicated angles. Explain your reasoning.*

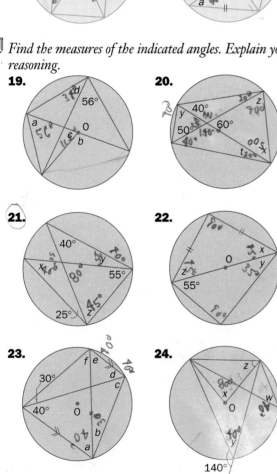

19.

20.

21.

22.

23.

24.

Applications and Problem Solving

25. *Given:* minor arc AD = minor arc BC
Prove: △ACB ≅ △BDA

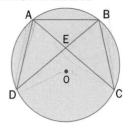

26. *Given:* AB ∥ DC
Prove: AC = BD

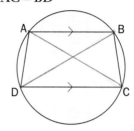

27 Points A, B, and C lie on a circle with centre O. ∠ABC = 45°. Prove that AO ⊥ CO.

28. Two circles intersect at X and Y. Two lines, AXB and CXD, are drawn through X to intersect one circle at A and C and the other circle at B and D. Prove that ∠AYC = ∠BYD.

29. Given that AB = CD, write a two-column proof to prove that two central angles subtended by congruent chords are congruent.

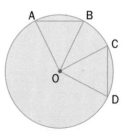

30. Write a flow proof to prove that, if two central angles are congruent, then the chords that subtend these angles are congruent.

31. Write a paragraph proof to prove that two inscribed angles subtended by equal arcs are congruent.

32. Stagehands Theatre stagehands are taught two methods to find the centre of a circle quickly. They can use a carpenter's square or a sheet of paper.

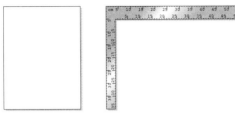

a) Describe how a stagehand could use a sheet of paper to find the centre of a circle.
b) How could a stagehand use a carpenter's square to find the centre of a circle?

33. Film production Film directors shoot a scene using several cameras. The director wants to shoot a scene from four different viewpoints.
a) Why will the cameras, in the positions shown, record the same scene?
b) Will the scenes look the same when they are shown? Explain.

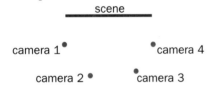

34. Similar triangles Two chords AB and CD intersect at E. By joining AC and BD, two triangles are formed.
a) Prove that $\triangle ACE \sim \triangle DBE$.
b) Write the three equal ratios of corresponding sides.
c) If AE = 4 cm, DE = 6 cm, and BE = 5 cm, find the length of CE, to the nearest tenth of a centimetre.

35. Navigation In some coastal areas, two beacons are used to warn ships of shallow and dangerous water in a circular region. In the diagram, beacons are located at X and Y. The measure of $\angle$XRY is given on the

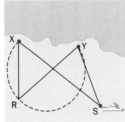

navigation charts as 50°. As a ship nears the region, the captain measures the angle between the two beacons and the ship, $\angle$XSY. What measures of $\angle$XSY assure the captain that the ship is not in the danger region? Explain your reasoning.

36. The points A, B, and C are on a circle such that $\triangle ABC$ is equilateral. The point P lies on the minor arc CA. The point D lies on the chord BP and BD = PC.
Prove:
a) $\triangle ABD \cong \triangle ACP$
b) $\triangle ADP$ is equilateral.
c) BP = AP + PC

37 RS is the diameter of a circle with centre O. T is any other point on the circle. RT is extended to Q so that TQ = OT. Prove that $\angle QOS = 3\angle TOQ$.

38 An angle is inscribed in a semicircle, and one arm of the angle is the same length as the radius, r. In terms of r, find the area of the region between the curve of the semicircle and the inscribed angle.

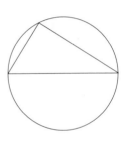

39. PQRS is a cyclic quadrilateral. PQ = PS and RQ = RS. Prove that the quadrilateral formed by joining the midpoints of adjacent sides of PQRS is a rectangle.

40. Can any rhombus be inscribed in a circle? Explain.

NUMBER POWER

a) Find three whole numbers, x, y, and z, that satisfy the following equation.

$$28x + 30y + 31z = 365$$

b) Explain your reasoning.

7.4 Cyclic Quadrilaterals

In some of his work, the Dutch artist M.C. Escher (1898–1972) tried to show the idea of infinity in two dimensions. In the coloured woodcut *Circle Limit III*, completed in 1959, he showed series of fish following each other, head to tail, along arcs inscribed in a circle. The fish seem to come from infinitely far away, become larger as they approach the centre of the circle, become smaller as they move away from the centre, and gradually fade into infinity.

Though Escher knew little about mathematics and constructed the woodcut using only simple instruments, he repeated the angles of intersection of the arcs with great accuracy. World-famous Canadian master geometer H. S. M. Coxeter, who knew Escher personally, has shown that Escher's *Circle Limit III* is mathematically perfect.

A set of points is called **cyclic** or **concyclic** if all of the points lie on the same circle. A polygon with all its vertices on the same circle is called a **cyclic polygon**. The pentagon ABCDE is a cyclic pentagon inscribed in the circle with centre O.

Explore: Use a Diagram

Draw a circle, centre O, and a cyclic quadrilateral ABCD. Join BO and DO. ∠A and ∠C are **opposite angles** of ABCD.
a) Let the measure of ∠A be x. What is the measure of the central ∠BOD subtended by the same arc as ∠A?
b) Let the measure of ∠C be y. What is the measure of the central ∠BOD subtended by the same arc as ∠C?

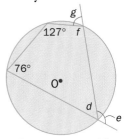

Inquire

1. What is the sum of the two central angles in terms of x and y?

2. How many degrees does this sum equal?

3. What is the sum of x and y in degrees?

4. What is the sum of the degree measures of ∠A and ∠C?

5. How could you determine the sum of the measures of ∠B and ∠D?

6. Write a statement about the sum of the opposite angles of a cyclic quadrilateral.

7. Find the measures of the indicated angles. Give reasons for your answers.

a)

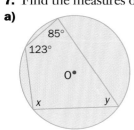

b)

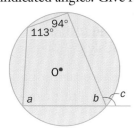

c)

8. What does each arc used in Escher's *Circle Limit III* have in common with each side of a cyclic quadrilateral?

In the Explore and Inquire questions, you proved the following.

Theorem
The opposite angles of a cyclic quadrilateral are supplementary.

The converse of the theorem is also true and will be proved in Example 4.
The proof of a corollary of the theorem is shown in Example 1.

Example 1   Exterior Angle of a Cyclic Quadrilateral
Prove that an exterior angle of a cyclic quadrilateral is equal to the interior opposite angle.

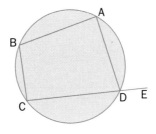

Given: Cyclic quadrilateral ABCD with CD extended to E
Prove: $\angle ABC = \angle ADE$
Plan: Use the fact that opposite angles in a cyclic quadrilateral are
           supplementary and the fact that $\angle CDE$ is a straight angle.
Proof:

Statements	Reasons
$\angle ABC + \angle ADC = 180°$	Opposite angles are supplementary.
$\angle ADE + \angle ADC = 180°$	Straight angle
$\angle ABC + \angle ADC = \angle ADE + \angle ADC$	Transitive property
$\angle ABC = \angle ADE$	Subtraction property

Corollary
An exterior angle of a cyclic quadrilateral is equal to the interior opposite angle.

Example 2   Finding Angle Measures
ABCD is a cyclic quadrilateral; O is the centre of the circle;
$\angle AOB = 110°$; $\angle DAO = 40°$. Find the measures of $\angle OAB$,
$\angle BCD$, and $\angle BCE$. Show your reasoning.

Solution
In $\triangle AOB$, the sum of the angles is $180°$, from the Triangle Angle Sum
Theorem.
So, $110° + \angle OBA + \angle OAB = 180°$
$\angle OBA + \angle OAB = 70°$
$\triangle AOB$ is isosceles, because OB and OA are radii.
So, $\angle OBA = \angle OAB$ from the Isosceles Triangle Theorem.
$\therefore \angle OAB = 35°$
$\angle BAD = 40° + 35°$
$= 75°$
$\angle BAD + \angle BCD = 180°$, because opposite angles of a cyclic quadrilateral are
supplementary.
$\therefore \angle BCD = 105°$
$\angle BCE = 75°$, because an exterior angle of a cyclic quadrilateral equals the opposite
interior angle.

So, $\angle OAB = 35°$, $\angle BCD = 105°$, and $\angle BCE = 75°$.

Every triangle is cyclic, because it is always possible to draw a circle through three non-collinear points. The centre of the circle is the point of intersection of the perpendicular bisectors of two sides of the triangle.

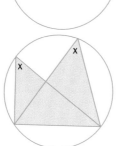

However, not every quadrilateral is cyclic. Examples 3 and 4 establish two methods for proving that a quadrilateral is cyclic.

In the previous section, it was proved that inscribed angles subtended by the same arc are congruent. The endpoints of an arc can be joined by a line segment. Also, the endpoints of an arc and the vertices of two subtended angles are the vertices of a cyclic quadrilateral. Therefore, another way to word this theorem is as follows.

Theorem
The line segment joining two vertices of a cyclic quadrilateral subtends equal angles at the other two vertices on the same side of the segment.

The converse of this theorem is also true, as shown in Example 3.

Example 3 Line Segment Subtends Two Equal Angles
Prove that, if the line segment joining two points subtends two equal angles at two other points on the same side of the segment, then the four points are cyclic.

Given: C and D are two points on the same side of AB.
$\angle ADB = \angle ACB$

Prove: ABCD is a cyclic quadrilateral.

Plan: Construct the circle that passes through A, B, and D.
Let E be the point of intersection of the circle and the line AC.
Consider the three possibilities where the circle can intersect AC.

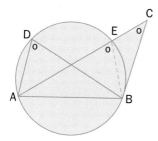

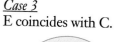

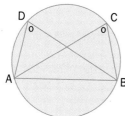

Case 1	*Case 2*	*Case 3*
C lies between A and E.	E lies between A and C.	E coincides with C.

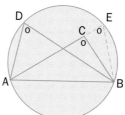

Proof: For Cases 1 and 2,

Statements	**Reasons**
$\angle ADB = \angle AEB$	Angles in a Circle Theorem
$\angle ADB = \angle ACB$	Given
$\angle AEB = \angle ACB$	Transitive property
EB ∥ CB	Transversal Parallel Lines Theorem

It is not possible for EB and CB to be parallel, since they intersect at B. Therefore, Case 1 and Case 2 cannot occur. The only possibility is Case 3, that is, C lies on the circle through A, B, and D.
∴ ABCD is a cyclic quadrilateral.

If the line segment joining two points subtends two equal angles at two other points on the same side of the segment, then the four points are concyclic.

Example 4 Opposite Angles Are Supplementary
Prove that if the opposite angles of a quadrilateral are supplementary, then the quadrilateral is cyclic.

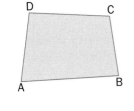

Given: Quadrilateral ABCD; $\angle A + \angle C = 180°$
Prove: Quadrilateral ABCD is cyclic.
Plan: Construct the circle that passes through A, B, and D.
Let E be any point on the arc BD not containing A.
If C is not on the circle, it can be inside or outside the circle.
Show that it is not possible for C to be inside or outside the circle.

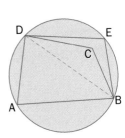   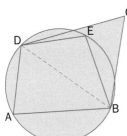

C lies inside the circle.   C lies outside the circle.

Proof:

Statements	**Reasons**
ABED is a cyclic quadrilateral.	Given
$\angle A + \angle E = 180°$	Opposite angles are supplementary.
$\angle A + \angle C = 180°$	Given
$\therefore \angle A + \angle E = \angle A + \angle C$	Transitive property
$\angle E = \angle C$	Subtraction property

Thus, BD subtends equal angles at E and C, which lie on the same side of BD.
$\therefore$ ABED is cyclic.
$\therefore$ C lies on the circle that passes through A, B, E, and D.
$\therefore$ ABCD is cyclic.

Note that the theorem proved in Example 4 is the converse of the theorem proved in the Explore and Inquire questions.

Converse
If the opposite angles of a quadrilateral are supplementary, then the quadrilateral is cyclic.

The following is a corollary.

Corollary
If an exterior angle of a quadrilateral is equal to the interior opposite angle, then the quadrilateral is cyclic.

The results of this section can be summarized as follows.

Cyclic Quadrilateral Theorem
- The opposite angles of a cyclic quadrilateral are supplementary.
- An exterior angle of a cyclic quadrilateral is equal to the interior opposite angle.
- The line segment joining two vertices of a cyclic quadrilateral subtends equal angles at the other two vertices on the same side of the segment.

Converse of the Cyclic Quadrilateral Theorem
- If the opposite angles of a quadrilateral are supplementary, then the quadrilateral is cyclic.
- If an exterior angle of a quadrilateral is equal to the interior opposite angle, then the quadrilateral is cyclic.
- If the line segment joining two points subtends two equal angles at two other points on the same side of the segment, then the four points are concyclic.

Example 5   Proving That Points Are Concyclic
Given: △DEF with DE = DF; ES and FT are the bisectors
   of ∠DEF and ∠DFE.
Prove: Quadrilateral TEFS is cyclic.
Plan: Prove △TEF ≅ △SFE, so that ∠FTE = ∠ESF
Proof:

Statements	Reasons
In △TEF and △SFE,	
∠TEF = ∠SFE	Isosceles Triangle Theorem
$\frac{1}{2}∠TEF = \frac{1}{2}∠SFE$	Division property
$∠FES = \frac{1}{2}∠TEF$	Definition of angle bisector
$∠EFT = \frac{1}{2}∠SFE$	Definition of angle bisector
∠EFT = ∠FES	Substitution property
EF = FE	Reflexive property
△TEF ≅ △SFE	ASA
∠FTE = ∠ESF	Congruent triangles
Quadrilateral TEFS is cyclic.	Converse of the Cyclic Quadrilateral Theorem

Practice

Find the values of the numbered angles in the diagrams.
Give reasons for your answers.

1.

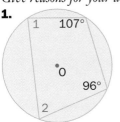

2.

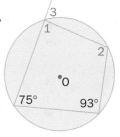

3.

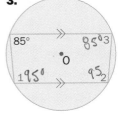

4.

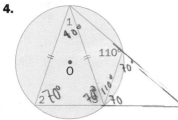

5.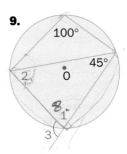

73°
107°
0
3 26°
86°
247°
1

6.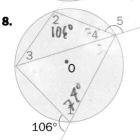

2
1
0
80°

7.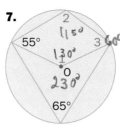

2
115°
55°   3 60°
130°
0
230°
65°

8.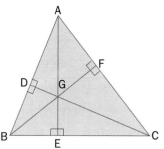

2
106°   4   5
3
0
74°
106°

9.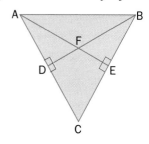

100°
45°
2
0
8
1
3

10.

5
1
35°
3 35
0   100°
280
30°
4

13.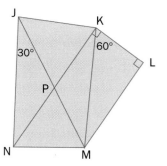

J
K
30°   60°
L
P
N   M

14.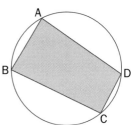

A
D   F
G
B   C
E

Name the cyclic quadrilaterals in the following diagrams. Give reasons for your answers.

11.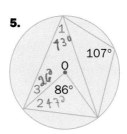

A   B
F
D   E
C

12.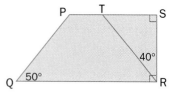

P   T   S
40°
Q 50°   R

Applications and Problem Solving

15. Algebra ABCD is a cyclic quadrilateral. If $\angle B = 2x + 8$, $\angle C = 3x - 4$, and $\angle D = 3x + 2$, find the measure of $\angle A$ in degrees.

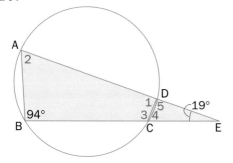

16. Determine the measures of angles 1, 2, 3, 4, and 5.

A
2
D
1 5   19°
94°   3 4
B   C   E

17. Write a flow proof to prove that, if an exterior angle of a quadrilateral is equal to the interior opposite angle, then the quadrilateral is cyclic.

18. Equal segments AC and BD bisect each other at P. Prove that ABCD is a cyclic quadrilateral.

19. Similar triangles
Given: Quadrilateral PQRS is cyclic.
Prove: △TPS ~ △TRQ

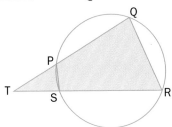

20. Two circles intersect at P and Q. Two lines, APB and CQD, meet the first circle at A and C and the second circle at B and D. Prove that AC ∥ BD.

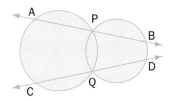

21. In △RST, RS = RT. The bisector of ∠RST meets RT at B. The bisector of ∠RTS meets RS at A. Prove that A, S, T, and B are concyclic points.

22. *Given:* Cyclic quadrilateral PQRS
XY ∥ QR
Prove: PXYS is a cyclic quadrilateral.

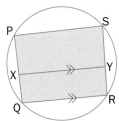

23. The diagonals of quadrilateral ABCD intersect at E such that ∠ADE = 64°, ∠CDE = 60°, ∠AEB = 106°, and ∠CBE = 42°.
a) Prove that ABCD is a cyclic quadrilateral.
b) Find the measure of ∠DBA.

24. *Given:* Parallelogram ABCD
Cyclic quadrilateral ABFE
Prove: CDEF is cyclic.

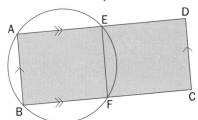

25. In isosceles trapezoid ABCD, AB = DC and AD ∥ BC. Write a two-column proof to prove that trapezoid ABCD is cyclic.

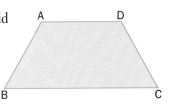

26. R, S, and T are points on a circle, and A, B, and C are points on the minor arcs RS, ST, and RT, respectively. Prove that ∠RAS + ∠SBT + ∠RCT = 360°.

27. △ABC is inscribed in a circle, and AB > AC. D is a point on AB, and AD = AC. The bisector of ∠A meets BC at E and the circle again at F. Prove that BDEF is a cyclic quadrilateral.

PATTERN POWER

1. Describe the pattern in words.

3	4	6	4
7	2	28	1
5	5	5	10
2	3	6	2
10	3		4

2. Find the missing number.

TECHNOLOGY

Exploring Tangent Properties Using Geometry Software

Complete the following explorations using geometry software or a graphing calculator with geometry capabilities. If suitable technology is not available, complete the equivalent paper-and-pencil explorations on pages 424–425.

A **tangent** is a line that intersects a circle at exactly one point. The point of intersection is called the **point of tangency**.

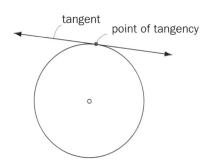

1 Perpendicular to a Radius at its Outer Endpoint

1. Construct a circle.

2. Construct a radius of the circle.

3. Construct a line perpendicular to the radius through the outer endpoint of the radius.

4. Construct the point of intersection of the perpendicular and the circle. Are there any other points of intersection? Compare your findings with those of your classmates.

5. Move the outer endpoint of the radius around the circumference to change the radius to different positions. Are there any other points of intersection each time? Compare your findings with those of your classmates.

6. Write a statement about the line perpendicular to a radius through the outer endpoint of the radius.

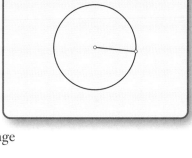

2 Tangent and Radius at Point of Tangency

1. Construct a circle.

2. Construct a point on the circle and a point outside the circle in a location such that a line passing through the two points would be nearly tangent to the circle.

3. Construct the line through the two points.

4. Construct the point of intersection of the line and the circle. If only one point of intersection is constructed, the line is tangent to the circle.

5. In most cases, two points of intersection will be constructed. To make the line tangent to the circle, move the point that you constructed outside the circle in step 2 until the two points of intersection become one.

6. Construct a radius of the circle to the point of tangency.

7. Measure the angles formed by the radius and the tangent to the circle. How are the measures of the angles related? Compare your findings with those of your classmates.

8. Write a statement about the measures of the angles formed by the tangent and the radius at the point of tangency.

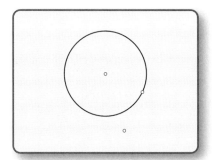

3 Lengths of Tangent Segments

1. Construct a circle.

2. Construct a radius of the circle.

3. Construct a tangent at the outer endpoint of the radius, that is, a line perpendicular to the radius through the outer endpoint of the radius.

4. Construct a second radius that is not on the same diameter as the first one, and a tangent at its outer endpoint.

5. Construct the point of intersection of the two tangents.

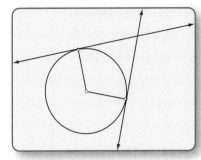

6. Measure the distance from the point of intersection to each point of tangency. This part of a tangent is known as a **tangent segment**. How are the lengths of the tangent segments related? Compare your findings with those of your classmates.

7. Move the outer endpoint of one radius to change the tangent segments to different lengths. How are the lengths of the tangent segments related each time? Compare your findings with those of your classmates.

8. Write a statement about how the lengths of tangent segments from an external point compare.

4 Angle Between a Tangent and a Chord

1. Construct a circle.

2. Construct a chord that is not a diameter.

3. Construct a tangent at one endpoint of the chord, that is, construct a radius to that point, and then, construct the line perpendicular to the radius through that point.

4. Measure the acute angle formed between the tangent and the chord.

5. Construct a point on the circle, on the opposite side of the chord from the angle you measured.

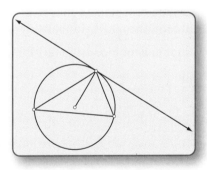

6. Using the point from step 5, construct and measure the inscribed angle subtended by the chord. How are the measures of the inscribed angle, and the acute angle formed between the tangent and the chord related? Compare your findings with those of your classmates.

7. Move the point of tangency to change the tangent to different positions. How are the measures of the angles related each time? Compare your findings with those of your classmates.

8. Write a statement about how the angle between a tangent and a chord, and the inscribed angle on the opposite side of the chord are related.

INVESTIGATING MATH

Exploring Tangent Properties

Complete the following paper-and-pencil explorations.

A **tangent** is a line that intersects a circle at exactly one point. The point of intersection is called the **point of tangency**.

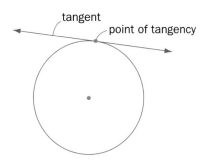

1 Perpendicular to a Radius at its Outer Endpoint

1. Draw a circle and a radius.

2. Construct a line perpendicular to the radius through the outer endpoint of the radius.

3. Are there any other points of intersection of the perpendicular and the circle?

4. Repeat steps 1 to 3 with another circle.

5. Compare your findings with those of your classmates.

6. Write a statement about the line perpendicular to a radius through the outer endpoint of the radius.

2 Tangent and Radius at Point of Tangency

1. Draw a circle and a tangent to the circle.

2. Construct a radius of the circle to the point of tangency.

3. Measure the angles formed by the radius and the tangent to the circle.

4. How are the measures of the angles related?

5. Repeat steps 1 to 4 with another circle.

6. Compare your findings with those of your classmates.

7. Write a statement about the measures of the angles formed by the tangent and the radius at the point of tangency.

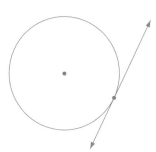

3 Lengths of Tangent Segments

1. Construct a circle.

2. Construct a radius of the circle, and a tangent at its outer endpoint.

3. Construct a second radius that is not on the same diameter as the first one, and a tangent at its outer endpoint.

4. Measure the distance from the point of intersection of the two tangents to each point of tangency. This part of a tangent is known as a **tangent segment**.

5. How are the lengths of the tangent segments related?

6. Repeat steps 1 to 5 with another circle.

7. Compare your findings with those of your classmates.

8. Write a statement about how the lengths of tangent segments from an external point compare.

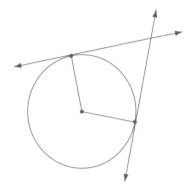

4 Angle Between a Tangent and a Chord

1. Draw a circle and a chord that is not a diameter.

2. Draw a tangent at one endpoint of the chord.

3. Measure the acute angle formed between the tangent and the chord.

4. On the opposite side of the chord from the angle you measured, construct and measure an inscribed angle subtended by the chord.

5. How are the measures of the angles related?

6. Repeat steps 1 to 5 with another circle.

7. Compare your findings with those of your classmates.

8. Write a statement about how the angle between a tangent and a chord, and the inscribed angle on the opposite side of the chord are related.

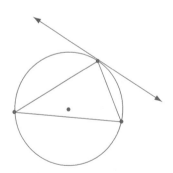

7.5 Tangents to a Circle

A solar eclipse occurs when the moon passes between the sun and the Earth and blocks the sun's rays from reaching the Earth. When there is a solar eclipse, some regions of the world experience a total eclipse, some regions, a partial eclipse, and other regions, no eclipse at all.

The diagram shows a cross section of a solar eclipse. AC and BD are tangents to the circles that represent the sun and the moon. AI and BH are tangents to the circles that represent the sun, the moon, and the Earth.

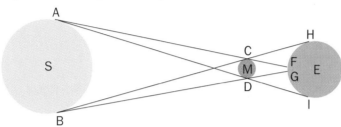

The region of the Earth on the minor arc FG experiences a total eclipse. The regions on the minor arcs FH and GI experience a partial eclipse. The region on the major arc HI does not experience an eclipse.

If a circle and a line lie in the same plane, there are three possibilities. As shown in the diagram, the line *l* does not intersect the circle. The line *s*, which is a secant, intersects the circle twice. The line *t* intersects the circle once, and only once, and is called a **tangent**. The point P, where *t* intersects the circle, is called the **point of tangency**. The word *tangent* comes from the Latin word *tangens*, which means touching.

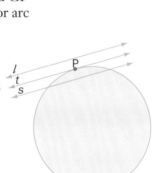

Explore: Use the Diagrams

Investigation 1
a) Draw a circle with centre O and radius OP.
b) Locate point Q on the circle and draw the line PQR. Measure ∠OPR.
c) Repeat part b) three times with point Q moved closer to P, but still on the circle.

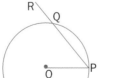

Investigation 2
a) Draw a circle with centre O and radius OR.
b) Draw the secant ST that intersects the circle at A and B and is perpendicular to OR at C.
c) Repeat part b) three times with point C moved closer to R.

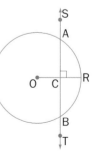

Inquire

1. In Investigation 1,
a) what does the length of PQ approach as Q moves closer and closer to P?
b) what value does the measure of ∠OPR appear to approach as Q moves closer and closer to P?
c) what appears to be the measure of ∠OPR when Q touches P?

2. In Investigation 2,
a) what does the length of AB approach as C moves closer and closer to R?
b) what happens to the length AB when C touches R?
c) what diagram results when C touches R?

3. Write a conjecture about the angle formed between a tangent to a circle and a radius drawn to the point of tangency.

Example 1   Tangent to a Circle

Prove that a tangent to a circle is perpendicular to the radius at the point of tangency.

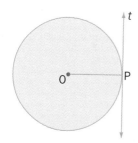

Given: Circle with centre O
          Tangent *t* with point of tangency P
Prove: $t \perp$ OP
Plan: Use an indirect proof. Assume that *t* is not perpendicular to OP. Draw the perpendicular OA from O to *t*. On *t*, mark the point B on the opposite side of A from P, such that AB = AP.

Proof:

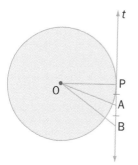

Statements	Reasons
In △OAB and △OAP,	
AB = AP	Construction
∠OAB = ∠OAP	Definition of perpendicular
OA = OA	Reflexive property
△OAB ≅ △OAP	SAS
OB = OP	Congruent triangles

But OP is a radius, so OB must be a radius.
So B lies on the circle, which means that *t* intersects the circle at two points, P and B. This statement contradicts the fact that *t* is a tangent, since a tangent intersects a circle exactly once. Therefore, the assumption that *t* is not perpendicular to OP is false, and so $t \perp$ OP.

The result of Example 1 can be stated in the following theorem.

Tangent Theorem, Part 1

A tangent to a circle is perpendicular to the radius at the point of tangency.

The converse to this theorem is also true, as shown in Example 2.

Example 2   Perpendicular to the Outer Endpoint of a Radius

Prove that, if a line is perpendicular to a radius at its outer endpoint, then the line is tangent to the circle.

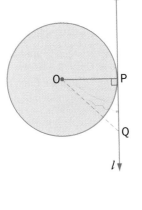

Given: Circle with centre O
           Point P on the circle
           Line l through P, with $l \perp OP$

Prove: l is a tangent to the circle at P.

Plan: Mark a point other than P on line l and show that the point lies outside the circle.

Proof: Let Q be any point except P on l. Join OQ.
           $\triangle OPQ$ is a right triangle. The hypotenuse is OQ.
           The hypotenuse is the longest side of a right triangle, so OQ > OP.
           Therefore, Q lies outside the circle. Q was any point except P on l, so any point except P on l lies outside the circle.
           Therefore, l is tangent to the circle at P.

From Example 2, we can state the converse of the theorem proved in Example 1.

Converse
If a line is perpendicular to a radius at its outer endpoint, then the line is tangent to the circle.

Example 3   Constructing Tangents

Prove that, from any point outside a circle, it is possible to draw two tangents to the circle.

Given: Circle with centre O
           Point P outside the circle.

Prove: There are two tangents to the circle from P.

Plan: Join OP. Bisect OP and label the midpoint C.
           With centre C and radius OC, draw a circle intersecting the original circle at A and B.
           Join PA and PB. Show that PA and PB are the tangents to the circle from P.

Proof: Join OA. Since $\angle OAP$ is an angle in a semicircle, $\angle OAP = 90°$.
           Since OA is a radius and $\angle OAP = 90°$, PA is a tangent, from the converse of the Tangent Theorem.
           Similarly, PB is a tangent.

Example 4 proves that the two tangent segments drawn to a circle from a point outside the circle are equal in length.

Example 4   Congruent Tangent Segments

Prove that the tangent segments to a circle from any external point are congruent.

Given: Circle with centre O; tangent segments PA and
           PB drawn from an external point P

Prove: PA = PB

Plan: Join OP, OA, and OB, and prove that triangles AOP and BOP are congruent.

Proof:

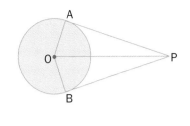

Statements	**Reasons**
In △AOP and △BOP,	
AO = BO	Radii
OP = OP	Reflexive property
∠PAO = ∠PBO = 90°	Tangent Theorem, Part 1
△AOP ≅ △BOP	HS
PA = PB	Congruent triangles

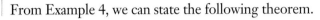

From Example 4, we can state the following theorem.

Theorem
The tangent segments to a circle from any external point are congruent.

The converse of this theorem is not true.

We can summarize the results of Examples 1, 2, and 4 as follows.

Tangent Theorem
- A tangent to a circle is perpendicular to the radius at the point of tangency.
- The tangent segments to a circle from any external point are congruent.

Converse of the Tangent Theorem
If a line is perpendicular to a radius at its outer endpoint, then the line is tangent to the circle.

Example 5   Finding Lengths
In △TSR, TS = TR, and the perimeter is 44 cm.
A, B, and C are points of tangency to a circle. SC = 6 cm.
Find the length of TR. Show your reasoning.

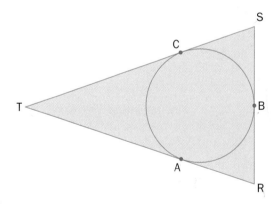

Solution
It is given that TS = TR.
From the Tangent Theorem, TC = TA.
Therefore, SC = RA.
From the Tangent Theorem, SC = SB and RA = RB.
So, SC = RA = SB = RB = 6
and SC + RA + SB + RB = 24
The perimeter of △TSR is SC + RA + SB + RB + TC + TA.
Therefore, 44 = 24 + TC + TA
$$\qquad\quad = 24 + 2TA$$
$$\quad 10 = TA$$
TR = TA + RA
$\quad$ = 10 + 6
$\quad$ = 16
So, the length of TR is 16 cm.

Example 6 will establish how the angle between a tangent and a chord and the inscribed angle on the opposite side of the chord are related.

Example 6 Tangent Chord Theorem

Prove that the angle between a tangent and a chord is equal to the inscribed angle on the opposite side of the chord.

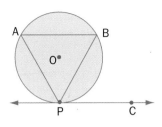

Given: Circle with centre O; tangent PC; chord PB;
∠BPC, the angle between the tangent and the chord;
∠PAB, an inscribed angle on the opposite side of the chord from ∠BPC.

Prove: ∠BPC = ∠PAB

Plan: Join OB and OP. Since ∠PAB is $\frac{1}{2}$∠POB, prove that ∠BPC is $\frac{1}{2}$∠POB.

Let ∠BPC = x.

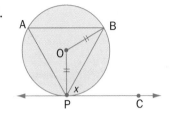

Proof:

Statements	**Reasons**
∠OPC = 90°	Tangent Theorem
∠OPB = ∠OPC − ∠BPC	B is in the interior of ∠OPC.
∠OPB = 90° − x	Substitution property
OP = OB	Radii
∠OBP = ∠OPB	Isosceles Triangle Theorem
∠OBP + ∠OPB + ∠POB = 180°	Triangle Angle Sum Theorem
∠OPB + ∠OPB + ∠POB = 180°	Substitution property
∠POB = 180° − 2∠OPB	Subtraction property
$\quad$ = 180° − 2(90° − x)	
$\quad$ = 180° − 180° + 2x	
$\quad$ = 2x	
∠PAB = x	Angles in a Circle Theorem
∠PAB = ∠BPC	Transitive property

Tangent Chord Theorem
The angle between a tangent and a chord is equal to the inscribed angle on the opposite side of the chord.

Example 7 Finding Angle Measures

Given ∠DFE = 70° and ∠CEF = 60°, find the measures of ∠ABC and ∠ADF. Show your reasoning.

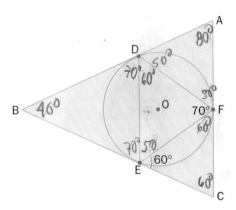

Solution
∠BDE = ∠DFE = 70°, from the Tangent Chord Theorem.
BD = BE, from the Tangent Chord Theorem.
∴ In isosceles △BED, the Isosceles Triangle Theorem gives ∠BED = 70°.
In △BED, the Triangle Angle Sum Theorem gives
$\qquad$ ∠DBE + 70° + 70° = 180°
$\qquad\qquad$ ∠DBE = 40°
∠DBE and ∠ABC are the same angle, so ∠ABC = 40°.
∠CEF = ∠EDF = 60°, from the Tangent Chord Theorem.
Because ∠ADB is a straight angle, ∠ADF + 70° + 60° = 180°
$\qquad\qquad\qquad\qquad\qquad\qquad$ ∠ADF = 50°

So, ∠ABC = 40° and ∠ADF = 50°.

Practice

In the diagrams, tangents have been drawn from P to the circles. Find the values of w, x, y, and z. Give reasons for your answers.

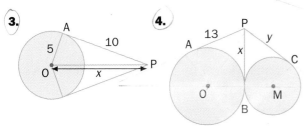

1.
A 12 P
x
13
O

2.
9
P z A
w x O
70°
y
B

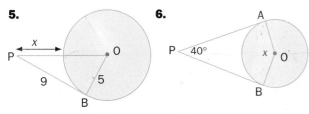

3.
A 10
5
O x P

4.
P
13 y
A x C
O M
B

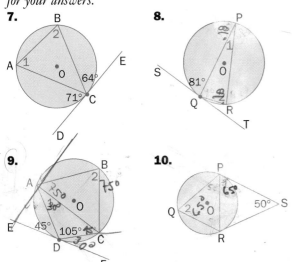

5.
x
P O
9 5
B

6.
A
P 40° x O
B

Find the measures of the indicated angles. Give reasons for your answers.

7.
B
2
A 1
O 64° E
71° C
D

8.
P
1
S O
81°
Q
R
T

9.
A 2 B 75°
250 O
30
E 45° 105° C
D 300
F

10.
P
5 65°
Q 25 O 50° S
R

11.
D
5 40°
70°
1 61° L
82° 58°
E K F

12.
A 66° E
3 51°
B O D
2 1
C F

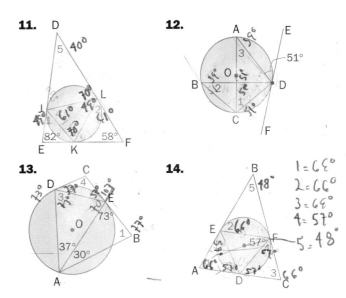

13.
C
D 4
3 5 E
O 73°
1 B
37°
30°
A

14.
B
5 48°
E 26°
57° F
A 51° 57° 3
D 66°

1 = 68°
2 = 66°
3 = 68°
4 = 57°
5 = 48°

Applications and Problem Solving

15. The points A, B, and C are points on a circle. The tangent at B is parallel to the chord AC. Write a flow proof to prove that △ABC is isosceles.

16. The points A, B, and C are on a circle. ∠ABC = 68° and ∠BCA = 47°. Find the measures of the angles in the triangle formed by tangents drawn to the circle at A, B, and C.

17. Q, R, S, and T are points in order on a circle. TR and QS intersect at X. Let *t* be the tangent at X to the circle that passes through T, Q, and X. Write a two-column proof to prove that *t* ∥ RS.

18. a) Find the radius, to the nearest tenth of a centimetre, of the largest circle that can be cut out of a square piece of paper with a diagonal length of 16 cm.
b) What is the area of the piece left over, to the nearest tenth of a square centimetre?

19. Two metal cylinders, each of diameter 8 cm, are bound together. How long is the band, to the nearest tenth of a centimetre?

20. Gong A gong, 80 cm in diameter, hangs by a chain from a hook, as shown. The total length of the chain is 60 cm. How far above the top of the gong is the hook, to the nearest tenth of a centimetre?

21. *Given:* AE and BC are both tangents to both circles.
Prove: AC ∥ BE

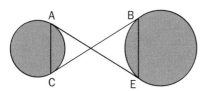

22. *Given:* CE is tangent to both circles at D.
Prove: AB ∥ FG

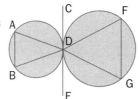

23. Space flight The space shuttle orbits the Earth at a distance of 250 km above the surface. If the radius of the Earth is approximately 6400 km, what is the distance from the shuttle to the horizon, to the nearest kilometre?

24. Two circles intersect at F and G. One of their common tangents has points of tangency at P and T. Write a paragraph proof to prove that ∠PFT and ∠PGT are supplementary.

25. Packaging A stack of round plates just fits inside a square box. Each plate has a radius of 20 cm.
a) Find the side length of the box.
b) Find the minimum horizontal distance from the edge of a plate to the nearest corner of the box, to the nearest tenth of a centimetre.

26. A circle is inscribed in isosceles triangle ABC, where AB = AC. Points D, E, F are the respective points of tangency of the lines AB, BC, and AC. AD = 5 cm, and the perimeter of the triangle is 62 cm. Find the length of each side of the triangle.

27. Algebra Find the lengths of AD, AF, and CE.

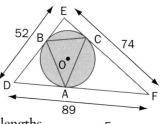

28. Algebra Find the lengths of OA and CD, and the perimeter of △DEF. Round answers to the nearest tenth.

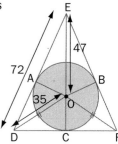

29. A circle is inscribed in right triangle ABC, where ∠B = 90°. Point D is the contact point for the tangent line AB. AD = 6 cm and DB = 3 cm.
a) Find the perimeter of the triangle.
b) Find the radius of the circle.

30. PA and PB are tangents, and Q is another point on the circle. What is the value of 2∠AQB + ∠APB?

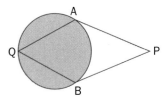

31. The two circles touch at one point and have two common tangents, as shown. If the radius of the smaller circle is 8 cm, what is the radius of the larger circle?

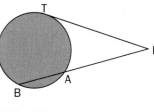

32 A tangent from an external point P is tangent to a circle at T. A secant through P intersects the same circle at A and B. Write a two-column proof to prove that $PT^2 = PA \times PB$.

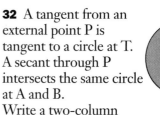

7.6 Arc Length and Sector Area

In a centre-pivot irrigation system, water is
applied to a field automatically by a series of
sprinklers that are mounted on a radial pipe.
The pipe is supported by a slowly moving row
of towers that rotate about a centre point,
where the water supply is located.

Explore: Interpret the Information

A **sector** of a circle
is a region bounded
by two radii and
their intercepted
arc. The central
angle is also known
as the **sector angle**.

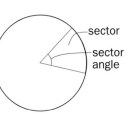

Suppose the length of the radial pipe for a
centre-pivot irrigation system is 400 m.
a) Calculate the area of field irrigated in a
360° rotation, to the nearest hectare.
b) Calculate the area of the sector irrigated,
to the nearest hectare, if its central angle is 90°; 180°; 270°.
c) Calculate the circumference of the circle formed by the irrigation
system, to the nearest 10 m.
d) Calculate the arc length of the sector irrigated, to the nearest 10 m,
if its central angle is 90°; 45°; 135°.

Inquire

1. What fraction of the area of a circle is a sector of the circle with a central angle of
a) 60°? **b)** 30°? **c)** 120°?

2. Write a formula for the area, A, of a sector of a circle with radius, r, and a central
angle of $m°$.

3. What fraction of the circumference of a circle is the arc of a sector of the circle
with a central angle of
a) 20°? **b)** 100°? **c)** 300°?

4. Write a formula for the arc length, l, of a sector of a circle with radius, r, and a
central angle of $m°$.

5. For the indicated sectors, calculate the area, to the nearest square centimetre, and
the arc length, to the nearest centimetre.

a)

10 cm

40°

b)

15 cm

160°

c)

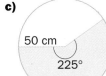

50 cm

225°

d)

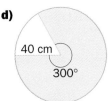

40 cm

300°

Example 1   Water Sprinkler

A water sprinkler turns back and forth through an angle of 100°. The water sprays out to a maximum distance of 25 m.
a) What is the length of the arc of the watered sector, to the nearest metre?
b) What is the area of the watered sector, to the nearest square metre?

Solution

a) The length, l, of an arc with a central angle of $m°$ is given by the formula

$$l = \frac{m}{360} \times 2\pi r$$

$$l = \frac{100}{360} \times 2\pi \times 25$$

$$\doteq 44$$

Estimate
$100 \times 6 \times 30 = 18\ 000$
$18\ 000 \div 400 = 45$

The length of the arc of the watered sector is 44 m, to the nearest metre.

b) The area, A, of a sector with a central angle of $m°$ is given by the formula

$$A = \frac{m}{360} \times \pi r^2$$

$$A = \frac{100}{360} \times \pi \times 25^2$$

$$\doteq 545$$

Estimate
$100 \times 3 \times 600 = 180\ 000$
$180\ 000 \div 400 = 450$

The area of the watered sector is 545 m², to the nearest square metre.

Example 2   Bicycle Chains

A chain on a bicycle connects two gear wheels with diameters of 21 cm and 9 cm. The centres of the gear wheels are 89 cm apart. Find the minimum length of chain needed, to the nearest centimetre.

Solution

Draw a diagram. Label the centres O and P, the points of tangency A, B, C, and D, and the points E and G on the circles, as shown.

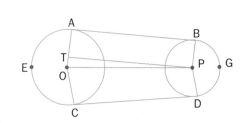

To find the minimum length of the chain, find and add the lengths of the two tangents AB and CD, and the lengths of the arcs AEC and BGD.

Join OA, OC, PB, and PD. A tangent to a circle is perpendicular to the radius at the point of tangency. So, ∠OAB, ∠PBA, ∠OCD, and ∠PDC are each 90°.
Draw PT perpendicular to OA at T.
ABPT is a rectangle, so PB = TA = 4.5 cm.
Then, OT = 10.5 cm − 4.5 cm = 6 cm

In the right triangle OTP, by the Pythagorean Theorem
$$OP^2 = OT^2 + TP^2$$
$$89^2 = 6^2 + TP^2$$
$$TP^2 = 89^2 - 6^2$$
$$TP \doteq 88.8$$

TP = 88.8 cm, to the nearest tenth of a centimetre.
So, AB = 88.8 cm. Similarly, CD = 88.8 cm.

In the right triangle OTP,

$$\cos\angle TOP = \frac{OT}{OP}$$

$$= \frac{6}{88.8}$$

$$\angle TOP \doteq 86.1°$$

So, $\angle TOP = 86.1°$, to the nearest tenth of a degree. Similarly, $\angle COP = 86.1°$.
So, $\angle AOC = 172.2°$
And reflex $\angle AOC = 360° - 172.2°$
$= 187.8°$.

The length of the arc AEC can now be found.

Arc AEC $= \dfrac{187.8}{360} \times 2\pi \times 10.5$

$\doteq 34.4$

So, arc AEC = 34.4 cm, to the nearest tenth of a centimetre.

Estimate

$200 \times 6 \times 10 = 12\,000$
$12\,000 \div 400 = 30$

```
187.8/360*2π*10.
5
        34.41614752
```

In $\triangle OTP$, $\angle TOP = 86.1°$ and $\angle OTP = 90°$.
So, $\angle TPO = 180° - (86.1° + 90°)$
$= 3.9°$
Then, $\angle OPB = 90° + 3.9°$
$= 93.9°$
Similarly, $\angle OPD = 93.9°$
So, reflex $\angle BPD = 187.8°$
And $\angle BPD = 360° - 187.8°$
$= 172.2°$

The length of the arc BGD can now be found.

Arc BGD $= \dfrac{172.2}{360} \times 2\pi \times 4.5$

$\doteq 13.5$

So, arc BGD = 13.5 cm, to the nearest tenth of a centimetre.

Estimate

$200 \times 6 \times 4 = 4800$
$4800 \div 400 = 12$

```
172.2/360*2π*4.5
        13.52455637
```

The sum of the four lengths is
$88.8 + 88.8 + 34.4 + 13.5 = 225.5$
So, the minimum length of chain needed is 226 cm,
to the nearest centimetre.

Estimate

$90 + 90 + 30 + 10 = 220$

Practice

Calculate the length of the indicated arc, to the nearest tenth of a centimetre.

1.

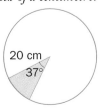

2.

3.

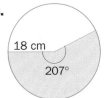

4.

Calculate the area of the shaded sector, to the nearest tenth of a square centimetre.

5.
6.

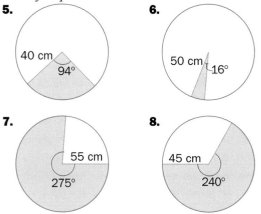

7.
8.

Find the measure of each sector angle indicated, to the nearest degree.

9.
10.

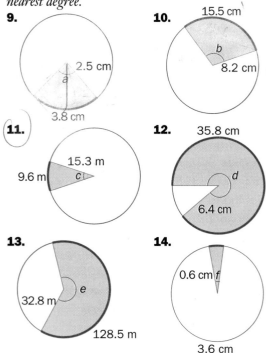

11.
12.

13.
14.

A circle has a radius of 15 cm. Find the length of the arc that subtends each sector angle. Round answers to the nearest tenth of a centimetre.

15. 125°   **16.** 230°   **17.** 42°
18. 89.3°   **19.** 17°   **20.** 308°

A circle has a diameter of 18 cm. Find the measure of the sector angle in the sector with each arc length. Round each angle to the nearest degree.

21. 48 cm   **22.** 22 cm   **23.** 14 cm
24. 5 cm   **25.** 30.5 cm   **26.** 47.3 cm

A circle has a radius of 5 cm. Find the area of the sector with each sector angle. Round each answer to the nearest tenth of a square centimetre.

27. 70°   **28.** 100°   **29.** 32°
30. 147°   **31.** 205°   **32.** 124°

Applications and Problem Solving

33. Pizza slices A large pizza with diameter 50 cm is cut into 12 equal sectors. A square pizza, with side length 45 cm, is cut into 16 equal squares. Which pizza slice, a sector or a square, has the greater area? How much greater is it, to the nearest square centimetre?

34. Windshield wiper The total length of a car's windshield wiper is 50 cm. The length of the blade is 30 cm. The blade swings through an angle of 145°. What is the area of the windshield cleaned by the blade, to the nearest square centimetre?

35. Electric cars In a technical studies competition, high school students design and build electric cars. The team whose car can complete the most laps of a track in an hour is the winner. Amy, Kenneth, Shuh Fen, and Sunil are working on an electric car. They are determining the length of the drive chain required. They know that the chain will be tangent to two sprockets and that the centres of the sprockets will be 70 cm apart. The back sprocket is 30 cm in diameter, and the front sprocket is 6 cm in diameter. Amy has produced a CAD drawing to represent the sprocket system.

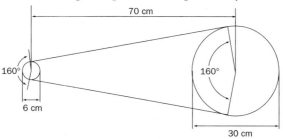

Determine the minimum length of chain, to the nearest centimetre, that the team will need for their car.

36. Gear wheels A chain connects two gear wheels of diameters 4 cm and 12 cm. The centres of the gear wheels are 54 cm apart. Find the minimum length of chain needed, to the nearest centimetre.

37. Write an expression, in simplest form, for the shaded area.

38. Three cylinders of diameter 20 cm are stacked and bound together as shown .

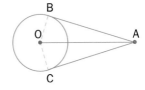

a) What is the sector angle formed by the part of each cylinder that is in contact with the band? Explain your reasoning.
b) Find the length of the band, to the nearest centimetre.

39. A circle is divided into three sectors. The smallest sector angle is 48°. The largest sector angle is 165°. If the arc length of the largest sector is 27.5 cm, find the arc length of the other two sectors, to the nearest tenth of a centimetre.

40. Communications satellite Canada launched the world's first domestic communications satellite into geostationary orbit. This satellite was called *Anik I*, after an Inuit word for brother. A geostationary satellite moves in a circular orbit approximately 42 000 km above the centre of the Earth. The radius of the Earth is approximately 6400 km.

a) Find the measure of the sector angle for the arc of the Earth's equator that is visible from a geostationary satellite, to the nearest degree.
b) Find the length of the arc, to the nearest kilometre.

c) Find the measure of the sector angle, to the nearest degree, if a satellite were 51 000 km above the centre of the Earth.
d) Will a satellite ever be able to "see" an arc of the Earth's equator with a 180° sector angle?

41. △ABC is an equilateral triangle with side length *a*. Find expressions for the perimeter and the area of the shaded region.

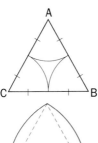

42. Engineering The rotor in a Wankel engine is shaped as shown. To create this design, start with an equilateral triangle of side length, *r*. Then, on each side of the triangle, draw an arc with radius, *r*, and with its centre at the opposite vertex of the triangle. Find an expression for the perimeter of the rotor.

43. Geography The southern border of Alberta is along the 49°N line of latitude. The northern border follows the 60°N line of latitude. The border between Alberta and Saskatchewan is at the 110°W line of longitude. If the radius of the Earth is approximately 6400 km, what is the length of the Alberta-Saskatchewan border, to the nearest hundred kilometres?

TECHNOLOGY

Exploring the Sums of the Interior Angles in Polygons

Complete Exploration 1 using geometry software and Exploration 2 using
spreadsheet software. If suitable software is not available, complete the Explore and
and Inquire parts of Section 7.7 on pages 439 and 440 using pencil and paper.

1 Number of Triangles in a Polygon

1. What is the sum of the interior angles in a triangle?

2. Construct the polygons listed in the table. Divide each polygon into triangles by
constructing diagonals from one vertex to each non-adjacent vertex. Copy and
complete the table.

Polygon	Number of Sides	Number of Triangles
quadrilateral		
pentagon		
hexagon		
heptagon		
octagon		
nonagon		
decagon		

3. What is the relationship between the number of sides of a polygon and the
number of triangles formed by drawing diagonals from one vertex?

2 Sum of the Interior Angles in a Polygon in Terms of Right Angles

1. Explain the formulas in this spreadsheet.

	A	B	C	D
1	Sides in Polygon	Triangles in Polygon	Sum of Interior Angles in Multiples of 180°	Sum of Interior Angles in Multiples of 90°
2				
3	3	=A3–2	=B3	=2*C3
4	=A3+1			
5				
6				
7				
8				
9				
10				

2. Complete the spreadsheet using the Fill Down feature.

3. Write a statement about the sum of the measures of the interior angles in
an n-sided polygon as a number of right angles.

7.7 Angles and Polygons

NASA's New Millenium Deep Space missions are conducted by refrigerator-sized, solar-powered probes that are able to carry out scientific investigations and explore the solar system. The first probe was named *Deep Space 1*. NASA plans to launch 10 to 15 such probes annually.

The main body of a Deep Space probe is in the shape of an octagonal prism. The base is a regular octagon, which is an example of a polygon.

A **polygon** is a closed plane figure made up of three or more line segments. The word polygon comes from the Greek word meaning "many-angled." A **convex polygon** is one in which a line segment joining any two points of the polygon has no part outside the polygon. For a **concave polygon**, this is not true.

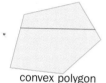
convex polygon

concave polygon

The Triangle Angle Sum Theorem states that the sum of the measures of the interior angles of a triangle is 180°. Another way of stating this is that the sum of the measures of the interior angles in a triangle equals two right angles. The theorem will now be used to develop a formula for the sum of the measures of the interior angles of a polygon with any number of sides.

Explore: Look for a Pattern

For a quadrilateral, the maximum number of diagonals that can be drawn from one vertex is one. For a pentagon, the maximum number is two.

Copy and complete the table by drawing each polygon and determining the maximum number of triangles that can be formed by drawing diagonals from one vertex.

Polygon	Number of Sides	Number of Triangles	Sum of Interior Angle Measures (degrees)	Sum of Interior Angle Measures (in Right Angles)
triangle	3	1	180	2
quadrilateral	4	2		
pentagon	5	3		
hexagon	6			
heptagon	7			
octagon	8			
nonagon	9			
decagon	10			

Inquire

1. What is the relationship between the number of sides of a polygon and the number of triangles formed by drawing diagonals from one vertex?

2. For a polygon with 20 sides,
a) how many triangles are formed by drawing the diagonals from one vertex?
b) what is the sum of the measures of the interior angles in degrees? in right angles?

3. For a polygon with n sides,
a) how many triangles are formed by drawing the diagonals from one vertex?
b) write an expression in terms of n to represent the sum of the measures of the interior angles in degrees.
c) write an expression in terms of n to represent the sum of the measures of the interior angles in right angles.

4. A **regular polygon** is a convex polygon with all sides equal and all interior angles equal. The base of a *Deep Space* probe is a regular octagon. What is the measure of each interior angle
a) in degrees?   **b)** in right angles?

The expressions you found in Inquire questions 3b) and 3c) can be stated formally in the following theorem.

> ### Interior Angle Sum Theorem
> The sum of the interior angles of any polygon with n sides is $180°(n-2)$ or $(2n-4)$ right angles.

The following corollary to this theorem describes the measure of each interior angle of a regular polygon.

> ### Corollary
> The measure of each angle of a regular polygon with n sides is
>
> in degrees
> $$\frac{180°(n-2)}{n}$$
>
> in right angles
> $$\frac{2n-4}{n}$$

Example 1   Finding Angle Measures
Find the measures of angles A, B, C, D, and E.

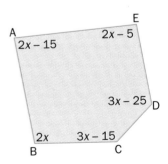

Solution
The polygon has 5 sides.
So, the sum of the interior angles is
$$180°(n-2) = 180°(5-2)$$
$$= 540°$$
Using the expressions for each angle measure, the sum of the angles is
$$(2x-15) + 2x + (3x-15) + (3x-25) + (2x-5) = 12x - 60$$

So, $12x - 60 = 540$
$$12x = 600$$
$$x = 50$$

$\angle A = 2x - 15$	$\angle B = 2x$	$\angle C = 3x - 15$	$\angle D = 3x - 25$	$\angle E = 2x - 5$
$= 2(50) - 15$	$= 2(50)$	$= 3(50) - 15$	$= 3(50) - 25$	$= 2(50) - 5$
$= 85°$	$= 100°$	$= 135°$	$= 125°$	$= 95°$

An **exterior angle** of a polygon is formed by extending one side of the polygon.

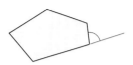

Example 2   Exterior Angle Sum

Prove that the sum of the measures of the exterior angles of any convex polygon, with one exterior angle at each vertex, is 360°.

Given: A convex polygon with n sides and one exterior angle drawn at each vertex

Prove: The sum of the measures of the exterior angles is 360°.

Plan: There are n interior angles and n exterior angles. Use the fact that each interior angle and its corresponding exterior angle form a straight angle.

Proof:

From the Interior Angle Sum Theorem, the sum of the interior angles of a polygon with n sides is $180°(n - 2)$ degrees.

Each interior angle and its corresponding exterior angle form a straight angle. There are n interior angles and n exterior angles, so there are n straight angles. The sum of the interior angles and exterior angles is $180° \times n$.

The sum of the exterior angles is

$$180° \times n - 180°(n - 2) = 180° \times n - 180° \times n + 360°$$
$$= 360° \text{ or } 4 \text{ right angles}$$

Exterior Angle Sum Theorem

The sum of the measures of the exterior angles of any convex polygon, with one exterior angle at each vertex, is 360° or 4 right angles.

In a regular polygon, all interior angles have the same measure and all exterior angles have the same measure. Therefore, the following is a corollary to the Exterior Angle Sum Theorem.

Corollary

The measure of each exterior angle of a regular polygon with n sides is

in degrees $\dfrac{360°}{n}$

in right angles $\dfrac{4}{n}$

Example 3 Regular Polygons Inscribed in a Circle

Given: AB is one side of a regular *n*-sided polygon inscribed in a circle.
D is any other vertex of the polygon.

Prove: The measure of ∠ADB is $\dfrac{180°}{n}$.

Plan: Draw the diagonals from D.
The sides of the polygon are chords of the circle, and all chords except
DC and DE subtend angles at D. Show that there are *n* – 2 equal angles
at D. Find ∠ADB by dividing ∠CDE by *n* – 2.

Proof:

$\angle CDE = \dfrac{180°(n-2)}{n}$, from the Interior Angle Sum Theorem.

Because the polygon is inscribed in the circle, the *n* sides of the polygon are
chords of the circle.

Because the diagonals from D form *n* – 2 triangles with a vertex at D, there are
n – 2 chords that subtend angles at D.

The polygon is regular, so the chords are equal. Therefore, the minor arcs AB,
BC, and so on, are equal.

The *n* – 2 angles subtended at D by the equal arcs are equal, by the Angles in a
Circle Theorem.

So, the measure of each of these angles is $\dfrac{180°(n-2)}{n} \times \dfrac{1}{n-2}$, or $\dfrac{180°}{n}$.

Therefore, $\angle ADB = \dfrac{180°}{n}$.

Practice

*Determine the measure of each numbered angle. Give
reasons for your answers.*

1.

2.

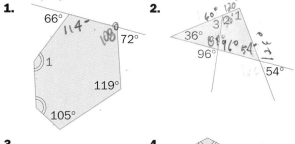

3.

4.

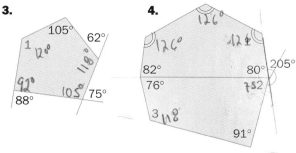

*Given the number of sides of a polygon, determine the
sum of the measures of the interior angles in degrees and
in right angles.*

5. 11   **6.** 23   **7.** 80
8. 37   **9.** *y*   **10.** 3*t*

*Given the sum of the interior angles, determine the
number of sides of the polygon.*

11. 1620°   **12.** 2340°   **13.** 3780°

*The measure of an interior angle of a regular polygon is
given. Determine the number of sides of the polygon.*

14. 144°   **15.** 156°   **16.** 160°
17. 176°   **18.** 157.5°   **19.** *m*°

*The measure of an exterior angle of a regular polygon is
given. Determine the number of sides of the polygon.*

20. 15°   **21.** 10°   **22.** 30°
23. 18°   **24.** 14.4°   **25.** *m*°

The number of sides of a regular polygon is given. Determine the measures of an interior angle and an exterior angle for each polygon. Round to the nearest hundredth of a degree, if necessary.

26. 40   **27.** 16   **28.** 25

29. 29   **30.** $3t$ **31.** $x + y$

Applications and Problem Solving

32. Algebra
Determine
the measures of angles
A, B, C, D, and E.

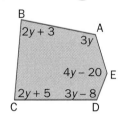

33. Algebra
Determine the
measures of angles P,
Q, R, S, T, and U.

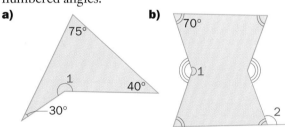

34. Concave polygons The Interior Angle Sum Theorem for polygons also applies to concave polygons. Determine the measures of the numbered angles.

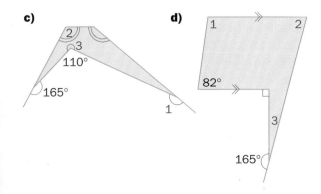

35. The regular hexagon ABCDEF is inscribed in a circle. What is the measure of

a) ∠ABF?

b) ∠ABD?

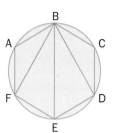

36. Use the diagram to find the following.

a) The sum of the measures of ∠1, ∠2, ∠3, ∠4, and ∠5.

b) The sum of the measures of ∠a, ∠b, ∠c, ∠d, and ∠e.

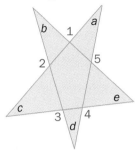

37. Ratio The measures of an interior angle and an exterior angle in a regular polygon are in a ratio of 8:1. Find the measures of the interior and exterior angles and the number of sides of the polygon.

38. Does the sum of the exterior angles of a concave polygon always add to 360°? Explain your answer.

39. Picture frame A picture frame is to be built in the shape of a regular octagon. Eight identical trapezoids will complete the frame, as shown. What are the measures of the interior angles of the trapezoids?

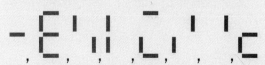

LOGIC POWER

The diagrams show 8 figures in a sequence.

What is the next figure in the sequence? Explain.

CONNECTING MATH AND BIOLOGY

Honeybees

Beekeeping exists in all the habitable parts of the world and produces over 900 million kilograms of honey a year from more than 50 million hives. Together, Canada and the United States have about 5 million hives. In the United States, the average annual honey yield per hive is about 20 kg. In Canada, the yield is about 65 kg, which is the highest national average in the world.

A typical beehive has between 20 000 and 30 000 bees. There are three types of bees in a hive — the queen, the drones, and the workers. The workers do everything for the hive, including the collection of pollen, nectar, and water. The workers convert nectar to honey.

1 Honeycomb Cells

Honeycomb cells are cylinders enclosed in regular hexagonal prisms. Assume that the sides of the prisms are tangent to the cylinders, as shown in the diagram.

The cell walls are made of wax. Since a hexagon tiles the plane, cell walls can be shared to reduce the amount of wax needed. The sharing of cell walls is important, since a typical hive has about 200 000 cells.

1. The cylinder of an average cell used by worker bees has a diameter of 4 mm and a height of 9 mm.
a) Calculate the volume of the cylinder, to the nearest hundredth of a cubic millimetre.
b) Calculate the volume of the hexagonal prism, to the nearest hundredth of a cubic millimetre.
c) Use the results from parts a) and b) to calculate the volume of wax needed for one cell.

2. A square also tiles the plane. Suppose that honeycomb cylinders were enclosed in square-based prisms. Calculate the volume of wax needed for one cell, to the nearest hundredth of a cubic millimetre.

3. An equilateral triangle also tiles the plane. Suppose that honeycomb cylinders were enclosed in prisms with equilateral triangles as bases. Calculate the volume of wax needed for one cell, to the nearest hundredth of a cubic millimetre.

4. Could a regular octagonal prism be used to enclose the cell cylinder? Explain.

2 Signalling the Distance to Food

Some worker bees have the job of foraging for food. Their search can extend up to 6000 m from the hive. When they find a good food source, they return to the hive and use dances on the vertical honeycomb surfaces to communicate the location of the food to other bees.

The round dance is used for food that is 10 m or less from the hive.

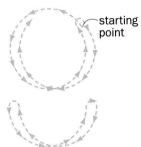

starting point

For food that is 10 m to 100 m away, the crescent dance is used.

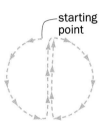

For food that is more than 100 m away, the wag-tail dance is used. In the wag-tail dance, the bee moves in a semicircle to one side, then turns sharply at the bottom and moves up the diameter to the starting point. Then, the bee moves in a semicircle in the opposite direction to complete the circle, and up the diameter to the starting point. The diameter is called the "straight run" of the dance.

starting point

During the wag-tail dance, a forager bee communicates the approximate distance to the food source by the number of straight runs made. The table gives the number of straight runs made in 15 s and the approximate distance to the food source.

Distance (m)	Straight Runs in 15 s
500	7
1000	5
3000	2
6000	1

1. Plot the points on a grid and draw the curve of best fit for the data.

2. Approximately how far away would the food source be if the forager bee made 3 straight runs in 15 s?

3. Approximately how far away would the food source be if the forager bee made 6 straight runs in 15 s?

3 Signalling the Direction of Food

The direction in which the dancing bee moves relative to the top of the honeycomb during the straight run gives the direction of the food source relative to the sun. The top of the honeycomb represents the direction of the sun.

This dance pattern shows that the food source is toward the sun.

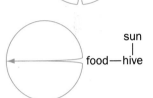

sun
|
food
|
hive

This dance pattern shows that the food source is 90° counterclockwise from the direction of the sun.

sun
|
food—hive

This dance pattern shows that the food source is 90° clockwise from the direction of the sun.

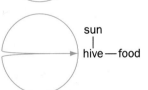

sun
|
hive—food

1. In what direction should the bees fly, relative to the sun, when a returning forager uses each of the following dance patterns?

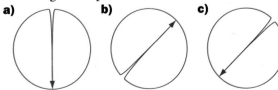

a)   **b)**   **c)**

2. Draw the dance patterns that would show each of the following directions to food sources.
a) 45° counterclockwise from the sun
b) 135° clockwise from the sun
c) 160° clockwise from the sun
d) 10° counterclockwise from the sun

Review

7.1 1. *Given:* ∠ABC = ∠DCB;
AB = DC
Prove: AC = DB

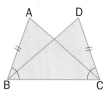

2. Two circles, with centres A and B, intersect at P and Q. AB and PQ intersect at T. Prove that PT = QT.

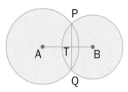

7.2 *Find the required angle measures and lengths, to the nearest tenth. O is the centre of the circle.*

3.

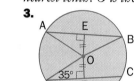

4.

a) ∠ABO   OD
b) ∠BOA

5. Water Pipe A circular water pipe, which runs horizontally under a road, has a diameter of 40 cm. The depth of the water in the pipe is 15 cm. Find the width of the water surface, to the nearest tenth of a centimetre.

7.3 *Find the measures of the indicated angles. Explain your reasoning.*

6.

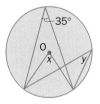

7.

8.

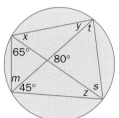

9.

10. *Given:* AE = BE
Prove: AB ∥ DC

7.4 *Find the measures of the indicated angles. Explain your reasoning.*

11.

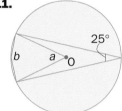

12.

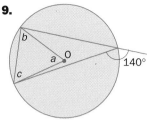

13. *Given:* AB = AC;
BE = CD
Prove: Quadrilateral DBCE is cyclic.

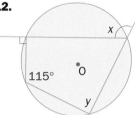

7.5 *Find the measures of the indicated angles. Explain your reasoning.*

14.

15.

Find the required lengths. Round answers to the nearest tenth of a centimetre.

16.

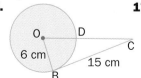

CD

17.

PQ

18. XP and XQ are tangents to one circle from X. XQ and XR are tangents from X to a second, smaller circle, which is outside the first circle and tangent to it. Prove that △XPR is isosceles.

7.6 *Calculate*
a) *the length of the indicated arc, to the nearest tenth of a centimetre*
b) *the area of the shaded sector, to the nearest square centimetre*

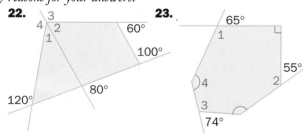

19. 50° 12 cm

20. 25 cm 210°

21. Apple pie A sector-shaped slice is cut from an apple pie with a diameter of 20 cm. The slice has a perimeter of 30 cm. Find the sector angle, to the nearest degree, and the sector area, to the nearest tenth of a square centimetre.

7.7 *Determine the measure of each numbered angle. Give reasons for your answers.*

22. 3 4 2 1 60° 100° 120° 80°

23. 65° 1 55° 4 2 3 74°

Given the number of sides of a polygon, determine the sum of the measures of the interior angles.
a) *in degrees*   **b)** *in right angles*
24. 25   **25.** 40   **26.** 2*m*

The measure of an exterior angle of a regular polygon is given. Determine
a) *the number of sides of the polygon*
b) *the measure of an interior angle of the polygon*
27. 72°   **28.** 30°   **29.** 22.5°

30. Traffic sign What is the measure of each interior angle of a stop sign?

Exploring Math

Investigating Inscribed Circles

If each side of a polygon is tangent to a circle, the circle is inscribed in the polygon.

A circle inscribed in a triangle is called the **incircle** of the triangle. The centre of the incircle is called the **incentre**. Use the following steps to construct an incircle.

- Draw any △ABC.
- Construct each angle bisector and find the point where the angle bisectors meet. This point is the incentre.
- Construct a perpendicular segment from the incentre to one side of the triangle. The length of the perpendicular segment equals the radius of the incircle.
- Use the incentre and the radius to construct the incircle.

1. Explain why the above construction of an incircle works.

2. A triangle has side lengths of 5 cm, 12 cm, and 13 cm. Calculate the length of the radius of its incircle, to the nearest tenth of a centimetre.

3. An equilateral triangle has a perimeter of 30 cm. What percent of the area of the triangle is the area of the incircle, to the nearest percent?

4. A circle is inscribed in a regular hexagon of side length 10 cm. What percent of the area of the hexagon is the area of the circle, to the nearest percent?

5. A circle of radius r is inscribed in a square. A smaller circle is inscribed in a corner of the square, so that the larger circle and two sides of the square are tangent to the smaller circle. Express the radius of the smaller circle in terms of r.

Chapter Check

1. *Given:* AB = AD; CB = CD
Prove: BE = DE

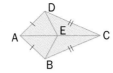

2. Prove that, if the opposite sides of a quadrilateral are equal, then the quadrilateral is a parallelogram.

3. Find the length of AB, to the nearest tenth of a centimetre.

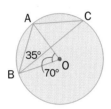

4. *Given:* ∠ABC = 35°
∠AOB = 70°
Prove: △ABC is isosceles.

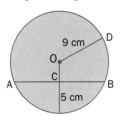

Find the measures of the indicated angles. Explain your reasoning.

5.

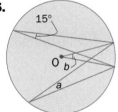

6.

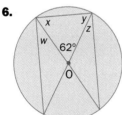

7.

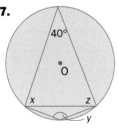

8.

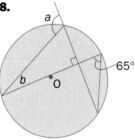

9. AB is a diameter of a circle, and C is a third point on the circle. X lies on the line segment BC, and Y lies on AB so that XY ⊥ AB. Prove that AYXC is a cyclic quadrilateral.

10. If PW = VW, name the cyclic quadrilateral. Explain your answer.

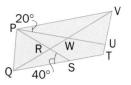

Find the measures of the unknown lengths and angles.

11.

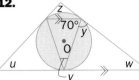

12.

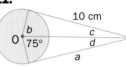

13. From a point P outside a circle with centre O, tangents are drawn to meet the circle at A and B.
a) Prove that PO is the right bisector of the chord AB.
b) Prove that ∠APB = 2∠OAB.

14. Find the measure of the indicated sector angle, to the nearest degree.

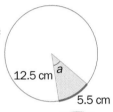

15. Calculate
a) the length of the indicated arc, to the nearest centimetre
b) the area of the shaded sector, to the nearest square centimetre.

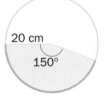

16. Clock hands The hour hand on a clock face is 8 cm long. From 01:00 to 02:00,
a) what is the arc length that the tip of the hand moves through, to the nearest tenth of a centimetre?
b) what is the sector area that the hand moves through, to the nearest tenth of a square centimetre?

Given the sum of the interior angles of a polygon, determine the number of sides of the polygon.
17. 1080°   **18.** 2520°   **19.** 3060°

20. Algebra
Determine the measures of angles D, E, F, G, and H.

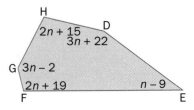

448   *Chapter 7*

Using the Strategies

1. There are three natural numbers that give the same result when they are added and when they are multiplied.

$$1 + 2 + 3 = 1 \times 2 \times 3$$

There is only one set of four natural numbers that has this property.

$$1 + 1 + 2 + 4 = 1 \times 1 \times 2 \times 4$$

There are three sets of five natural numbers, all less than 6, that have this property. What are they?

2. There were 100 applicants for a job. Ten had never taken a university course in history or geography. Seventy had taken at least one university course in history. Eighty-two had taken at least one university course in geography. How many of the applicants had taken at least one university course in history and at least one university course in geography?

3. About how many drops of milk are there in a one-litre carton of milk?

4. a) If $9x + 24 = A[x + B(x + C)]$ and A, B, and C are integers, find the values of A, B, and C.
b) If $-4x + 40 = A[x + B(x + C)]$ and A, B, and C are integers, find the values of A, B, and C.

5. Among nine similar coins, one is counterfeit and lighter than the others. Using a balance only twice, how can the counterfeit coin be identified?

6. a) Sketch a graph of distance from home plate versus time for the baseball in the following scenario.
The pitcher throws the baseball. The batter hits a long fly ball to right field. The ball hits the fence and is caught by the right fielder. The right fielder throws the ball to second base where it is caught by the shortstop.

b) Sketch a graph of the height of the ball versus time for the same scenario.

7. The sum of two numbers is 3. The product of the numbers is 2.
a) Find the numbers.
b) Find the sum of the reciprocals of the numbers.

8. The two concentric circles have centre O. The line PQ is tangent to the smaller circle at P. The point Q lies on the larger circle. The length of PQ is 4 cm. What is the area of the shaded region?

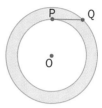

9. A rectangular floor is made up of identical square tiles. The floor is 40 tiles long and 30 tiles wide. If a straight line is drawn diagonally across the floor from corner to corner, how many tiles will it cross?

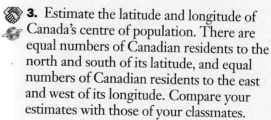

DATA BANK

1. The arc that connects Calgary and Glasgow lies on a circle with its centre at the centre of the Earth. What is the central angle for this arc, to the nearest degree? Assume that the radius of the Earth is 6370 km.

2. For a trip from Vancouver to Winnipeg,
a) what percent of the shortest driving distance is the shortest flying distance?
b) what percent of the shortest driving time is the shortest flying time? State your assumptions.

3. Estimate the latitude and longitude of Canada's centre of population. There are equal numbers of Canadian residents to the north and south of its latitude, and equal numbers of Canadian residents to the east and west of its longitude. Compare your estimates with those of your classmates.

CHAPTER 8

Coordinate Geometry and Trigonometry

I n 1972, Canada became the first country to use satellites for communications within its own borders. The *Anik A-1* satellite carried radio and television programs to all parts of the country. The satellite was in a geostationary orbit, which means that it moved in time with the Earth's rotation and stayed above a fixed point on the Earth's surface.

Anik E-2, launched in 1991, carries the bulk of Canada's television signals. This satellite is in a geostationary orbit 35 880 km above a point on the Earth's equator, at a longitude of 107.3°W. Canada has five teleports for uplinking signals from TV and radio stations to geostationary satellites. The teleports are in Montreal, Toronto, Calgary, Edmonton, and Vancouver.

1. The radius of the Earth is about 6370 km. To the nearest kilometre, how far does *Anik E-2* travel in one day?

2. At what velocity is *Anik E-2* revolving about the Earth's axis, to the nearest metre per second?

3. At what velocity is a point on the Earth's equator revolving about the Earth's axis, to the nearest metre per second?

4. How many times faster, to the nearest tenth, is Anik E-2 revolving than a point on the Earth's equator?

5. The velocity, v metres per second, of a satellite about the Earth's axis is related to the distance from the centre of the Earth, r metres, and the acceleration of gravity, g metres per second per second, by the following equation.

$$v = \sqrt{gr}$$

a) Solve the equation for g.
b) Calculate g, at the location of the satellite, to the nearest hundredth of a metre per second per second.
c) The value of g at the Earth's surface is about 9.8 m/s^2. How many times greater is this value than the value of g at the location of the satellite, to the nearest whole number?

6. Which Canadian teleport is closest to a longitude of 107.3°W?

Quilting

Quilts with traditional designs are made by sewing together many matching square blocks. Each block has a design made from small pieces of fabric stitched together. Many traditional designs use triangular and quadrilateral-shaped pieces on the square blocks.

To help determine the exact size and shape of the pieces, quilters may draw the pattern of the block on grid paper. The diagram shows one block of a maple leaf design on a grid.

Recall that, for two points $P_1(x_1, y_1)$ and $P_2(x_2, y_2)$,

- the slope of P_1P_2, $m = \dfrac{y_2 - y_1}{x_2 - x_1}$

- the midpoint of P_1P_2, M, is $\left(\dfrac{x_1 + x_2}{2}, \ \dfrac{y_1 + y_2}{2} \right)$

- the distance from P_1 to P_2, $d = \sqrt{(x_2 - x_1)^2 + (y_2 - y_1)^2}$

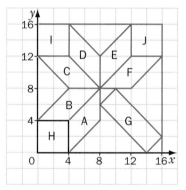

1 Slopes

1. a) Find the slope of each side of parallelogram A and parallelogram C.
b) How are the slopes of the opposite sides of a parallelogram related?
c) Is the result from part b) true for each type of quadrilateral in the maple leaf design?
d) What is the slope of a horizontal line? a vertical line?

2. a) Find the slope of each diagonal of square H.
b) How are the slopes related?
c) At what angle do the diagonals meet?
d) Are the results from parts b) and c) true for each type of quadrilateral in the design?

2 Midpoints

1. a) Find the midpoints of both diagonals of parallelogram F.
b) How are the midpoints related?
c) Is the result from part b) true for each type of quadrilateral in the design?

3 Distances

1. a) Find the exact length of each side of rectangle G.
b) How are the lengths of opposite sides related?
c) Is the result from part b) true for each type of quadrilateral in the design?

2. a) Find the exact length of each diagonal of square J.
b) How are the lengths related?
c) Is the result from part b) true for each type of quadrilateral in the design?

4 Equations

1. Write an equation for the line on which each of the following lies.
a) the shorter diagonal of parallelogram E
b) the shorter diagonal of parallelogram B

2. Write an equation in the slope and y-intercept form for the line on which each of the following lies.
a) the diagonal of square I with a negative slope
b) the longer diagonal of parallelogram A

Warm Up

State the slope of a line that is parallel to each given line.

1. $y = 3x + 1$ **2.** $y = -x + 4$
3. $y = 1.4x - 3.2$ **4.** $y = -5x - 2$
5. $2x + y - 6 = 0$ **6.** $3x - y + 1 = 0$
7. $x - 2y + 8 = 0$ **8.** $10x + 5y - 4 = 0$

State the slope of a line that is perpendicular to each given line.

9. $y = 2x + 3$ **10.** $y = -3x - 5$
11. $y = -\dfrac{1}{2}x + 7$ **12.** $y = \dfrac{2}{3}x - 4$
13. $x - y + 6 = 0$ **14.** $3x + 4y + 12 = 0$
15. $5x - 2y + 4 = 0$ **16.** $x - 5y = 0$

Write an equation for each line, in the slope and y-intercept form.

17.   **18.**

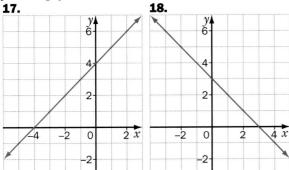

19.   **20.**

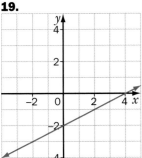
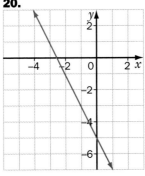

Find the x-intercept and the y-intercept for each line.

21. $3x + y - 6 = 0$ **22.** $x - 2y + 5 = 0$
23. $2x - 3y + 12 = 0$ **24.** $x + 0.5y + 4 = 0$
25. $5x + 3 = 0$ **26.** $2.5y - 15 = 0$

Solve each system of equations.

27. $x + y = 3$
    $2x - y = 0$
28. $2x + 3y = 1$
    $3x + 2y = -1$
29. $y = 3x - 1$
    $y = 4x - 3$
30. $2y = 5x + 1$
    $y = 2x - 1$

Mental Math

Order of Operations

Calculate the mean of each pair of numbers.

1. $5, 11$ **2.** $4, -6$ **3.** $-2, 8$ **4.** $-3, -7$
5. $7, 4$ **6.** $0, -9$ **7.** $-1, -6$ **8.** $3, -12$

Calculate the exact answer.

9. $\sqrt{(4-1)^2 + (7-3)^2}$ **10.** $\sqrt{(4-10)^2 + (2+6)^2}$

11. $\sqrt{(2+1)^2 + (3+4)^2}$

12. $\sqrt{(2+3)^2 + (6-(-6))^2}$

13. $\sqrt{(-3+5)^2 + (-4-5)^2}$

Squaring Numbers Ending in One or Two

To square a number ending in 1, multiply the numbers that are 1 above and 1 below the number. Then, add 1.
For 31^2, think $30 \times 32 = 960$
              $960 + 1 = 961$

Estimate
$30 \times 30 = 900$

So, $31^2 = 961$.
To find 3.1^2 or 310^2, first find 31^2, and then place the decimal point.
So, $3.1^2 = 9.61$ and $310^2 = 96\ 100$.

Calculate.

1. 21^2 **2.** 41^2 **3.** 91^2 **4.** 101^2
5. 5.1^2 **6.** 7.1^2 **7.** 810^2 **8.** 610^2

To square a number ending in 2, multiply the numbers that are 2 above and 2 below the number. Then, add 4.
For 32^2, think $30 \times 34 = 1020$
              $1020 + 4 = 1024$
So, $32^2 = 1024$.

Calculate.

9. 22^2 **10.** 52^2 **11.** 82^2 **12.** 102^2
13. 9.2^2 **14.** 6.2^2 **15.** 420^2 **16.** 720^2

17. Explain why the rules for squaring numbers ending in 1 or 2 work.

18. Write and test a similar rule that can be used to square numbers ending in 3.

19. Which rule would you use to square numbers ending in 9? ending in 8? Explain.

TECHNOLOGY

Exploring Geometric Properties Using Geometry Software

Complete the following explorations with geometry software. If suitable software is not available, construct and measure manually.

1 Midsegment of a Triangle

1. Construct any triangle.

2. Construct the midpoints of two sides of the triangle.

3. Join the two midpoints with a line segment, which is known as the midsegment.

4. Observe the figure you created, and predict two relationships between the midsegment and the third side of the original triangle.

5. Measure angles and lengths to check your predictions.

6. Use the drag property, or construct other triangles manually, to test whether your predictions hold for other triangles. Compare your findings with those of your classmates.

2 Midpoints of the Sides of a Quadrilateral

1. Construct any quadrilateral.

2. Construct the midpoints of the sides of the quadrilateral.

3. Join adjacent midpoints with line segments.

4. Observe the inner quadrilateral you created, and make a conjecture about its type.

5. Measure angles and lengths to check your conjecture.

6. Use the drag property, or construct other quadrilaterals manually, to test whether your conjecture holds for other quadrilaterals. Compare your findings with those of your classmates.

3 Diagonals of a Parallelogram

1. Construct any parallelogram.

2. Construct the diagonals of the parallelogram.

3. Observe the intersecting line segments you created, and predict a relationship between them.

4. Measure lengths to check your prediction.

5. Use the drag property, or construct other parallelograms manually, to test whether your prediction holds for other parallelograms. Compare your findings with those of your classmates.

4 Midpoint of the Hypotenuse of a Right Triangle

1. Construct any right triangle.

2. Construct the midpoint of the hypotenuse.

3. Observe the position of that midpoint relative to the vertices of the right triangle, and make a conjecture.

4. Measure distances to check your conjecture.

5. Use the drag property, or construct other right triangles manually, to test whether your conjecture holds for other right triangles. Compare your findings with those of your classmates.

8.1 Connecting Coordinate Geometry and Plane Geometry

A baseball diamond can be represented on a coordinate grid by placing the origin at home plate, with first base on the *x*-axis. The distance between the bases is 27.4 m. The pitcher's mound is on the diagonal from home plate to second base and is 18.4 m from home plate.

Explore: Use the Diagram

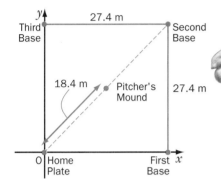

a) What are the coordinates of home plate and the three bases?
b) What are the slopes of the sides of the diamond? the diagonals of the diamond?

Inquire

1. a) How are the slopes of perpendicular lines related?
b) Are the diagonals of the diamond perpendicular?
c) Are the two sides that meet at first base perpendicular? Explain.

2. a) What are the coordinates of the midpoint of each diagonal of the diamond?
b) Do the diagonals bisect each other? Explain.

3. What is the distance from home plate to the point of intersection of the two diagonals, to the nearest tenth of a metre?

4. Is the pitcher's mound at the point of intersection of the diagonals?

Example 1 Verifying a Right Triangle

a) Verify that A(−1, 2), B(3, 0), and C(1, −4) are the vertices of a right triangle.
b) Is △ABC isosceles? Justify your answer.

Solution

a) Draw the triangle on a coordinate grid. ∠B appears to be a right angle, so find the slopes of AB and BC.

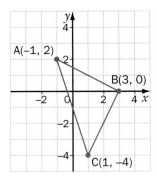

For AB,

$$m = \frac{y_2 - y_1}{x_2 - x_1}$$

$$m_{AB} = \frac{0 - 2}{3 - (-1)}$$

$$= \frac{-2}{4}$$

$$= -\frac{1}{2}$$

For BC,

$$m = \frac{y_2 - y_1}{x_2 - x_1}$$

$$m_{BC} = \frac{-4 - 0}{1 - 3}$$

$$= \frac{-4}{-2}$$

$$= 2$$

The product of the slopes of perpendicular line segments is −1, so find $m_{AB} \times m_{BC}$.

$$m_{AB} \times m_{BC} = -\frac{1}{2} \times 2$$

$$= -1$$

So, AB and BC are perpendicular.
A, B, and C are the vertices of a right triangle.

b) If △ABC is isosceles, exactly two of its side lengths are equal. Since ∠ABC is a right angle, the only possible equal sides are AB and BC. Use the distance formula to find the side lengths.

For AB,

$$d = \sqrt{(x_2 - x_1)^2 + (y_2 - y_1)^2}$$

$$AB = \sqrt{(3 - (-1))^2 + (0 - 2)^2}$$

$$= \sqrt{(4)^2 + (-2)^2}$$

$$= \sqrt{20}$$

$$= 2\sqrt{5}$$

For BC,

$$d = \sqrt{(x_2 - x_1)^2 + (y_2 - y_1)^2}$$

$$BC = \sqrt{(1 - 3)^2 + (-4 - 0)^2}$$

$$= \sqrt{(-2)^2 + (-4)^2}$$

$$= \sqrt{20}$$

$$= 2\sqrt{5}$$

So, AB = BC.
Since exactly two of its side lengths are equal, △ABC is isosceles.

Example 2 Diagonals of a Parallelogram

Verify that the diagonals of the parallelogram with vertices W(−2, 1), X(3, 3), Y(4, −1), and Z(−1, −3) bisect each other.

Solution

If the diagonals have the same midpoint, then they bisect each other. Use the formula for midpoint to find the midpoint of each diagonal.

$$\left(\frac{x_1 + x_2}{2}, \frac{y_1 + y_2}{2} \right)$$

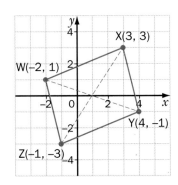

The midpoint of WY is $\left(\dfrac{-2+4}{2},\dfrac{1+(-1)}{2}\right)=(1,\ 0)$.

The midpoint of XZ is $\left(\dfrac{3+(-1)}{2},\dfrac{3+(-3)}{2}\right)=(1,\ 0)$.

The diagonals have the same midpoint.
The diagonals of the parallelogram bisect each other.

In Examples 1 and 2, coordinate geometry was used to verify properties of specific geometric figures. Coordinate geometry can also be used to prove general statements. Both uses are shown in Example 3. This example deals with the **midsegment** of a triangle, which is a segment that connects the midpoints of two of its sides.

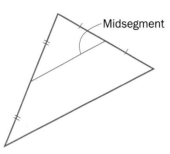
Midsegment

Example 3   Midsegments of Triangles
a) The vertices of a triangle are A(−3, 6), B(1, −6), and C(5, 2). If M is the midpoint of AB and N is the midpoint of AC, verify that MN is parallel to BC and that MN is half the length of BC.
b) If △PQR is any triangle, with K the midpoint of PQ and L the midpoint of PR, prove that KL is parallel to QR and is half its length.

Solution

a) Use the midpoint formula, $\left(\dfrac{x_1+x_2}{2},\dfrac{y_1+y_2}{2}\right)$, to find the coordinates of M and N.

The midpoint of AB is $\left(\dfrac{-3+1}{2},\dfrac{6+(-6)}{2}\right)=(-1,\ 0)$.

The midpoint of AC is $\left(\dfrac{-3+5}{2},\dfrac{6+2}{2}\right)=(1,\ 4)$.

So, the midpoints are M(−1, 0) and N(1, 4).

If MN is parallel to BC, then these two segments have the same slope. Find the slopes of MN and BC.

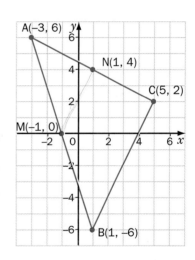

For MN,

$$m=\frac{y_2-y_1}{x_2-x_1}$$
$$m_{MN}=\frac{4-0}{1-(-1)}$$
$$=\frac{4}{2}$$
$$=2$$

For BC,

$$m=\frac{y_2-y_1}{x_2-x_1}$$
$$m_{BC}=\frac{2-(-6)}{5-1}$$
$$=\frac{8}{4}$$
$$=2$$

Since the slopes are equal, MN is parallel to BC.

Use the distance formula to find the lengths of MN and BC.

For MN,

$$d = \sqrt{(x_2 - x_1)^2 + (y_2 - y_1)^2}$$
$$= \sqrt{(1-(-1))^2 + (4-0)^2}$$
$$= \sqrt{4+16}$$
$$= \sqrt{20}$$
$$= 2\sqrt{5}$$

For BC,

$$d = \sqrt{(x_2 - x_1)^2 + (y_2 - y_1)^2}$$
$$= \sqrt{(5-1)^2 + (2-(-6))^2}$$
$$= \sqrt{16+64}$$
$$= \sqrt{80}$$
$$= 4\sqrt{5}$$

So, MN is half the length of BC.

b) Draw any triangle PQR on a set of coordinate axes. Because the properties of the triangle do not depend on its position, choose a position that is convenient. In coordinate geometry proofs, it is usually easiest to place a vertex of a figure at the origin and at least one side of the figure on a positive axis, or to place the centre of the figure at the origin. Assign general coordinates to P, Q, and R, and use these coordinates to complete the proof.

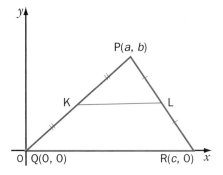

K is the midpoint of PQ, so the coordinates of K are $\left(\dfrac{a+0}{2}, \dfrac{b+0}{2}\right)$ or $\left(\dfrac{a}{2}, \dfrac{b}{2}\right)$.

L is the midpoint of PR, so the coordinates of L are $\left(\dfrac{a+c}{2}, \dfrac{b+0}{2}\right)$ or $\left(\dfrac{a+c}{2}, \dfrac{b}{2}\right)$.

K and L have the same y-coordinate, $\dfrac{b}{2}$, so KL is parallel to the x-axis.

As QR lies on the x-axis, KL is parallel to QR.

The length of a horizontal line segment is the difference in the x-coordinates of the endpoints.

So, $KL = \dfrac{a+c}{2} - \dfrac{a}{2}$
$$= \dfrac{c}{2}$$

The length of QR is c, so $KL = \dfrac{1}{2}QR$.

Therefore, KL is parallel to QR and is half its length.

The general statement proved in Example 3b) can be expressed as the following theorem.

Triangle Midsegment Theorem
If a segment joins the midpoints of two sides of a triangle, then the segment is parallel to, and half the length of, the third side.

Example 4 Midpoints of the Sides of a Quadrilateral

Prove that the figure formed by joining the midpoints of the sides of any quadrilateral is a parallelogram.

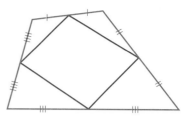

Solution

Position one vertex of the quadrilateral at the origin and one side along the positive x-axis. Let the coordinates of the vertices of the quadrilateral be $K(0, 0)$, $L(a, b)$, $M(c, d)$, and $N(e, 0)$. Let W, X, Y, and Z be the midpoints of the sides of the quadrilateral.

First, find the coordinates of W, X, Y, and Z using the midpoint formula $\left(\dfrac{x_1 + x_2}{2}, \dfrac{y_1 + y_2}{2}\right)$.

For W, the midpoint of KL, $\left(\dfrac{a+0}{2}, \dfrac{b+0}{2}\right) = \left(\dfrac{a}{2}, \dfrac{b}{2}\right)$

For X, the midpoint of LM, $\left(\dfrac{a+c}{2}, \dfrac{b+d}{2}\right)$

For Y, the midpoint of MN, $\left(\dfrac{c+e}{2}, \dfrac{d+0}{2}\right) = \left(\dfrac{c+e}{2}, \dfrac{d}{2}\right)$

For Z, the midpoint of KN, $\left(\dfrac{0+e}{2}, \dfrac{0+0}{2}\right) = \left(\dfrac{e}{2}, 0\right)$

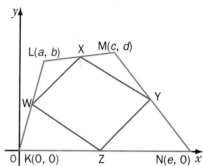

Now, find and compare the slopes of opposite sides of quadrilateral WXYZ.

For WX,
$$m = \frac{y_2 - y_1}{x_2 - x_1}$$
$$m_{WX} = \frac{\dfrac{b+d}{2} - \dfrac{b}{2}}{\dfrac{a+c}{2} - \dfrac{a}{2}}$$
$$= \frac{\dfrac{d}{2}}{\dfrac{c}{2}}$$
$$= \frac{d}{c}$$

For ZY,
$$m = \frac{y_2 - y_1}{x_2 - x_1}$$
$$m_{ZY} = \frac{\dfrac{d}{2} - 0}{\dfrac{c+e}{2} - \dfrac{e}{2}}$$
$$= \frac{\dfrac{d}{2}}{\dfrac{c}{2}}$$
$$= \frac{d}{c}$$

For YX,
$$m = \frac{y_2 - y_1}{x_2 - x_1}$$
$$m_{YX} = \frac{\dfrac{b+d}{2} - \dfrac{d}{2}}{\dfrac{a+c}{2} - \dfrac{c+e}{2}}$$
$$= \frac{\dfrac{b}{2}}{\dfrac{a-e}{2}}$$
$$= \frac{b}{a-e}$$

For ZW,
$$m = \frac{y_2 - y_1}{x_2 - x_1}$$
$$m_{ZW} = \frac{\dfrac{b}{2} - 0}{\dfrac{a}{2} - \dfrac{e}{2}}$$
$$= \frac{\dfrac{b}{2}}{\dfrac{a-e}{2}}$$
$$= \frac{b}{a-e}$$

Since their slopes are the same, WX and ZY are parallel.
Since their slopes are the same, YX and ZW are parallel.

Since both pairs of opposite sides are parallel, the figure formed by joining the midpoints of the quadrilateral is a parallelogram.

Note that there can be various ways of completing the same proof. In Example 4, WXYZ was proved to be a parallelogram by showing that both pairs of opposite sides were parallel. Other ways to prove that WXYZ is a parallelogram include showing that both pairs of opposite sides have equal lengths, that two opposite sides are parallel and equal in length, or that the diagonals bisect each other. Write a proof for Example 4 using one of these other ways.

Practice

1. The vertices of a triangle are A(0, 0), B(2, 4), and C(4, 0). Verify that $\triangle ABC$ is isosceles.

2. A quadrilateral has vertices at O(0, 0), P(3, 5), Q(8, 6), and R(5, 1). Show that OPQR is a parallelogram.

3. Given the points X(1, 4), Y(−2, 2), and Z(3, 1), show that $\triangle XYZ$ is a right triangle.

4. The vertices of a triangle are K(2, 6), L(4, 10), and M(8, −2). Let P be the midpoint of KL and Q be the midpoint of LM. Show that PQ is parallel to KM.

5. Show that the quadrilateral with vertices at P(2, 3), Q(5, −1), R(10, −1), and S(7, 3) is a rhombus.

6. A parallelogram has vertices at A(−2, −2), B(3, 3), C(7, 4), and D(2, −1). Show that the diagonals bisect each other.

7. The vertices of a quadrilateral are K(−1, 0), L(1, −2), M(4, 1), and N(2, 3). Verify that KLMN is a rectangle.

8. Given A(0, 0), B(2, 3), C(5, 1), and D(3, −2), show that the diagonals of ABCD are perpendicular to each other.

9. Show that the quadrilateral with vertices at O(0, 0), P(3, 5), Q(13, 7), and R(5, 1) is a trapezoid.

10. Verify that the quadrilateral with vertices P(−2, 2), Q(−2, −3), R(−5, −5), and S(−5, 0) is a parallelogram.

Applications and Problem Solving

11. Show that the triangle with vertices at A(0, 0), B($\sqrt{3}$, −1), and C($\sqrt{3}$, 1) is equilateral.

12. Given A(0, 0), B(−1, $\sqrt{3}$), C(0, 2$\sqrt{3}$), D(2, 2$\sqrt{3}$), E(3, $\sqrt{3}$), and F(2, 0), verify that ABCDEF is a regular hexagon.

13. The sides of a triangle have the equations $y = -\frac{1}{2}x + 1$, $y = 2x - 4$, and $y = \frac{1}{3}x - 4$. Verify that the triangle is an isosceles right triangle.

14. A triangle has vertices K(−2, 2), L(1, 5), and M(3, −3). Verify that
a) the triangle has a right angle
b) the midpoint of the hypotenuse is the same distance from each vertex

15. Consider the general case parallelogram, PQRS, positioned with three vertices at P(0, 0), Q(a, b), and S(c, 0).
a) What are the coordinates of R?
b) Prove that the diagonals of any parallelogram bisect each other.

16. The **centroid** of a triangle is the point of intersection of the three medians. A triangle has vertices at X(0, 0), Y(4, 4), and Z(8, −4).
a) Write an equation for each of the three medians.
b) Use the equations to verify that (4, 0) is the centroid of $\triangle XYZ$.

17. Find the coordinates of the centroid of the triangle with vertices at A(0, 0), B(2, 6), and C(6, 2).

18. The sides of a parallelogram have the equations $x = 0$, $y = \frac{1}{6}x + 3$, $x = 6$, and $y = \frac{1}{6}x - 2$. Verify that the diagonals intersect at the point (3, 1).

19. Use each diagram to prove that the quadrilateral formed by joining the midpoints of the sides of a rectangle is a rhombus. Which method do you prefer? Why?

a) origin at one vertex of the rectangle

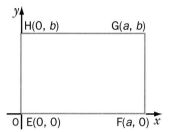

b) origin at the centre of the rectangle

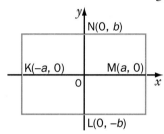

20. Prove that, in a right triangle, the length of the median from the right angle to the hypotenuse is half the length of the hypotenuse.

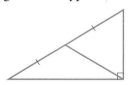

21. Prove that the diagonals of any square are perpendicular to each other.

22. Construction To ensure that a rectangular frame has four right angles, builders often check that the two diagonals have equal lengths. Prove that the diagonals of any rectangle are equal in length.

23. Prove that one median of an isosceles triangle is always perpendicular to one of the sides.

24. Prove that the line joining the midpoints of adjacent sides of any quadrilateral is parallel to one of the diagonals of the quadrilateral.

25. Pocket billiards The game of pocket billiards is played on a rectangular table. Suppose that a ball is on the centre spot exactly in the middle of the table. From this position, there are two directions in which the ball can be hit into a pocket at the right-hand end.

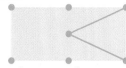

a) Prove that these two directions are not perpendicular.

b) If the table were square, would the two directions be perpendicular? Explain.

26. Show that, for a triangle with vertices (x_1, y_1), (x_2, y_2), and (x_3, y_3), the coordinates of the centroid are $\left(\dfrac{x_1 + x_2 + x_3}{3}, \dfrac{y_1 + y_2 + y_3}{3} \right)$.

27. Prove that the midpoints of the sides of a kite are the vertices of a rectangle.

28. Prove that the medians of any equilateral triangle are equal in length.

29. For a trapezoid, the midsegment is defined as the segment joining the midpoints of the non-parallel sides. Prove that the midsegment of any trapezoid is parallel to the bases and half as long as the sum of their lengths.

30. A triangle has vertices A(0, 0), B(6, 4), and C(12, −4).

a) Verify that the centroid of △ABC is at (6, 0).

b) The **orthocentre** of a triangle is the point at which the three altitudes intersect. Verify that $\left(\dfrac{56}{9}, \dfrac{14}{3} \right)$ is the orthocentre of △ABC.

c) The **circumcentre** is the point at which the three perpendicular bisectors of the sides of a triangle intersect. Verify that $\left(\dfrac{53}{9}, -\dfrac{7}{3} \right)$ is the circumcentre of △ABC.

d) Verify that the centroid, the orthocentre, and the circumcentre of △ABC are all collinear.

INVESTIGATING MATH

Exploring the Division of Line Segments

Recall that a single point, the midpoint, divides a line segment into two equal parts.
Two points can divide a line segment into three equal parts, three points can divide a line segment into four equal parts, and so on.
A line can be divided into n equal parts by $n - 1$ points.

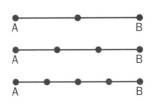

1 Division of Horizontal Line Segments

1. Graph the line segment with the given endpoints. Count units to find the coordinates of the points that divide each line segment into three equal parts.
a) A(2, 0) and B(5, 0)   **b)** C(1, 3) and D(7, 3)
c) E(–3, 2) and F(9, 2)   **d)** G(–10, –4) and H(–1, –4)

2. Describe how the coordinates of the points that divide a horizontal line segment into three equal parts can be found from the coordinates of the endpoints.

3. Graph the line segment with the given endpoints. Count units to find the coordinates of the points that divide each line segment into four equal parts.
a) M(1, 0) and N(5, 0)   **b)** P(0, 2) and Q(8, 2)
c) R(–4, 1) and S(8, 1)   **d)** T(–8, –2) and U(8, –2)

4. Describe how the coordinates of the points that divide a horizontal line segment into four equal parts can be found from the coordinates of the endpoints.

5. Graph the line segment with the given endpoints. Count units to find the coordinates of the points that divide each line segment into five equal parts.
a) X(3, 0) and Y(8, 0)   **b)** K(1, 5) and L(11, 5)
c) V(–5, 2) and W(10, 2)
d) G(–12, –6) and H(8, –6)

6. Describe how the coordinates of the points that divide a horizontal line segment into five equal parts can be found from the coordinates of the endpoints.

7. Use the pattern to write a rule for finding the coordinates of the points that divide a horizontal line segment into n equal parts.

8. If a horizontal line segment has the endpoints O(0, 0) and P(a, 0), what are the coordinates of the points that divide the line segment into each of the following numbers of equal parts?
a) 3   **b)** 4   **c)** 5
d) 6   **e)** 8

1. Graph the line segment with the given endpoints. Count units to find the coordinates of the points that divide each line segment into three equal parts.
a) F(0, 1) and G(0, 4)
b) K(2, 2) and L(2, 8)
c) A(3, −5) and B(3, 4)
d) E(−1, −12) and F(−1, 0)

2. Describe how the coordinates of the points that divide a vertical line segment into three equal parts can be found from the coordinates of the endpoints.

3. Graph the line segment with the given endpoints. Count units to find the coordinates of the points that divide each line segment into four equal parts.
a) X(0, 2) and Y(0, 6)
b) V(1, 4) and W(1, 12)
c) M(2, −6) and N(2, 6)
d) I(−3, −9) and J(−3, 7)

4. Describe how the coordinates of the points that divide a vertical line segment into four equal parts can be found from the coordinates of the endpoints.

5. Graph the line segment with the given endpoints. Count units to find the coordinates of the points that divide each line segment into five equal parts.
a) O(0, 0) and P(0, 5)
b) B(−1, 2) and C(−1, 12)
c) S(−2, −6) and T(−2, 9)
d) D(3, −9) and E(3, 11)

6. Describe how the coordinates of the points that divide a vertical line segment into five equal parts can be found from the coordinates of the endpoints.

7. Use the pattern to write a rule for finding the coordinates of the points that divide a vertical line segment into n equal parts.

8. If a vertical line segment has the endpoints O(0, 0) and P(0, b), what are the coordinates of the points that divide the line segment into each of the following numbers of equal parts?
a) 3   **b)** 4   **c)** 5   **d)** 7   **e)** 10

1. The line segment AB has the endpoints A(1, 2) and B(7, 5). Graph the segment.
a) Draw line segments that represent the rise and the run for AB.
b) Divide the rise into three equal parts.
c) Divide the run into three equal parts.
d) Show how your results from parts b) and c) can be used to divide AB into three equal parts.
e) Use the Pythagorean theorem to check that AB has been correctly divided into three equal parts.
f) State the coordinates of the points that divide AB into three equal parts.

2. Find the coordinates of the points that divide the line segments with each of the following pairs of endpoints into three equal parts.
a) X(−1, 4) and Y(5, −2)
b) M(3, 3) and N(−6, −9)

3. Find the coordinates of the points that divide the line segments with each of the following pairs of endpoints into four equal parts.
a) C(−4, 1) and D(0, −3)
b) M(2, 3) and N(−6, −9)

4. Find the coordinates of the points that divide the line segments with each of the following pairs of endpoints into five equal parts.
a) P(0, 5) and Q(5, 0)
b) G(4, 10) and H(−6, −5)

5. Write a rule for finding the coordinates of the points that divide a sloping line segment into n equal parts.

6. If a line segment has the endpoints O(0, 0) and P(a, b), what are the coordinates of the points that divide the line segment into each of the following numbers of equal parts?
a) 3   **b)** 4   **c)** 5   **d)** 6   **e)** n

8.2 Division of a Line Segment

Architects sometimes use steps or a staircase as a central feature in the design of a building. Canadian architect Arthur Erickson coined the term "stramps" to refer to the integrated steps and ramps he included in the design of Robson Square in Vancouver. The stramps were intended to give all people equal access to the front of the provincial law courts.

The mathematical principle behind the construction of steps is the equal division of a line segment.

Explore: Look for a Pattern

A staircase includes risers and treads.

We can describe a staircase in terms of its riser height and tread depth.

tread depth

riser height

A staircase is to be built to span a horizontal distance of 4.0 m and to rise vertically 2.4 m. Copy and complete the table to show how the depth of each tread and the height of each riser would vary with the number of steps in the staircase.

Number of Steps	Diagram	Tread Depth (m)	Riser Height (m)
1			
2			
3			
4			
n			

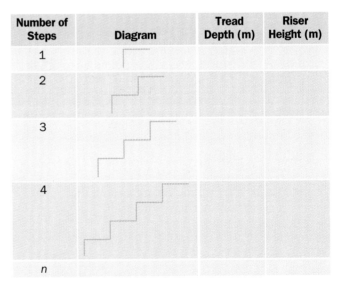

Inquire

1. If the staircase had 10 steps, what would be
a) the tread depth?   **b)** the riser height?

2. If the stairs are actually built with a tread depth of 25 cm,
a) how many steps are in the staircase?
b) what is the riser height, in centimetres?

3. Suppose a set of three steps spans a horizontal distance of
84 cm and rises 60 cm vertically.
a) Find the tread depth and the riser height, in centimetres.
b) Suppose a line segment is drawn from the bottom of the
stairs, A, to the top of the stairs, B, to intersect the corners of
steps at C and D. Into how many parts do the points C and
D divide the segment AB?

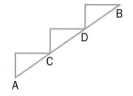

c) If a coordinate grid is superimposed so that A is at the
origin, as shown, and one unit on the grid represents 1 cm,
what are the coordinates of B? what are the coordinates of C
and D?

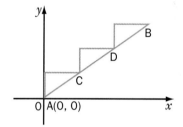

d) If the coordinates of A and B are not changed, but these
points are connected by four steps, as shown, what are the
coordinates of K, L, and M?

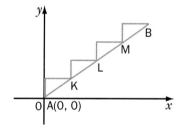

For the line segment with endpoints F(2, 6) and G(4, 10),
the coordinates of the midpoint M can be found using the
midpoint formula $\left(\dfrac{x_1 + x_2}{2}, \dfrac{y_1 + y_2}{2} \right)$.

$$\left(\dfrac{2+4}{2}, \dfrac{6+10}{2} \right) = (3, 8)$$

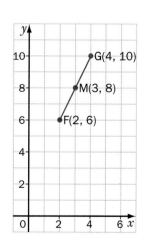

Another way to find the midpoint of the line segment with endpoints F(2, 6) and G(4, 10) is to visualize the segment FG as connecting the top and bottom of a set of steps. There is one division point, M, and two steps. Each step has a tread depth of 1, which is half the horizontal distance from F to G. Each step has a riser height of 2, which is half the vertical distance from F to G. Knowing the tread depth and the riser height of the imaginary stairs, we can find the coordinates of M from the coordinates of either F or G.

Using F, the coordinates of M are (2 + 1, 6 + 2) = (3, 8)

Using G, the coordinates of M are (4 − 1, 10 − 2) = (3, 8)

Note that, in finding the coordinates of the midpoint, we divided the horizontal and vertical distances from one endpoint to the other by 2. This is the number of congruent line segments. In general, for n congruent line segments, we can divide the distances by n.

Example 1   Dividing a Line Segment into Congruent Parts

Determine the coordinates of the points that divide the line segment joining A(−3, 6) and B(7, −9) into five congruent parts.

Solution

The horizontal distance from A to B is
$$|x_2 - x_1| = |7 - (-3)|$$
$$= 10$$

The horizontal distance between division points is $\frac{10}{5}$ or 2.

The vertical distance from A to B is
$$|y_2 - y_1| = |-9 - 6|$$
$$= 15$$

The vertical distance between division points is $\frac{15}{5}$ or 3.

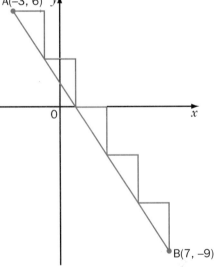

Starting from A, the first division point is 2 units to the right of A and 3 units below A. The coordinates of this division point are (−3 + 2, 6 − 3) or (−1, 3).

The coordinates of the next division point are (−3 + 2(2), 6 − 2(3)) or (1, 0).

The final two division points are (−3 + 3(2), 6 − 3(3)) or (3, −3), and (−3 + 4(2), 6 − 4(3)) or (5, −6).

So, the points that divide AB into five congruent parts have the coordinates (−1, 3), (1, 0), (3, −3), and (5, −6).

Check.
Find one of the division points by moving to the left and upward from B. The third division point from B has the coordinates
(7 − 3(2), −9 + 3(3)) = (1, 0)

Example 2   Ski Lift

A ski lift has five equally-spaced support towers. From the first tower to the last, the lift spans a horizontal distance of 120 m and rises 90 m vertically. Model the cable using coordinates. Determine the coordinates of the cable at each support tower.

Solution

Draw a diagram.
Let the points at which the cable is supported by the towers be A, B, C, D, and E. Let the coordinates of A be (0, 0). Then, the coordinates of E are (120, 90). There are three support towers between A and E, so AE is divided into four congruent parts.

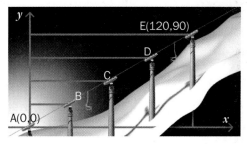

The horizontal distance between the cable positions at successive support towers is $\dfrac{|120-0|}{4} = 30$.

The vertical distance between the cable positions at successive support towers is $\dfrac{|90-0|}{4} = 22.5$.

The coordinates of B are (0 + 30, 0 + 22.5) or (30, 22.5).
The coordinates of C are (0 + 2(30), 0 + 2(22.5)) or (60, 45).
The coordinates of D are (0 + 3(30), 0 + 3(22.5)) or (90, 67.5).
So, the coordinates of the cable at each of the five support towers are (0, 0), (30, 22.5), (60, 45), (90, 67.5), and (120, 90).

Check that the calculation method gives the correct coordinates for E.
(0 + 4(30), 0 + 4(22.5)) = (120, 90)

Note that the coordinates of A used in Example 2 were chosen for convenience. Other coordinates could be used. Suppose, for example, that point A is 500 m above sea level. The coordinates chosen for A might then be (0, 500), so that E is at (120, 590). The coordinates of the division points would then be B(30, 522.5), C(60, 545), and D(90, 567.5).

Practice

Determine the coordinates of the points that divide the line segment joining the two given points into the given number of congruent parts.

1. F(0, 2), G(0, 8) into 2 parts
2. X(3, 0), Y(9, 0) into 3 parts
3. B(−1, 2), C(−9, 2) into 4 parts
4. L(−4, 2), M(−4, −4) into 3 parts
5. U(3, −1), V(6, −1) into 2 parts
6. D(−3, −2), E(−3, 0) into 5 parts

Determine the coordinates of the points that divide the line segment joining the two given points into the given number of congruent parts.

7. A(2, 4), B(6, 18) into 2 parts
8. C(4, 5), D(12, 17) into 4 parts
9. E(0, −1), F(3, 8) into 3 parts
10. G(0, 10), H(−10, 0) into 5 parts
11. W(−3, −8), X(3, 4) into 6 parts
12. Y(4, 2), Z(−3, 7) into 2 parts
13. R(8, 2), S(5, 1) into 3 parts
14. T(0, 4), U(4, 9) into 5 parts
15. I(−2, 1), J(3, 7) into 3 parts
16. K(−12, −8), L(−2, −6) into 4 parts
17. M(2, 4), N(8, −16) into 4 parts
18. P(−12, 4), Q(3, −22) into 6 parts

19. Find the coordinates of the third division point from A when the line segment with endpoints A(0, 1) and B(10, 16) is divided into five congruent parts.

20. Find the coordinates of the second division point from C when the line segment with endpoints C(−11, 1) and D(10, −8) is divided into three congruent parts.

21. Find the coordinates of the fourth division point from E when the line segment with endpoints E(12, 110) and F(60, 50) is divided into six congruent parts.

22. Find the coordinates of the second division point from X when the line segment with endpoints X(−3, −5) and Y(−8, −2) is divided into four congruent parts.

Applications and Problem Solving

23. Radicals Find the coordinates of the fourth division point from P when the line segment with endpoints P($\sqrt{8}$, $\sqrt{20}$) and Q(−$\sqrt{18}$, $\sqrt{125}$) is divided into five congruent parts.

24. Working backward A line segment XY is divided into four congruent parts. If X is at (1, 1) and the first division point from X is at (3, 4), what are the coordinates of Y?

25. Sequences a) Find the coordinates of the points that divide the segment with endpoints K(−4, 19) and L(6, −1) into 5 congruent parts.
b) List the x-coordinates of K, the four division points, and L from least to greatest.
c) List the y-coordinates of K, the four division points, and L from greatest to least.
d) What type of sequence did you write in parts b) and c)? Explain.

26. Working backward The two points that divide the segment AB into three congruent parts are C(3, −2) and D(−1, 4). If C is between A and D, what are the coordinates of A and B?

27. Elevator The floor of an elevator is at a height of 0 m on the ground floor of a hotel and at a height of 45 m on the 11th floor. What is the height of the floor of the elevator on the 7th floor of the hotel?

28. a) Use midpoints to find the coordinates of the points that divide the segments with the following endpoints into the given numbers of congruent parts. Describe your method in each case.
A(2, 3), B(6, 11) into 4 parts
X(−6, 9), Y(2, −7) into 8 parts
b) Could you use midpoints to divide a segment into three congruent parts?

29. Hydro lines In one part of the countryside, a hydro-electric corridor rises 100 m in a span of 500 m. The hydro lines in this section are supported by 6 equally spaced towers.
a) If a cable on the first support tower in this section is considered to be at (0, 0), what are the coordinates of the same cable on the sixth tower, at the top of the section?
b) Determine the coordinates of the same cable on the four intermediate towers.
c) Find the straight-line distance, to the nearest metre, between the locations of the cable on two successive towers.
d) Because of the sagging of the hydro lines, the actual length of cable between towers is 115% of the straight-line distance. Find the length of cable, to the nearest metre, between two successive towers.

30. Locks The Welland Canal was built to allow ships to travel between Lake Erie and Lake Ontario by avoiding Niagara Falls. Lake Erie is 99.5 m higher than Lake Ontario and, to raise or lower the ships, the canal has 8 locks along its course. Locks 4, 5, and 6 are next to each other like giant steps and they raise the ships by a total of 42.6 m in a distance of 785.4 m. If, in a side-view diagram showing the locks, the point at which a ship enters lock 4 when travelling south is considered to be the origin, determine the coordinates of the points that represent the ship's entry into locks 5 and 6.

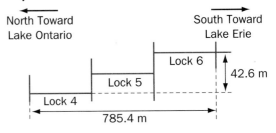

31. Ski lifts Creekside Lift at Whistler carries skiers up a vertical distance of about 650 m in 6-person gondolas, which travel at a rate of about 5.09 m/s. The time taken for the trip up the slope is approximately 6.73 min.
a) What is the straight-line distance travelled by the lift up the slope, to the nearest ten metres?
b) Determine the horizontal distance between the terminal at the lower end of the lift and the terminal at the top, to the nearest ten metres.
c) The lift has 25 support towers between the terminals. If the lower terminal is considered to have coordinates (0, 0), what are the coordinates of the cable at the tenth tower below the upper terminal? What assumption did you make in determining your answer?

32. Construction A set of stairs in a new theatre is to be banked at an angle of 35°.

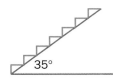

a) If the horizontal span of the stairs is 5 m, what is the vertical height, to the nearest tenth of a metre?
b) Use coordinates to model the cross section of the stairs. If there are 20 steps, determine the coordinates of the point at the back edge of the eighth step up. Assume that the coordinates of the vertex are (0, 0).

33. Division of a line segment is often written as a ratio. For example, X divides the line segment AB in the ratio 2:3.

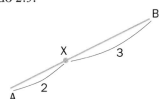

a) Determine the coordinates of X, if the coordinates of the endpoints are A(2, 6) and B(32, 66).
b) Find the coordinates of Y, if Y is between A and X, and Y divides AX in the ratio 2:1.

34. The line $y = mx$ intersects the line segment with endpoints P(–2, 7) and Q(10, 10) at the point R. Find the value of m if the ratio of PR:RQ is
a) 2:1   **b)** 1:4

35. A line segment has endpoints A(–2, 15) and B(13, –15). A point C is between A and B. Find the coordinates of C if the ratio of AC:BC is
a) 1:2   **b)** 2:3   **c)** 3:2   **d)** $m:n$

36. a) The vertices of a triangle are O(0, 0), P(4, 0), and Q(0, 6). Show that the three medians of △OPQ intersect at a single point and that this point divides each median in the ratio 2:1.
b) Prove that this property of medians is true for any triangle.

WORD POWER

Copy the diagram.

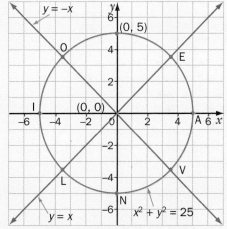

Name the points (0, 5) and (0, 0) with different letters so that the names of each of the following sets of points can be arranged to form the name of a country. Name each country.
a) the points 5 units from the origin
b) the points on the axes
c) the points with coordinates (0, 5), (5, 0), $\left(\dfrac{-5\sqrt{2}}{2}, \dfrac{5\sqrt{2}}{2}\right)$, and $\left(\dfrac{-5\sqrt{2}}{2}, \dfrac{-5\sqrt{2}}{2}\right)$

8.3 Distances Between Points and Lines

Alberta is Canada's main oil-producing province, but there are significant oil fields elsewhere in Canada. One of the latest to be exploited is Hibernia, which is under the Atlantic Ocean on the Grand Banks. The Hibernia drilling platform is located 315 km east-southeast of St. John's, Newfoundland.

Oil is transported to shore from an offshore oil platform by oil tankers. The platform must also receive regular visits from supply ships.

Explore: Use the Diagram

A radar operator on an oil platform is monitoring the positions and courses of ships on a radar screen. In the diagram, the innermost ring represents a distance of 5 km from the platform, P. Each successive ring represents an additional 5-km distance from the platform.
a) What is the scale of the diagram?
b) Draw the diagram and trace the positions of the labelled points.

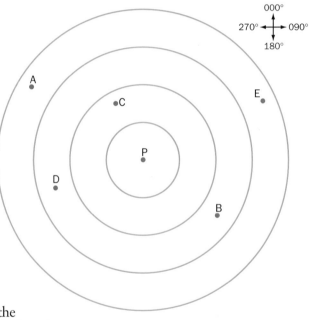

Inquire

1. Use the diagram to estimate the closest distance, in kilometres, that each of the following ships will come to the platform.
a) ship A, on a course of 180°
b) ship B, on a course of 270°
c) ship C, on a course of 120°

2. In question 1, if the closest distance from a ship to the platform is drawn as a line segment, at about what angle does this segment meet the line that represents the course of the ship?

3. If ship D is on a course of 045° and ship E is on a course of 225°,
a) how are the lines that represent their courses related?
b) about how far apart will they be, in kilometres, when they are closest together?

4. In question 3, if the closest distance between the ships is represented by a line segment, at about what angles does this segment meet the courses of the two ships?

Example 1   Distance From the Origin to a Line
Determine the shortest distance from the origin to the line $y = 2x - 10$, to the nearest tenth.

Solution

The shortest distance is the perpendicular distance OA from the point O(0, 0) to the line $y = 2x - 10$.

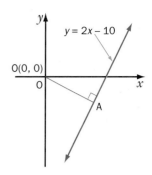

To find the length of OA, first find the coordinates of A.
The slope of $y = 2x - 10$ is 2.
Since $y = 2x - 10$ and OA are perpendicular, the product of their slopes is -1.
So, the slope of OA is $-\dfrac{1}{2}$.

Recall that, in the slope and y-intercept form, $y = mx + b$, m is the slope, and b is the y-intercept.

To find an equation for OA, use the point-slope form and substitute known values.
$$y - y_1 = m(x - x_1)$$
$$y - 0 = -\frac{1}{2}(x - 0)$$
$$y = -\frac{1}{2}x$$

To find the coordinates of A, solve the following system of equations.
$$y = 2x - 10 \quad \text{(1)}$$
$$y = -\frac{1}{2}x \quad \text{(2)}$$

The coordinates of A can also be found graphically.

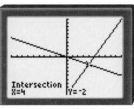

Substitute $-\dfrac{1}{2}x$ for y in (1).
$$y = 2x - 10$$
$$-\frac{1}{2}x = 2x - 10$$
$$-2\frac{1}{2}x = -10$$
$$x = 4$$

Substitute $x = 4$ in (2).
$$y = -\frac{1}{2}x$$
$$= -\frac{1}{2}(4)$$
$$= -2$$

The solution to the system can be checked by substitution in (1) and (2).

The coordinates of A are (4, −2).

Use the distance formula to find the distance from O(0, 0) to A(4, −2).
$$d = \sqrt{(x_2 - x_1)^2 + (y_2 - y_1)^2}$$
$$OA = \sqrt{(4-0)^2 + (-2-0)^2}$$
$$= \sqrt{20}$$
$$\doteq 4.5$$

The shortest distance from the origin to the line $y = 2x - 10$ is 4.5, to the nearest tenth.

Example 2   Distance From Any Point to a Line

Find the distance from the point P(–1, 3) to the line $x + y - 5 = 0$, to the nearest hundredth.

Solution

Find the coordinates of Q, the point of intersection of the
line $x + y - 5 = 0$ and the perpendicular from P.
The line $x + y - 5 = 0$, or $y = -x + 5$, has slope –1.
So, the perpendicular PQ has slope 1.
An equation of the line passing through P(–1, 3) with slope 1 can be
determined using the point-slope form, as follows.

$$y - y_1 = m(x - x_1)$$
$$y - 3 = 1(x - (-1))$$
$$y - 3 = x + 1$$
$$-4 = x - y$$

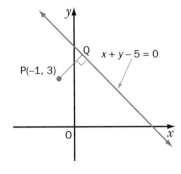

To find the coordinates of Q, solve the following system of equations.

$$x + y - 5 = 0 \quad (1)$$
$$x - y = -4 \quad (2)$$

Rearrange (1): $x + y = 5$
Write (2): $x - y = -4$

Add: $2x = 1$
Solve for x: $x = 0.5$

Substitute $x = 0.5$ in (2).
$$x - y = -4$$
$$0.5 - y = -4$$
$$-y = -4.5$$
$$y = 4.5$$

The coordinates of Q are (0.5, 4.5).   *Remember to check the coordinates of Q in (1) and (2).*

Use the distance formula to find the distance from P(–1, 3) to Q(0.5, 4.5).

$$d = \sqrt{(x_2 - x_1)^2 + (y_2 - y_1)^2}$$
$$= \sqrt{(0.5 - (-1))^2 + (4.5 - 3)^2}$$
$$= \sqrt{1.5^2 + 1.5^2}$$
$$\doteq 2.12$$

The distance from P(–1, 3) to the line $x + y - 5 = 0$ is 2.12, to the nearest hundredth.

Example 3   Playing Billiards

The game of billiards originated in France in 1429. A billiards table
measures 120 cm by 240 cm. The balls are 5 cm in diameter. Imagine a
centimetre coordinate grid superimposed on the table. The #8 ball is
situated at C(150, 60), and the #1 ball at A(40, 40). If the #1 ball is hit by
the cue ball directly toward the corner pocket at B(240, 120), will it hit
the #8 ball and be deflected from its path?

Solution

Sketch a graph showing the given information.
Write an equation for the line joining the #1 ball
at A(40, 40) and the corner pocket at B(240, 120).

$$m = \frac{y_2 - y_1}{x_2 - x_2}$$
$$= \frac{120 - 40}{240 - 40}$$
$$= 0.4$$

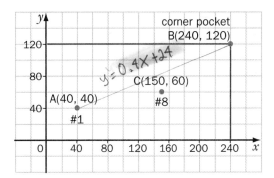

Use the point-slope form to write an equation
for the line AB.

$$y - y_1 = m(x - x_1)$$
$$y - 40 = 0.4(x - 40)$$
$$y - 40 = 0.4x - 16$$
$$y = 0.4x + 24$$

Find the shortest distance from the #8 ball at
C(150, 60) to the line $y = 0.4x + 24$.
The line $y = 0.4x + 24$, has a slope of 0.4.
So, the perpendicular CD from the #8 ball to
this line has a slope of −2.5.
Use the point-slope form to write an equation for CD.

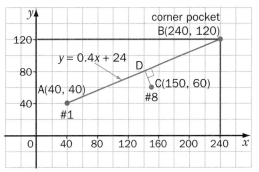

$$y - y_1 = m(x - x_1)$$
$$y - 60 = -2.5(x - 150)$$
$$y - 60 = -2.5x + 375$$
$$y = -2.5x + 435$$

Solve the following system of equations graphically or algebraically to
find the coordinates of the point D.

$$y = 0.4x + 24 \qquad (1)$$
$$y = -2.5x + 435 \qquad (2)$$

The coordinates of D are approximately (141.7, 80.7).

Use the distance formula to find the distance from
C(150, 60) to D(141.7, 80.7).

$$d = \sqrt{(x_2 - x_1)^2 + (y_2 - y_1)^2}$$
$$= \sqrt{(150 - 141.7)^2 + (60 - 80.7)^2}$$
$$= \sqrt{8.3^2 + (-20.7)^2}$$
$$\doteq 22.3$$

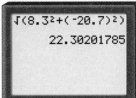

So, the shortest distance between the centres of the two balls will be about 22.3 cm.

Since each ball has a diameter of 5 cm, at the shortest distance the two balls will be
about 17.3 cm apart.
The #1 ball will not strike the #8 ball and so will not be deflected from its path to the pocket.

Example 4 Distances Between Parallel Lines

The equations of two lines are $y = 2x + 3$ and $y = 2x - 4$. Find the vertical distance, the horizontal distance, and the shortest distance between the two lines. Round distances to the nearest tenth, if necessary.

Solution

Draw a diagram to show the graphs and the required distances. Parallel lines do not become closer together or further apart, so the three distances do not vary from one part of the diagram to another. It is convenient to find the vertical distance on the y-axis. The vertical distance between the lines is the difference between their y-intercepts. The y-intercept of $y = 2x + 3$ is 3. The y-intercept of $y = 2x - 4$ is -4. The difference between the y-intercepts is $|3 - (-4)|$ or 7.

It is convenient to find the horizontal distance on the x-axis. The horizontal distance between the lines is the difference between their x-intercepts. The x-intercept of a line is the value of x when $y = 0$.

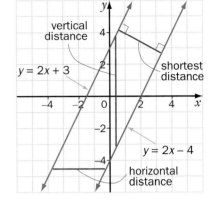

For $y = 2x + 3$,
$$0 = 2x + 3$$
$$-\frac{3}{2} = x$$

For $y = 2x - 4$,
$$0 = 2x - 4$$
$$2 = x$$

The difference between the x-intercepts is $\left|-\frac{3}{2} - 2\right|$ or $\frac{7}{2}$.

To find the shortest distance between the two lines, choose a point on one of the lines and find the shortest distance from that point to the other line. One point on the line $y = 2x + 3$ is (0, 3).

Find AB, the length of the perpendicular from (0, 3) to the line $y = 2x - 4$.

Since the slope of $y = 2x - 4$ is 2, the slope of AB is $-\frac{1}{2}$.

Using the point-slope form, an equation for AB is
$$y - y_1 = m(x - x_1)$$
$$y - 3 = -\frac{1}{2}(x - 0)$$
$$y = -\frac{1}{2}x + 3$$

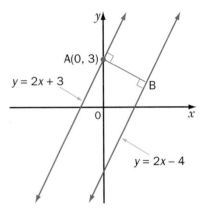

Solving the following system of equations graphically or algebraically gives (2.8, 1.6) as the coordinates of B.

$$y = 2x - 4 \qquad (1)$$
$$y = -\frac{1}{2}x + 3 \qquad (2)$$

The distance from A(0, 3) to B(2.8, 1.6) is given by

$$d = \sqrt{(x_2 - x_1)^2 + (y_2 - y_1)^2}$$
$$= \sqrt{(2.8 - 0)^2 + (1.6 - 3)^2}$$
$$= \sqrt{2.8^2 + (-1.4)^2}$$
$$\doteq 3.1$$

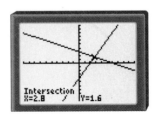

So, the vertical distance between the lines is 7, the horizontal distance is $\frac{7}{2}$, and the shortest distance is 3.1, to the nearest tenth.

Practice

Find the slope of a line that is perpendicular to the line with each of the following equations.

1. $y = 4x - 1$
2. $y = -3x + 2$
3. $y = \dfrac{1}{2}x$
4. $y = -\dfrac{5}{2}x + 8$
5. $x + y = 2$
6. $2x - 3y = 4$
7. $3x + y + 1 = 0$
8. $6x - 3y + 5 = 0$

Write an equation for the line that passes through the given point and has the given slope.

9. $(1, 2); m = 1$
10. $(3, -1); m = -2$
11. $(4, 0); m = \dfrac{2}{3}$
12. $(-3, -4); m = -\dfrac{1}{2}$
13. $(-2, 2); m = -\dfrac{4}{3}$
14. $(0, 0); m = \dfrac{6}{5}$

Find the exact value of the shortest distance from the origin to each line. Express radical answers in simplest radical form.

15. $y = x - 4$
16. $y = x + 6$
17. $y = 3x - 9$
18. $y = -2x - 5$
19. $y = -2$
20. $x - 3 = 0$
21. $y = \dfrac{2}{3}x - 13$
22. $y = -\dfrac{1}{2}x - 5$

Find the shortest distance from the origin to each line, to the nearest tenth.

23. $x - y = 3$
24. $x + y + 2 = 0$
25. $x + 2y = 4$
26. $3x - 4y = -6$
27. $6x + 8y - 5 = 0$
28. $4x = 6y + 13$
29. $2x + 3y = 9$
30. $x - 5y + 11 = 0$

Find the shortest distance from the given point to the given line. Round to the nearest tenth, if necessary.

31. $(2, 2)$ and $y = x + 1$
32. $(5, 0)$ and $y = 0.5x + 5$
33. $(3, 1)$ and $x + y = -2$
34. $(-3, 0)$ and $x - y = -10$
35. $(3, -1)$ and $2x - y + 3 = 0$
36. $(-1, 2)$ and $x - 4y + 1 = 0$
37. $(0, -1)$ and $5x + 2y + 3 = 0$
38. $(-2, -1)$ and $2x + y + 3 = 0$

Determine the vertical distance, the horizontal distance, and the shortest distance between the following pairs of parallel lines. Round distances to the nearest hundredth, if necessary.

39. $y = x + 5$ and $y = x - 2$
40. $y = 2x + 3$ and $y = 2x - 2$

41. $y = 0.5x - 4$ and $y = 0.5x + 10$
42. $3x + y = 5$ and $3x + y = 11$
43. $x + 2y = 8$ and $x + 2y = -4$
44. $3x - y = 3$ and $9x - 3y = -12$
45. $2x + 5y + 7 = 0$ and $4x + 10y - 12 = 0$
46. $11x - 7y + 12 = 0$ and $55x - 35y = 0$

Applications and Problem Solving

47. Find the distance from $(-2, -2)$ to the line joining $(5, 2)$ and $(-1, 4)$, to the nearest hundredth.

48. A line has y-intercept of 8 and x-intercept of -12. What is the shortest distance from the origin to this line, to the nearest tenth?

49. Calculate the distance from the point $K(-10, -13)$ to the line $8x - 5y + 15 = 0$. Explain the answer in terms of the relationship between the point and the line.

50. Measurement a) For the triangle whose vertices are $A(1, -1)$, $B(0, 5)$, and $C(-3, 0)$, determine the length of each altitude.
b) Calculate the area of $\triangle ABC$, to the nearest hundredth.

51. Measurement a) Find the distance from the point of intersection of the lines $2x + 3y = 10$ and $3x - y = 4$ to the line $5x - 6y = 1$, to the nearest hundredth.
b) Find the area of the triangle formed by the three lines, to the nearest hundredth.

52. Measurement In the quadrilateral ABCD, AB lies on the line $y = \dfrac{1}{2}x + 4$, and CD lies on the line $y = \dfrac{1}{2}x - 1$. The segments BC and AD both equal the shortest distance between the two lines. If $AB = 2BC$,
a) what type of quadrilateral is ABCD?
b) what is the exact area of ABCD?

53. Measurement Find the area of the trapezoid with vertices $K(-4, 3)$, $L(-1, 4)$, $M(10, 1)$, and $N(-5, -4)$.

54. Pipelines The longest crude-oil pipeline in the world is the one from Edmonton, Alberta, to Buffalo, New York, a distance of 2858 km. In one region, the pipeline follows the path given by $y = 2.7x + 20$, where each unit on the grid represents 1 km. A city in that region is centred at (50, 15) and has radius 5 km. If by-laws require that the pipeline cannot be within 50 km of an urban area, will this part of the pipeline need to be rerouted?

55. Billiards A bank shot in billiards is one in which the ball is hit so that it bounces off a cushion (a side of the table). The radius of each ball is 5 cm, and the table measures 120 cm by 240 cm. The centre of the #1 ball is at (120, 50), and the centre of the #8 ball is at (200, 100).

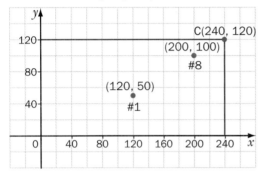

a) Determine the equation of the direct path from the #1 ball to the corner pocket at (240, 120).
b) Show that if the #1 ball is hit along the direct path toward the corner pocket, it will hit the #8 ball.
c) If a bank shot is attempted, and the #1 ball first strikes the cushion at (155.29, 0), determine the equation of the path of the ball after it bounces off the cushion. Assume that the angle of approach equals the angle of deflection, as shown.

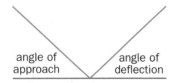

d) Show that, after it bounces off the cushion, the #1 ball is headed into the corner pocket.
e) Will the bank shot miss the #8 ball?

56. Tunnels A vertical cross-sectional view of a mine shows a tunnel that is sloping downward. Its floor can be modelled by the equation $y = 0.8x + 2.5$ and its roof by the equation $y = 0.8x + 4.4$. In this view, each unit on the grid represents 1 m.
a) What is the height of the tallest person who could walk down this tunnel?
b) If part of the tunnel were flooded, what would be the distance across the top of the water surface?
c) Could a fork-lift, which has a height of 1.75 m, be driven into the mine via this tunnel? Justify your answer.

57. Technology One way to find the shortest distance between the parallel lines $y = x + 2$ and $y = x - 2$ is to graph the lines and graph a line that is perpendicular to them, such as $y = -x$. Finding the coordinates of both points of intersection, and then using the distance formula, gives the distance between the parallel lines. Use this method to find the distance between each of the following pairs of lines, to the nearest tenth.
a) $y = x + 2$ and $y = x - 2$
b) $y = 2x + 1$ and $y = 2x - 3$
c) $x - y = 5$ and $x - y = -4$
d) $3x + 2y = 1$ and $3x + 2y = 7$

58. Write an equation for the line that bisects the acute angle formed by the lines $12x - 5y + 7 = 0$ and $3x - 4y - 12 = 0$.

59. Find the coordinates of the point(s) on the x-axis that are 4 units from the line $3x - 4y = 12$.

60. Write equations for two lines that meet each of the following sets of conditions. Compare your equations with your classmates'.
a) slope is $\frac{1}{2}$; shortest distance from origin is $\sqrt{13}$
b) slope is -3; shortest distance from origin is $\sqrt{5}$
c) slope is $-\frac{3}{4}$; shortest distance from (−2, −1) is 5
d) slope is 2; shortest distance from (1, 3) is $2\sqrt{5}$

61. Pattern For a line that does not pass through the origin and that has equal x- and y-intercepts, how is the shortest distance of the line from the origin related to the x-intercept?

Exploring the Concept of a Locus

A **locus** is a set of points determined by a given condition. For example, if a dog is attached by a 10-m leash to a post in the middle of a large yard, then the locus of the furthest points that the dog can reach is a circle with radius 10 m.

Using coordinate geometry, equations can be used to describe loci.

1. a) Draw a diagram that shows six points that are exactly 2 units from the x-axis.
b) How would you change your diagram to show all the points that are exactly 2 units from the x-axis?
c) Write an equation, or equations, to describe the points in part b), that is, the locus of points that are exactly 2 units from the x-axis.

2. a) Use a diagram to represent all the points that are equidistant from the origin and the point (6, 0).
b) Write an equation to describe this locus.

3. a) How are the lines $y = x + 5$ and $y = x - 7$ related?
b) Draw a diagram to show the two lines and all the points that are equidistant from them.
c) Write an equation to describe this locus.

4. a) Use a diagram to represent the locus of points that are equidistant from both axes.
b) Write an equation, or equations, to describe this locus.

5. a) Does a linear equation represent the locus of points that are equidistant from the vertices of a rectangle? Explain.
b) What is the locus of points that are equidistant from the vertices A(1, 8), B(6, 6), C(2, −4), and D(−3, −2) of the rectangle ABCD?

8.4 The Equation of a Circle

Joining all the points that are the same distance from a fixed point produces a circle. We are still learning about many of the circles that occur naturally in our universe. The spectacular rings of Saturn are formed from billions of particles of ice and rock that range in size from tiny specks to the size of a small car. These particles move in circular patterns around the planet.

Explore: Draw a Graph

a) Set up a table of values to include 12 points that satisfy the relation $x^2 + y^2 = 25$. Make sure that you include positive and negative values of x and y.

b) When $y \neq 0$, why are there two values of y for each value of x?

c) Graph the relation. If necessary, extend the table of values until the shape of the graph is complete.

Inquire

1. Is the relation $x^2 + y^2 = 25$ a function? Explain.

2. What is the centre of the graph of $x^2 + y^2 = 25$?

3. What is the radius of the graph of $x^2 + y^2 = 25$?

4. a) Graph the relation $x^2 + y^2 = 9$.
b) Find the centre and the radius of the graph.

5. a) Predict the centre and the radius for the graph of the relation $x^2 + y^2 = 16$.
b) Graph the relation to check your predictions.

6. Predict the centre and the radius for the graph of the relation $x^2 + y^2 = r^2$.

7. On a cross section through the planet Saturn in the plane of the rings, the inside edge of the innermost ring can be modelled by the equation
$$x^2 + y^2 = 4489$$
where one unit on the coordinate grid represents a million metres.
a) Where is the origin located in relation to Saturn?
b) What is the radius of the inside edge of the innermost ring?

A **circle** is the locus of points in the plane that are a fixed distance from a fixed point.
The equation of the circle with centre (0, 0) and radius r is
$$x^2 + y^2 = r^2$$
For example, the circle with centre (0, 0) and radius 6 has the equation
$$x^2 + y^2 = 36$$

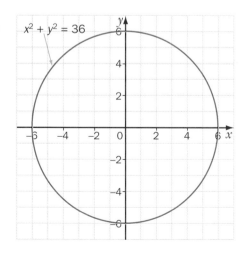

Some circles are not centred at the origin.

Example 1　Centre Not at the Origin

Determine the equation of the circle with centre $C(1, 2)$ and radius 3.

Solution

Draw a diagram.
Choose any point $P(x, y)$ on the circle.
Use the distance formula to represent the distance from $C(1, 2)$ to $P(x, y)$.

$$d = \sqrt{(x_2 - x_1)^2 + (y_2 - y_1)^2}$$
$$CP = \sqrt{(x - 1)^2 + (y - 2)^2}$$

Since $CP = 3$,

$$\sqrt{(x - 1)^2 + (y - 2)^2} = 3$$

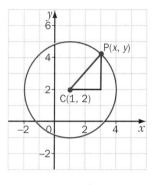

Squaring both sides gives $(x - 1)^2 + (y - 2)^2 = 9$.
The equation of the circle with centre $(1, 2)$ and radius 3 is
$(x - 1)^2 + (y - 2)^2 = 9$.

The steps shown in Example 1 can be generalized to give the equation of a
circle with centre (h, k) and radius r.

Consider the distance from a point on the circle $P(x, y)$ to the centre $C(h, k)$.

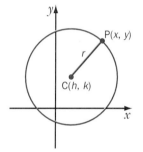

$$\sqrt{(x - h)^2 + (y - k)^2} = r$$
$$\text{So,} (x - h)^2 + (y - k)^2 = r^2$$

Example 2　Using the General Equation

Determine the equation of each of the following circles.
a) centre $(0, 0)$ with radius 10
b) centre $(5, -1)$ with radius 2

Solution

Use the equation of a circle in the form $(x - h)^2 + (y - k)^2 = r^2$.

a) $(x - 0)^2 + (y - 0)^2 = 10^2$
$\qquad x^2 + y^2 = 100$
The equation of the circle is $x^2 + y^2 = 100$.

b) $(x - 5)^2 + (y - (-1))^2 = 2^2$
$\qquad (x - 5)^2 + (y + 1)^2 = 4$
The equation of the circle is $(x - 5)^2 + (y + 1)^2 = 4$.

Example 3 Using the Centre and a Point on the Circumference
Determine the equation of the circle with centre C(–1, 2) and passing through P(3, 1).

Solution
Draw a diagram.
Use the equation of a circle in the form
$$(x - h)^2 + (y - k)^2 = r^2$$
$$(x - (-1))^2 + (y - 2)^2 = r^2$$
$$(x + 1)^2 + (y - 2)^2 = r^2$$
From the Pythagorean Theorem,
$$r^2 = (3 - (-1))^2 + (1 - 2)^2$$
$$= 4^2 + (-1)^2$$
$$= 17$$
So, the equation of the circle is $(x + 1)^2 + (y - 2)^2 = 17$.

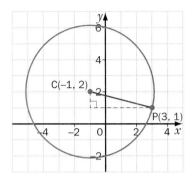

Example 4 Basketball
The centre circle on a basketball court has a radius of 1.8 m. The length of the
court is 26 m and the width is 14 m. A coordinate grid is placed on the court so
that the court is in the first quadrant, the origin is at one corner of the court,
and two sides of the court lie along the x- and y-axes. The side of each grid square
represents 2 m. Write the equation of the centre circle if
a) a longer side of the court is on the x-axis
b) a shorter side of the court is on the x-axis

Solution
a) Draw a diagram.
The centre of the circle is at the centre of the court, (13, 7).
The equation of the circle is
$$(x - h)^2 + (y - k)^2 = r^2$$
so, $(x - 13)^2 + (y - 7)^2 = 1.8^2$
$$(x - 13)^2 + (y - 7)^2 = 3.24$$
The equation of the centre circle is $(x - 13)^2 + (y - 7)^2 = 3.24$.

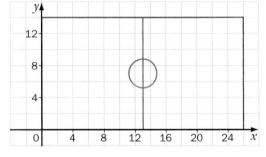

b) Draw a diagram.
The centre of the circle is at (7, 13).
The equation of the circle is
$$(x - h)^2 + (y - k)^2 = r^2$$
$$(x - 7)^2 + (y - 13)^2 = 3.24$$
The equation of the centre circle is $(x - 7)^2 + (y - 13)^2 = 3.24$.

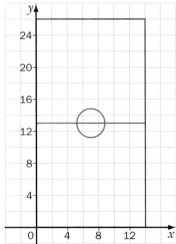

Practice

Write the equation of a circle with centre the origin and the given radius.
1. 5
2. 9
3. 2.5
4. $\sqrt{3}$
5. $2\sqrt{5}$
6. d

Write the equation for each of the following circles.
7. centre (0, 2), radius 5
8. centre (2, 4), radius 3
9. centre (−2, 3), radius 8
10. centre (5, −2), radius 4
11. centre (0, 0), radius $\sqrt{2}$
12. centre (−3, −8), radius 10
13. centre (−4, 0), radius $4\sqrt{2}$
14. centre (*a*, −*b*), radius *c*

Determine the equation of a circle with centre (0, 0) and the following property.
15. passes through (6, 8)
16. passes through (−4, 2)
17. passes through (−3, −3)
18. passes through (5, −1)
19. has an *x*-intercept of 6
20. has a *y*-intercept of 5

Determine the equation of each of the following circles.
21. centre (1, 0) and passing through (−2, −4)
22. centre (−1, −2) and passing through (3, 2)
23. centre (0, 1) and passing through (3, 0)
24. centre (2, 5) and passing through (2, −1)
25. centre (−3, 4) and passing through (−6, 6)
26. centre (11, −9) and passing through (18, 15)

Write the coordinates of the centre and find the radius of each circle.
27. $x^2 + y^2 = 49$
28. $x^2 + (y - 7)^2 = 9$
29. $(x + 5)^2 + y^2 = 1$
30. $(x - 3)^2 + (y - 4)^2 = 25$
31. $(x + 1)^2 + (y - 2)^2 = 4$
32. $x^2 + y^2 = 0.01$
33. $(x + 0.3)^2 + (y - 0.2)^2 = 0.25$
34. $(x - 312)^2 + (y + 458)^2 = 6400$
35. $2(x - 2)^2 + 2(y + 1)^2 = 32$
36. $(x - a)^2 + (y - b)^2 = c^2$

Applications and Problem Solving

37. Does each of the following points lie on the circle $(x + 4)^2 + (y - 3)^2 = 25$? Explain.
a) (0, 0)
b) (−4, 8)
c) (−6.5, 7.5)
d) $(\sqrt{8} - 4, \sqrt{17} + 3)$

38. A point (*k*, 2) lies on the circle $(x - 2)^2 + (y - 3)^2 = 12$. What are the possible values of *k*?

39. **Soccer** The centre circle on a soccer pitch has a radius of about 9 m. The length and the width of the pitch can vary. For one pitch, the length is 100 m and the width is 60 m.

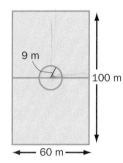

A coordinate grid is placed on the pitch, with the side length of each grid square representing 1 m. Write the equation of the centre circle if
a) the origin is at the centre of the circle
b) the origin is at one corner of the pitch, with a longer side along the positive *x*-axis and a shorter side along the positive *y*-axis
c) the origin is at one corner of the pitch, with a shorter side along the negative *x*-axis and a longer side along the negative *y*-axis

40. Find the equation of the circle that has a diameter with the following endpoints.
a) A(2, −5) and B(2, 5)
b) M(−1, 4) and N(3, −6)

41. Find the equation of the circle with centre at the origin and passing through the point of intersection of the lines $3x - 2y - 2 = 0$ and $4x + 3y + 20 = 0$.

42. **Geology** The Earth has a solid core, which is about 2400 km in diameter. The next layer is a liquid outer core, which is about 2300 km thick. The outermost layer, the mantle, is about 2900 km thick. Use a coordinate system to model a cross section through the Earth at the equator. Write the equations of the circles that represent the outer edge of each layer.

43. Satellites The equatorial radius of the Earth is about 6370 km. Geostationary satellites are positioned 35 880 km above the equator and travel along a circular path above a fixed point on the equator. Using the centre of the Earth as the origin, write an equation for the circular path of a geostationary satellite.

44. For the circle $(x + 5)^2 + (y - 8)^2 = 121$, determine the coordinates of the endpoints of the vertical diameter.

45. Chord property A circle has the equation $(x + 3)^2 + (y - 4)^2 = 58$.
a) Show that the line segment with endpoints A(0, −3) and B(4, 1) is a chord of the circle.
b) Write an equation for the perpendicular bisector of AB.
c) Show that the perpendicular bisector of the chord passes through the centre of the circle.

46. Measurement A circle has the equation $(x - 2)^2 + (y + 3)^2 = 30$. Find, to the nearest tenth,
a) the circumference of the circle
b) the area of the circle

47. Write the equation of the circle that passes through the point (a, b) and has
a) centre (0, 0)   **b)** centre (1, 2)

48. Basketball In basketball, the basket is a ring with a diameter of about 46 cm. At their closest points, the ring is about 15 cm from the backboard, as shown.

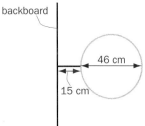

On a coordinate grid with the side of 1 square representing 1 cm, where is the origin if the equation of the ring is
a) $x^2 + y^2 = 529$?
b) $(x - 38)^2 + y^2 = 529$?
c) $x^2 + (y + 23)^2 = 529$?

49. Angle in a semicircle A circle has equation $x^2 + y^2 = 169$.
a) What are the coordinates of the endpoints A and B of the horizontal diameter?
b) Show that P(−5, 12) lies on the circle.
c) Verify that $\angle APB$ is a right angle.

50. Transformations Identify the transformation that maps the circle $x^2 + y^2 = 9$ onto each of the following circles.
a) $(x - 1)^2 + (y - 2)^2 = 9$
b) $(x + 3)^2 + (y + 4)^2 = 9$
c) $x^2 + (y - 1)^2 = 9$
d) $(x + 2)^2 + y^2 = 9$
e) $(x - h)^2 + (y - k)^2 = 9$

51. Find the equation of the circle that has its centre on the y-axis and passes through A(−5, 0) and B(3, 2).

52. An **annulus** is the region between two concentric circles.

Two concentric circles have their centres at the origin. The equation of the smaller circle is $x^2 + y^2 = 100$. If the area of the annulus equals the area of the smaller circle, then what is the equation of the larger circle?

53. Write the equation of the circle that passes through the points (2, 2), (−5, 3), and (−2, 4).

54. The centre of a circle lies on the line $y = x$. The circle passes through the points (−3, 0) and (0, −3). Write the possible equations for the circle.

55. Show that the equation $x^2 + y^2 - 10x + 12y - 3 = 0$ represents a circle. Find its radius and the coordinates of its centre.

56. Olympic flag Sketch the appearance of the 5 rings on the Olympic flag. Add a coordinate grid and write the equations of the 5 rings. Ask a classmate to draw the 5 rings using your equations. How close is the result to the appearance of the rings on the flag?

8.5 Intersections of Lines and Circles

The centre circle of a hockey rink has a radius of 4.5 m. A diameter of the centre circle lies on the centre red line.

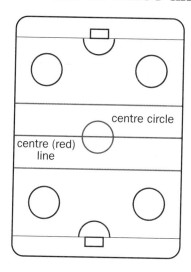

Explore: Draw a Graph

A coordinate grid is superimposed on the rink so that the origin is at the centre of the centre circle and the x-axis lies along the red line. The side length of each grid square represents 1 m.

a) Write the equation of the centre circle.

b) Graph the centre circle on grid paper.

Inquire

1. The puck is passed across the centre line along each of the following lines. Graph each line and find the number of points in which it intersects the centre circle. Find the coordinates of any points of intersection, rounding to the nearest tenth, if necessary.

a) $y = x$　　　**b)** $y = 8 - x$　　　**c)** $x = 4.5$

2. a) What is the maximum number of points in which a line and a circle can intersect?

b) What is the minimum number of points in which a line and a circle can intersect?

3. Without graphing each of the following lines, state the number of points in which it intersects the centre circle. Explain your reasoning.

a) $y = 6$　　　**b)** $y = -4.5$

c) $y = -1$　　　**d)** $y = 3x$

A line and a circle may or may not intersect. If they do intersect, the coordinates of the point(s) of intersection can be found by solving a system of equations graphically or algebraically.

Example 1 Finding Points of Intersection

Find the coordinates of the points of intersection of the line $y = x - 1$ and the circle $x^2 + y^2 = 25$.

Solution 1 Solving Graphically

Method 1 Graphing Manually
Use the y-intercept, -1, and the slope, 1, to graph the line $y = x - 1$. Use the centre, $(0, 0)$, and the radius, 5, to graph the circle $x^2 + y^2 = 25$.

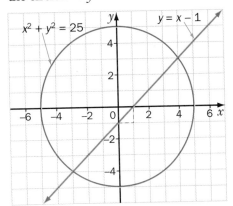

From the graph, the coordinates of the points of intersection appear to be $(-3, -4)$ and $(4, 3)$. Substitution shows that these coordinates satisfy both of the original equations.

Method 2 Using a Graphing Calculator
Graphing calculators accept equations in the form "$y = .$"
Solve the equation of the circle for y.
$$x^2 + y^2 = 25$$
$$y^2 = 25 - x^2$$
$$y = \pm\sqrt{25 - x^2}$$
So, in the same viewing window, graph $y = x - 1$,
$y = \sqrt{25 - x^2}$, and $y = -\sqrt{25 - x^2}$.

To make the circle look like a circle, use the Zsquare or equivalent instruction to make the units on the axes the same size. To find the points of intersection, use the Intersect or equivalent operation.

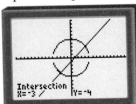
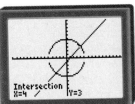

The coordinates of the points of intersection are $(-3, -4)$ and $(4, 3)$. These coordinates can be checked by substitution into the original equations.

Solution 2 Solving Algebraically

Solve the system of equations.
$$y = x - 1 \qquad (1)$$
$$x^2 + y^2 = 25 \qquad (2)$$
Substitute $x - 1$ for y in (2).
$$x^2 + (x - 1)^2 = 25$$
$$x^2 + x^2 - 2x + 1 = 25$$
$$2x^2 - 2x - 24 = 0$$
$$x^2 - x - 12 = 0$$
$$(x - 4)(x + 3) = 0$$
$$x - 4 = 0 \quad \text{or} \quad x + 3 = 0$$
$$x = 4 \quad \text{or} \quad x = -3$$

Substitute these values of x into (1).

For $x = 4$,   For $x = -3$,
$$y = x - 1 \qquad\qquad y = x - 1$$
$$= 4 - 1 \qquad\qquad\quad = -3 - 1$$
$$= 3 \qquad\qquad\qquad\ = -4$$

Check in (1).
For $(4, 3)$,
L.S. $= y$ **R.S.** $= x - 1$
$\quad\ = 3$ $= 4 - 1$
$\qquad\qquad\qquad\quad = 3$

For $(-3, -4)$,
L.S. $= y$ **R.S.** $= x - 1$
$\quad\ = -4$ $= -3 - 1$
$\qquad\qquad\qquad\quad = -4$

Check in (2).
For $(4, 3)$,
L.S. $= x^2 + y^2$ **R.S.** $= 25$
$\quad\ = 4^2 + 3^2$
$\quad\ = 25$

For $(-3, -4)$,
L.S. $= x^2 + y^2$ **R.S.** $= 25$
$\quad\ = (-3)^2 + (-4)^2$
$\quad\ = 25$

The coordinates of the points of intersection are $(4, 3)$ and $(-3, -4)$.

Example 2   Flight Path

A pilot is flying a small aircraft at 200 km/h directly toward the centre of an
intense weather system. She decides to change direction to avoid the worst of the
weather. Taking the aircraft as the origin of a coordinate grid, with the side
length of each grid square representing 1 km, the weather system can be
modelled by the relation $(x - 20)^2 + (y - 10)^2 = 49$. The new direction of the
aircraft is along the line $y = 0.2x$ in the first quadrant. Will the aircraft completely
avoid the weather system? If not, for what amount of time will the aircraft be
within the weather system, to the nearest tenth of a minute?

Solution

Graph both equations to find out whether the circle and the
line intersect.

They do intersect, so the aircraft will not completely avoid the
weather system. To find the amount of time the aircraft spends
within the weather system, first find the distance the aircraft
travels from when it enters to when it leaves the system.
Find the coordinates of the points of intersection.

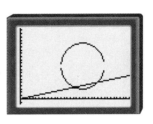

Method 1 Finding the Points Graphically

The coordinates of the points of intersection are
approximately (17.43, 3.49) and (24.87, 4.97).

Method 2 Finding the Points Algebraically
Solve the system of equations.
$$(x - 20)^2 + (y - 10)^2 = 49 \qquad (1)$$
$$y = 0.2x \qquad (2)$$
Substitute $0.2x$ for y in (1).
$$(x - 20)^2 + (0.2x - 10)^2 = 49$$
$$x^2 - 40x + 400 + 0.04x^2 - 4x + 100 = 49$$
$$1.04x^2 - 44x + 451 = 0$$
Solve this equation using the quadratic formula.
$$x = \frac{-b \pm \sqrt{b^2 - 4ac}}{2a}$$
$$= \frac{44 \pm \sqrt{(-44)^2 - 4(1.04)(451)}}{2(1.04)}$$

So, $x \doteq 24.87$ or $x \doteq 17.43$.
Substitute in (2).
For $x = 24.87$,   For $x = 17.43$,
$\quad y = 0.2(24.87)$ $\quad y = 0.2(17.43)$
$\quad\quad \doteq 4.97$ $\quad\quad \doteq 3.49$
The coordinates of the points of intersection are
approximately (17.43, 3.49) and (24.87, 4.97).

Use the distance formula to find the distance between the two points of intersection.

$$d = \sqrt{(x_2 - x_1)^2 + (y_2 - y_1)^2}$$
$$= \sqrt{(24.87 - 17.43)^2 + (4.97 - 3.49)^2}$$
$$\doteq 7.59$$

The aircraft will be within the weather system for a distance of about 7.59 km.

Estimate

$$\sqrt{7^2 + 1^2} = \sqrt{50}$$
$$\doteq 7$$

Use $\text{time} = \dfrac{\text{distance}}{\text{speed}}$ to find the amount of time within the weather system.

$$\text{time} = \frac{7.59}{200}$$
$$= 0.037\ 95$$

Convert this number of hours to minutes. $0.037\ 95 \times 60 = 2.277$
So, the aircraft will be within the weather system for 2.3 min, to the nearest tenth of a minute.

Recall that, if a line intersects a circle in two points, then the points are the endpoints of a chord of the circle.

chord

A line that intersects a circle in exactly one point is a tangent to the circle. The point of intersection is called the point of tangency.

tangent

Example 3   Tangents to a Circle
a) For what value(s) of c is the line $y = c$ tangent to the circle $x^2 + y^2 = r^2$?
b) Show that a tangent line is perpendicular to the radius of the circle at the point of tangency.

point of tangency

Solution
a) Draw a diagram.
$x^2 + y^2 = r^2$ is a circle with centre $(0, 0)$ and radius r.
The line $y = c$ is a horizontal line with y-intercept c.

Find the point(s) of intersection of the line $y = c$ and the circle by solving the system of equations.

$$x^2 + y^2 = r^2 \qquad (1)$$
$$y = c \qquad\qquad (2)$$

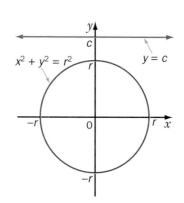

Substitute c for y in (1).

$$x^2 + c^2 = r^2$$
$$x^2 = r^2 - c^2$$
$$x = \pm\sqrt{r^2 - c^2}$$

Consider three cases for this solution.

486   *Chapter 8*

Case 1: If $c^2 > r^2$, then $r^2 - c^2 < 0$ and $\sqrt{r^2 - c^2}$ is not a real number, so there is no real solution for x.

Case 2: If $c^2 = r^2$, then $r^2 - c^2 = 0$ and so there is one solution, $x = 0$.

Case 3: If $c^2 < r^2$, then $r^2 - c^2 > 0$ and so there are two solutions, $x = \pm\sqrt{r^2 - c^2}$.

We are concerned with case 2, as a tangent has only one point of intersection with the circle.
If $c^2 = r^2$, then $c = \pm r$.
The line $y = c$ is tangent to the circle $x^2 + y^2 = r^2$ when $c = \pm r$.

b) The two tangent lines, $y = r$ and $y = -r$, are both horizontal lines.
At the point of tangency with either of these tangent lines, the radius
of the circle lies on the y-axis. The y-axis is a vertical line and so is
perpendicular to each of the tangent lines.

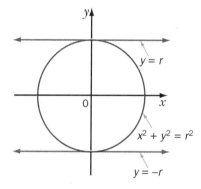

The equation of a tangent at any point on a circle can be determined
using the property that a tangent is perpendicular to the radius at
the point of tangency.

Example 4   Equation of a Tangent
Find the equation of the tangent to the circle $x^2 + y^2 = 25$ at the point P(3, 4).

Solution
Draw a diagram.
The circle $x^2 + y^2 = 25$ has centre O(0, 0) and radius 5.
The point P(3, 4) lies on this circle.

Find the slope of the radius OP.

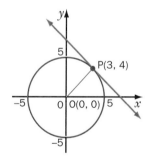

$$m_{OP} = \frac{y_2 - y_1}{x_2 - x_1}$$
$$= \frac{4 - 0}{3 - 0}$$
$$= \frac{4}{3}$$

Since the tangent is perpendicular to the radius at the point of tangency, and
perpendicular slopes have a product of -1, the slope of the tangent at P is $-\frac{3}{4}$.
Use the point-slope form to find the equation of the tangent at P(3, 4).
$$y - y_1 = m(x - x_1)$$
$$y - 4 = -\frac{3}{4}(x - 3)$$
$$4y - 16 = -3x + 9$$
$$3x + 4y - 25 = 0$$

The equation of the tangent to the circle $x^2 + y^2 = 25$ at the point P(3, 4) is $3x + 4y - 25 = 0$.

Example 5   Length of a Tangent

Find the exact length of a tangent from the point P(7, −6) to the circle $x^2 + y^2 = 9$.

Solution

Draw a diagram.

The circle has centre O(0, 0) and radius 3.

Draw a tangent from P(7, −6) to the circle. Let the point of tangency be M. Draw the segments OM and OP to complete △OMP. Because OM is a radius, its length is 3, and OM is perpendicular to the tangent MP. Use the distance formula to find the length of OP.

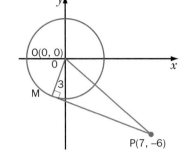

$$d = \sqrt{(x_2 - x_1)^2 + (y_2 - y_1)^2}$$
$$OP = \sqrt{(7 - 0)^2 + (-6 - 0)^2}$$
$$= \sqrt{49 + 36}$$
$$= \sqrt{85}$$

In △OPM, use the Pythagorean Theorem to find the length of MP.

$$MP^2 + 3^2 = (\sqrt{85})^2$$
$$MP^2 + 9 = 85$$
$$MP^2 = 76$$
$$MP = \sqrt{76}$$
$$= 2\sqrt{19}$$

The exact length of a tangent from the point P(7, −6) to the circle $x^2 + y^2 = 9$ is $2\sqrt{19}$.

Note that, in Example 5, there is a second tangent to the circle $x^2 + y^2 = 9$ from the point P(7, −6), as shown in the diagram.

However, because △OMP and △ONP are congruent, by the Hypotenuse-Side Theorem, the segments MP and NP are congruent. If coordinate geometry is used to find the lengths of MP and NP, they both equal $2\sqrt{19}$.

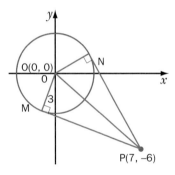

Practice

Find the coordinates of any point(s) of intersection of each line and circle.

1. $y = x$ and $x^2 + y^2 = 18$
2. $y = 3x - 5$ and $x^2 + y^2 = 25$
3. $y = x - 4$ and $x^2 + y^2 = 40$
4. $x - y = 10$ and $x^2 + y^2 = 10$
5. $y + 5 = 0$ and $x^2 + y^2 = 169$
6. $2y = x + 8$ and $x^2 + y^2 = 4$
7. $3x + 4y = 25$ and $x^2 + y^2 = 25$
8. $x + 2y + 15 = 0$ and $x^2 + y^2 = 90$

Find the coordinates of any point(s) of intersection of each line and circle. Where necessary, round answers to the nearest tenth.

9. $y = x$ and $(x - 2)^2 + (y - 3)^2 = 25$
10. $y = x + 2$ and $(x + 1)^2 + (y - 2)^2 = 13$
11. $y = x - 5$ and $(x + 3)^2 + (y + 1)^2 = 16$
12. $y = 2x$ and $(x - 4)^2 + (y + 3)^2 = 26$
13. $x + y = 0$ and $(x - 3)^2 + (y - 4)^2 = 25$
14. $y = x - 1$ and $(x + 2)^2 + (y - 2)^2 = 4$
15. $x = 0$ and $(x - 5)^2 + (y + 6)^2 = 36$
16. $y - 2 = 0$ and $(x - 6)^2 + y^2 = 9$
17. $2x - y + 3 = 0$ and $(x - 1)^2 + (y + 2)^2 = 36$
18. $0.5x + y + 4 = 0$ and $(x + 6)^2 + y^2 = 64$
19. $x - 9y + 53 = 0$ and $(x + 3)^2 + (y - 1)^2 = 41$
20. $x + 4y - 28 = 0$ and $(x + 1)^2 + (y + 1)^2 = 169$

Determine the length of the chord AB in each circle, to the nearest hundredth.

21.   **22.**

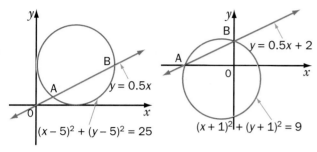

$(x-5)^2 + (y-5)^2 = 25$

$(x+1)^2 + (y+1)^2 = 9$

Determine the length of the chord with endpoints that are the points of intersection of the following. Round answers to the nearest tenth.

23. $(x+1)^2 + (y+1)^2 = 6$ and $y = x$

24. $(x-3)^2 + (y-4)^2 = 9$ and $y = 3$

25. $(x-5)^2 + y^2 = 16$ and $y = 2 - x$

26. $(x+2)^2 + (y-7)^2 = 36$ and $x - 2y + 5 = 0$

What are the equations of the horizontal lines that are tangent to each circle?

27. $x^2 + y^2 = 25$ **28.** $x^2 + y^2 = 49$

29. $x^2 + y^2 = 1$ **30.** $x^2 + y^2 = 900$

31. $x^2 + y^2 = \dfrac{9}{16}$ **32.** $x^2 + y^2 = 1.44$

What are the equations of the vertical lines that are tangent to each circle?

33. $x^2 + y^2 = 4$ **34.** $x^2 + y^2 = 64$

35. $x^2 + y^2 = 225$ **36.** $x^2 + y^2 = 8100$

37. $x^2 + y^2 = 0.25$ **38.** $x^2 + y^2 = 32$

For each circle, write an equation for the tangent at the given point.

39. $x^2 + y^2 = 2$ at $(1, 1)$

40. $x^2 + y^2 = 50$ at $(-5, 5)$

41. $x^2 + y^2 = 10$ at $(-1, 3)$

42. $x^2 + y^2 = 29$ at $(2, 5)$

43. $x^2 + y^2 = 13$ at $(2, 3)$

44. $x^2 + y^2 = 74$ at $(-5, -7)$

45. $x^2 + y^2 = 20$ at $(2, -4)$

46. $x^2 + y^2 = 34$ at $(-5, 3)$

47. The equation of a circle is $(x-2)^2 + (y-3)^2 = 20$.
a) What are the coordinates of the centre of the circle?
b) Show that the point $(4, 7)$ is on the circle.
c) Write an equation for the tangent at the point $(4, 7)$.

48. a) Show that the circle $(x+3)^2 + (y-4)^2 = 25$ passes through the origin.
b) Find the equation of the tangent at the origin.

For each circle, write an equation for the tangent at the given point.

49. $(x-1)^2 + (y-4)^2 = 17$ at $(0, 0)$

50. $(x+4)^2 + (y+2)^2 = 26$ at $(-3, 3)$

51. $(x+2)^2 + (y-3)^2 = 13$ at $(0, 6)$

52. $(x-3)^2 + (y-1)^2 = 25$ at $(6, -3)$

53. $(x-2)^2 + (y+3)^2 = 58$ at $(5, 4)$

54. $(x+5)^2 + (y+4)^2 = 20$ at $(-1, -2)$

Find the exact length of a tangent to the given circle from the given point. Express radical answers in simplest radical form.

55. $x^2 + y^2 = 1$; P(8, 1)

56. $x^2 + y^2 = 9$; P(4, -3)

57. $x^2 + y^2 = 16$; P(5, 9)

58. $x^2 + y^2 = 40$; P(5, -5)

59. $x^2 + y^2 = 25$; P(-6, -8)

60. $x^2 + y^2 = 50$; P(-8, 10)

Find the exact length of a tangent to the given circle from the given point. Express radical answers in simplest radical form.

61. $(x-2)^2 + (y-2)^2 = 14$; P(7, 7)

62. $(x+3)^2 + (y+2)^2 = 4$; P(-5, 2)

63. $(x-5)^2 + y^2 = 36$; P(8, -8)

64. $x^2 + (y+3)^2 = 39$; P(-2, -9)

65. $(x-4)^2 + (y-1)^2 = 17$; P(10, 0)

66. $(x+3)^2 + (y-2)^2 = 25$; P(8, 8)

Applications and Problem Solving

67. Verify that the line $y = 3x - 5$ passes through the centre of the circle $(x-15)^2 + (y-40)^2 = 225$.

68. The line $x + 3y - 5 = 0$ intersects the circle $(x-5)^2 + (y-5)^2 = 25$ in two points, A and B.
a) Find the coordinates of the endpoints of the chord AB.
b) Verify that the right bisector of the chord AB passes through the centre of the circle.

69. For the circle $x^2 + y^2 = 36$, verify that the perpendicular from the centre bisects the chord CD, with endpoints C(6, 0) and D(0, -6).

70. The line $5x + 9y = 66$ intersects the circle $(x + 1)^2 + (y - 2)^2 = 53$ at P and Q.
a) Find the exact length of the chord PQ.
b) Find the distance from the centre of the circle to the chord PQ, to the nearest tenth.

71. Write an equation for the tangent to the circle $(x + 1)^2 + (y - 1)^2 = 4$ at the point $(1, 1)$.

72. Write an equation for the tangent to the circle $(x - 2)^2 + (y - 3)^2 = 16$ at the point $(2, -1)$.

73. In the figure, the circle has its centre at the origin and a radius of 5 units. Determine the exact length of the chord MN.

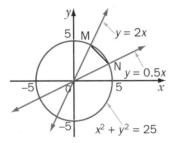

74. Two tangents intersect a circle at opposite ends of a diameter. How are the slopes of the tangents related? Explain.

75. Consider the set of all circles to which the x-axis and the y-axis are both tangent. Write equations to describe the locus of the centres of the circles.

76. Air-traffic control A radar screen has a range of 50 km. The screen can be modelled on a coordinate grid as a circle centred at the origin with radius 50.
a) Write the equation that describes the edge of the radar screen's range.
b) A small aircraft flies over the area covered by the radar at 180 km/h, on a path given by $y = -0.5x - 10$. Determine the length of time, to the nearest minute, that the plane is within radar range.

77. Machinery On an industrial engineer's design, a drive wheel is represented by the circle $(x - 2)^2 + (y - 5)^2 = 25$. The upper straight section of the drive belt is tangent to the drive wheel at the point $(5, 9)$. What equation represents the upper straight section of the drive belt?

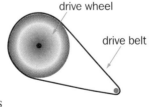

drive wheel

drive belt

78. Skidding A race car is driving around a curve that is an arc of the circle $x^2 + y^2 = 289$. If the car runs over an oil patch and skids off at the point $(8, 15)$, what is the equation of the linear path that it skids along?

79. Fireworks The sparks fly off a spinning firework along paths that are tangents. The world's largest Catherine wheel kept spinning for nearly 4 min when it was displayed at the Pyrotechnics Guild International Convention in Idaho Falls. Before it was lit, the outer coil of the Catherine wheel could be represented by the circle $x^2 + y^2 = 51.62$, with the wick at $(-4.1, 5.9)$, where the units are metres.
a) What was the diameter of this Catherine wheel, to the nearest tenth of a metre?
b) Write an equation that approximately represents the path of the first spark.

80. Radar The radar on a marine police launch has a range of 28 km. While the launch is at anchor in a bay, the radar shows a boat travelling on a linear path given by $y = 0.7x + 20$. If the boat is visible on the radar screen for 2 h, at what speed is it travelling, to the nearest kilometre per hour?

81. For each circle, write an equation for the tangent at the given point.
a) $x^2 + y^2 = 1$ at $\left(-\dfrac{1}{2}, \dfrac{\sqrt{3}}{2} \right)$

b) $2x^2 + 2y^2 = 5$ at $\left(\sqrt{2}, \dfrac{-\sqrt{2}}{2} \right)$

82. Working backward If the line $y = 7$ is tangent to a circle with its centre at the origin, what is the equation of the circle?

83. Working backward If the line $x = 8$ is tangent to a circle with its centre at $(-1, 3)$, what is the equation of the circle?

84. Transformations What are the equations of
a) the horizontal lines that are tangent to the circle $(x - h)^2 + (y - k)^2 = r^2$?
b) the vertical lines that are tangent to the circle $(x - h)^2 + (y - k)^2 = r^2$?

85. a) Find the equation of the tangent to the circle $x^2 + y^2 = 169$ at the point $(5, 12)$.

b) Explain how you can use the result from part a) to write the equation of the tangent to the same circle at the point $(-5, -12)$.

86. Find the equation of the tangent to the circle $x^2 + y^2 = r^2$ at the point $P_1(x_1, y_1)$.

87. If a circle has radius $\sqrt{10}$ units and has both the x- and y-axes tangent to it, what are the possible equations of the circle?

88. Three tangents to a circle are the x-axis, the line $x = -4$, and the line $x = 6$. If the centre of the circle is in the first quadrant, what is the equation of the circle?

89. Amusement park
A carnival ride has two rotating circular cars on the ends of a shaft. The cars have radius 5 m and the shaft is 20 m long. At one instant, the shaft can be modelled by the line $y = x$.

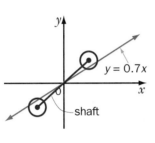

a) Determine the equation of each car at this instant.

b) The line $y = 0.7x$ represents a laser light shone from the centre of the shaft. Determine the length of the beam of light that crosses each car, to the nearest tenth of a metre.

90. The line $x + 2y - 10 = 0$ is tangent to a circle with centre at the origin. Find the equation of the circle.

91. Tangents are drawn to the circle $x^2 + y^2 = 100$ at the points $(6, k)$.
a) What are the possible values of k?
b) Find the equation of the tangent at each possible point $(6, k)$.

92. Given the circle defined by $x^2 + y^2 = r^2$, and the points $P(a, b)$ and $Q(-b, a)$ on the circle,
a) find the equation of the right bisector of the chord PQ
b) show that the right bisector of the chord PQ is a diameter of the circle

93. Given the circle, centre O, defined by $x^2 + y^2 = r^2$, and the points $P(p, q)$ and $Q(q, -p)$ on the circle,
a) find the midpoint, M, of PQ
b) find the slope of OM
c) find the slope of PQ
d) show that OM is perpendicular to PQ

94. A circle, centre O, is defined by $x^2 + y^2 = r^2$. The point $P(a, b)$ is outside the circle. T is the point of contact on the circle of a tangent from P.
a) Find the lengths of OT and OP.
b) Find the length of the tangent PT.

95. Given the circle, centre O, defined by $x^2 + y^2 = r^2$, and the point $T(a, b)$ on the circle,
a) find the slope of OT
b) find the slope of the tangent at T, perpendicular to OT
c) find an equation of the tangent to the circle at T

96. Two circles are tangent to each other if they intersect in exactly one point.
a) Verify that the circles $(x - 3)^2 + (y - 4)^2 = 25$ and $(x + 2)^2 + (y + 8)^2 = 64$ are tangent to each other.
b) If two circles are tangent to each other, how are their radii related to the distance between their centres?
c) Write the equation of a circle with radius 3 that is tangent to the circle $(x - 4)^2 + (y + 1)^2 = 16$ at the point $(0, -1)$. Is more than one answer possible? Explain.

97. The x- and y-axes are tangents to a circle of radius 8 with its centre in the first quadrant. The x-axis is also tangent to a circle of radius 2, which is tangent to the first circle, as shown. If the radius of the smaller circle intersects the x-axis at P, find
a) the length of OP
b) an equation for the smaller circle

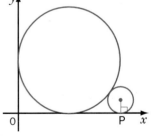

98. Visualization How many tangents can two circles in the same plane have in common? Illustrate your answer with appropriate diagrams.

COMPUTER DATA BANK

Air Travel

Use the *Airports* and *Aircraft* databases, from the Computer Data Bank, to complete the following.

1 Takeoff and Landing

1. On the basis of takeoff and landing runway length requirements, determine how many aircraft could use each of the following airports.
a) Thompson
b) Calgary International
c) Hay River
d) Prince George
e) Ottawa/Macdonald-Cartier International
f) Regina
g) Gander International
h) all airports in the database

2. a) How many aircraft require a greater length of runway for takeoff than for landing?
b) Why do you think a greater length of runway is required for takeoff than for landing?
c) Use your research skills to check your answer to part b).

3. a) For each aircraft, how could you determine the extra length of runway needed for takeoff as a percent increase over the length of runway needed for landing?
b) For the aircraft found in question 2, calculate the percent increase. Then, calculate the average percent increase.

2 Airport Categories

1. Sort the airports by category number. Then, use the other information given about the airports to help you predict the meaning of the category numbers. Explain your reasoning.

2. Use your research skills to check your prediction in question 1.

3 Comparing Aircraft

1. What percent of the aircraft can carry more than 300 passengers? 400 passengers? 500 passengers?

2. There are two types of aircraft in the database — turbofan and turboprop. What are the average wing span, length, height, and mass of each type, and how many aircraft are there of each type?

3. How many aircraft have a length to wing span ratio that is less than or equal to 1?

4 Mach Numbers

1. Of the aircraft with a Mach number given in the maximum speed field, which aircraft has the greatest number? Would you have predicted that? Explain. What is the greatest Mach number?

2. How many aircraft have a Mach number in both the maximum and cruise speed fields?

3. What is the difference between the Mach numbers for the aircraft found in question 2?

4. Use your research skills to determine the meaning of Mach number.

5 Flight Path

1. Devise a plan to do the following. Find all the aircraft with maximum speeds given in kilometres per hour. Then, determine the length of time, in minutes, that each plane would spend in a storm system, assuming that
• the aircraft is at the origin and is travelling into the first quadrant along a path $y = x$ at maximum speed
• the storm system is modelled by the relation $(x - 30)^2 + (y - 60)^2 = 500$ on a grid with one unit of length representing 1 km
Describe any calculated fields you would add.

2. Compare your plan with the plans of your classmates. Revise your plan, if necessary, and then carry it out. What is the least amount of time spent in the storm? the greatest?

8.6 Reviewing Trigonometry

The historic lighthouse at Cape Spear, Newfoundland, stands on a cliff on the easternmost point of the North American continent. The lighthouse operated from 1836 to 1955. From a point 1000 m offshore, the angle of elevation of the foot of the lighthouse is 4.3° and the angle of elevation of the top of the lighthouse is 4.9°.

Explore: Use a Diagram

The diagram represents the above information.

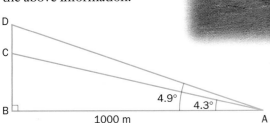

What is represented by
a) the line segment CD? **b)** the line segment BC?

Inquire

1. a) Use △ABC to write a trigonometric equation that expresses BC in terms of ∠BAC and AB.
b) Calculate BC, to the nearest tenth of a metre.

2. a) Use △ABD to write a trigonometric equation that expresses BD in terms of ∠BAD and AB.
b) Calculate BD, to the nearest tenth of a metre.

3. What is the height of the lighthouse, to the nearest tenth of a metre?

4. Another way to solve the problem is to use △ABC and calculate AC. Then, CD can be calculated using the obtuse △ACD. Name the trigonometric ratio and the trigonometric law that would be used to solve the problem in this way.

5. What is the angle of depression of point A from the top of the lighthouse? Explain.

Right triangles can be solved using the primary trigonometric ratios.

$$\text{sine } \theta = \frac{\text{opposite}}{\text{hypotenuse}}$$

$$\text{cosine } \theta = \frac{\text{adjacent}}{\text{hypotenuse}}$$

$$\text{tangent } \theta = \frac{\text{opposite}}{\text{adjacent}}$$

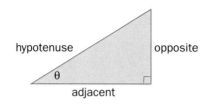

Example 1   Solving a Right Triangle

In $\triangle XYZ$, $\angle Y = 90°$, $\angle Z = 42°$, and $z = 8.4$ cm. Solve the triangle, rounding side lengths to the nearest tenth of a centimetre.

Solution

Draw a diagram.

$$\tan 42° = \frac{8.4}{x}$$

$$x = \frac{8.4}{\tan 42°}$$

$$\doteq 9.3$$

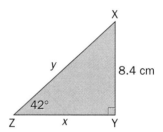

$$\sin 42° = \frac{8.4}{y}$$

$$y = \frac{8.4}{\sin 42°}$$

$$\doteq 12.6$$

$$\angle X = 180° - 90° - 42°$$

$$= 48°$$

In $\triangle XYZ$, $x = 9.3$ cm, $y = 12.6$ cm, and $\angle X = 48°$.

An **oblique triangle** is a triangle that does not have a right angle. Oblique triangles can be solved using the law of sines or the law of cosines.

For oblique triangle ABC, there are two forms of the law of sines

$$\frac{\sin A}{a} = \frac{\sin B}{b} = \frac{\sin C}{c} \quad \text{or} \quad \frac{a}{\sin A} = \frac{b}{\sin B} = \frac{c}{\sin C}$$

and three forms of the law of cosines

$$a^2 = b^2 + c^2 - 2bc \cos A$$
$$b^2 = a^2 + c^2 - 2ac \cos B$$
$$c^2 = a^2 + b^2 - 2ab \cos C$$

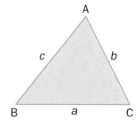

Example 2   Using the Law of Sines

In $\triangle PQR$, $\angle P = 105.2°$, $p = 23.2$ cm, and $r = 18.5$ cm. Solve the triangle, rounding side lengths to the nearest tenth of a centimetre and angles to the nearest tenth of a degree, if necessary.

Solution

Draw a diagram.

Use the law of sines to find the measure of $\angle R$.

$$\frac{\sin R}{r} = \frac{\sin P}{p}$$

$$\frac{\sin R}{18.5} = \frac{\sin 105.2°}{23.2}$$

$$\sin R = \frac{18.5 \sin 105.2°}{23.2}$$

$$\angle R \doteq 50.3°$$

$$\angle Q = 180° - 105.2° - 50.3°$$
$$= 24.5°$$

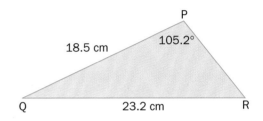

Use the law of sines to find q.

$$\frac{q}{\sin Q} = \frac{p}{\sin P}$$

$$\frac{q}{\sin 24.5°} = \frac{23.2}{\sin 105.2°}$$

$$q = \frac{23.2 \sin 24.5°}{\sin 105.2°}$$

$$\doteq 10.0$$

In $\triangle PQR$, $\angle R = 50.3°$, $\angle Q = 24.5°$, and $q = 10.0$ cm.

Example 3   Using the Law of Cosines

a) In $\triangle DEF$, $d = 2.5$ m, $e = 3.5$ m, and $\angle F = 59.4°$.
Find f, to the nearest tenth of a metre.
b) In $\triangle ABC$, $a = 9.6$ m, $b = 20.6$ m, and $c = 14.7$ m.
Find $\angle B$, to the nearest tenth of a degree.

Solution

a) Draw a diagram.
Use the law of cosines.
$$f^2 = d^2 + e^2 - 2de \cos F$$
$$= 2.5^2 + 3.5^2 - 2(2.5)(3.5)\cos 59.4°$$
$$f \doteq 3.1$$
So, $f = 3.1$ m, to the nearest tenth of a metre

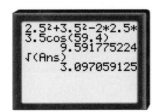

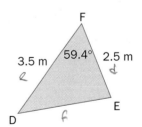

b) Draw a diagram.
Use the law of cosines.
$$b^2 = a^2 + c^2 - 2ac \cos B$$
so, $2ac \cos B = a^2 + c^2 - b^2$

$$\cos B = \frac{a^2 + c^2 - b^2}{2ac}$$

$$\cos B = \frac{9.6^2 + 14.7^2 - 20.6^2}{2(9.6)(14.7)}$$

$$\angle B \doteq 114.3°$$

So, $\angle B = 114.3°$, to the nearest tenth of a degree.

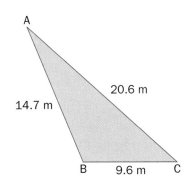

Example 4 Height of Mount Robson

The diagram shows the measurements that a surveyor made to find the height of Mount Robson above sea level. The points A, B, and C are all at the same elevation, 1200 m. The summit of the mountain is represented by R, and the point C is directly below R. Find the height of Mount Robson, to the nearest metre.

Solution

Find the measure of $\angle BCA$.
$$\angle BCA = 180° - 85.4° - 53.9°$$
$$= 40.7°$$

Use the law of sines to find x in $\triangle ABC$.
$$\frac{x}{\sin 53.9°} = \frac{2000}{\sin 40.7°}$$
$$x = \frac{2000 \sin 53.9°}{\sin 40.7°}$$
$$\doteq 2478$$

In $\triangle BCR$, $\dfrac{h}{2478} = \tan 48°$
$$h = 2478 \tan 48°$$
$$\doteq 2752$$

Since the elevation of A, B, and C is 1200 m, the height of Mount Robson is 2752 + 1200 or 3952 m, to the nearest metre.

Practice

Find the length of the indicated side, to the nearest tenth.

1.

A, b, B 56°, 15, C

2.

Q, 27°, P, 6.2, q, R

3.

K, 65°, 19, m, L, M

4.

X, 12, Z, x, 25°, Y

5.

E, D, d, 73°, 32.5, F

6.

W, 9.9, U, w, 50°, V

Find the length of the indicated side, to the nearest tenth.

11.

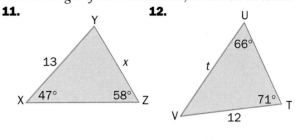

Y, 13, x, X 47°, 58° Z

12.

U, 66°, t, V, 71° T, 12

13.

B, 112°, 27°, A, a, 4.8, C

14.

E, 60.2°, f, 8.3, 75.9°, F, D

43.9°

15.

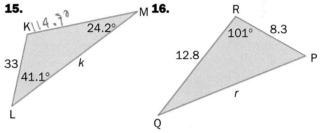

K 114.7°, 24.2°, M, 33, k, 41.1°, L

16.

R, 101°, 8.3, 12.8, P, r, Q

Find the measure of the indicated angle, to the nearest tenth of a degree.

7.

R, 38, T, 27, S

8.

D, B, 5.1, 3.5, C

9.

E, 7.4, F, 5.8, G

10.

W, 121, X, 187, Y

Find the measure of the indicated angle, to the nearest tenth of a degree.

17.

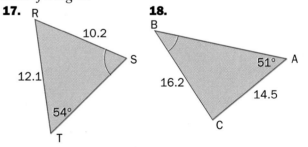

R, 10.2, 12.1, S, 54°, T

18.

B, 51°, A, 16.2, 14.5, C

19.

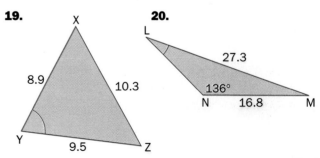

X, 8.9, 10.3, Y, 9.5, Z

20.

L, 27.3, 136°, N, 16.8, M

21.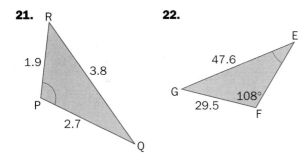

22.

37.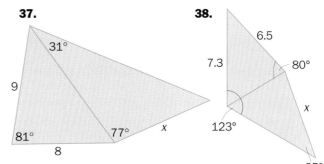

38.

Solve each triangle. Round answers to the nearest tenth, if necessary.

23. In △XYZ, ∠X = 90°, x = 9.5 cm, z = 4.2 cm
24. In △KLM, ∠M = 90°, ∠K = 37°, m = 12.3 cm
25. In △ABC, ∠A = 90°, ∠B = 55.1°, b = 4.8 m
26. In △DEF, ∠E = 90°, d = 18.2 cm, f = 14.9 cm

Solve each triangle. Round answers to the nearest tenth, if necessary.

27. In △ABC, ∠A = 84°, ∠C = 40°, a = 5.6 m
28. In △PQR, ∠R = 28.5°, p = 10.4 cm, r = 6.3 cm
29. In △LMN, ∠M = 62°, l = 16.9 m, m = 15.1 m
30. In △UVW, ∠W = 123.9°, ∠V = 22.2°, v = 27.5 km
31. In △XYZ, ∠X = 92.3°, y = 3.1 cm, z = 2.8 cm
32. In △FGH, f = 12.6 m, g = 8.5 m, h = 6.3 m

Find the length of the indicated side, to the nearest tenth.

33.

34.

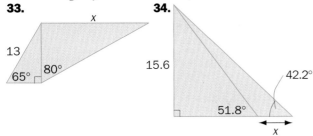

Find the measure of the indicated angle, to the nearest tenth of a degree.

39.

40.

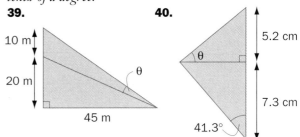

41.

42.

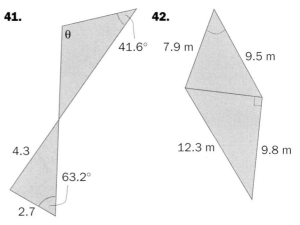

35.

36.

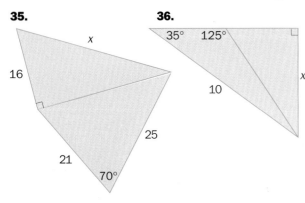

Applications and Problem Solving

43. Flagpole A steel flagpole in Surrey, British Columbia, is the world's tallest unsupported flagpole. When the angle of elevation of the sun is 64.1°, the flagpole casts a shadow that is 41.7 m long. Find the height of the flagpole, to the nearest tenth of a metre.

44. Escalator The world's longest escalator is in the subway system in St. Petersburg, Russia. The escalator is 330.7 m long and rises a vertical distance of 59.7 m. What is the angle of elevation of the top of the escalator when viewed from the bottom, to the nearest tenth of a degree?

45. Satellite In relation to two receiving towers, A and B, a communications satellite, C, is located as shown. How far is the satellite from tower A, to the nearest kilometre?

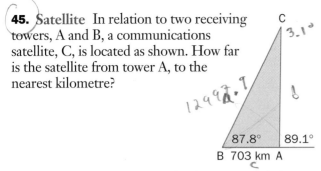

12992.7

46. Telecommunications A 150-m transmission tower stands on top of a hill. From a point on level ground some distance from the base of the hill, the angle of elevation of the bottom of the tower is 32° and the angle of elevation of the top of the tower is 37°. What is the height of the hill, to the nearest metre?

47. Model rockets Hobbyists often compete with their model rockets to determine which rocket flies the highest. On one test launch, a rocket was fired vertically upward. The angle of elevation to the top of the flight was measured from two points that were 20 m apart, on the same side of the launch site and collinear with it. The angles measured at the two points were 66.3° and 37.5°. How high did the rocket fly, to the nearest metre?

48. Peace Tower
To determine the height of the Peace Tower on Parliament Hill in Ottawa, measurements were taken from a baseline AB. It was found that AB = 50 m, ∠XAY = 42.6°, ∠XAB = 60°, and ∠ABX = 81.65°. Calculate the height of the Peace Tower, to the nearest metre.

49. Stikine Canyon
The Stikine Canyon in central British Columbia is often referred to as Canada's Grand Canyon. Two points X and Y are sighted from a baseline AB of length 30 m on the opposite side of the canyon. The angle measurements recorded from positions A and B were ∠XAY = 31.3°, ∠XBY = 18.5°, ∠ABX = 25.6°, and ∠BAY = 27.9°. Find the distance from X to Y, to the nearest metre.

50. Watch face The face of a watch is a regular hexagon with side length 12 mm. What is the shortest distance between two parallel sides of the watch face, to the nearest tenth of a millimetre?

51. a) Use the law of sines to find x, to the nearest tenth.
b) Use the sine ratio to find x, to the nearest tenth.
c) Explain why the two methods are equivalent in a right triangle.

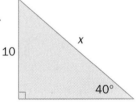

52. a) Use the law of cosines to find x, to the nearest tenth.
b) Use the Pythagorean Theorem to find x, to the nearest tenth.
c) Explain why the two methods are equivalent in a right triangle.

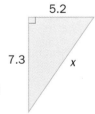

53. Measurement Find the area of △XYZ, to the nearest tenth of a square metre.

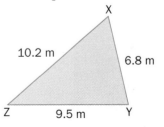

54. Geometry Use the law of cosines to prove that opposite angles in a parallelogram are congruent.

INVESTIGATING MATH

Constructing Triangles Using Side-Side-Angle (SSA)

If two triangles are constructed so that they have the same side lengths, then the two triangles are congruent (SSS). In other words, there is only one size and shape of triangle with a certain set of side lengths.

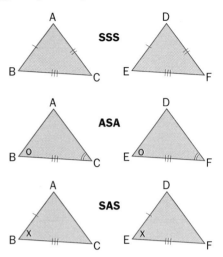

Similarly, if a triangle is constructed using two angles and the included side (ASA) or two sides and the included angle (SAS), only one size and shape of triangle is possible in each case.

You will now explore the construction of a triangle using two sides and a non-included angle, that is, the SSA case.

1 Exploring the SSA Case

Use the following steps to construct △ABC, where ∠A = 50°, AC = 6 cm, and CB = 5 cm.
• Draw a line segment at least 8 cm long for the base of the triangle. Mark and label point A at one end of the base.
• Use a protractor to draw an angle of 50° with vertex A. Mark and label the point C, 6 cm from A, as shown.
• To construct CB, use compasses with the radius set at 5 cm. With centre C, draw an arc to intersect the base.

1. a) How many possible locations are there for point B?
b) How many triangles can you construct using the given information?
c) Measure the approximate possible values of ∠CBA.

2. a) Keeping CB < AC, determine the approximate length of CB that would give one location for point B, and hence one △ABC.
b) What is the approximate measure of ∠B in the triangle from part a)?

3. a) If the length of CB is less than the value you found in question 2a), how many triangles can be drawn?
b) If CB is increased so that CB ≥ AC, how many triangles can be drawn?

4. Draw another base line, ∠A = 120°, and AC = 6 cm, as shown. If you try to complete △ABC by drawing an arc with centre C,
a) for what values of CB will no triangle exist?
b) for what values of CB will one triangle exist?
c) are there any values of CB for which two triangles will exist?

2 Making Generalizations

1. △ABC is constructed by first drawing the base line, an acute ∠A, and the side AC, or *b*.

a) If side CB, or *a*, is less than *b* and has a length that gives one position for point B and one △ABC, what must be the measure of ∠ABC? Explain.

b) For the triangle in part a), write an equation in the form *a* = ▦ to express *a* in terms of *b* and ∠A.

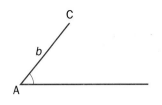

2. a) For the construction in question 1, if side *a* has a length that gives two possible positions for point B, how must the measures of ∠ABC in the two resulting triangles be related? Explain.

b) How are *a*, *b*, ∠A, and ∠B related in each triangle?

c) Write a compound inequality that relates *a*, *b*, and *b* sin A when there are two possible locations for B.

3. △ABC is constructed by first drawing the base, an obtuse ∠A, and the side AC, or *b*. How are sides *a* and *b* related if

a) one △ABC exists?

b) no △ABC exists?

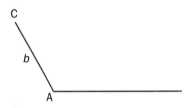

3 Applying the Concepts

Determine whether each set of SSA data defines no triangle, one triangle, or two possible triangles.

1. In △ABC, ∠A = 45°, AC = 12 cm, and CB = 10 cm.

2. In △ABC, ∠A = 80°, AC = 9 cm, and CB = 10 cm.

3. In △ABC, ∠A = 35°, AC = 10 cm, and CB = 3 cm.

4. In △ABC, ∠A = 30°, AC = 7 cm, and CB = 3.5 cm.

5. In △ABC, ∠A = 110°, AC = 5 cm, and CB = 4 cm.

6. In △PQR, ∠P = 60°, PR = 11.8 cm, and RQ = 13.5 cm.

7. In △XYZ, ∠X = 25°, XZ = 4.8 cm, and ZY = 3.2 cm.

8. In △KLM, ∠K = 139.5°, KM = 152 cm, and ML = 20 cm.

9. In △DEF, ∠D = 65.8°, DF = 8.5 cm, and FE = 8.1 cm.

10. In △UVW, ∠U = 30°, UW = 19.2 cm, and WV = 9.6 cm.

8.7 The Law of Sines: The Ambiguous Case

Canada has 1.3 million square kilometres of wetlands, or almost 25% of all the wetlands in the world. These marshes and swamps help to prevent flooding and act as natural water purifiers.

Wetlands provide a habitat for many species of animals and plants. Millions of waterfowl use wetlands as migration stops or nesting sites.

Explore: Draw a Diagram

A surveyor is preparing a map of a marsh, which is to be protected as a conservation area. She places flags at four points around the edge of the marsh and uses them in making various measurements. The flags at points B, C, and D lie in a line. ∠ADC measures 34°. The straight-line distance from A to D is 2 km, and from A to B is 1.3 km. The distance from A to C is also 1.3 km. Draw and label a diagram to show all the given information.

Inquire

1. In △ABD, write an equation of the form sin ∠ABD = ■ to express sin ∠ABD in terms of AD, AB, and sin ∠ADB.

2. In △ACD, write an equation of the form sin ∠ACD = ■ to express sin ∠ACD in terms of AD, AC, and sin ∠ADB.

3. Compare the equations from questions 1 and 2.
a) What can you conclude about how the values of sin ∠ABD and sin ∠ACD compare?
b) If you substituted known values into the equations and used a calculator to find the measures of ∠ABD and ∠ACD, how would the calculated results compare?

4. a) Is ∠ABD acute or obtuse?
b) Is ∠ACD acute or obtuse?
c) Can ∠ABD equal ∠ACD?
d) Complete the calculation described in question 3b).
Is the result the measure of ∠ABD or the measure of ∠ACD?

5. The diagram you drew shows an example of the ambiguous case of the law of sines. Explain why the word *ambiguous* is appropriate.

When two sides and the non-included angle of a triangle are given, the triangle may not be unique. It is possible that no triangle, one triangle, or two triangles exist with the given measurements.

Suppose that in △ABC, you are given the side lengths *a* and *b*, and the measure of ∠A, and suppose that ∠A < 90°. If *a* ≥ *b*, there is one triangle and one solution.

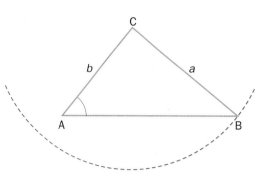

If *a* < *b*, there are three possibilities.

If *a* = *b* sin A, there is one triangle and one solution.
∠B = 90°

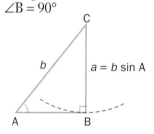

If *a* < *b* sin A, there is no triangle and no solution.

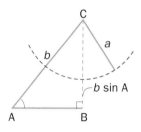

If *a* > *b* sin A, there are two triangles and two solutions.

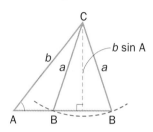

If ∠A ≥ 90°, there are two possibilities.

If *a* ≤ *b*, there is no triangle and no solution.

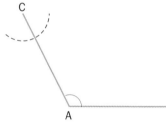

If *a* > *b*, there is one triangle and one solution.

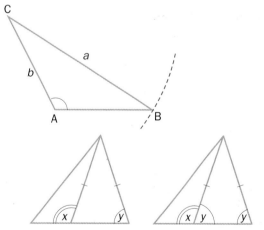

The situation in which there are two triangles and two solutions is shown in the diagram. In the isosceles triangle, the angles opposite the equal sides are equal.

Because they lie on a straight line, the adjacent angles *x* and *y* are supplementary. Thus, in the ambiguous case, the two possible values of ∠ABC are supplementary.

Recall that the sines of supplementary angles are equal. For example, sin 30° = 0.5 and sin 150° = 0.5.

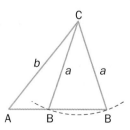

Example 1   The Ambiguous Case

Solve $\triangle ABC$ if $\angle A = 29.3°$, $b = 20.5$ cm, and $a = 12.8$ cm. Round side lengths
to the nearest tenth of a centimetre and angles to the nearest tenth of a degree, if necessary.

Solution

Draw a diagram.

Then $b \sin A = 20.5 \sin 29.3°$

$\qquad\qquad \doteq 10$

Because $b \sin A < a < b$, there are
two locations for point B, two
triangles ABC, and two solutions.

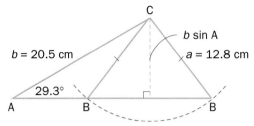

First, use the law of sines to find the
two possible measures for $\angle ABC$.

$\dfrac{\sin B}{b} = \dfrac{\sin A}{a}$

$\sin B = \dfrac{b \sin A}{a}$

$\qquad = \dfrac{20.5 \sin 29.3°}{12.8}$

So, $\angle B \doteq 51.6°$ or $\angle B \doteq 180° - 51.6°$

$\qquad\qquad\qquad\qquad\qquad \doteq 128.4°$

Solve both triangles ABC.

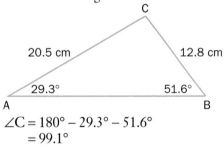

$\angle C = 180° - 29.3° - 51.6°$

$\qquad = 99.1°$

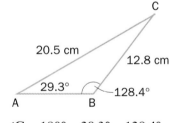

$\angle C = 180° - 29.3° - 128.4°$

$\qquad = 22.3°$

Use the law of sines or the law of cosines to find c.
Using the law of sines,

$\dfrac{c}{\sin C} = \dfrac{a}{\sin A}$

$c = \dfrac{a \sin C}{\sin A}$

$\quad = \dfrac{12.8 \sin 99.1°}{\sin 29.3°}$

$\quad \doteq 25.8$

Use the law of sines or the law of cosines to find c.
Using the law of sines,

$\dfrac{c}{\sin C} = \dfrac{a}{\sin A}$

$c = \dfrac{a \sin C}{\sin A}$

$\quad = \dfrac{12.8 \sin 22.3°}{\sin 29.3°}$

$\quad \doteq 9.9$

So, there are two solutions: $\angle B = 51.6°$, $\angle C = 99.1°$, and $c = 25.8$ cm
or $\angle B = 128.4°$, $\angle C = 22.3°$, and $c = 9.9$ cm.

Example 2   Chord of a Circle

A 15-cm line segment, PO, is drawn at an angle of 47° to a horizontal line segment, PT. A circle with centre O and radius 12 cm intersects PT at R and S. Calculate the length of the chord RS, to the nearest tenth of a centimetre.

Solution

Draw a diagram.

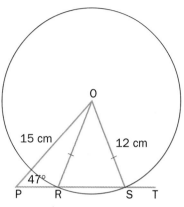

In $\triangle$POS, use the law of sines to find the measure of $\angle$PSO.

$$\frac{\sin \angle PSO}{PO} = \frac{\sin \angle OPS}{OS}$$

$$\sin \angle PSO = \frac{PO \sin \angle OPS}{OS}$$

$$= \frac{15 \sin 47°}{12}$$

$$\angle PSO \doteq 66.1°$$

In $\triangle$ROS, OR = OS, so $\angle$RSO = $\angle$SRO = 66.1°.

$\angle$ROS = 180° − 66.1° − 66.1°

      = 47.8°

Use the law of sines or the law of cosines to find the length of RS.
Using the law of cosines,

$$RS^2 = OR^2 + OS^2 - 2(OR)(OS) \cos \angle ROS$$

$$= 12^2 + 12^2 - 2(12)(12)\cos 47.8°$$

$$RS \doteq 9.7$$

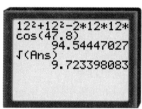

The length of the chord RS is 9.7 cm, to the nearest tenth of a centimetre.

Example 3   Triangles on a Coordinate Grid

Line segment AC, of length 5 units, lies on the line $y = \frac{4}{3}x$ and has endpoints A(0, 0) and C(3, 4). The segment makes an angle of about 53.1° with the positive x-axis.

a) If AB is horizontal, find the coordinates of the point B for these values of CB: CB = 2, CB = 4, CB = 4.5. Round to the nearest hundredth, if necessary.

b) Show that the answers from part a) are the points of intersection of the line $y = 0$ with the circles $(x - 3)^2 + (y - 4)^2 = 4$, $(x - 3)^2 + (y - 4)^2 = 16$, and $(x - 3)^2 + (y - 4)^2 = 20.25$.

c) Verify the answers from part a) by finding the points of intersection described in part b).

Solution

a) Draw a diagram.

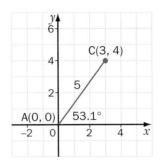

If AB must be horizontal, the point B must lie on the *x*-axis.

When CB = 2, the segment is not long enough to reach the *x*-axis from point C. There can be no point B that satisfies the condition that AB must be horizontal.

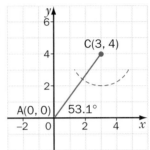

When CB = 4, the length of CB equals the vertical distance from the point C to the *x*-axis. So, there is one point B that satisfies the condition that AB must be horizontal. The coordinates of B are (3, 0).

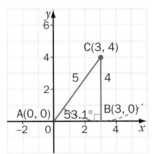

When CB = 4.5, its length is between the length of AC and the length of *b* sin A, which is 4, so there are two possible locations of point B. From the graph, the coordinates of the points appear to be about (1, 0) and (5, 0). More accurate coordinates can be found by finding the length of AB in each of the two possible triangles ABC.

Solving both triangles as shown in Example 1 gives the lengths of AB as 0.94 and 5.07, to the nearest hundredth. So, the coordinates of point B are (0.94, 0) or (5.07, 0).

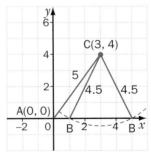

b) The arcs shown in the last three diagrams in part a) are all arcs of circles with centre C(3, 4). The radii of the circles are 2, 4, and 4.5, respectively. The equations of the circles are of the form $(x - h)^2 + (y - k)^2 = r^2$, where the coordinates of the centre are (h, k) and the radius is r.

As the values of r^2 are 2^2 or 4, 4^2 or 16, and 4.5^2 or 20.25, the equations of the circles are as follows.

$(x - 3)^2 + (y - 4)^2 = 4$

$(x - 3)^2 + (y - 4)^2 = 16$

$(x - 3)^2 + (y - 4)^2 = 20.25$

The coordinates of B are the points of intersection of the circles with the x-axis, which has the equation $y = 0$.

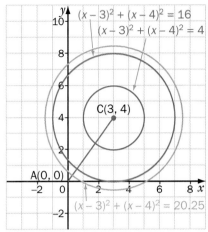

c) Solve each of the following systems of equations algebraically or graphically.

$(x - 3)^2 + (y - 4)^2 = 4$	$(x - 3)^2 + (y - 4)^2 = 16$	$(x - 3)^2 + (y - 4)^2 = 20.25$
$y = 0$	$y = 0$	$y = 0$

To solve algebraically, substitute 0 for y from the second equation into the first in each system.

$(x - 3)^2 + (0 - 4)^2 = 4$

$x^2 - 6x + 9 + 16 = 4$

$x^2 - 6x + 21 = 0$

The discriminant $b^2 - 4ac$

$= (-6)^2 - 4(1)(21)$

$= 36 - 84$

$= -48$

There are no real values of x.

$(x - 3)^2 + (0 - 4)^2 = 16$

$x^2 - 6x + 9 + 16 = 16$

$x^2 - 6x + 9 = 0$

$(x - 3)(x - 3) = 0$

The value of x is 3.

$(x - 3)^2 + (0 - 4)^2 = 20.25$

$x^2 - 6x + 9 + 16 = 20.25$

$x^2 - 6x + 4.75 = 0$

Use the quadratic formula.

$$x = \frac{6 \pm \sqrt{(-6)^2 - 4(1)(4.75)}}{2}$$

$$= \frac{6 \pm \sqrt{17}}{2}$$

$$\doteq 0.94 \text{ or } 5.06$$

Estimate

$$\frac{6 + 4}{2} = 5 \qquad \frac{6 - 4}{2} = 1$$

To solve graphically, to the nearest hundredth, use a graphing calculator.

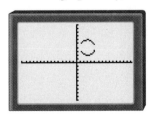

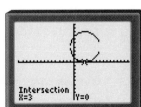

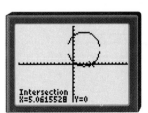

The algebraic or the graphical method verifies that, for AB to be horizontal, there is no point B such that CB = 2, there is one point B(3, 0) such that CB = 4, and there are two points B(0.94, 0) or B(5.06, 0) such that CB = 4.5.

Example 4   Streetlights

Along the road into a park, streetlights are placed 50 m apart. The light
from each streetlight can illuminate effectively up to 30 m away. From
the location of one of the streetlights, point A, a straight path leads off
the road at an angle of 25°.

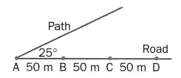

a) Determine the furthest distance from A along the path that receives
effective illumination from the streetlights, to the nearest metre.
b) What length of the path receives effective illumination from the light at B, to the
nearest metre?
c) What length of the path receives effective illumination from both the light at A
and the light at B?

Solution

a) The streetlight at A illuminates the first 30 m of the path.

Now consider the light from the streetlight at B.
Let P represent the point on the path that is 30 m from B.
In $\triangle APB$, $\angle A = 25°$ and $AB = 50$ m.

Since $50 \sin 25° \doteq 21.1$, and $21.1 < 30 < 50$, the point
P has two possible positions.
Use the law of sines to determine each value of $\angle APB$.

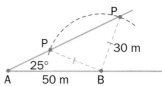

$$\frac{\sin \angle APB}{50} = \frac{\sin 25°}{30}$$

$$\sin \angle APB = \frac{50 \sin 25°}{30}$$

$$\angle APB \doteq 44.8° \text{ or } \angle APB = 180° - 44.8°$$
$$= 135.2°$$

The light at B effectively illuminates the furthest point from A
when $\angle APB$ is acute, that is, when $\angle APB = 44.8°$.

To find the longer distance AP, use the law of sines or the law
of cosines in the larger $\triangle APB$.

$$\angle B = 180° - 25° - 44.8°$$
$$= 110.2°$$

$$\frac{AP}{\sin 110.2°} = \frac{30}{\sin 25°}$$

$$AP = \frac{30 \sin 110.2°}{\sin 25°}$$

$$\doteq 67$$

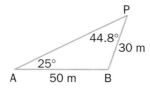

The furthest distance along the path that receives effective illumination from
streetlight B is 67 m from A, to the nearest metre.

Now consider the light from the streetlight at C.
Let Q represent a point on the path that is 30 m from C.
In $\triangle AQC$, $\angle A = 25°$ and $AC = 100$.

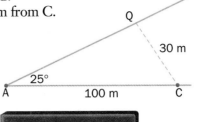

Since $100 \sin 25 \doteq 42.3$ and $30 < 42.3$, no
such $\triangle AQC$ exists.
So, the light from the streetlight at C does
not illuminate the path effectively.

Since all subsequent lights are even further from the path, they do not illuminate
the path effectively.
Therefore, the furthest distance from A along the path, that receives effective
illumination from the streetlights is 67 m, to the nearest metre.

b) As determined in part a), the light from B effectively illuminates a section of
the path between the two positions of point P. Let the two points be P_1 and P_2.
Then, $\angle AP_1B = 135.2°$ and $\angle AP_2B = 44.8°$.
Since $\triangle P_1BP_2$ is isosceles, $\angle BP_1P_2 = 44.8°$.

$\angle P_1BP_2 = 180° - 44.8° - 44.8°$
$\qquad = 90.4°$
Use the law of sines in $\triangle P_1BP_2$ to find the length of P_1P_2.

$$\frac{P_1P_2}{\sin 90.4°} = \frac{30}{\sin 44.8°}$$
$$P_1P_2 = \frac{30 \sin 90.4°}{\sin 44.8°}$$
$$\doteq 43$$

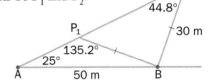

So, 43 m of the path, to the nearest metre, receives effective illumination from
the light at B.

c) From parts a) and b), we know that the light at B
effectively illuminates the 43-m length P_1P_2 of the path.
P_2 is about 67 m from point A. Therefore, P_1 must be
about 24 m from point A. Point A effectively illuminates
the first 30 m of the path. Therefore, beginning at P_1,
there must be about a 6-m length of the path that
receives effective illumination from both the light at A
and the light at B.

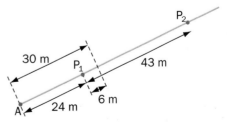

Practice

Find the measures of angles x and y, to the nearest tenth of a degree.

1. **2.**

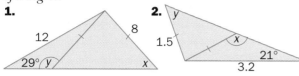

3. **4.**

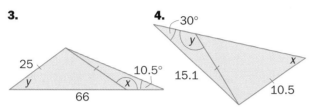

5. **6.**

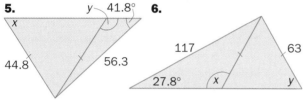

Determine the number of possible triangles that could be drawn with the given measures. Then, find the measures of the other angles in each possible triangle.

7. △ABC, where ∠A = 42°, a = 30 cm, and b = 25 cm

8. △ABC, where ∠B = 27°, b = 25 cm, and c = 30 cm

9. △PQR, where ∠P = 30°, p = 24 cm, and q = 48 cm

10. △KLM, where ∠M = 37.3°, m = 85 cm, and l = 90 cm

11. △UVW, where ∠W = 38.7°, w = 10 cm, and v = 25 cm

12. △ABC, where ∠B = 48°, c = 15.6 m, and b = 12.6 m

13. △XYZ, where ∠X = 120°, x = 40 cm, and z = 20 cm

14. △DEF, where ∠E = 144°, e = 10.5 m, and f = 12.5 m

Solve each triangle. Round angle measures to the nearest tenth of a degree and side lengths to the nearest tenth of a centimetre, if necessary.

15. △ABC, where ∠A = 45°, a = 30 cm, and b = 24 cm

16. △XYZ, where ∠Y = 32.7°, y = 54 cm, and x = 25 cm

17. △PQR, where ∠R = 40.3°, r = 35.2 cm, and q = 40.5 cm

18. △FGH, where ∠G = 105°, f = 3.5 cm, and g = 6.1 cm

19. △RST, where ∠T = 50.2°, s = 10.5 cm, and t = 7.1 cm

20. △DEF, where ∠E = 71.2°, e = 29.5 cm, and f = 30.3 cm

21. △BCD, where ∠C = 143°, d = 12.5 cm, and c = 8.9 cm

22. △LMN, where ∠L = 42.8°, l = 15.8 cm, and n = 18.5 cm

23. Calculate
a) the measures of ∠BCD and ∠BDA, to the nearest tenth of a degree
b) the length of CD, to the nearest tenth of a centimetre

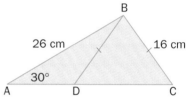

24. Find the length of MN, to the nearest tenth of a metre.

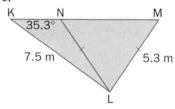

25. A circle with centre C and radius 5.5 cm intersects a line segment AB at points D and E. If ∠CAB = 48.9° and AC = 6.4 cm, what is the length of chord DE, to the nearest tenth of a centimetre?

26. A line segment PQ of length 13 units has endpoints P(0, 0) and Q(5, 12). PQ makes an angle of about 22.6° with the positive y-axis. If point R must be vertically above P, find the coordinates of R for each of the following lengths of QR. Round to the nearest hundredth, if necessary.
a) 5   **b)** 8   **c)** 4   **d)** 15

27. A circle with equation $(x + 1)^2 + (y - 3)^2 = 18$ intersects the x-axis at B and D. Point A has coordinates $(-6, 0)$, and $\angle CAB$ is about 31°.

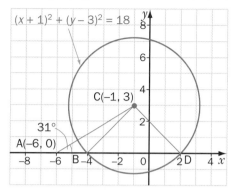

a) Use the law of sines to find the length of the chord BD.

b) Verify your answer by solving a system of equations to find the coordinates of B and D.

Determine the length of the chord AB in each circle, to the nearest hundredth.

28.

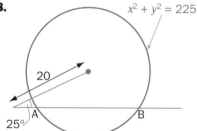

29.

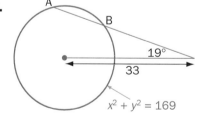

Applications and Problem Solving

30. Coordinate geometry Triangles are formed by the intersection of the lines $y = x$, $y = 2x$, $y = -2x$, and $y = -4$, as shown. Solve $\triangle ABC$ and $\triangle ABD$.

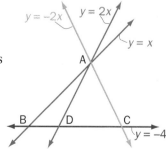

31. Forest fires A forest ranger spots a fire on a bearing of 050° from her station. She estimates that the fire is about 10 km away. A second station is due east of the first. A ranger in the second station thinks that the fire is about 8 km away from him. How far apart are the two stations, to the nearest kilometre?

32. Coordinate geometry The point $M(-2, 2)$ and the centre $C(4, 5)$ of the circle $(x - 4)^2 + (y - 5)^2 = 25$ lie on the line $y = \frac{1}{2}x + 3$. The circle intersects the line $y = 2$ at N and P.

a) Find the length of the chord NP by solving a system of equations.

b) Verify your answer using the law of sines.

33. Road work A mechanical digger is being used to dig a ditch for laying pipes under a road. The arm of the digger is articulated at A, and the two sections of the arm have lengths of 3.8 m and 2.7 m, as shown. If the operator keeps the first section fixed at 43° to the horizontal and then moves the second section to scoop out earth, what length of ditch will be worked in one swing of the second section, to the nearest tenth of a metre?

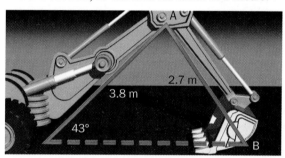

34. Navigation The light from a rotating offshore beacon can illuminate effectively up to a distance of 250 m. From a point along the shore that is 500 m from the beacon, the sight line to the beacon makes an angle of 20° with the shoreline. What length of the shoreline is effectively illuminated by the beacon, to the nearest metre?

35. Gardening An underground sprinkler system is laid at an angle of 34.5° to a fence. The sprinkler jets are 10 m apart and

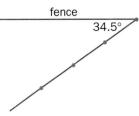

have a range of 12 m. Determine the length of the fence that gets wet from the sprinklers, to the nearest tenth of a metre.

36. Radar From a position 110 km northwest of a coastguard station, an oil tanker makes radio contact with the coastguard. The tanker is travelling due south at 25 km/h. The radar unit at the coastguard station has a range of 90 km. For what length of time can the coastguard expect the tanker to be visible on the radar screen, to the nearest tenth of an hour?

37. Satellite A satellite is in an orbit 1000 km above the surface of the Earth. A receiving dish is located so that the directions from the satellite to the dish and from the satellite to the centre of the Earth make an angle of 27°, as shown. If a signal from the satellite travels at 3×10^8 m/s, how long does it take to reach the dish, to the nearest thousandth of a second? Assume that the radius of the Earth is 6370 km.

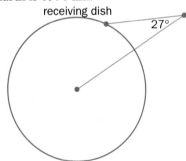

38. Show that the ratio of the areas of △ACD and △ACB is as follows.

$$\frac{\text{area } \triangle ACD}{\text{area } \triangle ACB} = \frac{\sin \ ACD}{\sin \ ACB}$$

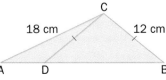

39. Landscaping Low-voltage lighting is a popular feature of landscaping. Two pathways meet at 30° to each other. One pathway has the lighting, and the first

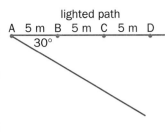

light is placed where the two paths meet, as shown. The distance between successive lights is 5 m, and each has a range of effective illumination of 6 m. For the second pathway, find, to the nearest tenth of a metre, the length that is
a) effectively illuminated
b) effectively illuminated by both light B and light C
c) effectively illuminated by light C but not by light B
d) effectively illuminated by light C but not by light A
e) effectively illuminated by light C or light D

40. Coordinate geometry Point A is at (−1, −1) and point B is at (0, 7). Point C must be vertically below B or horizontally to the right of B. Point C is a point of intersection of the line $y = x$ and the circle $(x − 3)^2 + (y − 4)^2 = 25$. Solve △ABC, rounding answers to the nearest tenth, if necessary.

41. Navigation Three ships, A, B, and C, are sailing along the same straight line on a course of 240°. Ship A is at the front and ship C brings up the rear. From ship A, the bearing of a navigation buoy is 025°. The buoy is 2.5 km from ship A and 2 km from ships B and C. To the nearest degree, what is the bearing of the buoy from ship C? from ship B?

LOGIC POWER

Paula has two pieces of fuse, each of which will burn completely from either end to the other end in 1 min. Without cutting or breaking these pieces of fuse, how can she use them to time 45 s?

The Ambiguous Case and the Law of Cosines

The ambiguous case may occur when two sides and a non-included angle (SSA) of a triangle are given. The number of triangles that can be constructed or solved may be two, one, or zero. In Section 8.7, triangles were solved from SSA data by first using the law of sines to find another angle.

The law of cosines also can be used. This method involves writing a quadratic equation in which the variable represents the length of the third side of the triangle. Solving this equation gives the length, or lengths, of the third side of the triangle, if one exists. Once the third side is known, the triangle, or triangles, can be solved.

1 Finding the Third Side

1. a) In $\triangle ABC$, $\angle A = 60°$, $b = 10$ cm, and $a = 5\sqrt{3}$ cm. Using the law of cosines,
$$a^2 = b^2 + c^2 - 2bc \cos A$$
$$(5\sqrt{3})^2 = 10^2 + c^2 - 2(10)c \cos 60°$$
Simplify and solve the quadratic equation to find the length of c.

b) How many triangles are possible? Explain.

For each of the following triangles,
a) *use the law of cosines to find the length of c, rounding to the nearest tenth of a centimetre, if necessary*
b) *state how many triangles are possible. Explain.*
2. In $\triangle ABC$, $\angle A = 60°$, $b = 10$ cm, and $a = 9$ cm.
3. In $\triangle ABC$, $\angle A = 60°$, $b = 10$ cm, and $a = 12$ cm.
4. In $\triangle ABC$, $\angle A = 60°$, $b = 10$ cm, and $a = 8$ cm.

2 Solving Triangles

a) *Use the law of cosines to determine whether each set of measurements will give one triangle, two triangles, or no triangle.*
b) *Solve the triangles that exist. Round side lengths to the nearest tenth of a centimetre and angle measures to the nearest tenth of a degree, if necessary.*
1. In $\triangle ABC$, $\angle A = 37°$, $a = 3$ cm, and $c = 4$ cm.
2. In $\triangle DEF$, $\angle D = 65°$, $d = 7$ cm, and $f = 9$ cm.
3. In $\triangle RST$, $\angle S = 70°$, $s = 6$ cm, and $t = 5$ cm.
4. In $\triangle WXY$, $\angle X = 30.5°$, $x = 2.1$ cm, and $y = 5.2$ cm.
5. In $\triangle LMN$, $\angle M = 41.2°$, $m = 6.5$ cm, and $n = 8.9$ cm.
6. In $\triangle ABC$, $\angle A = 30°$, $a = 5.7$ cm, and $b = 11.4$ cm.
7. In $\triangle PQR$, $\angle R = 150°$, $r = 8.4$ cm, and $q = 5.9$ cm.
8. In $\triangle FGH$, $\angle G = 102.5°$, $g = 9.8$ cm, and $f = 10.9$ cm.

CONNECTING MATH AND FASHION

Styles of Tying Shoelaces

There are several ways to lace shoes. Some people prefer how one particular lacing style looks and always lace their shoes that way. The most popular style varies from one part of the world to another.

The three styles shown are
a) the North American method

b) the European method

c) the method used by some shoe stores

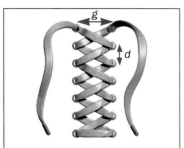 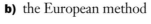  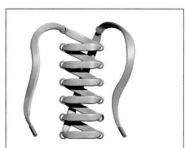

In the diagrams, the number of pairs of eyelets is 7, d represents the distance between successive eyelets on the same side, and g represents the gap between corresponding left and right eyelets.

1 Developing a Formula

1. For each of the lacing methods, develop a formula in terms of d and g for determining the length of shoelace required for a shoe with 7 pairs of eyelets. Assume that the length of lace required to tie a bow is the same for all of the methods, and exclude this length from the formula.

2. If $g = 6$ cm and $d = 2$ cm, which lacing method requires
a) the shortest length of shoelace?
b) the longest length of shoelace?

3. Explain why you think some shoe stores use method c) for tying shoelaces.

2 Developing a More General Formula

1. For each of the lacing methods, develop a formula in terms of n, d, and g for determining the length of shoelace required for a shoe with n pairs of eyelets. Again, exclude the length of lace needed to tie the bow.

2. If $n = 4$, $g = 4$ cm, and $d = 2$ cm, which lacing method requires
a) the shortest length of shoelace?
b) the longest length of shoelace?

3. If $n = 3$, $g = 4$ cm, and $d = 2$ cm, which lacing method requires
a) the shortest length of shoelace?
b) the longest length of shoelace?

4. If $n = 2$, $g = 4$ cm, and $d = 2$ cm, which lacing method requires
a) the shortest length of shoelace?
b) the longest length of shoelace?

5. If $n = 2$, and d and g are any length, are the answers the same as in question 4? Explain.

3 Comparing With Other Styles

Shown below are two other styles of lacing shoes.
The one on the right is known as Canadian straight-lacing.

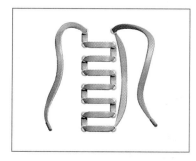 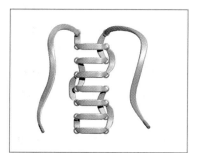

1. a) For each of these lacing methods, develop a formula in terms of n, d, and g for determining the length of lace required when n is even.
b) How do the lengths compare for these two methods?

2. If $n = 4$, $g = 4$ cm, and $d = 2$ cm, how do the lengths of the laces for these methods compare with the lengths for the North American, European, and shoe-store methods?

3. Why might a shoe manufacturer be interested in knowing
a) how people prefer to lace their shoes?
b) the length of the shoelace needed to lace a shoe in a certain way?

Review

8.1 **1.** Verify that the vertices A(–2, 3), B(1, 6), and C(2, 2) are *not* the vertices of an equilateral triangle.

2. Show that a quadrilateral with vertices K(2, –5), L(7, –3), M(1, 4), and N(–4, 2) is a parallelogram.

3. A square has vertices at U(–2, 1), V(2, 3), W(4, –1), and X(0, –3). Show that the diagonals perpendicularly bisect each other.

4. Given △DEF with vertices D(–4, –1), E(4, 3), and F(0, –5), show that
a) △DEF is isosceles
b) the line segment joining the midpoints of the equal sides is parallel to the third side and half the length of the third side

5. Prove that, in a parallelogram, the diagonals bisect each other.

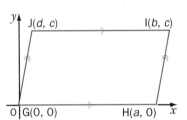

8.2 *Determine the coordinates of the points that divide the line segment joining the two given points into the given number of congruent parts.*
6. S(–2, 8), T(2, –4) into 2 parts
7. F(–3, –1), G(6, 5) into 3 parts
8. M(3, 5), N(–2, –10) into 5 parts
9. J(–5, –3), K(7, –8) into 2 parts
10. V(13, 3), W(–5, –3) into 4 parts
11. C(–4, 6), D(4, –3) into 3 parts

12. Ladder A vertical cross section of a ladder with six equally-spaced rungs is drawn on a coordinate grid, as shown. The second rung from the bottom is at (5, 4). What are the coordinates of the ends of the ladder?

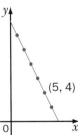

8.3 *Find the shortest distance from the origin to each line. Express radical answers in simplest radical form.*
13. $y = x + 5$ **14.** $y = -2x + 1$
15. $y = \frac{1}{3}x - 4$ **16.** $x + y = 8$
17. $x + 2y = 10$ **18.** $x + 2y + 2 = 0$

Find the shortest distance from the given point to the given line. Round to the nearest tenth, if necessary.
19. (1, 4) and $y = x - 5$
20. (–2, 2) and $2x + y = 8$
21. (–1, –3) and $x + 3y - 9 = 0$

Determine the vertical distance, the horizontal distance, and the shortest distance between the following pairs of parallel lines. Round distances to the nearest hundredth, if necessary.
22. $y = 3x - 1$ and $y = 3x + 5$
23. $y = 0.25x + 1$ and $y = 0.25x - 6$
24. $x + 2y = 10$ and $x + 2y = -2$

8.4 *Write the equation of each circle.*
25. centre (0, 0), radius 3
26. centre (3, 7), radius 7
27. centre (–7, –3), radius 6
28. centre (6, –3), radius 12
29. centre (–4, 5), radius $\sqrt{5}$
30. centre (11, –12), radius $3\sqrt{3}$

For each circle, write the coordinates of the centre and find the radius.
31. $x^2 + y^2 = 121$
32. $(x - 1)^2 + y^2 = 0.25$
33. $(x + 3)^2 + (y - 4)^2 = 81$
34. $(x - 3.5)^2 + (y + 6.5)^2 = 64$

Determine the equation of each circle.
35. centre (0, 0) and passing through (–8, 6)
36. centre (0, 0) and passing through (0, 9)
37. centre (2, 1) and passing through (5, 1)
38. centre (–1, 3) and passing through (5, –5)
39. centre (4, –1) and passing through (0, 6)
40. centre (–5, –5) and passing through (1, 1)

8.5 **a)** *Find the coordinates of any point(s) of intersection of each line and circle. Where necessary, round answers to the nearest tenth.*
b) *If there are two points of intersection, find the length of the chord that has these endpoints.*
41. $y = 3x + 10$ and $x^2 + y^2 = 12$
42. $x - 3y = 10$ and $x^2 + y^2 = 10$
43. $y = -x + 1$ and $(x - 1)^2 + (y + 4)^2 = 8$
44. $y = -x - 4$ and $(x + 3)^2 + (y + 2)^2 = 13$
45. $x + 2y + 1 = 0$ and $(x + 2)^2 + (y - 3)^2 = 5$

What are the equations of the vertical and horizontal lines that are tangent to each circle?

46. $x^2 + y^2 = 400$ **47.** $x^2 + y^2 = 225$

For each circle, write an equation for the tangent at the given point.

48. $x^2 + y^2 = 17$ at $(1, 4)$

49. $(x + 5)^2 + (y + 2)^2 = 13$ at $(-8, 0)$

Find the exact length of a tangent to the given circle from the given point. Express radical answers in simplest radical form.

50. $x^2 + y^2 = 34$; P$(-7, -11)$

51. $(x + 2)^2 + (y - 6)^2 = 17$; P$(4, 13)$

Solve each triangle. Round answers to the nearest tenth, if necessary.

52. In △DEF, ∠D = 90°, ∠E = 25°, f = 4.8 cm

53. In △KLM, ∠K = 90°, k = 12.4 cm, l = 8.8 cm

54. In △XYZ, ∠X = 125.8°, x = 31.3 m, y = 8.2 m

55. In △STU, s = 12.4 m, t = 18.8 m, u = 10.2 m

56. In △PQR, p = 19.4 cm, q = 15.1 cm, and r = 17.3 cm. Find ∠P, to the nearest tenth of a degree.

57. Natural arch
Percé Rock is a natural rock arch on the shore of the Gaspé Peninsula in Quebec. To find its height, measurements were taken at low tide, as shown in the diagram. What is the height of Percé Rock, to the nearest metre?

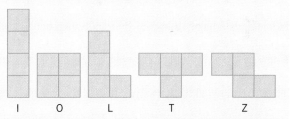

Determine the number of possible triangles that can be drawn with the given measures. Find the measures of the other angles in each possible triangle.

58. △GHI, where ∠G = 20°, g = 2 cm, h = 5 cm

59. △XYZ, where ∠X = 43°, x = 2 m, y = 4 m

60. △ABC, where ∠B = 104°, c = 1.4 m, b = 3.9 m

61. △KLM, where ∠L = 26°, m = 6.5 m, l = 4.2 m

62. Calculate the measures of ∠QRS and ∠QSP, to the nearest tenth of a degree, and the length of RS, to the nearest tenth of a centimetre.

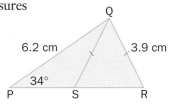

Exploring Math

Tetrominoes

Polyominoes are shapes formed by joining identical squares along their edges. The domino, which is made up of two squares, can have only one shape.

A triomino, which is made up of three squares, can have two shapes.

Tetrominoes are made up of four squares and can have the following five shapes.

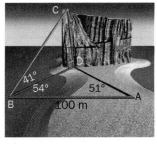

On the 7-by-7 grid shown, squares have been shaded so that no group of shaded squares forms the I shape, either vertically or horizontally. The maximum number of squares that can be shaded without shading the I shape is 37, as shown.

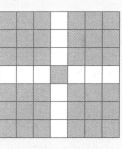

Determine the maximum number of squares that can be shaded on a 7-by-7 grid without shading the following shapes. Allow for all possible orientations; for example, an upside down T shape is still considered a T shape.

1. the O shape

2. the L shape

3. the I, O, and Z shapes

4. the I, O, T, Z, and L shapes

Chapter Check

1. Verify that the vertices A(−6, 1), B(2, −5), C(6, 1), and D(2, 4) are the vertices of a trapezoid.

2. The midpoints of the sides of quadrilateral RSTU, with vertices R(−4, 1), S(−2, 5), T(2, 1), and U (2, −7), are joined to form a quadrilateral. Show that the quadrilateral formed is a parallelogram.

3. Prove that, in a right triangle, the midpoint of the hypotenuse is the same distance from each vertex.

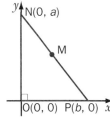

Determine the coordinates of the points that divide the line segment joining the two given points into the given number of congruent parts.

4. A(−5, −5), B(7, 3) into 4 parts
5. X(0, −3), Y(−2, 9) into 2 parts
6. M(−5, 4), N(10, −5) into 3 parts
7. S(1, −8), T(−4, 6) into 5 parts
8. J(−2, −4), K(5, −1) into 2 parts
9. G(2, −5), H(−2, 10) into 3 parts

Find the shortest distance from the origin to each line. Express radical answers in simplest radical form.

10. $y = x + 3$ **11.** $y = 0.5x − 3$
12. $2x − y + 7 = 0$ **13.** $x + 3y = 9$

Find the shortest distance from the given point to the given line. Round to the nearest tenth, if necessary.

14. (3, 1) and $3x + y = −2$
15. (−5, 0) and $2x + 4y = 6$

Determine the vertical distance, the horizontal distance, and the shortest distance between the following pairs of parallel lines. Round distances to the nearest hundredth, if necessary.

16. $y = 4x + 1$ and $y = 4x − 2$
17. $y = \frac{1}{3}x − 2$ and $y = \frac{1}{3}x + 3$
18. $3x + 2y = 6$ and $3x + 2y = 0$

Write the equation of each circle.

19. centre (0, 0), radius 8
20. centre (−2, 7), radius 9
21. centre (4, −8), radius $\sqrt{10}$

For each circle, write the coordinates of the centre and find the radius.

22. $(x − 5)^2 + y^2 = 169$ **23.** $(x + 6)^2 + (y − 4.5)^2 = 10$

Determine the equation of each circle.

24. centre (0, 0) and passing through (8, 0)
25. centre (0, 0) and passing through (−3, −4)
26. centre (4, −2) and passing through (0, 1)
27. centre (−2, −3) and passing through (−4, 2)

a) *Find the coordinates of any point(s) of intersection of each line and circle. Round answers to the nearest tenth, if necessary.*
b) *If there are two points of intersection, find the length of the chord that has these endpoints.*

28. $y = −2x + 10$ and $x^2 + y^2 = 40$
29. $y = −\frac{2}{3}x + 4$ and $(x + 2)^2 + (y − 1)^2 = 14$
30. $y = x − 1$ and $(x − 1)^2 + (y + 1)^2 = 5$

For each circle, write an equation for the tangent at the given point.

31. $x^2 + y^2 = 34$ at (−3, 5)
32. $(x + 5)^2 + (y + 5)^2 = 5$ at (−4, −2)

33. Find the exact length, expressed in simplest radical form, of a tangent from the point P(−1, 6) to the circle $(x − 3)^2 + (y + 1)^2 = 8$.

Solve each triangle. Round answers to the nearest tenth, if necessary.

34. In △ABC, ∠A = 90°, a = 2.5 m, c = 0.8 m
35. In △XYZ, ∠X = 90°, ∠Z = 28.7°, y = 50.2 cm
36. In △PQR, p = 38.4 m, q = 25.2 m, r = 19.3 m
37. In △GHI, ∠G = 88.8°, g = 42.7 cm, h = 30.1 cm

Determine the number of possible triangles that could be drawn with the given measures. Then, find the measures of the other angles in each possible triangle.

38. △ABC, where ∠A = 125°, a = 3 m, b = 5 m
39. △STU, where ∠S = 29°, s = 3.5 cm, t = 6 cm
40. △XYZ, where ∠X = 96°, x = 2.5 m, y = 0.8 m
41. △FGH, where ∠G = 41°, g = 7.2 cm, h = 9.9 cm

42. The distance between the centres of the circles, A and B, is 60 m. Each circle has a radius of 40 m. Point C lies on the circle with centre B. ∠BAC = 41°. What are the possible lengths of AC, to the nearest metre?

Using the Strategies

1. On the six tests that she wrote, Kelly had an average of 87%. Her highest mark was 95%, which she achieved on only one of the tests. What is the lowest percent she could have achieved on one of the tests?

2. Tom and Alicia bought identical boxes of stationery. Tom used his to write 1-page letters. Alicia used hers to write 3-page letters. Tom used all the envelopes and had 50 sheets of paper left over. Alicia used all the paper and had 50 envelopes left over. How many sheets of paper were in each box?

3. A circle with radius 3 cm intersects a circle with radius 4 cm. At the points of intersection, the radii are perpendicular. What is the difference in the areas of the non-overlapping parts of the circles?

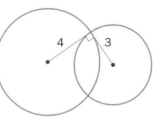

4. A, B, C, and D are whole numbers. The same number results when 4 is added to A, 4 is subtracted from B, C is divided by 4, and D is multiplied by 4. If A, B, C, and D add to 100, what are the values of A, B, C, and D?

5. The perimeters of a regular hexagon and an equilateral triangle are equal. What fraction of the area of the hexagon is the area of the triangle?

6. In how many different ways can four different keys be arranged on a key ring?

7. The powers of 3 are 3^0, 3^1, 3^2, 3^3, ..., or 1, 3, 9, 27, ... Using only addition or subtraction of powers of 3, the numbers 5, 26, and 35 can be expressed as follows.
$5 = 3 + 1 + 1$
$26 = 27 - 1$
$35 = 27 + 9 - 1$
Using only addition and subtraction, how many whole numbers from 1 to 50 cannot be expressed using three or fewer powers of 3?

8. What is the 53rd digit in the decimal form of $\frac{1}{7}$?

9. About how many take-out cups of coffee are sold in your province on a weekday?

10. In $\triangle ABC$, the perimeter is numerically equal to the area. The inscribed circle has centre O. What is the numerical value of the radius of the circle?

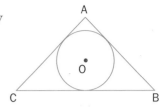

11. The points A, B, Q, D, and C lie on a circle. $\angle BAQ = 41°$ and $\angle DCQ = 37°$. What is the sum of the measures of $\angle P$ and $\angle AQC$?

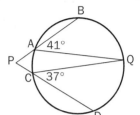

D A T A   B A N K

1. You are a travel agent arranging a tour of ancient sites in Rome and Athens for a group of students. The group is leaving Edmonton on a Saturday and arriving home on the following Saturday. The group is changing flights in London, England, in both directions. Draw up a detailed itinerary for the trip, allowing for time zone changes, so that the group spends about the same amount of time in Rome as in Athens. Indicate the sites that the group will visit in each city and the time to be spent at each site.

2. The northernmost point in Canada is Cape Columbia on Ellesmere Island. The latitude of Cape Columbia is 83°N. If a B747-400 aircraft flew from Cape Columbia around the 83°N parallel and back to Cape Columbia, how long would the flight take, to the nearest tenth of an hour? Assume that the radius of the Earth is 6370 km.

3. Which Canadian province has the greatest ratio of electricity generated to electricity consumed? Give possible reasons.

Chapter 5

1. For $f(x) = x^2 - 3$ and $g(x) = x - 1$, find the following. Write each function in simplest form and state any restrictions on the variable.

a) $(f + g)(x)$ **b)** $(f - g)(x)$ **c)** $(fg)(x)$ **d)** $\left(\dfrac{f}{g}\right)(x)$

e) $f(x) + 2g(x)$ **f)** $2g(x) - f(x)$

2. For $f(x) = x^2$ and $g(x) = |x|$, find
a) $(f \circ g)(x)$ and $(g \circ f)(x)$, if they exist
b) the domain and range of f, g, $f \circ g$, and $g \circ f$

3. Find the inverse of $h(x) = 5x - 2$.

4. Determine if $g(x) = \sqrt{\dfrac{x+1}{2}}$ and $k(x) = 2x^2 - 1$ are inverses of each other.

5. Graph $y = x^3 - 2x^2 - 5x + 6$ and determine
a) the domain and range
b) any real zeros and the y-intercept
c) the approximate coordinates of any relative maximums or relative minimums
d) the intervals where $f(x) > 0$ and where $f(x) < 0$
e) any symmetry and the end behaviour

6. Graph $f(x) = |x - 3| - 4$ and
a) determine the domain and range
b) determine the values of any real zeros
c) determine the values of x for which $f(x) \geq 0$
d) describe any symmetry

7. Graph $g(x) = \dfrac{x}{x+3}$ and determine
a) the equations of any asymptotes
b) the domain and range

8. Graph $y = \sqrt{x + 3}$ and determine the domain and range.

Solve and check.
9. $|2x - 1| - 4 = 0$ **10.** $\sqrt{3k} - \sqrt{k+3} = 0$

Solve. Graph the solution.
11. $\dfrac{m+2}{m-2} \leq 0$ **12.** $2w \geq \sqrt{w+3}$

Chapter 6

1. Seating One rectangular table seats 6 people. Two rectangular tables joined in a row seat 10 people. Three rectangular tables joined in a row seat 14 people.

a) Make a conjecture about the number of people who can be seated when n rectangular tables are joined in a row.
b) Test your conjecture for six rectangular tables.

Give an example that supports each conjecture. Then, give one counterexample to show that the conjecture is false.
2. Every integer has an opposite.
3. A quadrilateral with four equal sides has four right angles.

4. Prove deductively that the difference between the squares of consecutive whole numbers is equal to the sum of the whole numbers.

What values of k make each compound statement true?
5. k is a multiple of 4, and k is between 15 and 50.
6. k is an odd number between 0 and 20, or k is a factor of 24.

7. Fitness survey While leaving a gym, 65 people are surveyed about the machines they use for their cardiovascular workout. A treadmill is used by 36. A rowing machine is used by 24. A stationary bicycle is used by 40. A treadmill and a stationary bicycle are used by 20. A rowing machine and a stationary bicycle are used by 12. A treadmill and a rowing machine are used by 3. No one uses all three machines.
a) Display the information in a Venn diagram.
b) How many of those surveyed use a treadmill, but neither of the other machines?

8. a) Determine if the following statement is true. If a quadrilateral is a kite, then the longer diagonal bisects the shorter one.
b) Write the converse, and determine if it is true.
c) Write the contrapositive, and determine if it is true.

9. In $\triangle PQR$, PR is not equal to PQ, and S is the midpoint of QR. Use indirect reasoning to prove that PS is not perpendicular to QR.

Chapter 7

1. *Given:* AC and DB bisect each other at E.
Prove: ABCD is a parallelogram.

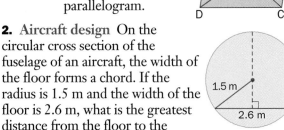

2. Aircraft design On the circular cross section of the fuselage of an aircraft, the width of the floor forms a chord. If the radius is 1.5 m and the width of the floor is 2.6 m, what is the greatest distance from the floor to the ceiling, to the nearest tenth of a metre?

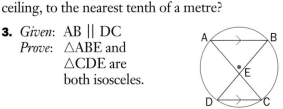

3. *Given:* AB ∥ DC
Prove: △ABE and △CDE are both isosceles.

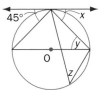

⬚ *Find the measures of the indicated angles. Explain your reasoning.*

4.

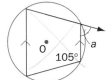

5.

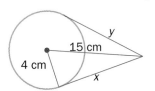

6. *Given:* △ABC and △CDE are isosceles triangles.

Prove: ABDE is a cyclic quadrilateral.

7. Find the indicated lengths. Round answers to the nearest tenth of a centimetre, if necessary.

8. In a circle with a diameter of 18 cm, a sector has a sector angle of 75°. Find the length of the arc that subtends the sector angle, to the nearest tenth of a centimetre, and the area of the sector, to the nearest tenth of a square centimetre.

9. Determine the measures of an interior angle and an exterior angle of a regular polygon with 18 sides.

Chapter 8

1. The vertices of a kite are G(2, 5), H(5, 1), I(8, 2), and J(7, 5). Show that
a) the diagonals are perpendicular
b) one, and only one, of the diagonals bisects the other diagonal

Determine the coordinates of the points that divide the line segment joining the two given points into the given number of congruent parts.
2. A(−3, −5), B(6, 4) into 3 parts
3. S(0, 1), T(10, −3) into 4 parts

Find the shortest distance from the given point to the given line. Round to the nearest tenth, if necessary.
4. (5, 4) and $x + y = 5$
5. (−3, 1) and $x − 2y = 1$

Write the equation of each circle.
6. centre (0, 0), radius 3
7. centre (−1, 5), radius 4
8. centre (0, 0) and passing through (4, −3)
9. centre (4, 2) and passing through (2, −2)

For each line and circle,
a) *find the coordinates of any point(s) of intersection*
b) *when there are two points of intersection, find the length of the chord between them*
Round answers to the nearest tenth, if necessary.
10. $y = −x + 5$ and $(x + 2)^2 + (y − 3)^2 = 8$
11. $y = x − 4$ and $(x − 2)^2 + (y + 4)^2 = 12$

12. Find the exact length of a tangent to the circle $(x + 1)^2 + (y + 2)^2 = 20$ from point P(5, 0).

Solve each triangle. Round answers to the nearest tenth, if necessary.
13. In △JKL, ∠K = 125°, ∠L = 21°, $l = 8$ cm
14. In △ABC, ∠A = 43.5°, $b = 12.5$ cm, $c = 10.8$ cm

15. Child's swing A swing seat is suspended from a horizontal bar by two 1.7-m chains. A father, standing directly behind the swing seat, pushes his child on the swing seat. When the father looks up at the bar to where the chains are attached, the angle of elevation is 40°, and his eyes are 2.2 m from where the chains are attached to the bar. What possible horizontal distance(s), to the nearest tenth of a metre, could the swing seat be from the father when it is at his eye level?

CHAPTER 9

Personal Finance

From 1759 to 1858, the official money in British North America consisted of British pounds, shillings, and pence. In 1858, the decision was made to change to the decimal system, already in use in the United States, and the dollar replaced the pound.

The graph shows the approximate value of one Canadian dollar in US funds for its first 100 years.

1. What event caused the Canadian dollar to climb to US$1.45 in the 1860s?

2. What caused the dollar to drop from 1914 to 1920?

3. What caused the drop in 1930?

4. What caused the drop from 1935 to 1940?

5. In the first 100 years, about what percent of the time was the Canadian dollar
a) worth more than the US dollar?
b) worth less than the US dollar?
c) the same value as the US dollar?

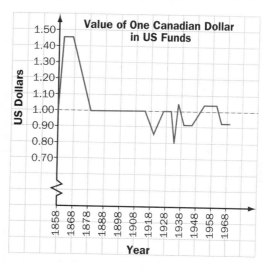

GETTING STARTED

Comparison Shopping

1 Comparing Unit Prices

Part of planning for a sound financial future is learning to spend wisely. A wise consumer shops around for the best prices. This is true, not only for major purchases such as homes and cars, but also for everyday purchases such as food.

1. a) What does the term **unit price** mean?
b) For each size of each item in the table, calculate the price of one unit.

Item	Size	Price
Olive Oil	250 mL	$3.60
	500 mL	$5.99
Tomato Ketchup	375 mL	$1.99
	1.25 L	$4.49
Orange Juice	946 mL	$1.89
	1.89 L	$3.19
Bleach	900 mL	$1.29
	1.8 L	$1.69

c) Can you make a good judgement about which size of each item is the better buy without comparing unit prices? Explain.

2. For each item, which size is the better value?

3. a) What trend do you see in the table between the unit price and the size of the item?
b) Why do you think this trend exists?

4. Give two reasons why a person might not buy the larger size of a product, even though the unit price is lower.

2 Buying at a Supermarket

The table shows the prices of the same brand of some items at three different supermarkets.

Item	Quality Store	EconoFoods	Foodmart
Bagels	$1.99 for 6	$3.99 for a family pack of 18	20¢ each
Oranges	$2.95 per dozen	10 for $2.25	25¢ each
Detergent	$7.97 for 8 L	$4.85 for 5 L	$11.49 for 10 L
Cream Cheese	$1.89 for 250 g	$1.69 for 200 g	$3.59 for 500 g

1. Which supermarket has the best buy for each item?

2. What assumptions are you making in choosing the best buy?

3. What factors, other than the price, might you consider when deciding on the best buy?

4. What factors, other than lower prices, might affect a customer's decision to choose one supermarket over another?

Warm Up

Estimate.
1. $5.85 + $3.89 + $4.12 + $25.05
2. $62.30 × 1.5
3. $8 ÷ 1.95
4. $32.29 − $4.78 − $0.97
5. $9.09 × 8.1 × 4.79
6. 0.1($7.41 + $3.82)
7. $750 − $62.81 − $56.74

Evaluate.

8. $224 × 0.1
9. $32 782 × 0.01
10. $4563 × 0.001
11. $8.46 ÷ 0.1
12. $4.48 ÷ 0.01
13. $15.62 ÷ 0.001
14. $21.50 × 1.1
15. $421 × 1.01

Express each fraction as a decimal and then as a percent.

16. $\dfrac{3}{10}$
17. $\dfrac{1}{4}$
18. $\dfrac{1}{2}$
19. $\dfrac{17}{100}$
20. $\dfrac{4}{5}$
21. $\dfrac{8}{25}$
22. $\dfrac{11}{20}$
23. $\dfrac{5}{4}$

Express each percent as a decimal.

24. 75%
25. 7%
26. $4\dfrac{1}{2}\%$
27. $2\dfrac{3}{4}\%$
28. 125%
29. 0.5%

Estimate.

30. 9% of 625
31. 61% of 3580
32. 25% of $2107
33. 65% of $4
34. 33% of $2.98
35. 26% of $19 485
36. 20% of $4221
37. 2% of $842

Determine each amount.

38. 20% more than $4044
39. 10% less than $260
40. $600 increased by 15%
41. $48 decreased by 25%
42. $\dfrac{1}{2}\%$ of $88
43. $\dfrac{1}{10}\%$ of $270

In each of the following, which is the larger percent?

44. $2 out of $20, or $3 out of $10
45. $8 out of $40, or $4 out of $24
46. $18 out of $192, or $1.20 out of $23

Mental Math

Evaluate.

1. 10% of $87.50
2. 1% of $25
3. 5% of $12
4. 3% of $16
5. 20% of $240
6. 25% of $520
7. $\dfrac{1}{2}\%$ of $300
8. 12.5% of $480
9. 7.5% of $200
10. 1.5% of $12

Express each as a percent.

11. $5.50 out of $100
12. $8 out of $50
13. $6.50 out of $50
14. $2.40 out of $48
15. $3.62 out of $3620
16. $1.90 out of $190
17. $1.20 out of $240
18. $0.50 out of $200

Multiplying Numbers That Differ by 10 and End in 5

To multiply two numbers that differ by 10 and end in 5, square their mean and subtract 25.
For 25 × 35, the mean is 30.
$30^2 = 900$
$900 − 25 = 875$
So, 25 × 35 = 875

Calculate.

1. 15 × 25
2. 45 × 55
3. 95 × 105
4. 135 × 125

To calculate 250 × 350 or 2.5 × 3.5, determine 25 × 35, and then place the decimal point.
250 × 350 = 87 500
2.5 × 3.5 = 8.75

Calculate.

5. 550 × 650
6. 850 × 750
7. 3.5 × 4.5
8. 9.5 × 8.5

9. Use algebra to explain why the above rule for multiplying numbers that differ by 10 and end in 5 works.

10. a) Modify the method to write a rule for multiplying two numbers that differ by 20 and end in 5. Test the modified method.
b) Use algebra to explain why the modified method works.

INVESTIGATING MATH

Foreign Exchange

1 Converting Currencies

To answer the following questions, use your research skills to find today's foreign exchange rates or use the rates shown in the table.

1. Michel plans to visit Greece, Sweden, Denmark, and Spain.
a) What is the name of the currency of each of these countries?
b) What is the equivalent amount to CDN$1000 in each of these currencies?

2. Patricia has saved CDN$800 to spend on a trip to Seattle, Washington. How many American dollars does she receive in exchange for her Canadian dollars?

3. While vacationing in Denver, Colorado, Jerri noticed the sale price of a car was US$25 000. How much is this in Canadian dollars?

4. Lianne inherited £25 000 sterling from a relative in Britain.
a) How much is this in Canadian dollars?
b) Lianne plans to study in Paris, France. How much is her inheritance in French francs?

5. Remo lives in Chicago, Illinois. He is planning to visit Whistler, British Columbia, and is researching the cost of accommodation. He finds that hotels can vary from CDN$90 to CDN$350 each night. Remo wants to stay for five nights, and has saved US$500 for accommodation. What is the highest price he can afford to pay per night, in Canadian dollars?

6. Judy is planning a trip to Japan in four years time. She is saving regularly and has estimated the cost of transportation, food, and accommodation, in Canadian dollars. Can she rely on the estimates? Explain.

7. Lief is planning a visit to Venezuela and Argentina.
a) Express CDN$100 in the currency of each country.
b) If Lief has 3500 bolivars left when he leaves Venezuela, about how many pesos will he receive in exchange for them in Argentina?

Foreign Exchange Rates

Country	Currency	Canadian Dollars Per Unit
Argentina	Peso	1.5269
Britain	Pound sterling	2.5517
Denmark	Krone	0.2309
France	Franc	0.2621
Germany	Mark	0.8794
Greece	Drachma	0.0051
Spain	Peseta	0.0104
Sweden	Krona	0.1923
United States	Dollar	1.5257
Venezuela	Bolivar	0.0026

2 Buying and Selling

1. Carli was organizing a trip to Berlin, Germany. When she asked for the exchange rate for the German mark, the bank representative asked her, "Are you buying or selling German marks?" Explain the significance of the question.

2. Peter lives in Lethbridge, Alberta, and went on a shopping trip to Great Falls, Montana. That day, the stores in Great Falls were accepting Canadian currency at an exchange rate of 68%. The same day, Connie travelled from Portland, Oregon, to Victoria, British Columbia, and was offered an exchange rate of 140% on her American dollars. Explain how these two rates occur.

3. One day, the value of the Canadian dollar was US$0.67. Two weeks later, the value of the Canadian dollar rose to US$0.69. How did this change affect
a) the price of Canadian goods being exported to the United States?
b) the price of American goods being imported into Canada?

9.1 Earning Income

British North America adopted its own decimal system of coinage in 1858. The coins of the Province of Canada, formed in the 1841 union of Upper Canada and Lower Canada, consisted of silver 5¢, 10¢, and 20¢ pieces, and bronze cents. All of these coins became legal tender in the Dominion of Canada after Confederation. In 1937, a completely new set of coinage was introduced, with designs closely resembling those used today.

Explore: Interpret the Graph

The bar graph shows the average cash income for Canadian households, in each province, for one year.

a) In which province was the average cash income the least? the greatest?

b) In which provinces did the average cash income exceed the average Canadian cash income?

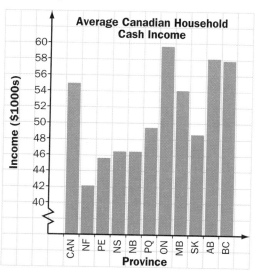

Inquire

📙 **1.** Why are average incomes in some provinces lower than in others?

📙 **2.** Does a lower income represent a lower standard of living? Explain.

🌎 **3. a)** Use your research skills to find the latest figures for the average cash income for Canadian households by province.

b) Use your data to draw a bar graph similar to the one shown.

📙 **c)** Compare your bar graph with the one shown. Write a description of the similarities and the differences in the two graphs.

Gross income is the amount of money earned through employment. There are various methods of calculating an employee's gross income. Some positions have an annual salary, while others have an hourly rate of pay. Most sales positions have some form of commission built into the employee's payment scheme.

Example 1   Earning an Hourly Rate

Suhanna, a financial assistant, is paid $15.50/h for a 37.5-h week. She is paid time-and-a-half for overtime. One week she worked 45 h. What was her gross income for the week?

Solution

Total number of hours worked in the week = 45
Regular number of hours in the week = 37.5
Number of hours of overtime = 45 − 37.5
$$= 7.5$$
Number of regular hours equivalent to overtime hours = 1.5×7.5
$$= 11.25$$

Total number of regular hours is $37.5 + 11.25 = 48.75$
Hourly rate of pay is $15.50.
Gross income = total number of hours worked × hourly rate of pay
$$= 48.75 \times \$15.50$$
$$= \$755.63$$

Estimate
$50 \times 15 = 750$

Suhanna's gross income for the week was $755.63.

Many employees in restaurants earn an hourly wage plus tips or gratuities. Often, the employees who wait on tables are required to give part of their tips to those employees who do not earn tips directly.

Example 2   Earning Gratuities

Tom has a choice of two restaurants at which to work. At Plato's, he will be paid $8/h, and tips average $25 per day. At Donalda's, he will be paid $7.25/h and receive tips averaging $40 daily, but 25% of tips are given to the kitchen staff. If Tom works 35 h per week, spread over 5 days, how much can he expect to earn at each restaurant?

Solution

At Plato's:
Gross Income = pay for regular hours + tips
$$= 35 \times \$8 + 5 \times \$25$$
$$= \$405$$

Estimate
$30 \times 10 + 125 = 425$

At Donalda's:
Gross Income = pay for regular hours + 75% of tips
$$= 35 \times \$7.25 + 0.75 \times 5 \times \$40$$
$$= \$403.75$$

Estimate
$40 \times 7 + 150 = 430$

Tom can expect to earn $405 at Plato's restaurant and $403.75 at Donalda's.

Many sales positions involve commission as an incentive for the salesperson. Some salespeople receive **straight commission**, that is, they receive a percent of the total value of their sales but no salary. Other salespeople receive a **salary and commission**. Some sales positions pay commission only on sales above a predetermined **sales quota**, which is a set amount sometimes called their sales base. As a further incentive, some sales positions involve **graduated commission**, where the rate of commission increases as the sales increase.

Example 3   Earning Commission

Rajan, Eric, and Lucy are all sales representatives, but they are paid in different ways. Rajan is paid straight commission of 5% of his total sales. Eric is paid a base salary of $250 a week, plus 2% commission on sales above his sales quota of $5000. Lucy is paid graduated commission of 2.5% on sales up to $3000, plus 6% on sales in excess of $3000. If each person's sales for one week are $12 000, what is each person's gross income?

Solution

Rajan:
Total sales are $12 000.

$$\text{Gross Income} = 5\% \text{ of } \$12\ 000$$
$$= 0.05 \times \$12\ 000$$
$$= \$600$$

Eric:
Total sales are $12 000.
Eric is paid commission on sales above his sales quota of $5000, so he earns commission on $12 000 − $5000, or $7000.

$$\text{Gross Income} = \text{Salary} + \text{Commission}$$
$$= \$250 + 2\% \text{ of } \$7000$$
$$= \$250 + 0.02 \times \$7000$$
$$= \$390$$

Lucy:
Total sales are $12 000.
Her sales in excess of $3000 are $9000.

$$\text{Gross Income} = 2.5\% \text{ of } \$3000 + 6\% \text{ of } \$9000$$
$$= 0.025 \times \$3000 + 0.06 \times \$9000$$
$$= \$615$$

Rajan's gross income is $600, Eric's gross income is $390, and Lucy's gross income is $615.

Employees in some situations are paid for each item they produce or each service they provide. This method of earning income is called **piecework.**

Example 4   Earning Income by Piecework

Tanya works at a service station, cleaning cars. She is paid $22 per car and cleans an average of 6 cars each day. If she works 5 days per week, what is her average gross income for one week?

Solution

Tanya cleans, on average, 6 cars a day.
She works 5 days a week.
Average number of cars cleaned in one week $= 6 \times 5$
$$= 30$$
Tanya is paid $22 per car.
Gross Income $= 30 \times \$22$
$$= \$660$$
Tanya's average gross income for one week is $660.

Practice

Round answers to 2 decimal places, where necessary.

Overtime is calculated at time-and-a-half. How many regular hours are equivalent to each number of overtime hours?

1. 10   **2.** 6   **3.** 15
4. 19   **5.** 3.5   **6.** 12.5

7. Reiko's gross annual income is $43 680.
a) What is her gross monthly income?
b) What is her gross weekly income?
c) What is her hourly rate of pay, if she works 35 h each week?

8. Raymond is paid $9/h, plus time-and-a-half for overtime on hours in excess of 40 h each week. If he worked 50 h last week, what was his gross income for the week?

Find the gross weekly income for each restaurant employee.
9. Gabriella works 40 h per week at $9/h. Her tips average $200 per week.
10. Chas works six 5-h shifts per week. He is paid $8.80/h, and tips average $20 per shift.
11. Li works 7.5 h per day, 5 days a week. She is paid $9.90/h, and tips average $30 daily.

Find the gross monthly earnings for each of the following commissioned sales.

	Rate of Commission	Total Monthly Sales
12.	17%	$4789
13.	2.5%	$222 800
14.	34%	$5765
15.	0.05%	$720 000

16. Aziz has the option of taking a position as a computer operator at a weekly salary of $675, or working a 40-h week at $16.90/h.
a) Which option generates the greater gross weekly income?
b) How much more would he earn from this option in a year?

17. During a 2-week period, Zoraida worked 64 h at her regular hourly rate and 3 h of overtime at time-and-a-half. On the weekend, she worked 16 h at double time. If Zoraida's regular hourly rate is $22/h, calculate her gross income for the 2-week period.

18. April is self-employed and teaches piano at $15 per half-hour lesson. She has 26 students who take one lesson each week, and she teaches 40 weeks each year. What is her gross income for the year?

19. Nirmala sells photography equipment and earns a salary plus commission. She is paid $14.85/h, plus 15% commission on total sales. Last week, she worked 35 h and sold $4800 worth of equipment. Calculate Nirmala's gross earnings for the week.

Applications and Problem Solving

20. Pay raise Chet is guaranteed 40 h of work each week. His hourly rate is $17.50. If he is awarded a 3% pay increase on the first anniversary of his employment, by what amount will his gross salary increase for a 2-week period?

21. Waiting tables Bonnie is a waitress and is paid $8.25/h for a 35-h week. She receives 15% of the total tips earned by all the staff. Last week, the tips totalled $1569. What was her gross income for that week?

22. Home business Louis weaves upholstery fabric in his home. Each week, he is paid $250 to weave 50 m of fabric. For every metre in excess of 50 m, he is paid $7.50. One week, Louis produced 73 m of fabric. What were his gross weekly earnings?

23. Computer sales Elmo sells computer equipment and is paid a base salary of $500, plus 4% on sales above his quota of $5000. If he sells $7200 of computer equipment in one week, what is his gross income for the week?

24. Financial services Nadia is a sales representative in a financial planning services company. She earns 12% on her first $3000 of sales, 15% on the next $2000, and 19% on all other sales. In December, she sold $15 850 worth of products and services. What was Nadia's gross monthly income if, in addition to the regular commission, the manager included a 2% bonus on total sales?

25. Delivering pizzas Myrna delivers pizzas. She works 3 days each week and is paid $2 for each delivery.
a) Would you describe her method of payment as a salary, an hourly rate of pay, commission, or piecework? Explain.
b) If she delivers 235 pizzas in one week, what is her gross income for that week?
c) By what other method does a pizza delivery person receive income for delivering pizzas?

26. Magazine sales Adriana sold magazine subscriptions worth $243 and received $36.45 in straight commission. What rate of commission was she paid?

27. Keyboarding Anton is offered a part-time job keying documents at a law firm. He is given two payment options.
Option A: $2.15 per page (Anton averages 120 pages per week.)
Option B: $345 per week
a) What is the difference in the gross weekly income earned for each option?
b) What are the advantages and the disadvantages of each method of payment?

28. Retail clothing Liam works in the retail business, selling men's clothing. He earns a monthly base salary of $2000, plus 6.5% commission on his total sales. His total sales for each of the last four months were $3000, $2885, $5088, and $5227.
a) Find his gross monthly earnings for each of the four months.
b) Draw a bar graph to show his earnings for the four months.

29. Advertising sales The Zinger Advertising Company has three plans for paying its sales representatives each month.
Plan A: $750, plus 15% commission on all sales
Plan B: 20% on sales up to $5000, 25% on sales from $5000 up to $10 000, 30% on sales of $10 000 and over
Plan C: 25% straight commission on all sales
a) Calculate the gross monthly income on sales of $12 500 using each of the plans.
b) On the same set of axes, draw a line graph to show gross income versus sales, for sales up to $15 000 in one month, for each plan.
c) At what value in sales does Plan B begin to pay the highest gross income?

9.2 Net Income

Tax Freedom Day is the day of the year on which Canadians start to work for themselves. Until that day, gross earnings are equal to the amount paid out in taxes to the federal, provincial, and municipal governments. Some of the taxes, such as income tax, sales tax, and property tax, are very visible. Other taxes are hidden in the price of certain consumer products, such as gasoline. Tax Freedom Day varies in different provinces because provincial tax rates vary.

Explore: Use a Table

The table shows the Tax Freedom Day for each province in one year.

For Newfoundland, Tax Freedom Day was June 8. From January 1 to June 7, there are 158 days, which is 43.3% of the 365 days in the year. Thus, the average household in Newfoundland spent 43.3% of its gross income on federal, provincial, and municipal taxes.

a) Which province had the highest taxes?

b) How did your province rank?

Province	Tax Freedom Day
British Columbia	June 30
Alberta	June 12
Saskatchewan	June 17
Manitoba	June 23
Ontario	June 26
Quebec	June 24
New Brunswick	June 18
Nova Scotia	June 9
Prince Edward Island	May 28
Newfoundland	June 8

Inquire

1. What percent of gross income did the Tax Freedom Day represent for Alberta? for British Columbia?

2. For the year shown, the average Canadian household income was $56 322, and the average amount paid out in taxes was $27 017. What was Tax Freedom Day for Canada that year?

3. Use your research skills to find the current Tax Freedom Day data. What is the current Tax Freedom Day for your province? If you earn a gross income of $40 000, about how much can you expect to spend on all types of taxation?

As well as income tax, there are two other statutory deductions that employers must withhold from their employees' gross income. These are the employee contributions to the Canada Pension Plan (CPP) and to Employment Insurance (EI). Some employees also have deductions for a registered pension plan, union or professional fees, and health insurance plans. All payroll deductions are shown on the employee's pay slip. The net amount, after all deductions are subtracted from the gross income, is the amount that the employee actually receives as **net income**.

WEEK END	EMPLOYEE SIN	REGULAR EARNINGS	OVERTIME EARNINGS	GROSS PAY
Aug 31	321 654 987	323.75	37.00	360.75

DEDUCTIONS

Description	Current	Year to Date
CPP	11.54	356.83
EI	9.74	311.04
Income Tax	79.20	2535.20

TOTAL DEDUCTIONS	100.48		**NET PAY**	260.27

The **Canada Pension Plan** (CPP) contribution is money that the government collects toward an employee's future pension. When the employee reaches the qualifying age, the government guarantees a minimum income based on the person's contributions to the plan. One year, the CPP contributions were 3.2% of gross income between $3500.01 and $36 900. The first $3500 of a person's income is the **basic CPP exemption** and is not subject to CPP contributions.

Employment Insurance (EI) is an insurance plan, supported by employee and employer premiums, and by federal government contributions. If employees have paid the minimum number of required premiums, then the plan provides some income during periods of unemployment. One year, the EI premiums were 2.7% of gross income, up to a maximum premium of $1053.

Example 1 Calculating CPP and EI
Roman's gross income is $925 biweekly. Calculate his CPP contribution and his EI premium for each pay period.

Solution

Gross Annual Income = $26 \times \$925$

$\qquad\qquad\qquad = \$24\,050$

Biweekly means every two weeks.

Estimate

$30 \times 900 = 27\,000$

Canada Pension Plan (CPP) contribution:

Contributory earnings = Gross Annual Income – Basic CPP Exemption

$\qquad\qquad\qquad = \$24\,050 - \$3500$

$\qquad\qquad\qquad = \$20\,550$

Annual CPP contribution = 3.2% of $20 550

$\qquad\qquad\qquad = 0.032 \times \$20\,550$

$\qquad\qquad\qquad = \$657.60$

Estimate

$0.03 \times 20\,000 = 600$

Biweekly CPP contribution = $657.60 \div 26$

$\qquad\qquad\qquad = \$25.29$

Estimate

$660 \div 30 = 22$

Employment Insurance (EI) premium:

Biweekly EI premium = 2.7% of $925

$\qquad\qquad\qquad = 0.027 \times \$925$

$\qquad\qquad\qquad = \$24.98$

Estimate

$0.03 \times 900 = 27$

Roman's biweekly CPP contribution is $25.29, and his EI premium is $24.98.

The amount of income tax deducted from an employee's gross pay depends on the employee's income and tax credits. Employees must pay two levels of income tax, federal and provincial. The rates for one year are shown in the tables.

Federal Tax Table		
Annual Taxable Income		
Over	Not Over	Tax Rate
$0	$29 590	17%
$29 590	$59 180	26%
$59 180		29%

Provincial Tax Table	
Province	Provincial Tax Rate*
British Columbia	50.5% of basic federal tax
Alberta	45.5% of basic federal tax
Saskatchewan	50% of basic federal tax
Manitoba	52% of basic federal tax

*Some provinces charge provincial surtaxes, but the percents shown provide reasonable estimates of provincial tax rates.

Taxable income is gross income minus any **tax-exempt deductions**: union or professional dues, Registered Pension Plan (RPP) contributions, Registered Retirement Savings Plan (RRSP) contributions, and child care expenses.

Basic personal tax credits are deductions granted for each person that the employee supports.

Several steps are needed to find an employee's federal and provincial taxes. The following is an outline of how to determine these amounts.

Step 1: Calculate the person's tax credits.
Tax credits = basic personal tax credit + CPP contribution + EI premium

Step 2: Find the person's annual taxable income.
Annual taxable income = gross annual income – tax-exempt deductions

Step 3: Determine the person's basic federal tax, using the rates given in the Federal Tax Table. Then, use the basic federal tax to calculate the provincial tax, using the rates given in the Provincial Tax Table.
Basic Federal Tax = Federal tax on taxable income – 17% of tax credits

The employee's net annual income can be found by deducting CPP contributions, EI premiums, federal and provincial income tax, and all other voluntary deductions from the employee's gross annual income.

Example 2   Calculating Net Annual Income

Dina lives and works in Calgary. Her annual salary is $35 000. Her basic personal tax credit is $6456. Each week she has the following tax-exempt deductions taken from her gross income: $5.50 for professional dues and $60 to a Registered Retirement Savings Plan. She also has $8 per week deducted for medical insurance.

a) Calculate Dina's annual deductions for CPP and EI.
b) Find the total amount of income tax that Dina will have deducted in a year.
c) Determine her net annual income.

Solution

a) *CPP contribution:*
Contributory earnings = gross annual income − basic CPP exemption
$$= \$35\ 000 - \$3500$$
$$= \$31\ 500$$
Annual CPP contribution = 3.2% of \$31 500
$$= 0.032 \times \$31\ 500$$
$$= \$1008$$

> **Estimate**
> $0.03 \times 30\ 000 = 900$

EI premium:
Annual EI premium = 2.7% of \$35 000
$$= 0.027 \times \$35\ 000$$
$$= \$945$$
Dina's annual deduction for CPP is \$1008 and for EI is \$945.

b) *Annual Taxable Income:*
Annual taxable income = gross annual income − tax-exempt deductions
$$= \$35\ 000 - 52(\$60 + \$5.50)$$
$$= \$31\ 594$$

> **Estimate**
> $35\ 000 - 50 \times 70 = 31\ 500$

Federal Tax:
Using the Federal Tax Table,
Federal tax = 17% of \$29 590 + 26% of (\$31 594 − \$29 590)
$$= 0.17 \times \$29\ 590 + 0.26 \times \$2004$$
$$= \$5551.34$$

> **Estimate**
> $0.2 \times 30\ 000 + 0.25 \times 2000 = 6500$

Tax credits = basic personal tax credit + CPP contribution + EI premium
$$= \$6456 + \$1008 + \$945$$
$$= \$8409$$
Basic federal tax = federal tax − 17% of tax credits
$$= \$5551.34 - 0.17 \times \$8409$$
$$= \$4121.81$$

> **Estimate**
> $5600 - 0.2 \times 8000 = 4000$

Alberta Provincial Tax:
Provincial tax = 45.5% of basic federal tax
$$= 0.455 \times \$4121.81$$
$$= \$1875.42$$

> **Estimate**
> $0.5 \times 4000 = 2000$

Total income tax = basic federal tax + provincial tax
$$= \$4121.81 + \$1875.42$$
$$= \$5997.23$$
Dina will have a total of \$5997.23 deducted for income tax in a year.

c) Total deductions = CPP + EI + income tax + tax-exempt deductions + any other deductions
$$= \$1008 + \$945 + \$5997.23 + 52(\$5.50 + \$60 + \$8)$$
$$= \$11\ 772.73$$

> **Estimate**
> $8000 + 50 \times 70 = 11\ 500$

Net annual income = gross annual income − total deductions
$$= \$35\ 000.00 - \$11\ 772.73$$
$$= \$23\ 227.27$$
Dina's net annual income is \$23 227.27.

Practice

Use the rates given on pages 533 and 534 for CPP, EI, and income tax calculations, or use your research skills to find the current rates. Round answers to 2 decimal places, where necessary.

How many pay periods are there per year for an employee paid at each of the following time intervals?
1. weekly
2. monthly
3. biweekly
4. semi-monthly

For questions 5 to 11, find the employee's Canada Pension Plan contribution that is required for each pay period.
5. Corinne is paid $1305 semi-monthly.
6. Kostas earns $586 each week.
7. Atholl is paid $2267 monthly.
8. Greg is paid $1856 every two weeks.
9. Paul is paid $11.25/h and works 38 h per week. He is paid weekly.
10. Mara's annual income is $34 000. She is paid semi-monthly.

For questions 11 to 16, find the employee's Employment Insurance premium for each pay period.
11. Todd is paid $408 per week.
12. Shai earns $28 650 per year and is paid biweekly.
13. Barb is paid $2175 per month.
14. Helga earns a salary of $39 000 and is paid semi-monthly.
15. Raj is paid $18/h and works a 38 h week with no overtime. He is paid weekly.
16. Daniel earns $18.70/h and works a 37.5-h week with no overtime. He is paid biweekly.

Use the Federal Tax Table to find the federal tax for each employee.
17. Steve has an annual taxable income of $26 800.
18. Martine's annual taxable income is $18 305.
19. Jose has an annual taxable income of $32 138.
20. Carmen's annual taxable income is $48 220.
21. Jackie's annual taxable income is $65 160.

Find the provincial tax payable by each employee.
22. Paul lives in Alberta and his basic federal tax is $3620.50.
23. Ellen lives in British Columbia. Her basic federal tax is $2815.17.
24. Leah lives in Manitoba, and her basic federal tax is $4907.36.
25. Mohammed lives in Saskatchewan, and his basic federal tax is $3015.89.
26. Heather lives in Alberta. Her basic federal tax is $1987.56.

For questions 27 and 28, find the annual deductions for CPP and EI, the taxable income, and the basic federal tax for each employee.
27. Kerri earns a monthly income of $3500. She pays monthly union dues of $25.50 and has a monthly RRSP contribution of $200 deducted from her pay. Her basic personal tax credit is $6456.
28. Jack is paid $1150 every two weeks. His basic personal tax credits are $8809.

Applications and Problem Solving

29. Ski instructor Sonya works in Whistler, British Columbia, as a ski instructor, and is paid $2625 every month. Her basic personal tax credit is $6456.
a) Calculate Sonya's annual deductions for CPP and EI.
b) Determine her total amount of income tax.

30. Marcus works in Winnipeg and has a semi-monthly gross income of $1950. His basic personal tax credit is $6456. He pays 2% of his gross income into a registered pension plan.
a) Calculate his annual deductions for CPP and EI.
b) Determine his total amount of income tax.
c) Find his net annual income.

31. Oil engineer Carla is an engineer and works for a large oil company in Alberta. She has a basic personal tax credit of $6456. Her gross income is $4818.21 per month. She has professional dues of $57, registered pension plan contributions of $500, and $23 for a health insurance plan deducted from her gross income each month. Calculate her net annual income.

32. Bernice lives in Saskatoon. Her basic personal tax credit is $6456. Her biweekly gross income is $1554. Each pay period, $17 in union dues and $60 for a Registered Retirement Savings Plan are deducted from her earnings. What is her net annual income?

33. Computer sales Felix is a sales representative for a computer store in Vancouver. His gross monthly earnings are $1250, plus 10% commission on any sales above his monthly sales quota of $35 000. His sales average $52 300 per month.
a) Calculate his gross income for an average month.
b) If his basic personal tax credits are $11 836, and he contributes 2% of his gross earnings to a registered pension plan, determine his net annual income.

34. For each employee, employers must pay a matching contribution to the CPP and 1.4 times the employee's EI premium. These amounts are not deductions from employees' earnings.
a) Where does the money come from?
b) Why does the government require employers to pay these contributions?
c) Do you think these contributions and premiums are taken into account when an employer presents a wage or salary package to a potential employee? Explain.

35. Canada Pension Plan In 1998, the Canada Pension Plan contribution was 3.2% of gross earnings between $3500.01 and $36 900. The federal government plans to increase the contribution rate gradually to a total of 10.1% from the employee and employer by the year 2016.
a) For an annual gross salary of $35 000, how much more will the employee's CPP contribution be in 2016 than in 1998?
b) Suggest reasons why the government might feel that increases to CPP deductions are necessary.

36. Use your research skills to investigate the tables used by the payroll department of a company.
a) What is a net claim code?
b) How are net claim codes assigned?
c) When might a 0 net claim code be assigned?

37. Employment Insurance Find out how a person goes about collecting employment insurance benefits after becoming unemployed.
a) What is the procedure?
b) What criteria must be satisfied to be eligible?
c) How much money can a person expect to receive each week?
d) For how long can an unemployed person receive these payments?

38. Income tax Draw a graph showing the total amount of income tax deducted versus taxable income in a year. Use taxable incomes of up to $75 000 and your provincial tax rate. Assume only CPP contributions and EI premiums are deducted from the gross income, and that the basic personal tax credit of $6456 applies.

LOGIC POWER

The diagram represents 16 flower beds in a botanical garden and the grass-covered paths that run between them. The paths are all the same width, and the path along one side of each flower bed is 20 m long.

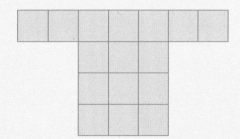

Tabitha uses a lawn tractor to cut the grass on the paths once a week.
1. Copy the diagram and use it to find the route that Tabitha should follow to travel the shortest possible distance when she cuts the grass. She may have to travel along some paths more than once.
2. Find the shortest distance she can travel.

9.3 Interest and Annuities

Paying interest on money borrowed, and earning interest on money invested, has been going on for thousands of years. Interest rates have varied. Around 1800 B.C., Hammurabi, King of Babylonia, developed a system of laws known as the Code of Hammurabi. The code dealt with many matters, including interest rates that could be charged. The code permitted a maximum interest rate of 33% per year for loans of grain and 20% per year for loans of silver. In twelfth century England, people with the best credit paid 50% per year for loans.

The formula for **simple interest** is $I = Prt$, where I is the interest, P is the principal, r is the annual rate of interest, and t is the time in years. Interest paid at regular intervals and added to the principal for the next interest period is called **compound interest**.

Explore: Use a Table

Serena invests $1000 in a one-year Guaranteed Investment Certificate (GIC) that pays interest at 5.5% per annum. The amount of the GIC at the end of the year is the total of the principal and interest. At the end of each year, Serena reinvests the amount of the GIC at the same rate. Copy and complete the table to show the growth of the $1000 GIC over a 6-year period.

Year	Principal ($) (at the beginning of the year)	Interest Rate (%)	Amount ($) (at the end of the year)
1	1000.00	5.5	1055.00
2	1055.00	5.5	1113.03
3		5.5	
4		5.5	
5		5.5	
6		5.5	

Inquire

1. What is the total amount of interest earned on Serena's GIC in 6 years?

2. If the $1000 had earned simple interest for 6 years at 5.5% per annum, how much interest would it have earned?

3. Compare the simple interest on Serena's $1000 over 6 years with the compound interest on Serena's $1000 over 6 years. Describe situations in which people might prefer simple interest to compound interest.

4. If you had borrowed $100 in twelfth century England, and paid the loan back after 4 years, how much would you have paid if the interest was
a) simple?   **b)** compounded annually?

Two kinds of Canada Savings Bonds are regular Canada Savings Bonds and compound Canada Savings Bonds. Regular Canada Savings Bonds earn simple interest. Each year the interest is deposited into the owner's bank account or mailed to the owner. Compound Canada Savings Bonds earn compound interest. The whole amount of the bond is paid when it is cashed.

Consider the growth of one $500 Canada Savings Bonds of each type, with interest at 6%, over a 5-year period. The simple interest formula can be used to find the value of each bond at the end of each year. A graph of the data from the tables shows that the regular savings bond is growing in a linear pattern, whereas the compound savings bond is growing more quickly, in the pattern of an exponential function.

	Regular Savings Bond				Compound Savings Bond		
Year	P ($)	I ($)	A ($)	Year	P ($)	I ($)	A ($)
1	500	30	530	1	500	30	530
2	500	60	560	2	530	31.80	561.80
3	500	90	590	3	561.80	33.71	595.51
4	500	120	620	4	595.51	35.73	631.24
5	500	150	650	5	631.24	37.87	669.11
6	500	180	680	6	669.11	40.15	709.26
7	500	210	710	7	709.26	42.56	751.82
8	500	240	740	8	751.82	45.11	796.92

$I = Prt$
$= 500 \times 0.06 \times 2$
$= 60$

$\leftarrow I = Prt$
$= 530 \times 0.06 \times 1$
$= 31.80$

The formula for compound interest is
$$A = P(1 + i)^n$$
where A is the amount, P is the principal, i is the rate of interest per compounding period, and n is the number of compounding periods. The interest rate per period, i, is found by dividing the annual rate by the number of compounding periods per year.

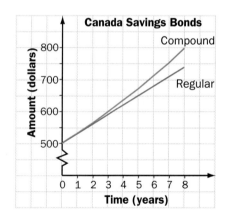

Canada Savings Bonds

Compounding Period	Number of Periods in one Year	Interest Rate for the Period (where r is the annual interest rate)
semi-annually	2	$\dfrac{r}{2}$
quarterly	4	$\dfrac{r}{4}$
monthly	12	$\dfrac{r}{12}$
daily	365	$\dfrac{r}{365}$

Example 1 Calculating Compound Interest

Lloyd arranged a personal loan of $2500 at 10.75% per annum compounded quarterly. He made no payments for 2 years.

a) What was the amount owing on the loan at the end of 2 years?

b) How much interest was Lloyd charged for the 2 years?

Solution

a) $P = \$2500$

$i = \dfrac{10.75\%}{4}$, since there are four interest periods per year.

$n = 8$, since there are 4×2 interest periods in 2 years.

$A = P(1 + i)^n$

$= 2500\left(1 + \dfrac{0.1075}{4}\right)^8$

$= 3090.87$

The amount owing after 2 years was $3090.87.

b) Interest = Amount − Principal

$\qquad = \$3090.87 - \$2500$

$\qquad = \$590.87$

Lloyd was charged $590.87 interest for the 2 years.

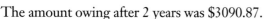

Example 2 Comparing Amounts with Different Compounding Periods

Tara has $1000 to invest. The current rate of interest is 4% per annum. Calculate the amount at the end of the year for Option A: compounding annually, Option B: compounding monthly, and Option C: compounding daily.

Solution

Option A: $P = \$1000$, $i = 4\%$, $n = 1$

$A = P(1 + i)^n$

$A = 1000(1 + 0.04)^1$

$\quad = 1000(1.04)$

$\quad = 1040$

Option B: $P = \$1000$, $i = \dfrac{4\%}{12}$, $n = 12$

$A = P(1 + i)^n$

$= 1000\left(1 + \dfrac{0.04}{12}\right)^{12}$

$= 1040.74$

Option C: $P = \$1000$, $i = \dfrac{4\%}{365}$, $n = 365$

$A = P(1 + i)^n$

$= 1000\left(1 + \dfrac{0.04}{365}\right)^{365}$

$= 1040.81$

The amount at the end of one year is $1040.00 with interest compounding annually, $1040.74 with interest compounding monthly, and $1040.81 with interest compounding daily.

Registered Retirement Savings Plans (RRSPs) are designed to help people save for their retirement. Many people choose to invest in RRSPs because these plans provide a method of deferring some of the taxes on income. The principal invested in an RRSP, and the interest earned on it, is only taxable when it is withdrawn. Many different types of investments are available within RRSPs. Guaranteed funds pay a fixed rate of interest for an agreed term. Other types of investments, such as mutual funds, earn variable rates of interest.

Example 3   Comparing RRSP Investments

By the end of his first year working full time, George had saved $2000. He decided to invest the money in an RRSP. He chose to invest in a 5-year guaranteed fund. Bank A offered an interest rate of 8% per annum, compounded quarterly, for the 5-year term. For the same term, Bank B offered 8.5% compounded annually. At which bank would George's RRSP investment earn more interest? How much more?

Solution

Bank A: $P = \$2000$, $i = \dfrac{8\%}{4}$, $n = 20$

$A = P(1 + i)^n$
$= 2000(1 + 0.02)^{20}$
$= 2971.89$

Interest = Amount − Principal
$= \$2971.89 - \$2000$
$= \$971.89$

At Bank A, George's $2000 RRSP investment would earn $971.89 interest by the end of the 5-year term.

Bank B: $P = \$2000$, $i = 8.5\%$, $n = 5$
$A = P(1 + i)^n$
$= 2000(1 + 0.085)^5$
$= 3007.31$

Interest = Amount − Principal
$= \$3007.31 - \$2000$
$= \$1007.31$

At Bank B, George's $2000 RRSP investment would earn $1007.31 interest by the end of the 5-year term.

$\$1007.31 - \$971.89 = \$35.42$

So, George's RRSP investment would earn $35.42 more interest at Bank B.

An **annuity** is a sequence of equal payments made at equal intervals of time. For example, if you deposit $100 each month into an RRSP plan, you are saving in the form of an annuity. If you pay a car loan off at $250 each month for 36 months, you are paying an annuity. If you receive $3500 from an investment every 6 months for 10 years, you are receiving an annuity.

Example 4 Calculating the Amount of an Annuity

Stephanie wants to buy a car when she graduates from college. She decides to deposit $750 on October 15, and additional $750 amounts on the 15th of the following April, October, and April, into a savings account that pays 5% per annum compounded semi-annually. What amount will Stephanie have in her account at the end of two years?

Solution 1

Consider each deposit separately and use the compound-interest formula.

The interest rate per 6-month period is $\dfrac{5\%}{2}$ or 2.5%.

First $750, compounded semi-annually, after 2 years:
$A = P(1 + i)^n$, where $P = \$750, i = 0.025, n = 4$
$= 750(1 + 0.025)^4$
$= 827.86$

Second $750, compounded semi-annually, after 1.5 years:
$A = P(1 + i)^n$, where $P = \$750, i = 0.025, n = 3$
$= 750(1.025)^3$
$= 807.67$

Third $750, compounded semi-annually, after 1 year:
$A = P(1 + i)^n$, where $P = \$750, i = 0.025, n = 2$
$= 750(1.025)^2$
$= 787.97$

Fourth $750, compounded semi-annually, after 0.5 years:
$A = P(1 + i)^n$, where $P = \$750, i = 0.025, n = 1$
$= 750(1.025)^1$
$= 768.75$

The total amount at the end of two years is $827.86 + \$807.67 + \$787.97 + \$768.75 = \$3192.25$
Stephanie will have $3192.25 in her account at the end of two years.

Solution 2

Use a table or spreadsheet and the simple-interest formula for each 6-month period.

6-Month Period	Principal, P ($)	Interest, I ($)	Amount, A ($)
1	750	18.75	768.75
2	768.75 + 750	37.97	1556.72
3	1556.72 + 750	57.67	2364.39
4	2364.39 + 750	77.86	3192.25

Stephanie will have $3192.25 in her account at the end of two years.

Practice

The rate of interest is 8% per annum. What is the interest rate for each compounding period?
1. semi-annually
2. quarterly
3. monthly
4. daily

How many interest periods are there in each of the following?
5. compounding semi-annually for 3 years
6. compounding quarterly for 2 years
7. compounding annually for 5 years
8. compounding monthly for 4 years
9. compounding monthly for 6 months
10. compounding quarterly for 18 months
11. compounding daily for the month of August
12. compounding daily for March and April

If the rate of interest is 6% per annum, what is the interest rate per period and the number of periods in each situation?

13. compounding quarterly for 3 years
14. compounding semi-annually for 6 years
15. compounding annually for 10 years
16. compounding monthly for one year
17. compounding daily for the month of June

The rate of interest is 9% per annum. Find the amount owing on a loan of $2000 in each case.

18. interest compounded semi-annually for 3 years
19. interest compounded quarterly for 2 years
20. interest compounded annually for 5 years
21. interest compounded daily for 60 days

The rate of interest is 4.5% per annum. Find the interest earned on an investment of $500 for each compound situation.

22. semi-annually for 4 years
23. monthly for 1.5 years
24. quarterly for 2.5 years
25. daily for 45 days

Find the amount of each RRSP investment.

26. $3000 at 4.5% per annum, compounded annually, for a 5-year term
27. $1800 at 5% per annum, compounded quarterly, for a 3-year term
28. $2500 at 6% per annum, compounded semi-annually, for a 2-year term

Applications and Problem Solving

29. Michel borrowed $2000 from the bank at 8.5%, compounded semi-annually. If he made no payments, find the amount owing three years later.

30. Education fund When his daughter was born, Brian invested $5000 to help provide for her education. If the investment earns an average of 8% compounded quarterly, how much will it be worth in 18 years?

31. Annuity Pierre deposited $200 into his savings account at the beginning of each month for 6 months. If the account pays interest at 3% per annum, compounded monthly, how much is in his account at the end of the sixth month?

32. RRSP Amber won $7500 and decided to invest the money in an RRSP. She put the money in a guaranteed fund for a 4-year term at 7%, compounded quarterly. At the end of that term, interest rates rose by 1%, so she re-invested the whole amount for another 4-year term, again with interest compounded quarterly. What was the value of her investment at the end of the eight years?

33. You have $1000 to invest for 3 years. Consider three options, all of which have a rate of interest of 5.5% per annum.
Option A: compounded semi-annually
Option B: compounded quarterly
Option C: compounded monthly
a) Predict which option will earn you the most interest. Explain.
b) How much more interest is earned by the best option than by the worst option?

34. Annuity Marla opened a savings account on January 1 with a deposit of $500. The following July 1, January 1, and July 1, she made three more deposits of $500 each. The account paid interest at 4.75% per annum, compounded quarterly.
a) What amount was in her account at the end of the second year?
b) How much interest had she earned by the end of the second year?

35. Functions a) Consider an investment of $100. Construct a table of values of the amount of the investment for a period of 12 years, with interest at 8% per annum calculated
• as simple interest
• with interest compounding quarterly
b) Construct broken-line graphs on the same set of axes for an investment calculated each way.
c) Do both graphs represent functions? Explain.
d) Describe each graph. Explain why each is the shape it is.

36. Working backward How much should be invested now at 8%, compounded semi-annually, to give an amount of $5000 in four years time?

37. Inflation If the average annual rate of inflation is 4%, about how long would it take for a pair of roller blades to double in price?

TECHNOLOGY

Financial Calculations Using a Graphing Calculator

Some graphing calculators have the capability of performing financial calculations.

Before starting, set the mode to show two decimal places.

Enter any four of the following five values and use the calculator to determine the fifth.
Number of payment periods
Annual interest rate, %
Present value, $
Payment, $
Future value, $

As well, enter the following two values.
Payments per year
Compounding periods per year

The three values above that are amounts of money are entered and calculated as positive values, if they represent money being received, or as negative values, if they represent money being paid. The approach used depends upon whether the situation is approached from the borrower's or the lender's point of view. The consumer can be a borrower or lender (investor).

1 No Payments Made

To determine how much money you need to invest at 5.75% per annum, compounded semi-annually, for the investment to accumulate to $8000 in 5 years, enter the following values.
Number of payment periods = 5 × 2
Annual interest rate, % = 5.75
Present value, $: to be determined
Payment, $ = 0   No payments are actually made.
Future value, $ = 8000
Payments per year = 2
Compounding periods per year = 2

```
N=10.00
I%=5.75
•PV=-6025.48
PMT=0.00
FV=8000.00
P/Y=2.00
C/Y=2.00
PMT:END BEGIN
```

The present value is –$6025.48, indicating that you need to invest $6025.48.

1. How much money must be invested today at 6.25% per annum, compounded quarterly, for the investment to accumulate to $10 000 in 10 years?

2. Adam borrows $4500 from his grandfather, to be repaid in one payment of $5500. He is paying his grandfather 3.9% per annum, compounded annually. When is Adam due to repay the loan?

3. Belinda borrows $3000, to be repaid in one payment of $3500 in 2 years. What annual rate of interest, compounded semi-annually, is she paying?

4. Gio has $500 to invest and two investment options. One is to invest at 7% per annum, compounded annually. The other is to invest at 6.75% per annum, compounded monthly. Gio wants his investment to grow to $1000 as quickly as possible. Predict which option grows to $1000 more quickly. Check your prediction, and explain the results.

2 Monthly Payments Made

1. A $15 000 loan at 6.75% per annum, compounded quarterly, is to be repaid in monthly payments of $300. To determine the amount still outstanding after 4 years, Karen enters the following values.
Number of payment periods = 4 × 12
Annual interest rate, % = 6.75
Present value, $ = 15 000
Payment, $ = −300
Future value, $: to be determined
Payments per year = 12
Compounding periods per year = 4

```
N=48.00
I%=6.75
PV=15000.00
PMT=-300.00
•FV=-3139.27
P/Y=12.00
C/Y=4.00
PMT:END BEGIN
```

The future value is −$3139.27. Is Karen's calculation correct? Does the future value she found indicate that a further $3139.27 must be paid, or that the loan has been overpaid by $3139.27? Explain how to check the reasonableness of the calculations.

2. An annuity of $25 000 earning 7.2% per annum, compounded monthly, pays $750 monthly. What is the value of the annuity after 4 years of payments?

3. Home entertainment A family wants to buy a home entertainment system for $9734, including taxes. They plan to pay for it over 3 years, making $300 monthly payments. What annual rate of interest, compounded monthly, allows them to purchase the entertainment system? Is this rate reasonable given the current rates of interest for loans? If not, what adjustments to their repayment plans could be made?

4. Wayne plans to buy a second-hand car in two and a half years. He estimates that he will need $15 000. To accumulate this amount, he plans to makes monthly payments to an investment that earns 6.5% per annum, compounded semi-annually. How much should his monthly payment be?

5. Markita invested in an annuity when she was first employed in full-time work at age 23. She invested $200 each month at 5.75% per annum, compounded monthly.
a) Calculate the value of her annuity 37 years later, when she was 60.
b) If Markita had not started her annuity until she was 35 years old, at what annual rate of interest would her $200 monthly payments have given her the same amount at age 60 as in part a)?
c) If Markita had not started her annuity until she was 35 years old, and had been able to invest at 8% per annum, compounded semi-annually, what monthly payment would have given her the same amount at age 60 as in part a)?
d) Is it advantageous to invest early? Explain.

TECHNOLOGY

Calculating Annuities Using a Spreadsheet

1 Annuity Remaining

Anita obtained a bank loan of $12 000. The bank charges interest at 11% per annum, compounded monthly. Anita is reducing her loan by making monthly payments of $400. She uses a spreadsheet to determine how much she still owes after two years of payments.

	A	B	C	D	E
1	Month	Opening Balance, $	Interest, $	Payment, $	Closing Balance, $
2	1	12000.00	=B2*.11/12	400.00	=B2+C2-D2
3	=A2+1	=E2			
4					
5					
24					
25					

1. Interpret the following parts of Anita's spreadsheet.
a) the column headings   **b)** the number of rows
c) the numerical entries   **d)** the formulas

2. Use spreadsheet software and the Fill Down feature to find how much of the annuity remains after two years of payments have been made.

3. When will Anita pay off the loan, assuming the interest rate and the payments do not change?

4. Use spreadsheet software to determine the amount remaining in each annuity after one year of equal monthly payments.
a) $40 000 with interest at 9% per annum, compounded monthly, and monthly payments of $750
b) $65 000 with interest at 8.5% per annum, compounded monthly, and monthly payments of $1150
c) $25 000 with interest at 10.5% per annum, compounded monthly, and monthly payments of $700

2 Annuity Payments

A spreadsheet can be used to determine the equal monthly payments that can be paid from an annuity for a set length of time. You can enter different payments until you find the one that gives a closing balance of less than $1 after the set length of time.

1. What equal monthly payments can be paid from each annuity?
a) $40 000 earning 8% per annum, compounded monthly, with a life of 6 years
b) $20 000 earning 10% per annum, compounded monthly, with a life of 5 years
c) $85 000 earning 9.5% per annum, compounded monthly, with a life of 8 years
d) $100 000 earning 6.5% per annum, compounded monthly, with a life of 10 years

9.4 Effective Annual Rate of Interest

The ancient Greek philosopher Theophrastus wrote of one usurer who charged an interest rate of 25% per day. Most other usurers were charging 48% a month. It remains true today that, to borrow or invest wisely, it is important to compare interest rates.

To compare different interest rates compounded over different time periods, either determine the amount from the same principal after one year, or compare the effective annual rates of interest.

The **nominal interest rate** is the "stated" or "named" rate of interest of an investment or a loan. The nominal interest rate is usually a compounded rate.

The **effective annual interest rate** is the simple interest rate that would produce the same interest in a year as the nominal interest rate.

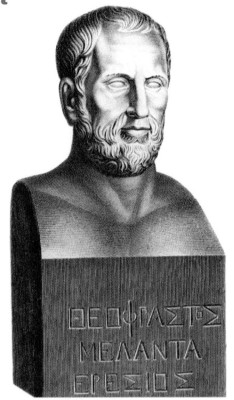

Explore: Use a Table

Copy and complete the table to find the amount at the end of one year, rounded to the nearest cent, for each $100 investment.

	Principal ($)	Nominal Annual Interest Rate (%)	Compound Period	Amount ($)
A	100	4	semi-annually	
B	100	5	quarterly	
C	100	9.76	semi-annually	
D	100	9.65	quarterly	

Inquire

1. How much interest is earned in one year for each investment?

2. For each investment, calculate the simple interest rate that would give the same amount as in the table after one year. Express each answer as a percent, to two decimal places.

3. From your answer to question 2, is it possible for investments with different nominal rates to have equal effective annual rates?

4. a) If you borrowed $100 from a usurer in ancient Greece who charged simple interest of 48% a month, how much would you owe in interest at the end of 12 months?
b) What is the effective annual interest rate for this loan?

5. a) If you borrowed $100 from the usurer in ancient Greece who charged simple interest of 25% a day, how much would you owe in interest at the end of a 365-day year?
b) What is the effective annual interest rate for this loan?

When comparing investments with different interest rates and compounded over different time periods, it is useful to compare their effective annual interest rates.

Example 1   Calculating the Effective Annual Interest Rate

What is the effective annual interest rate of an investment earning a nominal interest rate of 3.75% per annum, compounded quarterly?

Solution

Assume a principal of $100.
The number of compound periods is 4.
Interest rate for each period is $\dfrac{3.75\%}{4}$.
Amount of the investment at the end of one year is given by

$A = 100(1 + i)^n$, where $i = \dfrac{0.0375}{4}$, and $n = 4$.

$$= 100\left(1 + \dfrac{0.0375}{4}\right)^4$$

$$= 103.80$$

The amount of $100 invested at 3.75% per annum, compounded quarterly, is $103.80.

Interest = Amount − Principal
$\qquad$ = $103.80 − $100
$\qquad$ = $3.80

If the interest earned in one year on an investment of $100 is $3.80, then the simple interest rate is 3.8% per annum.
An investment earning interest at the rate of 3.75% per annum, compounded quarterly, is the same as an investment earning simple interest at the rate of 3.8% per annum.
Thus, a nominal interest rate of 3.75% per annum, compounded quarterly, is equivalent to an effective annual interest rate of 3.8%.

Example 2   Deciding on the Better Investment

Shelagh has $1000 to invest. Which option is better?
Option A: 5.95% per annum, compounded monthly
Option B: 6% per annum, compounded semi-annually

Solution

Option A: $1000 at 5.95% per annum, compounded monthly

$A = P(1 + i)^n$, where $P = \$1000$, $i = \dfrac{5.95\%}{12}$, and $n = 12$.

$$= 1000\left(1 + \dfrac{0.0595}{12}\right)^{12}$$

$$= 1061.15$$

Interest earned is $1061.15 − $1000 or $61.15.
In one year, the $1000 earns $61.15.
$61.15 is 6.115% of $1000.
The effective annual interest rate of option A is 6.115%.

Option B: $1000 at 6% per annum, compounded semi-annually

$A = P(1 + i)^n$, where $P = \$1000$, $i = \dfrac{6\%}{2}$, and $n = 2$.

$\quad = 1000(1 + 0.03)^2$

$\quad = 1060.90$

Interest earned is $1060.90 − \$1000$ or $60.90.

In one year, the $1000 earns $60.90.

$60.90 is 6.09% of $1000.

The effective annual interest rate of option B is 6.09%.

Although the nominal annual interest rate of option A is less than that of B, its effective annual interest rate is greater. Thus, option A is the better investment.

Practice

Round answers to 2 decimal places, where necessary.

The nominal interest rate is 8% per annum. Find the effective annual interest rate for each compounding situation.

1. semi-annually

2. quarterly

3. monthly

What is the effective annual interest rate for each of the following investments?

4. $100 invested at 12% per annum, compounded quarterly

5. $500 invested at 6% per annum, compounded semi-annually

6. $1000 invested at 8.25% per annum, compounded monthly

Find the effective annual interest rate equivalent to each of the following nominal rates.

7. 5% per annum, compounded semi-annually

8. 7.5% per annum, compounded quarterly

9. 5.88% per annum, compounded semi-annually

10. 4.25% per annum, compounded monthly

Applications and Problem Solving

11. Is it better to invest at 5.25% per annum, compounded semi-annually, or at 5% per annum, compounded daily? How much more interest would you earn on an investment of $1000 at the better rate?

12. a) Predict which is the better investment, A or B.

A: $2000 at 8.5% per annum, compounded quarterly, for 2 years

B: $2000 at 8% per annum, compounded monthly, for 2 years

b) Check your prediction by finding the effective annual interest rate for each investment.

13. Car loan Chad needs to borrow $10 000 to buy a car. The car dealership will finance the loan at 12% per annum, compounded quarterly. Chad's bank will give him a car loan at 10.75% per annum, compounded monthly. Which loan has the lower effective annual interest rate?

14. Credit cards To attract new customers a credit card company is offering a nominal interest rate of 6.9% per annum, compounded monthly, on any unpaid balance. What is the effective annual interest rate?

15. Credit cards A credit card statement gives the interest rate for the next period in two forms as shown below.

Annual	%	Daily
18.40		0.05041

a) How are the two rates related?

b) What is the related monthly rate of interest?

c) The interest charged on an unpaid balance compounds monthly. What is the effective annual interest rate?

16. Phone bills A telephone company charges interest at 1.5% per month on bills that are not paid by the due date. What effective annual interest rate is the company charging?

17. RRSP Dara is comparing two investment options for her $3000 RRSP deposit this year.
Option A: a guaranteed rate of 6.9%, compounded semi-annually, for a 5-year term
Option B: a guaranteed rate of 7.2%, compounded annually, for a 2-year term
a) Find the effective annual interest rate for each option.
b) Why might Dara decide that the option with the lower effective annual rate is the one she prefers?

18. Use a nominal interest rate of 12% per annum for the following.
a) Copy and complete the table.

Number of Compounding Periods Per Year	Effective Annual Interest Rate
1	
2	
3	
4	
6	
12	
24	
52	

b) Draw a graph to show how the effective annual interest rate changes as the number of compounding periods increases.
c) Use your graph to estimate the effective annual interest rate if interest is compounded daily at 12%.
d) What would the effective annual interest rate be if interest were compounded every minute? Explain.

19. Technology The financial functions of some graphing calculators include a menu option that can be used to calculate the effective annual interest rate. For example, for a nominal interest rate of 3.75% per annum, compounded quarterly, the effective annual interest rate is 3.803 064 737%, as shown.

Use a graphing calculator to find the effective annual interest rate for each of the following nominal interest rates.
a) 7.5% per annum, compounded quarterly
b) 10.4% per annum, compounded semi-annually
c) 9.25% per annum, compounded monthly
d) 6.2% per annum, compounded daily

20. An investment of $200 amounts to $226.86 after 2 years, with interest compounded semi-annually. If the effective annual interest rate on the investment is 6.5%, what is the nominal interest rate, to the nearest tenth of a percent?

WORD POWER

Start with the letter A. Add the letters below one at a time in the order shown, and make a new word each time you add a letter. Rearrange the letters to make each new word, if necessary. Plural words ending in S are not permitted.

T R E M S Y

9.5 Consumer Credit

If you purchase an item and agree to pay for it at a later date, you are using consumer credit. You will probably pay more for the item because of interest charges.

Individuals and organizations who buy on credit have a credit rating. A **credit rating** is an assessment by lending institutions of the individual's or organization's ability to pay. This assessment is based on the individual's or organization's past record of debt paying, on character and assets, and on the present ability to repay debt.

Explore: Interpret the Information

A television cost $599, including taxes. Elton bought the television on an instalment plan of 12 monthly payments of $54.90.
a) What was the cost of the television on the instalment plan?
b) How much more was this cost than the original price of the television?

Inquire

1. Why would a store prefer Elton to use the instalment plan, rather than pay cash?

2. The store used an interest rate of 10% per annum. How was the monthly payment calculated?

3. a) Use your research skills to find the credit rating of the federal government of Canada and of your provincial government. Identify the organizations that calculate credit ratings.
b) Use your research skills to identify the organizations that determine the credit ratings of individuals in Canada. Determine where credit ratings are stored.

When you buy an item on an instalment plan, the total cost of the item is the list price of the item plus taxes plus a finance charge. If you make a down payment when you purchase the item, the finance charge is the interest calculated only on the outstanding balance.

Example 1 Calculating the Instalment Cost

Tara bought a computer system with a retail price of $1799, including taxes. She paid 25% down and financed the balance. She agreed to pay the store $132.50 each month for 12 months.
a) What amount was financed?
b) What was the finance charge?
c) What did the computer system cost Tara?

Solution

a) Cost of computer system including taxes = $1799

Down payment = 25% of $1799
$$= 0.25 \times \$1799$$
$$= \$449.75$$

Estimate

25% of 2000 = 500

Amount to be financed = retail price − down payment
$$= \$1799 - \$449.75$$
$$= \$1349.25$$
The amount financed was $1349.25.

Estimate

1800 − 450 = 1350

b) Tara paid $132.50 for 12 months.

Total of the monthly payments = $132.50 × 12
$$= \$1590$$

Estimate

150 × 10 = 1500

Finance charge = total monthly payments − amount to be financed
$$= \$1590 - \$1349.25$$
$$= \$240.75$$
The finance charge was $240.75.

Estimate

1600 − 1350 = 250

c) Total cost = down payment + total monthly payments
$$= \$449.75 + \$1590.00$$
$$= \$2039.75$$
The computer system cost Tara $2039.75.

Estimate

450 + 1600 = 2050

The credit card is a very popular form of consumer credit. The repayment terms and the interest charges vary depending on the issuer of the credit card. Usually, the cardholder repays each month any amount between the minimum payment required and the entire balance. The **due date** is the day of the month by which the payment should be made.

For most retail-chain, department-store, and oil-company charge accounts, interest is calculated on the balance due after any payments have been deducted from the previous balance and any new purchases have been added.

Example 2   Calculating Interest on a Retail Charge Account

The table shows the summary of a customer's account with a department store for a six-month period. Monthly credit charges are 1.5% of the balance due.

Month	Previous Balance −	Payment Made +	Purchases Charged →	Balance Due +	Credit Charge →	New Balance
January	$562.80	$300.00	$197.28			
February		$200.00	$56.90			
March		$150.00	$273.26			
April		$250.00	$103.85			
May		$200.00	$24.95			
June		$100.00	$98.00			

a) Complete the table by finding the balance due, credit charge, and new balance for each month.

b) How much interest was charged, in total, for the six-month period?

Solution

a) For January:

Balance due = previous balance − payment made + purchases

$\quad$ = $562.80 − $300.00 + $197.28

$\quad$ = $460.08

Credit charge = 1.5% of balance due

$\quad$ = 0.015 × $460.08

$\quad$ = $6.90

New balance = balance due + credit charge

$\quad$ = $460.08 + $6.90

$\quad$ = $466.98

Estimate

$$0.015 \times 500 = 7.5$$

Enter these amounts into the table, and continue with similar calculations for each month to complete the table.

Month	Previous Balance	− Payment Made	+ Purchases Charged →	Balance Due	+ Credit Charge →	New Balance
January	$562.80	$300.00	$197.28	$460.08	$6.90	$466.98
February	$466.98	$200.00	$56.90	$323.88	$4.86	$328.74
March	$328.74	$150.00	$273.26	$452.00	$6.78	$458.78
April	$458.78	$250.00	$103.85	$312.63	$4.69	$317.32
May	$317.32	$200.00	$24.95	$142.27	$2.13	$144.40
June	$144.40	$100.00	$98.00	$142.40	$2.14	$144.54

b) Total credit charges = $6.90 + $4.86 + $6.78 + $4.69 + $2.13 + $2.14

$\quad$ = $27.50

For the six-month period, the total interest charged was $27.50.

Estimate

$$7 + 5 + 7 + 5 + 2 + 2 = 28$$

Holders of bank credit cards can buy goods and obtain cash advances up to the credit limit for which they have been approved. Monthly statements showing all transactions that have been charged to the credit card account are sent to the cardholder.

With many of these credit cards, there are no interest charges on purchases if the balance is paid by the due date. If the balance is not paid in full by the due date, then interest charges appear on the next statement. The interest is calculated using simple interest for the number of days from the date that a purchase was posted to the account up to, but not including, the current statement date.

Interest is always charged on cash advances from the date on which the cash was advanced. To pay off the full amount you owe, you can phone the bank and ask for your payout balance that day. By paying that amount on the same day, you will stop any further interest being accumulated.

Example 3   Calculating Interest on a Bank Credit Card

Bjork received the following bank credit card statement on October 23. Interest is charged at a daily rate of 0.0504% on any unpaid balance and on cash advances from the date of posting up to, but not including, the statement date. The minimum payment is 5% of the new balance, to the nearest dollar.

a) Calculate the interest charge. **b)** Calculate the total purchases.
c) Calculate the new balance. **d)** Calculate the minimum payment due.
e) If Bjork pays $200 on November 10 and decides to pay off the outstanding balance on November 15, how much will she have to pay?

Card Number	Previous Statement	This Statement	Payment Due By
102304506	SEP 18	OCT 18	NOV 10

Posting Date	Description	Amount
SEP 25	Dave's Discs, Edmonton, AB	53.29
OCT 10	Payment received – Thank you	100.00
OCT 15	Martine's, Edmonton, AB	85.99

Previous Balance	+	Interest	+	Purchases/ Debits	–	Payments/ Credits	→	New Balance
203.54								

Solution

a) Interest on previous balance:

$I = Prt$

$\quad = \$203.54 \times 0.000\,504 \times 30$

$\quad = \$3.08$

> **Estimate**
> $200 \times 0.0005 \times 30 = 3$

There are 30 days from the previous statement date up to, but not including, this statement date.

Interest on purchase posted on September 25:

$I = Prt$

$\quad = \$53.29 \times 0.000\,504 \times 23$

$\quad = \$0.62$

> **Estimate**
> $50 \times 0.0005 \times 20 = 0.5$

There are 23 days from Sep 25 up to, but not including, Oct 18.

Interest on purchase posted on October 15:

$I = Prt$

$\quad = \$85.99 \times 0.000\,504 \times 3$

$\quad = \$0.13$

> **Estimate**
> $100 \times 0.0005 \times 3 = 0.15$

There are 3 days from Oct 15 up to, but not including, Oct 18.

Total interest $= \$3.08 + \$0.62 + \$0.13$

$\qquad\qquad\quad = \$3.83$

The interest charge is $3.83.

b) Total purchases $= \$53.29 + \$85.99$

$\qquad\qquad\qquad = \$139.28$

The total of Bjork's purchases is $139.28.

c) New balance = previous balance + interest + purchases – payments

$\qquad\qquad = \$203.54 + \$3.83 + \$139.28 - \$100.00$

$\qquad\qquad = \$246.65$

> **Estimate**
> $200 + 140 - 100 = 240$

Bjork's new balance is $246.65.

d) Minimum payment = 5% of new balance

$\qquad\qquad\qquad = 0.05 \times \$246.65$

$\qquad\qquad\qquad = \$12.33$

> **Estimate**
> $0.05 \times 240 = 12$

Bjork's minimum payment is $12, to the nearest dollar.

e) The outstanding balance from the statement dated October 18 is $246.65. The number of days from October 18 up to, but not including, November 10 is 22.

$I = Prt$
$= \$246.65 \times 0.000\,504 \times 22$
$= \$2.73$

Estimate
$$250 \times 0.0005 \times 20 = 2.5$$

Balance on November 10 = outstanding balance + interest − payment
$= \$246.65 + \$2.73 - \$200.00$
$= \$49.38$

Estimate
$$250 - 200 = 50$$

From November 10 up to, but not including, November 15 is 5 days.

$I = Prt$
$= \$49.38 \times 0.000\,504 \times 5$
$= \$0.12$

Estimate
$$50 \times 0.0005 \times 5 = 0.125$$

Balance on November 15 = $49.38 + $0.12
$= \$49.50$

To pay off her outstanding balance on November 15, Bjork will have to pay $49.50.

Practice

Round answers to 2 decimal places, where necessary.

1. Michel bought a bicycle for $329, including taxes. He agreed to pay 12 monthly instalments of $31.26.
a) How much did Michel pay for the bicycle?
b) What was the finance charge?

2. Anik would like to buy a guitar that costs $2200, including taxes. She has $500 for a down payment, and the store allows her to pay off the balance in 24 monthly payments of $80.
a) What amount is to be financed?
b) How much is the finance charge?
c) How much will the guitar cost Anik?

The credit charge on a department store's charge card is 1.4% per month. Calculate the credit charge for one month for each of the following balances.
3. $682.00   **4.** $302.87
5. $59.45   **6.** $732.49

The credit charge on a gasoline company's charge card is 1.5% per month. Find the credit charge and the new balance for each customer.

	Balance Due	+	Credit Charge	→	New Balance
7.	$392.00				
8.	$63.45				
9.	$48.25				
10.	$82.51				

One bank credit card charges daily interest at 0.045%. Find the interest charge for each transaction for the number of days indicated.
11. $328.14 for 30 days
12. $86.10 for 21 days
13. $605.88 for 14 days
14. $425.63 for 31 days
15. $1204.58 for 10 days

Fern uses a credit card that charges daily interest at 0.042%. She has an unpaid balance from the previous month, and her current statement date is April 15. Find the interest charge for each of the following items.
16. purchase for $75.00, posted on April 1
17. purchase for $129.99, posted on March 28
18. cash advance of $100.00, on April 12
19. purchase of $672.25, posted on April 5
20. the previous balance of $238.52

Find the new balance for each credit card statement.

	Previous Balance	+ Interest	+ Purchases	− Payments →	New Balance
21.	182.10	2.80	49.50	120.00	
22.	610.00	7.69	0.00	400.00	
23.	493.72	9.72	247.50	250.00	
24.	805.00	12.75	120.00	500.00	
25.	532.47	10.24	86.00	27.00	

Applications and Problem Solving

26. Instalment buying Justin bought a computer system for $3699, including taxes. He made a down payment of 15% of the price and paid the balance in monthly instalments of $99 over 3 years.
a) How much was his down payment? **b)** How much was the finance charge?
c) How much did he actually pay for the computer system?

27. Which method of financing a purchase will cost less? Explain.
A: a small down payment, plus equal payments spread over 6 months
B: a large down payment, plus equal payments spread over 12 months

28. Department store credit The table shows Derek's department-store charge card account summary for a four-month period. Monthly credit charges are 1.25% of the balance due. Copy and complete the table to find the new balance at the end of January.

Month	Previous Balance	− Payment Made	+ Purchases Charged	→ Balance Due	+ Credit Charge	→ New Balance
October	$138.53	$100.00	$223.85			
November		$150.00	$158.37			
December		$150.00	$418.44			
January		$300.00	$42.10			

29. Bank credit card Paula received her bank credit card statement on September 12. Interest is charged at a daily rate of 0.0479% on any unpaid balance and on cash advances from the date of posting up to, but not including, the statement date. The minimum payment required is 3% of the previous month's balance, to the nearest dollar.
a) Calculate the interest charge.
b) Calculate the total purchases.
c) Calculate the new balance.
d) Calculate the minimum payment due.
e) If Paula made the minimum payment on the due date, how much would she have to pay to pay off her outstanding balance on November 5?

Card Number	Previous Statement	This Statement	Payment Due By
102304506	AUG 09	SEP 09	SEP 30

Posting Date	Description	Amount
AUG 12	Rainbow Creek, Vancouver, BC	75.00
AUG 13	Chateau Jaune, Victoria, BC	208.00
AUG 30	Payment – Thank you	600.00
SEP 06	Cash Advance	200.00

Previous Balance	+ Interest	+ Purchases/ Debits	− Payments/ Credits	= New Balance
203.54				

30. Some stores advertise, "No payments until one year from now." Jamie is considering buying a racing bicycle, retailing at $1350, including taxes. His options are to take a bank loan for 2 years at 11% per annum, compounded semi-annually, or to take the store's offer of no payments until one year from now, and then to pay 12 monthly payments of $135.
a) Describe the advantages and disadvantages of each option.
b) What assumptions did you make?

31. Explain when it makes sense to make a payment between due dates on a bank credit card and when it does not.

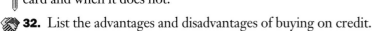

32. List the advantages and disadvantages of buying on credit.

9.6 Housing Costs

A **mortgage** is an agreement between a money lender and a borrower to purchase property. The security for the mortgage is the property being bought. The **mortgagor** is the person borrowing the money, and the **mortgagee** is the person or business lending the money. A mortgage is usually repaid in equal periodic payments that include the principal and the interest. To **amortize** a mortgage means to repay the mortgage over a given period of time in equal periodic payments. The period of time is known as the **amortization period**. The **term** of a mortgage is the length of time that the mortgage agreement is in effect.

Explore: Use a Table

The table shows monthly mortgage payments for different interest rates. Each monthly payment is a blend of principal and interest.

Monthly payment for each $1000 of Mortgage Debt				
	Amortization Period			
Interest Rate (%)	10 years	15 years	20 years	25 years
6	$11.07	$8.40	$7.12	$6.40
6.25	$11.19	$8.53	$7.26	$6.55
6.5	$11.31	$8.66	$7.41	$6.70
6.75	$11.43	$8.80	$7.55	$6.85
7	$11.56	$8.93	$7.69	$7.00
7.25	$11.68	$9.07	$7.84	$7.16
7.5	$11.81	$9.21	$7.99	$7.32
7.75	$11.94	$9.34	$8.13	$7.47
8	$12.06	$9.48	$8.28	$7.63

Suppose you need a mortgage of $120 000, and the current interest rate is 7% for a term of 5 years. How much will your mortgage payments be each month if your mortgage is amortized over a period of
a) 15 years?   **b)** 25 years?

Inquire

1. If you have a $100 000 mortgage, amortized over 25 years, and your monthly payments are $670, what rate of interest are you paying?

2. How much more would your monthly payments be if the $100 000 mortgage was amortized over 20 years instead of 25 years?

3. Hedda needs an $80 000 mortgage. She is considering two options.
Option A: a 3-year term at 6.25% amortized over 20 years
Option B: a 5-year term at 6.75% amortized over 25 years
Which option has the lower monthly payments?

4. Even though the monthly payments are higher, why might a person choose a shorter amortization period?

The amount of money you have as a down payment helps determine the kind of mortgage for which you qualify. If you have a down payment of at least 25% of the price of the house, you may qualify for a conventional mortgage.

When you approach a lending institution for a mortgage, your income and expenses will be analyzed to determine whether you can afford the mortgage payments.

Banks use computers to determine the monthly mortgage payments. You may use the Amortization Table found on page 590 or a graphing calculator to do this. Because of the rounding involved, some discrepancies occur in the amounts. The graphing calculator result is more accurate.

Example 1 Calculating Monthly Mortgage Payments

Felix bought a house for $175 000. He paid down 25% of the price of the house and arranged a 5-year mortgage at 6.75% per annum, amortized over 25 years, on the balance of the price.

a) How much was Felix's down payment?
b) How much was his monthly mortgage payment?

Solution

a) Price of house = $175 000
Down payment = 25% of $175 000
      = $43 750
Felix's down payment was $43 750.

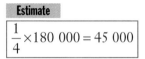

Estimate

$$\frac{1}{4} \times 180\ 000 = 45\ 000$$

b) Balance to be financed = price of the house − down payment
         = $175 000 − $43 750
         = $131 250

Estimate

$175\ 000 − 45\ 000 = 130\ 000$

Method 1: Using a Table
From the table, the monthly payment for each $1000 of mortgage debt at 6.75%, amortized over 25 years, is $6.85.
$131 250 = 131.25 × $1000
Monthly mortgage payment = $6.85 × 131.25
          = $899.06
Felix's monthly mortgage payment was $899.06.

Estimate

$7 × 130 = 910$

Method 2: Using a Graphing Calculator
Number of payment periods = 25 × 12
Annual interest rate, % = 6.75
Present value, $ = 131250
Payment, $: to be found
Future value, $ = 0
Payments per year = 12
Compounding periods per year = 2

By Canadian law, the interest rate on mortgages is compounded semi-annually, so the C/Y value entered must be 2.

The payment is −$899.13, so Felix must pay $899.13 as his monthly mortgage payment.

Another expense involved in owning a house is **property tax**. Property tax is levied by municipalities on real estate. The money collected is used to pay for the services provided by the municipality. These services include schools, libraries, garbage pickup, police and fire protection, and road maintenance.

The rate at which property tax is calculated is called the **mill rate** and is determined each year by the municipality when it sets its budget. The mill rate is the amount of tax levied annually for each $1000 of assessed value of the property. The mill rates for residential properties, apartment buildings, and commercial properties may be different.

A **mill** is a monetary denomination of one tenth of a cent, or one thousandth of a dollar. A mill rate of 3.5 mills taxes a property at $\dfrac{35}{1000}$ of a dollar for each dollar of assessed property value, or $35 for each $1000 of assessed value.

$$\text{Property tax} = \dfrac{\text{assessed value}}{1000} \times \text{mill rate}$$

Example 2   Calculating Property Taxes

The assessed value of a house is $129 550. If the residential mill rate is 22.375, what is the annual property tax on the house?

Solution

$$\text{Annual property tax} = \dfrac{\text{assessed value}}{1000} \times \text{mill rate}$$

$$= \dfrac{\$129\ 550}{1000} \times 22.375$$

$$= \$2898.68$$

Estimate
$20 \times 130 = 2600$

The annual property tax on the house is $2898.68.

When you own a house, your **monthly housing costs** are the monthly mortgage payment plus the monthly property tax.

Example 3   Calculating Housing Costs

Catherine has just renewed the mortgage on her house. She arranged a 5-year $95 000 mortgage at 7.25% per annum, amortized over 20 years. Her house has an assessed value of $165 000, and the residential mill rate in her municipality is 12.5970. Find her monthly housing costs.

Solution

From the Amortization Table on page 590, the monthly payment for each $1000 of mortgage at 7.25% per annum, amortized over 20 years, is $7.84.

$$\text{Monthly mortgage payment} = \dfrac{\text{mortgage amount}}{1000} \times \$7.84$$

$$= \dfrac{95\ 000}{1000} \times \$7.84$$

$$= \$744.80$$

Estimate
$100 \times 7.8 = 780$

$$\text{Annual property tax} = \dfrac{\text{assessed value}}{1000} \times \text{mill rate}$$

$$= \dfrac{\$165\ 000}{1000} \times 12.5970$$

$$= \$2078.51$$

Estimate
$170 \times 12 = 2040$

$$\text{Monthly property tax} = \dfrac{\$2078.51}{12}$$

$$= \$173.21$$

$$\text{Monthly housing costs} = \text{monthly mortgage payment} + \text{monthly property tax}$$

$$= \$744.80 + \$173.21$$

$$= \$918.01$$

Catherine's monthly housing costs are $918.01.

Practice

Where necessary, use the Amortization Table on page 590 to determine monthly payment for each $1000 of mortgage debt. Round answers to 2 decimal places, where necessary.

Calculate the amount of each down payment.
1. 25% down on a price of $200 000
2. 5% down on a price of $147 500
3. 5% down on a price of $99 900
4. 12.5% down on a price of $165 000

Calculate the monthly mortgage payment for a mortgage of $125 500, with each of the following rates and amortization periods.
5. 6.25% per annum, amortized over 25 years
6. 8% per annum, amortized over 10 years
7. 7.25% per annum, amortized over 15 years
8. 9.75% per annum, amortized over 20 years

Find the monthly payment for each mortgage.

	Principal ($)	Interest Rate (%)	Amortization Period
9.	90 000	8	20 years
10.	150 000	7.25	25 years
11.	146 000	6.5	15 years
12.	283 500	8.5	10 years
13.	312 474	6.75	25 years

The residential mill rate for a town is 32.0665. Calculate the annual property tax for each assessed value.
14. $79 000
15. $152 800
16. $235 000
17. $255 000
18. $426 500
19. $65 300

The mill rate for commercial properties in a city is 42.0061. What is the annual property tax for properties with each assessed value?
20. $4 235 000
21. $954 000
22. $27 500 000
23. $820 000
24. $1 532 000
25. $10 550 000

Applications and Problem Solving

26. A $100 000 mortgage loan is taken at 6.5% per annum, amortized over 25 years.
a) What is the monthly payment of the loan?
b) Assuming that the interest rate remains the same over the amortization period of the loan, what is the total amount paid for the loan?
c) What is the total interest paid for the loan?

27. Sarah would like to buy a condominium priced at $199 900. She has saved $55 000 for a down payment and has been offered a 3-year mortgage on the balance at 7.5% per annum, amortized over 20 years.
a) What is the amount to be financed?
b) What would her monthly mortgage payment be?

28. Hector wants to buy a bungalow priced at $175 000. His down payment is 28% of the selling price.
a) What amount of mortgage does Hector need to finance?
b) If he takes a 5-year mortgage at 7% per annum, amortized over 25 years, what is the monthly payment?
c) If the interest rate remains the same over the amortization period, what will be the total cost of the bungalow?
d) How much interest will Hector pay in total?

29. The assessed value of an office building is $742 000. If the commercial mill rate is 26.2118, what is the annual property tax for that building?

30. **Education funding** One year the combined residential mill rate for the City of Edmonton was 15.1888. This mill rate was the sum of the school mill rate of 7.1084 and the municipal mill rate of 8.0804. A house in Edmonton had an assessed value of $107 850.
a) What was the annual property tax for that house?
b) How much of the annual property tax did the schools receive?

31. One year, the residential mill rate for the City of North Vancouver was 6.545 15. If the home owner lived in the property, a grant of $470 was given to those under 65 years of age, and a grant of $745 was given to those 65 years of age and over. Winnie owns and lives in a single family home that was assessed that year at $275 600. If Winnie was 42 years old that year, what was her annual property tax?

32. One year, the residential mill rate for the City of North Vancouver was 6.545 15. The circle graph shows how the residential property taxes were distributed. If the assessed value of a single family dwelling was $354 000, how much of the annual property tax went to
a) the municipality?
b) schools?

Residential Property Tax Distribution

Municipal 49%
Other 8%
Schools 43%

33. Mala just renewed the $125 862 mortgage on her house for a one-year term at 6.5%, amortized over 15 years. Her house has an assessed value of $185 000, and the residential mill rate is 8.3015. Find her monthly housing costs.

34. Property conversion Jarvis owned a single family dwelling assessed at $224 000. He decided convert his property into business premises, consisting of a bakery and a cafe. The converted property was reassessed at $350 000. That year, the residential mill rate was 5.447 12 and the business mill rate was 17.220 05. By how much did Jarvis's property tax increase that year?

35. Mae needs to renew her mortgage. The principal will be $84 525, and she is considering whether to take a one-year term at 6.25% per annum or a three-year term at 6.75% per annum. In each case, the amortization period is 25 years.
a) How much less will she need to budget for monthly mortgage payments over the first year if she chooses the one-year term?
b) Suggest reasons why she might choose the three-year term mortgage instead.

36. Working backward What is the mill rate for condominiums, if a condominium assessed at $144 500 receives an annual property tax bill for $962.35? Round your answer to 4 decimal places.

37. The consumer has many options to consider when planning to buy a home. Find out about the following types of mortgages: open, closed, variable-rate, high-ratio, and government-assisted. Write a few sentences describing the advantages and disadvantages of the different types.

38. Abdul bought a small farm for $112 000. He paid 25% down and obtained a 7-year mortgage for the balance at 8.5% per annum, amortized over 10 years.
a) If the interest rate remained the same for the 10 years, how much did he pay for the farm altogether?
b) If Abdul had been able to negotiate 0.25% off the mortgage rate, how much would he have saved over the 10 years?
c) If he had been able to increase his down payment by $10 000, how much would he have saved over the 10 years?

39. Equity a) What does the term *equity* mean?
b) How can home-owners increase the equity in their home?
c) How could the equity in a home decrease?

40. a) Use your research skills to find the mill rate for each type of property in your municipality. Choose one local example of each type of property and find its assessed value. (The assessed value of properties is public information and may be available in your public library or from local municipal offices.)
b) Calculate the annual property tax on each of your choices.

NUMBER POWER

A winning lottery number was 832. Over 80 but under 100 people picked the winning number and shared a jackpot of $658 000. How many people shared the jackpot, and how much did each person get, if they each got a whole number of dollars?

9.7 Balancing a Budget

The word **budget** comes from the French word *bouqette*, meaning bag or billfold. In order to control their spending, people used to put their money into bags or envelopes. A budget is a spending plan. It is a record of money earned (income) and of money spent (expenditure).

Explore: Interpret the Graph

The circle graph represents the federal government's spending budget. On which category did the federal government spend
a) the most money?
b) the least money?

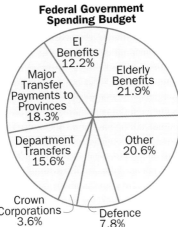

Federal Government Spending Budget

EI Benefits 12.2%
Elderly Benefits 21.9%
Major Transfer Payments to Provinces 18.3%
Department Transfers 15.6%
Other 20.6%
Crown Corporations 3.6%
Defence 7.8%

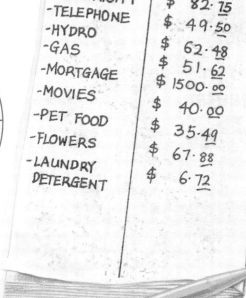

ITEM	AMOUNT
–GROCERIES	$175.00
–ELECTRICITY	$82.75
–TELEPHONE	$49.50
–HYDRO	$62.48
–GAS	$51.62
–MORTGAGE	$1500.00
–MOVIES	$40.00
–PET FOOD	$35.49
–FLOWERS	$67.88
–LAUNDRY DETERGENT	$6.72

Inquire

1. One year, the total spending of the federal government was about $140 billion. Approximately how much was spent on
a) EI benefits?   **b)** defence?

2. Suggest some services not included in the federal budget that would be included in a provincial budget; in a municipal budget.

3. From what sources do the various levels of government get the money in their budgets?

4. Why are government budgets important to Canadians?

5. Why is a circle graph the most appropriate type of graph for displaying budget data?

> A **balanced budget** is one in which the total expenditure equals the total income.
> **Fixed expenses** occur regularly and are difficult to control. Some fixed expenses in a family budget might be rent or mortgage, cable TV, and car payments.
> **Variable expenses** also occur regularly but can be controlled. Some variable expenses for a family are food, transportation, entertainment, and personal spending.
> **Occasional expenses** occur only once or twice in a year, or unexpectedly. Some occasional expenses for a family are holiday travel, home renovations, gifts, and charitable donations.

Example 1   Completing a Personal Budget

One year, Sylvana's net income from employment was $19 642, and she received $1137 from an investment. Her total annual expenses were as follows: rent $7200, utilities $560, food $2870, telephone $305, cable TV $179, home insurance $155, car licence $90, car insurance $965, car repairs $255, gasoline $780, clothing $1458, entertainment $2600, reading material $123, and personal care products $140. She spent a total of $350 on gifts and went on a vacation that cost her $600.
a) Complete an annual budget statement for Sylvana.
b) Was it a balanced budget?
c) What percent of her net income was Sylvana able to save, to the nearest percent?

Solution

a)

Sylvana's Annual Budget Statement

Income

Item	Amount
Net Employment Income	$19 642
Investments	$1 137
Gifts	
Other	
Total	$20 779

Expenditures

Fixed Expenses		Variable Expenses		Occasional Expenses	
Item	Amount	Item	Amount	Item	Amount
Shelter	$7200	Food	$2870	Home Repairs	
Utilities	$560	Clothing	$1458	Home Furnishings	
Car Licence	$90	Gasoline	$780	Charitable Donations	
Car Insurance	$965	Entertainment	$2600	Gifts	$350
Home Insurance	$155	Education/Reading	$123	Travel	$600
Cable TV	$179	Personal Care	$140	Personal Business	
		Telephone	$305	Car Repairs	$255
Other		Other		Other	
Total	$9149	Total	$8276	Total	$1205

Total Expenditures = $18 630

Balance = total income − total expenditures

$= \$20\ 779 - \$18\ 630$

$= \$2149$

b) Since total income and total expenditures were not the same, the budget was not balanced.

c) Percent available for saving $= \dfrac{2149}{20\ 779} \times 100\%$

$ \doteq 10\%$

Sylvana was able to save about 10% of her net income.

When changes occur in income or expenditures, a budget can be used to see where spending habits can be altered to maintain a balanced budget.

Example 2   Revising a Budget

Daniel is a student living at home. He has a part-time job that gives him a net income of $1200 each month. His monthly expenses are: telephone $22, room and board $400, entertainment $300, transportation $90, clothing $100, books $50, and snacks $100. Daniel would like to buy a used car. He estimates monthly expenses for a car to be: loan payment $200, gas $50, licence $7.50, repairs $50, and parking $15.

a) Make up a budget statement of Daniel's current monthly expenses.

b) Suggest some adjustments Daniel could make to his budget so that he is able to buy the car. Complete Daniel's revised budget statement.

Solution

a)

Daniel's Monthly Budget Statement

Income

Item	Amount
Net employment income	$1200
Total	$1200

Expenditures

Fixed Expenses		Variable Expenses	
Item	Amount	Item	Amount
Shelter	$400	Clothing	$100
		Telephone	$22
		Entertainment	$300
		Education/Reading	$50
		Snacks	$100
		Transportation	$90
Total	$400	Total	$662

Total Expenditures = $1062

Balance = total income − total expenditures

$= \$1200 - \$1062$

$= \$138$

b) With his current budget, Daniel has a surplus of $138. If he buys the car, he can reassign the $90 budgeted for transportation. So, with his present budget he has $228 available.
Total estimated monthly car expenses
= $200 + $50 + $7.50 + $50 + $15
= $322.50
If Daniel buys the car, monthly deficit
= $228 − $322.50
= −$94.50
Daniel cannot alter his fixed expenses. So, in order to balance his budget, Daniel needs to reduce his variable expenses to make up the $94.50. For example, he could deduct $50 from clothing, $30 from entertainment, and $14.50 from snacks as shown in the revised budget statement.

Daniel's Monthly Budget Statement

Income

Item	Amount
Net employment income	$1200
Total	$1200

Expenditures

Fixed Expenses		Variable Expenses	
Item	Amount	Item	Amount
Shelter	$400	Clothing	$50
Car Loan	$200	Telephone	$22
Licence	$7.50	Entertainment	$270
Parking	$15	Education/Reading	$50
		Snacks	$85.50
		Gas	$50
		Car Repairs	$50
Total	$622.50	Total	$577.50

Total Expenditures = $1200

Balance = total income − total expenditures

$= \$1200 - \$1200$

$= \$0$

Practice

Refer to the budget statement in Example 1. In which category would each of the following items be included?

1. magazines
2. $5000 inheritance
3. mortgage
4. hydro
5. cosmetics
6. take-out food
7. CDs
8. birthday present
9. groceries
10. dry cleaning
11. $50 donation to Heart Fund
12. fitness club membership
13. new sofa
14. pair of jeans

Classify each budget as balanced, having a deficit, or having a surplus. For those that have a surplus, express the surplus amount as a percent of the total income.

	Total Income	Total Expenditures
15.	$8 621.56	$8 621.56
16.	$25 649.50	$23 981.40
17.	$16 802.00	$16 945.00
18.	$35 500.00	$32 793.54

19. Clive has a net monthly income of $628.50 from his part-time job. He lives at home and pays $300 a month for his room and board. If he budgets $200 for entertainment, and $80 for clothing, how much does he save each month?

20. Aisha has a net monthly income of $2358. Her expenses are: rent $600, food $400, transportation $85, phone $43, clothing $200, and entertainment $250. She is saving the balance towards a trip to New Zealand.
a) Construct a budget statement to show Aisha's income and expenditures.
b) How much does she save each month?

Applications and Problem Solving

21. Holly's net income for one month is $2745. Her monthly expenses are given in the table.

Item	Amount	Item	Amount
Rent	$500	Car Loan	$300
Cable	$35	Student Loan	$400
Utilities	$100	Food	$300
Phone	$35	Clothing	$250
		Gasoline	$150

a) How much money will Holly have left after she deducts these amounts from her net monthly income?

b) Holly decides to budget the balance as follows:
savings 25%
recreation and miscellaneous expenses 60%
increase to her car loan payment 15%
Construct a balanced budget for Holly's income and expenditures.
c) Draw a circle graph to show Holly's spending budget.

22. **Shared expenses** Maurice has a net monthly income of $2415.76. He shares an apartment with two friends. The monthly rent is $1200, shared equally. Maurice's other monthly expenses are transportation $120, YMCA membership $30, and student loan payment $125.
a) The chart shows the other apartment expenses for each month of the previous year.

			Item		
Month	Hydro	Gas	Food	TV	Phone
Jan	$92	$120	$422	$22	$35
Feb	$88	$140	$453	$22	$35
Mar	$82	$110	$422	$22	$35
Apr	$70	$90	$426	$22	$35
May	$64	$58	$464	$22	$35
Jun	$66	$32	$422	$22	$35
Jul	$41	$22	$422	$22	$35
Aug	$56	$18	$422	$22	$35
Sep	$72	$56	$422	$22	$35
Oct	$84	$83	$422	$22	$35
Nov	$86	$100	$378	$22	$35
Dec	$122	$140	$247	$22	$35

Find the average monthly expense for each item and Maurice's share of each.
b) Construct a budget to show Maurice's monthly income and expenditures.
c) If Maurice decides to divide the balance of his money equally between savings, clothing, and entertainment, how much does he budget for each item?

23. The table gives a guide to the percent of net income that people spend on each item.

Item	Percent of Net Income
Shelter	20%–30%
Food	15%–25%
Transportation	10%–20%
Clothing	8%–12%
Entertainment/Personal	7%–10%

Use the table to make a budget for each of the following people.
a) Linda has an annual net income of $25 680. She has her own apartment, drives a car, and likes to entertain and travel.
b) Liam has a net weekly income of $425. He shares an apartment with his brother. Liam's hobbies are skiing and canoeing. He loves music and likes to attend rock concerts. He has no car, but would like to buy one in the future.

24. Variance Carlos has a monthly net income of $2153.60. Last month, he monitored his spending carefully so that he could compare it with his budget.

Item	Budgeted Amount	Actual Amount
Rent and Utilities	$750.00	$776.41
Food	$400.00	$362.50
Clothing	$200.00	$261.69
Transportation	$153.60	$148.00
Savings	$150.00	$150.00
Recreation/Miscellaneous	$500.00	$455.00

a) Calculate the percent that each budgeted amount is of his net income.
b) Use the percents to construct a circle graph to represent Carlos' budget.
c) Variance is the difference between the budgeted amount and the actual amount. Use a plus sign to indicate a surplus and a negative sign to indicate a deficit. Find the variance for each item in Carlos' budget.

25. Visualization The circle graph shows how Kostas spends his net income of $2000 each month.

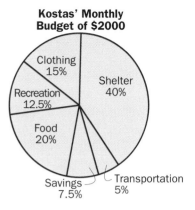

Kostas' Monthly Budget of $2000

a) Construct Kostas' monthly budget statement.
b) Kostas received a net monthly pay increase of $150. He wants to buy a car. The monthly loan for the car would be $195, and the monthly running costs would be $150. Create a new budget statement for Kostas to reflect the changes needed in his spending so that he can afford the car.
c) Draw a circle graph to show Kostas' revised budget.

26. Write a paragraph in support of, or disagreeing with, the following statement.
"Everyone's budget must reflect their income and their lifestyle."

27. To make a budget work, it is important to be realistic, and to review and revise it frequently.
a) Explain why each of these strategies is important.
b) Why is it difficult for many people to stick to a budget?

28. There are many ways to stretch your budget. For example, you could walk instead of taking the bus. You could buy food in bulk or join a wholesale superstore. What other financial tips can you suggest?

29. Prepare a budget for one of the following, based on your own estimates of the income and expenditures involved.
• the monthly budget of the president of a successful company
• a family vacation to Florida
• running a school dance

Financial Statements

Wise consumers keep careful records of the financial activities related to each of their bank accounts, and verify periodically that their records agree with those provided by the bank. By doing this, consumers can ensure that any errors are corrected as soon as possible.

1 Understanding a Bank Statement

Each month, Marina's bank sends her a statement of the transactions that have been cleared through her bank account. Below is Marina's bank statement for the month of October.

Date	Description of the Transaction	Debits	Credits	Balance
Sept 30	Balance Forward			1665.18
Oct 1	Direct Debit	65.80		1599.38
Oct 3	Cheque 431	144.00		1455.38
Oct 3	Instant Teller Withdrawal	200.00		1255.38
Oct 6	Cheque 430	780.00		475.38
Oct 15	Direct Deposit		1020.56	1495.94
Oct 19	Instant Teller Withdrawal	100.00		1395.94
Oct 27	Instant Teller Transfer	600.00		795.94
Oct 31	Direct Deposit		1020.56	1816.50
Oct 31	Service Charge	9.50		1807.00

1. a) What will be the opening balance of Marina's November statement?
b) Explain what the terms *debit* and *credit* mean.

2. a) Explain the difference between a *direct debit* and an *instant teller withdrawal*.
b) Look at your own bank statement, or ask family members about their statements. If the terms *direct debit* and *instant teller withdrawal* are not used in your statement, what corresponding terms are used?

3. Cheque 431 appears on the statement before cheque 430. Explain why.

4. Is it possible for a negative quantity to appear in the balance column? Explain.

5. The bank offers two options for service charges on Marina's type of account:
Option A: a monthly flat fee service charge of $9.50
Option B: a service charge of $1.00 for each direct debit and $0.60 for each other debit transaction.
Which option do you think is the better one for Marina, based on this month's statement?

2 Reconciling a Bank Statement with a Personal Transaction Record

Marina keeps a detailed record of her banking activities in the personal transaction record provided with her cheque book. Read the following transaction record carefully, interpreting each entry. Compare the two statements, noting any differences.

D-Deposit	DC-Debit Card	ABM-Teller Machine	AP-Automatic Payment	TT-Telephone Transfer	O-Other			
Date	Cheque Number	Transaction Type	Description of Transaction	Payment/ Debit	✔	Payment/ Debit Credit	Balance Forward	
							1665.18	
Oct 1	430	cheque	rent	780.00			885.18	
Oct 1		DC	Foodland	65.80			819.38	
Oct 1	431	cheque	dentist	144.00			675.38	
Oct 3		ABM	cash	200.00			475.38	
Oct 15		D	pay			1020.56	1495.94	
Oct 19		ABM	cash	100.00			1395.94	
Oct 27		ABM	transfer to savings	600.00			795.94	
Oct 31		D	pay			1020.56	1816.50	
Oct 31	432	cheque	Bob's Books	85.92			1730.58	
Nov 1	433	cheque	rent	780.00			950.58	
Nov 2		ABM	cash	200.00			750.58	
Nov 8		D	gift			100.00	850.58	

When Marina received her bank statement for October, she carefully checked that it agreed with her personal transaction record. Since the bank statement came in the mail, she did not receive it until November 9. Therefore, she had items noted in her personal record that did not appear on the October bank statement. That evening, she used the following steps to **reconcile** her account.

• Check that each item listed on the bank statement matches an entry on the personal record, using the column with the check mark heading to keep track.
• Correct any entries in the personal record that you are certain are your errors, and adjust the balance as needed.
• If any items from the bank statement have been missed on the personal record, enter them.

Marina had not recorded the service charge, so she added a new entry to her personal record, below her last entry, as follows.

Oct 31		0	service charge	9.50			841.08	

Marina then did a statement reconciliation as follows:

Balance on bank statement $= 1807.00$

Add Deposits/Credits made since the statement date $= 100.00$

Sub Total $= 1907.00$

Subtract Payments/Debits made since the statement date $= (85.92 + 780.00 + 200.00)$

Final Balance $= 841.08$

Since this final balance matched the new balance in Marina's personal record, the account was reconciled. If the two amounts had not matched, Marina would first have checked all her entries, her calculations, or any items she had failed to cross-check. If there were items on the bank statement for which she could not account, she would have contacted the bank for clarification or correction.

1. Describe at least three types of errors that might be found in a personal transaction record.

2. How might an error occur on the bank statement?

3. Richard opened a new chequing account on February 2. On March 8, he received the following bank statement for the month of February.

Date	Description of the Transaction	Debits	Credits	Balance
Feb 2	Deposit		500.00	500.00
Feb 8	Instant Teller Withdrawal	100.00		400.00
Feb 12	Cheque 001	78.00		322.00
Feb 14	Deposit		126.00	448.00
Feb 20	Instant Teller Withdrawal	100.00		348.00
Feb 21	Cheque 002	88.59		259.41
Feb 28	Service Charge	5.95		253.46

Richard had kept his own personal transaction record for this account, as follows.

D-Deposit DC-Debit Card ABM-Teller Machine AP-Automatic Payment TT-Telephone Transfer O-Other

Date	Cheque Number	Transaction Type	Description of Transaction	Payment/ Debit	✔	Payment/ Debit	Balance Forward
Feb 2		D	cash			500.00	500.00
Feb 5	001	cheque	Don's Discs	78.00			422.00
Feb 8		ABM	cash	100.00			322.00
Feb 14		D	pay cheque			126.00	448.00
Feb 15	002	cheque	shoes	88.95			359.05
Feb 20		ABM	cash	100.00			259.05
Feb 25	003	cheque	jeans	54.69			204.36
Mar 1		D	pay cheque			328.00	532.36
Mar 3		ABM	cash	100.00			432.36

a) Richard made one error in his personal transaction record. Copy the record and check off each item from the bank statement. Correct the error and subsequent balances.
b) Reconcile the bank statement with Richard's personal transaction record.

3 Keeping Small Business Account Records

Ben is the treasurer of the badminton club. At the beginning of the fiscal year, he made the following financial transactions.

Date	Transaction
Sept 10	Received 20 membership fees at $15 each.
Sept 12	Paid $45 to have meeting schedule word-processed and duplicated.
Sept 13	Bought $80.95 worth of equipment.
Sept 15	Bought a first-aid-kit for $28.
Sept 16	Bought $50 of refreshments for the welcome-back party.
Sept 17	Received a donation of $100 from a sponsor.

1. Copy and complete Ben's account register for the club's finances.

Date	Description of Transaction	Debits	Credits

2. If you were on the club's committee, would you recommend opening a bank account for club funds or keeping the cash locked in a safe? Explain.

CONNECTING MATH AND TRANSPORTATION

So You Want to Buy a Car!

A car is the first major purchase that many people make. There are many factors to consider when choosing a car, and most of them deal with affordability.

1 Which Car to Buy?

1. If you choose to buy a new car from a car dealership, what costs do you need to consider other than the sticker price of the car?

2. Which of the costs that you listed in the previous question also apply if you buy a used car?

3. Describe three different ways of finding a used car. Give one advantage and one disadvantage of each source.

4. What does the "black book" value of a used car mean? Describe two attributes that can make a used car worth more than its black book value.

5. Choose a new car that you would like to own.
a) Estimate its price.
b) Use your research skills to find the actual price from two different retailers.
c) What equipment is standard and what is optional on the car of your choice? How much extra would you have to pay for the options that you would like?
d) Find out approximately how much it would cost to drive your new car away from the dealership. (Assume that you pay the full cash price for the car.)

2 Financing a Car Purchase

Most people finance their car purchase either through a car dealership or by obtaining a bank loan. They usually make a cash down payment and then pay off the balance in instalments.

1. Ghita plans to buy a used car for $12 500. She has $2500 saved for a down payment.
a) The car dealership offers her the option of paying off the balance in 24 monthly instalments of $495. How much extra will she pay for the car if she chooses this option?
b) Ghita's bank will give her a car loan with interest at 8.5% per annum, compounded quarterly, for a term of two years. The amount will be divided by 24 to obtain the monthly instalments. What will her monthly payments be if she takes the bank loan?
c) Which source of financing costs Ghita less, the car dealership or the bank? Do some research to find out whether this is generally the case.

2. If you financed the purchase of the car you chose in Exploration 1, above, what would the monthly instalments be? State the values you have assumed for your down payment, the interest rate, and the number of years you would take to pay off the balance.

3. Some people choose to lease a car rather than buy one. Investigate and write a report on the advantages and disadvantages of leasing.

3 Operating Costs

Many factors affect how much it costs you to operate your car. How many kilometres do you drive per month? For what type of driving, city or highway, will the car be used? Does the car need frequent repairs?

1. What is the difference between fixed car expenses and variable car expenses? Give examples of each.

2. A major cost in operating a car is insurance. Find out and describe what the following terms mean: bodily injury, property damage, collision, comprehensive, liability, and deductible. What type(s) of car insurance are mandatory for driving a vehicle on a public road in your province? Use your research skills to estimate how much it would cost you to insure the car that you would like to purchase.

3. Depreciation is a frequently-overlooked car expense. One method of computing the annual depreciation is the double-declining balance method. For this method, divide 100% by the estimated life of the car, and then double the result to obtain the rate of depreciation. Use this method to find the value, at the end of the third year, of a new car purchased for $40 000 with an estimated life of 10 years.

4. a) Estimate the total operating costs in the first year after you purchased the car you chose in Exploration 1. State all the assumptions you made.

b) Do you think that the operating costs would increase or decrease in the second year, and by how much? Explain.

5. Prepare a report that categorizes and displays all the costs involved in owning and operating your car for a two-year period. Include all the assumptions you made.

Review

9.1 **1.** Gerri is paid $8.50/h for regular hours and time-and-a-half for hours in excess of 40 h per week. What is her gross income if she works 47.5 h one week?

2. Kurt is a waiter and earns $7.95/h. He averages $40 in tips for each 5-h shift that he works. One weekend he works 3 shifts. What is his gross income?

3. Gordon is a computer salesperson who is paid on a graduated commission basis. He earns 7% on the first $2000 of sales, 10% on the next $4000 of sales, and 15% on sales in excess of $6000. What is his gross income for a month in which he has $24 000 in sales?

4. Hedda picks apples on her uncle's farm each fall. For each kilogram of apples she picks, she is paid $0.10. How much does she earn for a weekend when she picks 908 kg?

9.2 *Use the Federal Tax Table on page 534 to find the federal tax for each of the following annual taxable incomes.*
5. $20 873.00
6. $15 095.46
7. $31 507. 33
8. $27 482.93

Find the amount of provincial tax payable by each employee.
9. MaeTze lives in Jasper, Alberta, and her basic federal tax is $2548.52.
10. Ben lives in Port Alberni, British Columbia, and his basic federal tax is $1976.84.
11. Natalya lives in Brandon, Manitoba, and her basic federal tax is $3010.55.

12. Laura works in Regina and earns an annual salary of $42 900. Her personal tax credit is $6456, and each month she has $50 deducted for a disability insurance plan and $200 for her RRSP.
a) Calculate her annual deductions for CPP and EI.
b) Determine her total income tax.
c) Find Laura's net annual income.

9.3 **13.** Find the amount of a $5000 Canada Savings Bond after 3 years, with interest at 4.5% per annum, compounded annually.

14. Find the interest charged on a loan of $2000 for 2 years, with interest at 7.25% per annum, compounded quarterly.

15. Marie invested $2500 in an RRSP for a two-year term at a guaranteed interest rate of 6.4% per annum, compounded quarterly.
a) Calculate the value of her investment at the end of the two-year term.
b) How much interest did she earn on this investment?

16. Jean opened a savings account with $1000. Six months later, and at six-month intervals after that, he made a total of five deposits of $300 into the account. The account paid interest at 3.75% per annum, compounded semi-annually.
a) What amount was in the account at the end of the third year?
b) How much interest had Jean's account earned?

9.4 **17.** If interest is compounded monthly at 4.5% per annum, what is the effective annual interest rate?

18. For an investment of $2000, which is the better option?
Option A: interest compounded quarterly at 6% per annum
Option B: interest compounded semi-annually at 5.5% per annum

19. Is it better to invest your savings at $5\frac{1}{4}$% per annum, compounded semi-annually, or at 5% per annum, compounded daily? Explain.

9.5 **20.** An exercise machine sells for $289, including taxes. The store offers an instalment plan of $50 down and six monthly payments of $41.83.
a) What is the instalment plan price?
b) What is the finance charge?

The credit charge on a retail store's charge card is 1.5% per month. Find the credit charge and the new balance for each of the following customers.

	Balance Owing	+	Credit Charge	→	New Balance
21.	$598.25				
22.	$108.50				
23.	$926.78				
24.	$1055.30				

25. Brad uses a credit card that charges daily interest at 0.045%. He has an unpaid balance from the previous month, and his current statement is dated November 14. Find the interest charge for each of the following items.
a) $38.00 posted on October 28
b) $100.00 posted on November 2
c) $250.75 posted on November 8

9.6 **26.** Mark bought a house for $86 000. He paid 25% down and obtained a 3-year mortgage for the balance at 6.75%, amortized over 25 years. What is his monthly mortgage payment? Refer to the Amortization Table on page 590.

27. Reka and Joe need to renew their mortgage. The principal will be $103 088, and they are considering a two-year term at 6% or a five-year term at 7%. The new mortgage will be amortized over 20 years. How much less will they need to budget for monthly mortgage payments if they choose the two-year term?

28. The assessed value of a house is $150 000. If the residential mill rate is 15.775, what is the annual property tax on the house?

9.7 **29.** Rita is sharing an apartment with her sister. Rita's net monthly income is $1749. At present, her monthly expenses are as follows.

Item	Amount	Item	Amount
Rent	$450	Food	$175
Car Loan	$250	Car Repairs	$50
Gas	$75	Parking	$15
Telephone	$12.40	Cable	$17.50
Clothing	$250	Recreation	$300
Personal Care	$45		

Any money Rita has left over, she saves. Rita would like to move out on her own. The rent on the apartment she would like is $750. Her telephone costs would be $35, and cable TV would be $30. She would like to save $75 per month.
a) Construct a budget statement for her present situation.
b) Suggest some adjustments to her current budget so that she could afford to move.

Exploring Math

Perfect, Abundant, Deficient, and Amicable Numbers

A **perfect number** is a counting number that is equal to the sum of all its proper divisors. A **proper divisor** of a number is less then the number itself.

The proper divisors of 6 are 1, 2, and 3.
$1 + 2 + 3 = 6$, so 6 is a perfect number.

An **abundant number** is a counting number the sum of whose proper divisors is greater than the number itself.

The proper divisors of 18 are 1, 2, 3, 6, and 9.
$1 + 2 + 3 + 6 + 9 = 21$, so 18 is an abundant number.

A **deficient number** is a counting number the sum of whose proper divisors is less than the number itself.

The proper divisors of 10 are 1, 2, and 5.
$1 + 2 + 5 = 8$, so 10 is a deficient number.

For two **amicable numbers** or **friendly numbers,** the sum of the proper divisors of one number equals the other number.

Identify the following numbers as perfect, abundant, or deficient.
1. 32   **2.** 52
3. 28   **4.** 58
5. 56   **6.** 50
7. 250   **8.** 112
9. 496   **10.** 264
11. 525   **12.** 804

13. Show that 220 and 284 are amicable numbers.

14. Show that 1184 and 1210 are amicable numbers.

15. Can two perfect numbers be amicable? Explain.

Chapter Check

1. Copy and complete the table. The employer pays time-and-a-half for hours worked in excess of regular hours each week.

	Hourly Rate	Regular Hours per Week	Hours of Overtime	Gross Weekly Income
a)	$15.00	35	7	
b)	$7.50	40	12	
c)	$12.90	37.5	0	
d)	$24.50	40	10	

2. Marion is paid $350 per week, plus 20% commission on sales in excess of $2000. One week, she had $6750 in sales. What was her gross income that week?

3. Bernie charges $3.00 per page for inputting data into a computer. What is his gross income if he inputs 103 pages one week?

4. Tosha lives in British Columbia and earns a monthly salary of $3000. Her personal tax credit is $6456, and she has $300 deducted from her pay each month for her RRSP.
a) Find her monthly CPP contribution.
b) Find her monthly EI premium.
c) Calculate her total annual income tax.

5. Find the interest earned on an investment of $1500 at 5.5% per annum, compounded annually, for four years.

6. Interest is charged at 4.5% per annum, compounded monthly. What is the total amount owing on a loan of $2000 after six months?

7. What is the effective annual interest rate charged on a loan, if the nominal rate is 9% per annum and interest is compounded semi-annually?

8. Instalment buying Mario bought an electronic keyboard that had a retail price of $429.31, including taxes. He made a down payment of 15% and paid off the balance in 18 monthly instalments of $25.21.
a) What was the instalment price?
b) What was the finance charge?
c) By what percent is the instalment price greater than the retail price?

9. RRSP Steve is 20 years old and hopes to retire when he is 55. He invests $6000 in an RRSP. If this investment earns interest at an average rate of 11% per annum, compounded semi-annually, what is its value in 35 years time?

10. Credit card Maggie uses a credit card that charges daily interest at 0.046%. She has an unpaid balance from the previous month, and the date of her current statement is May 04. Find the interest charge for each of the following items.
a) purchase for $89.00 posted on April 10
b) cash advance of $150.00 on April 15
c) purchase for $132.96 posted on April 18
d) previous balance of $320.45

11. Property tax A cottage has an assessed value of $95 000. If the mill rate for recreational property is 12.045, how much is the annual property tax on the cottage?

12. Housing costs Davon has a $115 000 mortgage at 7.5%, amortized over 25 years. His house has an assessed value of $162 000, and the residential mill rate in his municipality is 32.593. How much should he budget each month for his housing costs?

13. Meera has just started a new job as an engineer for a large oil company. Her gross monthly income is $4818.21. Her deductions each month are CPP $87.92, EI $95.88, income tax $1168.95, professional dues $57.00, RPP $484.48, health insurance $57.72.
a) Calculate Meera's net income per month.
b) Meera plans her budget by listing her predicted monthly expenses.

Item	Amount	Item	Amount
Rent	$500	Car Loan Payment	$350
Cable TV	$35	Student Loan	$400
Phone	$45	Food	$250
Clothing	$250	Car Operating Costs	$150
Hair Care	$100		

How much does Meera have left after she deducts these amounts?
c) Meera decides to budget the balance as follows: 25% savings, 60% recreation and miscellaneous, and 15% to pay off her car loan faster. Draw a circle graph to display her entire spending budget.

Using the Strategies

1. In the diagram the red horizontal, vertical, and diagonal line segments join two points. How many paths are there from A to B that consist of exactly 5 of these line segments?

2. Prove or find a counterexample to the following statement.

If the points D and E are in the interior of $\angle ABC$, and D is not on BE, then $\angle ABC = \angle ABD + \angle DBE + \angle EBC$.

3. Suppose that a domino covers two squares on a checkerboard. If the two squares in opposite corners of the checkerboard are removed, can the remaining portion of the board be completely covered with dominoes?

4. How many three-digit whole numbers do not contain any of the digits 1, 2, 4, 5, 6, 8, and 9?

5. A circular lawn has a radius of 10 m. The lawn needs re-sodding. Sod can be purchased in strips that are 40 cm wide. What is the approximate length of sod needed?

6. About what percent of the people in your city or town own at least one piece of apparel with a professional sports team name or logo on it?

7. In the diagram, $\triangle RST$ is isosceles, with RS = RT, and $\triangle ABC$ is equilateral. Express $\angle x$ in terms of $\angle y$ and $\angle z$.

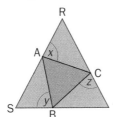

8. In the sum, D, E, and F represent different whole numbers. Find the values of D, E, and F.

9. The numbers 1, 4, 9, 49, and 144 are perfect squares and contain only the digits 1, 4, or 9. Find two other perfect squares that contain only the digits 1, 4, or 9.

10. What is the smallest value the expression $x^2 + 10x$ can have, if x is a real number?

11. Determine the pattern and find the next number in this sequence.

1, 256, 2187, 4096, 3125, 1296, ■.

12. The digits from 1 to 9 have been used to write three numbers, where the second number is twice the first number and the third number is three times the first number.

1 9 2
3 8 4
5 7 6

a) Another set of three numbers that satisfies the same conditions can be found by rearranging the digits in the three given numbers. What is the set of numbers?

b) There are two other sets of three numbers that satisfy the same conditions. One set is a rearrangement of the digits of the other set. What are the two sets of numbers?

DATA BANK

1. a) Is the percent of women in the Canadian population expected to increase or decrease?

b) In what age groups are women expected to outnumber men?

c) If you were working as a financial planner and specializing in helping people plan for retirement, how might the answer to part b) be useful to you?

2. Write two problems using data from the Data Bank. Have a classmate solve your problems.

3. In which Canadian province is the most spent, per person, on building and maintaining roads and highways? Give possible reasons.

Without solving, determine whether each system has no solution, one solution, or infinitely many solutions. Then, solve the systems with one solution graphically.

1. $y = -5x - 8$
   $x + 3y = 4$

2. $x - 5y = 3$
   $2x - 10y = -3$

3. $2x - y = -4$
   $3x + 2y = -20$

4. $y = 4 - 3x$
   $6x + 2y = 8$

Solve each system by substitution. Check each solution.

5. $x - 2y = 4$
   $2x - 3y = 7$

6. $y = 2x + 3$
   $4x + 5y = 8$

Solve each system by elimination. Check each solution.

7. $3x + 8y = -3$
   $5x + 8y = -5$

8. $11m + 3n = 25$
   $-11m + 7n = -15$

9. $3x - 4y = 10$
   $2x - 3y = 7$

10. $4x - 5y = -22$
   $5x + 6y = -3$

🖉 *Which method would you use to solve each system of equations? Explain. Then, solve and check each system.*

11. $y = 5x + 10$
   $y = -3x - 6$

12. $4x + 5y = -11$
   $3x + 2y = -3$

13. $5x + 6y = 7$
   $3x - 2y = 7$

14. $x + 5y = -8$
   $11x - 3y = 28$

Solve each system of equations. Check each solution.

15. $d + e = 5$
   $2d - e + f = 5$
   $4d = 12$

16. $x - y + z = -2$
   $2x + 3y - z = 1$
   $5x + 2y - z = -3$

17. Lake Superior The length of Lake Superior is 306 km more than its breadth. Three times the breadth is 208 km more than the length. What are the length and breadth of Lake Superior?

18. Apartment units There is a total of 168 bachelor, 1-bedroom, and 2-bedroom units in an apartment building. The number of 1-bedroom units is the same as the number of 2-bedroom units. Double the number of bachelor units is 36 more than the number of 1-bedroom units. How many units of each type are in the building?

Solve and check.

19. $p + 6 < -1$

20. $5h - 3 > 12$

21. $2(f - 1) \geq 6$

22. $3n - 1 \leq 11 + 2n$

23. $4(g - 3) + 5 \leq 5(4 - g) - 9$

24. $\dfrac{y}{3} + 1 > -3$

25. $\dfrac{3}{4}x - 8 \leq 1$

26. $\dfrac{m-1}{2} > \dfrac{4+m}{3}$

27. $\dfrac{d+5}{3} - \dfrac{1}{2} > \dfrac{5d}{6}$

Which of the given ordered pairs are solutions to the inequality?

28. $3x - 2y \leq -1$ (0, 0), (1, 6), (−5, 1), (−2, −2)

Graph each inequality.

29. $y \geq 3 - x$

30. $x + y < 4$

31. $3x - y > 4$

32. $8 - x + 5y \leq 3$

33. $y > \dfrac{4}{5}x + 2$

34. $\dfrac{x}{3} - \dfrac{y}{8} \geq -2$

Solve each system of inequalities by graphing.

35. $y < x + 2$
   $y > x - 1$

36. $y \leq 4$
   $y < x - 3$

37. $y \geq \dfrac{1}{4}x - 7$
   $y \geq 3x$

38. $x + y < 4$
   $x - y < -1$

39. $2x + y > 7$
   $x - 2y \geq 3$

40. $3x + y - 4 < 0$
   $2y - x + 1 \geq 0$

41. Charity baked goods At a charity bazaar, there are two baked-goods tables. All items at one table sell for $5 each, and all items at the other sell for $8 each. Renata can spend at most $40 on baked goods.
a) Write an inequality that represents the numbers of baked goods at each price Renata can buy.
b) State any restrictions on the variables.
c) Graph the inequality.

Without sketching each parabola, state
a) *the direction of the opening*
b) *the coordinates of the vertex*
c) *the equation of the axis of symmetry*
d) *the domain and range*
e) *the maximum or minimum value*

42. $y = -0.25x^2$

43. $f(x) = x^2 + 5$

44. $y = -(x - 1)^2 - 3$

45. $f(x) = 3(x - 5)^2$

46. $f(x) = 2(x + 3)^2 - 4$

47. $y = -0.5(x + 7)^2 + 2$

Write an equation that defines each parabola.

48. vertex (0, 3); passing through (1, 7)
59. congruent to $y = x^2$; opens down; vertex (−2, −3)
50. vertex (−2, 5); passing through (2, 13)
51. vertex (−3, −3); y-intercept 6

Find the coordinates of the vertex.

52. $y = x^2 - 10x + 12$

53. $y = -x^2 - 8x - 1$

54. $y = \dfrac{1}{3}x^2 - 2x$

55. $y = 2x^2 - 4x + 3$

56. Baseball The path of a baseball after a batter hit a pop-up can be modelled by the following function. For this function, $h(d)$ metres is the height of the ball and d metres is the horizontal distance of the ball from home plate, where it was hit.
$$h(d) = -0.07(d-10)^2 + 8$$
a) What was the maximum height of the ball?
b) What was the horizontal distance of the ball from home plate when it reached its maximum height?
c) What was the height of the ball when it was hit?
d) If the ball was caught 19.5 m from home plate, how far off the ground was the infielder's glove when the ball was caught, to the nearest tenth of a metre?
e) If no one had caught the ball, what would its horizontal distance from home plate have been when it hit the ground, to the nearest tenth of a metre?

57. Fencing A rectangular field is to be enclosed by 800 m of wire fencing.
a) What dimensions will give the maximum area?
b) What is the maximum area?

Solve by graphing.
58. $x^2 + x = 12$ **59.** $-x^2 = 15 - 8x$

Solve. Express radical solutions in simplest radical form.
60. $n^2 - 8n = 9$ **61.** $3a^2 = -5a + 2$
62. $k^2 - 21 = 100$ **63.** $3 + v^2 + 9v = 0$
64. $1 = 2b^2 - 5b$ **65.** $\dfrac{3}{y} + 1 = -\dfrac{2}{y^2}$
66. $5x^2 + 6x + 1 = 0$ **67.** $3n^4 + 8n^2 = 3$

Determine the nature of the roots.
68. $5c^2 - 8c + 7 = 0$ **69.** $4n^2 - 4n + 1 = 0$

Solve. Round answers to the nearest hundredth, if necessary.
70. $-3e + e^2 + 2 = 0$ **71.** $0 = t^2 + 7t - 1$

72. Write a quadratic equation with roots -5 and $\dfrac{2}{3}$.

73. Determine the values of k that give two distinct real roots for $2x^2 + 5x + k = 0$.

74. Factor $2p^3 - p^2 - 2p + 1$ completely.

Find the exact roots.
75. $x^3 - 3x^2 + 3 = x$ **76.** $0 = 2w^3 - 5w^2 + w + 2$

77. Flag Is it possible for a rectangular flag with a perimeter of 540 cm to have an area of 16 200 cm²? If so, find the dimensions.

78. Decorating The area of a rectangular floor is 35.75 m². A rug measuring 4 m by 5 m is centred on the floor, that is, the width of bare floor is the same on all sides of the rug. What is the width of bare floor?

79. For $f(x) = 4x^2 - 9$ and $g(x) = 2x - 3$, find the following. Write each function in simplest form and state any restrictions on the variable.
a) $(f + g)(x)$ **b)** $(f - g)(x)$ **c)** $(fg)(x)$ **d)** $\left(\dfrac{f}{g}\right)(x)$
e) $f(x) + 3g(x)$ **f)** $(gg)(x) + f(x)$

80. For $f(x) = \sqrt{x+3}$ and $g(x) = 5x$, find
a) $(f \circ g)(x)$ and $(g \circ f)(x)$, if each exists
b) the domain and range of f, g, $f \circ g$, and $g \circ f$

81. Show that $f(x) = 3 - x$ is its own inverse.

82. Graph $y = x^3 - 3x^2 - 9x - 5$ and determine
a) the domain and range
b) any real zeros and the y-intercept
c) the coordinates of any relative maximums or relative minimums
d) the intervals where $f(x) > 0$ and $f(x) < 0$
e) any symmetry and the end behaviour

83. Graph $f(x) = |x^2 - 4| - 5$ and
a) determine the domain and range
b) determine the values of any real zeros
c) determine the values of x for which $f(x) \geq 0$
d) describe any symmetry

84. Graph $g(x) = \dfrac{x^2 - 1}{x}$ and determine
a) the equations of any asymptotes
b) the domain and range

85. Graph $y = \sqrt{x - 2} + 3$ and determine the domain and range.

Solve and check.
86. $|2q - 3| + 1 = 3q$ **87.** $\dfrac{1}{x^2 - 1} = \dfrac{1}{x + 1}$

Solve. Graph the solution.
88. $|w - 2| > 2w - 10$ **89.** $\sqrt{g + 2} \leq \sqrt{g - 1} + 1$

90. Pattern One cube makes one step. Three cubes make two steps. Six cubes make three steps.
a) Sketch two diagrams to show the number of cubes that make four steps and five steps.
b) Make a conjecture about the number of cubes that make *n* steps.
c) Test your conjecture on six steps.

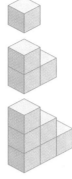

Give an example that supports each conjecture. Then, give one counterexample to show that the conjecture is false.

91. An angle smaller than an obtuse angle is an acute angle.

92. A whole number has two square roots.

93. a) Try the following several times by choosing different numbers. Then, make a conjecture about the result.
Choose a natural number. Add 5. Square the result. Subtract the square of the original number. Subtract 15. Divide by 10.
b) Prove your conjecture using deductive reasoning.

Show each solution set on a number line.
94. $n < 2$ and $n \geq -1$ **95.** $n \leq -4$ or $n > 0$
96. $n \leq 3$ and $n \leq -2$ **97.** $n > 8$ or $n > 3$

98. Health survey One hundred people are surveyed about what they are doing to improve their health. The results show 82 do not smoke, 33 exercise regularly, 28 eat less saturated fat, 20 exercise regularly and do not smoke, 15 eat less saturated fat and do not smoke, 10 exercise regularly and eat less fat, and 2 do all three.
a) Display the information in a Venn diagram.
b) How many of those surveyed do not smoke, but do neither of the others?

99. a) Determine if the following statement is true.
If a whole number is a factor of 24, then it is a factor of 12.
b) Write the converse, and determine if it is true.
c) Write the contrapositive, and determine if it is true.

100. In △ABC and △DEF, AC is equal to DF, AB is equal to DE, and ∠BAC is not equal to ∠EDF. Use indirect reasoning to prove that BC is not equal to EF.

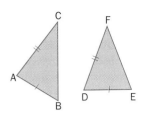

101. If AB = AF, and AC = AE, prove that ∠C = ∠E.

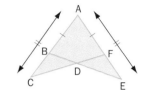

102. Road tunnel A tunnel under a river is built inside a cylinder. The road surface is 8.8 m wide and 1.9 m above the lowest point in the cylinder. What is the radius of the cylinder, to the nearest tenth of a metre?

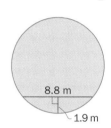

103. *Given:* A, B, and C are collinear; D, B, and E are collinear.
Prove: ∠DFA = ∠CFE

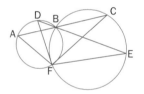

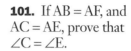
Find the measures of the indicated angles. Explain your reasoning.

104.
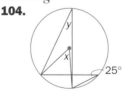

105.
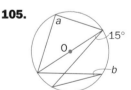

106.
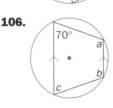

107.
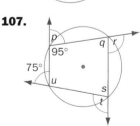

108. △ABC is an isosceles triangle with AB = AC. CE and BD are medians. Prove that BCDE is a cyclic quadrilateral.

Find the measures of the indicated lengths and angles.

109. **110.**

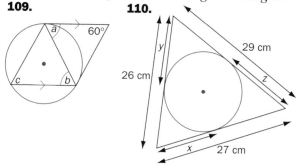

125. In △ABC, ∠A = 49.6°, a = 32.1 cm, and b = 21.9 cm. Find ∠C, to the nearest tenth of a degree.

126. Determine the length of chord AB, to the nearest hundredth.

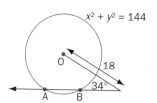

111. Pie slices A pie with a diameter of 24 cm is sliced into equal sectors, each with an arc length of 10.8 cm. What is the sector area of one slice, to the nearest tenth of a square centimetre?

The measure of an interior angle of a regular polygon is given. Determine the number of sides of the polygon.

112. 140° **113.** 168° **114.** 160°

115. Verify that P(–4, 3), Q(–1, –5), and R(2, 3) are the vertices of an isosceles triangle.

Determine the coordinates of the points that divide the line segment joining the two given points into the given number of congruent parts.

116. C(–7, –6), D(1, 6) into 4 parts
117. P(7, 5), Q(–2, 1) into 3 parts

Determine the vertical distance, the horizontal distance, and the shortest distance between the following pairs of parallel lines. Round distances to the nearest hundredth, if necessary.

118. $x - 4y = -8$ and $x - 4y = 4$
119. $y = -2x + 4$ and $y = -2x - 3$

Write the coordinates of the centre and find the exact radius of each circle.

120. $(x + 3)^2 + (y - 6)^2 = 36$
121. $(x - 4)^2 + y^2 = 10$

For each line and circle,
a) *find the coordinates of any point(s) of intersection*
b) *when there are two points of intersection, find the length of the chord between them*
Round answers to the nearest tenth, if necessary.

122. $y = 5x - 13$ and $x^2 + y^2 = 13$
123. $y = -2x - 2$ and $(x + 4)^2 + (y + 2)^2 = 10$

124. For the circle $(x + 2)^2 + (y - 4)^2 = 12$, write an equation for the tangent at (1, 2).

Calculate the gross weekly earnings of each employee.
127. Dan earns $12.50/h and works 37.5 h/week.
128. Katrina earns an annual salary of $42 250.
129. Kim earns $350 weekly, plus 2% of her weekly sales, which average $15 000.
130. Lina earns $13.25/h, with time-and-a-half for hours over 38 h, and works 42 h in one week.
131. Pat earns $2 per delivery, made 148 deliveries in a week, and averaged $1.50 tip per delivery.

132. Using CPP deductions of 3.2% of gross annual income between $3500.01 and $36 900, and EI deductions of 2.7% of gross income, calculate Garfield's CPP and EI deductions from his gross monthly income of $2800.

133. Lars deposited $200 in an account on January 1, and made additional $200 deposits on April 1, July 1, and October 1. The account paid 6% interest per annum, compounded monthly. How much was in the account at the end of the first year?

134. Find the effective annual interest rate that is equivalent to 5.5% per annum, compounded monthly.

135. Buying furniture A furniture store advertises a sofa and two chairs for $100 down and 30 monthly instalments of $100, excluding taxes. If the selling price is $2895, excluding taxes, what are the finance charges?

136. A home with a $110 000 mortgage, at 7.25% per annum, amortized over 20 years, is assessed at $165 000 with a mill rate of 7.1105. Use the Amortization Table on page 590 or a graphing calculator with finance functions to determine the monthly housing costs.

137. List eight expenses that most people who work and who own or rent a home must allow for when creating a budget.

Time Zones

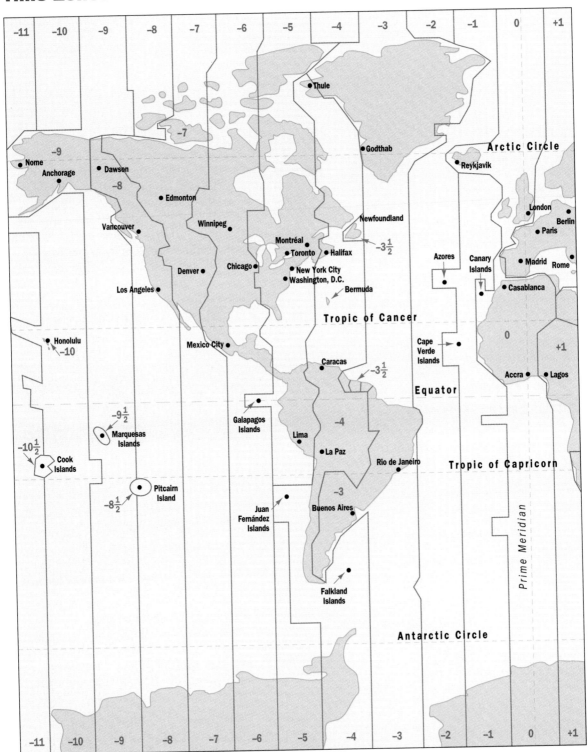

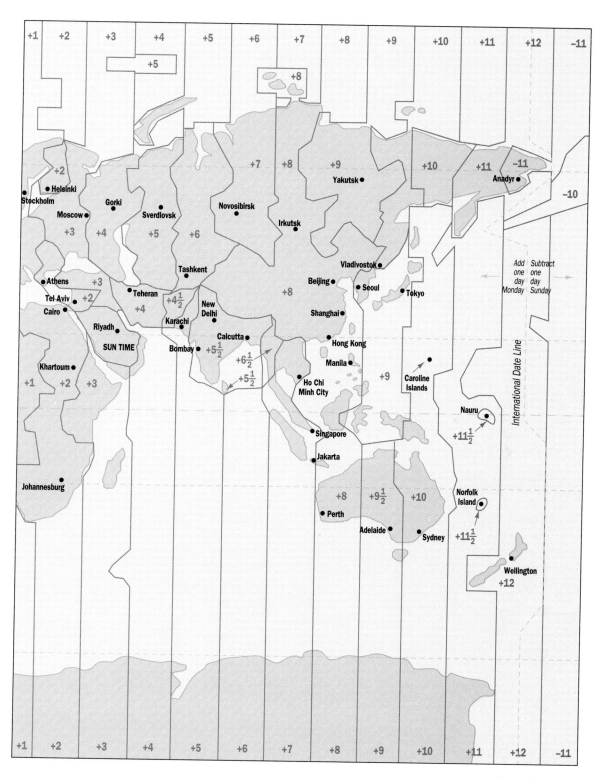

DATA BANK

Population Projections, by Region and for Selected Countries in 1997 and 2025

(millions of persons)

Region	1997	2025	Region	1997	2025
World	**5849**	**8039**			
Africa	**758**	**1454**	**Asia**	**3539**	**4785**
Eastern Africa	**234**	**480**	**Eastern Asia**	**1447**	**1696**
Ethiopia	60	136	China	1244	1480
Kenya	28	50	Dem. People's Rep. of Korea	23	30
Madagascar	16	35	Hong Kong	6	7
Malawi	10	20	Japan	126	121
Mozambique	18	35	Republic of Korea	46	53
Somalia	10	24	**South Eastern Asia**	**498**	**692**
Tanzania	32	62	Cambodia	11	17
Uganda	21	45	Indonesia	204	275
Zambia	9	16	Lao People's Dem. Rep.	5	10
Zimbabwe	12	19	Malaysia	21	32
Middle Africa	**88**	**188**	Myanmar	47	68
Angola	12	26	Philippines	71	105
Cameroon	14	29	Singapore	3	4
Dem. Rep. of the Congo	48	106	Thailand	59	69
Northern Africa	**165**	**257**	Vietnam	77	110
Algeria	30	47	**South Central Asia**	**1418**	**2100**
Egypt	65	96	Afghanistan	22	45
Morocco	28	40	Bangladesh	122	180
Sudan	28	47	India	960	1330
Tunisia	9	14	Iran	72	128
Southern Africa	**50**	**83**	Pakistan	144	269
South Africa	43	72	Sri Lanka	18	24
Western Africa	**222**	**447**	**Western Asia**	**175**	**297**
Burkina Faso	11	24	Iraq	21	42
Côte d'Ivoire	14	24	Israel	6	8
Ghana	18	36	Jordan	6	12
Mali	12	25	Saudi Arabia	19	42
Niger	10	22	Syrian Arab Republic	15	26
Nigeria	118	238	Turkey	63	86
Senegal	9	17	Yemen	16	40

Population Projections, by Region and for Selected Countries in 1997 and 2025

(millions of persons)

Region	1997	2025	Region	1997	2025
Europe	**729**	**701**	**Latin America**	**492**	**690**
Eastern Europe	**309**	**284**	**Caribbean**	**37**	**48**
Poland	39	40	Cuba	11	12
Romania	23	21	Dominican Republic	8	11
Northern Europe	**94**	**96**	Haiti	7	13
United Kingdom	58	60	**Central America**	**128**	**189**
Southern Europe	**144**	**137**	Guatemala	11	22
Greece	11	10	Honduras	6	11
Italy	57	52	Mexico	94	130
Portugal	10	9	**South America**	**327**	**452**
Spain	40	38	Argentina	36	47
Western Europe	**183**	**184**	Bolivia	8	13
France	59	60	Brazil	163	217
Germany	82	81	Chile	15	19
Netherlands	16	16	Colombia	37	53
			Ecuador	12	18
Former USSR	**286**	**290**	Peru	24	36
Belarus	10	10	Venezuela	23	35
Kazakhstan	17	20			
Russian Federation	148	131	**North America**	**302**	**369**
Ukraine	51	46	Canada	30	36
Uzbekistan	24	37	United States of America	272	333
Oceania	**29**	**41**			
Australia	18	24			
Melanesia	6	10			

Canadian Population Projections by Age Group

(thousands of persons)

		Total	Under 5 years	5-9 years	10-14 years	15-24 years	25-34 years	35-44 years	45-54 years	55-64 years	65-74 years	75 + years
2021	**Male**	19 165	1080	1102	1111	2317	2625	2656	2559	2664	1905	1147
	Female	19 534	1022	1042	1050	2194	2531	2594	2541	2719	2112	1729
2031	**Male**	20 362	1082	1131	1173	2410	2590	2834	2699	2467	2323	1653
	Female	20 855	1024	1070	1108	2280	2488	2753	2656	2515	2536	2424
2041	**Male**	21 110	1108	1137	1175	2499	2680	2799	2870	2598	2154	2090
	Female	21 742	1049	1075	1109	2364	2573	2711	2811	2625	2349	3076

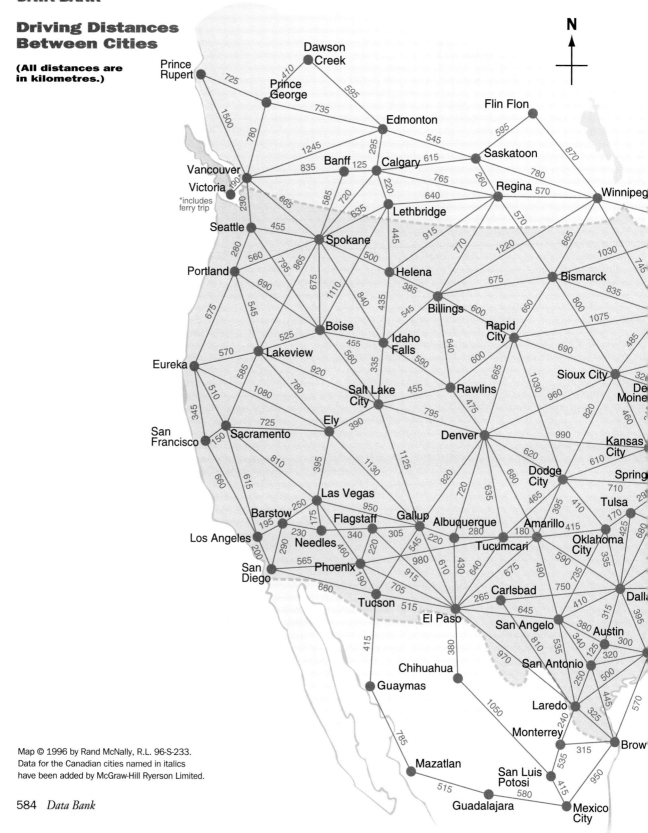

DATA BANK

Driving Distances Between Cities

(All distances are in kilometres.)

N

Prince Rupert

Dawson Creek

410 — Prince George

725

595

1500

780

735

Edmonton

Flin Flon

595

545

870

1245

835 — Banff — 125 — Calgary

295

615

Saskatoon

780

Vancouver

890

260

765

Regina — 570 — Winnipeg

Victoria

*includes ferry trip

230

665

585

720

220

640

Lethbridge

570

1030

745

Seattle — 455 — Spokane

445

915

665

280

560

795

865

500

770

1220

Bismarck

835

Portland

690

675

1110

840

435

Helena

385

675

650

800

1075

675

545

Billings

600

Rapid City

Boise

455

Idaho Falls

545

640

600

690

485

Eureka

570 — Lakeview

525

560

335

590

Rawlins — 475

Sioux City

32

De Moine

585

1080

780

920

Salt Lake City — 455

795

1030

960

820

460

345

510

725

Ely — 390

1125

Denver

Kansas City

San Francisco

150 — Sacramento

395

1130

820

720

635

680

620

610

Spring

810

Dodge City

465

395

410

710

Las Vegas

950

Gallup

Albuquerque

180

Tulsa

170

29

660

615

250

Barstow

175

Flagstaff

340

305

545

220

280

Amarillo — 415

Oklahoma City

08

Los Angeles

290

230

Needles

460

220

980

610

Tucumcari

590

735

335

200

565 — Phoenix

190

915

430

640

675

490

750

Dall

395

San Diego

660

705

Carlsbad

265

410

315

Tucson — 515

645

San Angelo

380

Austin — 300

El Paso

810

535

340

125

320

415

380

Chihuahua

970

San Antonio

250

500

445

075

Guaymas

1050

Laredo

325

240

Monterrey

Brow

315

Map © 1996 by Rand McNally, R.L. 96-S-233.
Data for the Canadian cities named in italics have been added by McGraw-Hill Ryerson Limited.

535

950

784 Data Bank

Mazatlan

515

San Luis Potosi

580

415

Guadalajara

Mexico City

Sept-Iles

St. John's

Charlottetown
Moncton

Sydney

*includes
ferry trip

Rivière
du Loup

Winnipeg

Quebec

Kapuskasing

Thunder
Bay

Halifax
Saint John

Montreal

Bangor

North
Bay

Sault
Ste. Marie

Ottawa

Boston

Syracuse

Mackinaw
City

Toronto

Albany

Minneapolis

Buffalo

New York

Madison

Detroit

Cleveland
Pittsburgh

Philadelphia

Chicago

Des
Moines

Indianapolis

Washington, D.C.

Springfield

Cincinnati

Kansas
City

St. Louis

Lexington

Charleston

Springfield

Nashville

Asheville

Raleigh

Tulsa

Memphis

Oklahoma

Little
Rock

Atlanta

Montgomery

Savannah

Dallas

Jackson

Tallahassee

Jacksonville

Austin

New
Orleans

Tampa

Houston

Miami

Brownsville

DATA BANK

Flying Distances Between Selected World Cities, in Kilometres

From Canada to USA

Calgary	Chicago	2222
	Los Angeles	1942
	New York	3245
	San Francisco	1637
Halifax	Boston	659
	Miami	2262
	New York	961
	Orlando	2409
Montreal	New York	522
	Orlando	2006
	Tampa	2095
Ottawa	Orlando	1941

From Canada to USA

Toronto	Boston	717
	Chicago	700
	Honolulu	7465
	Los Angeles	3492
	Miami	1988
	New York	574
	Orlando	1702
	San Francisco	3625
Vancouver	Honolulu	4350
	Los Angeles	1725
	San Francisco	1274
Winnipeg	Chicago	1137
	Honolulu	6124
	Orlando	2740

From Canada to Europe

Calgary	Glasgow	6473
	London	7012
Edmonton	London	6782
Halifax	Glasgow	4218
	London	4597
Montreal	Athens	7622
	Lisbon	5248
	London	5217
	Paris	5526

From Canada to Europe

St. John's	London	3741
Toronto	Dublin	5262
	Frankfurt	6340
	Glasgow	5280
	Lisbon	5737
	London	5735
	Paris	6015
	Rome	7110
	Zurich	6488

From Canada to Asia/Australia

Toronto	Hong Kong	13 048
	Sydney	16 753
	Tokyo	10 116
	Wellington	15 052

From Canada to Asia/Australia

Vancouver	Hong Kong	10 253
	Singapore	12 810
	Sydney	13 628
	Tokyo	7 533
	Wellington	11 937

From Canada to Mexico/Caribbean

Calgary	Puerto Vallarta	3467
Montreal	Acapulco	4003
	Barbados	3875
	Cuba	2590
	Haiti	3016
	Montego Bay	3042
	Nassau	2313
	St. Lucia	3755

From Canada to Mexico/Caribbean

Toronto	Acapulco	3541
	Barbados	3906
	Cancun	2605
	Cuba	2289
	Nassau	2080
	Puerto Plata	2790
Vancouver	Cancun	4472
	Puerto Vallarta	3543
Winnipeg	Montego Bay	3891

Within Europe/Asia/Australia

Athens	Beijing	7630
	Berlin	1801
	Madrid	2374
Beijing	Hong Kong	2018
	Tokyo	2103
	Zurich	8002
Berlin	Moscow	1619
	Paris	877
	Zurich	668
Calcutta	Beijing	3269
	Hong Kong	2745
	Singapore	2873
Glasgow	Berlin	1214
	London	566
	Paris	908
Hong Kong	London	9740
	Moscow	7252
	Singapore	2564
Lisbon	London	1585
	Paris	1452
	Zurich	1722
London	Athens	2391
	Beijing	8161
	Berlin	929
	Calcutta	7978
	Helsinki	1823
	Moscow	2508

Within Europe/Asia/Australia

Madrid	Berlin	1866
	London	1261
	Moscow	3446
Moscow	Athens	2227
	Beijing	5807
	Helsinki	898
	Lisbon	3913
	Tokyo	7500
Paris	Athens	2097
	Calcutta	7874
	Helsinki	1912
	London	343
	Madrid	1050
	Tokyo	9740
	Zurich	490
Rome	Athens	1040
	London	1444
	Moscow	2376
Singapore	Sydney	6316
	Wellington	8534
Sydney	Wellington	2218
Tokyo	Hong Kong	2855
	Moscow	7500
	Rome	9876
Zurich	Athens	1616
	London	777
	Rome	692

Flying Distances Between Selected Canadian Cities, in Kilometres

	Calgary	Edmonton	Halifax	Montreal	Ottawa	Regina	St. John's	Thunder Bay	Toronto	Vancouver	Whitehorse	Winnipeg
Edmonton	276											
Halifax	3768	3679										
Montreal	3003	2967	804									
Ottawa	2877	2848	953	151								
Regina	661	690	3099	2348	2219							
St. John's	4375	4216	880	1613	1766	3718						
Thunder Bay	1808	1779	1997	1222	1090	1131	2695					
Toronto	2686	2687	1287	506	363	2026	2122	909				
Vancouver	685	809	4426	3679	3550	1332	5005	2461	3343			
Whitehorse	1685	1527	4836	4239	4147	2196	5167	3169	4064	1484		
Winnipeg	1191	1187	2574	1816	1688	532	3220	600	1502	1863	2627	
Yellowknife	1273	1018	3742	3178	3098	1462	4067	2201	3057	1571	1103	1742

DATA BANK

Passenger Aircraft Operating Statistics

Aircraft	Number of Seats	Average Speed Airborne (km/h)	Average Flight Length (km)	Average Fuel Consumption (L/h)	Aircraft Operating Cost Per Hour (CDN $)
B747-100	410	834	4638	13 752	9 381
B747-400	400	867	8148	13 040	10 107
B747-200/300	369	851	5344	14 229	11 129
L-1011-100/200	305	801	2193	9 081	7 259
B-777	291	826	3944	7 711	5 991
DC-10-10	286	801	2403	8 453	7 274
DC-10-40	284	811	3159	10 020	6 691
DC-10-30	272	830	3829	9 937	8 370
A300-600	266	752	1812	6 325	7 319
MD-11	260	843	5235	9 085	9 050
L-1011-500	222	842	4820	9 289	6 806
B767-300ER	216	797	3751	6 019	5 166
B757-200	187	747	1878	3 967	3 767
B767-200ER	181	782	3436	5 421	4 564
MD-90	154	710	1258	3 093	2 444
B727-200	148	708	1194	4 876	3 423
A320-100/200	148	737	1772	3 089	3 036
B737-400	144	666	1130	2 998	3 009
MD-80	141	695	1284	3 498	2 904
B737-300	131	669	969	3 165	2 776
DC-9-50	121	602	555	3 399	2 750
B737-100/200	112	624	711	3 146	2 713
B737-500	110	663	917	2 813	2 471
DC-9-40	109	623	784	3 168	2 556
DC-9-30	100	626	753	3 096	2 499
F-100	97	618	805	2 669	2 654
DC-9-10	71	612	665	2 790	2 306
CRJ	50	805	755	1 465	1 580
DASH 8-300	50	532	304	808	1 640
DASH 8-200	37	546	304	780	1 436
DASH 8-100	37	500	304	689	1 357

Parabolic Dish Telescopes

Telescope	Location	Diameter of Dish (m)	Maximum Depth of Dish (m)
Canada-France-Hawaii Telescope	Hawaii	3.58	0.19
Hubble Space Telescope (primary reflector)	In Earth Orbit	4.27	0.75
Lovell Telescope	Jodrell Bank, England	76.2	15.85
Green Bank Telescope	West Virginia	42.7	6.23
Max-Planck Institute for Radio Astronomy Telescope	Bonn, Germany	100.0	20.83
Parkes Radio Telescope	New South Wales, Australia	64.0	9.85
Palomar Observatory	California	1.83	0.07
Palomar Observatory	California	5.00	0.09
Torun Centre for Astronomy	Poland	15.0	2.83
Torun Centre for Astronomy	Poland	32.0	5.71
United Kingdom Infrared Telescope	Hawaii	3.80	0.09

AMORTIZATION TABLE

Interest Rate (%)	Monthly Payment for Each $1000 of Mortgage Debt			
	Amortization Period			
	10 Years	15 Years	20 Years	25 Years
4	$10.11	$7.38	$6.04	$5.26
4.25	$10.23	$7.50	$6.17	$5.40
4.5	$10.34	$7.63	$6.30	$5.53
4.75	$10.46	$7.75	$6.44	$5.67
5	$10.58	$7.88	$6.57	$5.82
5.25	$10.70	$8.01	$6.71	$5.96
5.5	$10.82	$8.14	$6.84	$6.10
5.75	$10.94	$8.27	$6.98	$6.25
6	$11.07	$8.40	$7.12	$6.40
6.25	$11.19	$8.53	$7.26	$6.55
6.5	$11.31	$8.66	$7.41	$6.70
6.75	$11.43	$8.80	$7.55	$6.85
7	$11.56	$8.93	$7.69	$7.00
7.25	$11.68	$9.07	$7.84	$7.16
7.5	$11.81	$9.21	$7.99	$7.32
7.75	$11.94	$9.34	$8.13	$7.47
8	$12.06	$9.48	$8.28	$7.63
8.25	$12.19	$9.62	$8.43	$7.79
8.5	$12.32	$9.76	$8.59	$7.95
8.75	$12.45	$9.90	$8.74	$8.12
9	$12.58	$10.05	$8.89	$8.28
9.25	$12.71	$10.19	$9.05	$8.44
9.5	$12.84	$10.33	$9.20	$8.61
9.75	$12.97	$10.48	$9.36	$8.78
10	$13.10	$10.62	$9.52	$8.94
10.25	$13.23	$10.77	$9.68	$9.11
10.5	$13.37	$10.92	$9.83	$9.28
10.75	$13.50	$11.06	$10.00	$9.45
11	$13.64	$11.21	$10.16	$9.63
11.25	$13.77	$11.36	$10.32	$9.80
11.5	$13.91	$11.51	$10.48	$9.97
11.75	$14.04	$11.66	$10.65	$10.14
12	$14.18	$11.82	$10.81	$10.32
12.25	$14.32	$11.97	$10.98	$10.49
12.5	$14.46	$12.12	$11.14	$10.67
12.75	$14.59	$12.28	$11.31	$10.85
13	$14.73	$12.43	$11.48	$11.02
13.25	$14.87	$12.59	$11.64	$11.20
13.5	$15.01	$12.74	$11.81	$11.38
13.75	$15.15	$12.90	$11.98	$11.56
14	$15.29	$13.06	$12.15	$11.74

Math Standards

Mathematics as Problem Solving p. xvi
1 Solving Problems 1. 12 **2. a)** From left to right, top to bottom, the missing numbers are: 8; 23, 5, 16; 6, 20; 10; 25, 9 **b)** Yes. **3.** Fill the 5-L container and empty it into the 9-L container; then fill the 5-L container again and pour water into the 9-L container to fill it. There is now 1 L of water in the 5-L container. Empty the 9-L container, pour the 1 L of water from the 5-L container into the 9-L container, refill the 5-L container and pour it into the 9-L container. There are now 6 L of water in the 9-L container. **4. a)** The top vertex of each pyramid meets at the centre of the cube, with each face of the cube being a base of a pyramid. **b)** 20 cm by 20 cm by 10 cm **5.** pentagon, hexagon

Mathematics as Communication p. xvii
1 Writing Solutions 1. Answers may vary. **2.** Invert both timers. When the 5-min timer has expired, invert the 5-min timer again. When the 9-min timer has expired, there is still 1 min remaining on the 5-min timer. At this time, invert the 5-min timer, to time for the additional 4 min.
3 Writing and Interpreting Expressions
1. $E_k = \dfrac{1}{2}mv^2$ **b)** the bowling ball; It has the greater mass. **2.** slower

Mathematics as Reasoning p. xviii
1 Using Logic 1. 1 **2. a)** Melissa **b)** Paolo
2 Solving Problems 1. 15 years old and 45 years old **2.** 7 dimes and 10 quarters **3.** Jaleen: 17; Jamal: 14

Mathematical Connections p. xix
1 Animal Physiology 1. Mouse: 616.8 kJ/kg; Guinea pig: 320.2 kJ/kg; Rabbit: 178.4 kJ/kg; Monkey: 195.7 kJ/kg; Chimpanzee: 121.0 kJ/kg; Human: 83.7 kJ/kg; Pig: 42.2 kJ/kg; Horse: 17.7 kJ/kg; Elephant: 17.0 kJ/kg **2.** The relationship is not a direct variation. **3.** Answers may vary.
2 Human Physiology b) Oxygen consumption increases as heart rate increases. The relationship is close to linear. **c)** 0.95 L/min, 2.24 L/min **d)** 111 beats/min

Algebra p. xx
1 Writing and Evaluating Expressions
1. a) $m = 4l - 2.825$ **b)** 25.175 g **c)** 454.375 g
2. a) $A = 3x^2 + 16x - 12$ **b)** 1508 m² **3. a)** $A = 4y + 10$ **b)** 18 m²

ANSWERS

2 Simplifying Expressions 1. $\dfrac{2}{3}$ **2.** $\dfrac{x-5}{x+3}$ **3.** $\dfrac{2p+1}{3p+1}$
4. $\dfrac{(x+3)(x-2)}{(x+1)(x-1)}$ **5.** $\dfrac{(a-2)^2}{(a+1)(a-4)}$
6. $\dfrac{(5x+13)}{(x+1)(x+2)(x+3)}$

Functions p. xxi
1 Using Relationships 1. a) $d = 95t$ **b)** 527.8 m; 1583.3 m; 3958.3 m **2.** 7.2 s
2 Using Patterns 1. a) $5n + 1$ **b)** 751 **c)** 23 **2. a)** 20; 24 **b)** $4n + 4$ **c)** 104; 196; 452 **3. a)** 42; 50 **b)** $8n + 10$ **c)** 162; 290; 842 **4. a)** $P = 2s + 2$ **b)** 166; 294

Geometry From an Algebraic Perspective p. xxiii
1 Transforming a Triangle 1. a) A′(−1, 3), B′(−4, 1), C′(−5, 4) **b)** $x = 0$ **2. a)** A″(1, −3), B″(4, −1), C″(5, −4) **b)** $y = 0$ **3. a)** A‴(3, 1), B‴(1, 4), C‴(4, 5) **b)** $y = x$
4. a) A″″(3, −1), B″″(1, −4), C″″(4, −5) **b)** rotation 90° clockwise about the origin

Trigonometry p. xxiv
1 Finding Sides and Angles 1. $x = 18$ m **2.** 10.7 cm **3.** no
2 Problem Solving 1. 9.8 km **2. a)** H_1: 1875 m; H_2: 1089 m **b)** 822 m

Statistics p. xxv
1 Selecting Tires 1. Baron **2.** Answers may vary.
2 Purchasing Supplies 1. 156 **2.** Answers may vary.
3 Comparing Climates 1. Edmonton; Prince Rupert **2.** Prince Rupert; Toronto **3.** Toronto; There is not a lot of precipitation in the summer.
4. Prince Rupert; There is a lot of precipitation in the winter.

Probablility p. xxvi
1 Rolling Marbles 1. a) 1 **b)** 4 **c)** 6 **d)** 4 **e)** 1 **2. a)** 2 **b)** 8 **c)** 12 **d)** 8 **e)** 2
2 Rolling Dice 1. Regular dice: $\dfrac{1}{36}, \dfrac{1}{18}, \dfrac{1}{12}, \dfrac{1}{9}, \dfrac{5}{36}, \dfrac{1}{6}, \dfrac{5}{36}, \dfrac{1}{9}, \dfrac{1}{12}, \dfrac{1}{18}, \dfrac{1}{36}$; Irregular dice: $\dfrac{1}{36}, \dfrac{1}{18}, \dfrac{1}{12}, \dfrac{1}{9}, \dfrac{5}{36}, \dfrac{1}{6}, \dfrac{5}{36}, \dfrac{1}{9}, \dfrac{1}{12}, \dfrac{1}{18}, \dfrac{1}{36}$ **2.** Regular dice: $\dfrac{1}{6}$; Irregular dice: $\dfrac{1}{9}$

Discrete Mathematics p. xxvii
1 Telephone Numbers 1. a) 128 **b)** 640 **c)** 10 000 **d)** 6 400 000 **e)** 819 200 000 **2.** Answers may vary.
2 Selecting People 1. 20 **2.** 10

Investigating Limits p. xxviii

1. $f(2) = 1, f(4) = \frac{1}{3}$ **2.** The denominator is 0 when $x = 3$. **3.** 0.666 67, 0.588 23, 0.526 31, 0.502 51, 0.500 25; 0.400 00, 0.434 78, 0.476 19, 0.497 51, 0.499 75 **4.** 0.5 **5.** 0.5 **6.** 0.5 **7. a)** 4 **b)** −2

Mathematical Structure p. xxix

1 Investigating a Five-by-Five Grid **5.** 65 **6.** equal
2 Investigating Other Grids **2.** 111 **3.** 34; 15
3 Explaining Results **1.** Answers may vary.

Chapter 1

Systems of Equations p. 1
1. a) $(8, 4)$ **b)** 8; 4 **2. b)** $(8, 4)$ **3.** They are the same.

Getting Started pp. 2–3
Social Insurance Numbers **1.** 10; The next highest multiple of 10 is 10 greater than a multiple of 10. In this case, the check digit is 0. **2. a)** 9 **b)** 9 **c)** 2 **d)** 8 **3. a)** No; the check digit is incorrect. **b)** Yes; the check digit is correct. **c)** Yes; the check digit is correct. **4.** Answers may vary. 444 142 517; 535 253 520 **5. a)** $10 - m$ **b)** 10 **c)** m is the ones digit from step 4. Subtract m from 10 to find the check digit.
Warm Up **1.** $x + 2$ **2.** $2x + 8$ **3.** $3y - 5$ **4.** $-5a + 3$ **5.** $6x$ **6.** $-2c$ **7.** x **8.** $3n$ **9.** $x + 2y$ **10.** $3p - r$ **11.** 8 **12.** 2 **13.** −6 **14.** −5 **15.** 2 **16.** 12 **17.** $-\frac{1}{2}$ **18.** $\frac{3}{2}$ **19.** 4 **20.** −5 **21.** $-\frac{5}{3}$ **22.** −4 **23.** −1 **24.** −4 **25.** $x = 11 - 3y$ **26.** $x = 5y - 8$ **27.** $x = 2y - 4$ **28.** $x = 2y + 4$ **29.** $y = 3 - 2x$ **30.** $y = x - 2$ **31.** $y = \frac{-1 - 2x}{4}$ **32.** $y = \frac{3x - 4}{2}$

Mental Math
Evaluating Expressions **1.** 4 **2.** 1 **3.** −5 **4.** 12 **5.** 3 **6.** 8 **7.** 0 **8.** 3 **9.** −2 **10.** −1 **11.** 20 **12.** −9
Multiplying Special Pairs of Numbers **1.** 2016 **2.** 7221 **3.** 3024 **4.** 5609 **5.** 216 **6.** 4225 **7.** 12.24 **8.** 56.25 **9.** 6.16 **10.** 200 900 **11.** 902 100 **12.** 421 600
13. a) $100n^2 + 100n + 10x - x^2$ **b)** $100n^2 + 100n + 10x - x^2 = 100n(n + 1) + x(10 - x)$; The first term multiplies the tens digit by the next whole number. The second term multiplies the ones digits.

Investigating Math pp. 4–5
1 Ordered Pairs and One Equation **1. a)** $(1, 13)$, $(24, -10)$ **b)** $(5, -3)$ **c)** $(-2, -4)$, $(-12, 0)$ **d)** $(2, 3)$ **e)** $(-2, -10)$ **2. a)** 3, 9, 10, −2 **b)** 2, −9, 11, −2 **c)** −1, 5, 13, 10 **d)** 5, 3, −4, −7

2 Ordered Pairs and Two Equations **1. a)** $(1, 2)$ **b)** $(-3, 1)$ **c)** $(2, 3)$ **d)** $(6, -8)$ **e)** $(-2, -5)$ **f)** $(-4, 7)$ **2. a)** $(4, -3)$ **b)** $(6, 3)$ **c)** $(-1, 0)$ **d)** Answers may vary. $(0, 0)$
3 Problem Solving **1. a)** 38 **b)** Victoria: 17 m; Prince Rupert: 38 m **2. a)** 40 **b)** lynx: 16 kg; wolf: 40 kg **3. a)** The equations represent the same line on a coordinate grid. **b)** Answers may vary. $(-2, 3)$, $(-3, 4)$ **4.** The equations represent parallel lines on a coordinate grid. They do not intersect.

Section 1.1 pp. 11–12
Practice **1.** $(3, -1)$ **2.** $(-1, 6)$ **3.** $(4, -1)$ **4.** infinitely many solutions **5.** $(6, 0)$ **6.** $(-3, 4)$ **7.** no solution **8.** $(-2, -1)$ **9.** $(2, -1)$ **10.** $(-3, -2)$ **11.** $(4, 1)$ **12.** no solution **13.** $(5, -1)$ **14.** infinitely many solutions **15.** $\left(\frac{1}{2}, 2\right)$ **16.** $\left(2, \frac{3}{2}\right)$ **17.** $\left(-1, \frac{1}{2}\right)$ **18.** $\left(\frac{3}{2}, -\frac{5}{2}\right)$ **19.** $(1.5, -0.8)$ **20.** $(6.7, 1.7)$ **21.** $(3.9, -0.3)$ **22.** $(-2.7, 0.3)$ **23.** $(2.3, 3)$ **24.** $(-2.6, 5.1)$ **25.** one solution **26.** no solution **27.** infinitely many solutions **28.** one solution **29.** no solution **30.** no solution
Applications and Problem Solving **31.** Austria: 9; Germany: 16 **32. a)** $(20, 500)$ **b)** 20 **c)** Champion **33. a)** 3 mg **b)** 7 mg **34.** Montreal: 15 km/h; Victoria: 10 km/h **35. a)** $(50, 1000)$ **b)** 50 **c)** less than 50 **d)** greater than 50 **36.** north: 125 000; south: 5000 **37.** $(-6, 3)$ **38.** $(3, -1)$, $\left(5, -\frac{1}{3}\right)$, $(4, 0)$ **39.** parallelogram **40.** Answers may vary. **a)** $(0, 0)$, $(1, 1)$, $(1, 2)$ **b)** $(-2, 0)$, $(0, 4)$, $(1, 6)$ **41.** Answers may vary. **a)** $x + y = 6$ **b)** $2x + 2y = 8$ **c)** $x + 2y = 4$ **42. a)** $(3, 5)$ **b)** $(2, 3)$ and $(-1, 0)$ **43. a)** For less than 8 h/month, Plan A is least expensive. For between 8 h/month and 22 h/month, Plan B is least expensive. For greater than 22 h/month, Plan C is least expensive. **b)** For less than 11 h/month, Plan C is most expensive. For greater than 11 h/month, Plan A is most expensive. **44.** Answers may vary. **a)** $x + y = 5$, $2x + y = 8$ **b)** $x + y = 5$, $2x + 2y - 10 = 0$ **45.** A linear system can have one solution, no solution, or infinitely many solutions. It cannot have only two solutions. This system must have infinitely many solutions. **47. a)** $\left(-\frac{25}{2}, 9\right)$; $(48, 24)$; $(-16, -18)$

Computer Data Bank p. 13
1 Seating Capacity of New Vehicles **1.** 55 **2.** minivan **3. a)** Dodge Ram 1500 **b)** Mercury Grand Marquis **c)** Honda Odyssey, Isuzu Oasis, and Toyota Avalon **d)** GMC Yukon and Land Rover Discovery **2 Nations Around the World** **1. a)** 31, including

Canada **b)** 18, including Greenland **c)** 5, including China **2. a)** Europe **b)** Asia **c)** Africa and Europe **d)** Africa **3.** Asia, 10; South America, 5 **4.** 18.4% **5.** $23.388 billion **6.** Africa, 83%

3 Locating Craters on Earth 1. a) Oceania **b)** Africa **c)** Europe **d)** North America **e)** North America **f)** Europe **2. a)** Africa, 16; Asia, 19; Europe, 44; North America, 51; Oceania; 19, South America, 7

4 Summer Olympics 1. Answers will vary.
2. Answers will vary.

5 Camping in Western Canada 1. Provincial, 9524 **2.** Alberta, $8 703 187.20; British Columbia, $2 419 113.60; Manitoba, $1 073 404.80; Saskatchewan, $894 211.20; all four, $13 089 916.80

Section 1.2 p. 15
Applications and Problem Solving 1. 67 m **2.** 65 cm **3.** 20 s **4.** Timid swimmer and Bold swimmer cross in boat; Timid swimmer returns in boat; Timid swimmer and Bold cross in boat; Bold swimmer returns in boat; Bold swimmer and Timid cross in boat; Bold swimmer returns in boat; Bold swimmer and Timid cross in boat; Bold swimmer returns in boat; Bold and Bold swimmer cross in boat.
5. Train A is heading to the right, train B, to the left. Train A pulls into the siding with 20 cars, leaving 20 cars on the track. Train B pushes these cars back until it clears the way for train A to back out of the siding. Train B unhitches 20 of its cars. Train A picks them up and pulls them down the track. Train B backs its remaining 20 cars into the siding and train A backs down the track to pick up its 20 cars. Train A now pulls 60 cars - its 40 plus 20 from train B in the middle - to the right. Train B exits the siding, then backs up the track to get 20 cars from train A, pulling them forward and backing them into the siding. Train B backs up to collect its remaining 20 cars, pulls forward and hitches up the 20 cars from Train A in the siding, pulling them onto the track. Train A backs up to hitch up its 20 cars. Both trains proceed to their destinations.
6. 17.1 m **7.** $3\sqrt{2}$ cm **8.** (3, 10) and (9, 6) **9.** 24 **10.** 5.8 cm or 10 cm **13.** 1300 m

Investigating Math pp. 16–17
1 Expressions in Two Variables 1. a) $x + y$ **b)** $6x + 2y$ **c)** $5y - x$ **2. a)** $x - y$ **b)** $x + y$ **3. a)** $x + 7y$ **b)** $x + 15y$ **4. a)** $x + y$ **b)** $10x$ **c)** $5y$ **d)** $10x + 5y$ **5. a)** $10x + 25y$ **b)** $0.1x + 0.25y$ **6. a)** $x + y$ **b)** $0.07x$ **c)** $0.06y$ **d)** $0.07x + 0.06y$

2 Equations in Two Variables 1. $x + y = 8$ **2.** $y = x - 5$ **3.** $y = x^2 - 1$ **4.** $x - 2y + 1 = 0$ **5.** $l + w = 40$ **6.** $c - q = 6$ **7.** $g = 2t - 7$ **8.** $2b + 3t = 61$

3 Systems of Equations 1. $x + y = 7$, $x - y = 3$ **2.** $y = 2x$, $y = x - 4$ **3. a)** $x + y = 256$ **b)** $5x + 2y = 767$ **4.** $p + r = 295$, $p = r + 11$ **5.** $r = \frac{2}{3}c$, $c - r = 1700$ **6.** $b + f = 331$, $10b + 15f = 3915$ **7.** $q + l = 73$, $0.25q + l = 37$ **8.** $x + y = 180$, $y = 3x - 4$

Investigating Math pp. 18–20
1 Representing Equations 1. $x + y = 3$ **2.** $2x - y = -1$ **3.** $x + 3 = -2y$
3 Solving Systems by Substitution, I 1. $(4, -1)$ **2.** $(1, 3)$ **3.** $(-3, 1)$ **4.** $(2, 2)$
4 Solving Systems by Substitution, II 1. $(2, 1)$ **2.** $(2, -1)$ **3.** $(0, -1)$ **4.** $(1, 0)$

Section 1.3 pp. 25–27
Practice 1. $x = 8 - 3y$ **2.** $x = -4y - 13$ **3.** $x = 7y + 7$ **4.** $x = 2y - 1$ **5.** $y = 11 - 6x$ **6.** $y = -5x - 9$ **7.** $y = x + 2$ **8.** $y = 3x + 4$ **9.** $(3, 2)$ **10.** $(4, -5)$ **11.** $(5, 0)$ **12.** $(-2, 3)$ **13.** $(-2, -2)$ **14.** $\left(\frac{1}{2}, -1\right)$ **15.** $(-1, 1)$ **16.** $\left(\frac{7}{11}, -\frac{1}{11}\right)$ **17.** $\left(3, -\frac{6}{5}\right)$ **18.** $(-3, -4)$ **19.** $(1, 0)$ **20.** $\left(1, -\frac{1}{3}\right)$ **21.** $(1, 3)$ **22.** $\left(-1, \frac{2}{7}\right)$ **23.** $\left(\frac{4}{3}, \frac{11}{3}\right)$ **24.** $\left(-\frac{32}{5}, -\frac{18}{5}\right)$

Applications and Problem Solving 25. a) $(24, -18)$ **b)** $(-3, 2)$ **c)** $\left(\frac{3}{2}, 2\right)$ **d)** $\left(-\frac{5}{3}, \frac{1}{6}\right)$ **26.** If the system reduces to an impossible equation, there is no solution. If the system reduces to $0 = 0$, there are infinitely many solutions. Otherwise, there is one solution. **a)** no solution **b)** $(3, -1)$; one solution **c)** infinitely many solutions **d)** $(-1, -5)$; one solution **e)** no solution **f)** infinitely many solutions **27. a)** Fairweather Mountain is 3831 m higher than Baldy Mountain. The height of Fairweather Mountain is 329 m less than 6 times the height of Baldy Mountain. **b)** Baldy Mountain: 832 m; Fairweather Mountain: 4663 m **28.** $x = 34$, $y = 10$ **29. a)** $(5, 4)$ **b)** $(4, 5)$ **c)** $(-1, -5)$ **30.** 463, 289 **31.** 2.5 **32.** short span: 890 m; long span: 1780 m **33.** For less than 4.5 h, Quality is cheaper. For greater than 4.5 h, ABC is cheaper. **34.** owls: 14; pigeons: 3 **35.** 21°, 69° **36.** 323 adult tickets; 227 student tickets **37.** $6000 at 4%; $9000 at 5% **38. a)** 84 km **b)** 132 km **39.** "Macbet": 12 years; "Macbeth": 336 years **40.** 5% solution: 10 mL; 10% solution: 40 mL **41.** 18-carat gold: 100 g; 9-carat gold: 50 g **42.** 25 mL **43. a)** 1.8 h **b)** 135 km **44. a)** No; we get two equivalent equations, and cannot solve the

system. **b)** Yes; we get two different equations, and can solve the system. **45.** 68 **46. a)** $(1, 4, -2)$
b) $(2, -1, 3)$ **47.** -1 **48.** $\dfrac{1}{2}$ **49.** $x + y = q, x - y = r$

Section 1.4 p. 29
Applications and Problem Solving **1. a)** $\$14\,835$
b) $\$9.06$/km **c)** $\$0.031$ per passenger-kilometre **d)** 11:00
2. a) DC-9: 1.15 h; B737: 1.11 h **b)** DC-9: $\$4.58$/km;
B737: $\$4.35$/km **c)** DC-9: $\$0.038$ per passenger-kilometre; B737: $\$0.039$ per passenger-kilometre
3. Answers may vary. **4. a)** 191 000 **b)** Answers may vary. **c)** Answers may vary. **5.** 5915 km **6. a)** Jupiter
b) 45 591 km/h **c)** approximately 27 times faster than Earth; approximately 6 times faster than the sun
7. most crowded: Prince Edward Island; least crowded: Northwest Territories

Career Connection p. 30
1 Comparing Solubilities **1. a)** 16 °C **b)** 26 g/100 g
2. a) 13 °C **b)** 26 g/100 g **3. a)** no **b)** Yes; if it is not parallel, it must intersect. **4.** sodium chloride, ammonium chloride, and potassium iodide. The slopes of their graphs are positive.

Investigating Math p. 31
1 Equivalent Forms **1.** Answers may vary. $(1, 5)$, $(2, 4)$, $(3, 3)$ **2. a)** $2x + 2y = 12$ **b)** yes
3. a) $-3x - 3y = -18$ **b)** yes **4.** Yes; they represent the same line on a coordinate grid.
5. Answers may vary. **a)** $-x + y = -2$, $2x - 2y = 4$,
$3x - 3y = 6$ **b)** $-2x - y = -7$, $x + \dfrac{1}{2}y = \dfrac{7}{2}$, $4x + 2y = 14$
c) $2y = 8x - 6$, $3y = 12x - 9$, $4y = 16x - 12$
d) $2y = x + 5$, $4y = 2x + 10$, $6y = 3x + 15$
2 Equivalent Systems **1.** $(3, 4)$ **2.** $(3, 4)$
3. a) $4x - 2y = 4$, $-x - y = -7$ **b)** $(3, 4)$
4. They all have the same point of intersection.
5. Answers may vary. $2x + y = 10$, $x + 2y = 11$
3 Adding Equations **1.** $(2, 1)$ **2.** $2x + y = 5$ **3.** They all pass through $(2, 1)$. **4.** They are equivalent systems. They all have the same solution. **5.** They are equivalent systems. They all have solution $(3, -2)$.

Investigating Math pp. 32–33
1 Solving Systems by Addition **1.** $(2, 1)$ **2.** $(-1, 2)$
3. $(0, 1)$ **4.** $(1, 1)$
2 Solving Systems by Subtraction **1.** $(2, 1)$
2. $(-1, 1)$ **3.** $(0, 2)$ **4.** $(-1, -1)$
3 Solving Systems by Multiplication **2.** $(2, -1)$
3. $(1, 0)$ **4.** $(-2, -2)$

Section 1.5 pp. 38–40
Practice **1.** $(2, 6)$ **2.** $(-1, -3)$ **3.** $(-4, 1)$ **4.** $(3, -2)$
5. $(-2, 1)$ **6.** $(5, 3)$ **7.** $(1, -2)$ **8.** $(-2, -2)$ **9.** $(3, 1)$
10. no solution **11.** $(1, 0)$ **12.** infinitely many solutions
13. $(4, 2)$ **14.** $(-3, 2)$ **15.** $(-2, -3)$ **16.** $(0, -5)$ **17.** $(9, -4)$
18. $(-3, 8)$ **19.** $(4, 11)$ **20.** $(2, -1)$ **21.** $\left(\dfrac{1}{3}, 1\right)$ **22.** $\left(-2, \dfrac{1}{2}\right)$
23. $\left(\dfrac{5}{9}, \dfrac{1}{9}\right)$ **24.** infinitely many solutions **25.** $\left(\dfrac{4}{5}, \dfrac{3}{5}\right)$
26. no solution **27.** $(-1, -3)$ **28.** $(1, 6)$ **29.** $(-2, 3)$
30. $(2, 1)$ **31.** $(3, 4)$ **32.** $(5, 4)$ **33.** $(4, -2)$ **34.** $(4, 1)$
35. $(-1, -3)$ **36.** $(-0.2, 0.1)$
Applications and Problem Solving
37–42. Answers may vary. **43. a)** The total number of provinces is 10. Three times the number of provincial names with First Nations origins is equal to twice the number of provincial names with other origins.
b) 4 **44.** adult: 206 bones; baby: 350 bones **45.** $x = 32$, $y = 20$ **46.** $-28, 38$ **47.** boat: 16 km/h; current: 4 km/h
48. plane speed: 495 km/h; wind speed: 55 km/h
49. 200 km at 100 km/h and 270 km at 90 km/h
50. chicken sandwich by $\$0.75$ **51.** 2.7 m by 1.2 m
52. 30 min **53. a)** 3 V and 6 V **b)** 5 **54.** $(4, 6)$
55. $(3, 2), (0, -2), (-2, 4)$ **56.** A = 3, B = 2 **57.** $a = -2$,
$b = 3$ **58. a)** 10 **b)** 6 **59. a)** -2 **b)** 3 **60.** $(2, 5)$; The solution is not affected by multiplication by a constant. **61.** Answers may vary. $3x + 2y = 8$,
$5x - 7y = 65$ **62.** Answers may vary. **a)** $3x - 4y = -14$,
$4x - 3y = -7$ **b)** $2x + 3y = 13$, $4x + 3y = 5$
c) $2x - 3y = 4$, $4x + 9y = -2$

Section 1.6 pp. 44–46
Practice **1.** yes **2.** no **3.** no **4.** no **5.** yes **6.** no **7.** no
8. yes **9.** yes **10.** no **11.** $(2, 1, 3)$ **12.** $(0, 1, -2)$
13. $(2, -1, -3)$ **14.** $(-1, -2, -3)$ **15.** $(2, 3, 2)$ **16.** $(4, -3, 2)$
17. $(-2, 0, -7)$ **18.** $(5, 6, -2)$ **19.** $(-2, 4, 1)$ **20.** $(-3, -4, -2)$
21. $(4, 2, 5)$ **22.** $(3, -3, -2)$ **23.** $\left(-1, \dfrac{1}{3}, \dfrac{1}{2}\right)$ **24.** $\left(0, \dfrac{1}{4}, \dfrac{3}{4}\right)$
25. $\left(\dfrac{33}{4}, -\dfrac{17}{4}, \dfrac{9}{2}\right)$ **26.** $\left(\dfrac{27}{5}, \dfrac{7}{5}, -\dfrac{27}{5}\right)$ **27.** $(2, 3, 9)$
28. $(1, 2, -1)$ **29.** $(6, -5, 3)$ **30.** $(3, -1, 5)$ **31.** $(-2, -3, 4)$
32. $(-3, 0, -2)$ **33.** $(-3, 8, 1)$ **34.** $(4, -3, 1)$ **35.** $(3, 2, 4)$
36. $(-3, -2, -4)$ **37.** $(6, 8, 6)$ **38.** $(-4, -6, 12)$
39. $\left(\dfrac{1}{5}, 0, \dfrac{2}{3}\right)$ **40.** $\left(\dfrac{1}{2}, -\dfrac{1}{3}, \dfrac{1}{4}\right)$
Applications and Problem Solving **41. a)** The sum of the points won by the first, second, and third place finishers is 159. The second place finisher had 6 more points than the third place finisher. The first place finisher had 3 less than twice the number of points of the second place finisher. **b)** first: 81; second: 42;

third: 36 **42.** $x = 50$, $y = 55$, $z = 25$ **43.** 8, 14, 31
44. 20, 10, −5 **45.** 82°, 43°, 55° **46.** 120°, 40°, 20°
47. a) 3 gold, 6 silver, 4 bronze **b)** biathlon: 7.5-km
sprint and 15 km **48.** Saturn: 18, Uranus: 17,
Neptune: 8 **49.** 42 years **50.** Batman: $134 000;
Captain Marvel: $60 000; Superman: $144 000
51. 21 $5 bills, 18 $10 bills, 32 $20 bills
52. Canada: 240 000 km; United States: 20 000 km;
Mexico: 10 000 km **53.** British Columbia:
630 000 km²; Alberta: 350 000 km²; Manitoba:
350 000 km² **54.** $3000 at 4%, $9000 at 5%,
$8000 at 7% **55.** $a = -5$, $b = 200$, $c = 0$ **56.** $a = -1$,
$b = 100$, $c = 500$ **57.** 50 g of X, 30 g of Y, 20 g of Z
58. $a = 2$, $b = 4$, and $c = 7$ cannot be the side lengths of
a triangle, because $c > a + b$. **59. a)** Use elimination.
b) (2, 3, 1, 4) **60.** Answers may vary. $x + y + z = 4$,
$2x + y + z = 6$, $3x + y + z = 8$

Technology p. 47
1 Graphing Non-linear Equations **2. a)** The graphs
are congruent parabolas with different vertices and
different directions of opening. **b)** Graphs with a
positive coefficient of x^2 open up. Graphs with a
negative coefficient of x^2 open down. **4.** The graphs
start close to horizontal and then either increase to
positive infinity or decrease to negative infinity.
6. The graphs are cubics. The ones with a positive
coefficient of x^3 start in the 3rd quadrant and end in
the 1st quadrant. The ones with a negative coefficient
of x^3 start in the 2nd quadrant and end in the 4th
quadrant.
2 Solving Systems Containing Non-linear
Equations **1. a)** (−3, 7), (3, 7) **b)** (2, −2), (−2, −6)
c) (1, −1), (4, 5) **d)** (−0.62, 2.62), (1.62, 0.38)
2. a) (3, 8) **b)** (1, −2) **c)** (−1, 0.5) **d)** (−0.79, 0.42),
(1.44, 4.89) **3. a)** (2, 9) **b)** (2, −7) **c)** (0, 0), (−2, −8),
(2, 8) **d)** (0.84, 2.29) **4.** Answers may vary. **5. a)** 0
b) infinitely many **c)** 0 **d)** 1 **e)** 2 **f)** 2 **6. a)** $t_n = 36 + 4n$
b) $t_n = n^2 - n$ **c)** First quadrant; all the ordered pairs
have positive coordinates. **d)** (9, 72) **e)** The value of
term 9 is 72 for both sequences. **7. b)** 2063 **c)**
Answers may vary.

Connecting Math and Zoology p. 51
1 Interpreting the Graph **1.** 14 million years ago
2. a) 6% **b)** 94% **3. a)** 94% **b)** 6% **4.** 4 million years
ago
2 Solving Algebraically **1.** apes: $y = 5x - 20$;
monkeys: $y = -5x + 120$ **2. a)** (14, 50) **b)** the point
where the populations were equal
3 Critical Thinking **1.** Answers may vary. **2.**
Answers may vary. **3.** On the graph, the time for
"years ago" is positive instead of negative. This

reverses the signs of the slopes. **4.** They are equal.
The monkey population increased at the same rate as
the ape population decreased. **5.** No. It shows only
percents, not numbers.

Review pp. 52–53
1. (4, −1) **2.** (−4, 3) **3.** (2, 2) **4.** $\left(\frac{1}{2}, 5\right)$ **5.** (1.9, −2.2)
6. (0.1, 0.7) **7.** infinitely many solutions **8.** no solution
9. one solution **10.** no solution **11.** Sahara:
9 million km²; Australian: 4 million km²
12. a) d represents the number of dollars; p represents
the number of paddles **b)** (62.5, 1125) **c)** at least 63
13. (2, 2) **14.** (1, −1) **15.** (−1, 5) **16.** $\left(1, \frac{1}{3}\right)$ **17.** 75 kg of
24% nitrogen and 25 kg of 12% nitrogen **18.** (3, −2)
19. (1, 1) **20.** $5000 Canada Savings Bond; $10 000
provincial government bond **21.** Mount Pleasant: 16;
Centreville: 15 **22.** (−1, 2) **23.** (−2, 1) **24.** (3, 2)
25. (4, 1) **26.** (−4, −5) **27.** (1, 1) **28.** $\left(2, \frac{1}{2}\right)$ **29.** (−1, 2)
30. 36 cars, 9 vans **31.** (−2, −3) **32.** (3, 4) **33.** (0.6, −0.5)
34. wind speed: 40 km/h; plane speed: 280 km/h
35. (2, 1, −3) **36.** (2, 1, 4) **37.** (7, −1, 2) **38.** (1, 2, −2)
39. a) 13 **b)** 4 **c)** 33 **40.** Cross-Cedar Lake:
10 billion m³; Kinbasket Lake: 25 billion m³;
Williston Lake: 70 billion m³

Exploring Math p. 53
2. a) no **b)** 3, due to symmetry **3. a)** corner, middle
side, middle **b)** between corner and middle side,
between middle and corner, between middle and
middle side **c)** 6 **4.** no

Chapter Check p. 54
1. (4, 3) **2.** (−2, −3) **3.** (−1, 0) **4.** (1, −2) **5.** (−0.7, 3.7)
6. (2.4, 1.1) **7. a)** The lines intersect at one point.
b) The lines are parallel. **c)** The lines coincide.
8. (2, 2) **9.** $\left(-3, \frac{1}{2}\right)$ **10.** (−1, −1) **11.** (2, 1) **12.** (3, 2)
13. (2, −2) **14.** infinitely many solutions **15.** no solution
16. (−6, 4) **17.** $\left(\frac{2}{3}, \frac{1}{3}\right)$ **18.** $\left(-\frac{4}{7}, -\frac{2}{7}\right)$ **19.** (4, 1)
20. (2, 0, 3) **21.** (1, 2, −1) **22.** Lindros: 16; Modano: −8
23. Yukon: 3185 km; Mackenzie: 4241 km
24. 240 g of 30% fruit granola; 360 g of 15% fruit
granola **25.** Yellowknife: 111 days; Peace River:
93 days **26.** $4000 at 4%; $9000 at 6% **27.** wind
speed: 50 km/h; plane speed: 550 km/h **28.** Western
Canada: 21; Central Canada: 42; Eastern Canada: 16

Using the Strategies p. 55

1. $11 = 6^2 - 5^2$; $12 = 4^2 - 2^2$; $15 = 8^2 - 7^2$; $16 = 5^2 - 3^2$; $17 = 9^2 - 8^2$; $19 = 10^2 - 9^2$ **2.** Monday, Tuesday, Wednesday **3.** 400 **5.** 9 and 81 **6.** Answers may vary. **7.** 512 cm² **8.** 1049 **9.** 9 **11.** 192.5 cm³
Data Bank **1.** Answers may vary. **2. b)** 2011 **3.** Answers may vary.

Chapter 2

Linear Inequalities p. 57

1. a) 50 min **b)** 120 min **c)** 10 min **2.** 50 min **3. a)** no **b)** yes **c)** no **d)** yes **e)** yes **f)** no **4.** self-contained underwater breathing apparatus

Getting Started pp. 58–59

1. a) $250 \leq f \leq 21\,000$ **b)** $760 \leq f \leq 1520$ **2. a)** dolphin **b)** dolphin **c)** frog **d)** grasshopper **e)** dog **f)** cat **3. a)** yes **b)** no **4. a)** yes **b)** yes **5. a)** grasshopper **b)** 91.4% **6. a)** $10\,000 \leq f \leq 20\,000$ **b)** 9.1% **7. a)** the soprano hitting high notes **b)** No; the frequency of a normal speaking voice is too low.
Warm Up **1.** < **2.** > **3.** ≤ **4.** ≥ **5.** ≥ **6.** ≥ **7.** > **8.** ≤ **9.** ≤ **10.** < **11.** ≤ **12.** ≥ **13.** $x \geq -3$ **14.** $x < 2$ **15.** $x > -4$ **16.** $x \leq -2$ **17.** $-1 \leq x \leq 7$ **18.** $-3 < x < 1$ **19.** $-2 \leq x < 4$ **20.** $-6 < x \leq -2$ **21.** same; order does not matter **22.** same; order does not matter **23.** same; order does not matter **24.** same; order does not matter
Mental Math
Equations and Inequalities **1.** $(3, 1)$ **2.** $(-2, -7)$ **3.** $(2, 2)$ **4.** $(-1, 1)$ **5.** $(0, -2)$ **6.** $(2, 3)$ **7–12.** Answers may vary. **7.** $(1, 2), (1, 3), (1, 4)$ **8.** $(2, -2), (2, -3), (2, -4)$ **9.** $(-1, 1), (0, 1), (1, 1)$ **10.** $(-1, 3), (0, 3), (1, 3)$ **11.** $(1, 3), (1, 4), (1, 5)$ **12.** $(-2, 7), (-2, 6), (-2, 5)$
Squaring Two-Digit Numbers Beginning in 5 **1.** 3364 **2.** 2601 **3.** 3136 **4.** 2809 **5.** 3025 **6.** 3481 **7.** 29.16 **8.** 291 600 **9.** 26.01 **10.** 270 400 **11.** 31.36 **12.** 348 100 **13.** 2601 **14.** 2809 **15.** 30 250 **16.** 33 640 000 **17.** 31.36 **18.** 3249 **19. a)** $100(25 + x) + x^2$; The first term represents adding 25 to the ones digit. The second term represents affixing the square of the ones digit.

Section 2.1 pp. 63–64

Practice **1.** $y < 2$ **2.** $w > -1$ **3.** $x \geq 3$ **4.** $z \leq -3$ **5.** $x > -2$ **6.** $t > -4$ **7.** $m \leq 3$ **8.** $n \geq 0$ **9.** $x > \frac{1}{2}$ **10.** $x < -\frac{2}{3}$ **11.** $y \leq -1$ **12.** $z \geq 5$ **13.** $x < 2$ **14.** $x > 1$ **15.** $x \leq 0$ **16.** $x \geq -\frac{1}{4}$ **17.** $x \leq 3$ **18.** $x > 2$ **19.** $x < -2$ **20.** $x > 1$ **21.** $y \geq -4$ **22.** $z \leq \frac{5}{4}$ **23.** $x > 4$ **24.** $x < \frac{5}{3}$ **25.** $x < 1$ **26.** $x > 1$

27. $y \leq -4$ **28.** $c \geq 2$ **29.** $x \leq 1$ **30.** $x > \frac{1}{3}$ **31.** $x \geq \frac{3}{2}$ **32.** $t < -\frac{3}{5}$ **33.** $y < -3$ **34.** $w > 2$ **35.** $x \geq \frac{3}{2}$ **36.** $z \leq -8$ **37.** $x > 3$ **38.** $x < -6$ **39.** $q \geq 2$ **40.** $n \geq 3$ **41.** $a > -2$ **42.** $x \geq 1$ **43.** $y < -1$ **44.** $n \geq -2$ **45.** $x > -\frac{1}{2}$ **46.** $x < 0$ **47.** $x < 1$ **48.** $x \leq \frac{3}{4}$ **49.** $z > 6$ **50.** $x \geq 1$
Applications and Problem Solving **51.** 8 **52.** 1.8 m **53.** $16 < x < 34$ **54. a)** $12.25 + 1.55n$ **b)** $12.25 + 1.55n \leq 20$; 5 **55. a)** $15t - 75$ **b)** $15t - 75 \geq 450$; 35 h **56.** 63 **57.** 2056 to 2066 **58. a)** $a < \frac{31\,000 + 1000}{5}$; $a < 6400$ **c)** An island must have an area greater than 0 km². **59. a)** $x > 7$ **b)** $x < 9$ **c)** $x > \frac{7}{3}$, because the area has to be greater than 0 **60.** $\frac{5}{2} \leq x \leq 3$ **61.** between 10:00 and 14:00 **62. a)** $x \leq -1, x > 0$ **b)** $x \neq 0$ **63. a)** $0 = 4$ **b)** no real values **c)** $4 > 0$ **d)** all real values **64. a)** graph of $y = x - 3$ to the left of $x = 2$ **b)** graph of $y = 2 - x$ to the left of $x = 5$ **c)** graph of $y = x + 4$ to the right of $x = -4$ **65.** Answers may vary. **a)** $1 + 2x \leq 3 + x$ **b)** $2(2x + 1) > -2(2 - x)$ **c)** $\frac{x - 2}{2} < \frac{x - 3}{3}$

Technology p. 65

1 Displaying a Solution **1.** $x > 3$ **2.** The calculator displays the solution on a coordinate grid instead of on a number line. **3.** $x > 3$ **5. a)** 1 **b)** The graph would not show if it was on the x-axis. **6.** The connected mode shows a small vertical piece of the graph that is not accurate. **7. b)** no
2 Solving Inequalities **1.** $x \geq 2$ **2.** $x < 3$ **3.** $x > 1$ **4.** $x \leq -3$ **5.** $x \geq 1$ **6.** $x \leq 4$ **7.** $x \geq -2$ **8.** $x < -3$ **9.** $x \leq 3$ **10.** $x > 2$ **11.** $x < -1$ **12.** $x \geq 3$ **13.** $x \leq -\frac{1}{2}$ **14.** $x > \frac{1}{3}$

Section 2.2 p. 67

Applications and Problem Solving **1.** 29 square units **2.** -100 **3.** 55 **4.** 11 111 111 100 000 000 000 **5.** 728 units **6.** 46 **7.** 37 **9.** 21 **10. a)** $\frac{n(n+1)}{2}$ **b)** 741 **c)** 1562 **11.** 1 000 000 **12. a)** 1, 8, 27 **b)** 4913; 970 299

Investigating Math pp. 68–70

1 Inequalities in One Variable **1. a)** Answers may vary. $(3, 2)$ **b)** Answers may vary. $(2, 2)$ **c)** equal **d)** less than **2. a)** yes **b)** Points that satisfy the inequality. They all have x-coordinates less than or equal to 3. **3. a)** no **b)** broken line **5. b)** $y < 2, y \le 2$, $y > 2, y \ge 2$

2 Linear Inequalities in Two Variables
1. b) Answers may vary. (1, 3) **c)** Answers may vary. (1, 4) **d)** equal **e)** greater than **f)** yes; no **g)** above; These points satisfy the inequality. **h)** The line would be broken for $y > x + 2$. **2. b)** Answers may vary. (2, 1) **c)** Answers may vary. (2, 0) **d)** equal **e)** less **f)** yes; no **g)** Below; these points satisfy the inequality. **h)** The line would be broken for $y < x - 1$. **4. a)** below **b)** below **c)** above **d)** above

3 Restricting the Variables
1. a) The graph of $b < 2a - 3$ does not include the points on the axes, and the graph does not extend above the x-axis or to the right of the y-axis. **b)** Only negative numbers are included in $b < 2a - 3$. **3. a)** no **b)** no **c)** yes **d)** no **7. a)** 4 **b)** 12 **c)** 1 **d)** 28

Technology p. 71
2 Solving for y and Graphing
1. $y > x - 2$ **2.** $y < x + 1$
3. $y \le -2x - 3$ **4.** $y \ge \dfrac{x-4}{2}$ **5.** $y > x - 3$ **6.** $y \le \dfrac{2x+6}{3}$
7. $y \ge \dfrac{3x+2}{2}$ **8.** $y > x - 1$ **9.** $y > 2(x + 1)$

Section 2.3 pp. 75–76
Practice   1. (2, 2), (1, −2), (0, 0) **2.** (0, 0), (−3, 8)
3. (5, −1) **4.** (2, 5), (−4, 0)
Applications and Problem Solving   35. a) $m > 0, n > 0$ **c)** Answers may vary. (16, 1), (15, 1), (14, 1)
36. a) $l \ge 2w - 1$ **b)** $l > 0, w > 0$ **d)** Answers may vary. (1, 1), (2, 3), (3, 5) **37. a)** $125d + 50b \ge 500$ **b)** $d \ge 0, b \ge 0$
38. a) $w + t \le 10$ **c)** yes, with 7 wins and 1 tie, for example; no, there are not enough games
39. a) $l + w > 2$ **40. a)** $\dfrac{1}{2}x + y \le 30$ **41. a)** the half plane that lies below the boundary line $y = mx + b$ **b)** the half plane that lies above the boundary line $y = mx + b$ **c)** the half plane that lies below and includes the boundary line $y = mx + b$ **d)** the half plane that lies above and includes the boundary line $y = mx + b$ **e)** the half plane that lies above the boundary line $y = b$ **f)** the half plane that lies below and includes the boundary line $y = b$ **g)** the half plane that lies to the left of the boundary line $x = c$ **h)** the half plane that lies to the right and includes the boundary line $x = c$ **i)** the half planes that lie on either side of the boundary line $x = c$ **42. a)** $y \le 2x - 2$ **b)** $y > -2x - 3$ **44. a)** No, there is only one intercept. **45.** No, the point is on the line. **47.** Answers may vary. $x + y \ge -11$

Computer Data Bank p. 77
1 Comparing Nations   1. 34 **2.** 182 **3.** 5, including New Zealand **4.** 108 **5.** 188, including Canada **6.** 38, including Australia **7.** 4 **8.** 15 **9.** 61 **10.** Answers will vary. **11.** Answers will vary. **12.** 56 **13.** 20 **14.** 203
2 Forested Areas in South America   1. $y \le 0.67x$; $283\,560 \le x \le 8\,511\,965$ **3.** vertical line segment from $912\,050$ km^2 to the boundary line **4.** $0 \le y \le 611\,073.5$ **5.** Answers will vary.
3 Standard of Living   1. Answers will vary. **2.** Answers will vary. Using GDP per capita, United Arab Emirates is the highest, Democratic Republic of Congo is the lowest, and Canada is the 9th.

Section 2.4 p. 79
1. Empty the 7-L container into the 19-L container. Fill the 19-L container from the 13-L container, leaving 1 L in the 13-L container. Fill the 7-L container from the 19-L container. Empty the 7-L container into the 13-L container. There is now 8 L of water in the 13-L container. **2.** Vancouver vs. Boston; Toronto vs. Calgary; Edmonton vs. Detroit; Chicago vs. Montreal **3.** $g = 3$, $h = 22$ **4.** 6, 1, 10, 8; 5, 9, 2; 4, 7; 3 **5. a)** one thousand **b)** one billion **6.** Double the pile of 7 from the pile of 11; double the pile of 6 from the resulting pile of 14; double the pile of 4 from the resulting pile of 12. **7.** Tonya **8.** Sharif **9.** Donna

Section 2.5 pp. 85–87
Practice   1. (−1, 0), (−2, −2), (1, 3) **2.** (4, 2), (5, −1)
3. (0, 0), (2, 3), (−3, −3) **4.** (0, 3), (4, −2), (0, 4)
5. (3, 2), (10, 9) **6.** (0, 0), (−4, −2) **7.** $y \ge 3 - x, y \ge x - 1$
8. $x + y \ge 3, x - y \ge 3$ **9.** $x + y < 4, y \ge 3x + 1$
10. $y < \dfrac{1}{2}x + 1, y < x + 1$ **11. a)** $y \ge 1 - x, y \ge x + 2$
b) $y \le 1 - x, y \ge x + 2$ **12. a)** $y < 1 - x, y < x + 2$
b) $y > 1 - x, y < x + 2$ **13. a)** $y > 1 - x, y \ge x + 2$
b) $y > 1 - x, y \le x + 2$
Applications and Problem Solving   46. b) (5, 0), (6, 0), (4, 1), (5, 1), (3, 2), (4, 2), (2, 3), (3, 3), (1, 4), (2, 4), (3, 4), (0, 5), (1, 5), (2, 5), (0, 6), (1, 6), (0, 7), (0, 8) **47. a)** $2w + t \ge 80, w + t \le 82$ **b)** $w \ge 0, t \ge 0$
48. Graph the system $x + y < 8, x + y > 4, x \ge 0, y \ge 0$.
49. $12x + 15y \le 90, x + y \ge 6, x \ge 0, y \ge 0$, where x represents the \$12 pizzas, and y represents the \$15 pizzas; (6, 0), (7, 0), (5, 1), (6, 1), (4, 2), (5, 2), (3, 3), (2, 4), (1, 5), (0, 6) **50.** $10x + 15y \ge 180, x + y \le 14$, $x \ge 0, y \ge 0$ **51.** part c); If you isolate y in the other systems, they are the same. **54. a)** infinitely many solutions; One of the four regions determined by the boundary lines will be the solution set. **b)** infinitely

many solutions; The solution set consists of the boundary line together with a half plane, or just the boundary line itself. **c)** infinitely many solutions or no solutions; The solution set consists of a half plane in the event that the inequality signs do not conflict. **d)** infinitely many solutions; The solution set consists of the half plane above the upper boundary line, the half plane below the lower boundary line, or the strip between the boundary lines, if there are solutions.

55. all real numbers **56. a)** $y \leq \frac{2}{3}x - 2$, $y \geq -2x - 4$

b) $y > 3x - 3$, $y \geq \frac{1}{2}x + 2$ **59. a)** Answers may vary.

$0 \leq x \leq 2$, $0 \leq y \leq 2$ **b)** 4 **60. a)** 6 **b)** 18
61. a) $x + y \leq 12\ 000$, $0.04x + 0.05y > 500$, $x \geq 0$, $y \geq 0$
b) \$9999; If she invests more than \$9999 at 4%, she will not earn more than \$500 in interest.
62. a) irregular pentagon **b)** 29.5 m²

63. a) $j + w \leq 8$, $\frac{j}{10} + \frac{w}{6} \geq \frac{1}{2}$, $\frac{j}{10} + \frac{w}{6} \leq 1$, $j \geq 0$, $w \geq 0$
b) Answers may vary. (5, 1), (1, 5), (6, 2)
64. Answers may vary. **a)** $0 \leq x \leq 50$, $-20 \leq y \leq 50$
b) $-20 \leq x \leq 10$, $-30 \leq y \leq 5$ **c)** $0 \leq x \leq 10$, $0 \leq y \leq 40$
d) $-50 \leq x \leq 0$, $0 \leq y \leq 30$ **65. a)** $x + y \geq 50$,
$0.35x + 0.12y \leq 10$, $x \geq 0$, $y \geq 0$ **b)** 17.4 g **66. a)** Shade between the solid lines $y = 4$ and $y = -4$. **b)** Shade to the right of the broken line $x = 1$ and to the left of the broken line $x = -1$. **67. b)** The points on the line $y = 2x + 2$ that are on and below the line $x + y = 8$.

Section 2.6 p. 89
Applications and Problem Solving **1. a)** corner pieces: 4, side pieces: $4m - 8$, inner pieces: $(m - 2)^2$
b) corner pieces: 4, side pieces: 152, inner pieces: 1444 **2.** corner pieces: 4, side pieces: 128, inner pieces: 1015 **3.** 3 333 333 266 666 667 **4. a)** 2002, 3003, 4004, 5005, 6006 **b)** If the second factor in the product is $n \times 7$, the product is $1000n + n$. **c)** 14 014
5. a) $y = 4x + 6$; 42, 23, 214 **b)** $y = x^2 + 2$; 66, 11, 227

c) $y = 2x - 1$; 9, 19, 64 **d)** $y = \frac{x+3}{2}$; 7, 37, 51

6. 49; In each row, the sum of the middle two numbers equals the sum of the outer two numbers.
7. a) 35 **b)** $n^2 + 2n$ **c)** 960; 2600 **8.** 8 **9.** 17, 10 **10.** 5
11. a) equal **b)** The sum is divisible by 9. **c)** Answers may vary. 111 211 111; 12 222 122 221; 211 211 121 121 112

Investigating Math pp. 90–91
1 Maximum and Minimum Values **1.** $x \geq 3$, $x \leq 7$, $y \geq 2$, $y \leq 6$ **2. a)** A: 21; B: 13; C: 25; D: 33 **b)** D; 33

c) B; 13 **3. a)** Answers may vary. E(7, 4); F(3, 4); G(5, 3); H(5, 4) **b)** E: 29; F: 17; G: 21; H: 23; None of these values is less than the minimum or greater than the maximum. **4.** the vertices **5. a)** maximum = 22 at B(5, 4); minimum = 0 at O(0, 0) **b)** maximum = 28 at C(7, 0); minimum = −6 at A(0, 6) **c)** maximum = 12 at A(0, 6); minimum = −21 at C(7, 0)
6. a) maximum = 26 at C(5, 3); minimum = 0 at O(0, 0)
b) maximum = 12 at D(6, 0); minimum = −35 at A(0, 5)
c) maximum = 25 at A(0, 5); minimum = −6 at D(6, 0)
7. a) maximum = 43 at B(5, 7); minimum = 0 at O(0, 0)
b) maximum = 32 at C(8, 4); minimum = −8 at A(0, 4)
c) maximum = 12 at A(0, 4); minimum = −10 at D(5, 0)
2 Graphing Polygonal Regions, I **1.** (1, 2), (1, 7), (8, 2), (8, 7) **a)** maximum = 51; minimum = 12
b) maximum = 4; minimum = −22 **2.** (0, 0), (8, 0), (2, 6), (0, 6) **a)** maximum = 20; minimum = 0
b) maximum = 8; minimum = −24 **3.** (2, 0), (10, 0), (10, 8), (8, 8), (2, 2) **a)** maximum = 80; minimum = 8
b) maximum = 20; minimum = −8 **4.** (0, 2), (5, 2), (8, 5), (8, 9), (3, 9), (0, 6) **a)** maximum = 15; minimum = −1 **b)** maximum = −1; minimum = −24
3 Graphing Polygonal Regions, II **1.** (0, 0), (4, 0), (2, 4), (0, 5) **a)** maximum = 20; minimum = 0
b) maximum = 8; minimum = −15 **2.** (0, 0), (3, 0), (8, 10), (0, 2) **a)** maximum = 28; minimum = 0
b) maximum = 3; minimum = −42 **3.** (0, 0), (5, 0), (5, 3), (2, 6), (0, 5) **a)** maximum = 13; minimum = 0
b) maximum = 16; minimum = −5 **4.** (10, 0), (6, 8), (2, 4) **a)** maximum = 20; minimum = 0
b) maximum = 12; minimum = −20
4 Technology **1.** Yes. Graph the inequalities.
2. Graph the first three inequalities, and set the viewing window to show only the first quadrant.

Connecting Math and Business pp. 92–93
1 Radio Advertising **2.** (0, 0), (8, 0), (4, 6), (0, 10)
3. 0, 64 000, 68 000, 60 000 **4.** 68 000 **5.** 4 between 06:00 and 09:00 and 6 between 16:00 and 18:00
2 More Business Applications **1. a)** $x + y \geq 10\ 000$, $x + y \leq 15\ 000$ **b)** $x \geq 3000$, $x \leq 4000$ **d)** (3000, 7000), (3000, 12 000), (4000, 6000), (4000, 11 000) **e)** $3x + 1.2y$
f) maximum = \$25 200; minimum = \$17 400 **2.** 10 h at the hardware store, 5 h at the fitness centre
3. 12 Mogul and 8 Speed **4.** 5 regular and 6 deluxe
5. a) 80 classic and 20 deluxe **b)** No. The feasible region has no outside boundary. The store can buy as many dishwashers as it can sell.

Review pp. 94–95
1. $y < 6$ **2.** $w > 2$ **3.** $x \geq -1$ **4.** $z \leq 2$ **5.** $k > -2$ **6.** $t > -8$
7. $m \leq 4$ **8.** $n \geq -4$ **9.** $x > -4$ **10.** $y < 0$ **11.** $m \leq -1$

12. $z > 11$ **13.** $b > 8$ **14.** $q > 1$ **15.** $h \le 2$ **16.** $n \le 4$
17. $m \le 3$ **18.** $w < 2$ **19.** $x < 17$ **20.** $z \le 1$ **21.** $y \le -2$
22. $n < 3$ **23.** $x > 8$ **24.** $w \le -9$ **25.** $m < 2$ **26.** $p \le -2$
27. $x > 0$ **28.** $w \le 5$ **29.** $y > -2$ **30.** $k \le 4$ **31.** more than
255 tickets **32. a)** $x \ge 7$ **b)** $x < 9$ **33.** $(-1, 6), (3, 13)$
34. $(-1, -5), (2, -9)$ **55. a)** $2x + 3y \le 18$ **b)** $x \ge 0, y \ge 0$
56. a) $\frac{2}{3}x + y \le 10$ **b)** $x \ge 0, y \ge 0$ **57.** $(15, 21)$
58. $(0, -3), (-2, 1)$ **59.** $y \ge x + 1, y \ge 2 - x$
60. $x + y \le 2, x - y \le 5$ **61.** $y > 1 - x, y \le 2 + 0.5x$
62. $2x + y < 2, y < x + 5$ **73.** $x + y < 12, x - y \ge 6$;
$(6.0), (7.0), (8.0), (9.0), (10.0), (11.0), (7.1), (8.1),$
$(9.1), (10.1), (8.2), (9.2)$

Exploring Math p. 95
1. scalene triangle **2.** isosceles triangle **3.** equilateral
triangle **4.** rhombus **5.** square **6.** rectangle
7. parallelogram **8.** rectangle **9.** parallelogram
10. rhombus **11.** rectangle **12.** rectangle **13.** regular
hexagon **14.** irregular hexagon **15.** square **16.**
scalene, isosceles, and equilateral triangles; square;
regular hexagon **17.** yes **18.** no

Chapter Check p. 96
1. $m < 17$ **2.** $w > 4$ **3.** $x \ge -3$ **4.** $n \le 3$ **5.** $k > -5$
6. $t > -11$ **7.** $m < -5$ **8.** $z \ge -8$ **9.** $h \le -11$ **10.** $y < 13$
11. $x > -1$ **12.** $z < 11$ **13.** $m \le 4$ **14.** $w < 2$ **15.** $g > -6$
16. $z \le -3$ **17.** $y \le 12$ **18.** $n < \frac{1}{3}$ **19.** $x \ge 25$ **20.** $m > 7$
21. $q < 1$ **22.** $w \le \frac{1}{2}$ **23.** $h < 8$ **24.** $k \ge -15$ **25.** $p < 0$
26. $y < 5$ **27.** $(1, 1), (-1, 6), (0, 0)$ **28.** $(0, 0)$ **29.** $(-2, 3)$
60. $200 + 25x \le 4000$; at most 152 people
61. a) $0.4x + y \le 20$

Using the Strategies p. 97
1. $D = 1$; $F = 9$ **2.** Move the 2nd and 3rd counters to
the right end. In the new configuration, move the 3rd
and 4th counters to fill the gap made on the previous
move. In the new configuration, move the 6th and 7th
counters to fill the gap made on the previous move.
Move the first and second counters to fill the gap
made on the previous move. **3.** Answers may vary.
4. $E = 10$; $F = 14$ **5.** 7 **6. a)** $\frac{h(x - 2b)}{x + b}$ **b)** $y = 1, x = 15$
7. 9 km **8.** A: 60 kg; E: 61 kg; B: 62 kg; D: 63 kg;
C: 64 kg **9.** 25° **10.** X = 2; Y = 7 **11.** 1¢, 2¢, 4¢, 7¢
Data Bank 1. Answers may vary. **2.** Answers may
vary. **3.** Answers may vary.

Chapter 3

Quadratic Functions p. 99
Height: 0, 45, 80, 105, 120, 125, 120, 105, 80, 45, 0
1. 125 m **2.** 5 s **3.** 10 s **4.** 40 km

Getting Started pp. 100–101
Number Games 1. c) 40 **d)** 40, 2000; 41, 1999; 42,
1996; 43, 1991; 44, 1984, 39, 1999; 38, 1996; 37,
1991; 36, 1984 **f)** no **g)** $y = -x^2 + 80x + 400$ **2. c)** 35
d) 35, 75; 36, 76; 37, 79; 38, 84; 39, 91; 34, 76; 33, 79;
32, 84; 31, 91 **f)** no **g)** $y = x^2 - 70x + 1300$
3. a) $m = 100 - n^2 + 50n$; The equation gives a greater
amount of money, \$725, for $n = 25$.
b) $m = 400 + n^2 - 20n$; The equation has no
maximum. Since there is no limit on the value of n,
there is no limit on the value of m.
Warm Up 1. Domain: {1, 2, 3, 4, 5};
Range: {2, 4, 6, 8, 10} **2.** Domain: {5, 8, 12, 15, 28};
Range: {4, 7, 11, 14, 27} **3.** Domain: {1, 4, 8, 22, 53};
Range: {1} **4.** function; Domain: R; Range: $y \ge 0$
5. not a function; Domain: $x \ge 0$; Range: R **6. a)** -4
b) -1 **c)** -7 **d)** 2 **e)** -19 **f)** -2 **g)** 0.5 **h)** 71 **7. a)** 0 **b)** 1 **c)** 1
d) 9 **e)** 9 **f)** $\frac{1}{4}$ **g)** $\frac{1}{4}$ **h)** 2.25 **8. a)** -1 **b)** 4 **c)** -4 **d)** 11 **e)** 44
f) $\frac{5}{4}$ **g)** -4 **h)** 15.25 **9.** $x^2 - 3x$ **10.** $x^2 + 2x$ **11.** $x^2 - 3x$
12. $x^2 + 4x$ **13.** $x^2 - \frac{1}{2}x$ **14.** $x^2 - \frac{5}{2}x$ **15.** $x^2 - 14x$
16. $x^2 - 3x$ **17.** $x^2 - 6x$ **18.** $x^2 + 10x$ **19.** $x^2 + 0.3x$
20. $x^2 + 60x$ **21.** $x^2 - \frac{5}{2}x$ **22.** $x^2 - 30x$ **23.** 1 **24.** 2
25. 2 **26.** 3 **27.** 2 **28.** 4
Mental Math
Evaluating Expressions 1. 7, 19, 7, 19 **2.** 1, 1, 17, 17
3. 2, 0, 6, 42 **4.** 1, -3, -3, -24 **5.** 4, 7, 15, -1.25
6. -3, 3, 3, 9 **7.** 10, 2, 26, 5 **8.** -3, -4, 0, 5
Multiplying in Two Steps 1. 220 **2.** 609 **3.** 324 **4.** 143
5. 900 **6.** 1005 **7.** 377 **8.** 650 **9.** 2952 **10.** 2550
11. 1750 **12.** 3857 **13.** 31.5 **14.** 102.6 **15.** 34.83
16. 0.0288 **17.** 70.2 **18.** 0.1825
19. a) $100xm + 10xn + 10ym + yn$
b) $100xm + 10xn + 10ym + yn$
c) $100xm + 10xn + 10ym + yn$
d) All three expressions are equivalent.

Investigating Math pp. 102-103
1 Exploring $y = |x|$ 2. up **3.** All values of y are greater
than or equal to 0. **4. a)** y-axis **b)** $x = 0$ **5.** $(0, 0)$ **6. a)** R
b) $y \ge 0$
2 Comparing $y = |x|$ and $y = |x| + q$ 2. The three
graphs are congruent, with the same domain and axis

of symmetry, but a different range and vertex.
3. a) $(0, 0)$, $(0, 3)$, $(0, -7)$ **b)** $x = 0$ **c)** Domain: R; Range:
$y \geq 0$, $y \geq 3$, $y \geq -7$ **4. a)** $[0, 3]$ **b)** $[0, -7]$ **5. a)** $(0, 11)$;
Domain: R; Range: $y \geq 11$ **b)** $(0, -10)$; Domain: R;
Range: $y \geq -10$ **c)** $(0, -22)$; Domain: R; Range: $y \geq -22$
d) $(0, 44)$; Domain: R; Range: $y \geq 44$

3 Comparing $y = |x|$ and $y = |x - p|$ **2. a)** $(0, 0)$,
$(4, 0)$, $(-6, 0)$ **b)** $x = 0$, $x = 4$, $x = -6$ **c)** Domain: R;
Range: $y \geq 0$ **3. a)** 4 units to the right **b)** 6 units to the
left **4. a)** $(9, 0)$, $x = 9$ **b)** $(-7, 0)$, $x = -7$ **c)** $(11, 0)$,
$x = 11$ **d)** $(-13, 0)$, $x = -13$

4 Comparing $y = |x|$ and $y = |x - p| + q$ **2. a)** $(0, 0)$,
$(1, 5)$, $(6, -3)$ **b)** $x = 0$, $x = 1$, $x = 6$ **c)** Domain: R;
Range: $y \geq 0$, $y \geq 5$, $y \geq -3$ **3. a)** $[1, 5]$ **b)** $[6, -3]$
5. a) $(0, 0)$, $(-5, 6)$, $(-8, -7)$ **b)** $x = 0$, $x = -5$, $x = -8$
c) Domain: R; Range: $y \geq 0$, $y \geq 6$, $y \geq -7$ **6. a)** $[-5, 6]$
b) $[-8, -7]$ **7. a)** $(3, 4)$, $x = 3$ **b)** $(-2, -5)$, $x = -2$
c) $(11, -3)$, $x = 11$ **d)** $(-13, 6)$, $x = -13$

5 Comparing $y = |x|$ and $y = a|x|$ **2. a)** up: $y = |x|$,
$y = 2|x|$, $y = 0.5|x|$; down: $y = -|x|$, $y = -2|x|$,
$y = -0.5|x|$ **b)** the sign of the coefficient **3. a)** $(0, 0)$
b) $x = 0$ **c)** Domain: R; Range: $y \geq 0$, $y \leq 0$, $y \geq 0$, $y \leq 0$,
$y \geq 0$, $y \leq 0$ **4.** reflection in the x-axis **5.** vertical
stretch **6.** vertical shrink

6 Combining Transformations **1. a)** $(0, -9)$ **b)** $x = 0$
c) Domain: R; Range: $y \geq -9$ **d)** up **e)** stretch **2. a)** $(0, 7)$
b) $x = 0$ **c)** Domain: R; Range: $y \leq 7$ **d)** down **e)** stretch
3. a) $(0, -2)$ **b)** $x = 0$ **c)** Domain: R; Range: $y \leq -2$
d) down **e)** congruent **4. a)** $(3, 6)$ **b)** $x = 3$ **c)** Domain: R;
Range: $y \geq 6$ **d)** up **e)** stretch **5. a)** $(-4, 0)$ **b)** $x = -4$
c) Domain: R; Range: $y \leq 0$ **d)** down **e)** congruent
6. a) $(-6, -3)$ **b)** $x = -6$ **c)** Domain: R; Range: $y \leq -3$
d) down **e)** congruent **7. a)** $(7, 0)$ **b)** $x = 7$ **c)** Domain: R;
Range: $y \geq 0$ **d)** up **e)** shrink **8. a)** $(5, -8)$ **b)** $x = 5$
c) Domain: R; Range: $y \leq -8$ **d)** down **e)** shrink

7 Exploring Intercepts **1. a)** y-intercept: 2,
x-intercepts: none **b)** y-intercept: -3, x-intercepts: 3,
-3 **c)** y-intercept: 1, x-intercept: 1 **d)** y-intercept: 5,
x-intercept: -5 **e)** y-intercept: 5, x-intercepts: none
f) y-intercept: 2, x-intercepts: 2, 4 **g)** y-intercept: 5,
x-intercepts: none **h)** y-intercept: 1, x-intercepts: -1,
-5 **i)** y-intercept: 0, x-intercept: 0 **j)** y-intercept: 2,
x-intercept: 1 **k)** y-intercept: 6, x-intercept: -2
l) y-intercept: 0, x-intercept: 0 **m)** y-intercept: -3,
x-intercept: -1 **n)** y-intercept: -6, x-intercept: 3
o) y-intercept: 1, x-intercepts 0.5, -0.5 **p)** y-intercept:
-2, x-intercepts: none **q)** y-intercept: 7, x-intercepts:
none **r)** y-intercept: 2, x-intercepts: -1, -5
s) y-intercept: 1, x-intercepts: -0.5, 2.5 **t)** y-intercept:
-5, x-intercepts: none **2. a)** one **b)** 0, 1, or 2
c) There is no relationship between the number of
x-intercepts and the value of p. If $aq > 0$, then there

are no x-intercepts. If $q = 0$, then there is one
x-intercept. If $aq < 0$, then there are two x-intercepts.

Section 3.1 pp. 109-111
Practice **1. a)** up **b)** $(0, 5)$ **c)** $x = 0$ **d)** Domain: R;
Range: $y \geq 5$ **e)** min: 5 at $x = 0$ **2. a)** up **b)** $(0, -2)$
c) $x = 0$ **d)** Domain: R; Range: $y \geq -2$ **e)** min: -2 at $x = 0$
3. a) down **b)** $(0, -1)$ **c)** $x = 0$ **d)** Domain: R; Range: $y \leq$
-1 **e)** max: -1 at $x = 0$ **4. a)** down **b)** $(0, 3)$
c) $x = 0$ **d)** Domain: R; Range: $y \leq 3$ **e)** max: 3 at $x = 0$
5. a) up **b)** $(0, 0)$ **c)** $x = 0$ **d)** Domain: R; Range: $y \geq 0$
e) min: 0 at $x = 0$ **6. a)** down **b)** $(0, 0)$ **c)** $x = 0$
d) Domain: R; Range: $y \leq 0$ **e)** max: 0 at $x = 0$ **7. a)** up
b) $(0, 2)$ **c)** $x = 0$ **d)** Domain: R; Range: $y \geq 2$ **e)** min: 2 at
$x = 0$ **8. a)** down **b)** $(0, 0)$ **c)** $x = 0$ **d)** Domain: R; Range:
$y \leq 0$ **e)** max: 0 at $x = 0$ **9. a)** down **b)** $(0, -3)$ **c)** $x = 0$
d) Domain: R; Range: $y \leq -3$ **e)** max: -3 at $x = 0$
10. a) up **b)** $(0, 1)$ **c)** $x = 0$ **d)** Domain: R; Range: $y \geq 1$
e) min: 1 at $x = 0$ **11. a)** down **b)** $(0, 7)$ **c)** $x = 0$
d) Domain: R; Range: $y \leq 7$ **e)** max: 7 at $x = 0$
12. a) down **b)** $(0, -6)$ **c)** $x = 0$ **d)** Domain: R; Range:
$y \leq -6$ **e)** max: -6 at $x = 0$ **13.** The graph of $y = x^2 - 4$ is
the graph of $y = x^2$ translated 4 units downward.
14. The graph of $y = -x^2 + 5$ is the graph of $y = -x^2$
translated 5 units upward. **15.** The graph of $y = 3x^2$ is a
vertical stretch of the graph of $y = x^2$ by a factor of 3.
16. The graph of $y = -\frac{1}{3}x^2$ is a vertical shrink of the
graph of $y = -x^2$ by a factor of $\frac{1}{3}$. **17.** The graph of
$y = 2x^2 - 2$ is the graph of $y = 2x^2 + 7$ translated 9 units
downward. **18.** The graph of $y = -0.25x^2$ is the
reflection of the graph of $y = 0.25x^2$ in the x-axis.
19. a) $y = -2x^2 + 3$ **b)** $y = 2x^2 - 3$ **c)** $y = 2x^2 + 3$
d) $y = -2x^2 - 3$ **20. a)** down **b)** $(0, 0)$ **c)** Domain: R;
Range: $y \leq 0$ **d)** max: 0 at $x = 0$ **21. a)** up **b)** $(0, -11.4)$
c) Domain: R; Range: $y \geq -11.4$ **d)** min: -11.4 at $x = 0$
22. a) down **b)** $(0, 4.7)$ **c)** Domain: R; Range: $y \leq 4.7$
d) max: 4.7 at $x = 0$ **23. a)** up **b)** $(0, -3)$ **c)** Domain: R;
Range: $y \geq -3$ **d)** min: -3 at $x = 0$ **24. a)** down
b) $(0, -8.3)$ **c)** Domain: R; Range: $y \leq -8.3$ **d)** max: -8.3
at $x = 0$ **25. a)** up **b)** $(0, 9.9)$ **c)** Domain: R; Range:
$y \geq 9.9$ **d)** min: 9.9 at $x = 0$ **26. a)** up **b)** $(0, 3.5)$
c) Domain: R; Range: $y \geq 3.5$ **d)** min: 3.5 at $x = 0$
27. a) down **b)** $(0, -0.5)$ **c)** Domain: R; Range: $y \leq -0.5$
d) max: -0.5 at $x = 0$ **28.** $(2, 13)$ **29.** $(2, -1)$ **30.** $(2, -2)$
31. $(2, -2)$ **32. a)** $(0, -9)$ **b)** y-intercept: -9, x-intercepts:
-3, 3 **33. a)** $(0, 1)$ **b)** y-intercept: 1 **34. a)** $(0, 4)$
b) y-intercept: 4, x-intercepts: -2, 2 **35. a)** $(0, -8)$
b) y-intercept: -8, x-intercepts: -2, 2 **36. a)** $(0, 16)$
b) y-intercept: 16, x-intercepts: none **37. a)** $(0, 18)$
b) y-intercept: 18, x-intercepts: -3, 3 **38. a)** $(0, -3)$

b) y-intercept: -3, x-intercepts: none **39. a)** $(0, 5)$
b) y-intercept: 5, x-intercepts: $-1, 1$ **40. a)** $(0, 8)$
b) y-intercept: 8, x-intercepts: $-4, 4$ **41. a)** $(0, -1)$
b) y-intercept: -1, x-intercepts: $-2, 2$ **42.** $-1.4, 1.4$
43. $-1.7, 1.7$ **44.** no x-intercepts **45.** $-2.2, 2.2$
46. $-1.4, 1.4$ **47.** $-2.4, 2.4$ **48.** $y = 5x^2$ **49.** $y = -6x^2$
50. $y = -8x^2 - 7$ **51.** $y = 0.2x^2 + 3$ **52.** $y = 0.1x^2 - 2.5$
53. $y = -0.6x^2 + 6.5$ **54.** $y = 4x^2$ **55.** $y = -2x^2$
56. $y = 3x^2 - 7$ **57.** $y = -x^2 + 3$ **58.** $y = -0.5x^2 - 5$
59. $y = \dfrac{1}{6}x^2 + \dfrac{3}{2}$ **60.** $y = 2x^2$ **61.** $y = -0.5x^2 - 2$
62. $y = -x^2 + 5$ **63.** $y = 2x^2 - 8$

Applications and Problem Solving **64.** -15
65. -7.5; The parabola is symmetric about the y-axis.
66. $y = -\dfrac{2}{3}x^2 + 6$ **67. a)** $A = \dfrac{1}{2}h^2$ **c)** $(0, 0)$ **d)** Domain:
$h > 0$; Range: $A > 0$ **68. b)** Domain: $x \geq 0$; Range: R
c) No; the vertical line test fails. **69. b)** 2 m **c)** 150 m
d) 17 m **70. b)** first quadrant; t and h must be greater
than or equal to 0 **c)** 5.2 s **d)** 12.9 s **71. a)** $(2, 2)$,
$(-3, 7)$ **72. a)** $A \leq s^2$ **73. a)** $y = x^2 + 2$ **b)** $y = -x^2 - 1$
c) $y = 2x^2 - 3$ **d)** $y = -0.5x^2 + 4$ **74. a)** $y = -\dfrac{9}{12\,100}x^2$
b) $y = -\dfrac{9}{12\,100}x^2 + 49$ **75. a)** $n = 2p^2 - 4$ **b)** $n = -2p^2 + 4$
c) They are reflections in the x-axis. **76. a)** $A = \pi r^2$
c) No; the radius must be non-negative. **d)** $r \geq 0$,
$A \leq 0$ **77. a)** $A = 400 - s^2$ **b)** 16 **d)** $0 \leq s \leq 16$,
$144 \leq A \leq 400$ **79. a)** no relationship; always one
y-intercept **b)** If $aq > 0$, then there are no x-intercepts.
If $q = 0$, then there is one x-intercept. If $aq < 0$, then
there are two x-intercepts.

Section 3.2 p. 113
Applications and Problem Solving **1.** Great Bear
Lake: 31 792 km² **3. a)** 15 000 km **b)** Answers may
vary. **4. a)** 1255 **5. a)** 8 m **b)** 16 **6.** Beginning at the
top and moving left to right, place the numbers in the
order 2, 6, 3, 7, 8, 5, 9, 4, 1. **7.** O = 1, N = 8, E = 2,
T = 7 **8.** three, four, five **9.** 13 **10.** 7, 5, 8; 6, 1, 4; 3,
2, 9 **11.** $8 - 7 = 1$; $20 \div 5 = 4$; $9 - 6 = 3$

Section 3.3 pp. 118-121
Practice **1. a)** up **b)** $(-5, 0)$ **c)** $x = -5$ **d)** Domain: R;
Range: $y \geq 0$ **e)** min: 0 at $x = -5$ **2. a)** down **b)** $(-1, 0)$
c) $x = -1$ **d)** Domain: R; Range: $y \leq 0$ **e)** max: 0 at
$x = -1$ **3. a)** up **b)** $(3, 0)$ **c)** $x = 3$ **d)** Domain: R; Range:
$y \geq 0$ **e)** min: 0 at $x = 3$ **4. a)** up **b)** $(-2, 4)$ **c)** $x = -2$
d) Domain: R; Range: $y \geq 4$ **e)** min: 4 at $x = -2$
5. a) down **b)** $(2, -5)$ **c)** $x = 2$ **d)** Domain: R; Range:
$y \leq -5$ **e)** max: -5 at $x = 2$ **6. a)** up **b)** $(-3, -5)$ **c)** $x = -3$
d) Domain: R; Range: $y \geq -5$ **e)** min: -5 at $x = -3$

7. a) up **b)** $(-6, 2)$ **c)** $x = -6$ **d)** Domain: R; Range: $y \geq 2$
e) min: 2 at $x = -6$ **8. a)** up **b)** $(5, -4)$ **c)** $x = 5$
d) Domain: R; Range: $y \geq -4$ **e)** min: -4 at $x = 5$
9. a) down **b)** $(-4, 3)$ **c)** $x = -4$ **d)** Domain: R; Range:
$y \leq 3$ **e)** max: 3 at $x = -4$ **10. a)** down **b)** $(6, -1)$ **c)** $x = 6$
d) Domain: R; Range: $y \leq -1$ **e)** max: -1 at $x = 6$
11. a) up **b)** $(5, 0)$ **c)** $x = 5$ **d)** Domain: R; Range: $y \geq 0$
e) min: 0 at $x = 5$ **12. a)** down **b)** $(-4, 0)$ **c)** $x = -4$
d) Domain: R; Range: $y \leq 0$ **e)** max: 0 at $x = -4$
13. a) up **b)** $(2, 1)$ **c)** $x = 2$ **d)** Domain: R; Range: $y \geq 1$
e) min: 1 at $x = 2$ **14. a)** down **b)** $(-1, -2)$ **c)** $x = -1$
d) Domain: R; Range: $y \leq -2$ **e)** max: -2 at $x = -1$
15. a) up **b)** stretched by a factor of 2 **c)** $(1, 0)$ **d)** $x = 1$
e) min: 0 at $x = 1$ **16. a)** down **b)** shrunk by a factor of
0.5 **c)** $(-7, 0)$ **d)** $x = -7$ **e)** max: 0 at $x = -7$ **17. a)** down
b) stretched by a factor of 2 **c)** $(4, 7)$ **d)** $x = 4$ **e)** max: 7
at $x = 4$ **18. a)** up **b)** stretched by a factor of 4
c) $(-3, -4)$ **d)** $x = -3$ **e)** min: -4 at $x = -3$ **19. a)** down
b) stretched by a factor of 3 **c)** $(5, 6)$ **d)** $x = 5$ **e)** max: 6
at $x = 5$ **20. a)** down **b)** shrunk by a factor of 0.4
c) $(8, -1)$ **d)** $x = 8$ **e)** max: -1 at $x = 8$ **21. a)** up

b) shrunk by a factor of $\dfrac{1}{3}$ **c)** $(-6, -7)$ **d)** $x = -6$

e) min: -7 at $x = -6$ **22. a)** up **b)** shrunk by a factor of
0.5 **c)** $(-1, -5)$ **d)** $x = -1$ **e)** min: -5 at $x = -1$ **23. a)** up
b) stretched by a factor of 2.5 **c)** $(-1.5, -9)$ **d)** $x = -1.5$
e) min: -9 at $x = -1.5$ **24. a)** down **b)** stretched by a
factor of 1.2 **c)** $(2.6, 3.3)$ **d)** $x = 2.6$ **e)** max: 3.3 at
$x = 2.6$ **25. a)** $y = -3(x + 1)^2 + 2$ **b)** $y = 3(x - 1)^2 + 2$
c) $y = 3(x + 1)^2 - 2$ **d)** $y = -3(x - 1)^2 - 2$ **32. a)**
y-intercept: 4, x-intercept: 2 **b)** Answers may vary.
$(4, 4)$, $(3, 1)$ **33. a)** y-intercept: -5, x-intercepts: $-5, 1$
b) Answers may vary. $(2, 7)$, $(3, 16)$ **34. a)** y-intercept:
8, x-intercepts: 2, 4 **b)** Answers may vary. $(1, 3)$,
$(3, -1)$ **35. a)** y-intercept: -3, x-intercepts: $-3, -1$
b) Answers may vary. $(-2, 1)$, $(1, -8)$ **36. a)**
y-intercept: -18, x-intercepts: none **b)** Answers may
vary. $(-1, -9)$, $(-2, -6)$ **37. a)** y-intercept: -6,
x-intercepts: $-3, 1$ **b)** Answers may vary. $(-1, -8)$,
$(2, 10)$ **38.** y-intercept: -2, x-intercepts: 0.7, -2.7
39. y-intercept: -2, x-intercepts: $-0.4, 2.4$
40. y-intercept: -3, x-intercepts: 0.5, 1.5
41. y-intercept: -47, x-intercepts: none
42. y-intercept: 1, x-intercepts: -0.5
43. y-intercept: $-\dfrac{2}{9}$, x-intercept: $\dfrac{1}{3}$ **44.** y-intercept:
4, x-intercept: -4 **45.** y-intercept: -2.5, x-intercepts:
$-1, -5$ **46.** $y = (x - 7)^2$ **47.** $y = -(x + 5)^2$
48. $y = 2(x - 3)^2 - 5$ **49.** $y = -3(x - 6)^2 + 7$
50. $y = -0.5(x + 1)^2 - 1$ **51.** $y = 1.5(x + 8)^2 + 9$
52. $y = (x - 1)^2 + 5$ **53.** $y = -(x + 3)^2$ **54.** $y = 3(x - 4)^2 - 2$
55. $y = -2(x - 2)^2 - 3$ **56.** $y = 0.4(x + 3)^2 - 3$

57. $y = 5(x - 4.5)^2$ **58.** $y = -4(x - 3)^2$
59. $y = 2(x + 5)^2 - 6$ **60.** $y = (x + 4)^2 - 5$
61. $y = -(x - 3)^2 + 2$ **62.** $y = -(x - 1)^2 + 6$
63. $y = 3(x + 2)^2 + 3$ **64.** $y = -2(x + 5)^2 - 3$
65. $y = \dfrac{1}{2}(x - 6)^2 + 4$ **66.** $y = 2(x - 1)^2 + 2$
67. $y = -(x + 2)^2 + 3$ **68.** $y = \dfrac{1}{2}(x - 2)^2 - 4$
69. $y = -\dfrac{1}{4}(x + 4)^2 - 1$

Applications and Problem Solving **70.** 4 **71.** -11
72. $x = -1$; This is halfway between the x-intercepts.
73. $x = -3$ **74. a)** 83 m **b)** 6 s **75.** $a = 2$, $q = 4$
76. $a = -1$, $q = -4$ **77.** $a = -2$, $q = 5$ **78. a)** 10 m
b) 20 m **c)** 40 m **d)** 7.5 m **e)** No; the player would need to be able to reach 5.1 m, which is impossible.
f) $h(d) = -0.025d^2$ **79. a)** 38.5 m **b)** 1 m **c)** 5 s
d) 25 m **80. a)** 6 m **b)** 20 m **c)** 2 m; 2 m **d)** 38 m
e) 2.76 m **81. a)** Domain: $s \geq 0$; Range: $d \geq 0$ **b)** (0, 0), $(-30, 0)$ **c)** 24 m; 78 m **d)** Answers vary. 30 km/h or 40 km/h **e)** Answers may vary. 10.8 m at 30 km/h or 19.5 m at 40 km/h **82. b)** The part in the first quadrant since t and h must be greater than or equal to 0. **c)** 253 m **83. b)** (0, 0), (1, 0); No games will be played if there are no teams or one team.
c) $g = t(t - 1)$ **d)** $g = t(t - 1)$ **84. a)** The graphs are the same. **b)** $(x - p)^2 = (p - x)^2 = x^2 - 2px + p^2$
85. (1, 6), $(-2, -3)$ **86. a)** $m = n$ **b)** $m > n$ **c)** $m < n$
87. a) $A = (x - 2)^2 + 3$ **c)** 2 m **d)** 0 **e)** Shade above the parabola $A = (x - 2)^2 + 3$. **88. a)** $y = -3(x - 2)^2 - 1$
b) $y = 3(x + 2)^2 + 1$ **c)** $y = -3(x + 2)^2 - 1$
89. a) 17, 19, 23 **b)** 289 **90. a)** $(-30, 0.36)$, $(30, 0.36)$
b) $y = 0.0004x^2$ **c)** $y = 0.0004(x + 30)^2 - 0.36$
d) $y = 0.0004(x - 30)^2 - 0.36$ **e)** 0.16 cm
91. $y = 2(x - 1)^2 + 3$

Section 3.4 p. 123
Applications and Problem Solving **1.** Scott: 6; Ivan: 11; Enzo: 4 **2.** \$3500 **3.** $(-2, 4)$ **4.** WNWWWNN; 43 km **5.** 6 cm by 4 cm

Computer Data Bank p. 124
1 Long Jump **1.** Answers will vary. **2.** For the start of the path at the origin, $p = 3.96$ and $q = 0.79$.
3. a) Substitute values for all the variables except a into $y = a(x - p)^2 + q$, and solve for a. **b)** -0.050
4. Answers will vary. **6.** For the parabola opening down, from least flat to most flat
2 Winning Distances **1.** Answers will vary.
3. Answers will vary.

Investigating Math p. 125

1 Making Squares **2. a)** $x^2 + 4x + 4 = (x + 2)^2$
b) $x^2 + 6x + 9 = (x + 3)^2$
2 Completing the Square **1.** 16
2. $x^2 + 8x + 16 = (x + 4)^2$ **3. a)** 25;
$x^2 + 10x + 25 = (x + 5)^2$ **b)** 36; $x^2 + 12x + 36 = (x + 6)^2$
4. the square of half the coefficient of x **5. a)** 49 **b)** 64
c) 100 **d)** 225 **6. a)** $x^2 + 14x + 49 = (x + 7)^2$
b) $x^2 + 16x + 64 = (x + 8)^2$ **c)** $x^2 + 20x + 100 = (x + 10)^2$
d) $x^2 + 30x + 225 = (x + 15)^2$

Section 3.5 pp. 130-134
Practice **1.** 49 **2.** 36 **3.** 1 **4.** 81 **5.** 25 **6.** 100 **7.** 2.25
8. 6.25 **9.** 0.25 **10.** 0.25 **11.** 0.16 **12.** 0.000 625
13. 1.44 **14.** 46.9225 **15.** $\dfrac{1}{9}$ **16.** $\dfrac{1}{144}$ **17.** $y = (x + 3)^2 - 6$;
$(-3, -6)$; $x = -3$; Points may vary. (0, 3), (1, 10)
18. $y = (x - 2)^2 - 5$; $(2, -5)$; $x = 2$; Points may vary.
$(0, -1)$, $(1, -4)$ **19.** $y = (x + 5)^2 + 5$; $(-5, 5)$; $x = -5$;
Points may vary. (0, 30), (1, 41) **20.** $y = (x - 1)^2 + 2$;
(1, 2); $x = 1$; Points may vary. (0, 3), (2, 3)
21. $y = (x + 6)^2 - 8$; $(-6, -8)$; $x = -6$; Points may vary.
(0, 28), (1, 41) **22.** $y = (x - 4)^2 - 4$; $(4, -4)$; $x = 4$;
Points may vary. (0, 12), (1, 5) **23. a)** $y = x^2 - 4$
b) $y = -x^2 + 4x$ **c)** $y = x^2 - 4x$ **d)** $y = x^2 + 4x$ **e)** $y = -x^2 + 4$
f) $y = -x^2 - 4x$ **24.** $(1, -9)$; $x = -1$; y-intercept: -8,
x-intercepts: -2, 4; $y \geq -9$ **25.** (3, 1); $x = 3$; y-intercept: 10, x-intercepts: none; $y \geq 1$ **26.** $(-2, -4)$; $x = -2$;
y-intercept: 0, x-intercepts: -4, 0; $y \geq 4$ **27.** (6, 4);
$x = 6$; y-intercept: 40, x-intercepts: none; $y \geq 4$
28. $y = -(x - 4)^2 + 5$; (4, 5); $x = 4$; Points may vary.
$(0, -11)$, $(1, -4)$ **29.** $y = -(x + 4)^2 + 9$; $(-4, 0)$; $x = -4$;
Points may vary. $(-7, 0)$, $(-1, 0)$ **30.** $y = -(x + 2)^2 - 3$;
$(-2, -3)$; $x = -2$; Points may vary. $(0, -7)$, $(1, -12)$
31. $y = -(x + 1)^2 + 1$; $(-1, 1)$; $x = -1$; Points may vary.
$(-2, 0)$, (0, 0) **32.** $(-1, 4)$; $x = -1$; y-intercept: 3,
x-intercepts: -3, 1; $y \leq 4$ **33.** $(-2, -8)$; $x = -2$;
y-intercept: -12, x-intercepts: none; $y \leq -8$ **34.** (4, 4);
$x = 4$; y-intercept: -12, x-intercepts: 2, 6; $y \leq 4$
35. (5, 0); $x = 5$; y-intercept: -25, x-intercept: 5; $y \leq 0$
36. min: -7 at $x = -3$ **37.** max: 5 at $x = -2$ **38.** max: 16 at $x = 4$ **39.** min: 0 at $x = 6$ **40.** min: -30 at $n = -5$
41. max: 13 at $t = -3$ **42.** min: -28 at $x = 7$ **43.** max: -3 at $k = -5$ **44.** min: 1 at $x = -1$ **45.** max: 6 at $x = 5$
46. max: 7 at $x = -3$ **47.** max: -1 at $x = 3$ **48.** min: -2 at $x = 2$ **49.** min: 2 at $x = 1$ **50.** max: 8 at $x = 2$ **51.** max: 0 at $x = 1$ **52.** min: -1.25 at $x = -1.5$ **53.** min: -2.25 at $x = 0.5$ **54.** max: 7 at $x = 3$ **55.** max: -0.875 at $x = 0.75$
56. max: 6.25 at $x = -2.5$ **57.** max: 0.97 at $x = 0.1$
58. max: -1.92 at $x = -0.2$ **59.** min: 1.5 at $x = -1$
60. max: $\dfrac{4}{3}$ at $x = \dfrac{2}{3}$ **61.** min: -0.18 at $x = 0.6$

64. $-3.5, 0$ **65.** $-1.7, 1$ **66.** -0.3 **67.** $-1.3, 1.3$ **68.** no x-intercepts **69.** $0, 2.9$

Applications and Problem Solving
70. a) y-intercept: 3, x-intercepts: $-1, -3$; $(-2, -1)$
b) y-intercept: 2, x-intercepts: $-2, 1$; $(-0.5, 2.25)$
c) y-intercept: 9, x-intercept: 1.5; $(1.5, 0)$
d) y-intercept: -2, x-intercepts: $-0.5, 2$; $(0.75, -3.125)$
e) y-intercept: 3, x-intercepts: 0.5, 1.5; $(1, -1)$
f) y-intercept: 6, x-intercepts: $-2, 1$; $(-0.5, 6.75)$
71. a) $y = x^2 - 8x + 35$ **b)** 4 **72. a)** $y = 375 - 10x - x^2$
b) -5 **73.** $5, -5$ **74.** 17, 17 **75.** 17, 17 **76. a)** 20 m
b) 100 m **c)** 200 m **77. a)** 4.25 m **b)** 5 m **c)** 2 m
78. a) Earth: 7 m, Jupiter: 4 m, Mars: 14.5 m,
Neptune: 6.2 m **b)** Earth: 1 s, Jupiter: 0.4 s, Mars:
2.5 s, Neptune: 0.83 s **79. a)** 46 m **b)** 480 m **c)** 17 m
80. a) 84 m **b)** 75 m **c)** 31 m **81. a)** 100 m by 100 m
b) 10 000 m² **82.** 10 m by 30 m **83.** 15 m by 30 m
84. a) $R(x) = (2000 - 100x)(8 + x)$ **b)** (6, 19 600) **c)** \$14
d) 1400 **85.** \$30 **86. a)** 12.5 cm² **b)** 21.125 cm²
87. a) 176.6 m **b)** 8.5 s **88.** 50 cm² **89. a)** They are
reflections in the x-axis. **b)** They are opposites.
90. a) The graph is a straight line. **b)** The parabola has
an axis of symmetry of the y-axis. **91.** $y = x^2 - 2x - 3$
92. $y = -2x^2 + 4x + 6$ **93.** No; the graphs never
intersect. **94.** $b = 0$; If $f(x) = f(-x)$ for all x, then the
axis of symmetry is $x = 0$ and this means that $b = 0$.
95. a) $k = 9$ **b)** $k < 9$ **c)** $k > 9$ **96. a)** $k = -8$ **b)** $k > -8$
c) $k < -8$ **99.** Answers may vary. **a)** $y = x^2 - 6x + 8$
b) $y = -x^2 - 6x + 7$ **c)** $y = 2x^2 - 4x + 22$
d) $y = -0.5x^2 + 6x - 18$

Investigating Math p. 135
1 Relating $y = ax^2 + bx + c$ to the Axis of
Symmetry **1. a)** $a = 1, b = -4, c = 0$; $x = 2$ **b)** $a = 1$,
$b = -4, c = 3$; $x = 2$ **c)** $a = 1, b = 6, c = 0$; $x = -3$ **d)** $a = 1$,
$b = 6, c = -5$; $x = -3$ **e)** $a = -1, b = 8, c = 0$; $x = 4$
f) $a = -1, b = 8, c = -4$; $x = 4$ **g)** $a = 0.5, b = -3, c = 0$;
$x = 3$ **h)** $a = 0.5, b = -3, c = 2$; $x = 3$ **i)** $a = -2, b = -4$,
$c = 0$; $x = -1$ **j)** $a = -2, b = -4, c = -7$; $x = -1$ **2.** No; if
the value of c changes, the axis of symmetry does not
change. **3.** Divide the negative of b by twice a.
4. $x = -\dfrac{b}{2a}$ **5. a)** $x = -2$ **b)** $x = 8$ **c)** $x = -6$ **d)** $x = 4.5$
e) $x = -2$ **f)** $x = -2$ **g)** $x = -2$ **h)** $x = 2.5$ **i)** $x = -3$
j) $x = -1.5$ **k)** $x = 0.75$ **l)** $x = \dfrac{4}{3}$

2 Relating $y = ax^2 + bx + c$ to $y = a(x - p) + q$
1. the x-coordinate **2.** Substitute the coordinate into
the equation to find the other coordinate.
3. a) $(-3, -5)$ **b)** $(-6, 35)$ **c)** $(1, -7)$ **d)** $(-10, -50)$
e) $(-0.75, -2.75)$ **f)** $(3, -1)$ **4.** The coordinates of the
vertex are (p, q). **5.** Divide the negative of b by twice a.

6. $p = -\dfrac{b}{2a}$ **7.** Find $p = -\dfrac{b}{2a}$ and then substitute

$x = -\dfrac{b}{2a}$ in the equation $ax^2 + bx + c = a(x - p)^2 + q$ to

find q. **8. a)** $y = (x - 3)^2 - 9$ **b)** $f(x) = 2(x + 1)^2 - 7$
c) $y = -5(x - 2)^2 + 22$ **d)** $f(x) = -(x + 1.5)^2 + 0.25$
e) $y = (x + 2.5)^2 - 4.25$ **f)** $f(x) = 3(x - 0.5)^2 - 0.75$
g) $y = -1.5(x - 1)^2 + 2.5$ **h)** $y = 0.4(x + 1.25)^2 - 0.625$

Technology pp. 136-137
1 Comparing Graphing Calculator and Manual
Methods **1. a)** $(0, 5)$; y-intercept: 5, x-intercepts:
none **b)** $(0, -3)$; y-intercept: -3, x-intercepts: $-1.7, 1.7$
c) $(0, 4)$; y-intercept: 4, x-intercepts: $-2, 2$ **d)** $(0, 8)$;
y-intercept: 8, x-intercepts: $-2.8, 2.8$ **2. a)** $(0, -9)$;
y-intercept: -9, x-intercepts: $-2.1, 2.1$ **b)** $(0, 2)$;
y-intercept: 2, x-intercepts: none **c)** $(0, 12)$;
y-intercept: 12, x-intercepts: $-2, 2$ **d)** $(0, 4)$;
y-intercept: 4, x-intercepts: $-2.6, 2.6$ **3. a)** $(2, -3)$;
y-intercept: 1, x-intercepts: 0.3, 3.7 **b)** $(-2, 1)$;
y-intercept: 9, x-intercepts: none **c)** $(-3, 1)$;
y-intercept: -8, x-intercepts: $-4, -2$ **d)** $(1, 6)$;
y-intercept: 5.5, x-intercepts: $-2.5, 4.5$ **e)** $(4.5, 0)$;
y-intercept: 5.1, x-intercept: 4.5 **f)** $(-5, 0)$; y-intercept:
-5, x-intercept: -5 **4. a)** $(2.5, -9.25)$; y-intercept: -3,
x-intercepts: $-0.5, 5.5$ **b)** $(3, 5)$; y-intercept: -4,
x-intercepts: 0.8, 5.2 **c)** $(-1, 6)$; y-intercept: 5,
x-intercepts: $-3.4, 1.4$ **d)** $(-3.5, 24.5)$; y-intercept:
12.25, x-intercepts: $-8.4, 1.4$ **e)** $(0.75, -3.125)$;
y-intercept: -2, x-intercepts: $-0.5, 2$ **f)** $(-7, 21.5)$;
y-intercept: -3, x-intercepts: $-13.6, -0.4$
5. a) $(1.5, 2.3)$; y-intercept: 0, x-intercepts: 0, 3
b) $(-1, 1)$; y-intercept: 0, x-intercepts: $-2, 0$
c) $(-2.5, -0.6)$; y-intercept: 0, x-intercepts: $-5, 0$
d) $(0.4, 0.04)$; y-intercept: 0, x-intercepts: 0.75, 0
e) $(1.3, -0.9)$; y-intercept: 0, x-intercepts: 0, 2.5
f) $(-0.9, 2.8)$; y-intercept: 0, x-intercepts: $-1.8, 0$
6. a) $(4.58, -6.30)$; y-intercept: 0, x-intercepts: 0, 9.17
b) $(0.18, 0.16)$; y-intercept: 0, x-intercepts: 0.36, 0
c) $(-1.14, -0.42)$; y-intercept: 1, x-intercepts: -1.75,
-0.52 **d)** $(0.56, 1.03)$; y-intercept: 0.8, x-intercepts:
$-0.64, 1.77$ **e)** $(-291.67, -510.42)$; y-intercept: 0,
x-intercepts: $-583.33, 0$ **f)** $(-242.13, -243.25)$;
y-intercept: -1.12, x-intercepts: $-484.82, 0.56$
g) $(0.21, -24.90)$; y-intercept: -25, x-intercepts: none
h) $(-31.73, 54.66)$; y-intercept: 2.3, x-intercepts:
$-64.15, 0.69$

2 Problem Solving **1. a)** 2.1 m **b)** 4.43 m **c)** 3.05 m
2. a) 0.09 mm²/h; 3.57 h **b)** The number of cells was
decreasing. **c)** 7.14 h **3. a)** 1.46 **b)** $x = 0.83$
4. a) 32.33 m **b)** 54.9 m **c)** 32.08 m **5. a)** $y = x^2 - 4$ and

$y = |x^2 - 4|$ are the same for $x \le -2$, $x \ge 2$; $y = x^2 - 4$ and $y = |x^2 - 4|$ are reflections in the x-axis for $-2 < x < 2$ **b)** $y = x^2 - 4$ and $y = 4 - x^2$ are reflections in the x-axis **c)** $y = |x^2 - 4|$ and $y = |4 - x^2|$ are identical

Section 3.6 p. 139
Applications and Problem Solving **1. b)** 23rd month **c)** $y = 100(x - 11)^2 - 12\,100$ **2.** 5 months sooner **3.** 14 **4. a)** 276 **b)** 312 **5. b)** 5 s **c)** 122.5 m **d)** $h(t) = 49t - 4.9t^2$ **e)** $0 \le t \le 10$, $0 \le h \le 122.5$ **6.** 49 **7.** 10 **8.** To follow this plan, eventually Ray must save more in a month than what he earns.

Connecting Math and History pp. 140-142
1 Falling Objects **1.** 5, 125, 50; 6, 180, 60 **2.** $f = 5t^2$
3. 245 m; 320 m **4.** 10 m/s² **5.** $\dfrac{1}{2}$ of g **6.** Answers may vary.
2 The Path of a Cannonball **1. a)** 60, 90, 120, 150, 180 **2. c)** 45 m **d)** 3 s **e)** $h(t) = 30t - 5t^2$ **f)** 44.2 m; 28.8 m **g)** 6 s **3. a)** $h(t) = 50t - 5t^2$ **b)** 125 m **c)** 5 s **d)** 100.8 m **e)** 10 s
3 Distances Travelled by a Cannonball **1. a)** $H = D\sin A$ **b)** $h(t) = D\sin A - 5t^2$ **c)** $h(t) = vt\sin A - 5t^2$ **2. a)** 75 m **b)** yes **c)** 80 m; 8 s **3. a)** $d = D\cos A$ **b)** $d = vt\cos A$ **c)** 554 m **4.** 355 m; 106 m **5.** no
6. a) $v = \dfrac{d}{t\cos A}$ **b)** 64 m/s

Career Connection p. 143
1. The tallest building in Canada, the CN Tower, is 553 m, which is 53 m taller than the fountain of lava. **2. b)** 151 m **c)** 5.5 s **d)** The lava may fall on land that is below the crater, and therefore take longer to get to the ground. **e)** The equation is only a model of the situation. It does not account for any external factors that might affect the way the lava falls. **3.** British Columbia: 1.9 cm; Alberta: 2.8 cm; Saskatchewan: 2.9 cm; Manitoba: 2.8 cm

Review pp. 144-145
1. The graph of $y = x^2 - 3$ is a translation of the graph of $y = x^2$, 3 units downward. **2.** The graph of $y = -4x^2$ is a vertical stretch of the graph of $y = -x^2$ by a factor of 4. **3. a)** up **b)** $(0, 4)$ **c)** $x = 0$ **d)** Domain: R; Range: $y \ge 4$ **e)** min: 4 at $x = 0$ **f)** y-intercept: 4, x-intercepts: none **4. a)** down **b)** $(0, -2)$ **c)** $x = 0$ **d)** Domain: R; Range: $y \le -2$ **e)** max: -2 at $x = 0$ **f)** y-intercept: -2, x-intercepts: none **5. a)** up **b)** $(0, 0)$ **c)** $x = 0$ **d)** Domain: R; Range: $y \ge 0$ **e)** min: 0 at $x = 0$ **f)** y-intercept: 0, x-intercept: 0 **6. a)** down **b)** $(0, 3)$ **c)** $x = 0$ **d)** Domain: R; Range: $y \le 3$ **e)** max: 3 at $x = 0$ **f)** y-intercept: 3, x-intercepts: 1, -1 **7. a)** down **b)** $(0, 0)$ **c)** Domain: R; Range: $y \le 0$

d) max: 0 at $x = 0$ **8. a)** down **b)** $(0, 3.5)$ **c)** Domain: R; Range: $y \le 3.5$ **d)** max: 3.5 at $x = 0$ **9. a)** down **b)** $(0, -7)$ **c)** Domain: R; Range: $y \le -7$ **d)** max: -7 at $x = 0$ **10. a)** up **b)** $(0, 3)$ **c)** Domain: R; Range: $y \ge 3$ **d)** min: 3 at $x = 0$ **11.** -2.6, 2.6 **12.** -1.4, 1.4 **13.** no x-intercepts **14.** -2.1, 2.1 **15.** $y = 2x^2$ **16.** $y = -3x^2 - 2$ **17.** $y = -5x^2$ **18.** $y = x^2 - 5$ **19. a)** 2.13 m **b)** 12 m **c)** 1.2 m **20. a)** down **b)** stretched by a factor of 3 **c)** $(3, 1)$ **d)** $x = 3$ **e)** Domain: R; Range: $y \le 1$ **f)** max: 1 at $x = 3$ **21. a)** up **b)** not stretched or shrunk **c)** $(-7, -2)$ **d)** $x = -7$ **e)** Domain: R; Range: $y \ge -2$ **f)** min: -2 at $x = -7$ **22. a)** up **b)** shrunk by a factor of 0.5 **c)** $(-1, 5)$ **d)** $x = -1$ **e)** Domain: R; Range: $y \ge 5$ **f)** min: 5 at $x = -1$ **23. a)** down **b)** not stretched or shrunk **c)** $(-3, -1)$ **d)** $x = -3$ **e)** Domain: R; Range: $y \le -1$ **f)** max: -1 at $x = -3$ **24. a)** up **b)** not stretched or shrunk **c)** $(-1, -1)$ **d)** $x = -1$ **e)** Domain: R; Range: $y \ge -1$ **f)** min: -1 at $x = -1$ **25. a)** down **b)** stretched by a factor of 4 **c)** $(1, 0)$ **d)** $x = 1$ **e)** Domain: R; Range: $y \le 0$ **f)** max: 0 at $x = 1$ **26. a)** down **b)** stretched by a factor of 2 **c)** $(4, -3)$ **d)** $x = 4$ **e)** Domain: R; Range: $y \le -3$ **f)** max: -3 at $x = 4$ **27. a)** up **b)** shrunk by a factor of 0.25 **c)** $(-2, 1)$ **d)** $x = -2$ **e)** Domain: R; Range: $y \ge 1$ **f)** min: 1 at $x = -2$ **28. a)** $(3, 0)$ **b)** min: 0 at $x = 3$ **c)** y-intercept: 9, x-intercept: 3 **d)** Answers may vary. $(1, 4)$, $(2, 1)$ **29. a)** $(-2, -4)$ **b)** min: -4 at $x = -2$ **c)** y-intercept: 0, x-intercepts: -4, 0 **d)** Answers may vary. $(1, 5)$, $(2, 12)$ **30. a)** $(3, -8)$ **b)** min: -8 at $x = 3$ **c)** y-intercept: 10, x-intercepts: 1, 5 **d)** Answers may vary. $(2, -6)$, $(3, -8)$ **31. a)** $(-2, 9)$ **b)** max: 9 at $x = -2$ **c)** y-intercept: 5, x-intercepts: -5, 1 **d)** Answers may vary. $(-4, 5)$, $(-3, 8)$ **32.** -4.2, 0.2 **33.** -0.2, 2.2 **34.** $y = 2(x - 3)^2 + 4$ **35.** $y = (x - 2)^2 - 3$ **36.** $y = 2(x + 3)^2 - 4$ **37.** $y = -4(x - 1)^2 + 3$ **38.** $y = \dfrac{1}{2}(x + 2)^2 + 1$ **39. a)** 13 m **b)** 0.9 m **c)** 4.9 s **d)** 8.9 m **40.** 16 **41.** 49 **42.** 6.25 **43.** 0.09 **44.** $y = (x + 2)^2 - 3$; $(-2, -3)$; $x = -2$; Points may vary. $(0, 1)$, $(1, 6)$ **45.** $y = (x - 5)^2 - 10$; $(5, -10)$; $x = 5$; Points may vary. $(0, 15)$, $(1, 6)$ **46.** $y = -(x + 3)^2 + 4$; $(-3, 4)$; $x = -3$; Points may vary. $(0, -5)$, $(1, -12)$ **47.** $y = -(x + 2)^2 + 7$; $(-2, 7)$; $x = -2$; Points may vary. $(0, 3)$, $(1, -2)$ **48.** $(-3, -9)$; $x = -3$; y-intercept: 0, x-intercepts: -6, 0; $y \ge -9$ **49.** $(4, -4)$; $x = 4$; y-intercept: 12, x-intercepts: 2, 6; $y \ge -4$ **50.** $(-2, -5)$; $x = -2$; y-intercept: -9, x-intercepts: none; $y \le -5$ **51.** $(-4, -1)$; $x = -4$; y-intercept: 15, x-intercepts: -5, -3; $y \ge -1$ **52.** $(2.5, -3.25)$ **53.** $(0.5, -3.75)$ **54.** $(-2, 3)$ **55.** $(-1.5, 10.5)$ **56.** $(-0.25, -1.25)$ **57.** $(-1.5, 1.125)$ **58.** no x-intercepts **59.** -0.3, 1 **60.** -0.5, 0 **61.** -1.6, 1.6 **62. a)** 4.5 m **b)** 4 m **c)** 2.5 m **63.** 6, -6 **64. a)** 150 m by 150 m **b)** 22 500 m²
Exploring Math **1.** Player 1 takes 1 counter, leaving

8. Player 2 takes 1, 2, or 3 counters, leaving 7, 6, or 5. Player 1 takes 3 counters if Player 2 left 7, 2 counters if Player 2 left 6, and 1 counter if Player 2 left 5. There are now 4 counters left for Player 2. Player 2 takes 1, 2, or 3 counters, leaving 3, 2, or 1. Player 1 can take all the remaining counters, and win.
2. Player 1 takes 1, 2, or 3 counters, leaving 7, 6, or 5. Player 2 takes 3 counters if Player 1 left 7, 2 counters if Player 1 left 6, and 1 counter if Player 1 left 5. Therefore, there are now 4 counters left for Player 1. Player 1 takes 1, 2, or 3 counters, leaving 3, 2, or 1. Player 2 can take all the remaining counters, and win.
3. F, F, F, S, F, F, F, S, F, F, F, S, F **4. a)** first player **b)** Take 2 counters. **c)** Any first move that results in a number of counters divisible by 4 results in a win for the first player. **5. a)** second player **b)** Take away the number of counters that will result in a number divisible by 4. **c)** Any second move that results in a number of counters divisible by 4 results in a win for the second player. **6. a)** first player **b)** second player **c)** first player **d)** second player

Chapter Check p. 146
1. a) up **b)** $(0, -1)$ **c)** $x = 0$ **d)** Domain: R; Range: $y \geq -1$ **e)** min: -1 at $x = 0$ **2. a)** down **b)** $(0, 5)$ **c)** $x = 0$ **d)** Domain: R; Range: $y \leq 5$ **e)** max: 5 at $x = 0$ **3. a)** down **b)** $(0, 0)$ **c)** $x = 0$ **d)** Domain: R; Range: $y \leq 0$ **e)** max: 0 at $x = 0$ **4. a)** down **b)** $(0, -3)$ **c)** $x = 0$ **d)** Domain: R; Range: $y \leq -3$ **e)** max: -3 at $x = 0$ **5.** no x-intercepts **6.** $-3.2, 3.2$ **7.** $-1.6, 1.6$ **8.** $-2.4, 2.4$ **9.** $y = -4x^2$ **10.** $y = -0.5x^2 - 3$ **11.** $y = 3x^2$ **12.** $y = 2x^2 - 5$ **13. a)** up **b)** neither stretched nor shrunk **c)** $(-3, -1)$ **d)** $x = -3$ **e)** Domain: R; Range: $y \geq -1$ **f)** min: -1 at $x = -3$ **14. a)** up **b)** stretched by a factor of 3 **c)** $(1, 0)$ **d)** $x = 1$ **e)** Domain: R; Range: $y \geq 0$ **f)** min: 0 at $x = 1$ **15. a)** down **b)** stretched by a factor of 2 **c)** $(5, -2)$ **d)** $x = 5$ **e)** Domain: R; Range: $y \leq -2$ **f)** max: -2 at $x = 5$ **16. a)** down **b)** shrunk by a factor of 0.5 **c)** $(-2, 3)$ **d)** $x = -2$ **e)** Domain: R; Range: $y \leq 3$ **f)** max: 3 at $x = -2$ **17. a)** $(1, 0)$ **b)** min: 0 at $x = 1$ **c)** y-intercept: 1, x-intercept: 1 **d)** Answers may vary. $(2, 1)$, $(3, 4)$ **18. a)** $(-1, -4)$ **b)** min: -4 at $x = -1$ **c)** y-intercept: -3, x-intercepts: $-3, 1$ **d)** Answers may vary. $(2, 5)$, $(3, 12)$ **19. a)** $(5, -9)$ **b)** min: -9 at $x = 5$ **c)** y-intercept: 16, x-intercepts: 2, 8 **d)** Answers may vary. $(1, 7)$, $(3, -5)$ **20. a)** $(-6, 18)$ **b)** max: 18 at $x = -6$ **c)** y-intercept: -54, x-intercepts: $-9, -3$ **d)** Answers may vary. $(-2, -14)$, $(-1, -32)$ **21.** $-4.1, 0.1$ **22.** $0.3, 3.7$ **23.** $y = (x + 3)^2 + 1$ **24.** $y = -2(x + 5)^2 + 4$ **25.** $y = -2(x - 1)^2 + 4$ **26.** $y = \dfrac{4}{9}(x + 3)^2 + 1$ **27.** $y = (x + 4)^2 - 8$; $(-4, -8)$; $x = -4$; Points may vary. $(0, 8)$, $(1, 17)$

28. $y = (x - 4)^2 - 7$; $(4, -7)$; $x = 4$; Points may vary. $(0, 9)$, $(1, 2)$ **29.** $y = (x - 2)^2 + 1$; $(2, 1)$; $x = 2$; Points may vary. $(0, 5)$, $(1, 2)$ **30.** $y = -(x + 5)^2 + 21$; $(-5, 21)$; $x = -5$; Points may vary. $(0, -4)$, $(1, -15)$ **31.** $(-4, -14)$; $x = -4$; y-intercept: 2, x-intercepts: $-0.3, -7.7$; $y \geq -14$ **32.** $(5, -25)$; $x = 5$; y-intercept: 0, x-intercepts: 0, 10; $y \geq -25$ **33.** $(-3, -1)$; $x = -3$; y-intercept: $(0, -10)$, x-intercepts: none; $y \leq -1$ **34.** $(-3, 2)$; $x = -3$; y-intercept: $(0, 11)$, x-intercepts: none; $y \geq 2$ **35.** $(3.5, -11.25)$ **36.** $(0.5, 12.25)$ **37.** $(-1, 9)$ **38.** $(-1.25, 1.875)$ **39. a)** 3 m **b)** 3.2 m **c)** 2.7 m **40. a)** 86 m **b)** 2 m **c)** 8 s **41.** \$12

Using the Strategies p. 147
1. A: 11 kg, B: 13 kg, C: 14 kg, D: 9 kg, E: 7 kg **2. a)** Astros: 2, 0, 1, 1, 2, 4; Bears: 2, 0, 1, 1, 3, 7; Colts: 2, 2, 0, 0, 7, 1 **b)** Astros: 2, Bears: 2; Colts: 2, Astros: 0; Colts: 5, Bears: 1 **3.** 34 **5.** 11 **6.** 12 km **7.** by rows: 19, 22, 7; 4, 16, 28; 25, 10, 13 **8.** 9 **9. a)** 60 or 48 **10. a)** 68 **b)** no
Data Bank 1. a) $y = 0.0144x^2 - 0.09$ **b)** 5.76 cm **2.** Answers may vary. 2036 **3.** Answers may vary. Northwest Territories

Chapter 4

Quadratic and Polynomial Equations p. 149
1. $s^2 = 16$ **2.** $s = \pm 4$ **3.** -4; speed is non-negative **4.** 4 m/s **5. a)** 2 m/s **b)** 6 m/s **c)** 1.2 m/s

Getting Started pp. 150-151
1 The Sum of Consecutive Squares 2. The sum of the term numbers is equal to the term number of the result. **3. a)** t_{19} **b)** t_{43} **4.** $t_n^2 + t_{n+1}^2 = t_{2n+1}$
2 The Difference Between Alternate Squares 2. The sum of the term numbers is equal to the term number of the result. **3.** $t_{n+2}^2 - t_n^2 = t_{2n+2}$
3 Four Consecutive Fibonacci Numbers 1. The product of the first and last numbers is equal to the difference between the squares of the middle two numbers. **2.** $t_n \times t_{n+3} = t_{n+2}^2 - t_{n+1}^2$
Warm Up 1. $3x(x - 1)$ **2.** $2xy(2x + 5y)$ **3.** $(y + 1)(y + 7)$ **4.** $(s + 2)(s - 3)$ **5.** does not factor **6.** $(c + 5)^2$ **7.** does not factor **8.** $(2a + 1)(2a - 1)$ **9.** $(3v - 1)(v + 4)$ **10.** $(2x - 5)^2$ **11.** $2(t - 1)(t - 12)$ **12.** does not factor **13.** ± 1 **14.** ± 3 **15.** ± 2 **16.** ± 5 **17.** 0, 1 **18.** $0, -2$ **19.** $0, -4$ **20.** 0, 3 **21.** $2\sqrt{5}$ **22.** $3\sqrt{6}$ **23.** $2\sqrt{15}$ **24.** $4\sqrt{6}$ **25.** $6\sqrt{2}$ **26.** $20\sqrt{3}$ **27.** $42\sqrt{2}$ **28.** $8\sqrt{13}$ **29.** $21\sqrt{11}$ **30.** $\sqrt{2}$ **31.** $\sqrt{3}$ **32.** $2\sqrt{2}$ **33.** 5 **34.** $2\sqrt{10}$ **35.** $2\sqrt{5}$ **36.** $\dfrac{3 - 2\sqrt{3}}{2}$

37. $-\dfrac{1}{2}$ **38.** $2+\sqrt{5}$ **39.** 5 **40.** $\dfrac{-1-\sqrt{7}}{3}$ **41.** $x+2$

42. $x-3$ R–1 **43.** $x+1$ **44.** $3x+5$ R1 **45.** x^2+3x+1
46. $4x+1$ R2 **47.** $3x+4$ **48.** $5x-1$ **49.** x^2+2x+1 R–2
50. x^2-4x+4 R3

Mental Math
Simplifying and Evaluating Square Roots **1.** $2\sqrt{2}$
2. $3\sqrt{2}$ **3.** not possible **4.** $2\sqrt{3}$ **5.** not possible **6.** $2\sqrt{6}$
7. $3\sqrt{3}$ **8.** $2\sqrt{11}$ **9.** $3\sqrt{5}$ **10.** $5\sqrt{2}$ **11.** $3\sqrt{7}$ **12.** $4\sqrt{5}$
13. 7 **14.** not possible **15.** 11 **16.** 9 **17.** 4 **18.** 6 **19.** 8
20. 8 **21.** 9 **22.** 5 **23.** 10 **24.** 5
Subtracting in Two Steps **1.** 25 **2.** 25 **3.** 54 **4.** 28 **5.** 39
6. 36 **7.** 64 **8.** 61 **9.** 87 **10.** 86 **11.** 81 **12.** 83 **13.** 1.9
14. 1.9 **15.** 2.6 **16.** 10.8 **17.** 17.6 **18.** 16.7 **19.** 350
20. 380 **21.** 290 **22.** 470 **23.** 530 **24.** 880

Section 4.1 pp. 155-156
Practice **1.** $-3, 2$ **2.** $4, 1$ **3.** $-5, -1$ **4.** -2 **5.** no real
roots **6.** $-5, 1$ **7.** ± 2 **8.** $0, -3$ **9.** ± 3 **10.** no real roots
11. 1 **12.** no real roots **13.** $0, 5$ **14.** $2, -1$ **15.** 3 **16.** -4,
1 **17.** no real roots **18.** $1, 2$ **19.** $-1, 1.5$ **20.** $-0.5, 3$
21. no real roots **22.** -0.5 **23.** $0, 2.5$ **24.** $-2.9, 0.6$
25. $1.3, -0.5$ **26.** 2.7 **27.** $-0.6, 0.4$ **28.** $-0.8, 0.5$
29. $-1.6, 3.6$ **30.** no real roots **31.** $0, -3.3$ **32.** -1.7
33. $1, 3$ **34.** $-3, 1$ **35.** no real roots **36.** 3 **37.** 1
38. $-0.5, -1.5$ **39.** 1 **40.** $-7, 1$
Applications and Problem Solving **41.** $w = 8$ m,
$l = 9$ m **42.** 20 m **43.** 45 m **44.** 11 cm by 3 cm
45. 6 m, 8 m **46.** 12 cm, 5 cm **47.** 5 m **48.** 35 m by
65 m **49.** $l = 26$ m, $w = 14$ m **50.** 4.8 cm by 6.4 cm
51. 14, 16 or $-16, -14$ **52.** 18.3 m by 9.1 m **53.** 7, 8, 9
54. a) $x^2-x-12=0$ **b)** $4, -3$ **c)** opposites **55. a)** $-0.3, 2$
56. a) $-0.5, 2$ **57. a)** $c < 0$ **b)** $c = 0$ **c)** $c > 0$ **58. a)** $c = 49$
b) $c < 49$ **c)** $c > 49$ **59. a)** $b = \pm 10$ **b)** $b < -10, b > 10$
c) $-10 < b < 10$ **60. a)** $b = 0$ **b)** $0, -b$ **61. a)** $x \le -4, x \ge 4$
b) $-5 \le x \le 5$

Section 4.2 pp. 160-162
Practice **1.** $-1, -2$ **2.** $-3, 1$ **3.** 5 **4.** $2, -3$ **5.** $-\dfrac{1}{2}, 3$
6. $-\dfrac{4}{3}, \dfrac{1}{2}$ **7.** $0, -9$ **8.** $0, 4$ **9.** $x^2-2x-6=0$
10. $2y^2-3y+2=0$ **11.** $3z^2+4z+3=0$
12. $x^2+2x-3=0$ **13.** $4m^2-3m=0$ **14.** $2x^2-x-2=0$
15. $3x^2+2x-6=0$ **16.** $8x^2-x-13=0$ **17.** $x^2-5=0$
18. $y^2+2y-1=0$ **19.** $2t^2+3t-4=0$
20. $10x^2-6x+15=0$ **21.** $-3, -4$ **22.** $1, 2$ **23.** $-2, 3$
24. 4 **25.** $-7, 5$ **26.** $9, -2$ **27.** $-2, \dfrac{1}{2}$ **28.** $\dfrac{1}{3}, 1$ **29.** $-5, -\dfrac{1}{2}$
30. $\dfrac{2}{3}, -3$ **31.** $-\dfrac{1}{2}, \dfrac{3}{2}$ **32.** $\dfrac{3}{5}, 1$ **33.** $0, -2$ **34.** $0, 3$ **35.** $0, -\dfrac{2}{3}$

36. $0, \dfrac{8}{5}$ **37.** $0, 4$ **38.** $0, -\dfrac{4}{3}$ **39.** $-3, 5$ **40.** $7, 3$ **41.** $-3, 1$
42. $\dfrac{3}{2}$ **43.** $0, \dfrac{2}{5}$ **44.** $2, 18$ **45.** $-6, -2$ **46.** $0, 6$ **47.** $-1, 2$
48. $5, 1$ **49.** $-\dfrac{2}{3}, 2$ **50.** $-3, -2$ **51.** $-3, 2$ **52.** $-\dfrac{4}{3}, 3$
53. $-1, -\dfrac{1}{2}$ **54.** $-2, \dfrac{8}{3}$ **55.** $x^2+8x+15=0$
56. $x^2-4x+4=0$ **57.** $x^2-9=0$ **58.** $2x^2-7x-4=0$
59. $9x^2-9x+2=0$ **60.** $8x^2+10x-3=0$
61. $x^2+5x=0$ **62.** $3x^2-4x=0$ **63.** $0, 1$ **64.** $-\dfrac{1}{2}, 2$
65. $-4, 2$ **66.** $\dfrac{1}{2}$ **67.** $-4, 3$ **68.** $\dfrac{8}{3}, 6$

Applications and Problem Solving
69. a) $0 = -5t^2+9t+2$ **b)** 2 s **70.** 5, 11 or $-11, -5$
71. 9, 10 or $-10, -9$ **72.** -2 or 3 **73.** 16, 18 or $-18, -16$
74. 0 or -10 **75.** 9 cm by 4 cm **76.** $\dfrac{3}{2}$ or $\dfrac{2}{3}$ **77.** -1 or 2
78. 18 m by 1 m **79.** 20 cm by 122 cm **80.** $\dfrac{8}{3}$ m by 6 m
81. 8 cm, 15 cm **82.** 11 **83.** 4 **84.** 0.5 m
85. a) 70 mm by 135 mm **b)** The dimensions of a
Canadian \$20 bill are 70 mm by 153 mm.
86. a) -3; one **b)** $-3, -3$; two equal roots
87. $x^2-(p+q)x+pq=0$ **88. a)** $-4y, -y$ **b)** $3y, -\dfrac{y}{2}$ **c)** $\dfrac{y}{2}$
d) $-2y, \dfrac{y}{4}$ **e)** $0, -\dfrac{y}{5}$ **f)** $0, \dfrac{7y}{3}$ **89. a)** $6x^2-x-2=0$
b) Yes. Multiply the equation by any non-zero
constant. **90. a)** 10 **b)** $-\dfrac{1}{3}$ **91. a)** $x^2+4x+4=0$
b) $x^2-5x+6=0$ **c)** $2x^2-x-3=0$

Section 4.3 pp. 165-167
Practice **1.** ± 9 **2.** ± 8 **3.** $\pm\dfrac{5}{2}$ **4.** ± 4 **5.** ± 5 **6.** ± 6 **7.** ± 4
8. ± 10 **9.** ± 1 **10.** ± 0.5 **11.** ± 6 **12.** ± 4 **13.** ± 4 **14.** ± 3 **15.** ± 2
16. ± 7 **17.** ± 1.1 **18.** ± 0.7 **19.** ± 1 **20.** ± 5 **21.** ± 3.87
22. ± 4.47 **23.** ± 6.32 **24.** ± 2.45 **25.** ± 4.12 **26.** ± 3.46
27. ± 3.16 **28.** ± 3.61 **29.** ± 0.76 **30.** ± 1.67 **31.** ± 0.82
32. ± 4.12 **33.** $\pm 2\sqrt{3}$ **34.** $\pm 5\sqrt{3}$ **35.** $\pm 3\sqrt{5}$ **36.** $\pm 3\sqrt{2}$
37. $\pm 2\sqrt{2}$ **38.** $\pm 6\sqrt{3}$ **39.** $\pm\dfrac{\sqrt{15}}{3}$ **40.** $\pm\dfrac{2\sqrt{10}}{5}$ **41.** $\pm\dfrac{\sqrt{2}}{2}$
42. $\pm\dfrac{\sqrt{13}}{2}$ **43.** $\pm\dfrac{3\sqrt{2}}{2}$ **44.** $\pm\dfrac{3\sqrt{5}}{2}$ **45.** 1 **46.** $-5, 1$
47. $-2, 0$ **48.** $-1, 7$ **49.** $-1, 0$ **50.** $1, -\dfrac{1}{3}$ **51.** $-1, 4$
52. $-3, 4$ **53.** $-3, -7$ **54.** $-\dfrac{5}{4}, \dfrac{7}{4}$ **55.** $-10, 6$ **56.** $5, -4$

57. $-\dfrac{2}{3}$ 58. $2, -\dfrac{3}{2}$ 59. $-\dfrac{5}{2}, -\dfrac{9}{2}$ 60. $0, \dfrac{6}{5}$ 61. $0.75, 0.25$

62. $0.01, -0.21$ 63. $-0.15, -0.85$ 64. $\dfrac{2}{3}, -\dfrac{1}{3}$ 65. $\pm\sqrt{3}+5$;

6.73, 3.27 66. $\pm2\sqrt{2}-3$; $-0.17, -5.83$ 67. $\dfrac{\pm\sqrt{5}+1}{3}$;

1.08, -0.41 68. $\dfrac{\pm2\sqrt{5}-3}{4}$; $0.37, -1.87$ 69. $\pm\dfrac{\sqrt{7}}{2}-3$;

-1.68, -4.32 70. $\dfrac{\pm3\sqrt{2}+5}{2}$; 4.62, 0.38

Applications and Problem Solving
71. a) $28 - x^2 = 19$; $x = 3$; 3 m by 3 m b) $28 - x^2 = 19$; $x = \pm3$ c) A flower bed can only have positive dimensions. 72. ±12 73. ±5 74. a) $2w$ b) $2w^2$ c) $2w^2 = 800$; $w = 20$; 20 cm by 40 cm 75. a) $2\sqrt{10}$ s b) 6.3 s 76. a) 2 s b) 10.5 s 77. ±4 78. ±2.5 79. ±2.65 80. -14 or 20 81. $\pm\dfrac{1}{2}$ 82. a) $\pm\dfrac{10\sqrt{7}}{7}$ b) ±3.78 83. 9 84. 4 85. 11 cm by 11 cm 86. 3.5 cm 87. a) 4 cm by 4 cm, 8 cm by 8 cm b) 3 cm by 3 cm, 9 cm by 9 cm 88. a) $\pm\dfrac{5}{3}$ b) ±3 c) $\pm\dfrac{\sqrt{10}}{2}$ d) $\pm\dfrac{\sqrt{17}}{2}$ e) $\pm\sqrt{10}$ f) $\pm\sqrt{2}$ g) ±1 h) $\pm2\sqrt{2}$ i) $\pm\dfrac{3\sqrt{11}}{11}$ 89. a) ±2 b) ±1.4 c) ±2.8 d) ±0.7 e) 1.5, 2.5 f) $-0.3, -1.7$ 90. No. The equation reduces to $3 = 1$ if the left side is expanded and simplified. This is impossible. 91. a) 8.5 cm b) 72 cm² 92. a) $-3 < x < 3$ b) $x \le -5$, $x \ge 5$ 93. No. A square must always be non-negative.

Section 4.4 pp. 172-173
Practice 1. $1; (x + 1)^2$ 2. $25; (x + 5)^2$ 3. $16; (t - 4)^2$ 4. $49; (w - 7)^2$ 5. $\dfrac{9}{4}; \left(m + \dfrac{3}{2}\right)^2$ 6. $\dfrac{49}{4}; \left(x + \dfrac{7}{2}\right)^2$ 7. $\dfrac{25}{4}; \left(p - \dfrac{5}{2}\right)^2$ 8. $\dfrac{121}{4}; \left(q - \dfrac{11}{2}\right)^2$ 9. $\dfrac{4}{9}; \left(x + \dfrac{2}{3}\right)^2$ 10. $\dfrac{1}{9}; \left(d - \dfrac{1}{3}\right)^2$ 11. $\dfrac{1}{16}; \left(x - \dfrac{1}{4}\right)^2$ 12. $\dfrac{1}{100}; \left(r + \dfrac{1}{10}\right)^2$ 13. $0.49; (x + 0.7)^2$ 14. $0.0009; (x - 0.03)^2$ 15. $0, -6$ 16. $9, 11$ 17. $-\dfrac{2}{3}, -\dfrac{4}{3}$ 18. $-\dfrac{1}{2}, -\dfrac{7}{2}$ 19. $1 \pm 2\sqrt{2}$ 20. $4 \pm 2\sqrt{3}$ 21. $-\dfrac{5}{2}, \dfrac{3}{2}$ 22. $\dfrac{1 \pm \sqrt{7}}{3}$ 23. $\dfrac{-3 \pm \sqrt{3}}{4}$ 24. $\dfrac{-6 \pm \sqrt{6}}{4}$ 25. $1.6, -0.6$ 26. $-0.3, -0.5$ 27. $-3 \pm \sqrt{5}$ 28. $2 \pm \sqrt{15}$ 29. $-4 \pm \sqrt{23}$

30. $5 \pm 2\sqrt{7}$ 31. $\dfrac{7 \pm \sqrt{13}}{2}$ 32. $\dfrac{5 \pm \sqrt{17}}{2}$ 33. $\dfrac{-1 \pm \sqrt{13}}{2}$ 34. $10 \pm 4\sqrt{6}$ 35. $\dfrac{-4 \pm \sqrt{6}}{2}$ 36. $\dfrac{3 \pm \sqrt{3}}{3}$ 37. $\dfrac{-5 \pm \sqrt{5}}{4}$ 38. $\dfrac{-2 \pm \sqrt{10}}{3}$ 39. $\dfrac{-3 \pm \sqrt{57}}{12}$ 40. $2, -\dfrac{1}{3}$ 41. $\dfrac{-1 \pm \sqrt{31}}{5}$ 42. $\dfrac{-1 \pm \sqrt{6}}{5}$ 43. $-1 \pm 3\sqrt{3}$ 44. $\dfrac{1 \pm \sqrt{10}}{3}$ 45. $0.41, -2.41$ 46. $3.73, 0.27$ 47. $1.45, -3.45$ 48. $2.19, -3.19$ 49. $3.58, 0.42$ 50. $0.34, -2.34$ 51. $-0.72, -2.78$ 52. $4.10, -1.10$ 53. $-0.13, -3.87$ 54. $3.81, -1.31$

Applications and Problem Solving
55. 40 m by 110 m 56. 4.3 cm 57. 3.6 m by 5.6 m 58. 8.1 m by 6.1 m 59. 11.2 m 60. 7.4 cm by 5.4 cm 61. -15 or 14 62. 1.45 63. a) $7 \pm 2\sqrt{3}$ b) 10.464, 3.536 64. $1 \pm 3\sqrt{3}$ 65. 23.7 cm by 29.7 cm 66. a) $\dfrac{-7 \pm 3\sqrt{5}}{2}$ b) $\dfrac{9 \pm \sqrt{73}}{2}$ c) $2 \pm \sqrt{6}$ d) $-3 \pm 2\sqrt{2}$ 67. a) $\dfrac{1 \pm \sqrt{5}}{2}, x \ne 0$ b) $\dfrac{5 \pm \sqrt{73}}{4}$, $z \ne -\dfrac{1}{2}$ c) $\dfrac{1 \pm 2\sqrt{34}}{3}, y \ne \pm\sqrt{15}$ d) $\dfrac{3 \pm \sqrt{89}}{8}, x \ne \pm1$ 68. a) 4.1 s b) 2 s 69. a) Let x represent the number of 10¢ increases. The number of loaves sold is $50 - 2x$. The price of each loaf is $1.50 + 0.1x$. The total revenue is $(50 - 2x)(1.50 + 0.1x)$. For revenue of \$80, solve $(50 - 2x)(1.50 + 0.1x) = 80$, which reduces to $0.2x^2 - 2x + 5 = 0$. b) 5 c) \$2 d) between \$1.80 and \$2.20 70. ±7 71. a) $-1 \pm \sqrt{k + 1}$ b) $\dfrac{1 \pm \sqrt{k^2 + 1}}{k}$ c) $\dfrac{k \pm \sqrt{4 + k^2}}{2}$ 72. a) $x^2 - 5 = 0$ b) $x^2 - 6x + 7 = 0$ c) $x^2 + 2x - 11 = 0$ d) $4x^2 - 24x + 23 = 0$ 73. 5, 9 74. $x = \dfrac{-b \pm \sqrt{b^2 - 4c}}{2}$

Section 4.5 pp. 178-180
Practice 1. $-5, -1$ 2. $-4, 2$ 3. $3, -1$ 4. $5, 7$ 5. -2 6. 1 7. $1, \dfrac{1}{2}$ 8. $3, -\dfrac{1}{5}$ 9. $4, -\dfrac{3}{2}$ 10. $\dfrac{1}{3}$ 11. $\dfrac{3}{4}, -\dfrac{3}{2}$ 12. $-\dfrac{1}{2}, \dfrac{2}{3}$ 13. $\pm\dfrac{3}{2}$ 14. $-\dfrac{5}{2}, -\dfrac{3}{2}$ 15. $0, \dfrac{5}{2}$ 16. $-\dfrac{5}{3}, -2$ 17. $-2 \pm \sqrt{2}$ 18. $3 \pm \sqrt{10}$ 19. $2 \pm \sqrt{3}$ 20. $1 \pm \sqrt{2}$ 21. $-2 \pm \sqrt{3}$

22. $\dfrac{1\pm\sqrt{17}}{2}$ **23.** $\dfrac{1\pm\sqrt{15}}{7}$ **24.** $\dfrac{-1\pm\sqrt{5}}{2}$ **25.** $\dfrac{-4\pm\sqrt{22}}{2}$

26. $\dfrac{1\pm\sqrt{21}}{2}$ **27.** $\dfrac{-1\pm\sqrt{6}}{2}$ **28.** $1\pm\sqrt{5}$ **29.** $\pm\dfrac{2\sqrt{3}}{3}$

30. $\dfrac{2\pm\sqrt{7}}{3}$ **31.** 0, 1.6 **32.** 1.3, −0.3 **33.** 3.4, −1.4

34. 3.9, −0.9 **35.** 6.6, −0.6 **36.** 2.8, −1.3 **37.** −0.3, −2
38. 10.7, 1.3 **39.** 6.2, 0.8 **40.** 1.9, 0 **41.** 0.65, −4.65
42. −1.16, 5.16 **43.** 1.31, −0.13 **44.** 1.67, −0.5
45. −0.04, −1.05 **46.** −12.44, 9.94 **47.** −3, 5
48. 20, −2.78 **49.** −1.61, 5.61 **50.** 6.16, −0.16
51. 2, −1.5 **52.** −1, −2 **53.** 0, −10 **54.** $7\pm\sqrt{58}$

55. $-1\pm\sqrt{7}$ **56.** $\dfrac{1\pm\sqrt{13}}{2}$ **57.** $\dfrac{1\pm\sqrt{33}}{2}$ **58.** $4\pm2\sqrt{7}$

Applications and Problem Solving **59. a)** 2.25 m

b) 3.8 s **60.** 82 m **61.** 1160 m **62.** $\pm\dfrac{9}{2}$ **63.** 56 m by

116 m **64.** 600 km/h **65.** −24 or 25 **66.** 75 km/h
67. −29, −27 or 27, 29 **68.** 2.5 km/h **69.** 2.8 cm
70. 10 km/h **71.** 12 cm, 16 cm **72. a)** 7.5 cm

b) 6562.5 cm³ **73. a)** 0, $-\dfrac{3}{4}$ **b)** $-\dfrac{11}{4}$, 2 **c)** $-\dfrac{1}{4}$, $-\dfrac{1}{2}$

74. 10 km/h **75.** 13 cm by 8 cm **76. b)** 17.72 cm
77. a) 110; $160 **b)** $120; 130 **78. a)** 1. Multiply both
sides by $4a$. 2. Add b^2 to both sides. 3. Subtract $4ac$
from both sides. 4. Factor the perfect square
trinomial on the left-hand side. 5. Take the square
root of both sides. 6. Subtract b from both sides. 7.
Divide both sides by $2a$. **b)** Yes. Terms are added and
subtracted from both sides to make the left side a
perfect square. **c)** 1. $36x^2 + 24x - 48 = 0$
2. $36x^2 + 24x - 48 + 4 = 4$ 3. $36x^2 + 24x + 4 = 52$
4. $(6x+2)^2 = 52$ 5. $6x + 2 = \pm\sqrt{52}$ 6. $6x = -2 \pm\sqrt{52}$

7. $x = \dfrac{-2\pm\sqrt{52}}{6}$, which reduces to $x = \dfrac{-1\pm\sqrt{13}}{3}$

79. 3.58 units **80. a)** 6, 10 **b)** $s = \dfrac{p^2 - p}{2}$ **c)** 11

d) No. The solution to the quadratic must be an
integer. **81.** $b^2 - 4ac$ is a perfect square.

82. $b^2 - 4ac = 0$ **83.** 2.2 cm **84. a)** $-8y$, $-\dfrac{y}{2}$ **b)** $\left(-1\pm\sqrt{2}\right)y$

85. a) $40x^2 + 2x - 3 = 0$ **b)** $x^2 - 6x + 4 = 0$
c) $4x^2 - 4x - 11 = 0$

Section 4.6 pp. 185-186
Practice **1.** $3i$ **2.** $5i$ **3.** $9i$ **4.** $i\sqrt{5}$ **5.** $i\sqrt{13}$ **6.** $i\sqrt{23}$
7. $2i\sqrt{3}$ **8.** $2i\sqrt{10}$ **9.** $3i\sqrt{6}$ **10.** $-2i$ **11.** $-2i\sqrt{5}$ **12.** $5i\sqrt{y}$
608 *Answers*

13. $6ix$ **14.** $3ix^2\sqrt{2}$ **15.** $2iz^2\sqrt{5z}$ **16.** 6 **17.** 6
18. $2ix^2y\sqrt{10xy}$ **19.** $-i$ **20.** 1 **21.** i **22.** −20 **23.** −5 **24.** i
25. −12 **26.** 64 **27.** 18 **28.** −2 **29.** 5 **30.** 6 **31.** −12
32. −50 **33.** 40 **34.** $7 - 2i$ **35.** $3 - 11i$ **36.** $2 - 5i$
37. $1 + 6i$ **38.** $-2 + 13i$ **39.** $5i - 11$ **40.** $-3 - i$
41. $24 - 3i$ **42.** $14 - 17i$ **43.** $-12i + 7$ **44.** $8 - 6i$
45. $3i - 6$ **46.** $-12i - 20$ **47.** $8 - 2i$ **48.** $14 + 2i$
49. $29 - 3i$ **50.** $-7 - 19i$ **51.** 26 **52.** $-3 + 4i$ **53.** $-7 - 24i$
54. $-2i$ **55.** 4 **56.** $\pm3i$ **57.** $\pm2i$ **58.** $\pm2i\sqrt{5}$ **59.** $\pm2i\sqrt{3}$
60. $\pm2i\sqrt{2}$ **61.** $\pm3i\sqrt{2}$ **62.** $-1\pm i$ **63.** $2\pm2i$

64. $\dfrac{-5\pm i\sqrt{7}}{2}$ **65.** $\dfrac{3\pm i\sqrt{3}}{2}$ **66.** $\dfrac{1\pm 3i\sqrt{3}}{2}$ **67.** $\dfrac{3\pm 3i\sqrt{3}}{2}$

68. $\dfrac{-3\pm i\sqrt{15}}{4}$ **69.** $\dfrac{2\pm i\sqrt{2}}{3}$ **70.** $\dfrac{-5\pm i\sqrt{15}}{10}$ **71.** $\dfrac{2\pm i}{5}$

72. $\pm i\sqrt{6}$ **73.** $\pm i$ **74.** $\dfrac{1\pm i\sqrt{11}}{2}$ **75.** $1\pm i$ **76.** $\dfrac{-1\pm i\sqrt{23}}{6}$

77. $\pm2i\sqrt{2}$ **78.** ±2 **79.** $\pm i$ **80.** ±1, $\pm2i$ **81.** $\pm\sqrt{3}$, $\pm\sqrt{2}$

82. $\pm\sqrt{3}$, $\pm i\sqrt{2}$ **83.** ±1, $\pm\dfrac{\sqrt{6}}{3}$ **84.** $\pm i$, $\pm\dfrac{i\sqrt{6}}{2}$ **85.** $\pm\dfrac{\sqrt{6}}{2}$,

$\pm i\sqrt{2}$ **86.** $\pm\dfrac{\sqrt{2}}{2}$, $\pm\dfrac{i\sqrt{2}}{2}$ **87.** 0, $\pm\dfrac{2}{3}$

Applications and Problem Solving **88. a)** $a^2 + b^2$; real
b) 74 **c)** $(3 + 4i)(3 - 4i) = 25$, $(4 + 3i)(4 - 3i) = 25$
89. a) i, $-1 + i$, $-i$ **b)** $-i$, $-1 - i$, i **c)** $3i$, $-9 + 3i$, $72 - 51i$
d) $2 + i$, $5 + 5i$, $2 + 51i$ **90. a)** -1, $-i$, 1, i, -1, $-i$, 1, i, -1,
$-i$, 1 **b)** The pattern -1, $-i$, 1, i repeats. **c)** Divide n by
4. If the remainder is 1, $i^n = i$. If the remainder is 2,
$i^n = -1$. If the remainder is 3, $i^n = -i$. If the remainder
is 0, $i^n = 1$. **d)** 1; −1; i; −i **91. a)** $s = 3$, $t = 4$ **b)** $s = 3$,
$t = -1$ **c)** $s = 2$, $t = 1$ **92. b)** An error message appears.
93. a) $x^2 + 4 = 0$ **b)** $x^2 - 2x + 2 = 0$ **c)** $4x^2 - 12x + 13 = 0$
94. a) 1 s and 9 s **b)** 5 s **c)** no **95.** No. Imaginary roots
occur in complex conjugate pairs. **96. a)** 2; equal
b) 2, −1; equal **c)** 0, 2, −1; equal **d)** $\pm i$, $\pm\sqrt{2}$; equal
e) 0, $\pm i$, $\pm\sqrt{2}$; equal **97.** 12, 14 or −14, −12

Section 4.7 pp. 189-190
Practice **1.** two equal real roots **2.** two distinct real
roots **3.** two imaginary roots **4.** two imaginary roots
5. two distinct real roots **6.** two equal real roots
7. two imaginary roots **8.** two distinct real roots
9. two distinct real roots **10.** two imaginary roots
11. two imaginary roots **12.** two distinct real roots
13. two equal real roots **14.** two distinct real roots
15. two imaginary roots **16.** two equal real roots
17. two distinct real roots **18.** two distinct real roots
19. two equal real roots **20.** two imaginary roots

21. two distinct real roots 22. two distinct real roots
23. two imaginary roots 24. two imaginary roots
25. two imaginary roots 26. two distinct real roots
27. 2 28. 0 29. 2 30. 1 31. 0 32. 1 33. $k = 9$ 34. $k < 1$,
$k \neq 0$ 35. $k < -2$ 36. $k < \dfrac{2}{3}$ 37. $k > \dfrac{3}{4}$ 38. $k = \pm\dfrac{1}{2}$

39. $k < -\dfrac{4}{3}$ 40. $k > \dfrac{9}{16}$ 41. $k > -\dfrac{4}{3}$ 42. $k = 2$

43. a) $m > -\dfrac{4}{3}$, $m \neq 0$ b) $m = -\dfrac{4}{3}$ c) $m < -\dfrac{4}{3}$

Applications and Problem Solving 44. a) 16, 15
b) no c) $\dfrac{55}{2}, \dfrac{7}{2}$ 45. a) 5 m by 20 m or 10 m by 10 m

b) no 46. a) no b) 11 cm by 11 cm c) 9 cm by 13 cm
47. Yes, after 2 s. 48. a) 6000 at \$26 or 6500 at \$24
b) No. The discriminant is negative and the function
has no zeros. c) prices from \$20 to \$30
49. two distinct real roots; If $ac < 0$, then $b^2 - ac > 0$,

since $b^2 > 0$ and $-ac > 0$. 50. $\dfrac{1}{2}$ 51. $25i$ and $-6i$

52. a) If $a = k$, then $b = -k^2 - 1$ and $c = k$, where $k \neq 0$,

then the equation $ax^2 + bx + c = 0$ has roots k and $\dfrac{1}{k}$.

b) Answers may vary. $x^2 - 2x + 1 = 0$ has roots 1 and 1;

$3x^2 - 10x + 3 = 0$ has roots 3 and $\dfrac{1}{3}$ 53. a) $k < -8$, $k > 8$

b) $k = 2$ c) $-4 < k < 4$ 54. a) $\left(-\dfrac{1}{2}, 5\right), \left(-\dfrac{3}{2}, 7\right)$ b) no

55. a) $-2\sqrt{6} < m < 2\sqrt{6}$ b) $m = \pm 3\sqrt{3}$

Career Connection p. 191
1 Defining the Dimensions of a Package
1. a) 6.25 cm by 10 cm by 16 cm; 7.2 cm by 11.4 cm
by 18.3 cm **b)** 843 cm²; 1072 cm² **2.** 5.8 cm by 9.4 cm
by 15.0 cm
1 Research **1-5.** Answers may vary. **1.** math, design,
economics **2.** artistic, advertising, consumer
awareness **3.** A package with a colour and shape that
stands out and is attractive may influence a buyer.
5. all companies that package goods for display in
stores

Investigating Math pp. 192-193
1 Exploring the Relationships **1. b)** 5, 4; 9; 20; 1,
$-9, 20$ **c)** 2, -6; -4; -12; 1, 4, -12 **d)** 3, $\dfrac{1}{2}$; $\dfrac{7}{2}$; $\dfrac{3}{2}$; 2, -7, 3

e) $-\dfrac{1}{2}, -1$; $-\dfrac{3}{2}$; $\dfrac{1}{2}$; 2, 3, 1 **f)** $\dfrac{2}{3}, -3$; $-\dfrac{7}{3}$; -2; 3, 7, -6

g) 0, -8; -8; 0; 1, 8, 0 **h)** 4, -4; 0; -16; 1, 0, -16
2. a and b **3.** $-\dfrac{b}{a}$ **4.** c and a **5.** $\dfrac{c}{a}$ **6. a)** sum $= -6$,

product $= 8$ **b)** sum $= 3$, product $= -4$ **c)** sum $= \dfrac{3}{2}$,

product $= -\dfrac{5}{2}$ **d)** sum $= -\dfrac{9}{5}$, product $= 0$ **e)** sum $= -\dfrac{1}{2}$,

product $= \dfrac{9}{4}$ **f)** sum $= -\dfrac{2}{3}$, product $= -\dfrac{8}{3}$ **g)** sum $= 0$,

product $= \dfrac{9}{2}$ **h)** sum $= -\dfrac{3}{2}$, product $= 2$ **i)** sum $= \dfrac{3}{4}$,

product $= \dfrac{1}{4}$

2 Using Algebra **1. a)** $r_1 + r_2 = -\dfrac{b}{a}$ **b)** equal

2. a) $r_1 \times r_2 = \dfrac{c}{a}$ **b)** equal **3.** sum of roots $= -\dfrac{b}{a}$;

product of roots $= \dfrac{c}{a}$

3 Working Backward **1. a)** $x^2 - 2x + 3 = 0$
b) $x^2 + x + 5 = 0$ **c)** $x^2 + 2x - 2 = 0$ **d)** $x^2 - 3 = 0$
e) $x^2 + 4x = 0$ **f)** $4x^2 - 12x + 1 = 0$ **g)** $2x^2 - x + 2 = 0$
h) $6x^2 + 4x - 3 = 0$ **i)** $10x^2 + 4x + 3 = 0$
2. a) $x^2 - 8x + 15 = 0$ **b)** $x^2 - 3x - 4 = 0$
c) $3x^2 + 7x - 6 = 0$ **d)** $2x^2 + x = 0$ **e)** $16x^2 - 24x + 9 = 0$
f) $9x^2 - 1 = 0$ **g)** $x^2 - 5 = 0$ **h)** $x^2 - 2x - 1 = 0$
i) $x^2 - 4x - 14 = 0$ **j)** $x^2 + 4 = 0$ **k)** $x^2 - 2x + 10 = 0$
l) $4x^2 - 8x + 1 = 0$
4 Problem Solving

1. a) $-\dfrac{2}{3}$ **b)** -2 **2.** $\pm 33, \pm 12, \pm 3$ **3.** ± 9 **4.** -14

5. $x^2 - 2x - 9 = 0$ **6.** 1 **7. a)** $k = 1$ **b)** $k = -\dfrac{1}{5}$ **c)** $k = -\dfrac{4}{9}$

d) $k = 5$ **8. a)** $\dfrac{1}{r_1} + \dfrac{1}{r_2} = \dfrac{r_1 + r_2}{r_1 r_2} = \dfrac{-\dfrac{b}{a}}{\dfrac{c}{a}} = -\dfrac{b}{a} \times \dfrac{a}{c} = -\dfrac{b}{c}$

b) $r_1, r_2, c \neq 0$

Connecting Math and Esthetics pp. 195-196

1 Investigating ϕ **1. a)** $\phi = \dfrac{1+\sqrt{5}}{2}$ **b)** 1.618

2. a) $\dfrac{3+\sqrt{5}}{2}$ **b)** 2.618 **c)** $2.618 - 1.618 = 1$

d) $\dfrac{3+\sqrt{5}}{2} - \dfrac{1+\sqrt{5}}{2} = 1$; equal **3. a)** $\dfrac{-1+\sqrt{5}}{2}$ **b)** 0.618

c) $1.618 - 0.618 = 1$ **d)** $\dfrac{1+\sqrt{5}}{2} - \left(\dfrac{-1+\sqrt{5}}{2}\right) = 1$;

equal **4. a)** $\dfrac{1}{\phi - 1} = \dfrac{1}{\dfrac{1+\sqrt{5}}{2} - 1} = \dfrac{1}{\dfrac{-1+\sqrt{5}}{2}} = \dfrac{2}{-1+\sqrt{5}}$

$$= \frac{2(1+\sqrt{5})}{4} = \frac{1+\sqrt{5}}{2} = \phi \text{ b) } 2 - \frac{1}{\phi^2} = 2 - \frac{1}{\frac{3+\sqrt{5}}{2}}$$

$$= 2 - \frac{2}{3+\sqrt{5}} = 2 - \frac{2(3-\sqrt{5})}{4} = 2 - \frac{3\sqrt{5}}{2} = \frac{1+\sqrt{5}}{2}$$

$= \phi$ **5. a)** $t_6 = \phi^5$, $t_{22} = \phi^{21}$, $t_n = \phi^{n-1}$ **b)** $\frac{3+\sqrt{5}}{2}$ **c)** t_3

d) $2 + \sqrt{5}$ **e)** t_4 **f)** t_5, t_{10}, t_{n+2} **g)** Fibonacci sequence

2 Geometry and ϕ **1.** $EF = \sqrt{5}$, $AE = 1$, $AF = 1 + \sqrt{5}$,

$AB = 2$, $\dfrac{AF}{AB} = \dfrac{1+\sqrt{5}}{2} = \phi$ **2.** $AC^2 = AB^2 + BC^2 = AB^2$

$+ \left(\dfrac{1}{2}AB\right)^2 = \dfrac{5AB^2}{4}$, $AC = \dfrac{\sqrt{5}AB}{2}$, $CD = CB = \dfrac{1}{2}AB$,

$AE = AD = AC - CD = \dfrac{\sqrt{5}AB}{2} - \dfrac{1}{2}AB = \dfrac{\sqrt{5}-1}{2}AB$,

$\dfrac{AB}{AE} = \dfrac{AB}{\dfrac{\sqrt{5}-1}{2}AB} = \dfrac{2}{\sqrt{5}-1} = \dfrac{2(\sqrt{5}+1)}{4} = \dfrac{1+\sqrt{5}}{2}$

$= \phi$ **3.** $a^2 = 1^2 + 1^2 - 2(1)(1)\cos 108°$, $a \doteq 1.618 \doteq \phi$

3 Fibonacci Numbers and ϕ **1.** $377, 610$ **2. a)** $\dfrac{5}{3}$ **b)** $\dfrac{13}{8}$

c) The denominator and numerator are consecutive terms of the Fibonacci sequence.

d) $1 + \cfrac{1}{1+\cfrac{1}{1+\cfrac{1}{1+\cfrac{1}{1+\cfrac{1}{1+\cfrac{1}{1+1}}}}}}$

3. a) 2, 5, 7, 12, 19, 31, 50, 81, 131, 212 **b)** 2.5, 1.4, 1.7143, 1.5833, 1.6316, 1.6129, 1.62, 1.6173, 1.618; ϕ **c)** Answers may vary. **i)** 1, 10, 11, 21, 32, 53, 85, 138, 223, 361 **ii)** 10, 1.1, 1.9091, 1.5238, 1.6563, 1.6038, 1.6235, 1.6159, 1.6188; ϕ

4 ϕ **in Architecture, Design, and Nature** **1.** 18 m **2.** approximately ϕ **3.** approximately ϕ

Technology p. 197
1 Solving Algebraically **1.** 4, −1 **2.** 2, −5 **3.** −1, −5

4. 6, 1 **5.** 8 **6.** ±0.7 **7.** $\dfrac{1}{2}$, −1 **8.** $\dfrac{3}{2}$, −$\dfrac{2}{3}$ **9.** 0, −$\dfrac{3}{7}$

10. −$\dfrac{1}{3}$, −2 **11.** 3, −5 **12.** 1, −4 **13.** 2, −$\dfrac{4}{3}$ **14.** −8, $\dfrac{1}{2}$

15. −$\dfrac{33}{10}$, 3 **16.** −2 ± $\sqrt{11}$ **17.** 3 ± $\sqrt{5}$ **18.** $\dfrac{5 \pm \sqrt{17}}{2}$

19. $\dfrac{-7 \pm \sqrt{145}}{4}$ **20.** $\dfrac{-5 \pm \sqrt{13}}{6}$ **21.** $\dfrac{6 \pm \sqrt{105}}{3}$

22. $\dfrac{-31 \pm \sqrt{2611}}{15}$ **23.** $\dfrac{1 + 3\sqrt{5}}{2}$ **24.** $\dfrac{1 + 3\sqrt{19}}{10}$

25. −1 ± $\sqrt{5}$ **26.** $\dfrac{1 \pm 3\sqrt{19}}{10}$ **27.** $\dfrac{-7 \pm \sqrt{113}}{3}$ **28.** 2, 1

29. ±3 **30.** $\dfrac{1 \pm \sqrt{13}}{3}$

2 Nature of the Roots **1. a)** −1 ± $2i\sqrt{3}$ **b)** Answers may vary. **2.** $\dfrac{3}{2}$, 1 **3.** $\dfrac{-3 \pm i\sqrt{11}}{4}$ **4.** ±$\dfrac{i\sqrt{3}}{5}$ **5. a)** 0, ±i
b) ±1, ±i **c)** ±$\sqrt{5}$, ±$i\sqrt{3}$

Section 4.8 pp. 202–203
Practice **1.** −3 **2.** −2 **3.** 0 **4.** 12 **5.** 0 **6.** −4 **7.** −3
8. −24 **9.** 6 **10.** −2 **11.** −18 **12.** 22 **13.** −23 **14.** 85 **15.** 5
16. $\dfrac{9}{2}$ **17.** −9 **18.** 0 **19.** 1 **20.** 4 **21.** −2 **22.** 0 **23.** −7
24. −3 **25.** 0 **26.** −55 **27.** 12 **28.** 10 **29.** −1 **30.** 11
31. −10 **32.** −16 **33.** −45 **34.** 0 **35.** 22 **36.** 70 **37.** 136
38. 0 **39.** 11 **40.** −3 **41.** 19 **42.** 0 **43.** −$\dfrac{3}{8}$ **44.** 6 **45.** $\dfrac{8}{3}$
46. −37 **47.** 2 **48.** 4 **49.** −1 **50.** 3 **51.** $m = 2, n = -3$
52. $p = 1, q = 2$ **53.** $v = 6, w = -11$
Applications and Problem Solving **54.** 7 **55.** −20
56. a) 14 **b)** When the height is $\dfrac{7}{2}$ units, the area is
14 square units. **57. a)** 12 **b)** When $n = -\dfrac{1}{2}$, the product
of the two numbers is 12. **58. a)** 77 **b)** 77 **c)** equal;
$h(500) = h(-500)$ **59. a)** −0.017d + 0.45 R25 **b)** When
the horizontal distance is 50 m, the height is 25 m.
c) −0.017d − 0.06 R−2.3 **d)** No. The hammer cannot
have a negative height. **60.** 1, 4 **61. a)** $ba^2 + ca + d = 0$

b) $a = \dfrac{-c \pm \sqrt{c^2 - 4bd}}{2b}$ **62. a)** −$Q(x)$, R

b) $\dfrac{P(x)}{x-b} = Q(x) + \dfrac{R}{x-b}$. Multiply both sides by −1.

$$\frac{P(x)}{b-x} = -Q(x) + \frac{R}{b-x}$$ **63. a)** $x^2 - 3x - 4 = 0$
b) $x^3 - 2x^2 - 8x + 3 = 0$ **c)** $8x^4 - 4x^3 + 2x^2 - x + 1 = 0$

Section 4.9 pp. 209-211
Practice   1. yes **2.** no **3.** no **4.** yes **5.** yes **6.** no **7.** no
8. yes **9.** yes **10.** no **11.** yes **12.** yes **13.** yes **14.** yes
15. no **16.** yes **17.** no **18.** yes **19.** $P(-1) = 0$ **20.** $P(2) = 0$
21. $P(3) = 0$ **22.** $P(-3) = 0$ **23.** $P(-2) = 0$ **24.** $P(-5) = 0$
25. no **26.** no **27.** yes **28.** yes **29.** yes **30.** yes **31.** yes
32. no **33.** yes **34.** yes **35.** no **36.** yes **37.** no **38.** yes

39. yes **40.** no **41.** no **42.** yes **43.** $P\left(-\dfrac{1}{2}\right) = 0$

44. $P\left(\dfrac{3}{2}\right) = 0$ **45.** $P\left(\dfrac{1}{3}\right) = 0$ **46.** $P\left(-\dfrac{1}{3}\right) = 0$

47. $P\left(-\dfrac{2}{3}\right) = 0$ **48.** $P\left(\dfrac{2}{3}\right) = 0$ **49.** no **50.** yes **51.** yes

52. yes **53.** no **54.** no **55.** $(x-1)(x-2)(x-3)$
56. $(x+1)(x+3)(x+4)$ **57.** $(x-2)(x+3)(x-3)$
58. $(x+3)(x^2+x-1)$ **59.** $(z+2)(z+4)(z-5)$
60. $(x+1)(x-4)(x+4)$ **61.** $(x-4)(x^2+2x+2)$
62. $(k-3)(k+4)(k+5)$ **63.** $(x-5)(x^2+5x-2)$
64. $(x-3)(x+1)(x+6)$ **65.** $(2x-1)(x-1)(x-3)$
66. $(y+1)(2y+1)(2y-3)$ **67.** $(x+2)(3x-1)(x-3)$
68. $(x+2)(3x-2)(x-2)$ **69.** $(x+4)(2x+3)(x+1)$
70. $(x-2)(2x^2+x+5)$ **71.** $(3x+5)(2x-1)(x-3)$
72. $(p+2)(2p+1)(2p-1)$ **73.** $(3w-1)(2w^2+6w-5)$
74. $(x+1)(x-1)(4x+3)$
Applications and Problem Solving   75. a) $h(h-1)^2$
b) 0.5 m by 0.5 m **76. a)** $l(3l-4)(l+1)$ **b)** 9.8 m by 5.6 m
77. a) $(h+2)(h+1)(3h-1)$ **b)** 4 m by 3 m by 5 m
78. a) $(x+4)(x+2)(x+1)(x-3)$
b) $(x+3)(x+2)(x+1)(x-1)(x-2)$
79. a) $(2x+1)^2(2x-1)$ **b)** $(2x+1)(2x-1)(2x-3)$
80. They are consecutive integers starting at -3.
81. $P(-y) = y^2(y^2-1) - y^2(1+y^2) + y^2 + y^2$
$= y^4 - y^2 - y^2 - y^4 + y^2 + y^2 = 0$ **82. a)** 3 **b)** -72
83. 2 m by 2 m by 3 m **84. a)** $(x-2), (x+4), (3x+1)$
b) No. A cubic polynomial has only three factors.
85. $m = 3, n = -8$
86. $P(a) = a^3 - a^3 + ba^2 - a^2b + ca - ac = 0$
87. The edge length of the larger cube is 2 more than
the edge length of the smaller cube.
88. a) $(x-1)(x^2+x+1)$ **b)** $(x+1)(x^2-x+1)$
c) $(x-3)(x^2+3x+9)$ **d)** $(x+4)(x^2-4x+16)$
e) $(2x-1)(4x^2+2x+1)$ **f)** $(4x+1)(16x^2-4x+1)$
g) $(x+y)(x^2-xy+y^2)$ **h)** $(x-y)(x^2+xy+y^2)$
i) $(2x+5)(4x^2-10x+25); (3x-4)(9x^2+12x+16)$
j) $(x^2+y^3)(x^4-x^2y^3+y^6)$ **89. a)** yes; yes;
$P(-1) = P(1) = 0$ **b)** yes; no; $P(-1) = 0, P(1) \neq 0$
90. $r+3$ **91. a)** neither **b)** both **c)** $x+y$ **d)** $x-y$ **e)** neither

f) both **g)** $x+y$ **h)** $x-y$ **i)** $x+y$ is a factor of $x^n + y^n$ if n
is odd; $x-y$ is a factor of $x^n - y^n$ if n is odd; $x+y$ and
$x-y$ are factors of $x^n - y^n$ if n is even; neither $x+y$ nor
$x-y$ is a factor of $x^n + y^n$ if n is even **j)** $x-y, x+y$
k) $x+y$ **92.** If there is more than one zero, there must
be 3 zeros. Since they are all integers, the factors must
be of the form $x-m$ or $m-x$, where m is an integer.
When these three factors are multiplied, the
coefficient of x^3 will be ± 1. **93. a)** $P(1) = 0$; thus
$a + b + c + d = 0$ **b)** yes **c)** no **d)** yes

Technology pp. 212-213
1 Cubic or Third-Degree Functions and Equations
4. With the exception of the region between any local
maximum or minimum values, when $a > 0$ the cubic
function increases from left to right and when $a < 0$
the cubic function decreases from left to right.
5. the y-intercept **6. a)** $-2, 1, 3$ **b)** Yes. The x-
intercepts occur when $y = 0$. **7. a)** 3 **b)** 2 **c)** 1 **d)** 1 **e)** 3
f) 1 **g)** 2 **h)** 1 **8. a)** 1, 2, 3 **b)** 2, 3 **c)** 0, 2 **9.** No. The
term involving x^3 will dominate all others in the cubic
function for sufficiently large (positive) x and for
sufficiently small (negative) x. Thus, the function will
assume both negative and positive values and, since it
is continuous, it must cross the x-axis at least once.
2 Quartic or Fourth-Degree Functions and
Equations   4. If $a > 0$, the function decreases from
the left and then increases again to the right. If $a < 0$,
the function increases from the left and then
decreases again to the right. **5.** the y-intercept
6. a) $-3, -1, 1, 2$ **b)** Yes. The x-intercepts occur when
$y = 0$. **7. a)** 4 **b)** 2 **c)** 0 **d)** 1 **e)** 2 **f)** 2 **g)** 0 **h)** 4 **i)** 3 **j)** 1
8. a) 0, 1, 2, 3, 4 **b)** 0, 2, 3, 4 **c)** 0, 2, 4 **9.** No. There
could be two pairs of equal roots.
3 Quintic or Fifth-Degree Functions   1. If the
function is expanded, the highest power of x is 5.
2. $0, \pm 1, \pm 2$; These values of x produce $y = 0$. **5. a)** 2
distinct real roots, 3 equal real roots **b)** 1 distinct real
root, 2 pairs of equal real roots **c)** 2 equal real roots,
1 distinct real root, 2 imaginary roots **d)** 2 pairs of
equal real roots, 1 distinct real root
4 Functions in the Form $y = x^n$ 1. b) All have a
similar shape to the parabola. **c)** $(0, 0), (-1, 1), (1, 1)$
d) The solutions are $x = 0$, and all graphs pass
through the origin. **2. b)** All increase from left to
right, without any maximum or minimum values.
c) $(0, 0), (-1, -1), (1, 1)$ **d)** The solutions are $x = 0$,
and all graphs pass through the origin.

Section 4.10 pp. 219-221
Practice   1. $-1, 4, -5$ **2.** 2, 7, -6 **3.** 0, $-3, 8$ **4.** $-6, 3$
5. 0, $-3, 2$ **6.** 0, $-4, -3$ **7.** 0, 2, 2 **8.** 0, ± 3 **9.** $-3, \pm 1$

10. $3, \pm2$ **11.** $-4, 1, 1$ **12.** $\pm4, 3$ **13.** $-1, 2, 3$ **14.** $-2,$ $3, 3$ **15.** $1, 2, 3$ **16.** $-5, \pm1$ **17.** $-5, -1, 4$ **18.** $-2, -2, 5$
19. $1, 1, 7$ **20.** $-3, 2, 6$ **21.** $-3, -2, 5$ **22.** $-4, 3, 5$
23. $-1, 2, 4$ **24.** $1, 1, 3$ **25.** $-6, -1, -1$ **26.** $-2, -1, 4$
27. $-\dfrac{1}{2}, 1, 3$ **28.** $-\dfrac{1}{4}, \dfrac{1}{3}, -1$ **29.** $\dfrac{2}{3}, \dfrac{1}{2}, \dfrac{1}{2}$ **30.** $0, 4, -\dfrac{2}{5}$
31. $0, -\dfrac{1}{2}, 2$ **32.** $0, 3, \dfrac{1}{3}$ **33.** $0, \pm\dfrac{2}{3}$ **34.** $0, -\dfrac{1}{4}, \dfrac{1}{4}$
35. $-3, -1, -\dfrac{1}{2}$ **36.** $\dfrac{2}{3}, 1, 1$ **37.** $-1, \dfrac{2}{5}, 2$ **38.** $-1, -1, \dfrac{7}{2}$
39. $-\dfrac{5}{2}, -\dfrac{1}{2}, 1$ **40.** $\dfrac{1}{2}, 1, 5$ **41.** $-2, \dfrac{1}{3}, 1$ **42.** $-\dfrac{1}{4}, \dfrac{1}{2}, 3$
43. $-\dfrac{1}{2}, 3, 3$ **44.** $-2, \pm\dfrac{2}{3}$ **45.** $1, \dfrac{4}{3}, \dfrac{3}{2}$ **46.** $\dfrac{1}{2}, \pm1$

47. a) $0, \pm2\sqrt{2}$ **b)** $0, \pm2.83$ **48. a)** $3, \dfrac{-3\pm\sqrt{13}}{2}$
b) $3, 0.30, -3.30$ **49. a)** $4, 1\pm\sqrt{3}$ **b)** $4, 2.73, -0.73$
50. a) $-5, 1\pm\sqrt{6}$ **b)** $-5, 3.45, -1.45$ **51. a)** $-3, -1\pm\sqrt{7}$
b) $-3, 1.65, -3.65$ **52. a)** $-2, \dfrac{-3\pm\sqrt{17}}{2}$ **b)** $-2, 0.56,$
-3.56 **53.** $0, \pm\dfrac{5\sqrt{2}}{2}$ **54.** $2, \pm\dfrac{\sqrt{5}}{2}$ **55.** $1, \dfrac{1\pm\sqrt{61}}{6}$
56. $-3, \dfrac{-1\pm\sqrt{10}}{3}$ **57.** $-4, \dfrac{-1\pm\sqrt{33}}{4}$ **58.** $3, \dfrac{-2\pm\sqrt{29}}{5}$
59. $0, \pm i$ **60.** $-1, \dfrac{1\pm i\sqrt{7}}{2}$ **61.** $2, \dfrac{1\pm i\sqrt{7}}{2}$
62. $-2, 1\pm i\sqrt{3}$ **63.** $1, -1\pm\sqrt{5}$ **64.** $-5, \dfrac{-3\pm i\sqrt{3}}{3}$
65. $-1, \dfrac{-1\pm\sqrt{3}}{3}$ **66.** $0, \pm\dfrac{i\sqrt{15}}{5}$ **67.** $4, \pm\dfrac{i\sqrt{10}}{2}$
68. $1, \dfrac{2\pm i\sqrt{2}}{3}$ **69.** $-2, \dfrac{-3\pm i\sqrt{31}}{4}$ **70.** $3, \dfrac{-3\pm i\sqrt{23}}{8}$

Applications and Problem Solving **71.** $\dfrac{1}{2}, \dfrac{1}{2}, \dfrac{1}{2}$
72. $\dfrac{1}{2}, -\dfrac{2}{3}, -\dfrac{2}{3}$ **73.** $\dfrac{1}{5}, -\dfrac{1}{3}, -\dfrac{1}{2}$ **74.** $\dfrac{1}{3}, \pm\dfrac{3}{2}$ **75.** $\dfrac{1}{3}, \dfrac{-3\pm\sqrt{5}}{2}$
76. $-\dfrac{3}{2}, \dfrac{3\pm3i\sqrt{3}}{4}$ **77.** $0, \pm\dfrac{\sqrt{6}}{3}$ **78.** $2, 2, -\dfrac{3}{4}$ **79.** $1, \pm i$
80. $0, \dfrac{3\pm\sqrt{5}}{2}$ **81. a)** $k = 3; -4, 3$ **b)** $k = -5; -\dfrac{1}{3}, 1$
82. a) 4 **b)** $0, 2, 2$ **83. a)** $x^3 - 6x^2 + 3x + 10 = 0$

b) $x^3 + 3x^2 - 10x - 24 = 0$ **c)** $x^3 - 3x^2 + x + 1 = 0$
d) $x^3 - 2x - 4 = 0$ Yes. Multiply each equation by any non-zero constant and the roots remain the same.
84. $-9, -8, -7$ **85.** $0, -1, 2, 3$ **86.** $-3, -2, 1, 2$
87. $-2, -2, 3, 3$ **88.** $\pm1, \pm\sqrt{3}$ **89.** $-3, 2, 1\pm\sqrt{3}$
90. $\pm1, \pm i$ **91.** $-1, -1, -1, \dfrac{1}{2}$ **92.** $1, 2, -\dfrac{1}{2}, -\dfrac{1}{2}$
93. 2 cm by 3 cm by 7 cm **94.** 3 cm by 3 cm by 15 cm
95. 5 cm by 20 cm by 25 cm **96.** 12 cm by 12 cm by 7 cm **97.** $-3, \pm1, \pm2$ **98.** 5 m by 20 m by 1 m
99. Answers may vary. $x^3 - 7x^2 + x - 7 = 0$ **100.** Yes. Multiply the equation by any non-zero constant to get a different graph. **101.** 100 m by 300 m by 300 m
102. 6 cm by 9 cm by 20 cm **103.** 4 m by 3 m by 0.25 m **104. a)** $y = x^3 + x^2 - 5x - 5$
b) $y = 2x^3 + 2x^2 - 10x - 10$; Multiplying the right-hand side by 2 does not affect the roots, but changes the y-intercept to -10. **105.** n must be odd, since imaginary roots always occur in pairs. **106. a)** never true; Imaginary roots occur in conjugate pairs.
b) always true; Take into account repeated and imaginary roots. **c)** sometimes true; for example, $x^4 + 1 = 0$ **d)** sometimes true; for example, $(x - 1)(x - \sqrt{5})(x + \sqrt{5})$ **e)** sometimes true; for example, $(x - \sqrt{2})^4 = 0$ **f)** never true; Imaginary roots occur in conjugate pairs and an imaginary number never equals its conjugate.

Technology p. 222
1 Solving Algebraically **1.** $-5, -3, 2$ **2.** $-8, 6, 9$
3. $-5, -4, 1, 3$ **4.** $-6, -5, -3, 1$ **5.** $-5, -\dfrac{5}{2}, -1$
6. $-\dfrac{7}{3}, -\dfrac{1}{2}, \dfrac{2}{3}$ **7.** $\pm\dfrac{1}{2}, 2, 4$ **8.** $\dfrac{1}{4}, \dfrac{1}{3}, \dfrac{2}{3}, \dfrac{3}{2}$ **9.** $-2, -1.41, 1.41$
10. $-0.54, 2.07, 4.97$ **11.** $\pm1.73, \pm2.24$ **12.** $-1.65,$ $\pm0.45, 3.65$ **13.** $-3.65, 1.65, 4.5$ **14.** $0, -1, \pm0.63$
15. The number of roots found was equal to the degree of the equation in each case.
2 Nature of the Roots **1. a)** $-1, -1, -1$ **b)** $3, -1\pm i\sqrt{2}$
c) $3, 4, 3$ The graphing calculator does not show repeated roots or imaginary roots. **2.** Answers may vary. Use the pencil-and-paper method. **3.** $-1, -1, -1,$
-1 **4.** $-2, -2, \dfrac{3}{2}$ **5.** $\dfrac{1}{2}, \dfrac{1\pm2i\sqrt{2}}{3}$ **6.** $\pm\sqrt{2}, \dfrac{1}{3}, \dfrac{1}{3}$
7. $1, 1, -1, \pm i$ **8.** $\pm i, \pm i\sqrt{2}$
3 Problem Solving **1.** 12, 14, 16, 18 or $-18, -16,$ $-14, -12$ **2.** 35 m, 21 m

Investigating Math pp. 223-228
1 Exploring Linear Functions, $y = mx + b$ **1. a)** 9, 11, 13; 2, 2, 2 **b)** 6, 10, 14; 4, 4, 4 **c)** $-5, -8, -11; -3,$

−3, −3 **2.** The differences are equal to *m*. **3.** The constant term is the value of y when $x = 0$.
4. a) $y = 2x + 3$ **b)** $y = 5x - 4$ **c)** $y = -6x + 2$
d) $y = -0.5x + 5$ **5. a)** $3m + b$, $4m + b$; m, m, m, m
b) A unit increase in the x-coordinate produces an increase or decrease in the y-coordinate of an amount equal to the slope.

2 Exploring Quadratic Functions, $y = ax^2 + bx + c$
1. a) 13, 21; 6, 8; 2, 2 **b)** 11, 20, 33; 1, 5, 9, 13; 4, 4, 4
c) −1, 4, 15, 32, 55; 5, 11, 17, 23; 6, 6, 6 **2.** They are equal. **3.** The second difference is equal to $2a$.
4. a) $5a + b$, $7a + b$; $2a, 2a, 2a$ **b)** The second difference is equal to $2a$, which gives the value for a. The first entry in the first difference column is equal to $a + b$, which gives the value for b. The y-value when $x = 0$ is equal to c. **5. a)** 5, 9, 13, 17; 4, 4, 4 **b)** 1 **c)** 2 **d)** 3
e) $y = 2x^2 + 3x + 1$ **6. a)** $y = x^2 + 2x + 3$
b) $y = 4x^2 - x - 2$ **c)** $y = -2x^2 + 3x + 4$ **d)** $y = -x^2 + 4x$

3 Exploring Cubic Functions, $y = ax^3 + bx^2 + cx + d$
1. a) 9, 25, 57, 111; 6, 16, 32, 54, 4, 10, 16, 22; 6, 6, 6
b) −4, −5, 6, 41, 112, 231; −1, 11, 35, 71, 119; 12, 24, 36, 48; 12, 12, 12 **2. a)** 3rd column **b)** The third difference is equal to $6a$. **3. a)** $27a + 9b + 3c + d$, $64a + 16b + 4c + d$; $7a + 3b + c$, $19a + 5b + c$, $37a + 7b + c$; $6a + 2b$, $12a + 2b$, $18a + 2b$; $6a$, $6a$
b) When $x = 0$, the value of y is equal to d. The third difference is equal to $6a$. The first entry in the second difference column is $6a + 2b$, from which b can be found. When $x = 1$, the value of y is $a + b + c + d$. Use this to find c. **4. a)** −3, 1, 11, 27; 4, 10, 16; 6, 6 **b)** 1
c) −1 **d)** −3 **e)** −2 **f)** $y = x^3 - x^2 - 3x - 2$
5. a) $y = x^3 + 2x^2 - 4x + 3$ **b)** $y = 2x^3 + x^2 + 3x + 2$
c) $y = -x^3 + 4x^2 + x - 4$ **d)** $y = -3x^3 + 5x - 8$

4 Problem Solving **1.** $y = x^2 - 3x + 7$ **2.** $y = -2x + 6$
3. $y = x^3 + x^2 - x - 1$ **4.** $y = -3x + 5$ **5.** $y = 5x^2 + 2$
6. $y = -2x^3 + 9x^2$ **7.** $y = 3x^3 - 4x^2 - 6x$
8. $y = -3x^2 + 4x - 5$ **9.** 1, 16; 3, 3, 3, 3, 3; 0, 0, 0, 0; 0, 0, 0; $y = 3x + 1$ **10.** −1; 1, 3, 5, 7, 9; 2, 2, 2, 2; 0, 0, 0; $y = x^2 - 1$ **11.** 3, 1, −5; −2, −6, −10, −14, −18, −22; −4, −4, −4, −4; $y = -2x^2 + 3$ **12.** 1; 1, 7, 19, 37, 61; 6, 12, 18, 24; 6, 6, 6; $y = x^3 + 1$ **13.** 0; 0, 10, 32, 66, 112; 10, 22, 34, 46; 12, 12, 12; $y = 2x^3 - x^2 - x$ **14.** 5, 8; 3, 5, 1, −9, −25, −47; 2, −4, −10, −16, −22; −6, −6, −6, −6; $y = -x^3 + 4x^2 + 5$ **15. a)** $n = 5d + 6$ **b)** 81 **c)** 25
16. a) $n = \dfrac{l^2 + l}{2}$ **b)** 55 **c)** 14 **17.** −54, −79, −108

18. a) $n = 2p^3 - 3p - 1$ **b)** 8 **c)** 1969
19. a) $V = p^3 + 3p^2 + 2p$, $p \geq 1$ **b)** 10 **c)** 9240 cm³
d) $p(p + 1)(p + 2)$ **e)** 1 cm by 2 cm by 3 cm; 2 cm by 3 cm by 4 cm; 3 cm by 4 cm by 5 cm; 4 cm by 5 cm by 6 cm; 5 cm by 6 cm by 7 cm; 6 cm by 7 cm by 8 cm **f)** No. For example, the following dimensions fit the pattern of the first 6 given volumes: 1 cm by 1 cm by 6 cm; 2 cm by 2 cm by 6 cm; 2 cm by 5 cm by 6 cm; 2 cm by 6 cm by 10 cm; 3 cm by 7 cm by 10 cm; 4 cm by 7 cm by 12 cm

Technology pp. 229-231
1 Linear Functions **1. a)** $y = 2x + 4$ **b)** $y = -x + 2$
c) $y = -12x + 11$ **d)** $y = \dfrac{1}{2}x - 2$ **2. a)** $n = -8p + 13$
b) −123 **c)** 35
2 Quadratic Functions **1. a)** $y = x^2 - 3x + 2$
b) $y = 2x^2 + x - 6$ **c)** $y = -3x^2 - x + 9$ **d)** $y = -4x^2 + 6x$
2. a) $n = 4p^2 + 2p - 3$ **b)** 269 **c)** 12 **3.** $n = p^2 + \dfrac{2}{3}p + \dfrac{1}{9}$
4. a) Substitute the points into the equation $y = ax^2 + bx + c$, then solve the system of three equations for a, b, and c. **b)** $y = x^2 - 2x - 1$
3 Cubic Functions **1. a)** $y = x^3 - 3x^2 - x + 2$
b) $y = x^3 + 2x^2 + 3x - 1$ **c)** $y = -x^3 - x^2 + 4x + 5$
d) $y = -2x^3 + 4x + 6$ **2. a)** $n = 2p^3 - 8$ **b)** 424 **c)** 20
4 Using Finite Differences **1. a)** linear; $n = 3p - 7$, $p \geq 1$ **b)** cubic; $n = 2p^3 - 3p + 1$, $p \geq 1$ **c)** quadratic; $n = -4p^2 - 5$, $p \geq 1$ **2. a)** 1, 7, 19, 37 **b)** quadratic
c) $h = 3r^2 - 3r + 1$ **d)** 271 **e)** 15 **3. a)** 14, 30, 55 **b)** cubic
c) $n = \dfrac{1}{3}l^3 + \dfrac{1}{2}l^2 + \dfrac{1}{6}l$ **d)** 385 **4. a)** 5 points **b)** Answers may vary.
5 Scatter Plots and Lines of Best Fit **1. b)** 57 000
c) 2011 **d)** Answers may vary. **e)** about −4.3 **f)** the decrease in Armed Forces in thousands per year
2. b) $37 billion; $49 billion **c)** $84 billion **d)** Answers may vary. **e)** about 1.7 **f)** the increase in education spending in billions of dollars per year

Review pp. 232-233
1. −3, 1 **2.** no real roots **3.** −4, 1 **4.** 2, 2 **5.** no real roots **6.** −5, −1 **7.** 3, 6 **8.** $\dfrac{3}{2}, \dfrac{3}{2}$ **9.** $\pm\dfrac{3}{2}$ **10.** −3, $\dfrac{5}{2}$ **11.** 4 cm by 9 cm **12.** 4, −7 **13.** 2, 3 **14.** −5, −2 **15.** −3, $\dfrac{1}{2}$ **16.** −9, $\dfrac{3}{2}$ **17.** 0, $\dfrac{3}{8}$ **18.** 1, $\dfrac{4}{3}$ **19.** 1, −4 **20.** 3, −2
21. $x^2 - 4x - 5 = 0$ **22.** $2x^2 - 9x + 4 = 0$ **23.** 5 m by 45 m
24. ±5 **25.** ±8 **26.** −7, 11 **27.** −10, 4 **28.** $\pm 5\sqrt{2}$ **29.** $\pm 2\sqrt{3}$
30. $\pm 2\sqrt{2}$ **31.** $\pm\dfrac{3\sqrt{2}}{2}$ **32.** 2 **33.** 4, −2 **34.** $-4 \pm \sqrt{11}$
35. $\dfrac{-5 \pm \sqrt{21}}{2}$ **36.** $\dfrac{3 \pm \sqrt{17}}{2}$ **37.** $\dfrac{5 \pm \sqrt{61}}{2}$
38. $\dfrac{-3 \pm \sqrt{21}}{2}$ **39.** $\dfrac{-5 \pm \sqrt{13}}{6}$ **40.** $\dfrac{-1 \pm \sqrt{31}}{6}$ **41.** $2 \pm \sqrt{2}$

42. $-\dfrac{1}{6}$, 1 **43.** 2.5 m **44.** 6, −7 **45.** $\dfrac{1}{2}$, 3 **46.** $\dfrac{2}{7}$, 1

47. $-\dfrac{1}{2}, \dfrac{3}{2}$ **48.** $5 \pm \sqrt{34}$ **49.** $-3 \pm \sqrt{3}$ **50.** $\dfrac{3 \pm 3\sqrt{33}}{16}$

51. $\dfrac{-5 \pm \sqrt{73}}{6}$ **52.** 0.74, −0.90 **53.** 0.33, −0.75

54. $\dfrac{1}{2}$, 4 **55.** $\dfrac{-1 \pm \sqrt{41}}{2}$ **56.** 650 km/h **57.** 7i

58. $3i\sqrt{2}$ **59.** $2yi$ $\dfrac{-1 \pm \sqrt{41}}{2}$ **60.** −50 **61.** 8 **62.** −3

63. $12 - 3i$ **64.** $-2 - 6i$ **65.** $-25 + 19i$ **66.** $-5 - 12i$

67. $\pm 4i$ **68.** $\pm 3i$ **69.** $-1 \pm i\sqrt{6}$ **70.** $\dfrac{5 \pm i\sqrt{11}}{2}$

71. $\dfrac{-1 \pm i\sqrt{2}}{2}$ **72.** $\dfrac{1 \pm i\sqrt{11}}{3}$ **73.** $\pm\sqrt{5}$, $\pm\dfrac{i}{2}$

74. $\pm\dfrac{\sqrt{6}}{3}$, $\pm\dfrac{i\sqrt{6}}{3}$ **75.** $-2i, -4 - 2i, 12 + 14i$

76. two distinct real roots **77.** two imaginary roots
78. two equal real roots **79.** two distinct real roots
80. two equal real roots **81.** two imaginary roots
82. $k < \dfrac{9}{4}$ **83.** $k = \dfrac{25}{8}$ **84.** $k > \dfrac{9}{8}$ **85.** Yes; 15 cm by 8 cm
86. 6 **87.** 7 **88.** −2 **89.** 14 **90.** 11 **91.** 4 **92.** 7 **93.** $P(1) = 0$
94. $P(-2) = 0$ **95.** $P\left(-\dfrac{3}{2}\right) = 0$ **96.** $P\left(\dfrac{1}{3}\right) = 0$
97. $(x + 1)^2(x - 3)$ **98.** $(x + 4)(x^2 + x - 1)$
99. $(x + 1)(2x - 1)(x - 1)$ **100.** $(y - 1)(y + 4)(3y + 4)$

101. $0, \pm 3$ **102.** $-1, -1, 2$ **103.** $-2, \dfrac{1}{2}, 3$ **104.** $\dfrac{2}{3}$, 1

105. $1 \pm \sqrt{2}$, 1 **106.** $-2, \dfrac{2 \pm \sqrt{7}}{2}$ **107.** $\pm 4i, -1$

108. $3, -1 \pm i\sqrt{3}$ **109.** 5 cm by 20 cm by 25 cm

Exploring Math 1. a) $-4 - 3i$; rotation of 180°
b) $3 - 4i$; rotation of 270° counterclockwise
c) $4 + 3i$; rotation of 360° **d)** $8 + 6i$; vertical stretch by
a factor of 2 **e)** $12 + 9i$; vertical stretch by a factor of 3
f) $16 + 12i$; vertical stretch by a factor of 4 **2. b)** $2 + 5i$
e) The sum is the diagonal of the parallelogram.
3. a) $5 - 2i$ **b)** $-7 + 7i$ **c)** $-2 - 2i$ **d)** $-3 + 0i$

Chapter Check p. 234

1. −4, 2 **2.** 1, −3 **3.** $\dfrac{1}{2}$, 5 **4.** $\dfrac{-3 \pm i\sqrt{23}}{4}$ **5.** −5, 3

6. 3, 8 **7.** $-4, \dfrac{1}{2}$ **8.** $-\dfrac{1}{3}, \dfrac{2}{3}$ **9.** −3, 2 **10.** 1, 2 **11.** $x^2 + 4x = 0$

12. $8x^2 - 2x - 3 = 0$ **13.** ± 12 **14.** $\pm\dfrac{\sqrt{7}}{2}$ **15.** −11, 1

16. 2, 6 **17.** 4 **18.** −3, 6 **19.** $\dfrac{1 \pm \sqrt{22}}{3}$; 1.90, −1.23

20. $\dfrac{1 \pm \sqrt{6}}{5}$; −0.29, 0.69 **21.** −2, −2 **22.** $-1, -\dfrac{2}{5}$

23. $-\dfrac{2}{3}, \dfrac{1}{6}$ **24.** $-\dfrac{1}{3}, \dfrac{3}{4}$ **25.** $\dfrac{3 \pm \sqrt{37}}{2}$ **26.** $\dfrac{4 \pm \sqrt{11}}{5}$

27. $\dfrac{-7 \pm \sqrt{13}}{6}$ **28.** $-1, \dfrac{7}{4}$ **29.** 0.19, 3.47 **30.** 2.67, −1

31. $6i$ **32.** $4i\sqrt{3}$ **33.** −45 **34.** $13 - 8i$ **35.** $-2 + 8i$
36. $27 + 24i$ **37.** 50 **38.** $\pm 3i\sqrt{2}$ **39.** $\pm i$ **40.** $\pm 2i$
41. $\dfrac{5 \pm i\sqrt{3}}{2}$ **42.** $\dfrac{-3 \pm \sqrt{31}}{4}$ **43.** $\pm\dfrac{\sqrt{2}}{2}$, $\pm i\sqrt{3}$

44. two imaginary roots **45.** two distinct real roots
46. two equal real roots **47.** two distinct real roots

48. $k < \dfrac{25}{4}$ **49.** $k > 4$ **50.** 14 **51.** −10 **52.** 0 **53.** −2

54. $m = -4, n = -9$ **55.** $P(5) = 0$ **56.** $P(-3) = 0$

57. $P\left(\dfrac{2}{3}\right) = 0$ **58.** $P\left(\dfrac{1}{4}\right) = 0$ **59.** $(x + 6)(x - 1)(x - 3)$

60. $(x + 1)(3x - 1)(x - 4)$ **61.** $0, -2, -2$ **62.** $3, \pm 2$
63. $-2, -2, 2$ **64.** $-1, 3 \pm 2\sqrt{2}$ **65.** $-2, -1 \pm 2i$

66. $8, 1, \dfrac{1}{3}$ **67.** 27 cm by 10 cm **68.** 3.5 m **69.** 12 km/h

Using the Strategies p. 235

1. 8 **2. a)** 35 cm²; 440 cm²; $n^2 + 2n$ cm² **b)** 43 cm;
58 cm; 99 cm **3.** 528 km from Vancouver at 15:36
4. 1.8 **5.** 0, 0, 0, 6, 6, 6 **6.** last row sum: 21; last
column sum: 22 **8.** $\dfrac{qst}{prx}$ **9.** 13 cm, 14 cm, 15 cm

10. Q **11.** 10 240 **12.** Danielle: 3 or 4, Jessica: 5; For
the products 15, 20, 24, and 28, the possible pairs of
numbers are (1, 15), (3, 5), (1, 20), (2, 10), (4, 5),
(1, 24), (2, 12), (3, 8), (4, 6), (1, 28), (2, 14), and (4, 7).
If either one had 15, 20, 10, 24, 12, 8, 6, 28, 14, or 7,
she would know what the other's number was, so the
pairs including those numbers can be eliminated.
This leaves two pairs: (3, 5) and (4, 5). Since Jessica
doesn't know what Danielle's number is, Jessica must
have the 5.
Data Bank 1. a) Dash 8-100 **b)** yes **3. a)** Quebec
b) Manitoba

Cumulative Review, Chapters 1–4 pp. 236-237

Chapter 1 1. (−14, −41) **2.** $\left(\dfrac{1}{2}, -3\right)$ **3.** (−1, 1) **4.** (1, 0)

5. $(2, 2)$ **6.** infinitely many solutions **7.** $(-3, -4)$
8. $\left(0, \dfrac{1}{2}\right)$ **9.** $(5, 4, 1)$ **10.** $(1, 3, 2)$ **11. a)** 7 mg **b)** 3 mg
12. 600 g portobello, 400 g shiitake **13.** 20 km/h, 4 km/h **14.** 4 par 3 holes, 11 par 4 holes, 3 par 5 holes
Chapter 2 **1.** $n < -3$ **2.** $w > 6$ **3.** $d \geq 5$ **4.** $k \leq 5$
5. $m > 5$ **6.** $y \geq -8$ **7.** $x \leq -6$ **8.** $h > 3$ **9.** $p > 2$ **10.** $q \leq 7$
11. $c < 0$ **18.** $(3, -1)$ **25.** $2y - 900 \leq 10\,300$; $y \leq 5600$
26. a) $x + 2y \leq 3.5, x \geq 0, y \geq 0$ **27.** $9 < l + w < 11$
Chapter 3 **1. a)** down **b)** $(0, 0)$ **c)** $x = 0$ **d)** domain: all real numbers, range: $y \leq 0$ **e)** x-intercept: 0, y-intercept: 0 **2. a)** up **b)** $(0, -3)$ **c)** $x = 0$ **d)** domain: all real numbers, range: $y \geq -3$ **e)** x-intercepts: $\pm\sqrt{3}$, y-intercept: -3 **3. a)** up **b)** $(-3, 0)$ **c)** $x = -3$ **d)** domain: all real numbers, range: $y \geq 0$ **e)** x-intercept: -3, y-intercept: 9 **4. a)** down **b)** $(2, 1)$ **c)** $x = 2$ **d)** domain: all real numbers, range: $y \leq 1$ **e)** x-intercepts: 1, 3, y-intercept: -3 **5. a)** up **b)** $(4, 3)$ **c)** $x = 4$ **d)** domain: all real numbers, range: $y \geq 3$ **e)** x-intercepts: none, y-intercept: 11 **6. a)** down **b)** $(-5, -2)$ **c)** $x = -5$ **d)** domain: all real numbers, range: $y \leq -2$ **e)** x-intercepts none, y-intercept: -77 **7.** x-intercepts: $-4.4, -1.6$, y-intercept: 7 **8.** x-intercepts: 2.6, 5.4, y-intercept: -7 **9.** $y = x^2 - 4$ **10.** $y = -2(x - 1)^2 + 5$
11. $y = -(x - 5)^2 + 4$ **12.** $y = 2(x + 1)^2 + 2$
13. $y = -(x + 1)^2 - 2$; $(-1, -2)$, $x = -1$, $(0, -3)$, $(1, -6)$
14. $y = 0.5(x - 4)^2 - 7$; $(4, -7)$, $x = 4$, $(0, 1)$, $(2, -5)$
15. a) 18.2 m **b)** 38 m **c)** 5.3 m **16.** \$22

Chapter 4 **1.** $-1, \dfrac{3}{2}$ **2.** 3, 4 **3.** ± 6 **4.** $-2, 8$ **5.** $-\dfrac{1}{2}, 4$

6. $-4, 3$ **7.** $\dfrac{1}{3}$ **8.** $\dfrac{-1 \pm i\sqrt{7}}{4}$ **9.** $\dfrac{-1 \pm i\sqrt{35}}{2}$ **10.** $-8, 6$

11. $-5, -\dfrac{2}{3}$ **12.** $\dfrac{1 \pm \sqrt{13}}{2}$ **13.** $-2, 6$ **14.** $-2 \pm 2\sqrt{2}$

15. two distinct real roots **16.** two equal real roots
17. two imaginary roots **18.** two distinct real roots
19. $-0.67, 0.14$ **20.** $1.67, -1.07$ **21.** $2x^2 - 5x - 3 = 0$
22. $k > \dfrac{9}{4}$ **23.** 0 **24.** 0 **25.** $(x + 1)(x - 4)(x - 5)$

26. $(x + 1)(4x - 3)(x - 3)$ **27.** $2, \dfrac{3 \pm \sqrt{5}}{2}$ **28.** $-1, 6, 6$

29. $1, 1 \pm i$ **30.** $\pm 3, \dfrac{1}{2}$ **31.** base: 6 cm, height: 8 cm

32. 80 km/h

Chapter 5

Functions p. 239
1. R^3: 1.94×10^{32}, 1.26×10^{33}, 3.31×10^{33}, 1.19×10^{34}, 4.71×10^{35}, 2.92×10^{36}; T^2: 5.78×10^{13}, 3.76×10^{14}, 9.99×10^{14}, 3.53×10^{15}, 1.40×10^{17}, 8.65×10^{17}; $\dfrac{R^3}{T^2}$: 3.36×10^{18}, 3.35×10^{18}, 3.31×10^{18}, 3.37×10^{18}, 3.36×10^{18}, 3.38×10^{18} **2. a)** They are all almost equal. **b)** 3.355×10^{18} **3. a)** $T = \sqrt{\dfrac{R^3}{k}}$ **b)** 2.65×10^9 s; 5.21×10^9 s **4. a)** $R = \sqrt[3]{kT^2}$ **b)** 5.90×10^{12} m

Getting Started pp. 240–241
1. a) $y = x - 3, y = \dfrac{1}{2}x, y = x + 9, y = -\dfrac{1}{2}x + 6$, $y = \dfrac{1}{6}x + 2, y = -\dfrac{1}{6}x + 4$ **2. a)** $y = -x^2 + 4, y = -\dfrac{1}{4}x^2 + 4$, $y = x^2 + 4, y = \dfrac{1}{4}x^2 + 4$ **3. a)** $y = -4x^2 + 36, y = 4x^2$, $y = -2x^2 + 18, y = 2x^2 + 18, y = 18, y = 18x + 18$, $y = -18x + 18$

Warm Up **1.** $5x + 1$ **2.** $3x^2 + 6x - 7$ **3.** $13x + 15$
4. $-x^2 - 3$ **5.** $3x^2 + x - 2$ **6.** $2x^3 - 7x^2 + 7x - 2$ **7.** $x - 2$
8. $3x - 2$ **9.** $4\sqrt{x} + 1$ **10.** $-8\sqrt{x} + 1$ **11.** $3x + 2\sqrt{x} - 1$
12. $-8x + 10\sqrt{x} - 3$ **13.** $x + 4\sqrt{x} + 4$ **14.** $9x - 6\sqrt{x} + 1$
15. $\dfrac{x + 2\sqrt{x} + 1}{x - 1}$ **16.** $\dfrac{2x - 5\sqrt{x} + 2}{x - 4}$ **17.** $y = \dfrac{x - 2}{3}$
18. $y = \dfrac{2}{x} - 2$ **19.** $y = \dfrac{3}{x + 5}$ **20.** $y = \dfrac{x - 5}{x - 2}$ **21.** 2
22. 4 **23.** 1 **24.** 0 **25.** 4 **26.** 1 **27.** 6 **28.** 9 **29.** 6 **30.** -2
31. $\dfrac{1}{2}$ **32.** -6 **33.** $-\dfrac{3}{2}$ **34.** 1 **35.** 11 **36.** $-\dfrac{1}{4}$ **37.** $x \neq 0$
38. $x \neq 1$ **39.** $x \neq -\dfrac{1}{2}$ **40.** $x \neq 0$ **41.** $x \neq \pm 3$ **42.** $x \neq -2, 3$
Mental Math
Evaluating Functions **1. a)** -5 **b)** 1 **c)** 16 **2. a)** -2 **b)** -1
c) 0 **3. a)** 3 **b)** 9 **c)** 9 **4. a)** -1 **b)** $-\dfrac{2}{3}$ **c)** $-\dfrac{1}{4}$
Dividing Using Compatible Numbers **1.** 24 **2.** 11 **3.** 9
4. 13 **5.** 9 **6.** 12 **7.** 12 **8.** 29 **9.** 18 **10.** 22 **11.** 19
12. 12 **13.** 1.2 **14.** 1.3 **15.** 1.9 **16.** 0.21 **17.** 0.09
18. 160 **19.** 220 **20.** 230 **21.** 410 **22. a)** m, m, m

Section 5.1 pp. 247–250
Practice **1. a)** $(f + g)(x) = 4x + 2$
b) $(f - g)(x) = 2x - 10$ **c)** $(fg)(x) = 3x^2 + 14x - 24$
d) $\left(\dfrac{f}{g}\right)(x) = \dfrac{3x - 4}{x + 6}$, $x \neq -6$ **2. a)** $(f + g)(x) = 3x + 11$

b) $(f-g)(x) = -x + 5$ c) $(fg)(x) = 2x^2 + 19x + 24$

d) $\left(\dfrac{f}{g}\right)(x) = \dfrac{x+8}{2x+3}, x \neq -1.5$ **3. a)** $(f+g)(x) = 3x - 6$

b) $(f-g)(x) = -x - 4$ c) $(fg)(x) = 2x^2 - 11x + 5$

d) $\left(\dfrac{f}{g}\right)(x) = \dfrac{x-5}{2x-1}, x \neq 0.5$ **4. a)** $(f+g)(x) = 3x - 6$

b) $(f-g)(x) = x - 2$ c) $(fg)(x) = 2x^2 - 8x + 8$

d) $\left(\dfrac{f}{g}\right)(x) = 2, x \neq 2$ **5. a)** $(f+g)(x) = 10 - 5x$

b) $(f-g)(x) = 10 + 5x$ c) $(fg)(x) = -50x$

d) $\left(\dfrac{f}{g}\right)(x) = \dfrac{-2}{x}, x \neq 0$ **6. a)** $(f+g)(x) = -4x + 4$

b) $(f-g)(x) = 4x + 14$ c) $(fg)(x) = -36x - 45$

d) $\left(\dfrac{f}{g}\right)(x) = \dfrac{-9}{4x+5}, x \neq -1.25$ **7. a)** $(f+g)(x) = 0$

b) $(f-g)(x) = 6x$ c) $(fg)(x) = -9x^2$ d) $\left(\dfrac{f}{g}\right)(x) = -1,$

$x \neq 0$ **8. a)** $(f+g)(x) = 2x - 5$ b) $(f-g)(x) = -5$

c) $(fg)(x) = x^2 - 5x$ d) $\left(\dfrac{f}{g}\right)(x) = \dfrac{x-5}{x}, x \neq 0$ **9. a)** 7

b) -7 c) -6 d) -2.5 **10. a)** 11 b) 3 c) 7 d) $\dfrac{1}{3}$ **11. a)** 17

b) 3 c) 22 d) 0.5 **12. a)** 1 b) 1 c) -6 d) -2 **13. a)** 19 b) 3

c) 36 d) 0 **20. a)** $(f+g)(x) = x^2 + x - 1$

b) $(f-g)(x) = x^2 - x + 1$ c) $(fg)(x) = x^3 - x^2$

d) $\left(\dfrac{f}{g}\right)(x) = \dfrac{x^2}{x-1}, x \neq 1$ **21. a)** $(f+g)(x) = x^2 + x + 3$

b) $(f-g)(x) = x^2 - x - 5$ c) $(fg)(x) = x^3 + 4x^2 - x - 4$

d) $\left(\dfrac{f}{g}\right)(x) = \dfrac{x^2-1}{x+4}, x \neq -4$

22. a) $(f+g)(x) = 2x^2 + 3x - 1$

b) $(f-g)(x) = -2x^2 + 3x - 1$ c) $(fg)(x) = 6x^3 - 2x^2$

d) $\left(\dfrac{f}{g}\right)(x) = \dfrac{3x-1}{2x^2}, x \neq 0$

23. a) $(f+g)(x) = 2x^2 + 2x + 2$ b) $(f-g)(x) = 2x^2 - 2x - 8$

c) $(fg)(x) = 4x^3 + 10x^2 - 6x - 15$ d) $\left(\dfrac{f}{g}\right)(x) = \dfrac{2x^2-3}{2x+5},$

$x \neq -2.5$ **24. a)** $(f+g)(x) = x^2 + x + 1$

b) $(f-g)(x) = -x^2 + x - 1$ c) $(fg)(x) = x^3 + x$

d) $\left(\dfrac{f}{g}\right)(x) = \dfrac{x}{x^2+1}$ **25. a)** $(f+g)(x) = 2x^2 - 2x$

b) $(f-g)(x) = 2x^2 - 6x$ c) $(fg)(x) = 4x^3 - 8x$

d) $\left(\dfrac{f}{g}\right)(x) = x - 2, x \neq 0$ **26. a)** $(f+g)(x) = x^2 - x$

b) $(f-g)(x) = x^2 - 3x + 2$ c) $(fg)(x) = x^3 - 3x^2 + 3x - 1$

d) $\left(\dfrac{f}{g}\right)(x) = x - 1, x \neq 1$ **27. a)** $(f+g)(x) = -2x^2 + 3x$

b) $(f-g)(x) = -2x^2 - 3x$ c) $(fg)(x) = -6x^3$

d) $\left(\dfrac{f}{g}\right)(x) = -\dfrac{2}{3}x, x \neq 0$ **28. a)** $(f+g)(x) = 2x^2 + 5x$

b) $(f-g)(x) = 2x^2 + x - 10$

c) $(fg)(x) = 4x^3 + 16x^2 + 5x - 25$

d) $\left(\dfrac{f}{g}\right)(x) = x - 1, x \neq -2.5$

29. a) $(f+g)(x) = x^2 - 3x + 14$

b) $(f-g)(x) = -x^2 + 3x + 10$ c) $(fg)(x) = 12x^2 - 36x + 24$

d) $\left(\dfrac{f}{g}\right)(x) = \dfrac{12}{x^2-3x+2}, x \neq 1, 2$

30. a) $(f+g)(x) = 4x^2 + 2x - 2$ b) $(f-g)(x) = 4x^2 - 2x$

c) $(fg)(x) = 8x^3 - 4x^2 - 2x + 1$

d) $\left(\dfrac{f}{g}\right)(x) = 2x + 1, x \neq 0.5$ **31. a)** 0 b) 2 c) 0 d) 3

32. a) 1 b) 2 c) 0 d) $\dfrac{11}{6}$ **33. a)** -5 b) 9 c) 0 d) $-\dfrac{8}{9}$ **34. a)** 2

b) 2 c) 1 d) $\dfrac{1}{4}$ **35. a)** 3 b) 0 c) 0 d) 6

36. a) $(f+g)(x) = \dfrac{2x+1}{x^2+x}, x \neq 0, -1$

b) $(f-g)(x) = \dfrac{-1}{x^2+x}, x \neq 0, -1$ c) $(fg)(x) = \dfrac{1}{x^2+x},$

$x \neq 0, -1$ d) $\left(\dfrac{f}{g}\right)(x) = \dfrac{x}{x+1}, x \neq 0, -1$

37. a) $(f+g)(x) = \dfrac{5x+5}{(x+3)(x-2)}, x \neq -3, 2$

b) $(f-g)(x) = \dfrac{-x-13}{(x+3)(x-2)}, x \neq -3, 2$

c) $(fg)(x) = \dfrac{6}{(x+3)(x-2)}, x \neq -3, 2$

d) $\left(\dfrac{f}{g}\right)(x) = \dfrac{2(x-2)}{3(x+3)}, x \neq -3, 2$

38. a) $(f+g)(x) = \dfrac{2x^2-5x}{(x-1)(x-4)}, x \neq 1, 4$

b) $(f-g)(x) = \dfrac{-3x}{(x-1)(x-4)}, x \neq 1, 4$

c) $(fg)(x) = \dfrac{x^2}{(x-1)(x-4)}, x \neq 1, 4$

d) $\left(\dfrac{f}{g}\right)(x) = \dfrac{x-4}{x-1}$, $x \neq 0, 1, 4$

39. a) $(f+g)(x) = \dfrac{3x^2-4x}{x^2-16}$, $x \neq \pm 4$

b) $(f-g)(x) = \dfrac{-x^2+12x}{x^2-16}$, $x \neq \pm 4$

c) $(fg)(x) = \dfrac{2x^2}{x^2-16}$, $x \neq \pm 4$

d) $\left(\dfrac{f}{g}\right)(x) = \dfrac{x+4}{2(x-4)}$, $x \neq 0, \pm 4$

40. a) $(f+g)(x) = 4\sqrt{x}$, $x \geq 0$ **b)** $(f-g)(x) = 2\sqrt{x}$, $x \geq 0$

c) $(fg)(x) = 3x$, $x \geq 0$ **d)** $\left(\dfrac{f}{g}\right)(x) = 3$, $x > 0$

41. a) $(f+g)(x) = 3\sqrt{x}+3$, $x \geq 0$
b) $(f-g)(x) = -\sqrt{x}+3$, $x \geq 0$

c) $(fg)(x) = 2x+6\sqrt{x}$, $x \geq 0$ **d)** $\left(\dfrac{f}{g}\right)(x) = \dfrac{\sqrt{x}+3}{2\sqrt{x}}$, $x > 0$

42. a) $(f+g)(x) = 2\sqrt{x}$, $x \geq 0$ **b)** $(f-g)(x) = -4$, $x \geq 0$

c) $(fg)(x) = x-4$, $x \geq 0$ **d)** $\left(\dfrac{f}{g}\right)(x) = \dfrac{\sqrt{x}-2}{\sqrt{x}+2}$, $x \geq 0$

43. a) $(f+g)(x) = 3\sqrt{x}$, $x \geq 0$
b) $(f-g)(x) = \sqrt{x}-2$, $x \geq 0$
c) $(fg)(x) = 2x+\sqrt{x}-1$, $x \geq 0$

d) $\left(\dfrac{f}{g}\right)(x) = \dfrac{2\sqrt{x}-1}{\sqrt{x}+1}$, $x \geq 0$ **44. a)** $4x-1$ **b)** $-7x+18$

c) $4x^2-12x+9$ **45. a)** $-x^2+13$ **b)** $4x^2+3$
c) $-2x^4+2x^2+12$ **46. a)** $4x^2-3x-9$ **b)** $-8x^2+x+3$
c) x^2+6x+9 **47. a)** $-2x^2+2$ **b)** $2x^2-2$ **c)** 2, $x \neq \pm 1$
48. $7-3x-4x^2$ **49.** $5x-4$ **50.** $7x^2-9x-9$
51. $9-4x+x^2$ **52.** $-2x+4$ **53.** $-4x^2-5x+2$

Applications and Problem Solving **54. a)** $r(x) = 450$, $p(x) = 15x - 562.5$ **b)** $t(x) = 15x - 112.5$ **c)** $x \geq 37.5$; Joseph works at least a regular 37.5 h week every week. **d)** \$532.50 **55. a)** 3 **b)** -3 **c)** 40 **d)** No. g is not defined at $x = 1$. **56. a)** $w(x) = 2x+1$ **b)** 11 m

57. a) $r(x) = 2x^2$ **b)** $c(x) = \dfrac{\pi x^2}{8}$ **c)** $w(x) = \dfrac{(16+\pi)x^2}{8}$

58. a) $C(x) = 3x^2+6x$ **b)** x by $3x+6$, $3x$ by $x+2$
59. a) $B(x) = x^2$ **b)** $V(x) = 0.21x^3$ **c)** 2 555 000 m^3
60. a) $A(s) = s^2$ **b)** $P(s) = 4s$ **c)** $s > 0$; The side length of a square must be positive. **d)** $r(s) = \dfrac{s}{4}$ **e)** 80 m, 400 m^2

61. a) $B(r) = \pi r^2$ **b)** $h(r) = 3r$ **c)** $V(r) = 3\pi r^3$ **d)** 3233 cm^3

62. a) $A(r) = \pi r^2$ **b)** $B(r) = \dfrac{\pi r^2}{64}$ **c)** $C(r) = \dfrac{63\pi r^2}{64}$

d) 111 cm^2 **63.** Find $(m+n)(x)$, then find $(m+n)(3)$, or find $m(3)$ and $n(3)$, then find $m(3)+n(3)$. **64. a)** 2, -2; -3, 3; The values in each pair are the negatives of each other. **b)** The values are both 0. **c)** $(f-g)(x)$ is the negative of $(g-f)(x)$. **65.** $(fg)(x) = (gf)(x)$; Multiplication is commutative. **66.** Either $f(x) = 0$, $g(x) = 0$, or both. **67. a)** $\left(\dfrac{f}{g}\right)(x)$ has a restriction at

$x = 0$, while $h(x)$ does not. **b)** $\left(\dfrac{f}{g}\right)(x)$ has a restriction

at $x = 0$, while $h(x)$ does not. **c)** $\left(\dfrac{f}{g}\right)(x)$ has a

restriction at $x = -9$, while $h(x)$ does not.
68. The graphs are reflections in the x-axis.
69. a) $f(x) = 2x+3$, $g(x) = x^2-4$ **b)** +A1^2+2*A1−1
c) B: 5, 1, 7, −1; C: −3, −3, 0, 0; D: 2, −2, 7, −1
70. a) quadratic **b)** quadratic **c)** quadratic **d)** neither
71. Answers may vary. $f(x) = 3x+5$, $g(x) = 2x-7$
72. a) $(fg)(x) = x^2-4$ **b)** The domain is the same. The range for $f(x)$ and $g(x)$ is all real numbers. The range for $(fg)(x)$ is $y \geq -4$. **73.** $h(x) = x-1$
74. $h(x) = x^2+x-2$ **75.** Subtract values of $f(x)$ from values of $(f+g)(x)$ with equal x-coordinates.
76. $f(g(x)) = 6x-4$ **77.** Answers may vary.

Section 5.2 pp. 256–259
Practice **1.** 4 **2.** 2 **3.** 2 **4.** 5 **5.** 7 **6.** −3 **7.** 12 **8.** 0
9. a) $\{(5, 4), (4, 5), (3, 2), (2, 1), (1, 2)\}$ **b)** $\{(12, 7),$ $(7, 12), (2, -3), (0, -3), (-3, 0)\}$ **10. a)** $\{(2, 7), (1, 4),$ $(0, -3), (-1, -4)\}$ **b)** does not exist **c)** does not exist
d) does not exist **11. a)** $(3, 2), (0, -1)$ **b)** $(6, 8), (5, -1)$
c) $(-1, -1)$ **d)** $(-2, 8), (-5, -1)$ **12.** 9 **13.** 10 **14.** 11
15. 14 **16.** −19 **17.** −28 **18.** 14 **19.** 12
20. $(f \circ g)(x) = 2x+7$ **21.** $(g \circ f)(x) = 2x+3$
22. $(f \circ g)(x) = 500-5x$, $(g \circ f)(x) = 100-5x$
23. $(f \circ g)(x) = 144-24x+x^2$, $(g \circ f)(x) = 12-x^2$
24. $(f \circ g)(x) = 9$, $(g \circ f)(x) = 13$ **25.** $(f \circ g)(x) = 3x^2$, $(g \circ f)(x) = 9x^2$ **26.** $(f \circ g)(x) = x-10$, $(g \circ f)(x) = x+10$ **27.** $(f \circ g)(x) = x$, $(g \circ f)(x) = x$
28. $(f \circ g)(x) = -x^2$, $(g \circ f)(x) = x^2$
29. $(f \circ g)(x) = 9x^2+6x-1$, $(g \circ f)(x) = 3x^2-5$
30. $(f \circ g)(x) = -2x^2-2$, $(g \circ f)(x) = 2x^2-4x+5$
31. $(f \circ g)(x) = -4x^2+4x+3$, $(g \circ f)(x) = -2x^2+7$
32. $(f \circ g)(x) = |3x|$, $(g \circ f)(x) = 3|x|$
33. $(f \circ g)(x) = |x|$, $(g \circ f)(x) = |x+1|-1$
34. $(f \circ g)(x) = \sqrt{x+1}$, $(g \circ f)(x) = \sqrt{x}+1$

35. $(f \circ g)(x) = 2\sqrt{2x} - 1$, $(g \circ f)(x) = \sqrt{4x - 2}$
36. a) 11 **b)** $(h \circ h)(x) = x + 6$ **37. a)** -25
b) $(g \circ g)(x) = 9x - 16$ **38. a)** 1 **b)** $(f \circ f)(x) = x^4$
39. a) 3 **b)** $(f \circ f)(x) = x$ **40.** 16 **41.** 12 **42.** 121 **43.** 27
44. 64 **45.** -18 **46.** $(h \circ k)(x) = 3(x - 1)^2$
47. $(k \circ h)(x) = (3x - 1)^2$ **48.** $(h \circ h)(x) = 9x$
49. $(k \circ k)(x) = (x^2 - 2x)^2$ **50.** does not exist
51. $(h \circ g)(x) = 3\sqrt{x} + 2$, R: $y \geq 2$
52. $(h \circ k)(x) = \sqrt{|x|} - 1$, R: $y \geq -1$ **53.** $y = 0$
54. $(f \circ g)(x) = 2 - |x - 1|$, R: $y \leq 2$
55. $(g \circ f)(x) = 2\sqrt{-x^2}$, R: $y \geq 0$ **56.** $(g \circ f)(x) = x + 1$,
R: all real numbers **57.** does not exist
58. $(f \circ g)(x) = \dfrac{-1}{x}$, $x \neq 0$, $(g \circ f)(x) = \dfrac{-1}{x}$, $x \neq 0$

59. $(f \circ g)(x) = \dfrac{1}{x^2}$, $x \neq 0$, $(g \circ f)(x) = -\dfrac{1}{x^2}$, $x \neq 0$

60. $(f \circ g)(x) = \dfrac{1}{5 - x}$, $x \neq 5$, $(g \circ f)(x) = \dfrac{3x + 5}{x + 2}$,

$x \neq -2$ **61.** $(f \circ g)(x) = \dfrac{x}{x - 1}$, $x \neq 1$, $(g \circ f)(x) = \dfrac{2x}{x - 2}$,

$x \neq 2$ **62. a)** $(f \circ g)(x) = \sqrt{3x}$, $(g \circ f)(x) = 3\sqrt{x}$
b) f: $x \geq 0$, g: all real numbers, $f \circ g$: $x \geq 0$, $g \circ f$: $x \geq 0$
c) $f \circ g$: $y \geq 0$, $g \circ f$: $y \geq 0$ **63. a)** $(h \circ k)(x) = \sqrt{x - 2}$,
$(k \circ h)(x) = \sqrt{x} - 2$ **b)** h: $x \geq 0$, k: all real numbers,
$h \circ k$: $x \geq 2$, $k \circ h$: $x \geq 0$ **c)** $h \circ k$: $y \geq 0$, $k \circ h$: $y \geq -2$
64. a) $(h \circ k)(x) = \sqrt{4x + 1}$, $(k \circ h)(x) = 4\sqrt{x} + 1$
b) h: $x \geq -1$, k: all real numbers, $h \circ k$: $x \geq -\dfrac{1}{4}$,
$k \circ h$: $x \geq -1$ **c)** $h \circ k$: $y \geq 0$, $k \circ h$: $y \geq 0$
65. a) $(f \circ g)(x) = \sqrt{x^2 - 4}$, $(g \circ f)(x) = x - 4$
b) f: $x \geq 2$, g: all real numbers, $f \circ g$: $x \geq 2$, $x \leq -2$, $g \circ f$:
all real numbers **c)** $f \circ g$: $y \geq 0$, $g \circ f$: all real numbers
66. a) $(h \circ k)(x) = \dfrac{1}{5x}$, $(k \circ h)(x) = \dfrac{5}{x}$ **b)** h: $x \neq 0$, k:
all real numbers, $h \circ k$: $x \neq 0$, $k \circ h$: $x \neq 0$ **c)** $h \circ k$: $y \neq 0$,
$k \circ h$: $y \neq 0$ **67. a)** $(f \circ g)(x) = \dfrac{1}{x - 2}$,

$(g \circ f)(x) = \dfrac{2 - x}{x - 1}$ **b)** f: $x \neq 1$, g: all real numbers,

$f \circ g$: $x \neq 2$, $g \circ f$: $x \neq 1$ **c)** $f \circ g$: $y \neq 0$, $g \circ f$: $y \neq -1$
68. a) $(f \circ g)(x) = 2|x|$, $(g \circ f)(x) = |2x|$ **b)** f: all real
numbers, g: all real numbers, $f \circ g$: all real numbers,
$g \circ f$: all real numbers **c)** $f \circ g$: $y \geq 0$, $g \circ f$: $y \geq 0$

Applications and Problem Solving **69. a)** $s(d) = 8d$
b) 8000 schillings **c)** $d(s) = \dfrac{s}{8}$ **d)** \$125

70. a) $v_1(c) = 0.8c$ **b)** $v_2(v_1) = 0.9v_1$ **c)** $v_3(v_2) = 0.9v_2$,
$v_4(v_3) = 0.9v_3$ **d)** $v_4(c) = 0.5832c$ **e)** \$37 908 **f)** \$52 500
71. a) $l(x) = \sqrt{x}$ **b)** $r(l) = 3l$ **c)** $r(x) = 3\sqrt{x}$
d) 15 square units **e)** 64 square units **72. a)** $A(s) = s^2$

b) $s(d) = \dfrac{\sqrt{2}}{2}d$ **c)** $A(d) = \dfrac{d^2}{2}$ **d)** 72 cm²

73. a) $d(t) = 330t$ **b)** $A(d) = \pi d^2$ **c)** $A(t) = 108\ 900\pi t^2$
d) 3420 m² **e)** 1.7 s **74. a)** $s(x) = x - 250\ 000$
b) $p(s) = 0.03s$ **c)** $(p \circ s)(x) = 0.03(x - 250\ 000)$ **d)** The
composition represents the bonus Connor gets for
sales over \$250 000. **e)** \$3750 **75. a)** $s(c) = 625c$

b) $c(b) = \dfrac{b}{25}$ **c)** $i(n) = \dfrac{n}{2}$ **d)** $s(i) = 250i$ **e)** Israeli

shekels: 1250; Norwegian krones: 2500; Belgian
francs: 12 500; South Korean won: 312 500
76. a) $g(d) = 0.09d$ **b)** Answers may vary. Use a cost of
\$0.50. $c(g) = 0.5g$ **c)** $c(d) = 0.045d$ **d)** \$38.25

e) $d(c) = \dfrac{200}{9}c$ **f)** 666.7 km **77. a)** $s(p) = \dfrac{p}{3}$

b) $A(s) = \dfrac{\sqrt{3}}{4}s^2$ **c)** $A(p) = \dfrac{\sqrt{3}}{36}p^2$ **d)** 43 cm²

78. a) $D = 0.75c$ **b)** less **c)** 300% **79.** $(f \circ f)(x) = \dfrac{2x + 1}{x + 1}$,

$x \neq 0, -1$ **Answers may vary for 80–83.**
80. $f(x) = 3x$, $g(x) = x$ **81.** $f(x) = 2x$, $g(x) = x + 1$
82. $f(x) = \dfrac{1}{x}$, $g(x) = x - 4$ **83.** $f(x) = x^2 + 1$,

$g(x) = x - 1$ **84.** $t = \dfrac{q(1 - r)}{1 - p}$ **85.** $x = -1$

86. $(f \circ g)(x)$: $y \leq 0$, $(g \circ f)(x)$: $y \geq 0$ **87. a)** $S = 0.7R$
b) $T = 1.15S$ **c)** $T = 0.805R$ **d)** \$40.25 **88. a)** $j(r) = 0.8r$
b) $s(r) = 0.6r$ **c)** $j(s(r)) = s(j(r)) = 0.48r$; The first
composition means the sale discount is calculated
before the employee discount. The second
composition means the employee discount is
calculated before the sale discount. **d)** No. See part c.
e) $m(r) = r - 5$; $j(m(r)) = 0.8r - 4$; $m(j(r)) = 0.8r - 5$;
Yes. The two composite functions are different.

89. a) $A = \pi r^2$ **b)** $r = \dfrac{C}{2\pi}$ **c)** $A = \dfrac{C^2}{4\pi}$ **d)** 796 cm²

90. No. $f \circ g \neq g \circ f$ in general. **91.** $g(x) = 1 - x$
92. a) always true **b)** never true **c)** never true
d) sometimes true **93.** Answers may vary. $f(x) = 2x - 1$,

$g(x) = x^2$ **94.** Answers may vary. $f(x) = x$, $g(x) = x^2$
95. a) $(h \circ g \circ f)(x) = 3$ **b)** $(g \circ f \circ h)(x) = 24$
c) $(f \circ g \circ h)(x) = 60$ **d)** $(f \circ f \circ f)(x) = 125x$
e) $(f \circ g \circ f)(x) = 25x + 45$ **f)** $(g \circ g \circ g)(x) = x + 27$
96. $f(x) = 1$ or $f(x) = x^2$ **97. a)** no **b)** x: $-9, -4, -1, 0,$
$1, 4, 9$; $f \circ f$: is undefined, for all values of x,
except 0. **c)** The graph consists of only one point:
$(0, 0)$. This does not show on the graphing
calculator.

Technology p. 260
1 Reviewing Reflections **2.** $(-1, -2), (4, -4), (5, -1)$
3. $(1, 2), (-4, 4), (-5, 1)$ **4. a)** The image point of (x, y)
reflected in the x-axis is $(x, -y)$. **b)** The image point of
(x, y) reflected in the y-axis is $(-x, y)$. **5. a)** y-axis
b) x-axis
2 Exploring the Mapping $(x, y) \rightarrow (y, x)$ **3.** $(4, 4)$
4. equal **5.** $90°$ **6.** $1, -1$ **7.** yes **8.** yes **9.** $(-1, -1)$;
equal; $90°$; $1, -1$; yes; yes **10.** the line $y = x$ **11.** $(4, 1)$,
$(5, -2), (-4, -3)$
3 Problem Solving **1. a)** 2 **b)** 0 and undefined
2. a) no **b)** 1 and -1

Section 5.3 pp. 268–270
Practice **1.** $f^{-1} = \{(2, 0), (3, 1), (4, 2), (5, 3)\}$
2. $g^{-1} = \{(-3, -1), (-2, 1), (4, 3), (0, 5), (1, 6)\}$
3. $f^{-1} = \{(3, -2), (2, -1), (0, 0), (-2, 4)\}$; function
4. $g^{-1} = \{(-2, 4), (1, 2), (3, 1), (-2, 0), (-3, -3)\}$; not a
function **5.** $x = \dfrac{y-2}{3}$ **6.** $x = \dfrac{12-3y}{2}$ **7.** $x = \dfrac{3-y}{4}$
8. $x = 4y - 3$ **9.** $x = 2(y + 5)$ **10.** $x = \pm\sqrt{y - 3}$
11. $f^{-1}(x) = x + 1$ **12.** $f^{-1}(x) = 2x$ **13.** $f^{-1}(x) = x - 3$
14. $f^{-1}(x) = \dfrac{3}{4}x$ **15.** $f^{-1}(x) = \dfrac{x-1}{2}$ **16.** $f^{-1}(x) = 3x - 2$
17. $g^{-1}(x) = \dfrac{2}{5}(x + 4)$ **18.** $h^{-1}(x) = 5(x - 1)$
19. $f^{-1}(x) = x - 2$ **20.** $f^{-1}(x) = \dfrac{1}{4}x$ **21.** $f^{-1}(x) = \dfrac{x+2}{3}$
22. $f^{-1}(x) = x$ **23.** $f^{-1}(x) = 3 - x$ **24.** $f^{-1}(x) = 3x + 2$
25. $f^{-1}(x) = \dfrac{x+5}{2}$; function **26.** $f^{-1}(x) = 4x - 3$;
function **27.** $f^{-1}(x) = 4(x - 3)$; function **28.** $f^{-1}(x) = 5 - x$;
function **29.** yes **30.** yes **31.** yes **32.** no **33.** no **34.** no
35. yes **36. a)** $f^{-1}(x) = \pm\sqrt{x+3}$ **c)** f: D: all real
numbers, R: $y \geq -3$; f^{-1}: D: $x \geq 0$, R: all real numbers
37. a) $f^{-1}(x) = \pm\sqrt{x-1}$ **c)** f: D: all real numbers, R: $y \geq 1$;
f^{-1}: D: $x \geq 1$, R: all real numbers **38. a)** $f^{-1}(x) = \pm\sqrt{-x}$

c) f: D: all real numbers, R: $y \leq 0$; f^{-1}: D: $x \leq 0$, R: all
real numbers **39. a)** $f^{-1}(x) = \pm\sqrt{-x-1}$ **c)** f: D: all real
numbers, R: $y \leq -1$; f^{-1}: D: $x \leq -1$, R: all real numbers
40. a) $f^{-1}(x) = \pm\sqrt{x+2}$ **c)** f: D: all real numbers, R:
$y \geq 0$; f^{-1}: D: $x \geq 0$, R: all real numbers
41. a) $f^{-1}(x) = \pm\sqrt{x-1}$ **c)** f: D: all real numbers, R:
$y \geq 0$; f^{-1}: D: $x \geq 0$, R: all real numbers **48.** no **49.** no
50. $f^{-1}(x) = \dfrac{x+3}{2}$; D: all real numbers, R: all real

numbers **51.** $f^{-1}(x) = \dfrac{2-x}{4}$; D: all real numbers, R:

all real numbers **52.** $f^{-1}(x) = \dfrac{x}{3} + 2$; D: all real

numbers, R: all real numbers **53.** $f^{-1}(x) = 2x + 6$; D: all

real numbers, R: all real numbers **54.** $f^{-1}(x) = \pm\sqrt{x}$
55. $f^{-1}(x) = \pm\sqrt{x-2}$ **56.** $f^{-1}(x) = \pm\sqrt{x+4}$
57. $f^{-1}(x) = \pm\dfrac{\sqrt{2(x+1)}}{2}$ **58.** $f^{-1}(x) = \pm\sqrt{x} + 3$

59. $f^{-1}(x) = \pm\sqrt{x} - 2$ **60. a)** $f^{-1}(x) = \sqrt{x}$

c) f: $x \geq 0, y \geq 0$; f^{-1}: $x \geq 0, y \geq 0$ **61. a)** $f^{-1}(x) = \sqrt{x+2}$
c) f: $x \geq 0, y \geq -2$; f^{-1}: $x \geq -2, y \geq 0$
62. a) $f^{-1}(x) = -\sqrt{x-4}$ **c)** f: $x \leq 0, y \geq 4$; f^{-1}: $x \geq 4, y \leq 0$
63. a) $f^{-1}(x) = \sqrt{3-x}$ **c)** f: $x \geq 0, y \leq 3$; f^{-1}: $x \leq 3, y \geq 0$
64. a) $f^{-1}(x) = \sqrt{x} + 4$ **c)** f: $x \geq 4, y \geq 0$; f^{-1}: $x \geq 0, y \geq 4$
65. a) $f^{-1}(x) = -\sqrt{x} - 3$ **c)** f: $x \leq -3, y \geq 0$; f^{-1}: $x \geq 0, y \leq -3$
66. $f^{-1}(x) = \dfrac{1}{x}$ **67.** $f^{-1}(x) = \dfrac{1}{x-2}$ **68.** $f^{-1}(x) = \dfrac{1}{x} - 3$

69. $f^{-1}(x) = \dfrac{1-2x}{x+1}$ **70.** $f^{-1}(x) = \dfrac{2x}{1-x}$

71. $f^{-1}(x) = \dfrac{1}{x-1}$ **72.** $f^{-1}(x) = x^2$; $x \geq 0$

73. $f^{-1}(x) = x^2 + 2$; $x \geq 0$ **74.** $f^{-1}(x) = 3 - x^2$; $x \leq 3$
75. $f^{-1}(x) = \pm\sqrt{x^2 - 9}$ **76. a)** $f^{-1}(x) = \pm\sqrt{x-3}$ **c)** $x \geq 0$
e) f: D: all real numbers, R: $y \geq 3$; f^{-1}: D: $x \geq 3$, R: all

real numbers **77. a)** $f^{-1}(x) = \pm\dfrac{\sqrt{2x}}{2}$ **c)** $x \geq 0$ **e)** f: D: all

real numbers, R: $y \geq 0$; f^{-1}: D: $x \geq 0$, R: all real

numbers **78. a)** $f^{-1}(x) = \pm\sqrt{x+1}$ **c)** $x \geq 0$ **e)** f: D: all
real numbers, R: $y \geq -1$; f^{-1}: D: $x \geq -1$, R: all real

numbers **79. a)** $f^{-1}(x) = \pm\sqrt{-x}$ **c)** $x \geq 0$ **e)** f: D: all real numbers, R: $y \leq 0$; f^{-1}: D: $x \leq 0$, R: all real numbers

80. a) $f^{-1}(x) = \pm\sqrt{1-x}$ **c)** $x \geq 0$ **e)** f: D: all real numbers, R: $y \leq 1$; f^{-1}: D: $x \leq 1$, R: all real numbers

81. a) $f^{-1}(x) = \pm\sqrt{x+2}$ **c)** $x \geq 2$ **e)** f: D: all real numbers, R: $y \geq 0$; f^{-1}: D: $x \geq 0$, R: all real numbers

82. a) $f^{-1}(x) = 4 \pm \sqrt{x}$ **c)** $x \geq 4$ **e)** f: D: all real numbers, R: $y \geq 0$; f^{-1}: D: $x \geq 0$, R: all real numbers

83. a) $f^{-1}(x) = -5 \pm \sqrt{-x}$ **c)** $x \geq -5$ **e)** f: D: all real numbers, R: $y \leq 0$; f^{-1}: $x \leq 0$, R: all real numbers

Applications and Problem Solving **84. a)** $f(x) = 2\pi x$

b) $f^{-1}(x) = \dfrac{x}{2\pi}$ **c)** yes **d)** The inverse finds the radius given the circumference x. **85. a)** $f(x) = 4\pi x^2$, $x \geq 0$

b) $f^{-1}(x) = \sqrt{\dfrac{x}{4\pi}}$ **c)** $x \geq 0$, y all real numbers **d)** yes

e) The inverse finds the radius given the surface area x.

86. a) $c(d) = 50 + 0.15d$ **b)** $d(c) = \dfrac{c - 50}{0.15}$ **c)** The inverse finds the distance driven given the total cost a.

87. a) $s(p) = 0.7p$ **b)** $p(s) = \dfrac{s}{0.7}$ **c)** The inverse finds the original price given the sale price s. **88. a)** $u(c) = 0.7c$ **b)** $c(u) = 1.43u$ **c)** \$214.50 **89.** $(63 \times 2 + 10) \div 8 - 6 = 11$

90. a) $T(d) = 35d + 20$ **b)** $d(T) = \dfrac{T - 20}{35}$ **c)** 2 km

91. a) $E(s) = 400 + 0.05s$ **b)** $s(E) = 20(E - 400)$ **c)** The inverse represents the sales given Jana's total weekly earnings E. **92. a)** $128.6°$ **b)** $n(i) = \dfrac{360}{180 - i}$ **c)** decagon

93. b) $t(h) = \sqrt{\dfrac{80 - h}{5}}$ **c)** Yes. The domain of $h(t)$ is restricted to $t \geq 0$, so $t(h)$ is a function. **d)** the time of the fall given the height above the ground **e)** 3 s **f)** 4 s

94. a) $t \geq 0$ **b)** $t(d) = \sqrt{\dfrac{d^3}{830}}$ **c)** Yes. Since the domain is restricted to $t \geq 0$, the inverse is a function. **d)** 35 h **95.** No. $x \geq 0$ **96. a)** If a horizontal line crosses the original function at more than one point, the inverse is not a function. **b)** yes **97.** Answers may vary. $y = x$, $y = -x$, $y = 2 - x$, $y = 7 - x$ **98. a)** yes **b)** No, because then f would not be a function. **99.** 4 square units

100. a) Yes. It passes the vertical line test. **b)** The inverse of $y = k$ is $x = k$, a vertical line, which is not a function. **101.** The original function. The inverse function undoes the original function. The inverse of the inverse undoes the undoing, returning the original function.

Computer Data Bank p. 271

1 The "Average" Vehicle **3. a)** minivan; sport-utility vehicle; luxury car; pickup truck; large car; coupe; medium car; sports/sporty car; small car **b)** pickup truck; large car; luxury car; coupe and minivan; medium car; sport-utility vehicle; sports/sporty car; small car **c)** large car and minivan; coupe, luxury car, medium car, pickup truck, sports/sporty car, and sport-utility vehicle; small car **d)** luxury car; coupe and large car; sport-utility vehicle; medium car; pickup truck; minivan; sports/sporty car; small car **e)** small car, sports/sporty car, large car, medium car, coupe, luxury car, minivan, pickup truck, sport-utility vehicle **f)** small car, sports/sporty car, medium car, large car, coupe, luxury car, minivan, sport-utility vehicle, pickup truck **4.** Answers will vary. For example: None of the orders are identical. The closest orders are highway and city fuel efficiency, with two pairs of vehicles switched. The heaviest is not the longest or widest, nor does it have the greatest power; but the lightest is the shortest and narrowest, and has the least power. Small cars are always the least except in fuel efficiencies, where they are the greatest.

2 Acceleration Times Answers may vary because of rounding. **1.** Answers will vary. **2.** 103 **3.** 0 to 48 km/h: Buick Riviera, BMW 3-series, and Pontiac Sunfire; 0 to 96 km/h: BMW 3-series and Volvo S70/V70 **4.** Answers will vary. **5.** Answers will vary. **6.** 77.7% **7.** 23.3%

3 Buying a Vehicle **1.** Chevrolet Malibu, Ford Contour, Nissan 200SX, Plymouth Breeze, Pontiac Grand Am, Toyota Avalon **2.** Answers will vary. **3.** Answers will vary.

Technology p. 273

1 Analyzing Functions **1. a)** 1; negative, positive; 0 **b)** 1; positive, negative; 0 **c)** 2; positive, positive; 1 **d)** 2; negative, negative; 1 **e)** 3; negative, positive; 2 **f)** 3; positive, negative; 2 **g)** 3; negative, positive; 0 **h)** 3; positive, negative; 0 **i)** 4; positive, positive; 3 **j)** 4; negative, negative; 3 **k)** 4; positive, positive; 1 **l)** 5; negative, positive; 4 **m)** 5; positive, positive; 0 **n)** 5; positive, negative; 2 **o)** 5; negative, positive; 4 **2.** If the leading coefficients are opposite in sign, the end behaviours are opposite in sign. **3. a)** They are equal. **4. a)** They are opposite. **5. a)** 0, 1, 2, 3 **b)** The maximum number of turning points is one less than the degree of the function. **c)** 6

Section 5.4 pp. 281–284

Practice **1.** polynomial; degree 5 **2.** not polynomial **3.** not polynomial **4.** polynomial; degree 4 **5.** not polynomial **6.** polynomial; degree 3 **7.** not polynomial **8.** not polynomial **9.** D: all real numbers, R: all real numbers, maximum: (1.4, 0.4), minimum: (2.6, −0.4), y-intercept: −6 **10.** D: all real numbers, R: all real numbers, minimum: (0, 2), maximum: (2, 6), y-intercept: 2 **11.** D: all real numbers, R: $y \geq -9$, minimums: (−2.3, −9), (1.3, −9), maximum: (−0.5, 1.6), y-intercept: 0 **12.** D: all real numbers, R: $y \leq 9.6$, maximums: (−0.3, 6), (3.8, 9.6), minimum: (1.7, −9.8), y-intercept: 5 **13.** zeros: −3, −1, 2; $f(x) \geq 0$: $-3 \leq x \leq -1$, $x \geq 2$; $f(x) < 0$: $-1 < x < 2$, $x < -3$ **14.** zeros: −2, −1, 2, 3; $f(x) \geq 0$: $-2 \leq x \leq -1$, $2 \leq x \leq 3$, $f(x) < 0$: $x < -2$, $-1 < x < 2$, $x > 3$ **15.** zeros: −2, −0.3; $f(x) \geq 0$: $x \leq -2$, $x \geq -0.3$; $f(x) < 0$: $-2 < x < -0.3$ **16.** zeros: −3, −2, 1.1, 2; $f(x) \geq 0$: $x \leq -3$, $-2 \leq x \leq 1.1$, $x \geq 2$; $f(x) < 0$: $-3 < x < -2$, $1.1 \leq x \leq 2$ **17. a)** D: all real numbers, R: $y \geq -4$ **b)** −2, 0, 2 **c)** 0 **d)** minimums: (−1.4, −4), (1.4, −4), maximum: (0, 0) **e)** symmetric about the y-axis **f)** positive, positive **18. a)** D: all real numbers, R: all real numbers **b)** 0, 3 **c)** 0 **d)** maximum: (0, 0), minimum: (2, −4) **e)** no symmetry **f)** negative, positive **19. a)** D: all real numbers, R: all real numbers **b)** −3, 0, 3 **c)** 0 **d)** minimum: (−1.7, −10.4), maximum: (1.7, 10.4) **e)** symmetric in the origin **f)** positive, negative **20. a)** D: all real numbers, R: $y \geq 0$ **b)** 0 **c)** 0 **d)** minimum: (0, 0) **e)** symmetric about the y-axis **f)** positive, positive **21. a)** D: all real numbers, R: all real numbers **b)** 0, 4 **c)** 0 **d)** minimum: (0, 0), maximum: (2.7, 9.5) **e)** no symmetry **f)** positive, negative **22. a)** D: all real numbers, R: all real numbers **b)** −0.6, 0, 3.6 **c)** 0 **d)** maximum: (−0.3, 0.3), minimum: (2.3, −8.3) **e)** no symmetry **f)** negative, positive **23. a)** D: all real numbers, R: all real numbers **b)** −2, −1, 1 **c)** −2 **d)** maximum: (−1.5, 0.6), minimum: (0.2, −2.1) **e)** no symmetry **f)** negative, positive **24. a)** D: all real numbers, R: all real numbers **b)** −1 **c)** 4 **d)** none **e)** no symmetry **f)** negative, positive **25. a)** D: all real numbers, R: $y \geq 5$ **b)** none **c)** 5 **d)** minimum; (0, 5) **e)** symmetric about the y-axis **f)** positive, positive **26. a)** D: all real numbers, R: $y \leq 6$ **b)** −1.6, 1.6 **c)** 6 **d)** maximum: (0, 6) **e)** symmetric about the y-axis **f)** negative, negative **27. a)** D: all real numbers, R: all real numbers **b)** −2, 0, 2 **c)** 0 **d)** maximum: (−1.5, 5.9), minimum: (1.5, −5.9)

e) symmetric in the origin **f)** negative, positive **28. a)** D: all real numbers, R: all real numbers **b)** 0, 1.6 **c)** 0 **d)** minimum: (0, 0), maximum: (1.2, 3.2) **e)** no symmetry **f)** positive, negative **29. a)** D: all real numbers, R: all real numbers **b)** −2, 0, 2 **c)** 0 **d)** maximum: (−1.2, 3.1), minimum: (1.2, −3.1) **e)** symmetric in the origin **f)** negative, positive **30. a)** D: all real numbers, R: all real numbers **b)** −1, 1 **c)** −1 **d)** maximum: (−1, 0), minimum: (0.3, −1.2) **e)** symmetric in the origin **f)** negative, positive **31. a)** D: all real numbers, R: all real numbers **b)** −1, 2, 3 **c)** 6 **d)** maximum: (0.1, 6.1), minimum: (2.5, −0.9) **e)** no symmetry **f)** negative, positive **32. a)** D: all real numbers, R: $y \geq -2.2$ **b)** −2, −1, 1, 2 **c)** 4 **d)** minimums: (−1.6, −2.3), (1.6, −2.3), maximum: (0, 4) **e)** symmetric about the y-axis **f)** positive, positive **33. a)** D: all real numbers, R: all real numbers **b)** −1, 2, 4 **c)** 8 **d)** $f(x) > 0$: $-1 < x < 2$, $x > 4$; $f(x) \leq 0$: $x \leq -1$, $2 \leq x \leq 4$ **e)** no symmetry **f)** negative, positive **34. a)** D: all real numbers, R: all real numbers **b)** −3, −1, 2 **c)** 6 **d)** $f(x) > 0$: $x < -3$, $-1 < x < 2$; $f(x) \leq 0$: $-3 \leq x \leq -1$, $x \geq 2$ **e)** no symmetry **f)** positive, negative **35. a)** D: all real numbers, R: $y \geq -9$ **b)** −2, 0, 1, 3 **c)** 0 **d)** $f(x) > 0$: $x < -2$, $0 < x < 1$, $x > 3$; $f(x) \leq 0$: $-2 \leq x \leq 0$, $1 \leq x \leq 3$ **e)** no symmetry **f)** positive, positive **36. a)** D: all real numbers, R: $y \leq 3.1$ **b)** −3, 0, 1 **c)** 0 **d)** $f(x) > 0$: $0 < x < 1$, $f(x) \leq 0$: $x \leq 0$, $x \geq 1$ **e)** no symmetry **f)** negative, positive **41.** $x < -1$, $x > 3$ **42.** $-2 < x < 3$ **43.** $x \leq -1$, $x \geq -\frac{1}{3}$ **44.** $-\frac{3}{2} \leq x \leq \frac{1}{2}$ **45.** $x < -4$, $x > 3$ **46.** $-2 \leq x \leq 5$ **47.** $x \neq -2$ **48.** $x \leq \frac{1}{2}$, $x \geq 3$ **49.** $x < -2$, $-1 < x < 1$ **50.** $x \geq 0$ **51.** $-\frac{1}{2} < x < 0$, $x > 3$ **52.** $x \leq -1$, $\frac{1}{2} \leq x \leq 2$ **53.** $x < -3$, $0 < x < 3$ **54.** $-1 \leq x \leq 1$, $x \geq 2$ **55.** $x \leq -3$, $-1 \leq x \leq 5$ **56.** $-\frac{3}{2} < x < 0$, $x > 2$

Applications and Problem Solving **57. a)** $-2 \leq x \leq 1$ **b)** $x < -2$, $x > -1$ **c)** $x < -3$, $-1 < x < 1$ **d)** $-3 \leq x \leq -2$, $x \geq -1$ **58. a)** $-2.3 \leq x \leq 1.3$ **b)** $x < -1.1$, $1.2 < x < 3.9$ **c)** $-1 \leq x \leq 0.5$ **d)** $-2 < x < -0.5$, $x > 0.5$ **59. b)** The zeros are the same, but the maximum is higher and the minimum is lower for the second function. **60. b)** 17 m **61. a)** $V = 2\pi r^3$ **c)** $r \geq 0$, $V \geq 0$ **62. a)** $A(x) = 14x^2$, $V(x) = 3x^3$ **b)** $\frac{14}{3}$ **c)** $0 < x < \frac{14}{3}$; $x > \frac{14}{3}$ **d)** For part b, find x to satisfy $A(x) - V(x) = 0$. For part c, find x to satisfy $A(x) - V(x) > 0$ and $A(x) - V(x) < 0$. **63. a)** Answers may vary. $t \geq 0$

c) 110 lm **d)** 27°C **64. a)** $V(w) = w(w + 5)(w - 2)$
b) $w > 2$ **d)** 9000 m^3 **e)** 28 m **65. a)** $y = x$: 0; negative,
positive; $y = x^2$: 0, positive, positive; $y = x^3$: 0; negative,
positive; $y = x^4$: 0; positive, positive; $y = x^5$: 0; negative,
positive; $y = x^6$: 0; positive, positive **b)** If n is even,
$y = x^n$ looks like $y = x^2$. If n is odd, $y = x^n$ looks like
$y = x^3$. **66.** $w \geq 7, l \geq 12$ **67.** Add the y-values for
corresponding x-values of $y = x^2 - 2$ and $y = x$ to find
the y-values of $y = x + x^2 - 2$. **68.** Subtract the y-values
of $y = x^3 + 2$ from the y-values of $y = x$ for
corresponding x-values to find the y-values of
$y = x - (x^3 + 2)$. **69. a)** $V(x) = x(11 - 2x)(9 - 2x)$
c) 1.6 cm **d)** 72 cm^3 **e)** 0 cm $< x < 1.1$ cm,
2.3 cm $< x < 4.5$ cm **70. b)** 26 **c)** 499
d) $-0.02x^3 - 5x^2 + 7900x - 200\ 000$ **e)** \$1 180 000,

288 trailers **71. a)** $V(x) = \dfrac{\sqrt{3}}{4}x^3$ **b)** $x > 0$

d) 54 cm^3 **e)** 3.6 cm **72. a)** function **b)** not a function
73. a) $-3 < x < -1, x > 1$ **b)** $x > 1$ **c)** The condition
$-3 < x < -1$ is discarded because it would result in
negative values for the width and the height.
74. Answers may vary. $x^2 + 1 < 0, -x^2 - x - 1 > 0$,
$x^2 + 4x + 5 \leq 0$ **75. a)** $x^2 - x - 2 \leq 0$ **b)** $2x^2 - 7x - 4 > 0$
76. $-7 \leq x < -5$ **77.** Answers may vary.

Technology p. 287

1 Verifying Equal Roots **1.** The roots are $-\dfrac{1}{3}, \dfrac{2}{3}, \dfrac{2}{3}$.

2. The roots are $-1, 2, 2$. **3.** The roots are $-\dfrac{4}{3}, \dfrac{8}{3}, \dfrac{8}{3}$.

2 Investigating Patterns **1. a)** $k(c) = -\dfrac{4}{27}c^3$

b) $k = -\dfrac{4}{27}$; The roots are $-\dfrac{2}{3}, -\dfrac{2}{3}, \dfrac{1}{3}$. **2. a)** $-\dfrac{1}{3}, \dfrac{2}{3}, \dfrac{2}{3}, \dfrac{4}{3}$,

$\dfrac{4}{3}, -\dfrac{2}{3}; -1, 2, 2; -\dfrac{4}{3}, \dfrac{8}{3}, \dfrac{8}{3}$; The equal roots are -2
times the distinct root. The equal roots are positive if
k is positive. The product of the roots is equal to k.

b) $k = \dfrac{500}{27}$ **c)** $\dfrac{10}{3}, \dfrac{10}{3}, -\dfrac{5}{3}$ **d)** $f(\dfrac{10}{3}) = 0, f(-\dfrac{5}{3}) = 0$

Section 5.5 pp. 295–298

Practice **1.** ± 3 **2.** ± 4 **3.** no solution **4.** $-7, 11$
5. $-28, 12$ **6.** $-8, 14$ **7.** $0, -10$ **8.** $-17, 13$ **9.** no

solution **10.** no solution **11.** $-3, 4$ **12.** $2, -\dfrac{10}{3}$

13. $-2, 5$ **14.** $-2, \dfrac{10}{3}$ **15.** no solution **16.** $-3, 1$ **17.** $0, 2$

18. $-20, 16$ **19.** $\dfrac{9}{2}, -\dfrac{3}{2}$ **20.** $-8, 7$ **21.** -1 **22.** $\dfrac{3}{2}$ **23.** no

solution **24.** 1 **25.** 3 **26.** 2 **27.** no solution **28.** $-\dfrac{1}{3}, 3$

29. $\dfrac{9}{2}, 9$ **30.** -1 **31.** 3 **32.** $0, \dfrac{12}{5}$ **33.** $4, -\dfrac{4}{3}$ **34.** $\dfrac{1}{6}$ **35.** 0

36. $-\dfrac{1}{2}, \dfrac{4}{3}$ **37.** $\dfrac{3}{2}, \dfrac{11}{4}$ **38.** $-4, 0$ **39.** no solution

40. $-\dfrac{7}{5}, 1$ **41.** $2, -2$ **42.** $-3 \leq x \leq 2$ **43.** no solution

44. $-\dfrac{7}{2}$ **45.** $m \geq -4$ **46.** $4, -\dfrac{2}{3}$ **47.** no solution

48. $-3 \leq x \leq 3$ **49.** $-2 < x < 2$ **50.** $x \leq -5, x \geq 5$
51. $y < -5, y > 5$ **52.** no solution **53.** $-5 < g < 5$
54. $x \leq -2, x \geq 2$ **55.** $a < -5, a > 5$ **56.** $x < -4, x > 12$
57. all real numbers **58.** all real numbers **59.** $x < -2$,
$x > 3$ **60.** $-2 < x < 8$ **61.** $-8 \leq x \leq 4$ **62.** $z < -3, z > 5$

63. $x < 2$ **64.** $x > 1$ **65.** $x \geq -7$ **66.** $x \leq 2$ **67.** $x > \dfrac{5}{2}$

68. no solution **69.** $-1 < x < 1$ **70.** $b \leq -\dfrac{3}{2}, b \geq 1$

71. $-3 \leq x \leq 0$ **72.** $x < -\dfrac{14}{3}, x > -\dfrac{6}{5}$ **73.** $-3 \leq x \leq 3$

74. $x < -3, x > 5$ **75.** $a \geq -2$ **76.** $x < -6, x > 4$ **77.** all

real numbers **78.** $-\dfrac{1}{2} < x < \dfrac{17}{2}$ **79.** all real numbers

80. $-3 \leq y \leq \dfrac{1}{3}$ **81.** $x < \dfrac{1}{4}$ **82.** $x \leq -5, x > 1$ **83. a)** D: all

real numbers, R: $y \geq -4$ **b)** $-6, 2$ **c)** $x \leq -6, x \geq 2$
d) symmetric about $x = -2$ **84. a)** D: all real numbers,
R: $y \geq -5$ **b)** $-2, 8$ **c)** $x \leq -2, x \geq 8$ **d)** symmetric about
$x = 3$ **85. a)** D: all real numbers, R: $y \geq 1$ **b)** no zeros
c) all real numbers **d)** symmetric about $x = -2$
86. a) D: all real numbers, R: $y \leq 0$ **b)** 5 **c)** $x = 5$
d) symmetric about $x = 5$ **87. a)** D: all real numbers,
R: $y \leq 3$ **b)** $-7, -1$ **c)** $-7 \leq x \leq -1$ **d)** symmetric about
$x = -4$ **88. a)** D: all real numbers, R: $y \geq -2$ **b)** -2.5,
-0.5 **c)** $x \leq -2.5, x \geq -0.5$ **d)** symmetric about $x = -1.5$
89. a) D: all real numbers, R: $y \geq -3$ **b)** $0, 2$ **c)** $x \leq 0$,
$x \geq 2$ **d)** symmetric about $x = 1$ **90. a)** D: all real
numbers, R: $y \leq 4$ **b)** $-6, 10$ **c)** $-6 \leq x \leq 10$
d) symmetric about $x = 2$ **91. a)** D: all real numbers,
R: $y \geq 0$ **b)** $-1, 1$ **c)** $x \neq \pm 1$ **d)** symmetric about the
y-axis **92. a)** D: all real numbers, R: $y \leq 0$ **b)** ± 3 **c)** no
values of x **d)** symmetric about the y-axis **93. a)** D: all
real numbers, R: $y \geq -4$ **b)** $\pm 2\sqrt{2}, 0$ **c)** $x < -2\sqrt{2}$,
$x > 2\sqrt{2}$ **d)** symmetric about the y-axis **94. a)** D: all
real numbers, R: $y \geq 0$ **b)** $0, 2$ **c)** $x \neq 0, 2$ **d)** symmetric
about $x = 1$ **95. a)** D: all real numbers, R: $y \leq 0$
b) $-6, 0$ **c)** no values of x **d)** symmetric about $x = -3$
96. a) D: all real numbers, R: $y \geq 0$ **b)** $0, -3$ **c)** $x \neq -3, 0$
d) symmetric about $x = -1.5$ **97. a)** D: all real
numbers, R: $y \geq -7$ **b)** $-4, 4$ **c)** $x < -4, x > 4$
d) symmetric about the y-axis **98. a)** D: all real
numbers, R: $y \geq 0$ **b)** $-3, 4$ **c)** $x \neq -3, 4$ **d)** symmetric
about $x = 0.5$

Applications and Problem Solving **99.** 06:40 to
07:20 **100.** $|x - 9| \leq 1.4$ **101.** $0 \leq d \leq 30$
102. maximum: 152 million km; minimum: 147
million km **103.** water **104.** 8 m **105.** $|s - 7| \leq 5$
106. a) $5 < s < 11$ **b)** The third side must be less than
the sum of the other two sides. **c)** no The solution is
different. **d)** Yes. The solution is the same. **107.** The
inverses are the reflections of the original functions in
the line $y = x$. **108.** They are the same. **109.** $m \geq 0$
110. a) $-5 \leq x \leq 1$ **c)** Answers may vary. **d)** Answers
may vary. Test them. **111. a)** $-2 \leq x \leq 3$ **b)** $-3 \leq x \leq 4$
c) $x \leq -4$ **d)** $x \geq \dfrac{3}{2}$ **e)** $x \leq -\dfrac{1}{2}$ **112. a)** $-3 \leq x \leq 5$
c) Answers may vary. **d)** Answers may vary. Test
them. **113. a)** all real numbers **b)** $x < -1$, $x > 4$
c) $-3 < x < 3$ **d)** $-2 \leq x \leq 0$ **e)** $x \leq -\dfrac{7}{2}$, $x \geq \dfrac{1}{2}$
114. a) The same for $x \geq -2$, reflection in the x-axis
for $x < -2$. **b)** The same for $x \geq \dfrac{1}{2}$, reflection in the
x-axis for $x < \dfrac{1}{2}$. **c)** the same **d)** The same for $x \leq -1$,
$x \geq 1$, reflection in the x-axis for $-1 < x < 1$. **e)** The
same for $f(x) \geq 0$, reflection in the x-axis for $f(x) < 0$.
115. $y = |2x| + 1$ **116. a)** $|x| < 2$ **b)** $|x - 2| \leq 2$
c) $|2x + 1| > 5$ **d)** $|x - 3| \geq 2$ **117.** No solution. A
positive quantity cannot be less than a negative
quantity. **118. a)** $m = \pm 1$ **b)** $m < -1$, $m > 1$
c) $-1 < m < 1$ **119.** Sometimes true; If $f(x) = x^2$, the
statement is true. If $f(x) = x + 2$, the statement is false.
120. a) -1, 5 **b)** -1, 5 **c)** same **d)** Answers may vary.
e) -2, 4 **f)** -5, -1 **g)** -5, -3 **h)** 0, $\dfrac{4}{3}$ **i)** -2, 1 **j)** 0, 3
121. a) $x \leq -3$, $x \geq 3$ **b)** $x \leq -3$, $x \geq 3$ **c)** $-3 < x < 3$
122. a) $|k| < 1$ **b)** $k < -3$ **c)** $k < -4$ **123. c)** the line
segment $y = x + 2$ for $-1 \leq x \leq 2$ **124.** Answers may
vary.

Section 5.6 pp. 308–312
Practice **1.** polynomial **2.** rational **3.** polynomial
4. other **5.** rational **6.** other **7.** rational **8.** other
9. rational **10.** polynomial **11.** rational
12. polynomial **13. a)** $x = 1$, $y = 0$ **b)** D: $x \neq 1$, R: $y \neq 0$
14. a) $x = -1$, $y = 0$ **b)** D: $x \neq -1$, R: $y \neq 0$ **15. a)** $x = 3$,
$y = 0$ **b)** D: $x \neq 3$, R: $y \neq 0$ **16. a)** $x = -4$, $y = 0$
b) D: $x \neq -4$, R: $y \neq 0$ **17. a)** $x = -3$, $y = 0$ **b)** D: $x \neq -3$,
R: $y \neq 0$ **18. a)** $x = 2$, $y = 0$ **b)** D: $x \neq 2$, R: $y \neq 0$
19. a) $x = 5$, $y = 0$ **b)** D: $x \neq 5$, R: $y \neq 0$ **20. a)** $x = 2$,
$y = 0$ **b)** D: $x \neq 2$, R: $y \neq 0$ **21. a)** $x = -2$, $y = 1$
b) D: $x \neq -2$, R: $y \neq 1$ **22. a)** $x = 1$, $y = 1$ **b)** D: $x \neq 1$,
R: $y \neq 1$ **23. a)** $x = -3$, $y = 1$ **b)** D: $x \neq -3$, R: $y \neq 1$
24. a) $x = -1$, $y = 2$ **b)** D: $x \neq -1$, R: $y \neq 2$ **25. a)** $x = 2$,

$y = 3$ **b)** D: $x \neq 2$, R: $y \neq 3$ **26. a)** $x = 2$, $y = -3$
b) D: $x \neq 2$, R: $y \neq -3$ **27.** D: $x \neq -2$, R: $y \neq -4$
28. D: $x \neq 3$, R: $y \neq -6$ **29.** D: $x \neq -1$, R: $y \neq 0$
30. D: $x \neq 2$, R: $y \neq 0$ **31.** D: $x \neq 3$, R: $y \neq 5$
32. D: $x \neq -2$, R: $y \neq -1$ **33. a)** $x = 0$, $y = 1$ **b)** D: $x \neq 0$,
R: $y \neq 1$ **34. a)** $x = 0$, $y = -2$ **b)** D: $x \neq 0$, R: $y \neq -2$
35. a) $x = 1$, $y = 0$ **b)** D: $x \neq 1$, R: $y \neq 0$ **36. a)** $x = 1$,
$y = 0$ **b)** D: $x \neq 1$, R: $y \neq 0$ **37. a)** $x = 1$, $y = 3$
b) D: $x \neq 1$, R: $y \neq 3$ **38. a)** $x = 1$, $y = -1$ **b)** D: $x \neq 1$,
R: $y \neq -1$ **39. a)** $x = -1$, $y = 2$ **b)** D: $x \neq -1$, R: $y \neq 2$
40. a) $x = -2$, $y = 2$ **b)** D: $x \neq -2$, R: $y \neq 2$ **41. a)** $x = \dfrac{3}{2}$,
$y = \dfrac{1}{2}$ **b)** D: $x \neq \dfrac{3}{2}$, R: $y \neq \dfrac{1}{2}$ **42. a)** $x = 2$, $y = -2$
b) D: $x \neq 2$, R: $y \neq -2$ **43. a)** -3 **b)** $x = -3$ **44. a)** 5
b) $x = 5$ **45. a)** ± 2 **b)** $x = \pm 2$ **46. a)** ± 1 **b)** $x = \pm 1$
47. a) 0, -2 **b)** $x = 0$, $x = -2$ **48. a)** -1, 2 **b)** $x = -1$, $x = 2$
49. -3, 2 **50.** -1 **51.** -2, 5 **52.** 0 **53.** no solution **54.** 0
55. ± 2 **56.** 5, 6 **57.** 1 **58.** all real numbers except $n = 1$
59. $\dfrac{-1 \pm \sqrt{17}}{2}$ **60.** $\dfrac{3}{2}$ **61.** $-\dfrac{5}{3}$, 2 **62.** $\dfrac{2}{5}$ **63.** -3, -1
64. -2, $\dfrac{9}{2}$ **65.** -3 **66.** -3 **67.** -1 **68.** no solution **69.** no
solution **70.** all real numbers except $x = -1$, $-\dfrac{1}{2}$
71. -1, 2 **72.** -2.7, 0.7 **73.** -1.5, 9.5 **74.** -4.7, -1.3
75. 0.2, 1.8 **76.** -0.1, 0.8 **77.** $x > 5$, $x < 0$ **78.** $x > 1$,
$x \leq -4$ **79.** $-5 < y < 3$ **80.** $x < 2$, $x \geq 7$ **81.** $x < -3$,
$x > -2$ **82.** $-6 \leq m < -1$ **83.** $x < -1$ **84.** $x > 5$
85. $a < -3$, $1 < a < 5$ **86.** $-2 < x < 1$, $x > 4$
87. $-4 \leq x \leq -2$, $x > 3$ **88.** $-1 < n \leq 6$, $n < -1$
89. $0 < x \leq 2$ **90.** $x < -2$, $-1 < x < 0$ **91.** $\dfrac{1}{2} < k \leq \dfrac{7}{11}$,
$k > 1$ **92.** $-5 \leq x < 1$ **93.** $x > \dfrac{3}{2}$ **94.** $c > 1$, $-4 < c < -3$
95. $w < -1$ **96.** $x \leq -1$, $2 < x \leq 4$
Applications and Problem Solving **97. a)** $x = -3$,
$x = 2$, $y = 0$ **b)** D: $x \neq -3$, 2, R: $y \leq -0.16$ and $y > 0$
98. a) $x = -4$, $x = -2$, $y = 0$ **b)** D: $x \neq -4$, -2, R: $y \neq 0$
99. a) $x = \pm\dfrac{3}{2}$, $y = 0$ **b)** D: $x \neq \pm\dfrac{3}{2}$, R: $y \leq -1$ and $y > 0$
100. a) $x = -4$, $x = 1$, $y = 0$ **b)** D: $x \neq -4$, 1, R: $y \leq \dfrac{-4}{25}$
and $y > 0$ **101. a)** $x = -3$, $y = 0$ **b)** D: $x \neq -3$, R: $y < 0$
102. a) $x = \dfrac{1}{2}$, $x = 3$, $y = 0$ **b)** D: $x \neq \dfrac{1}{2}$, 3, R: $y \leq \dfrac{-8}{25}$ and
$y > 0$ **103.** $-4 \leq x < -1$, $-1 < x < 7$ **104.** $x \leq 3$,
$4 \leq x < 5$, $x > 6$ **105.** $-8 < x < 0$, $1 < x < 4$
106. $x < -4$, $-1 < x < 0$, $x > 2$ **107.** $x < 0$, $x > 1$
108. $x < 0$, $x > 3$ **109.** 14 **110.** $\pm\sqrt{2}$
111. a) Laura: 75 km/h, Mariko: 80 km/h **b)** 08:00

112. Gersh: 6 km/h, Jason: 10 km/h **113.** 125 g
114. 62 km/h **115.** 6.9 km/h **116.** 2 units **117. a)** not

rational **b)** rational **118. a)** $R = \dfrac{R_1 R_2}{R_1 + R_2}$

b) $R_1 = \dfrac{R R_2}{R_2 - R}$ **c)** $R_2 = \dfrac{R R_1}{R_1 - R}$ **d)** 24 Ω **119.** 1, 2

120. Answers may vary. **121. a)** −6, −1 **b)** −3, −2, 1

c) ±1, ±2 **122.** $x = \dfrac{y}{yz - 1}$ **123.** $x = \dfrac{c + d}{2}$; or if $c = d$,

$x < c$ or $x > c$ **124. a)** −1 < x < 3 **b)** Answers may vary.
c) Answers may vary. **d)** Test them. **125. a)** $x < -4$, $x \geq 2$

b) $x < 1$, $2 < x \leq 4$ **c)** $x < -2$, $-1 < x < 2$, $x > 4$ **d)** $x < \dfrac{1}{2}$

e) $x < -1$, $-\dfrac{1}{2} \leq x < 0$, $x \geq 2$ **126. a)** $f = \dfrac{106\ 330}{343 \pm u}$

b) The + sign is used when the sound is moving
toward you, and the − sign is used when the sound is
moving away from you. **c)** 298 Hz; 323 Hz
127. b) $f(x)$ is undefined at $x = -1$ and $x = -2$.

128. $m = 2$, $n = 1$ **129.** Answers may vary. $f(x) = -\dfrac{5x}{x - 2}$

Technology p. 313
1 Exploring Rational Functions **1.** asymptotes:
$x = \pm 2$, $y = 1$; D: $x \neq \pm 2$, R: $y > 1$, $y \leq 0$; zeros: 0,
symmetry: about the y-axis **2.** asymptotes: $x = 0$,
$y = 1$; D: $x \neq 0$, R: $y < 1$; zeros: ±2, symmetry: about
the y-axis **3.** asymptotes: $x = -1$, $y = 1$; D: $x \neq -1$,
R: $y \geq 0$; zeros: 0, symmetry: none **4.** asymptotes:
$y = 1$; D: all real numbers, R: $0 \leq y < 1$; zeros: 0,
symmetry: about the y-axis **5.** asymptotes: $x = 0$,
$y = 1$; D: $x \neq 0$, R: $y > 1$; zeros: none, symmetry: about
the y-axis **6.** asymptotes: $x = \pm 3$, $y = 1$; D: $x \neq \pm 3$,
R: $y > 1$, $y \leq 0$; zeros: 0, symmetry: about the y-axis
7. asymptotes: $x = 0$, $y = 1$; D: $x \neq 0$, R: $y < 1$; zeros:
±1, symmetry: about the y-axis **8.** asymptotes: $x = \pm 1$,
$y = 1$; D: $x \neq \pm 1$, R: $y > 1$, $y \leq -1$; zeros: none,
symmetry: about the y-axis **9.** asymptotes: $y = 1$;
D: all real numbers, R: $-1 \leq y < 1$; zeros: ±1,
symmetry: about the y-axis **10.** asymptotes: $x = 0$,
$y = 1$; D: $x \neq 0$, R: $y \geq 0$; zeros: −2, symmetry: none

11. asymptotes: $x = 1$, $y = 1$; D: $x \neq 1$, R: $y < \dfrac{4}{3}$; zeros:

±2, symmetry: none **12.** asymptotes: $x = 1$, $x = 3$,
$y = 1$; D: $x \neq 1$, 3, R: $y \geq 0$, $y \leq -3$; zeros: 0, symmetry:

none **13.** $y = \dfrac{x^2 - 1}{x^2 - 1}$ has point discontinuities at ±1.

2 Exploring Transformations of Rational Functions
2. It moves up or down the graph. **4. a)** reflection in

the x-axis **b)** reflection in the line $y = 2$ **c)** reflection in
the line $y = -4$

Section 5.7 pp. 323–327
Practice **1.** D: $x \geq -2$, R: $y \geq 0$ **2.** D: $x \leq 3$, R: $y \geq 0$

3. D: $x \geq -\dfrac{1}{2}$, R: $y \geq 0$ **4.** D: $x \leq \dfrac{3}{2}$, R: $y \geq 0$

5. D: $x \geq -8$, R: $y \geq 0$ **6.** D: $x \geq 0$, R: $y \geq 0$ **7.** D: $x \geq 1$,
R: $y \geq 0$ **8.** D: $x \leq -1$, R: $y \geq 0$ **9.** D: $x \geq -3$, R: $y \leq 0$
10. D: $x \leq 2$, R: $y \leq 0$ **11.** D: $x \geq -3$, R: $y \geq 1$
12. D: $x \geq -1$, R: $y \geq -5$ **13.** D: $x \geq 4$, R: $y \geq -2$
14. D: $x \leq 2$, R: $y \geq -3$ **15.** D: $x \geq 0$, R: $y \geq -4$

16. D: $x \geq -\dfrac{5}{2}$, R: $y \geq 2$ **17.** D: $x \leq 1$, R: $y \geq 3$

18. D: $x \geq -2$, R: $y \leq 2$ **19.** D: $x \leq 5$, R: $y \leq 1$

20. D: $x \geq 0$, R: $y \leq -3$ **21.** D: $x \geq \dfrac{1}{2}$, R: $y \leq -1$

22. D: $x \geq 2$, R: $y \leq 5$ **23.** 25 **24.** 4 **25.** −3 **26.** 3
27. −13 **28.** no solution **29.** 4 **30.** 0 **31.** no solution
32. 9 **33.** 6 **34.** no solution **35.** 26 **36.** −1 **37.** no

solution **38.** 2 **39.** 7 **40.** −1 **41.** 2 **42.** $-\dfrac{1}{2}$ **43.** 5 **44.** $\dfrac{3}{2}$

45. 21 **46.** no solution **47.** 8 **48.** no solution
49. 25 **50.** 3 **51.** 2 **52.** 12 **53.** 1 **54.** 5 **55.** −2 **56.** 1
57. no solution **58.** 9, 21 **59.** 2 **60.** 2.4 **61.** −1.3
62. −0.5 **63.** 4.6 **64.** 3.6 **65.** −5.5 **66.** 0.9 **67.** 9.8

68. $-1 \leq x < 8$ **69.** $x \leq -2$ **70.** $-\dfrac{5}{2} \leq x \leq 2$ **71.** $x \leq \dfrac{4}{3}$

72. $0 \leq x \leq 3.5$ **73.** $1 < x \leq 4$ **74.** $3 \leq n \leq 9$ **75.** $t \geq 2$
76. no solution **77.** $0 \leq x \leq 2$ **78.** $x \leq 1$ **79.** $x > 5$

80. $x < -1$ **81.** $d \leq 3$ **82.** $\dfrac{1}{2} \leq x < 5$ **83.** $x \geq \dfrac{1}{2}$

84. $1 < x \leq 5$ **85.** $0 \leq c < 4$ **86.** $x \geq 5$ **87.** $1 \leq u < 5$
88. $0 \leq x \leq 1$ **89.** $0 < y < 9$ **90.** $0 \leq x \leq 1$ **91.** $0 \leq x < 2$,
$x > 4$ **92.** $0 \leq n < 3$, $x \geq 4$ **93.** $0 < x < 2$ **94.** $0 \leq x < 2$
95. $x > -2$ **96.** no solution **97.** $m > -1$ **98.** $-3 < x < -2$
99. $-2 < x \leq -1$ **100.** $t > 2$ **101.** $x \geq 3$
Applications and Problem Solving **102. a)** rational
b) rational **c)** radical **d)** rational **e)** radical **f)** rational
103. a) $-2 \leq x < 2.9$ **b)** $x < -6.8$ **c)** $x \geq 4.2$ **d)** $x \geq 16.8$
104. a) D: $x \leq -2$, $x \geq 2$, R: $y \geq 0$ **b)** D: $x \leq -2$, $x \geq 2$,
R: $y \leq 0$ **c)** D: $-3 \leq x \leq 3$, R: $0 \leq y \leq 3$ **d)** D: $-3 \leq x \leq 3$,
R: $-3 \leq y \leq 0$ **105. a)** 9 **b)** 6 **c)** 3 **106.** They are
reflections of each other in the x-axis. **107. a)** 3.7 cm
b) 137 cm^2 **108. a)** $y = x^2$, $x \geq 0$; function **b)** $y = x^2 - 2$,
$x \geq 0$; function **c)** $y = (x - 2)^2 + 1$, $x \geq 2$; function
109. a) 0 **b)** 2 **c)** 0, 2 **110.** C(7, 13), D(1, 13) or
C(7, −11), D(1, −11) **111.** C(2, 11) or C(2, −5)
112. a) 12 **b)** 45 **113.** P(12, 0) or P(−12, 0) **114.** P(0, 8)
or P(0, −8) **115. a)** 5 to the left, 5 to the right **b)** 3 up,
3 down **c)** 5 left, 3 up and 5 left, 3 down **d)** 5 right,
3 up and 5 right, 3 down **116.** The transformations

have the same effect. **117.** $\dfrac{19}{6}$ **118.** 147 **119. a)** 1 s

b) 4 m **120.** $\sqrt{n-4} \geq 5, n \geq 29$ **121. a)** $A = \dfrac{\sqrt{3}}{4}s^2$

b) $s = \dfrac{2\sqrt{A}}{\sqrt{\sqrt{3}}}$ **c)** 24 cm **122.** $\sqrt{n+2} \leq 10,$

$-2 \leq n \leq 98$ **123.** $a = b$ or $a = -b$ **124.** Squaring both sides of the equation or inequality can introduce extraneous solutions. **125. a)** $d = \sqrt{L^2 - 40\,000}$

b) $L > 200$ **d)** 150 m; the observer is 150 m horizontally from the balloon. **126. b)** Answers may vary. $d \geq 5$ **c)** 59 m **127. b)** 1280 km/h **c)** 5°C **128. b)** Answers may vary. $0 \leq a \leq 20, 0 \leq d \leq 450$ **c)** 316 km **d)** Answers may vary. **129.** 78 m **130. a)** 3 **b)** 16 **131. a)** $1 \leq x < 5$ **c)** Answers may vary. **d)** Answers may vary. Test them. **132. a)** $x \geq -1$ **b)** $3 \leq x \leq 7$

c) $-1 \leq x < 2$ **d)** $x \leq -3$ **e)** $-\dfrac{5}{4} < x < 5$ **f)** $x \geq 1$ **g)** $0 \leq x < 1$

h) $x \geq -4$ **i)** $-2 < x < 2, x > 3$ **133. a)** $b = \sqrt{w^2 - 2wh}$

b) $A = \dfrac{h}{2}\sqrt{w^2 - 2wh}$ **c)** $A = \dfrac{h}{2}\sqrt{100 - 20h}$ **e)** $0 < h < 5,$

$0 < A < 9.6$ **f)** 3.3 cm **g)** 9.6 cm^2 **134. a)** $\sqrt{x-2} < 3$

b) $\sqrt{2-x} < 3$ **135.** $-2 \leq x < 1, x > 1$ **136.** 0.25 **137.** 10 **138. a)** Let $y = \sqrt{x}$. Rewrite the expression as $y^2 + 2y + 1$ and factor: $(y + 1)^2$. Substitute $y = \sqrt{x}$: $(\sqrt{x} + 1)^2$. **b)** 1 **c)** 4, 9 **d)** 16 **e)** no solution **139.** Answers may vary. **140. a)** 5 **b)** 0 **c)** $x > 1$ **d)** $x \geq -10$ **141. a)** Answers may vary. **b)** 2 **c)** 3 **d)** 3

Connecting Math and Astronomy pp. 328–329
1 The Earth and the Moon 1. 9.8 N **2.** $W = 9.8m$
3. 588 N **4.** 1.6 N **5.** $W = 1.6m$ **6.** 96 N **7.** 5.1 m
8. a) 11 200 m/s **b)** 40 300 km/h **9. a)** 2400 m/s
b) 8500 km/h **10.** It would increase. **11.** 6370 km
2 Planets and the Sun 1. Mars: 3.7 N, Jupiter:
24.5 N, Saturn: 10.4 N, Pluto: 0.6 N, Sun: 274.1 N
2. a) 0.4 m **b)** 17.4 m **3.** no **4. a)** 5000 m/s

b) 35 500 m/s **5. a)** $\sqrt{\dfrac{Gm_1m_2}{F}}$ **b)** 24 800 km

6. a) $m_1 = \dfrac{Fd^2}{Gm_2}$ **b)** 3.3×10^{23} kg **7.** 3.4×10^{17} N

Review pp. 330–331
1. a) $(f + g)(x) = x + 8$ **b)** $(f - g)(x) = 3x + 2$

c) $(fg)(x) = -2x^2 + x + 15$ **d)** $\left(\dfrac{f}{g}\right)(x) = \dfrac{2x + 5}{3 - x}, x \neq 3$

2. a) $(f + g)(x) = 9x^2 + 3x - 2$ **b)** $(f - g)(x) = 9x^2 - 3x$

c) $(fg)(x) = 27x^3 - 9x^2 - 3x + 1$ **d)** $\left(\dfrac{f}{g}\right)(x) = 3x + 1,$

$x \neq \dfrac{1}{3}$ **3. a)** $(f + g)(x) = \dfrac{x^2 + 3x - 6}{x(x - 2)}$

b) $(f - g)(x) = \dfrac{x^2 - 3x + 6}{x(x - 2)}$ **c)** $(fg)(x) = \dfrac{3}{x - 2}$

d) $\left(\dfrac{f}{g}\right)(x) = \dfrac{x^2}{3(x - 2)}, x \neq 0, 2$

4. a) $(f + g)(x) = 3 - \sqrt{x}, x \geq 0$
b) $(f - g)(x) = -1 - 3\sqrt{x}, x \geq 0$
c) $(fg)(x) = -2x - 3\sqrt{x} + 2, x \geq 0$

d) $\left(\dfrac{f}{g}\right)(x) = \dfrac{1 - 2\sqrt{x}}{\sqrt{x} + 2}, x \geq 0$ **5. a)** 4 **b)** 9 **c)** -2 **d)** 0

6. a) 0 **b)** -5 **c)** 36 **d)** 6 **8. a)** $x^2 - 6x + 8$
b) $18 - 24x + 8x^2$ **c)** $2x^3 - x^2 - 2x + 1$ **9.** $\{(-2, 0),$
$(-4, -1), (6, 4), (8, 5)\}$ **10.** does not exist **11.** does not
exist **12.** does not exist **13.** 36 **14.** -4 **15.** 0 **16.** 16
17. $(f \circ g)(x) = 5 - 2x^2$ **18.** $(g \circ f)(x) = -4x^2 + 4x + 2$
19. $(f \circ f)(x) = 4x - 3$ **20.** $(g \circ g)(x) = -x^4 + 6x^2 - 6$
21. a) $(f \circ g)(x) = \sqrt{3x + 2}$ **b)** $(g \circ f)(x) = 3\sqrt{x + 2}$
c) f: D: $x \geq -2$, R: $y \geq 0$, g: D: all real numbers, R: all

real numbers, $f \circ g$: D: $x \geq -\dfrac{2}{3}$, R: $y \geq 0$, $g \circ f$:

D: $x \geq -2$, R: $y \geq 0$ **22. a)** $(f \circ g)(x) = 3|x| + 1$

b) $(g \circ f)(x) = |3x + 1|$ **c)** f: D: all real numbers, R: all
real numbers, g: D: all real numbers, R: $y \geq 0$, $f \circ g$:
D: all real numbers, R: $y \geq 1$, $g \circ f$: D: all real

numbers, R: $y \geq 0$ **23.** $(h \circ k)(x) = \dfrac{1}{1 - x^2}, x \neq 0, \pm 1;$

$(k \circ h)(x) = \left(\dfrac{x - 1}{x}\right)^2, x \neq 0, 1$ **24. b)** yes

25. $f^{-1}(x) = \dfrac{x - 2}{4}$ **26.** $f^{-1}(x) = \pm\sqrt{x + 5}$

27. $k^{-1}(x) = \pm\sqrt{x} - 7$ **28.** $g^{-1}(x) = 3 - \dfrac{2}{x}$ **29.** yes **30.** no

31. a) $f^{-1}(x) = \sqrt{3 - x}$ **c)** $x \geq 0$ **e)** f: D: all real
numbers, R: $y \leq 3$, f^{-1}: D: $x \leq 3$, R: $y \geq 0$ **32.** no
33. no **34.** no **35.** Yes, 3. **36. a)** D: all real numbers,
R: $y \geq -16$ **b)** zeros: $\pm 1, \pm 3$, y-intercept: 9
c) minimums: $(-2.2, -16), (2.2, -16)$, maximum: $(0, 9)$
d) $f(x) > 0$: $x < -3, -1 < x < 1, x > 3$;
$f(x) < 0$: $-3 < x < -1, 1 < x < 3$ **e)** symmetric about the

y-axis; positive, positive **37. a)** D: all real numbers, R: all real numbers **b)** zeros: $-1.1, -1, 0.8$, y-intercept: -2 **c)** maximum: $(-1.1, 0.0)$, maximum: $(0, -2)$ **d)** $f(x) > 0$: $-1.1 < x < -1, x > 0.8$; $f(x) < 0$: $x < -1.1$, $-1 < x < 0.8$ **e)** no symmetry; negative, positive **38. a)** D: all real numbers, R: $y \geq -1$ **b)** zeros: $0, \pm 1, 2$; y-intercept: 0 **c)** minimums: $(-0.6, -1), (1.6, -1)$, maximum: $(0.5, 0.6)$ **d)** $f(x) > 0$: $x < -1, 0 < x < 1$, $x > 2$; $f(x) < 0$: $-1 < x < 0, 1 < x < 2$ **e)** symmetric about $x = 0.5$; positive, positive **39. a)** D: all real numbers, R: all real numbers **b)** zeros: $-1, 1.6, -0.6$, y-intercept: 1 **c)** minimum: $(-0.8, -0.1)$, maximum: $(0.8, 2.1)$ **d)** $f(x) > 0$: $x < -1, -0.6 < x < 1.6$; $f(x) < 0$: $-1 < x < -0.6, x > 1.6$ **e)** no symmetry; positive, negative **40.** $x < -3, x > 0$ **41.** $x < -1$ **42.** -3, 11 **43.** 1 **44.** $\frac{2}{3}, 6$ **45.** $5, -3$ **46.** $x < -4, x > 10$

47. $q \leq -\frac{10}{3}, q \geq 2$ **48.** $x > \frac{3}{2}$ **49.** $-2 \leq d \leq 2$ **50. a)** D: all real numbers, R: $y \geq -2$ **b)** 1, 5 **c)** $x \leq 1$, $x \geq 5$ **d)** symmetric about $x = 3$ **51. a)** D: all real numbers, R: $y \leq 5$ **b)** $-6, 4$ **c)** $-6 \leq x \leq 4$ **d)** symmetric about $x = -1$ **52. a)** D: all real numbers, R: $y \geq -3$ **b)** ± 2 **c)** $x \leq -2, x \geq 2$ **d)** symmetric about y-axis **53. a)** D: all real numbers, R: $y \geq -2$ **b)** $\pm \sqrt{2}, \pm \sqrt{6}$ **c)** $x \leq -\sqrt{6}, -\sqrt{2} \leq x \leq \sqrt{2}, x \geq \sqrt{6}$ **d)** symmetric about the y-axis **54. a)** $x = 3, y = 0$ **b)** D: $x \neq 3$, R: $y \neq 0$ **55. a)** $x = -4, y = 1$ **b)** D: $x \neq -4$, R: $y \neq 1$ **56. a)** none **b)** D: $m \neq 3$, R: $y \neq 6$ **57. a)** none **b)** D: $p \neq -2$, R: $y \neq -6$ **58.** $x = -1, y = 2$, D: $x \neq -1$, R: $y \neq 2$ **59. a)** 0, 4 **b)** $x = 0, x = 4$ **60.** 3 **61.** 0, 7 **62.** $n < -3, n \geq 8$ **63.** $-4 < x < 3, x > 24$ **64.** D: $x \geq -2$, R: $y \geq 4$ **65.** D: $x \geq 1$, R: $y \leq 3$ **66.** 15 **67.** -2 **68.** 2 **69.** $-\frac{3}{4}$

70. $d > 2$ **71.** $-1 \leq n \leq 1$ **72.** $x \geq 8$ **73.** $w > -2$ **Exploring Math** **1. b)** Answers may vary. **2.** Answers may vary.

Chapter Check p. 332
1. a) $(f + g)(x) = 3x + 1$ **b)** $(f - g)(x) = 5x - 3$ **c)** $(fg)(x) = -4x^2 + 9x - 2$ **d)** $\left(\frac{f}{g}\right)(x) = \frac{4x - 1}{2 - x}, x \neq 2$
2. a) $(f + g)(x) = x^2 + 9x + 20$ **b)** $(f - g)(x) = x^2 + 7x + 10$ **c)** $(fg)(x) = x^3 + 13x^2 + 55x + 75$ **d)** $\left(\frac{f}{g}\right)(x) = x + 3$, $x \neq -5$ **3. a)** $(f + g)(x) = \frac{x^2 + 4x - 2}{(x + 2)(x - 1)}, x \neq -2, 1$
b) $(f - g)(x) = \frac{-2 - x^2}{(x + 2)(x - 1)}, x \neq -2, 1$

c) $(fg)(x) = \frac{2x}{(x + 2)(x - 1)}, x \neq -2, 1$
d) $\left(\frac{f}{g}\right)(x) = \frac{2(x - 1)}{x(x + 2)}$ **4. a)** $(f + g)(x) = 4\sqrt{x} + 2, x \geq 0$
b) $(f - g)(x) = -2\sqrt{x} + 4, x \geq 0$
c) $(fg)(x) = 3x + 8\sqrt{x} - 3, x \geq 0$
d) $\left(\frac{f}{g}\right)(x) = \frac{3x + 10\sqrt{x} + 3}{9x - 1}, x \geq 0, x \neq \frac{1}{9}$ **5. a)** -5 **b)** 1
c) 30 **d)** $-\frac{3}{4}$ **6. a)** -8 **b)** 7 **c)** -36 **d)** -4 **7.** $65 - 2x^2 - 3x$
8. $\frac{5 - x}{x + 5}, x \neq \pm 5$ **9.** 1 **10.** -16 **11.** 225
12. $(h \circ k)(x) = 3 - x^2$ **13.** $(k \circ h)(x) = x^2 - 10x + 27$
14. $(h \circ h)(x) = x$ **15.** $(k \circ k)(x) = x^4 + 4x^2 + 6$
16. a) $(f \circ g)(x) = \sqrt{3x} - 2$ **b)** $(g \circ f)(x) = \sqrt{3(x - 2)}$
c) f: D: all real numbers, R: all real numbers; g: D: $x \geq 0$, R: $y \geq 0$; $f \circ g$: D: $x \geq 0$, R: $y \geq -2$; $g \circ f$: D: $x \geq 2$, R: $y \geq 0$ **17. a)** $(f \circ g)(x) = |\sqrt{x} - 1|$
b) $(g \circ f)(x) = \sqrt{|x - 1|}$ **c)** f: D: all real numbers, R: $y \geq 0$; g: D: $x \geq 0$, R: $y \geq 0$; $f \circ g$: D: $x \geq 0$, R: $y \geq 0$; $g \circ f$: D: all real numbers, R: $y \geq 0$
18. $(f \circ g)(x) = \frac{1}{x + 3}, x \neq -3$; $(g \circ f)(x) = \frac{1}{x} + 3$,
$x \neq 0$ **19. a)** $f^{-1}(x) = x - \frac{2}{5}$ **b)** yes

20. a) $h^{-1}(x) = \pm \frac{\sqrt{3(x + 2)}}{3}$ **b)** no **21.** no **22.** yes

23. a) D: all real numbers, R: all real numbers
b) zeros: $-1, \frac{1}{2}, 3$, y-intercept: 3 **c)** maximum:
$(-0.3, 3.7)$, minimum: $(2, -9)$ **d)** $f(x) > 0$: $-1 < x < \frac{1}{2}$,
$x > 3$; $f(x) < 0$: $x < -1, \frac{1}{2} < x < 3$ **e)** no symmetry;
negative, positive **24. a)** D: all real numbers, R: $y \geq 0$
b) zeros: ± 2, y-intercept: 16 **c)** minimums: $(-2, 0)$,
$(2, 0)$, maximum: $(0, 16)$ **d)** $f(x) > 0$: all real numbers except $x = \pm 2$; $f(x) < 0$: no values of x **e)** symmetric about the y-axis; positive, positive **25.** $-3 \leq x \leq -\frac{3}{2}$,
$0 \leq x \leq 1$ **26.** $x < -\sqrt{3}, 0 < x < \sqrt{3}$ **27. a)** D: all real numbers, R: $y \leq 3$ **b)** 1, 7 **c)** $1 \leq x \leq 7$ **d)** symmetric about $x = 4$ **28. a)** D: all real numbers, R: $y \geq -2$
b) $\pm \sqrt{7}, \pm \sqrt{11}$ **c)** $x \leq -\sqrt{11}, -\sqrt{7} \leq x \leq \sqrt{7}, x \geq \sqrt{11}$
d) symmetric about the y-axis **29. a)** $x = 2, y = 0$
b) D: $x \neq 2$, R: $y \neq 0$ **30. a)** none **b)** D: $x \neq 1$, R: $y \neq 7$

31. a) -3 **b)** $x = -3$ **32.** 9 **33.** 1 **34.** $-\dfrac{5}{2}, \dfrac{1}{4}$ **35.** $-5, 2$
36. 4 **37.** ± 1 **38.** 7 **39.** 4 **40.** 0 **41.** 1 **42.** $b < -2, b > 8$
43. $-1 < g < 5$ **44.** $x \geq 1$ **45.** $-6 \leq e \leq -1$ **46.** $-3 \leq v < 3$
47. $-3 < b < 0, b > 2$ **48.** $q > 5$ **49.** $x \geq 1$

Using the Strategies p. 333
1. Cut 4 rods into lengths of 5, 5, 3. Cut 5 rods into lengths of 4, 4, 5. Cut 3 rods into lengths of 3, 3, 3, 4.
2. Beth had juice, lamb, and cheesecake. Barbara had salmon. **3.** $S = 4, R = -2$ or 6, $T = -6$ or 2 **4. a)** 37
b) Answers may vary. **c)** Yes. Answers may vary.
5. 24 km **6.** 7 **7.** Use the initial 4 tires for 12 000 km each, label the remaining 5 tires with the letters A, B, C, D, and E. Rotate the tires as follows, using each group for 3000 km: A, B, C, D; B, C, D, E; C, D, E, A; D, E, A, B; E, A, B, C **8.** 7 **9.** no **10.** 12
Data Bank **1.** Winnipeg to Regina: 95 km/h; Regina to Saskatoon: 65 km/h

Chapter 6

Reasoning p. 335
1. a) 06:30 to 20:00 **b)** 19:00 to 05:00 and 14:00 to 14:30 **c)** 20:00 to 22:00, 22:30 to 02:00, 02:30 to 05:00, 06:00 to 07:00 **2.** 22:00 to 22:30, 02:00 to 02:30, 05:00 to 06:00 **3. a)** 06:30 to 09:30, 12:00 to 13:00, 16:30 to 19:00 **b)** 23:00 to 05:00 **4.** Selina interpreted *or* as either, or both. Victor interpreted *or* as either, but not both.

Getting Started pp. 336–337
1 Patterns and Observations **1.** 20th **2.** $n + y + 1$
3. a) $n - x + 1$ **b)** $n - x + 1 + y$ **c)** $n + y + 1$
2 Using Logical Reasoning **1.** Mike and Tia; Carl and Amy; Hari and Sarah **2. a)** 1, 2, 3 **b)** 2, 5, 4
c) Mike and Tia; Carl and Amy; Hari and Sarah
3 A Logic Challenge Carys and Dianne are swimming. Andrew, Barb, and Erik are not swimming.
Mental Math
Complementary and Supplementary Angles **1.** $30°$
2. $70°$ **3.** $45°$ **4.** $75°$ **5.** $50°$ **6.** $18°$ **7.** $39°$ **8.** $7°$ **9.** $66°$
10. $86°$ **11.** $57°$ **12.** $22°$ **13.** $70°$ **14.** $130°$ **15.** $135°$
16. $140°$ **17.** $65°$ **18.** $105°$ **19.** $75°$ **20.** $85°$ **21.** $117°$
22. $68°$ **23.** $162°$ **24.** $121°$
Adding a Column of Numbers **1.** 150 **2.** 221 **3.** 299
4. 422 **5.** 440 **6.** 23.7 **7.** 31.3 **8.** 2390 **9.** 3010 **10.** 2255

Section 6.1 pp. 340–342
Practice **1.** The square of a number composed of n 1s consists of the digits 1 to n and $n - 1$ to 1 in order. $11\ 111^2 = 123\ 454\ 321$; $111\ 111^2 = 12\ 345\ 654\ 321$

2. The sum of the first n odd numbers is equal to n^2. $1 + 3 + 5 + 7 + 9 = 25$; $1 + 3 + 5 + 7 + 9 + 11 = 36$
3. The difference between the squares of the $(n + 1)$th and nth odd numbers is equal to $8n$. $11^2 - 9^2 = 40$; $13^2 - 11^2 = 48$ **4.** The last digit of the product of 11 and a two-digit number is the second digit of the two-digit number. The first digits are the sum of the two-digit number and the first digit of the two-digit number. $13 \times 11 = 143$; $99 \times 11 = 1089$ **5.** The sum of a two-digit number and the number consisting of the reverse of the digits of the two-digit number is 11 times the sum of the digits. $34 + 43 = 77$; $56 + 65 = 121$ **6.** The product of a number consisting of n 2s and 9 consists of 1, $(n - 1)$ 9s, and 8. $22\ 222 \times 9 = 199\ 998$; $222\ 222 \times 9 = 1\ 999\ 998$
7. The measures of opposite angles of intersecting lines are equal. **8. a)** In a triangle, the longest side is opposite the largest angle. **b)** In a triangle, the shortest side is opposite the smallest angle.
9. The line segment joining the midpoints of two sides of a triangle is parallel to the third side, and one half the length of the third side. **10. a)** The sum of the numbers in the nth row is $(n - 1)^3 + n^3$.
b) $26 + 27 + 28 + 29 + 30 + 31 + 32 + 33 + 34 + 35 + 36 = 341 = 5^3 + 6^3$
Applications and Problem Solving **11.** The sums of the two pairs of numbers at opposite corners of a rectangular array on a calendar page are equal. **12.** A figure with a diagonal made from n cross-stitches has $2n - 1$ cross-stitches.
13. a) 768, 3072 **b)** 45, 52 **c)** 256, 8192 **d)** U, B
e) N, O **14.** $98 = 79 + 19$ **15. a)** 6 **b)** $\dfrac{n(n-1)}{2}$ line
segments are required to join every pair of points when there are n points in a plane. **16. b)** There are $2n + 2$ hydrogen atoms for n carbon atoms in a straight-chain alkane. **17.** For a pendulum length of l centimetres, the period is $\dfrac{\sqrt{l}}{5}$ seconds **18. a)** 7
b) The maximum number of pieces for k cuts is $\dfrac{k(k+1)}{2} + 1$. **19.** 7, 8, 40; The numbers are arranged first according to the number of letters in the name of the number, and then in numerical order.
20. a) 1, 1, 2, 3, 5, 8, 13, 21, 34, 55, 89, 144 **b)** 4, 12, 33, 88 **c)** $t_2 + t_4 + t_6 + \ldots + t_{2k} = t_{2k+1} - 1$
21. a) $\angle 3$ is equal to $\angle 7$; $\angle 2$ and $\angle 6$, $\angle 1$ and $\angle 5$, $\angle 4$ and $\angle 8$; yes **b)** The sum of $\angle 3$ and $\angle 6$ is $180°$; $\angle 4$ and $\angle 5$; yes **22. a)** $x \triangle y$ means multiply the first number by one more than the second number.

Section 6.2 pp. 345–346
Practice 1. 8, 16; 12 **2.** 25 + 49 = 74, 9 + 1 = 10; 9 + 16 = 25 **3.** 4 − 1 = 3, 9 − 4 = 5; 25 − 16 = 9
4. $\sqrt{9} = 3$, $\sqrt{16} = 4$; $\sqrt{0.01} = 0.1$ **5.** $52 = 4^2 + 6^2$, $100 = 6^2 + 8^2$; $74 = 5^2 + 7^2$ **6.** $\sqrt{5^2} = 5$, $\sqrt{6^2} = 6$; $\sqrt{(-5)^2} = 5$ **7.** (2, 5), (3, 6); (2, −1)
Applications and Problem Solving 13. Prince Edward Island **14. a)** penguins **b)** Manx cats
15. a) $a = 1, b = 2, c = 3, d = 4$; $a = 5, b = 6, c = 7, d = 8$; $a = -5, b = 5, c = -7, d = 7$ **b)** positive real numbers
16. b) equilateral **17. b)** $A_1 = \dfrac{\pi d^2}{4}$; $A_2 = \pi d^2$
18. a) 1 + 2 = 3, 1 + 2 + 4 = 7; 1 + 2 + 4 + 8 = 15 **b)** $2^2 - 1 = 3$, $2^3 - 1 = 7$; $2^1 - 1 = 1$ **c)** $1^2 - 1 + 41 = 41$; $2^2 - 2 + 41 = 43$; $41^2 - 41 + 41 = 41^2$ **19.** equilateral triangle; quadrilateral with 3 equal angles and one not equal **20. a)** 2 + 7 = 9 but 7 − 2 = 5, 7 − 3 = 4 but 7 + 3 = 10; 2 + 2 = 4, 2 − 2 = 0 **b)** This is the only counterexample. **21. a)** $0 < y \leq 1.4$ **b)** $x = -1$ gives $y = -1$ **c)** Answers may vary.

Section 6.3 p. 349
Practice 1. Paulette lives in Alberta. **2.** All dogs have hearts. **3.** Stella is taller than Annisa. **4.** The sum of 11 and 12 is an odd number. **5.** The diagonals of PQRS bisect each other. **6.** The diagonals of KLMN intersect at right angles. **7.** △ABC has two equal angles. **8. a)** The final number is the original number.
Applications and Problem Solving 12. Their heights are also different. **13.** PQRS is a kite.

Section 6.4 pp. 354–356
Practice 1. statement **2.** not a statement **3.** statement **4.** not a statement **5.** statement **6.** 1, 2, 3, 6 **7.** 0, 2, 4, 6, 8 **8.** 1, 3 **9.** 0, 1, 4, 9, 16, 25, 36, 49 **10.** 2, 3, 5, 7, 11, 13, 17, 19 **11.** 1, 2, 3, 4, 6, 8, 9, 12, 18, 24 **12.** 0, 1, 2, 3, 4, 5, 6, 7, 8, 9, 12 **13.** 1, 2, 3, 6 **14.** 0, 1, 3, 5, 15 **15.** 1, 2, 3, 5, 6, 7, 9, 11, 18 **32.** $n \leq 1$ and $n \geq -4$ **33.** $n < 2$ and $n \geq -1$ **34.** $n < 3$ and $n > -1$ **35.** $n \leq 4$ and $n > -4$ **36.** $n < -2$ or $n \geq 2$ **37.** Answers may vary. $n > -4$ or $n > 2$ **38.** $n < 0$ or $n > 0$ **39.** $n \leq -1$ or $n \geq 1$ **40.** Paulo does not live in Edmonton. **41.** The number 3 is not the smallest prime number. **42.** Not all isosceles triangles have 3 acute angles. **43.** Ben is not older than Katerina. **44.** Deepak is not telling the truth. **45.** The Canucks did not win their game last night. **47.** 3, 5, 7, 11, 13, 17, 19 **48.** 2, 3, 4, 5, 6, 7, 8, 10, 11, 12, 13, 14, 16, 17, 18, 19 **49.** 1, 9, 15 **50.** There are no numbers that are even, odd, and prime. **51. b)** 6
Applications and Problem Solving 53. $n < 4$ **55.** $x \geq -1$ and $x < 4$ **56. a)** 151 **b)** 65 **c)** 63 **d)** 13 **57. b)** 109 **c)** 2 **58. b)** 218 **59.** Answers may vary. $x \geq 0$ or $x < 0$ **60.** $x \leq 5$ and $x \geq 5$ **61.** $x^2 < 0$ or $-x^2 > 0$ **62. a)** $x^2 \geq 0$ and $|x| \geq 0$ **b)** $x < 0$ and $x > 0$ **63. b)** 6 **c)** 43

Technology p. 357
1 Comparing Searches 1. G or H; I **2.** Logically, the searches have the same meaning. **3.** D **4.** AND and OR are associative.
2 Making Up Searches 1. mathematics AND NOT magic OR mathematics AND NOT cards

Section 6.5 pp. 361–362
Practice 1. If angles are opposite, then they are equal. **2.** If you are a Canadian at least 18 years old, then you may vote. **3.** If a figure is a quadrilateral, then it is a polygon. **4.** If a prime number is greater than 2, then it is odd. **5.** If an angle measures 90°, then its sine is 1. **6.** If a figure is a rectangle, then its diagonals bisect each other. **7.** If a person lives in Moose Jaw, then the person lives in Saskatchewan. **8.** If a triangle is a right triangle, then it has two acute angles. **9.** A polygon is a pentagon if and only if it has exactly five sides. **10.** A number is rational if and only if it can be expressed as a quotient of two integers. **11.** A number is prime if and only if it has no factors other than itself and one. **12.** A triangle is isosceles if and only if it has two sides of equal length. **13.** A trinomial is a perfect square trinomial if and only if it can be factored as the square of a binomial. **14.** If $x^2 = 36$, then $x = 6$; false, $x = -6$ **15.** If $|x| = 4$, then $x = -4$; false, $x = 4$ **16.** If $n + 1$ is an odd number, then n is an even number; true **17.** If a rectangle is a square, then it has 4 equal sides; true **18.** If a triangle is equilateral, then it has three equal sides; true **19.** If a quadrilateral is a trapezoid, then it has one pair of opposite sides that are parallel; true **20.** If the slope of a line is 3, then the equation of the line is $y = 3x + 1$; false, $y = 3x + 2$ **21.** true; If $x^2 = 16$, then $x = -4$, false; If $x^2 \neq 16$, then $x \neq -4$, true **22.** true; If $|x| = 3$, then $x = 3$, false; If $|x| \neq 3$, then $x \neq 3$, true **23.** true; If $2n + 1$ is odd, then n is even, false; If $2n + 1$ is even, then n is odd, false **24.** true; If n is a multiple of 3, then n is a multiple of 6, false; If n is not a multiple of 3, then n is not a multiple of 6, true **25.** true; If x is an odd number, then x^2 is an odd number, true; If x is an even number, then x^2 is an even number, true **26.** true; If the diagonals of a quadrilateral are equal, it is a rectangle, false; If the diagonals of a quadrilateral are not equal, it is not a rectangle, true **27.** true; If $x = 7$, then $3x - 5 = 16$, true; If $x \neq 7$, then $3x - 5 \neq 16$, true

Applications and Problem Solving 28. a) yes
b) If $x^2 > 0$, then $x < 0$; false **c)** If $x^2 \leq 0$, then $x \leq 0$;
true (for $x = 0$) **29. a)** no **b)** If $a = b$, then $a^2 = b^2$; true
c) If $a \neq b$, then $a^2 \neq b^2$; false **30. a)** yes **b)** If the
midpoint of AB is M(5, 10), then the endpoints of AB
are A(3, 8) and B(7, 12); false; A(5, 5) and B(5, 15)
have a midpoint of M(5, 10). **31. a)** that if you have
good taste, you will eat at their restaurant **b)** People
with good taste eat at other restaurants. **32. a)** If p is a
factor of c, then $x - p$ is a factor of $x^2 + bx + c$; $x - 3$ is
not a factor of $x^2 + 6x + 9$, but 3 is a factor of 9
b) If p is not a factor of c, then $x - p$ is not a factor of
$x^2 + bx + c$. **33.** Answers may vary. **34.** The
contrapositive must be true.

Technology p. 363
1 Testing If ... then Statements 1. false **2.** true
3. true **4.** false **5.** false **6.** false **7.** true **8.** true **9.** true
10. true **11.** true **12.** false
2 Solving Inequalities 1. If $12 - 3x \geq 23 - 14x$,
then $x \geq 1$. **2.** If $4x - 13 \leq -3x + 8$, then $x \leq 3$.
3. If $x^2 < x - 20$, then x is not a real number.
4. If $x^2 > -3x + 18$, then $x < -6$ or $x > 3$.
5. If $\dfrac{8}{x-3} > 4$, then $x > 3$ and $x < 5$. **6.** If $\dfrac{5}{x+4} \leq 2$,
then $x < -4$ or $x \geq -\dfrac{3}{2}$.

Investigating Math pp. 364–365
1 Congruent Triangles 1. a) AB = PQ, BC = QR,
$\angle$ABC = $\angle$PQR **b)** SAS **c)** AC = PR, $\angle$BAC = $\angle$QPR,
$\angle$BCA = $\angle$QRP **2. a)** $\angle$EDF = $\angle$KJL, DF = JL,
$\angle$DFE = $\angle$JLK **b)** ASA **c)** $\angle$DEF = $\angle$JKL, DE = JK,
EF = KL **3. a)** ZX = TR, $\angle$ZXY = $\angle$TRS, XY = RS
b) SAS **c)** $\angle$XYZ = $\angle$RST, YZ = ST, $\angle$YZX = $\angle$STR
4. a) PQ = UW, QR = WV, RP = VU **b)** SSS
c) $\angle$PQR = $\angle$UWV, $\angle$QRP = $\angle$WVU,
$\angle$RAQ = $\angle$VUW
2 Triangles With Common Points and Sides
1. a) AB = CD, BC = DA, AC = CA **b)** SSS
c) $\angle$ABC = $\angle$CDA, $\angle$BCA = $\angle$DAC, $\angle$CAB = $\angle$ACD
2. a) PR = TR, $\angle$PRQ = $\angle$TRS, RQ = RS **b)** SAS
c) $\angle$RQP = $\angle$RST, QP = ST, $\angle$QPR = $\angle$STR
3. a) WZ = YZ, $\angle$WZX = $\angle$YZX, ZX = ZX **b)** SAS
c) $\angle$ZXW = $\angle$ZXY, XW = XY, $\angle$XWZ = $\angle$XYZ
4. a) $\angle$EDF = $\angle$GHR, DF = HF, $\angle$DFE = $\angle$HFG
b) ASA **c)** FE = FG, $\angle$FED = $\angle$FGH, ED = GH
5. a) $\angle$DAC = $\angle$BCA, AC = CA, $\angle$DCA = $\angle$BAC
b) ASA **c)** AD = CB, $\angle$ADC = $\angle$CBA, DC = BA
6. a) UT = WT, TV = TV, VU = VW **b)** SSS
c) $\angle$UTV = $\angle$WTV, $\angle$TVU = $\angle$TVW,
$\angle$VUT = $\angle$VWT **7. a)** JM = LM, $\angle$JMK = $\angle$LMK,
MK = MK **b)** SAS **c)** $\angle$MKJ = $\angle$MKL, KJ = KL,

$\angle$KJM = $\angle$KLM **8. a)** $\angle$XYW = $\angle$ZYW, YW = YW,
$\angle$YWX = $\angle$YWZ **b)** ASA **c)** WX = WZ,
$\angle$WXY = $\angle$WZY, XY = ZY **9. a)** KL = NM,
$\angle$KLM = $\angle$NML, LM = ML **b)** SAS
c) $\angle$LMK = $\angle$MLN, MK = LN, $\angle$MKL = $\angle$LNM
10. a) $\angle$BAD = $\angle$CDA, AD = DA, $\angle$BDA = $\angle$CAD
b) ASA **c)** AB = DC, $\angle$ABD = $\angle$DCA, BD = CA

Section 6.6 p. 372
Practice 1. Less than 2 people were born in the
same month. **2.** There is a greatest whole number.
3. The sum of two odd integers is an odd integer.
4. Suspect A is guilty of the crime.

Computer Data Bank p. 373
1 True or False 1. true **2.** false, change 60
campsites to 30 **3.** true **4.** false, change national to
provincial
2 Facilities 1. Alberta $\dfrac{8}{51}$; British Columbia $\dfrac{87}{191}$,
Manitoba $\dfrac{1}{33}$; Saskatchewan $\dfrac{3}{23}$ **2.** Birds Hill, Grand
Beach, Spruce Woods, and Whiteshell **3.** 27 **4.** 161
5. Alberta
3 Hiking Trails $\dfrac{92}{103}$
4 Campsite Density 1. Answers will vary.
2. Answers will vary.
5 National Parks 47 087 662 ha, 5 231 962 ha
6 Planning a Visit 1. Answers will vary. **2.** Answers
will vary.

Connecting Math and Computers pp. 374–375
1 Determining the Output 1. a) 2 and 7 **b)** 7 and 18
c) 2 and 18 **d)** yes **2. a)** x, y **b)** x, z **c)** y, z **d)** yes
2 More Complicated Sorting Networks 1. a) 5 and
22 **b)** 29 and 51 **c)** 5 and 51 **d)** 22 and 51 **e)** 5 and 29
2. no **3.** yes

Review pp. 376–377
1. a) 8, 188, 2888, 38 888 **b)** 8 888 888 888 **2.** 144
3. a) 95, 191 **b)** 244, 730 **c)** 6561, 1 594 323 **d)** 44, 47
4. (−4, −7); (4, −7) **5.** 8 ÷ 4 = 2; 6 ÷ 4 = 1.5 **7.** 1; 0
9. 96 is divisible by 6. **10.** $\angle$R is a reflex angle.
11. Miko will go swimming tomorrow. **12.** In
$\triangle$KLM, each of the three angles measures 60°.
13. a) The result is the original number. **23. b)** 12
24. b) 30 **c)** 51% **d)** 68 **25.** true; If a prime number is
odd, then it is greater than 2, true; If a prime number
is even, then it is less than or equal to 2, true **26.** true;
If a polygon is a triangle, then it has three sides, true;
If a polygon is not a triangle, then it does not have
three sides, true **27.** true; If $\triangle$XYZ is obtuse, then
$\angle$X + $\angle$Y < 90°, false; If $\triangle$XYZ is not obtuse, then
$\angle$X + $\angle$Y $\geq$ 90°, true **28.** false; If $x > 0$, then $x^2 > 0$,

true; If $x \le 0$, then $x^2 \le 0$, false

Chapter Check p. 378

1. a) $6 + 12\ 345 \times 9 = 111\ 111$,
$7 + 123\ 456 \times 9 = 1\ 111\ 111$ **2. a)** 6, 10 **b)** The

number of angles formed by n rays is $\dfrac{n^2 - n}{2}$.

3. January; February **4.** 3; 2 **5.** $-1, 2, -3$; 1, 2, 3
9. Marcel is likely to get a speeding ticket. **10.** Sonya
is a teenager. **11.** The point P is in the third
quadrant. **12.** 1, 2 **13.** 2, 4, 6, 12 **14.** 1, 2, 3, 4, 5, 6, 7,
9, 11, 12 **15.** 0, 1, 2, 3, 4, 6, 8, 9, 12, 15, 18, 24
16. true; If $a + b$ is an odd number, then a and b are
consecutive natural numbers, false; If $a + b$ is an even
number, then a and b are not consecutive natural
numbers, true **17.** true; If $\triangle ABC$ contains two acute
angles, then it is a right triangle, false; If $\triangle ABC$ does
not contain two acute angles, then it is not a right
triangle, true **18.** false; If $x = 5$, then $x^2 = 25$, true;
If $x \ne 5$, then $x^2 \ne 25$, false **19.** $\angle x + \angle y = 180°$

Using the Strategies p. 379

1. 3 **3.** 6 km/h **4.** 9 square units **5.** D **6.** 1982 **7.** 12
8. 25 **9.** 13 **10.** 44 m² **11.** 35
Data Bank **1.** 7.2 m **2.** Answers may vary.
3. Answers may vary.

Chapter 7

The Circle

Getting Started pp. 382–383
1 Angle Relationships **1.** $w = 37°$, $x = 52°$, $y = 91°$,
$z = 52°$ **2.** $x = 72°$ **3.** $a = 67°$, $b = 65°$, $c = 48°$
4. $w = 33°$, $x = 37°$, $y = 33°$, $z = 110°$ **5.** $a = 54°$,
$b = 54°$, $c = 126°$, $d = 126°$, $e = 54°$ **6.** $d = 51°$, $e = 58°$,
$f = 71°$, $g = 122°$, $h = 58°$ **7.** $w = 50°$, $x = 92°$, $y = 38°$,
$z = 50°$ **8.** $a = 55°$, $b = 55°$, $c = 40°$, $d = 55°$, $e = 125°$,
$f = 95°$, $g = 85°$, $h = 85°$ **9.** $40°$ **10.** $30°$ **11.** $31°$
12. $44°$ **13.** $22°$ **14.** $11°$ **15.** $37°$ **16.** $35°$
2 Congruent Triangles Some answers may vary.
1. a) $AB = AD$, $BC = DC$, $CA = CA$ (SSS)
b) $\angle ABC = \angle ADC$, $\angle BCA = \angle DCA$,
$\angle CAB = \angle CAD$ **2. a)** $GI = GJ$, $\angle GHI = \angle GKJ$,
$\angle GIH = \angle GIK$ (AAS) **b)** $GH = GK$, $IH = JK$,
$\angle IGH = \angle JGK$ **3. a)** $\angle FDE = \angle FHG$,
$\angle FED = \angle FGH$, $DE = HG$ (ASA) **b)** $DF = HF$,
$EF = GF$, $\angle DFE = \angle HFG$ **4. a)** $PQ = RS$,
$\angle QPR = \angle SRP$, $PR = RP$ (SAS) **b)** $QR = SP$,
$\angle PRQ = \angle RPS$, $\angle RQP = \angle PSR$
5. a) $\angle ADB = \angle CBD$, $DB = BD$, $\angle ABD = \angle CDB$

(ASA) **b)** $AD = CB$, $AB = CD$, $\angle DAB = \angle BCD$
6. a) $\angle RTS = \angle UST$, $TS = ST$, $\angle SRT = \angle TUS$
(AAS) **b)** $\angle RST = \angle UTS$, $RS = UT$, $RT = US$
Mental Math
Angle Measures **1.** $a = 30°$, $b = 75°$ **2.** $a = 55°$,
$b = 75°$, $c = 50°$ **3.** $p = 70°$, $q = 110°$, $r = 70°$, $s = 110°$
4. $a = 30°$, $b = 70°$, $c = 70°$
Adding the First n Whole, Even, or Odd Numbers **1.** 66
2. 1225 **3.** 5050 **4.** 500 500 **5.** Multiply n by $n + 1$.
6. 56 **7.** 110 **8.** 650 **9.** 2550 **10. a)** 4 **b)** 9 **c)** 16 **d)** 25
11. Multiply n by itself. **12.** 81 **13.** 2500

Investigating Math p. 384
1 Writing Reasons **1.** addition property
2. transitive property **3.** subtraction property
4. division property **5.** multiplication property
6. distributive property **7.** transitive property
8. reflexive property **9.** transitive property
10. symmetric property **11.** symmetric property,
transitive property **12.** addition property
13. subtraction property, symmetric property,
transitive property **14.** substitution property, division
property **15.** substitution property, addition property
2 Solving Equations **1.** 11 **2.** 8 **3.** 3 **4.** $\dfrac{3}{2}$ **5.** $-\dfrac{1}{3}$

Section 7.1 pp. 389–392
Practice **1.** $BD = CD$; Definition of perpendicular;
Reflexive property; SAS; $\angle B = \angle C$ **2.** Given;
$\angle DBC = \angle DCB$; Given; Addition property; Isosceles
Triangle Theorem **3.** Given; $\angle PTQ = \angle RTS$;
Transversal Parallel Lines Theorem; $\triangle PTQ \cong$
$\triangle RST$; Congruent triangles **4.** Given; $OC = OC$;
Radii of a circle; HS; Congruent triangles
Applications and Problem Solving **15. a)** yes (ASA)
b) yes (HS) **c)** yes (SAS) **d)** no **e)** yes (AAS) **f)** yes (SSS)
22. BEC is a straight angle and $EC = BE$; AED is a
straight angle and $AE = ED$. **25.** $\triangle PQR \cong \triangle CBA$
26. no **27. a)** $x = 40°$ **b)** $\angle A = 75°$, $\angle B = 65°$,
$\angle C = 40°$, $\angle D = 75°$, $\angle E = 65°$, $\angle F = 40°$ **29.** no
30. $\dfrac{13}{20}$ or 65%

Computer Data Bank p. 393
1 Simple and Complex Craters **1.** If a crater has at
least one of the two central peak dimensions, it must
be complex. **2.** 76 simple, 80 complex
2 Simple Craters **1.** West Hawk **2.** Answers will
vary. **3.** For the parabola opening up in the fourth
quadrant, $p = 1.22$, $q = -0.34$ **4. a)** Substitute values
for all the variables except a into $y = a(x - p)^2 + q$, and
solve for a. **b)** 0.228 **5.** Answers will vary. **7.** For the
parabola opening up, from most flat to least flat

3 Simple Crater Characteristics   1. Answers will vary. **2.** Macha
4 Complex Crater Characteristics   1. Answers will vary. **2.** simple

Technology p. 394
1 Perpendicular Bisector of a Chord   4. It passes through the centre of the circle. **5.** It passes through the centre of the circle. **6.** The perpendicular bisector of a chord of a circle passes through the centre of the circle.
2 Perpendicular From the Centre of a Circle to a Chord   5. They are equal. **6.** They are equal. **7.** The perpendicular from the centre of a circle to a chord in the circle bisects the chord.
3 Line Segment From the Centre of a Circle to the Midpoint of a Chord   5. They are equal to 90°. **6.** They are equal to 90°. **7.** The line segment from the centre of a circle to the midpoint of a chord in the circle is perpendicular to the chord.

Investigating Math p. 395
1 Perpendicular Bisector of a Chord   4. It passes through the centre of the circle. **5.** It passes through the centre of the circle. **7.** The perpendicular bisector of a chord of a circle passes through the centre of the circle.
2 Perpendicular From the Centre of a Circle to a Chord   5. They are equal. **6.** They are equal. **8.** The perpendicular from the centre of a circle to a chord in the circle bisects the chord.
3 Line Segment From the Centre of a Circle to the Midpoint of a Chord   6. They are equal to 90°. **7.** They are equal to 90°. **9.** The line segment from the centre of a circle to the midpoint of a chord in the circle is perpendicular to the chord.

Section 7.2 pp. 400–401
Practice   1. true **2.** true **3.** false **4.** false **5. a)** 5.8 cm **b)** 10 cm **6.** 41.4 cm **7. a)** 1 cm **b)** 5.3 cm **8. a)** 10.8 cm **b)** 14.8 cm **9. a)** 14.2 cm **b)** 22 cm **10. a)** 8.5 cm **b)** 17.0 cm **11. a)** 5.2 cm **b)** 10.4 cm **12. a)** 6.4 cm **b)** 2.4 cm **13.** 6.2 cm **14. a)** 4.0 cm **b)** 4.5 cm **15.** 29° **16. a)** 48° **b)** 49°
Applications and Problem Solving   17. 13 cm **18.** 12 cm **19.** 5.3 cm **22.** Construct two chords using the points. The perpendicular bisectors of the chords intersect at the centre of the circle. **23.** 7.4 cm **24.** 3.6 cm **25.** 8.09 m **26.** 41.6 cm **27.** 26.2 cm **28.** longer chord **29.** 52 cm **30.** 10 cm **33.** No; The diameter of the hole is 20 cm, but the diagonal of the square is 21.2 cm. **34.** two, one on each side of the diameter **36.** 8.9 cm

Technology pp. 402–405
1 Central Angles Subtended by Equal Arcs   7. equal **8.** equal **9.** Central angles subtended by equal arcs are equal.
2 Inscribed Angles Subtended by the Same Arc   5. It stays the same. **6.** It stays the same. **7.** It stays the same. **8.** Inscribed angles subtended by the same arc are equal.
3 Inscribed Angles Subtended by Equal Arcs   9. equal **10.** equal **11.** equal **12.** Inscribed angles subtended by equal arcs are equal.
4 Inscribed Angles in a Semicircle   4. 90° **5.** 90° **6.** 90° **7.** 90° **8.** Inscribed angles subtended in a semicircle are equal to 90°.
5 Central and Inscribed Angles Subtended by the Same Arc   5. The central angle is twice the inscribed angle. **6.** The central angle is twice the inscribed angle. **7.** The central angle is twice the inscribed angle. **8.** The central angle is twice the inscribed angle subtended by the same arc.
6 Opposite Angles of a Cyclic Quadrilateral   4. supplementary **5.** supplementary **6.** supplementary **7.** The opposite angles of a cyclic quadrilateral are supplementary.
7 Applying to Chords   1. yes

Investigating Math pp. 406–407
1 Central Angles Subtended by Equal Arcs   4. equal **7.** Central angles subtended by equal arcs are equal.
2 Inscribed Angles Subtended by the Same Arc   4. equal **7.** Inscribed angles subtended by the same arc are equal.
3 Inscribed Angles Subtended by Equal Arcs   4. equal **7.** Inscribed angles subtended by equal arcs are equal.
4 Inscribed Angles in a Semicircle   4. They are equal to 90°. **7.** Inscribed angles subtended in a semicircle are equal to 90°.
5 Central and Inscribed Angles Subtended by the Same Arc   5. The central angle is twice the inscribed angle. **8.** The central angle is twice the inscribed angle subtended by the same arc.
6 Opposite Angles of a Cyclic Quadrilateral   4. They are supplementary. **7.** The opposite angles of a cyclic quadrilateral are supplementary.
7 Applying to Chords   1. yes

Section 7.3 pp. 412–414
Practice   1. ∠BAC, ∠BDC **2.** ∠BAC, ∠BDC, ∠BFC **3. a)** ∠ADB, ∠AOB, ∠ACB **b)** ∠CBD, ∠CAD **4. a)** ∠ADB, ∠AOB, ∠ACB **b)** ∠CBD,

∠CAD, ∠COD **5.** 40° **6.** 60° **7.** 35° **8.** 90° **9.** 120°
10. 86° **11.** $a = 50°$, $b = 100°$ **12.** $a = 20°$, $b = 140°$,
$c = 80°$ **13.** $a = 48°$, $b = 42°$, $c = 90°$ **14.** $x = 110°$
15. $a = 40°$, $b = 40°$ **16.** $a = 99°$, $b = 57°$ **17.** $a = 61°$,
$b = 29°$, $c = 29°$ **18.** $a = 40°$, $b = 40°$ **19.** $a = 56°$,
$b = 112°$, $c = 68°$, $d = 34°$ **20.** $t = 20°$, $x = 50°$, $y = 70°$,
$z = 70°$ **21.** $x = 40°$, $y = 25°$, $z = 60°$ **22.** $x = 45°$,
$y = 35°$, $z = 45°$ **23.** $a = 40°$, $b = 30°$, $c = 70°$, $d = 40°$,
$e = 40°$, $f = 70°$ **24.** $w = 40°$, $x = 80°$, $y = 40°$, $z = 50°$
Applications and Problem Solving **32. a)** Use the
sheet of paper to draw two chords and to find the
perpendicular bisector of the chords. The
intersection point of the perpendicular bisectors is
the centre of the circle. **b)** Use the carpenter's square
to construct two right angles on the circle. Extend
the arms of the angles to intersect the circle. The 4
intersection points form 2 diameters. The point of
intersection of the diameters is the centre of the
circle. **33. a)** The cameras are on a circle with the
scene as a chord. They all have the same filming
angle. **b)** No. **34. b)** $\dfrac{AC}{DB} = \dfrac{CE}{BE}$, $\dfrac{AC}{DB} = \dfrac{AE}{DE}$,

$\dfrac{CE}{BE} = \dfrac{AE}{DE}$ **c)** 3.3 cm **35.** $\angle XSY < 50°$

38. $\dfrac{(\pi - \sqrt{3})r^2}{2}$ **40.** No. Only a square has opposite

angles supplementary.

Section 7.4 pp. 419–421
Practice **1.** $\angle 1 = 84°$, $\angle 2 = 73°$ **2.** $\angle 1 = 87°$,
$\angle 2 = 105°$, $\angle 3 = 93°$ **3.** $\angle 1 = 95°$, $\angle 2 = 95°$, $\angle 3 = 85°$
4. $\angle 1 = 40°$, $\angle 2 = 70°$, $\angle 3 = 70°$ **5.** $\angle 1 = 43°$,
$\angle 2 = 47°$, $\angle 3 = 26°$ **6.** $\angle 1 = 160°$, $\angle 2 = 100°$
7. $\angle 1 = 130°$, $\angle 2 = 115°$, $\angle 3 = 60°$ **8.** $\angle 1 = 74°$,
$\angle 2 = 106°$, $\angle 3 = 37°$, $\angle 4 = 37°$, $\angle 5 = 143°$
9. $\angle 1 = 80°$, $\angle 2 = 55°$, $\angle 3 = 100°$ **10.** $\angle 1 = 80°$,
$\angle 2 = 80°$, $\angle 3 = 35°$, $\angle 4 = 30°$, $\angle 5 = 30°$ **11.** FDCE,
ABED **12.** PTRQ **13.** JKMN **14.** GFCE, GFAD,
GDBE, ABEF, BCFD, ACED
Applications and Problem Solving **15.** 82°
16. $\angle 1 = 86°$, $\angle 2 = 67°$, $\angle 3 = 113°$, $\angle 4 = 67°$,
$\angle 5 = 94°$ **23. b)** 14°

Technology pp. 422–423
1 Perpendicular to a Radius at its Outer Endpoint
4. no **5.** no **6.** The line perpendicular to a radius
through the outer endpoint of the radius is a tangent
to the circle.
2 Tangent and Radius at Point of Tangency
7. The angles are equal to 90°. **8.** The tangent and
the radius at the point of tangency are perpendicular.

3 Lengths of Tangent Segments **6.** equal **7.** equal
8. The lengths of the tangent segments from an
external point are equal.
4 Angle Between a Tangent and a Chord **6.** equal
7. equal **8.** The angle between a tangent and a chord,
and the inscribed angle on the opposite side of the
chord are equal.

Investigating Math pp. 424–425
1 Perpendicular to a Radius at its Outer Endpoint
3. no **6.** The line perpendicular to a radius through
the outer endpoint of the radius is a tangent to the
circle.
2 Tangent and Radius at Point of Tangency
4. The angles are equal to 90°. **7.** The tangent and
the radius at the point of tangency are perpendicular.
3 Lengths of Tangent Segments **5.** equal **8.** The
lengths of the tangent segments from an external
point are equal.
4 Angle Between a Tangent and a Chord **5.** equal
8. The angle between a tangent and a chord, and the
inscribed angle on the opposite side of the chord are
equal.

Section 7.5 pp. 431–432
Practice **1.** $x = 5$ **2.** $w = 20°$, $x = 70°$, $y = 9$, $z = 20°$
3. $x = 5\sqrt{5}$ **4.** $x = 13$, $y = 13$ **5.** $x = \sqrt{106} - 5$
6. $x = 140°$ **7.** $\angle 1 = 64°$, $\angle 2 = 71°$ **8.** $\angle 1 = 18°$,
$\angle 2 = 81°$ **9.** $\angle 1 = 30°$, $\angle 2 = 75°$ **10.** $\angle 1 = 65°$,
$\angle 2 = 65°$ **11.** $\angle 1 = 49°$, $\angle 2 = 61°$, $\angle 3 = 70°$,
$\angle 4 = 61°$, $\angle 5 = 40°$ **12.** $\angle 1 = 51°$, $\angle 2 = 39°$, $\angle 3 = 39°$
13. $\angle 1 = 77°$, $\angle 2 = 37°$, $\angle 3 = 73°$, $\angle 4 = 106°$
14. $\angle 1 = 66°$, $\angle 2 = 66°$, $\angle 3 = 66°$, $\angle 4 = 57°$, $\angle 5 = 48°$
Applications and Problem Solving **16.** 44°, 50°, 86°
18. a) 5.7 cm **b)** 27.5 cm² **19.** 41.1 cm **20.** 10 cm
23. 1806 km **25. a)** 40 cm **b)** 8.3 cm **26.** 18 cm, 18 cm,
26 cm **27.** AD = 33.5, AF = 55.5, CE = 18.5
28. OA = 19.3, CD = 29.2, perimeter = 202.2
29. a) 36 cm **b)** 3 cm **30.** 180° **31.** 16.3 cm

Section 7.6 pp. 435–437
Practice **1.** 12.9 cm **2.** 63.4 cm **3.** 65.0 cm
4. 261.5 cm **5.** 1312.5 cm² **6.** 349.1 cm²
7. 7259.5 cm² **8.** 4241.2 cm² **9.** 87° **10.** 108° **11.** 36°
12. 320° **13.** 224° **14.** 16° **15.** 32.7 cm **16.** 60.2 cm
17. 11.0 cm **18.** 23.4 cm **19.** 4.5 cm **20.** 80.6 cm
21. 306° **22.** 140° **23.** 89° **24.** 32° **25.** 194° **26.** 301°
27. 15.3 cm² **28.** 21.8 cm² **29.** 7.0 cm² **30.** 32.1 cm²
31. 44.7 cm² **32.** 27.1 cm²
Applications and Problem Solving **33.** sector;
37 cm² **34.** 2657 cm² **35.** 199 cm **36.** 133 cm

37. $\dfrac{(\pi - 2)r^2}{4}$ **38. a)** $120°$ **b)** 123 cm **39.** 8 cm,

24.5 cm **40. a)** $162°$ **b)** $18\,096$ km **c)** $166°$ **d)** No.

41. Perimeter: $\dfrac{\pi a}{2}$; Area: $\dfrac{(2\sqrt{3} - \pi)a^2}{8}$

42. Perimeter $= \pi r$ **43.** 1200 km

Technology p. 438
1 Number of Triangles in a Polygon 1. $180°$
2. quadrilateral: 4, 2; pentagon: 5, 3; hexagon: 6, 4;
heptagon: 7, 5; octagon: 8, 6; nonagon: 9, 7; decagon:
10, 8 **3.** The number of triangles is 2 less than the
number of sides.
**2 Sum of the Interior Angles in a Polygon in Terms
of Right Angles 1.** =A3+1 adds 1 to the number in
cell A3; =A3−2 subtracts 2 from the number in cell
A3; =B3 copies the number in cell B3; =2*C3
multiplies the number in cell C3 by 2 **3.** The number
of right angles in an n-sided polygon in $2n - 4$.

Section 7.7 pp. 442–443
Practice 1. $\angle 1 = 137°$ **2.** $\angle 1 = 90°$, $\angle 2 = 120°$,
$\angle 3 = 60°$ **3.** $\angle 1 = 120°$ **4.** $\angle 1 = 126°$, $\angle 2 = 75°$, $\angle 3 = 118°$
5. $1620°$, 18 **6.** $3780°$, 42 **7.** $14\,040°$, 156
8. $6300°$, 70 **9.** $180°(y - 2)$, $2y - 4$ **10.** $180°(3t - 2)$,
$6t - 4$ **11.** 11 **12.** 15 **13.** 23 **14.** 10 **15.** 15 **16.** 18
17. 90 **18.** 16 **19.** $\dfrac{360}{180 - m}$ **20.** 24 **21.** 36 **22.** 12
23. 20 **24.** 25 **25.** $\dfrac{360}{m}$ **26.** $171°$, $9°$ **27.** $157.5°$, $22.5°$
28. $165.6°$, $14.4°$ **29.** $167.59°$, $12.41°$
30. $180° - \dfrac{120°}{t}, \dfrac{120°}{t}$ **31.** $\dfrac{180°(x + y - 2)}{x + y}, \dfrac{360°}{x + y}$

Applications and Problem Solving 32. $\angle A = 120°$,
$\angle B = 83°$, $\angle C = 85°$, $\angle D = 112°$, $\angle E = 140°$
33. $\angle P = 145°$, $\angle Q = 95°$, $\angle R = 140°$, $\angle S = 110°$,
$\angle T = 130°$, $\angle U = 100°$ **34. a)** $\angle 1 = 215°$
b) $\angle 1 = 220°$, $\angle 2 = 110°$ **c)** $\angle 2 = 130°$, $\angle 3 = 250°$
d) $\angle 1 = 98°$, $\angle 2 = 75°$, $\angle 3 = 15°$ **35. a)** $30°$ **b)** $90°$
36. a) $540°$ **b)** $180°$ **37.** $160°$; $20°$; 18 **38.** No, because
the vertices with reflex angles do not have exterior
angles in the usual sense. **39.** $112.5°$, $112.5°$, $67.5°$,
$67.5°$

Connecting Math and Biology pp. 444–445
1 Honeycomb Cells 1. a) 113.10 mm²
b) 124.71 mm² **c)** 11.61 mm² **2.** 30.90 mm²
3. 73.96 mm² **4.** No, because a regular octagon does
not tile the plane.

2 Signalling the Distance to Food 2. Answers may
vary. 2000 m **3.** Answers may vary. 750 m
3 Signalling the Direction of Food 1. a) directly
away from the sun **b)** $45°$ clockwise from the direction
of the sun **c)** $135°$ counterclockwise from the
direction of the sun

Review pp. 446–447
3. a) $35°$ **b)** $110°$ **4.** 6.7 cm **5.** 38.7 cm **6.** $x = 125°$
7. $x = 70°$, $y = 35°$ **8.** $m = 35°$, $s = 35°$, $t = 65°$, $x = 45°$,
$y = 35°$, $z = 35°$ **9.** $a = 80°$, $b = 50°$, $c = 50°$
11. $a = 50°$, $b = 155°$ **12.** $a = 115°$, $y = 90°$
14. $a = 144°$, $b = 216°$ **15.** $m = 55°$, $x = 55°$, $y = 60°$,
$z = 65°$ **16.** 10.2 cm **17.** 5.7 cm **19. a)** 10.5 cm
b) 63 cm² **20. a)** 91.6 cm **b)** 1145 cm² **21.** $57°$,
50 cm² **22.** $\angle 1 = 40°$, $\angle 2 = 60°$, $\angle 3 = 120°$,
$\angle 4 = 140°$ **23.** $\angle 1 = 115°$, $\angle 2 = 125°$, $\angle 3 = 106°$,
$\angle 4 = 142°$ **24. a)** $4140°$ **b)** 46 **25. a)** $6840°$ **b)** 76
26. a) $(360m - 360)°$ **b)** $4m - 4$ **27. a)** 5 **b)** $108°$
28. a) 12 **b)** 150 **29. a)** 16 **b)** $157.5°$ **30.** $135°$
Exploring Math 1. Any point on an angle bisector is
equidistant from the two arms of the angle. The
intersection of two bisectors is therefore equidistant
from all three sides. **2.** 2 cm **3.** 60% **4.** 91%
5. $(3 - 2\sqrt{2})r$

Chapter Check p. 448
3. 16.1 cm **5.** $a = 15°$, $b = 30°$ **6.** $w = 31°$, $x = 59°$,
$y = 59°$, $z = 31°$ **7.** $x = 70°$, $y = 140°$, $z = 70°$
8. $a = 115°$, $b = 25°$ **10.** PWSQ **11.** $a = 10$ cm, $b = 75°$,
$c = 15°$, $d = 15°$ **12.** $u = 40°$, $v = 40°$, $w = 40°$, $y = 70°$,
$z = 100°$ **14.** $25°$ **15. a)** 52 cm **b)** 524 cm²
16. a) 4.2 cm **b)** 16.8 cm² **17.** 8 **18.** 16 **19.** 19
20. $\angle D = 157°$, $\angle E = 36°$, $\angle F = 109°$, $\angle G = 133°$,
$\angle H = 105°$

Using the Strategies p. 449
1. 1, 1, 1, 2, 5; 1, 1, 2, 2, 2; 1, 1, 1, 3, 3 **2.** 62
4. a) (3, 2, 4), (1, 8, 3), (−3, −4, 2) **b)** (1, −5, −8),
(4, −2, −5), (−2, 1, −20) **5.** Divide the coins into
groups of three, and weigh one group against
another. If they balance, the third group contains the
counterfeit; if they do not, the lighter group contains
the counterfeit. From the identified group, weigh one
coin against another. If one is lighter, it is counterfeit.
If they balance, the one not weighed is counterfeit.
7. a) 1 and 2 **b)** 1.5 **8.** 16π cm² **9.** 60
Data Bank 1. $58°$ **2. a)** 81.2% **b)** Assume a driving
speed of 80 km/h and a flying speed of 800 km/h;
8.12%

Chapter 8

Coordinate Geometry and Trigonometry

p. 451 **1.** 265 465 km **2.** 3073 m/s **3.** 463 m/s

4. 6.6 times **5. a)** $g = \dfrac{v^2}{r}$ **b)** 0.22 m/s² **c)** 44 times

Getting Started pp. 452–453

1 Slopes **1. a)** A: 1 and undefined; C: 0 and −1
b) equal **c)** Yes. **d)** 0; undefined **2. a)** 1, −1 **b)** negative
reciprocals **c)** 90° **d)** No.
2 Midpoints **1. a)** (12, 10), (12, 10) **b)** equal **c)** yes
3 Distances **1. a)** $2\sqrt{2}, 6\sqrt{2}, 2\sqrt{2}, 6\sqrt{2}$ **b)** equal

c) yes **2. a)** $4\sqrt{2}, 4\sqrt{2}$ **b)** equal **c)** no
4 Equations **1. a)** $y = 12$ **b)** $x = 4$ **2. a)** $y = -x + 16$
b) $y = 2x - 8$

Warm Up **1.** 3 **2.** −1 **3.** 1.4 **4.** −5 **5.** −2 **6.** 3 **7.** $\dfrac{1}{2}$

8. −2 **9.** $-\dfrac{1}{2}$ **10.** $\dfrac{1}{3}$ **11.** 2 **12.** $-\dfrac{3}{2}$ **13.** −1 **14.** $\dfrac{4}{3}$ **15.** $-\dfrac{2}{5}$

16. −5 **17.** $y = x + 4$ **18.** $y = -x + 3$ **19.** $y = \dfrac{1}{2}x - 2$

20. $y = -2x - 5$ **21.** 2; 6 **22.** $-5; \dfrac{5}{2}$ **23.** −6; 4 **24.** −4; −8

25. $-\dfrac{3}{5}$; no y-intercept **26.** no x-intercept; 6 **27.** (1, 2)

28. (−1, 1) **29.** (2, 5) **30.** (−3, −7)
Mental Math
Order of Operations **1.** 8 **2.** −1 **3.** 3 **4.** −5 **5.** 5.5
6. −4.5 **7.** −3.5 **8.** −4.5 **9.** 5 **10.** 10 **11.** $\sqrt{58}$ **12.** 13
13. $\sqrt{85}$
Squaring Numbers Ending in One or Two **1.** 441
2. 1681 **3.** 8281 **4.** 10 201 **5.** 26.01 **6.** 50.41
7. 656 100 **8.** 372 100 **9.** 484 **10.** 2704 **11.** 6724
12. 10 404 **13.** 84.64 **14.** 38.44 **15.** 176 400
16. 518 400 **17.** A number ending in 1 is $10n + 1$.
$10n(10n + 2) + 1 = 100n^2 + 20n + 1 = (10n + 1)^2$;
A number ending in 2 is $10n + 2$.
$10n(10n + 4) + 4 = 100n^2 + 40n + 4 = (10n + 2)^2$
18. Multiply the numbers that are 3 above and 3
below the number. Then add 9. **19.** Use the rule for
numbers ending in 1 for numbers ending in 9. Use
the rule for numbers ending in 2 for numbers ending
in 8.

Technology p. 454
1 Midsegment of a Triangle **4.** trapezoid; The
midsegment is parallel to and one half the length of
the third side.
2 Midpoints of the Sides of a Quadrilateral
4. parallelogram
3 Diagonals of a Parallelogram **3.** The diagonals
bisect each other.

4 Midpoint of the Hypotenuse of a Right Triangle
3. The midpoint of the hypotenuse of a right triangle
is equidistant from the vertices of the triangle.

Section 8.1 pp. 460–461
Applications and Problem Solving **15. a)** $R(a + c, b)$

16. a) $y = 0$, $x = 4$, $y = -x + 4$ **17.** $\left(\dfrac{8}{3}, \dfrac{8}{3}\right)$ **25. b)** Yes;

the diagonals of a square are perpendicular.

Investigating Math pp. 462–463
1 Division of Horizontal Line Segments **1. a)** (3, 0),
(4, 0) **b)** (3, 3), (5, 3) **c)** (1, 2), (5, 2) **d)** (−7, −4),
(−4, −4) **3. a)** (2, 0), (3, 0), (4, 0) **b)** (2, 2), (4, 2), (6, 2)
c) (−1, 1), (2, 1), (5, 1) **d)** (−4, −2), (0, −2), (4, −2)
5. a) (4, 0), (5, 0), (6, 0), (7, 0) **b)** (3, 5), (5, 5), (7, 5),
(9, 5) **c)** (−2, 2), (1, 2), (4, 2), (7, 2) **d)** (−8, −6),

(−4, −6), (0, −6), (4, −6) **8. a)** $\left(\dfrac{a}{3}, 0\right), \left(\dfrac{2a}{3}, 0\right)$

b) $\left(\dfrac{a}{4}, 0\right), \left(\dfrac{a}{2}, 0\right), \left(\dfrac{3a}{4}, 0\right)$ **c)** $\left(\dfrac{a}{5}, 0\right), \left(\dfrac{2a}{5}, 0\right),$

$\left(\dfrac{3a}{5}, 0\right), \left(\dfrac{4a}{5}, 0\right)$ **d)** $\left(\dfrac{a}{6}, 0\right), \left(\dfrac{a}{3}, 0\right), \left(\dfrac{a}{2}, 0\right), \left(\dfrac{2a}{3}, 0\right),$

$\left(\dfrac{5a}{6}, 0\right)$ **e)** $\left(\dfrac{a}{8}, 0\right), \left(\dfrac{a}{4}, 0\right), \left(\dfrac{3a}{8}, 0\right), \left(\dfrac{a}{2}, 0\right), \left(\dfrac{5a}{8}, 0\right),$

$\left(\dfrac{3a}{4}, 0\right), \left(\dfrac{7a}{8}, 0\right)$

2 Division of Vertical Line Segments **1. a)** (0, 2),
(0, 3) **b)** (2, 4), (2, 6) **c)** (3, −2), (3, 1) **d)** (−1, −8),
(−1, −4) **3. a)** (0, 3), (0, 4), (0, 5) **b)** (1, 6), (1, 8),
(1, 10) **c)** (2, −3), (2, 0), (2, 3) **d)** (−3, −5), (−3, −1),
(−3, 3) **5. a)** (0, 1), (0, 2), (0, 3), (0, 4) **b)** (−1, 4),
(−1, 6), (−1, 8), (−1, 10) **c)** (−2, −3), (−2, 0), (−2, 3),

(−2, 6) **d)** (3, −5), (3, −1), (3, 3), (3, 7) **8. a)** $\left(0, \dfrac{b}{3}\right),$

$\left(0, \dfrac{2b}{3}\right)$ **b)** $\left(0, \dfrac{b}{4}\right), \left(0, \dfrac{b}{2}\right), \left(0, \dfrac{3b}{4}\right)$ **c)** $\left(0, \dfrac{b}{5}\right), \left(0, \dfrac{2b}{5}\right),$

$\left(0, \dfrac{3b}{5}\right), \left(0, \dfrac{4b}{5}\right)$ **d)** $\left(0, \dfrac{b}{7}\right), \left(0, \dfrac{2b}{7}\right), \left(0, \dfrac{3b}{7}\right), \left(0, \dfrac{4b}{7}\right),$

$\left(0, \dfrac{5b}{7}\right), \left(0, \dfrac{6b}{7}\right)$ **e)** $\left(0, \dfrac{b}{10}\right), \left(0, \dfrac{b}{5}\right), \left(0, \dfrac{3b}{10}\right), \left(0, \dfrac{2b}{5}\right),$

$\left(0, \dfrac{b}{2}\right), \left(0, \dfrac{3b}{5}\right), \left(0, \dfrac{7b}{10}\right), \left(0, \dfrac{4b}{5}\right), \left(0, \dfrac{9b}{10}\right)$

3 Division of Sloping Line Segments **1. f)** (3, 3),
(5, 4) **2. a)** (1, 2), (3, 0) **b)** (0, −1), (−3, −5)
3. a) (−3, 0), (−2, −1), (−1, −2) **b)** (0, 0), (−2, −3),
(−4, −6) **4. a)** (1, 4), (2, 3), (3, 2), (4, 1) **b)** (2, 7), (0, 4),

(−2, 1), (−4, −2) **6. a)** $\left(\dfrac{a}{3}, \dfrac{b}{3}\right), \left(\dfrac{2a}{3}, \dfrac{2b}{3}\right)$ **b)** $\left(\dfrac{a}{4}, \dfrac{b}{4}\right),$

$\left(\frac{a}{2}, \frac{b}{2}\right), \left(\frac{3a}{4}, \frac{3b}{4}\right)$ **c)** $\left(\frac{a}{5}, \frac{b}{5}\right), \left(\frac{2a}{5}, \frac{2b}{5}\right), \left(\frac{3a}{5}, \frac{3b}{5}\right),$

$\left(\frac{4a}{5}, \frac{4b}{5}\right)$ **d)** $\left(\frac{a}{6}, \frac{b}{6}\right), \left(\frac{a}{3}, \frac{b}{3}\right), \left(\frac{a}{2}, \frac{b}{2}\right), \left(\frac{2a}{3}, \frac{2b}{3}\right),$

$\left(\frac{5a}{6}, \frac{5b}{6}\right)$ **e)** $\left(\frac{a}{n}, \frac{b}{n}\right), \left(\frac{2a}{n}, \frac{2b}{n}\right), \left(\frac{3a}{n}, \frac{3b}{n}\right), \dots,$

$\left(\frac{(n-1)a}{n}, \frac{(n-1)b}{n}\right)$

Section 8.2 pp. 467–469

Practice   1. $(0, 5)$ **2.** $(5, 0), (7, 0)$ **3.** $(-3, 2), (-5, 2),$
$(-7, 2)$ **4.** $(-4, 0), (-4, -2)$ **5.** $(4.5, -1)$ **6.** $(-3, -\frac{8}{5}),$
$(-3, -\frac{6}{5}), (-3, -\frac{4}{5}), (-3, -\frac{2}{5})$ **7.** $(4, 11)$ **8.** $(6, 8),$
$(8, 11), (10, 14)$ **9.** $(1, 2), (2, 5)$ **10.** $(-2, 8), (-4, 6),$
$(-6, 4), (-8, 2)$ **11.** $(-2, -6), (-1, -4), (0, -2), (1, 0),$
$(2, 2)$ **12.** $(\frac{1}{2}, \frac{9}{2})$ **13.** $(7, \frac{5}{3}), (6, \frac{4}{3})$ **14.** $(\frac{4}{5}, 5), (\frac{8}{5}, 6),$
$(\frac{12}{5}, 7), (\frac{16}{5}, 8)$ **15.** $(-\frac{1}{3}, 3), (\frac{4}{3}, 5)$ **16.** $(-\frac{19}{2}, -\frac{15}{2}),$
$(-7, -7), (-\frac{9}{2}, -\frac{13}{2})$ **17.** $(\frac{7}{2}, -1), (5, -6), (\frac{13}{2}, -11)$
18. $(-\frac{19}{2}, -\frac{1}{3}), (-7, -\frac{14}{3}), (-\frac{9}{2}, -9), (-2, -\frac{40}{3}),$
$(\frac{1}{2}, -\frac{53}{3})$ **19.** $(6, 10)$ **20.** $(3, -5)$ **21.** $(44, 70)$

22. $(-\frac{11}{2}, -\frac{7}{2})$

Applications and Problem Solving

23. $(-2\sqrt{2}, \frac{22\sqrt{5}}{5})$ **24.** $(9, 13)$ **25. a)** $(-2, 15), (0, 11),$
$(2, 7), (4, 3)$ **b)** $-4, -2, 0, 2, 4, 6$ **c)** $19, 15, 11, 7, 3, -1$
d) arithmetic **26.** $A(7, -8), B(-5, 10)$ **27.** 27 m
28. a) $(3, 5), (4, 7), (5, 9); (-5, 7), (-4, 5), (-3, 3),$
$(-2, 1), (-1, -1), (0, -3), (1, -5)$ **b)** No.
29. a) $(500, 100)$ **b)** $(100, 20), (200, 40), (300, 60),$
$(400, 80)$ **c)** 102 m **d)** 117 m **30.** $(261.8, 21.3),$
$(523.6, 42.6)$ **31. a)** 2060 m **b)** 1950 m **c)** Assume the
support towers are equally spaced; $(1200, 400)$
32. a) 3.5 m **b)** $(2, 1.4)$ **33. a)** $(14, 30)$ **b)** $(10, 22)$
34. a) 1.5 **b)** 19 **35. a)** $(3, 5)$ **b)** $(4, 3)$ **c)** $(7, -3)$

d) $\left(-2 + \frac{15m}{m+n}, 15 - \frac{30m}{m+n}\right)$

Section 8.3 pp. 475–476

Practice   1. $-\frac{1}{4}$ **2.** $\frac{1}{3}$ **3.** -2 **4.** $\frac{2}{5}$ **5.** 1 **6.** $-\frac{3}{2}$ **7.** $\frac{1}{3}$ **8.** $-\frac{1}{2}$
9. $y = x + 1$ **10.** $y = -2x + 5$ **11.** $2x - 3y - 8 = 0$
12. $x + 2y + 11 = 0$ **13.** $4x + 3y + 2 = 0$ **14.** $y = \frac{6}{5}x$

15. $2\sqrt{2}$ **16.** $3\sqrt{2}$ **17.** $\frac{9\sqrt{10}}{10}$ **18.** $\sqrt{5}$ **19.** 2 **20.** 3

21. $3\sqrt{13}$ **22.** $2\sqrt{5}$ **23.** 2.1 **24.** 1.4 **25.** 1.8 **26.** 1.2
27. 0.5 **28.** 1.8 **29.** 2.5 **30.** 2.2 **31.** 0.7 **32.** 6.7 **33.** 4.2
34. 4.9 **35.** 4.5 **36.** 1.9 **37.** 0.2 **38.** 0.9 **39.** $7; 7; 4.95$
40. $5; 2.5; 2.24$ **41.** $14; 28; 12.52$ **42.** $6; 2; 1.90$
43. $6; 12; 5.37$ **44.** $7; 2.33; 2.21$ **45.** $2.6; 6.5; 2.41$
46. $1.71; 1.09; 0.92$

Applications and Problem Solving   47. 6.01 **48.** 6.7
49. 0; The point is on the line. **50. a)** $3.94, 5.58, 3.78$
b) 11.5 **51. a)** 0.38 **b)** 0.14 **52. a)** rectangle **b)** 40

53. 60 **54.** Yes. **55. a)** $y = \frac{7}{12}x - 20$

c) $y = 1.42x - 220.5$ **e)** Yes. **56. a)** 1.9 m **b)** 2.375 m
c) No. **57. a)** 2.8 **b)** 1.8 **c)** 6.4 **d)** 1.7

58. $99x - 77y - 121 = 0$ **59.** $(\frac{32}{3}, 0), (-\frac{8}{3}, 0)$

60. Answers may vary. **61.** It is $\frac{\sqrt{2}}{2}$ times the

x-intercept.

Investigating Math p. 477

1. c) $y = 2, y = -2$ **2. b)** $x = 3$ **3. a)** parallel
c) $y = x - 1$ **4. b)** $y = x, y = -x$ **5. a)** No, only the
centre of the rectangle is equidistant from the

vertices. **b)** $(\frac{3}{2}, 2)$

Section 8.4 pp. 481–482

Practice   1. $x^2 + y^2 = 25$ **2.** $x^2 + y^2 = 81$
3. $x^2 + y^2 = 6.25$ **4.** $x^2 + y^2 = 3$ **5.** $x^2 + y^2 = 20$
6. $x^2 + y^2 = d^2$ **7.** $x^2 + (y - 2)^2 = 25$
8. $(x - 2)^2 + (y - 4)^2 = 9$ **9.** $(x + 2)^2 + (y - 3)^2 = 64$
10. $(x - 5)^2 + (y + 2)^2 = 16$ **11.** $x^2 + y^2 = 2$
12. $(x + 3)^2 + (y + 8)^2 = 100$ **13.** $(x + 4)^2 + y^2 = 32$
14. $(x - a)^2 + (y + b)^2 = c^2$ **15.** $x^2 + y^2 = 100$
16. $x^2 + y^2 = 20$ **17.** $x^2 + y^2 = 18$ **18.** $x^2 + y^2 = 26$
19. $x^2 + y^2 = 36$ **20.** $x^2 + y^2 = 25$ **21.** $(x - 1)^2 + y^2 = 25$
22. $(x + 1)^2 + (y + 2)^2 = 25$ **23.** $x^2 + (y - 1)^2 = 10$
24. $(x - 2)^2 + (y - 5)^2 = 36$
25. $(x + 3)^2 + (y - 4)^2 = 13$
26. $(x - 11)^2 + (y + 9)^2 = 625$ **27.** $(0, 0), 7$
28. $(0, 7), 3$ **29.** $(-5, 0), 1$ **30.** $(3, 4), 5$
31. $(-1, 2), 2$ **32.** $(0, 0), 0.1$ **33.** $(-0.3, 0.2), 0.5$
34. $(312, -458), 80$ **35.** $(2, -1), 4$ **36.** $(a, b), c$
Applications and Problem Solving   37. a) yes **b)** yes
c) no **d)** yes **38.** $2 \pm \sqrt{11}$ **39. a)** $x^2 + y^2 = 81$
b) $(x - 50)^2 + (y - 30)^2 = 81$ **c)** $(x + 30)^2 + (y + 50)^2 = 81$
40. a) $(x - 2)^2 + y^2 = 25$ **b)** $(x - 1)^2 + (y + 1)^2 = 29$
41. $x^2 + y^2 = 20$ **42.** $x^2 + y^2 = 1\,440\,000;$
$x^2 + y^2 = 12\,250\,000; x^2 + y^2 = 40\,960\,000$

43. $x^2 + y^2 = 1\ 785\ 062\ 500$ **44.** $(-5, 19), (-5, -3)$
45. b) $y = -x + 1$ **46. a)** 34.4 **b)** 94.2
47. a) $x^2 + y^2 = a^2 + b^2$
b) $(x - 1)^2 + (y - 2)^2 = (a - 1)^2 + (b - 2)^2$
48. a) at the centre of the ring **b)** at the closest point on the backboard **c)** at the top of the ring
49. a) $(-13, 0), (13, 0)$ **50. a)** $[1, 2]$ **b)** $[-3, -4]$ **c)** $[0, 1]$
d) $[-2, 0]$ **e)** $[h, k]$ **51.** $x^2 + (y + 3)^2 = 34$
52. $x^2 + y^2 = 200$ **53.** $(x + 2)^2 + (y + 1)^2 = 25$
54. $(x - h)^2 + (y - h)^2 = 2h^2 + 6h + 9$ **55.** radius: 8;
centre: $(5, -6)$

Section 8.5 pp. 488–491
Practice 1. $(3, 3), (-3, -3)$ **2.** $(0, -5), (3, 4)$
3. $(-2, -6), (6, 2)$ **4.** no points of intersection
5. $(12, -5), (-12, -5)$ **6.** no points of intersection
7. $(3, 4)$ **8.** $(3, -9), (-9, -3)$ **9.** $(-1, -1), (6, 6)$
10. $(2, 4), (-3, -1)$ **11.** no points of intersection
12. $(0.2, 0.4), (-1, -2)$ **13.** $(0, 0), (-1, 1)$ **14.** no points
of intersection **15.** $(0, -2.7), (0, -9.3)$ **16.** $(3.8, 2)$,
$(8.2, 2)$ **17.** $(0.5, 4.0), (-4.1, -5.2)$ **18.** $(0.7, -4.4)$,
$(-13.5, 2.8)$ **19.** $(1, 6), (-8, 5)$ **20.** $(-9.0, 9.2)$,
$(10.9, 4.3)$ **21.** 8.94 **22.** 4 **23.** 4.9 **24.** 5.7 **25.** 6.8
26. 6.9 **27.** $y = 5, y = -5$ **28.** $y = 7, y = -7$ **29.** $y = 1$,
$y = -1$ **30.** $y = 30, y = -30$ **31.** $y = -\dfrac{3}{4}, y = \dfrac{3}{4}$

32. $y = 1.2, y = -1.2$ **33.** $x = 2, x = -2$ **34.** $x = 8, x = -8$
35. $x = 15, x = -15$ **36.** $x = 90, x = -90$ **37.** $x = 0.5$,
$x = -0.5$ **38.** $x = 4\sqrt{2}, x = -4\sqrt{2}$ **39.** $y = -x + 2$
40. $y = x + 10$ **41.** $x - 3y + 10 = 0$ **42.** $2x + 5y - 29 = 0$
43. $2x + 3y - 13 = 0$ **44.** $5x + 7y + 74 = 0$
45. $x - 2y - 10 = 0$ **46.** $5x - 3y + 34 = 0$ **47. a)** $(2, 3)$
b) $x + 2y - 18 = 0$ **48. b)** $3x - 4y = 0$ **49.** $x + 4y = 0$
50. $x + 5y - 12 = 0$ **51.** $2x + 3y - 18 = 0$
52. $3x - 4y - 30 = 0$ **53.** $3x + 7y - 43 = 0$
54. $2x + y + 4 = 0$ **55.** 8 **56.** 4 **57.** $3\sqrt{10}$ **58.** $\sqrt{10}$
59. $5\sqrt{3}$ **60.** $\sqrt{114}$ **61.** 6 **62.** 4 **63.** $\sqrt{37}$ **64.** 1 **65.** $2\sqrt{5}$
66. $2\sqrt{33}$

Applications and Problem Solving
68. a) $(5, 0), (2, 1)$ **70. a)** $\sqrt{106}$ **b)** 5.1 **71.** $x = 1$
72. $y = -1$ **73.** $\sqrt{10}$ **74.** equal **75.** $y = x, y = -x$
76. a) $x^2 + y^2 = 2500$ **b)** 33 min **77.** $3x + 4y - 51 = 0$
78. $8x + 15y - 289 = 0$ **79. a)** 14.4 m
b) $4.1x - 5.9y + 51.62 = 0$ **80.** 23 km/h
81. a) $x - \sqrt{3}y + 2 = 0$ **b)** $4x - 2y - 5\sqrt{2} = 0$
82. $x^2 + y^2 = 49$ **83.** $(x + 1)^2 + (y - 3)^2 = 81$
84. a) $y = k + r, y = k - r$ **b)** $x = h + r, x = h - r$
85. a) $5x + 12y - 169 = 0$ **b)** $5x + 12y + 169 = 0$
86. $x_1 x + y_1 y = x_1^2 + y_1^2$
87. $(x - \sqrt{10})^2 + (y - \sqrt{10})^2 = 10$;

$(x + \sqrt{10})^2 + (y - \sqrt{10})^2 = 10$;
$(x + \sqrt{10})^2 + (y + \sqrt{10})^2 = 10$;
$(x - \sqrt{10})^2 + (y + \sqrt{10})^2 = 10$
88. $(x - 1)^2 + (y - 5)^2 = 25$
89. a) $(x - 5\sqrt{2})^2 + (y - 5\sqrt{2})^2 = 25$;
$(x + 5\sqrt{2})^2 + (y + 5\sqrt{2})^2 = 25$ **b)** 9.4 m **90.** $x^2 + y^2 = 20$
91. a) ± 8 **b)** $3x + 4y = 50; 3x - 4y = 50$
92. a) $y = \dfrac{a + b}{a - bx}$ **93. a)** $\left(\dfrac{p + q}{2}, \dfrac{-p + q}{2}\right)$ **b)** $\dfrac{-p + q}{p + q}$

c) $\dfrac{-p - q}{q - p}$ **94. a)** $OT = r, OP = \sqrt{a^2 + b^2}$

b) $PT = \sqrt{a^2 + b^2 - r^2}$ **95. a)** $\dfrac{b}{a}$ **b)** $-\dfrac{a}{b}$ **c)** $ax + by = a^2 + b^2$
96. b) The distance is equal to the sum of their radii.
c) $(x - 3)^2 + (y + 1)^2 = 9; (x + 3)^2 + (y + 1)^2 = 9$. Yes;
there are two possible answers. **97. a)** 16
b) $(x - 16)^2 + (y - 2)^2 = 4$ **98.** $0, 1, 2, 3,$ or 4

Computer Data Bank p. 492
1 Takeoff and Landing 1. a) 36 **b)** 120 **c)** 36 **d)** 60
e) 92 **f)** 69 **g)** 109 **h)** 1 **2. a)** 114 **3. b)** 49.89%
2 Airport Categories 1. Answers will vary.
3 Comparing Aircraft Some answers may vary due to rounding. **1.** $19.5\%, 8.1\%, 0.8\%$ **2.** 93 turbofans, average wing span 42.0 m, average length 49.0 m, average height 13.7 m, average mass 161 t; 30 turboprops, average wing span 23.2 m, average length 23.0 m, average height 7.0 m, average mass 19 t **3.** 22
4 Mach Numbers 1. British Aerospace Concorde, Mach 2.00 **2.** 12 **3.** 7 at 0.03, 5 at 0.04
5 Flight Path 1. Answers will vary. **2.** 0.8 min, 2.0 min

Section 8.6 pp. 497–499
Practice 1. 22.2 **2.** 2.8 **3.** 8.0 **4.** 25.7 **5.** 111.2
6. 12.9 **7.** $44.7°$ **8.** $43.3°$ **9.** $38.1°$ **10.** $49.7°$ **11.** 11.2
12. 12.4 **13.** 2.4 **14.** 11.6 **15.** 73.1 **16.** 16.5 **17.** $73.7°$
18. $44.1°$ **19.** $68.0°$ **20.** $25.3°$ **21.** $110.2°$ **22.** $36.1°$
23. $y = 8.5$ cm, $\angle Y = 63.8°$, $\angle Z = 26.2°$ **24.** $\angle L = 53°$,
$l = 9.8$ cm, $k = 7.4$ cm **25.** $\angle C = 34.9°$, $a = 5.9$ m,
$c = 3.3$ m **26.** $\angle D = 50.7°$, $\angle F = 39.3°$, $e = 23.5$ cm
27. $\angle B = 56°$, $b = 4.7$ m, $c = 3.6$ m **28.** $\angle P = 52.0°$,
$\angle Q = 99.5°$, $q = 13.0$ cm **29.** $\angle L = 81.2°$, $\angle K = 36.8°$,
$k = 10.2$ m **30.** $\angle U = 33.9°$, $u = 40.6$ km,
$w = 60.4$ km **31.** $x = 4.3$ cm, $\angle Y = 46.6°$, $\angle Z = 41.1°$
32. $\angle F = 115.9°$, $\angle G = 37.4°$, $\angle H = 26.7°$ **33.** 66.8
34. 4.9 **35.** 31.0 **36.** 5.7 **37.** 6.0 **38.** 7.2 **39.** $9.7°$
40. $39.0°$ **41.** $104.3°$ **42.** $49.3°$
Applications and Problem Solving 43. 85.9 m

44. $10.4°$ **45.** $30\,964$ km **46.** 728 m **47.** 23 m
48. 73 m **49.** 13 m **50.** 20.8 mm **51. a)** 15.6 **b)** 15.6
c) since $\sin 90° = 1$ **52. a)** 9.0 **b)** 9.0
c) since $\cos 90° = 0$ **53.** 31.3 m²

Investigating Math pp. 500–501
1 Exploring the SSA Case **1. a)** 2 **b)** 2 **c)** $67°$, $113°$
2. a) 4.6 cm **b)** $90°$ **3. a)** none **b)** 1 **4. a)** $CB \le 6$
b) $CB > 6$ **c)** No.
2 Making Generalizations **1. a)** $90°$ **b)** $a = b \sin A$
2. a) supplementary **b)** $\dfrac{a}{\sin A} = \dfrac{b}{\sin B}$
c) $b \sin A < a < b$ **3. a)** $a > b$ **b)** $a \le b$
3 Applying the Concepts **1.** two **2.** one **3.** none
4. one **5.** none **6.** one **7.** two **8.** none **9.** two **10.** one

Section 8.7 pp. 510–512
Practice **1.** $x = 46.7°$, $y = 133.3°$ **2.** $x = 130.1°$, $y = 49.9°$
3. $x = 18.3°$, $y = 161.7°$ **4.** $x = 46.0°$, $y = 134.0°$
5. $x = 56.9°$, $y = 123.1°$ **6.** $x = 120.0°$, $y = 60.0°$
7. one; $\angle B = 33.9°$, $\angle C = 104.1°$ **8.** two; $\angle C = 33.0°$,
$\angle A = 120°$; or $\angle C = 147.0°$, $\angle A = 6.0°$ **9.** one;
$\angle Q = 90°$, $\angle R = 30°$ **10.** two; $\angle L = 39.9°$,
$\angle K = 102.8°$; or $\angle L = 140.1°$, $\angle K = 2.6°$ **11.** none
12. two; $\angle C = 66.9°$, $\angle A = 65.1°$; or $\angle C = 113.1°$,
$\angle A = 18.9°$ **13.** one; $\angle Z = 25.7°$, $\angle Y = 34.3°$
14. none **15.** $\angle B = 34.4°$, $\angle C = 100.6°$, $c = 41.7$ cm
16. $\angle X = 14.5°$, $\angle Z = 132.8°$, $z = 73.3$ cm
17. $\angle Q = 48.1°$, $\angle P = 91.6°$, $p = 54.4$ cm; or
$\angle Q = 131.9°$, $\angle P = 7.8°$, $p = 7.4$ cm **18.** $\angle F = 33.7°$,
$\angle H = 41.3°$, $h = 4.2$ cm **19.** no triangle
20. $\angle F = 76.5°$, $\angle D = 32.3°$, $d = 16.7$ cm; or
$\angle F = 103.5°$, $\angle D = 5.3°$, $d = 2.9$ cm **21.** no triangle
22. $\angle N = 52.7°$, $\angle M = 84.5°$, $m = 23.1$ cm; or
$\angle N = 127.3°$, $\angle M = 9.9°$, $m = 4.0$ cm
23. a) $\angle BCD = 54.3°$, $\angle BDA = 125.7°$ **b)** 18.7 cm
24. 6.0 m **25.** 5.3 cm **26. a)** $(0, 12)$ **b)** $(0, 18.24)$ or
$(0, 5.74)$ **c)** not possible **d)** $(0, 26.15)$ **27. a)** 6
28. 24.78 **29.** 14.64
Applications and Problem Solving **30.** $AB = 4\sqrt{2}$,
$AC = 2\sqrt{5}$, $BC = 6$, $\angle ABC = 45°$, $\angle ACB = 63.43°$,
$\angle CAB = 71.57°$; $AB = 4\sqrt{2}$, $BD = 2$, $DA = 2\sqrt{5}$,
$\angle ABD = 45°$, $\angle ADB = 116.57°$, $\angle DAB = 18.43°$
31. 9 km or 4 km **32. a)** 8 **b)** 8 **33.** 1.5 m **34.** 365 m
35. 20.4 m **36.** 3.6 h **37.** 0.004 s **39. a)** 12.0 m
b) 12.0 m **c)** 2.2 m **d)** 6.0 m **e)** 6.6 m **40.** $AB = \sqrt{65}$,
$BC = 7$, $CA = \sqrt{2}$, $\angle B = 7.1°$, $\angle A = 37.9°$, $\angle C = 135°$;
$AB = \sqrt{65}$, $BC = 7$, $CA = 8\sqrt{2}$, $\angle A = 37.9°$,
$\angle B = 97.1°$, $\angle C = 45°$ **41.** $286°$, $14°$

Investigating Math p. 513
1 Finding the Third Side **1. a)** $c = 5$ **b)** one; there is

one solution to the quadratic equation. **2. a)** $c = 2.6$ or
7.4 **b)** two; there are two solutions to the quadratic
equation. **3. a)** $c = 13.3$ **b)** one; there is one positive
solution to the quadratic equation. **4. a)** no solution
b) zero; there is no solution to the quadratic equation.
2 Solving Triangles **1. a)** two triangles **b)** $b = 5.0$ cm,
$\angle B = 89.6°$, $\angle C = 53.4°$; or $b = 1.4$ cm, $\angle B = 16.4°$,
$\angle C = 126.6°$ **2. a)** no triangle **3. a)** one triangle
b) $r = 5.4$ cm, $\angle R = 58.5°$, $\angle T = 51.5°$ **4. a)** no
triangle **5. a)** two triangles **b)** $l = 3.9$ cm, $\angle L = 23.2°$,
$\angle N = 115.6°$; or $l = 9.5$ cm, $\angle L = 74.4°$, $\angle N = 64.4°$
6. a) one triangle **b)** $c = 9.9$ cm, $\angle C = 60°$, $\angle B = 90°$
7. a) one triangle **b)** $p = 2.8$ cm, $\angle P = 9.4°$, $\angle Q = 20.6°$
8. a) no triangle

Connecting Math and Fashion pp. 514–515
1 Developing a Formula **1. a)** $l = g + 12\sqrt{d^2 + g^2}$

b) $l = 6g + 2\sqrt{d^2 + g^2} + 5\sqrt{4d^2 + g^2}$

c) $l = 6g + 6\sqrt{d^2 + g^2} + \sqrt{36d^2 + g^2}$

2. a) North American **b)** shoe store **3.** Answers may
vary.
2 Developing a More General Formula

1. a) $l = g + 2(n - 1)\sqrt{d^2 + g^2}$

b) $l = (n - 1)g + 2\sqrt{d^2 + g^2} + (n - 2)\sqrt{4d^2 + g^2}$

c) $l = (n - 1)g + (n - 1)\sqrt{d^2 + g^2} + \sqrt{(n-1)d^2 + g^2}$

2. a) North American **b)** shoe store **3. a)** North
American **b)** European and shoe store **4.** The lengths
are all equal. **5.** When $n = 2$, the formulas all simplify
to the same formula: $l = g + 2\sqrt{d^2 + g^2}$.

3 Comparing With Other Styles
1. a) $l = (n - 1)(2d + g)$; $l = (n - 1)(2d + g)$ **b)** equal
2. The length is less than all three other methods.
3. Answers may vary.

Review pp. 516–517
6. $(0, 2)$ **7.** $(0, 1)$, $(3, 3)$ **8.** $(2, 2)$, $(1, -1)$, $(0, -4)$,
$(-1, -7)$ **9.** $(1, -5.5)$ **10.** $(8.5, 1.5)$, $(4, 0)$, $(-0.5, -1.5)$
11. $\left(-\dfrac{4}{3}, 3\right)$, $\left(\dfrac{4}{3}, 0\right)$ **12.** $(7, 0)$, $(0, 14)$ **13.** $\dfrac{5\sqrt{2}}{2}$

14. $\dfrac{\sqrt{5}}{5}$ **15.** $\dfrac{6\sqrt{10}}{5}$ **16.** $4\sqrt{2}$ **17.** $2\sqrt{5}$ **18.** $\dfrac{2\sqrt{5}}{5}$

19. 5.7 **20.** 4.5 **21.** 6.0 **22.** 6; 2; 1.90 **23.** 7; 28; 6.79
24. 6; 12; 5.37 **25.** $x^2 + y^2 = 9$
26. $(x - 3)^2 + (y - 7)^2 = 49$ **27.** $(x + 7)^2 + (y + 3)^2 = 36$
28. $(x - 6)^2 + (y + 3)^2 = 144$ **29.** $(x + 4)^2 + (y - 5)^2 = 5$

30. $(x - 11)^2 + (y + 12)^2 = 27$ **31.** $(0, 0)$, 11
32. $(1, 0)$, 0.5 **33.** $(-3, 4)$, 9 **34.** $(3.5, -6.5)$, 8
35. $x^2 + y^2 = 100$ **36.** $x^2 + y^2 = 81$
37. $(x - 2)^2 + (y - 1)^2 = 9$ **38.** $(x + 1)^2 + (y - 3)^2 = 100$
39. $(x - 4)^2 + (y + 1)^2 = 65$ **40.** $(x + 5)^2 + (y + 5)^2 = 72$
41. a) $(-2.6, 2.3)$, $(-3.4, -0.3)$ **b)** 2.8 **42. a)** $(1, -3)$
43. a) $(3, -2)$ **44. a)** $(-5, 1)$, $(0, -4)$ **b)** 7.1 **45. a)** $(-3, 1)$
46. $x = \pm 20$, $y = \pm 20$ **47.** $x = \pm 15$, $y = \pm 15$
48. $x + 4y - 17 = 0$ **49.** $3x - 2y + 24 = 0$ **50.** $2\sqrt{34}$
51. $2\sqrt{17}$ **52.** $\angle F = 65°$, $e = 2.2$ cm, $d = 5.3$ cm
53. $m = 8.7$ cm, $\angle L = 45.2°$, $\angle M = 44.8°$
54. $\angle Y = 12.3°$, $\angle Z = 41.9°$, $z = 25.8$ m
55. $\angle S = 37.6°$, $\angle T = 112.2°$, $\angle U = 30.2°$
56. $\angle P = 73.2°$ **57.** 70 m **58.** two triangles;
$\angle H = 58.8°$, $\angle I = 101.2°$; or $\angle H = 121.2°$, $\angle I = 38.8°$
59. no triangle **60.** one triangle; $\angle C = 20.4°$,
$\angle A = 55.6°$ **61.** two triangles; $\angle M = 42.7°$,
$\angle K = 111.3°$; or $\angle M = 137.3°$, $\angle K = 16.7°$
62. $\angle QRS = 62.7°$, $\angle QSP = 117.3°$, RS = 3.6 cm
Exploring Math 1. 40 **2.** 33 **3.** 33 **4.** 27

Chapter Check p. 518

4. $(-2, -3)$, $(1, -1)$, $(4, 1)$ **5.** $(-1, 3)$ **6.** $(0, 1)$, $(5, -2)$
7. $(0, -5.2)$, $(-1, -2.4)$, $(-2, 0.4)$, $(-3, 3.2)$
8. $(1.5, -2.5)$ **9.** $\left(\dfrac{2}{3}, 0\right)$, $\left(-\dfrac{2}{3}, 5\right)$ **10.** $\dfrac{3\sqrt{2}}{2}$ **11.** $\dfrac{6\sqrt{5}}{5}$
12. $\dfrac{7\sqrt{5}}{5}$ **13.** $\dfrac{9\sqrt{10}}{10}$ **14.** 3.8 **15.** 3.6 **16.** 3; 0.75; 0.73
17. 5; 15; 4.74 **18.** 3; 2; 1.66 **19.** $x^2 + y^2 = 64$
20. $(x + 2)^2 + (y - 7)^2 = 81$ **21.** $(x - 4)^2 + (y + 8)^2 = 10$
22. $(5, 0)$, 13 **23.** $(-6, 4.5)$, 4 **24.** $x^2 + y^2 = 64$
25. $x^2 + y^2 = 25$ **26.** $(x - 4)^2 + (y + 2)^2 = 25$
27. $(x + 2)^2 + (y + 3)^2 = 29$ **28. a)** $(2, 6)$, $(6, -2)$
b) 8.9 **29. a)** $(0.8, 3.4)$, $(-0.8, 4.6)$ **b)** 2 **30. a)** $(-1, -2)$,
$(2, 1)$ **b)** 4.2 **31.** $3x - 5y + 34 = 0$ **32.** $x + 3y + 10 = 0$
33. $\sqrt{57}$ **34.** $b = 2.4$ m, $\angle B = 71.3°$, $\angle C = 18.7°$
35. $\angle Y = 61.3°$, $z = 27.5$ cm, $x = 57.2$ cm
36. $\angle P = 118.7°$, $\angle Q = 35.1°$, $\angle R = 26.2°$
37. $\angle H = 44.8°$, $\angle I = 46.4°$, $i = 30.9$ cm **38.** no
triangle **39.** two triangles; $\angle T = 56.2°$, $\angle U = 94.8°$;
or $\angle T = 123.8°$, $\angle U = 27.2°$ **40.** one triangle;
$\angle Y = 18.6°$, $\angle Z = 65.4°$ **41.** two triangles;
$\angle H = 64.4°$, $\angle F = 74.6°$; or $\angle H = 115.6°$,
$\angle F = 23.4°$ **42.** AC = 38 m or AC = 52 m

Using the Strategies p. 519

1. 51% **2.** 150 **3.** 7π **4.** A = 12, B = 20, C = 64, D = 4
5. $\dfrac{2}{3}$ **6.** 3 **7.** 17 **8.** 5 **10.** 2 **11.** 78°
Data Bank 2. 5.6 h

Cumulative Review, Chapters 5–8 pp. 520–521

Chapter 5

1. a) $(f + g)(x) = x^2 + 3x - 4$ **b)** $(f - g)(x) = x^2 + x - 2$
c) $(fg)(x) = x^3 + x^2 - 5x + 3$ **d)** $\left(\dfrac{f}{g}\right)(x) = x + 3$, $x \neq 1$
e) $f(x) + 2g(x) = x^2 + 4x - 5$
f) $2(gg)(x) - f(x) = x^2 - 6x + 5$ **2. a)** $(f \circ g)(x) = -x^2$;
$(g \circ f)(x) = x^2$ **b)** f: D: all real numbers, R: $y \leq 0$;
g: D: all real numbers, R: $y \geq 0$; $f \circ g$: D: all real
numbers, R: $y \leq 0$; $g \circ f$: D: all real numbers, R: $y \geq 0$
3. $y = -3x - 6$ **4.** Yes. **5. a)** D: all real numbers, R: all
real numbers **b)** -2, 1, 3; 6 **c)** maximum: $(-0.8, 8.2)$,
minimum: $(2.1, -4.1)$ **d)** $f(x) > 0$: $-2 < x < 1$, $x > 3$;
$f(x) < 0$: $x < -2$, $1 < x < 3$ **e)** no symmetry; negative,
positive **6. a)** D: all real numbers, R: $y \geq 0$
b) 1, 5 **c)** $f(x) \geq 0$: all values of x **d)** symmetric about
$x = 3$ **7. a)** $x = -3$, $y = 1$ **b)** D: $x \neq 3$, R: $y \neq 1$
8. D: $x \geq -3$, R: $y \geq 0$ **9.** no solution **10.** 1.5
11. $-2 \leq m < 2$ **12.** $-3 \leq w \leq 1$

Chapter 6

1. a) 10, 12 **b)** $2n + 2$ people can be seated at n square
tables joined in a row. **2.** -1 is the opposite of 1. 0 has
no opposite. **5.** 16, 20, 24, 28, 32, 36, 40, 44, 48
6. 1, 2, 3, 4, 5, 6, 7, 8, 9, 11, 12, 13, 15, 17, 19
7. b) 13 **8. a)** true **b)** If the diagonals of a quadrilateral
are perpendicular, with the longer one bisecting the
shorter one, then the quadrilateral is a kite; true
c) If the diagonals of a quadrilateral are not
perpendicular, and the longer one does not bisect the
shorter one, then the quadrilateral is not a kite; true

Chapter 7

2. 2.2 m **4.** $x = 230°$ **5.** $a = 40°$, $b = 35°$, $c = 35°$,
$d = 15°$, $e = 15°$ **6.** $a = 75°$ **7.** $x = 45°$, $y = 45°$, $z = 45°$
9. $x = 14.5$ cm, $y = 14.5$ cm **10.** $a = 8$ cm, $b = 8.5$ cm,
$c = 3$ cm **11.** 11.8 cm, 53.0 cm² **12.** 160°, 20°

Chapter 8

2. $(0, -2)$, $(3, 1)$ **3.** $(-1, 4)$, $(0, 1)$, $(1, -2)$, $(2, -5)$
4. $(2.5, 0)$, $(5, -1)$, $(7.5, -2)$ **5.** 2.8 **6.** 2.7 **7.** $x^2 + y^2 = 9$
8. $(x + 1)^2 + (y - 5)^2 = 16$ **9.** $x^2 + y^2 = 25$
10. $(x - 4)^2 + (y - 2)^2 = 20$ **11. a)** $(0, 5)$
12. a) $(4.0, -1.2)$, $(5.0, -5.8)$ **b)** 4.7 **13.** $2\sqrt{5}$
14. $y = 3.3$ m, $\angle Y = 69.9°$, $\angle Z = 20.1°$ **15.** $\angle J = 34°$,
$j = 12.5$ cm, $k = 18.3$ cm **16.** 0.7 m or 2.6 m

Chapter 9

Personal Finance p. 523
1. US Civil War **2.** World War I **3.** The Great Depression **4.** World War II **5. a)** 30% **b)** 30% **c)** 40%

Getting Started pp. 524–525
1 Comparing Unit Prices **1. a)** the price of a specified unit of a product **b)** olive oil: $0.0144/mL, $0.0120/mL; tomato ketchup: $0.0053/mL, $0.0036/mL; orange juice: $0.0020/mL, $0.0017/mL; bleach: $0.0014/mL, $0.0009/mL **c)** Answers may vary. **2.** olive oil: 500 mL; tomato ketchup: 1.25 L; orange juice: 1.89 L; bleach: 1.8 L **3. a)** The larger size has a lower unit price. **b)** Answers may vary. **4.** Answers may vary. The person may not need the larger size, or may not have enough storage space.
2 Buying at a Supermarket **1.** bagels: Foodmart; oranges: EconoFoods; detergent: EconoFoods; cream cheese: Foodmart **2.** Answers may vary. You assume quality is the same, and in products such as bagels and oranges, you assume size is the same. **3.** Answers may vary. quality **4.** Answers may vary. quality, location, selection
3 Warm Up **Estimates may vary for 1.–7.** **1.** $39
2. $93 **3.** $4 **4.** $26 **5.** $360 **6.** $1.10 **7.** $630
8. $22.40 **9.** $327.82 **10.** $4.563 **11.** $84.60 **12.** $448
13. $15 620 **14.** $23.65 **15.** $425.21 **16.** 0.3, 30%
17. 0.25, 25% **18.** 0.5, 50% **19.** 0.17, 17% **20.** 0.8, 80% **21.** 0.32, 32% **22.** 0.55, 55% **23.** 1.25, 125%
24. 0.75 **25.** 0.07 **26.** 0.045 **27.** 0.0275 **28.** 1.25
29. 0.005 **Estimates may vary for 30.–37.** **30.** 60
31. 2400 **32.** $500 **33.** $3 **34.** $1 **35.** $5200 **36.** $800
37. $17 **38.** $4852.80 **39.** $234 **40.** $690 **41.** $36
42. $0.44 **43.** $0.27 **44.** $3 out of $10 **45.** $8 out of $40 **46.** $18 out of $192
Mental Math
1. $8.75 **2.** $0.25 **3.** $0.60 **4.** $0.48 **5.** $48 **6.** $130
7. $1.50 **8.** $60 **9.** $15 **10.** $0.18 **11.** 5.5% **12.** 16%
13. 13% **14.** 5% **15.** 0.1% **16.** 1% **17.** 0.5%
18. 0.25%
Multiplying Numbers That Differ by 10 and End in 5
1. 375 **2.** 2475 **3.** 9975 **4.** 16 875 **5.** 357 500
6. 637 500 **7.** 15.75 **8.** 80.75 **9.** The numbers are $10x + 5$ and $10x - 5$. Their product is $(10x + 5)(10x - 5) = 100x^2 - 25$. **10. a)** Drop the 5 from the larger, and add to the smaller, multiply and subtract 75. **b)** The numbers are $10x - 5$ and $10(x + 1) + 5$. Their product is $100x^2 + 100x - 75$, or $100x(x + 1) - 75$.

Investigating Math p. 526
1 Converting Currencies **1. a)** drachma, krona, krone, peseta **b)** 196 078 drachma; 5200 krona; 4331 krone; 96 154 peseta **2.** $524.35 **3.** $38 142.50
4. a) $63 792.50 **b)** 243 390 francs **5.** $152.57 **6.** No. The exchange rate may change in four years.
7. a) 38 462 bolivar; 65 pesos **b)** 6 pesos
2 Buying and Selling **1.** The bank pays less if you are selling than they charge if you are buying. This is how they make money. **2.** 71% represents a Canadian dollar worth US71¢. 132% represents a US dollar worth $1.32 Canadian. **3. a)** increased **b)** decreased

Section 9.1 pp. 530–531
Practice **1.** 15 **2.** 9 **3.** 22.5 **4.** 28.5 **5.** 5.25 **6.** 18.75
7. a) $3640 **b)** $840 **c)** $24/h **8.** $495 **9.** $560
10. $384 **11.** $521.25 **12.** $814.13 **13.** $5570
14. $1960.10 **15.** $360 **16. a)** the 40-h week **b)** $52
17. $2211 **18.** $15 600 **19.** $1239.75
Applications and Problem Solving **20.** $42
21. $524.10 **22.** $422.50 **23.** $588 **24.** $3038.50
25. a) piecework **b)** $470 **c)** tips **26.** 15% **27. a)** He would earn $87 more for Option B. **b)** Answers may vary. Option A: pays less, but Anton can improve his keyboarding; Option B: pays more, but no room for improvement **28. a)** $2195, $2187.53, $2330.72, $2339.76 **29. a)** A: $2625; B: $3000; C: $3125
c) $15 000

Section 9.2 pp. 536–537
Practice **1.** 52 **2.** 12 **3.** 26 **4.** 24 **5.** $37.09
6. $16.60 **7.** $63.21 **8.** $55.08 **9.** $11.53 **10.** $40.67
11. $11.02 **12.** $29.75 **13.** $58.73 **14.** $43.88
15. $18.47 **16.** $37.87 **17.** $4556 **18.** $3111.85
19. $5692.78 **20.** $9874.10 **21.** $14 457.90
22. $1647.33 **23.** $1421.66 **24.** $2551.83
25. $1507.95 **26.** $904.34 **27.** CPP: $1068.80; EI: $1053; taxable income: $39 294; basic federal tax: $6095.11 **28.** CPP: $844.80; EI: $807.30; taxable income: $29 900; basic federal tax: $3332.51
Applications and Problem Solving **29. a)** CPP: $896; EI: $850.50 **b)** $6219.38 **30. a)** CPP: $1068.80; EI: $1053 **b)** $11 861.03 **c)** $31 881.17 **31.** $35 389.06
32. $27 485.41 **33. a)** $2980 **b)** $26 881.28 **34. a)** the employer's earnings **b)** Answers may vary. **c)** Answers may vary. **35. a)** $582.75 **b)** Answers may vary.
36. Net claim code is a category on which the amount of tax deduction is based. **b)** Codes are based on the personal tax credit an employee expects to have.
37. Answers may vary. **38.** Answers may vary.

Section 9.3 pp. 542–543
Practice   1. 4% **2.** 2% **3.** 0.667% **4.** 0.022% **5.** 6
6. 8 **7.** 5 **8.** 48 **9.** 6 **10.** 6 **11.** 31 **12.** 61 **13.** 1.5%; 12
14. 3%; 12 **15.** 6%; 10 **16.** 0.5%; 12 **17.** 0.016%; 30
18. $2604.52 **19.** $2389.66 **20.** $3077.25
21. $2029.81 **22.** $97.42 **23.** $34.85 **24.** $59.18
25. $2.78 **26.** $3738.55 **27.** $2089.36 **28.** $2813.77
Applications and Problem Solving   29. $2567.36
30. $20 805.70 **31.** $1210.54 **32.** $13 589.85
33. a) Option C **b)** $2.18 **34. a)** $2122.35 **b)** $122.35
35. a) $108, $116, $124, $132, $140, $148, $156,
$164, $172, $180, $188, $196; $108.24, $117.17,
$126.82, $137.28, $148.59, $160.84, $174.10,
$188.45, $203.99, $220.80, $239.01, $258.71 **c)** Yes.
There is only one y-value for each x-value. **d)** Simple
interest gives a straight line. The amount of interest
is the slope, and it does not change. Compound
interest gives a curve. Since the interest is increasing,
the slope is increasing. **36.** $3653.45 **37.** about
18 years

Technology pp. 544–545
1 No Payments Made   1. $5378.54 **2.** 5.25 years
3. 7.86% **4.** 7% compounded annually
2 Monthly Payments Made   1. Yes. $3139.27 must
still be paid. **2.** –$8261; The annuity has run out.
3. 6.87% **4.** $462.32 **5. a)** $306 837.52 **b)** 10.84%
c) $329.52 **d)** Yes. The earlier you start, the more
interest you earn.

Technology p. 546
1 Annuity Remaining   1. Answers may vary.
2. $4254.52 **3.** after 3 years **4. a)** $34 371.59
b) $56 394.89 **c)** $18 938.81
2 Annuity Payments   1. a) $701.33 **b)** $424.94
c) $1267.43 **d)** $113.55

Section 9.4 pp. 549–550
Practice   1. 8.16% **2.** 8.24% **3.** 8.30% **4.** 12.55%
5. 6.09% **6.** 8.57% **7.** 5.06% **8.** 7.71% **9.** 5.97%
10. 4.33%
Applications and Problem Solving   11. 5.25%
compounded semi-annually; $1.92 **12. a)** A
b) A: 8.77%; B: 8.30% **13.** the bank loan **14.** 7.12%
15. a) The annual rate is the daily rate times 365.
b) 1.53% **c)** 20.03% **16.** 19.56% **17. a)** Option A:
7.02%; Option B: 7.2% **b)** Answers may vary. She
may think the interest rate will go down. **18. a)** 12%,
12.36%, 12.49%, 12.55%, 12.62%, 12.68%, 12.72%,
12.73% **c)** 12.75% **d)** 12.75% **19. a)** 7.71% **b)** 10.67%
c) 9.65% **d)** 6.40% **20.** 6.4%

Section 9.5 pp. 555–556
Practice   1. a) $375.12 **b)** $46.12 **2. a)** $1700 **b)** $220
c) $2420 **3.** $9.55 **4.** $4.24 **5.** $0.83 **6.** $10.25
7. $5.88; $397.88 **8.** $0.95; $64.40 **9.** $0.72; $48.97
10. $1.24; $83.75 **11.** $4.43 **12.** $0.81 **13.** $3.82
14. $5.94 **15.** $5.42 **16.** $0.44 **17.** $0.98 **18.** $0.13
19. $2.82 **20.** $3.11 **21.** $114.40 **22.** $217.69
23. $500.94 **24.** $437.75 **25.** $601.71
Applications and Problem Solving   26. a) $554.85
b) $419.85 **c)** $4118.85 **27.** Answers may vary.
28. $298.51 **29. a)** $7.01 **b)** $483 **c)** $93.55 **d)** $3
e) $93.07 **30. a)** The store's offer is less expensive.
b) Answers may vary.

Section 9.6 pp. 560–561
Practice   1. $50 000 **2.** $7375 **3.** $4995 **4.** $20 625
5. $822.03 **6.** $1513.53 **7.** $1138.29 **8.** $1174.68
9. $745.20 **10.** $1074.00 **11.** $1264.36 **12.** $3492.72
13. $2140.45 **14.** $2533.25 **15.** $4899.76
16. $7535.63 **17.** $8176.96 **18.** $13 676.36
19. $2093.94 **20.** $177 895.83 **21.** $40 073.82
22. $1 155 167.75 **23.** $34 445 **24.** $64 353.35
25. $443 164.36
Applications and Problem Solving   26. a) $669.82
b) $200 946 **c)** $100 946 **27. a)** $144 900 **b)** $1157.17
28. a) $126 000 **b)** $882.52 **c)** $313 756 **d)** $138 756
29. $19 449.16 **30. a)** $1638.11 **b)** $766.64
31. $1333.84 **32. a)** $1135.32 **b)** $996.30 **33.** $1218.41
34. $4806.86 **35. a)** $307.42 **b)** Answers may vary.
36. 6.6599 **38. a)** $152 188 **b)** $1293.60 **c)** $4784

Section 9.7 pp. 565–566
Practice   1. education/reading **2.** gifts **3.** shelter
4. utilities **5.** personal care **6.** food **7.** entertainment
8. gifts **9.** food **10.** clothing or personal care
11. charitable donations **12.** personal care **13.** home
furnishings **14.** clothing **15.** balanced **16.** surplus of
6.5% **17.** deficit **18.** surplus of 7.6% **19.** $48.50
20. b) $780
Applications and Problem Solving   21. a) $675
22. a) Hydro: $76.92, $25.64; Gas: $80.75, $26.92;
Food: $410.17, $136.72; TV: $22, $7.33; Phone: $35,
$11.67 **c)** $510.83 **24. a)** 34.8%, 18.6%, 9.3%, 7.1%,
7.0%, 23.2% **c)** –$26.41, +$37.50, –$61.69, +$5.60,
$0, +$45

Investigating Math pp. 567–569
1 Understanding a Bank Statement   1. a) $1807
b) Debit is an amount subtracted from an account,
and credit is an amount added to an account.
2. a) Direct debit is the use of your bank card in a
store or a bill payment taken directly from your
account; instant teller withdrawal is the withdrawal of

money from a bank machine. **3.** It was cashed first.
4. Yes, if the bank allows overdrafts. **5.** Option A
**2 Reconciling a Bank Statement with a Personal
Transaction Record** **1.** Answers may vary.
2. Answers may vary. **3. a)** The error was writing
$88.95 instead of $88.59 for cheque 003.

Connecting Math and Transportation
pp. 570–571
1 Which Car to Buy **1.** freight and dealer
preparation, taxes, licence, possibly dealer options
4. "Black book" value is the average retail price of the
given model, with stated options, in good condition.
2 Financing a Car Purchase **1. a)** $1880 **b)** $493
c) the bank
3 Operating Costs **1.** fixed: depreciation, insurance,
licence; variable: gas, maintenance **3.** $20 480

Review pp. 572–573
1. $435.63 **2.** $239.25 **3.** $3240 **4.** $90.80
5. $3548.41 **6.** $2566.23 **7.** $5528.81 **8.** $4672.10
9. $1159.58 **10.** $998.30 **11.** $1565.49
12. a) CPP: $1068.80; EI: $1053 **b)** $9613.01
c) $28 165.19 **13.** $5705.83 **14.** $309.08
15. a) $2838.51 **b)** $338.51 **16. a)** $2704.43 **b)** $204.43
17. 4.59% **18.** Option A **19.** $5\frac{1}{4}$% compounded
semi-annually **20. a)** $300.98 **b)** $11.98 **21.** $8.97;
$607.22 **22.** $1.63; $110.13 **23.** $13.90; $940.68
24. $15.83; $1071.13 **25. a)** $0.29 **b)** $0.54 **c)** $0.68
26. $441.86 **27.** $58.89 **28.** $2366.25
Exploring Math **1.** deficient **2.** deficient **3.** perfect
4. deficient **5.** abundant **6.** deficient **7.** deficient
8. abundant **9.** perfect **10.** abundant **11.** deficient
12. abundant **13.** sum of proper factors of 220: 284;
sum of proper factors of 284: 220 **14.** sum of proper
factors of 1184: 1210; sum of proper factors of 1210:
1184 **15.** No. Since the proper factors of any perfect
number add to the number itself, they cannot add to
any other number.

Chapter Check p. 574
1. a) $682.50 **b)** $435 **c)** $483.75 **d)** $1347.50 **2.** $1300
3. $309 **4. a)** $86.67 **b)** $81 **c)** $6503.62 **5.** $358.24
6. $2045.42 **7.** 9.2% **8. a)** $518.18 **b)** $88.87 **c)** 20.7%
9. $254 579.50 **10. a)** $0.98 **b)** $1.31 **c)** $0.98 **d)** $4.42
11. $1144.28 **12.** $1281.30 **13. a)** $2866.26 **b)** $786.26

Using the Strategies p. 575
1. 10 **3.** no **4.** 18 **5.** 785 m **7.** $x = 2y - z$ **8.** D = 1,
E = 4, F = 8 **9.** 441, 1444 **10.** −25 **11.** 343
12. a) 219, 438, 657 **b)** 327, 654, 981 and 273, 546, 819
Data Bank **1. a)** increase **b)** 55+ years

Cumulative Review, Chapters 1–9 pp. 576–579

1. one solution; (−2, 2) **2.** no solution **3.** one solution;
(−4, −4) **4.** infinitely many solutions **5.** (2, −1)
6. $(-\frac{1}{2}, 2)$ **7.** (−1, 0) **8.** (2, 1) **9.** (2, −1) **10.** (−3, 2)
11. (−2, 0) **12.** (1, −3) **13.** $(2, -\frac{1}{2})$ **14.** (2, −2)
15. (3, 2, 1) **16.** (−1, 1, 0) **17.** length: 563 km,
breadth: 257 km **18.** bachelor: 48; 1-bedroom: 60;
2-bedroom: 60 **19.** $p < -7$ **20.** $h > 3$ **21.** $f \geq 4$
22. $n \leq 12$ **23.** $g \leq 2$ **24.** $y > -12$ **25.** $x \leq 12$ **26.** $m > 11$
27. $d < \frac{7}{3}$ **28.** (1, 6), (−5, 1), (−2, −2) **41. a)** $5x + 8y \leq 40$
b) $x \geq 0, y \geq 0$ **42. a)** down **b)** (0, 0) **c)** $x = 0$
d) D: all real numbers, R: $y \leq 0$ **e)** maximum: 0
43. a) up **b)** (0, 5) **c)** $x = 0$ **d)** D: all real numbers, R:
$y \geq 5$ **e)** minimum: 5 **44. a)** down **b)** (1, −3) **c)** $x = 1$
d) D: all real numbers, R: $y \leq -3$ **e)** maximum: −3
45. a) up **b)** (5, 0) **c)** $x = 5$ **d)** D: all real numbers, R:
$y \geq 0$ **e)** minimum: 0 **46. a)** up **b)** (−3, −4) **c)** $x = -3$
d) D: all real numbers, R: $y \geq -4$ **e)** minimum: −4
47. a) down **b)** (−7, 2) **c)** $x = -7$ **d)** D: all real numbers,
R: $y \leq 2$ **e)** maximum: 2 **48.** $y = 4x^2 + 3$
49. $y = -(x + 2)^2 - 3$ **50.** $y = \frac{1}{2}(x + 2)^2 + 5$
51. $y = (x + 3)^2 - 3$ **52.** (5, −13) **53.** (−4, 15) **54.** (3, −3)
55. (1, 1) **56. a)** 8 m **b)** 10 m **c)** 1 m **d)** 1.7 m **e)** 20.7 m
57. a) 200 m by 200 m **b)** 40 000 m² **58.** −4, 3 **59.** 3, 5
60. −1, 9 **61.** $-2, \frac{1}{3}$ **62.** ±11 **63.** $\frac{-9 \pm \sqrt{69}}{2}$
64. $\frac{5 \pm \sqrt{33}}{4}$ **65.** −1, −2 **66.** $-\frac{1}{5}, -1$ **67.** $\pm \frac{1}{\sqrt{3}}$
68. no real roots **69.** real, equal **70.** 1, 2 **71.** −7.14,
0.14 **72.** $3x^2 + 13x - 10 = 0$ **73.** $k < \frac{25}{8}$
74. $(2p - 1)(p + 1)(p - 1)$ **75.** 3, ±1 **76.** $-\frac{1}{2}, 1, 2$
77. Yes. 180 cm by 90 cm **78.** 0.75 m
79. a) $(f + g)(x) = 4x^2 + 2x - 12$
b) $(f - g)(x) = 4x^2 - 2x - 6$
c) $(fg)(x) = 8x^3 - 12x^2 - 18x + 27$
d) $\left(\frac{f}{g}\right)(x) = 2x + 3, x \neq \frac{3}{2}$
e) $f(x) + 3g(x) = 4x^2 + 6x - 18$
f) $(gg)(x) + f(x) = 8x^2 - 12x$
80. a) $(f \circ g)(x) = \sqrt{5x + 3}$, $(g \circ f)(x) = 5\sqrt{x} + 3$
b) f: D: $x \geq -3$, R: $y \geq 0$; g: D: all real numbers,
R: all real numbers; $f \circ g$: D: $x \geq -\frac{3}{5}$, R: $y \geq 0$;

$g \circ f$: D: $x \geq -3$, R: $y \geq 0$ **82. a)** D: all real numbers, R: all real numbers **b)** -1, 5; -5 **c)** maximum: $(-1, 0)$; minimum: $(3, -32)$ **d)** $f(x) > 0$: $x > 5$; $f(x) < 0$: $x < -1$, $-1 < x < 5$ **e)** no symmetry; negative, positive
83. a) D: all real numbers, R: $y \geq -5$ **b)** -3, 3 **c)** $x \leq -3$, $x \geq 3$ **d)** symmetric about the y-axis **84. a)** $x = 0$, $y = x$ **b)** D: $x \neq 0$, R: all real numbers **85.** D: $x \geq 2$, R: $y \geq 3$

86. $\dfrac{4}{5}$ **87.** 2 **88.** $w < 8$ **89.** $g \geq 2$ **90. b)** $\dfrac{n(n+1)}{2}$ cubes

make n steps. **92.** 4 has square roots -2 and $+2$; 0 has only one square root of 0 **93. a)** The result is one greater than the original number. **98. b)** 45
99. a) false **b)** If a whole number is a factor of 12, then it is a factor of 24; true **c)** If a whole number is not a factor of 12, then it is not a factor of 24; false
102. 6.0 m **104.** $x = 50°$, $y = 25°$ **105.** $a = 90°$, $b = 15°$
106. $a = 110°$, $b = 110°$, $c = 70°$ **107.** $p = 85°$, $q = 75°$, $r = 105°$, $s = 85°$, $t = 95°$, $u = 105°$ **109.** $a = 60°$, $b = 60°$, $c = 60°$ **110.** $x = 12$ cm, $y = 14$ cm, $z = 15$ cm
111. 64.8 cm^2 **112.** 9 **113.** 30 **114.** 18 **115.** PQ = $\sqrt{73}$, QR = $\sqrt{73}$; Thus, PQ = QR and $\triangle$PQR is isosceles.

116. $(-5, -3)$, $(-3, 0)$, $(-1, 3)$ **117.** $(1, \dfrac{7}{3})$, $(4, \dfrac{11}{3})$

118. 3; 12; 2.91 **119.** 7; 3.5; 3.13 **120.** $(-3, 6)$, 6
121. $(4, 0)$, $\sqrt{10}$ **122. a)** $(2, -3)$, $(3, 2)$ **b)** 5.1 **123. a)** no points of intersection **124.** $3x - 2y + 1 = 0$ **125.** 99.1°
126. 13.07 **127.** \$468.75 **128.** \$812.50 **129.** \$650
130. \$583 **131.** \$518 **132.** CPP: \$80.27; EI: \$75.60
133. \$830.62 **134.** 5.64% **135.** \$205 **136.** \$960.06

A

absolute value The absolute value of a number is its distance from zero on a real number line.

absolute value equation An equation with a variable within the absolute value symbol.

$|x + 3| + 1 = x$ is an absolute value equation.

absolute value function A function with a variable within the absolute value symbol.

$f(x) = |x| + 1$ is an absolute value function.

absolute value inequality An inequality with a variable within the absolute value symbol.

abundant number A natural number the sum of whose proper divisors is greater than the number itself.

acute angle An angle whose measure is between 0° and 90°.

acute triangle A triangle with three acute angles.

algebraic expression A mathematical phrase made up of numbers and variables, connected by operators.

alternate angles Two angles between two lines and on opposite sides of a transversal.

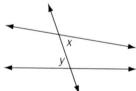

∠x and ∠y are alternate angles.

altitude of a triangle The perpendicular distance from one vertex to the opposite side.

amicable numbers Two natural numbers for which the sum of the proper divisors of one number is equal to the other number.

amortization period The period of time in which a mortgage would be fully repaid with equal periodic payments.

annuity A sequence of equal payments made at equal intervals of time.

area The number of square units contained in a region.

Argand plane A diagram in which complex numbers can be represented geometrically in the complex plane, where the horizontal axis is the real axis and the vertical axis is the imaginary axis.

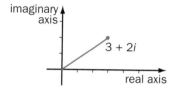

asymptote A line that a curve approaches more and more closely.

axes The intersecting number lines used for reference in locating points on a coordinate plane.

axiom A statement that is accepted to be true without proof.

axis of symmetry A line that is invariant under a reflection.

B

balanced budget A spending plan in which the total expenditure equals the total income.

biconditional statement A statement that can be written in *if and only if* form.

binomial A polynomial consisting of two terms.

$x^2 - 4$ is a binomial.

bisect Divide into two equal parts.

boundary line A line that divides the coordinate plane into two parts or regions.

boundary point of a number line A point that divides a number line into two parts or regions.

break-even point In business, the point at which the cost and revenue are equal.

budget A spending plan, or a record of money earned and of money spent.

C

capacity The largest amount that a container can hold.

central angle An angle formed by two radii of a circle.

Central angle AOC is subtended by arc AC and by chord AC.

centroid The point of intersection of the three medians of a triangle.

circle The set of all points in the plane that are equidistant from a fixed point called the centre.

circumcentre The point of intersection of the three perpendicular bisectors of the sides of a triangle.

circumference The perimeter of a circle, or the length of this perimeter.

chord of a circle A line segment with its endpoints on a circle.

coefficient A number or symbol immediately preceding a variable in a term. In $3x^2$, the coefficient of x^2 is 3.

co-interior angles Two angles between two lines and on the same side of a transversal.

collinear points Points that lie in the same straight line.

common factor A term that is a factor of two or more terms. The common factor of $4x$ and $6x$ is $2x$.

commutative property The property defined by $a + b = b + a$, and $ab = ba$.

complementary angles Two angles whose sum is $90°$.

complex conjugates Two numbers in the form $a + bi$ and $a - bi$, where a and b are real numbers and $i = \sqrt{-1}$.

complex number A number of the form $a + bi$, where a and b are real numbers and $i = \sqrt{-1}$.

composition of functions $f(x)$ and $g(x)$ The function whose value at x is $f(g(x))$ or $(f \circ g)(x)$.

composite number A whole number that is greater than 1 and is not prime.

$6 = 1 \times 2 \times 3$, so 6 is a composite number.

compound inequality An expression that involves two conditions of inequality.

$1 < x \leq 8$ is a compound inequality.

compound interest Interest that is calculated at regular intervals and is added to the principal for the next interest period.

compound statement A statement formed by connecting two or more statements with a connective, such as *and*, *or*, *not*, ...

concave polygon A polygon in which at least one line segment joining vertices of the polygon lies outside the polygon.

conclusion In a conditional statement, the part following "...*then*...".

conditional statement A compound statement that is written in the form "*If...then...*".

congruent figures Figures with the same shape and size.

conjecture A generalization, or educated guess, made using inductive reasoning.

continuous function A function that can be graphed with a line or smooth curve, and that has a domain with an infinite number of elements.

contrapositive A statement formed by negating the hypothesis and the conclusion of the converse of a conditional statement.

converse A statement formed by interchanging the hypothesis and the conclusion of a conditional statement.

convex polygon A polygon in which a line segment joining any two vertices of the polygon has no part outside the polygon.

coordinate plane A one-to-one pairing of all ordered pairs of real numbers with all points of a plane. Also called the Cartesian coordinate plane.

coordinates An ordered pair, (x, y), that locates a point on a coordinate plane.

corresponding angles Four pairs of angles formed by two lines and a transversal. In the diagram, the pairs of corresponding angles are:

$\angle 1$ and $\angle 5$
$\angle 2$ and $\angle 6$
$\angle 3$ and $\angle 7$
$\angle 4$ and $\angle 8$

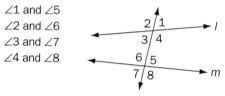

corollary An additional statement that follows simply from a theorem already proved.

cosine ratio For an acute angle in a right triangle, the ratio of the length of the adjacent side to the length of the hypotenuse

counterexample An example that shows that a conjecture is false.

cubic equation A polynomial equation of degree 3.

cubic function A function of degree 3.

cyclic quadrilateral A quadrilateral with all of its vertices on the same circle.

D

decagon A polygon with 10 sides.

deductive reasoning The process of demonstrating that, if certain statements are true, then other statements can be shown to follow from them.

deficient number A natural number the sum of whose proper divisors is less than the number itself.

degree of a polynomial The largest sum of the exponents of the variables in any one term of the polynomial.

The degree of $5x^4y + 4x^2y + 2xy$ is 5.

dependent variable In a relation, a variable whose value is determined by the independent variable.

diagonal A line segment with endpoints on two non-adjacent vertices of a polygon.

diameter of a circle A chord that passes through the centre of the circle.

direct proof A proof that begins with given information and deductively reaches a conclusion.

discontinuous function A function whose graph contains at least one break.

discriminant The quantity $b^2 - 4ac$ for the quadratic equation $ax^2 + bx + c = 0$.

distributive property The property defined by $a(b + c) = ab + ac$.

domain of a function The set of numbers for which a function is defined. The set of all first coordinates of the ordered pairs in a function.

double root One of a pair of equal roots of the same equation.

E

effective annual interest rate The simple interest rate that would produce the same interest in one year as the nominal interest rate.

equilateral triangle A triangle with all sides equal.

equivalent equations Equations that have the same solution over a given domain.

even-degree function A function whose degree is an even number.

$f(x) = x^4 + 2x^2 + 1$ is an even-degree function.

exterior angle An angle contained between one side of a polygon and the extension of the adjacent side.

extraneous root A solution to an equation, found algebraically, that does not satisfy the original equation.

F

factor A number or polynomial that is multiplied by another number or polynomial to give a product.

factoring Finding the factors of a number or expression.

factor theorem A polynomial $P(x)$ has $x - b$ as a factor if and only if $P(b) = 0$.

fractal A geometric figure that has self-similarity, is created using a recursive process, and is infinite in structure.

function A rule that assigns to each element in the domain a single element in the range.

G

golden ratio The ratio of the length to the width of a golden rectangle, approximately 1.6:1.

golden rectangle A rectangle that is pleasing to the eye. The ratio of the length to the width is approximately 1.6:1.

golden triangle An isosceles triangle in which the ratio of the length of one of the equal sides to the base is the golden ratio.

graduated commission A pay scheme in which the rate of commission increases as sales increase.

gross income An amount of money earned through employment.

H

half-plane The region of a plane on one side of a given boundary line.

heptagon A polygon with 7 sides.

hexagon A polygon with 6 sides.

hypotenuse The side opposite the right angle in a right triangle.

hypothesis In a conditional statement, the part following "*If...*".

I

image point A point that corresponds to an object point under a mapping.

imaginary unit The number i, which is a solution to the equation $i^2 = -1$.

incentre The point at which the angle bisectors of a triangle intersect.

incircle A circle inscribed in a triangle.

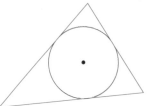

independent variable In a relation, a variable whose value may be freely chosen and which determines the value(s) of the dependent variable.

indirect proof A method of proof in which a desired conclusion is assumed to be false. If this assumption leads to a contradiction, then it can be concluded that the assumption was incorrect and the desired conclusion is true.

inductive reasoning A type of reasoning in which a pattern is observed in a set of data and the pattern is used to make an educated guess, or generalization, about the data.

inequality Two expressions related by an inequality symbol ($>$, $\geq$, $<$, $\leq$, or $\neq$).

$$4x \geq 8 \text{ is an inequality.}$$

inscribed angle An angle that has its vertex on a circle and is subtended by an arc of the circle.

Inscribed angle ABC is subtended by arc AC.

integer A number in the sequence ..., -3, -2, -1, 0, 1, 2, 3, ...

integral zero theorem If $x = b$ is an integral zero of a polynomial $P(x)$ with integral coefficients, then b is a factor of the constant term of the polynomial.

intercept A point at which a graph crosses or touches the x-axis or y-axis.

interior angle An angle formed inside a polygon by two adjacent sides of the polygon.

interval A restricted set of values of a variable.

$$-3 \le x < 2 \text{ is an interval.}$$

inverse function A function, f^{-1}, defined by $f^{-1}(b) = a$ if $f(a) = b$.

irrational number A real number that cannot be expressed in the form $\frac{a}{b}$, where a and b are integers and $b \ne 0$.

isosceles triangle A triangle with two equal sides.

iteration A repeated application of a mathematical procedure, with the result of one step being used as the input value of the subsequent step, and so on.

K

kite A quadrilateral with two pairs of adjacent sides equal.

L

law of cosines The relationship between the lengths of the three sides and the cosine of an angle in any triangle.

$$a^2 = b^2 + c^2 - 2bc \cos A$$

law of sines The relationship between the sides and their opposite angles in any triangle.

$$\frac{\sin A}{a} = \frac{\sin B}{b} = \frac{\sin C}{c}$$

leading coefficient The coefficient of the highest-order term in a polynomial.

linear equation An equation of degree 1. Its graph is a line.

$$y = 5x + 4 \text{ is a linear equation.}$$

line of symmetry A mirror line that reflects an object onto itself.

locus A set of points determined by a given condition.

lowest common denominator (LCD) The least common multiple of the denominators of two or more rational expressions.

The lowest common denominator of $\frac{4}{5x}$ and $\frac{3}{10y}$ is $10xy$.

M

major arc A part of a circle that is greater than half the circumference.

mapping A pairing of each element in the domain of a function with each element in the range. A correspondence of points between an object and its image.

mean The average of a set of values. The mean is found by dividing the sum of a set of numbers by the number of numbers in the set.

median of a triangle The line segment joining a vertex to the midpoint of the opposite side.

midsegment of a triangle The line segment joining the midpoints of two of the sides of a triangle.

mill rate The amount of tax levied annually for each $1000 of assessed value of a property.

minor arc A part of a circle that is less than half the circumference.

monomial A number, a variable, or a product of numbers and variables.

mortgage An agreement between a money lender and a borrower to purchase property.

mortgagee A person or business that lends money for a mortgage.

mortgagor A person or business that borrows money to buy a property.

N

natural number A number in the sequence 1, 2, 3, 4, 5, 6, …

negation The opposite of a statement, often formed using the word *not*.

net income The amount an employee receives after all deductions are subtracted from the employee's gross income.

nominal interest rate The stated, or named, rate of interest of an investment or loan.

nonagon A polygon with 9 sides.

non-linear equation An equation whose graph is not a straight line.

oblique triangle A triangle that is not right-angled.

obtuse angle An angle whose measure is greater than 90° but less than 180°.

octagon A polygon with 8 sides.

odd-degree function A function whose degree is an odd number.

$$f(x) = x^3 + 2x^2 + 3x - 1 \text{ is an odd-degree function.}$$

ordered pair A pair of numbers, such as $(-3, 6)$, used to name a point on a graph.

origin The intersection of the x- and y-axes on a Cartesian coordinate grid. Described by the ordered pair $(0, 0)$.

orthocentre The point of intersection of the three altitudes of a triangle.

P

parabola The graph of a quadratic function for which the domain is the set of real numbers.

parallel lines Two lines in the same plane that never meet.

parallelogram A quadrilateral with opposite sides parallel.

pentagon A polygon with 5 sides.

perfect number A counting number that is equal to the sum of its proper divisors.

$$6 = 1 + 2 + 3 \text{ is a perfect number.}$$

perfect square A whole number that can be expressed as the square of a whole number.

25 is a perfect square.

perfect square trinomial A trinomial that can be factored as the square of a binomial.

$$a^2x^2 + 2abx + b^2 = (ax + b)^2$$

perimeter The distance around a closed plane figure.

perpendicular bisector The line that intersects a line segment at right angles, dividing it into two congruent parts.

perpendicular lines Lines that intersect at right angles.

piecework A method of earning income in which a worker is paid for each item produced or each service provided.

point discontinuity A point on a graph at which a function is not defined.

point of tangency The point of intersection of a tangent and a circle.

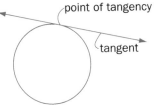

polygon A closed plane figure formed by at least three line segments.

polynomial An expression of the form $a_nx^n + a_{n-1}x^{n-1} + \ldots + a_1x^1 + a_0$, where the coefficients $a_n, a_{n-1}, \ldots, a_0$ represent real numbers, a_n is not zero, and the exponents are non-negative integers.

$$3x^5 + 4x^4 - 2x^3 + x^2 - 5x - 1 \text{ is a polynomial.}$$

postulate A fact that is assumed to be true without proof.

prime number A number with exactly two factors — itself and 1

2, 5, and 7 are prime numbers.

probability The ratio of the number of favourable outcomes to the number of possible outcomes.

proper divisor A number that divides evenly into a given number.

Pythagorean theorem The relation that expresses the area of the square drawn on the hypotenuse of a right triangle as equal to the sum of the areas of the squares drawn on the other two sides.

Q

quadrant One of the four regions formed by the intersection of the x-axis and the y-axis.

quadratic equation An equation in the form of $ax^2 + bx + c = 0$, where a, b, and c are real numbers and $a \neq 0$.

quadratic formula The formula for finding the roots of a quadratic equation in the form $ax^2 + bx + c$, where $a \neq 0$.

$$x = \frac{-b \pm \sqrt{b^2 - 4ac}}{2a}$$

quadratic function A function defined by a quadratic equation of the form $y = ax^2 + bx + c$.

quadrilateral A polygon with 4 sides.

quartic function A function of degree 4, such as $y = x^4 + 3x^3 - 2x^2 - 1$.

quintic function A function of degree 5.

R

radical equation An equation that has a variable in a radicand.

$\sqrt{x + 1} + 2 = 4$ is a radical equation.

radical function A function that has a variable in a radicand.

$f(x) = \sqrt{x - 3}$ is a radical function.

radical inequality An inequality that has a variable in a radicand.

$\sqrt{x + 1} - \sqrt{5 - x} > 0$ is a radical inequality.

radical sign The symbol $\sqrt{}$, which indicates the principal or non-negative root of an expression.

radicand An expression under a radical sign.

radius A line segment that joins the centre of a circle and a point on the circumference.

range The set of all second coordinates of the ordered pairs of a relation. The set of all values of a function $f(x)$.

rational equation An equation that contains one or more rational expressions.

$\dfrac{3}{x - 4} = 2$ is a rational equation.

rational function A function of the form $f(x) = \dfrac{g(x)}{h(x)}$, where $g(x)$ and $h(x)$ are polynomials and $h(x) \neq 0$.

$f(x) = \dfrac{1}{x + 1}$ is a rational function.

rational inequality An inequality that includes rational expressions.

rational number A number that can be expressed in the form $\dfrac{a}{b}$, where a and b are integers and $b \neq 0$.

rational zero theorem If $x = \dfrac{b}{a}$ is a rational zero of a polynomial $P(x)$ with integral coefficients, then b is a factor of the constant term of the polynomial and a is a factor of the coefficient of the highest-degree term.

real numbers All the rational and irrational numbers.

real zeros The x-intercepts of the graph of a function.

reciprocals Two numbers that have a product of 1.

2 and $\dfrac{1}{2}$ are reciprocals.

rectangle A parallelogram with four right angles.

reflection A transformation that maps an object onto an image by a reflection in a line.

regression line An accurate line of best fit usually determined with a computer or a graphing calculator.

regular polygon A polygon in which all sides and all angles are equal.

relation A set of ordered pairs.

relative maximum A point that does not have the greatest y-coordinate of any point of a function, but no nearby point has a greater y-coordinate.

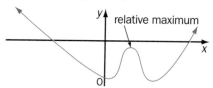

relative minimum A point that does not have the least y-coordinate of any point of a function, but no nearby point has a lesser y-coordinate.

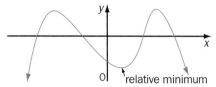

remainder theorem When a polynomial $P(x)$ is divided by $ax - b$, and the remainder is a constant, then the remainder is $P\left(\dfrac{b}{a}\right)$.

restriction on a variable A condition placed on the value(s) of a variable.

rhombus A parallelogram in which all sides are equal.

right triangle A triangle with one right angle.

root of an equation A solution to the equation.

rotation A transformation that maps an object onto its image by a turn about a fixed point.

sales quota An amount of sales that a salesperson is expected to make before the salesperson starts to earn commission.

scalene triangle A triangle with no sides equal.

scatter plot The result of plotting data that can be represented as ordered pairs on a graph.

secant A line that contains a chord.

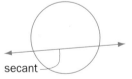

sector A region of a circle bounded by two radii and their intercepted arc.

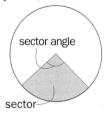

sector angle An angle formed by two radii of a circle. Also known as a central angle.

sequence An ordered list of numbers.

similar figures Figures with corresponding angles equal and corresponding lengths proportional.

simple interest Interest calculated using the formula

$$\text{Interest} = \text{Principal} \times \text{Rate} \times \text{Time}$$

sine ratio For an acute angle in a right triangle, the ratio of the length of the opposite side to the length of the hypotenuse.

slope The ratio $\dfrac{\text{rise}}{\text{run}}$. For a non-vertical line containing two distinct points (x_1, y_1) and (x_2, y_2), the slope is $\dfrac{y_2 - y_1}{x_2 - x_1}$.

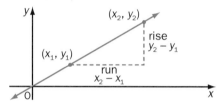

sphere The set of all points in space that are the same distance from a given point.

square pyramid A pyramid with a square base.

square root One of two identical factors of a number.

standard form of a quadratic equation A quadratic equation written in the form $ax^2 + bx + c = 0$, where a, b, c are real numbers and $a \neq 0$.

standard form of a quadratic function A quadratic function written in the form $y = a(x - p)^2 + q$.

statement A sentence that is either true or false.

straight angle An angle whose measure is 180°.

straight commission Income that is a percent of the value of sales.

supplementary angles Two angles whose sum is 180°.

system of equations Two or more equations studied together.

$x + y = 3$ and $3x - y = 1$ is a system of equations.

T

table of values A method of organizing values of a relation.

tangent ratio For an acute angle in a right triangle, the ratio of the length of the opposite side to the length of the adjacent side.

tangent to a circle A line that intersects a circle at exactly one point.

taxable income The amount obtained by subtracting tax-exempt deductions from gross income.

tax-exempt deductions Union or professional dues, Registered Pension Plan contributions, Registered Retirement Savings Plan contributions, and child care expenses that are deducted from gross income to obtain taxable income.

term of a mortgage The length of time that a mortgage agreement is in effect.

transformation A mapping of points of a plane onto points of the same plane.

translation A transformation that maps an object onto its image so that each point in the object is moved the same distance in the same direction.

transversal A line that intersects two lines in the plane in two distinct points.

trapezoid A quadrilateral with one pair of parallel sides.

triangle A polygon with 3 sides.

trinomial A polynomial consisting of three terms.

$x^2 + 2xy + y^2$ is a trinomial.

turning points Relative maximums or relative minimums of a graph.

V

variable A letter or symbol, such as x, used to represent a number.

Venn diagram A diagram that uses overlapping circles inside a rectangle to model statements.

vertex of a parabola The point where the axis of symmetry of a parabola intersects the parabola.

volume The number of cubic units contained in a solid.

W

whole numbers Numbers in the sequence 0, 1, 2, 3, 4, 5, ...

X

x-axis The horizontal line used as a scale for the independent variable in the Cartesian coordinate plane.

x-coordinate The first value in an ordered pair.

x-intercept The x-coordinate of a point where a line or curve crosses the x-axis.

Y

y-axis The vertical line used as a scale for the dependent variable in the Cartesian coordinate plane.

y-coordinate The second value in an ordered pair.

y-intercept The y-coordinate of a point where a line or curve crosses the y-axis.

Z

zero of a function Any value of x for which the value of the function $f(x)$ is 0.

zero product property For any real numbers a and b, if $ab = 0$, then $a = 0$ or $b = 0$, or $a = 0$ and $b = 0$.

APPLICATIONS INDEX

TECHNOLOGY INDEX

INDEX

Photo Credits

v Ian Crysler; **vi top** Canapress Photo Service; **vi bottom** Corel Corporation/#73011; **vii** Canadian Olympic Association/Claus Andersen; **viii** Ian Crysler; **ix top** Courtesy of The Bata Shoe Museum; **ix bottom** Ian Crysler; **xvi** Ian Crysler; **xvii** Zigy Kaluzny/Tony Stone Images; **xix** Corel Corp./#16042; **xx** Reprinted by permission of the Royal Canadian Mint; **xxi** Thomas Kitchin/First Light; **xxiii** Nicole A. Higa, Punahou School, Honolulu, Hawaii; **xxvii** Dick Hemingway; **xxviii** Ian Crysler; **xxix** Ian Crysler; **1 left, bottom right, bottom centre** R. W. Ford; **1 top right** Wolfgang Weber / Government of the NWT; **1 top centre** Don Ford; **1 background** Tourism Newfoundland and Labrador; **5** Thomas Kitchin / First Light; **6** Canapress Photo Service; **13** Ron Watts/First Light; **14** Corel Corp. / #167065; **17** Canapress Photo Service; **18-19** Ian Crysler; **21** Thomas Kitchin/First Light; **21** Jim Brandenberg / First Light; **28** Canadian Airlines International; **30** Petroleum Communication Foundation; **34** Canapress Photo Service; **41** HBC Museum Collection, Manitoba Museum of Man and Nature; **48** TrizecHahn Corporation; **50** K. Wothe/First Light; **51** Canapress/Bill Cooke; **56-57** Doug Pemberton/Vancouver Aquarium; **58** Canapress Photo Service; **60** Mike Ridewood/Canapress Photo Service; **66** Photographer: Cylla von Tiedemann. Courtesy of Stratford Festival Archives; **69** Ian Crysler; **70** Tom Hanson/Canapress Photo Service; **72** Ray Giguere/Canapress Photo Service; **77** New Zealand Tourism Board; **78** Don Ford; **80** Jeff Vinnick/Vancouver Canucks; **91** Ian Crysler; **92-93** Photo by Jason Hughes, Mix 99.9 FM in Toronto; **98-99** Corel Corporation / #230064; **102** Ian Crysler; **104** David Clark / Province; **112** Canapress/Frank Gunn; **114** Corel Corporation / #73011; **124** Thomas Zimmermann/Tony Stone Images; **126** Canadian Space Agency; **136-137** Courtesy National Parks Service, Utah; **140** The Bettmann Archive; **143** Kevin Schafer/Corbis; **148-149** Corel Corp./#204064; **150** Courtesy of Dole Foods; **152** Bob Torrez/Tony Stone Images;

157 Canadian Olympic Association/Ted Grant; **163** Jim Tuck, Memorial University of Newfoundland; **168** Mimmo Jodice/Corbis; **174** Canadian Sport Images; **181** (C) 1996 Bernt Wahl/Dynamic Software; **187** Canada's Sports Hall of Fame; **191** Courtesy of Compaq Canada; **196** Jim Winkley; Ecoscene/Corbis; **197** Ian Crysler; **198** Reprinted by permission of Catherine Bond-Mills. Photo by Peter J. Thompson/Thompson Sport Images; **204** Noe Zamel; **214** Richard Elliott/Tony Stone Images; **238-239** NASA; **240** Ian Crysler; **242** Drawing courtesy of Warren Hill, Michael Blake, and John F. Clark; **251** Corel Corp./#227064; **261** Canadian Olympic Association/Claus Andersen; **271** Courtesy of Ford Motor Company of Canada Ltd.; **274** Canadian National Exhibition Archives; **288** NASA; **299** Daylight HMI Fresnel Light courtesy of Strand Lighting (Canada) Ltd.; **314** Corel Corp./#312015; **328** NASA; **334-335** Kazuaki Iwasaki/First Light; **336** Ian Crysler; **338** COMSTOCK/Russ Kinney; **350** National Archives of Canada/C10968; **357** Ian Crysler; **373** Steve Short/First Light; **374** Courtesy of Compaq Canada Inc.; **380-381** Corel Corp./#22026; **385** Corbis-Bettmann; **393** © Terence Dickinson; **396** Bombardier Aerospace; **408** Canadian Sport Images/Sandy Grant; **426** NASA; **433** Raymond Gendreau/Tony Stone Images; **439** NASA; **444** Saskatchewan Agriculture and Food; **450-451** Photo courtesy of Telesat Canada; **452** Quilt block/photo by Catherine J.M. Rostron, President, Canadian Quilters' Association/association canadienne de la courtepointe 1998/99; **454** Ian Crysler; **455** Toronto Blue Jays Baseball Club; **462** Ian Crysler; **464** Photo by Robert G. Sherrin, originally published in The Capilano Review, No. 40, 1986; **470** Hibernia Management and Development Company Ltd.; **477** Mary Agnes Challoner; **478** NASA; **483** Duomo/Layton/ Image Bank; **492** D. Lawrence/First Light; **493** Don Ford; **500-501** Ian Crysler; **502** Don Ford; **513** Ian Crysler; **514 left, centre** Courtesy of The Bata Shoe Museum; **514 right** Don Ford; **522-523** National Currency Collection, Bank of

Canada, photography James Zagon, Ottawa;
527 National Currency Collection, Bank of
Canada, photography James Zagon, Ottawa;
532 Revenue Canada; Reproduced with
permission of the Minister of Public Works and
Government Services Canada, 1998; **538** Erich
Lessing/Art Resource, NY; **547** Corbis-Bettmann;
557 Tom Tracy/Tony Stone Images; **570-571**
Jon Riley/Tony Stone Images; **580-581** From
MATHPOWER™, Nine, Western Edition, by
George Knill. Reprinted by permission of
McGraw-Hill Ryerson.; **582-583** Source:
UNFPA - State of the World Population Report
1997; **583** Statistics Canada, Population
Projections for Canada, Provinces and Territories,
1993-2016, Catalogue No. 91-520 and pages.
Statistics Canada information is used with the
permission of the Minister of Industry, as Minister
responsible for Statistics Canada. Information on
the availability of the wide range of data from
Statistics Canada can be obtained from Statistics
Canada's Regional Offices, its World Wide Web
site at http://www.statcan.ca, and its toll-free access
number 1-800-263-1136.; **586** From
MATHPOWER™, Nine, Western Edition, by
George Knill. Reprinted by permission of
McGraw-Hill Ryerson.; **588** Reprinted by
permission of Air Transport Association of
America; **589** Courtesy of the Canada-France-
Hawaii Telescope, Mauna Kea, Hawaii;

Technical Art by Tom Dart, First Folio Resource
Group, Inc.

Illustration Credits

2 Micheal Herman; **14** Michael Herman ;
31 Michael Herman; **46** Michael Herman;
48 Michael Herman; **110** Deborah Crowle;
111 Deborah Crowle; **122** Bernadette Lau;
132 Deboarah Crowle; **133** Deborah Crowle;
230 Bernadette Lau; **285** Deborah Crowle;
335 Deborah Crowle; **343** Clarence Porter;
347 Bernadette Lau; **358-359** Bernadette Lau;
366 Clarence Porter; **414** Deborah Crowle;
467 Michael Herman; **496** Michael Herman;
499 Michael Herman; **511** Michael Herman;
514 Michael Herman; **515** Michael Herman;
517 Michael Herman; **551** Clarence Porter;
562 Bernadette Lau; **584-585** Teco Rodrigues